THE KID

ALSO BY BEN BRADLEE, JR.

Guts and Glory: The Rise and Fall of Oliver North

*Prophet of Blood: The Untold Story of Ervil LeBaron and the
Lambs of God* (with Dale Van Atta)

*The Ambush Murders: The True Account of the Killing of Two
California Policemen*

For more information, please visit BenBradleeJr.com.

THE KID

THE IMMORTAL LIFE
OF
TED WILLIAMS

BEN BRADLEE, JR.

LITTLE, BROWN AND COMPANY
New York Boston London

Little, Brown and Company
Hachette Book Group
237 Park Avenue, New York, NY 10017
littlebrown.com

First Edition: December 2013

Little, Brown and Company is a division of Hachette Book Group, Inc. The Little, Brown name and logo are trademarks of Hachette Book Group, Inc.

The publisher is not responsible for websites (or their content) that are not owned by the publisher.

The Hachette Speakers Bureau provides a wide range of authors for speaking events. To find out more, go to hachettespeakersbureau.com or call (866) 376-6591.

Library of Congress Cataloging-in-Publication Data

Bradlee, Ben, Jr.
    The kid : the immortal life of Ted Williams / Ben Bradlee, Jr.—First edition.
        pages cm.
    Includes bibliographical references and index.
    ISBN 978-0-316-61435-1
    1. Williams, Ted, 1918–2002.   2. Baseball players—United States—Biography.   I. Title.
    GV865.W5B73 2013
    796.357092—dc23
    [B]   2013028253

10 9 8 7 6 5 4 3

RRD-C

Printed in the United States of America

For Jan, Joe, Anna, and Greta.
And in memory of Matt Herrick.

Contents

THE KID

Author's Note

When I was a boy growing up in the mid-1950s outside Boston, Ted Williams was my hero. My bedroom was plastered with pictures of the Kid clipped from *Sports Illustrated* or *Sport* magazines, and I especially liked a large, framed, pen-and-ink drawing done by the artist Robert Riger in 1955 showing Williams in baseball repose, leaning on two bats, presumably waiting his turn to hit.

Like thousands of kids my age, I was captivated by Ted's peerless batting skill and by the way he always seized and held the spotlight. He was the only reason to follow the abysmal Red Sox teams of that era. When I went to games, I was struck by the way the atmosphere at Fenway Park changed each time he came to bat. There would be an anticipatory murmur from the crowd when Ted stepped into the box. He'd knock some real or imagined dirt from his spikes, dig in, wiggle his hips, grind his hands on the handle of the bat, and hold it tight against his body, ready to face the pitcher. People never even considered leaving their seats when Williams was hitting. His at bats were events, and he himself was the main event in Boston sports from 1939 to 1960 and well into his retirement.

With his dramatic, tempestuous persona, Ted made as much news off the field as on: always feuding with newspapermen, outraged over perceived slights, spitting or gesturing at hostile fans, going off not just to one war but to two as a Marine Corps fighter pilot, getting married and divorced three times. He even made news fishing, once catching a 1,235-pound black marlin off the coast of Peru and putting on annual fly-casting exhibitions in the off-season.

I got Ted's autograph once, waiting outside the players' parking lot at Fenway Park with scores of other kids. Williams stopped to sign that day, which he didn't always do. He insisted on imposing some order on the unruly scene before him, and he made us take turns. I still have the ball he signed for me, on the sweet spot, of course, the ink on the signature now fading badly with the passage of more than fifty years.

And I happened to be at the ballpark on Sunday, September 21, 1958, when Ted, enraged by a rare strikeout, flung his bat in disgust, only to have it sail into the box seats near the Red Sox dugout and strike an elderly woman in the head. Mortified, Williams rushed to the first-aid room to apologize to the bloodied lady, explaining that he had lost control of the bat because the handle had sticky resin on it. The woman, a Ted fan, saw how anguished he was and consoled *him,* saying she knew it had been an accident.

Melodrama of that sort always seemed to attend Williams. He knew how to make an entrance—and an exit, as when he took his leave from baseball by hitting a majestic home run on his last time at bat on September 28, 1960.

I kept following Ted in his retirement, with interest. He took a visible job with Sears, Roebuck, advising the chain on a line of sports and outdoor equipment. He had a syndicated column. He was inducted into the Hall of Fame the first time he was eligible, in 1966. He published his autobiography in 1969, which I remember devouring. He made a surprise return to baseball as manager of the lowly Washington Senators that same year. He wasn't particularly good at managing, but the game was better for having him back. He stayed engaged in baseball as a fan, and signed on with the Red Sox as a hitting coach. In that capacity, Williams would make godlike annual appearances at spring training, where he would hold court before worshipful young players—and the writers, whom he had outlasted and bent to his will.

Being Ted Williams seemed like a full-time job. He plied the memorabilia circuit, but not aggressively. He returned to Fenway Park for Old-Timers' Games and to be honored on various occasions. He had highways and tunnels named after him. And in 1991, on the fiftieth anniversary of his signature achievement—batting .406—President George H. W. Bush feted him at the White House along with Joe DiMaggio, whose fifty-six-game hitting streak in 1941 was also recalled with awe. Then Ted returned solo later in the year to receive the Medal of Freedom from Bush. Those celebrations, however poignant, paled in comparison to the nationally televised spectacle of Williams, eighty and frail, returning to Fenway Park for the 1999 All-Star Game and what everyone understood would be his farewell to Boston. Living members of baseball's All-Century Team joined that year's All-Stars in one of the game's most memorable tableaux, swarming around Williams in adulation and refusing to leave the field despite appeals to do so by the public-address announcer.

So it seemed Ted never really left the sporting scene. When he died in 2002, I read the obituaries, the special sections, and the tributes and was struck by how much interest there still was in his life, by how many different people he had touched in different ways, and by what a rich, extraordinary life he had led. I was familiar with the Williams genre— the dozen or so previous books on the Kid, the vast majority of which had been written by adoring sportswriters who had concentrated almost exclusively on his baseball exploits. I'd read most of them as a boy when they came out—short books like *Ted Williams: The Eternal Kid,* by Ed Linn (1961), *Ted Williams,* by Ray Robinson (1962), and *The Ted Williams Story* by Gene Schoor (also 1962). Williams himself improved on the spare, early books with his autobiography, *My Turn at Bat,* ghost-written by John Underwood. *My Turn* captured Ted's voice, but was limited in scope, as autobiographies often are, and Williams barely delved into his personal life at all. He also had thirty-three more years to live after the book was published.

In subsequent years, several coffee-table books about Ted appeared, most of them glowing hagiography. In 1991, Columbia University English professor Michael Seidel produced the solid and serious *Ted Williams: A Baseball Life,* though it received little national attention. In 1993, Ed Linn greatly expanded his small 1961 book into the worthy *Hitter: The Life and Turmoils of Ted Williams.* The best piece of writing on Ted in this period, however, was not a book but a long piece in *Esquire* magazine by the estimable Richard Ben Cramer, published in 1986. Cramer, who died of cancer in 2013, precisely captured Ted's vernacular—and a hint of his deep-seated anger: the Kid spoke in loud and profane staccato bursts, veering from one subject to another. It was an ultimately sympathetic portrait of a troubled man who tried to be the best at what he did, a man who wanted fame but not celebrity and who was the absolute master of his own his-way-or-the-highway universe.

This was basically the state of "Ted lit"—plentiful but thin—when I began work on this biography more than a decade ago now, in the fall of 2002. Before long, Leigh Montville's *Ted Williams: An American Hero* appeared. Montville, a former sports columnist at the *Boston Globe* and a colleague of mine when he was there, is a gifted writer—and much faster than I am. His book, published in 2004, just twenty-one months after Williams's death, raised the bar in Ted lit substantially.

I decided not to skimp on the central baseball part of Ted's life but nevertheless to concentrate my efforts on areas that had been far less chronicled, such as his troubled childhood, his anger and its source, his kindness to sick children and others down on their luck, his war service, his dealings with the sportswriters who covered him (a dynamic essential to understanding Williams), his love and mastery of fishing as an example of his striving for excellence in everything he undertook, his relationships with his wives, other women, and his children, his vibrant second act in retirement, and finally a detailed examination of the dark cryonics affair, which, sadly, dominated the Williams postmortems.

What I discovered in my many years of research surprised me. Ted, it turned out, had gone to considerable lengths to conceal the fact that he was Mexican-American out of fear that his baseball career might be jeopardized by the prejudice of the day. In addition, the Williams war years seemed even more remarkable when compared to the virtually unfathomable prospect of a modern superstar athlete putting his career aside to serve in two wars. Yet it was curious that historians glossed over the fact that Williams initially sought a deferment in World War II and actively tried to avoid being recalled for Korea.

Ted's boiling anger—rage, really—particularly piqued my curiosity: where it came from, how he managed it, and how he failed to manage it. On the field he was able to use it as a tonic to fuel hitting tears—often using the press as his foil. At other times he used it to manufacture a controversy or portray himself as the maligned victim of ink-stained wretches, most of whom actually gave him rave notices. But in his personal life, the anger often made him dysfunctional and unable to sustain relationships with loved ones. He'd had three wives and a handful of serious relationships with other women, two of whom, I learned, he'd proposed to. He'd lived with another woman for nearly twenty years at the end of his life, and hardly anything was known about that relationship. And he'd had three children: a daughter by his first marriage, Bobby-Jo, whom he'd grown estranged from, and a son and daughter from his third marriage, John-Henry and Claudia.

The first Mrs. Williams, Doris Soule, had died in 1987. Tracking down Lee Howard, Ted's second wife, in October of 2002 and persuading the former Chicago model to publicly discuss her life with Williams for the first time gave me an early insight into the joy and misery of loving the Kid. But the most important breakthrough came in the spring of 2004, when, after nearly two years of saying no, Ted's two daughters agreed, quite separately, to give me their first substantive interviews about growing up with their famous father.

Bobby-Jo, speaking for two days in Florida with her husband, Mark Ferrell, at her side, was still traumatized by the fact that Ted's body had been frozen, or cryonically preserved, a decision driven by John-Henry that might have remained a deep family secret had she not alerted the press. Bobby-Jo had threatened to go to court to try to get her father's remains taken out of the Arizona cryonics facility that held them on the grounds that his will specified he had wished to be cremated, but she'd been forced to drop her challenge when she ran out of money. She spoke of how hard it had been to please her father when she was growing up, of his bouts of anger, which were so intense she thought he was mentally ill, and of her gradual isolation and estrangement from Ted as an adult—aided and abetted, she thought, by John-Henry as he came to play a more dominant role in his father's life. Bobby-Jo was a wounded, fragile figure, and before long she went underground, moving to Tennessee and cutting herself off completely from many of her friends.

Claudia, after initially appearing more distrustful than Bobby-Jo, ended up speaking with me extensively. We had sixteen formal interviews over sixteen days spanning 2004 through 2006. Many of these sessions were in Ted's Florida house, and she came to allow me to remain in the house by myself, free to rummage around as I pleased through his papers, records, scrapbooks, letters, journals, wartime pilot's logs, and fishing logs. This sort of stuff is a biographer's dream and yielded nuggets such as Ted's private address book, containing names of many people I'd never heard of but who ended up providing useful insights about Williams when interviewed; letters from people such as Richard Nixon, Bob Feller, and John Updike; copies of little-known speeches Ted delivered while working for Sears, Roebuck; and various audio- and video-tapes of Williams interviews, one dating back to 1946. Claudia also shared Ted's private family photos, tape recordings, and videos with me, and helped persuade her mother—Ted's third wife, Dolores Williams—to give me her first interview. Like Bobby-Jo, Claudia provided important insights into growing up with Ted—his view of women, his anger, his insecurity, and his record as a father. But perhaps the most significant thing she supplied was her family's first full explanation, including many new details, of the cryonics affair.

I think Claudia's main motivation in cooperating with me to the extent that she did was that she thought I would give John-Henry a fair hearing, and I made every effort to do that—to go beyond the way he'd been caricatured in the press as Ted's scheming bad seed. Like his sisters, John-Henry himself had initially declined to talk to me, then he agreed, but contracted leukemia and became too ill to be interviewed. He died in March of 2004, less than two years after his father. Then he had his body frozen at the same cryonics facility in Arizona that held Ted's remains.

After having little to do with any of his children as they grew up, Williams reached out to John-Henry, in particular, at the end. Ted wanted to make up for all the years he'd been absent, and in the process he overcompensated by ceding total control of his affairs during the final decade of his life to his untested son, who was then just coming of age, in his early twenties. John-Henry eagerly seized the reins with a mixture of exploitation, love, and devotion. The last part of the book is the story of a father and a son discovering each other during a difficult but poignant period of symbiotic dependency.

Researching and writing this book took me more than a decade. After six-hundred-odd interviews, uncounted hours of research in archives and among the private papers given to me by the Williams family, after looking closely at that signed baseball more than a few times and thinking hard about the man I'd briefly met as a boy and the man I was meeting now, I felt ready to let go of this Ted Williams tale, the story of an exceptional, tumultuous, and epic American life—an immortal life.

Ben Bradlee, Jr.
August 2013

Introduction

The Kid appeared in the small room on the night of July 5, 2002. Video cameras rolled, and the flashbulbs popped—just as if he were making another star turn of the sort he had made so many times throughout his celebrated life.

About thirty people had anxiously awaited the arrival of Ted Williams—the great Teddy Ballgame himself: American icon, last of the .400 hitters, war hero, world-class fisherman, perfectionist, enfant terrible. Yet this was no press conference, no card show, no charity event or meet and greet, where Ted would wave and say a few words to the faithful.

For he was dead, after all. Quite dead.

Williams had passed away some twelve hours earlier in Florida, at the age of eighty-three, and then been secretly flown on a small chartered jet to Scottsdale, Arizona, outside Phoenix. There his body had been loaded onto an ambulance and taken, in a motorcade, to the place where this small crowd awaited him, in an operating room at a company called the Alcor Life Extension Foundation, located just a mile from the Scottsdale airport.

Alcor was then, and remains today, the leading practitioner of cryonics, a fringe movement that freezes people after they die in the hope that medical technology will someday advance to the point where it will be possible to stop or reverse the aging process and cure now-incurable diseases. At that point, cryonics—not to be confused with cryogenics, the mainstream science that studies how various materials react to extremely low temperatures—aspires to thaw out its frozen charges and bring them back to life. Alcor froze its first "patient," as it calls its customers, in 1976. By the time Ted arrived, twenty-six years later, the group said it had frozen forty-nine people and had 590 living "members"—those who'd signed up to undergo the procedure when they die and who paid $400 in annual dues in the meantime, while they waited.

On Alcor's macabre menu, people have two basic options. The first is called a whole-body procedure, in which the entire body is frozen. The second is known as the neuro, in which only the head is frozen and preserved after being severed from the torso, which is then cremated or buried. A third variation provides for freezing both the torso and the head separately. Alcor stores both the bodies and the heads in huge, Thermos bottle–like tanks known as Dewars, which are filled with liquid nitrogen cooled to minus 321 degrees Fahrenheit.

In 2002, the whole-body procedure cost $120,000, the neuro $50,000. Among cryonicists, the neuro was becoming the preferred option. It was cheaper, for one thing, though Alcor liked to say that both procedures were easily affordable through life insurance. Most important for Alcorians, the head contains the brain, which they consider by far the most important organ in the body because it holds the memory. When the patient comes back to life, or is "reanimated," in cryospeak, he (the believers are overwhelmingly male) will want to remember from whence he came. Furthermore, the brain is the hardest organ to replace. With stem cell research and other advances on the horizon, it will be possible to regenerate tissue, and therefore simply grow a new body beneath your old head. Or so the hope goes.

Inside the Alcor operating room, it took five or six people to lift Ted out of the Ziegler case — the airtight metal container that airlines require for shipping bodies — in which he'd arrived. Under instructions from Alcor, a Florida mortician had filled the box with ice, a cryonics staple applied to the body immediately after death in order to keep it as cool as possible and to help preserve vital organs.

Ted's body was placed on the operating table, faceup. Attendants quickly pressed fresh bags of ice against his skin, especially around the head, neck, and groin. The table was surrounded by a custom-made six-inch-high white plastic wall to contain the ice and to keep excess fluids from spilling onto the floor during the upcoming operation, which would last about four hours. Technicians then began connecting the major blood vessels to a perfusion machine, which would replace the blood with so-called cryoprotectant solutions. These chemicals, similar to antifreeze, were designed to help prevent the formation of ice crystals, which could cause further cell damage before the intense cooling process could begin.

The Alcor staff then started to drain blood and water from Ted's body in what Alcor called a washout, replacing them with glycerol and another cryoprotectant known as B2C, which was used for the head only. Then, using a perforator, a standard neurological tool that looks like an electric drill, a surgeon and his assistant bored two small holes on either side of Ted's skull so that the surface of the brain could be examined during the perfusion process to guard against swelling. Small wire sensors were inserted into each hole to be used to detect cracking of the skull during the freezing process later.

A green-and-white tube popped out of the perfusion machine, disrupting the washout process and causing "lots" of Williams's blood to surge over the protective plastic wall on the operating table and spill onto the floor, according to the OR notes, which were taken in an informal style by the lay girlfriend of one of the Alcorians.[1] About forty-five minutes later, the surgeon "shut down some tube accidentally" on the machine, and the pressure ratcheted up too quickly, the notes reported, causing the mix of blood and chemicals to pump through Ted's system at too high, and then at too low, a level. An "enormous amount of arterial leakage," with blood flowing from Williams's left eye, was also noted.[2]

Soon the surgeon announced that he was ready to perform the "cephalic isolation." This meant Ted Williams's head was now ready to be cut off. The surgeon took out a carving knife and began to cut— starting below Ted's neck, slicing through tissue and bone, working his way down through the sixth cervical vertebra, at the top of the spine. At one point, the going slow, the surgeon remarked that he wished he had an electric knife. Finally, he switched to a bone saw to finish the job, and at 9:17 p.m. mountain time, the head of the greatest hitter who ever lived had been sliced off.

After Ted's head was severed, it was put into a small plastic container and taken to an adjoining room known as the "neuro cool-down area." There it was placed into a small Dewar connected to a larger Dewar filled with liquid nitrogen. The larger Dewar then began pumping nitrogen gas cooled to minus 202 degrees at a high velocity into the smaller Dewar containing Ted's head. This went on for about three hours. The goal was to cool all parts of the head below the glass transition temperature, minus 191 degrees, as quickly as possible, after which it would be vitrified, or reach an ice-free state.

Over the next two weeks, a head would normally be placed in a cylindrical tank known as an LR-40 and gradually cooled further, to minus 321 degrees, the temperature at which it would be deemed fit for permanent storage. But in this case, the Alcorians chose to put Ted's head inside what they called their Cryostar, an intermediate cooling facility where heads were sometimes stored during the freezing process. The Cryostar was supposed to limit the cracking of the brain that normally occurred as the head was frozen, but the machine was malfunctioning, causing its temperature to fluctuate. As a result, Ted's brain may have been subjected to more cracking, not less.

The procedure took more than three hours to complete. Ted's torso was taken to what Alcor called its whole-body cooling bath, a large, thermally insulated rectangular box filled with silicone oil cooled by dry ice. Two drums of oil were at the foot of the bath, connected by a pipe. The torso was wrapped in protective plastic and strapped to a wire-mesh stretcher before being lowered into the oil bath. A lid was placed over the bath, and a pump circulated the oil amid chunks of dry ice, cooling the torso to minus 110 degrees at a rate of 32 degrees per minute. Then Ted's body was removed and deposited in a large Dewar, where, like his head, it would be cooled further over a period of two weeks.

Each Dewar is ten feet tall, a little more than three feet in diameter, and weighs about 5,400 pounds when full. The capacity is four bodies and five heads. The bodies are wrapped in insulated bags and put inside an aluminum container called a pod. Four pods ring the inside circumference of a Dewar, and in the middle is the "neuro column," which consists of five large cans about the size of lobster pots, each resting on a shelf, one on top of the other. Each can contains a head.

An eyebolt is screwed into the bone below the neck to make it easier to handle the head when necessary. The heads lie upside down, resting on a can of Bumble Bee tuna, or if a head is larger than normal, perhaps a can of Dinty Moore beef stew. "They wanted the heads resting on something, not just setting at the bottom of the stockpot," said Cindy Felix, a former facilities operations manager at Alcor. "It's amazing some of the things they did. They were so high-tech in some areas but almost medieval in others—like the tuna can."[3]

Whole bodies, those with the heads still attached, hang in the Dewars upside down. "We protected the head by putting it at the bottom, so that the last thing to be uncovered and thawed in the worst-case scenario is the brain, because we care about the identity and the personality, and most of that is encoded in the brain," said Tanya Jones, then Alcor's chief operating officer.[4]

After Ted's long procedure was over, the Alcorians were tired but jubilant. Here was the celebrity who could transform cryonics and give it some legitimacy, the kind of boost Walt Disney's preservation might have given the movement—had it actually happened and not merely been urban legend.

Of course, for the moment, at least, the company couldn't say anything because of patient confidentiality rules. And John-Henry Williams, Ted's son, was keeping them to that. Holding a sweeping power of attorney and health proxy for his father, John-Henry, thirty-three, had become a cryonics disciple. He'd been in secret talks with Alcor for more than a year about freezing Ted when the time came and had given the company strict instructions not to tell anyone his father was there. Alcor executives hoped they could eventually persuade John-Henry to let them go public—perhaps in return for a price concession. Meanwhile, Ted—his head now in a pot, his torso in a pod—settled in to await what would be his greatest comeback ever.

The fundamental question of whether Williams wanted his body to be in the place it now was—an Arizona cryonics facility—and decapitated, at that, was very much in doubt. He had never submitted an application to Alcor or signed up for the cryonics procedure himself, as is standard practice among the facility's other clients. John-Henry had only faxed Alcor a completed application on his father's behalf about six hours after Ted was pronounced dead. Moreover, Ted's will, last revised in 1996, had specified that he wanted to be cremated, not frozen, and he had told scores of friends and associates over the years, at least one as late as 2002, that his wishes were to have his ashes scattered off the Florida Keys, where he had fished for years, along with the ashes of his beloved dog, a Dalmatian named Slugger, who had died in 1999.

John-Henry knew that Ted's will specified he wished to be cremated, and he also knew that his half sister, Bobby-Jo Williams Ferrell, was vehemently against the idea of her father being frozen. She had told John-Henry so directly when he asked her to consider cryonics for Ted a year before. Bobby-Jo had also notified Alcor by e-mail on the day Williams died, when his body was still in Florida, that she opposed the procedure.

The preparation of Ted's 1996 will, which was a revision of earlier drafts he had made over the years, was overseen by Eric Abel, a Williams family attorney. John-Henry had confided in Abel about his plans to freeze Ted several years before his death, and Abel had advised him on the issue. Abel said he counseled John-Henry that because of Ted's stated preference for cremation in his will, it would be prudent for John-Henry to get something in writing from his father, preferably notarized, saying that he now wanted to be cryonically preserved. But after Ted died and his body was flown to Alcor, Abel said he didn't know if John-Henry had obtained such a statement, nor did he ask him if he had.[5]

Besides facing opposition from Bobby-Jo on freezing Ted, John-Henry also encountered resistance from his younger sister, Claudia Williams. But Claudia said she gradually came around to the idea, and that while their father was initially dismissive of cryonics, she and John-Henry were able to convince him and gain his approval in November of 2000 during a private meeting in Ted's hospital room, shortly before he had a pacemaker installed to boost his failing heart. Claudia and her brother also felt they could dispose of his body as they saw fit. "As far as I was concerned, our father had died, and John-Henry and I could do whatever we wanted with our father," she said.[6]

Having no idea Williams had been frozen, his many fans were left to ponder the Kid's legacy: his magnificent .406 mark in 1941, achieved on the last day of the season, when Ted, in perhaps the defining moment of his career, declined the invitation of his manager to sit out the final day of the year to protect his .39955 average, which would have been rounded to .400, and proceeded to go 6–8 playing both games of a doubleheader; and his consistent flair for delivering other dramatic moments—such as winning the 1941 All-Star Game for the American League with a three-run homer in the bottom of the ninth inning, surviving a fiery crash landing in his jet after getting shot down by enemy gunfire in Korea, and hitting a home run on his last time at bat in 1960. They remembered Williams as the driven perfectionist; his swagger, style, and panache in the batter's box—a shade under six foot four, skinny and loose, hips swaying back and forth, bat cocked close to his body, hands grinding, then unleashing, at the last possible second, his perfect, slightly uppercut swing—and the what-ifs of how much grander his final numbers would have been had he not lost nearly five seasons in his prime fighting two wars, tempered by the realization that serving in the wars had also enhanced his legacy immeasurably. And they recalled the way he loped around the bases in his distinctive home-run trot, head always tucked way down; the way his explosive, often dark persona regularly made more news than his exploits on the field as he feuded with, gestured toward, and spat at a small faction of fans who delighted in taunting him and as he carried on a running war with the sportswriters who, he felt, had pried unjustifiably into his life and knocked him unfairly; and how despite such crude outbursts, Williams consistently demonstrated a basic sense of generosity and kindness, especially through his work for the Jimmy Fund, a charity for children with cancer, for which he raised millions of dollars over the years.

Ted was an original; not a traditional, modest, self-effacing hero but brash, profane, outspoken, and guileless. Self-taught and inquiring, he excelled as a Marine fighter pilot and became one of the most accomplished fishermen in the world. For better *and* worse, he was always his own man, never a phony—characteristics that helped him outlast his critics and win widespread affection and admiration as he aged. He had three favorite songs, which he played in his mind to help him fall asleep: "The Star-Spangled Banner," "The Marines' Hymn," and "Take Me Out to the Ball Game."

On visits to Boston long after he retired, Williams was struck by how people fawned and fussed over him, puzzled that he seemed more popular in retirement than he was during his playing days. The best evidence of this was his reception at the 1999 All-Star Game at Fenway Park. Ted, by then fragile and ailing, was driven out on the field in a golf cart to a thunderous ovation, and then, in a memorable scene, swarmed by a new generation of All-Star players who knew they were in the presence of baseball royalty. The players lingered, wanting to soak in the moment and bask in Williams's glow.

Of course all the obituaries listed Ted's key batting statistics, representing the spine of his twenty-two-year career: the .344 lifetime average, six batting titles (he led the league two more years, in 1954 and 1955, but injuries and walks prevented him from getting enough at bats to qualify for the batting titles in those years), two Most Valuable Player awards, two Triple Crowns, and 521 homers. He was selected an All-Star eighteen times.

Out of 7,706 at bats, Ted had nearly three times as many walks (2,021) as strikeouts (709), and he retired with a .482 on-base percentage—baseball's best ever. That meant he reached base nearly every other time he came up. He was second in all-time slugging percentage at .634, behind Ruth's .690. He led the league in homers four times and RBIs four times, in runs scored six times, walks eight times, slugging percentage eight times, and on-base percentage twelve times.

Ted's .388 average in 1957, at age thirty-nine, was nearly as remarkable as his .406 year. Though injured, he won the batting title, then promptly did it again in 1958, at the age of forty. "If in the end I didn't make it as the greatest hitter who ever lived—that long ago boyhood dream—I kind of enjoy thinking I might have become in those last years the greatest old hitter who ever lived," Ted wrote in his autobiography, *My Turn at Bat*.

During each Williams at bat, something between a hush and a buzz suddenly filled the air as the crowd shifted from autopilot engagement to edge-of-the-seat anticipation. "I was looking around for a story one day, and someone said there was this blind guy on the first-base line," remembered Tim Horgan, who covered the Red Sox for the *Boston Herald* and then the *Boston Evening Traveler* in the 1950s. "I went up to the man and said, 'Pardon me for asking, but why do you come to the park? Why not listen to the game on the radio?' He said, 'I love the sounds of the game when Ted comes up.'"[7]

Red Sox fans and the rabid press corps that covered the team seemed as captivated by Ted's personality as they were by his slugging. He was a prickly prima donna whose much-chronicled "rabbit ears" had an unerring ability to zero in on even a few scattered boos amid all the cheers. He seemed immune to receiving praise but generally couldn't tolerate criticism. On the field, his moods ranged from sheer joy and exuberance during his rookie year in 1939 to rage and petulance later in his career.

Williams reasoned that he was an expert at what he did, was trying his best to do even better, and thus resented any criticism. From 1940 to his last game in 1960, he swore off the time-honored baseball convention of tipping his hat to the fans. Once, after a spring training game in Miami in 1947, Ted appeared to doff his cap as he crossed home plate after hitting a home run. So alert was the press to Williams's every move that the *Boston Globe*'s beat writer at the time, Hy Hurwitz, rushed to the clubhouse after the game and asked Ted if he had, in fact, tipped his hat. He denied that he had and said he was merely mopping his brow. Whereupon Hurwitz famously wrote: "It was the heat, not the humility."[8]

The self-made, intellectually curious Williams was ahead of his time in regarding hitting as a science worthy of study, experimentation, and technical analysis. He coddled the blunt instruments of his success: his bats. He boned them. He cleaned them with alcohol every night. He weighed them meticulously on small scales to make sure they hadn't gotten slightly heavier through condensation. And, acting on the improbable suggestion of a teenage boy from Chelsea, Massachusetts, he even heated his bats to keep their moisture content low.

If anyone could get under Ted's skin, it was reporters, a group he contemptuously called the Knights of the Keyboard. For most of Ted's career, Boston had between seven and nine daily newspapers, plus another half dozen or so from the surrounding communities, not to mention the New York and national press. It was the post–*Front Page* era, but Ted was still prime fodder for intense tabloid and circulation wars in Boston, his every move dissected, debated, analyzed, second-guessed, and, of course, photographed.

A voracious consumer of his own press, Ted ignored all the positive coverage and focused only on the negative. "There were 49 million newspapers in Boston, from the *Globe* to the Brookline Something-or-Other, all ready to jump us," he whined in *My Turn at Bat.*[9] He was particularly sensitive about any stories that he felt delved unnecessarily into his private life, accused him of failing to hit in the clutch, or suggested that he was more interested in his own performance than that of the team.

It was natural for writers to despise Williams and fear him, because he treated them like dirt. But they also knew Ted was great copy, and if they could get him to talk, he was usually a terrific interview because he spoke with unvarnished candor. He was not above stirring the pot with reporters to give him something to be mad at if he felt he was losing his edge. He often said he hit better if he was mad. "He nurtured his rage," as the writer Roger Kahn once put it.

If Ted had been quiet for a while, and perhaps not hitting as well as he normally did, the writers would learn to expect that he'd pick a fight with one or several of them, pop off, then usually go on a tear at the plate.

If Ted's rages on and off the field dominated his public persona, his dedicated charitable work underscored his innate kindness. Once, after the Red Sox finished playing a night game in Washington, Ted chartered a plane and flew down to Raleigh, North Carolina, to spend five hours visiting a sick child, then flew back to Washington in time for an afternoon game the next day.

Every time Williams made a charitable visit on behalf of the Jimmy Fund or another organization, he would insist that no press coverage be allowed. If he saw a reporter or photographer, he would turn around and leave. He had a genuine, generous spirit and feared that press coverage might make people think he had some ulterior motive, such as trying to improve his churlish image. "He did not want to be thought of as a phony, I think," said Tim Horgan.

In retirement, the public Ted blossomed. He was quickly inducted into the Hall of Fame, and in his acceptance speech made a totally unexpected, bald political statement that called on the lords of Cooperstown to lift their color ban and induct the old Negro League stars. The statement was courageous, earned Ted enormous goodwill among black players, and underlined his basic sense of fairness and decency. Later, he returned to baseball and did a turn as a manager for the Washington Senators, pursued big-time fishing and hunting around the world, made annual spring training forays to Florida on behalf of the Red Sox to work with young hitters, took bows at the White House, made his peace with the fans and press of Boston, dabbled in the memorabilia market, and was a goodwill ambassador for baseball. Unlike many old-timers who cling to their era while belittling and resenting modern players, Ted remained a fan of the game, heaped praise on current stars, and forged relationships with players such as Tony Gwynn and Nomar Garciaparra.

His private life, during and after baseball, was much more problematic. If, during his career, Ted was able to manipulate the rage that simmered inside him and turn it into an on-field positive, off the field his inability to control his anger hurt him immeasurably in maintaining relationships—especially with his wives and children.

If he failed to perform a given task up to his own high standard, or if a friend or loved one did something in what he felt was an inept or shoddy manner, Ted would ignite. He could also be set off if he wasn't in control of a situation, or was not being accorded what he felt was proper deference. If the telephone rang at an inopportune or intrusive time, he might rip it from the wall and fling it across the room.

After seeing a lifetime's worth of these explosions close-up, Bobby-Jo Williams Ferrell concluded that her father had some kind of mental illness: "My dad was sick. And it's a damn shame that because he was Ted Williams, and because nobody wanted to tell him like it was, including myself, he suffered and progressively became more ill by the years. And I think even especially after he quit managing, he got worse and worse and worse."[10]

Gnashing of teeth was a telltale sign that Ted was getting ready to go off. "He would clench his teeth so hard it was like he was having a seizure," said Jerry Romolt, a memorabilia dealer who became a friend to Williams. "A fulmination. Then it would pass."[11]

That was the thing: the storms always passed, and usually quickly. But the price of being in Ted's orbit was that you had to endure the foul weather. "Sometimes he'd get so ticked off at me that the damnedest things would come out of his mouth, and then he would feel bad about it, but he would never apologize," said former Red Sox shortstop Johnny Pesky. "He was a proud guy. Every time you'd ask him a question, he'd look at you and say, 'Why are you so goddamn dumb?' He said that about pitchers, too, and they didn't like it."[12] His language made even some other ballplayers blush. "He'd say things that I shudder to think about and would never repeat," said Milt Bolling, a Red Sox shortstop from 1952 to 1957.[13] If you called him on his behavior, or decided that absorbing a steady diet of such outbursts was too much to take, then so be it, good-bye, you were out. But if you could accept that the eruptions were just *Ted being Ted,* that he really meant no harm, and that he could in fact be charming and engaging after the storm had blown over and act as though nothing had happened, then you were in, and Ted was your loyal friend for life.

Bobby Doerr, the old Red Sox second baseman and dear friend to Ted, felt Williams's lash while fishing and on many other occasions, but accepted him unconditionally. "He'd be like a maniac," Doerr said. "Ted fought embarrassment. Anytime he was embarrassed over anything—if it was baseball, he'd throw the bat in the air; fishing, he'd break a rod; golf, he'd throw the club. He fought embarrassment terribly because he was a perfectionist."[14]

Would Doerr ever tell him he was out of line? "No—you never said anything to Ted. It wasn't going to do any good." Doerr was far from alone. Johnny Pesky, also one of Ted's closest friends on the team, thought most of his teammates were simply awestruck by Ted. "We were like a bunch of kids looking up to a schoolteacher," Pesky said. "Some of the guys called him God. They'd say, 'God has spoken.' "[15]

Williams had few close friends, but would embrace and cultivate friendships with perfect strangers. He preferred the company of the "little people" to hanging around other celebrities or swells. "If I said this guy was a reporter and he could make you or break you, Ted would have nothing to do with the guy," said Dave McCarthy, a former New Hampshire state trooper who became a confidant of Ted's and a trustee of his estate. "But if I said, 'I'd like you to meet a janitor who likes bone fishing,' he'd talk all night. He was genuine about that. That's what I loved about him."[16]

Ted realized his behavior was a burden to others. "He said, 'The people that really love me have had to endure more than you can possibly imagine, because I can't control my temper,'" recalled Steve Brown, a Florida filmmaker and fisherman who became a confidant of Ted's toward the end of his life.[17]

Some friends struggled with the notion that they were enabling Ted's abusive conduct by not intervening. One was Elizabeth "Betty" Tamposi, daughter of the late Sam Tamposi, a longtime pal of Williams's who was a Red Sox limited partner and real estate developer in New Hampshire and Florida. After long being exposed to the kind and humanitarian side of Ted, Betty Tamposi was startled to witness his abusive conduct, sometimes exacerbated by drinking. Once, enraged by something, he furiously beat his dog in frustration. Another time, she watched as he humiliated the woman he lived with late in life, Louise Kaufman, in front of others at a restaurant. "I think there were a lot of people that enabled behavior of Ted's that was unacceptable," concluded Tamposi, who served as an assistant secretary of state under President George H. W. Bush.[18]

The Red Sox themselves coddled and enabled Williams in several ways: moving the right-field fences in for him, letting him maintain rules that kept reporters out of the clubhouse for a period of time after games, tolerating his spitting and various other on-field flameouts, and looking the other way when he missed two months of one season just so he could get a better divorce deal.

And what was Ted Williams angry about, exactly? Most who knew him well thought the cause was rooted in resentment of his unhappy childhood in San Diego. His mother, May, was a well-known Salvation Army zealot, out all day and much of the night saving souls, leaving Ted and his younger brother, Danny, to fend mostly for themselves. His father, Sam, was a ne'er-do-well who ran a small photo shop, drank excessively, and showed little interest in either of his sons.

And unlike many professional ballplayers—most of them, probably—Ted was embarrassed that he never went to college and had no formal education beyond high school. In 1991, on the fiftieth anniversary of his .406 year, Harvard University wanted to give him an honorary degree, but he turned it down, feeling that he would have been out of place among the intelligentsia in Harvard Yard.

"It's too bad he didn't get to go to college," said Dave Sisler, a Red Sox pitcher in the late '50s and the son of Hall of Famer George Sisler. "He was very, very smart. I went to Princeton, and was around some guys with big IQs. I bet if he took the test, he would have done very well."[19]

Ted certainly was inquisitive. He bought a set of encyclopedias in middle age and couldn't wait to delve into them. He liked verbal jousting and a good argument, which he would often start on a given subject—after marshaling his facts in advance, the better to sandbag his opponent.

But facts were only part of it.

Bob Costas, the television broadcaster, interviewed Ted several times and found him "curious about excellence. 'How do you do what you do? Whatever it is you do, how do you do it?' Curt Gowdy [the longtime Red Sox announcer] said he was the most capable man he ever knew. My [own] impression was if Ted was walking down the street and you said to him, 'Over there is the best carpenter who ever lived,' he'd have gone over and talked to the guy."[20]

Williams would end up repeating some of his parents' mistakes. He was repeatedly unfaithful and an absentee father himself. When Ted was introspective, he'd talk about his failures, according to Steve Brown. "He never talked about his accomplishments. He was humble. He looked at his failures very heavy. His biggest was as a father. He felt he'd never been a good father. He felt he had many areas to make up for."

Added Manuel Herrera, one of Ted's cousins: "Ted's exact words to me were: 'As a father, I struck out. I was for shit as a father. I was never there. I was always gone. I had my commitments. I just didn't do the job.' It was obscure to him. He didn't know how to do it. I think Ted tried to compensate for being a lousy father by trying to help other kids."[21]

Gino Lucero, a cousin on May Williams's side of the family, said, "Ted was a great hero, and he was dysfunctional. When he was pissed, he was lethal. You had this anger thing that he courted, that he embraced. No matter how distasteful it was, he embraced it.

"He was a kid who wanted to fit in, and here's his mom banging tambourines on a street corner and spreading the Gospel. Ted always gravitated to his friends' fathers. Think about it. His dad had a photo business. His dad was never home. His dad was a drinker who showed no interest in Ted. How many men are screwed up because they were never validated by their fathers?"[22]

Manuel Herrera thought Ted hid his fears with anger: "We were driving back from LA once. I said, 'Why were you so hard on the people in Boston?' He says, 'You know, I was afraid.' 'What were you afraid of?' 'I really don't know what I was afraid of, but I didn't want them to know I was poor, didn't have a good home, didn't have the intangibles. I didn't want them to know my private life, so I backed them away with my anger. But despite all that they loved me.'"

The news of Williams's passing hit hardest in Boston, where city flags were ordered flown at half-staff and talk radio began to give voice to a sense of communal grieving and remembering. At the Ted Williams Tunnel, which runs under Boston Harbor and had been dedicated in 1995, condolences were posted on electronic message boards. Newspapers ran updated obituaries of Williams that had been filed years ago; some papers ran special commemorative sections. Wondrous archival footage of the Kid in his prime aired on cable channels and on newscasts across America.

President George W. Bush, the über–baseball fan who had once owned the Texas Rangers and whose father, President George H. W. Bush, revered Ted, said of Williams's nearly five-year-long military service as a Marine Corps pilot in both World War II and Korea: "Ted gave baseball some of its best seasons—and he gave his own best seasons to his country."

Bob Feller, who once had said that trying to get his blazing fastball by Williams was "like trying to get a sunbeam by a rooster," called Ted "the greatest hitter I ever faced." And Yogi Berra, the old Yankees catcher, who used to enjoy needling Williams and trying to distract him as he stood in the batter's box waiting to hit, echoed Feller and scores of others in concluding that Ted "sacrificed his life and career for his country. But he became what he always wanted to be: the greatest hitter ever."

At the National Baseball Hall of Fame and Museum in Cooperstown, New York, events scheduled for the day Ted died were canceled. Officials placed a wreath under Ted's plaque and flowers under his life-size statue, which stands next to Babe Ruth's in the entrance to the museum. Around Major League Baseball, stadiums held moments of silence and lowered their flags. At Fenway Park in Boston that night, where the Red Sox were playing the Detroit Tigers, the grounds crew carved Ted's number, 9, into the left-field grass. A lone bugler played taps at the base of the 9 as a Marine honor guard carried the flag. Both teams stood along the baselines in tribute, the Red Sox with black armbands on their right sleeves. A long-stemmed red rose was placed in the right-field bleachers on seat 21, row 37, section 42, where Ted had hit a massive 502-foot home run in 1946, crushing the straw hat of the man sitting in the seat.

Ty Cobb may have hit for a higher average, and Babe Ruth with more power, but nobody combined power and average the way Williams did. He was a pure hitter—not a fielder or a complete player—and never pretended or aspired to be anything else. "They don't pay off on fielding," as he once explained it.

Williams pioneered the use of a lighter bat—once considered heresy for sluggers—arguing that bat speed, not heft, was the key to power. Over the course of his entire career, Ted studied pitchers intently for their tendencies and quizzed hitters about what a pitcher threw to them in what situation. "Ted always said: 'I don't guess what they throw. I *figure* what they're going to throw,'" said Tom Wright, a backup outfielder and pinch hitter for the Sox from 1948 to 1951.[23]

And his hitting credo was simple: get a good pitch to hit. Critics said he followed this rule to the extreme by refusing to chase a pitch that was even an inch off the strike zone, thereby hurting his team by having its best hitter often pass up an opportunity to drive a runner home. But Ted made the slippery-slope counterargument: that if he chased a pitch an inch from the plate, it would only encourage pitchers to throw two inches outside the zone, then three inches, and so on. History has vindicated Ted's approach, and there is now broad acceptance of the value of reaching base, or having a high on-base percentage—a statistic that was not appreciated and barely even kept in Williams's day.

His eyesight was exceptional, and his command of the strike zone so renowned that opponents often complained that the umpires effectively gave him four strikes. The umps loved Ted because he never showed them up by arguing a call. One oft-told story, perhaps apocryphal, has it that when a catcher beefed about a pitch that had been called a ball, the umpire told him: "Mr. Williams will let you know when your pitcher throws a strike."

A small minority of Ted's teammates was less charitable, and resented his aloof, individualist persona and his temper tantrums, but most liked and admired him enormously, even worshipped him. "You're not going to like everybody or be liked by everybody," said Ted Lepcio, a Red Sox infielder from 1952 to 1959. "Geniuses have their own intricacies, and maybe that best describes Ted. He had a hard time understanding why guys like me couldn't hit better. I think he had a hard time relating to nonperfectionists."[24]

Of Ted's many nicknames, the Kid was his favorite, followed closely by Teddy Ballgame. Johnny Orlando, the longtime Sox clubhouse attendant, had first called Williams the Kid after he arrived at his first spring training in 1938. Never lacking in self-confidence when discussing his hitting prowess, Ted wouldn't hesitate to use either nickname or to refer to himself in the third person.

"He was really in love with himself," said Jimmy Piersall, the splendid

Red Sox outfielder who played from 1952 to 1958. "He'd be in that mirror talking, saying 'Teddy Ballgame'; I think he kissed the mirror right in the clubhouse."[25]

Asked by the writer Cleveland Amory following his .406 year in 1941 what he could possibly do for an encore, Ted was ready with his answer: "I wanna be an immortal," he said.[26]

1

Shame

Ted was always ashamed of his upbringing.

Ashamed of his mother, the Salvation Army devotee and fixture of Depression-era San Diego who seemed far more committed to her street mission than she was to raising her two sons.

Ashamed of his largely absent and indifferent father, who ran a cheesy downtown photo studio that catered to San Diego's sailors and their floozies, and who had a fondness for the bottle.

Ashamed of his younger brother—a gun-toting petty miscreant always one step ahead of the law—who bitterly resented Ted's fame and success.

This sense of shame manifested itself in a reluctance to talk about his family with friends, outsiders, and especially reporters—at least until he was much older and out of baseball.

But there was one aspect of his family life that Ted for many years decided to conceal outright. It was one of the most interesting parts of his background, an important element that did not emerge publicly until near the end of his life: the fact that he was half Mexican—on his mother's side.

Based on Ted's All-American appearance and his white-bread last name, this was an improbable revelation, but that did not stop Hispanic activists from claiming him as one of their own. Not long before he died, Williams became the first inductee into the fledgling Hispanic Heritage Baseball Museum Hall of Fame.

May Williams was the second of eight children born to Pablo Venzor and the former Natalia Hernandez, a native of Chihuahua, Mexico. Pablo, a mason, married Natalia in 1888. Natalia had a brother who worked in the Mexican government, and the family, feeling vulnerable to Pancho Villa and the coming revolution, emigrated from Chihuahua to Santa Barbara, California, in 1907.

As immigrants often do in their effort to assimilate in a new country, some of the Venzors sought to play down their roots south of the border and claimed a Basque, or "Basco," heritage with a strain variously said to have been French or Spanish. May's younger sister Sarah Venzor Diaz, who died in 1999 at the age of ninety-four, went so far as to tell writer Bill Nowlin: "We have no Mexican heritage in our family. We are Basque." And she suggested that attempts by writers to delve into Ted's Mexican background were a slur against him.[1]

Yet genealogical research reveals that May's Mexican roots extended back at least three generations—as far as records could be traced. No records on Pablo's side could be found, but interviews with surviving Venzor family members reveal nothing to indicate that his lineage is not cemented in Mexico as well. The Venzors' sensitivity probably reflected the fact that in Mexico, those with European or Anglo roots are often more socially esteemed than those with "indio," or indigenous, roots. This tension was also evident in the next generation of Venzors—Ted's cousins and May's nieces and nephews.

"We were fruit pickers," said Frank Venzor, son of May's younger brother Paul, speaking of the extended family.

"My dad was no fruit picker," replied Frank's sister Carolyn Ortiz.

"The hell he wasn't," said Frank, who, in a private interview later, sarcastically offered the Venzor family line on their Mexican roots: "We're not fruit pickers per se. We're Basques. We don't come from Mexico. We just happened to be passing through. My uncle Bruno would say, 'I ain't no Mexican! I'm a French Canadian!'"[2]

If those sentiments represented normal immigrant sensitivity to what the Venzors perceived as the garden-variety prejudice of the day, Ted thought he had much more at stake. Coming of age as a baseball player in the 1930s, he decided then to hide his Mexican heritage for fear that deeply ingrained prejudice in baseball would hurt his career. He maintained silence on the topic throughout his tenure with the Red Sox and beyond.

"Ted didn't want anyone to know he was part Mexican," said longtime friend Al Cassidy, the executor of Ted's estate. "It concerned him. He was afraid they wouldn't let him play. He'd say, 'It was an entirely different time back then.'"[3]

In late 1939, after Ted's sensational rookie season with the Red Sox, he returned home to San Diego for a visit, the conquering hero. But when a gaggle of his relatives on the Mexican side of the family gathered to meet him at the train station, Ted beat a hasty retreat after spotting the ragtag group from afar.

According to one of Ted's relatives who was there, Williams took "one look at this big group of Mexicans, and he says, 'Oh, my goodness, my career is down the drain if I'm seen with these people,' and he walks away."[4]

Carolyn Ortiz said that when she was about twelve, "Aunt May called and told us Ted was going to be coming through Santa Barbara and he'd stop for a visit. Well, you would have thought the pope was coming. My aunt Jeanne painted the house inside and out. They had us kids cleaning and making all kinds of preparations. But when the day came, he didn't show up. He never even called. That's the way he was."[5]

Several years later, a host of Venzors traveled to Los Angeles to watch Ted and the Red Sox play an exhibition game against the Los Angeles Angels, then a Pacific Coast League team. When the Venzors hollered and waved at him from the stands, Ted made a motion to indicate that he would see them later, but he never did. "All the family went to root him on and he didn't have the guts to come over and say hi to them," said Ted's cousin Rosalie Larson.[6]

Another cousin, Salvador Herrera, used to spar with Ted about denying his roots. "Ted was a Mexican," Herrera said. "He was embarrassed to be a Mexican. He wanted to be an American, a gringo. I said, 'You asshole, you're a Mexican! Say you're a Mexican and say the Mexicans are the best hitters in the world.' I used to push his button. He laughed and he'd say, 'I'm Basco.' He wanted people to think he was Basque. But he was Mexican, just like me. He just laughed me off. He'd say, 'Don't tell nobody' and hang up the phone."[7]

Years after he retired, Ted did say in his book: "If I had my mother's name, there is no doubt I would have run into problems in those days, the prejudices people had in Southern California."[8] In *My Turn at Bat*, published in 1969, he even misspelled his mother's maiden name as "Venzer," and devoted just one line to her heritage, saying she was "part Mexican and part French." Herrera thought the misspelling was deliberate. "Venzer with an *e*, that's the way Basque people spell it. Hispanics, it's Venzor with an *o*." Yet no reporter developed this theme or dug into his Mexican heritage until Nowlin explored some of the Venzor family lineage in an article for the *Boston Globe Magazine* published in June of 2002, a month before Ted died.*

The Venzors were a colorful collection of cowboys, longshoremen, evangelicals, bricklayers, sandlot ballplayers, and truck drivers. And many of them had serious drinking problems.

The patriarch, Pablo Venzor, was a stonemason and a sheepherder. Occasionally he would also get work as an extra at Flying A Studios, a onetime Hollywood outpost in Santa Barbara, but he finally quit in a huff after being cast as a Mexican peon once too often. Pablo died in 1920 at the age of fifty-two.[9]

His widow, Natalia, never remarried and would outlive her husband by thirty-four years. Natalia chopped wood, rolled her own Bull Durham cigarettes, and never learned to speak or write English. She raised eight children (two others died in childbirth) and also watched over most of them as adults from the family's Santa Barbara base at 1008 Chino Street. Son Bruno lived next door at 1006 Chino, son Paul was at 1002, youngest daughter, Jeanne, lived across the street, and daughter Mary lived several blocks away, at 1716 Chino.

The oldest of Natalia's brood, born in 1889, was Pedro Venzor, known as Pete. A World War I veteran, Pete was a working cowboy at Santa Barbara's Tecolote Ranch, whose owners would stage grand barbecues that attracted California political notables and Hollywood cowboys like Will Rogers, Gene Autry, and Tex Ritter. Several of Pete's siblings worked stints at Tecolote at various times, and Ted visited the ranch as a boy.

Ted's mother, May, was born next, on May 8, 1891, though there is confusion about her place of birth. On her 1913 marriage license, she wrote that she was a native of Mexico. But in 1918, on Ted's birth certificate, she wrote that she was born in El Paso, Texas, though the city has no record of that. (On the 1920 US census she said her native language was Spanish.)

The next Venzor child, Mary, was born in Mexico in 1893, according to her marriage license. Thus it appears more likely that in 1891, the

---

* Salvador Herrera said the Venzors were Mexican through and through. "They were almost Apaches, man," he added, referring to the darkness of their skin. "There are a lot of Hispanics who don't want to be Hispanics. I see that every day." Teresa Cordero Contreras, May Williams's niece, recalled that in 1936, she and her older sister Madeline Cordero were in San Diego to help May out around the house. The Corderos' skin is dark, and after a disagreement one day, Ted angrily told Madeline to "go back to the reservation."

Venzors were still in Mexico and that May was born there, too. In 1895, son Daniel arrived.

May and Mary were "inseparable," according to Mary's daughter Teresa Cordero Contreras, the youngest of twelve children, who said the sisters always stayed in close touch until Mary's life ended tragically in 1943, when she and her daughter Annie were murdered by Annie's husband, who then killed himself.[10]

Daniel was killed in World War I on November 11, 1918, the day the armistice was signed. This made Natalia a Gold Star Mother, and provided benefits that financed the purchase of her home at 1008 Chino in 1920.[11]

The Venzor sibling who had the greatest influence on Ted's baseball development was Saul, born in 1903. He was a longshoreman and an accomplished ballplayer himself, a pitcher who managed the local semi-pro team, the Santa Barbara Merchants. Saul was about six foot five, with arms that dangled down to his knees and huge hands.

When May brought young Ted to Santa Barbara for visits, the boy would gravitate to his uncle Saul and pester him to play catch. Saul would turn these sessions into tough-love tutorials. The driveway at 1008 Chino was slanted; Saul would stand at the top and put Ted at the bottom, and challenge him to stand in there and see if he could hit any of the nineteen different pitches that Saul boasted he threw.

Saul would taunt and tease Ted, belittling his ability. "Ted picked his brain on how to throw a curve," said Manuel Herrera, Salvador's brother. "Saul wouldn't let Ted pitch to him, told him he wasn't mature enough yet." Sometimes Ted would cry in frustration after the driveway sessions, wishing he were bigger and stronger.[12]

Natalia thought her son was being too harsh. "Grandma used to lean out the window and say, 'Leave that kid alone,'" remembered Dee Allen, Saul's daughter. "May would, too. My dad liked to do things and do them right. He would challenge Ted, to teach him."[13]

Ted had seen Saul pitch in a sandlot game once and was duly impressed. Saul had gotten into a bases-loaded, no-outs jam. He then called time, walked over to the opposing team's bench, and took bets that he would get out of the inning without that team scoring a run. Saul collected the bets, then went back out and retired the side without further damage. "Ted was there and saw this, and told the story at a family barbecue," said David Allen, Dee's husband.[14]

According to unconfirmed Venzor family lore, Saul also struck out Babe Ruth in 1935, after Ruth had retired and barnstormed through

Santa Barbara. "Saul did this while he was playing with a bunch of rag-tag Mexicans," said Salvador Herrera with some sense of awe.

Ted was closest to the next Venzor, Sarah, because she had come to San Diego and done yeoman duty helping to raise him as May worked the streets for the Salvation Army, and also because it was Sarah who would take care of May in her final days in Santa Barbara.

After Natalia, the Venzor matriarch, died, Sarah took over the main house at 1008 Chino, along with her husband, Arnold Diaz, a musician who had a mariachi band. Sarah became the backbone of the family and its chief caretaker. She would tend to her brothers when they went off on benders, and after her sister Mary and niece Annie were murdered, Sarah helped raise Annie's son, Manuel Herrera, and his twin sister, Natalie.

For many years, Sarah served as Ted's point of contact with the family. "Ted would say to Sarah, 'I'm coming on such and such a date, and don't you dare tell anyone that I'm there.' He didn't want to see any of the other relatives," said Ruth Gonzalez, May's first cousin.[15]

If Ted called for Sarah and someone else answered the phone, he couldn't keep track of who was who. "Ted called one day out of the blue," Dee Allen recalled. "'Hello, this is Ted; who's this?' 'This is Dee.' 'Who's Dee?' 'I'm Saul's daughter.' He asked what Sarah needed. Whatever I felt needed to be done — a new roof, windows, a wooden fence — I got bids for all that stuff and sent them to his office. Ted was a hard person to get into. You could only get so close. He wouldn't allow it."

Ted also enjoyed his uncle Bruno Venzor because they both liked to fish. Bruno was an excitable, happy-go-lucky sort who had a stutter. He drove a cement truck and also played some baseball, but not as seriously as his brother Saul. Once, when Bruno was pitching, he kept laughing at the hitters, and an irritated Saul yanked him from the game. Bruno was active in the Elks club and liked to dress up in Western duds. Arnold Diaz called him the sheriff of Chino Street.[16]

May's life calling, superseding all else, was to be a foot soldier in the Salvation Army. Founded in England in 1865, the Army is an evangelical Christian group that considers itself a church but functions as a relief and social service organization whose adherents forswear drinking, smoking, drugs, and gambling. It rose to prominence by targeting and converting alcoholics, the homeless, drug addicts, unwed mothers, and prostitutes to Christianity. These were the kinds of people May tended to in a colorful mission that ranged from San Diego south to Tijuana and north to Los Angeles.

May was a beloved figure, a star of the street. Indeed, in San Diego during the Depression, "no woman was better known than Salvation May," wrote Joe Hamelin of the *San Diego Union* in a 1980 series the newspaper published about Ted. "In Salvation Army bonnet and flowing garb, she patrolled the streets in the '20s and '30s, collecting for the poor. Some thought her almost saintly. Others thought her eccentric, or simply a 'nut.' . . . She knew everyone, and everyone knew her. She would take a downtown office building, start on the top floor, and work her way down without missing an office. There was no tougher job in Depression time than raising funds for charity. No one was better at her craft than May."[17]

According to Alice Rasmussen, a colleague of May's in the Army: "She knew all the people in all the right places, and a lot of people in the wrong places, too. She had access to the mayor, the chief of police, business leaders, and she would go into the red light district—there was white slavery in those days—and minister there as well."

Kenny Bojens, who eventually became a sports columnist for the local paper, would run into May as she trolled the downtown bars making collections. "I used to run around with a legend of sorts, Gentleman Joe Morgan, the *Union*'s police reporter," Bojens said in the 1980 *Union* series. "May used to call us her 'Sunshine Boys.' I remember this one night we were in a night club, the College Inn at Fourth and C, and we were flat broke. May came in, said, 'How are my little Sunshine Boys tonight?' and God-blessed the dickens out of us like she'd always do, and asked for a donation. I said, 'May, we don't even have the price of a beer,' which in those days was about 15 cents. And she reached down into her purse and said, 'Well, let the Army buy you one.' "

Another colleague was Alice Psaute, a lifelong Salvationist who made the rounds with May when she was a young woman. "We'd go to prize-fights, and in intermissions we'd go around with a tambourine and try to collect money," Psaute said. "The smoke was so thick you could cut it with a knife. We'd also go to the county jail for meetings on Sunday morning. I played the violin. It made them better so they could get out sooner. May went to the jail many times."[18]

So popular and influential was May that in 1924, John D. Spreckels, the richest man in San Diego, quietly paid off the note on the Williamses' house at 4121 Utah Street, where Ted grew up, in the city's North Park section. May had acquired the six-room house in December of 1923 for $4,000, agreeing to $20 monthly payments, plus interest, until the note was paid off. But by August 1, 1924, the note was discharged, courtesy of

Spreckels, a sugar-refining industrialist, philanthropist, and publisher of both the *San Diego Union* and the *San Diego Evening Tribune*.

When Ted became a star, May would unabashedly trade on his celebrity for the greater good of the Army, telling startled bank or bar patrons, "I'm Ted Williams's mother. Empty your pockets."[19] Worse, as far as Ted was concerned, she'd work Lane Field after he signed his first pro contract to play for the San Diego Padres of the Pacific Coast League, collecting money in the stands with her tambourine.

Bill Starr, a catcher with the Padres in 1937, told writer Ed Linn about "the time one of the players asked Ted if he knew that his mother had been walking around the stands collecting money and telling everybody Ted Williams was her son. Ted looked down at the floor and didn't say anything for a long time. And then he said, 'I know. She embarrasses me.' The whole clubhouse went absolutely silent. Everybody felt so bad for him."[20]

"I was embarrassed about my home, embarrassed that I never had quite as good clothes as some of the kids, embarrassed that my mother was out in the middle of the damn street all the time," Williams wrote in *My Turn at Bat*. "Until the day she died she did that, and it always embarrassed me, and God knows I respected her and loved her."[21]

May had entered the Salvation Army training college in Chicago in 1909, when she was eighteen. She graduated in 1911, was appointed a lieutenant, and sent to Hawaii. She made captain in 1912, but after marrying Ted's father, Samuel Stuart Williams, in 1913, she was demoted back to envoy status because her husband was not a Salvationist—she'd "married out," as the Army called it, and therefore could no longer be an officer.

May Williams was lean and tall—about five foot ten. She won awards for selling the most copies of the Army's newspaper, *War Cry*. She was an accomplished musician, playing piano, guitar, and banjo as well as cornet in the Army band. She was an eccentric presence, sometimes wearing sunglasses in church, as if she were a street celebrity. She'd use magic— making a quarter disappear in a sleight-of-hand trick—to get people's attention before asking them for a donation. Eventually, the *San Diego Sun* editorialized that "to thousands of San Diegans, rich and poor, Mrs. Williams IS the Salvation Army."

Sam Williams was born on April 5 of either 1886 or 1888—records conflict—in Ardsley, New York, today a suburb of New York City. He was the only child born to the former Elizabeth Miller and Nicholas Williams, a barber.

They divorced, and Nicholas Williams later married a British woman, Margaret Higgins. Nicholas and Margaret produced three daughters, all born in Yonkers, New York: Veacy, who was also known as Mae and Vivian, born in 1893; Alice, born in 1895; and Effie, born in 1899 — these were Sam Williams's half sisters and Ted's aunts.

Effie Williams married John Smith, a short, stocky fireman who worked in Mount Vernon, New York, in Westchester County. In the summer of 1939, his rookie year with the Red Sox, Ted, on instructions from his mother, came to visit his aunt Effie when the team was in New York playing the Yankees. Smith jumped at the chance to bring Ted down to the firehouse to meet the fellas. Edward Donovan, whose father worked for the department, was there the day Ted came.

"I was fifteen," said Donovan, recounting the moment with rich detail, as if it had happened yesterday. "My father called the house and said, 'Brother—they called me Brother—come down; I want you to meet a ballplayer. This is Ted Williams.' Ted shook my hand and he said, 'When you gonna get in shape, kid?' I was kind of fat."[22]

It was a big event. All the firemen congregated around. Ted walked behind a fire engine, picked up a broom, and started swinging it. It was a beautiful swing, Donovan thought. Ted answered questions with "Yes, sir" or "No, sir." The firemen, mostly Yankees fans, asked Williams if he thought the Red Sox had a chance to win that year. Ted said, "Oh, yeah, I think we're gonna win."

"Ted charmed everybody. It was what you call awe-inspiring. He was so tall! And skinny! I don't know how he could hit those home runs. I don't think he was more than a hundred and sixty-five pounds."

Whenever he could in the ensuing years, Donovan would drive down to Yankee Stadium to see Ted play, armed with insider tidbits from John Smith, such as which pitcher gave Ted the toughest time (Ted had confided that it was Eddie Lopat, of the White Sox and later the Yankees). "For a dollar and ten cents we'd get great seats. Hot dogs were a nickel."

Ted seemed to like his uncle John, who was obsessed with keeping his firehouse, Engine 6, clean. He also liked to play the horses. According to Donovan, in 1949, Ted bought John a new white Ford. John went to Boston to pick it up and gave Eddie a ride in it when he got home. The car had plates that read ES41. ES stood for Effie Smith, and the 41 was a nod to Ted's .406 year. "Ted would always ask how Aunt Effie was doing," Donovan said. "He really cared for his aunt. He always called no matter where he was."

But of his three aunts, Ted was closest to Alice, according to Roselle Romano, a Miami Beach retiree who lived near the sisters and got to know them well when they moved to Florida from Westchester County later in life.

"Alice was a spitfire," Romano said. "She'd curse you out like a sailor. Vivian and Effie were very much alike. Two ladies. But Alice! What a mouth she had."[23]

Alice told Romano that Ted had spent extended time with her in Mount Vernon as a young man. "He was always with Alice. They would all go into Manhattan to go clubbing. Alice said, 'He came to me. When he left California he came to me.' That's exactly how she put it. They had a lot of his plaques in their house."

Alice would also go out and visit Ted in San Diego. In October of 1941, she was photographed with May outside Lane Field, where Ted, fresh off his .406 season, was on a barnstorming tour with Jimmie Foxx, his Red Sox teammate. Romano recalled that Alice returned home from one trip to San Diego with a dog named Cap that was part coyote. "He was a nasty thing," she said.

Alice had been the first of the sisters to move to Miami Beach, where she bought a house on 181st Street with her husband, Phil Sheridan, a retired New York City police captain. Then, in the late 1950s, John and Effie decided to come down, too, and bought a place on 177th Street, two houses away from Roselle and her husband, Gennaro, known as Gin. The Romanos were from Fort Lee, New Jersey, just over the George Washington Bridge from New York.

John and Effie only used their house in the winter, so Effie invited her sister Veacy, whom Romano called Vivian, to use the place when she and John weren't there. Vivian moved down permanently after her husband, a Con Edison machinist named Tom Grey, died.

The three sisters were petite, none taller than five foot three or so. "John had an Oldsmobile," said Roselle. "Four doors. John, Effie, Alice, and Vivian sat in the front seat. That's how small they all were."

Alice was a brassy blonde, Effie a prim redhead. Vivian dyed her hair red. Effie, though the youngest of the three sisters, was the first to die, in 1971. Vivian died in 1978, Alice in 1984. After they passed, Roselle learned that the sisters were all actually ten years older than they had always said they were.

They were proud of Ted, their famous nephew, but didn't drop his name. They allowed it to just come up in conversation.

"My husband almost fell off the chair," Roselle said. "One day they start talking about Ted Williams. They said he was their brother's child, and their brother had left New York to go to San Diego. They were all crazy for Ted. They'd go down and visit him in the Keys. Three or four times a year, maybe. They were very glad to see one another. Ted to me looks exactly like Vivian. They'd stay for a few days. They were very excited when Ted had his first child."

Roselle said the sisters thought May Williams was an overbearing wife to their brother, Sam, and that she neglected Ted and his brother. "They said she was an absolute horror. They came back, and they were telling me Ted was so infuriated because him and his brother were out in the dark playing baseball because his mother never came home to cook for them. They were very fond of their brother, Sam. They said he was kind and nice. They thought May overpowered him, and him and the boys had to fend for themselves."

The sisters didn't discuss their childhoods much, other than to say that their mother had died shortly after giving birth to Effie and that their father never remarried. In various documents, Effie and Vivian said they worked as bookkeepers, while Alice described herself as a carpet weaver. "They said they were English," Roselle said. "They bought everything fresh every day. Nobody could cook like those girls. The only thing in the freezer was Howard Johnson's coffee ice cream. Some days we drove to Fort Lauderdale and we'd go to a fashion show. And we'd have lunch. They were fashionable. They had more money than me. In the afternoon we used to sit on the screen porch and have light conversation. They thought I lived in a circus. Nobody came to their house unless they were invited. I'm Italian—people always in and out."

Of the three sisters, only Alice drove. One night in Miami Beach, she drove the wrong way down a one-way street. After that, she lost her license, and Roselle had to drive the sisters around wherever they went. Alice grew eccentric as she aged, and took to eating a box of candy before dinner. "They were little square cakes with icing, like an inch square," said Roselle.

Ted wrote in his autobiography that his father ran away from home at the age of sixteen to enlist in the Army, and—impossibly—served in the Spanish-American War. Sam's military records show he enlisted in December of 1904, which would have made him sixteen, but if he was born in 1886, the earliest of the birth dates that he variously cited, he obviously could not have served in the Spanish-American War, which was fought in 1898. Nevertheless, Sam was smitten by Teddy Roosevelt, and over the years, either flatly told people he had been one of Roosevelt's Rough Riders at San Juan Hill or failed to correct the impression that he'd been there.

Although Sam hadn't been in Cuba, he had served in the Philippines seven years later, part of the Fourteenth Cavalry's drive to quash the Moro Rebellion. There he saw combat and served under Major General Leonard Wood, who had been Roosevelt's commanding officer at San Juan Hill. Thus the Rough Rider braggadocio, while unfounded, was at least rooted in a link to Wood, the man who really did lead the charge up the hill.

Sam's infatuation with Roosevelt was apparently the inspiration for his choice of Teddy as the true first name for his older son. He passed on his own name, Samuel, for Ted's middle name.* According to his military records, Sam was just five foot five and three-quarters, so Ted would eventually tower over him by nearly a foot. "Years later I used to kid my dad when we walked together: 'Come on, Shorty, let's keep up,'" Ted wrote.[24]

Sam's stint in the Army was his heyday. "I remember he had a sword, a big saber he used to let me swing, and he always liked to shoot guns and ride horses," Ted wrote. "I've got pictures of him: a little guy, posing behind a horse that was lying down, getting ready to shoot over the horse, and another of him at attention, standing real straight with a bugle slapped against his side."[25]

Sam made corporal in October of 1907, two months before he was discharged. He liked the Army so much he decided to reenlist for a second three-year tour in 1908, drawing tamer duty this time — in Hawaii. It was there that he met May Venzor, the budding Salvationist.

Following his discharge in 1911, Sam, perhaps trying to impress May, enrolled in a Salvation Army training program. It was a bad match, and he soon dropped out, but May didn't hold it against him. They kept courting, and before long, he asked for her hand. May accepted — at great sacrifice to her career. In the scheme of things, May decided that didn't matter, so on May 13, 1913, she and Sam were wed in Santa Barbara.

---

* In another biographical error in *My Turn at Bat,* Ted wrote that the Samuel "was for my mother's brother who was killed the last day of World War I." Actually, that was Daniel Venzor; May had no brother named Samuel.

The couple first lived in Los Angeles, where Sam took a job as a street-car conductor. By 1915, they had moved to San Diego, where Sam opened a photo studio downtown, at 820 5th Street, in a second-floor walk-up above a restaurant. He took passport shots and catered to sailors and their girlfriends. At least at first, May was involved in the business, helping her husband with various chores.

Three years later, on August 30, 1918, Ted was born at San Diego's Sunshine Maternity Home. Before Ted, May had had two other children, both of whom apparently died at birth.* On Ted's birth certificate, his name was originally written "Teddy Samuel Williams," but the typed "Teddy" is crossed out and replaced with a handwritten "Theodore." Ted said he had later done this himself because he did not like the name Teddy. And the original birth date was typed in as August 20, but the "20" is crossed out and replaced with a handwritten "30." August 20 may have been the correct date, since the attending physician, J. M. Steade, filled out his portion of the certificate the next day, August 21. Yet compounding the confusion as Ted came of baseball age were references in the San Diego papers to his birthday falling on October 30. May had tried to straighten out the mix-up—at least for the record—years earlier, in 1920, by filing an affidavit with the county clerk, saying that the correct date of birth was August 30 and that "the child's name should be given as 'Theodore Samuel Williams.'"[26] Ted would later explain to *Boston Globe* sportswriter Harold Kaese that he was born in late August but moved his birth date back to October because he did not want the distraction of celebrating a birthday during baseball season.[27]

When May and Sam Williams arrived in San Diego in 1915, the city was a benign backwater with a population of about fifty-five thousand and a downtown fraying at the edges. San Diego could lay claim to being the birthplace of California: in 1769 the Franciscan priest Junípero Serra made it the first European settlement in the area and built a beautiful network of Spanish missions. But the tides of history and geography worked against the city's emergence as an important political or economic center. The end of the Mexican-American War in 1848 established the international boundary just south of San Diego, the gold rush passed the city by, and the railroads found San Francisco and Los Angeles to be more felicitous end points for their east-west lines. Until 1919, San Diego had to be content with just a spur line from Los Angeles.

---

* On Ted's birth certificate, replying to the question "Number of children born to this mother, including present birth," May had written "3." And to the next question, "Number of children of this mother now living," she wrote "1."

That year, the city finally got its rail link to the East. None of the railroads had been willing to take on the prospect of laying tracks across the hazardous mountains and gorges rising out of San Diego, but in 1905, John D. Spreckels, the industrialist-philanthropist who paid off the Williams family's mortgage in appreciation of May's Salvation Army work, underwrote the project. It took fourteen years to build, at a loss of many millions of dollars, and came to be called the Impossible Railroad. But by the time it was built, the connection with the eastern United States seemed moot, as Los Angeles and San Francisco were much better established centers of commerce, and the automobile was emerging as a more convenient mode of travel with the establishment of a coast-to-coast highway system.

Still, San Diego was given a substantial shot in the arm and international attention in 1915 when it hosted a world's fair to help celebrate the completion of the Panama Canal. Officially known as the Panama-California Exposition, the fair drew tens of thousands of people to see the grand neo-Spanish buildings designed by the architect Bertram Goodhue and the transformation of fourteen-hundred-acre Balboa Park, named for Vasco Núñez de Balboa, the first white man known to have crossed the Isthmus of Panama and sight the Pacific.[28]

Teddy Roosevelt, William Jennings Bryan, Thomas Edison, and Henry Ford all came to San Diego for the celebration. Balboa Stadium was built, along with museums and key elements of urban infrastructure that served as a boon to economic development. A menagerie of animals left over from the fair would become the nucleus for the famed San Diego Zoo, the world's largest. The exposition was so successful it lasted for two years, through the end of 1916.

The United States' entry into World War I the following year brought a spike in military activity in San Diego with the opening of Camp Kearny and facilities at North Island and Fort Rosecrans. The Navy had built a coaling station at Point Loma in 1907 and used that as a foundation to greatly expand its presence. Later, the Navy choose San Diego as the base for the Pacific Fleet. A Marine Corps base was launched in 1919 and the Naval Training Center in 1921.

The fair ignited a "smokestacks versus geraniums" debate about how the city should develop, but it was the military and tourists—attracted by San Diego's near-perfect temperate climate and its proximity to Mexico—who would shape the city more than anything else. San Diego promoted its ties to a romantic Spanish past and collaborated on development projects with neighboring Tijuana, the better to position itself as the gateway to Mexico. Tijuana became a major tourist attraction during Prohibition, thanks to Agua Caliente, its luxurious casino resort, which featured a racetrack and a championship golf course. Hundreds of thousands of Southern Californians seeking the high life passed through San Diego on their way to Tijuana, the Las Vegas of its day, until Mexico banned gambling in 1935. Many tourists liked enough of what they saw in San Diego, though, and the city's population nearly doubled in the '20s, reaching about 148,000 by 1930.

"When I was a kid," Ted would tell the writer David Halberstam in 1988, "I'd see a falling star and I'd say, 'Make me the greatest hitter who ever lived.' "[29]

The center of young Williams's world then, a refuge from the angst and sadness of home, was the University Heights playground. Also known as North Park, it was located just a block and a half from his house, and for seven years, when he was between the ages of nine and sixteen, Ted spent part of virtually every day there. North Park had lights and stayed open till 9:00 p.m. — a good thing, given his parents' prolonged absences.

The proprietor of the playground, the man who would become the most important baseball influence in Williams's early life, was Rod Luscomb. Luscomb was eleven years older than Ted. Blond, about six foot three, two-hundred-plus pounds, and friendly, he'd played baseball at the University of Arizona and briefly as a pro in the Class D California State League: Williams would recall him as "my first real hero."[30]

Luscomb at first paid little attention to the tall and awkward boy who kept following him around, asking questions about pitching and hitting. But he was impressed when he saw the kid hit — the smooth hip turn, the strong roll of the wrists.

When Rod did his chores around the playground, Ted would be nipping at his heels, all chatter. "He hung [on] to me like a little puppy," Luscomb told *Time* magazine's Ed Rees in 1950, in an interview that was part of nearly one hundred pages of unpublished notes and files that Rees and several other correspondents assembled for an April 10, 1950, *Time* cover story on Williams.* "He would look up and say with his eyes full of excitement, 'Hey, Lusk, if I get big arms like Jimmie Foxx, and I

---

* The files were in Ted's papers, which were made available to me.

could throw like DiMaggio and run like Jesse Owens, think I'd make the big leagues?'" Sure he could, Rod would tell him. But then Ted would point to his bony arms and say, "How in hell am I gonna get big arms?" Push-ups, Rod would advise—and Ted would do them, commencing a routine of fifty to one hundred fingertip push-ups a day that he would follow until the end of his professional career. He'd also squeeze a handball constantly to strengthen his wrists.*

One day, when he was about twelve or thirteen and Luscomb was wetting down the infield, Ted, all uncorrupted bluster, said to him: "Lusk, some day when I get a million bucks in the big leagues, I'm gonna build myself a ballpark with cardboard fences all around. Then I'm gonna knock 'em down with homers."[31]

The park helped provide some structure to Williams's life, given the infrequent presence of his parents. But there were limits. Luscomb would arrive at the park at 2:30, and a few times, he noticed that Ted was already there. That meant the boy was playing hooky, since school didn't get out until three o'clock. Ted tried to explain that he was only trying to get a jump on the other kids so he could get in more at bats, but Luscomb bluntly told Ted he'd have nothing to do with him if he cut school again.

Ted obeyed, but he did have one other ethical lapse. Once, when Luscomb was getting out of the shower, he overheard Ted and a pal discussing whether to steal a new baseball they had spotted in Rod's locker. When the friend went ahead and swiped it, at Ted's urging, Rod walked around the corner, caught them red-handed, and banned Ted from the playground for two weeks.[32]

Ted and Luscomb played a game on the handball court they called big league. They'd hit a softball against a wall, getting singles, doubles, triples, or homers depending on where they hit it and how well they placed their shots. But what most interested Ted was extended batting practice—hardball—and Luscomb was happy to indulge him. They would play nine-inning games, and each would pitch to the other for three innings at a time. Imaginary fielders would be in their designated positions. A ball landing beyond a designated line would be a single, farther out a double, farther than that a triple, and out of the park was a home run. The score was usually close—6–5, 4–3, 7–5, or 3–2—and

---

* Williams told *Sports Illustrated* for its August 1, 1955, issue: "There wasn't anything about it that I was going to be a great baseball player or anything in the future. It was just something that I liked to do. I was a funny looking kid, a string bean, a terribly scrawny looking thing. I certainly had no muscles. My mother used to get notes from the health officer, 'This kid is underweight; tonsils need checking.'"

each player won about an equal number of games. They pushed each other and threw hard. Rod liked to exploit a weakness of Ted's at the time—a slow, inside curve—and Ted would bark at him when he threw the pitch: "Hell, Lusk, get back to the bull pen and warm up!"[33]

Sometimes, Ted would hit Luscomb so hard that Rod would try and cheat in a little and move closer to the plate to reduce the distance he had to throw. When Ted noticed, he'd drill a couple back through the box, forcing Luscomb to retreat.

"I was so eager to play, and hitting a home run off Rod Luscomb in those makeshift games was as big a thrill for me as hitting one in a regular game," Ted wrote. "We played for blood."[34]

These early one-on-one jousts with Luscomb were central to Ted's emerging view of baseball as more of an individual test of will than a competition between two teams. "I'm sure that during this time the little game between the pitcher and the batter was coming to light for me," he wrote. "It's so important, the real crux of baseball, and so many hitters seem to miss it. You're not playing the Cincinnati Reds or the Cleveland Indians, you're playing that pitcher—Johnny Vander Meer, Bob Feller, Bob Lemon, whoever he is—and he's the guy you concentrate on."[35]

Williams always believed there was no such thing as a natural hitter. Yes, you had to have good eyesight and strong wrists, but after that, there was only one way to really be great: through hard work and practice.

"I would never have gained a headline for hitting if I hadn't kept everlastingly at it, and thought of nothing else the year round," Ted told Joe Cashman, Red Sox beat writer for the *Boston Evening American* and *Daily Record* in July of 1941, during the midst of his .406 season. "I never passed up an opportunity to watch the leading Coast League hitters in action. I read every word of advice about hitting uttered by big league stars. And when I wasn't sleeping or eating I was practicing swinging. If I didn't have a bat, I'd take any piece of wood, or make a bat of paper and swing it. If I didn't have a ball to swing at, I swung at stones, marbles and even peanuts and pop corn thrown at me by pals."[36]

Or he'd just swing with an imaginary bat. If he passed a storefront that had a big, clear window, he liked to stop, take a few swings, and check his reflection out. When he did this, he'd be in his own world, oblivious to the merchants inside bemused by the vainglorious displays. The truth was, Ted didn't want to just *be* good. He wanted to *look* good, too. "I wanted to have a great-looking swing," he acknowledged. "That was important to me. Everybody wants to look good."[37]

The Williams-Luscomb sessions attracted notice. Ted's pals would often gather and watch, as would some Triple-A players on their way to the majors, such as Earle Brucker, Lee Stine, and the Coscarart brothers, Pete and Joe, all of whom lived in San Diego.

In the heat of the competition, Ted might pop off and snarl at Luscomb. "We'd argue, boy, we'd argue," Ted wrote. "I was always the kind of kid who spoke his mind, just blurted it out, without thinking of the consequences or what anybody might think."[38]

But Luscomb didn't think Ted impudent. "He always wore a grin on his face," Rod told *Time*'s Rees. "That's the first thing I think of now when I recall him as a boy. Also, I greatly admired the qualities he had—aside from his ball-playing abilities. Honest, good-natured and loyal to his friends—he's a lot better man than many. He was pretty sensitive too. Things would bother him deep down, although he wouldn't let on. I'm sure a lot of his trouble with the press can be laid to this."

Luscomb didn't think Ted was a leader. Or a showboater. He seemed to take as much delight in hitting a homer off Rod in their private games as he would hitting a drive in a weekend sandlot game before a few hundred fans. He did what Luscomb told him to do. When Rod said he thought Ted was going to the movies too much, that his eyes might get strained, Ted stopped going—unless a movie starring Olivia de Havilland, his favorite actress, was playing. And when Luscomb suggested he eat more to fill out his scrawny frame, Ted went on an eating binge that lasted for years, though to no great effect.

When Ted finally left the playground for high school and pro ball, Luscomb picked up the bats his pupil had used and was struck by one thing. All the dirt smudges from the balls striking the bats were in the same place: the thickest part of the bat on the side opposite the label, at the heart of the sweet spot. In the seven years they played almost daily, Luscomb said he had never seen Ted break a bat by hitting a ball in the wrong place.[39]

Williams would never forget Rod. When he got to the big leagues, he would write Luscomb letters that included diagrams of the various ballparks he was playing in and where some of his hits had landed. And he would complain about the fickle fans who cheered him one minute and booed him the next. When Rod got Parkinson's disease in the 1960s, Ted sent him letters of cheer and sympathy; in 1966, while being inducted into the Hall of Fame, he cited Rod's role in his development, and in 1969, Ted sent his mentor a warmly inscribed copy of his autobiography. Luscomb died in 1977, a letter from Williams taped to the wall near his bed in a San Diego hospital.[40]

May didn't altogether discourage Ted's interest in sports. She bought him a baseball glove (a Bill Doak model), a shotgun, and a tennis racket. But she hoped sports would be Ted's hobby, not his passion, and she tried to hold the line as his baseball increasingly encroached on her religious realm.[41] When he turned six, in a ceremony similar to a baptism, May had had Ted formally "dedicated" to the Army, hoping he would follow in her footsteps and make a career of it. For a while, Ted was a "Corps cadet" and participated in a program for Salvationist youth that involved Bible study, going to group meetings with other kids, and attending Sunday services. But Ted would hide whenever it was time to go to church, and May couldn't find him. And by the time he was nine, Ted, while swinging a stick or a bat, would repeatedly say to his mother, "This is the way I'm gonna do it, Mom. I'm gonna be a Babe Ruth." Not surprisingly, when he came home with the blasphemous idea that he could earn $5 a game by playing ball on Sundays for a local club called, of all things, the Texas Liquor House team, she vetoed the plan with fury. "No Sunday playing, and no tie-up with demon-rum!" May said.[42] For a long time, Ted respected her wishes—in the face of ridicule from his pals—until finally May relented and allowed him to play on Sundays—as long as it was not for the liquor team. Ted started playing for another sandlot club for $3 a game.

This ballpark allowance did not mean a broader recess from his mother's convictions. May took Ted on her street rounds, insisting that he march in the Army band.

"Oh, how I hated that," Ted recalled. "I never wore a uniform or anything, but I was right at that age when a kid starts worrying about what other kids might think, especially a gawky introverted kid like me, and I was just so ashamed. Today I'd be proud to walk with those people, because they are truly motivated, but then I'd stand behind the bass drum, trying to hide so none of my friends would see me." He said the dedication ceremony simply "didn't take. The thing was I had to go so damn often. I just hated it.

"My mother was strictly Salvation Army. As a result, strictly non-family." She "was gone all day and half the night, working the streets.... These were Depression years, and we had a housekeeper I think we paid seven or eight dollars a week, I forget exactly, but none of them lasted long and they were all lousy, couldn't get a job anywhere else, the bottom of the barrel."

Ted wrote that he gave May "a lot of credit" for working so hard and tirelessly helping others, "but the thing a kid remembers is that he never saw his mother or father very much. Many nights my brother, Danny, and I would be out on that porch past ten o'clock waiting for one of them to come home. I was maybe eight at the time, and Danny was six."[43]

That was the key point. For May, charity did not begin at home. She was so absorbed with doing the Lord's work, tending to others, that she neglected her own two sons and husband, causing resentment against her to fester in all three of them.

Bobby Doerr—the Hall of Fame Red Sox second baseman, a dear friend and teammate of Ted's—remembered that when they played together on the 1936 Padres, Ted envied Doerr's stable home life in Los Angeles. "We'd play all day games and afterwards he'd say, 'Well, I guess I'll go home and scramble eggs for supper,'" Doerr said. "There'd be nobody home. When we came to Los Angeles, and he had dinner with us, he used to love my mother and father. He told me how lucky I was to have parents like that. My dad was always talking with Ted. Ted thought that was impressive—that anyone would give him the time of day. He didn't get the kind of love that he could see we had in our family."[44]

"His biggest thing was the hunger he went to bed with, literally, because his mother was busy feeding orphans in Tijuana," said Steve Brown, the Florida filmmaker and fisherman who became a good friend to Ted at the end of his life. "His mother never showed him love, yet she showed those street urchins love like you wouldn't believe. That's what made him turn against religion. Any God that could have a woman so on fire for street urchins and couldn't have her tuck in her own kids and even feed them—he didn't want any part of that kind of God."[45]

But May was stubborn. "She thought she was right that she was going to preach the Word, and if her kids weren't going to listen, too bad," said Rosalie Larson, May's niece. "I think if I were the kids, I would have resented that."

Another niece, Dee Allen, had a different take: May didn't see it as neglect if the Lord wanted her to put the unfortunate first. "I don't think May saw she was neglecting her sons, because she was doing something for God."

John Cordero, son of Mary Venzor Cordero—the third of the Venzor siblings, born two years after May—dreaded the visits to San Diego because he said May would exploit him and his brother and look down on them because their skin was so dark.

"My aunt May was that way," said Cordero. "She'd call my mother and say, 'Can I use your boys down here for a couple weeks?' We'd go down and mow the lawns and clean up. Their yard was awful. The grass was seven or eight inches tall. Hedges were awful, the fence was falling down. They had a dog at one time. A German shepherd. They got rid of him because he was too mean. The garbagemen couldn't get in there. I told my mom, 'I can't stand my aunt May.' She said, 'Why?' I said because May's neighbor would ask who we were, and she'd tell her, 'They're not family, they're friends of Danny.' Then she'd point down toward Tijuana, as if we were from Mexico. She'd say to us, 'Don't call me aunt, call me May.'"[46]

Cordero said Ted would avoid talking to him and his brother. "We slept in the room with Danny. My brother and I slept in one twin bed; Danny was in the other. Ted had a new room that had been built in the back. We'd be in the kitchen. Ted wouldn't come in. If we were in the backyard and he was going to go out, he'd go out the front door. He wanted to avoid us. We never saw him. At nighttime, he'd stay in his room." And Ted's father was not much better. "My uncle Sam would come home. Nothing. 'Hi, Uncle Sam.' 'Don't call me Uncle Sam.'"

When May would visit her family in Santa Barbara, after Ted was all grown up, her brothers and sisters had so many children and grandchildren she couldn't keep track of who was who. "'Now, whose child is this?' she'd say when she met anyone in the family," said Salvador Herrera, whose mother was May's niece. "'Now, how are you, sonny boy? Are you going to church regularly? Do you believe in the Word?' May would talk to you. In her talk she'd bring up stuff about the Bible. In Corinthians it says so and so. She'd be telling you what life is all about, how you should be in the face of the Lord. May was staunch."

She'd drive the two-hundred-odd miles from San Diego to Santa Barbara in her old Packard and arrive tooting the horn. She'd tell stories about her famous son, recite the Bible, and play hymns on her guitar, leading sing-alongs.

By early 1950, May was starting to behave erratically. One day, neighbors noticed her watering her lawn barefoot while in her pajamas. And she told *Time* that Danny was actually a better ballplayer than Ted, and that he would soon be playing for the Padres. Ted, she suggested, owed his success more to God than anything else. It was "God's will that he

become a baseball player, and the reason he is so good is that God coop-
erates," May said.

Salvador's brother, Manuel Herrera, lived with May in Santa Barbara
during the last few years of her life. He'd talk to her before she went to
sleep, and she'd tell him the stories of her life.

"She told me, 'Yes, precious, I was the angel of Tijuana.' She had one
thing in her life: to save the world from sin," Manuel said. "We sang old
Baptist hymns. Her favorite was 'The Old Rugged Cross.' Someone
tried to play a rock 'n' roll song once, and she said, 'No, precious, we
don't want to hear that.' She could kill you with kindness and that smile
from cheek to cheek. She could penetrate your soul."[47]

When Manuel asked May to tell him how she came to be called the
angel of Tijuana, she told him it was because she had once convinced
Tijuana's jail commander to release a group of thirteen- and fourteen-
year-old American boys being held in filthy conditions.

When May died in 1961, at the age of seventy, Ted flew in and took
charge of the funeral arrangements, limiting those who could attend the
Salvation Army service to just her siblings. This irritated Manuel and
other members of the extended Venzor clan who knew and loved May
and wanted to pay their respects. Ted took over the top floor of the Santa
Barbara Inn so no one would bother him. He received one of May's
brothers, Bruno Venzor, in his room for breakfast. Bruno brought along
his son, Daniel. When they entered Ted's room, they found him in his
undershorts, quietly swinging a bat, gazing at his reflection in the window. "He found it relaxing, I guess," said Daniel Venzor, Ted's cousin.

After the funeral, Ted drove his rented white Ford Galaxie over to a
Venzor family reception on Chino Street to hold court with "the Mexicans," as Ted referred to the Venzors privately. Manuel remembered an
emotional scene in which Ted and his uncle Saul Venzor talked about the
old days when Saul pitched to Ted in the driveway. "Saul said, 'You did
pretty good in the big time.' They smiled at each other. 'I knew what you
taught me,' Ted said. Saul asked him what a palm ball, fork, and a split
pitch were. Ted said, 'That's a damn good question. All they are is curves.'"

Later, when Ted went through May's personal effects at her home in
San Diego, he tore up every family picture he came across, Manuel said.
"That was there: hate, unhappiness. Later I sent him a picture of May
when she was a young girl with her Salvation Army guitar. He thanked
me for it."[48]

If he'd considered it further, Ted might have concluded that he was
indebted to his mother in some ways. May's dedication—obsession,

even—with the Army at the expense of her family was similar to Ted's relentless drive to be the best hitter in the world—to the exclusion of everything else in his life.

"May and Ted had the same single-minded determination to do what they had to do, and everything else suffered as a result," said Ted's nephew and namesake, Ted Williams. "But that determination gave them the strength to overcome obstacles."

There was also Ted's compassion—his willingness to do most anything to help a sick child or others who were down on their luck. Jim Vinick, a Springfield, Massachusetts, businessman who acquired the rights to make a movie of Williams's life, said Ted told him he thought he'd been influenced by his mother in that regard.

"One of the things he conveyed to me was that he felt that he had some of his mother's genes, in the fact that she was a very compassionate person and a nurturer," Vinick said. "And he felt that his attitude toward children or sickness" was shaped by his mother.[49]

Of course when Ted went to the playground, he wasn't just playing ball with Rod Luscomb. He had a gang of friends with him most of the time—guys like Wilbert Wiley, Joe Villarino, Del Ballinger, Roy Engle, Swede Jensen, and Ted Laven. All were ballplayers who wanted to be out there every day. They took advantage of San Diego's sublime climate to stretch baseball out into a twelve-month season. All became devoted to Ted and helped build his legend at the grass roots.

There was always a game, always action. Two Mexican-American families, the Tallamantes and the Villarinos, were baseball fixtures at the park in the early '30s, as Ted and his gang were coming up. Each family had at least five brothers, and the Tallamantes' father, known at the playground as Dad Tallamante, was out playing with his charges into his fifties. "Those two tribes were very instrumental in baseball at University Heights," said Jensen. "Between the two of them, they could make a baseball team."[50]

Among Ted's crew, his stalwart at the playground was Wiley, whom Williams described in *My Turn at Bat* as "my first real boyhood pal." The son of a streetcar conductor, Wiley had a paper route delivering the *San Diego Evening Tribune*. Ted would help Wilbert with his route, and then they'd go off to the playground and pitch to each other.

"Wilbur," Ted wrote, misspelling his friend's name, "was a little smaller than me, but a little better and a little stronger. We'd play with however many balls we could round up and a bat that was taped up good. We'd hit three or four and go chase them and hit some more."[51]

Wiley was amazed at Ted's power. "When he'd hit, guys would say, 'Where in the Sam Hill does that skinny drink of water get his power from?' Ted was unusually strong in his hands and wrists. When I used to hang around his house, I'd see him take a dining room chair and place six or seven big Life magazines on it and get down on one knee and pick the chair up by one leg and raise it up.... When he was 10, 11, 12, he was such a scrawny kid that nobody dreamt he would turn out to be what he was in major league baseball."[52]

Ted may have been scrawny, but he could handle himself in a pinch, Wiley said. "No one would ever want to tangle with him. That guy could really fight. I mean, he was good. He got into scrapes around that playground every once in a while.... He could throw those fists and they were fast."[53]

It was while playing against Wiley that Ted had a playground epiphany of sorts. "Know what was the biggest thing that ever happened to me in baseball?" Ted told *Time*'s Ben Williamson in 1950. "Well, it wasn't getting picked up by the Red Sox, or the first homer I ever hit for Boston. It was when I was playing with a kid named Wilbert Wiley. We were pals in San Diego and we would take turns pitching to each other. I was 14 then and he was a year or so older—and we'd have some small fry chasing the balls we hit out in a vacant sandlot. Well, Wilbert would always tell me what he was going to throw—fast ball, curve and so on. He had a pretty good roundhouse. And one day I told him never mind calling out what he was going to throw. I said, 'Come on, throw what you like.' Well, I could hit anything he threw up there. I could time them right. Boy, I was all swelled up over that. I could hit anything. I knew right then that I was a good hitter."

Joe Villarino was one of the baseball Villarinos who were fixtures at University Heights. Joe lived five blocks from Ted and would spend forty years working for San Diego Gas and Electric. One of his favorite memories was the day he hit a home run and Ted greeted him at home plate, all smiles. "That was the day of my life," Villarino said. "Ted said, 'If there'd been another coat of paint on the fence, it wouldn't have gone over! He'd hit one the inning or two before. I think that ball's still going."[54]

Del Ballinger moved to San Diego from Monterey, California, when he was thirteen. He had been a batboy for the San Francisco Seals of the Pacific Coast League and lived near Ted, on Nevada Street. Del told Ed Linn that the first time his father took him to the playground, "I heard a lot of noise and looked through the swings and slides—I'll never forget this—and saw this big, tall string bean hitting the ball a mile, and all the other kids were chasing after it.... This was his life. Ted never shagged for anybody. Nobody wanted him to. Everybody loved to see him hit." But Del said Ted's legs were so skinny he was nicknamed Birdlegs on the playground, which he hated.[55]

Roy Engle was a big, strapping catcher who would become the captain of Ted's high school team. "We played together on the playground all the time," Engle recalled. "Ted lived at that ballpark, and if he could get somebody to throw the ball to him he'd be happy. I think we all realized Ted was just a little bit different than we were."[56] Engle also played football, and in 1939 he would become a member of USC's national championship team. "He was the guy I admired," Ted said of Engle. "He was so strong. Everything he hit was a line drive.... I couldn't hit it anywhere near as hard as he did."[57]

Swede Jensen was the shortstop on Ted's high school team and later played for the San Diego Padres in the Pacific Coast League. "North Park was our main getout," Jensen said. "It was a wonderful meeting place. Ted was loud and boisterous. When he started to laugh, he'd fill the place with laughter, wherever he was." Swede lived on Iowa Street, and he and Ted would often walk to school. Ted would never be without his bat, and he'd always be sure to stop and swing at any bush that dared to be blooming in his path.

Ted Laven would tell the *Boston Globe* years later that when Williams first showed up at North Park he was a right-handed hitter: "He was nine or ten years old and always hit from the right side. How he became a left-handed batter is a funny story. We use to play on a softball diamond. The left field fence was only 150 feet away, and we had a rule that if you hit the ball over the fence you were out.... The right field fence was something like 350 feet away, as I remember. Well, Ted decided he could swing from the left side and have plenty of room to swing. From that day on, Ted was a left-handed batter."[58] Williams himself never related that story. In speaking of his beginnings as a hitter he would say that even though he was right-handed, he'd picked up a bat one day and begun swinging it left-handed, and he'd stayed with it because it felt comfortable. But in hindsight he thought he'd have been a better hitter right-handed, because hitting lefty, his power hand, his right, was farther away from the ball at contact, thereby diminishing his power.[59]

Some just watched the playground show. Bud Maloney, who would become a sportswriter for the *San Diego Union*, was five years younger than Ted—an avid baseball fan and an early observer of Williams's coming of age at University Heights. "I was a shy little kid," Maloney said. "I just simply watched. I never talked to Ted."[60] As Ted's sandlot career began to take off, that meant watching him not just at University Heights but at other parks around town. "Almost at every field for some years there was a story that Ted hit a ball here that went over the fence of some guy's backyard. For years Ted was talked about. He was renowned."

The emerging acclaim made it easy to find shaggers—playground urchins who were more than happy to chase after the long balls Ted would blast hither and yon. One regular was Ben Press, who went on to become a noted tennis pro in the San Diego area. Press lived a few doors down from Ted, on Utah Street. "Rod would take and throw balls to Ted, and he'd hit them over the fence, and we'd chase them for him," recalled Press. "We did that for hours every day. I was in awe of Ted." Williams would usually borrow a quarter from his mother to pay Press or other neighborhood kids for their trouble.[61]*

Looking back, Ted thought he spent all those early years at the playground more for the love of the game than out of any overarching ambition to be a pro ballplayer, which he had grave doubts he could become anyway, given his skinny frame.

He didn't follow the major leagues closely. "I was out *doing* it," he wrote. "That's all I cared about. If there was any player I thought about imitating, it was Bill Terry. He was having big years for the Giants then, and when I'd be playing, or just swinging a bat, I'd say to myself, OK, Terry's up, last of the ninth, two men on, two-two count. Giants trailing three to one—announcing the game the way kids do—here's the pitch...Terry *swings*...And I'd treat myself to another home run."[62]

Terry had hit .401 in 1930, when Williams was twelve, leaving a strong and lasting impression on the boy. "The only players I had ever heard of were Ruth and Gehrig," Ted said. "And then I read that Bill Terry had hit .400, and that really excited me. Four hundred! I don't think I even knew what you had to do to hit .400, but I could tell that it was something wonderful. I knew I wanted to do that, too."[63]

---

* At the time, some of the best tennis in San Diego was being played on the courts on the south side of the North Park playground (the ball field was on the north side). Maureen Connolly, who in 1953 would become the first woman to win tennis's grand slam, was just starting out and played at University Heights. Ted played with Connolly occasionally, as well as with Press and Joe Villarino, but he had to give up the game after he broke too many strings and May told him they couldn't afford the thirty-five cents it cost to get the racket restrung each time. Press said Ted had talent. "He would've probably been just as good at tennis as he was at baseball. I always marveled because he did the same thing in tennis as he did in baseball: he hit it in the middle of the racket. He did it pretty much every time."

★   ★   ★

Ted did discover life outside the playground. His early heroes were not ballplayers but rather George Washington, Napoleon Bonaparte, and Charles Lindbergh. He was particularly intrigued by aviation. And when Lindbergh flew across the Atlantic in 1927 after spending several months that year in San Diego overseeing the construction and testing of his *Spirit of St. Louis,* Ted basked in the reflected glory with other San Diegans.

San Diego's role in Lindbergh's historic Atlantic crossing had spurred the city to stake a claim in the aerospace industry, and in 1935, the Consolidated Aircraft Corporation moved its headquarters to San Diego from Buffalo, New York. Once in California, it built one of the largest airframe factories in the world and soon became the city's largest civilian employer.

Ted would draw pictures of Lindbergh and his plane. "I never drew a picture of Ruth...or any ballplayer," he said. "But I drew pictures of Lindbergh—and George Washington and Napoleon. Those three guys."[64]

Another passion was marbles, and Ted learned the intricacies of the game, throwing around terms like *aggies, immies,* and *puries.* He'd play a game called Boston with Joe Villarino. You drew a big circle in the dirt, got on your knees, and tried to shoot the other guy's marbles out of the circle. His obsessive play made for holes in the knees of his pants and the toes of his shoes.

On Saturday mornings Joe and Ted would hike up into the hills and go rabbit hunting, swim, and look for Huck Finn–like adventure. "One day," Villarino remembered, "we was walking around this trail and a rattlesnake come out and Ted shot it with a .45 he had. We laid it aside, and when we came back, he wrapped him around his neck and shoulders and carried it home.

"Another time, at Dobie's Pond, there was a kid in trouble. He was about eight or nine. We was about fourteen or fifteen. The kid was kinda splashing around. Ted went in and got him. He didn't make a big deal of it. He didn't like to be in the limelight too much."

Saturday afternoons during football season, Ted liked to get home in time to listen to the USC games on the radio. He loved Irvine "Cotton" Warburton, a San Diego boy who was the team's All-American quarterback in 1933. "On Saturday night we'd listen to Benny Goodman," Ted wrote. "Swing bands were the thing then. I still prefer swing to anything else."[65]

His favorite radio program was *Gang Busters,* which, with the cooperation of J. Edgar Hoover, dramatized closed FBI cases. Originally launched in 1935 and called *G-men,* the show featured the dramatic sound effects of screeching tires, police sirens, and tommy guns.[66]

Ted was a fire buff, an early sparky.[67] He became a fixture at his neighborhood fire station, playing pinochle with the firemen. When an alarm sounded and the truck responded, they'd put a fireman's hat on young Ted and let him hop aboard. Williams would hang on to the rear of the truck with one arm, lean out, face to the wind, and wave his arm, shouting with glee.[68]

Ted also liked to hang out at the Majestic Malt Shop, not far from his house, where you could buy ten-inch-high malts for a quarter, and at Doc Powelson's drugstore, across from Herbert Hoover High School, which Williams would graduate from. He often mixed his malts with eggs in his perpetual quest to gain weight. ("Let's malt up," Ted would say to Wilbert Wiley or some other friend.)

There was also time for mischief—though nothing too serious. Once, Ted and his brother climbed a nearby water tower, got stuck, and the fire department was called to get them down. On Halloween, Ted would join his pals in greasing the trolley tracks in order to wreak havoc on the streetcars. One year, the group pilfered some fruit from downtown storefronts with the intention of using it to raise hell that night. The police caught them. Most were apologetic and let go, but Ted was a smart aleck, so he was hauled in to the station. The cops ended up playing pinochle with him and driving him home at midnight, charmed.[69] But beyond such childish pranks, Williams was straight as an arrow—never smoked a cigarette as a kid, always in bed by 10:00 p.m.

Improbably, Ted tried piano lessons for a while, but that didn't take. And he dabbled at odd jobs.[70] Once, he reported to an employment office and spent several hours tossing barrels onto a truck for thirty cents an hour.[71] In 1934, he worked as a lifeguard under Art Linkletter at a YMCA camp that May sent him to.[72] He drove a delivery truck for a bakery that sponsored a sandlot team he played on. He even did a stint as an elevator operator and waiter at the U.S. Grant Hotel in San Diego, where, according to the hotel's proprietor, Edward S. Bernard, Ted "never dropped a room service order, never spilled ice water on hotel guests and never was impolite."[73]

Ted couldn't afford his own car, but he loved to cruise around town with those who could. Bill Skelley, a teammate of Ted's on the 1937 Padres, had a maroon 1929 Chrysler roadster, and they'd glide down Broadway with the top down or zip through Balboa Park. When they passed a golf course where someone was getting ready to tee off, Ted would reach over and honk the horn to try to disrupt the golfer. "Just fooling around," Skelley said.[74]

Girls? Forget it. "I never went out with girls, never had any dates, not until I was much more mature-looking," Ted wrote. "A girl looked at me twice, I'd run the other way."[75]

Ted did go to his senior prom in January of 1937, double-dating with his friend Bob Breitbard. "I had an old '27 Chevy, green with orange wheels," Breitbard said. "I was ashamed of that thing. My brother had a Dodge with four doors. Later model. So we went in style. It was the first time I'd ever seen Ted in a tie. Ted took Alberta Camus, a girl in our class. She was fairly attractive. As far as I know, I don't think he ever had a date before that one. We didn't think that much about girls. Hell, the fellas hung out together."[76]

Yet there was no anxiety when it came to voicing his opinion: Williams was high-strung, filled with nervous energy, always biting his fingernails. Ted's friends found him candid to a fault, unvarnished. If he didn't like someone, he would tell him so, to his face, rather than gossip behind his back. "I don't care for you, fella," he might say.

Ted's booming voice could be heard above any din. And he used it to good effect, often to shout out an odd greeting cry— *"Ta-ta-weedo"* — when he saw a friend, say, a hundred feet away. No one knew what this meant—it was just a colorful eccentricity. Ben Press remembered that Ted would also use this whoop in triumph when he blasted a home run or hit a winning shot in tennis. A variation that he liked to use in his junior high school metal shop class was: *"Pow-ho-we-hah!* My muscles are bulging!"* according to friend Jerry Allen. "Everyone laughed at that and thought it was funny," Allen said. "My teacher would laugh, too, but he'd tell us he hoped we never yelled like that."[77]

Such yelps were precursors to another odd scream Ted would use when he reached the minor leagues—and continued to use in his first year with the Red Sox, 1939, before his early ebullience started to fade. To amuse himself during bouts of boredom in the field as he waited to bat again, when a fly ball was hit his way Ted would slap his behind and yell, "Hi-yo, Silver!" as he took off to run for it.

Sam Williams toiled away in relative obscurity. Compared to May, who was well liked and a real presence in San Diego, Sam didn't leave much of a footprint in town. In 1923, he did reach out and formally fraternize, joining the Freemasons, a group he would stay active in for the rest of his life.[78]

In 1931, Sam was named a deputy US Marshal at a salary of $1,440 a year.[79] This was "the best job he ever had, his biggest claim to fame," Ted wrote.[80] "It was kind of a political appointment because he had done something for Governor Merriam when Merriam got elected. Strings were pulled."

Actually, Frank Merriam, a Republican, did not become governor until three years later, so more likely the appointment was arranged as a favor to the politically connected May.

On February 2, 1932, Sam the marshal made news for participating in a Prohibition-era raid of a bootlegging ring that had been smuggling what was described as "rare liquor" from Tijuana to San Diego. Sam and three other officers struck an Eliot Ness–like pose for the *San Diego Evening Tribune,* holding their contraband with grim visages.

One of the perks of the marshal's job was an Oldsmobile, complete with a siren on top, which Sam could drive home and which he delighted in showing off. May's niece Teresa Cordero Contreras remembered Sam letting her and her siblings horse around in the car. "He'd come in the police car over the house, and he'd do the siren for us. We pressed a little red button on the dashboard. I was just a little kid."

In 1934, Sam took another position in law enforcement, becoming jail inspector for the state of California, a $2,160-a-year job that would keep him almost constantly on the road over the next five years. He was based in Sacramento and seemed to take an activist approach, notably in Fresno, where he made recommendations to ease overcrowding at the Fresno County jail.[81]

Ted was sixteen and blooming as a baseball player when Sam went to Sacramento. He became the star of his high school team, and professional scouts were tracking him hard. Until this point, when the promise of money was in the air, Sam had shown zero interest in Ted's baseball, beyond once threatening to beat his son for skipping school to play an American Legion game.[82]

But when the scouts materialized, Sam got religion. "By this time my dad was in on the act....He got the idea I was the second coming of Ruth," Ted remembered. Sam started buying Ted steaks on game days, which the boy thought slowed him down. "But I was pleased he was interested so I ate the steaks."[83]

Still, to Ted, Sam's belated and materialistic interest in his baseball stung. "In the real crises of my life he never once gave me any advice," Ted wrote.[84] He tried to get Sam's attention but couldn't. He even learned photography, his father's former profession, because he hoped it would give them something to talk about. But it was all to no avail.

"His father could have cared less," said Steve Brown, the Florida filmmaker and fisherman. "He said, 'I thought I could impress him,' but it wouldn't have mattered. Ted didn't understand his father at all. How he could have no concerns for his sons. He shared nothing with them. He'd come in the house and let May make all the decisions. Ted said his dad would get up in the middle of a meal, leave, and not come back for two days. Ted told me he was an alcoholic. That the only time his father would talk to him was when he was drunk."[85]

So Ted searched out surrogate fathers. Chief among these was Les Cassie Sr., the father of Ted's friend Les Cassie Jr. The Cassies lived across the street from the Williamses.

"Ted was at our house a lot," said Les junior. "My mother and dad treated Ted like me, like just another one of their sons."[86]

The elder Cassie, who was superintendent of construction for the San Diego schools, would play checkers with Ted, but they bonded over fishing. Les junior wasn't interested in the sport, so his dad would take Ted down to the beach at Coronado and teach him surf casting. They'd catch croakers, corbina, and maybe some perch starting in the early evening, and they wouldn't come home until two or three o'clock in the morning. By the time he was sixteen, Ted could cast farther than anyone else on the beach.

It was Mr. Cassie who gave Ted the only present he received when he graduated from high school: a fountain pen. And it was Mr. Cassie whom Ted would ask to drive with him across the country to Florida for spring training in 1939, when he joined the Red Sox. Ted promised then that if the Sox ever made it to the World Series, Mr. and Mrs. Cassie would be his guests at Fenway Park. In 1946, Ted delivered on that promise.

"The night they clinched, he called and said, 'Are you coming?'" said Les junior. "It was the high point of my dad's life. He introduced him to everyone back in Fenway Park, everyone from [Red Sox owner] Tom Yawkey to the ushers."

Ted wrote in his book: "I loved Mr. Cassie. The nicest, dearest man.... When Mr. Cassie died, I felt as bad as when my own father died."[87] Williams would later say he always regarded Les junior as a brother, and the feeling was mutual.[88] "We just seemed to hit it off real good," Cassie said. "Right from the start we used to eat lunch together, carry a brown sack, sit on the steps of the auditorium. We'd talk baseball day after day."

Two other neighbors, Johnny Lutz and Chick Rotert, also played paternal roles in Ted's life.

When he was only five, Ted had dragged his small bat across the street and asked Lutz to pitch to him.[89] Lutz was a poultry retailer and competitive marksman who would take Ted on hunting trips across the border in Mexico. Ted thought Lutz was the best shot he ever saw; Williams, however, needed more patience with a gun. "Once he missed," Lutz recalled, "he would become so disgusted that he would just shoot off the rest of the round wildly."[90]

Later, Lutz, on whose kitchen table Ted signed his first professional contract, grew concerned that the boy wasn't being adequately cared for. Once, on a hunting trip to the Imperial Valley, Ted said he was hungry. So they stopped and ate, and Ted had four eggs, a stack of toast, a stack of pancakes, and six bottles of a soft drink. Lutz said he and his wife found it pathetic to see Ted and Danny, when they were only eight and six, sitting on the curb until 11:00 p.m. or midnight waiting for one of their parents to come home.[91]

Chick Rotert, a former game warden who'd had two of his fingers shot off in World War I, was actually the first person to take Ted fishing. He showed the boy pictures of bass he'd caught from local lakes, then took him out to experience the real thing. Eventually Ted got himself a $3.95 Pflueger Akron reel and a Heddon bamboo rod. "I practiced casting until I knew what I was doing, standing on the porch in the evenings, maybe waiting for my mother to come home, casting into the yard or out to the street."[92]

During a 1934 deep-sea outing from Point Loma, Ted and his party caught ninety-eight barracuda and gave them all away to people gathered on the docks, hungry in the Depression. The trip helped fuel Ted's love of fishing, which would become a lifelong passion. Soon he was fishing with his friends, not just Mr. Cassie, Johnny Lutz, and Chick Rotert. Ted and Del Ballinger liked to take the streetcar to Ocean Beach, and on the way home the conductor would make them sit in the back because the fish they caught smelled so bad.[93]

Meanwhile, Ted and Sam Williams continued to drift apart. "My dad and I were never close," Ted said. "I was always closer to my mother, always feeling I had to do right by her, always feeling she was alone, and knowing for years afterward how hard she had worked with nothing to show for it. I loved my dad, it wasn't that I didn't love him, but he didn't push very hard. He was just satisfied to let things go as they were. He was a quiet man. He never smiled much."[94] Nevertheless, until Williams died, he kept a picture of his father smoking a pipe and holding a baby—Ted himself—on display in his house. "He was always very sad he never got to know his father," said John Sullivan, one of Ted's caretakers at the end.[95]

Cousin Gino Lucero thought Ted's anger, which he would mostly aim toward his mother later in life, was misdirected. "All this anger that Ted vented toward his mom and used playing ball and flying jets—it's his dad. I don't think he even knew it. I think the only anger he had at his mom was the embarrassment she caused him. But here's a guy—his whole youth was spent looking for a father figure. This guy was hungry for a dad that would play catch with him, a dad that would come to his games. I think Ted felt his dad didn't love him. There was no example of validation. Nothing Ted didn't know himself. We're all in denial about our dysfunctions. But there's no denying, in psychiatry, the importance of a father."

In 1939, the state legislature decided to eliminate Sam's position as jail inspector, and he was out of a job. By this time, he and May were also out of business. The relationship had been strained for years. May was turned off by Sam's drinking, smoking, prolonged absences, and general indifference to her, while Sam was put off by her obsession with the Salvation Army and what he saw as her indifference to him.

They officially separated on April 21, 1939 (coincidentally, the day Ted made his major-league debut in Boston), according to the divorce complaint May brought against Sam in February of 1941. The separation occurred after Sam ran off with a woman who had been his secretary, Minnie Mae Dickson. The oldest of seven children, Minnie had grown up in Sedalia, Missouri, the daughter of a cattle rancher. She had snow-white hair, which she would often highlight with a pink or purple rinse. She was married once before Sam came into her life. "She loved clothes," said her niece Beverly Schultz. "Her hats and purses and shoes always matched. Real snappy dresser. Probably that was why Sam was attracted to her. She was kind of heavyset but always carried herself nicely, and she was well put together. She was involved in Christian Science but didn't like to talk about it." They settled in the San Francisco area and opened another photo studio there.

May was devastated and tried to persuade Sam to come back, according to her younger sister Sarah Diaz. "She was just heartbroken, but there was nothing she could do," Sarah said. "She even went up there and tried to make up with him, with Samuel. No, he had this woman, so there was nothing she could do."[96]

May let Sam have it in her 1941 divorce complaint, saying he had been "guilty of extreme cruelty in the wrongful infliction of grievous mental suffering." She also said he had "willfully neglected" to provide for her and was still not doing so. Sam initially failed to answer the complaint, but the following year, it was he, not May, who filed a motion to make the divorce final. His motion was granted, and the divorce became official on May 14, 1942.

The divorce, certainly rare in those days, pained Ted, but he didn't blame his father. "Whenever anybody ever wrote about my dad, they seemed to delight in calling him a 'wanderer' or a 'deserter of the family,' but that's a lot of bull," he wrote. "He stuck it out with my mother for twenty years, and finally he packed up, and I'd probably have done the same. My mother was a wonderful woman in many ways, but gee, I wouldn't have wanted to be married to a woman like that. Always gone. The house dirty all the time. Even now I can't stand a dirty house.* She was religious to the point of being domineering, and so narrow-minded. My dad smoked, usually a pipe, and she didn't like that and never stopped complaining about it. I remember one time he came home sick, he'd been drinking wine or some of that lousy beer, and God, you'd think it was the end of the world the way my mother carried on. My mother had a lot of traits that made me cringe."[97]

As an adult, Ted rarely saw his father, but he did provide for him. He regularly sent funds that Sam used to supplement the threadbare income he earned from his photo business. Ted also bought his father a small house in Walnut Creek, California, across the bay from San Francisco, where Sam had settled with Minnie Dickson. The couple had married following Sam and May's divorce.

"It was a little three-room house with a walnut tree in the yard," said Beverly Schultz. "There was a living room, a bedroom, and a kitchen. I kept thinking that a big baseball star owned the house, and I wondered

---

* Ted and his brother were not blameless when it came to mess. According to Mary Cordero's son John, "We were called down to help because Ted and Danny wouldn't do anything around the house. Danny one time bought a white rat and brought him in the house. May said to get rid of the rat. He put him in the garage, [and he] got out and multiplied. May told us to get rid of the rats. We went in there, they'd jump on us and bite us, so we just closed the garage off and said to hell with it."

why he didn't buy his father a bigger house. I assumed they were probably not real close. But at least Ted took some care of his father."[98]

Though he had received considerable financial support from Ted,
including one $6,000 payment in the late 1940s, which he used to buy
new cameras and other supplies for his Williams Photo Studio on Main
Street in Walnut Creek, Sam was not above using the press to try and
leverage more support from his famous son. On January 9, 1950, Sam
told the *Oakland Post Enquirer* that because someone who owed him
$3,500 had defaulted on the loan, he was in danger of losing his house
and his business. He'd had a stroke two years before, he added. "We just
went broke when the note wasn't paid, that's all," Sam said. Minnie was
quoted as saying they had asked Ted for help.

The story went national immediately; some papers also published a
picture of Sam and Minnie gazing forlornly at a photo of Ted and his
new infant daughter, Bobby-Jo. While the implication was obviously
that the rich ballplayer was ignoring his nearly destitute father, Williams's
agent, Fred Corcoran, mounted a quick damage-control operation and
let it be known that Ted had been taking care of Sam for years. It wasn't
long before the Boston press was rallying to the Kid's defense.

As he was growing up, and feeling frustrated and saddened by his parents' neglectful behavior, Ted could find no solace in his younger
brother, Danny, who was a classic juvenile delinquent.

Daniel Arthur Williams was born July 20, 1920, almost two years
after Ted. Danny was shorter than his brother, a shade under six feet, and
darker.

To compensate for May and Sam's indifference, Ted had baseball—
and his surrogate fathers, who helped look out for him and whose
authority he respected—as a touchstone. But Danny had an incorrigible
bent that always challenged authority, and he had no singular talent or
passion to fall back on.

Early on, Danny turned to shoplifting and petty crime. Once, he bra-
zenly stole his mother's prize cornet and hocked it at a pawnshop, only to
have May spot it one day as she walked by the store. Before long, he took
to carrying a gun or a knife[99] and swiping candy and cigarettes. "Danny
would steal stuff, and they'd put him in a juvenile home called Anthony
Home," Joe Villarino said. "He'd go in and out of there. Danny started
smoking when he was six or seven years old. Ted and Danny, they didn't
get along too good. One time I was over there and Ted was running

away and Danny took a knife out of his pocket and threw it at him. Ted ducked around the door, and it missed him. Then I got the hell out of there."[100]

By the time he was a teenager, Danny had become a fixture on the San Diego police blotter, and occasionally his name would appear in the paper for some caper or other, to May's great shame. If he had a court date, he would ignore it and not show up. Once, Danny led San Diego police on a high-speed chase and ditched them—with his mother and cousin Teresa Cordero Contreras in the car with him. "One day Danny drove me and Aunt May to the grocery store," Contreras said. "Pretty soon a cop came up behind him. He was going too fast, but instead of pulling over, he stepped on the gas and started leading the cop on a chase! He was trying to lose him, and he did. He just pulled into some garage and the cop passed by. I was so scared I couldn't even think. May was saying 'Stop, Danny, stop!'" When his father had the US Marshal's job, Danny would sometimes commandeer his dad's car for joyrides to Santa Barbara, its siren wailing. "They'd catch him and send him back to San Diego," recalled Danny's cousin John Cordero, chuckling.[101]

"I know he was a thorn in my mother's side, always getting into scrapes," recalled Ted. "Nothing really serious, but one jam after another—piling up traffic tickets, maybe stealing a bicycle, or owing money on a truck and trying to clear out without paying....For me, respecting authority was no problem, not then or now. I never got into jams with the police or anything. But some guys have absolutely no respect for authority, and Danny was one of them."[102]

Rod Luscomb once took a loaded gun from Danny and had to chase him out of the playground several times for shouting obscenities at young girls. "Ask any cop in San Diego who was the most notorious juvenile delinquent in the city, and I'll bet you he names Danny," Luscomb told *Time* in 1950.

Gradually, Danny's crimes grew more serious and brazen. Once, when Ted brought home a new car, Danny stripped off its tires and sold them. In 1941, after Ted paid to renovate the Utah Street house, Danny stole all the new furniture and hocked it, prompting May to have him arrested.[103] And according to Daniel Venzor and Manuel Herrera, when Danny was in his early twenties, he was charged with rape in Santa Barbara, but his lawyer got him off after convincing the judge that the evidence might have been tainted.

"My being in the public eye probably made it tougher for him," Ted recalled. "He never had too many advantages. He never had the outlets for expression I did. His life was just an existence."[104] Danny plainly resented his brother's success and would do anything to get attention. Nevertheless, as the years went by and Ted's fame grew, Danny would trade on his brother's celebrity, using it to get free drinks at bars. And with pure chutzpah, he even sent a telegram directly to Red Sox owner Tom Yawkey asking for money.[105]

In 1940, Danny and Helen Mildred Hansen, a high school sweetheart he'd married, had a son named Daniel. Then, in February of 1942, with World War II on, Danny enlisted in the Army. This was a time when Ted, coming off his .406 season the previous year, had obtained a deferment as the sole supporter of their mother. But if Danny gained any measure of satisfaction from enlisting before Ted, the regimented military life didn't suit him. He couldn't take orders, and he frequently went AWOL to visit his wife and son.

By August of 1943, Danny had been dishonorably discharged, and his marriage was over.[106] He barely got to know his son. In the late 1940s, Danny met a girl named Betty Jean Klein when she was a dirt-poor fifteen-year-old from Texas. Before long, they were married, and in 1950, they had a son, Samuel Stuart Williams, named after Danny's father.

"My dad had a troubled life," said Sam Williams, who works as the sports editor for a weekly newspaper in Northern California. "I think it was hard for him to live in Ted's shadow. He had a pretty good temper, and that's why he got into trouble, I think. If we did something he told us not to do, he was strict. Fathers were stricter back then. We would get spanked."[107]

In 1951, a second son arrived. He was given the first name John and the middle name Theodore, after Ted. Growing up, the boy resisted being called Ted, but when people seemed to insist on referring to him that way he stopped fighting it. "The name's haunted me all my life," said Ted, the namesake nephew, now a graphic designer living in Oakland. "When I was younger I never talked about it, but finally gave in to it because that's what people wanted to hear."[108]

Danny found work as a commercial painter — MY EXPERIENCE IS YOUR PROTECTION, his business card said — and took his young family on the road, moving between San Diego, Chicago, and Texas, where his wife's family lived. Ted thinks his father was trying to stay one step ahead of the bill collectors.

On the long drives across country, Danny would always keep his gun close by. "He strapped it to the steering column of the car. He said, 'The

car is my house, and you're allowed to carry a gun in your house.' He
had a casual respect for the law," son Ted said, laughing. "He didn't like
rules. And he'd invoke Ted's name whenever he got in trouble."

Always short of cash, Danny kept causing problems. One day, he stole
and sold a new television May had received from Ted. By the late '50s,
Danny had contracted leukemia, and his behavior grew even more
erratic. On a visit to the family homestead in Santa Barbara, he even
pulled a gun on May, apparently in a half-baked robbery attempt.

Salvador Herrera witnessed this: "I seen Danny pull a gun on his
mother. He was dying of cancer, bone marrow. He was fuckin' nuts. He
wanted money and said, 'Give me that goddamn purse.' I couldn't
believe he pulled that fuckin' gun out. May said, 'Oh, praise Jesus! Praise
Jesus!' That was crazy shit. Danny was a fuckin' gangster."

Ted's relationship with his brother was always distant, to say the least.
When he was with the Red Sox and would send money home to his
mother, Ted knew that she was giving much of it to Danny. Bobby
Doerr recalled watching Ted read letters from his mother in the Fenway
Park clubhouse: "I'd watch his face turn red. She'd be writing him and
usually asking for money, and he knew the money was probably going to
the brother."

Ted also knew that while he had had mentors and others to help him
in life, Danny didn't. "I know Danny suffered because of it," Ted wrote.
"I have to think poor Danny had a tormented life."

At the three public schools he attended—Garfield Elementary, Horace
Mann Junior High, and Herbert Hoover High School—Ted was an
indifferent student at best. He would carry his bat in to school with him
and store it under his desk during the day.

Leila Dickinson Bowen taught for thirty-one years at Garfield Elementary, and in 1928 one of her fifth-grade students was ten-year-old Ted
Williams. She knew him as Teddy. "He had those sharp elbows and he
used them," Bowen said. "He'd run out to the playground and shout 'first
ups!' and if he didn't get them, he'd take off his cap and throw it as hard as
he could down on the ground. Then, he'd cry....But, that quick, he'd
break out in a smile. He was a good boy, never a discipline problem."[109]

Another Garfield teacher told May Williams she thought Ted was
underweight and not eating enough. May asked how that could be since
she was giving her son thirty-five cents a day for lunch in the school caf-
eteria. A nurse investigated and determined that Ted was giving his
money away to kids who couldn't buy lunch for themselves.[110]

At Hoover, besides the usual subjects, Ted's courses included the non–college track typing, print shop, wood shop, and one offering called simply "metal." He compiled a grade point average of 2.06, and would have been below 2.0 but for phys ed.[111]

"I was a lousy student," he wrote. "I always took subjects I wouldn't have a lot of homework in. I took shop. I was lucky I didn't cut my fingers off. I wish I had then the inquisitive mind I have now. I feel like I've missed so much, and I'm always hammering at myself trying to catch up."[112] Under his high school yearbook picture there was one word: *baseball.*

At print shop, where they learned how to set type on a press, Ted was best known as the class clown. He'd often drop a match in a metal trash can containing the flammable printing detritus, then run off laughing and whooping.

When Ted graduated from Hoover, in February of 1937, the principal gave him a prize for being one of the school's best typists, along with his friend and Hoover classmate Bob Breitbard. "We did thirty-two words per minute without an error," said Breitbard. "We thought we were hot stuff."

Ted was a fan of Hoover's principal, Floyd Johnson. Ted credited Johnson as an important influence. "He was a man of high principles and he'd tell me that I'd get out of life and baseball...just what I put into it. Well, I've tried to put everything into it."[113] Williams would stop by Johnson's office regularly to talk about baseball and fishing. He'd relax and feel free to put his feet on the principal's desk. Concluded Johnson: "This was not impudence on Ted's part, because to him all folks on the campus were just the same—faculty, principal, or kids."[114]

Ted's junior high school included ninth grade, so when he entered Hoover—in February of 1934, on a staggered seasonal schedule—he was a tenth grader. A month earlier, baseball tryouts were held, and Ted's performance that day must stand as one of the best of all time—indeed, the tale has been told thousands of times.

Les Cassie Jr. was there. He met Ted at the tryout, in fact: "This long, tall kid came in. We were just practicing in a big open area. Ted sat on the porch of the print shop, behind where we were working out. He was just finishing up the ninth grade, so he wasn't eligible to come out for the varsity yet till he hit the tenth grade. That was going to be the next Monday. There must have been a hundred kids out there. Anyway, Ted yells over to our coach, Wos [Wofford] Caldwell, 'Hey, Coach, let me hit!' Finally, Caldwell, who was pitching, said, 'All right, get up there and hit.'"

Williams wore three pairs of socks at the tryout to make his skinny legs look bigger, but once he swung the bat, all eyes turned from him to the sky.[115]

"Ted hit the first ball on top of the lunch arbor," recalled Cassie. "That was a series of benches with a roof over it where kids ate lunch, behind the right-field fence. No one had ever hit a ball up there. Must have carried three hundred and fifty feet. He hit the next pitch over there, too. Back-to-back, twice. Caldwell said, 'What's your name, kid?' Ted said, 'My name's Ted Williams, and I'll be back here Monday.'"

Despite his splashy debut, Ted was not a regular in his first year; Caldwell apparently didn't want to rush him. He only played in six games, getting six hits in eighteen at bats for a .333 average.[116]

That summer of 1934, and the following summer, Ted supplemented his relatively spare high school season with an extensive sandlot schedule, which served to vastly improve, and showcase, his game. He played American Legion ball for the Padre Serra Post team and for a variety of other clubs in county, independent, and semipro leagues, among them San Diego Market, Central, Walter Church Service Station, Cramer's Bakery, and the North Park Merchants. The clubs played full schedules against each other, and some would also challenge Navy teams from whichever ship was docked in the San Diego harbor, such as the *Lexington* or the *Saratoga*. The Navy had plenty of equipment, of course, so Ted and his pals would usually pilfer extra balls and bats, with the tacit blessing of the fleet.[117]

"I remember my first home run," Ted said. "Came against a guy named Hunt in a Sunday game at North Park. Just a poopy fly ball to center, but it made it over the fence. There I was, a little 15-year-old standing in against guys 25 to 30 and this guy could really throw hard. I could barely get the bat around on it, and I hit that homer."[118]

The Sunday contests were intense and could draw hundreds of fans at various parks around town. Ted would usually get $3 a game, plus a couple of milk shakes and hamburgers afterward. Occasionally a team might spring for $25 to get a Pacific Coast League player who had an off day. In one Sunday game, Ted homered off Hall of Famer Grover Cleveland Alexander, who had retired in 1930 and become a boozy barnstormer on the semipro circuit.[119]

The teenager's clutch hitting helped build his reputation. One of his sandlot managers, Travis Hatfield, recalled an instance when the team's pitcher had to leave for military school after eight innings in a scoreless game. "So Ted pipes up, 'Let him go, I'll pitch the ninth.'" Hatfield said.

"Well, the other team gets a run off Ted and we came to bat, trailing by a run. Our first batter got out, second one got on and Ted had a chance to come up. The third batter went out and the fans started to leave. Ted looked up and waved them back to their seats. 'It's not over yet,' Ted was yelling at them. And it wasn't. He poked one out for a home run and we won, 2–1. Boy, did he have a big grin galloping around the bases."[120]

Back at Hoover for his junior year, Ted broke out, hitting .588 in fifteen games and fifty-one at bats, including seven home runs.[121] Caldwell would buy a milk shake for each player who hit a homer—a perfect reward for the "malt-up" Kid. That year, Hoover went 12–3. The *San Diego Union* of April 23, 1935, said young Williams was "pounding the apple like a Babe Ruth." Ted would have had even more home runs but for a unique ground rule at Hoover High. The baseball field was on a football field and had home plate in a corner of one of the end zones. It wasn't more than 275 feet down the right-field line. So the local ground rule was that anything hit over the fence to the right of a pole in right-center, known as the barber pole, was only a double.[122] "Ted hit some of the longest two-base hits in the history of world," recalled Bud Maloney, the sportswriter and early Williams observer. "The ball would still be going up when it went over the fence."*

One of the highlights of the season occurred when Hoover traveled up to Los Angeles to play a doubleheader against Santa Monica. The start of the first game was delayed so that Babe Herman, the former Brooklyn Dodger who had hit .393 with thirty-five homers five years earlier but was then holding out as a Pittsburgh Pirate, could finish taking batting practice. "We were sitting in the dugout while Babe Herman was hitting," former neighbor Del Ballinger said. "And Ted is beating on his wrist, and he'd say, 'Oh, I wish I had power like that. I wish I was that big and strong.' And then Ted got up in the game and hit two balls farther than Babe Herman! I mean, seven miles farther. He hit them farther as a high school boy. I said, 'Ted, you're a doozy.' He never seemed to realize how good he was."[123]

Williams mostly played the outfield and first base, but had also emerged as a strong pitcher. He went 4–2 his junior year as the number two starter.[124] In his senior season he became Hoover's lead pitcher and went 12–1, once striking out nineteen against Redondo. Another time,

---

* Like many ballplayers, Ted was superstitious. He gave the batboy, Coach Caldwell's son Bill, a special rabbit's foot and insisted that Bill rub Ted's bat with it each time before he hit.

he pitched both games of a doubleheader, going nineteen innings, striking out twenty-one, and allowing three runs.[125]

Childhood pal Wilbert Wiley always touted Ted as a pitcher: "When you got up to bat, he'd throw you that breaking stuff and I'll tell you, it did break. And he had...a palm ball. A few players still remember that. It'd come out of his hand like a knuckler. He'd give all the motions of throwing a fastball and that thing would slip out and...you'd swing when the ball was halfway there."[126]

Ted told the Boston writer Joe Cashman in 1941 that the reason he took up pitching was to try and disguise his poor fielding. "I was an awkward, sloppy fielder and couldn't run any faster than a snail," he said.[127] Caldwell tried hard to improve Ted's speed. In one drill, the coach stood at home plate with a switch in his hand. He gave Ted a head start, halfway to first base, and told him to take off running. By the time Ted approached second, Caldwell would usually catch Williams and whip his behind with the switch until they reached home.[128]

When he made his high school's all-league team in 1936, the *San Diego Union* referred to Ted as "T. Samuel Williams, elongated chucker."[129] The school paper called him "Hoover's Dizzy Dean."[130] But it was in hitting where he was making his mark. In 1936, his senior season, his average dropped from the prodigious .588 he'd hit the year before to .402 (33–82), perhaps because of all the pitching he did.[131] But he still showed explosive power, belting seven home runs over two days and three games at the annual high school baseball tournament sponsored by the 20-30 Club of Pomona, a business group in Los Angeles County.

The invitational tournament was a major event. More than thirty teams from around Southern California played over several adjoining diamonds, and Ted's homers would spill over into other games, interrupting play. Governor Frank Merriam was there to throw out the first ball in the 1936 championship game. Introduced to Merriam, Ted offered a breezy, "Hi, Guv!"

Jackie Robinson and his Pasadena high school team were playing in the Pomona tournament that year, though not against Hoover and Ted. Race was no great obstacle at the high school level in those days. Hoover's rival, San Diego High, had black players. And in 1935, Ted had a memorable game against one of Southern California's leading pitchers, Willie "Emperor" Jones, of Santa Ana. Jones, who was described in the sporting-press parlance of the day as a "whirlwind Negro pitcher," was touched for two homers by Ted in a March 16 game.

There were black players on the sandlots, too. Satchel Paige made an appearance in February of 1935, pitching a three-hit shutout against the Texas Liquor House club, further entertaining about one thousand fans by stepping to the microphone to sing. "Singin' Satchel Paige," the *San Diego Union* called him, raving that "the elongated colored twirler exhibited blinding speed and miraculous control."[132]

Rather than court trouble, opposing pitchers would often simply walk Ted, and that infuriated him. "If we had a threat going, they'd walk him," said Hoover teammate Roy Engle. "He used to get so upset at that. He threatened to quit one time. It used to irk him something terrible to get a walk." Del Ballinger said Ted would actually break down and "cry like a baby."[133]

As a result of Williams's baseball prowess and outsize persona, his friends and other schoolmates would talk about him constantly.[134] But perhaps the leader of Ted's Hoover cult was Ray Boone, the journeyman major leaguer from 1948 to 1960 who finished his career with Williams and the Red Sox. Boone, whose son and grandsons also played in the majors, was the batboy on Ted's American Legion team and several years behind him at Hoover. Ray and his pals would get on their bikes and follow Ted wherever he was playing.

"We watched Ted play every Friday at Hoover High," Boone said.[135] "We never missed him. He was our big leaguer. We idolized him. I used to kid him he was a better hitter at Hoover than he was at Boston. When I got to Cleveland I was always waiting for the Red Sox to come to town. One day, taking batting practice, I wondered if I should go over and tell Ted I went to Hoover. I decided not to, because I figured, what if he said he doesn't give a damn? Then later at Fenway, I had a great game, hit two homers. After I made an out and ended the inning, I was rounding first. Ted was trotting in from left field and passed me. Without even looking up, he said, 'They can't get old Hoover out, can they?' That stuck with me a long time."

Major-league scouts, or "bird dogs," covering San Diego had been tracking Ted for some time. The most ardent suitor had been Herb Benninghoven. Benninghoven worked for San Diego Gas and Electric, ran a Sunday sandlot team, and moonlighted on behalf of the St. Louis Cardinals. He started showing up at Ted's games, watching from a distance with field glasses. Afterward, Herb might drive Ted home, and they'd talk baseball, or he'd invite the boy over to his house. His wife was always cooking and baking something good.[136]

Benninghoven's chief competition for Ted was Elmer Hill, assistant chief of the San Diego fire department, who served as the bird dog for Bill Essick, a leading scout for the New York Yankees. Essick had first seen Ted the day he hit a long home run for his American Legion team when he was fifteen. The ball soared over the fence and across the street, smashing through a storefront window. The next day, Essick and Hill appeared at the Williams house, and Ted and his mother assumed they were the store owners looking to get reimbursed for the shattered glass.

"Essick was as anxious as anybody to get me," Ted wrote.[137] "I'll never forget what he said: 'Ted, if I didn't think you were going to be a New York Yankee, I'd never sign you.' Maybe he said that to everybody, but that sure impressed me. I think he offered $200 a month, and a $500 bonus if I made the team at [Class A] Binghamton, New York, but the story is my mother asked for a $1,000 bonus and Essick refused."

Still, Hill and Essick kept after Ted, watching him play periodically. One Sunday, Elmer Hill, who also pitched for the semipro Cramer's Bakery team, was scheduled to pitch against Benninghoven's Cardinal-affiliated team, the Juniors. Ted was playing for the Juniors that day, and Hill had Essick come down.

"I had a good day and pitched a one hitter, struck out Ted 3 times," Hill wrote a friend in a 1957 letter on file at the Hall of Fame in Cooperstown. "Nevertheless, Bill liked what he saw, and after the game I took him to Ted's home to talk contract."

Ted was acutely aware of his family's circumstances and ashamed of his dirty, dingy home. "When he was being courted by scouts who came to the house, Ted would move from one side to another to hide a hole in a chair, and once he was appalled when a mouse ran across a baseboard," said John Underwood, Ted's ghostwriter for *My Turn at Bat*.[138]

Sam Williams, newly interested in his son's baseball career now that scouts were about, wondered what might be in it for him and May. "After talking to the parents for a while it was easy to see that Mr. Williams was thinking about a bonus," wrote Hill.[139]

Essick offered $250 a month and $400 monthly if Ted made the Yankees' Pacific Coast League affiliate in Oakland. With Major League Baseball having no team west of Saint Louis at the time, the Pacific Coast League, then playing at the Double-A level, was the leading venue for baseball along the West Coast and indeed west of the Mississippi. The

Oakland option sounded a lot better to the Williamses than Binghamton, across the country and thousands of miles from home. According to Hill, by the end of the meeting it was agreed upon in principle that Ted would sign with the Yankees the following year, after he finished high school. "Bill told them he would leave the contract with me, and when they were ready I would sign him," Hill wrote.

The Detroit Tigers had also sent their area scout, Marty Krug, down to take a look at Ted, but Krug thought the kid was too skinny to make it as a pro. Ted said Krug had May Williams in tears with his assessment. "He had told her I had a lot of good moves, but I was so scrawny a year of professional baseball would kill me. Literally kill me," Ted wrote.[140] Sam had personally vetoed one team that was interested in signing Ted, the Los Angeles Angels of the Pacific Coast League, because he didn't like the team's manager, Truck Hannah. It seems Sam went to see Hannah without Ted, but Hannah said Ted was the one he was interested in talking to, not his father. "My dad didn't like his attitude," Ted wrote.[141]

Meanwhile, in January of 1936, a significant new alternative emerged when San Diego was awarded a franchise in the Pacific Coast League. The owner of the new San Diego Padres was H. W. "Hardrock" Bill Lane, a former semipro ballplayer who'd made a fortune in the goldfields of Alaska and the Yukon. Lane had owned the PCL's Hollywood Stars, but was forced to share local Wrigley Field with the better-established Los Angeles Angels. When Wrigley management said they would double his rent, Lane bolted for an eager San Diego, which built him a new ballpark on the waterfront in three months, using WPA funds. It was a spacious wooden stadium with a capacity of 11,500. The import of the Padres deal was clear to May Williams: if her son had to play professional baseball, here was a chance to keep him at home.

Benninghoven and Essick persisted on behalf of the Cardinals and Yankees, however. Early in 1936, Benninghoven invited Ted to a regional tryout the Cardinals were staging in Fullerton, California, which would be overseen by Branch Rickey. Rickey was pioneering scouting and player development in the major leagues and had built a vast farm-team system for the Cardinals. At the tryouts, the speed-conscious Rickey required recruits to run race after race with numbers pinned to their backs. But the day before the tryout, Ted was hit by a pitch on his thigh, just above the knee. Slow anyway, Ted was made even less mobile by the injury, and he largely went through the motions. Rickey showed no interest in him.

Benninghoven was still able to get Williams an offer from the

Cardinals, but Ted figured that Saint Louis was not the quickest way to the majors. "They would have probably sent me to Oshkosh or Peoria or someplace, because they had a huge farm system and you could get lost," he concluded.[142]

Ted's last game for Hoover High was on May 22, 1936. The following month, Williams and some other local high school standouts who had finished their eligibility but had not yet graduated were invited to informal workouts by the Padres, who were drawing well and had become an immediate source of civic pride for San Diego.

Bobby Doerr was playing second base for the Padres that year and vividly remembered the first time Ted stepped onto Lane Field: "He was standing right in front of me, maybe fifteen feet away," Doerr recalled. "I was on the right side of the batting cage. All the old players were standing around waiting to hit, mostly ex–major leaguers. I can remember this just like it was yesterday—Ted standing there, big skinny kid, six foot three, one forty-seven. He was all excited, Ted. Frank Shellenback was our manager, and he was throwing batting practice. He said, 'Let the kid get in there and hit a few.' The old guys started grumbling. He must have hit six or seven balls. Seems to me he hit one over, or against, the fence. That was a good poke. We didn't have many who could hit like that. I remember one of the older guys said, 'This guy will be signed before the week's out.' "

On June 22, the high schoolers were invited to play for the Padres in an exhibition game against a Navy All-Star team. Late in the game, Ted was sent to left field. He got up once and singled.[143]

"By now the pressure's on pretty good for me to sign with San Diego," Ted wrote. "It was a new team. . . . A few of the politicians got into it, talking to my mother, and my mother liked the idea because she wanted me close to home."[144]

But Elmer Hill and Bill Essick thought they were still in the driver's seat on behalf of the Yankees—after all, they had that agreement in principle from the year before. Moreover, Sam Williams had just called Hill to say that Ted would sign with the Yankees if Hill would increase his monthly payments by a mere $25. "I told him I was sure that would be agreeable, but I would like to contact Bill [Essick] first," Hill wrote in his 1957 letter. "I talked to Ted, and his mother, and they all agreed that they would be happy to sign for the additional 25."

That was on June 25. When Hill picked up the paper the next morning, he learned that Ted had signed with the Padres.

"I was fuming plenty, called Ted's dad, told him the least he could do, was wire Essick and explain," Hill wrote. "This he did. Bill sent me his wire which I still have. It seemed that the same evening after they talked to me agreeing to terms, they had a visit from Bill Lane and Frank Shellenback. I don't know for sure what the deal was, but it was rumored that Mr. Williams was offered a couple hundred bucks for signing, and grabbed it."

But according to Ted, the family had actually come to an agreement with the Padres on June 20, two days before he played in the exhibition game against the Navy All-Stars. He said his mother got the team to agree not to sell or trade Ted, even to a big-league team, until he was twenty-one. And he could not be demoted to a lower minor league. The Padres offered $150 a month, considerably less than the Yankees, but Ted said he chose the local team for May's sake, and because the club made a minor concession that nonetheless was meaningful to the cash-strapped Williams family: they would pay him for the entire month of June, even though they were making the deal on the twentieth. "That was my bonus," Ted wrote.[145]

2

"Fairyland"

A key factor in the decision to sign with the Padres was the comfort level that May Williams felt with the club's owner, Bill Lane, who himself had scouted Ted at Hoover at the urging of an umpire friend. May "was a Salvation Army woman and Mr. Lane...was a big Salvation man," said George Myatt, who played shortstop for the Padres in 1936 and 1937. "So they were real good friends."[1]

To further soothe May, Lane had Cedric Durst, who had played with the mighty 1927 Yankees and was then a courtly forty-year-old center fielder for the Padres, pay a visit to her house and testify to the fact that professional ballplayers weren't all heathens and louts. Durst, a clean-living, nonswearing family man, was also assigned to be Ted's room-mate on the road and watch over him. "He was the designated go-between between the team ownership and Ted's mother," recalled Durst's daughter, Autumn Durst Keltner.[2] "She was apprehensive of Ted at such a young age going off somewhere, so my dad was a facilitator of goodwill."

After Ted signed with the Padres, Lane told him: "I know you were a pitcher in high school, but you can forget pitching from now on," Ted recalled for Joe Cashman in 1941.[3] "I'm taking you because I think you're going to be a great hitter. So concentrate on your hitting."

Williams was thrilled. He'd always wanted to be known as a hitter anyway, not a pitcher.

On Saturday, June 27, 1936, two days after signing his Padres contract, Ted appeared inside the clubhouse at brand-new Lane Field. Carrying a battered suitcase in his right hand, he stopped, looked around at his new teammates—a combination of up-and-coming hotshots and former major leaguers on the wane—then slowly closed the door behind him.

Many of the players stopped to size Williams up as he made his entrance. He was still only seventeen years old, tall and reed-thin, a Huck Finn–Li'l Abner amalgam who was the rawest-looking rookie imaginable.

Manager Frank Shellenback greeted the kid and introduced him around. Finally, Ted sat himself down next to Bud Tuttle, a left-handed pitcher, and said, "When do we hit?"[4]

There was a carnival atmosphere at the ballpark that day as Ted dressed for his first game as a pro. The Padres, playing the Sacramento Solons, were trying to create a fun, family-oriented environment for their new fans. They staged a fungo-hitting contest; the opposing catchers took turns seeing who could throw the most balls from home plate into a barrel at second base; and shortstop George Myatt ran a seventy-five-yard race against Sacramento second baseman Joe Dobbins.[5]

Ted was all wide-eyed as he walked around Lane Field, which was 339 feet down the left-field line, 355 to right, and 480 to dead center. The prevailing winds were favorable for a left-handed power hitter because they blew off San Diego Bay out toward right field.

After signing his contract on the twenty-fifth, Ted had gone down to the University Heights playground and invited some neighborhood kids out to the ballpark to see his first game. Now he spotted the group in the stands, preened for them in his new uniform—which had the number 19 on the back—waved, and yelled, "Hi, gang! Look at me!"[6]

The game started, and before long Shellenback sent Ted up as a pinch hitter against the Solons' Henry "Cotton" Pippen. He took three strikes right down the middle, too "petrified" to swing, as he recalled.[7] That showing could not have inspired much confidence in Ted on the part of the manager, so for the next several days, Williams found himself relegated to throwing batting practice.

Then on July 3, in Los Angeles, the Padres were getting blown out by the Angels, 12–3. San Diego was using up its pitchers quickly and was facing a doubleheader each of the next two days, to boot. Ted overheard Shellenback rather desperately ask one of his coaches, Eddie Mulligan, "Damn it, Eddie, who am I going to put in there? I'm using up all my pitchers."[8]

Ted saw a chance to play, even though Bill Lane had just told him in June his pitching days were over. Williams sidled up to Mulligan and said, "Tell him to put me in, Eddie. I can pitch. I'm ready." Mulligan relayed the suggestion to Shellenback. Lacking a better option, the manager agreed to have the kid go warm up.

Rather than just take the mound, Ted entered the game pinch-hitting for the pitcher he would replace. Facing the Angels' Glen Babler, Williams cracked a long single off the right-field fence at Wrigley Field for his first hit as a professional. That started a rally, and the Padres scored five runs to make it 12–8. Then Ted went in to pitch the seventh inning—his catcher was Harold Doerr, Bobby's older brother—and retired the side in order.

Williams got up again in the top of the eighth and hit another single to right, but when he went back out to pitch the bottom of the eighth, he gave up two screaming home runs ("I can still hear the swish of the line drives past my ears," he said in 1941[9]) before Shellenback came out with the hook. "Skip, I think you've got me playing the wrong position," Ted told his manager.[10]

As he neared the dugout after being lifted, Ted took off his glove and flung it. He aimed for the bench, but the glove sailed into the stands, according to Bobby Doerr. "Ted fought embarrassment all the time, and he was embarrassed he didn't do better pitching," Doerr said.[11]

But the pitching fiasco was just a blip on Ted's screen, dissolving before the overarching reality that he was now a pro ballplayer taking his first road trip, a boy on a train with men, lapping up new sights, smells, and experiences like the exuberant naïf he was.

Mondays were usually off days in the Pacific Coast League, a day when a team would take the train to the next city, where they would sometimes play as many as seven games. Doerr remembered the image of Ted the Monday after his first game in San Diego. He showed up at the train station, nervously waiting as the Padres prepared to leave for Los Angeles and then Oakland. "There's Ted, prancing up and down the platform, all excited," Doerr said.

Doerr was only eighteen, but he already had two years of pro ball under his belt. He'd grown up in Los Angeles, dropped out of school when he was sixteen, and joined the Hollywood Stars in 1934, two years before Bill Lane moved the team to San Diego. Ossie Vitt, Doerr's manager during his first season, had taught him how to order and tip in a restaurant.[12] Vitt had said it was important to act like a big leaguer and use fifteen cents of his $2.50 daily meal allowance as a tip. Now Doerr passed on to Ted some of the baseball savoir faire he'd learned.

Williams needed all the road wisdom he could get. The first time he walked into the train's dining car on the way to Los Angeles and had to order from a menu, he didn't know what to do. He'd never been to anything fancier than a coffee shop or malt shop, where the selections were posted on a wall. This first dining-car experience left an indelible impression on Ted, according to Louise Kaufman, his lover for more than forty years, who was living with Ted when she died in 1993. "Part of *The Natural* where the kid was on the train in the dining car, going to where he was going—that was taken from Ted Williams's life right there," Kaufman told the writer Ed Linn in an unpublished interview.[13] "It's one of his favorite stories. He says, 'My God, and here I was on the train in a dining car.... And my God, to read a menu. Who knows how to read a menu if you never saw one?' He was a child."

Cedric Durst had his hands full tamping down the boy's rough edges. He found his roommate over the top and loud but likable and good-natured. Durst would watch in amazement as his charge entered a restaurant, screamed out a greeting to a teammate on the other side of the room, gave another a friendly but pulverizing slap on the back, and lifted a piece of bread off the plate of a third. When Ted ordered food, he always acted as if he were in a hurry, Doerr said, often telling a waitress he had a train to catch. Doerr was never sure what the rush was.

Ted ate like a horse. "My God, he'd put away two T-bone steaks and a platter of rolls for breakfast," recalled teammate George Myatt. When the Padres arrived in Oakland, Bill Lane confronted Ted in the lobby of the Hotel Leamington.

"Kid," said Lane, "you're leading the list!"[14]

"What list?" said Ted.

"The overeaters' list," the owner said, explaining that Williams was consistently signing for more than his $2.50 daily meal allowance.

Ted waved the owner off. "Well, I just can't eat on $2.50 a day. Take it out of my check." Lane never did.

As a roommate, Ted had his eccentricities. One morning at six thirty, Durst was awakened by a great hullabaloo. "Jeezem, I was almost scared to death," he told *Time* magazine's Ed Rees in 1950.[15] "Ted was jumping up and down on his bed and shouting. 'Christ!' I said, 'What's the matter, kid?' Ted just smiled and said, 'Boy, it's great to be young and full of pep!' 'Yeah,' I said, 'but not so early in the morning.'" Then Durst rolled over and tried to go back to sleep as Ted roared with laughter.

Another quirk Durst discovered was that Ted would talk in his sleep—about hitting, of course. "What a hit!" he would say, or "Boy, what power!" Or, "Big arms are what I need. Big arms!"[16]

Ted liked to go to the movies on the road, usually westerns with Gene

Autry, but only the team batboy, Ralph Thompson, would go with him, because Ted would often act out and cause a scene himself. "If the theater didn't start the movie on time, he'd get up on his feet and start hollering and raising hell," Thompson recalled.[17] "As a kid, I didn't care. I was happy to go. His actions didn't bother me any. He was always good to me. He paid my way in. The other players wouldn't go anywhere with him, though. They'd be embarrassed."

Ted also discovered pinball machines and played them too much for his mother's liking;[18] May had the Padres stop her son from using his meal money for such frivolous pursuits. Durst said Ted would also generously use what cash he had to front for other players if they were broke.

Other rules of the road that Ted learned on that first trip included the fact that on the train, the starting players got the lower births and the scrubs got the uppers. And the veterans felt it was their right to haze rookies, especially such an inviting target as Ted. Doerr recalled that on an early trip, several of the older players with a few drinks under their belts decided to grab, tug, and aggressively horse around with the sleeping rookie. Finally Ted escaped by taking his bedcovers and going into the women's bathroom, left vacant in the car the Padres had taken over. When he played for the Red Sox, Ted would continue this ladies' room maneuver on train trips, but by then it was to assert a star's privacy prerogative.

Yet Ted didn't mind the hazing—he was having the time of his life.

"I never had so much fun," Ted remembered.[19] "It was like a fairyland to me. Everything was new. The train ride was new. The Pullman. Riding up to Sacramento, riding up to Oakland and to Frisco, and riding up on the train to Portland, all through the Cascades, Mount Shasta, and Jesus, going into Seattle. And seeing all the players and seeing them up close and getting that experience to be a professional ballplayer. Oh, Jesus, yes, I thought I was in fairyland. It was all like a dream for a year and a half."[20] He was beginning to experience the perks of his chosen profession and see some of America doing it. After always worrying about how he would afford his next bat, he could soon order his own bats whenever he wanted to and would have an endless supply of baseball's most vital piece of equipment.[21]

Frank Shellenback was impressed early on by Williams's work ethic, drive, and determination. After home games Ted would ask Shellenback for a couple of old baseballs. When the manager asked what he did with them, Ted said he used them for extra batting practice after dinner at the park near his house. Shellenback found that hard to believe, having seen

Ted come in to Lane Field at ten in the morning for extra hitting in addition to the regular workout every day. As Shellenback told the *Boston Herald*'s Arthur Sampson in 1949, one evening he drove to Williams's neighborhood to investigate and saw the rookie "driving those two battered baseballs all over the field. Ted was standing close to a rock which served as a plate. One kid was pitching to him. A half dozen others were shagging drives. The field was rough and stony. The baseballs I had given him were already showing signs of wear. The stitching was falling apart. The covers were rough as sandpaper. Blood was trickling from Williams's hands as he gripped a chipped bat. But he kept swinging. And hitting. Ted made himself the great ballplayer he is today."[22]

Williams's dedication to his hitting far surpassed the attention he gave to his fielding—which was to say, none at all. His "When do we hit?" remark to Bud Tuttle the day he started with the Padres reflected Ted's one-dimensional view of the game as well as a sense of arrogance on the part of a rookie so young, coarse, and inexperienced.

Ted would balk at shagging, taking ground balls, or otherwise working on his fielding. "He did little more many times than simply wave at balls hit to left field in the San Diego park," recalled Jack Orr, a sportswriter for the *San Diego Evening Tribune*.[23]

The first time Ted started a game in left in 1936, George Myatt, the Padres' shortstop and captain, caught the rookie with his back to the infield.

"I'd see the signs . . . and give the signs to the outfielders," Myatt said. "Once, right after the sign had been given . . . I turned around real fast. There Ted is, standing with his back to the hitter. He had his glove in his hands and he was swinging his glove like it was a bat. I called time and went out and called him a few names, told him there was something else to this game besides swinging a bat."[24]

When a ball skipped through Ted's legs, and he just casually jogged after it early that first season, his manager benched him. "I didn't speak to him about it at the time," said Shellenback, a former spitball pitcher who compiled a 296–177 record in nineteen Pacific Coast League seasons.[25] "I merely took him out of the lineup the next day. For five days in a row he came to me in the morning and followed me all over the field. 'Am I going to play today, Skipper?' he would inquire. When I'd say 'no,' he would add, 'How about tomorrow?' I'd say, 'Maybe,' and walk away. At the end of about five days of this, Ted was about ready to burst a blood vessel. I knew that I had punished him severely by keeping him out of the lineup. . . . So I finally put him back in the lineup with the comment that he could stay there as long as he hustled. And he never gave me any cause to criticize him again."

Ted's hustle may have improved after that incident, but his fielding skills, and fundamental indifference to the defensive part of the game, generally did not. Shellenback would order him to report early for spring training in 1937 so that Durst could work with him on improving his fielding. Durst also arranged for a track coach to try to improve Ted's speed on the bases.[26]

But after the season got under way, Ted's poor fielding persisted, causing the veteran players to grouse and warn him to shape up. Earl Keller, the beat writer for the *Tribune,* got wind of the grumbling and decided to publicly scold Ted. "If Ted Williams, 18-year-old outfielder with the San Diego Padres is to make the grade in the diamond sport, he has one thing to learn," Keller wrote. "Ted must get it in his head that fielding is just as important as hitting. The young flyhawk believes all he has to do is get up to the plate and hit the ball, but that's where he's wrong. The veterans on the Padres team are trying to convince Ted of this fact, and the sooner they do, the sooner the youth will make good."[27]

Keller, who would stay on as a *Tribune* sportswriter for forty-six years, probably intended those words to serve more as paternal advice than as harsh rebuke, for he was a reliable Padres booster and a friend to most of the players—especially Ted, whom he'd been tracking since high school. There was not even a hint of an adversarial relationship between Williams and the writers who covered him in San Diego. Boston would be a different story.

"There was no particular pressure on me playing in San Diego," Ted said later, reflecting on his first season. "I didn't know what pressure was. I was nervous—not because I was born there, but because it was a whole new experience playing before crowds, professional baseball."[28] After getting two hits in the game he pitched in on July 3, Ted went up as a pinch hitter in the first game of the July 4 doubleheader against Los Angeles. Then he started the second game, going 1–5 on the day. He also played both games of a doubleheader the next day and went a combined 0–6. He only got up seven more times the rest of the month, collecting one hit. Shellenback was opting to bring him along slowly.[29]

Then in early August, when the Padres were playing in Portland, Cedric Durst went down with a groin injury, creating an opportunity for Ted. He played in three consecutive doubleheaders between August

7 and August 9, going 6–17, including two doubles.[30] The press took notice. Monroe McConnell wrote in the *Union* that "young Ted Williams...has been delivering like a veteran and Padre fans probably will see more of him."[31]

Shellenback was probably impressed with this miniburst and display of power, but there was a VIP sitting in the stands in Portland for those games who really took notice of Ted: Eddie Collins. Collins had been a superb second baseman for twenty-five years with the Philadelphia Athletics and the Chicago White Sox, and was then on the verge of being inducted into the Hall of Fame. In 1933, Collins had advised multimillionaire Tom Yawkey, his old friend from prep school, to buy the Boston Red Sox, and Yawkey, after acquiring the team, had brought Collins to Boston with him as general manager and part owner.

Collins rarely made scouting trips, but had decided to take the train out to the West Coast that summer and spend some time watching the Padres, with whom the Red Sox had a working agreement. Specifically, Collins had taken options on Bobby Doerr and George Myatt and now had to decide whether to exercise them before they expired. He'd joined the Padres in Seattle for games against the Indians, then come down the coast for a series against the Portland Beavers.

But in the Portland series, it was Williams, not Doerr or Myatt, who made an impression on Collins.

"The announcer yelled, 'Williams hitting for San Diego,'" the general manager later recounted.[32] "I looked down on the field and nearly broke out laughing when I got a peek at the gawky bean pole who was striding toward the plate. But I didn't laugh when I saw him swing at the ball and line a double over the first sacker's head. There was nothing remarkable about the hit. There was certainly nothing impressive about the appearance of the hitter. But there was something about the way he tied into that ball which all but shocked me out of my seat. It was as though a shock of electricity had just passed through my body. In that fleeting moment, as he swung at that ball, I became so convinced that here was one of the most natural hitters in baseball history. I'd have staked my life on it.

"I tried to tell myself a little later that I must be mistaken: that if Williams was the extraordinary prospect I believed him to be, he'd be playing regularly instead of infrequently as a pinch hitter, and there'd be an army of scouts present with his name on their lips. But my judgment wouldn't listen to that argument. So I decided to have another peek at the kid in action and then began making inquiries about him."

In his mind's eye that first day, Collins told an interviewer in 1950, Williams had stood out "like a white horse in a herd of black ones."[33]

Another person impressed by Williams in that Portland series was Johnny Pesky, the future Red Sox shortstop who would become Ted's lifelong friend. Pesky was then the clubhouse boy for the Beavers. He shined Ted's shoes and watched in awe as Williams took batting practice, belting balls out of the park against a smoke-belching foundry in the distance. "He was just a kid, small, skinny, gangly," Pesky remembered. "I don't think he weighed one-sixty by then. I remember he had a great swing."[34]

Collins followed the Padres down to San Francisco for a series against the Mission Reds and then arranged to meet Bill Lane in Los Angeles to discuss his pending options for Doerr and Myatt. Collins said he would take Doerr, even though he'd watched the second baseman make four errors in the first game of the August 8 doubleheader against Portland. (Doerr said he was unnerved, knowing the GM was in the stands.) Collins passed on Myatt and also acquired the rights to Padres catcher Gene Desautels. When Lane asked if there was anyone else on the team who interested him, Collins said he was intrigued by Ted.

"Williams?" asked Lane incredulously. "Why that's preposterous. He's just a child, only a couple months out of high school. He couldn't be more crude. . . . He looks pretty good at bat at times. That's why I'm keeping him around. But he's years away and may never make it. I wouldn't think of sticking you with him."

"Don't do me any favors," said Collins. "Name your price and I'll take him."

"To be perfectly frank about it, Eddie, I can't sell him at this time. I promised his parents when I signed him up that I'd keep him this year. And I would anyway. You see, he's not shown anything to date which would warrant me asking a good price for him. I feel, though, as you apparently do, that he may become a standout. So I want to keep him until I can get some real money for him. However, I promise you that I'll let you know and give you a chance to bid before sending him to the majors."[35]

That was good enough for Collins, who thought Lane was a man of his word. Collins called Joe Cronin, the player-manager for the Red Sox, to tell him he'd bought Doerr and reached an understanding with Lane on a kid named Ted Williams. "The . . . boy is only seventeen, but he's got the most beautiful swing I ever saw," Collins told Cronin.[36]

Ted played sparingly the rest of the month, but on August 31, in a benefit game at Lane Field against a local semipro All-Star team, he hit a home run, a double, and two singles.[37]

The next day, the regular left fielder, Ivey "Chick" Shiver, suddenly announced he was quitting the team—and baseball—to take a job as a football coach at Georgia College. Shellenback decided to have Ted take Shiver's place for the remaining two weeks of the season.

Williams, who had just turned eighteen, responded, hitting .305 the rest of the way, with six doubles and two triples. He played with exuberance. His hat often fell off as he ran the bases, and he found it hard to conceal his delight whenever he tagged one. "When he connected, you could count his teeth from second base," wrote Monroe McConnell in the *Union*.[38]

Ted was still raw, but he was improving. Though the Padres were eliminated in the first round of the playoffs against the Oakland Oaks, Ted hit his first professional home run in that series—on September 15, off Wee Willie Ludolph, who was also known as the Oakland Ghost. Williams's average for the season was .271. He had appeared in forty-two games and got twenty-nine hits in 107 times up.[39] He wasn't selective enough at the plate, Shellenback thought—too eager to swing at whatever was thrown up there to him, especially the soft stuff favored by some of the older Coast League pitchers who'd lost their fastball but could still change speeds effectively.

Herm "Old Folks" Pillette, an archetypical junkballer for the Padres who was known for starting the day with a half cup of whiskey, gave Ted a valuable lesson on how to hit pitchers of his ilk: wait for the off-speed pitch, then tee off on it.

"Here is where being surrounded by older players helped me," Ted said.[40] "The opposition pitchers, they were starting to slow up on me a lot, a little slow ball and I'd be out in front and hit a ground ball or something. I just wasn't waiting on the ball. So Herm Pillette, who pitched for the Detroit Tigers in the 1920s—he was on the Padres, he said, 'What are they throwing you?'

"I said, 'Some little crappy curve ball.'

"He said, 'Why don't you go up there and kind of lay for one of those, just kind of lay for it a little bit?'

"Well, I did—and I got a line drive to right field. I said, 'Hell, if this keeps up . . .' Pillette got me *thinking* at a young age about having an idea about what the pitcher was throwing. Then once you hit one of those slow curves the pitchers say, 'I can't do that anymore.' So you get the pitch *you* want. I could never forget what happened when it went right for me. Like for example, looking for the curve ball, here it comes. Bang!"

It wasn't just the tip from Pillette; it was Ted's hunger to receive it that was striking. He had an innate baseball curiosity. He was constantly pumping pitchers about what they would throw in certain situations and pressing other hitters about their experiences against a given pitcher. He would absorb the information, process it, then use it.

Durst and other Padres were amazed by Ted's ability to read pitchers' tendencies. After a few times around the league, Durst recalled, "Ted was predicting what so and so would throw in a given situation: 'He'll get two and nothing on me, and then he'll throw me a slow, inside curve and I'll murder it.' Here was a kid just out of high school telling us things like that. He wasn't bragging. He was thinking out loud."[41]

Reflecting back years later, Durst concluded that "Ted was the greatest hitter I ever saw and that includes Babe Ruth. When it came to day in and day out hitting, I'd have to take Ted. I never saw anyone who had the memory of every pitch a pitcher threw like Ted did....He'd say, 'Next time I hit against that guy, I'll knock the ball out of the park,' and sure enough he would."[42]

Besides Durst and Doerr, Ted also learned from a variety of other Padres, including pitchers Wally "Preacher" Hebert, Bud Tuttle, and Howard Craghead, first baseman George McDonald, second baseman Jimmie Reese, shortstop Myatt, outfielder Vince DiMaggio (Joe's older brother), and catcher George Detore. They retained vintage Ted stories for the rest of their lives, many of which were mined by San Diego writer Bill Swank for his colorful oral history of the Padres, *Echoes from Lane Field*.

Tuttle, who was Ted's roommate in 1937, was something of a Renaissance man. He would go on to dabble in sportswriting, serve as a publicity agent for Jayne Mansfield, and crank out scores of forgettable books and screenplays. He recalled that on train trips to Portland and Seattle, the train would stop in the small Northern California town of Dunsmuir for fifteen minutes. "There was a lady on the platform with a small wagon. She had home-made ice cream and everyone wanted some. As we pulled into the depot, Ted would climb out the window and drop to the platform and get ice cream for both of us. It sure was good on hot days as there was no air conditioning on the train at that time."[43]

Williams introduced Tuttle to his father after Sam went to see the

Padres play when they came through Sacramento in 1937. Sam was still based in the state capital then for his job as a jail inspector. "He was proud of Ted," Tuttle said. "He was thrilled. Ted hit a home run when he was there at the Sacramento stadium and oh, his father was just so happy and he reached clear over the fence to shake Ted's hand when he came by afterward."[44]

Howard Craghead, who was nicknamed the Professor because he had a degree in philosophy from Fresno State College, once asked Ted what pitches he had difficulty with. "Can't tell the difference," Ted said. "They all look like they are hanging out in front of the plate on a string."[45]

"[Ted] had the prettiest swing of anybody I ever saw!" said George McDonald, who had dropped out of high school in 1935 with Bobby Doerr to join the Hollywood Stars. "When I saw him later, when he was hitting .400, his swing wasn't as pretty as when he was young."[46]*

Jimmie Reese, who played for the New York Yankees in 1930 and 1931 and roomed with Babe Ruth, remembered that Ted enjoyed his own reflection. "Ted Williams used to stand in front of a mirror in the clubhouse and take different poses with the bat. He went to take those poses and everybody said, 'Look at what that busher's doing.' But it turned out he wasn't crazy."[47]

Doerr also recalled the shadow hitting and that once, while demonstrating his technique on the slippery marble floor of a San Francisco hotel lobby, Ted swung so hard he fell.[48]

George Detore, the Padres catcher in 1937, taught Ted some of the rites of the game and a lesson about team play. Once, in Portland, Ted was outraged when Padres pitcher Dick Ward bowled over the Beavers catcher on a play at the plate, hurting him. Ted shouted at his teammate Ward: "That's just dirty baseball and you ought to have your block knocked off! I won't stand for that kind of work!"

"You won't stand for it?' piped up someone on the Padres bench. "What are you going to do about it?"

"I'll show you right now," replied Williams, the next man to bat, consumed with a need for fairness. "I'm going up there and strike out."

Detore told Williams that if he did so, he shouldn't "come back to the bench; just put on your street clothes and go home."

---

* McDonald liked to debunk a story told about Ted from the Padres years—that he'd struck the world's longest home run when a ball he hit out of Lane Field went into the railroad yards and landed directly on a Los Angeles–bound freight car. It was he, not Ted, who hit that ball, McDonald insisted to Bill Swank.

With a different sort of fairness on his mind, the Portland pitcher tried to bean Ted, who ducked out of the way. Williams shouted at the pitcher, asking him why he did it, since Ted hadn't done anything. The pitcher said he'd do it again, which he did. Ted dusted himself off and knocked the next pitch more than four hundred feet over the right-field fence. Back on the bench, Ted asked again why he'd been thrown at if he didn't do anything wrong.

Detore explained: "Oh yes, you did. You were wearing the same uniform as the rest of us. Whenever one of us gets in a jam, you're involved, remember that. And when you get into trouble, we're all for you. The uniform's the thing, kid. You can't get out of it when a quarrel starts. Always keep that in mind."[49]

As the new year began, Padres beat writer Earl Keller raised expectations for Ted in the 1937 season. "If you want to make a little extra money to put in the old sock," he wrote, "bet it on young Teddy Williams to be taken as the outstanding major league prospect after this year's Pacific Coast League baseball race is finished.... There wasn't a manager who didn't say Williams had the makings of a great slugger after they saw him in action the later part of the 1936 season."

Keller interviewed May Williams for his story, and May reported that "Teddy is drinking more milk and putting on weight steadily. Every night after he comes home from school he gets a bat and practices swinging for 30 or 40 minutes. The boy really is confident of making good and we all are sure he will go places."[50]

May's reference to her son coming home from school served as a reminder that Ted really was still a boy who hadn't graduated from Hoover High yet. After the 1936 season ended, as his Padres teammates — all grown men — fanned out to various jobs, Ted had headed back to Hoover to finish up his final semester.

Before the '37 season began, the Padres sold Vince DiMaggio to the Boston Bees, the National League franchise that would soon be renamed the Braves and that ran a distant second to the Red Sox in the hearts and minds of Bostonians. The DiMaggio move might have been expected to make Ted a lock as a starter, but Frank Shellenback decided to stick to his go-slow program for Williams. So Ted began the year on the bench, behind Cedric Durst, Tommy Thompson, and Hal Patchett.

Ted grew restless and bored. At a game in Seattle early in the year, he noticed in the clubhouse that the visiting batboy had a kit to blow bubbles through a pipe. Languishing in the dugout, Ted asked the batboy for his kit. Together, they soaped up some water in a bucket and Ted began blowing huge bubbles onto the field. When the umpires finally determined the source of the distraction, Ted was tossed from the game.[51]

Lefty O'Doul, who had touted Williams to Earl Keller, helped get Ted's confidence back on track. O'Doul, who had hit .398 with thirty-two home runs for the 1929 Philadelphia Phillies, had been managing the Seals in his hometown of San Francisco since 1935. He'd sent Joe DiMaggio up to the Yankees, and by 1937, O'Doul had another DiMaggio on his team—Joe's younger brother, Dominic. By 1940, Dominic would be playing center field for the Red Sox alongside Ted, and the two would become lifelong friends.

O'Doul was known as a great teacher of the game, especially of hitting. He'd seen enough of Williams in 1936 to be impressed, and now, early in 1937, at Lane Field against the Padres, O'Doul left the visitors' dugout to get a close look at Ted taking batting practice.

Dominic DiMaggio remembered the moment clearly more than sixty years later. "Lefty O'Doul left our dugout in San Diego," DiMaggio said.[52] "He was our manager, who I had a great deal of admiration for. Ted was batting in batting practice. He said, 'I've got to talk to this kid.' He ran off to the other side and waited for Ted to get through hitting. He took more than his allotted swings, and when he got through, Lefty called him over and talked to him, said something to him. Then of course [he] came back to the dugout.

"That was a no-no. You didn't fraternize with the opposition. Especially the manager with the opposing player. He came back in the dugout and all the old-timers were like, 'What the heck is this all about, Lefty? What did you say to the kid?' He said, 'I just told him to never let anyone ever fool around with his batting style.' He said, 'He's going to be one of the greatest hitters we've ever seen.' That was it."

O'Doul kept up his drumbeat for Ted. When the Padres visited San Francisco, and he was mired in a slump, Ted picked up a paper at the Pickwick Hotel. Its headline declared, WILLIAMS GREATEST HITTER SINCE WANER, Ted recalled in his book. "At first I wondered who the Williams was that it was talking about."[53]

He later asked O'Doul if he had been the one who'd spoken to the reporter.[54] "'Yes,' he told me, 'I said it, and I meant it, kid. You're the tops. You're headed straight for the majors and you're going to knock 'em dead up there with your hitting. That goes, though, only if you stick to your present style. Don't let anybody change your stance and your swing. Attempts will be made to, you can bet on that. Ignore them.... Just go on the way you are.' " Ted told the *Boston Evening American*'s Cashman that until that point, he felt he had ability but lacked confidence. "I might never have acquired it, either, if O'Doul hadn't given it to me."

Through eighty games into late June, Ted was playing irregularly, batting .259 with two homers in just 116 at bats. Then he went on a tear, cracking six home runs over the next week, including an inside-the-park job on June 22 to the deepest part of Lane's vast center field. By July, Shellenback had made him a regular, and Ted continued to hit. By the end of August, he had seventeen homers and was batting .283.[55]

Then on August 31, with O'Doul and his Seals in town, Ted hit a prodigious home run in the eighth inning to break open a tight game and lead the Padres to a 4–2 win. Ted's homer "fairly screamed" as it went over the right-field fence, recalled the *Union*'s Monroe McConnell.[56] Then "the ball cleared the railroad tracks beyond bordering Pacific Highway, took one hop into a railway freight house, and was retrieved by workmen who ran far back into the shed and indulged in a wild scramble to retrieve it. There have been some mighty homers at Lane Field since, but none in the memory of veteran scribes that has even closely approached that one for sheer power." After the game, O'Doul told Earl Keller of the *Tribune* he'd like to have Ted play for him next year. "That kid is the best prospect this circuit has seen since Joe DiMaggio," O'Doul said. "I would like to be his teacher."[57] The next day, Ted hit two more homers as the Padres beat the Seals again, 10–5.[58]

The Padres finished the year strong, sweeping Sacramento and Portland in the playoffs to win the Pacific Coast League championship. Williams performed solidly in the eight playoff games, batting .333, including a double, a triple, and a home run. He was the hitting star in three of the games. Ted finished the regular season with 23 home runs, 98 runs batted in, and an average of .291. He appeared in 138 of the Padres' 178 games, collecting 132 hits in 454 at bats. Somewhat predictably, his fielding percentage was the lowest among Coast League outfielders, with seven errors, 213 putouts, and ten assists.

Eddie Collins of the Red Sox had been monitoring Ted's progress closely during the 1937 season, along with Billy Evans, who had been appointed Boston's farm director the previous year. Twice during the summer of '37, Collins had called Lane and asked if he would be willing to deal Ted. Lane had put him off each time, reassuring Collins that he would have the chance to match any bid and that they'd be in touch after the season. Now Williams's strong showing and promise were generating interest from about twelve major-league teams. The teams' scrutiny of Ted and courting of Lane came to a head at the midwinter baseball meetings in early December at the Palmer House in Chicago.

Detroit was especially interested, as were Ted's old hero, Bill Terry of the New York Giants, and Casey Stengel, who was going to be manager of the Boston Bees the following season, 1938. Stengel had been out of baseball in '37, but had watched many Coast League games from his home in California and was high on Ted. He came up with an offer of cash and several minor-league players for Williams that Frank Shellenback liked, and the Padres manager urged Lane to do the deal with Stengel and the Bees. At that point several other teams also made offers, but Lane told all interested parties that he had promised Collins and the Red Sox the right of first refusal.

The *Boston Globe* reported at the time that one of the teams chasing Williams was the Yankees.[59] That wasn't surprising, given Bill Essick's pursuit of Ted while he was still in high school. But another Yankees scout, Joe Devine, had weighed in with a negative report on Ted earlier in the 1937 season. "Williams shows possibilities as a hitter, has good power," Devine wrote, while going on to say that Ted "is a very slow lad, not a good outfielder now, just an average arm. There is no doubt Williams will never be fast enough to get by in the majors as an outfielder. His best feature now is that he shows promise as a hitter, but good pitching so far has stopped him cold."[60]

Lane sent word to Collins, who was in Chicago at the meetings, that he was ready to go ahead with the deal for Ted.[61] But Collins then ran into a problem with Red Sox owner Tom Yawkey. Having spent millions of dollars acquiring talent like Joe Cronin and Jimmie Foxx only to fall well short of winning a pennant, Yawkey had decided to change tactics and play for the long haul by developing a first-rate farm system. He said he was through buying other teams' players and wanted to develop his own. Collins had agreed with this decision in principle. So when Collins now told him he wanted to buy Williams, Yawkey balked, pointing out that this would violate the new policy they were trying to implement. Collins argued that they had to make an exception in this case: Williams was that good. But Yawkey continued his objections, not so much because of the money but because they would immediately be breaking their new policy. Collins went to the mat, stressing that he himself had discovered Williams and tracked him. They weren't relying on the opinion of some unknown scout here.

Finally, Yawkey yielded—and apparently not a minute too soon. Convincing Yawkey had taken quite a long time, and Lane had grown impatient at not hearing back from Collins. According to writer Arthur Sampson's 1950 account, Lane decided he'd waited long enough—he'd satisfied his promise to give the Red Sox an opportunity to compete for Williams and they hadn't responded in time. Lane had started to leave the lobby of the hotel to go upstairs to meet another team interested in Ted when Collins stepped off the elevator saying he was ready to deal. If Collins could give him $25,000 and come up with a batch of players acceptable to Shellenback, he could have Ted, Lane said.

Collins realized the cash would be no problem, but the Red Sox didn't have any decent minor leaguers at the time. That was why they were going to revamp their entire farm system. So he had Billy Evans quickly acquire the rights to four solid Double-A players who were agreeable to Shellenback—Dom Dallessandro, Al Niemiec, Bunny Griffiths, and Spencer Harris. The deal was apparently finalized at 11:45 p.m. on December 6, just before a midnight deadline that had been imposed by Lane.[62]

The Red Sox were thrilled and thought they'd stolen Ted. "One thing I am sure of," said Evans, a former major-league umpire, in a 1954 interview with the *Boston Globe:* "Williams was the least expensive great baseball player I ever brought into the majors. . . . We knew it was a steal and would have gone much higher. Anywhere up to $100,000, if necessary. But we didn't have to. We had friendly relations with the San Diego owner, and he was an honorable man. . . . The day we clinched the deal we knew for sure we had the best prospect of the era."[63] Later, Joe Cashman reported that Lane had turned down more money for Ted from other clubs.[64] The Tigers, he wrote, had offered $30,000 and the Giants $31,000. Moreover, Collins told Cashman, he had paid Lane more for Bobby Doerr than for Ted, "and Dom DiMaggio cost us far more than Teddy and Bobby together."

Boston's acquisition of Williams was announced on December 7, 1937, and Ted himself was given the news by Earl Keller. He was stunned, but provided the *Tribune* a politic quote: "Go on, you're kidding me. Boy, this is the happiest day of my life. If the Red Sox give me a chance, I'll make good."[65]

But privately, he would write years later in his book, "I was sick. The Red Sox didn't mean a thing to me. A fifth, sixth-place club, the farthest from San Diego I could go. I sure wasn't a Boston fan. I might have been a New York Giant fan, with Mel Ott and Arky Vaughan and those guys, or a Detroit fan, with Greenberg and Charley [*sic*] Gehringer, but *Boston*. Then Eddie Collins came to visit us."[66]

The Williamses steered Collins to the only decent chair in their living room, an old mohair number that, as Ted recalled, had a hole in it through which the springs were visible. (They covered the hole with a five-cent towel.) Collins's mission was to sell the Red Sox to Ted and his family and to get his name on a contract, which would have to also be approved by his mother and father, since the player was still a minor. Collins said the Sox were on the rise. They'd been spending a lot of Tom Yawkey's money to build a team. They had Cronin, Foxx, Lefty Grove, Doc Cramer, Joe Vosmik, and now young Bobby Doerr at second. Collins said he was prepared to offer Ted a two-year contract: $3,000 for the first year, $4,500 for the second.

"I thought to myself, 'Gee, he wants to give me all this money, and here I'm only hitting .290, and I could do so much better," Ted wrote. "What if I'd been hitting .320?"[67] Still, he wanted to leap at the offer and sign immediately. But Sam Williams began haggling and insisting on a bonus for him and May, at which point an embarrassed Ted left the room.

May and Sam demanded that $5,000 of the $25,000 the Red Sox were paying Lane be given to them. They said that when Ted first signed with the Padres, Lane had promised them that they would receive a portion of whatever price the boy might fetch from a big-league team. Collins realized this wasn't his fight. He knew nothing of what Lane may have promised the couple, so he left San Diego with Ted unsigned.

Lane took the position that he had promised the Williamses nothing, and wasn't going to give them a penny of the $25,000 now. So May and Sam decided that they were effectively free agents who could peddle their son to other interested teams.

As Collins told Joe Cashman in 1941, "Ted's mother and father thought my offer was fair enough, but before accepting, they wanted to make sure they couldn't do better. You see, they had talked with the Tiger, Yankee and Cardinal scouts before Ted joined San Diego, and they thought those clubs could still bid for their son."[68] But when the Williamses began entering into discussions with other teams, and when some of those clubs prepared to try to sign Ted, American League president Will Harridge and baseball commissioner Kenesaw Mountain Landis learned of the moves and grew alarmed. If another team were allowed to sign Williams after the Red Sox had duly acquired his rights from the Padres, it would be a fundamental challenge to the game's bedrock reserve clause. Landis and Harridge ordered Collins to go back to San Diego and do whatever it took to get Williams signed, posthaste. "Don't come back without the signed contract, no matter what it costs you," Landis told Collins.[69]

Cashman said Collins went back to San Diego and saw Ted and May. Ted was again quite willing to sign, but May persisted in her demands and said her husband had to be satisfied as well. Sam was still living in Sacramento, doing his stint as a jail inspector, so Collins located him for a further to-and-fro.

But by mid–February of 1938, the issue was still unresolved, and Ted was scheduled to report to Sarasota, Florida, for spring training with the Red Sox in early March.

On February 15, May raised the stakes, bluntly telling reporters that there was no chance of Ted signing until Lane came through with a $5,000 check for her and Sam.[70] After another fruitless meeting with May, Collins emerged to tell the writers gathered outside the Williams house that the "next move is up to the Williams family. . . . I hate to think that Williams's career might be ruined because of money. The lad has a brilliant future and, in my opinion, he's one in a million. He has all the chance in the world to become a great player and I know he will. I have done all I can and I feel everything will turn out okay."

Two days later, the impasse was resolved when Collins, under increasing pressure from Landis and Harridge, agreed to pay the Williamses $2,500—from Red Sox funds.[71]

All sides seemed satisfied. Lane could say he stood fast and didn't have to give up a piece of his payment for Williams, while May and Sam, their marriage dissolving, could nonetheless say they'd received a reasonable compromise. They didn't care where the money came from. As for the Red Sox, they got their man.

Ted signed his two-year contract worth $3,000 and $4,500 and went off to chase his dream.

3

Sarasota and Minneapolis

I n 1938, the Boston Red Sox spring training headquarters was in Sarasota, on Florida's Gulf Coast. After Ted signed his contract, Eddie
Collins called Bobby Doerr and asked him to chaperone Williams
across the country.

Doerr had played infrequently in Boston the previous season but was
projected as the starting second baseman that year. Not even twenty yet,
Doerr was mature beyond his years, especially compared to Williams.
The two had gotten to know each other on the '36 Padres. Ted had
never been east of California before, and Collins thought it advisable
that the voluble rookie have a temperate traveling companion on the
long transcontinental train ride. But for several days in late February and
early March, just before Doerr and Williams were to meet and embark
on their trip, torrential rains swept through Southern California. Bridges
and railroads were washed away, lakes formed in the Mojave Desert,
communications were cut, more than two hundred people were killed,
and property damage exceeded $50 million.

With the phone lines down, Ted was able to find a ham radio operator
in San Diego who contacted a colleague in Los Angeles near Doerr's
home. Bobby decided they would have to go their separate ways and
hope for the best. "I said, 'You go the best way you can go, and I'll go
the best way I can.' We couldn't do more about it," Doerr recalled.[1]

Doerr set out on a bus from Los Angeles to the desert city of Indio, in
California's Coachella Valley, and there boarded a train bound for El
Paso. Also traveling with Doerr was Max West, a power-hitting out-
fielder who was joining the Boston Bees as a rookie, and Babe Herman,

the former Brooklyn Dodger who had hit .393 in 1930 and whom Ted, while still in high school, had watched take batting practice.

Carrying $200 he had borrowed from a bank, Williams was able to get out of San Diego by train, and his first connection was in El Paso, where he chanced to meet Doerr, Herman, and West.[2]

"We rode together on the train the rest of the way," Doerr remembered. "We were back at one end. Ted was pumping Babe Herman on hitting. He was so loud that the women at the other end of the car kept telling the conductor to tell him to be quiet. But that didn't stop Ted. He was swinging pillows for a bat and going on and on talking."

When Ted arrived at Payne Park in Sarasota, he was greeted by Johnny Orlando, the irascible Red Sox equipment manager, better known, in the parlance of the day, as the "clubhouse boy." Orlando had been working in the team's clubhouse since 1926 and would quickly hitch his surly star to Williams's, becoming, over the years, Ted's manservant. Orlando would always remember Ted's first appearance, the day he gave the rookie his most enduring nickname: the Kid.

"Sarasota in 1938 was a hayshaker town," Orlando told the *Boston Evening American* in 1960. "You could shoot a cannon up Main Street from Five Corners and you'd only hit maybe a rattlesnake. The Ringling Brothers winter training headquarters were almost as big a tourist attraction as the Red Sox in spring training. That is, until 1938 when Ted Williams arrived for his first tryout in the majors."[3]

When Ted walked in, Orlando said, "he's got a red sweater on, his shirt open at the neck, a raggedy duffle bag. His hair's on end like he was attached to an electric switch. If anyone ever wanted a picture of a raw rookie, this was the time to take the shot."

"Where you been, Kid?" Orlando asked him. Ted mumbled something about getting tied up in New Orleans. It was the morning of March 9. Ted and Doerr had arrived the night before, and though many of the players had been in camp for a week, team officials of course knew of the flood in California, and May Williams had wired ahead of her son's progress. Also taking the field that day was another heralded rookie, third baseman Jim Tabor of the University of Alabama. Some regulars were still trickling in.

Orlando said he gave Williams the biggest shirt and pair of pants he had and took him out to the field. But the shirt wasn't long enough to tuck in his pants. Manager Joe Cronin, sitting in the first-base stands, saw him walk onto the field and yelled: "Hey, busher, this is the big leagues; stick your shirttail in!"

Ted seethed and asked Orlando, "Who's the wise guy up there?"

"That's Joe Cronin, your manager, Kid."

Later that morning, Doerr introduced Ted to Cronin. "I said, 'Joe, I want you to meet Ted Williams,'" Doerr remembered. "Ted's response was, 'Hiya, sport.'

"He was excited, and it just popped out. I thought at the time that would give him his ticket to Minneapolis." The Minneapolis Millers were the Red Sox's top farm team in the American Association.

Cronin, then only thirty-one, was nonetheless starting his sixth season as a player-manager. At the time considered one of baseball's premier shortstops, he had broken in with the Pittsburgh Pirates in 1926 and, in 1928, been traded to the Washington Senators, where he blossomed, hitting .346 with 126 RBIs by 1930. In 1933, Washington owner Clark Griffith named Cronin his player-manager at the age of twenty-six, and Cronin had led the team to the World Series.

In 1934, Griffith introduced his niece, a team secretary named Mildred Robertson, to Cronin, and they married later that year. But at the end of the 1934 season, Griffith stunned baseball, and presumably his own family, by selling his new nephew-in-law to the Red Sox for the then-unheard-of sum of $225,000. A Hall of Famer and lifetime .301 hitter, Cronin would remain the Red Sox's regular shortstop until 1942, when he took himself out of the every-day lineup to make way for Johnny Pesky. He remained the manager until 1948, when he joined the front office and succeeded Eddie Collins as general manager. In 1959 he was named president of the American League and served in that capacity until 1973.

Back in Sarasota, at the end of the morning workout, Cronin called Ted over and told him to step into the batting cage and hit. He hadn't planned to have Williams bat until the afternoon, but five movie newsreel companies were in camp shooting footage, and they asked to see the rookie hit, so the manager obliged.

Cronin stood behind the cage and watched as Herb Pennock, his pitching coach, got ready to pitch to Williams. Pennock, who had been a Hall of Fame lefty over twenty-three seasons for the Philadelphia Athletics, Red Sox, and Yankees, told Ted not to hit any balls back through the box.

"I'll try and pull 'em," the Kid said.

"Yes, but where's your hat?" one of the newsreel photographers called out.[4] He didn't want to look like a bush leaguer in the newsreels, did he? Strangely, Williams had stepped into the box without his cap, the baseball equivalent of being half naked.

As he yanked the folded hat from his hip pocket and put it on, a chastened Ted tried to recover with a wisecrack: "Is this all it takes to be a big leaguer? And I thought it was going to be tough."[5]

"Just another college boy," chirped the catcher, Moe Berg, wryly. The irony and humor of this remark by Berg — a true baseball anomaly who was a Phi Beta Kappa from Princeton and spoke a dozen languages fluently — was perhaps lost on Ted, who stepped out of the box, glared at Berg, and replied: "Looks like there's at least one agitator in camp.[6] How are ya, Adge?"[7] Thereafter Williams would refer to the erudite Berg, who would soon become an acclaimed spy for the Office of Strategic Services during World War II, as Adge whenever he saw him.

Standing next to Cronin behind the cage was Jack Malaney, Red Sox beat writer for the *Boston Post.* Cronin and Malaney were friendly, and the reporter would later work under Cronin as the team's PR man.

Cronin noticed that most everyone on the field had stopped what they were doing and turned to watch as Williams prepared to hit. Sensing the drama of the moment, Cronin, who had a good rapport with most of the writers and was attuned to their needs, dictated a mock lead paragraph for Malaney's morning story:

"A hush went over the ballpark at the Red Sox training camp this morning. All eyes were focused on one man. Even the veterans stopped and gazed and the photographers got ready to shoot. For Ted Williams, the Pacific Coast phenom, was about to make his first appearance at the bat in a big league uniform."[8]

Malaney used Cronin's lead verbatim in the March 10 *Post,* between quotation marks, explaining in the second paragraph that Cronin had then told him: "Now that's the way I would start my story tonight if I were writing it." If Malaney was having fun and not playing it straight, the headline over his piece picked up the lead directly, with no apparent irony: WILLIAMS HUSHES WHOLE SOX CAMP, it said. PACIFIC COAST PHENOM CYNOSURE OF ALL EYES IN SARASOTA DEBUT — LONG, LOOSE SWINGER.

Malaney wrote that in reality, "Skipper Joe" was, in fact, as interested as everybody else in watching the Kid hit, and that "it did seem as if everybody hushed up for the occasion.... Williams did not disappoint. Immediately he smashed three solid blows into right field, one of them a terrific line drive over first base, and another a long fly to right. The young man is to be colorful. He was that as soon as he got into uniform. He is a long string bean with a baby face. He handles the bat in toothpick fashion. He is a big, loose swinger, but he whips that bat. He is a pop-off kid, which the crowd soon discovered."

After the morning workout, Ted went into the clubhouse and asked no one in particular: "Now what do we do?" Someone told him to get a sandwich and a bottle of milk, then there would be another workout.

"Work out again in these suits?" Ted asked indignantly.

"What do you think we do, get two uniforms a day?" replied Jim Bagby Jr., a second-year pitcher who had a harelip.

Then Ted started panning the rainy Florida weather. "Why, this place is under a foot of water," he complained. Whereupon Gene Desautels, his former teammate on the Padres, reminded him he had just arrived from flooded Southern California.

Speaking to reporters after the morning workout, Cronin had this initial assessment of Ted: "I liked the way Williams handles that bat. He's quite a kid. He holds it back there, handles it like a whip, and has a great pair of wrists."

On March 13, in the Red Sox's first game of the spring training season against the Cincinnati Reds, Cronin started Ted in right field and had him hit third, but Williams went 0–4 and looked "a trifle nervous," one writer thought.[9] He fared better in an intrasquad game on March 16, stroking a double to drive in a run and drawing a walk. The following day against the Boston Bees, Ted entered the game as a pinch hitter, but was fooled by Ira "Speed Boy" Hutchinson and struck out.

Williams was clearly attracting more attention off the field than on. On March 18, the Associated Press moved a story on its feature wire headlined UNSHAVEN BOSTON ROOKIE GETS BILLING AS ANOTHER JOE DIMAGGIO. Ted revealed he'd yet to take a razor to his face, and gave it the aw-shucks routine when asked to compare himself to DiMaggio. "I'm just a punk trying to get along," he said. He thought he should have hit better in the Coast League, but then added, curiously: "I've got a lazy disposition and when the jockeys out there started riding me I got discouraged and for awhile just didn't give a darn."

Finally, assessing his chances to make the Red Sox, he said it would be difficult to crack the starting outfield of Doc Cramer, Ben Chapman, and Joe Vosmik, "and if I can't get in games pretty regularly, I'd rather they'd ship me to the minors for another season. I guess I could stand some more experience."[10]

That's exactly what the Red Sox had decided, and in making those remarks—perhaps his first since arriving that had a modicum of humility—Ted probably saw the handwriting on the wall. Though there would be no official announcement for three more days, the *Boston Globe*'s Hy Hurwitz wrote on the afternoon of March 18 for his paper's evening edition that Williams, whom he referred to as Babyface, would be farmed out. "The cocky Coast youngster is lacking in experience," Hurwitz wrote in a "Diamond Dots" notes item that was easy to miss.

But the news could have surprised no one. The Red Sox, after all, had just traded for Vosmik, an All-Star left fielder, in the off-season. In center field they had Cramer, who had hit .305 the previous year, and in right field, they had Chapman, who'd hit .307.

The truth was, Ted's mouth had been louder than his bat. He'd tried to disguise his own raging insecurity with false bravado and bluster, challenging baseball's tradition that a rookie should be seen and not heard. He had offended everyone from the "Royal Rooters"—the elderly die-hard Boston fans who stayed with the team at the Sarasota Terrace Hotel—to the Red Sox regulars and veterans, who responded by hazing and riding him mercilessly.

After panning Florida on his arrival, Ted even had the temerity to criticize Boston and Fenway Park, which the faithful in his midst considered heresy of the highest order.[11]

If he failed to hit, he'd make a flippant, nonsensical remark; he'd question why he was fooling around playing baseball in the first place or say he probably should quit and get a real job.

Not all Ted's outrageous remarks were reported at the time. In a 1959 article reflecting on Williams's career, Bill Cunningham, who in 1938 wrote for the *Boston Post* and was considered the city's leading sports columnist, said he witnessed an early Ted rant during that brief spring training stint in Sarasota. Spotting a gaggle of writers and photographers on one side of the clubhouse interviewing some of the veteran players, Ted said, to no one in particular, and in a loud voice: "What are all the writers and photographers doing down there around those old men?" Cunningham wrote. "Why aren't some of 'em up here looking at some real ball players?" Earlier, when Ted had tried to approach the irascible Lefty Grove as if he were a long-lost friend—"How are ya, Lefty, old kid?"—Grove brushed the upstart back: "Better not fool with me or you'll get hurt."[12] Now Williams unloaded. "From what that old Lefty Grove showed me out there today he couldn't pitch third string in the Coast League."

Bobby Doerr had tried to tell Ted on the trip across country how great Jimmie Foxx was. "I said to Ted, 'Wait til you see Foxx hit these shots.' Ted said, 'Yeah, wait til he sees *me* hit.' Ted was impressive, but he was an excitable kid."[13] Now Williams let loose on the man who would become the second player in Major League Baseball history to hit five hundred home runs, beaten only by Babe Ruth. "And what's so hot about this Foxx? I've been reading about him, and expected to see something, but I hit three balls out there today farther than anything he got hold of. But you can't expect any sense from writers. They're all alike. They don't know anything. They try to tell you how to play, when they never played themselves. It's the same on the Coast. I thought it might be different over here."[14]

Furthermore, Williams continued to radiate his indifference to fielding. He did his "Hi-yo, Silver, away!" routine while chasing balls in the outfield. Cronin once caught him swinging his imaginary bat in the outfield and shouted to him, "Hey, Bush, never mind practicing this [mimicking a swing]; practice this [bending to scoop up a ground ball]." And Doc Cramer gave up trying to teach Ted how to play the outfield after a few days. "They wanted me to teach Williams how to field up there," Cramer told writer Peter Golenbock. "Ted said, 'They ain't paying me to field. I'm going to get paid for hitting. The hell with this.' You couldn't do much with him. I did help him a little bit. He couldn't catch a ground ball. Used to go right between his legs."[15]

In one brief introspective passage in his book, Ted chalked up some of his bizarre behavior in Sarasota to the fact that he was "a kid away from home, really for the first time in his life, feeling alone, a little scared and seeking attention."[16]

On March 21, the Red Sox made it official and announced that Ted was being optioned out to Minneapolis. Though his departure was inevitable, Ted had perhaps hastened it by again calling an unamused Cronin "Sport" the day before.[17]

Ted was given a bus ticket and told to join the Millers at their training camp across the state, in Daytona Beach. Johnny Orlando remembered escorting the Kid to the bus stop. Orlando, ever the Williams apologist, thought the older players had been overly harsh on the rookie from the outset, riding him almost immediately with barbs like "Hey, Kid, how you gonna like it back in the minors?"

"It wasn't like it is today," Orlando said. "A veteran will help a rookie now. Those days, they gave him the short end of the stick. They really got under his skin. They irritated him until he finally blew his stack. He really let loose the day he got his walking papers back to the minors. 'I'll be back and I'll make more money in one year than the three of you combined!'" Ted shouted at Chapman, Vosmik, and Cramer. Then Williams asked Orlando how much he thought each of the veterans made. Orlando guessed $12,000, maybe $15,000.

Then Orlando asked him how much money he had. Ted didn't answer directly, but said he had enough. "So I told him, 'Kid, I got a finif [$5]. I'll split it with you. That'll buy you a good steak. Just go out and have a good year. You've got a lot of time coming up for you in the big leagues.' "[18]

Chapman later laughed off Ted's parting shot at Vosmik, Cramer, and himself: "It didn't bother me. I took it with a grain of salt. He was a young kid. Let him have his fun." But what had seemed like a spiteful outburst would turn out to be not just petulance but prophecy: "What he said came true. You can't condemn him. That guy was one of the greatest hitters you ever looked at. Oh boy, could he swing a bat. When he said what he did about the three of us, I thought, 'He might be right.' "[19]

If Ted was disappointed at his demotion, his mood seemed to have brightened by the time his bus pulled into Daytona Beach.

On a lark, he borrowed a bicycle from a Western Union messenger and rode it all around the station, hooting and hollering "and frightening women and little children," it was reported.[20] For a Minnesota press corps already overheated by the Millers' acquisition of Williams—"one of the greatest hitting prospects ever to come along," wrote Halsey Hall of the *Minneapolis Journal*—this arrival scene set the tone for the portrayal of Ted as an ebullient, puckish, Peter Pan–type character who, in the sporting-press vernacular of the day, was quickly labeled a "screwball."[21] But a screwball with talent, clearly. Reporters began gravitating to him as a hitting prodigy with color, whose exploits and persona made him an endless font of good copy.*

After Ted's first day in camp, Dick Hackenberg of the *Minneapolis Star* pronounced the young slugger "tickled to death to be with the Millers" and said he "talks a blue streak, wants to know all about Minneapolis and Minnesota, when the duck hunting season opens, the fishing [and] would like to get his hands on the guy who started 'this second DiMaggio business.' "[22]

The next day, the *Minneapolis Journal* reported that Ted was "rattling the fences" and "would not pose for a picture doing anything but swinging a bat. He likes to use a 44 ounce bat in practice and then switches to his own 34-ouncer for the game. He doesn't care for any other sports but baseball. He's the happiest, pokingest lad in camp. Although he has been

---

* In their early features on Williams, many reporters covering the Millers somehow settled on Francis, not Samuel, as Ted's middle name and would stay with the error all season. "Theodore Francis" would become one of their favorite affectionate monikers for the Kid.

here less than a week, he is everybody's friend." The only downer in this upbeat report with no byline came at the end, when it was noted that Ted "is no ball of fire in the outfield."[23]

The Kid still had difficulty channeling his exuberance. Early one morning he walked down the hall of the Millers' spring training hotel to rouse a teammate by jumping on him—only it turned out to be not a teammate at all but future Hall of Fame umpire Jocko Conlan, then apprenticing in the American Association.

"Get up, Bush, let's go!" Ted screamed, pouncing on the umpire.

"Get out of here, you big skinny punk!" Conlan yelled, as he recounted the story in his memoir, *Jocko*.[24]

"You're not Bush," said Ted. "You're not even a ballplayer. You're too old to be a ballplayer."

"Who are you?" Conlan demanded.

"I'm Ted Williams. I hit twenty-three home runs in San Diego and I'll hit forty in this league."

"You better wait till this league gets started. Maybe you won't even be here."

"Is that so? You watch me. I'm a great hitter."

Later that summer, Conlan would be umpiring a game behind the plate in Minneapolis. There was a big crowd, and Ted had already hit two long home runs. Then he came to bat in the ninth with the bases loaded, two outs, the Millers down by a run, and the count at three and two. Conlan ended the game by calling Williams out on a pitch at the knees.

The crowd screamed for the ump's head, and Millers manager Donie Bush, who'd been coaching third base, came running in to argue, shouting at Conlan that the pitch had been down around Ted's ankles.

"And then Williams did something I'll never forget, and it is one of the reasons I consider him a great friend of mine in baseball," Conlan wrote. "He looked at Donie Bush and he shook his head. 'No Donie,' he said. 'It was a good pitch. It was a perfect strike right at the knees. I should have hit it.' I could have thrown my arms around him. I walked off the field and I thought, 'What a man.' I never had anyone else in my career do anything like that."

Ted hit it off well with Bush, a five-foot-six, 140-pound firebrand who'd had a sixteen-year big-league career as a slick-fielding, light-hitting shortstop, mainly for the Detroit Tigers. He'd also managed in the majors for seven years, taking the 1927 Pirates to the World Series, where they were swept by the magnificent Yankees. "I knew the minute I saw him that he was the greatest hitter I'd seen in 20 years," Bush would say of Ted years later.[25]

Having had his ears pinned back at Sarasota, Ted tried a more self-effacing tack with the press in Minneapolis, admitting to one reporter that he hadn't been ready for the big leagues and that he still had much to learn as a hitter: "I am glad I am going to spend a year under Donie Bush because I think he can make me a good hitter....It would have been nice to have crashed the major leagues at 19. But I'm not ready."[26]

Ted had been in the Millers camp for five days when suddenly Rogers Hornsby, generally considered to have been baseball's greatest right-handed hitter, appeared. Hornsby was putting on a clinic for the Millers and another minor-league club, the Chattanooga Lookouts of the Southern Association, but then decided to stay on for a while, entering into talks with Millers owner Mike Kelley about a possible role as a utility player for Minneapolis.

The Rajah, as Hornsby was known, was then forty-one and had just finished twenty-three seasons in the big leagues, most recently as the pinch-hitting manager of the St. Louis Browns. During his career, he had hit over .400 three times, including .424 in 1924, the highest average of the modern era. He'd won six straight batting titles from 1920 to 1925, and from 1921 to 1925 he had averaged an astonishing .402. A second baseman with speed, Hornsby had a lifetime average of .358, second only to Ty Cobb's, with 301 career home runs. No banjo hitter, he.

Hornsby never smoked or drank, and he wouldn't read or go to the movies for fear of hurting his eyes. He had a cold, contentious personality and wouldn't respect authority figures. He was also a compulsive gambler at the racetrack and had clashed on this issue with Commissioner Landis, who was unsympathetic to any players gambling after dealing with the Black Sox scandal of 1919. Hornsby told Landis it was nobody's business what he did off the field.

The mere fact that Hornsby was at a minor-league camp and willing to consider a utility role for the Millers was testament to his continuing love for the game as well as to the fact that his barbed persona was wearing out its welcome in the majors. But he was a good teacher, and he loved to talk about hitting for hours with anyone willing to listen and work hard.

And that was Ted, of course, the ultimate hitting inquisitor, whose curiosity and thirst for batting wisdom had not been—and never would be—sated. He had questions, and the Rajah had answers.

Ted was respectful of Hornsby, who was twenty-two years his elder and soon to be a Hall of Famer, but he called him Raj, not Mr. Hornsby. ("Hi, Raj!" he shouted one day, hoping to engage Hornsby in a game of pepper. "Want to stop a few?" Hornsby didn't.[27]) Williams fell in quickly as a Hornsby acolyte. He would stay after practice and take extra hitting with the Rajah, and they'd have contests to see who could hit harder and with greater accuracy. Ted had more power, but Hornsby could still hit one line drive after another. It was quite a scene: two once and future hitting masters dissecting and perfecting their craft.

"I liked Hornsby because he talked to me, a kid of 19, and boy I picked his brains for everything I could," Ted remembered. "We'd talk hitting and I'd ask personal questions I had no business asking." Like how much money he'd lost at the track. (Hornsby apparently didn't answer that question, but he told Ted he'd won $78,000 one day.)

"Get a good ball to hit" was what Hornsby preached to Ted, and that became the Williams mantra, his main rule to live by in hitting. If he had known this in theory before, he hadn't fully digested it until now. Earlier in his career, getting walked would send him into a deep funk and was something to be avoided at all costs, even if he had to hit a ball out of the strike zone. Now, ahead of his time, Williams began to view a base on balls in a different light: a walk *was* as good as a hit, as the cliché said; getting on base helped your team and ultimately made you a better hitter by letting pitchers know you would insist on not chasing balls that weren't strikes.

After two weeks, Hornsby left the Millers to take a job with the Baltimore Orioles as a coach and pinch hitter.[28] Staying with a minor-league team as a utility player made no sense, and Donie Bush had no desire to be overshadowed by an irascible legend known for getting prickly whenever his advice wasn't accepted. But for Ted, the time and tutorials with Hornsby had been serendipitous and invaluable.

"I thought Hornsby was great," Ted wrote in his book.[29] "He wasn't a very diplomatic guy. If he had a dislike about anything, he came out with it.... I mean, even if the owner of the club said something he disagreed with, Hornsby would say, 'What the hell do you know about it?' He was all the time getting into wringers for what he said."

The Rajah had an opinion about young Williams, too. "He'll be the sensation of the major leagues in three years," Hornsby told reporters as he left Daytona Beach.[30]

After about ten days with the Millers, Williams had performed respectably but hadn't quite lived up to the hype generated by the Minneapolis press corps, either. And he was the goat of the final exhibition game, a 4–3 loss to Chattanooga. Batting in the seventh inning with the bases loaded, he failed to run out a ground ball he thought would go foul but stayed fair, and then dropped a fly ball with two outs, allowing the Lookouts to continue the inning and score two decisive runs.

When the regular season began, the Millers had to play their initial twelve games on the road, first against Indianapolis, then against Louisville, Columbus, and Toledo. In his first game, Ted, wearing the number 19 again and batting cleanup, went 0–5, though he ripped one ball on a line that the right fielder made a good catch on. He went hitless in the next two games, and during the third game, when a passing train sounded its whistle, a frustrated Williams said wistfully, "That's what I want to be, an engineer. I'm no good for baseball."[31]

But things started looking up in Louisville, the next stop. Showing patience, Ted walked five times in the first game, went 2–5 with a double in the second, then broke out in the third game by hitting two massive home runs that were said to be perhaps the longest in American Association history.[32] Ironically, both stayed inside massive Parkway Field. The first ball soared about 470 feet to right-center, and the second rose 450 feet in the air, slightly left of dead center, before it rolled up against the wall 512 feet away. Both balls were hit so far that Ted could jog home without a play at the plate. On his next time up, with center fielder Nick Tremark playing so deep as to be barely discernible from the press box, Ted lined a single to right. His homers accounted for the only Millers runs in a 6–2 loss.

Williams was hitting his stride. Over the next six games on the rest of the road trip, he collected eight hits, including another home run and three doubles, and had his average up to .270 by the time the club arrived in Minneapolis for its home opener. The Millers—or the Kels, as they were also called in the local press, after team owner Mike Kelley—were 6–6.

The Millers played their home games at Nicollet Park, a quaint ball field built in 1896 at the corner of 31st Street and Nicollet Avenue, across from the city's streetcar barns. The park was made to order for left-handed power hitters like Ted: only 279 feet and ten inches down the right-field line, 330 to the power alley in right-center, 432 to dead center, and 334 down the left-field line. The right-field fence was thirty feet high, and it had netting on top as a further constraint against balls flying onto Nicollet Avenue and shattering the plate-glass windows of Minken's department store and the President's Café. But the windows at those establishments would still prove especially vulnerable during Ted's time in town.

The Millers and their crosstown American Association rivals, the St.

Paul Saints, provided the only source of serious baseball for much of the upper Midwest in those years.[33] Local idiosyncrasies included the requirement that Sunday doubleheaders be stopped promptly by 6:00 p.m. and the fact that Mike Kelley was inexplicably allowed to keep his menacing dog, a Dalmatian, in right field, in fair territory. Kelley had trained the dog to growl threateningly if any player wearing a visitor's uniform chased a ball into the area. Highlights of the summer for fans were the holiday doubleheaders between the Millers and Saints, with perhaps a morning game at Nicollet and an afternoon game across the river in Saint Paul.

Ted gave the crowd something to remember at the home opener. He went 3–5 with a gigantic home run that soared over the fence and onto the roof of a building on the far side of Nicollet Avenue. He drove in four runs, scored three, and led the Millers to a 14–4 win over the Louisville Colonels.

The Kid owned the town from that day on.

"Ted Williams hit one so high and fast yesterday that he rode over the city on it," wrote Halsey Hall in his account of the game for the *Journal*. "He rode right into his new baseball home, into the hearts of opening day fans."[34]

Journal sports columnist Dick Cullum went further, saying, "There was not a fan in the park who did not form an immediate attachment to gangling Ted. He is as loose as red flannels on a clothes line, but as beautifully coordinated as a fine watch when he tenses for action. He is six feet and several inches of athlete and the same number of feet and inches in likeable boyishness. He is positively splashed with class, up to that rare point where he looks good making mistakes. You see a lot of players you THINK will make the big league grade...but once in a while you have one quick glance of a natural and you KNOW he will make it, and not as just an average big leaguer, but as a star. That would be Ted Williams. He's a dead mortal cinch."[35]

Ted kept hitting, and he embraced his new status as star and toast of the town with relish. He began to assert his new freedom from home, his independence, and his financial wherewithal.

He bought his first car—a red Buick convertible—washed it almost every day, and, behind the wheel, raced around the city. "I thought I was gonna get killed," remembered Sid Hartman, longtime sports columnist for the *Minneapolis Star Tribune,* who met Ted that summer of '38 while working at the ballpark selling peanuts and popcorn. "He just said, 'C'mon, let's take a ride, I got a new car....' He took the town over. He was a good-looking young kid, a lot of women chasing him."[36]

Women were a new phenomenon. Ted had been all left feet in that department and still was. At first he had his roommate at Minneapolis's Sheridan Hotel—Millers catcher Jimmy Galvin—field calls from groupies and decline any overtures. "No, Ted ain't in, and he don't want no dates!" Galvin would say as Ted sat nearby, listening to the radio full blast.[37]

But as the summer wore on and his celebrity blossomed, Ted, who had volunteered to Boston reporters in Sarasota that he was "still a virgin," decided to dip a toe into the dating waters. It was still awkward, but at least his sense of cluelessness about girls began to dissipate.

"I met what amounted to the first girl I ever got interested in, and dated her that summer, and was so self conscious I never even put my arm around her, never kissed her," Ted wrote in his book.[38] "I don't remember how I met her now, probably the ballpark. For a young ballplayer there's never any shortage of available girls around a ballpark. A lot of them move pretty hard, and after a while a ballplayer learns to move pretty good himself."

Williams was discreet about the identity of his first crush, and though it's been widely reported to have been Doris Soule, the Minnesota woman who would become his first wife, it was not. They wouldn't meet until the end of 1940.

The Millers didn't want him hanging out with hell-raisers like Jim Tabor, the Alabama third baseman who had been with Williams at Sarasota and was now in Minneapolis as well. They thought they might be able to tamp down some of Ted's rough edges if they had him rent a room from Wally Tauscher, an older pitcher who was married and had a family. Living next door to the Tauschers was Jack Bean, who was four years younger than Ted. His father, John, was a gregarious salesman for an ice cream company and an avid hunter. Williams prevailed on the elder Bean to take him hunting, and they got friendly.*

"My father was an Irishman, a first-class bullshitter, so they became close friends," remembered Jack, who married Mitzi Gaynor, the singer, dancer, and actress. "Ted got to know him and liked him. Ted had that

---

* Surprisingly, Ted was apparently tapped for babysitting duty occasionally by a family who lived near the Beans. Elizabeth Harris surfaced after Williams died and wrote the San Diego Union to brag that "not everyone can say, 'Ted Williams was my baby-sitter.' When he played in Minneapolis, Ted lived across the street from our home. My parents had him baby-sit on several occasions. They said he was a tease—he would hide my toys!"

need, because he had no male influences except baseball people....He had dinner or lunch at our house whenever he wanted."

Jack found Ted entertaining but untamed and crude. "He was a wild kid. He just wouldn't listen to anybody. He wasn't interested in acting like a man; he just wanted to hit home runs. He didn't drink or smoke, and girls were a great delicacy, but he didn't know very much about them. Ted was such an oddball; he'd say anything."[39]

That was in evidence one night when John Bean took Ted to dinner at the home of a friend of his, Marty Hoffman, a Woolworth's executive who was dying to meet the young ballplayer. Hoffman's son Tom recalled the scene at the dinner table:

"According to our family custom, the food would go counterclockwise. You'd pass the dishes. Now keep in mind, Ted did not speak in a talking voice. It was practically a yell when he opened his mouth. The food would come, and if it was mashed potatoes, he'd say, 'No, thanks!' And then he'd take two big helpings and smack them on his plate. Then the roast beef would come around. 'No, thanks!' And he'd fill his plate with the roast beef. Then the mixed nuts, and he'd take about two or three spoonfuls after saying, 'No, thanks.' Of course we got a big kick out of that."

At the end of the evening, as the elder Hoffman, who was rotund, said good-bye to his guest, Ted smacked him in the stomach hard and said, "Thanks for the dinner, Whale Belly!" Tom said his father laughed uproariously.

Ted stayed in touch with the Hoffmans and would come back to listen to the swing music Tom collected. "We had Artie Shaw, Benny Goodman, all this kind of stuff," Tom said. "We're out there playing the record, and Ted's beating on a pillow...like he's playing the drums. Just listening to the music."[40]

Ted made more friends in the small town of Princeton, some fifty miles north of Minneapolis, near prime hunting and fishing country. One off day, Ed Shave, a local outdoor writer, took Williams to Princeton and introduced him to John Kallas, proprietor of the Kallas Café. Kallas was a Greek immigrant who ran a mom-and-pop establishment that served good food and was a social center for the community. His teenage sons, Jim and Tony, ran the soda fountain. Jim followed baseball, but he did a double take when he saw Ted walk through the door of the restaurant. "I told my brother, 'Do you know who that is coming through the door? That's Ted Williams!'" Jim remembered. "My brother said, 'You're crazy.' Dad took him hunting and fishing. Ted took to him like a dog took to water."[41] Before long, Ted would come up and stay at the Kallas home or at their cabin at nearby Green Lake. At the café, Mrs. Kallas would feed him her trademark pheasant with thick gravy, and he'd eat undisturbed in the kitchen.

The first time they went fishing, John got four or five northern pikes and Ted couldn't get a bite.[42] He was competitive, and he asked John for tips. Later Ted came back to go duck hunting. "Ted was from California and had never gone duck hunting," recalled Frank Weisbrod, who was part of those early forays. Weisbrod worked nights as a baker and would go hunting during the day. "He made some mistakes at first. He didn't know the distance the shells would travel. He was shooting from too far away. So we'd tell him whatever we knew. Give him some tips. Eventually he became an excellent shot."[43]

By mid-July, Ted was hitting .310 with 24 home runs and 78 runs batted in, and he was a unanimous selection for the American Association All-Star team. His hitting ability had been on display for all to see, along with refreshing and endearing displays of exuberance, as when he would gallop from the dugout to his position in right field screaming "Yahoo!" like a man-child playing cowboys and Indians, or when he would take out the red handkerchief he carried in his hip pocket and wave it to the fans to acknowledge applause.

Yet there also had been startling displays of immaturity, self-absorption, and lack of concentration. He continued his pattern of shadow hitting—swinging an imaginary bat out in right field in between pitches—jawing with fans, doing jumping jacks, even turning his back on the infield.

Rival players were appalled by all this and jeered the rookie mercilessly. One opponent was Sammy Baugh, the football Hall of Famer, who had completed his first season with the Washington Redskins in 1937. Slingin' Sammy had signed a baseball contract with the St. Louis Cardinals before starting with the Redskins, and in the summer of 1938 was playing minor-league ball with the Columbus Red Birds. "My best memory of being in Columbus was seeing this 19-year-old phenom for Minneapolis named Ted Williams," Baugh told writer Dennis Tuttle. "He'd go out to right field, stick his glove in his back pocket and turn his back on the pitcher and start doing jumping jacks.... These old-school guys, many of them on their way back down from the majors...they were raising hell, saying 'get him out of here!' They hated Williams. Here was a young kid who didn't give a fuck about anything. Nothing bothered that cocky bastard....But you know, that crazy sonofabitch would get up there and knock a goddamn board off the fence in the outfield. Everybody knew he was crazy. Everybody also knew he was going to be great."[44]

In one game against Milwaukee, the Brewers had the tying run at second base when Donie Bush happened to look out to right field and see Williams swinging his imaginary bat. But this time, his glove wasn't even on. It was lying on the grass next to him, a useless appendage. Bush stopped the game, sprinted out to Ted, and yelled, "What's the idea! This run means the ball game!" Not to worry, the Kid replied. "That guy never hits to right field."[45]

His teammates weren't thrilled by Ted's antics, either, according to Wilfred "Lefty" LeFebvre, a pitcher from Rhode Island who had just graduated from the College of the Holy Cross and who eventually became a pal of Ted's. The day after graduating, LeFebvre signed a contract with the Red Sox for $600 a month and was soon pitching at Fenway Park. But by June he found himself in Minneapolis for further seasoning.

"Ted was a young guy, big and cocky as a son of a gun," LeFebvre remembered. "The old-timers didn't like him. You know, he would talk an awful lot, but he could back it up at the plate. I think that was what really got to some of the guys. He was a peculiar guy, always yelling, 'Yahoo! Yahoo!' He was just having fun playing baseball." And LeFebvre knew Williams did some good deeds for impaired children in Minneapolis. There was more to the loud and garrulous Californian than many knew.*

LeFebvre was amused by Ted's eccentricities. Williams would suggest that they go for a ride in his convertible, then would suddenly pull over and want to eat. He'd order a chicken sandwich, smell it, then call the owner over and demand to know if the chicken was fresh. Assured that it was, Ted would then inhale the sandwich and stand up to leave before LeFebvre had barely touched his food.

Then there was the time a champion Minneapolis softball team challenged the Millers to a softball game. "Ted laughed at them and said it was a kids' game," LeFebvre said. "We went to play them and Ted said to the pitcher, 'I'll bet you five dollars that you can't strike me out.' The

---

* LeFebvre would witness this kindness on a personal level several years later. He had a son with Down syndrome. At a Red Sox family event, Ted went out of his way to talk to the boy, bring him food, and spend time with him—without knowing he was Lefty's son. "That meant so much to me, Ted waiting on him like that," LeFebvre said.

pitcher said, 'You're on.' The guy struck him out. So the next time up, Ted bets him ten dollars that he'd hit a home run. The pitcher said, 'You're on.' Well, he hit that softball three hundred ninety feet, over the fence. He jumped around the bases like a jackrabbit."[46]

Ted's on-field behavior could have been written off as merely wacky and colorful as long as it didn't hurt the team, but sometimes it did.

In a home game on July 23 against the Toledo Mud Hens, he had his back turned and was gazing at the scoreboard when a ball was hit right to him. Center fielder Stan Spence, seeing that Williams was otherwise occupied, raced over and made a great catch, nearly colliding with his teammate. "I never saw the ball, just heard Stan Spence's footsteps, and he almost knocked me down making a hell of a play on a ball that should have been mine," Ted admitted.[47]

Donie Bush yanked Williams from the game immediately and chewed him out. In the clubhouse later, Millers third baseman Jim Tabor grabbed Ted and threatened to beat the daylights out of him, but Bush intervened and told Tabor: "Leave him alone. He's only a kid."[48]

Two days later, at home against Columbus, Ted went out to the outfield without his sunglasses and promptly dropped a fly ball after losing it in the sun, leading to three runs for the Red Birds. An enraged Bush ran out from the dugout, handed the Kid his sunglasses, and dressed him down for all to see. Humiliated, Ted went into a sulk. For the rest of the game, he merely jogged after base hits to right field and would lob the ball back in, allowing runners to take an extra base. In one case, he again wasn't paying attention when a ball was hit, and he didn't even realize it had gone past him until fans and teammates started screaming at him. When the Millers trailed by thirteen runs, he was laughing with Red Birds players and failed to run out a fly ball. By the time he came up to bat in the ninth, Ted was roundly booed by the home crowd, and the papers gave him hell the next day.

Ted was now too far along in baseball, one step from the majors, to pretend that defense didn't exist. Even Rogers Hornsby, as an aside to his lectures on hitting, had warned the Kid that hitting was not the only part of the game. But as Dick Johnson and Glenn Stout put it in their elegant coffee-table book on Williams, *Ted Williams: A Portrait in Words and Pictures*, "Ted was like some strange, slugging idiot savant: hitting was everything."[49]

Reflecting on these mental lapses in his autobiography, Ted said he was slow to make the transition from viewing baseball with childlike delight to treating it as a serious livelihood. "It takes some guys longer to find things out," he said. "I had gotten into some rotten habits."[50] He recalled playing a sandlot game on Mission Bay when he was fifteen and watching a flock of geese fly by and thinking how beautiful they were, when all of a sudden a fly ball landed right behind him that he never saw. "By the time I got to Minneapolis, I had these lapses of concentration pretty much built in. Playing the field was too much like being a spectator to suit me. If I wasn't slapping my butt and yelling, 'Hi-ho, Silver!' chasing a fly ball, I was sitting down between batters or talking to some fan and the crack of the bat would catch me looking the wrong way."

His temper was an issue, too. One afternoon against Saint Paul, hecklers were giving him a hard time in right field. After catching a fly ball for the third out of the inning and before running into the dugout, Ted went over to the offending fans and whipped the ball at them, only to strike an innocent bystander. Owner Mike Kelley later told Sid Hartman of the *Star Tribune* that he had to pay out $1,500 to the injured fan.[51]

On September 4, after popping up a ball he thought he should have crushed, Ted, in a grand show of disgust, flipped his bat end-over-end, dangerously high into the air. ("It's all in the wrist," Ted quipped later.[52]) But that outburst was only the beginning. When Ted reached the dugout he smashed a five-gallon watercooler with his left fist, sending shattered glass and water everywhere. "His wrist was all cut up and bleeding," outfielder Fabian Gaffke said. "He was lucky. If he'd ripped an artery, his career was over."[53]

Other gaffes had happy endings.

Ground balls were never Ted's forte in the outfield, and one afternoon he let two skip through his legs, then struck out twice, to boot. After the second strikeout, with the Millers trailing in the late innings, Ted was so mad he went right to the clubhouse and started to take his uniform off, thinking he wouldn't get up again. "I was half undressed when the batboy came running in yelling for me to get back out there," Ted wrote in his book. "We had staged a big rally. The score was 6–4, two men on, two out and I was due up. I was still fumbling with my buttons when I got there, and wouldn't you know it, I hit the first pitch out of the park and we won, 7–6. It was that kind of year."[54]

Of course dealing with the zany, mercurial Williams would have been enough to tax any manager, and Donie Bush was no exception. At one point, Bush grew so frustrated that he went to Mike Kelley and threatened to resign if Williams wasn't shipped out. But Kelley, reinforced by the Red Sox, quickly called that bluff and let Bush know that a choice between letting go the greatest hitting talent to come along in years and a highly replaceable manager was no choice at all. Apart from that minicrisis, Bush handled Williams skillfully and shrewdly.

After one midseason slump, Ted told Bush he was fed up and needed to go home to San Diego to chill out for a while. The manager thought the best way to deal with this outrageous request was by humoring the rookie, so he told him to go ahead and leave.

"Donie Bush got so he could get to me with a little psychology," Ted wrote, recalling the incident.[55] "When I was having my troubles and packed my trunk one time and told him I was going home, he didn't blow up at all, he just said, 'OK, Ted, I'll line up the transportation and when you've had a nice visit you can come back.' I went right to my room and unpacked that trunk."

Ted had a breezy, irreverent relationship with his manager. One day, after hitting a double and getting fed up with Bush's constant screaming from his third-base coaching perch about how big a lead to take, Ted finally yelled: "Take it easy, Skip. I got here by myself. I'll get home by myself."[56]

"What a headache he was!" Bush later said of Ted. "He did some daffy things. . . . But you had to like him."[57]

"If Donie hadn't put up with me as a raw kid in 1938, I wouldn't be here today or perhaps even in baseball," Ted would say twenty years later on a trip back to Minneapolis in the off-season. "He was great to me, and I'll never forget him for going along with me."[58]

In 1939, Ted's first year with the Red Sox, Bush was in a Saint Louis hospital recovering from major surgery. Though visitors were barred, every time the Red Sox came to Saint Louis to play the Browns, Ted would come by the hospital and try, unsuccessfully, to visit him. Ted wrote Bush a letter after one failed visit, saying he had tried to see him, then added: "I guess you saw enough of this busher last year, eh?"[59]

Overriding all Williams's bizarre behavior was his astonishing hitting. He finished the season with an average of .366, 43 home runs, and 142 runs batted in to win the American Association's Triple Crown. He also led the league in runs scored (130) and total bases (370).

In addition to posting those gaudy numbers and maturing at least a little, Ted thought two other important things had happened that summer to fuel his development as a hitter.

On August 3, in Milwaukee, he was struck in the head with a ball thrown by the Brewers' "Wild Bill" Zuber. This was apparently the first time Ted had been beaned. He was knocked out cold, sustained a concussion, and had to be carried off the field. There seemed little doubt it was a purpose pitch, as he had been 2–2 with four RBIs to that point against Zuber.

After being hospitalized for two days, he returned on August 6 in Kansas City, intent on proving to himself that he could dig in again without fear. Facing Kemp Wicker, who had pitched for the Yankees the year before and was considered one of the best left-handers in the American Association, Ted grounded out his first two times up, then hit a home run and a double, knocking in four runs. "That was when I knew that I would never worry about how I was going to react to a beaning," Ted said. "I was proud of myself."[60]

Another revelation that season was the value of using a lighter bat. This went against then-conventional wisdom, which held that power hitters by definition always used heavy bats. Williams would pioneer a countertheory: it was not the weight of the bat but the whip and speed at which it collided with the ball that generated power. Using a lighter bat could generate more whip as well as conserve a hitter's energy and strength in the dog days of summer.

"It was real hot in Minneapolis, hotter than anything I had been used to on the West Coast," Ted said. "I was on base all the time, an average of two and a half times a game, just swinging and sweating all the time, and as thin as I was, began to get tired. One muggy hot night in Columbus, I happened to pick up one of Stan Spence's bats. Geez, I thought. 'What a toothpick. Lightest bat in the rack...' "[61] He asked Spence if he could borrow it, then got up with the bases loaded. Behind on the count two strikes, he swung at a pitch low and away and hit it 410 feet over the center-field fence.

"That really woke me up. From then on, I always used lighter bats, usually 33 or 34 ounces, never more than 34, sometimes as light as 31. In the earlier part of the year I'd go for the heavier ones with better wood. You're stronger then, the pitchers are still working to get their stuff down, to get their control."[62]

Toward the end of his sensational season, the press was full of speculation about what he would do with the Red Sox the following year, but Ted shocked local reporters with a counterintuitive comment: maybe he wasn't ready to leave just yet. "I want to stay right here in Minneapolis with the Millers for another year at least," he said. "I'm not ready for the major leagues. Another year under Donie Bush will do me a lot of good."[63]

The Millers finished the season with a 78–74 record, in sixth place and out of the playoffs. To try and recoup some of the money they would have earned in the postseason, the older players organized a barnstorming tour for two weeks. They would travel to backwoods towns in Minnesota and the Dakotas, following the trail of festivals and carnivals, challenging the top local talent. The veterans asked Ted to join them, knowing he'd be the top draw, and Williams agreed.

Ted "did that for us," catcher Otto Denning told Ed Linn. "We made twenty dollars a game, and in those days twenty bucks was like a thousand now. He was one hell of a wonderful person."

The first game was in Worthington, Minnesota, and when the Millers arrived, there was a full house screaming for Williams's head. It seems Ted had told a local sportscaster that the first stop of the barnstorming tour would be "some jerk town called Worthington."

"Everybody was booing him," Denning said. "You know how he quieted them? He hit a home run in his first time at bat that went out of the park and over some cow barns. It must have gone 500 feet. For the rest of the game they cheered every move he made."[64]

Lefty LeFebvre was on the trip, along with Ted's landlord, pitcher Wally Tauscher, and Stan Spence. They rode with Ted in his red Buick.

One day as they were traveling to the next stop, LeFebvre remembered, Ted asked Tauscher to drive his car while he sat in the front passenger seat. He'd brought his shotgun on the trip, along with a case of shotgun shells he'd been given by a Millers sponsor. He propped the shotgun up between his legs and rolled the window down. As they sped through the countryside, if Ted saw an animal of some kind that he deemed a suitable target, he'd whip the gun out the window, take aim, and blast away at it.

"I think we were in South Dakota, way out there, and Ted was firing away out the window," LeFebvre said. "Boom! Boom! Boom! He'd stop for a while, and then he would see something, and boom again! I thought we were going to get pinched. I think he killed a couple of cats, a dog on a farm, maybe a cow, too. He was a wild man."[65]

At one stop, Ted bet and lost $400 at a carnival wheel game, but the operator of the game was apparently controlling the wheel with his foot. According to Otto Denning, Tauscher insisted that Ted go to the local district attorney and report the sharpie, and he was able to get $200 of his money back.[66]

Ted drove home to San Diego for the winter, eager more than anything else to show off his new car to friends. Joe Villarino and the boys were duly impressed, as were the regulars at Ted's neighborhood fire station, where he'd take the car to hose it down and buff its sheen.

As for where he'd be playing baseball next season, if there had been any doubts, the Red Sox removed them on December 15, 1938, by announcing that they had traded their starting right fielder, Ben Chapman, to Cleveland for Denny Galehouse and Tommy Irwin. Ted was bound for Boston to replace Chapman.

The Red Sox were grateful to Minneapolis for bringing their young star along. At baseball's winter meetings, Boston owner Tom Yawkey handed Mike Kelley, his Millers counterpart, an envelope. Inside it was a $10,000 check with a note that read: "Thanks, Mike, for making a ballplayer out of Ted Williams."[67]

4

Big Time

On March 1, 1939, Williams set out from his San Diego home in style, climbing into his Buick convertible for the long cross-country drive to Sarasota and the start of his big-league adventure.

It would be a year in which Ted would establish himself as a singular talent on the field and almost as big an attraction off it, as the press—seduced by the Kid's refreshing, guileless persona—touted him as an American original. Williams professed to be fresh off the "haystack circuit," even posing as a Huck Finn–like rube for a Boston newspaper and, in a tableau of innocence, delighting Fenway fans by doffing his cap—lifting it right off his head by the button. But he would back up his showmanship by hitting like a seasoned All-Star, weathering slumps and rebuffing pitchers who tried to test him with baseball's requisite rite of passage: the knockdown pitch.

Ted would establish a beachhead in a Boston hotel and forge friendships with a handful of non–big shots, like a state cop and managers of a restaurant and movie theater. But in his first year, he would rely most on his Red Sox family: clubhouse man Johnny Orlando, Bobby Doerr (his link to California), slugger Jimmie Foxx, catcher Moe Berg, and pitchers Charlie Wagner and Elden Auker. Ted's bosses—player-manager Joe Cronin and Tom Yawkey, the thirty-six-year-old owner—offered him detached guidance.

Thus far the six-year Yawkey regime had been characterized by failed—and what were then thought to be profligate—attempts to buy a pennant. Yawkey had first purchased two pitchers from the Yankees in 1933 for $100,000: George Pipgras and Bill Werber. Then he acquired

Lefty Grove, Rube Walberg, and Max Bishop from the Philadelphia Athletics for $125,000 and two players. Cronin was obtained from the Washington Senators for a staggering $225,000 and an infielder in 1934; then came Foxx in 1935 for $150,000 and a journeyman pitcher.

In 1934, Yawkey further pampered his players by instituting a bonus system, boosting pay by a certain percentage of their salaries if the club finished third—then double that if it finished second and triple if it won the pennant. Critics called this coddling and noted that the incentives seemed to do little good, as the team finished fourth in 1934, fourth in 1935, sixth in 1936, and fifth in 1937 before improving to second in 1938.

But inspired by the arrival of Williams, Yawkey had high hopes for 1939, and the owner would cap off the spring training season by exercising a personal prerogative. As the Red Sox headed north for the start of the season, he had his team stop and play an exhibition game against the Cincinnati Reds in an unlikely locale: Florence, South Carolina, where there was no suitable ball field and local officials had to fashion one from scratch.

The Florence site was a home game of sorts for Yawkey because it was near his twenty-thousand-acre oceanfront former rice plantation in Georgetown, where he spent most of the year. He brought in several carloads of his high-ranking employees and their families to see his club in action. Not invited were the one hundred or so black field hands who comprised the backbone of the estate or the madam who ran the Sunset Lodge, a high-class bordello in Georgetown famed throughout the South, which Yawkey had financed and continued to patronize himself.

The reclusive Yawkey's time in Georgetown amounted to a largely secret world in which he lived the life of a gentleman-sportsman perpetually at ease—hunting, fishing, and partaking of the Sunset's services whenever he wished. Over the years, Yawkey would offer the same pleasures to his guests, including Ted and other favored members of the Red Sox. Yawkey's hidden life in Georgetown offered a window into the culture of paternalism, generosity, and subtle racism with which he ran his ball club.

Williams didn't want to make the trip from San Diego to Florida alone, so he asked one of his surrogate fathers, Les Cassie Sr., if he'd like to come along, then stay on in Sarasota awhile to watch some workouts. It's doubtful Ted even considered asking his own father. But Cassie, the neighbor who had taught Ted surf casting and given him his only high school graduation present, was delighted, and he arranged to take leave of his job as superintendent of construction for the San Diego schools.

On the road, Ted picked up a virus, as he was prone to do, and when he reached New Orleans he was running a temperature of 102. A doctor advised him to lay low and rest for a few days. So by the time he arrived in Sarasota, March 7, he was two days late and still looking a bit peaked.

The Boston press corps, always lusting for good spring training copy, had been on high alert for the Kid's arrival. This was the second year in a row that he'd come to Sarasota late, and the writers seemed skeptical of his story that Arizona had been cooler than normal this year and that he'd probably picked up the bug there. Couldn't he have called or wired manager Joe Cronin to let him know he'd be late? That never occurred to him, Ted said. He offered up the avuncular Mr. Cassie as his alibi witness, who corroborated everything, and the writers seemed mollified.

Ted told a few reporters whom he bumped into while checking in at the Sarasota Terrace Hotel that he was too tired to work out that afternoon. "I'll be out there tomorrow showing the boys how it should be done," he said.[1]

But Cronin, on learning that Williams had arrived, sent a clubhouse boy to the hotel with instructions for him to get over to the park pronto. So Ted pulled himself together, drove to the field, got in uniform, and made his entrance.

"Hi, Joe, how's the old boy?" Ted said brightly, greeting Cronin.[2]

"Hello, Theodore; pick up a bat," replied the manager, disarmed and charmed at the same time.

Ted got in the cage against pitching coach Herb Pennock in a reprise of the scene a year earlier, when he took his first major-league licks. There was less anticipation this time, given Williams's epic minor-league season and the fact that he was a known quantity. But there was still plenty of curiosity and interest as players and spectators stopped what they had been doing to watch. Pennock was still nervous about being drilled by a line drive. He reminded Williams to pull the ball, and pitched inside to make sure he did.

After the session, in which Ted, peaked or not, cracked several long drives, Cronin took him aside for a pep talk: Circumstances were different this year. He was succeeding Ben Chapman as the regular right fielder and, to symbolize that, he would inherit Chapman's number, 9. He should be aware that he was going to be playing in a wonderful baseball town and for a top owner in Tom Yawkey. It was time to bear down and get serious. According to Jack Malaney, the *Boston Post* beat writer who retained his closeness to Cronin, the manager's exact words were: "You're in a great city and you're working for the best man in baseball. You've got a lot of ability and have had enough schooling. You know what it's all about now. This is serious business and there is no place in the game for clowning. I hope you take advantage of the chance you've got."[3] Ted assured Cronin that he would.

But there was a fine line between clowning and letting Ted be Ted. It was clear that Williams's sunny, somewhat daffy persona was central to his emerging stardom, and Cronin found himself criticized by some writers for trying to rein in the color that they craved.

"Peace is repulsive to Williams," wrote the *Boston Evening American*'s Austen Lake.[4] What "the 1939 Red Sox need, more than temperance and dull docility, is a couple emotional buckaroos like Ted to keep life constantly at the boil."

The writers celebrated color almost as much as ability, and Ted had both. That was a bonanza. One story, headlined TED WILLIAMS REPLICA OF RUTH, cheered the rookie's off-the-field "Ruthian idiosyncrasies" as much as his potential to succeed the Babe on merit.[5]

Reporters lapped up the Kid's on-field chatter and locker-room banter and worked it into their stories and notes items. One get-acquainted interview gives a good sense of why he made such rich copy:

WRITER: The roster says your name is Theodore S. Williams.
TED: That's right.
WRITER: What's the *S* for?
["Screwball; what did you think?" piped up Doc Cramer, the center fielder.]
TED: It's for Samuel.
WRITER: You think you'll hit up here?
TED: Who's going to stop me?[6]

Cramer, who had not warmed to Williams, was annoyed by his constant banter when they were in the outfield and threatened to put cotton in his ears.

Yet Cramer and Williams (who early in the season would get into an unpublicized clubhouse brawl at Fenway Park[7]) often warmed up together before games and liked to throw the ball as hard as they could.

Harold Kaese, then the beat writer for the *Boston Evening Transcript* and later for the *Boston Globe,* watched this display with interest and noted that they threw harder than some of the pitchers did. Ever the fledgling pitcher, Ted occasionally liked to mix in his knuckleball.

Williams gravitated to Jimmie Foxx, "Double X," whose eye-popping muscles and long home runs now held the rookie spellbound. Foxx, a right-handed-hitting first baseman who had broken in with Connie Mack's Philadelphia Athletics in 1925 and was regarded as one of the game's great sluggers, went out of his way to be kind and generous to Ted. "Right now I'll promise you that Teddy Williams will hit," Foxx told reporters a few days into spring training.[8]

Knowing that Williams wanted to bulk up and get stronger, clubhouse attendant Johnny Orlando advised him to drink buttermilk. Ted said he couldn't stand the stuff, but when Orlando told him that Foxx used it, Williams began drinking a pint after every practice.[9]

Another early adviser was Moe Berg, the Princeton-educated backup catcher and linguist, who'd needled Ted a year ago but had now been asked by Cronin to watch over him and ease his passage to acceptance by the veterans. Ted peppered Berg with questions about the various pitchers in the league and what they would throw in certain situations. Berg became fond of Ted and looked upon him with wry amusement.

"He liked me as a player and a kid," Ted told Nicholas Dawidoff, author of *The Catcher Was a Spy: The Mysterious Life of Moe Berg.* "I think he liked my young, enthusiastic approach to it all."[10] But Ted thought Berg wasn't enthusiastic enough. "Moe was only 16 years older than I was, but he was much more subdued than the average guy even of that age. Not a lot of pep or vinegar."

Berg didn't play much and didn't care if he did. "Gentlemen," he would say, coming off the bench to enter a game, "does everyone still get three strikes out there?" He liked the camaraderie of baseball and enjoyed being on the team, but he was essentially biding his time. Cronin was willing to tolerate Berg's insubordination and indifference because Moe was a brilliant character whom he could learn from and whose company he enjoyed. It seemed that one of Berg's roles was to serve as Cronin's Pygmalion.

An inveterate newspaper reader, Berg would start his days in Boston at Old South News, a newsstand on the corner of Washington and Milk Streets, downtown. He'd buy all of the major Boston papers and several from New York and Washington. Often he'd go out to Harvard Square in Cambridge and pick up some of the foreign journals.* Berg was so serious about his newspapers that he would often bring them into the dugout if he hadn't finished reading a particular story that interested him. One day the Red Sox were on the field warming up before a game when Cronin spotted Berg in the dugout still reading his paper. When the manager asked him what in God's name he was doing, Berg looked up briefly and replied: "You lead your life and I'll lead mine, and next year we'll beat the Yankees."[11]

Ted got off to a good start, hitting a triple and a single in each of the first two intrasquad games, followed by a 2–6 showing in a twelve-inning loss to the St. Louis Cardinals in Saint Petersburg. His confidence was high. "I haven't seen any pitching yet from these big leaguers to scare me," he wrote home to his parents. "I can see the ball all right and I've been hitting it."[12]

On a free night, Ted could often be found at the movies—usually at westerns. One night in Sarasota, when the villain had the hero cornered and took out his gun, ready to shoot, Ted stood up in the theater and yelled: "Go on and shoot, you skunk! You just haven't got the nerve!"[13] The story quickly made its way back to Cronin, who received it with a mixture of amusement and chagrin. He was dismayed that Ted would still enter hotel lobbies and do an imitation of a pig squealing or saunter into fine restaurants in an open collar when a tie was required. Cronin thought it high time that Ted stop acting like a rube and master at least some of the big-league social graces.

On their way north, the Red Sox stopped in Atlanta to play an exhibition game on April 1 against the Atlanta Crackers of the Southern Association. The right-field portion of the park was oddly designed— almost as though it were a prison compound. It had a succession of three fences, each rising higher than the one before it, like steps. The farthest fence had been too far for Crackers batters, so management had built a second fence in front of it; when the second fence had also proved too challenging, they had built the third, closer still.

---

* One day that spring, some players were quizzing the learned Berg about the prospects for war in Europe. Ted piped up: "Germany and Russia will go in together if there's any fighting." Berg assured Ted that would never happen. Germany and the Soviet Union signed a nonaggression pact five months later, in August of 1939, and World War II began shortly thereafter. The pact remained in effect until 1941, when Germany invaded the Soviet Union.

During batting practice, Johnny Orlando goaded Ted by telling him that Babe Ruth had once cleared all three fences with a home run. "I wanted to get him worked up so he'd give the crowd a show," Orlando said.[14] His first three times up, Williams struck out. On his fourth appearance, in the seventh inning, he tripled in three runs. But in the eighth, he struck out with two men on and went back to right field seething. Then a short fly ball was hit out to Ted in foul territory. After dropping it, he became so enraged that he picked the ball up and heaved it out of the park — over the last fence he'd been trying to reach with his bat — and onto Ponce de Leon Avenue.

Cronin immediately yanked Ted from the game. He "disappeared into the clubhouse wearing a sheepish grin," the Globe's Gerry Moore reported, adding that Cronin planned a "nice fatherly talk" with the rookie back at the hotel.[15] The Sox lost, 10–9.

Williams was back in the lineup for a rematch with the Crackers the next day, and this time "the glorious screwball…problem child," as Moore called him, smacked one over that last fence and made a "spectacular fielding play," to boot, as the Sox won, 3–0.[16] Entering the dugout after his home run, Ted said he gave Orlando "a hard look."[17]

Five days later, the Red Sox arrived in South Carolina by train for the Cincinnati Reds game scheduled by Yawkey in Florence.

Yawkey was no stranger to Florence. According to his friends and associates, after he bought the Red Sox, at age thirty, he would take the train down to South Carolina after the season ended and get off in Florence, which is some seventy miles north of his estate in Georgetown. The estate consisted of thirty-one square miles of marshland, managed wetlands, pristine beach, and forests spread out over North, South, and Cat Islands. Today the varying habitats support more than two hundred species of birds, including peregrine falcons, golden and bald eagles, and the federally endangered red-cockaded woodpecker.

Yawkey had inherited all this, along with the rest of his wealth, from his uncle, William Hoover Yawkey. Born into a genteel New York family and educated at Yale and a fancy prep school before that, Tom was the son of Thomas and Augusta Austin. After his father and mother both died when he was young, Tom was taken in by his mother's brother, William Yawkey, the heir to a mining, oil, and timber fortune who also owned the Detroit Tigers. Tom was seven. Yawkey later adopted his nephew and gave him the last name Yawkey. When William died suddenly in 1919, he left half his $40 million estate, as well as two $500,000 trust funds, to Tom Yawkey, who was then only sixteen. The will provided that most of the proceeds be withheld until he reached the age of thirty, in 1933. That was the year he bought the Red Sox.

Tom loved the baseball life he had soaked up hanging around his uncle, and would pick up William's habit of drinking heavily with executives, managers, and favored players. Ty Cobb had been especially pampered by the elder Yawkey, and Cobb reportedly was at William's bedside when he died. Cobb, a mercurial avowed racist and frequent plantation guest, then lavished his attention on young Tom and encouraged him to buy a major-league team of his own as soon as his ship came in.

Tom Yawkey had been married since 1925 to Elise Sparrow of Birmingham, Alabama, but the marriage was troubled. Elise, a former Miss Alabama and Broadway showgirl, was an effusive socialite who loved to party, while Yawkey was a virtual recluse who preferred to quietly hunt, fish, and tend to his Red Sox. But Yawkey, by all accounts, also liked to patronize houses of ill repute, and while in Florence, he made the acquaintance of one Hazel Weisse, a former Indiana schoolteacher who had decided there was an easier way to make a living.

Yawkey grew fond of Hazel, and around 1935, he came to her with a business proposition. The International Paper Company was opening a plant in Georgetown. The city fathers were concerned that scores of factory workers with too much time on their hands might terrorize the fragile belles in town. Instead it was thought prudent that a cathouse be established to enable the workers to channel their energy in alternative directions. So acting as both a friend and civic leader, Yawkey asked Hazel if she would move to Georgetown to establish the business, and he offered to finance the venture. Hazel accepted, and before long the Sunset Lodge was up and running just south of town, along Route 17.

According to Phil Wilkinson, a biologist who lived on the Yawkey estate for eleven years beginning in 1966 and helped his boss manage the wildlife on the property, Yawkey told him the money he gave Hazel was a loan, and that she "quickly" repaid it, with interest.[18]

Hazel told her friends—including Ralph Ford Jr., whose parents owned a fine local grocery where the plantation owners shopped; George Daniels, her Charleston-based financial adviser; and Bettye Roberts, who bought the Sunset Lodge after it closed in 1969—that she was fully indebted to Yawkey financially.

"She'd say, 'If it hadn't been for Tom,'" Roberts recalled. "He would pay handsomely for the girls, unlike other dignitaries like the sheriff, who did not pay. The girls were real happy when they went out to

Mr. Yawkey's place. They made good money. When the Red Sox would come down, all the girls would go to his plantation and entertain. Not just for the night but for a couple of days. That's what she told me."

Yawkey would frequently visit Sunset Lodge as well. And whereas Hazel had a rule that dogs were not allowed, she would waive that requirement for the Red Sox owner, who would sometimes appear with his Labrador retriever. "The dog stayed at the foot of the stairs until Yawkey finished his business," Roberts said. "He was lord and master there. Hazel thought he was very generous. Anything she needed, he saw to it that she got it. Like they needed more electricity, and he took a transformer from his plantation and had it installed so she could have enough power. She needed a stronger current for air-conditioning. It was during the war that Yawkey did this for her. During the war you could not come by a transformer, and you had to have some pull to get it."[19]

The Sunset Lodge complex was fifteen acres, consisting of a main house with four bedrooms and several outbuildings with apartments. In the main house, there was a jukebox for dancing and a cigarette machine. Both would only take dollar bills. Hazel generally kept eighteen girls on the premises but might cut back to a dozen during slower times of the year. The clientele was upscale—mostly businessmen, lawyers, doctors, and politicians. "She wouldn't let any drunks come in," said Roberts. "She'd take ship captains but not the ordinary sailor. I guess when you're in that business you can read people pretty well."

George Daniels, who served as Hazel's financial adviser from 1954 to 1974, when she died of cancer, said Weisse told him that after backing her financially, Yawkey "went to the sheriff and told him to lay off, and that she would run a very fine establishment. She was a very fascinating person, with a heart big as a whale. She did a tremendous amount of charitable things in Georgetown anonymously. She ran a very tight house of prostitution and insisted that the girls conduct themselves accordingly. They were meticulously examined regularly by one of the local doctors."[20]

Ralph Ford, whose father was Yawkey's best friend in Georgetown, said that after a night of drinking and carousing at Sunset, Yawkey would often come by the Ford house and roust him from bed. Ralph junior played the organ and piano, and Yawkey would demand that he get up and play for him. When he was old enough, Ford was invited each year to Hazel's birthday party at Sunset, which was considered the social event of the year in Georgetown. "It was all men," Ford said. "We supplied the food from Ford's store. The girls were on the house. There were doctors, lawyers, politicians. The Social Register of Georgetown. Most of the men's wives knew. They were right proud to have their husbands invited, as I recall."

According to Ford, Yawkey did most of his philandering with the Sunset girls between 1939, when he was separated from Elise, and 1944, when he was divorced and married Jean Hollander. Yawkey had met Jean in New York, where she worked as a model for Jay Thorpe, a high-end women's clothing store on West 57th Street.[21] Elise took Tom shopping at the store one day, and she asked Jean to model a dress for her. After Tom and Elise separated, he began courting Jean, who also volunteered at the Red Cross. When she came to Boston to see Yawkey, she would wear her Red Cross uniform in an effort to travel incognito.[22] They dated for about five years, but Tom would not marry Jean until Elise remarried first. Tom and Jean—both dressed in hunting clothes—were wed on Christmas Eve of 1944 in Georgetown at C. L. Ford & Sons, Inc., reputed to be the finest grocery store south of S. S. Pierce in Boston.

"The Ford family did not care for Jean because they thought she went after Tom for his money," said Ralph. "Maybe she did, but she blended into his life down here. No makeup, hunting and fishing—let herself go to pot. Back in New York she looked like a model again."

But Yawkey continued to visit Sunset Lodge. "Tom went to Sunset frequently between wives and even after," said Ford. "He was a whore-hopper. He was oversexed but shy, too. He built his own whorehouse so he wouldn't have to be shy. Tom would talk about his whoring. He made no bones about it."

Jean Yawkey took a dim view of Tom's Sunset dalliances but apparently tolerated them. Once, he took her there just to show her the operation. "Jean was highly insulted," Ford said.[23] To others, Mrs. Yawkey offered a more positive spin about her husband and Sunset. "She said this was Tom helping the lady out," said John Harrington, who ran the Red Sox after Jean's death in 1992, on behalf of her JRY Trust, until the team was sold in 2002.[24]

Yawkey often blurred the owner-player relationship and sought out friendships with players he especially liked, such as Joe Cronin, Jimmie Foxx, Lefty Grove, and Mike "Pinky" Higgins. Yawkey worshiped Ted and undoubtedly would have liked to have had something comparable with him. Williams resisted that, but according to Harrington, friends and associates of Yawkey in South Carolina, and people who used to live on his estate, Ted was a visitor to Georgetown over the years, along with other members of the Red Sox, including Cronin, Grove, and Foxx.*

Once, when Cronin was visiting, Yawkey decided to get up a sandlot game in front of his house, and he sent word to have the field hands come over to fill out the teams. Wallace Lawrimore, whose father, Hampton, lived on the property with his family and worked as Yawkey's chief mechanic from the early 1930s to the early '50s, was appointed the scorekeeper. Wallace was then six.

"I drew numbers in the sand. It was on South Island. They had the colored people that was working. Yawkey said to send people over. 'Throw down your shovel!' My daddy played first base. Cronin was on his team. He couldn't remember Daddy's name so he called him Skidmore, for his slide. Yawkey pitched for one team and Captain Gibson pitched for the other team. Williams wasn't there that day."

Jim Gibson was the overseer who managed the Yawkey estate. The black field hands usually called him Captain Jim. Wallace's dad was Captain Hamp.

Yawkey encouraged his field hands to play baseball on their own and equipped them with bats, balls, and gloves. He even made a crude diamond, where they practiced. "They had a real field on the plantation that Mr. Yawkey had fixed up for the colored boys," Wallace said. "They had a pretty good team. This was on the plantation side. Mosquito Creek cut it off—across that they called the plantation side. It was about five miles from the Yawkey house. But two, three, or four times they played on the lawn in front of Yawkey's house."[25]

Phil Wilkinson, Yawkey's biologist in residence, recalled a later Williams visit, around 1970. "Ted was by himself. I rode around with him and Mr. Yawkey. Mr. Yawkey drove. One of my impressions was they were good friends. They'd maintained their friendship after Ted was out of the game. Both of them were avid fishermen, but they both had different ideas about it. They would hassle on technique, and neither would give in to the other."

Wallace Lawrimore vividly remembered the April 6, 1939, game in Florence between the Red Sox and the Reds. "Daddy carried two car-

---

* Besides his players, Yawkey would invite friends to visit, such as chief Yankees scout Paul Krichell, who signed Lou Gehrig, and Ed Barrow, who managed the Red Sox from 1918 to 1920 before moving to the Yankees front office, where he was credited with building a dynasty in the era of Ruth, Gehrig, and DiMaggio.

loads of family to the game. We all went up to the dugout to tell Cronin we wanted some passes to get in. I got a program from that day, with all the players' autographs."

The one ball field Florence had was deemed unsuitable for a major-league game because the fences were too short, so it was decided to build a field from scratch at the local fairgrounds. They laid down a coating of dirt for the infield and put up some circus-style bleachers for the 2,285 spectators who showed up, but when it came time for the game, gale-force winds blowing out toward left field drove the dirt everywhere, and conditions made the game virtually unplayable. It was called in the ninth inning, with the score tied 18–18, because they ran out of baseballs. Ted went 1–2 before leaving the game in the third inning after complaining of chills and a fever.

Several days later, Gerry Moore of the *Globe* summed up spring training and provided a succinct theme for the coming season in a piece perfectly headlined: TED WILLIAMS THE ANSWER TO A SPORTS WRITER'S PRAYER.

Not only does Ted "show promise of becoming one of the greatest hitters of all time, but he just exudes that intangible quality known as color, the number one object of every sports writer's search," Moore wrote. "Everything about Williams shuns the orthodox. His six foot three inch 175 pound string-bean physique, his inimitable nonchalance in fielding his right field position, his constant boyish chatter, seldom possessing any meaning, both on and off the field and last, but by no means least, his frequent flair for committing eccentric or what is known in the baseball world as 'screwball acts.' "

Whatever his off-the-field eccentricities, "he can still powder that onion, as the boys say in the bleachers, and if he continues to break down the fences the way he has been doing around the whistle stop circuit, all his extraneous comment and conduct will only enhance his big league luster. There's quite a future for this inimitable kid who will be seeing his first major league game when he plays against the Yankees in the house that the man who he may succeed built, a week from Tuesday."

Drenching rains on April 18 and 19 washed out two attempts to start the season at Yankee Stadium, so the Red Sox were forced to cool their heels at the Commodore Hotel in midtown Manhattan. Finally, on April 20, the skies cleared enough to play, and opening day was on. Ted recalled that he watched, transfixed, as the Yankees greats took batting practice: Lou Gehrig, who was already sick with the disease that would kill him, though no one knew it yet; DiMaggio, Frank Crosetti, Tommy Henrich, Bill Dickey, Joe Gordon. "I'm watching them, studying them all, and I remember so distinctly...I said to myself, 'I know I can hit as good as these guys.' "[26]

It was damp and chilly, and a crowd of 30,278 had gathered to see Yankees ace Red Ruffing versus thirty-nine-year-old Lefty Grove. Ted thought Yankee Stadium was just as he'd seen it in the movie newsreels, its aura perhaps enhanced only by the attendance of Ruth himself. Batting sixth, "butterflies running up and down my spine," Williams stepped into the box.

"How tall are you, kid?" asked catcher Bill Dickey as he flashed the sign to Ruffing.

"Six foot three," said Ted, glancing back at Dickey nervously.

"Gee," said Dickey, who was six two.

"Strike one!" said the umpire.[27]

Two more pitches and Ted was on his way back to the dugout, an ignominious strikeout victim in his first major-league at bat. When he returned to the bench, angry and embarrassed, veteran Sox pitcher John "Black Jack" Wilson came and sat down next to him. They'd been needling each other all spring, and Ted had assured Wilson that he would wear Ruffing out. "Whattaya think of this league now, Bush?" Wilson chirped.[28]

"Screw you!" said Ted. "This is one guy I know I'm going to hit, and if he puts it in the same place again, I'm riding it out of here."

Next time, Ruffing left a pitch up, and Ted drilled it about four hundred feet off the right-center-field fence, just a foot from being a home run. After he reached second base, Joe Gordon came over, smiling. They'd played against each other in 1937 in the Coast League. "You nervous?" asked Gordon. "Boy, am I," said Ted. "Nervous as hell."

Ted struck out again and popped up on his next at bats, but he handled several chances in right field cleanly, his first putout a line drive by Gehrig. The Sox lost, 2–0.

When the team returned to Boston for its home opener against Connie Mack's Philadelphia A's on April 21, Ted's stack of fan mail was the largest of any player's. When he was introduced on his first at bat, he got the loudest ovation, and the fans in the right-field bleachers quickly adopted him as their own, chanting "Slugger! Slugger!" each time he came up.[29] Ted went 1–5 as the Red Sox won, 9–2. He said he was surprised that the home opener was considered so important that the governor of the Commonwealth of Massachusetts, Leverett Saltonstall, would throw out the first ball.

In his third game, Ted had a double and a single, but it was his fourth game, on Sunday, April 23, that served as his true Fenway Park coming-out party. In his first time up against Philadelphia's LeRoy "Tarzan" Parmelee, Ted scorched a ball into the right-center-field bleachers, just to the right of the outfield triangle, about 430 feet away, for his first home run. Burt Whitman of the *Boston Herald* called it "as harshly hit a line drive as anybody ever sent into that sector, not excepting even Babe Ruth and the ever-present Jimmie Foxx."

On his second time up, Ted hit a long fly off the wall in left-center that missed being another home run by inches. The blow came off Cotton Pippen, the pitcher who had struck Williams out on three pitches in his first at bat for the San Diego Padres, when he was too scared to swing. In the fifth inning, he scalded a line-drive single to right, again off Pippen. In the sixth, he singled to center, knocking in a run, to make it 8–6 Red Sox.

In the eighth, Ted actually flashed some leather, making a nice running catch of a short fly to right-center. In the ninth, with Boston now losing 12–8 and all twelve thousand fans staying in their seats only to await Ted's final at bat, to see if he could go 5–5, the Kid lined a ball to left field into a stiff east wind, but it was caught at the wall by Bob Johnson. As he ran back into the dugout, the crowd accorded Ted a grand ovation—and then promptly left the park, in a display that would be emblematic of much of Williams's career: in the eyes of the fans, his performance was often considered more important than the game itself.

"Those present yesterday unquestionably saw the official unveiling of a new major league star," wrote Whitman in the *Herald,* adding that Ted "won the customers to him as a strong magnet attracts wee pieces of steel."[30]

After watching Williams slug for three games, Connie Mack was awed: "My goodness gracious, how that boy can hit," Mack told Arthur Sampson of the *Herald.* "It wouldn't surprise me if he becomes another Babe Ruth. I never saw anything like it. It doesn't seem to make any difference where you pitch him. We gave him all sorts of stuff—high balls, low balls, inside pitches, outside pitches, fast balls, curve balls and slow balls. He hit them all as if each one was just what the doctor ordered. Goodness gracious, I never have seen such a good-looking young boy."

Ted basked in the early rave reviews, and, assessing his first week in the majors a few days later, said he saw no reason he couldn't hit as well as he did in Minneapolis the previous year. "I promise you you'll see plenty of homers over the left centerfield fence at Fenway Park," he boasted.[31]

In Boston, Ted initially lived at the Canterbury Hotel, a small, inexpensive establishment near Fenway Park and Kenmore Square. But his room was near a rail line, and when trains went by, the whole building shook, so he moved nearby to the better-appointed Shelton Hotel, still reasonable at $6 or $7 a night. The hotel would remain his in-season home, off and on, until it closed in 1954.

Jimmie Foxx also lived at the Shelton. Occasionally, pitcher Elden Auker would invite Ted and Foxx out to his apartment in nearby Brookline for one of the fried chicken dinners prepared by his wife, Mildred. "Ted would eat everything in sight," Auker remembered. "He never put on weight, not until he left baseball. We'd just talk about things. Maybe the game, just laughing, having dinner together. Ted loved that chicken. He was always asking about it."[32]

While Ted reached out and forged some relationships in Boston, he mostly stayed to himself. "I have never cultivated 'important' people, perhaps because I did not feel comfortable in a necktie crowd," he wrote in his book.[33] "My friends were the guys who delivered the magazines, the highway cop, the guy who took care of my car and wanted a ticket now and then, the clubhouse boy, the guy who ran the theater."

And the theater guy saw plenty of Ted. Williams was a serious movie buff. He'd clip the schedule from the newspaper and sometimes see two or three films a day, baseball permitting. John Wayne westerns were his staple, and they were often featured at a theater in the Allston section of Boston. Ted would usually sit in the back row and drape his legs over the seat in front of him. One day, the manager of the theater, John Buckley, tapped him on his shoulder and said: "Where the hell you think you are, home? Take your feet down."[34] As the movie ended and the patrons were filing out, Buckley recognized the customer he'd challenged as Ted. They ended up going out for a milk shake and becoming lifelong friends.

Williams had strong likes and dislikes that effectively made him a loner. He wanted to see a certain type of movie when he wanted to see it, get it over with, get home early, and go to bed. Unlike most of his teammates, he didn't drink or smoke; he couldn't stand even the smell of tobacco. He liked to hunt and fish, the individualist's recreation.

"Eating is a real sore spot with me," Ted said.[35] "I don't want to hear, 'Let's wait awhile,' because all of a sudden it's nine o'clock, and when I eat late, I can't sleep well and I don't feel well the next day. I don't believe there was ever a ballplayer who ate in his room as often as Ted Williams."

And he had little desire to socialize beyond his small circle — or even within it. "I'd ten times rather sit home and watch a good TV program than go out to some phony-baloney cocktail party and listen to a lot of bull. I think a lot of people are like that but are afraid to admit it."

If Williams did go out to eat during his first season, it was usually at Jimmy O'Keefe's, a hangout for politicians and athletes in Boston's Back Bay neighborhood. There he became friendly with the manager, Bill Greeley. One night, Greeley suggested they go eat at a place he knew called the Lafayette House in Foxborough, about thirty miles south of Boston. It was quiet there, and they served big portions of beef. On the way home, a state policeman pulled Ted over for speeding. Greeley piped up, trying to defuse the situation: "This is the new man with the Red Sox."[36] The trooper gave Ted a lecture but let him off with a warning.

A few days later, Ted was driving back to the Lafayette House by himself when the same cop stopped him. This time it was just a social call. John Blake was the officer's name. He recognized the Red Sox rookie's shiny Buick with the California plates. "We got to talking and I got to thinking what a lonely job he had, so I invited him to have dinner with me," Ted said.[37] Blake thought Ted was just being polite and never expected anything to come of the invitation, but a few days later, Williams did follow up, and the two met for another meal.[38] It wasn't long before they were fishing together, and Ted was invited to the state police shooting range for target practice. He scored 295 out of 300 possible points from twenty-five yards, Blake said. The two men also started boxing together. They became "friends for life," Ted wrote.[39]

Looking for a travel roommate during spring training, Ted had gone to Cronin and asked him who didn't drink or smoke. Cronin pointed to Charlie Wagner. A right-handed pitcher, he was known as Broadway Charlie because he dressed stylishly and liked the bright lights.

"We were good roommates," Wagner said. "We both got to bed early and got up early. After the games we separated. He went his way. I didn't ask him where he was going, and he didn't ask me. That's why we got along."

One night in their room at the Chase Hotel in Saint Louis, Ted was swinging a bat in front of the mirror. He had two bats and, unsatisfied with both, was shaving their handles down, then swinging each one, trying to get them just so. After one mighty swing, Ted's bat crashed into Wagner's bedpost, the bed collapsed, and Wagner was sent sprawling to the floor. "Boy, what power!" Ted said.

He stayed close with Johnny Orlando, the clubhouse attendant who had watched over him that first spring in Sarasota and had spotted him five bucks on his way down to the minors. On an off day early in the 1939 season, Ted chartered a boat in Gloucester, north of Boston, and went fishing with Orlando and the clubhouse kids who worked for him. They caught a couple of tuna, and everyone had a swell time, except for Orlando, who got seasick.[40]

Williams also nurtured his new fans, patiently signing autographs after the game and spending extra time with kids. Sometimes after a game he'd take a gaggle of them off to the amusement park at nearby Revere Beach, where they'd ride the roller coaster and eat hot dogs and ice cream.

As the month of May began, Ted was in bed with what was reported as a "heavy grippe." This was his third bout with illness since being waylaid in New Orleans on the way to Sarasota in early March. After spring training, as the Red Sox barnstormed their way north with the Cincinnati Reds, the feverish Williams had been ordered to bed by trainer Win Green. Green and Cronin had lectured him as though he were a child on the basic need to take care of himself and guard against a chill in the cold northern climes. Now *Globe* columnist Victor Jones weighed in and essentially told Ted to grow up: "It's all right to be a kid when you're young," Jones wrote, "but Ted Williams ought to realize he's got the responsibilities that go with membership on a pennant challenging club and stay out of bed, even if it means wearing a hat during New England's spring."[41]

By May 4, Ted was out of sick bay and ready to make his debut in what would become his favorite park to hit in, Briggs Stadium in Detroit. He arrived early to check out its friendly right-field dimensions—325 feet to the base of the triple-tiered grandstand—and to watch some of the Tigers stars—such as Hank Greenberg, Charlie Gehringer, and Rudy York—take batting practice.

They hit some pretty fair shots, but none approaching the scale of what Williams was about to hit in the game itself. Coming to bat in the second inning against Roxie Lawson, Ted limbered up by lacing the first pitch over the right-field roof, 120 feet high, but just foul. No player had ever hit a ball over the roof at Briggs Stadium, so that display got Tigers historians, press-box graybeards, and many in the small Thursday afternoon crowd of 5,550 stirring.

Then Jim Bagby, the Red Sox pitcher with a harelip who was also an active bench jockey, began yelling out to Greenberg that he was playing Williams too close in at first base. "Hank, you had better get back!" Bagby shouted.[42] "You don't know this guy, you better get back!" Greenberg paid no attention. Finally, Bagby called out: "All right, Hank, if you want to look like me and talk like me, stand right where you are!" Ted, who then lined out to center fielder Barney McCosky, delighted in telling that story over the years.

On his next time up, in the fourth inning, with Joe Cronin on base, York tried to get the rookie off balance by asking him how many home runs he'd hit for Minneapolis the previous year. Ted respectfully said it didn't matter because York must have hit more when he played for Toledo, the Tigers farm team in the American Association. He worked the count to three and two, then unloaded on a high fastball and drove it on top of the roof in right-center. Gerry Moore reported in the *Globe* that "the most dependable Detroit historians immediately tabbed that blow as the longest homer ever hit here, surpassing previous granddaddies propelled by Lou Gehrig and Sunny Jim Bottomley."

In the fifth, with one out and Foxx and Cronin aboard, Ted dug in against Bob Harris, a rookie just up from Toledo. Harris's first three pitches were balls. Now York piped up again.

"You're not hitting, are you Kid?" the catcher asked.[43]

"I sure as hell am," Ted replied, having just been flashed the green light by Cronin.

The pitch came, and Williams crushed a rising line drive. The ball screamed out to right field in a heartbeat, flew over the roof, fair by a dozen feet, and landed across adjoining Trumbull Avenue, bouncing against a taxi garage on one hop.

"The reaction of the Detroit writers, fans and players alike was almost indescribable," Gerry Moore wrote. "Greenberg looked with positive awe and admiration at the smiling Ted as he rounded first base. York just stood at home plate and scratched his head." As Williams crossed home, the catcher also muttered: "Darned if you weren't telling the truth."

On his last time up, he flied to right after receiving what Moore called "the greatest ovation we have ever heard a visiting athlete receive here."

The Kid was making his mark. Before the game, Hank Greenberg, then acknowledged as one of the great hitters in the game, had offered to bet Williams that he wouldn't hit .320 that year. But afterward he sent word into the Sox dressing room through a Detroit writer that he wanted to take the offer back, and asked Ted to come out early the next day at batting practice to give him a few tips. Foxx put the icing on the cake for Ted, calling out to him as they were leaving the clubhouse: "Hey, Kid, wait for me.... I want to see if I can get inoculated with some of that power.... Yes sir, there goes the Kid that makes us a real pennant contender."[44]

News of Ted's show in Detroit rippled through the American League, and at least one rival manager decided to change tactics against him. Bobby Doerr recalled that at the team's next stop in Saint Louis, Browns manager Fred Haney pointedly told Williams directly that he would be knocked down.

At Sportsman's Park, visiting players had to walk through the Browns clubhouse to get to theirs. As Doerr and Ted passed through, Haney spotted them. He had managed Doerr in the Coast League, but now he ignored his former player, walked right up to Ted, and said: "I've seen how well you hit. Let's see how you hit sittin' on your ass."[45]

"When the game started," Doerr told writer Mike Blake, "the first pitch to Ted was right near his ear and knocked the big guy down. Ted got up, didn't even dust off his uniform, took his stance and on the next pitch, drove it against the right field screen for a double. The next time up, the first pitch knocked him down and on pitch two, Ted drove it into Grand Boulevard for a home run. That was that."

Ted gained confidence each time he faced a pitcher. "The first time around the league, the first western trip we made, he might have struck out ten times in the four towns, and his average was pretty low," recalled Cronin. "But he kept saying, 'Don't worry. Don't worry. I'll hit these guys.' He kept his confidence.... He knew what he wanted and he knew he was gonna do it. Wasn't any doubt about it."[46]

Williams capped an eventful May by hitting a homer in each game of a Memorial Day doubleheader split with the Yankees at Fenway Park before a packed house of thirty-five thousand people, ten thousand more having been turned away. The first blow, off Red Ruffing, was said by Gerry Moore of the *Globe* to have been the longest home run ever witnessed at Fenway, landing seventy-five feet up in the right-field bleachers, just to the left of the runway separating that section of the park from the grandstand. "Even Ruffing couldn't conceal his amazement as Teddy loped around the bases in his usual grinning style, and the crowd went entirely nuts."[47] Ted said later: "It was the longest home run I ever hit. I couldn't even feel the contact, the swing was that sweet."[48]

With June came an extended slump, however, and Ted went into a funk. He told Johnny Orlando that he wished he were back in Minneapolis.

"So I told him right to his kisser: 'Kid, you're gonna be all right,'" Orlando said. "'You'll hit .335 for the year. You keep swinging and you'll have 35 home runs, and if the guys ahead of you keep getting on base, you'll drive in 150 runs.' He said, 'If I do...I'll buy you a Cadillac.'"[49]

By late June, Ted was still only hitting in the .270s, but he was hitting for power. By the July 4 benchmark, he was leading the league in RBIs with sixty-four and was third in home runs with twelve. Meanwhile, a rare five-game sweep of the Yankees by the Red Sox between July 5 and July 9 in Yankee Stadium had Boston buzzing and pushed any talk of individual disappointments aside. Before the series started, Ted spoke up for the team, telling Tommy Henrich of the Yanks: "It's all right for you guys to think you're tough, but it's about time somebody quit agreeing with you."[50]

Williams wasn't selected for the All-Star team—the only time in his career that would happen. He said he wasn't sore at the snub, noting that when the team was picked, his average was still under .300. He would use the break to go visit his aunts and uncle in nearby Westchester County, then return to New York to watch the All-Star Game at Yankee Stadium from Tom Yawkey's box, next to the American League dugout.

By mid-July, Ted had worked his average up above .310, and he was feeling frisky. Before a game on July 17 in Detroit, he walked over to Tigers starter Bobo Newsom, one of the league's leading pitchers, as he was warming up and told him: "I'm going to give you a going over!"[51]

"Why, you rookie!" snorted Newsom. "You couldn't hit me with a banjo."

His first time up, Ted homered and later touched Newsom for a double. When he reached second base, Ted looked in at the pitcher and wagged his fingers, as if to say he'd been foolish to doubt him. "Fresh busher!" said Bobo afterward in the clubhouse.

A few days later, at Comiskey Park in Chicago, Williams, after striking out, threw a mini-tantrum, kicking the ground, heaving his bat, and punching the air. As the White Sox fans hooted at him, Ted doffed his cap and curtsied extravagantly. Seeing home plate umpire Bill Summers whip off his mask and walk briskly toward Ted, Cronin rushed from the dugout and, trying to save his star from being run from the game, screamed at him: "Busher!" followed by a string of other invectives. The dressing-down may have averted an ejection, but didn't seem to have much effect curbing Ted's erratic behavior. Later in the game, after another disappointment, Ted punted his glove some fifty feet in the air while walking out to his position in right field. After the game, Williams told *Boston Evening American* columnist Austen Lake that Cronin had taken him aside and said, "Kid, don't get in uproars. It'll sour the fans on you. They'll think you're a crackpot and start to hoot you. Right now, everybody's pulling for you. Keep 'em on your side." Ted said Cronin was right, "but shucks, I was only funnin'!"

Of course this sort of exuberance, color, and candor was music to the press's ears. Before the first game of a doubleheader on July 18 in Chicago, Ted had told the *Globe*'s Hy Hurwitz, "I've got to get a home run out there today. It's the only western city that I haven't hit for the circuit so far." After belting a curveball from Clint Brown more than four hundred feet and collecting five other hits in the two games, Ted said: "That leaves only New York and Washington to conquer and I'll take care of those towns on my next visit."[52]

Similarly, the *Globe*'s Gerry Moore had asked Williams earlier that month in Philadelphia if it wasn't about time for him to hit his first homer at Shibe Park. "You're darn right!" he replied. "I'll hit one for you today."[53] He did, and as he crossed the plate, he waved to Moore in the press box.

He went on to give Austen Lake a series of candid predictions, including that he'd lead the league in hitting and home runs before 1942 and that he was a "cinch" to hit three homers before the end of that very week. He said his greatest satisfaction thus far was the day earlier in July when Cronin installed him as the cleanup hitter—behind Foxx. Lake said that Ted was relishing the attention he was getting from reporters, autograph seekers, and photographers and was gracious to all of them, especially the latter. He was "posturing interminably for the picture men. He loves it!" Lake wrote. Ted admitted as much. "Boy! Maybe this doesn't give me a kick. I'm a kid from the haystack circuit. I never had nothin' like this!"[54]

It was true that Williams was often willing to go to great lengths for photographers, especially those who worked for the Hearst-owned *Daily Record*. Like any tabloid worth its salt, the *Record* knew how to play a good picture, and when it got one, would offer it up to the rest of the Hearst papers around the country. On May 22, during yet another bout with the grippe, Ted posed for a hokey but endearing page 1 *Record* shot in which he was fishing from a goldfish bowl while lying in his bed. Three months later, there was Ted on the cover of the August 4 *Record,* dressed as a latter-day Huck Finn: barefoot, wearing overalls over a white shirt with the sleeves rolled up, standing along the banks of the Charles River with a bamboo fishing rod over his right shoulder, waving happily. He had on a straw hat and had tied a red handkerchief around his neck. Inside the paper, he was shown sitting on the grass, waiting for an imaginary fish to bite while sucking on a piece of honeysuckle.

"We like Williams because he's regular," said *Record* photographer Bruce McLean in a copy block that accompanied his Huck Finn photos. "I'm telling you, you just can't help liking that kid, and every photographer will tell you the same thing."[55]

By the beginning of August, Ted was on a tear, hitting .327 with 16 homers and 85 RBIs, as was Jimmie Foxx, who was at .358 with 24 homers and 74 RBIs. The press began to characterize the two sluggers as a mini Murderers' Row who helped and admired one another while waging a friendly competition to see who could hit the longest homers and knock in the most runs.

Ted accorded Foxx his proper deference and respect. "I'm lucky to be working with such a real guy as Jimmie Foxx," he said. "You know, a lot of people ask me who I want to pattern myself after. Well, when it comes to hitting a baseball, Jim is the one man I want to follow, but even if he never hit a baseball, he'd still be the one I'd like to pattern myself after as a man."[56]

Foxx, for his part, said he had been helped by having Williams hit behind him so that pitchers were forced to throw to him.[57] Ted's effervescence amused Double X, particularly when the rookie engaged in an exaggerated hand-pumping routine when greeting him after a home run. Williams was also giving him motivation, lest Foxx get outhit by someone he affectionately referred to as a "fresh busher."

Though Ted tolerated that comment coming from Foxx, by now he was getting defensive at any implication that he was still a minor leaguer. His record had proved otherwise, he thought. "I'm not a busher, and I hate that word," he told the Associated Press for an early August feature.[58]

"Sure, you're a busher," said third baseman Jim Tabor, overhearing the conversation. "What else are you?"

"I'm not a busher!" Ted screamed back. "I'm a big league ballplayer and don't call me a busher."

He took more kindly to another traditional baseball term. "Screwball?" He smiled. "Sure, they call me a screwball and say I make wisecracks. But let me tell you, I may be a screwball to some people and I do have a lot of fun. But when I get out there on the field, I'm plenty serious."

The same day that story appeared, August 8, Williams demonstrated why people were still using both words to describe him.

After popping up with the bases loaded in a 9–2 win over the Athletics at Fenway Park, Ted loped down the line and had only barely reached first base when the ball dropped between two fielders. He should have been on second, so Cronin sent in a pinch runner and benched him. John Gillooly wrote in the *Record* that Williams's baserunning apathy was the result of being "obviously stung" that Foxx had taken over the lead in their RBI race following two home runs earlier in the game.[59] But Gerry Moore of the *Globe* reported that Cronin and Ted had a long talk after the benching, during which Cronin learned that "some outside circumstance of a private nature" had been the cause of his disinterested and lax play.[60]*

Ted made amends in a doubleheader against the Athletics the next day. In the first game, he showed a sense of humor, sprinting to first base after he bounced a ball back to the pitcher. The crowd loved it, laughing and cheering. Then he won the second game with a ninth-inning bases-loaded single off the left-field wall to drive in two runs for a 6–5 come-from-behind victory.

One issue that vexed Williams and that he decided to speak out about was Fenway Park's long right field, which he felt was unfairly cutting down on his home runs. He had a point, especially when comparing Fenway to his favorite American League destinations—Yankee Stadium, which was 314 feet down the line in right, and Briggs Stadium in Detroit, which was 325 feet. But the way he argued his case made it appear that he was more interested in his own well-being than the team's.

"I should be doing a lot better and I know I would be if I played my home games in another park except Fenway," Ted told Hy Hurwitz of

---

* This was apparently a reference to the fact that his parents had separated. The separation had occurred in April, but it's possible Ted did not learn of it until later.

the *Globe*. "Why, I'm really delighted to leave Boston, even though the fans, the management, and everybody has just been wonderful to me. Because now that I'm going on the road, I'll really start hitting that ball.

"I feel that I have a chance to be one of the greatest hitters in baseball, but I won't unless they shorten right field at Fenway Park. Why, I wanted to be the greatest first year player in the game and I believe I'd have done it easily if I didn't have to play 77 games in Boston."[61] Ted went on to name the great sluggers and said they were all helped by favorable home fences. He reiterated that he didn't want to leave Boston, but "I'm the guy that counts most to myself. I'm in this game to make a lot of dough and I want to get it fast. The best way for me to get it is to hit more home runs and drive in more runs than anyone in the game. I won't do it at Fenway Park if the fence stays out as far as it is now."

Ted said a shorter fence would add twenty to twenty-five points to his average. He wanted to beat Joe DiMaggio's rookie records, and said that Fenway was tougher for him than Yankee Stadium was for DiMaggio. If they moved the fence in twenty-five feet, Ted concluded, he'd be "crazy" to want to play for anyone else but Boston.

Red Sox owner Tom Yawkey loved Williams and delighted in needling him or otherwise horsing around with his young star. In a July game at Detroit, Yawkey had stationed himself in the right-field stands, and, masquerading as a Tigers fan, heckled Williams mercilessly. In the clubhouse after the game, Yawkey said to Ted, sympathetically: "That fellow in the bleachers was certainly riding you today."[62] "Yeah," Ted snapped. "He was plenty loud, the cheap punk. I'd like to have busted him in the puss." Yawkey broke up laughing and confessed. The following month in Cleveland, Williams had a room directly below Yawkey's at the Lake Shore Hotel. Yawkey called out the window to him, waited until he looked up, then doused him with a pitcher of ice water.[63]

But understanding that in the matter of the right-field fence Williams was in no mood to joke, Yawkey agreed with his star and began to take steps to rectify the situation. On September 24, six days before the end of the season, the Red Sox made the official announcement on Fenway Park's new dimensions: the distance down the right-field foul line would be shortened from 332 to 302 feet, and bull pens for the home and visiting teams would be moved from the sidelines to right and right-center field, thereby shortening the fence at the base of the right-field bleachers from 402 to 380 feet. It would still be a poke even at that range, especially as the new fence would angle out gradually as it approached the deepest point in the ballpark in right-center, 420 feet from home plate.

In making the announcement, the Red Sox said nothing about the purpose of the change, but it was widely interpreted in the press as a move to help·Ted. The newspapers quickly labeled the shortened right field "Williamsburg," and Ted seemed to embrace the designation by gleefully posing for pictures with construction workers as they built the new fence in the off-season. "Boy, won't I be glad to see those shorter fences!" he said following the announcement.

The team finished with a solid season, 89–62, but still ended up in second place, seventeen games behind the Yankees, who won 106 games and captured their fourth straight American League pennant. But the second-place finish took no luster off Ted's season. He was Rookie of the Year by acclamation at a time when there was no such official award, finishing with an average of .327, 31 home runs (14 at Fenway, 17 on the road), and 145 RBIs. He thus achieved his goal of besting the great DiMaggio's rookie line of .323, 29 homers, and 125 RBIs. Ted's RBI total topped the American League, the first time a rookie had led in that category, and he finished fourth in the Most Valuable Player balloting behind DiMaggio, Bob Feller, and Foxx. His fourteen Fenway homers were eight more than all other left-handed batters combined hit in Boston.

The day before the season ended with a September 30 doubleheader against the Yankees in New York, Williams reflected on his year by writing to Earl Keller, the San Diego reporter who had covered him when he was in high school and with the Padres.

"Well Earl, I guess there's no one in the world happier about me having a good year my first year than myself," Ted wrote on Commodore Hotel stationery. "I hoped all last winter that I'd have this kind of a year. Really though, Earl, the big leagues is easier to play in than the minors, and I really see very little difference in the pitching. There's a few, like Feller, Bridges, Ruffing, and a few others that are really tough, but outside of that, it's the same. Everything is just a little better. A little better pitching, fielding, backgrounds. Even the steaks are better up here. Mr. Yawkey, the owner of the Red Sox, and Joe Cronin have treated me great. So have all the other fellows, especially Jim Foxx. . . . Boy, a fellow doesn't realize what cities these are until he's in them a while. Today I went to the top of the Empire State Building, and as soon as I looked over the hundred-odd stories, I just went 'Oh!' The cars look like flies. Well Earl, I guess I've popped off enough, so I'll close. As ever, Ted."

All in all, Williams felt no one could have had a better, happier first year in the big leagues than he did. "The fans in right field were yelling with me and for me all the time, really crowding in there to see what I would do next, and that year, nobody tipped his hat more than I did," Ted wrote in his book.[64] "I mean, right off my head, by the button. Nothing put on, nothing acted, just spontaneous."

He also wrote he was "unaware, I suppose, that my troubles were just beginning."

5

The Writers

There seemed no troubles on the horizon for Ted that winter of 1940, as spring training neared. He had a pleasant off-season, eschewing San Diego to return to Minneapolis and his minor-league glory days. He hunted and fished and stayed in baseball shape by working out at the University of Minnesota's indoor cage.

He returned to Boston in January to have his tonsils taken out and later to attend the Boston baseball writers' annual dinner. They had voted him the Red Sox's Most Valuable Player of 1939, and, to everyone's surprise, Williams showed up to receive his prize wearing a tuxedo. He spoke off-the-cuff and charmed the crowd. "Thank God I ain't got any notes," Ted said. "This is really the greatest and happiest honor I've ever achieved in my short baseball career."[1]

Meeting later in his hotel room with a reporter, Ted fretted that he weighed only 187 pounds, and he showed off an array of muscle magazines he'd been consulting in an effort to get stronger. But he betrayed no lack of confidence about the upcoming season, and he fairly salivated over those shortened Fenway fences in "Williamsburg."

"Last year I hit 14 home runs in this park," Ted said. "This year, at a conservative estimate, and I mean really the most conservative one, I ought to hit at least 20. That fence has shortened the right field bounds by 20 feet, and at least 10 of the balls I hit last year missed being homers by just about that much, do you see what I mean?"[2]

Everyone did, and expectations were raised higher still on April 13, three days before the Red Sox were to open the season in Washington, when Ted put on a show in batting practice before a rained-out exhibition game against the Boston Braves at Fenway. He hit fifteen balls into

Williamsburg, including seven of the first eight thrown to him, despite the cold, foul weather. Further underscoring the perception that the shortened fences were made for him and that he would take full advantage of the new dimensions, Williams posed after the workout for a *Boston Sunday Advertiser* photographer, pointing to right field. The photo ran prominently the next day under the headline HOWDY, BOSTON— THAT'S MY SPOT.[3]

Besides Williamsburg, there were two other significant changes for Ted in 1940. First, he would be playing left field, not right. The left fielder the previous year, Joe Vosmik, had been sold to the Dodgers, and Dominic DiMaggio, Joe's younger brother, had been acquired from the San Francisco Seals in the Coast League to play right field. Ted would have less ground to cover in left and a shorter distance to throw, the thinking went, and those keen eyes of his would be spared the harsh glare of the sun field.

Second, he would switch places with Jimmie Foxx in the batting order and hit third rather than fourth. Joe Cronin felt Foxx would protect Ted, since opponents would be less willing to pitch around Williams with Double X waiting on deck. But if Cronin thought this would help the team, Ted was thinking more about how the change would affect him: "Heck sakes, there goes my runs-batted-in championship," he said when the move was announced.[4]

The comment foreshadowed a fundamental shift in Ted's mood, and it was not long before the attractive, boyish charm and innocence that Williams had radiated all during the previous season—as well as that winter and spring, right through his batting-practice show on April 13—faded altogether and Williams unveiled his dark side.

He got off to a bad start, getting only two hits in five games the first week the Red Sox were home. After a few fans jeered him for early hitting and fielding miscues, the highly sensitive Ted overreacted and told a few teammates that he would never tip his cap again.

When some reporters wrote that he was not hustling on every play, Ted was outraged and started a vendetta against the writers. He began to brood and sulk and complain that he was underpaid. Some teammates got angry with him. Fans also reacted negatively to this churlish behavior, and when more than a month passed without Ted hitting even one home run into Williamsburg, resentment grew among some of the patrons. A faction decided that Williams was a spoiled child undeserving of the special treatment the Red Sox had accorded him.

On the team's first western trip, Ted confessed to Harold Kaese of the

Boston Evening Transcript that he was in a funk. "I wish I had a disposition like Jimmie Foxx's," Williams said. "I've got a rotten disposition."[5]

Cronin decided he had to address Williams's darkening mood. The manager told the *Boston Globe*'s Gerry Moore that Ted's fixation with hitting was adversely affecting his "hustle and concentration" and therefore the team's chances at the pennant. "Nobody wants to see the Kid become a great star more than I do," Cronin said. "That's why I must impress on him that all great stars...first of all have been great team players....Ted is still only a boy and I know he wants to win as much as anybody on our club. He's just so wrapped up in hitting, that he forgets himself now and then."[6]

Not that Williams wasn't hitting. As of May 21, he was batting .347, but he only had two home runs, none yet in Williamsburg. The failure thus far to meet the fans' power expectations—and those he himself had so publicly set—was probably the chief source of Ted's problem. But whatever it was, Cronin thought it had to be nipped in the bud. He told Harold Kaese in a May 22 story that he had decided to bench Ted.

"I didn't want to do this," Cronin said. "I don't want Williams to get this kind of reputation, but there's no other way."[7] Kaese added that owner Tom Yawkey had become "sick and tired of watching the Kid go through the motions. He as well as nearly every player and coach on the team talked to him and tried to wake him up. It was no go....If it continues, if he sulks and complains on the bench, one of his teammates undoubtedly will punch him on the nose. The players, an ideal group of hustlers, are down on him."

After listing the possible causes of Ted's gloom—his bad start at home, the booing by some Fenway fans, his low home-run production, and the likelihood that he would lose any chance at the RBI title as a result of hitting third—Kaese concluded his article with a cheap shot: "Whatever it is, it probably traces to his up-bringing. Can you imagine a kid, a nice kid with a nimble brain, not visiting his father and mother all of last winter?"

Kaese himself had second thoughts about that non sequitur and wired his paper to have it removed, but in a composing-room snafu, it was left in. Kaese apologized to Ted the next day and always regretted that the gratuitous remark had run.[8] But to Williams, this was an unpardonable sin, representing an unacceptable invasion of his privacy. The Kaese story was a pivot point, turning what had been a simmering feud with sportswriters into a vitriolic campaign that he chose to wage his entire career.

Still, Ted couldn't seem to stop talking with reporters about almost anything that popped into his mind—an undisciplined habit that would always cause him difficulty. Speaking with syndicated writer Harry Grayson in late May about all the pressures he was feeling, Williams contrasted his lot with that of his uncle John Smith, the Westchester County fireman whom Ted had visited several times. Being a firefighter wouldn't be a bad life, Ted said, thinking out loud. It was a throwaway line, offered in jest, but Grayson took it and snidely played it straight— that Williams would rather chuck his baseball career and become a fireman—as part of a larger piece about the Kid's malaise.

The Grayson story focused further attention on Ted's state of mind and gave rival bench jockeys plenty of ammunition. At a June 3 game at Fenway, for example, Chicago White Sox manager Jimmy Dykes screamed when Williams came to bat that "Teddy wants to be a fireman!"[9] Dykes then had his players whistle to imitate siren noises. When Williams finally hit his first home run into one of the new bull pens at Fenway, the *Globe* took caustic note with a banner headline: TED LOCATES WILLIAMSBURG.

Nevertheless, on June 4, perhaps realizing that was going too far, the *Globe*'s Victor Jones wrote what would become the first of several sympathetic columns penned by various Boston writers over the next several weeks that seemed an attempt to save Williams from himself. "This sure is a mighty tough world for a kid of 21, particularly a sensitive kid like you, if he can't get in the dumps occasionally," wrote Jones in what was effectively an open letter to the struggling Red Sox star. "The trouble is that a guy in your position, no matter what his age, can't afford the common luxury of a sulk or a 'mad.' Whether you like it or not, you are a public character, and as such you've got to stand the gaff....You're a great kid, a great ballplayer with maybe 20 years of major league ball ahead of you. Don't go and spoil it all."

But Ted seemed bent on doing just that. The morning of August 13, he was in the clubhouse at Fenway Park, packing his equipment and getting ready to fly down to New York to meet his teammates for a doubleheader against the Yankees later that afternoon. He'd been out of the lineup for several days with lower back pain and had stayed home while the team was on the road. He was hitting .333 with 14 homers and 68 RBIs. The Red Sox, who in mid-June were in first place, had long since faded from contention.

Austen Lake, the *Boston Evening American* columnist, walked into the clubhouse. Trying to avoid Lake, Ted, dressed in blue overalls, walked out toward the field and sat down in a box seat. Lake followed him outside. Williams seemed in a foul mood, and Lake asked, "What's the matter with you, Ted?" Then it all poured out.

Venting for the next twenty minutes, he said that he had asked Cronin and Yawkey—many times—to trade him. He couldn't stand Boston's fans, its press, and the city itself. He also said he would have to be paid "plenty" more next year than the $12,500 he was making now, declaring that he'd earned it. "And you can print the whole rotten mess just as I said it," Ted insisted. "I don't like the town. I don't like the people and the newspaper men have been on my back all year. Why?"[10]

The headline on the story was TED WILLIAMS BLASTS BOSTON, WANTS TO BE TRADED TO YANKS. The first paragraph said: "Young Ted Samuel Williams, adolescent Red Sox outfielder, detests Boston!" The second paragraph: "Theodore wants to be traded to some other major league town." He rejected Detroit, Cleveland, and Chicago as cities where he might go, saying he'd hold out first. Asked if he wanted to go to New York, Ted fell silent, and Lake inferred that was his destination of choice.

"Plainly," Lake wrote, Ted had been "nursing his torrent of spleen" during the week that he had spent alone in Boston while injured. "He felt what he did with a vast conviction. He didn't like Boston's streets, the way the houses were built, the parks, the people, the Riverway. Phooie! But most of all he didn't like the human crows who perch on the rim of the ballpark and write typographical sneers."

Lake said he had considered not printing what Ted had told him, so that he and the team might work out their differences in private, but decided that "the situation is such that inevitably the ulcerous condition will have to be lanced publicly." Williams's private behavior and thoughts were his own business, Lake wrote, "except where he wants to get away and is saturated with that desire, or where he detests the uniform he wears and abhors the people he represents. That is a public matter." Lake said he had nonetheless offered to let Ted take whatever he wanted back, and have it be off the record, but again Williams said that everything could be printed.

"They pay you on your record," Ted said. "The bleachers can boo, the newspapers can sneer, but right out there [pointing to the field] is where you get the dough or you don't, and I'm going to get mine."

Not surprisingly, the story reverberated. Tom Yawkey—furious with Williams—denied that Ted had ever asked to be traded. "No player in baseball is greater than the game itself, and Teddy Williams will discover that fact to his sorrow unless he mends his way," Yawkey said.[11] He also let it be known that Ted was essentially on his own in dealing with the press. "While I don't condone his feud with newspapermen and any fans away from the ballpark, I've decided to let him work out the situation on his own after talking to him once on that matter and getting no results."[12]

Ted thought the team could have done more to help him deal with the writers, though it was debatable how much the Red Sox could actually control their volatile star. And some critics would conclude that Yawkey and the team's management had no interest in helping Ted with the press, especially in the second half of his career, since his ability to command headlines and dominate coverage served to deflect attention from the consistently poor teams the Red Sox fielded in the 1950s.

After the Lake story appeared, Cronin, like Yawkey, also denied that Ted had ever approached him demanding a trade. And Jimmie Foxx told the writers he thought Ted was "a spoiled boy. How long it will take for him to grow up remains to be seen. But he'll have to grow up the hard way now."[13]

Doc Cramer, who'd had a rocky relationship with Williams, nonetheless tried to give him a boost. "You know who's the best, don't you?" Cramer told Ted privately. "You know who's the best in the league? You are."[14] But then Williams made another intemperate remark, telling Associated Press writer Eddie Brietz that if there were free agency in baseball, and if each team made him the same offer, he'd sign with the Dodgers. "I know I'd be a hero in Brooklyn," Ted proclaimed.[15]

The Red Sox played out the string, gliding toward what would be a fourth-place finish. On a lark, Cronin decided to have Williams pitch the last two innings in a 12–1 loss to the Tigers at Fenway Park on August 24. He allowed three hits and one run, walked none, and struck out Rudy York on three pitches. The move seemed to be an attempt by Cronin to placate angry fans with some pure entertainment in one of the worst losses of the year.

On September 4, Ted probably reached his nadir during a doubleheader at Fenway against the Athletics. The Sox won both games, but Williams was pouting again. He'd misjudged a liner that went over his head for a double, got picked off first base, and failed to run out a fly he thought would go foul but dropped in safely. In the seventh inning of the afternoon game, Ted decided to take out his frustrations by picking up a foul ball he had retrieved and throwing it as hard as he could at a bunch of photographers, who in those days were allowed on the field to take up positions in foul territory. The group was huddled near third base, and the ball Ted threw hit one of them in the back. None was expecting it because the ball had been out of play. "As it happened, no damage was done and Ted was merely shown up as about the most unattractive ballplayer we've had here in a long, long while," wrote the *Globe*'s Vic Jones, who had written Williams the sympathetic open letter in June.[16]

Reflecting back years later on his dealings with the press that season, Ted wrote in his book that he was "still a kid, high strung and prone to tantrums," and he felt like he was being "persecuted.... If there were eight or ten reporters around my locker, I'd spot a guy who'd written a bad article about me and I'd say, 'Why should you even come around me, that crap-house stuff you've been writing.' So that would embarrass *him,* and he'd get mad, and then off we'd go.... Before this, I was willing to believe a writer was my friend until he proved otherwise. Now my guard's up all the time, always watching for critical stuff. If I saw something, I'd read it twenty times, and I'd burn without knowing how to fight it."[17]

Ted finished 1940 with more than respectable numbers: a .344 average, with 23 home runs and 113 RBIs. His average was 17 points higher than it was in his rookie year, but his power production was off, with eight fewer homers and 32 fewer RBIs compared to 1939. Of his 23 homers in 1940, only nine were at Fenway and just four of those went into the new bull pens.[18] But the story of 1940 was not a set of numbers that, however good, came in below expectations. The story of the year was Ted's psychic tailspin, an evolving public meltdown that had played out in, and been shaped by, Boston's newspapers.

It marked the first season of what would become a career-long jihad waged by Ted against the baseball writers—his so-called Knights of the Keyboard. In fact, this was not a feud as such but a conflict largely manufactured by Williams to fuel his drive to excel. Though his press was overwhelmingly positive, he would seize on a negative story or column to portray all writers as a contemptible lot bent on invading his privacy and stirring up public opinion against him. The newspapers became a bogeyman that Williams constructed to feed the fire of antagonism that was central to his ability to perform well. He always said he hit best when he was angry, and that was generally true.

The interplay between Ted and the writers would become an important window into his character and one of the longest-running dramas in his career. Now, reporters who had fawned over Ted during his rookie year and even for part of the 1940 season had to recalibrate their relationship with him. In the process, the rules of engagement between newspapers and baseball began to change.

Between 1939 and 1960, the years spanning Ted's career with the Red Sox, Boston had eight major newspapers, or nine if one counted both the morning and evening editions of the *Boston Globe*, which had separate staffs and circulations. The morning papers were the *Post*, the *Herald*, the *Record*, the *Daily Globe*, and the *Christian Science Monitor*. The evening journals were the *American*, the *Transcript*, the *Traveler*, and the *Evening Globe*. Two of the papers folded while Williams was still playing: the *Transcript* in 1941, and the *Post* in 1956.

The *Record* and the *American* were tabloids owned by the Hearst chain, and they operated out of the same building. The papers competed against each other but on Sundays jointly published the *Boston Sunday Advertiser*. The *Herald* owned the *Traveler*.

The *Post* and *Record* dominated the city in 1940, with circulations of 369,000 and 329,000 respectively. The *Traveler* ranked third with 211,000, while figures for the others ranged between 117,000 and 168,000 — except for the *Transcript*, which had only 28,000 customers.

But those 28,000 were highly prized by advertisers, representing as they did the vanguard of Boston's dwindling but still disproportionately influential and moneyed Brahmin elite. The role of the *Transcript* in the city's life was celebrated by Cleveland Amory in his classic novel about the blue bloods in the most class-conscious city in America, *The Proper Bostonians*. "Daily except Sunday, just at tea-time — when the Proper Bostonian mind is traditionally at its most receptive stage — the *Transcript* was quietly laid, never tossed, on the doorsteps of the best people in Boston," Amory wrote. "Not to read the *Transcript* was unthinkable. It was never a newspaper in the vulgar sense of the word.... The loyalty of its readers was proverbial. In the wind of its editorial opinion they swayed, said the poet T. S. Eliot, 'like a field of ripe corn.' "

Legend had it that when three reporters showed up one day to see the owner of a grand Beacon Hill town house, they received this introduction from the attending servant: "Two reporters from the papers, sir, and a gentleman from the *Transcript*."

The *Transcript* saw itself as a bulwark against the encroaching yellow journalism flaunted by the *Post* and the *Record*. "The *Transcript* marches in the van of progress without sacrifice of dignity and self-respect...," the paper said when marking its centennial edition on July 24, 1930. "It differentiates solids from froth, the permanent from the passing, substance from shadow."

Just eleven years later, however, the *Transcript* closed its doors, its circulation down to 15,788 Proper Bostonians, only nine of whom chose to heed the paper's final appeal to send $500 to the National Shawmut Bank if the journal were to be kept afloat. But Boston then was still one of the most competitive newspaper cities in the country. The battles for circulation were intense, the journalism shallow and parochial.

The *Post*—which in its heyday in the late 1920s had a circulation of 628,000, larger than any other broadsheet in the country at the time—set the sensationalist tone for Boston at the start of the '40s with a steady diet of crime, sex, and sports, pushed hard in the same direction by Hearst's *Record* and *American*. The *Post* had supplanted the *Globe* as the favored paper of the Boston Irish by aggressively courting Catholics, who had become a majority in the city by the 1920s.

The *Post, Record,* and *American* were militantly Democratic. The *Herald* and its *Traveler* in the evening catered to a more upscale, suburban Republican clientele. The *Globe* tried to position itself as an enlightened, middle-of-the-road paper serving both the upper and the working classes. It saw itself as the *Post* and Hearst antidote, and adopted an aloof, don't-rock-the-boat line geared toward the family, which often cost it scoops. The *Globe* took the somewhat self-deluding line that *Post* and Hearst scoops were suspect to begin with, not to mention here today and gone tomorrow, at least as far as the more refined sensibilities of *Globe* readers were concerned. It stressed features, sports, and politics.

The *Christian Science Monitor* emphasized foreign news, and most of its circulation was outside New England. It was not a competitive factor locally, but the *Monitor's* longtime Red Sox beat writer Ed Rumill was respected and influential, not least because he was one of the few writers Ted liked and favored.

From 1851 to 1956, the Boston papers were concentrated downtown on a two-hundred-yard stretch of Washington Street, along what was called Newspaper Row. The row was known as the "Fleet Street of America" but had more journalists per square foot than its London counterpart and teemed with traffic through the horse-and-buggy era, then trolleys and cars. Before radio and through the late '30s, up to fifty thousand people would pack the area on Election Night to get results. Office boys and artists posted the latest news on blackboards or bulletin boards. If the night ran long, the papers provided music, entertainment, and political analysis over loudspeakers. Candidates would hop from paper to paper giving interviews.

Entertainers would also work the row during the day, hoping to attract publicity. In the '20s, Houdini performed for a lunchtime crowd, drawing gasps and cheers when he freed himself from a straitjacket and chains while hanging by his feet. There were many other attractions and distractions, ranging from watering holes aplenty to indulgences of the flesh. Reporters wanting sex were accommodated by a prostitute who nominally worked as a waitress in a greasy spoon headquartered in one of the *Post*'s buildings.

If there was one place that personified the dominant Boston journalism ethos of the day, it was probably the building at One Winthrop Square that housed Hearst's *Record* and *American*. Walking inside, one saw a huge framed poster featuring a portrait of William Randolph Hearst himself, along with the patriarch's guidelines to good newspapering. These included "Pay LIBERALLY for big, exclusive stuff and encourage tipsters. . . . Make a paper for the NICEST KIND OF PEOPLE, for the great middle class. Don't print a lot of dull stuff that they are supposed to like and don't. . . . Try to get scoops in pictures. They are frequently almost as important as news. . . . Pictures of pretty women and babies are interesting."

It was understood, of course, that "the nicest kind of people" were white. When a reporter called the city desk after responding to the scene of a murder, he would be asked, "Is it dark out there?" Meaning, was the murder victim black? If the answer was yes, there would be no story. The reporters were virtually all men, and the few women who cracked the ranks were mostly steered to "sob-sister" duty, turning out popular tearjerker stories that usually featured the widows and orphans of murder victims or of soldiers killed at war. The star sob sister at the *American* during World War II was Kitty Donovan. Gorgeous and a stylish writer to boot, Donovan turned out daily propaganda pieces about how awful the Germans were, under the standing headline DIARY OF A GERMAN HOUSEWIFE. The stories were pure fiction.

One of the framed Hearst admonitions was to "please be accurate," but that was taken with a large grain of salt. "Mr. Hearst did allow an awful lot of fakery," Frank "Mugsy" McGrath, a former night city editor at the *American,* told reporter Dave O'Brian for his 1982 *Boston Phoenix* article on the local history of Hearst. "There was stiff competition, so you did have to imagine a few things from time to time. Reporters would sometimes spend a month on the scene of a big murder, and the papers would be demanding fresh angles and startling news leads every day. We'd all get together after work and swap stories and leads."

One legendary trafficker in tall tales back in the day was ace Hearst crime reporter Bob Court, who used to delight in bragging about all the fabricated stories he'd written. His favorite was the time he had planted a woman's bloodstained panties at a crime scene for police to discover. On another occasion, running late to a murder scene with deadline for the first edition looming, Court stopped to phone in a totally fictitious account of the crime. Asked by McGrath how he could do that, Court replied, "Oh, that'll keep 'em happy for the first edition. We'll correct the story for the next one."

The *Record* and *American* newsrooms looked nothing like the antiseptic interiors of today's newspapers, whose carpeted quiet is as conducive to issuing insurance policies as it is to gathering the news. With the *Record* and *American* presses located just below the newsroom, above all there was noise and stifling heat year-round. Reporters sitting at their typewriters literally sweated. There was also the constant clacking of wire service machines and copy paper strewn about the floor, along with cigarette butts, many still smoldering. Cigarette and cigar smoke filled the air, along with shouts of "Boy!" from editors calling for copyboys.

The city editor of the *Record* from the mid-'20s to the '60s was Eddie Holland. Holland's first job was selling vegetables off a truck. He never went to college and didn't like the notion of college graduates working as reporters because he thought they were too polite to ask difficult questions. "He wanted street-smart reporters who would dig and who didn't mind embarrassing people," his son Bob Holland, a former reporter and photo editor at the *Record,* told O'Brian.

Reporters with no college education were one thing, but that could be a liability in an editor, George Frazier, the late columnist for the *Globe,* once suggested cheekily. "When I went to the *Record-American* as a columnist," Frazier wrote in reference to the paper that grew out of the 1961 merger of the *Record* and the *American,* "I was aware that its devotees moved their lips while they read. What I didn't realize was that the editors did too."

In the '30s, '40s, and '50s, Major League Baseball was by far the dominant sport in the country. It would often take up a third of the front page of newspapers in Boston, New York, Chicago, and Philadelphia.[19]

Before television, writers such as Ring Lardner, Damon Runyon,

Grantland Rice, Westbrook Pegler, Paul Gallico, and, later, Red Smith and Jimmy Cannon were key cogs in the machine that fashioned baseball legend and lore. What they wrote shaped glorious public perceptions of the players, who remained at a certain distance and remove that the arrival of TV would forever change. And to be a baseball writer assigned to cover one of the big-league teams was a highly prized position. "The sportswriters loved the game, their jobs, and the prestige it gave them on the paper," wrote David Halberstam in *Summer of '49*, his book about the 1949 pennant race between the Red Sox and the Yankees.[20] "Trying to get a position as a beat baseball writer was like waiting for a Supreme Court justice to retire. It was a position held for life."

The writers wore suits. When covering road games, they'd play poker on the trains with the players and among themselves. Some great yarns came out of those trips, but in the fraternal milieu, it was understood that the stories would stay in-house, never to turn up in print.

On average, the writers were a generation or more older than the players they covered. Before World War II, the vast majority of them had not gone to college, and in the '40s, their salaries ranged between $5,000 and $7,000 per year. But you couldn't beat the perks. In what seems a quaint anachronism today, it was common practice at least into the '60s for the ball clubs to pay all the expenses of the writers when the teams traveled. The reporters would stay at the best hotels, order from room service, and eat at fine restaurants. Moreover, they spent six weeks in Florida for spring training on the teams' tab. In return for such largesse, the clubs of course expected—even demanded—favorable coverage, and they received it. On the rare occasions when they did not, the teams would not hesitate to assert their economic leverage over the papers.

In 1947, Boston Braves manager Billy Southworth was arrested for drunk driving. To try to keep the news out of the papers, the Braves, or Southworth himself, supplied the police with a false name. When the *Globe's* Hy Hurwitz, in a then-rare burst of enterprising zeal, got wind of the story and began poking around, Braves PR man Billy Sullivan, who later became the founder of the Boston Patriots pro football team, protested vehemently to the *Globe*. He argued that no writer whose expenses the Braves covered should even be contemplating stories like that.* Tim Horgan, who covered Williams and the Red Sox in the 1950s for the *Boston Herald* and *Evening Traveler*, said the Red Sox once got a

---

* This incident was one reason why the *Globe* became the first paper in Boston to stop having the teams pay the expenses of its writers on the road, according to notes by Harold Kaese, the former *Transcript* writer who by then had become a leading *Globe* columnist.

colleague of his at the *Traveler* fired for writing a story the team deemed too critical of catcher Birdie Tebbetts.[21]

Before Tom Yawkey bought the Red Sox in 1933, the Boston press had been inclined to favor the National League Braves because Braves president Emil Fuchs showered the writers with food and drink and gave them Christmas presents. This changed under Yawkey, who had plenty of money to throw around, and by the time Ted arrived on the scene in 1939, the Red Sox were firmly established as the leading team in town. But manager Eddie Collins tried to economize on Yawkey's behalf and ordered that writers' expenses be curbed, while the Braves increased the team's publicity budget to the point where it later even included gambling money for writers on the road. The result was divided loyalties among the writers as to which team treated them better, and thus which was more deserving of their favorable notices.[22]

The accepted reporting convention of the day was to write spare, runs-hits-and-errors stories that focused only on what happened in the game.* Criticizing management, flawed strategy, or inept play, or otherwise rocking the boat, was considered off-limits. Scoops were discouraged— and often shared—because they made those who didn't get them look bad. In addition, there was collaboration in the writing of stories and sharing of quotations.

Another conspirator in the collaborative process was the Western Union telegraph operator who wired the reporters' stories to the papers. "We had telegraph operators who would write half the stories," Horgan said. "He'd be sending your story, and if he saw you didn't have something that another guy had, he'd just stick that in your piece....It was like a big club. Everyone was in it, and no one was going to get hurt."

Some stories were wildly embellished or altogether untrue. Russ Kemmerer, who pitched for the Red Sox in the mid-'50s, thought this was the natural by-product of so many newspapers competing with one other and looking for their own angles. "Each paper had to find a way to deal with the same game, make it interesting enough to sell papers and at the same time mention the score," wrote Kemmerer in a memoir of his time in the big leagues. "One paper had this heartwarming story of how my sick three-year-old son had seen me pitching on television and crawled out to the kitchen to get his mother to watch the game. Another told a story of how General Manager Joe Cronin ripped up my contract

---

* Another financial connection between the clubs and the writers was the job of official scorer at the games. Writers could earn an extra $50 or more for that assignment, which was coveted and rotated among the beat reporters.

and doubled my salary. One related that Red Sox owner Tom Yawkey had given me a bonus check for $1,000. They all sounded great! Sadly enough, none of them was true."[23]

Yawkey assumed the press was basically corrupt, interested in little more than hospitality, and in return for that would remain compliant. Indeed, the willingness of the Red Sox and other teams to pay the writers' expenses, and the newspapers' ready acceptance of the arrangement, established a corrupt foundation for the player-reporter relationship. In addition, some reporters were personally corrupt—part of a culture that was built on sloth and collaborating with one another, not competing.

Writers who were on the take had nonbaseball "accounts," as they were called—clients who paid them to write stories, usually short items. The sponsors included racetracks, boxing promoters, wrestling promoters, dog tracks, or anyone else who wanted publicity. The papers, which knew of the practice and encouraged it, could thus pay their writers less, knowing they would supplement their salaries through such after-hours pursuits.[24]

With Williams's arrival in 1939, Yawkey had made a token effort to improve ties with the writers by hiring a public relations man, Ed Doherty. But Doherty was so hostile to reporters that he effectively served as the anti–press agent. Doherty "considered the writers parasites and made no attempt to conceal his contempt for them," wrote Al Hirshberg, who covered the Red Sox of that era for the *Post* and the *Herald*. "His standard reply to anything but routine questions was, 'How the hell do I know?'"[25]

Partly as a result of Doherty's antagonism, loyalties and affinities fluctuated. By the mid-'40s, relations between the writers and the team ranged from congenial to extremely tense. In late 1946, when the Red Sox clinched the pennant in Cleveland, a long-running feud between manager Joe Cronin and the *Evening American*'s Herb "Huck" Finnegan boiled over. There had been bad blood between the two for a while, and Cronin felt the hard-drinking and irascible Finnegan had been insufficiently appreciative of his leadership.

"Well, what do you say now, you fuckin' bastard?" Cronin asked Finnegan when they chanced to run into each other in the elevator back at the hotel.

"You'll never win another one!" replied Finnegan defiantly.[26]

That night the Red Sox refused to include the writers in the team celebration. Though Yawkey paid for a separate press party, the moment was a watershed in Red Sox–press relations, and they got steadily worse.

"The Red Sox just didn't know how to make the press work for them, and the result was a multitude of unnecessary problems," Hirshberg recalled.[27] Later, in choosing a successor to Doherty, the team under-scored its disregard, or contempt, for the press by selecting aging bull-pen coach Larry Woodall, who also couldn't stand reporters. Woodall made it his business at spring training to circulate among rookies and instruct them not to talk to the Boston writers because they couldn't be trusted.[28]

At first, the writers had thoroughly enjoyed their repartee with Williams. He was new, immensely talented, raw, spirited, amusing, clever, and, of course, he talked nonstop. He'd received a charmed press his rookie year, but in 1940, as he brooded and sulked, he began to lash out at the writers with increasing frequency. One of Williams's favorite maneuvers was to give a scoop to an out-of-town writer—the better to antagonize his real or perceived enemies in the local press corps. Like the fans, reporters found Williams easy to provoke, and then his public rages would become fair game to report. "I remember one time I asked him how he could talk to the writers the way he did," said Don Buddin, who played shortstop for the Red Sox from 1956 to 1961. "He said, 'Son, if you hit .350, you can do a lot of things.'"[29]

This new adversarial dynamic would be further fueled, especially after World War II, by the arrival of younger and better-educated writers who were not interested in writing one-dimensional stories about the game only. Readers were beginning to demand a more personal, behind-the-scenes treatment of their heroes, an approach Ted thought an unacceptable invasion of his privacy. In addition, while the number of major dailies in Boston began to decrease, each paper was starting to assign two or three writers to the Red Sox beat, and sheer repetition was no longer an option. Moreover, the number of suburban dailies that covered the team proliferated. Soon the Boston chapter of the Baseball Writers' Association of America was the largest in the country, after New York's.

By far the leading Boston sports journalist of the day—the most widely read, the most outrageous, and the most brilliant, even in the nonsports realm—was Dave Egan, a columnist for the *Record* whose nom de plume (chosen for reasons unknown) was the Colonel. And this leading light had a vendetta against Ted, to whom he referred as "T. Williams Esquire."

Egan was about five foot seven, 150 pounds, and dapper. He always wore a suit and tie topped off with a stylish fedora. An elegant writer, he was a provocateur, a contrarian who delighted in cutting against the grain seven days a week. If Ted was the darling of Boston, Egan decided he had to knock him down. He was a populist rabble-rouser who targeted the haves on behalf of—he liked to think—the have-nots. And in addition to all that, he was a drunk. (When the Colonel was hors de combat, writers at the other papers would hear about it, and press-box parlor games ensued to guess who the ghostwriter of the column would be that day.)

Egan was far more educated than his brethren on the sports pages. Born in Newport, Rhode Island, in 1901, the son of a milkman who fathered sixteen other children, Egan won a scholarship to Harvard, sailed through in three years, cum laude, and went on to Harvard Law School, graduating in 1925. He practiced law for a year and then went to work as a sportswriter for the *Globe,* where he had been a night office boy and had done some writing while in college.

Egan ranged widely and colorfully. When a dog wandered onto the floor of the Boston Garden once during a Celtics game, the Colonel linked the moment to his antagonism toward referees, writing that the refs had "whistled him in off the street." He referred to New York mayor Fiorello La Guardia as "the Little Flower with the Big Pot." In 1943, when a cabdriver struck Boston Braves manager Casey Stengel one rainy night in Kenmore Square and broke his leg, Egan suggested that the cabbie should be hailed as Man of the Year.[30] Yet Egan was far from without moral compass and dignity. His concern for racial justice and equality placed him well ahead of his time. In 1942, five years before Jackie Robinson broke the color line with the Brooklyn Dodgers, Egan called on Major League Baseball to integrate, and he continued to pressure the Red Sox until his death in 1958. The following year, Boston became the last team in baseball to have a black player. For his efforts, Egan was honored by the Boston chapter of the NAACP in 1948.

The core of the Egan indictment against Ted was that he was the consummate greedy individualist, "just not suited for a bicycle built for nine," a man whose boorish on-field behavior set a poor example for young people. But his harshest charge, the one that frosted Williams the most, was that he failed in the clutch. The ultimate evidence for this, the Colonel would later claim, was that in the ten most important games of Ted's career—the seven World Series games of 1946, the playoff game for the pennant against the Cleveland Indians in 1948, and the final two games of the 1949 season against the New York Yankees, in which the flag was on the line—he hit just .205. Williams's defense, of course, was that it was unfair to cherry-pick ten games and ignore the countless other times when he *did* come through. Egan couldn't have cared less.

A chronic beef of Ted's, and of other players who were the target of Egan's slashing prose, was that the Colonel rarely showed up in the clubhouse to allow the players he had ripped to confront him—unlike the beat writers, who were there every day. Still, Ted always read Egan carefully. At Fenway, it would be one of the jobs of Larry Corea, a clubhouse boy who worked under Johnny Orlando, to make sure Williams got his daily *Record*. "Ted used to send me out to get the *Record* at about 5:00 p.m. to see what the Colonel wrote," said Corea.[31] When the team was on the road, Williams would have his pals at home call and read him what the Colonel had written. If it was bad, Ted's anger would usually help him go on a tear. Then he'd want to know if Egan had mentioned any of the good things he'd done. Invariably, there would be nothing, reinforcing Ted's theory that the Colonel was simply out to get him.

Egan always felt that much of his so-called feud with Ted was simply good business for both of them. He knew that writing about Williams attracted more readers, and he felt that all the ink he gave Ted was instrumental in making him baseball's first six-figure ballplayer. So the Colonel thought Ted feigned his outrage. Egan generally confined his criticism of Williams to his actions and behavior on the field. Off the field, when Ted was criticized for seeking a draft deferment in 1942, with World War II on, when he was off fishing when his first child was born, and when he was recalled for service in Korea, the Colonel came to Williams's defense.

If Egan helped shape, even manipulate, public perceptions about Ted, he also directly affected Williams's views of the writers as a whole. It didn't matter to Ted that the vast majority of his press was favorable; when the Colonel unloaded on him, it was as if all the nice notices had never appeared.

After Ted popped off to Austen Lake—lashing out at Boston and saying that he had demanded to be traded—Egan wrote that "Williams is the prize heel ever to wear a Boston uniform." When Ted was being honored by the Red Sox before going off to Korea in 1952, Egan again blasted him. "It seems disgraceful to me that a person such as Williams now is to be given the keys to the city. We talk about juvenile delinquency, and fight against it, and then officially honor a man whom we should officially horsewhip for the vicious influence that he has had on childhood in America."

Some of the things Egan wrote about Ted were so harsh that the Hearst Corporation, owner of the *Record,* got nervous. *Record* publisher Pat Curran confided to Red Sox broadcaster Curt Gowdy, who took over as the voice of the team in 1951, that a Hearst lawyer had instructed him to have Egan tone it down. "Pat told me one day that a lawyer from Hearst came to him with a warning, saying, 'Listen, this kid playing for the Red Sox, this Williams, it's almost impossible for someone to win a libel/slander case against a newspaper, but we've gone over some of Egan's columns, and this kid's got a great case,'" Gowdy said. "This was somewhere in the fifties. So I went and told Ted, and I said, 'Look, you've got a great case here. You ought to sue 'em.' He said, 'I wouldn't lower myself to do that.' That's the way he was."[32]

Bob Ajemian, then a young baseball reporter at the *American,* said Egan's barbs against Ted made the jobs of the beat reporters much harder. "The bile Egan delivered, Williams would take it out on me and the other writers. Egan would write from the bunker. He was a figure in the locker room, which he never visited. GIs like me would dig out the information from the players in the locker room and take the abuse, and Egan would take the information while never going into combat himself."

Ted would later mellow a bit in his attitude toward the press, but never toward Egan. Once, surrounded by a group of writers toward the end of the 1954 season, Williams was in a reflective mood about the interplay between ballplayers and reporters. Recalled George Sullivan, a former reporter for the *Traveler,* "He said, 'You know, there are a lot of jerks in your business but a lot in mine, too.'" Then Williams added, "'There's one SOB that if someone came in that door and said, 'Dave Egan just dropped dead,' I'd say, 'Good.'"[33]

Reflecting back on their time with Ted and the press, Williams's teammates are virtually all sympathetic with the pressures inflicted on him by celebrity in general and by the Boston reporters in particular.

All the writers looked for a fresh story on Williams because that's what their editors thirsted for, the only thing that would satisfy insatiable reader demand for all things Ted. As John Lardner — the humorist, reporter, and critic — once put it: "By the time the press of Boston has completed its daily treatment of Theodore S. Williams, there is no room in the papers for anything but two sticks of agate type about Truman and housing, and one column for the last Boston girl to be murdered on a beach."

"When he would sit in the dugout, he'd see them coming, and he'd ask them, 'What kind of goddamn rumors are you going to start today?'" said Tex Clevenger, who pitched for the Red Sox in 1954.[34]

Added outfielder Jimmy Piersall: "One day a writer in KC said both me and Ted were mentally ill, and Ted got up and spat at him. [The writer] was a fuckin' prick."[35]

Charlie Maxwell, a substitute outfielder in the early '50s, had another story: "One time there was a Boston writer who was ragging on Ted. In the clubhouse there were buckets of water and ammonia to keep us cool. The writer said some not-so-nice things to Ted, and Ted asked him to leave. He didn't, and Ted picked up the bucket and dumped it over his head. The writer just turned and walked away. If he had walked away the first time, it wouldn't have happened."[36]

One of the things that struck the *Globe*'s Clif Keane about Williams was his unpredictability. "You never knew what it was going to be from the middle of a sentence," Keane told Ed Linn. "No idea what to expect....I might walk in the dressing room. He might say, 'Did you see the fight last night, Clif? Hell of a fight.' [Then] he might look at me and say, 'What the hell smells around here?...Did somebody shit in here? Oh, never mind. It's only the sportswriters.'"[37]

The players seemed to enjoy watching Ted give the writers what for in a manner that most of them would never even have contemplated. When the reporters came into the clubhouse after the game, the players would groan audibly, Ajemian remembered. "When Ted would tear into us, the other players would be amused and enjoy it. It was something they wouldn't do. Few players would take reporters on. They admired Ted for doing it."

Ajemian, like his colleagues, noted that Williams was more approachable if he had a bad game rather than a good game. "Coming around after a good game was easy. He was struck by the fact you'd come after a bad game and ask questions. Even though he'd still give you a bad time, you could read signs of approval. It reflected his personal code of really being demonstrably down on weasels and behaving somewhat differently toward those who would take more of a dare or risk."

Ed Linn, who wrote two books about Williams, felt that in dealing with writers, Ted played to his bad-boy stereotype and appeared harsher than he really was. "If you ask a question that shows you know something about him and about baseball, you will get a thoughtful, forthright answer; if you ask a general question, you will get a short answer," Linn wrote in a 1958 *Sport* magazine profile of Ted. "And yet, through it all, there is a sense that Williams is really putting on an act, that he is only doing what he knows is expected of him. A mannerly Ted Williams would be as much of a disappointment to a writer in search of a colorful story as a sober Joe E. Lewis. Williams would deny it indignantly, but he was a great showman."[38]

That didn't mean his outbursts were always without justification. Once, Ajemian wrote a piece that was critical of Ted for taking a walk in a key situation when the tying run was at second. When Williams saw him later, he lit into him: "Hey, you bush cocksucker, get over here! What the fuck do you know about the strike zone? What do you know about the discipline of taking a pitch?" Ajemian said he took the heat and said nothing, and on reflection, decided that Ted had a point. "He had an astuteness that became more publicly winning later. People came to see him as someone who thought things through. He always brought some adroitness to his thinking." But for all the times teammates privately enjoyed the way Ted treated the writers, or watched the show in silent amazement, there was at least one occasion when a player called Ted on his behavior. According to Harold Kaese's notes, in August of 1948, following a Red Sox victory over the Indians at Fenway Park, Ted popped off at the scribes for no apparent reason. Afterward, shortstop Vern "Junior" Stephens said to Williams: "Why don't you smarten up?"

"Oh, you're Irish, too," Ted told Stephens, apparently using "Irish" as a synonym for "wiseguy."

"And you're colored," replied Junior.

Ted stalked off to the showers. Complimented by the writers on what they considered a snappy comeback, Stephens said: "Somebody's got to tell him off sometimes."

Williams of course expected his teammates and friends to keep his confidences and never dish about him to the press. Pal Jim Carroll, a Boston liquor distributor, got in trouble once for getting too cozy with Huck Finnegan, of the *American*. One day in 1958, Finnegan, trolling for a story, called Carroll and asked him how Ted was feeling. Actually, Carroll said, he had dysentery. Finnegan promptly blew the story up, and Ted called Carroll, furious, demanding to know why he had confided in the reporter. "Now you have it all over Boston that I was shitting my pants the whole month of August!" said Ted. "It almost cost me my friendship," Carroll said.[39]

Others thought Ted's distrust of the writers bordered on paranoia. Recuperating in the hospital from a fractured elbow in 1950, Ted was urged to walk over to the window and wave to a flock of kids who were

gathered outside hoping to get a glimpse of him, remembered Jim
Cleary, another friend, who was in the room at the time. "Ted didn't
want to because he said the press would say he was giving kids the finger," Cleary said.[40]

Williams considered Curt Gowdy a good friend and once sought his
advice on dealing with the press. Gowdy found Williams fundamentally
naive about the way the media worked. Ted didn't understand or accept
the premise that the public would be interested in the personal life of a
star of his magnitude and that therefore writers would want to ask him
about his life off the field. "We'd talk," Gowdy said. "He asked me,
'Maybe you can help me—what I don't understand is why they write
about my mother, my brother, my dad. That's my personal business. It's
my family. If I strike out with the bases loaded or drop a fly ball that costs
the game, then hell, they can get on me all they want. I accept that.' And
I'd say, 'Ted, that's just the way it is. It may not be fair. But you're a star,
you're in a goldfish bowl, and it's the same way with Sinatra and everybody, and they're going to do it. So you've just got to accept it. And he
said, 'I don't want to accept it.' You couldn't convince him. 'Fuck them!'
he'd say."*

As sensitive as Williams was about his own notices, he also paid careful attention to what the press wrote about his teammates and resented it
if he was upstaged. That was one reason there was friction between him
and Piersall, who, Ted felt, was too much of a publicity hound. And
when Mickey McDermott, the hard-throwing and colorful left-handed
pitcher, came up in the late '40s and a newspaper headline proclaimed
him a star, Williams called McDermott over and said: "Bush, don't let
that write-up go to your head. You're not the star here. I am." Another
time, McDermott was given Ted's uniform pants by mistake and noticed
that they had stars embroidered inside the waistband. When Williams
discovered the mix-up, he again admonished McDermott: "Come here,
Bush. Don't make me tell you again. Hand over those pants. *I'm* the
star."[41] (McDermott found himself back in Ted's good graces in 1953,
after the pitcher got into a brawl in the clubhouse with *Globe* beat writer
Bob Holbrook. Williams applauded and said to him, "Way to go. You're
the first player to pop a writer in 20 years."[42])

---

* Gowdy told me he'd noticed that Ted was much more receptive to radio (and, later,
television) reporters than he was to the writers. "I said to him, 'Look, why are you being
so nice to these guys when you're brutal with the press?' And he says, 'These radio guys
boost baseball where the press tears it down.' He was always good to the little radio
announcers, guys from Bangor, Maine, or Rhode Island."

Ted would use the press as his all-purpose whipping boy and, rather than take responsibility for his own behavior, blame the writers. In August of 1956, in the aftermath of another spitting episode, Austen Lake called Ted on this point. "Each time this scaramouche foams into one of his copyrighted tantrums he uses a rubber stamp excuse: 'The Boston sports writers drive me daffy,'" Lake wrote. "No blame to himself! He shrugs off responsibility for his hooliganisms by saying the writers are persecuting him maliciously. Nothing is further from fact. . . . It's half past time the writers told the stark naked truth about this Johnny-jump-up, who paints himself a martyr to sports page oppression."

Then, delving into Ted's psyche, Lake speculated that Ted had substituted the writers for the adults who had failed him in his childhood. "As a psychotic personality who grew up from a nerve-frazzled childhood, among eccentric adults and an insecure atmosphere, he built a protective wall around himself to shut out what, in his junior sight, was a hostile world run by adult tyrants," Lake wrote. "It stunted his spiritual development. So he clung to this adolescent obsession and in time, as he became an adult himself, substituted the tyrants of his childhood with a similar set of tyrants, the sportswriters. We stand as carping critics, symbols of censure, the disciplinary eyes, the thought police, antagonists. He had to have a new set of antagonists to replace the old, obsolete set."[43]

Though there was quite a drop-off in impact after Egan, the two other leading Boston columnists in that era were Lake and Bill Cunningham of the *Post* and later the *Herald*. Together they comprised what was known in local sports circles as the Big Three.

"Egan was an entertainer, Cunningham a spellbinder, Lake a preacher," wrote Harold Kaese in an appraisal of the three men following Lake's death in 1964.[44]

Cunningham, a former All-American football player at Dartmouth, was a tall, extroverted, pompous dandy who usually wore a blue beret and a sleeveless yellow sweater and carried a walking stick. He had famously panned Ted in 1938 after he was sent down to the minors, and the following spring, when Ted was up for good, he had an unpleasant encounter with the columnist. Cunningham or his editors had decided that a make-good column on the rookie he had written off twelve months earlier would be appropriate. Cunningham, however, didn't seem too enthused about the prospect, and apparently he had had one too many on the day of the encounter.

"The elevator door opens, and out pops Cunningham wearing a

porkpie hat, and it was obvious he had been drinking," recalled pitcher Elden Auker. "He walks straight over to Ted and interrupts us, saying, 'C'mon, kid, let's get this over with. I have to interview you because the people in Boston want to know what this kid coming up from Minneapolis is like.' Ted just looked at him and said, 'I'm sorry, Mr. Cunningham, I don't talk to sportswriters after they've been drinking.' Well, you could see the steam coming out of him as he walked away."[45] Despite that incident, Cunningham generally liked Williams and would often come to his defense when he was under attack over the years.

Lake, like Cunningham, had once starred in football—first as a halfback at Lafayette College, in Pennsylvania, and then in Buffalo and Philadelphia, where he played professionally. He served as a college football referee until shortly before his death.

Nicknamed the Duke, Lake worked with Egan in the Hearst building that housed the *Record* and the *American,* but the two were unfriendly rivals and sometimes feuded publicly. Although it was Lake to whom Ted gave his pivotal rant in August of 1940—the story that would permanently change the tenor of his tenure with the Red Sox—Lake, unlike Egan, was never obsessed with Williams and seemed more interested in the interplay between the star and his fans. He once wrote that the murmur of the crowd when Ted came to bat was "like the autumn wind moaning through an apple orchard."[46]

Besides the Big Three, the longest-serving, most influential, and most colorful beat writers and columnists who covered Williams included Hy Hurwitz, Harold Kaese, Clif Keane, and Roger Birtwell—all of the *Globe*—Joe Cashman of the *Daily Record,* and Ed Rumill of the *Christian Science Monitor.* These men were characters and players in their own right, and they had a significant role both in shaping public perceptions of Williams and in framing Ted's own view of the press and the world around him.

Few writers had as many ups and downs or jousts with Ted as Hurwitz, a former Marine who was just a shade over five feet tall. Hurwitz had joined the *Globe* as a copyboy in the late '20s, when he was a senior at Boston's English High School. He covered Ted throughout his career, and they served in World War II at the same time, from 1942 to 1946.

Hurwitz and Ted were thrown together in earnest in 1946, when the *Globe* announced that Williams, for the hefty sum of $1,500 per week, would write a column at the end of the Red Sox's pennant season. The paper did not announce that Hurwitz, also the *Globe*'s Red Sox beat reporter, would be the ghostwriter. Each dreaded the daily meeting, in which Ted would riff on some subject or other and then Hurwitz would produce the column, entitled TED WILLIAMS SAYS. According to Al Hirshberg, around the seventh inning of every game, Hurwitz would say to his colleagues in the press box: "In two more innings I'm going to have to go down to listen to that big sonofabitch." Ted, for his part, would sit on the bench and complain to teammates: "In two more innings I'm going to have to talk to that no-good little bastard."[47]

One of the most colorful characters among the writers of the day was the *Globe*'s Clif Keane, who was known as the Che Guevara of Boston's sporting press. Short, paunchy, balding, and bespectacled, Keane constantly pushed the boundary between friendly ribbing and overly harsh needling. He carried out his often riotous repartee with the deft timing and delivery of a stand-up comedian, but he softened his blows if the targets were people he liked.

When Roger Maris was chasing Ruth's record in 1961 and the Yankees were making their last visit of the season to Fenway Park, the New York writers told Keane that Maris was in the bunker and not talking to anyone. "Really?" said Keane. He walked over to the Yankees dugout, spotted his target, and called out, "Hey, Maris, you shoemaker! You busher! Who would want to talk to you?" Maris laughed and said, "Come on, Clif, I'll give you a story."[48] And Keane got a scoop.

Baseball was Keane's realm, but occasionally his editors gave him an assignment off the diamond. Once, he was dispatched to cover a dog show—unfamiliar turf, to say the least. He filed a routine story, then later learned that one of the leading dogs in the show had died of a heart attack. Keane called in a perfunctory paragraph to be added to the end of his story. The next day *Globe* editor Larry Winship called Keane in and chewed him out, telling him that the drama of the dog dying should have led the story, not ended it. Keane was unmoved. "Larry," he explained, "the dog died and I buried it."[49]

Keane grew up in the Dorchester section of Boston and was married to a *Globe* classified ad taker. He joined the paper's sports staff in 1939. He always called Williams Bush, tossing Ted's familiar greeting right back at him. Ted once threw a ball toward Keane in jest, but the ball hit a pebble and bounced up to shatter Keane's eyeglasses. Williams apologized and offered to buy him a new pair of glasses. Keane declined and said, "I'll get you, but I'll get you between the eyes."[50]

Roger Birtwell was a Boston Brahmin (Phillips Exeter Academy and Harvard, class of '23) who spoke with the lockjawed, languid manner characteristic of the city's self-styled aristocracy. Before joining the *Globe* in 1942, Birtwell, who was known as the Rajah, had worked in New York for the *Daily News,* the *World-Telegram*, and the *Herald Tribune*. He wore blue suits, often with his slippers for extra comfort. Before tapping out a story, he would back a spool of copy paper up to his typewriter, roll it out to the desired length, then write his piece to order. He was infamous for showing up at Fenway Park around the sixth inning, sidling up to a colleague in the press box, and saying, "Yeeeeaaas, could you catch me up a bit?" After some requisite eye rolling, the fellow scribe would give Birtwell his fill, and the Rajah—partly out of enthusiastic gratitude and partly to rev himself up for the task at hand—would say, "Ye-e-es! Ye-es! Yes!" with increasing near-orgasmic intensity as he scribbled out his notes on what had transpired.

In February of 1955, when Ted was threatening to retire as part of a financial ploy to shield income from his first wife during tense divorce proceedings, he said he had signed contracts to take fishing trips in Peru and Nova Scotia that May and June—proof, he said, that he would not be playing ball in the summer. Birtwell found the concept of a fishing contract amusing, and wrote a tongue-in-cheek story saying that he, too, would not be working during those months because "I've signed a contract to go fishing for flounders in the Hampton River. By the way, with whom do I sign the contract—the flounders?"[51]

Not all Ted's relationships with the press corps were antagonistic. He was friendly with the *Record*'s Joe Cashman and would keep up with him in retirement. Mindful of Williams's ambition to be the greatest hitter who ever lived, Cashman liked to say that he considered Ted only the second-greatest hitter—after Rogers Hornsby. Ted thought that was still pretty good company, and once when he called the writer's house to make dinner plans, Ted said: "This is the second-greatest hitter who ever lived calling."[52] When Cashman died in 1993 at the age of ninety-two, Williams sent a telegram offering his condolences.*

Williams kept his soft, kind side well hidden, but Cashman saw it revealed on several occasions. Once, after a reporter died suddenly, Ted called his paper and inquired after his financial status, saying he was prepared to cover the funeral expenses if necessary. Williams was thanked and told that wouldn't be necessary.[53]

---

* Perhaps unbeknownst to Williams and his teammates, the old-school Cashman served as a legman for Dave Egan, feeding the columnist raw, behind-the-scenes stuff that Cashman himself would never write.

The writer who was probably closest to Williams was someone who worked for the least influential paper in town. Ed Rumill of the *Christian Science Monitor* had covered the major leagues for forty-five years, and every World Series from 1930 to 1972, by the time he retired. Rumill was also a regular in the *Sporting News,* a forum he needed to enhance his visibility, since few ballplayers saw the *Monitor*—though the Red Sox did buy nine copies a day because it was the only paper in Boston that carried the minor-league standings and scores.

Rumill's significance was that he was a confidant of Ted and Tom Yawkey and thus a reliable barometer of the thinking of the two most important figures on the Red Sox. Rumill often served as a middleman between Ted and the rest of the writers, passing on quotes from Williams whenever he refused to speak to other reporters, which was not infrequently. Rumill would also show up at the ballpark hours before game time and meet Tom and Jean Yawkey in the last row of the grandstand to talk and perhaps have a libation or two.

Rumill played baseball himself, in the amateur Boston Park League, and in the late '30s Yawkey permitted him to throw batting practice for the Red Sox. This was a different kind of writer, one whom Ted thought he could trust. Rumill introduced his mother to Williams, and she would become a regular visitor to Fenway Park on Wednesday afternoons, when the Red Sox hosted their "Ladies Days." Ted would always wave to her or stop by and chat.

Rumill was six foot three and looked so much like Ted that fans often approached him and asked for his autograph. Over the years, on the numerous occasions when Ted went into the bunker and refused to talk to the writers over some perceived slight or another, he never stopped talking to Rumill. So Rumill would agree to serve as a pool reporter for the frozen-out scribes, carrying their questions to the Great Man. Recalled Phil Elderkin, a columnist for the *Monitor* who was a friend of Rumill, "Ed talked him into this. He'd say, 'Ted, you gotta do this. They have families and obligations. They're trying to do a job.' Ted went along with it. He pretended to be mad about a lot of things."[54]

One night in Philadelphia in 1954, Williams hit one of his tape-measure home runs out of Connie Mack Stadium and onto the roof of a neighboring apartment building. It was career home run number 362, putting him one ahead of his archrival, Joe DiMaggio. Rumill knew the ball would be an important keepsake for his pal, so he bolted from the press box and ran outside to the apartment building. He tracked down the fan who had come up with the ball and arranged for him to cough it up in exchange for another ball, autographed by Ted.

In the off-season, Rumill would visit Williams in the Florida Keys, where Ted would later take up residence, and the two would have long talks. Once, Ted confided to Rumill that he had paid the hospital bill for a Boston writer who had a medical problem but couldn't cover the cost, Elderkin said. And when Rumill himself got in a financial jam, Ted insisted on giving him a loan, the writer later told a friend.

For the writers, their daily encounters with Williams were a tumultuous mixture of riveting theater, sheer excitement, and resentment at having to absorb a matinee idol's torrent of bile and abuse. But their front-row seat also gave them a fascinating perspective on the development and evolution of Ted's mercurial and fragile persona.

They learned his moods and eccentricities, what approach he might favor, how he would play them off against each other, how he could be extraordinarily kind to people, and how, for all his raging at the press, he devoured everything that was written about him. They also learned how he craved fame but not the inconvenience of celebrity—a naïveté that betrayed a basic misunderstanding of a writer's role in ferreting out information about him, an outsize personality whom the public thirsted to know more about.

Bob Ajemian of the *American* was a young reporter thrown into the Williams fray in the late '40s and early '50s. He had grown up in suburban Boston as a great fan of Ted's. "We were all just crazy about him.... But to be with him in the locker room was scary. He radiated so much energy and appeal, and he intimidated us. His voice was unique. He spoke with certitude. 'What the fuck do you know?' He was a transcendent figure. You didn't want to be on the wrong side of him. The press was largely afraid of him. He would berate you publicly and loudly, as opposed to taking someone aside for a private beef."

Ajemian thought Ted was not a team leader the way Joe DiMaggio was. "If you walked into the Yankee locker room, people skirted Joe differently than you'd skirt Ted. Joe took a loss very hard and radiated that. Williams radiated superb individual performance. Individuality was the dominant theme of his career. Yet his teammates regarded him with reverence. He had tremendous standing. He owned the town."[55]

Bud Collins, the longtime television commentator and tennis writer for the *Boston Globe*, remembered well his first encounter with Williams.

It was 1955, and Collins was a cub reporter for the *Herald*. Eager to show what he could do, the young journalist burst into the clubhouse after the game, unaware that reporters were barred for fifteen minutes, a Williams-inspired team rule that Ted took delight in personally enforcing. "What's that cocksucker doing in here!" thundered Ted from across the room as he spotted Collins.[56] Jack Fadden, the trainer, quickly hustled Collins into an adjoining room, explaining the fifteen-minute rule and telling him not to worry: Ted treated everyone that way.*

Collins eventually got to know the Kid and engaged him a bit. One familiar postgame ritual with Williams was to ask him what kind of pitch he'd hit for a home run. "Fastball, cock high," Ted would usually respond.† (Recalled the *Herald*'s Tim Horgan, "If I could get a quote out of TW that was printable through all the four letter words, I was golden.")

Collins said occasionally Ted would approach *him* to comment on something he had written. "Once, he came up and said, 'You probably don't think I read that piece of shit you wrote because we were on the road. Well, let me tell you something: when you rip somebody, someone always makes sure he sees it.'" Another time, Collins was assigned to interview a group of fans in the bleachers about what they thought of some of the moves Red Sox management had been making—sort of a Fenway man-in-the-street feature. The next day Williams complained to him that the hoi polloi had no authority to comment. "What the hell do you think a bunch of fuckin' Armenians know about baseball?" Ted demanded.

Collins witnessed several Ted meltdowns. After one, Jimmy Piersall, the Red Sox outfielder who had been hospitalized with a nervous breakdown in 1952, whispered in Collins's ear: "They'd put me away for acting like that guy."

And Bud was there in 1958 the day Ted, angered after striking out,

---

* In retirement, Ted warmed up to Collins. In 1969, as manager of the Washington Senators, Ted, seeing Collins for the first time in years, called out cheerfully: "Are you still writing that shit?" And as he took up tennis later in life, Williams became a fan of Bud's TV commentary.

† Bob Ajemian thought that Williams went beyond the token, customary observation that such and such a pitcher had good stuff; that he was often expansive and enthusiastic in his comments about the pitchers he faced. "Ted would praise other pitchers, and the other pitchers of course loved that. I always thought he was praising pitchers to not be thrown at." It was true that Williams was rarely drilled, but that may also have been because pitchers concluded that it was counterproductive, since whenever Ted was knocked down he would usually get up and hit a rope somewhere.

threw his bat, only to have it sail into the box seats and strike an elderly lady in the head. After the game, Collins hustled over to ask general manager Joe Cronin if the team was worried about being sued. "There'll be no lawsuit," Cronin said definitively.

"How can you be so sure?" asked Collins.

"Because this woman happens to be my housekeeper, and she loves Ted Williams," Cronin replied.

Perhaps no sportswriter has the perspective on Williams that George Sullivan—formerly of the *Traveler* and later the *Record*—does. That's because Sullivan first got to know Ted when he was a Red Sox batboy in 1949, before he went on to college and made what Williams viewed as the heretical decision to become a dreaded writer.

One day he was in the Sox dugout when Ted was up. "Williams hit one about fourteen rows into the bleachers over the visiting team bull pen," Sullivan said. "The bench went wild. The first words from the other players were, 'What kind of a pitch was it?' He was cussing. He's very unhappy. 'Son of a bitch, I never should have swung at that.' He said it was off the plate. I thought, 'Whoa, wait a minute. The guy's won a ball game and he's bitching about it?' It jarred me. I was only fifteen. Jesus, this is not the way you play the game. Frankly, I wondered if he was so self-centered that he wasn't a team player. I hated to even think of it, because the guy was my idol."

But Sullivan wasn't jarred enough to stop being enthralled with Ted, and the two got to know each other. Sometimes, on days when Williams had to go to the WBZ studios for an interview show he had committed to, he would offer to take George to his house in nearby Cambridge. "He'd say, 'Let's go!' He had a Cadillac. He drove me home to my corner, Putnam Square, on Mass Ave and Trowbridge Street. Kerry Corner. I wanted to make sure my pals saw who was driving me home."

One of Sullivan's strangest encounters with Ted came at Fenway. As he approached the ballpark one day, he heard an alarming sound. "Near the service entrance there was a corrugated door. The door was open. I hear an explosion. I thought it was a car backfiring. I hear it again. Then it sounded like it was coming from inside the ballpark. I walked onto the field, and I saw the damnedest thing I ever saw. There were dead pigeons all over the field. I heard a shot again, and I saw Ted in old clothes with a rifle out in the visitors' bull pen. I'm a city kid. I'd never seen anyone shoot a weapon. I watched him for a couple minutes. I was mesmerized. Finally I had to go do my chores. Then I hear the *clump, clump* of cleats coming down the runway. It's Ted. With his arms around my shoulders, I thought, 'Look out, he has a favor to ask.' He said, 'Hey, old buddy, when you have a chance, grab a few barrels and go out and get those pigeons.' I filled a bunch of barrels, and that's how I learned to swear. Every one I picked up I used one of the cuss words Ted taught me."

In the summer of 1954, between his junior and senior years at Boston University, Sullivan was working full-time for the *Traveler* sports section. One day, the regular Red Sox beat writer called in sick. "Arthur Siegel, the sports editor, looked at the ceiling and said, 'What's this business coming to? I'm going to have to send you to cover the Red Sox today.'

"So I went to Fenway. I had never been in the clubhouse since I was a batboy, and now I had my ticket in. I went in before the game, and Mel Parnell spotted me. Mel's a wonderful guy and he gave me a hug. Ted was in the trainer's room.

"Parnell yelled at Ted, 'Look who's here!'

"Ted said, 'Well, Jesus Christ! Son of a bitch! What are you doing now?'

" 'Ted, I'm a sportswriter.'

"He dropped my hand like it had a disease. He said, 'You used to be a good kid! Where did you go wrong?' That was the beginning of phase two of my relationship with Ted."

Sullivan took his first road trip with the Sox in 1956—first to Washington for a series against the Senators, then up to New York, where they would play the Yankees. In Washington, he had breakfast with Jimmy Piersall, and Piersall mentioned that he and Ted weren't speaking. The two had a rocky relationship, and it wasn't the first time they'd feuded. Sullivan thought he had a good scoop, but he had to get Ted's side of the story first. He waited until the team arrived in New York and Williams was picking up the key to his room in the hotel lobby.

"I went up to him and said, 'Tell me about you and Piersall,' " Sullivan said. "He hit the roof. We were good friends, but he starts using the four-letter words right in the lobby. I learned as a batboy he did not respect you unless you returned the insults in kind. So I filed that away, and whatever he was saying to me now I was giving back to him in spades. I wanted him to respect me. We went toe-to-toe on Piersall. We were turning the room blue, and a little old lady turned heel right in the lobby and beat it out of there. It was like a class B western movie. Finally, Ted stormed off, and I wrote my story. I had a scoop."

Sullivan and his hero clashed again later that summer of '56, after Ted hit his four hundredth career home run in the second game of a twi-night doubleheader against Kansas City at Fenway.

Williams had been stuck at 399 for eight days, and the fans were on him a bit.

"So he finally hits the home run, and as he rounded the bases, the boos became cheers," Sullivan remembered. "The press box was hanging over the field back then. As he crossed the plate he cocked his head up at us and pursed his lips as if to spit, but I don't think he did spit. Then it looked like he said, 'Fuck you.' After the game I went down. I waited to grab him until the writers had left and he was alone. I went over and congratulated him. Then I said, 'Did you say something to the press box when he you crossed the plate?' He said, 'Yeah, I spit at you bastards.' He boomed it out. Everything in the locker room stopped. I said, 'No, Ted, you did not spit, you said something.' He turned beet red. He said, 'You're right, I didn't spit. I meant to spit at you bastards, but I was afraid I'd hit the on-deck guy coming up.' As soon as Ted stomped off all the writers came running over. 'What happened? What happened?' I told them."

Sullivan was still young, only twenty-two, learning the ways of the press and angry at Williams for apparently forgetting that they had once been friends. Now Ted was just lumping him in with the other writers and abusing him. "I waited outside the locker room for Ted. I didn't want any witnesses this time. I was taking this personally. Ted sees me, and it's like nothing had ever happened. He was all smiles. I said, 'Tell me, what was that crap that just went on? Were you talking about me, too, or just the other guys?' He put his arms around my shoulders, and he said he wasn't talking about me specifically. It was just sportswriters. He said, 'Don't take it personally.' "

For all Williams's rage and bluster, Sullivan remained forever impressed by his quiet acts of kindness, especially toward children sick with cancer. This was widely known among the writers, but it was rarely written about because Ted demanded that it not be. "Williams would be getting dressed and a writer would have been tipped off that Ted had been to a hospital at three in the morning to visit some kid," Sullivan said. "Williams had circulated his private number to some hospitals so they could call him if a kid was in serious trouble, and he'd told them if he can get there he will. So the writer would say, 'Ted, I heard you were at Children's at three in the morning.' Ted's neck would get red and he'd start sputtering and he'd say, 'Yeah, I was there, but if you write one word about it it's your ass, because I'll never do it again.' So he put the writer in a box, and of course it was never written."

Why did he insist on anonymity? "He didn't want to grandstand.... He had a thing for privacy like no one I've ever seen."

Following the upheavals of 1940, there would be many more outbursts, fulminations, obscene gestures, and spitting episodes as Williams's career unfolded, but in the end, he was able to gradually turn public opinion in his favor. The crowd could lash out at him if he made an error or behaved churlishly, and the boos would grow even louder after fans saw they could provoke the thin-skinned Kid into some outrageous response. So it was in 1950, after he gave them the finger, and in 1956, after he spat at them.

But in each case, after Ted took his medicine with a fine or a half-baked apology that the team forced him to issue, the fans would welcome him back and bathe him in their cheers and applause. The 1950 reception was especially meaningful to Williams. "I got an ovation that I'll never forget," he said years later. "It was one of my biggest thrills in baseball. I learned that night that New England fans really were for me and cared about me."

Ted's central claim that it was the malevolent writers who prompted the harsh treatment from the crowd was spurious at best, but gradually fans seemed to conclude that Williams was right. They came to accept Ted's fragile psyche and his insistence that he was being persecuted. They admired his independence, his individuality, and his determination to buck convention, stick to his guns, and do things his own way—even if that stubbornness hurt him in the short term.

When the fans again welcomed Ted back after he spit at them in 1956, even some in the press began to take note of the shift in public opinion and questioned whether they had overstepped their bounds.

"The tide has begun to turn in this case of the Boston sports writers versus Ted Williams, and the verdict is becoming increasingly favorable to Ted as public opinion starts to make itself felt," wrote the *Lowell Sun* in an editorial. "If there has been a case of injustice done by a group of sportswriters to a great sports figure, this is it. Time after time they picked Williams apart, they have tormented him, they have knifed him, roasted him, flayed him, tortured him, and have obviously taken what can only be called a sadistic glee in doing so. It is sports journalism at its lowest."

In 1957, when Williams was defying nature and batting close to .400 late in August at the age of thirty-nine, the Fenway crowd nearly rioted when a decision by the official scorer, the *Globe*'s Hy Hurwitz, initially went against Ted. Williams hit a line drive that Tigers shortstop Harvey Kuenn dropped and Hurwitz deemed an error. Spectators shouted insults at the press box and raised their fists menacingly. An hour after the game, fans were still lingering to jeer the writers as they walked out. Hurwitz later changed his decision and gave Ted a hit after talking with Kuenn, who said the ball had had a lot of topspin on it.

During a three-week newspaper strike that same month, fans flooded the sports departments with calls wanting to know first what Ted did and then what the Sox score was.

The *American* responded to the shifting public mood in January of 1958 by running a fifteen-part series entitled "The Case for Ted Williams." The series totaled eighteen thousand words and was prompted by letters objecting to criticism of Ted and demanding more positive treatment.* The *Herald* followed with a flattering seven-week serial about Williams's life by cartoonist Vic Johnson—forty-nine strips in all.

The warm communal feeling toward Ted held through to the end of his playing days in 1960 and would grow exponentially in his retirement. He became a beloved figure. Visiting Boston later in life, Williams would always be struck by how fans showered him with unabashed affection of the sort he'd not been able to sustain in his playing days.

He would take great satisfaction from this and delight in the fact that he had outlasted the bastards: the writers.

---

* The *American* ripped off the title of its series from a *Look* magazine article the previous year that carried the same headline.

6

.406

T ed wintered in Minnesota again, and in November of 1940, he met
the girl who would become his first wife.

After a day of duck hunting outside Princeton, the small town
fifty miles north of Minneapolis that he had been frequenting since he
played for the Millers in 1938, Williams walked into his favorite haunt
in town, the Kallas Café. He was fresh from the woods and gamy, wearing boots, a cap with earflaps, and pants with a hole in the seat. Sitting
down at the counter, Ted asked the proprietor's son, Jim Kallas, if he
knew any cute girls.

Kallas wasted little time before calling up a former high school classmate and girlfriend, Doris Soule, and asking her to come down to the
café. "I didn't say who I had down there," Kallas said. "I just told her
point-blank to come down the store and have a Coke—that's it. When
she came in, I left."[1]

Ted towered over the petite Doris, who was five foot three and 108
pounds but quite buxom. She had blue eyes, brown hair, and a whole-
some, angular face; sort of a poor man's Dorothy Lamour.

Doris was a Princeton native whose parents had divorced when she
was a little girl. Her father took off for California, not to be heard from
again, and she and her younger brother, Donald, were raised by their
mother, Ruby, who worked as a secretary at the local bank. They lived
with Ruby's parents, and Doris was close to her grandfather, a black-
smith, and her grandmother, a piano teacher.

Doris couldn't have cared less about baseball and was not impressed by
the cocky, unkempt Ted after their initial meeting. "You know, on that
first date, I just couldn't stand him," Doris told a reporter in 1942.[2] "We

had arguments all that first evening and I told him I never wanted to see him again. But I guess when Ted fixes on an idea he stays with it. He came right back the next day as if nothing had happened and I hadn't sent him away at all."

Before long, Ted had Doris out on a frozen lake, where he was teaching her to ice-fish. They would hack through ice five feet thick, then Ted would go over the fine points of firing a speargun into the dark water. At night, he'd come over to the Soule house and play cards. It would be Ted and Doris against Donald and Ruby. Ted barely knew Doris's family, but that didn't stop him from filling the air with four-letter words.

"My mother and I used to whip 'em at whist all the time," Donald Soule recalled.[3] "Ted had such a foul mouth, and my house was a very pious place. He used to swear, and every time he swore we used to make him put a coin [on] the table. At intermission time, there was always enough money in the jar to buy ice cream. So he'd go downtown and buy a couple quarts of ice cream and we'd go and finish the game."

Doris also had a salty tongue, though nothing like Ted's. She was twenty-one, four months younger than Williams. At the time, she was living downstate in Rochester, working as a cashier in a restaurant near the Mayo Clinic.

"Doris was very likable, very popular," said Ramona Mitchell, another Princeton girl who was living in Rochester at the time. "She drank a lot after she got out of high school. We used to party a lot.

"I can remember Ted when she introduced me. He was laying on the bed at Doris's house, and he didn't even get up to acknowledge the introduction. He wasn't my favorite person. Another thing that used to aggravate me is he always used to walk in late to the movie theater. He was a celebrity in town. He'd be wearing those buckled overshoes. You could hear him coming. Ted, I could take him or leave him. Nobody's better than I am. He put on airs, you know."[4]

Growing up in Princeton, Doris had always been a performer. She and her friend and neighbor, Jean Holetz, would sing each other love songs with a washcloth and bowl of water nearby, the better to sprinkle their faces with faux tears as a tune reached its emotional climax. A cheerleader, Doris took piano lessons from her grandmother, played E-flat alto saxophone in the high school band, and loved to dance the Charleston. Neither of their families was well-off: they shared an outdoor toilet that was part of a garage, and she and Jean would light bonfires between their houses at night and roast potatoes, then play tag under the streetlights.[5]

Another friend of Doris's was Jane Ross, whose father was the town mortician. Doris and Jane had the run of the funeral home, and it was there that Doris sneaked her first cigarette by climbing into an empty casket and closing the lid. She wasn't spooked by being around corpses. "She used to say, 'Shoot, you don't have to be afraid of the dead ones— it's the live ones you have to watch out for!'" remembered Doris and Ted's daughter, Bobby-Jo.[6]

By the end of that winter, Ted and Doris had progressed to the point where he invited her to come to Boston in the spring for the baseball season. Doris lined up a job as a hotel cashier and eagerly awaited her big-city debut.

But Ruby Soule worried about the transition for her daughter, especially in light of something an ex-beau had remarked upon before Doris left. "One of the boyfriends she had was talking to my mother and me," said Donald Soule. "He said, 'You know, you ought to tell Doris she's drinking too much. She shouldn't drink that way.'"

On January 23, 1941, Ted interrupted his winter of hunting and romance to appear before a draft board in Minneapolis. Only vaguely aware that Hitler was by then rampaging across Europe, Williams proceeded to register for conscription into the military under the terms of the Selective Training and Service Act signed into law the previous September by President Franklin D. Roosevelt. The legislation required that men ages twenty-one to thirty register with their local draft boards. Ted drew number 648 under the law's lottery system, which meant that he stood to become the 648th man called into service in his Minneapolis district. But a board official said it was unlikely that Ted would be called before the end of the upcoming baseball season, and he indicated there was a possibility he could be deferred and classified 3A, since he was then the sole supporter of his mother.

Williams said he was "willing to serve my country if they want me," but pointedly added that he would "like to cash in on another season's salary."[7] If that sentiment didn't exactly square with the nascent patriotic zeal taking shape in the country as World War II approached, few seemed to notice or take offense, and the draft board did, in fact, give him a 3A classification, entitling him to a deferment because his service would create a hardship for a dependent, his mother.

Ted returned to his girlfriend and the outdoor life, oblivious not only to foreign affairs but also, it seemed, to baseball. By the end of February, when his Red Sox teammates had gathered for spring training in Florida,

Ted was a no-show. He surfaced on March 1, calling Eddie Collins to report that he was in the wilds of northern Minnesota hunting wolves with a group of friends. The countryside was so remote that he'd lost track of the time and had only now been able to reach a phone. He asked for a few more days to consider the contract offer that the team had made, and Collins agreed. Ted was technically not late for camp, Collins and Joe Cronin explained, rather lamely, to reporters, because only those players who'd signed their contracts had received notices spelling out when to report.

Two days later, Ted and Collins agreed on a contract worth a reported $18,500—a $6,000 raise over the previous year—and Ted got in his car for the long drive to Sarasota. When he arrived, four days later, the Red Sox had just left for a three-game exhibition trip to Tampa and Miami. Ted walked into the nearly empty clubhouse at Payne Park and came upon clubhouse attendant Vince Orlando, Johnny's younger brother, asleep on a training table. Williams tiptoed over to the table and upended it with a loud roar, sending Orlando sprawling to the floor. "It scared the hell out of me," Orlando remembered later.[8]

Williams had the field to himself over the weekend, so he took batting practice until the blisters bloomed on his hands. When his teammates and the writers returned, Ted held court on his wolf-hunting adventure in Minnesota: "It seems as though after hunters out there get tired of shooting ducks and pheasants...they go after wolves on which the state pays a bounty," he explained to a rapt audience. "It's easy to track the gray wolves, but pretty hard to get a shot at them. I didn't get any, but some of the fellows with me came up with three or four."

Addressing the baseball season, Ted pledged to go all out. "I'd rather play ball than eat, sleep or hunt," he said. "The fans want a ballplayer to give everything he has. That's my aim, not only this year but every year. That's my greeting to Boston baseball fans. See you later. I think it's my turn to hit."[9]

Ted had greeted the writers with smiles and handshakes all around, not exactly offering a mea culpa for his poisonous behavior the previous year but plainly chastened and hoping to be given a fresh start. Asked by the *American*'s Huck Finnegan to account for his 1940 funk, Ted put a new spin on his pop-off session with Austen Lake, during which he had said he wanted out of Boston: "One of the writers came to me last year and we had a good, heart-to-heart talk. One of those off-the-record talks. I had plenty of worries and was upset. I told him everything, never thinking he was going to print it. Then, blooie, all over the paper. What a let-down. And, so I figured to myself, 'you can't trust any of these birds,' and I guess I acted that way. But I know you can trust most of them, so I'm willing to call it quits if they are. Wipe the whole slate clean and start the year right."[10]

The writers seemed amenable. Finnegan wrote that Ted seemed like the "laughing boy" and "personality kid" once more. And the *Transcript*'s Harold Kaese, who had ignited Williams last season with his low blow about the Kid failing to visit his parents, now suggested that he and his brethren in the press bore part of the responsibility. "Maybe we're largely to blame, those of us who wrote.... We should have handled the Kid as a psychologist would."[11]

Even Colonel Egan seemed in a forgiving mood. First, he ran a long interview with Eddie Collins in which Collins raved about Ted and said that "last year he reminded me of a friendly puppy who had been hurt in some way and so became distrustful of everybody, including his friends. He is only a boy and he could not understand how anybody could dislike him."[12] Then, a week later, Egan ratified the new détente between Williams and the writers. "The main argument was between Ted and the newspapermen," wrote the Colonel. "So far as this sports writer is concerned, it is finished, and a new and more satisfactory chapter in the life of the young man is about to begin."[13]

Sensing the friendlier, more convivial atmosphere, Ted relaxed and spoke with the same disarming certitude and confidence that he had during his rookie year. "All right, I ask you: how can they stop me from hitting?" he said, chatting with Kaese about the 1941 season. "They can't, that's all.... They couldn't stop me my first year and they couldn't stop me my second. They won't stop me my third.... My second year was better than my first. I'll tell you why. I hit higher, .344 to .327, I struck out less, and I got more walks. I made more hits and I scored more runs. I was on base more. I didn't hit so many home runs and I didn't knock in so many runs. So what? I was batting third instead of fourth. I had more chance to bat in runs my first year because Foxx batted ahead of me.... And remember, I was hitting in the toughest park in the league for a left hand hitter.... I was the best hitter on the Red Sox last year, wasn't I?...What's more, I got the biggest raise in baseball, except for maybe Greenberg. I guess that shows what the Red Sox thought of me."[14]

Ted's aplomb was tempered somewhat by injury. He twisted his right ankle stepping in an outfield gully while chasing a fly ball, then aggravated the injury in an exhibition game on March 19 by catching a spike sliding into second base while trying to stretch a single into a double.

Williams was sidelined for a few weeks, sitting out exhibition games but still taking regular batting practice. One workout companion was Hall of Famer Paul Waner, who lived in Sarasota and had been released by the Pittsburgh Pirates. Ted and Waner (who in 1941 would play for the Brooklyn Dodgers and then the Boston Braves) talked hitting with gusto every day.[15]

After some initial confusion on a diagnosis, it was finally announced on April 5 that Williams had a slight fracture of one of the small bones in his ankle and would be out for five to six weeks. "Bullshit," Ted told the writers, promising to be back far sooner.

Tom Yawkey had insisted that Williams go to Birmingham, Alabama, to be examined by his wife's brother-in-law, Dr. L. E. Sorrell. Arriving home at Boston's Back Bay station on the Colonial Express train after a thirty-six-hour ride from Alabama, the Kid was upbeat and bantered with the pack of writers and photographers gathered to meet him. " 'I kept telling everybody that the ankle wasn't getting any better, but I guess they wanted to wait until we got to Birmingham to see some doctor they knew."[16] He said the ankle didn't hurt when he hit, only when he ran, so the Red Sox held him out of the opening day lineup on April 15 and relegated him to pinch-hitting duty for the first two weeks of the season.

Ted saw a silver lining to the injury. He never hit well in the early part of the season anyway because of the cold weather. Now he'd bide his time until it got warmer, and in the meantime he'd keep sharp by hitting against Joe Dobson, the pitcher whom the Red Sox had acquired in a trade with Cleveland.

"I got the most batting practice of my life, and the best, because Dobson had a hell of a curve and a good overhand fastball, and he always bore down," Ted later wrote. "Every day that his arm would hold out, and the blisters on my hands would hold out, we'd go out there like it was all out war, one-on-one."[17] Back in the lineup, Williams hit .436 for the month of May and .536 from May 17 to June 1. May 15, in hindsight, was one of the most significant dates of the season, for that was the day Ted and Joe DiMaggio each started hitting streaks. DiMaggio's, of course, would last for fifty-six games, a wondrous skein in which he hit .409 and defined his magnificent career. Williams's was a more modest twenty-three and lasted until June 8, but during that time he hit .487 and launched himself on the path to .400.

It was the first time that the two men came to be linked in the public imagination as the dominant players of their era. Ted was still only twenty-two and starting his third season; Joe was twenty-six and in his sixth year with the Yankees, but the summer of 1941 would be their gateway to baseball immortality. Lively debates began in Boston, New York, and around the country—debates that would span Williams's and DiMaggio's lifetimes and beyond—as to which man was the better hitter, the more valuable to his team, the more reliable in the clutch, the better leader.

Ted got the edge in two early Red Sox–Yankees meetings, going 7–11 in a three-game series at Yankee Stadium on May 23, 24, and 25, and 3–5 in a Memorial Day doubleheader at Fenway Park that sixty thousand fans turned out to try to get tickets for. DiMaggio had four errors in the doubleheader and barely kept his streak alive in the second game, thanks to a windblown fly muffed by Red Sox right fielder Pete Fox.

By June 1, Ted was hitting .430, and there was talk in the papers that not only could Williams be the first to hit .400 since Bill Terry in 1930, but perhaps he had a chance to break the .440 mark set by Hugh Duffy of the old National League Boston Beaneaters in 1894. As it happened, Duffy was then the seventy-four-year-old first-base coach for the Red Sox and one of Ted's biggest boosters.

"I can say this about Teddy," Duffy told the *Globe*'s Hy Hurwitz. "I have never seen a hitter better than Williams in all my life, and that goes for Cobb, Ruth, Hornsby and all the rest." Duffy said Ted came to him quite often "for a check-up." But there was little that he could tell him other than to not think about setting any records, lest he lose his rhythm. "All Teddy has to do is keep swinging in that lazy natural way of his and he'll hit a million."[18]

In 1941, the notion of hitting .400 was not considered the exalted accomplishment that it is today. Between the start of baseball's modern era, in 1900, and the beginning of the 1941 season, seven players had achieved .400 or higher twelve times. In the 1800s, nineteen players had done it twenty-two times.

Baseball historians informally place nineteenth-century players in a different category because the rules of the game were far different then. For example, hitters could use bats that had a flat side; they could call for low or high pitches; and a strike zone was not defined until 1887. In the 1887 season, walks were counted as hits, a rule that helped fully ten players reach the .400 mark or higher that year. In the modern era, Nap Lajoie's .426 average in 1901 came with an asterisk because there was no foul strike rule. Until 1903 in the American League, foul balls that were not caught did not count as strikes, giving the hitter a significant advantage. Between Bill Terry's .401 in 1930 and the beginning of the 1941 season, only four players had made serious runs at .400: Al Simmons of the A's (.390 in 1931), Arky Vaughan of the Pirates (.385 in 1935), Luke Appling (.388 in 1936), and Joe DiMaggio (.381 in 1939).

On June 7, the Associated Press did a feature on Williams for its national audience, noting the .436 tear he was on while proclaiming that "the Kid has grown up." Ted reflected on his bitterness of the previous year and said he was through feuding with writers and fans. He said both he and the fans got sore that he didn't hit as many homers as they thought he would in a smaller Fenway. "Everyone thought I'd hit 80 homers and I guess I thought I would too.... Boy, it got so I hated to go out and meet people.... But that's all over now. I'm just trying to get along. It's a dream I've always had—the way I'm hitting now. Boy, I'm just busting the cover off that ball."[19]

At the end of June, Babe Ruth himself weighed in to tout Ted. "When I first saw Ted Williams swinging a bat I knew he would be one of the best," the Babe told Grantland Rice. "He's loose and easy, with a great pair of wrists. Just a natural. Williams ought to be one of the first hitters in many years to pass .400."[20]

On July 1, DiMaggio hit in his forty-fourth straight game, tying the record that had been established by Wee Willie Keeler in 1897. This sent the press into overdrive and would eclipse any attention given to Ted over the next three weeks or so—except for July 8, when the elite players from the American and National Leagues gathered in Detroit for the annual All-Star Game. Ted, who was batting .405, took the train out from Boston along with his teammates Doerr, Foxx, Cronin, and Dominic DiMaggio—all of whom had also been selected to play in what was only the major leagues' ninth midsummer showcase. The game was bigger then, with a far more intense feel and rivalry than today's languid exhibitions have.

Williams loved the All-Star Game, and that year's venue, Briggs Stadium, was his favorite park to hit in. He'd bought a new 8mm movie camera for the occasion and used it to pan across the crowd of 54,674—and to film some of the ballplayers, too, including Dominic's older brother Joe. "I want to study his style," Ted told the writers, giving the Yankee Clipper his due at the height of his streak. "DiMaggio is the greatest hitter I ever saw and probably will see during my career....I have to tie into a pitch to get power. DiMaggio is stronger. He hits the ball hard in any direction. And then there's the matter of temperament. I've been down on myself, but I never heard of Joe getting unsettled."[21]

In the starting lineup, Williams was to bat cleanup behind DiMaggio. In the fourth inning, Ted laced a line drive to right field, which Bob Elliott of the Pittsburgh Pirates misjudged, and the ball went sailing over his head for a double, driving in a run that gave the American League an early lead. But by the ninth inning, the Nationals were ahead 5–3, thanks to Pirates shortstop Arky Vaughan belting successive two-run homers, first in the seventh and then in the eighth.

Frankie Hayes of the Athletics opened the last of the ninth for the Americans against right-hander Claude Passeau of the Cubs by popping up to second base for the first out. Ken Keltner of the Indians followed with a smash to shortstop, which Eddie Miller, who had entered the game for Vaughan, couldn't handle cleanly, giving Keltner time to reach first safely. The Yankees' Joe Gordon then stroked a clean single to right, and Cecil Travis walked to load the bases for the great DiMaggio.

The crowd roared with anticipation, as Joltin' Joe, who by then had hit in forty-eight straight games, stepped to the plate. DiMaggio fouled the first pitch off, swung and missed at the second, then hit a tailor-made double-play ball to short. Miller fielded the ball cleanly, and flipped it to Dodgers second baseman Billy Herman for the force-out, but Herman's relay to first was wide, enabling DiMaggio to reach safely. Keltner scored.

So with the AL now trailing 5–4, Ted was up. National League manager "Deacon" Bill McKechnie of the Reds came out to the mound to talk with Passeau and summoned the catcher and infielders in as well. Famed broadcaster Red Barber gave the moment a little more of a drum-roll for his national radio audience: "How do you like this for a setting? Two out. The tying run at third, the winning run at first, last half of the ninth inning, and the .400 hitter of today at the plate, Ted Williams....I wouldn't have missed this for anything."

Rather than go to a left-hander, or walk Williams to get to the on-deck batter, Dom DiMaggio, McKechnie decided to allow Passeau to pitch to Ted, no doubt mindful of the fact that in the eighth inning the Cubs right-hander had struck Williams out. Ted had thought that called third strike was low. As the conference at the mound continued, Williams asked home plate umpire Babe Pinelli where the pitch had been. At the knees, Pinelli replied.

"Then I stood back and sort of gave myself a fight talk," Ted told J. G. Taylor Spink of the *Sporting News* after the game. "I said, 'Listen you big lug. He outguessed you last time and you got caught with your bat on your shoulder for a called third strike. You were swinging late when you fouled one off, too. Let's swing, and swing a little earlier this time, and see if we can connect.'"[22]

Passeau's first pitch was high and outside. Williams fouled off the second, straight back. Then came another ball, high and tight. With the count two and one, Passeau threw a slider, letter high, and Ted was sitting on it. He swung with all his might—"no cut-down protection swing, an all-out home run swing, probably with my eyes shut," he said later—and smashed a towering drive to right field. The only question was whether it would be fair or foul. There was a brisk wind blowing across the field from left to right, but the ball was crushed so hard the breeze couldn't alter its path much before it struck the facing of the third tier, about twenty feet fair. The ball bounced back to right fielder Enos Slaughter, who picked it up and stuffed it in his back pocket as a souvenir.[23]

Of course, hitting a game-winning home run in such a circumstance "was the kind of thing a kid dreams about and imagines himself doing when he's playing those little playground games we used to play in San Diego," Ted wrote in his book. "Half way down to first, I stopped running and started leaping and jumping and clapping my hands, and I was just so happy I laughed out loud. I've never been so happy and I've never seen so many happy guys.... I had hit what remains to this day the most thrilling hit of my life."[24]

After he finished skipping around the bases, Ted was mobbed at the plate by delirious teammates, including both DiMaggio brothers and starting pitcher Bob Feller of the Indians, who raced out of the dugout dressed in his street clothes. The bedlam moved to the clubhouse, where the American League manager, Del Baker of the Tigers, planted a big kiss on Ted's left cheek, and the photographers made him do it again. The Red Sox brass—Tom Yawkey, Eddie Collins, and Joe Cronin— glad-handed their star, as did Will Harridge, the American League president. Bill McKechnie, the rival manager, also stopped by to pay homage. "Ted, you're just not human," he said.

The writers demanded more detail from Ted, of course. "I had a funny feeling after I struck out in the eighth that I was going to get up there at least one more time and hit one," he said. "And when that one came up fast and about elbow high, I said to myself, 'This is it.'

"Confidence is a great thing. You have to have it in our game and that's how it was with me that last trip to the plate.... There ain't nothing like hitting a homer.... Wasn't it a pip?"

Then Ted paused and added: "I know one thing. The happiest woman in America right now is my mother."[25]

May Williams had been listening to the game on the radio and had sent Ted a telegram before the game, which he did not receive until afterward. "Congratulations on being on All Star team," it said. "We're pulling for American League and thinking of you, my wonderful son." It was signed "Mother."

Little more than an hour after his All-Star Game heroics, Ted was not out painting the town but back in his hotel room alone, writing a letter to Doris Soule. A reporter, Gerry Moore of the *Globe,* decided to take a chance and knock on the door of room 1812 of the Book Cadillac Hotel. "Come in, the door's open," Ted called out cheerfully.

Moore found the Kid ebullient, eager for company, and talking in staccato bursts—mostly about his mother. "Do you know the biggest kick I get out of this whole thing? I'm tickled for my mom's sake because she was listening." He showed Moore the telegram she had sent him, then read from a letter May had written, which he'd received just the day before. "Dear Son," it began. She hoped he was well. She'd bought a schedule of his games but was having problems deciphering it to know where he was when. But she was pleased he was hitting so brilliantly. "San Diego is thrilled.... There have been some lovely articles about your hitting." She added in a postscript that she was "glad you're getting along so well with the sports writers."

The All-Star Game served as a loud exclamation point in that summer of '41, a season long regarded by many baseball historians as the sport's greatest ever. There was DiMaggio, whose streak would extend for another eight games—until July 17—ending a two-month run of drama that riveted the nation, fan and nonfan alike. There was Ted, who in the second half of the season dug in to prove that his All-Star heroism was no fluke. He eagerly reclaimed the national spotlight later in the summer as DiMaggio's acclaim receded and his own march to .400 showed no signs of abating. Lefty Grove finally won his three hundredth career game, for the Red Sox, at the same time as the leader of a new pitching generation, Bob Feller, won twenty-five games for the Cleveland Indians. And the Brooklyn Dodgers emerged as baseball's Cinderella team, edging out the St. Louis Cardinals for the National League pennant only to be heartbroken by Mickey Owen's dropped third strike, which paved the way for the Yankees to win the World Series.

Baseball was a generation removed from the *Field of Dreams* era but was still bathing in its halcyon days and in the aura of Ruth, who had retired in 1935. A few concessions were starting to be made to the future, such as the beginning of night play, but expansion was more than a decade away, and this was still old-time hardball.

"School kids grew up learning their geography by knowing the ten cities and sixteen teams in the American and National Leagues," Dom DiMaggio wrote in his memoir of the 1941 season, *Real Grass, Real Heroes*. "It was that wonderful sameness, year in and year out. We could always count on baseball to be the same warm and sunny game, on the same fields, in the same cities. We loved baseball not only for itself but for the secure feeling of community it gave you. We felt a loyalty to baseball, because it was loyal to us."[26]

Players were still leaving their gloves on the field at the end of an inning, before they came in to bat. They'd be tossed in the shallowest part of the outfield, just beyond the infield, and when play resumed, the gloves were obstacles that the players had to contend with while ranging under pop-ups.

All travel was still done by train, and teams could take between ten days and two weeks to go only as far west as Saint Louis and only as far south as Washington, just below the Mason-Dixon Line. The major-league teams would lease three cars on a train, and the hierarchy of the players was evident in who was assigned to be in what car. Rookies were assigned to the third car, the one that swayed the most when the train went around a bend.

"If you were assigned an upper berth in the third car, you knew you had a long way to go before you acquired any seniority on that ball club," wrote Dominic. "Your goal was to progress to the point where you could be assigned to Lower 7, Car A. Car A was the front car, the one that remained the steadiest of the three. A lower berth was always preferable to an upper, and the seventh Pullman berth was in the middle of the car, the smoothest riding part of the car because it wasn't over the wheels. When you were assigned Lower 7, Car A, you knew you had established yourself as an important member of the team."[27]

Generally, the players loved train travel. "Ballplayers from the 1940s will tell you to a man that when baseball teams started flying, a certain bonding that held teams together went out of major league baseball," Dominic added. "We got to know each other as only you can when

May Williams, young
Salvationist. (May
Williams Collection)

Young Ted.
(May Williams
Collection)

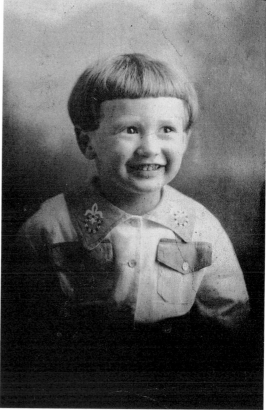

Young Sam Williams. (May Williams Collection)

Ted's childhood home at 4121 Utah Street. (San Diego Hall of Champions Sports Museum)

May with her two boys, Ted (left) and Danny (right). (May Williams Collection)

May, second guitarist from right (with glasses), and the Salvation Army band. (May Williams Collection)

Ted's uncles, from left to right: Pete, Saul, and Paul Venzor, with their mother, Natalia, in Santa Barbara, circa 1954. (Courtesy of Rosalie Larson)

With his prom date, Alberta Camus, January 1937. (May Williams Collection)

At age seventeen. (May Williams Collection)

Pitching for Herbert Hoover High School, circa 1935. (May Williams Collection)

With Red Sox general manager Eddie Collins and San Diego Padres owner Bill Lane after signing his contract with the Padres on June 25, 1936. (San Diego History Center)

With the Padres, 1937. (San Diego Hall of Champions Sports Museum)

Enjoying the fruits of duck hunting with then girlfriend Doris Soule in Minnesota, 1940. (Ted Williams Family Enterprises)

Hauling in his kill in Minnesota, late 1939. (Ted Williams Family Enterprises)

With his three aunts, the half sisters of Sam Williams, in San Diego, circa 1939. (May Williams Collection)

Ted, 1941.
(May Williams
Collection)

Danny Williams,
Ted's brother, at work
on his car. (May
Williams Collection)

With the Minneapolis Millers, 1938. (National Baseball Hall of Fame Library)

At Boston's Back Bay station, April 1939, arriving in the city for the first time. (*Boston Globe* photograph)

Swinging in 1939, his rookie year with the Red Sox. (National Baseball Hall of Fame Library)

Happily crossing home plate at Fenway, 1939. (Courtesy of the Trustees of the Boston Public Library / Leslie Jones Collection)

Flashing some leather in a posed shot during his rookie season. (Courtesy of the Griffin Museum of Photography)

At the Boston
baseball writers'
dinner, 1939.
(Leslie Jones
photograph)

In Chicago, 1939,
checking out the
other side of the
camera. (Rogers
Photo Archive)

Hamming it up with Jimmie Foxx, 1939. (National Baseball Hall of Fame Library)

Helping with the construction of "Williamsburg" in early 1940, after Tom Yawkey ordered that the right-field fence at Fenway Park be moved in to accommodate Ted. (Brearley Collection)

Limbering up, circa 1941. (National Baseball Hall of Fame Library)

you're on a train together for 24 hours, or 36 or more. You came together as a group, and when you went out onto that field, you came together as a team....We were heroes on those trains. We'd roll into a station and look out the window and see kids yelling up to us and pointing out to their buddies, 'There's Williams!' Who wouldn't be happy to sign autographs in that kind of enthusiasm?"[28]

Most of the trains would leave around midnight. The dining cars were formal: tables for four were set with white tablecloths and a center-piece of fresh flowers; waiters wearing white jackets served fine food. Air-conditioning was just being introduced, so more often than not a large block of ice was stationed at one end of a car in front of a fan.

The trips strengthened the bond between Dominic and Ted, the pre-cursor to what would become an even stronger lifelong friendship when their playing days were over. During Joe's streak, when the Red Sox were playing at home, Ted would get updates from the Fenway score-board operator, Bill Daley, on whether the Clipper had gotten his hit yet, then he would shout out the news to Dominic over in center field.

Even in the absence of Joe DiMaggio news, Ted would usually keep up a running repartee throughout the game with Daley, who would poke his head through an opening in the scoreboard. The Fenway tele-graph operator, Hartwell McIsaac, knew that the Kid liked to keep up on who was doing what around the majors, so when something of inter-est happened, McIsaac would call Daley, who would then relay it to Williams. Williams would chatter with delight after he hit a home run or mutter in frustration if a pitcher had good stuff and he was having a hard time handling it. If Daley posted a number showing how many runs the Yankees or some other team had scored in an inning, Ted would ask him how they'd increased their tally.

Dominic became a keen observer of Ted. He noticed, for instance, that when a relief pitcher was brought in and Williams was next up, he would—against the rules—inch in as close as he could to the batter's box while the reliever was warming up, the better to size up his stuff.

And Williams was always quizzing Dominic about what the opposing pitcher was throwing. "If I led off the game by making an out, I would be headed past Ted on my way back to the dugout while he was on his way to the on-deck circle. As Johnny Pesky stepped into the batter's box, Ted would be giving me the third degree: 'Where was that last pitch, Dommie? What's he throwing? What did you hit?'

"His timing was always the worst in that situation. I was fed up with myself and in no mood to talk about it, so I'd tell him in my disgust, 'I don't know.' To Williams, ignorance was worse than not getting a hit. 'How the hell can you not know?' he'd bark. 'What kind of a dummy are you? No wonder you didn't get a hit. Don't be so damned dumb!' "[29]

Williams probably spent more time that summer with his roommate, pitcher Charlie Wagner, than with anyone else—which meant that no one else had as intimate a sense of Ted's obsessions. "Ted was a very intense guy and he used to psych himself up for games," Wagner recalled. "The better he hit the moodier he'd get because he was psyching himself. In the room the morning before a game he'd walk around talking out loud about the pitcher and what he was going to do to the guy. He loved to stand in front of a mirror like he was swinging a bat."[30] He'd get up early, listen to the radio, then get the papers and study the box scores. Williams would pay special attention to what the pitchers did, how long they lasted, how many runs and walks they gave up. Then he would do fingertip push-ups, telling Wagner that he could do twenty-five more than however many Broadway Charlie could do. Some days, Wagner and Ted would go fishing together at a lake in Framingham, about twenty miles west of Boston, a relaxing way for Ted to contemplate the contest to come before getting to the park at noon for a three o'clock game.

As it happened, the Red Sox began the second half of their season in Detroit, so Ted, still dining out on his All-Star heroics, didn't have far to report for duty. But on July 12, he reinjured his right ankle sliding back into first base. X-rays showed no new chip or break. Still, it was sore, so Williams was confined to pinch-hitting duty for the next ten days.

When he returned to the lineup on July 22, his ankle heavily taped and his average down to .393, Ted learned that Joe Cronin had shifted him from batting third in the order to cleanup. Williams was happy with the change—hitting fourth figured to boost his RBI chances. Batting third with Cronin and then Foxx behind him, he'd seen good pitches. But at cleanup, with Foxx in decline as a power hitter batting fifth, pitchers opted to be more selective with the pitches they threw Ted. This was a mixed bag in his quest for .400—he got fewer chances for hits but more walks, thus keeping his total number of official at bats down.

The next day, July 23, at Fenway Park, White Sox manager Jimmy Dykes unveiled the first-ever shift against Williams to try to plug holes on the right side of the field, where the pull-hitting Ted smacked the ball most often. The outfield tilted way right: the third baseman played where the shortstop normally played, the shortstop swung around to the right side of second base, the second baseman moved deep in the hole onto the outfield grass, and the first baseman hugged the line. Ted saw the new alignment and started laughing. "Dykes, you crazy son of a bitch, what the hell are you doing?" he yelled.[31] Ted hit one down the left-field line and went 4–10 in two games against the shift, and Dykes abandoned it.

Williams stayed hot, and by August 13 he was hitting .413. He was full of confidence when he held court with a group of writers around the batting cage at Shibe Park in Philadelphia. "I'll tell you why I'm hitting .400," Ted said. "It's a cinch. I got confidence this year for the first time. When I came up two years ago, I thought it would be swell if I could have a pretty fair season. You know, hit around .300 and get a homer now and then. Before I knew it, I was hitting .330, but I really didn't think I was that good. I finished that first year at .327, I led the league in runs batted in and I hit more homers than DiMaggio, but I still did not feel sure of myself. Last year I missed the batting title by six or eight points, and I found myself wondering if I was as good as DiMaggio, Appling, Greenberg and those other guys. I told myself I was a sap for thinking that way, and I guess it worked. I don't believe there's such a thing as a natural hitter. If that's all there was to it, a guy could lay off all winter and come back in the spring as good as he was the previous mid-season. Nobody can do that. Natural hitter, my ass."[32]

It was the kind of stark, introspective quote that made Williams such good copy, and it was something that the painfully shy, inarticulate DiMaggio would never say.

Ted held steady for the rest of August, dipping only slightly to .407 at the end of the month, when he celebrated his twenty-third birthday.

As the final month of the season began, and the excitement built over whether Ted could maintain the .400 plateau, there was a spate of national attention on Williams. He appeared on the cover of *Life* magazine and was featured in a photo spread inside that amounted to a baseball cheesecake layout. He was pictured bare-chested, in undershorts, doing a frame-by-frame breakdown of his famous swing as his washboard abs and long, rawboned arms strained.

The Boston papers began running house ads requesting readers not to call in asking how Williams did that day, because the switchboards were getting jammed. "We'll give you all you can possibly read...and more!" said the *Post*. The *Globe* ran a daily feature showing day-by-day comparisons between Ted that year and Bill Terry in 1930, when the latter had hit .401.

Feisty and having fun, on September 1, Ted appeared at Fenway early, showing off a new .22 revolver and a Zipper rifle to his teammates.[33] When the park was empty, he walked out to the field and, standing in front of the Red Sox dugout, took aim at one of the red lights under the word *strike* on the scoreboard, which was positioned on the left-field wall about 350 feet away. He fired, and the glass shattered. He went on to hit three home runs against Washington that day in a Labor Day doubleheader to take over the American League home-run lead with thirty-four.

In a back-to-reality moment that same day, President Roosevelt announced that the United States was prepared to join the Allies at war.

Momentous events that summer, such as Hitler's invasion of the Soviet Union and the sinking of the *Bismarck,* had even penetrated baseball's cocoon to become a prime topic of clubhouse conversation. Throughout that month, FDR made more strident denunciations of Hitler and his "insane forces of violence," but the country wasn't at war yet, and many remained absorbed by baseball and Ted's chase for .400.

The day after the Washington doubleheader, a fourteen-year-old from South Brewer, Maine, Billy Kane, hitchhiked 250 miles to Fenway Park to see Williams play only to find that there was no game scheduled. He was found sleeping in an aisle of the park by police officers. Back at the station, when the kid told his story, a few cops went over to the Shelton Hotel and got the almost-ready-for-bed Ted to come down to the station and meet the boy. The next day, Billy was Ted's guest for a game against the Yankees. The papers loved the story and played it big.

When the Yankees clinched the American League pennant early, on September 4, it only focused more attention on Williams as the fortunes of the Red Sox and other AL teams became irrelevant. And as the Sox came into Yankee Stadium on the sixth for their final series of the year, Ted was again baldly honest about his goals and ambitions, speaking in a manner that would be unusual for a player today.

"I'll be the happiest fellow in the world if I hit .400," he told the writers. "I want to be talked about. I want to be remembered when I leave baseball. Who are the players they talk about and remember: Babe Ruth because he hit 60 home runs, Rogers Hornsby because he hit .424. Hack Wilson because he batted in 190 runs, and DiMaggio because he hit in 56 straight games. Those are the best, top performances in baseball. They're what I'm aiming at."[34]

The following day, Yankee Stadium fans gave Ted a standing ovation after he came to bat for the four hundredth time of the season, thereby qualifying for the batting title. By now it seemed like fans of every team—including the most intense haters of the Red Sox—were rooting for the Kid to break the barrier. Indeed, the previous month, when Ted singled and then was walked four times by Yankees pitchers, they had booed the home team lustily.

On an off day, September 11, Williams drove down to Providence, Rhode Island, from Boston for a batting exhibition, and four thousand people turned out to cheer him on. The night before, the retired Babe Ruth had attracted twelve hundred. Yet occasionally the bad-Ted persona from last year slipped out.

Asked by the *Globe*'s Louis Lyons how he felt about Boston fans now, Ted said: "They're like any other fans. They follow what the baseball writers say."

Williams was not just leading the league with his average but contending for the Triple Crown as well. On September 15, he smacked a three-run homer at Fenway off John Rigney, his thirty-fifth of the year, giving him 116 RBIs—tied for second with Joe DiMaggio and six behind the leader, Charlie Keller of the Yankees.

The next day, Ted flew off to New York to appear on the nationally syndicated *We the People* radio program. On Ted's arm when he appeared at the airport for the afternoon American Airlines flight was Doris Soule, who had spent the summer under the radar, working as a cashier at Boston's Parker House hotel, but now was making her public debut. The writers and photographers on hand to record Ted's every move swarmed around Doris, the first girl to be seen accompanying the Kid, but the couple flew off before anyone could determine who she was.

Doris was initially described as an "oh-so-beautiful brunette," part of "an intriguing romantic mystery," until she flew back the next day, alone, and identified herself for the pack of reporters staked out awaiting her arrival after midnight.[35] Was Ted in love with her? Doris was asked. "Just say we are good friends," she replied with a smile. Well, did *she* love Ted? At that, her eyes closed and she declined to answer. Did she realize she was the envy of "many girls"? No she didn't, said Doris. She refused to say where she was from or how they'd met, but said she'd known Ted for about a year.

The shocker for the writers came when Doris allowed that she "hated" baseball. "I like practically all sports except baseball," she said. "I have seen only two games this season. The reason was to see Ted." She liked fishing a lot better, and noted that she was with Ted earlier in the summer when he'd caught a 374-pound tuna off Plum Island, north of Boston.

As for Ted and the radio show in New York, he'd been "*wonnnderful*,"

Doris said. Asked by *We the People* announcer, Harry von Zell, to account for his success that year, Williams had replied: "I am not popping off anymore. I am just popping everything out of the ballpark."

On September 21, following the last home game of the year, Ted's average stood at .406. There was an off day on the twenty-second and then six more games, three in Washington and three in Philadelphia. Williams vowed to play in all six. "If you hit .400, it's got to be because you played a whole season," he said.

Joe Cronin announced that after a doubleheader in Washington on the twenty-fourth, the Red Sox would go right to Philadelphia so that Williams could get all the batting practice he needed during two off days on the twenty-fifth and twenty-sixth before the final series against the Athletics. There had originally been a game scheduled for the twenty-sixth, but A's owner and manager Connie Mack decided to play it on Sunday as part of a doubleheader finale that he hoped would draw a large crowd for the Williams denouement.

"We all want to see Ted stay right up there and it ought to help him to get in some batting practice on the off days at Shibe Park Thursday and Friday," Cronin told Burt Whitman of the *Herald*. Whitman figured Ted needed five hits in the last six games to stay above .400, provided he got his usual complement of walks.[36]

In the first Washington game, Williams went 1–3 with a walk, and his average dropped a point, to .405. The hit came on a 420-foot fly ball to left-center that old friend Doc Cramer dropped while on the run. The official scorer ruled it a double, though the *Globe* called the hit "tainted."*

In the first game of the next day's doubleheader, Williams faced knuckleballer Dutch Leonard, who was going after his nineteenth win. Williams was never able to hit the knuckler as well as he felt he should have, and he went 0–3, walking twice, fouling out, grounding out, and flying out; his average dropped three more points, to .402.[37]

In the second game, the Nationals' starter was Dick Mulligan, a left-handed rookie who was pitching in his first major-league game. Ted felt at a disadvantage going up against late-season call-ups he knew nothing about. First time up, a dazzling curve buckled Williams for a called third strike. Next, Ted drilled a grounder that gave second baseman Jimmy

---

* Washington pitcher Sid Hudson told me that he'd been trying to help Ted make history, having told him before the game that he'd throw "nothing but fastballs today unless I'm in a jam, then you're on your own. I did it because I wanted to see if he could get up to .400." Nevertheless, Hudson added, "every time I threw a fastball, I threw the best one I had. . . . I just did it, and that's it. I didn't think about it."

Bloodworth enough trouble to allow Williams to make it to first safely, according to umpire Bill Grieve. Grieve first started to raise his thumb in the out call, then signaled safe, drawing boos from the crowd. Ted failed his last two times up, thus submitting a 1–7 line for the day, the one hit plainly a gift. As the team left for the final series in Philadelphia, his average was down to .401.

The two off days before the first game, on Saturday, September 27, gave Ted ample time to brood and fret. The lighting was a complicating factor for Williams at this time of year at Shibe Park. Early in the afternoon, the sun was on the pitcher's mound while the plate was in shadow, making it hard to follow the flight of a pitch. Ted continued to vow that he would play all three games—"A batting record's no good unless it's made in all the games of the season"[38]—but Cronin, citing the shadow problem, said he would reserve the right to pull Williams for the second game of the doubleheader, on Sunday, if the .400 mark was assured.

"You got to admire the Kid for being so courageous about it, but I can tell you one thing: I may yank him in that second game Sunday if he's got his hits," Cronin told the writers. "We go on the new time Sunday and with the first game starting at 1:30, it'll be pretty dark when that second game gets underway. I feel that I have obligations, and I may decide to take him out of that second game, even if he doesn't like it."[39]

In the Saturday game, the A's Connie Mack started Roger Wolff, a rookie pitching only his second big-league game. Mack, the dignified owner-manager who directed the game from the dugout while dressed in a business suit, a white shirt with a starched collar, and a fedora, knew Ted disliked going up against pitchers he hadn't faced before. To make it worse for Williams, Wolff was a right-handed knuckleballer.

His first time up against Wolff, in the second inning, Ted walked on a three-and-two pitch. In the fourth, he doubled to deep right-center. But after that he flied to right, popped up to first, and struck out swinging. The 1–4 dipped his average below .400, to .39955, the first time he'd dropped under .400 since July 24.

Though the statisticians would have rounded his .39955 average up to .400, and though he could have sat out the last two games, Ted knew that history wouldn't look kindly on that option, so it was really no option at all. As he'd said, he would play the doubleheader and achieve the mark by getting his hits—or he wouldn't achieve the mark at all.

That night, Williams tried to quiet his nerves by walking the streets of Philadelphia with Johnny Orlando at his side to offer encouragement.

"We walked for over three hours, and my feet were burning," Orlando recalled. "Ted didn't drink, so from time to time I'd run into a barroom to get a drink, and he'd wait outside until I got finished.... During the whole conversation all he kept repeating over and over was how determined he was to hit .400."[40] Williams stopped twice for ice cream.[41]

When they returned to the Benjamin Franklin Hotel, it was 10:30 p.m., half an hour past Ted's normal bedtime. He ran into Joe Cronin, who was sitting on a couch in the lobby with Tom Daly, a coach. Williams sat down and talked with his manager. Cronin again gave Ted an out, saying he could sit it out tomorrow if he wished, but Williams dismissed the suggestion out of hand.

Ted went to his room, where Charlie Wagner was waiting up for him. They talked about which pitchers he might face the next day. In those days managers did not announce their starters in advance—an effort to minimize any edge that gamblers might try to gain. Williams was "sky high emotionally," Wagner recalled.

The next morning they got up early, ate breakfast in the hotel, and went out to the park in a cab together. "The ride out was quiet," Wagner said. "I remember thinking how fast the cabbie was driving and that we'd probably get killed before we got there, the way he was flying through intersections."[42]

By the start of the game, at 1:30 p.m., 10,268 fans were on hand at Shibe Park, where the capacity at the time was about thirty-three thousand. It was eighty-two degrees, mostly cloudy, and the wind was blowing mildly from the southwest at thirteen miles per hour, a nonfactor.[43]

Hoping to keep Williams off balance, Connie Mack again decided to start two rookies who'd been called up earlier that month: Dick Fowler in the first game and Fred Caligiuri in the second. Both were right-handers.

"I remember Connie Mack saying, 'Don't do him any favors. Try to get him out,'" recalled Caligiuri.[44] "I was just a wide-eyed rookie, so I listened to him. I was more nervous because I'd just got married, and my wife was there. I had bigger things to worry about than Williams and .400. We tried to pitch him outside. We tried to change up speeds on him. You keep throwing him the fastball, and he'll make you pay."

In eight previous games against the Red Sox, A's pitchers had walked Ted fourteen times.[45] But now Mack had decided to pitch to him. As Williams stepped into the box for his first time up, leading off the second inning, A's catcher Frankie Hayes let him know of his manager's decision directly.

"Ted, Mr. Mack told us if we let up on you he'll run us out of base-ball," Hayes said. "I wish you all the luck in the world, but we're not giving you a damn thing."

As the crowd gave Ted a loud, prolonged cheer, home plate umpire Bill McGowan called time, walked around the plate, bent over, and began dusting it off. Without looking up, he said to Williams: "To hit .400, a batter has got to be loose. He has got to be loose."[46]

That was a highly unusual remark for a nominally neutral umpire to make to a player, but the umps plainly liked Ted. They respected his great skill, his keen batting eye, his obvious command of the strike zone, and, perhaps most of all, the fact that he virtually never argued with them or tried to show them up. Williams liked to leverage his good rela-tionships with the umpires and would often pump them for information about how rival pitchers were doing: Who had they seen in the previous series they'd worked? And what pitches were being thrown to what hit-ters in what situations? "It was like having a personal scouting system," said Vince Orlando, Johnny's brother.[47] "The league got wind of this later and made the umpires stop it."

The first two pitches from Fowler were balls. Then Ted scorched a grounder to the right of first baseman Bob Johnson into right field for a single. He was back up to .4008.

His second time up, in the fifth, Williams drove a 1–0 pitch over the right-field wall and onto the street, about 440 feet away, for his thirty-seventh home run of the season. His average now stood at .4022. In the sixth, facing lefty Porter Vaughan, Ted again lashed a grounder past Johnson for his third straight hit to creep up to .4035. In the seventh, Ted smacked a line drive over the head of Johnson, who by then was like a target in a shooting gallery. Four for four, and up to .4048. His final time up, Williams hit a hard grounder to second baseman Crash Davis, which Davis bobbled for an error. So at the end of the two-hour-and-two-minute game, which the Red Sox won 12–11, Ted stood at .4039.

Between games, his teammates all congratulated him, knowing that no matter what happened in the second game he was virtually assured of reaching his goal. Jack Malaney of the *Boston Post* came down to the clubhouse to update Cronin on what Ted's average was, in case the man-ager wanted to pull him. But Williams, as he'd promised, said he would finish, though the suspense was largely gone. Even if he went 0–4 in the final, he'd still be over .400.

The crowd gave him a standing ovation when he dug in against Caligiuri to lead off the second inning of the second game, and they cheered him again when he spanked a grounder in the hole between first and second (.4052). His next time up, in the fourth, Williams absolutely crushed Caligiuri's 2–0 pitch, and years later he would call it the hardest-hit ball of his career. It was a wicked, rising line drive that reached the top of the right-field wall in a heartbeat before slamming into a loud-speaker mounted on the wall, knocking a hole in it, and dropping back to the playing field for a ground-rule double.

Ted got one more at bat, in the seventh (the game was called after eight innings because of darkness), and improbably lofted a routine fly to left fielder Elmer Valo, the only ball of the day that he did not hit hard.

It was a stunning performance. Having eschewed a rounded .400, Williams had bravely put everything on the line and knocked out six clean hits in eight trips to the plate to finish at .4057, officially .406. It was a day that would define his playing career and shape his legacy.

The press raved. Burt Whitman in the *Herald* called it "one of the most spectacular last-day batting splurges in the history of major league baseball."[48] "All hail Thumping Theodore Samuel Williams," wrote Malaney in the *Post*.[49]

One of the happiest people in the clubhouse afterward was Cronin. "Imagine that Kid getting four singles, a double and a homer the closing day of the season when the chips are down," he said. "I tell you, I never came closer to bawling right out loud on a baseball diamond [than] when Ted got that third hit. I really filled right up. I was so happy that the Kid had done the trick without asking or being given any favors. I guess I was no different from the whole rest of the club. For if ever a ballplayer deserved to hit .400, it's that same Ted. A dozen times in the last three weeks he has refused to protect his average by dropping down a bunt. He just kept swinging up there to the very finish."

Bill McGowan, the home plate umpire who'd given Ted the sotto voce advice to stay loose, also sung Williams's praises unabashedly and wanted to dispel any notion that the A's pitchers had been going easy on him. "Don't let anyone tell you that those kid pitchers weren't bearing down on Ted," said McGowan. "For instance, that single Ted hit in the seventh inning against that young left hander, Porter Vaughan, was as beautiful a curveball as I've ever seen."[50]

After the game, Ted seemed restrained in his joy, almost subdued, but it was obvious he was swelled with pride at his accomplishment. Before the writers arrived in the clubhouse, he took Johnny Orlando aside and said simply: "I'm a good hitter."

"He said it just like he had proved something to himself," Orlando said.[51] Then he kissed the bat he'd used in the two games. An AP photographer saw that and asked him to do it again for posterity, and Ted obliged. To his roommate, Charlie Wagner, who had pitched in the first game, Williams expressed satisfied surprise: "Geez," he said. "I hit .406."[52]

A reporter asked Ted if he thought he had a chance at being elected MVP. "Gee," he replied with a wide smile, "do you think there's any chance? Even if I don't, I'll be satisfied with that thrill out there today. I wasn't saying much about it, but I never wanted anything more in my life."[53]

Outside, at least two thousand Philadelphians waited near the Red Sox clubhouse and spilled out onto 21st Street to honor the visiting hero.[54] Ted was pinned against a wall and happily signed hundreds of autographs until police finally shoved him into a cab, which drove him to the train station.

Besides Ted's illustrious .406 batting average, he led the league in home runs (37), runs scored (135), walks (147), on-base percentage (.553), and slugging percentage (.735). His 120 RBIs were five short of DiMaggio's leading 125, so that narrowly cost him the Triple Crown.

His average had been remarkably consistent, falling below .400 only from April 30 to May 24 and from July 11 to July 24. Ted had a substantially higher average at home, where he hit .428, than on the road (.380). Williams liked Fenway for its good green background, its lack of shadows, and the short left-field wall, which enabled him to wait longer on a pitch and still hit it. "I always said to myself: 'If you swing a little late it won't be the worst thing in the world, because there's that short fence, the defense isn't there, and slices or balls hit late can still go out,'" Ted wrote in his book.[55]

Williams is the only .400 hitter, at least in the modern era, not to get the benefit of the sacrifice fly rule, which does not charge a batter with a time at bat if he hits a fly ball that scores a runner from third base. The rule was on the books from 1908 until 1931, on again in 1939, and off from 1940 to 1954. While no one at the time kept track of the number of sacrifice flies Williams hit in 1941, statisticians would determine years later that he hit six. So if those six at bats had been deducted from his total, he would have had an average of .411.

Another hurdle that Ted had to overcome was his lack of speed. Only five of his 185 hits were infield hits, or so-called leg hits.

But fueling Williams's road to .406, on the other hand, were his 147 walks—far more than any of his twentieth-century predecessors in the .400 club—which enabled him to be charged with many fewer times at bat. With just 456 official plate appearances, Williams was the only .400 hitter in the modern era to have fewer than 500 at bats and the only one to have fewer than 200 hits.

YEAR	PLAYER	AB	H	BB	BA
1901	Nap Lajoie	544	232	24	.426
1911	Joe Jackson	571	233	56	.408
1911	Ty Cobb	591	248	44	.420
1912	Ty Cobb	553	226	43	.409
1920	George Sisler	631	257	46	.407
1922	George Sisler	586	246	49	.420
1922	Ty Cobb	526	211	55	.401
1922	Rogers Hornsby	623	250	65	.401
1923	Harry Heilmann	524	211	74	.403
1924	Rogers Hornsby	536	227	89	.424
1925	Rogers Hornsby	504	203	83	.403
1930	Bill Terry	633	254	57	.401
1941	Ted Williams	456	185	147	.406

Another factor was his average relative to that of the rest of the league. When Bill Terry—the last .400 hitter before Williams—posted his .401 mark in 1930, the league batting average was .303, meaning that Terry's average was 32 percent higher than the norm. When Ted hit .406, the league average was down to .266, meaning that Williams hit 53 percent higher—a much greater feat than Terry's in a far more competitive era.[56]

The late Stephen Jay Gould—renowned Harvard University evolutionary biologist, science historian, baseball statistics maven, and ardent Yankees fan—crunched Williams's 1941 numbers against those of the previous .400 hitters and concluded that Ted's feat was "the greatest achievement in twentieth-century hitting...a beacon in the history of excellence, a lesson to all who value the best in human possibility."[57]

★   ★   ★

Several days later, Ted and Jimmie Foxx flew to San Diego to join a team of major leaguers and Pacific Coast League players on a brief barnstorming tour through Southern California.★

Several thousand people and a brass band turned out at Lindbergh Field on October 3 to greet their hometown hero. As a city official launched into a windy speech, Ted shifted his feet nervously, scanned the crowd for familiar faces, and spotted Rod Luscomb, his mentor at the University Heights playground.

"Hi, Rod!" Ted yelled as the city official droned on. "Come the hell up here!"[58] Williams walked over to the rope line and escorted Luscomb up to the platform.

Ted was embarrassed at all the fuss and said only a few words. Foxx assured the crowd that "you will find that Ted still wears the same size hat despite his success. The only thing that's bigger is the bat that he waves in front of opposing pitchers."[59] Then there was a parade to the civic center downtown, followed by another program at Williams's old playground in University Heights.

That night there was a reception at Ted's house, and Luscomb wanted to talk hitting with his former pupil. Had he changed his swing at all?

"Wait a minute, I'll get a bat and show you," replied Ted eagerly. "Hey, Ma, got a bat for me?" May Williams could come up with nothing. "A helluva house," Ted said. "Haven't even got a bat here." So Ted proceeded to shadow-hit, taking full imaginary cuts to demonstrate how his swing had evolved, the throw rug gathering under his feet as he swung and as May's guests watched, transfixed.

Before the first game the following day at Lane Field, Ted put on a show in batting practice, smashing four over the right-field fence onto Pacific Highway. Ted and Foxx each hit homers for their team, the San Diego All-Stars, who were managed by Cedric Durst, Williams's old teammate from the Padres.

On November 11, Joe DiMaggio was named the American League's Most Valuable Player. The sportswriters had voted, and DiMaggio garnered 291 points compared to Ted's 254. Colonel Egan called the

---

★ The tour had been organized by Foxx, who needed the money after losing $45,000 in a golf-club venture in Florida. Williams had wanted to go fishing and skip the tour but agreed to go as a favor to Foxx, knowing of his financial problems. The trip didn't generate as much money as Foxx had hoped, so when it was over, Ted returned the $2,500 he had been guaranteed to his teammate.

decision a "crying sin and shame," and a *Sporting News* fan poll concluded, by a margin of 55 to 26, that the award should have gone to Williams.

But Ted didn't squawk. He acknowledged that the streak was a singular accomplishment—and besides, the Yankees had won the World Series. In any event, he was keeping his head down in Minnesota, back for another winter of hunting and romance. The activities took place in that order, if Doris Soule's plaintive poem of November 28, commemorating the first anniversary of their meeting, was any indication:

> It's just a year ago today
> That Ted and I first met,
> And yet I cannot think of it
> Unless my eyes are wet
>
> For here I sit just drinking Cokes
> And waiting for the phone,
> While Ted sits on some blasted lake,
> I sit here all alone.
>
> I think of Ted — Ted thinks of ducks
> Oh — vicious life I lead!!!
> Sometimes I wish that I could be
> A "Mallard" in the weeds.
>
> For then attention I would get
> If only with a gun
> For as it is now everyday
> I just see him on the run
>
> But after all an anniversary
> Doesn't mean so much
> Especially when there's such a thing
> As an open season on ducks!!

Nine days later, Pearl Harbor was bombed, and shortly thereafter, the United States declared war against Japan. Three days after that, the United States declared war upon Germany and Italy. World War II was on. Doris suddenly had a new worry about her man, and Ted geared up for a vastly different 1942.

7

3A

On the morning of Pearl Harbor, Ted had been out hunting ducks. When he returned to his room at the Gagen Hotel in Princeton, Minnesota, he heard the news on the radio.

"Frankly, none of this war talk had meant a damn to me up to then," Williams later wrote.[1] "I had read where some admiral had said if the Japanese got too frisky we could take them in six months, so I'd pretty much dismissed them as a threat. Hitler had been giving Europe fits, and things were looking bad all over, but it hadn't sunk in on me yet. All I was interested in was playing ball, hitting the baseball, being able to hunt, making some money."

In other words, he was self-absorbed. He certainly didn't react to Pearl Harbor the way Bob Feller did, which was to enlist in the Navy two days later.

With the notable exception of Hank Greenberg, few pro ballplayers had been called up in 1941, when the US role in the war was confined to financial and logistical support of Great Britain and the Allies under the Lend-Lease program. Greenberg had been drafted into the Army in May and released two days before Pearl Harbor. After the bombing, he signed back up and would serve until mid-1945.

But Feller and Greenberg were baseball anomalies. Among major leaguers, there was no mass rush to enlist following Pearl Harbor, especially after President Roosevelt told Commissioner Landis that baseball should carry on with its schedule for the sake of the nation's morale and sense of normalcy.

Williams thus felt he had been granted at least some latitude to savor the grandeur of his luminous 1941 season.

"All right," he told the writer Cleveland Amory in a piece for the *Saturday Evening Post,* "so I think I'm one helluva hitter. Well, all I'm asking is, suppose I stop thinking it, then who do you suggest is going to?"

Amory, fresh out of Harvard and five years away from publishing his seminal satire, *The Proper Bostonians,* was charmed and disarmed by Ted as he watched him prance around the room where they met, a suite at the Shoreham Hotel in Washington, swinging a wet towel as he spoke. At one point, Williams stopped, gazed down at the hotel guests gathered by the swimming pool, and said, "How would you like to be really rich?"

Amory was struck by Ted's naked ambition, his rebelliousness, his disdain for mediocrity, and by what Bob Feller told him when the writer called to ask how good Williams really was: "The pitcher never lived who could throw it by him."

Among the many stories Ted told Amory, one stood out as particularly delightful. A few years earlier, following the dedication of the Hall of Fame in Cooperstown, and apparently soon after the contretemps over his throwaway line about wanting to be a fireman, Ted had secretly visited the new shrine to baseball.

"As soon as he got the chance, the Kid stole away all by himself and wandered into the little building where he longs someday to be remembered," Amory wrote. "For a long time he stood in awe among the various busts, plaques, records and bats. He read every line. After he had gone out he thought no one had seen him. He was even sure of it. But a few days later, back in Boston, he received a letter at his hotel. On the head of the envelope was a name and after it the words, 'Chairman, Cooperstown Committee, Cooperstown, N.Y.' The Kid could not believe it—it was sooner than even he had expected. He tore it open." But a town father was merely writing to inform Ted that he had been named Cooperstown's honorary fire chief.

In 1941, Williams's draft board in Minneapolis had classified him 3A because he was the sole supporter of his mother. Though May and Sam Williams would not be officially divorced until May 14, 1942, they had been separated since April of 1939, when Sam had run off with Minnie Dickson and settled in the San Francisco area. Ted's father had not seen fit to send May any money since then, and Danny Williams was of no help to his mother. Moreover, Danny was preparing to enlist, so the responsibility for May's support—the Salvation Army paid her little or nothing, and she was in poor health—had fallen totally on Ted. He'd been giving her money since he first joined the Red Sox and often had the team send her his payroll checks directly.

In November of 1941, Ted's draft board had asked him to have his mother submit affidavits attesting to her financial and medical condition. This apparently prompted May to conclude that Ted either would be or had already been reclassified 1A: eligible for induction. When a San Diego paper quoted her as saying that Ted had, in fact, been called up, a spokesman for Hennepin County Draft Board 6, in Minneapolis, denied the report, saying Ted was still 3A.

But Pearl Harbor changed the military and political calculus for the Hennepin County board and hundreds of others across the country. About four weeks later, after Pearl Harbor, Ted was notified that he was 1A. He was ordered to report for a physical in Minneapolis on January 8.

In his initial public comments about his reclassification, Williams was chipper and seemingly enthused about going off to war, cracking that it would be fun to serve with Hank Greenberg. "If they can't put me in Hank's company, I hope they put me in Company B," said Ted. "You know old Company B: 'B there when they go and B there when they come back.' "[2]

But that quote was just for public consumption. Privately, Ted was miffed, and he couldn't understand why his draft status had been changed. He plainly was the sole supporter of his mother and could easily document that. She depended on him, Pearl Harbor or no Pearl Harbor, so on the same day that he told the writers he hoped he could be in Company B, Williams consulted a lawyer.

The lawyer, Wendell Rogers, was a Selective Service adviser appointed by the governor of Minnesota. Rogers was supposed to serve as an honest broker between draftees and the government regarding the circumstances of individual cases. Williams asked Rogers if the draft laws had changed as a result of Pearl Harbor. Rogers said he didn't think so. They discussed his situation, and Rogers asked Ted if he wanted him to appeal the 1A classification to a state appeals board. Williams said yes.

On January 8, Ted appeared before his draft board and passed an initial Army physical as a scrum of reporters and photographers recorded the event. The *Record* of the ninth ran a front-page picture of Ted getting his eyes examined. "I guess they need more men," a more subdued Williams remarked.

Within a week, the Red Sox announced they had received written word from Ted that he would have his final Army physical at Fort Snelling in Saint Paul on January 25 and probably be inducted into the service soon after that. Ted added that it was doubtful he'd be able to make the January 28 dinner given by the Boston baseball writers, who had voted to give him their MVP award for 1941.

So as far as the public and the Red Sox knew, Williams was bound for the Army. His appeal effort was a secret. That changed on January 23, two days before the final physical at Fort Snelling was to have taken place, when local draft board spokesman William Price announced that Williams's case had been successfully appealed and his induction postponed indefinitely. Price said a board agent had asked the state appeals panel to consider whether May Williams would be left without support if Ted was drafted. "Williams did not appeal the case himself," said Price, charitably.[3]

The press made little of Price's announcement, treating it as a pro forma exercise by Williams that had little chance of success, and despite the hyperpatriotic milieu, refrained at this stage from any suggestion that Ted was a slacker. Then on January 28, Williams called Eddie Collins to let the Red Sox know that the state appeals board had turned him down, voting 5–0 to keep his 1A classification intact.[4] The reasons for this reversal would soon be made clear, but neither the draft officials nor the Red Sox made the decision public. As far as the fans knew, Ted was still 3A.

Ted went back to confer with Wendell Rogers to see if he was at the end of the line or whether any other options remained. Rogers introduced Williams to John Fagre, another Selective Service lawyer. Like Rogers, Fagre concluded that Ted deserved to be 3A, so they went to their boss, Minnesota Selective Service director Colonel J. E. Nelson, to discuss the case.

After the meeting, as Williams recounted it later, Rogers and Fagre told him they were informed by Nelson that "ordinarily this would be a 3A case, but this case is an exception."[5] When asked why, Nelson didn't explain. The colonel did say that Williams had a final recourse, which would be to appeal his case to Washington, where it would be heard by a national Selective Service board that reported to the president. Nelson would authorize this step if Williams could convince the appeals agent in Minnesota, Herbert Estrem, of the merits of his case, and if Estrem would then agree to file the appeal on his behalf. When Estrem looked into May Williams's situation, he learned that she was officially considered disabled, that she'd undergone a recent operation (paid for by Ted) and needed more medical attention, and furthermore, that Ted had invested in annuities for his mother and paid to have her house remodeled. Correspondence with relevant authorities convinced him she had no means of support besides Ted.

Estrem concluded that the local board would not have changed Ted's 3A classification if he had been earning an average salary. He thought officials incorrectly assumed that because he was well paid as a star baseball player he had enough money saved to take care of his mother and thus could be shifted to 1A. "Yet I discovered that like many other youths of his age, Williams has spent much of his money, and taxes had taken [a] considerable [amount of it], along with the support he gave his mother," Estrem would tell reporters later. "The result was he actually had very little money, certainly not enough to continue support for his mother were he called into the Army as a private."

Estrem had also taken note of President Roosevelt's decision to allow baseball to continue during the war and concluded that "not only Williams but many others were in a ticklish situation and...some definite ruling had to be forthcoming from Washington....I decided to appeal to the President, still believing Williams should be in class 3A, and sent my certification that unusual hardship would take place for his mother were he not deferred."

Although Estrem filed the appeal, the law required that Williams not only had to approve it but also officially request it. When the two discussed taking the case to Washington, Estrem said that Ted was initially reluctant, apparently wary of bad press. "I had to ask him and he replied, 'I don't know as I would appeal. If I get called, I'll report for duty,'" Estrem said. But ultimately, Ted approved.[6] The presidential appeal was filed February 1—again in secrecy. Ted did not tell the Red Sox, who still had not announced that he'd been turned down by the state board.

Reporters already had the Kid virtually in boot camp. The *Sporting News* of January 29 ran a cartoon of Williams in uniform firing a rifle with the caption: "If Uncle Sam gives Ted a uniform, th' guy'll certainly be dressed to kill!" The *Globe's* Hy Hurwitz, who had just enlisted in the Marine Corps (a photograph of him wearing his uniform had been published in the paper), assumed in his notes column of February 3 that Ted would be inducted any day because he "hasn't a chance of being deferred."

Yet as the days rolled by, the writers got restless and sensed something was happening on the Williams front. By the seventh, the Red Sox had mailed out contracts to all its players for the 1942 season, including Ted.[7] "This should not be a tremendous problem to solve," Dave Egan wrote. "He is just a number that was drawn out of a barrel in Washington, and he should be treated exactly like every other number."[8]

But the general mood of the nonsports press was less egalitarian. The *Globe* held up to front-page ridicule local men who resisted joining up, and the paper was delighted to note that one of its columnists, Dorothy Thompson, had punched out a woman who had shouted "Heil Hitler" on the dance floor at a nightclub in New York. On February 26, the *Globe* did a piece about the sons of National Hockey League owners who were off to war.[9]

Meanwhile, Ted had been lying low in Minnesota. When his contract arrived, he couldn't believe the figure: $30,000—more than a 60 percent raise over the previous year. "The end of the rainbow," he called it later, and he put the document in his wardrobe trunk for safekeeping.[10] Ted's resolve to fight his reclassification and play the 1942 season was hardening. His 3A was legitimate. The law was the law. Egan had it right: he shouldn't be singled out as Ted Williams; he should be treated just like any other guy. So the morning of February 27, Ted called Eddie Collins to accept the terms of his new contract.

Then that afternoon, the news finally arrived from Washington, via Minnesota: Ted was officially 3A again. National Selective Service System director Lewis B. Hershey informed the Hennepin County Draft Board in Minneapolis that President Roosevelt's advisory panel had reversed the local board's induction notice and concluded that Williams's case for a deferment based on being the sole supporter of his mother was legitimate.

Though elated, Williams felt placed on the defensive when he commented about the ruling. "I had nothing to do with the draft deal," he told a reporter. "I just made a routine report. The appeal did not come from me." The headline over the United Press story in the *Evening Globe* of the twenty-seventh was: I HAD NOTHING TO DO WITH DRAFT DEAL— WILLIAMS. The story indicated that a national appeal was rare, and reported that Massachusetts had had no more than a dozen people appeal their draft status to the presidential board since the Selective Service law went into effect in 1940.

At spring training in Sarasota, the Red Sox reacted with ambivalence. Press-savvy Joe Cronin was delighted from a baseball standpoint but clearly worried that the writers and the public would conclude that the fix was in, that somehow Williams had been accorded special treatment at the urging of the Red Sox. Cronin felt compelled to stress that Ted would surely fight if eventually called upon to do so.

Eddie Collins told the *Globe*'s Harold Kaese that the team had not known that Ted appealed to the presidential board. "The news that Williams was placed in 3A by the president hit me like a bolt out of the blue," said Collins. "People who think the Red Sox had anything to do with Williams being deferred are crazy, that's all."

Kaese, reflecting the skeptical initial press reaction to the deferment, wrote that Ted had had plenty of challenges in his short career thus far. "If he clears this challenge of public opinion, that .406 batting average will seem puny by comparison."[11] Five out of six people interviewed by the *Globe* said they opposed the deferment. But the only serviceman in the group, a Marine, said whatever Washington decided was okay with him.

George Carens of the *Traveler,* usually a reliable pro-Williams voice, wrote that the general reaction to Ted's deferment is that "it smells." Carens added: "I personally do not think that Williams will be able to continue baseball while the roar of the crowd rises against him."

But Sam Cohen, the *Record* sports editor who loved Williams, wrote a rare editorial headlined THE KID MADE NO APPEAL, in which he argued that the decision was consistent with FDR's green light to baseball and that Ted had "talked gleefully about dropping his bat and taking up a gun and knocking some Japs out of the park."[12]

On February 28, recognizing they had a significant public relations problem on their hands, the Red Sox summoned the writers to the Sarasota Terrace Hotel for a faux press conference. There, Joe Cronin spoke by phone to Ted in Minnesota, and the Kid's words were piped in via speakerphone. This session, in which questions from reporters were not entertained, was to serve as a stopgap measure and allow Williams to offer some, but not all, details of what had happened on the draft front. Upon his arrival in Sarasota, he'd submit to a full cross-examination by the writers.

"Neither I nor any member of my family took any appeal to the ruling, which put me in class 1A," Ted began, saying that the initiative had come from Herbert Estrem, a member of his Minneapolis draft board. "He never discussed the matter with me, nor I with him."

Ted claimed he'd been "too stunned to think" about the deferment, and that "right up to Friday morning [the twenty-seventh] I expected an induction order at any minute and I was ready to go. Then came the president's decision. There's really nothing more I can say in the matter. I've been completely in the dark as to what was going on right from the start. I registered and filled out my questionnaire. I was put in class 3A without saying anything. Then I was placed in class 1A. I figured if that was where the board felt I belonged, then I belonged there. So I accepted the ruling without comment. What's happened since, while I daily awaited word to join the Army, was brought about by the agent of the board. That's the whole story. . . .

"If it had been finally ruled that I should enter the Army, it would have been all right with me. Now that it has been decided that I should go on supporting my mother, that's all right with me. I only hope folks won't think I brought about this change in my draft status. Gee, I had nothing to do with it. I want folks to like me. I'm not going to pop off. I'm always ready to do what the authorities think best. And now, Cronin, what are you expecting me to do?"

When Cronin suggested that he fly down to Florida to get there sooner, Ted replied: "Nothing doing; I'm coming in my own car."[13]

Ted added that "the quickest route to a solution of this whole matter is to earn some big dough this year, then just as soon as I lay down my bat in September or October, I'm in the Navy. And quick, too. I certainly do not feel I have committed any crime or done anything dishonest; and if I wasn't sincere I wouldn't be picking what is not going to be any bed of roses."

That last statement about wanting to "earn some big dough this year," delivered without any mention of his need to pay off the annuities he'd established for his mother, came off as harshly selfish at a time of national sacrifice, and the Red Sox were not pleased. Tom Yawkey issued a statement the next day saying that Ted's decision "in all likelihood will affect not only his entire baseball career but his life as well."[14] The owner's clear implication was that he hoped his star would enlist sooner rather than later.

Then Herbert Estrem came forward to make his first public comment about the Williams case and essentially corroborated Ted's account — except the part about not having discussed the case with him. Estrem said that after the 1A reclassification, Ted and his lawyer came to see him, and that the meeting had taken place at his initiative, not Ted's. "I am supposed to be a disinterested party seeing that both the government and Uncle Sam get a fair deal. I saw Williams only that one time. It was on my own initiative. I decided to appeal his case. Williams said he was not eager to enter his own appeal."[15]

The *Boston Post* sent a reporter to San Diego to try to determine the extent to which May Williams was reliant on her famous son for support. In the resulting March 3 story, which carried no byline, the *Post* reported that while it had been unable to contact May herself, neighbors defended Ted and the decision of the presidential board. They said that Mrs. Williams was, in fact, dependent on Ted for support; that she was in poor health; that she'd had one operation, which Ted paid for, and that she needed another. They said Ted had paid $2,500 to have May's house remodeled the previous year, that he had bought her $1,000 worth of furniture, and that he was sending her weekly support payments. They also said May had told them that Ted had written her with instructions not to do anything that would result in his being given special consideration, though she'd earlier filed an affidavit with his draft board attesting to his support of her.

Then Colonel Nelson, the Minnesota Selective Service director, weighed in. In a call to the Associated Press "just to set the record straight," he said he wanted it known that contrary to the impression left by Herbert Estrem, Ted had sought his deferment himself.[16] Nelson said he had conferred with Williams's attorney and told him the issue could not be appealed to the president without Ted himself asking for it. The attorney talked to Williams, who confirmed he wanted his case reviewed and then notified Estrem that he wished to appeal.

The conflict between Nelson's and Estrem's version of events, if there was one, seemed mostly about emphasis and about the technical, bureaucratic requirement that the man on whose behalf the appeal was being filed, Williams, had to officially request it.

Replying to the AP, Estrem said: "I think the word 'request' is too strong, although technically he did request it. That is the only way an appeal would be taken. . . . Of course the boy wanted to play baseball, but that was just one of the subjects on his mind when he conferred with me."

The Williams deferment quickly became topic A in Boston and beyond and would remain a major story in the papers for months. It had all the elements: a whiff of favoritism and the shirking of duty at a time of overwhelming national unity and surging patriotism; self-interest versus the national interest—all tempered by the facts of the case, which were undeniably on Williams's side. He was, in fact, the sole supporter of his mother and had been for some time. The law provided for a deferment under such circumstances, and thousands upon thousands of them had been duly awarded to anonymous men unburdened by Ted's brand of lightning-rod celebrity.

Colonel Egan kept up his egalitarian, against-the-grain defense of Ted, noting that in this case, the rule of law had been followed with a "meticulousness that is not present in Hitler's Germany." He condemned the reported man-on-the-street view—that Ted was getting special treatment. "It makes no difference that thousands of obscure men previously had been deferred in the same manner and for the same reason," Egan wrote, satirizing the reasoning of the uninformed unwashed. "This is a professional athlete! This is a demi-God of the diamond! This is an idol of the youth of America! So into the Army with him and to hell with the rights or wrongs of it!"[17]

But Quaker Oats, which had paid Ted $4,000 to endorse its cereal, thought the body politic had concluded that Ted's position was untenable and thus bad for business, so it canceled their contract. Williams seethed at the slight and would never eat a Quaker Oats product again.

Worried that there was additional money out there to be lost, Ted's business manager, James A. Silin, sent his client a telegram advising him to throw in the towel and enlist promptly. "Your baseball career as well as your patriotism and your future happiness for many years to come are at stake," Silin wrote Ted. "If you enlist, you will gladden the hearts and stir the Americanism of thousands of kids to whom you have been and should always remain an idol. Don't let those kids down, Teddy. If you accept deferment from the Army, you will ruin the greatest baseball career of all time."[18] Silin gave a copy of his wire to the papers, a move that may have shortened his tenure in the Kid's employ.

Then Joe Cronin, concerned about the prevailing winds, wrote his star and suggested he visit Mickey Cochrane, the former Tigers catcher, who had enlisted in the Navy and landed softly at Naval Station Great Lakes, where he was running the athletic program. Ted agreed, flew into Chicago, and drove up to the base, on the shores of Lake Michigan. Cochrane drove Ted around in his new Lincoln Continental "all decked out in his Navy uniform, buttons shining like mad, and he gave me the big pitch," Williams recalled. "I met a few of the guys, and I'm weakening. I'm about to enlist right now.

"Then he says, 'Gee, it's going to be awful tough to play ball. You try to play ball this summer, they'll boo you out of every park in the big leagues.' Boy, I saw fire. I said to myself, 'I don't give a damn who they boo or what they do. I've heard plenty of boos. I'm going to play ball if I can.' "

Then Ted said Tom Yawkey "got into the act" by telling him he did not think it would be smart for him to go to spring training. "That was the first mistake the Red Sox made with me. I made up my mind I was going to go anyway. All I could think about was that big contract, and the very fact that I was entitled to be 3A, and now for the first time in my life I would be able to get my mother out of hock a little."[19]

After returning to Minnesota, Williams announced on March 5 that he intended to play out the season, after which he would enlist. "While deferred from the draft in a 3A classification, I made certain financial commitments," he said in a statement issued by the Red Sox. "I must carry through with them. Therefore, despite a strong urge to enter the service now, I have decided to play ball with the Red Sox this summer. That will enable me to fulfill my obligation to my family and make everything right all around."[20]

His statement came the same day that columnist Bill Cunningham cast fundamental doubt on Ted's 3A claim and warned that he had "better have a challenge-proof excuse, if he wants to hold his head up among men for the rest of his days."[21] A few days later, Cunningham suggested that Tom Yawkey take over payments to Ted's mother, then fire his left fielder if he refused to go to war.

By March 9, two days after Williams had set out by car from Minnesota, expectations were running high in Sarasota for his expected arrival the next day. Writers from Boston, New York, and Chicago had gathered, along with half a dozen newsreel cameramen.[22] Also waiting for Ted was a raft of fan mail, including one letter containing two blank sheets of paper that were yellow — the color of cowardice.[23]

He arrived at 6:50 p.m. on March 10, completing a three-day, 1,700-mile drive from Minnesota, which included three hours wasted in Nashville trying to cash a check when no one believed he was the real Ted Williams.

The clubhouse was nearly empty. He picked out one of Dom DiMaggio's bats and took it out to swing on the field, alone except for Johnny and Vince Orlando. No one else noticed at first, then trainer Win Green spotted him from the hotel. The press was alerted.

Cronin greeted him briefly in the locker room, saying, "Hi, Meat." Then Williams showered and emerged to face about a dozen writers, with whom he knew he had to speak in detail. "Glad to see you fellows again," he began. "I hope the people in Boston will be glad to see me. I realize I'm sitting on the hot seat. I suppose I'm a so-and-so in Boston. But if that's the case, I'll have to try and grin and bear it. I think I can too, because I know in my heart I'm entitled to deferment and right in taking the course I've chosen. I'm not popping off. Everything I say is honest."

Ted revealed that he had stayed an extra day in Minnesota in order to speak by phone with American League president William Harridge, who gave Ted his blessing and advised him to keep his chin up. Williams said he'd handled his appeal by the book and described his financial situation in detail, saying he'd spent more than he made in 1939, broke even in 1940, and saved a little last year. With his savings, he'd invested $6,000 in three annuities for his mother, which he said he'd lose if he didn't keep up payments by playing this year.

"Baseball is awfully important to me," he said. "This war, of course, is more important, but I just feel I'm as much entitled to this season of baseball as anyone in the country with a legitimate classification for dependency.... I'm Ted Williams. That's why I've been getting all this. I'll bet you there are 100 cases the same as mine in the big leagues. But do you hear any popping off about them? No sir. Just on Ted Williams."

He said he'd made every decision on his own. "And I guess I'm pretty much all alone right now.... I know it's going to be tough. But I'm sure that if the fans can learn all the facts and will look at them fairly, they'll be pulling for me before the season is over."[24]

Williams checked into the Sarasota Terrace Hotel, where they paid their respects by assigning him room 406.[25]

The early fan reaction was pro-Ted. In the Red Sox's 6–5 exhibition loss to the Reds in Sarasota the following day, Williams emerged to make his first public appearance of the spring by pinch-hitting in the sixth. On being introduced, he was received with "thunderous applause" from the pro-Sox crowd of eight hundred people, reported Joe Cashman in the *Record,* with not a dissenter audible. He drove one ball four hundred feet, but foul, before striking out on a 3–2 pitch at his ankles.

A more significant test came four days later in Tampa, during another game against the Reds. The game was played before 3,747 people, almost half of whom were soldiers from nearby bases. The soldiers cheered Williams loudly, swarming around him before the game to the point where he couldn't take batting practice. Ted signed hundreds of autographs, then was asked to do a radio interview that would be sent to the troops overseas. The soldiers mobbed him after the game, too, delaying the team bus. This buoyed Williams's spirits considerably — after all, soldiers were the most important constituency, and if they were with him, civilians would seem to have less cause to be upset.

Over breakfast with Huck Finnegan of the *American* a week later, Ted said he'd received about two hundred letters so far, with reaction to his deferment split fifty-fifty. He noted that those against him seemed to be less educated than those who were for him. "I've noticed that the mudslingers border on the illiterate side; that the encouraging letters come from well-bred persons," he said. So far, so good in spring training, but he expected trouble up north, especially in Washington, Detroit, and Cleveland. "But I'll just keep my mouth shut and tend to my knitting, I mean my hitting," he said, smiling.[26]

Still, the harsh early reaction to his deferment in many of the papers and from some fans who wrote to him would stay with Williams for the rest of his life. "What a howl!" he remembered years later. "You would have thought Teddy Ballgame bombed Pearl Harbor himself. Unpatriotic. Yellow. Those were the milder epithets."[27]

The reaction that Williams cared about most, of course, was that of Red Sox fans, and among those, he confided to the *Globe*'s Gerry Moore as the team made its way north, the only group he couldn't tolerate not being with him was the kids.

His first Fenway Park appearance of the year came on April 12 in the annual exhibition game against the Boston Braves. It was bitterly cold, and there were snow flurries, but a crowd of nine thousand turned out and roared its approval of Ted, drowning out a smattering of boos. Out in the bleachers, six hundred soldiers, sailors, and Marines seemed unanimously for him.

"That was swell," Ted said of the reaction. "It certainly was great. They were ninety-eight percent for me, weren't they?"

Williams's acute rabbit ears had pinpointed the few dissenters: two kids in the left-field grandstand and a guy in the bleachers. "I could hear them," he said. "That fellow in right had a loud voice, and those kids in left gave it to me all through the game." The *Globe*'s Harold Kaese had gone down to interview the kids, and Kaese told Ted that one of them had said he had two brothers off in the Army, stationed in Australia.

"There'll be people like that," Williams replied philosophically. "They'll feel pretty bitter, maybe, and say things, but it's great to know that most of the fans in Boston are for me."

The writers concluded that Ted had cleared a huge hurdle. They all had been waiting for the first Fenway reaction as a guidepost for the season's story line. "Ted's in now," a reporter, overheard by Kaese, had remarked in the press box. "All he's got to do is mind his p's and q's, and throw in some base hits and homers."[28]

On opening day—two days later—Ted received more applause from the seventeen thousand fans in attendance, and that only ratified the exhibition verdict. Ted responded by hitting the fifth pitch of his first at bat over the bull pen into the bleachers for a three-run homer. He got two more hits, five RBIs on the day, and even threw out a runner trying to leg out a double as the Sox beat the Athletics, 8–3.

Colonel Egan called the opening day reception a vindication—not of Ted, who, he said, needed none, but of New England and "John Quincy Public." The fans were "telling the world that we do not tar and feather men and ride them away on a rail," Egan wrote. "That we will not be stampeded into doing an injustice by the loud voices of a few zealots; that we can use our heads for more than a hat rack, and can think things through correctly. It was an exhibition of good, old fashioned common sense."[29]

The Red Sox won two more games from the A's to sweep the series and then set out for New York, where fifty thousand people, including two thousand soldiers, filled Yankee Stadium. In his first road test, Williams was cheered. This was added evidence of popular support for Ted's decision to play ball and, more broadly, for wartime baseball. FDR had been right: the country did need touchstones of normalcy as its servicemen fought battles around the world. Baseball was proving to be a tonic for the masses, not simply an indulgence for the players.

Still, news from the sports page paled against the life-and-death dispatches from the war unfolding daily on the front page. April 18 brought one of the first welcome headlines in months: sixteen American B-25 bombers based on the USS *Hornet* in the Pacific had successfully pierced Japanese air defenses and bombed Tokyo. The country felt a surge of pride. REMEMBER PEARL HARBOR read the *Globe* headline.[30] Less than three weeks later, aircraft carriers from the United States and Japan clashed off New Guinea in the Battle of the Coral Sea, a precursor to the Battle of Midway a month later. While America lost the carrier *Lexington,* it sank a light Japanese carrier and gained a strategic victory by preventing Tokyo from landing troops to take Port Moresby, in New Guinea. With war fever running high, the Armed Forces were taking out recruiting ads in the papers saying: "If you are itching to be in the thick of the fight, and you'd like to slip those Japs and Nazis a man-sized dose of their own medicine, then here's your chance to do something about it."[31]

In this climate, Williams began to rethink his position. He'd made his decision, made his stand. He had responsibilities to his mother and had therefore been entitled to his 3A. He wasn't going to forsake it or be pushed. He would act on his timetable, not someone else's. He hadn't completed a loop around the league yet, but the fans in Boston and New York had greeted him warmly and respected his decision. To a certain extent, he had already made his point. He didn't want to overplay his hand, and he wanted to do the right thing. Yet he still had to earn enough money to pay off those annuities for his mother. Maybe there was a way to enlist while still being allowed to play out the year to meet his financial obligations.

On April 29, following a loss to the Tigers at Fenway Park, Williams was introduced to Lieutenant Robert "Whitey" Fuller of the Navy by Red Sox publicist Ed Doherty. Fuller, a former sports publicist for Dartmouth College, urged Ted to take a discreet look at the Navy's V-5 flight preparation program at Naval Air Station Squantum in Quincy, just south of Boston. Ted agreed, and on the morning of May 6—unbeknownst to any reporters—the two men drove down to Squantum as the Battle of the Coral Sea raged in the Pacific.

Ted spent three hours at the base, talking baseball and aviation with the enlisted men. He climbed into the cockpit of a hornet-yellow training plane, played with the gadgets, looked over the instrument panel, and pulled on the pilot's stick. If he liked, they told him, he now was eligible to become a Naval aviator, because the educational requirements for that program had just been lowered so that high school graduates could apply. Commander James A. Voit of San Diego sat with him in the cockpit. Voit had known of Ted in their hometown, but they hadn't met. Voit needled Williams that he'd only hit six home runs as of that day. The Kid also visited a gunnery class, a machine shop, and a hangar, and had lunch at the officers' mess.

Ted was impressed. Here was a chance to rekindle his childhood fondness for aviation—in a most dramatic fashion. (One of his most vivid memories was of the Navy's USS *Shenandoah,* a two-million-cubic-foot dirigible that arrived in San Diego in 1924.) He liked Voit and the rest of the fellows he'd met. He liked their work, their mission, and their soft sell. Unlike Mickey Cochrane out at Great Lakes, they weren't pushing him. They were letting him make up his own mind. In principle, he was sold, and on the drive back to Fenway Park for a game against the White Sox, Ted signed an application to join the Navy. But nothing could be announced until he passed his physical and an aptitude test. So the Navy and Williams agreed to sit on the news for about two weeks, until the Red Sox returned from a road trip.

After a win over the White Sox that afternoon, Ted repaired to his room on the eighth floor of the Shelton Hotel. That night, the Red Sox were supposed to leave for Philadelphia for the start of a twelve-day tour that would also take them to Chicago, Saint Louis, Detroit, and Cleveland. But Williams's mind was racing. He called his confidant, clubhouse man Johnny Orlando, and summoned him to his room. When Orlando arrived, Williams hadn't packed for the road trip and was sitting in a chair in the middle of the room, trying out a new fishing rod he'd just bought. He was casting out an open window.

"To hell with everything," Ted said. "I'm going into the Navy right now."

Orlando counseled against doing anything rash: Ted should keep playing as long as he could. Try and finish out the season. Things were in turmoil, and the Navy wasn't even ready for him yet. But Ted said he was tired of the distractions and the controversy. He'd made up his mind.

Then there was a knock on the door. It was Eddie Collins. The GM had somehow gotten wind of trouble brewing with Williams. Ted repeated everything he'd told Orlando. He was quitting and joining the Navy now. He had just wanted to finish out the year to earn enough money to pay off those three annuities.

Collins advised Ted not to enlist now. "Eddie didn't want to keep him out of the service, but he realized, too, that the wild rush to join the Armed Forces had created a traffic jam and the Kid should wait," Orlando recalled. But Collins told him that the Red Sox would make up any earnings shortfall whether he finished the season or not, so that he could meet his obligations to his mother. "Consider it taken care of," he said.[32]

This was a significant statement by the team, which, had it been made earlier, might have persuaded Williams to enter the service months ago and rendered the Red Sox's public relations concerns moot. In any case, the financial assurances from Collins eased Ted's mind greatly and were all he needed to hear to resolve his immediate predicament: he quickly packed his bag, then he and Orlando hurried to the train station for the trip to Philadelphia.

Williams was booed lustily at Shibe Park, but it no longer seemed to be because he was 3A—it was just that he was the leading enemy villain again. He'd been hitless until the ninth inning of the third and final game of the series, and the hooting had increased with each out he'd made. Then, when he belted a two-run homer out of the park entirely and onto a roof across 20th Street, the crowd of twenty-five thousand stood and cheered, in what *Traveler* writer John Drohan called "an interesting study in mob psychology." Ted said of the earlier fan treatment: "They booed me because I didn't hit. Well, if I haven't been a good hitter, they wouldn't have bothered to boo me."[33]

Ted's mind was now made up: he planned to take his physical and his aptitude test on the morning of May 22, after the Red Sox returned from Cleveland. Assuming he passed, he'd announce his enlistment later that day. He'd hoped the Navy would let him play out the year, but if he was called up before the season ended, he now had Collins's promise that the team would bridge whatever gap he might still have in the annuity payments due to his mother.

On the train ride home the night of the twenty-first, Williams hinted at his plans to Huck Finnegan of the *American*. He said he'd received an anonymous letter recently accusing him of being a " 'yellow so-and-so.... You make enough money in a month to keep your mother for three years.'

"I'm not yellow," Ted said. "I'll fight. But I don't want to be rushed into things. I'm going to help my country before this thing is over. Probably a lot sooner than people realize."[34]

When the team train pulled into Boston the next morning, Ted reported to the Naval Aviation Cadet Selection Board at 150 Causeway Street, near North Station. None of his teammates or Red Sox officials knew what he was about to do. He'd written his mother to tell her two days before.

He passed his three-hour physical and aptitude test with flying colors. Then, before being sworn in, Ted called Dave Egan to give him the scoop. Though the Colonel would become his avowed enemy in later years, Ted was grateful for Egan's numerous defenses of the way he'd comported himself on the draft issue, so Egan and a *Record* photographer showed up and got exclusive pictures of the swearing-in. The next day the Colonel and Williams were shown on the front page of the *Record*, smiling as Ted pointed at a recruiting poster.

Asked by Egan why he chose aviation, Ted quipped, "Hell, I've been up in the air for three years. Now I'm beginning to like it!" And why the Navy as opposed to the Army? "Haw! My girl thinks I look sweet in navy blue."[35]

At 6:10 p.m. that evening, Navy officials announced to the rest of the press that Ted Williams had enlisted in the Navy as a seaman second class. It was unclear when he'd have to go in, but he was promised nothing and asked for no favors. "I just want to be in this thing," he said. When someone asked why he'd chosen a branch of the service that could lead to combat, Ted replied, "I like to hit!"

Though everyone knew his eyesight was exceptional, Williams told the writers he'd fretted that a childhood injury he'd sustained to his right eyeball while swatting walnuts with his brother, Danny, might somehow have caused him to fail the eye exam. But the Navy doctors found his eyesight to be twenty-fifteen. That meant that "a certain letter which the average man can read at a maximum of 20 feet, Ted can read at 30 to 35 feet," explained Lieutenant Frank R. Philbrook in briefing the press on Ted's examinations. He said that of Naval aviation applicants Williams's age, only four or five out of one hundred had eyesight that acute, and he added that Williams's depth perception was unusually good—a significant attribute for a pilot.

Ted's blood pressure, pulse rate, and reflexes were all excellent. And "his nerves are very steady," Philbrook reported.*

Though Williams was found to have been well above normal for a high school graduate in aptitude and mechanical tests, Ted said he was worried about that part of the equation. "Like a lot of other kids, I didn't take the right kind of courses in high school," he remarked. "Didn't take the right kind of math or nothing."

Although Ted was making $30,000 per year with the Red Sox, he would be making only $105 a month from the Navy during training and $245 a month when he was commissioned. Still, Williams pronounced himself "tickled to death to be in this thing.... The minute I got in the cockpit of that plane in Squantum, I knew what I wanted." Then he added, softly, "I've tried to do the right thing from the start. I didn't want to be pushed into anything by anybody. I knew I was right all the time. Then this thing came along. It was just what I wanted.... All I want is to get into it and do my best to throw a few curves at the enemy.... I'd like to get into one of those big bombers and lay a few eggs just for the thrill of it before it's over."[36]

---

* One possible obstacle had been narrowly cleared. The tallest a Naval aviator could be was six foot four, and Ted had been measured at six foot three.

Doris Soule surfaced in the next day's *American* to praise her man. "I'm very proud of Ted," she said, "but I'm also frightened. I hope he will be safe, and I hope the war will be over before he gets a chance to fight." She denied reports she and the Kid were about to wed before he went off to war. She said they were not even engaged, and besides, the Navy did not allow its aviators to marry until they were commissioned. While Ted enlisted, Doris did her bit by donating blood to the Red Cross.

The enlistment was breathlessly hailed in the papers. Jerry Nason of the *Globe* wrote that Ted had now "batted 1000 as an American." Austen Lake of the *American* said Ted had "stood up to the measure of American manhood." And Colonel Egan, no doubt grateful for his scoop, also pronounced Ted a man, and he added: "Here's a prediction about Williams. He'll survive whatever hazards and whatever adventures may lie ahead, however long the war may last, for he was originally constructed to ride out all the storms of life. Then he'll come back into baseball, even more of a man. And then he'll become the greatest figure that the game has ever known, which includes a guy by the name of Ruth."

Before long, Williams made an arrangement with the Navy that would ensure he could finish out the season: he signed up for an indoctrination course in math, physics, and navigation. The class of 250 men met for four hours three nights a week at Mechanic Arts High School in Boston. Johnny Pesky, who had followed Ted's lead in deciding to enlist, also attended. The first night, Lieutenant F. T. Donahue surprised Ted by inviting him to come up and address his classmates.

"I only hope I prove myself worthy to go through with you," Ted told the group. "I give you my word I'll do my best."[37]

By June, the United States had decisively won the Battle of Midway in what would later be viewed as the most significant Naval engagement in the war against the Japanese. Tokyo lost four aircraft carriers and a heavy cruiser, and America began to assert its strategic superiority in the Pacific. Williams read of the exploits of Navy and Marine aviators, some of whom would soon be serving as his instructors.[38]

Ted's enlistment, on his own terms and played out to boffo reviews in the papers, had short-circuited whatever isolated fan bleatings that remained over his 3A status, so any fans who wanted to razz the Kid now had to revert to garden-variety heckling over a misplayed ball, an 0–4 day, or some other demonstrable imperfection. Still, that was often sufficient to get a rise out of the hypersensitive and still immature

Williams. The "wolves," as Ted liked to call those fans who baited him from the nearby left-field grandstands at Fenway, seemed especially ready to engage him during a doubleheader on July 1 against the Washington Senators, and he gave them every reason to. The day had begun innocently enough, and Ted seemed in good spirits, chatting with the *Globe*'s Gerry Moore about the effects of twilight and night baseball on hitting. He'd gone 1–3 in the first game and made a nice running catch, contributing to a 3–2 Red Sox win.

But in the first inning of the second game, Stan Spence of the Senators blooped a hit into short left between Pesky, the shortstop, and Williams. A heckler called out from the left-field stands: "Why don't you get off that dime, Ted?"[39] Frosted, Williams glowered at the fan. As the game progressed, his mood grew darker. He seemed to be sulking and going through the motions. By his second time at bat, it "became noticeable he wasn't giving his best," Jack Malaney wrote in the *Post*. After he flied out to center, Ted flung his bat high in the air as he trotted down to first and was booed as he veered back to the dugout after the catch.

His next time up, with runners on first and second, Williams took two strikes right down the middle without even moving his bat. It looked like he intended to take three and sit down to make some kind of perverse protest against fan hazing. Then he intentionally fouled a pitch off in the general direction of the wolves in left. On the fourth pitch, he swung in a lazy, half-baked manner, as if intending to flick another foul at his tormentors, but the ball took off to deep left-center. Surprised, Williams jogged down toward first base and then into second, eschewing a possible triple if he'd run hard. Both runners scored. When Bobby Doerr singled, Ted moved leisurely over to third, then scored on a fielder's choice as the crowd hooted him with a full-throated jeer. When he reached the dugout, Joe Cronin was in his face: "What's the matter? Don't you want to play? Get out of here, then!" And he waved his star into the clubhouse.

It was the third time in his short career that Ted had been pulled from a game by Cronin for one transgression or another, but this was the first time he'd actually appeared disinterested at the plate. This time, Williams knew he didn't have a leg to stand on and berated himself for being a fool as he dressed. He left before the game was finished. The next day, Cronin fined him $250, and Ted fell on his sword.

"I know it was all my fault and Joe did the right thing in taking me out of the game," Williams told the writers. "I'm just thick-headed enough, screwy enough and childish enough to let those wolves in left field get under my skin. Some day I'm going to bring 25 pounds of raw hamburger out there and invite those wolves down to enjoy it....I guess I was just kind of unconscious out there yesterday. I was too lackadaisical. I was going to take three strikes right down the gut. Then I decided I'd try and hit a few line drives at those wolves in left field. I was probably the most surprised guy in the park when I looked up and saw I had hit the fence."

Williams, as was his wont, took umbrage at almost any criticism, especially if he was performing well. Despite all the distractions of the draft controversy, Ted was hitting .336, and he noted that he was leading the league with 17 home runs and 75 RBIs. "What do they want?" he demanded. It was a question from the individual's prism, not the team's. The Red Sox had now won twenty-one of their last twenty-six to draw within three games of the Yankees, from nine and a half in mid-June. And New York was about to come to Fenway for a big three-game series.

The Yankees won two of the three games, and the Red Sox then faded, finishing a distant second to New York. In their end-of-the-year meditations on the season, some of the writers concluded that the early July series was pivotal and blamed Williams's self-indulgence for striking a discordant note at just the wrong time.

Indeed, his selfish and petulant display made it easy for some of the writers who had just sung Ted's praises for enlisting in the Navy to jump off his bandwagon. The Colonel flogged him, saying: "He's not a Splendid Splinter. He's just a splinter." Egan suggested that Ted reconsider his decision to be a Naval aviator and become a commando instead, for "he is a born saboteur."[40]

In the end, Williams put up phenomenal numbers—an average of .356, with 36 homers and 137 RBIs—and won the Triple Crown. But the writers voted to give the Most Valuable Player award to Yankees second baseman Joe Gordon, whose statistics paled by comparison: Gordon had batted .322, hit 18 home runs, and knocked in 103. Gordon was given 270 total points to Williams's 249, and was first on 12 of 24 ballots compared to Ted's 9 of 24. The Globe's Harold Kaese concluded that Ted had lost on "character, disposition, loyalty, and effort."[41]

The announcement came in early November, as Williams was preparing to go off to war. One final piece of business he took care of was to take out a $10,000 life insurance policy in which he named his mother as his beneficiary.[42] His first assignment would be a stint in the Navy's V–5 Civilian Pilot Training Program at Amherst College, in western Massachusetts.

Ted knew he'd be passed over in the MVP balloting by the writers, who mostly detested him, but he was gracious in defeat. "I was glad Gordon got it," he said. "I really think he kept the Yankees up there. Yeah, I wanted it, but I knew I wasn't going to get it, and got it out of my mind. . . . There's a bigger game to think about now."

8

World War II

In the service, Williams did not want to get by on, or trade on, his celebrity. Now that he'd started his commitment, he actually looked forward to the challenge of establishing his military bona fides out of the spotlight, on his own merits. So he was more than a bit chagrined by the fact that the first impression he created when officially reporting for duty in the Navy at Amherst College was that of a puerile personality looking for special attention and treatment.

He had taken a trip to Chicago and arrived back in Boston by train at 3:00 a.m. on November 16. Breakfasting several hours later at the Shelton Hotel, Ted chanced to meet old friend Hugh Duffy, his .400 mentor.

Duffy, who also resided at the Shelton, was surprised to see Ted, assuming that he'd already left for Amherst. Williams said he wasn't due there until two o'clock that afternoon, "Eastern War Time." Further conversation made it apparent that Ted was under the mistaken impression that Amherst was merely a suburb of Boston, not a full ninety miles west of the city. Duffy volunteered to explore train connections from Boston to Springfield, some twenty-five miles from the rustic college town, or to Pittsfield, even farther west, but returned with the news that no connections could come close to getting Williams to his final destination by 2:00 p.m. So while Ted feverishly packed his bags, Duffy arranged for a limousine that could reach Amherst by the appointed hour.[1]

Most of the twenty-nine other Naval Aviation Cadets enrolled in the Civilian Pilot Training Program at Amherst had made far more modest arrivals, via train or bus. Now here was Williams, pulling up in a limo, as if wishing to underscore the fact that he had just won the American League Triple Crown and hit .406 the year before that. Immediately placed on the defensive, Ted waved off various wiseacres who asked about his choice of transport with a mea culpa about not having known where Amherst was, exactly, and having to get there posthaste. Then he quickly set about the process of becoming one of the boys. He was assigned a room in one of the dorms, Genung House, with Joe Coleman, a rookie pitcher for the Athletics. Three other major leaguers were also in residence: Johnny Sain and Buddy Gremp of the Braves and Ted's Red Sox teammate Johnny Pesky. (Pesky was officially listed in Navy records under his true name, John M. Paveskovich.)

The Civilian Pilot Training Program had been launched in early 1939 by Franklin Delano Roosevelt with the goal of providing pilot training to twenty thousand college students a year. The program was designed to provide a shot in the arm for civilian aviation, with the understanding that it would have a military application as well.

In the run-up to World War II, it became clear to the various branches of the US military that its ability to fight a two-front war would be severely limited by a shortage of pilots and training aircraft. Italy and Nazi Germany had already started similar programs and generated thousands of pilots for their war machines, so the military effectively co-opted the Civilian Pilot Training Program and facilitated its graduates' entry as pilots in the Army Air Forces, Navy, and Marine Corps. At its height, the program was operating in 1,132 colleges and 1,460 flight schools.

At Amherst, besides the thirty V-5 cadets, there were also fifteen members of the Army Air Forces' enlisted reserve on campus. The small college, known for its prep school–educated undergraduates, was starting its third year running the eight-week program. There was classroom instruction in math, physics, navigation, meteorology, and the like, as well as a rigorous program of physical training, swimming, and scaling the obstacles and barriers of a commando course. Flying lessons were conducted eighteen miles down the road, at the airport in Turners Falls.

The programs amounted to a proving ground for the students. In the case of the Naval cadets, if they passed muster at Amherst, they would be sent on to preflight school in North Carolina to continue their training and, at that point, officially deemed to be in the Navy. If they washed out, they would be sent back to their draft boards for induction into another service branch. For now, the cadets wore service-neutral generically tailored forest-green uniforms. (A request from Ted for a better fit went unheeded.)

There was considerable curiosity in Boston and beyond about how the Kid was faring in the Armed Forces, so officials at Amherst agreed to set aside December 1 as a day when newspapermen could come out and observe an entire day of the training regimen.

Reveille for the cadets was at 6:45, after which they had ten minutes to dress, wash, shave, and get to breakfast. Then they returned to make their beds and clean their rooms. By 8:00 a.m. they were in the gym for calisthenics, followed by maneuvers on the commando course and then swimming.

"It's great here and I'm really crazy about every bit of it," Ted declared to the assembled reporters. "I'll admit I dreaded coming here because I never have had to take orders before and always did as I pleased, came and went as I wanted to and lived my own life. But I'm really stuck on it all, and I think you know me well enough to know that I'd say so if I didn't like it."

Ted's instructors all sang his praises to the writers: he was eager to learn and expected no favors. "Ted Williams has the making of a super pilot," said Ensign John C. Edgren, adding that the famed Williams temper had so far been a nonissue.[2] "On the contrary, his conduct has been exemplary. Frankly, his superiors are amazed at his attitude. He has been working like a Trojan ever since he reported."

He had six hours of flying to his credit up to that point and was preparing to make his first solo run in a few days. "I was fighting the training ship the first few times I was given the controls," Ted said, "but now I'm handling them instinctively."

Swimming was another matter. Sure, he'd grown up on the water in San Diego, but he revealed to the writers that he'd been afraid to go the beach because he was so skinny. He could swim, but he couldn't do the breast stroke, which the Navy insisted on so that the cadets could always see what was going on around them in the case of a mishap at sea.

Johnny Pesky did his part to cement the emerging Williams-is-adapting-well story line: "Why Ted is going after this flying stuff as hot and heavy as he did about hitting," the shortstop said as number 9 stood nearby, listening.

"Well, I'm not getting .400 in this flying course yet, but I'm going to do it," Williams replied. "Flying is the last thing I'm worrying about. It's a cinch if you just keep thinking and applying yourself. I like it so much that I'd quit baseball for it." That was it—the writers had their story: WILLIAMS WOULD QUIT BASEBALL TO FLY PLANES read the headline in the *Record* over the Associated Press story describing the day at Amherst.

Both the brass and the writers knew Ted was humoring them and merely ingratiating himself with the Navy. (In the next breath, he said the reason he was rooming with young Joe Coleman of the Athletics was "so I can find out what he's got. I'll probably have to hit against him some day.") But never mind. He'd said he might quit the big leagues to become a pilot, so the writers went with it.

Far more demanding than flying was the classroom work, especially math: "Pesky and I, and I guess the rest of the ballplayers here, have grown very rusty about our math because, no doubt, we have been out of school much longer than the rest of the class.... Therefore I crack that math book every time I get the chance. You have to know what mathematics are all about to be a Navy flier."

In fact, Pesky was having problems on several fronts. He was struggling in the classroom, couldn't swim a lick, and had great difficulty flying.[3] The first time he took off, he'd hit the right rudder so hard that the plane almost veered into a lake. The first time he landed, the plane struck the ground with such force that he'd popped up and slammed his head on the roof of the cockpit. Pesky "flew an airplane like he had stone arms," Ted wrote in his book. "One time at Amherst on a real windy day, we were flying Cubs. If you hold a Cub too tight, the wind blows you off the runway. You have to crab, or you have to slip. Poor John lines up the runway and, *whoosh,* the wind blows him away. Around he goes. He tries again and the wind takes him again. He made eight approaches that day. It looked like they were going to have to shoot him down."[4]

Although flying came a lot easier to Williams, he stumbled, too. Once, he was buzzing a bit low over the Connecticut River: "Two of us were flying Cubs and I didn't see some power lines across the river—we were flying upriver—and I just barely cleared at the last second."[5] Summing up the experience, he said, "I damn near killed myself."

In their dispatches from Amherst, the writers noted two other things about the military Williams: as part of his uniform, he was required to wear a necktie, which he'd always shunned. He said it had taken him a while to get used to it, but now it didn't bother him a bit. And the military requirement that he address his superiors as "sir" was becoming so routine that Ted even extended the greeting to some of the reporters. "It was odd for a scribe who had traveled with him since he joined the Sox to hear Ted say, 'It has been nice seeing you again, SIR,' as happened at Amherst," wrote Jack Malaney in the *Sporting News.*[6]

Dr. Warren K. Green, a Harvard-educated astronomy professor who was in charge of Amherst's pilot program, said after the press session that there would not be another. "That was the only day we'll exploit him," Green said of Williams. "He's a Naval Aviation Cadet now, not a ball-player. . . . He's a great boy, and I predict he'll be just as great a flier as he was a batter."[7]

Williams plunged into his daily routine and into campus doings. He enjoyed being around students, and even took time to learn the Amherst fight songs. The Navy WAVES (Women Accepted for Volunteer Emergency Service) based at nearby Smith College were a nice bonus. He had a quick, inquisitive mind, and enjoyed stretching it to absorb heretofore foreign concepts, such as celestial navigation. Pesky, for one, marveled at Ted's learning style. "The guy's perception was uncanny. He mastered complex problems in 15 minutes which took the average cadet an hour."[8]

He so wanted to immerse himself in service life, and to be treated like everyone else, that he spurned an invitation to attend the annual dinner of the New York chapter of the Baseball Writers' Association of America in January.*

One day, Ted's zeal for the task at hand landed him in sick bay. During a competition to see who could do the most chin-ups and push-ups, and to determine who could swim the fastest, Ted came up with a hernia. He had to go to the Chelsea Naval Hospital, outside Boston, for an operation and convalesce until March before he could rejoin his class at its next stop—the Navy Pre-Flight School at the University of North Carolina, Chapel Hill.

"I'll never forget getting off the train in Chapel Hill, just at dusk, and marching up in front of the administration building with the other recruits," Ted remembered. "The cadets already there were hanging out the windows watching us, and as we passed, one guy hollered, 'OK Williams, we know you're there, and *you're going to be sor-ry.*' I never was sorry. All of it was absolutely different from anything I'd ever been through, and even the hairiest times were interesting."[9]

Among the cadets at Chapel Hill then was a future president of the United States: George Herbert Walker Bush. Bush and Williams met only briefly at the time but would become friends later in life. "I was there in the First Battalion," said Bush, who while attending prep school at Phillips Andover Academy, outside Boston, had loved to go in to

---

* The New York writers, perhaps trying to rectify what had been widely seen as an injustice when the Yankees' Joe Gordon was voted the American League MVP over Williams in November, had selected Ted as their "Player of the Year."

Fenway Park to watch Ted. "Everybody was excited that the big hero was coming."[10]

The Navy Pre-Flight School had nothing to do with flight. If the physical regimen at Amherst—calisthenics, swimming, and the commando course—had been rigorous, the drill at Chapel Hill was akin to an all-sports marathon designed to build physical and mental stamina. "They really ran us through the wringer there—up by the light of the moon, double time all day, and to bed with the owls," Pesky told columnist Austen Lake in 1952.[11] "Drill till your tongue bulged.... Sports, hikes, inspections, fatigue. We played all games to test us for versatility— boxing, football, wrestling, swimming, soccer and baseball. The object was to find if we had a nerve cracking point. Some did! A lot of guys, knowing Ted's reputation as a pop-off, waited for him to explode. But he never blew any fuses or got a single bad behavior demerit. If anything, he took a little stiffer discipline than the others, sort of stuff like, 'Oh, you're the great Ted Williams, huh? OK, Mister.' Ted took it all."

Williams enjoyed the novelty of trying different sports, especially boxing. He'd always been a fight buff and admired the toughness and courage of boxers. Now he tried his hand in the ring himself, and the instructor, Lieutenant Al Wolff, thought him skilled and polished. Along with Pesky and the other major leaguers from Amherst, Ted of course joined the Chapel Hill baseball team, the Cloudbusters. Later that summer, the mayor of Boston, Maurice Tobin, prevailed upon the Navy to spring Ted from Chapel Hill for a few days so that he could join a group of service All-Stars on July 12 for an exhibition game against the Boston Braves at Fenway Park. The game would support Tobin's annual charity drive benefiting impoverished children. And a featured attraction, generating more interest than the game itself, was to be a hitting contest between Ted and Babe Ruth. It was the first time the Kid and the Babe had ever met or appeared together. Ruth had a soft spot for Boston because he'd broken in with the Red Sox in 1914 and retired with the Braves in 1935.

Ruth, managing the service team, flew up from New York the day before and stopped in at a doubleheader at Braves Field. Renewing acquaintances with his old pals in the press box, the Bambino tried to boost the gate for the following day. "I'll be out there swinging, you can tell the fans!" he boomed to the writers, though perhaps in deference to Ruth's rustiness and age (he was forty-eight), the writers were calling the match with Ted not a home-run contest but a "distance hitting contest."[12] Some eighteen thousand fans turned out early to watch the festivities, which included appearances by the Army and Coast Guard bands, a drill by a group of WACs, a softball game between city and state officials, and the introduction of thirty retired major leaguers.[13]

Williams, in his Navy dress blues, arrived in the clubhouse before Ruth. Mayor Tobin and a thicket of lesser Boston pols swarmed around the Kid, asking for his autograph on baseballs. Ted cheerfully obliged, signing his name on remote areas of the balls. "I'll leave the honor space for the Babe," he said, referring to the narrow spot between the seams.

Johnny Orlando presented him with two new bats from the factory in Louisville. Told they weighed thirty-five ounces, Williams asked the clubhouse boy to shave them down to thirty-three. He fielded a few calls from the front office and bantered excitedly with the writers about Ruth. "All I've got to say is, if the Babe, at 50 years, without a bat in his hand for a year, can hit one into the right field stands, he's a wonder," said Ted.

Then the other guest of honor strolled into the room. "Hiya, Kid!" boomed the Babe, a black cigar smoldering in his mouth.

"A very great pleasure indeed," replied Williams, both awestruck and tongue-tied.

"You remind me a lot of myself," Ruth continued. "You love to hit. You're one of the most natural ballplayers I've ever seen. And if ever my record is broken, I hope you're the one to do it."

The Babe repaired to Bobby Doerr's locker and stripped to his shorts. He chatted happily with the writers, old-timers, and assorted hangers-on while signing a batch of balls in the sweet spot left for him by Williams. He claimed his weight was down to 231 pounds from the 247 he'd last played at with the Yankees in 1934. Then Johnny Orlando brought him his pin-striped uniform, which bore the number 3, and gave Ted his road-gray flannels. After they finished dressing, they posed for pictures grabbing a bat hand over hand, choosing up sides to see who would hit first.

Williams emerged on the field first to a loud cheer, but it paled next to the sustained ovation given the Babe when he waddled out of the dugout. As the preliminary ceremonies played out, Ted sat in the dugout and told John Drohan of the *Traveler* that he wasn't thinking much about baseball now. "I rarely look at a box score these days," he said. "I couldn't even tell you how much the Yankees are leading by. And you know, when I was playing ball, I had all those things figured out to the Nth degree. But I figure I'm in a bigger game now, one that requires my full and complete attention."

Before the hitting contest began, Ruth stepped to the microphone and proved he'd lost none of his showman's flair. "Boston's my starting town," he told the adoring crowd. "I was mighty sorry to leave for New York. Of course, I got lots more dough when I went there." He paused for laughter, then concluded, "But here's the town I love."

Ruth would bat after Williams. "I ain't had a bat in my hand since last September at Yankee Stadium," the Babe told Ted, lowering expectations.

"You've got nothing on me, Babe!" replied Ted, who'd taken a few licks for the Cloudbusters.

Williams stood in against right-hander Red Barrett of the Braves and launched the third pitch fifteen rows up into the right-field bleachers, bringing the crowd to its feet. Ted looked "very natural and loose as ever at the dish," wrote Fred Barry of the *Globe*. "He still has the knack." Of the next fifteen pitches, Ted delivered two more homers into the same vicinity.

Then it was Ruth's turn. On his second swing, he took a mighty cut—and fouled the ball off his ankle. He hobbled around in pain, and the ankle swelled up on him. After a few more futile hacks, he was forced to quit and limped back to the dugout. It was a dismal anticlimax to what had been the promoters' unfair construct: the Home Run King, after all, was way over the hill at forty-eight, and Ted, the would-be successor entering his prime, was only half Ruth's age.

Ruth gamely managed his service All-Star team from the first-base coaching box and had a bird's-eye view when Williams, coming up in the seventh inning of a tie game, crushed a three-run homer into the center-field bleachers, leading the service team to a 9–8 win over the Braves. This time, as he crossed the plate, Williams abandoned his usual pose of studied indifference to the cheering crowd. He looked up into the stands, smiled, and tipped his cap.

In the clubhouse afterward, Ruth was ashamed of his hitting performance. "See that uniform down there on the floor?" he said to the *Globe*'s Mel Webb. "It was the last I ever shall put on. I started right here in Boston...and I finished right here today." But by that evening, the Babe was out of the dumps and in a gregarious mood at Boston's Hotel Kenmore. He entertained patrons in the bar with a boisterous rendition of "Let Me Call You Sweetheart" and lavished praise on Ted, who had already returned to Chapel Hill.[14]

Ruth and Williams would have another encounter just two weeks later. Babe reneged on his pledge to Mel Webb and agreed to put on the uniform for what this time really would be his final appearance in a ball game. Following a game between the Yankees and Indians at Yankee Stadium on July 28, Ruth agreed to manage a combined Yankees-Indians team called the Yanklands in an exhibition game against Ted's Chapel Hill Cloudbusters to benefit the Baseball War Relief and Service Fund.

Though they were now on opposing sides, Williams and Ruth again met in the clubhouse before the game. Wearing his khaki Navy uniform this time, Williams asked his hero to sign a ball for him—the first and only time in his life that he would ask someone for an autograph. A photo was taken of Ted lighting Ruth's cigar as the Babe gave Williams the signed ball. It was inscribed "To my pal Ted Williams from Babe Ruth" and would become one of Ted's most prized possessions.*

There were 27,281 fans at Yankee Stadium to watch the Yanklands play the Cloudbusters, featuring Williams in left field, Johnny Pesky at short, and Johnny Sain pitching. The Cloudbusters won 11–5, the highlight of the game being when Ruth inserted himself as a pinch hitter in the sixth. As the Bambino strode to the plate, umpire Ed Rommel suggested sotto voce to Cloudbusters catcher Alex Sabo, who had played two seasons for the Washington Senators, that after flashing the signs to Sain he let Ruth know what pitch was coming. Sabo did, without telling Sain. The information no doubt helped the Babe turn on one pitch and hit a long, loud foul, but in the end he took a walk.[15]

Among those in attendance that day was American League president Will Harridge. Harridge was sitting next to the commanding officer of Chapel Hill, who had accompanied the Cloudbusters to New York. When Williams was introduced to loud cheers, the commander was prompted to give Harridge a glowing endorsement of the young cadet. As Harridge related the remarks the following day to Jack Malaney of the Boston Post, the commander said of Williams: "You are going to be surprised at the boy we will turn back to you when activities are over. He is one of the finest young men we have in the entire school. He is liked equally well by the officers and the men. In fact, he is idolized by the men for what he has proven to be.... I understand he had ideas of his own in baseball which he insisted on carrying out. There hasn't been any of that since we've had

---

* The ball was stolen from his house in the late 1970s. Williams offered a $5,000 reward to anyone who could help him recover the ball, to no avail. Then, in 2006, four years after Ted's death, someone tried to sell the ball on the memorabilia market, and Williams's daughter Claudia was alerted. She filed a lawsuit against the Chicago-area auction house that planned to sell the ball and successfully negotiated for its recovery in return for agreeing not to prosecute the seller or the auction house.

him....Ted Williams has different ideas on life now, and I am sure his Naval training has added greatly to a remarkable personality."[16]

Ted finished Chapel Hill in mid-September, at which point he was given a choice of resuming his flight training in Chicago or in rural Indiana.

"The line for Chicago was from here to the end of the block," remembered Pesky. "The line for Indiana was much shorter. Ted grabbed me and said, 'We don't want to go to Chicago. The goddamn writers will be all over us.' I didn't give a shit where I went, so I went with him to Indiana. If Ted would have asked me to jump off the Mystic River Bridge, I think I would have."[17]

The Bunker Hill Naval Air Station consisted of eighteen hundred acres south of the town of Peru, in north-central Indiana. This would be where Ted got down to flying in earnest—practicing takeoffs and landings on four five-thousand-foot runways and one twenty-five-hundred-square-foot concrete mat. He was still a relative novice in the air, with thirty-five hours to his credit at Amherst, just fifteen of those solo, and none at Chapel Hill, much of which had effectively been a sports camp. At Bunker Hill, he would get ninety-nine hours of flying, including sixty solo.

Arriving at the base, Williams was struck by the sheer number of planes he saw in the air. "The day we got there it looked like a flying circus," he remembered in his book. "The air was black with planes. We'd been told, 'Always stay 1,000 feet away from any other airplane and 1,000 feet above the terrain, and make nice, easy 45 degree turns.' But here we see about 150 planes in the air, all flying around each other, maybe 200 feet apart....I said to Johnny Pesky, 'What the hell's going on?' They were all coming in at the end of their flying period. They'd gone out separately, but they were coming in together. Awful."[18]

The routine at Bunker Hill was similar to the one at Amherst, only with more flying. And now, Williams was made commander of his seventy-man company at cadet barracks 30-A, responsible for rousing his men at 5:30 a.m. and getting them down to the mess hall on time. "The Williams Company is one of the most ship-shape on the station," an Associated Press dispatch in December reported.[19]

The flying was now more technical and challenging: there were precision landings, aerobatics, formation and night flying, inverted spins, snap rolls, and slow rolls. Williams was a quick learner and continued to show himself to be a skilled pilot, though he did have another close call. During his first time in a Navy SNV, a variable-pitch prop, Ted, flying with an instructor, nearly put the plane in a ditch. Taking off once, he had the prop in too high a pitch and the flaps up when they should have been down. "We would never have made it off the mat," he wrote in his book. "We'd have gone right into the boondocks, no doubt about it. But the instructor was in the back seat and he broke his watch scrambling to get the flaps down and the prop back in low pitch."[20]

Despite that setback, Williams was given good marks and finished his flight instruction more than two weeks ahead of schedule. Pesky, on the other hand, continued to struggle. Ted tried to help, in his own impatient way. "He said, 'Come on, Johnny, why can't you get this, you've got a high school diploma,'" Pesky recalled, chuckling. "I said, 'Ted, I'm not you. I don't have your get-up-and-go, your mind is quicker, and I didn't hit .400, either.' That kind of shut him up. But he said, 'Yeah, but after you get it, you'll retain it. I may forget it, but you remember everything.' I said, 'You pig's ass, you never forget anything.'"[21]

The powers that be decided it would be best if Pesky was eased out of the cockpit and redirected into another Navy specialty. "In an airplane he was a menace to himself and everybody else, but he was certainly officer material, so they moved him into O.C.S. and he actually got his rank before I did," Williams said.[22]

After a year and three tours together through Amherst, Chapel Hill, and Bunker Hill, the two friends parted. Ted moved on to intermediate flight training in Pensacola, Florida. He told Pesky he was determined to get his wings. "If it takes ten years, I'll qualify," Williams proclaimed.[23]

Williams arrived at his new post on December 7, 1943.

Naval Air Station Pensacola, known as the cradle of Naval aviation, is located on the Gulf of Mexico at the western tip of the Florida Panhandle near the Alabama state line, about an hour east of Mobile. Established as a Navy yard in 1826, NAS Pensacola was selected as the country's first Naval Air Station in 1914, and during World Wars I and II it served as the central training facility for Naval air operations. After Pearl Harbor, Pensacola vastly expanded its mission, and by mid-1943 it had produced nearly twenty thousand pilots—including many from Allied countries such as Great Britain, Australia, Canada, and New Zealand. In 1944, twelve thousand more would be turned out.

Bunker Hill, which had looked like a "flying circus" to Ted, was tame compared to tumultuous Pensacola, where the air was thick and loud with all manner of training aircraft, from single-engine monoplanes to flying boats and floatplanes, humming day and night. The air station consisted of a central training base, known as Main Side, where arriving cadets received their basic orientation, and six outlying fields, all within a forty-mile radius, where the aspiring pilots received specialized training in various aspects of flying. Main Side oozed tradition: its history dated back to the nineteenth century, when its primary mission was to suppress the slave trade and curb piracy in the Gulf and the Caribbean. The airfield consisted of a large circular landing mat with four runways, each four thousand feet long. Tall oak trees draped with Spanish moss formed the backdrop for decorous old houses, where the senior officers lived. The arriving cadets shared a barracks known as Transient Quarters with those about to get their wings as commissioned officers. The new arrivals were thus able to instantly take the measure of men who had reached the goal they were still striving for. The graduating cadets had successfully endured months of formation flying, night flying, free and fixed gunnery, aerobatics, dive-bombing, and more to become newly minted Naval aviators.

A year into Ted's service, there was still considerable interest, especially in Boston, as to how he was faring in the Navy. So four days before Christmas, Huck Finnegan of the *American* arrived in Pensacola to begin work on what would turn into no less than a thirteen-part series starting in early January. Though Finnegan would later become a harsh Williams critic, he was then a reliable supporter to whom the Kid felt comfortable unburdening himself.

It had snowed in Pensacola that December for the first time in forty-four years, and there was still a chill in the air when Finnegan arrived at Saufley Field, twelve miles from Main Side, where Ted was now working on formation flying. At one point, three young men in advanced flight training with Ted were killed in a landing mishap. "They tried some sort of hotshot landing," Williams recalled years later. "They went in and they were all killed. They were great guys. Young guys."[24] Ted was also being exposed to "pressure chamber" tests. That involved going up to eighteen thousand feet without oxygen and forty thousand feet with it to see if he experienced sinus trouble or "the bends." Williams later confided to Johnny Pesky that on one test run, he'd blacked out at seventeen thousand feet, and his plane had gone into a dive for fifteen thousand feet before he regained consciousness and pulled it back up at treetop level. The incident didn't make the papers until Pesky casually mentioned it to a writer years later.[25]

Williams was friendly and outgoing to Finnegan. Though still wary of calling attention to himself, he seemed eager to have a visitor and was hungry for news about Boston and the Red Sox, so it wasn't difficult for Finnegan to get his subject in a talkative mood.

"Gee, I miss baseball," Ted began, his earlier professed flirtation with a career in flying now formally withdrawn. "You know, I get the feeling sometimes that I'll never get the chance to play it again. When I look at my roomies, I realize I'm no kid. They're all 20 and 21. I'm 25. And this war won't be over in a hurry." Then he veered away from any self-indulgent wistfulness and returned to the importance of the war. "You know something? I won't be satisfied with this life until I get myself a Zero,"* he said. "I'm not fooling. Boy, I thought I got the thrill of a life-time when I hit that three-run homer in the '41 All Star game. Downing a Zero would cap that a hundred times. Lousy Japs—attacking Pearl Harbor and spoiling everything." That priceless quote, delivered with exuberant guilelessness, gave Finnegan the title of his series—"Ted Williams Wants a Zero"—and would soon cause the Kid some annoyance.

Of course, Ted's wish to bag himself a Zero was predicated on the assumption that first he would get his wings and second he would be assigned combat duty. What if he were made an instructor? Finnegan asked. "Yeah, I thought of that," Williams replied. That's why, he announced, he'd decided that he wanted to be a Marine. "You don't pick your spots there. Orders come from Washington in a sealed envelope. You don't know—nobody knows what's to become of you. But in the Navy, you have a selection—that is, if you can make it. And if I wound up an instructor, the wolves would say, 'I knew it. In the bag. He'll never leave the country.' That's why I want to make the Marines. I'll have no say in the matter. They can send me to the Southwest Pacific, anywhere they wish. And whatever they do, I'll have a clear conscience. Ted Williams, Marine lieutenant, flying a fighter. Boy, wouldn't that be something?"[26]

After dinner, in the dark, Ted took Finnegan to the hangars of Sauf-ley Field and showed him the various kinds of planes he had flown to date. There was the Piper Cub that he had started on at Amherst. It flew about seventy miles an hour and only weighed about 750 pounds, Ted said, stopping to lift one by the tail—with one hand. Then he pointed out an N2S trainer, which he had flown at Bunker Hill. It weighed a ton and could go one hundred miles an hour. Now he was flying an SNV, a low-winged plane with fixed landing gear that he said weighed two tons and went 120. "Rides much smoother than a lighter plane," Ted said. "Difference between a light automobile and a heavy one."

---

* The Mitsubishi A6M, a Japanese fighter aircraft.

Then he told of another near miss he'd had—the same mistake he'd made at Bunker Hill. "You know, I almost killed myself the other day. Just about to take off when the instructor saw my wing flaps weren't down. If I had taken off I wouldn't have been able to gain altitude, and the Sox would have had a gold star on their flag. Wouldn't the newspapermen have loved that!" He howled with laughter before turning serious. Ted concluded that he was "still in a D league as far as flying is concerned. In baseball, you can make a mistake on a pitch, and you've got two strikes left. In this game, one miscue can be fatal."[27]★

At the end of their evening, around 9:15, Ted walked Finnegan to the bus stop. Waiting on the bench were a sailor and "three Negroes," Finnegan reported. "How about a regular Pensacola cheer for Ted Williams?" the writer suggested.

"Who's Ted Williams?" a black woman asked.

"Just a drop in the bucket," said Williams, starting back to his barracks.[28]

On Christmas Day, Ted accepted an invitation to dine with an officer, Lieutenant Forrest Twogood, and his wife, along with their guests. Finnegan tagged along. During dinner, Ted held forth on a variety of topics, including his stormy relationship with the writers and the limited amount of time a major leaguer has to make his mark and his money.

"Dough's all that counts," Williams said.[29] "Who's going to care about me when I can't swing a bat? It doesn't lake them long to forget you....A big leaguer's got about 10 years to pile it up. If he doesn't, nobody's going to kick in to him when he's through. I'm not reaching for the moon. But I've come down from $250 a day to $2.50 a day, and that's a sharp drop. I've lost one year of baseball already and might lose three more. How do I know I'll be any good when I go back?"

Finnegan then went to interview Ted's commander at Saufley, a Marine named Major Graham J. Benson, of Lexington, Kentucky. Benson, remarking that he would be "very disappointed" if Ted were not commissioned in the Marine Corps, rated the ballplayer highly.

"Frankly, I like his work," Benson said. "I had heard of his pop-off reputation in baseball, and was looking for some sign of temperament. But...his conduct has been exemplary. He's had chances to pop too." Once, said Benson, Ted had missed an exam on ground and air traffic procedures known as course rules. When Benson called him in and

---

★ To editors at the *American,* that story was no laughing matter. When Finnegan wrote about this in the third installment of his series, the piece carried the headline WILLIAMS NEAR DEATH ON TAKE-OFF MISTAKE, as if the incident had just happened and he was on life support in the hospital.

asked for an explanation, Ted didn't offer any excuses. He said he'd just been absorbed in a navigation problem and forgotten about the test. He was assigned duty as a messenger for punishment and carried out the assignment without objection.[30]*

By the time Finnegan's series started running, on January 9, 1944, Williams had moved on to another station within the Pensacola complex, Whiting Field, where he was learning to fly by instruments. Whiting was a new facility that had been constructed in haste several miles inland, amid the black, piney woods. The base's red earth turned to mud during the winter rainy season. Ted and the other cadets would go up with instructors in whiny, vibrating SNVs fitted with a dark canvas curtain that would shut out all outside light as well as the view of the horizon, which a pilot uses as his anchor when flying by sight. The cadets practiced landings without being able to see the landing strip, and they flew in intricate patterns, recalibrating their instincts and learning to trust what the instruments told them about their altitude and attitude even if their body felt something different. All this was first simulated on the ground in what was called the Link Trainer, a machine that replicated the experience of flying at various speeds, altitudes, and angles. From the safety of the trainer, cadets would be informed by their instructors if they had passed or failed, a failure often being the equivalent of actually crashing and burning.

Another training device in the same building was more fun—a 1940s-vintage video game of sorts called the Simulated Aerial Combat Machine. A cadet would get into a faux cockpit at one end of what looked like a movie theater and look out at a screen showing films of attacking enemy planes. The idea was to fire off your guns at the planes and hit as many as you could. The whole exercise was accompanied by the dramatic theater-in-the-round sound of screaming planes and bursting bullets. When the lights came on, the cadets would rush to find out how many Japanese fighters they'd shot down.[31]

As the Finnegan series was unfolding back in Boston, a copy of the second installment, published on January 10—the one in which Ted was quoted as saying he "won't be satisfied with this life until I get myself a Zero"—found its way to the bulletin board outside the Whiting mess

---

* While Finnegan was still visiting, Ted was assessed his first demerit—not one but five, just for failing to make his bed one morning. This had him in a funk. Ted explained that his formation had been called twenty minutes earlier than usual and he hadn't had time to tend to his bed.

hall. The clipping had probably been mailed to Pensacola by the parents of a cadet who'd excitedly written home about training with the great Williams. But the cadet who posted the article apparently did so with puckish intent, for as Ted walked in for chow that evening, he was serenaded by hundreds of his peers chanting, "Teddy wants a Zero! Teddy wants a Zero!"—louder and louder, until Williams abruptly stood up from his meal and stalked out of the hall in anger.

Now flying the SNJ-4 and SNJ-5 combat trainers, Williams further revealed his superb reflexes, coordination, and natural feel for the plane. He flew more smoothly than other cadets, most of whom would return from a training flight with their fuel tanks nearly empty. Such throttle jockeys were like drivers who stepped on the gas and braked more than they needed to. Ted, on the other hand, would have about a third of a tank left, conserving fuel by slowly and steadily making adjustments and corrections on the throttle with his hands, cutting the RPMs, and controlling the pitch of the prop.

Another aspect of flying in which Williams's exceptional hand-eye coordination served him well was gunnery. A plane would tow a cloth sleeve around ten or twelve feet long and five feet wide approximately one hundred yards behind it. A group of four cadets, flying a thousand feet above, would then make dives toward the tow plane and try to shred the sleeve with as many bullets as they could. The proper technique was to lead the target slightly, as a skeet shooter does.

"Ted might have twenty to twenty-three hits, and the rest of us might have six to eight," recalled Dick Francisco, a Marine fighter pilot who trained with Williams at Pensacola. "In gunnery he was way better than the average pilot. Sometimes the instructor would demonstrate, and Ted would get far more than the instructor as well."[32]

Perhaps not surprisingly, the recollections of Ted's instructors of his performance as a pilot were more exalted than his actual marks and fitness reports. During his first two months at Pensacola, he'd been rated below average on such skills as landings and field approaches. But in the final two months, from mid-February to late April of 1944, preceding his scheduled commissioning in May, Williams had stepped it up and earned an average mark of 3.53 on a scale of 0 to 4 in the key measurement of "officer-like qualities."*

* The breakdown was: Intelligence, 3.7; Judgment, 3.4; Initiative, 3.6; Force, 3.5; Moral Courage, 3.6; Cooperation, 3.6; Loyalty, 3.5; Perseverance, 3.4; Reactions in Emergencies, 3.4; Endurance, 3.5; Industry, 3.6; and Military Bearing and Neatness of Person and Dress, 3.6.

His 3.53 rating put him in the above-average range of 3.5 to 3.7, short of the "outstanding" range of 3.8 to 3.9. "Cadet Williams has shown a good attitude while in this squadron," concluded Lieutenant A. B. Koontz in the "remarks" section of the evaluation. "He has been enthusiastic, industrious and cooperative. While in this squadron his progress has been satisfactory and he has performed all duties in an efficient manner. He possesses a good moral and military character and is above average officer material. I would like to have him in my squadron."

Two key decisions faced by the cadets were whether to receive their commission in the Navy or Marine Corps and what kind of plane they wished to fly. None of the choices was guaranteed. Getting into the Marines was competitive and depended on the needs of the services at the time; only a fraction of a graduating class — perhaps 20 percent — would be designated for the Corps. Ted talked it over with one of his classmates, Raymond Sisk. "Ted said, 'What do you think? Shall we go for the Marines?' I said, 'Sure, why not?'" Sisk recalled. "I was kind of fed up with the Navy at that point — a lot of chickenshit. I figured you'd be a man in the Marines." But it was more about the Corps' esprit for Ted. He basically bought into his pal Dick Francisco's view that if you hadn't served a hitch in the Marines, you still owed your country a military obligation.

Choosing a plane was thought to be a crapshoot. Cadets often assumed they would be denied their first choice, so they might try to game the system by saying a plane was their second or third choice when actually it was their first. But Ted played it straight. He wanted to be a fighter pilot and so chose fighter, scout, and torpedo, in that order. He got his first choice.

"We didn't hear anything at first," Sisk said. "Finally they posted the names. They accepted thirty of us as Marines. The ones they took were mainly college graduates. Ted was probably taken for his name, but he was also a good pilot."

On May 2, 1944, Ted was commissioned and received his wings in a pomp-and-circumstance ceremony at Main Side attended by a full Navy band. Wearing a specially fitted gleaming new white officer's uniform with starred epaulets, he officially accepted an appointment as a second lieutenant in the Volunteer Marine Corps Reserve. He had graduated forty-ninth in a class of 159 and was given a final mark of 3.186 when his entire five months at Pensacola were factored in. That put him at the high end of the "below average" range of 2.50 to 3.19, but he still finished in the top third of his class. The cadet who was ranked first only had a mark of 3.598, in the middle of the "above average" range. However, Naval and Marine Corps historians say that during World War II it was common for even the best pilots to receive mediocre grades and fitness reports. Said Hill Goodspeed, a historian at the National Naval Aviation Museum in Pensacola, "You have some of the foremost fighter pilots to come out of World War II getting average grades, so average was not an uncommon score. I'd say the grading was tough."[33]

The first enlisted man Williams encountered after the commissioning ceremony had to salute him. That was a glorious moment. Meanwhile, watching the ceremony in the audience with great pride had been Doris Soule, who'd been patiently waiting for her man for more than three years. She was there not only to witness a milestone in Ted's life but also to collect on his promise that they would be married as soon as he became an officer and thus eligible to wed under Navy regulations. Two days after the commissioning, Ted and Doris were married. Soon the couple rented a house off the base, in Pensacola proper, and got themselves a German shepherd they named Slugger—naturally. Red Sox owner Tom Yawkey sent down an engraved silver service for the couple. Doris took a job in a local beauty salon.[34]

Ted's idea of the perfect honeymoon was to take his new bride fishing in the Everglades.[35] Williams chose the most remote area he could find and happily fished away, but Doris refused to leave their cabin because she was afraid of the snakes. Ted assured her there were no snakes, but Doris was (quite literally) unmoved. Finally he talked her into coming out to join him one day. As they headed down a path toward his favorite spot, Doris suddenly let out a scream. An enormous snake had just slithered across the path. Back to the cabin she went.

After commissioning, the next logical assignment for Williams, given his training to date and his skills as a pilot, would have been to go to the Naval Air Station in Jacksonville, Florida, for final operational, or combat, training before being sent off to the Pacific Fleet. But then he learned he'd received different orders: to become an instructor and remain at Pensacola. As the United States was increasingly in control of the Pacific theater and thus the war against Japan by mid-1944, and since there was a backlog of pilots developing in Pensacola and elsewhere, the assignment effectively meant that he would not see combat in World War II.

Though Ted would claim in his book that he had chosen to become an instructor "because it would mean extra flight training and I figured I would need all I could get if we were going into combat," he actually had no choice in the matter, according to several people he served with as well as Naval officials.[36] "The choice of instruction or combat was made by someone else," said Goodspeed. And of course, Williams had explicitly told Huck Finnegan for his series in the *American* that he wanted to choose the Marine Corps, since they would make the instructor/combat decision for him, thereby ensuring that the "wolves" would know he had clean hands if he remained stateside.

"Everyone wanted to see combat," agreed Dick Francisco. "We were young, patriotic, hated Japs, the usual gung-ho stuff. Marines a little more so. To this day a guy doesn't join the Marines to be stationed in the US. He wants to fight."

The Marine Corps could have calculated that keeping Williams in the United States as an instructor would bolster the morale of the cadets he taught while boosting Armed Services public relations at home. It would also avoid the horrific headlines that could have ensued had he been sent off to combat and killed in action. But other celebrities and prominent people were accorded no such deference. The actor Tyrone Power was a Marine aviator and saw action in Okinawa, while FDR's son James Roosevelt was a Marine Raider, part of an elite unit that conducted amphibious light-infantry warfare during World War II, often behind enemy lines. Those who served with Ted at the time said that another factor in the instructor decision might have been that an overzealous Pensacola commander wanted to keep Ted in Florida so he could play in the base's highly competitive baseball league—a banal but perhaps persuasive hypothesis.

When Ted began his stint as an instructor, he was assigned to Bronson Field, one of the outlying stations in the Pensacola complex, twelve miles west of the city, near the Alabama line. Bronson, which mostly trained fighter pilots, had been Ted's last post, or final station, as it was called, before he was commissioned, and he had begun playing for the base's ball team, known as the Bronson Bombers.

Besides Ted, the Bombers had three other major leaguers on their roster: Bob Kennedy, a third baseman for the White Sox; Nick Tremark, who had played for the Brooklyn Dodgers in the mid-1930s; and Ray Stoviak, who'd had a cup of coffee with the Phillies in 1938. The Bombers would play two or three games a week, usually drawing a few thousand fans each time. Mostly they would play against the other bases within the Pensacola complex, but they would also play against other service teams in the region, some from as far away as Texas.

At Bronson Field, Ted served under a lieutenant commander who did not try to conceal the fact that one of his top priorities was to field a winning ball team. The commander "made no bones about it," recalled Ken Carroll, an instructor with Williams at the time and a former semi-pro ballplayer who was on the Bombers.[37] "He wanted a team to beat the Main Station. I don't know if he was unhappy being assigned to an out-lying field or what. It may have been a political thing with him."

Williams's roommate at Whiting Field, Karl Smith, who subsequently became Ted's lifelong friend, was convinced it was baseball that kept Ted out of combat. "Every base was competitive with the other bases, and every base had a baseball team, so everybody wanted Ted as an instructor.... That's the one thing that kept him out of combat in World War II." Others recalled Williams's commander rescheduling training sessions in order to make certain pilots available for games.

When it came to military baseball during World War II, the acknowledged powerhouse was the Naval Station Great Lakes teams organized by former Tigers catcher Mickey Cochrane, who had tried to woo Ted to the base, outside Chicago, in 1942. Cochrane's teams won 166 games and lost twenty-six over the first three wartime seasons and featured, at various times, such major-league pitchers as Bob Feller, Virgil Trucks, Denny Galehouse, and Schoolboy Rowe, as well as position players such as Pinky Higgins, Billy Herman, Walker Cooper, Ken Keltner, Johnny Mize, and Gene Woodling.

Right behind Great Lakes in its baseball prowess was the Norfolk Naval Training Station, in Virginia. Norfolk was home to Gene Tunney, the former heavyweight champion who by then was a lieutenant commander in charge of physical training in the Navy. Tunney's job was to recruit athletes, coaches, and phys ed teachers to oversee conditioning at Navy bases around the country. When the "athletic specialists," as they were called, showed up for Tunney's eight-week training course, the base commander, Captain Harry McClure, who favored baseball, had his pick of prime professional talent. McClure proclaimed that the ball games they were playing were "point-blank proof to our enemies that they cannot succeed in overhauling our way of life," and his Norfolk roster included Williams's Red Sox pals Charlie Wagner and Dom DiMaggio, the Yankees' Phil Rizzuto, Walt Masterson of the Senators, and Eddie Robinson of the Indians.

Many major leaguers found safe sinecures in the Army as well, including Tex Hughson of the Red Sox, Harry "the Hat" Walker of the Cardinals, Pete Reiser of the Dodgers, Red Ruffing of the Yankees, and, most notably, the Yankee Clipper himself, Joe DiMaggio. It was Hughson who, reflecting later on his wartime experience, famously said: "I tell them I fought World War II with a baseball bat and glove."*

Ted was always uninterested in service baseball and, to his credit, never exploited it in an effort to stay out of harm's way.[38] "I didn't have my heart in it at all, and I played lousy," Williams recalled. "By this time I was more interested in flying. It was going to be my job for the duration, and I was also enjoying the pleasures of Florida fishing for the first time."†

He'd read an article in *Field & Stream* magazine about the fight that Florida snook put up when they're caught. Intrigued, one day Ted and a friend saved their gas ration stamps and drove down to Everglades City to fish the canals there. On his second or third cast, he caught a fifteen-pound snook that took off harder and faster than any fish he'd ever encountered in fresh water. By the next day, Ted and his pal had caught 110 pounds of snook and sold them off at a fish market along the Tamiami Trail for eleven cents a pound.

"It was the first and only time I ever sold a fish. I made up my mind right there that after the war I was going to come down a week early before spring training just to fish the Florida waters. As it turned out, a week wasn't enough. I stretched it to two weeks, then a month, and before I knew it, I was a Florida resident."[39]

Once, when a Bronson Bombers game was rained out, Bob Kennedy

---

* When it was reported in the spring of 1944 that 280 professional ballplayers were still assigned to domestic Army bases, some never having even finished basic training, the Army deflected the heat by simply transferring the players overseas—mostly to Hawaii. The Army Air Forces' Seventh Air Force club, based in Honolulu, boasted the likes of DiMaggio and Ruffing, their Yankees teammate Joe Gordon, and Johnny Beazley of the Cardinals. The Navy waited another year, until the war was almost over, before pronouncing the "deliberate concentration of professional or publicly known athletes within the continental United States for the purpose of exploiting their specialties...detrimental to general morale." But months earlier—in the summer of 1944—Admiral Chester Nimitz, commander in chief of the Pacific Fleet, had moved to counter the growing Army baseball presence in Hawaii by transferring some of the better Navy players there, including Virgil Trucks, Schoolboy Rowe, Johnny Vander Meer, Pee Wee Reese, and Dom DiMaggio. By September, Nimitz had challenged the Army to an Army-Navy "World Series."

† Though lackadaisical in his play, there were brief moments when Williams offered those in attendance a glimpse of what he could do if he tried. In one game, he hit a ball so far that it landed among a group of alligators in a marsh near the base.

and Ted hired a flat-bottomed boat and went out fishing in the Gulf. "We came up on this alligator in shallow water," Kennedy remembered. "Ted said, 'Let's get the son of a bitch!' I said, 'You gotta be kidding me.' Next thing I know, Ted jumps into the water, and he's got the head, I got the tail. We throw him into the boat, get him back on shore, and then throw him in the trunk of the car. He was close to six feet. We drove back to Ted's place that night. He had a little house off base. We put the alligator in a fenced backyard. He didn't tell Doris. They had a little police-dog pup named Slugger. The next day Doris let the dog out and sees the damn alligator. Luckily she got the dog back in, then she called Ted at the base, screaming."[40]

Williams and Kennedy began spending more time together. Once, after Kennedy got married, he and his wife, Claire, went out to dinner with the Williamses. "At dinner Ted said to Claire, 'Are you and Bob going to have kids?'" Kennedy said. "She said she hoped so. Then Ted said, 'By God, if my wife ever gets pregnant, I'm gonna kick her right in the belly!' That sounds terrible, but it was an offhand remark. He didn't mean anything by it.... Doris just looked at him." Williams also liked to debate religion with Kennedy, who was a strong believer. Once, Ted asked Bob if he believed in God. "Certainly," replied Kennedy. "Oh, bullshit!" said Ted. "No one will ever prove to me there's a God."

Williams generally played center field for the Bronson Bombers. Len Poth, a Navy carrier pilot, was a pitcher on the team. One thing that drew the two men together was their exceptional eyesight. On road trips they would see who could be the first to read the letters on the license plates of cars approaching from the opposite direction. "We played for ten cents a shot. The other guys didn't have the same kind of eyes we did, and they'd say, 'Damn it, you're making it up.'"[41]

As an instructor, Williams would fly seven days straight and get the eighth day off. He got high marks from those he taught. Recalled Frank Maznicki, who had been to Boston College and would go on to play pro football with the Chicago Bears, "He explained everything very well. He explained it so well that it was pretty easy to do. The other cadets I was with thought he was good, too."[42]

Williams also earned a reputation for standing up for his students. As a surplus of pilots built up later in the war, he resisted pressure to thin the ranks by giving failing grades to an assigned number of them. Recalled Johnny Pesky, "Ted refused to wash them out, even though he was hauled on the carpet.... He said, 'If I think a kid'll make a competent flier, I won't wash him,' and he didn't. I never met a Marine pilot who trained under Ted who didn't say, 'There's a right Joe.' "[43]

Williams didn't mingle with his fellow officers much and wasn't always sensitive to protocol when he did. According to Bob Kennedy, when a group of baseball-crazed senior commanders asked to socialize with Ted once at the Main Side officers' club, he had one drink with them and excused himself. "Good night, boys," he said. "It's past my bedtime."[44]

In May of 1945, after more than a year of instructor duty at Bronson Field, Williams suddenly received orders to report the following month to Naval Air Station Jacksonville for combat training before being shipped out to the Pacific to join the fleet. The timing of the transfer seemed curious. The war against Japan was nearing an end, with the decisive Battle of Okinawa, the largest amphibious assault in the Pacific, then in progress and tipping in the Allies' favor.

Seven years later, in 1952, the *Boston Globe* would report that Williams's transfer to Jacksonville was punitive, a reaction to Pensacola's commanders exploiting him for baseball. Citing an unnamed Marine general as her source, reporter Ruth Montgomery wrote that while most of his peers were being sent off to combat, Williams had been assigned to be a flight instructor because his commanding officer "couldn't bear to part with such a terrific ballplayer."

She said the situation only came to the attention of Marine Headquarters in Washington when House majority leader John McCormack asked permission for Williams to leave Pensacola to attend "a special Irish celebration" in McCormack's home city of Boston. When a general saw the request and then called for Ted's service record, he hit the roof. "We're not running a war to provide any pink teas for congressmen!" Montgomery quoted the general as saying.[45] "Why wasn't this fighter pilot sent into combat long ago?" Shortly afterward, Williams was shipped off to Jacksonville.

In Jacksonville, Williams continued to hone his skills, learning how to fly the F4U Corsair and setting a base gunnery record for student pilots.[46] Williams also had a serious scare in Jacksonville when he crashed his plane while practicing a carrier landing in an incident that wasn't publicized at the time. It was his fifth near miss since he began flight training at Amherst. After the accident, an unhurt Ted was hauled out of his plane by a Navy fireman from Boston, Jim Dunn. Recalled Dunn's son Jimmy, "When he took his helmet and goggles off, my dad saw that it was Ted Williams. He said, 'Hey, I've seen you play ball up in Boston.' Ted said, 'Yeah, I've played there.'"[47]

Despite the flap over his Pensacola ball playing, Ted was virtually forced onto the Jacksonville base's team. The Fliers, as they were known, also had Charlie Gehringer, the famed Tigers second baseman, on their roster. (Gehringer, who had played his last season in 1942, wanted only to coach, but said he was made to play by the base commanding officer, an ardent sports fan, who otherwise threatened to "send you so far they won't know where to find you.")

One day Karl Smith, Ted's pal from Pensacola, appeared. "I came back after my first tour of combat," Smith said, "and I was at the Naval Air Station in Jacksonville, and the first day on the base I saw him, and he said, 'Hey, Bush, where the hell you been?' I says, 'Out trying to win this war while you been playing ball here,' and he died laughing. . . . I got shot down over Tokyo, and he wanted to hear every damn word of it. . . . He felt he really didn't get to do what he set out to do: that was to be a fighter pilot."

On August 3, Williams received his orders for the Pacific and was given a month's leave before he had to report to his departure point—San Francisco. On August 6, the United States dropped the atomic bomb on Hiroshima and, three days later, on Nagasaki. On September 2, when Williams was in San Francisco, Japan surrendered, and the war was officially over.

But once orders were in the pipeline, the ship of state turned slowly. Ted was obligated to continue on to Hawaii, arriving on September 4 for what would be a final four months of duty marked by anticlimactic boredom, sporadic ball playing, and mounting impatience to be released. The war, after all, was finished: he would see no action, and he had no desire to be kept on as a mere baseball prop, even in paradise.

Which seemed to be mostly what the Navy had in mind when it ordered Williams and the other major leaguers in its Hawaii employ to stage another "World Series," this time with those attached to American League teams on one side and those attached to National League teams on the other. Though Ted was indifferent to the series and was plagued by a bad cold, Johnny Pesky, who was in Honolulu and suited up for the Americans, felt certain that his pal would rise to the occasion during a key moment in one game. The AL was trailing 5–4 in the ninth when Ted came up with one out and runners on first and second.

Pesky said, "There were about 30,000 servicemen packed into the stands at Furlong Field, and you can imagine how they were rooting and yelling. This was their spot. In the better seats, there was enough gold braid to start a mint, admirals galore, with four-stripers—captains, and such lesser lights as commanders, draped in the back.

"I've seen Ted enough times up at the platter in the clutch to know his thoughts. I watched him. He was gripping that bat so hard that I expected to see sawdust falling around his feet. He was wiggling around and setting his stance. It was that old determination I had seen so many times."

Pesky still wasn't worried when Braves lefty Lou Tost got two strikes on Ted. But then Tost jammed him, and Williams popped up weakly to the catcher, the ball rising no more than thirty feet in the air.

"Ted didn't wait for the catch," Pesky continued. "The second he saw what he had done, he tossed that bat into the air, and I mean into the air, as high as he could throw it. There was a Navy photographer kneeling down who didn't see the bat go up. Detroit's Dick Wakefield was the next hitter, and when he saw what was coming down near the photographer, he yelled and then stuck out his own bat to prevent the photographer from getting hit.

"The crowd booed and shouted at Williams. As he headed toward the bench, Ted gave some of the photographer equipment a kick that sent it airborne. Silently, Williams continued to the bench.

"Ted Williams hasn't changed a bit!" Pesky concluded.[48]

On November 25, 1945, Ted and some sixteen hundred other servicemen gathered in Pearl Harbor, where it all had begun. They climbed aboard the USS *Texas*—a 573-foot battleship that had seen duty in World War I and had shelled Axis-held beaches in the North African campaign of World War II before being sent to the Pacific for the battles at Iwo Jima and Okinawa—then set sail for home.

Nine days later, on December 4, they arrived in San Diego, a port of call no longer home to Williams but part of his emotional fabric nonetheless. Waiting on the docks, amid the cheering throng, were two people who represented the past and future of Ted's life: his aging mother, "Salvation May" Williams, and his new wife, Doris Williams.

On January 12, 1946, Ted was officially relieved of active duty after three years and two months of service.

9

1946

As 1946 began, postwar America was exultant, euphoric, and eager for the return of a prosperous normalcy. Much of this giddy optimism was channeled into the resumption of Major League Baseball, which was eager to replace the cast of also-rans that had stocked its rosters in the war years and reinstall its varsities. Led by Ted, who was now twenty-seven, and Joe DiMaggio, more than three hundred players who had been off with the Armed Forces were now back home, preparing to reclaim their former positions with the start of spring training.

Attendance would soar in the coming season as fans (a good number of them back from overseas themselves) flocked to see their favorite returning stars. Twelve of the sixteen teams, including the Red Sox, would set attendance records, and overall, 18.5 million fans came out to watch big-league baseball, a new high.

Boston's prospects looked brighter than they had in years. The Red Sox had finished seventh among the eight American League teams in 1943, fourth in 1944, and seventh again in 1945. Now the Sox's nucleus of Ted, Dom DiMaggio, Johnny Pesky, and Bobby Doerr was back, as were pitchers Tex Hughson, Joe Dobson, and Mickey Harris. The pitchers would be joined by Dave "Boo" Ferriss, who in his rookie season in 1945 had gone 21–10. There were other changes: Jimmie Foxx had retired, Jim Tabor had been sold to the Phillies, Joe Cronin was now the manager only, and Rudy York, the powerful, right-handed-hitting first baseman, had been obtained in an off-season trade with the Tigers and was expected to tattoo the wall at Fenway.

News of Ted trickled back to Boston from San Diego, where he had stayed since arriving from Hawaii. Lacking a home base after being away for three years, he and Doris had moved in with May Williams and stayed at the family homestead for a few months. It was Ted's first extended stay in San Diego since he'd joined the Red Sox, a chance to reconnect with his divorced mother and to have May get to know Doris.

Joe Cronin came to San Diego to visit Ted and reported back to the team's beat writers that he had found his star enthusiastic about the upcoming season, hoping to play in 150 games and confidently predicting that the Red Sox would win the pennant. Then the *Globe*'s Hy Hurwitz flew out for his own assessment after Ted signed a $40,000 contract for the '46 season—a $10,000 raise from 1942. Hurwitz found Ted chipper, cryptically noting without elaboration that after three years of military life Williams "appeared to have a far greater respect for his fellow humans."

Ted told Hurwitz that he now weighed 195, seventeen pounds more than what he played at in 1942, but he promised to be down to 185 by the end of spring training. "I've been living an easy life, sitting on my big fat duff," he said. "I've got fat and bumpy. I haven't any wind. But I'm not worried. I'll get into physical condition easily. I'm not an old man, you know. The main thing is to get back my swing and the old eye on the ball.... I can hardly wait to start swinging again."[1]

In early February, Ted and Doris set out from San Diego by car for the long drive across country to Florida. They wanted to arrive early and do some fishing before Williams joined his teammates in Sarasota. Joining them for the trip was another San Diegan, Earle Brucker, a former catcher, now coach for the Philadelphia Athletics, and his wife. To a *Sporting News* reporter, Brucker dished that it had been quite a ride with the Kid, then held forth about Ted's eccentricities, calling him "the most nervous man in the world...like a humming bird on a hot griddle."[2] In the mornings, they would get up early and drive. Ted would be at the wheel, of course, driving fast but skillfully and safely. They would go maybe fifty or a hundred miles before stopping for breakfast. Ted would jump out of the car, hurry into the restaurant, and place his order of orange juice, eggs over, and coffee before Doris, Brucker, and his wife had even set foot in the establishment. Then Williams would go over to the magazine rack and flip through anything dealing with hunting or fishing. When his orange juice arrived, he'd return to the table, gulp it down, and go back to the magazines until his eggs were served. Then he'd inhale the eggs, toast, and coffee, and as soon as he was finished, he would stand up and say, "Let's go!" even though his traveling companions usually hadn't even been served yet. Back on the road, Williams would demand that the others join him in contests to see who could first read the letters and numbers of license plates on approaching cars, and he would incessantly question Brucker about the new pitchers who had come into the league during the war.

After fishing for ten days, Ted made his usual dramatic and tardy entrance in Sarasota on February 25. He and Doris pulled in to Payne Park at 1:00 p.m., a few hours after the first morning workout. The writers and photographers swarmed them. Before long, Ted had dispatched Doris off to Boston in their car to apartment-hunt. Then, trailed all the while by the press, he launched into a four-hour star turn of constant motion, chatter, wisecracking, complaining about the chigger bites all over his legs from fishing, posing for pictures, ordering new bats, talking up the Sox's chances this year—and, of course, hitting.

Since Williams had not played nearly as much baseball in the service as most other major leaguers, he regarded the 1946 spring training season as essential to getting his batting eye and rhythm back. His hands were soft from not swinging a bat ad nauseam, so he would have to develop blisters and then a layer of calluses (batting gloves would not come into regular use until the 1960s, after Ted retired). He would use a thirty-seven-ounce bat to help build his strength and hone his reflexes so that his customary thirty-three ounces would feel like a feather by opening day. He'd continue to sweat off the extra pounds he'd put on during the war, and he told the writers he'd started the process by playing handball with some old pals in San Diego.

Ted was friendly to the writers but still wary of them. When a *Time* magazine reporter told him he seemed more approachable now, Williams had a curt reply: "I'm always nice enough in the spring, until I read what those shitheads write about me."[3]

Before long, Ted let it be known that he had his groove back. "I really think I'm hitting the ball farther than I ever did," he told Huck Finnegan of the *American* after smashing a few bombs over the right-field wall in Sarasota. "I haven't got that old wrist snap yet, but I'll have it by opening day.... The ball looks big to me. My eyes seem sharp as ever. On the whole I'm well satisfied with my stay here."

So was Joe Cronin. "You're looking at the greatest hitter who ever lived," the manager told Finnegan. "Yes, I've seen Ruth and all the rest, but Williams is number 1."[4]

The more Ted played, and the more success he had, the more confidence he developed and the more he felt entitled to tell the world how good he was. There would be his garden-variety batting-cage braggadocio, which he would display by demanding that Pesky or Doerr or Dom DiMaggio tell him whether he was not the greatest hitter who ever lived. And before they could even robotically answer, "Sure, Ted," Williams would say, "Damn right."[5] But he went a step further in an early April interview, telling Grantland Rice that, yes, he did in fact think he was the greatest hitter who ever lived.

After pronouncing Williams a likely candidate to surpass Ty Cobb's lifetime .366 record—even though Williams was much more of a power hitter than Cobb—Rice said that the most interesting thing about Ted was not his hitting but "his philosophy of competition and life in general."

First, Williams pointedly disagreed with Rice's contention that the greatest hitters were simply born that way and that working hard left room for only marginal improvement. He also passionately preached the power of positive thinking, reiterating his belief that the reason he didn't win the batting title his rookie year was because he simply didn't *think* he was as good as the likes of Joe DiMaggio and Jimmie Foxx, even though he was. That had been a "big mistake." Now, he said, "it's my angle you are only going to be as good as you think you are. You've got to have that target to aim at. . . . I can tell you I'm shooting at nothing less than a .400 season. I still tell you I think I'm the greatest hitter baseball has ever known. Why? Because I have to think that way to ever be the greatest hitter. Suppose I'm wrong? Then what? I'll still hit pretty well and I'll still keep on thinking I'm the best. They can't arrest me for that. If you are aiming at a target, why not pick the top one?"[6]

Ted's chutzpah notwithstanding, perhaps the most intriguing story of the spring had been the emergence of a fledgling professional baseball league in Mexico, which by the end of March had successfully staged guerrilla signings of several American major leaguers, notably Vern "Junior" Stephens, the power-hitting St. Louis Browns shortstop, and veteran Dodgers catcher Mickey Owen.

The Mexican challenge had been brewing since February, when five brothers—all import-export tycoons who claimed to be worth between $30 million and $50 million—began threatening to break up the American professional baseball monopoly. The leaders of this fraternal initiative, Jorge and Bernardo Pasquel, were colorful, gun-toting characters predictably portrayed in the American press as Mexican bandito caricatures. When the Pasquels announced that they intended to make six-figure offers to Ted Williams, Bob Feller, Hank Greenberg, and Stan Musial, they had the full attention of A. B. "Happy" Chandler, the former Kentucky governor and senator who had become commissioner of baseball in 1945.

The Pasquels' timing was good. They knew that the returning major leaguers who had been off at war were thirsting to make up for lost earnings and that Chandler was also confronting baseball's first stirrings of labor unrest. Dom DiMaggio of the Red Sox, for instance, resentful that Boston had merely tried to renew his contract for his prewar salary of $10,000, consulted a lawyer to determine if he was actually bound to the Red Sox or could become a free agent and sell his services to the highest bidder.[7]

Players who were demoted to the minors after serving their country at war sued under the GI Bill of Rights, which required that service personnel had to be rehired at their former jobs for at least a year unless they were physically impaired. And in April, the American Baseball Guild would be formed in Boston, a first attempt at a union that would establish a minimum salary and the right of arbitration.

It was in this climate that Ted agreed to an early March meeting with Bernardo Pasquel in Cuba, where the Red Sox had gone to play an exhibition game against the Washington Senators. The meeting was brokered by *Globe* writer Roger Birtwell, who wrote a colorful front-page account of the session, which took place over a rickety wooden table in a Havana barroom.

Birtwell, who had a ghostly complexion and spoke with a fey, aristocratic accent, described Pasquel as "a mustached Mexican out of the pages of O. Henry." The meeting came about when Pasquel told Birtwell he was prepared to pay Williams $500,000 for three years if he jumped to Mexico. After some more conversation about the brothers' grandiose plans, which included building a fifty-thousand-seat stadium in Mexico City, Birtwell went down to the hotel lobby and staked out Ted, hoping to arrange a meeting for him with Pasquel, which he would then witness and have the scoop on.

When Ted appeared, shortly after 11:00 p.m., Birtwell was waiting and told him of Pasquel's offer. "Ted," the writer said, "you're going to meet this chap eventually. You might as well meet him now."

"Where is he?" Williams bellowed, whereupon Pasquel materialized and, speaking broken English, engaged the Kid in some preliminary small talk. Ted noticed that Pasquel wore several diamond rings and sprayed out saliva as he spoke.

"Have you signed Bob Feller?" Williams asked.

"Why not?" replied Pasquel cryptically.

"Well, if you've got Feller, I'm going to stay in the American League," Williams cracked.

Birtwell wasn't sure either man was understanding the other, so he hustled them off to a bar, where he would snag an interpreter. But to Birtwell's and Pasquel's dismay, Joe Cronin and clubhouse man Johnny Orlando were there having a drink. Williams tried to introduce Pasquel to Cronin, but the manager wanted no part of the Mexican entrepreneur and refused to shake his hand.

Pasquel secured the services of an interpreter and led Williams off to a corner table. Birtwell sat down with Cronin and Orlando. "Oblivious of dark-eyed senoritas who frolicked about the vicinity of the table, Pasquel went to work on Williams with great vim," wrote Birtwell. "He talked earnestly and rapidly, constantly grabbing Williams by the shoulders and arms."

Cronin watched this scene unfold while plotting to disrupt it. He ordered Orlando to crash the meeting and just tell Pasquel that he was Williams's interpreter. Orlando walked over, but Pasquel refused to let him sit down. Then Cronin himself got up and, waving off a flurry of protests from Pasquel, sat down grimly.

"I am having private talk!" Pasquel shouted. Cronin said nothing. "I will talk to you any time you wish but this talk he is [*sic*] private."

"What's so secret about it?" Cronin asked. When Pasquel lodged another volley of complaints, Cronin tried a different tack. "How many teams you got in your league?" The Mexican was dead silent for a few seconds, whereupon Cronin finally gave up and left.

Pasquel and Ted continued their conversation, talking earnestly for another ten minutes. Back at the hotel, Williams told Birtwell that Pasquel had said, "I could name my own figure and my own terms. He said that since I was under a contract for this year he would not make me an offer for this season but he wants me next year. He invited me and my wife to come down to Mexico as his guests in the fall. He promised me short right-field fences and said they've got winds down there that always blow toward the outfield."[8]

When news of the approaches to Williams, Feller, and Musial surfaced, Commissioner Chandler reacted harshly. He called the Mexican League an "outlaw" venture and threatened that anyone in organized baseball who jumped his contract and was not back with his club by opening day would be barred from returning for five years. The Pasquels countered that Chandler was running an illegal monopoly that effectively placed his players in peonage.

Baseball survived the legal skirmish that ensued, though not before the major leagues' antitrust exemption and its foundational reserve clause were given an uncomfortable vetting. The Pasquels continued to court Ted through much of 1946, but neither he nor any other superstar ever assented to their pitch, and the Mexican League would fade as a threat.

The Pasquel overture and a slew of other postwar offers to get involved in various endorsement deals or get-rich-quick schemes had persuaded Williams that he needed a business manager. He had fired James Silin after Silin leaked to the press his advice in 1942 that the Kid drop his 3A claim and enlist promptly for service in World War II. Ted consulted a friend, John Corcoran, who ran a Ford dealership outside Boston. Corcoran said he had just the man for the job: his brother Fred, who was promotional manager of the Professional Golfers' Association.

Ted met Fred Corcoran in Chicago and explained his problem. He had a lot of people pestering him with offers to do this and that. He didn't want to be bothered, and he needed a reliable agent to sift through the offers. He would continue to negotiate his contract with the Red Sox himself. The two men talked for a while and hit it off. Finally, Ted asked Corcoran what his fee would be.

"I'll take fifteen percent," said Corcoran.

Williams thought he heard "fifty" and agreed, betraying his naïveté.

"Not fifty," Corcoran said, correcting him. "Fifteen."

Ted laughed. "Whatever you say. If you want to make it fifty, that's all right with me."[9]

Corcoran assured him that 15 percent was satisfactory, and they shook hands on the arrangement. By that evening, Corcoran had secured an endorsement deal for Ted with Wilson Sporting Goods, and he soon would form Ted Williams Enterprises to obtain stakes in car dealerships and other ventures.

Williams and the Red Sox broke fast. On opening day in Washington, April 16, in front of President Harry Truman, Ted hit a 430-foot missile into the center-field bleachers that *Washington Post* columnist Shirley Povich called the hardest-hit ball at Griffith Stadium in a decade. Truman and his military retinue rose from their box to follow the flight of the ball, the president applauding, then tipping his hat and even bowing to Williams in appreciation as the Kid, head down, trotted around third and approached home plate. The homer, which followed three batting-practice shots over the right-field fence, paced the Sox to a 6–3 win over the Senators.[10]

Boston won its first five, lost three out of four, then began building another winning streak in Philadelphia. The fan schizophrenia that often attended Ted both at home and away was on full display at a doubleheader in Shibe Park on April 28. Left-field wolves were in good voice, calling him DP for having hit into three double plays against the Yankees at home on the twenty-fourth and "Mr. Williams, sir," mocking his officer rank during the war. But when the Red Sox had completed a sweep and were leaving the field after the second game, quite a different spectacle unfolded: some twenty-five hundred adoring, frenzied fans, mostly kids, ran onto the field and surrounded Williams as he reached the pitcher's mound on his way to the dugout from left field. They began pawing at him, reaching for his hat and glove, ripping his shirt open. Ted tried to escape but couldn't, engulfed in a scrum that gradually pushed its way back out to left field. Finally, a burly policeman saw what was happening, bulled his way through the crowd, and cut a path for Ted to flee. Emerging from the clubhouse later and hopping into the car of a friend, Williams was mobbed again.

It was Sinatraesque ball-field bobby-soxer treatment. "I honestly thought they were going to tear me in shreds," Ted said afterward, his body bruised from the pummeling he took. "They were tearing away at my uniform when the cop saved me. I had visions of doing a nudist race into the clubhouse. Somehow I managed to save my glove. But boy, I had to fight for it."[11]

Ted stayed in a groove, blasting his second home run of the season four days later in Boston to give the Red Sox a ten-inning win against the Tigers, 5–4. While nearly everyone at Fenway stood and cheered the homer, one up-and-coming politician in attendance sat on his hands, brooding. John F. Kennedy, then a gaunt, twenty-eight-year-old World War II veteran running for Congress in Boston, had just lost a bet that Williams would *not* hit a home run.*

Ted and his team continued on a tear. Over the first nine games in May, Williams hit four home runs and his average on the season stood at .427. The *Globe* began running a daily box called "Williams vs. Williams," comparing his batting pace in 1941, the .406 year, with the current

---

* JFK apparently considered Fenway Park fertile campaign ground. He returned on June 8 for another game against the Tigers and was pictured in the next day's *Herald* posing with Ted, Joe Cronin, and Army sergeant Charles A. MacGillivary, a Boston native and Congressional Medal of Honor winner for his heroism at the Battle of the Bulge. Ten days later, Kennedy easily won the Democratic nomination in a ten-man field, then coasted to victory in the November general election.

season's. The Red Sox, meanwhile, were flying high in first place and took a fourteen-game winning streak to New York for a big three-game series against the Yankees.

The Sox won the first game, 5–4, before a Ladies Day crowd of 64,183, but dropped the second, 2–0, ending their streak at fifteen. Ted did not distinguish himself in the loss, and again put his petulance on display for all to see. After taking a called third strike that he felt was outside, Williams pouted in left field, kicking several divots, and then lost a routine fly ball in the sun after forgetting to bring out his sunglasses. The Yankees fans unloaded on him, as did Dave Egan, who had ventured down to New York for the series.

After chiding Williams for taking the third strike and for his "amateurish outfielding," the Colonel proclaimed that despite the current standings, "the Yankees are the team to beat and I furthermore tell you that the Red Sox are not the team to beat them." That was because Ted's "fads, foibles and fancy fandangoes" created too many divisive distractions. The Red Sox, Egan asserted, were "divided into two detachments. The one consists of eight fellows mostly named Joe, whose hearts are bursting with the desire to win a pennant. The other consists of Ted Williams, who will rack up a nice, fat batting average for Ted Williams, and drive in a large total of runs for Ted Williams and, meanwhile, undermine the spirit of a team which deserves better."[12]

Ted must have seethed at that bit of Egan bile, especially since there was no indication it was true. A month later, the Red Sox, having ripped off another long winning streak, stood at 41–9, leading the Yankees by ten games. Ted hit over .500 for the first nine games in June, and on June 9, he capped the surge with a titanic blow off the Tigers' Fred Hutchinson that landed thirty-seven rows up in the right-field bleachers at Fenway.★

On July 9, the All-Star Game came to Fenway Park for the first time. That seemed appropriate in 1946, since the Red Sox had placed eight men on the American League squad, including four starters, and were still comfortably in first place. Bob Feller was to start for the Americans;

★ The ball was initially estimated to have gone 450 feet, but in the mid-'80s, the Red Sox decided to scientifically measure the clout and concluded that it had traveled 502 feet. They marked the spot by painting the seat where it had landed red, to make it stand out in the green bleachers, and pronounced it the longest ball ever hit at Fenway Park. Latter-day Sox sluggers such as Mo Vaughn and David Ortiz have called the distant red seat impossible to reach, even in the steroids era, and dismissed it as management propaganda designed to enhance the Williams mythos.

for the Nationals, it was Claude Passeau, the Cubs right-hander whom Ted had taken deep to glory in the 1941 game.

There was unusually high interest in the first postwar All-Star Game, now that the real stars were back. (The powers that be had decided to skip the game altogether in 1945.) Williams always looked forward to the showcase, especially this year, his first since 1942. He put on a grand exhibition in batting practice, bantering happily with friend and foe alike.

He spotted Truett "Rip" Sewell, the puckish Pirates pitcher, who had rejuvenated his career in recent years by throwing a blooper ball, or "eephus" pitch. Sewell threw the pitch overhand in a twenty-foot arc, the way a softball pitcher might throw one underhand in a game of slow-pitch. Fans delighted in watching batters flail away at the bloopers, mostly ineffectively, as they had to supply all their own power. Reveling in the enchanted reaction to his eephus pitch from the crowds, who behaved as if they were watching a circus act, Sewell had come to see himself as a showman as much as a pitcher.

"Hey, Rip!" Ted yelled at Sewell. "You wouldn't throw that damn crazy pitch in a game like this, would you?"

"Sure, I'm gonna throw it to you," Rip replied.

"Man, don't throw that ball in a game like this."

"I'm gonna throw it to you, Ted. So look out."[13]

Passeau walked Ted in the first inning, undoubtedly not wanting to get burned again, but Charlie Keller of the Yankees followed with a home run to give the Americans an early 2–0 lead. Leading off the fourth against Kirby Higbe of the Dodgers, Williams hit a laser that took about three seconds to reach the center-field bleachers, some 420 feet away. As he rounded second, Ted caught a glimpse of slick-fielding Marty Marion, the Cardinals shortstop, winked at him, and said: "Don't you wish you could hit like that, kid?" Marion, who was nine months older than Williams, just smiled.[14]

The game devolved into a laugher for the American League. As for Williams, he put on a hitting clinic: he followed his fourth-inning homer with two sharp singles, one of which drove in a run. By the bottom of the eighth, the AL was up 8–0, and National League manager Charlie Grimm decided it was showtime — he called for Rip Sewell.

Sewell was greeted rudely with three singles and a sacrifice fly, then Williams came to the plate with two men on. Sewell smiled at Ted, recalling their pregame dialogue. Ted shook his head, as if to say no, don't do it. But Sewell nodded yes, he would.

Rip went into his full windup, as if he were going to throw his fastball, such as it was, but came with the blooper. Ted, bug-eyed, swung from his heels but fouled it off. He stepped out of the box, got back in, and stared out at Sewell, who again nodded at him. Once more came the blooper, but this time Ted let it drift outside for a ball. Then with Williams sitting on another blooper, Sewell snuck a fastball down the middle for a strike. The count was one and two.

Now Sewell thought he had the advantage because Ted wouldn't know what to expect. He wound up and let the blooper fly. It rose high, then dropped right down the chute for what would have been a strike. Williams was ready. As the ball floated down, Ted, acting on a pregame tip·from Yankees catcher Bill Dickey, skipped forward with two short hops, propelling himself slightly out of the batter's box to get almost a running start. He uncoiled a fierce uppercut swing—from his waist up through his shoulders—and drove the ball high and deep to right field in a splendid arc. It landed in the American League bull pen.

In the six years that Sewell had been throwing the blooper, no one had come close to hitting a home run off him. As the 34,906 fans rose to cheer Ted's blow, they also erupted "into a paroxysm of laughter," the *New York Times*'s John Drebinger reported, underscoring the carnival atmosphere that attended Sewell and his blooper pitch.[15] Ted also laughed in sheer delight as he rounded the bases, but again found time to ask Marty Marion at shortstop if he didn't wish he could hit like that. Sewell, ringmaster of his own burlesque, savored the moment, too, laughing along with the crowd, following Williams around the bases and talking to him.

" 'Yeah,' I told him, 'the only reason you hit it is because I told you it was coming,' " Sewell later said. "I got a standing ovation when I walked off the mound after that inning. We'd turned a dead turkey of a ball game into a real crowd pleaser."[16]

Listening on the radio out in San Diego had been May Williams. It was quite festive on Utah Street as neighbors and newspapermen crowded around May to congratulate her and to get her reaction to Teddy's heroics. How did she feel about her son going 4–4 and becoming the first player to drive in five runs in an All-Star Game? "All my prayers were answered," said May, predictably. It was all "perfectly marvelous.... He's a wonderful boy."[17]

Ted's dazzling performance triggered a new round of gushing over his hitting prowess. Both Charlie Grimm and Steve O'Neill, the rival All-

Star managers, called Ted the greatest hitter ever, as did a host of awe-struck players, former players, and writers, who filed glowing dispatches from Boston.

Then five days later, at Fenway, Williams put on another spectacular exhibition in a doubleheader against the Cleveland Indians, a day that would mark a significant turning point in his career. In the first inning, facing right-hander Steve Gromek, Williams lashed a line drive at second baseman Johnny Conway, which was hit so hard that Conway staggered out into right field after leaping to catch it. In the third inning, with the Red Sox trailing 5–0, Ted came up with the bases loaded and belted a curve from Gromek into the back of the Cleveland bull pen in right-center for a grand slam. Then, leading off the fifth against Don Black, Williams clubbed another homer, this one into the runway separating the right-field grandstand from the bleachers. After a mere single in the seventh, Ted returned in the eighth to face Jonas "Jittery Joe" Berry, with two men on and the Red Sox now down 10–8. Jittery Joe jammed Williams, who nonetheless was able to turn on the ball and muscle it off his fists into the lower right-field grandstand for a three-run homer that won the game for his team, 11–10. The 31,581 fans roared in celebration of Ted's three-homer, eight-RBI, one-man-team display, while from his third-base coaching perch, manager Joe Cronin greeted his star by leaping around in a "hysterical" manner, according to Burt Whitman's account in the *Herald*.[18]

After Williams, still sizzling, began the second game of the double-header by lacing a double down the right-field line with the bases loaded, Indians player-manager Lou Boudreau implemented a serpentine scheme he'd hatched between the two games. Boudreau knew that Williams pulled the ball to the right 85 percent of the time, so the next time Ted came up there was no one on base, and Boudreau—who had rivaled Williams's hitting in the first game with four doubles and a home run—shifted his defenders into a drastic realignment that blanketed the right side of the field. He moved his first baseman and right fielder close to the foul line. He put his second baseman forty feet back on the outfield grass, about fifteen feet from the line. Boudreau himself, normally the short-stop, went over to where the second baseman usually played, only shaded more toward first, in the hole. The third baseman moved slightly to the right of second, the center fielder shaded toward right-center, and the left fielder came in to the edge of the outfield grass, about thirty feet behind where a shortstop might normally play.

"Gee, I had to laugh when I saw it," Ted recalled. "What the hell's going on?[19] In effect, they are now telling me, 'Go ahead, hit to left field, have yourself a single. We'll sacrifice singles to take away your doubles and home runs any day.' They're tickled to death if I go to left because the only thing they're really afraid of is the long ball."

Boudreau knew the shift would play directly to Ted's ego and that to try and hit to left would be to disrupt the natural arc of a swing that was designed to drive a pitch in the air to right field. Sure, Ted could presumably drop a bunt to the vacated left side of the infield and reach base any time he wished, but he would not, Boudreau calculated, for he would consider it humiliating: he was a power hitter whom the fans paid to watch go for the long ball. So Boudreau felt Williams would take up the challenge and try to blast the ball through his realigned fielders. The shift could not prevent a home run, of course, but by plugging certain power alleys and gaps, it could turn what otherwise would be line-drive singles or doubles into outs.

After settling himself, Ted dug in against Indians pitcher Red Embree and promptly drilled a grounder to Boudreau. The ball probably would have gone for a hit in a normal defense, but Boudreau, in the hole between first and second, gobbled it up for the out. Williams walked his next two times up, as the Cleveland pitchers seemingly ignored their new defense and continued to work him outside.

After the game, Ted and Joe Cronin argued over how to deal with the shift.

"Ted, push the ball to left and Boudreau will have to put all those guys back where they belong," the manager said.

"The heck I will," Williams replied. "All my power is toward right, and I'll jam the ball through them."

They kept arguing, but Ted was insistent: he was a natural pull hitter and would not interfere with his swing.[20]

So Williams ignored the shift and kept swinging away, pulling the ball the way he always had, but Boudreau's defense, which was soon adopted with variations by most teams in the league and used for at least the next decade, began to erode his average—not precipitously, but noticeably. His 1946 mark before the shift was .354; after the shift it was .327.

By September, as the season wound down, the shift had had its desired effect of getting under Ted's skin, and he openly acknowledged it was hurting him. "It has cost me a lot of hits," Ted wrote in his column for the *Globe*. "It takes time to break away from your natural habit. Hitting to the opposite field is a science. Players who have accomplished this skill have required many long hours of practice. That's what I'm going to have to do."[21]

But despite statements like that, Ted could never shake a fundamental ambivalence over how to cope with the shift. He knew he should hit to left, that it only made sense to take what his opponents were so tantalizingly offering him — if only to force them back to a conventional defense so that he could resume pulling the ball freely. But he was loath to meddle with the mechanics of his swing, to artificially alter its rhythm and flow. He was, after all, the Natural, and style was important to Williams. He liked looking good at what he did; he liked smashing the ball to right, the way a classic left-handed pull hitter should. The notion of punching singles to the opposite field was anathema to him.

Boudreau was not the first to devise a lopsided defense against Williams. Chicago White Sox manager Jimmy Dykes had tried it on July 23, 1941, but abandoned it when Ted drilled one down the left-field line. Three days later, another Indians manager, Roger Peckinpaugh, tried a variant of the shift but also dropped the idea after Ted singled and doubled. And in 1926, there is a record of the Boston Braves using a less pronounced shift against another slugging Williams of the day — the Phillies' Cy Williams. Still, it was Boudreau's shift that was the most effective, and variations endure to the present day.

The shift, and how Ted should cope with it, inspired a cascade of commentary in the press for the rest of 1946 and in the ensuing years, as well as lively debate among fans, hitting experts, and other observers. It had all the elements of a great story: there were good arguments on both sides for whether Williams should change his approach; and his reactions — at first blind stubbornness and an insistence that he would forge ahead and swing as he always had, but then a willingness to recalibrate and reanalyze the problem — were revealing of his character and reignited old arguments about Ted being more of an individualist than a team man. Among fans, the shift also provoked animated strategic and tactical discussions, and until they grew used to seeing it, the spectacle of watching six of the nine defensive players move over to the right side of the field produced a certain whimsical enchantment. (This feeling was certainly not dispelled when, in a game later that summer of '46 against Boudreau's Indians, a dwarf leaped from the Fenway box seats and ran out on the field to assume the vacant third-base position.*)

---

* During spring training in 1947, a Dallas minor-league team playing an exhibition game against the Red Sox put seven of its nine players in the right-field bleachers when Ted came to bat, leaving only its pitcher and catcher in play.

There seemed considerable evidence to suggest that Ted, with his superb bat control, could hit to left if he wanted to. San Diego friends from childhood recalled that when they played on the sandlot, because the right-field fence was too short, Ted hit to left without trouble. Then there was the time he'd drilled a foul ball at hecklers in the left-field stands at Fenway Park. But Ted insisted he could not just flip a switch and begin hitting to the opposite side at will. "The story you read was: 'Williams is too proud, he's too stubborn, Williams isn't trying to beat it,'" Ted wrote in his book. "The hell I wasn't. I was just having a hard time hitting to left field. Every spring after that I'd experiment, shifting my feet, trying to drop balls into left field, plunking them into short center, seeing what could be done. But I was having a hard time."[22] Before long, the writers were prodding a cast of hitting greats— including Ruth, Cobb, Hornsby, Tris Speaker, Paul Waner, Harry Heilmann, and Al Simmons—to give Ted advice on what to do about the shift. This advice was often conflicting.

But the first meaningful guidance Williams received that summer after Boudreau unveiled his razzmatazz came from one Bert Dunne, a San Francisco advertising executive and boyhood chum of Joe Cronin's. Dunne had gone to Notre Dame, where he served as Knute Rockne's publicist and also compiled a .519 batting average for the baseball team. When he joined John McGraw's New York Giants after graduation, Dunne had the temerity to tell the legendary McGraw that the older man did not know the first thing about hitting technique. Dunne soon found himself demoted to the Eastern League, where he developed a sore arm that forced him to quit the game prematurely. Nearly two decades later, he'd written a well-received instructional baseball book for preteen and young teenage boys called *Play Ball, Son!*

Through his friendship with Cronin, Dunne had been hanging around the Red Sox since 1939, Williams's rookie season. One night after a game in Detroit that year, Dunne approached Moe Berg, who was hitting .210 at the time, and told the catcher that he had certain mechanical defects in his swing. If he corrected these flaws, he could raise his average by at least forty points. Dunne argued that the mechanics of hitting—the proper stance, stride, hand position, and swing—could be taught to anyone. The erudite Berg vehemently disagreed, saying Dunne was not accounting for differences in talent and physical size. The two argued for five straight hours, and "it was a brilliant duel," Cronin wrote in his introduction to *Play Ball, Son!*

Other Red Sox players became interested in the Dunne-Berg debate, and Cronin decided to test their ideas further by filming many of his players' swings and batting technique. The result? "We found Bert's theories fundamentally sound," Cronin said. Williams, of course, spent more time analyzing clips of his swing than anyone else, and the manager concluded that this paid dividends, especially in his .406 year. "Ted believes in style, as Bert Dunne does," Cronin added. "Ted watched the pictures, then went before the mirror in his room and swung the bat for hours on end. I am absolutely convinced that Williams added at least thirty points to his average in 1941 by his practice swings."[23]

Dunne decided to make a movie based on his *Play Ball, Son!* book, and in May of 1946, he screened it for some of the Red Sox—including Ted, Cronin, Bobby Doerr, and Boo Ferriss—in a Philadelphia hotel room. Ted, in fact, watched the film three times and pronounced it "the greatest teaching picture ever made."[24] What intrigued Williams most was a part of the film in which Dunne had kids batting off tees that had been crudely adapted from simple toilet plungers.

Ted decided to use this as a practice tool himself. He went to a hardware store, bought three plungers, three broomsticks, and a garden hose. He sawed off the broomsticks to knee-high, waist-high, and letter-high lengths and attached each to the rubber base of the plunger after removing the wooden handle the device came with. Then he slipped a small length of hose over the top of each broom, atop which he could place a baseball.

"The beauty of the Tee was that I could move it around," Williams wrote in a little-noticed chapter he provided for a sequel to *Play Ball, Son!* called simply *Play Ball!*, which Dunne wrote in 1947. "For instance, I wanted to hit low outside balls. I just moved the Tee to the corner of the plate and went to work. Then I moved the Tee for the low-inside ball. I did the same for the belt-ball Tee and the letter-ball Tee."

Dunne, of course, was delighted that Williams adopted his tee method—even more so after Ted told him he'd be willing to make a film using the tee to show boys how he hit the ball. "Dunne almost hit the sky, so intense was his excitement," wrote *New York Times* sports columnist Arthur Daley in a preface for *Play Ball!* "Here he would have the greatest hitter in baseball using the Tee and telling the boys of America: 'Make one of these Tees yourself—and go out and practice hitting.'"

Ted wrote in *Play Ball!* that his decision to make the film was actually triggered by a curious encounter he'd had with an older man outside the Fenway Park clubhouse after the doubleheader of July 14, 1946, the day he'd hit three home runs in the first game and Boudreau debuted the shift in the second. Williams was elated, thinking more of the first game and the possibility of another .400 season than of any dark implications related to the shift. As he was about to get into his car, someone said, "I beg your pardon, Mr. Williams."

"I turned quickly because the voice had a rare charm and was quite different from some of the 'raazzberry' voices I had heard from the left field stands," Ted wrote. "I said, 'Yes, sir?' and eyed an old gentleman. He could have been seventy, but he had such a well-preserved look that he could pass for fifty."

The man cleared his throat and asked: "Sir, could you please tell me whether or not you are a natural hitter? I mean, were you born a great hitter or did you develop yourself into a great hitter?"

Williams looked for the needle. Maybe one of his teammates had turned this fellow loose on him as a gag. It wasn't the kind of question he normally entertained in the parking lot after a three-homer game. "You've got me," Ted finally said. "I don't know what you mean by a natural hitter."

"This, sir," Williams quoted the man as replying quietly. "I understand that you are a great student of the art and science of hitting. I understand that you practice swinging before a mirror, that you seek to interpret certain definite mathematical laws, that you endeavor to harmonize the mechanical aspects of the swing until you achieve a composite of rhythm, style, power, and beauty."

Ted said the words came at him "like Bob Feller's fastball" and threw him off balance, but he recovered enough to answer: "I study hitting. I study stance, stride, hand action, and the rest. I practice religiously. In fact I live to hit. Of course nature has to give a man good eyesight, strength in his hands, wrists, and forearms, and a lot of other things before he can hit a ball in the major leagues."

The man thanked him for the answer and said he admired that Williams had added hard work to the natural ability he'd been given. He said he would tell his grandson, whom he thought had natural ability as a hitter but had yet to demonstrate an adequate work ethic. Then the man said to Ted, "Sir, why don't you tell some of your secrets to the boys of America? I am sure you would make them happy."

"How?" said Williams.

"Make a motion picture of your hitting secrets," said the man before smiling, bowing, and walking away.[25]

Dunne followed Ted for several months in 1946 and took five thousand feet of film, showing him in practice, in games, and in the clubhouse. He cut four thousand feet from the final print and gave the outtakes to Williams and Cronin as a present. The film, now a cult classic, was called *Swing King* and released in 1947.

The result was as much a minidocumentary on Ted as it was a T-ball instructional. There were revealing glimpses of Williams's hitting fundamentals, broken down. His stance, for example, was twenty-seven inches wide, his stride a controlled six inches, and he stood just twelve inches from the plate. A close-up of his hands gripping a cocked bat showed his fingers slightly overlapped, like a golfer's. When he started his swing, the hands held back until the hips pivoted, then they slashed through the strike zone, the front arm leading the way and the back hand and arm supplying the power. Furthermore, Dunne told Arthur Daley, who had become an admirer of Dunne's and devoted three of his Sports of the Times columns to him in 1946 and 1947, that Williams consistently hit an outside pitch when it was two inches in front of the plate, a ball down the middle nine inches in front, and an inside pitch fourteen inches in front. Those measurements never changed for low, belt-high, or letter-high balls, he added.[26]

In a chapter he devoted to the filming of *Swing King* in *Play Ball!*, Dunne wrote that Ted told him at the time that he feared the Boudreau shift could lower his batting average by as much as fifty points.[27] With teams now likely to pitch Williams inside so that he could more frequently hit into the teeth of the stacked defense in right, Dunne concluded that the only way for Ted to beat the shift would be for him to stand farther back from the plate, draw his back foot away from the plate still more while the pitch was in flight, and take an inside-out swing with the hands ahead of the bat. This way the angle of the bat through the strike zone would naturally drive the ball to left field.*

Dunne's tutorials flew largely under the radar. But the shift, and Ted's initial determination to forge ahead and try blasting the ball through it, became such a press cause célèbre that it was not long before some of the Hall of Famers of the era came forward to offer their views.

Babe Ruth rose to Williams's defense. He recalled that when the Indians had tried to shift against him, he'd taken advantage by hitting five singles to left, whereupon the fans, used to seeing the

---

* Williams took Dunne's advice seriously, and before *Swing King* was released in early 1947, he told Arthur Daley for the February 16 edition of the *Times:* "Bert Dunne knows more about hitting than any man in the country—including myself." Coming from the Kid, this was high praise indeed—especially the afterthought.

Sultan swat, "booed the shit out of me." He further said it would be "bullshit" for Ted to alter his natural power swing to right by hitting to left.[28] But Al Simmons, long a mainstay of Connie Mack's A's who never liked Ted, said the shift merely exposed Williams's weakness as a hitter, while Ty Cobb and Tris Speaker claimed no team would have dared try that defense on them because they would have hit to left all day.

"Well, Cobb was a great athlete," Williams reflected, "in my estimate the greatest of all time, but he was an entirely different breed of cat. He was a push hitter. He choked up on the bat, two inches from the bottom, his hands four inches apart. He stood close to the plate, his hands forward. At bat he had the exact posture of the punch hitter that he was. When he talked hitting, he talked Greek to me.... Cobb was up high with his stance, slashing at the ball, pushing at it; I was down with a longer stroke. The arc of my swing was much greater than Cobb's. I was anything but a push hitter."[29]

Cobb and Williams, both supremely confident and even arrogant, kept up a running dialogue over the issue for the next several years. At the 1947 World Series between the Yankees and Dodgers, Cobb, after being introduced to Ted by Grantland Rice, buttonholed him for a talk about the shift outside a stadium restaurant. Cobb had just written Ted a letter on the fine points of spray hitting. As Williams recalled the conversation in his book, the Georgia Peach said: " 'Boy, Ted, if they ever pulled that drastic shift on me —' and he laughed and kind of shuddered, seeing with his mind's eye the immortal Ty Cobb ripping line drives into those wide-open spaces in left field."

But Cobb was not content to keep his thoughts private, and in May of 1951 he went public with his criticism of Ted, telling the Associated Press: "Williams has fine ability, but he cannot be classed as a great hitter. No player can be called a truly great hitter unless he can hit to all fields." Then that July, Cobb wrote Williams another letter, perhaps wanting to tone down his public remarks but continuing his lecture about combating the shift.

Bobby Doerr was with Ted when he received Cobb's letter, around the time of the All-Star Game in Detroit. As the two were riding from the airport to their hotel the day before the game, Doerr said Ted pulled the letter from his pocket and read it out loud, but again rejected Cobb's advice. "I don't want to do anything to change what I'm doing now," Doerr recalled Ted saying. "I'm hitting .340 now. Why should I change something and then lose something that I've got?" Then, Doerr said,

Ted took the letter "and crumpled it up and threw it out the window of the cab."[30]*

The bottom line for Williams was that he would not fundamentally change or overhaul his classic swing; he was paid to slug, and a player has to do what he does best. And he was getting increasingly frustrated at other advice he was receiving from mere mortals: "advice from newspapermen who can't hit, from pitchers, and from .250 hitters."[31] But Bert Dunne, former Pirates great Waner, and several others convinced him that he at least had to adapt; he had to go to left often enough to make the defenses more honest. He began following their advice in 1947, and by the end of that season, Boudreau was praising Ted for being "cute" enough to go to left at least occasionally, and he predicted that opposing teams would have trouble "getting Ted's goat from now on. The whole idea of the shift was to bother Williams psychologically. He was stubborn in 1946."[32]

By the early '50s, Ted was proving he could go to the opposite field on a regular basis, and opponents reconsidered the shift. The Yankees were the first to abandon it, in 1951, and others gradually followed suit over the course of the decade, as Ted's bat speed declined slightly with age and he became less of a natural pull hitter anyway.

Williams guessed that without the shift, his lifetime batting average of .344 would have been up to fifteen points higher; he said it was the second baseman playing in short right field who caused him the most difficulty and erased most of his hits. But he noted that he still won four batting titles after the shift was implemented, lost another by just two-tenths of a percentage point, and lost a sixth because he lacked the requisite number of official at bats — a title he would have won had present rules on a walk not counting as an at bat been in effect.

The Red Sox had built a big lead early in 1946 and would never look back. After the halfway point of the season, they were never less than ten games ahead of their nearest pursuer. By early September they were up by sixteen games, and they seemed on track to break the record of 107 wins set by the 1932 Yankees. Then they lost six in a row.

Finally, on September 13 in Cleveland, the Sox clinched their first pennant since 1918 when Ted hit the only inside-the-park home run of

---

* Doerr loved that story and told it often. "Can you imagine what that letter would be worth today in the memorabilia business?" he asked the writer David Halberstam, chuckling. "Ty Cobb writing to Ted Williams on how to beat the shift? One million? Two million?"

his career. Facing Boudreau's shift, Williams deliberately drove the ball over the head of left fielder Pat Seerey, who had been playing about twenty feet behind shortstop. The ball rolled all the way to the wall, four hundred feet away, and by the time it was retrieved and thrown back in, Ted had easily scored what turned out to be the game's only run.

Now Red Sox traveling secretary Tom Dowd could break out the champagne he'd been lugging from Washington and Philadelphia to Detroit and Cleveland, waiting for the team to clinch. Owner Tom Yawkey led the victory party for the players at the team hotel— excluding the writers, for whom the team staged a separate party. This enraged the newspapermen, and when Yawkey made an appearance at the press gathering, Austen Lake of the *American* engaged him in a shouting match. This followed another confrontation earlier in the day between sworn enemies Joe Cronin and the *American's* Huck Finnegan after Finnegan assured Cronin he'd never win another pennant.

Notably absent from the players' party was Williams, who, characteristically, had decided to go his own way and meet up with a Cleveland fishing buddy to spend the evening tying flies. When the writers demanded to know why Ted wasn't celebrating with his teammates, Dowd lied and said the Kid was visiting a dying veteran in a Cleveland hospital. When that story quickly unraveled, Dave Egan pounced and wrote that this was further evidence Ted cared only about himself and not his team; that there was one set of rules for Williams and another for the other Red Sox players.*

Yet there was no doubt that the double standard was reinforced by the press. On August 27, Ted got in a car accident. Williams, accompanied by his wife and two friends, had been driving his new Ford to East Douglas, Massachusetts, near Worcester, where the Red Sox were scheduled to play an exhibition game against the Cleveland Indians. Another car suddenly swerved in front of Ted's car and struck it head-on. No one was seriously hurt, but the bang-up prompted Pearl Harbor–size headlines in the papers.

Four days later, at Fenway Park, Williams, increasingly frustrated by

---

* Yawkey had given credence to the latter charge just the day before, when Bob Feller revealed that he had offered to pay Williams $10,000 to be the headliner for an off-season barnstorming tour of prominent American Leaguers that the pitcher was organizing, only to have Yawkey sabotage the plans by agreeing to pay Ted $10,000 not to participate. The Sox owner didn't want to take a chance that his star would get hurt, but he didn't object to his other players signing up if they wished. They wanted to, but Feller, irked by Yawkey's stance on Williams, refused to invite any of the other Red Sox.

the effects of the shift and a lingering slump in which he'd hit only .272 for the month of August, was roundly booed for getting into an unseemly snit after being robbed of a home run by Athletics right fielder Elmer Valo. In the third inning, into the teeth of a fierce east wind, Ted had scorched a ball that Valo had caught in front of the bull pen. The day before, Valo had made a more remarkable catch of another drive by Ted that by all rights should have been another home run. Then, at the start of the sixth inning, with the Red Sox leading the Athletics, 3–2, Williams, still pouting after the second Valo catch, halfheartedly hit a ground ball, which he failed to run out. The crowd let him have it, and Cronin, heading to the dugout from his third-base coaching position, lectured Ted on his way out to left field.

Williams played most of the seventh inning with his arms folded in left, continuing to sulk. When Valo hit a fly ball to him to end the inning, Ted, after catching it, heaved the ball up in the air, then took his glove and threw it after the ball. The wolves naturally howled still louder at this display. Cronin waited for him in the dugout and chewed him out again, but he said after the game he would take no further action.

At least one of Williams's teammates was angered by his antics and called him on it. Rudy York, the slugging first baseman who had come over from Detroit in the off-season, confronted Williams in the clubhouse.

"We're about to win this pennant," York later recalled telling Williams, "and everybody's in it together. All we got to do is play our best and we got it in the bag. Anybody who loafs on this ball club has got to answer to me. I'm about washed up, and you've got a long way to go. I'm not aiming to let a pennant slip away from me now, and I'm not aiming to see you let it slip away, either."[33]

York, who liked to chain-smoke Camels in the dugout while studying opposing pitchers to determine when they tipped their pitches, said, "Williams was a good friend of mine, and he took it in the right spirit. I always did say he was the greatest hitter I ever saw step in the box."

The Red Sox played out the string to finish 104–50, twelve games ahead of Detroit and fully seventeen ahead of the reeling third-place Yankees. Williams remained in the spotlight as the subject of long profiles in the September issues of *Sport, Collier's,* and *Life* magazines. The *Life* piece did nothing to dispel the notion that Ted cared only about hitting. "They'll never get me out of the game running into a wall after a fly ball," he told writer John Chamberlain.[34] "I'll make a damn good try, but you can bet your sweet life I won't get killed. They don't pay off on fielding."

Ted's final batting line—a .342 average with 38 home runs and 123 runs batted in—was not enough to lead the league in any one category but would be deemed impressive enough to win him the American League's Most Valuable Player award. His series of late-season contretemps soon faded in importance as the excitement of Boston being in its first World Series in twenty-eight years began to build.

The National League season ended in a tie for first place between the St. Louis Cardinals and the Brooklyn Dodgers, forcing a three-game series to determine the pennant winner.

Williams, in his column, picked the Cardinals to win. He thought the fact that both teams were having to fight to the finish would help keep them sharp for the World Series. The Red Sox had clinched early, and for the last month "just fiddled around," Ted wrote in his book. "It had been the kind of season that positively breeds overconfidence."[35]

With the onset of cool weather in October, Williams had again contracted what had become an almost annual virus. "They never could find out what the hell that was, and they tested me for everything," he said years later.[36] After a course of antibiotics, he felt even more weakened. Like many players returning from three years off at war, Williams would acknowledge later that he was fatigued, his body still not yet fully reacclimated to the rigors of a seven-month season. He had done most of his hitting in the spring and early summer and had tailed off in the late summer and early fall. He hadn't hit a ball out of the park since September 11 in Detroit.

Waiting for the Cardinals-Dodgers winner, the Red Sox decided to try to keep their edge by playing an exhibition series at Fenway Park against a handpicked group of leading American Leaguers that included Joe DiMaggio and Hank Greenberg. It was a cold, raw day, and only 1,996 people turned out to watch the first game on October 1, when DiMaggio was forced to take the field in a Boston uniform after his Yankees flannels did not arrive on time. In his third at bat, Williams, facing five-foot-eight Washington Senators left-hander Mickey Haefner, was struck on the tip of his right elbow. The pitch wasn't deliberate—it was simply a curve that didn't curve. Ted had seen the ball spinning toward him and thought it would break in, but it never did, and he couldn't get his elbow out of the way in time.

X-rays showed no break but revealed a bad bone bruise, which was painful and swelled quickly. "Shoosh," Ted wrote in his book, "the elbow went up like a balloon. It turned blue. The World Series was to begin three days later, but I couldn't take batting practice for two days."

Les Cassie Sr.—Ted's old San Diego neighbor who had driven him across the country to spring training in 1939 and was now in Boston, collecting on Williams's promise to invite him to the first World Series he appeared in—was alarmed. He phoned Les junior and said: "His elbow is three times as big as it's supposed to be. He's all stuffed up with antibiotics. I don't see how he can play."[37] The papers splashed news of Ted's injury on the front page, next to dispatches from Germany and the Nuremberg trials, in which Nazi leaders had been found guilty of crimes against humanity.

By October 3, the Cardinals had dispatched the Dodgers in two straight, and the Red Sox knew they would be heading to Saint Louis. Dr. Ralph McCarthy, the team physician, announced that Williams would be in the lineup when the Series began on Sunday the sixth, but he would not have proper use of his elbow for at least a week. "It's going to hurt him every time he swings," McCarthy said.[38] Williams spent the next three days in the trainer's room getting whirlpool treatments.

Hundreds of fans turned out at Trinity Place station in the Back Bay section of Boston on the evening of the third to give their heroes a proper sendoff as Williams and his teammates boarded the eight-car "Red Sox Special" for the twenty-four-hour trip to Saint Louis.

Just before the train was scheduled to pull out, Dave Egan launched a maliciously timed bombshell designed to make maximum mischief on the eve of the Series: Ted, the Colonel claimed, was on the trading block. The Detroit Tigers had already offered to swap pitcher Hal Newhouser and outfielder Dick Wakefield for him, while the Yankees, not to be outdone, had offered Joe DiMaggio himself as well as third baseman Bill Johnson and catcher Aaron Robinson. Delighting in tweaking Ted, Egan played off Williams's status as a *Globe* columnist. "I hate to scoop a brother journalist," the Colonel began, "particularly one who is laboring bravely under the handicap of an injured writing arm, but this is to inform journalist Ted Williams that left-fielder Ted Williams is up for sale to the highest bidder."[39]

Egan cited no basis for his story and did not otherwise explain how he knew it to be so. He merely asserted he "has the facts . . . and knows them to be the facts." He said the Red Sox had been fed up with Ted's behaving like a "spoiled brat" in August and September and interpreted his comportment to mean he wanted out. Moreover, since Williams had not yet officially ruled out jumping to the Mexican League at the end of the season, the team worried it could receive nothing of value for its star player if he took that option. The Colonel predicted it would be the Yankees who would land Williams and that DiMaggio had signaled as much when he put on a Boston uniform the other day at Fenway Park.

Egan's column was the talk of the train ride to Saint Louis as the players and members of the front office passed copies of the *Record* around. Ted, of course, devoured every word and smiled broadly as his teammates ribbed him about it, but he declined comment to the writers. Sox general manager Eddie Collins said he knew nothing about any trade for Ted, then, oddly, added that he didn't want to be quoted as saying so. Tigers manager Steve O'Neill, who was on board the train as a guest of the Red Sox, said he had not heard that his team had made any offer for Williams.[40]

When the Red Sox took the field at Sportsman's Park to practice the day before the Series was to start, Williams made his first comment on Egan's column, saying he'd quit or jump to Mexico before going to New York. "I'd hate to be traded to the Yankees," he said. "I don't like New York. I just don't want to play there." He said nothing about Detroit, perhaps feeling he didn't have to, since it was well known that Williams considered Briggs Stadium one of his favorite parks to hit in.

Meanwhile, the rest of the Red Sox hierarchy—Joe Cronin and Tom Yawkey—were less equivocal than Collins had been in denying Egan's column. Cronin said, "The idea of trading Williams is silly—ridiculous. We have never discussed such a thing."[41] Added Yawkey: "I wouldn't trade him for Yankee Stadium or Briggs Stadium. If he ever is sold, however, the press won't name the club nor will the press name the price. I'm still running the ball club."[42]

Taking his first batting practice since being plunked on the elbow, Williams felt better than he thought he would, and he certainly put on a show. He hit three homers on top of the right-field roof and crashed two balls against the right-field screen. "When I give it that little extra— either throwing or hitting—it hurts," Ted told the writers.[43] But the pain did not prevent him from giving it that little extra, he added.

The Red Sox were heavy favorites to win the Series, but many of the Cardinals were cocky, and some openly talked trash. Stan Musial would make Ted "look sick" in the Series, predicted pitcher Red Barrett.[44] "Do we fear Williams? Of course we don't," added reliever Ted Wilks. "We pitched against him in the South this spring and got him out and we'll stop him again."

Not all the Cardinals were so impudent. Joe Garagiola, the rookie catcher and Saint Louis native, was a great admirer of Ted's and remembered well listening to him abuse the Browns on the radio as he was growing up. Now Garagiola found himself behind the plate in game 1 of the World Series when the Great Man himself stepped into the box. "All of a sudden there he was right in front of me," Garagiola recalled. "I didn't know whether to throw the ball to the pitcher or ask for an autograph. The first pitch was an inside fastball, and he followed it all the way into my mitt. 'That ball was inside,' he said to me. 'Yes, sir,' I said to him, and that was all I could say."[45]

The first time Williams came up, Cardinals manager Eddie Dyer ordered his team into a modified Boudreau shift, despite having said before the Series that he would play it straight against Ted. Shortstop Marty Marion remained at his position, while third baseman Whitey Kurowski ran across the diamond to play second, second baseman Red Schoendienst shifted to the hole in short right, and first baseman Stan Musial hugged the line. The left fielder played center while the center and right fielders divided right. If Dyer's goal was to get into Ted's head, he apparently succeeded. "I never expected it," Williams wrote in his column the next day. "Brother, did they pull a fast one on me."

Ted, facing left-hander Howie Pollet, then grounded out sharply to the newly aligned Schoendienst. He walked in the third, lashed a single over Kurowski's head into right-center in the sixth, and walked in the eighth. The game was tied after nine innings, 2–2. In the tenth, Ted fouled out to Musial before Rudy York ripped a home run to the left-field bleachers to give the Red Sox a 3–2 win in the first game.

The Cardinals came back strong the next day, winning 3–0 behind lefty Harry "the Cat" Brecheen. Ted went for the collar—grounding out to Musial, striking out swinging, lining out to Schoendienst in short right (a hit without the shift), and then popping up awkwardly to shortstop Marion when he tried to go to left. Williams "looked pitiful" on that last at bat, Schoendienst told the writers afterward, provocatively.

The scene shifted to Boston for the next three games. On the train ride home, Ted sat with Johnny Orlando and trainer Win Green and brooded about having gone 1–7 in Saint Louis, and also about the Egan story. "Do you think they'll trade me?" he asked.[46] "I'd like to know. I want to get straightened out." He did seem pleased to pass around a telegram he'd received from a new fan after the second game. "Don't forget, I'm a National Leaguer, but I'm for you," said the wire from Bing Crosby. (Ted and Crosby, it had been reported, were considering making a baseball movie together in the off-season.)

The Red Sox cruised to a 4–0 win in game 3 on the strength of brilliant pitching by Boo Ferriss and a three-run blast in the first inning by Rudy York, his second home run of the Series. One of the highlights of the game, for Fenway fans and the press, was a bunt by Ted in the third inning. With two out, nobody on, and the wind blowing in from right field, Williams decided the time was right for a bunt, which he successfully pushed down the line, past third base, and into left field for a single.

Boisterous TED BUNTS headlines in the papers rivaled the game itself for attention, and the writers seemed captivated by the moment.* Williams failed to see the humor in the headlines and felt it was an attempt by the press to ridicule him—which, to some extent, it was.[47]

Besides the bunt, Ted was walked intentionally, struck out swinging with a man in scoring position, and lined out to Enos Slaughter down the right-field line to lead off the eighth inning. After the game, Joe Cronin, responding to Harold Kaese's column in the *Globe* that morning, which suggested it was the manager who wanted to trade Ted, issued a definitive statement on behalf of the team: Williams would not be dealt. The fans, meanwhile, had clearly weighed in on the trade issue. When the Kid first came to bat—the first time the home crowd had a chance to render any opinion since the Egan story broke—he was greeted with waves of applause and cheers.

Williams was touched by the reception and told Bill Grimes of the *American* after the game: "I want to stay in Boston. This is my town. The fans were wonderful to me today." He also went out of his way to try to knock down the criticism—fueled by the Colonel—that he was out for himself. "I have been accused of being an individual player," he said. "This is NOT true. I am strictly a team player. If it looks to the fans as though I'm trying to show any individuality, it's only because I've had a poor day. Believe me when I tell you, I want the Red Sox to win and I

---

* "Ted Williams bunted yesterday and it was the biggest thing around here since Bunker Hill," wrote Red Smith in his syndicated column on October 10. "The Kid's bunt was bigger than York's home run. Thirty-four thousand, five hundred witnesses gave off the same quaint animal cries that must have been heard at the bonfires in Salem when Williams, whose mission in life is to hit baseballs across Suffolk County, pushed a small, safe roller past third base."

am willing to sacrifice anything for a victory."[48] Somewhat typical for Williams was his decision to give away the six tickets he was allotted for each of the three World Series games at Fenway Park: he had his wife go to Kenmore Square before the games and give the tickets to the first six GIs she saw.[49] He felt no need to tell the press about the token of appreciation for the fans.

The Cardinals again rebounded in game 4, crushing Tex Hughson and five other Red Sox pitchers for twenty hits in a 12–3 laugher. Ted went 1–3, with a walk.

In the pivotal fifth game, the Sox broke on top in the first inning when Williams, batting with runners on first and second, singled to right to knock in a run. The Sox took a 3–1 lead into the bottom of the seventh, then blew it open when Mike Higgins doubled to drive in a run and the usually reliable Marty Marion at shortstop threw wildly to second with the bases loaded, allowing two more runs to score. Boston won, 6–3, with Joe Dobson going all the way and holding the Cardinals to just four hits.

After his first-inning single and RBI, Ted failed to get a hit in his next four times up. He grounded to Marion at short, struck out swinging with a runner on second, was called out on strikes two innings later with another runner at second, and fouled out to the catcher in the eighth — again while a runner was at second. Despite this display of futility after the solid start, Williams felt the fans' love all day long. They cheered wildly at anything he did—even his Ks. "It has been said that Ted's shell-like ears have been offended by comments from the electorate in the past," Red Smith wrote. "If so, he heard celestial pipes today....He went away in the knowledge that his immortality was secure."[50]

Whatever psychic benefit the home crowd adoration may have given Williams was mitigated by the torrent of abuse Saint Louis fans showered on him at Sportsman's Park during game 6. It started in batting practice with shrieks of "When are you gonna get a home run, Williams?" Ted ground his teeth in anger and mumbled, "I hear you, you..." according to the *American,* which omitted the curse word, as required of a family newspaper.

Williams walked in the first and popped up to Musial in the fourth. When he struck out in the sixth, "the howls of derision that came from the left field stands were never equaled in Boston," the *American* reported.[51] The Cardinals did their damage with three runs in the third inning off Mickey Harris and added another in the eighth. And when Ted came to bat in the ninth with nobody on, his team trailing 4–1, the

Cardinals patrons twisted the knife, screaming for a pinch hitter. Williams responded with a single between Schoendienst and Marion, who this time was lined up on the first-base side of second.

The 4–1 score held up as Saint Louis again got a sterling pitching performance from Harry Brecheen to force a seventh and deciding game. The Red Sox looked to have had the Cat on the ropes in the first two innings, but both times he'd escaped trouble, notably by getting Rudy York to hit into an inning-ending double play with the bases loaded in the first. The Red Sox's only run came in the seventh, on a sacrifice fly by Bobby Doerr.

In his column, Williams had high praise for Brecheen. "What makes him so effective is that you don't know which spot he's going to pitch to," Ted said. "He's high when you think he'd be low, and he's inside when you're looking for him to be outside.... After the first two innings, the Cat played with us like he would a mouse."[52]

Predictably, the Boston papers began looking for scapegoats. "As matters stand, Ted Williams is an enormous bust," wrote the *Globe*'s Kaese, noting that Williams had just five hits and one RBI through six games.[53] None of the other Red Sox were hitting particularly well, either: of the regulars, only Doerr was batting over .300.

Williams unburdened himself to Grantland Rice, the syndicated columnist, after game 6, conceding that he had been trying to outguess the Cardinals pitchers too much. "They've been smarter than I am," Ted said. "They've outguessed me." Rice, who was emerging as the Kid's Series confidant, called this "a pretty honest statement" and went on to consider Williams's psyche. He called the conventional wisdom that Ted is conceited "entirely incorrect. The main trouble is that Ted suffers from an inferiority complex. He also admits that he does things he knows he shouldn't do, and doesn't do things he knows he should." Williams told Rice that Red Sox fans had been swell to him during the three World Series games in Boston, "where I was a flop. I wanted to lift my cap to their applause. For some reason, I couldn't do it. And I knew I was wrong. I'd rather win, or help to win this Series, for Tom Yawkey alone, than anything I ever did. I'll probably lose it."[54]

This was a startling admission, which seemed to underscore Williams's insecurity. That night he was sitting alone with his thoughts in his room at the Chase Hotel when a writer stopped by and knocked on his door, which was slightly ajar. There was no response. The room was dark. The writer peered inside and could see Ted sitting at the window, silhouetted against the lights from the city below. Unsettled by the scene, he left without disturbing Williams, and the next day he told Rice what he'd seen. "I'll see he doesn't sit alone in the dark tonight," Rice replied.

With an off day scheduled to give the Cardinals more time to print and sell tickets for game 7, Ted stewed in his own juices, but he seemed upbeat during the Red Sox workout. Some of his teammates were stirred by the news that the losers' share in the Series would be $2,094 per player, or less than the $2,500 each umpire would earn. "We can't let that happen," said Rudy York. "If we're not worth more than the umpires, we shouldn't be in the business."

When batting practice began, and it was Ted's turn to step in the cage against pitcher Mace Brown, many of the Red Sox stopped to watch number 9, hoping he'd find his groove and set the proper tone for the team. After a few languid swings to get loosened up, Williams began talking quietly to himself. Hy Hurwitz of the *Globe* pressed against the cage to listen.

"There's a 3–2 count on me, the bases are full, and it's the last of the ninth with two out," Ted said to psych himself, just as a Little Leaguer might. "Throw me a low fast one, and I'll blow it out of the park."

Brown delivered it low and hard, and Williams drilled the ball over the pavilion roof in right field and out onto Grand Avenue, where fans were waiting in line to buy tickets.

Then the chatter began. "Now you're swinging," said Bobby Doerr from behind the cage. "You're not pushing it the way you have been. You've got your shoulders into it."

"Attaboy, Teddy," chimed in York. "Cut at all of them that way and you won't be an out man."

Williams kept ripping the ball for the next fifteen minutes—line drives, rising line drives, deep, towering fly balls, many of them home runs. His teammates "began to acquire new confidence that they'd be better paid than the umpires," Hurwitz wrote. Said one unnamed player: "Hits like that tomorrow and somebody's gonna get murdered."

Back in the clubhouse, Brown said to Williams: "You hit the ball good, Ted, and I had good stuff out there today."

"You're darn right you had good stuff. Are you sure I hit the ball good?" Ted replied, the insecurity creeping back in.[55] But when the writers came around looking for quotes, Williams put his bravado back on, saying he'd gotten good wood on the ball today and had a feeling he "might break loose tomorrow."[56]

That night, Williams was again alone in his hotel room when Grant-land Rice called and insisted they go out to dinner. Ted quickly agreed. He was glad to have company, so he took Rice and a writer pal that the columnist brought along to a restaurant in South Saint Louis that served a good steak. Rice, sensing the Kid's vulnerability, tried to get Williams to relax by talking about hunting and fishing. But Ted, who had two glasses of wine with his meal, only wanted to talk about the seventh game. "I'd give anything in the world if we could win that game tomorrow," he said.

"And if you could get a couple of home runs?" Rice asked.

"I wouldn't care if I didn't get a single, unless it could mean winning the game," Williams replied. "Naturally I'd like to get four singles. Or four home runs. But if I struck out four times, I'd be happy — if we could just win. Tom Yawkey...Joe Cronin...all the fellows on the ball club...have waited so long for this. I hate like hell to think they might miss it." Rice thought Ted meant he hated to think the Red Sox might lose because of him.[57]

It was sunny and warm the day of the deciding game, in the mid-seventies. Boo Ferriss was starting for the Red Sox; slight right-hander Murry Dickson for the Cardinals.

The Sox opened with a run in the top of the first. Wally Moses led off with a single, Pesky singled Moses over to third, and Dom DiMaggio hit a sacrifice fly to score Moses. Williams then hit a bomb more than four hundred feet to dead center, but the ball lingered in the air just long enough to allow center fielder Terry Moore, who had been positioned in right-center in the shift, to race over and make a beautiful catch.

Williams made a nice defensive play of his own in the bottom of the first, fielding Red Schoendienst's leadoff single cleanly and throwing him out at second when he tried to leg out a double. But in the bottom of the second, with a runner on third and one out, Ted didn't appear aggressive enough in left field, catching a fly ball of medium depth and not even attempting to throw the runner tagging at third out at the plate.

Leading off the fourth, with the score 1–1, Williams crushed another four-hundred-foot drive, to left-center, and this time left fielder Harry "the Hat" Walker raced over to make another fine catch, nearly colliding with Moore. "Ted turned disgustedly toward the bench, his cup of woe overflowing," wrote Austen Lake in the *American*.[58]

The Cardinals got to Ferriss for two runs in their half of the fifth. Ted, batting with two outs and a runner on first in the sixth, flied to right.

The score remained 3–1, Saint Louis, until the Red Sox came to bat in the eighth inning. Utility infielder Rip Russell, pinch-hitting for catcher Hal Wagner, singled to lead off. Outfielder Catfish Metkovich then pinch-hit for pitcher Joe Dobson, who had replaced Ferriss in the fifth, and doubled. With runners on second and third and no one out, Cardinals manager Eddie Dyer pulled Murry Dickson and brought in Harry Brecheen — again. The Cat had pitched nine innings just two days earlier, after throwing another nine in the winning game 2.

Brecheen struck out Wally Moses and got Johnny Pesky to line out to right field. That brought Dom DiMaggio up, and Dyer went out to the mound to confer with Brecheen. First base was open, but DiMaggio knew he would not be intentionally walked with Williams on deck. Brecheen pitched carefully to DiMaggio, a right-handed batter, nibbling the corners, staying out of the heart of the strike zone. With the count three and one, Dom guessed Brecheen would come with his most effective pitch, a screwball on the outside corner. He guessed correctly and laced the ball off the top of the right-field fence, about two feet from a home run.

"When I got to first base, I thought if I could just get to third they're going to be very careful, because Ted Williams is hitting behind me," DiMaggio recalled. "If they make the slightest passed ball, I'm going to score. Well, that was a bad mistake, because as soon as I turned first base and dug for more, I popped my hamstring."[59]

DiMaggio was lucky to hobble into second safely, much less reach third, but two runs had scored, tying the game. DiMaggio had to leave the game and was replaced by outfielder Leon Culberson.

Now Williams dug in against Brecheen for what was easily his most important at bat of the Series. The momentum was back with the Red Sox, and the go-ahead run was at second, waiting to be knocked in. It was a pivotal situation, a moment when the hitting star of the team was expected to deliver. But it didn't happen. Ted merely popped up to Schoendienst to end the inning.

In the bottom of the eighth, the Cardinals quickly capitalized. Enos "Country" Slaughter led off with a single to center. Red Sox reliever Bob Klinger retired the next two batters and then faced Harry Walker. Slaughter noticed Klinger was not holding him close enough at first, so he took off for second with a big jump. Walker swung away and hit a soft liner that fell between Williams and Culberson, who had replaced DiMaggio in center. The ball landed just as Slaughter was reaching second, and he raced ahead, the play unfolding before him.

Culberson retrieved the ball, but without the sense of urgency that the situation required. Then, making things worse, his relay to Johnny Pesky lacked the requisite zip. Slaughter, well aware that Culberson's arm was weaker than DiMaggio's, had made up his mind even before he hit second that he was going to try and score, and he was flying around third by the time Pesky, in a play that lives on in baseball lore, hesitated slightly before firing to the plate. He was not nearly in time to nail the sliding Slaughter. "I'm the goat," Pesky said afterward, bravely, and so it has played in the books, but in truth, Culberson shared much of the blame for Slaughter's mad dash because of his lackadaisical approach to Walker's hit—as did Klinger, for not holding Slaughter on first properly to begin with.

The Red Sox had their chances in the ninth when York and Doerr led off with consecutive singles, but the next three men went down quietly, and the Cardinals won, 4–3. Ted never got a chance to redeem his eighth-inning failure.

It had been a thrilling World Series, but the blame game began immediately. The *Globe*'s Harold Kaese said the Sox were beaten by "the three W's: World Series inexperience, winning the pennant too early, and Williams's batting slump." Cardinals shortstop Marty Marion was more specific: "We won the Series by stopping Williams," Marion said, and that seemed to be the consensus in the Saint Louis clubhouse.[60]

Cardinals manager Eddie Dyer revealed to the *Globe*'s Roger Birtwell that his team had systematically drawn up a plan to stop Williams. Since it was a foregone conclusion that the Red Sox would win the pennant, the Cardinals had dispatched two of their scouts, Ken Penner and Tony Kaufmann, to follow Boston starting in August. Penner and Kaufmann were to gather daily information on all the Red Sox but pay particular attention to Williams. (National League president Ford Frick provided Saint Louis with money to hire another scout, and the Dodgers, after losing to the Cardinals in the playoffs, turned over their dossier on Williams, which corroborated what the others had found.)

"Williams was the key man," said Dyer.[61] "We came to the conclusion that the best thing to do was pitch him tight, but we needed more than that. We could not put every pitch to him in the same place." Dyer, Penner, and Kaufmann concluded that Ted was fundamentally a guess hitter: he would study opposing pitchers closely and learn their tendencies in a given situation so that when he faced that circumstance, he would be looking for a certain pitch from a certain pitcher. So the Cardinals told their pitchers what Williams would be expecting from them in a variety of situations and then ordered them to keep him off balance by throwing something different.

The plan worked. Williams did not get one extra-base hit in the Series, scattering just five singles over five games and striking out five times for a .200 batting average. He did reach base five more times through walks. And a combination of good defense and the shift took away several potential extra-base hits on balls that Ted hit on the nose, but that was part of Dyer's plan, too.

When it was all over, Ted gave the Cardinals their due, singling out Brecheen. "Brecheen, the Cat, was the big hero of the Series," he said in his column. "I think his mere presence on the field inspired the Cardinals. . . . I had hoped my bat would do the talking for me in the Series, but it was tongue-tied by some great Cardinal pitching."[62]

When the writers and photographers were allowed in the clubhouse, Williams sat woefully on the bench in front of his locker, hunched over, staring at the floor, disconsolate. Pitcher Mickey Harris sat next to him and struck a similar pose, and the two were pictured in a bleak tableau in the next day's *Globe*.

Ted was the last player to dress and the last to leave the clubhouse, having lingered in the shower, where, according to a consoling Johnny Orlando, he "cried like a baby. . . . Cried because he knew he'd been a flop."[63] Outside, scores of Cardinals fans were lying in wait for him, hurling invective inside. "Where's Williams?" they screamed. "Where's Superman?"[64] When he finally came out, the fans had formed two raging lines on either side of the door, forcing Ted to run the gauntlet of abuse. Police stood by, watching only to make sure he was not assaulted.

Williams took the insults impassively, yearning now only for the train and the privacy of his own compartment for the long ride back to Boston. He gave his Series check to Orlando as a tip for the season, and in a coat pocket he discovered twelve tickets—six each for the last two games—which he had forgotten to give away.

When the team finally reached the train, Ted made his way to his room, shut the door, and wept.[65] After a time, when he looked out the window, he saw scores of people gawking at him, a mix of glee and malice in their eyes.

Williams wrote that his year had ended "in a frustration that grew, like the importance of the .400 season, to a terrible dimension as the years passed. Who was to know at the time I would not get another chance? The first World Series Ty Cobb played in he batted .200, but he got two more chances. The first World Series Stan Musial played in he batted .222, but he got three more chances. Babe Ruth hit .118 in the 1922 Series, but he played in six [sic] others.... This was it for me."[66]

10

1947–1948

Williams lay low all winter, fishing and brooding over his World Series washout. "It was a long winter," he said. "I had been humiliated."[1]

He flew to Boston in early February to sign his 1947 contract and to attend the annual dinner of the Boston baseball writers. Ted usually enjoyed the harmless hoopla that attended his contract sessions each year, when the writers would fuss over him and often throw out wild guesses about how much of a raise he was going to get, what his total number would be, and where that would put him among baseball's elite. Given the loss to the Cardinals last fall and his own prominent role in it, Williams assumed there might be some grousing that his new salary would represent ill-gotten gains. But business was business.

Ted was aware that in January, Bob Feller, the Indians ace, had signed a precedent-setting contract that introduced the concept of attendance-escalator clauses. In addition to his base salary, he would receive another $7,500 if home attendance reached 700,000, and another $7,500 for every 100,000 fans over 700,000.[2] Ted figured he could draw more people to Fenway Park (not to mention around the league) as an every-day player than Feller could to Cleveland Stadium by pitching every fourth day, so he wanted to take the same approach.

Williams and Feller were friendly, and Ted admired the pitcher's aggressive approach to business—including the fact that he had incorporated himself as "Ro-Fel" and earned tens of thousands of extra dollars in endorsements, speeches, and radio deals.*

---

* Ted had agreed to appear on one of Feller's radio shows, and in return, as Feller told the writer Michael Seidel years later, he agreed to pitch to Williams in future games—not pitch around him—unless first base was open or there were runners in scoring position.

When Ted sat down with Eddie Collins, they quickly agreed on a $65,000 base salary (representing a $25,000 raise from 1946) with escalators topping out at a total of $75,000 if Fenway attendance reached 1.25 million, a figure the team would easily surpass. The writers didn't pick up a whiff of the escalator provisions, and they generally pegged the salary at $70,000. Collins called it the highest base salary ever paid in baseball, except for Ruth's.

The writers' dinner was a mob scene, infested with scores of hangers-on and assorted vacuum cleaner, furniture, and haberdashery salesmen trying to sell their wares to Ted and the other stars on hand—such as Tigers pitcher Dizzy Trout and World Series heroes Enos Slaughter and Harry Brecheen. Ted, wearing a tie for the occasion on the advice of his business manager, Fred Corcoran, was presented the writers' award as the team's MVP for 1946, but he said he felt guilty accepting it given his Series flop.

Grantland Rice, the syndicated writer and Williams devotee, tried to buck his pal up in a *Sport* magazine open letter. "I have an idea that this new season of 1947 may be your best year," Rice wrote. "In a way, baseball needs you more than you need baseball. For we have all too few colorful characters left who can catch the fancy of the crowds. This is the year to show the mobs that you belong with the great hitters of all time. Forget the World Series, just as Ruth, Cobb and Wagner forgot their flops. I can't recall another ballplayer who ever had the chance you have this season to steal the show."[3]

Ted reported to Sarasota for spring training "jacked up," he said, to atone for his Series failure.[4] There was still a lot of talk about how best to combat the Boudreau shift, and, to that end, Williams began working with Paul Waner on hitting to left.

That spring there was more significant news away from Sarasota: Jackie Robinson broke baseball's color barrier on April 15 as a Brooklyn Dodger. Ted—who had crossed paths with Robinson in 1936 on the Southern California high school baseball circuit, when both were named to the All-Star team in the tournament sponsored by the 20-30 Club of Pomona—admired Jackie's guts and sent him a letter of congratulations. Years later, Robinson's widow, Rachel, told writer Bill Nowlin: "Jack was very impressed that someone of that stature took the time to do that. That was the kind of person Ted Williams was."[5]

In July, Larry Doby was called up by the Cleveland Indians, thus becoming the first black ballplayer in the American League. Whenever the Red Sox played the Indians, Williams would go out of his way to make Doby feel welcome, offering hitting tips around the batting cage and chatting with him as they passed each other coming on and off the field.

"He'd just say, 'Congratulations! Good luck!'" Doby said. "He just gave me a feeling of being welcome, which was important to me, especially when you had a lot of other people not saying anything. . . . I don't think he was that sort of person to make a spectacle of it, just a quiet kind of person, going about his business. Didn't have to make any big deal out of it. That's why I feel it was from the heart."[6]

Blacks, at least black ballplayers, were not foreign to Williams. He'd been hearing about the exploits of Negro League old-timers since he was a kid, when the father of one of his friends told him of seeing the great Walter Johnson pitch an exhibition contest in New Haven against a team of Negro League All-Stars, giving up a tape-measure homer to one player and losing the game, 1–0. (Williams had confirmed the story by asking Johnson himself about it after he arrived in the majors.[7]) At the age of fourteen, he'd gone to watch Satchel Paige pitch in San Diego and marveled at how hard he threw. He'd competed against black players in high school, and against Negro League barnstormers when he was in the Pacific Coast League.

One of the black players who went up against Ted when he was playing for the San Diego Padres was Buck O'Neil, the former Negro League star who went on to become a pioneering coach and scout in the major leagues. "Oh, man, he could swing that bat," O'Neil remembered. "He said to us then, when he was in the minor leagues, 'You guys can really play. I can learn a lot from you guys. When I got a chance to hit against Satchel Paige, that's when I knew I was ready.' He said that to all of us, just talking like guys after a game."[8]

The Boston press had taken note of Williams's popularity with black fans. In a notes column headlined TED WOULD GET SOLID COLORED VOTE, published a week before Robinson's debut, Huck Finnegan of the *American* reported from Knoxville, Tennessee, where the Red Sox were playing some exhibition games: "If Ted Williams ever ran for office down this-a-way he'd get the solid colored vote. How they idolize him. Bellhops in the hotels gape at him as if he had two heads. Fans at the ballparks start a-buzzin' and a rockin' when he comes to bat. And if he hits one, as he did in dear old Chattanooga, they rock and shout for 10 minutes."

Two years before Robinson debuted with the Dodgers, the Red Sox had had a chance to sign him—but declined. Tom Yawkey was not going to be the first owner to break baseball's color line; in fact, he would become the last.

In the spring of 1945, under pressure from the black press and a Boston city councilman named Isadore Muchnick, the Red Sox had reluctantly agreed to a tryout at Fenway Park for Robinson and two other prominent Negro Leaguers, Sam Jethroe and Marvin Williams. World War II had forced the major leagues to reevaluate their Jim Crow policies, since it was difficult to argue with the proposition that anyone willing to die for his country should have an equal chance to play baseball. But when the three men showed up on the appointed day, the Red Sox reneged on the agreement and closed their doors to the players without explanation.

The tryout had attracted no notice in the white press, but Dave Egan of the *Record* got wind of what was happening and decided to weigh in. "Here are two believe-it-or-not items exclusively for the benefit of Mr. Edward Trowbridge Collins, general manager of the Boston Red Sox," the Colonel wrote. "He is living in *anno domini* 1945, and not in the dust-covered year 1865. He is residing in the city of Boston, and not in the city of Mobile, Alabama.... Therefore we feel obliged to inform you that since Wednesday last three citizens of the United States have been attempting vainly to get a tryout with his ball team."[9]

The Sox folded quickly, opening Fenway to Robinson, Jethroe, and Williams the very morning Egan's story appeared. As manager Joe Cronin watched from the stands, coach Hugh Duffy and scout Larry Woodall put the players through a few paces. Robinson stood out, fielding cleanly at shortstop, flashing his speed, and peppering the left-field wall during batting practice. But the Red Sox never contacted the players again.

Cronin shifted his story over the years about what really happened with the Robinson charade, first saying Jackie wasn't good enough, then admitting the obvious — that the team had made a mistake — then suggesting that the issue was decided over his head. "Cronin told me the American League thought Boston wasn't a good fit, knowing how tribal we are here, and that the Dodgers would be the best fit," said John Harrington, who took over as CEO of the Red Sox following the death of Yawkey and his widow, Jean. "They had Montreal as their Triple-A farm team, and there was less racism in Canada. Boston's farm team was in Louisville, and that was a problem. So according to Joe, this was being orchestrated by the league."[10] Yawkey himself echoed this view, telling the *Boston Globe* in 1971, five years before he died, that Robinson's was a "special case." He said Dodgers owner Branch Rickey, who signed Robinson to a minor-league contract in late 1945 but had been preparing to do so for more than a year, "called me and told me he'd send Robinson to Boston and to take a look at him. Our situations were different and we thought Rickey and Brooklyn were in a better position to work Robinson into the major leagues. Rickey was the man to handle Robinson, and he did."[11]

By 1946, the year after the Robinson tryout, Yawkey had emerged as one of the most influential figures in baseball, and that year he was named by the new commissioner, Happy Chandler, to serve on a committee that would advise Chandler on significant emerging issues, like the attempts of "outsiders" to unionize the players as well as "the race question." Besides Yawkey, the members of the committee were National League president Ford Frick, American League president William Harridge, and three other owners: Larry MacPhail of the Yankees, Sam Breadon of the Cardinals, and Phil Wrigley of the Cubs.

Using contorted, catch-22, and separate-but-equal logic, the committee stonewalled and said the race issue should be put off for another day and studied further by an "executive council," which was precisely what this group was. Yawkey and the others wrote in their report that black players weren't good enough for the majors and that major-league teams could not sign and develop players without risking decimating the Negro Leagues. If that were to happen, many major- and minor-league teams that rented their parks to the black ballplayers would lose an important revenue source. And if blacks were to play in the majors in significant numbers, black fans could flock to the games, thereby driving away white fans and diminishing the value of existing franchises.

"Certain groups in this country, including political and social-minded drum-beaters, are conducting pressure campaigns in an attempt to force major league clubs to sign Negro players," the committee's report said. "Members of these groups are not primarily interested in professional baseball.... Professional baseball is a private business enterprise. It has to depend on profits for its existence, just like any other business. A situation might be presented, if Negroes participate in Major League games, in which the preponderance of Negro attendance in parks such as Yankee Stadium, the Polo Grounds and Comiskey Park could conceivably threaten the value of the Major League franchises owned by these clubs....

"These Negro leagues cannot exist without good players. If they cannot field good teams, they will not continue to attract the fans who click the turnstiles. Continued prosperity depends on improving standards of play. If the major leagues and big minors of Professional Baseball raid· these leagues and take their best players, the Negro leagues will eventually fold up, the investments of their club owners will be wiped out, and a lot of professional Negro players will lose their jobs. The Negroes who own and operate these clubs do not want to part with their outstanding players—no one accuses them of racial discrimination."

The committee stressed the need for solidarity on race, warning that "the individual action of any one club may exert tremendous pressures upon the whole structure of Professional Baseball, and could conceivably result in lessening the value of several major league franchises." This was clearly a finger pointed at Branch Rickey of the Dodgers, whom Yawkey et al. knew was well along in his plans to use Robinson to break baseball's color line. But Rickey had an ally in Commissioner Chandler, who ignored his committee's recommendation and the following year signed off on the call-up of Robinson. When the report was released to other owners and to the press, the section on race was deleted. Chandler apparently decided that to include the section would have been too provocative, and its existence did not become publicly known for at least another thirty-five years.[12]*

The arrival of Robinson, Doby, and other black players was far from enough impetus to stir the Red Sox to integrate. In 1948, the team had a chance to atone for the Robinson fiasco by signing Willie Mays, but again declined. George Digby, who had become the Red Sox's first southern scout in 1944, was urged to check out Mays, then a wispy seventeen-year-old racing around center field for the Birmingham Black Barons. Digby's tipster was Eddie Glennon, general manager of Birmingham's all-white club in the Double-A Southern League, the Barons. The Black Barons had ties with the white Barons, a Red Sox affiliate, and used their park when the white club went out of town.

"Mays was a young, skinny kid then, but he did everything you looked for—he could run, throw, and hit, and I could see he was gonna have some power in his swing," Digby recalled. "That's what made me think he was gonna be an All-Star."[13]

Glennon asked Digby how he liked Mays. Digby said he liked him fine. Glennon said the Sox could have him for $4,500. Digby: "So he said, 'Let's go call [Joe] Cronin.' He said, 'I got Cronin's home number,'

---

* Chandler had kept the original report and later released it along with his other personal papers, which are stored at the University of Kentucky.

so he called Cronin." Cronin then told Digby he would send Larry Woodall, the chief scout in Boston, down to take a look at Mays.

That was a sign the decision had already been made, for it was Woodall who had helped run the sham Robinson tryout. Woodall came to Birmingham as instructed but apparently didn't even watch Mays play. When it rained for three days, he got tired of waiting around and returned to Boston. "I'm not going to waste my time waiting on a bunch of niggers," Woodall is reported to have said.[14]

"The GM in Birmingham came in and said, 'Woodall didn't like him,'" Digby recalled. "I didn't talk any more to Cronin [about it]. He was my boss, and I wasn't going to contradict him; I wanted to keep my job. They didn't tell me anything. Cronin told Eddie Glennon they weren't ready for any black players."

It wasn't until 1959 that the Red Sox finally joined the rest of the major leagues and brought up a black player from the minors to play in Boston. This tardiness on race and its lingering effects put the team at a competitive disadvantage for years and was far more responsible for the extended World Series drought in Boston than the 1919 sale of Babe Ruth to the Yankees—the so-called Curse of the Bambino. As Jim Bouton, the ex-Yankees pitcher of *Ball Four* fame, would put it, the real culprit was the "Curse of the Albino."[15]

Williams would try to make the Sox's first black player, Elijah "Pumpsie" Green, a shortstop from California, as comfortable as possible by playing catch with him in front of the dugout during warm-ups before each game. "The spring of fifty-nine, when I first went to spring training with the Red Sox, my impression was like all others who meet the great Ted Williams, the best hitter of all time," said Green. "I was in awe. He went out of his way to help me. He'd ask questions and would spend extra time talking to me, especially about hitting. He'd talk to you as long as you'd stay and listen to him. Ted didn't make any extra effort because of my color. He treated you like you should be treated. Sometimes I could sense people trying to do too much. Ted was just a regular person."[16]

Williams's own Mexican roots, and his witnessing firsthand the discrimination that some of his family members were subjected to, likely shaped his views on race and the egalitarian ideal. "Ted was the most unbiased man I ever met," said Curt Gowdy, the longtime Red Sox broadcaster. "He didn't have a biased bone in his body."[17] Added Larry Taylor, a retired Marine Corps major general who became friendly with Williams late in life: "He was a guy that believed baseball was the ultimate meritocracy. It didn't matter where you came from or your background. He liked the Marine Corps for the same reason: they didn't care who you were—just what you did."[18]

Beyond race and the arrival of Jackie Robinson, there was another intriguing development that April of 1947—this one taking place behind closed doors—that could have drastically altered the arc of Williams's career.

One night, apparently during the Red Sox's first trip to New York, from April 22 through April 24, Tom Yawkey and Yankees co-owner Dan Topping were biding their time at Toots Shor's saloon when the conversation turned to the baseball icons of the day, Williams and Joe DiMaggio. As fans often did, they talked of how frequently DiMaggio's long outs in Yankee Stadium's vast left field would be home runs over the short wall at Fenway Park, and how easily Ted's deep flies in Fenway's cavernous right field would find their way into New York's short upper deck in right. The two stars were playing in the wrong home parks. The conversation grew more and more serious. Finally, after both Yawkey and Topping were well lubricated, they agreed to make the trade. They would sleep on it and confer again the next day.

But when Topping called Yawkey in the morning, the Red Sox owner was having second thoughts; his people back at Fenway didn't like the deal. DiMaggio had slumped the previous year, with numbers that paled next to Ted's .342 average with 38 homers and 123 RBIs. Plus the Clipper had had surgery in the off-season to remove a bone spur from his left heel and had yet to return to the lineup. Ted, who was making twice as much money as Joe, was twenty-eight and still in his prime, while DiMaggio was thirty-two and likely in decline.

"If you want to make the deal," Yawkey told Topping, "you've got to throw in your little left fielder," a reference to the rookie Yogi Berra, who was also a catcher. Yawkey, whose Red Sox were still trying to live down the sale of Babe Ruth to the Yankees in 1920, was probably looking for a graceful exit, knowing his demand for Berra would be a deal breaker, and it was. Topping refused.[19]

The Sox erected lights, and night baseball came to Fenway in 1947. Williams displayed increasing skill hitting to left field, doubling off the wall regularly, and on May 13, he hit his first two home runs into the screen in left. After Ted complained that the huge advertisements on the wall for Calvert liquor, GEM razor blades, and Liberty soap distracted him at the plate, the Sox took the ads down, so the wall was now an even more hitter-friendly clean green.

Yet both Williams and DiMaggio complained that balls weren't carrying as well as they used to. "The ball was deadened near the close of the '42 season and hasn't been hopped up since," Ted said in May. "What's the percentage going for the home run? Why, I can't even hit one into the bleachers in batting practice. I'll tell you this, and I mean it: I'm going to stop going for home runs and hit for average."

Another reason it was becoming more difficult to hit homers: opposing pitchers gave him little to hit, especially with men on base. Williams had been walked 156 times the previous year and was on pace to increase that total in 1947. And not only was it getting boring for fans at Fenway and around the league who came to see the Kid hit, but American League owners felt the walks to Williams were starting to hurt them at the gate. In a highly unusual move, they met around the All-Star break and agreed to order their pitchers to let Ted swing more often when the season resumed.[20]

In the All-Star Game itself, Ted singled and doubled off the Cardinals' Harry Brecheen to exact a small measure of revenge from the man who'd humbled him in the World Series, as the American League edged the Nationals, 2–1.

The Sox then kept it close for a while, but Boo Ferriss, Mickey Harris, and Tex Hughson, the mainstays of the pitching staff who in 1946 had combined for sixty-two wins, all went down with arm problems, and the team went on to finish in third place, fourteen games behind the Yankees. And while Ted hit .343 with 32 homers and 114 RBIs to win the Triple Crown, he was robbed of the MVP when the writers narrowly gave the award to DiMaggio. The Yankees had won the pennant, but Joe's statistics were again clearly inferior to Williams's: DiMaggio finished with a .315 average, 20 home runs, and 97 runs batted in, but compiled 202 votes to Ted's 201.*

---

* Three writers from each of the eight American League cities picked ten players in descending order of importance. A first-place vote was worth ten points; tenth place counted for one. Ted had been named on twenty-three of the ballots, meaning that one writer had left him off his ballot entirely. In his book, Williams wrongly named a Boston writer, Mel Webb of the *Globe,* as the culprit who had blanked him, but as it turned out, Webb didn't even have a vote. The three Boston writers who did vote—Joe Cashman of the *Record,* Burt Whitman of the *Herald,* and Jack Malaney of the *Post*—all listed Ted in first place. It had been a midwestern reporter who hadn't listed him at all, as the writer Glenn Stout noted in his book *Red Sox Century,* cowritten with Richard Johnson. And the vote was not only unfair but scandalous, it emerged. The *Sporting News* later revealed that the election results had been available to the writers a week before they were announced, and that some of them had used the inside information to wager hundreds of thousands of dollars on who the winner would be. Voting procedures were later changed, but too late to help Williams in 1947.

Ted tried to find solace in some pleasant family news: Doris was expecting, he announced. The *Traveler,* in a breathless story headlined MRS. TED WILLIAMS TRAINS FOR STORK LEAGUE DEBUT, revealed that Doris had made arrangements for her "confinement" in Boston in January.[21]

Since Ted's return from the war, he and Doris had lived quietly and modestly in a five-room apartment, the middle unit of a brown-shingled three-decker in Brighton, a blue-collar section of Boston. Tex Hughson, the pitcher, and his wife lived in another apartment in the same building. Word had quickly spread that Ted had moved into the neighborhood, and kids would always hang around outside the residence hoping to get an autograph.

Doris had indulged the insatiable Boston press and consented to several at-home-with-Ted features in the previous few years. The papers all agreed she was pretty, usually noting her icy blue eyes, husky voice, and petite stature: even in heels she stood an inch or two below Ted's shoulders. She liked to cook and bake, but said she had to prepare meals for six because Ted ate like a horse. She still rarely went to Fenway Park, but would listen to the games on the radio, both to gauge what kind of mood her husband might be in when he returned and to know when to start dinner, since Ted insisted on eating as soon as he walked in the door. They avoided talk about baseball—Ted didn't want to bring any of his problems home, and Doris didn't care for the game anyway. They both liked the movies, and they had the radio or record player on all the time, playing swing, jazz, or anything upbeat.

Doris seemed able to keep Ted's temper in check. She wasn't afraid to stand up to him, and might handle a tantrum with a droll put-down or by just keeping quiet and waiting for the storm to pass. But they both seemed to enjoy mixing it up, usually when fishing.

"He's always making me cast over again," Doris complained to a reporter. "He taught me, but he has no patience with me. And I have none with him.... We have some rows that literally rock the boat. Sometimes we fight because he won't go home and it gets so dark I have to light matches so he can see to bait the hook. Then he's always butting in when I have a bite, telling me how to haul the fish in. Usually I tell him to shut up."[22]

The Williamses wintered back in Doris's hometown of Princeton, Minnesota. On January 6, the Kid, dispensing with the annual contract-signing press extravaganza in Boston, sent the Red Sox a telegram from Princeton agreeing to the same exact terms for 1948 as he had in '47: a base salary of $65,000 with easily achievable attendance escalators topping out at $75,000.

Williams sent Doris on to Boston to prepare for the delivery of their baby, which was due on February 15. Doris would be staying with friends in Brighton while Ted would go down to Florida to resume fishing in warmer climes.

"I hope it's a boy," Ted told the *Globe* by phone.[23] "And I hope he breaks every record in baseball, as I've been trying to do since I first joined the Red Sox." Doris, for her part, said she wanted a girl.

The birth came suddenly, nearly three weeks ahead of schedule, on January 28. It was a girl, weighing five pounds and six ounces. The child was formally named Barbara Joyce, but they would call her Bobby-Jo. Williams's daughter would later say that her father called her Bobby-Jo because it reminded him of a boy's name, and he always wanted a son.

Ted, who had been planning to arrive in Boston to be with Doris the first week in February, was off fishing in the Everglades when the baby was born. Doris, her family, and their friends all tried to locate him — telegrams were sent, calls made. Finally a reporter in Miami tracked him down at a house in Everglades City and gave him the news.

That night, someone on the *Globe* sports desk called him. The reporter asked when Williams was going to come to Boston to be with Doris and his new baby. Ted, who considered virtually any call from a reporter an invasion of his privacy, was cranky and defensive. The conversation, which the paper recorded, wasn't pretty:

REPORTER: Hello, Ted. This is the *Globe*.
WILLIAMS: Yeah.
REPORTER: Have you been able to get a reservation to Boston?
WILLIAMS: Haven't tried.
REPORTER: Aren't you coming up to see the baby?
WILLIAMS: For Chrissake! What could I do up there?
REPORTER: Were you disappointed that it was a girl?
WILLIAMS: Nope.
REPORTER: Then you didn't care?
WILLIAMS: I didn't give a shit.
REPORTER: How's the fishing?
WILLIAMS: Pretty good.
REPORTER: I didn't get you up, did I?
WILLIAMS: Hell, no.
REPORTER: Where are you fishing, the creeks?

WILLIAMS: Yup.

REPORTER: What do you get?

WILLIAMS: Goddamn it! I've been down here three years and I've been telling you for three years what I get.

REPORTER: You never spoke to me before in your life.

WILLIAMS: Well, I told the goddamn sportswriters.

REPORTER: What do you get?

WILLIAMS: Fish.

REPORTER: Okay. Good luck.

WILLIAMS: Thanks.

REPORTER: Are you going out today?

WILLIAMS: Sure.

REPORTER: Okay. So long.

WILLIAMS: [Slams phone down]

A softer, sanitized version of this conversation was published in the *Globe* of January 29 in an article that carried no byline. The original transcript—which would make the rounds of the paper for years to come, always eliciting amusement—is contained in Harold Kaese's archives, under the cheeky headline BLESSED EVENT. In a column the same day, Kaese dug at Williams for not being at his wife's side when their daughter was born, claiming that "almost everybody in Boston seems to be mad about it." The support for that assertion was interviews with ten unnamed people, five of whom spoke in favor of Ted, five against. Still, Kaese concluded: "Everybody knows where Ted Williams was when his baby was born here yesterday. He was fishing....Once again, Williams finds himself standing in a corner wearing a dunce cap."[24]

But Doris, talking to writers by phone from her hospital bed the following day, didn't seem upset with her husband and stated the obvious: the baby had been born prematurely, far sooner than expected. Ted had been planning to be there for the birth. She explained that he had indeed tried to call the previous night, but she'd been asleep and he hadn't wanted to disturb her, adding that she hoped to hear from him today. She said their daughter had Ted's eyes and her mouth. Meanwhile, Doris was enjoying herself watching television, the first patient in Boston's Lying-in Hospital to be accorded this new perk.[25]

Furious with the Kaese column, Williams flew up to Boston three days later, on the night of February 1. The flight was delayed, and by the

time it arrived it was 1:45 a.m. Ted told the mob of reporters and photographers awaiting him that he'd learned of the birth about ten hours
after the fact and claimed he'd tried to make a plane reservation to get to
Boston but had not been able to get a flight until now. Asked if he'd pose
for pictures with the baby, Ted replied, "Nothing doing. I don't care
what people say about this, but there'll be no pictures taken in the hospital."[26] He said Doris and Bobby-Jo would soon move in with friends in
the area and he would return to Florida. As for those who thought he'd
behaved poorly, he was blunt: "To heck with public opinion," he said.
"It's my baby, and it's my life."

The crowd of reporters followed him over to the hospital, where the
Kid did allow himself to be photographed peering in through the glass
wistfully at little Bobby-Jo. "What a sweetheart," he murmured. "A little on the light side, but so was I....They tell me she has a temper,
too....I wonder where she got that?" Ted added, smiling. Now that his
family was growing, he would move out of his apartment and rent a big
house in upscale Newton, just west of Boston, so Doris and the baby
would have plenty of room. He'd hire a nurse, too. "That gal is going to
have everything she wants."[27]

Before long, the writers were ready to change the subject. They
wanted the Kid's reaction to two big off-season moves the Red Sox had
made.

First was the hiring of Joe McCarthy, the fabled former Yankees manager, to take over the dugout in Boston, replacing Joe Cronin, who'd
moved on to the front office as general manager. McCarthy had been
forced out of New York in May of 1946 because of complications arising
from his well-known battle with the bottle. Still, he had the highest
winning percentage of any major-league manager ever, and he'd won
nine pennants—one with the Cubs in 1929 and eight with the
Yankees—as well as seven World Series titles in New York, so it was
considered a coup for the Red Sox to have lured him out of retirement.
McCarthy was known for his insistence on discipline and professional-
ism, and the press was already speculating about whether he and Williams would clash and about whether, or how, McCarthy might try to
bring Ted to heel.

The second move was a blockbuster trade with the St. Louis Browns
in which Boston gave the Browns $375,000 and nine marginal players in
return for All-Star shortstop and slugger Junior Stephens and two
frontline starting pitchers, Ellis Kinder and Jack Kramer. Stephens was

considered the most important part of the deal, since he provided a potent bat to hit behind Williams and keep pitchers honest.[28]

"I'm hoping, of course, that Junior Stephens can pile up some 25 homers this year," Ted said.[29] "That certainly would help the team, wouldn't it?" As for McCarthy, the Kid didn't foresee any problems. "It's kind of queer for me to hear people asking me how I'll like McCarthy. That doesn't worry me a bit. I hope I play and conduct myself so that McCarthy will like me." McCarthy himself was also ready with a conciliatory off-season quote: "A manager who can't get along with a .400 hitter ought to have his head examined," he proclaimed.

But it was the baby story — Ted's perceived callousness toward his wife and his scorn for public opinion — that lingered in the news for weeks and became one of the defining episodes of his career.

The syndicated columnist Paul Gallico wrote an open letter to Ted, fanning the flames of the anti-Williams narrative: "You . . . were quoted out of Boston as saying to newsmen who interviewed you at Logan Airport upon your belated return from fishing in Florida to visit your wife and newborn daughter: 'To hell with the public — they can't run my life.' These, you must surely know, are the most famous of famous last words. . . . With them, you brand yourself as not only an ingrate, but a first class dolt. You are not a nice fellow, Brother Williams. I do believe that baseball and the sports pages would be better off without you."[30]

Ted did have his defenders, who argued that the press had no business butting in on his private life, including, surprisingly, Dave Egan as well as the *Globe*'s Jerry Nason. Yet the birth of his daughter was a public relations debacle that could easily have been avoided had Ted simply said how delighted he was to be a father and that he would certainly have been with his wife had he only known that the baby was going to arrive early. Once again, Williams wasn't wired to comply with PR norms. He'd felt cornered by a press he deemed out-of-bounds, and he wasn't about to pivot and curry favor with the sort he despised.

Ted also thought this episode illustrated the differences between playing in Boston and New York, arguing that DiMaggio and other Yankees stars got a pass and he didn't. "You can make a case out of anything if you want to, or you can be fair to a guy and not make a big how-do-you-do out of a little thing," he wrote in his book.[31] "I always thought the Yankee players were protected from this sort of thing, that even their real bad actors were written up in angelic terms by the New York press. You can protect a guy and everybody will love him, or you can dig at him and everybody will think he's an S.O.B. Of course, the

Yankees were winning—you get a good press when you're winning, and we were losing."

Joe McCarthy had always insisted that he and his Yankees wear jackets and ties off the field—another point of interest as spring training approached. How, people wondered, would he enforce his dress code on Ted, who of course was famous for disdaining ties? The manager surprised everyone in Sarasota with a disarming gesture: he greeted his star while wearing a shirt with an open collar.

Spring training was thus quickly defused of any tension and unfolded quite boringly, save for an entertaining diversion on March 9, when Ted accepted a challenge from Babe Didrikson Zaharias, the former Olympic track star turned golf champion, to compete with her in a driving contest at a local range. This publicity stunt, lapped up by writers and photographers alike, was engineered by Fred Corcoran, the agent for both Ted and Babe. Ted, who towered over and substantially outweighed Zaharias, sliced most of his drives out to the left, while Babe's were always down the middle and mostly longer. Soon she was coaching Williams on his swing—and needling him, too. "Let's see you chase this one," she'd say. Or: "Here's one for you to shoot at, Ted." After finishing his bucket of balls, the Kid cheerfully conceded. "You've got me beat," he said.[32]

Despite the big-name manager and the new reinforcements from Saint Louis, the Red Sox got off to a miserable start and were 14–23 at the end of May, in seventh place. Ted was hitting, at .374 with 11 home runs and 42 RBIs, but nobody else was. Responding, McCarthy dropped Mickey Harris and Boo Ferriss from the pitching rotation and installed rookie Billy Goodman at first base. The team took off, going 18–6 in June, as Ted hit .460 for the month. By late July, the Sox were in first place, and through August, the month Babe Ruth died, they fought for the top spot with the Yankees and the Indians. In September, with seven games left, the three teams were tied, with records of 91–56.[33]

Across town, meanwhile, the Boston Braves had clinched the National League pennant. The city was baseball-mad and preparing for a streetcar World Series. The rise of the Braves, who hadn't won a pennant since 1914, was an intriguing story. While Boston had long been dominated by the Red Sox, the balance of power started to change during the war years, when the Braves were acquired by three wealthy local contractors—Lou Perini, Joe Maney, and Guido Rugo—whom the press quickly dubbed "the Three Little Steam Shovels."

The Steam Shovels had plenty of money and weren't shy in spending it to build a respectable team and a loyal fan base. In 1946, they had hired away the successful Cardinals manager Billy Southworth, saw their attendance jump by nearly six hundred thousand to just under a million, and finished fourth. Though the Red Sox won the pennant that year, the Braves had been helped by their rival's success, when fans, unable to get into sold-out Fenway Park, instead tried Braves Field, which was within walking distance along Commonwealth Avenue.

The Braves had exciting new players, such as Bob Elliott, Warren Spahn, Earl Torgeson, Johnny Sain, and Tommy Holmes. They brought night baseball to Boston a year before the Red Sox did and aggressively marketed the team to the community with such initiatives as a new $50,000 scoreboard the size of a tennis court, a new press box, three troubadours who wandered the stands playing music, and fan appreciation days, when new cars were given away. Many of these ideas came from the Steam Shovels' indefatigable publicity man, Billy Sullivan, the future founding owner of the Boston Patriots. By 1947, the Braves had finished third and broken the million mark, drawing 1,277,361 fans. In the pennant year of '48, attendance went up to 1,455,439.

Back in the American League, what many consider to be one of the greatest pennant races ever approached its finale. With three days left, the Indians had pulled ahead by two games over both the Red Sox and the Yankees. Cleveland had three games at home against Detroit. Boston and New York had an off day, then played each other on October 2 and October 3 at Fenway. When the Tigers won their first game, the Indians' lead over the Yankees and Red Sox dropped to one.

A capacity crowd of thirty-five thousand watched Jack Kramer defeat Tommy Byrne of the Yankees. Boston's 5–1 victory was paced by Williams, who hit a homer and a double to drive in two runs. He also stole a base and was walked three times, twice intentionally.

The home run off Byrne was especially satisfying for Williams, since the New York pitcher delighted in needling Ted almost every time he faced him, trying to break his concentration. "Hey, Ted," Byrne would say. "How's the Boston press these days? Still screwing you? That's a shame. I think you deserve better. . . . By the way, what are you hitting? You don't know? Goddamn, Ted, the last time I looked it up it was .360 or something." Or later, when he knew Williams was having marital problems, Byrne would bellow, "Ted, how's the family?" Finally, Ted would turn to the catcher, Yogi Berra, and say, "Yogi, tell that son of a bitch to throw the ball!"[34]

Boston's win eliminated the Yankees, while in Cleveland, the Indians beat Detroit to maintain a one-game lead going into the final day. That meant the Red Sox needed to beat the Yankees and have Cleveland lose in order to tie the Indians. In the event of a tie, there would be a one-game playoff for the pennant in Boston.

After the game, Joe DiMaggio drove with his brother Dominic to spend the night at Dominic's home, in suburban Wellesley. The Red Sox center fielder was getting married on October 7, and his parents had flown in from San Francisco for a family dinner that night. The two brothers drove in silence. Joe was down because the Yankees had lost, but he was quiet and reserved under normal circumstances. Finally he turned to Dominic and said: "You knocked us out today, but we'll get back at you tomorrow. We'll knock you out. I'll take care of it personally." Dominic, who always played in Joe's shadow, pondered that for a moment, then replied: "You're forgetting I may have something to do with that tomorrow. I'll be there too."[35]

Since Joe had already had such great success, his parents were openly rooting for Dom. As it happened, both brothers delivered the next day. Joe doubled to drive in the Yankees' first run as New York jumped out to a 2–0 lead after two innings. Fans were dividing their attention between the game and the scoreboard, awaiting news from Cleveland, and roared in the second when they learned that the Tigers had scored four runs off Bob Feller. The Red Sox responded with five runs of their own, triggered by a Williams double. But Joe DiMaggio, despite being hobbled by his bad heel and a variety of other ailments, hit a double in the fifth, driving in two runs to bring the Yankees within one. Then Dominic, leading off the sixth, stroked a home run over the wall in left, igniting a pivotal four-run rally that gave the Red Sox a 9–4 cushion. Nevertheless, his brother didn't give up, singling in a run in the seventh and banging out another single in the ninth. But by then it was 10–5, and Yankees manager Bucky Harris raised the white flag by sending in a pinch runner for the Clipper. As Joe limped off the field, the sellout crowd gave him a long standing ovation—a generous, spontaneous gesture that DiMaggio would later call the greatest thrill of his career. Dominic joined in the tribute, doffing his cap from center field as Joe entered the dugout.

It had been another big game for Williams: two doubles and a sacrifice fly for two runs batted in and a walk. In the two Yankees games, he had reached base eight out of ten times. And the news remained good from Cleveland: the Tigers, behind Hal Newhouser, beat the Indians and the redoubtable Feller, 8–1, to force the playoff showdown in Boston on October 4.

When the Red Sox arrived at Fenway the next day, they were shocked to learn that Joe McCarthy had selected Denny Galehouse, a journeyman right-hander nearing the end of an ordinary career, to pitch the most important game of the season. Mel Parnell, the left-hander who last had pitched on September 30, had expected to get the start, and Ellis Kinder, more rested, was generally thought to be the second choice. But McCarthy — in what remains one of the most controversial decisions a Red Sox manager has ever made, a decision that is still debated among old-timers and baseball aficionados — eschewed Parnell, Kinder, and the rest of his starting rotation in favor of Galehouse, a reliever who had warmed up in the bull pen for six innings the day before in the 10–5 win over the Yankees.

Parnell wasn't the only one stunned. "McCarthy would always put the ball under your cap in your locker," Parnell explained. "That's how you knew you were pitching. We only had three days' rest back then. Finally McCarthy comes up to me and says, 'Kid, I've changed my mind. The elements are against a left-hander today. The wind's blowing out.' The wind *was* blowing out, but hell, I pitched a lot of games at Fenway Park with the wind blowing out. So he told the clubhouse boy to go out and get Galehouse. Galehouse was white as a ghost. He was shocked."[36]

In the first inning, Indians player-manager Lou Boudreau homered over the left-field wall to take Cleveland to a 1–0 lead. The Sox tied it in the first, but the roof fell in on Galehouse in the fourth, when he gave up four runs, three of them on a homer by Ken Keltner, after which the Indians cruised to an 8–3 win. Boudreau got four hits, including another homer. Gene Bearden, a left-handed rookie knuckleballer who'd gone 20–7 in 1948 before fading away to mediocrity, easily kept the Sox, and Ted, in check, giving up only five hits. Williams could manage only a single in four trips to the plate, and he dropped a fly ball in the eighth inning that led to the seventh Cleveland run.

McCarthy's decision to start Galehouse dominated the postgame commentary, deflecting attention from the failure of Williams and other Sox hitters to deliver in the pinch against Bearden's junky soft-serves. Ted hung around the clubhouse moping, waiting for the writers and almost everyone else to leave.

Finally, he showered and dressed and was walking through the training room when McCarthy approached him.

"Well, we fooled 'em, didn't we?" the manager said.[37]

"What do you mean, Joe?"

"Well, they said you and I couldn't get along, but we got along pretty good, didn't we?"

"Yeah, we did, Joe," Ted replied.

Williams won the batting title with a .369 average, and he had 25 homers, with 127 RBIs. Though he led the league in doubles and slugging percentage, critics noted that his home-run production was off sharply from his previous four years. Statistics maven Harold Kaese concluded that Ted had changed his swing too radically in order to beat the shift: "The Cleveland Indians won the pennant on July 14, 1946," the day Lou Boudreau installed the shift, he wrote.[38]

Boudreau was victorious in another way, too: he was the runaway winner of the American League MVP award. Ted finished third.

En route to his fourth batting championship in 1948, Ted made an intriguing change in his pregame preparation. Open to hitting-related ideas from all comers (except the media) as he turned thirty and looked to maintain his edge, Williams tinkered with the care and maintenance of his bats on the advice of quite an unlikely source: fourteen-year-old David Pressman from Chelsea, Massachusetts, a gritty immigrant city located just across the Mystic River from Boston.

Pressman loved baseball, which he played on the Chelsea sandlots, and he also had a scientific bent. One morning, after leaving his bat outside overnight, he noticed that it felt heavier and had less pop. He wondered if it had absorbed too much moisture from the damp ground. He went to the Chelsea post office to use the scales there and determined that his bat was two ounces heavier than it was when he kept it off the ground or when the weather was dry.

In the spring of 1948, Pressman decided to see if he could dry the bat out artificially by warming it. His house was heated by a coal stove. He went home, stoked up the furnace, and baked the bat over the embers of the coals for a while. When he went out to hit with the bat the next day, he found it was "perfect," and he returned to the post office scales to confirm that it had lost the two ounces it had gained from the moisture.

Pressman wondered if his favorite ballplayer, Ted Williams, might like to know about the experiment he had conducted, which suggested that heating a bat could extract moisture from it, restore its original weight, and perhaps enhance its performance. He read an article in one of the Boston papers about Frank "Tabby" Ryan of Hillerich & Bradsby, the Louisville company that manufactured the famed Louisville Slugger used by most major leaguers.

Pressman sat down and wrote to Ryan, the company's representative to the Red Sox and other teams, laying out his theory, and asked him to pass his letter on to Williams. The boy wanted the letter to look official, so he borrowed the official stationery used by his father, a lawyer.

"Next thing I knew, my father got a call from Ted himself, thinking it was my father who had given him the tip," Pressman recalled. "My dad said, 'You must want my kid. He's in school. He'll be home at two o'clock.' When I got home, I got a call from Ted. He said, 'That's really interesting. Can you come to Fenway? We're playing a doubleheader with the Tigers, and Virgil Trucks is pitching.'"

Pressman's discovery confirmed Williams's views on the virtues of a lighter bat. He'd had an epiphany on the subject when he was playing for the Minneapolis Millers back in 1938 and borrowed teammate Stan Spence's much lighter bat on a hot, muggy night in Columbus. He was tired, and Spence's bat felt like a feather, as if it were made of soft balsa wood. But Ted hit a 410-foot home run to center field with it.

When Williams broke into the majors, the big sluggers were all using heavy bats—between thirty-six and forty ounces. When Ted ordered lighter bats, John Hillerich, then the head of Hillerich & Bradsby, tried to talk him out of it. Ted insisted, arguing that the speed of his swing, its torque and whip, would generate more power than Hillerich's heavier bats alone.[39] A lighter bat also gave him more control. It allowed him to wait a fraction of a second longer before he committed to swinging at a pitch: if he could wait longer, he would not be fooled as often.

Williams had made his first visit to the factory in Louisville in the spring of 1941, with Bobby Doerr. They arrived half an hour before the plant gate opened, and Ted couldn't wait to get inside, examine the wood, and quiz the lathe operators who actually fashioned the bats from billets. He met an old-timer on the factory line named Fritz Bickel, who presented him with a choice billet from which he promised to construct a nice bat. Bickel pointed out that the wood had two knots in it, which helped make it harder. Ted gave Bickel $25 and would send him other gratuities over the ensuing years. Bickel would reciprocate by prowling the factory line looking for only the best wood for the Kid.[40]

The doubleheader Ted invited young David Pressman to attend took place on June 6. Pressman had never been to Fenway Park, and by the time he arrived, after being delayed by public transportation, the second game had already started. "Ted had made arrangements for me, but I had to sit in the clubhouse and wait a while," he recalled. "There was some leftover food. They gave me a tuna sandwich and a Coke. Ted came down during the game, and that's when I showed him my bat, which I'd brought along for him to see. He looked at it and said, 'This is a piece of shit.'

"He said he'd be hitting next inning and to come up to the dugout then. One of the batboys came down to get me." Pressman arrived in the dugout just in time to see Williams blast a home run off Fred Hutchinson. Then the next two batters, Stan Spence and Junior Stephens, also homered. "There were three home runs back-to-back," Pressman said. "I never saw such excitement." He saw Williams go 4–5 with a double and three RBIs as the Red Sox crushed the Tigers, 12–4.

In the clubhouse after the game, Ted and the teenager talked hitting. They discussed what generated power: the speed of the pitch and the speed of the swing. Pressman, who said he had consulted with older acquaintances at the Massachusetts Institute of Technology about the physics of hitting, told Williams about a third factor in generating power: the principle of restitution, in which both the bat and the ball compress and then expand at impact. They discussed the wisdom of using narrow-grain wood in a bat to promote flexibility: the more grain lines there are in the bat, the more it can compress and expand.

On the matter of heating the bat, Ted asked Pressman how he could do it. He didn't have access to a coal stove the way David did. Pressman suggested putting his bats in the clubhouse clothes dryer with some towels wrapped around them so they didn't bang around and get nicked up. (He had thought of the dryer idea beforehand because his uncle was in the dry cleaning business and once had the contract to clean the Red Sox uniforms.) Pressman advised Ted to check the bats every fifteen minutes and weigh them. When they stopped losing the weight they had gained from moisture, he should take them out of the dryer. Pressman said the Chelsea post office provided two scales for Williams to use. "When I told them the scales were for Ted, they sent them to him, no problem," Pressman said. "He then experimented with the dried bats and called me afterwards and said, 'This is incredible. This really works.' He said he was hitting the ball harder and farther. I was not surprised, because I'd already done it."

Since there were no rules against drying bats in Williams's day—and none today, for that matter—the practice was not cheating. Rather, it seemed to be an extension of the diligent and rigorous care with which Williams treated the tools of his trade. "I always worked with my bats, boning them down, putting a shine on them, forcing the fibers together," Ted wrote in his autobiography.[41] "Not just the handle—the whole bat. I treated them like babies. Weight tolerance got to be a big thing with me. The weight can change. Early in the season it's cold and damp and the bats lying around on the ground pick up moisture and get heavier. I used to take them down to the post office to have them weighed. Eventually, with the Red Sox, we got a little set of scales put in the locker room."

In 1949, the year after he started heating his bats, Williams told Pressman he wanted to try to scientifically measure how much harder he was hitting the ball with a dried bat compared to a nondried bat. Pressman's acquaintances at MIT said they could help.

On a day when the Red Sox were off, the MIT people showed up at Fenway Park around ten in the morning and set up three instruments, two on tripods and one on the ground, just to the left of the batting cage. MIT had been the center of American radar research during World War II, and the instruments were precursors of the radar gun, which would be widely used in baseball years later. Williams stepped into the box against Joe Dobson, a hard-throwing right-hander. Ted told him to bring it. Even though there was a batting cage, Birdie Tebbetts, the Red Sox starting catcher, was behind the plate, Pressman recalled, perhaps to increase the efficiency of the exercise and to more quickly return the balls Williams didn't swing at to Dobson.

"He had four bats, two of which were heated, two not, and he had numbers on the knobs marking which was which," Pressman remembered. "If he hit a ball on the screws, Ted would call out, 'Measure that one.' They would get the velocity results right away. There were very consistent findings of one hundred fifteen miles per hour for the non-heated bats versus one hundred and forty-eight for the heated bats."*

Pressman entered Harvard while continuing his interest in baseball. He got a key to Harvard's indoor batting cage, and on rainy days Ted

---

* That summer of 1949, when Pressman was at Fenway for a game against the Yankees as a guest of Ted's, Williams brought Joe DiMaggio over and introduced him. Said Pressman, "I was in the stands. Ted said, 'I want you to tell Joe about this whole baking thing.' So I did. Joe thought the whole thing was foolish and he had a deer-in-the-headlights look in his face as I told him this stuff. Then he just walked away. Ted said to him, 'The kid told you something. You should thank him in some way.'" So DiMaggio sent Pressman a Yankees hat. "Years later I met DiMaggio at Cooperstown," Pressman recalled, "and he said he remembered that and he signed the hat for me. Ted seemed annoyed by Joe's reaction at the time. Later, Ted told me, 'I want to tell you something about Joe D. He asked me a question about hitting at an All-Star Game, and I knew from the question he didn't know shit about hitting.'"

would call him and ask him to open up the facility early in the morning so he could come over and take batting practice. Williams would swing by Pressman's dorm at Lowell House in his Cadillac and pick him up, in full uniform.

Pressman graduated magna cum laude from Harvard in 1957 and wanted to pursue his dream of trying to play baseball professionally, but Ted told him to forget it. "He said, 'A Jewish kid like you should go to medical school,' and then he called my father and told him the same thing. And that's why I went to med school."

Pressman graduated from Columbia University medical school in 1961 and later became a cardiologist. The two men stayed in touch over the years. Ted volunteered to be a godfather to one of Pressman's sons, and Pressman would later enter into a memorabilia venture with Williams's son, John-Henry.

Ted maintained his interest in the way physics applied to baseball. In 1955, he would go over to MIT to meet with a professor who taught him about Bernoulli's principle, the aerodynamic law of physics that allows a plane's wings to produce lift and fly.[42] Named for the eighteenth-century Dutch-Swiss mathematician Daniel Bernoulli, the principle also explains why a curveball curves.

After their initial consultations about heating bats in 1948 and 1949, Pressman said he and Ted never discussed the issue again. "It was a done deal. He just did it. There were no further discussions, but as far as I know, he was using heated bats from 1948 to 1960, when he retired. Ted did say to me, 'Don't reveal this until I die,'" Pressman said. "He did not want other people to know what he was doing and have that same advantage. He was hitting for a very high average. He still wanted to win batting titles. Ted regarded this as a trade secret and didn't want anyone else to know."[43]

Yet some of Williams's teammates were aware of what he was doing, including Bobby Doerr, Johnny Pesky, and Jimmy Piersall.[44] "Johnny Orlando, the clubhouse boy, would put Ted's bats in a dryer," said Doerr. "I knew he was doing it. There was no rule against it, so there was no problem on that. We didn't think anything about it."[45] Piersall, the Red Sox center fielder from 1952 to 1958, said Orlando told him Williams was drying his bats. Then, occasionally, Piersall would see Ted go to the dryer himself to check on their progress.

"He felt he got better performance from the bats by drying them," Piersall said. "There was only one dryer. It was pretty big, though. He never said anything about it. I never considered doing it because I used to steal his bats anyway. If he thought it was an advantage to dry his bats, it must have been because he was such a great hitter. He hit the ball harder than anybody I ever saw."[46]

While Williams may not have discussed drying bats with his teammates, he did warn them not to let their bats lie on the ground, where they could absorb extra moisture. But most ignored him, thinking he was over the top in his scientific theories and his exactitude.

In the end, the benefit from all this was likely minor at best. In 1949, the first full year he used a heated bat, Ted's power production would spike. He hit 43 home runs and had 159 RBIs, compared to 25 and 127 respectively in 1948. But after that, there would be no discernible effect in his power numbers, except for 1957 — the year he hit .388 — when he struck 38 home runs, by far his largest total of the 1950s.

Two experts on the physics of baseball — Alan M. Nathan, professor emeritus of physics at the University of Illinois at Urbana-Champaign, who runs a website devoted to physics and baseball, and Patrick Drane, assistant director of the University of Massachusetts at Lowell's Baseball Research Center, which tests bats and balls for Major League Baseball and the NCAA — believe Williams probably received only marginal benefits from heating his bats. "I never say never, but all evidence that I have ever seen points to the fact that with heating or drying, you're probably not going to change much bat performance at all," said Nathan. "Ballplayers are notoriously superstitious about things. If Ted believed it helped him, who knows? You could imagine he tried it once and hit a long home run, and continued to do it that way. But I'm quite frankly very skeptical that performance would increase very much."[47]

"It sounds basically that what Williams was doing was using a scientific basis to take advantage of what's allowed," said Drane, whose master's thesis in mechanical engineering was about the effects of moisture content on wooden bats. In his research he found that moisture had a negligible effect on bat performance, but he said that further tests were needed to determine whether drying could improve performance. "A player typically will have more control with a lighter bat, and a really good player — if they have more control, it will make a difference in the length of long fly balls, and where the ball goes. During the season it gets more humid. Ted may have had a bat he was pretty happy with in April, then it got heavier. Drying it out, he was able to bring it back down to where he liked it. For someone that was meticulous about the weight, it could seem over the course of the summer it would be better to keep the bat he liked at the weight that he liked, so that's where drying it out would have some benefits. Ted Williams would potentially be able to hit the ball more squarely. But I don't see that equaling a hundred and forty-eight miles per hour with a heated bat and nonheated [at] a hundred and fifteen — that's a big difference."[48]

Nathan, a lifelong Red Sox and Ted Williams fan, said he thought both the 115 and 148 figures, which Pressman said the MIT people recorded, were "simply crazy numbers." Nathan said he had analyzed a total of 8,801 home runs from the 2009 and 2010 Major League Baseball seasons and found that the average batted-ball speed was 100.2 miles per hour. He said only seventy-three of the 8,801 home runs exceeded 110 miles per hour, and the highest recorded speed was 117.4 miles per hour.[49]

If Williams had truly hit a ball 148 miles an hour, it "would have gone farther than any baseball has ever gone," Nathan concluded.

11

1949–1951

Assessing 1948, Tom Yawkey and the Red Sox management viewed the season as an anomaly, almost a fluke. They certainly didn't blame McCarthy, and Yawkey went to absurd lengths to give his manager a vote of confidence. "I'd rather finish second with Joe McCarthy than first with someone else," the owner told Harold Kaese.[1]

The Sox felt the Indians had had a once-in-a-lifetime season and that the aging Yankees were in decline, so Boston decided to stand pat and make no major changes in the off-season. As spring training neared, most of the baseball cognoscenti seemed to vindicate this strategy by picking the Sox to win the American League pennant in 1949.

Following a March 11 workout in Sarasota, there was an interesting discussion about the fine points of hitting between the last two men to bat .400 in the American League—Ted and Harry Heilmann—which left Williams a bit rattled. The sensitive topic, still debated to this day, was the extent to which Ted should be willing to swing at a pitch that was off the plate. Heilmann, the former Detroit Tiger who had posted a .403 mark in 1923 and was at the time of the discussion the team's radio broadcaster, met with Ted in Joe McCarthy's office. Nicknamed Slug in his playing days for his lack of swiftness afoot, Heilmann was in a feisty mood and recorded the conversation, later reproduced by Austen Lake of the *American:*

HEILMANN: Ted, you say you'll be satisfied to hit .367 this year.

WILLIAMS: No, I'll settle for that, but I won't be satisfied unless I hit .400.

HEILMANN: Well, you'll never hit .400 again as long as you take those fourth-ball pitches low and outside. You have to learn to hit bad balls instead of taking free passes. All the great hitters had to hit off-center pitches.

WILLIAMS: Now, wait a minute. The greatest right-hand batter in the game told me—

HEILMANN: Yeah, Hornsby. He hit a flock of pitches a full foot outside the plate and rode 'em over the walls.

WILLIAMS: He must have had thirty-nine-inch arms if he did. I never saw a batter stand farther away from the plate. Anyhow, he told me the secret of hitting was waiting for the good pitch.

HEILMANN: Well, then you'll never again bat .400.

That was the end of the interview. Ted shrugged and walked off to his locker. Heilmann packed up his recording equipment and muttered: "Guy's the greatest natural batsman in history. Got everything but ability to accept advice."[*]

Another heel injury would keep DiMaggio out of the Yankees lineup until late June, yet the Red Sox couldn't make any hay. Ted's hitting kept the team afloat, but Boston generally underperformed over the first half, forcing McCarthy to make some moves—acquiring right fielder Al Zarilla, who had hit .329 in 1948, from the ever-accommodating St. Louis Browns for $100,000; bringing up two young fireballers, Mickey McDermott and Chuck Stobbs, to insert into the starting rotation in place of Jack Kramer and Tex Hughson, both of whom were suffering arm problems; and releasing Denny Galehouse, who would never pitch in the majors again. The Sox won ten of eleven in June to pull within five of New York by the time the Yankees arrived in Boston for a three-game series on June 28.

DiMaggio, always finely attuned to dramatic possibilities, chose that date to make his 1949 debut. The pain from off-season surgery, this time to remove a bone spur in his right heel, had finally dissipated, and Joe made a last-minute decision to fly up from New York that afternoon to join his teammates, who'd already arrived in Boston.

His performance over the next three days was extraordinary. In the first game, still limping slightly and wearing a specially constructed shoe, he singled and hit a two-run homer, took out Junior Stephens with

---

[*] Later in spring training, Williams proved he wasn't exclusively obsessed with hitting, suggesting that outfielders warm up before each inning by throwing balls to each other, the way infielders did. It was a logical idea—innovative then but seemingly obvious in hindsight—that would later be adopted.

a vicious slide at second, and robbed Williams in the ninth inning, running down a four-hundred-foot drive to the triangle in right-center, with a runner on third. The Yankees won, 5–4. The next day, he homered twice as the Yankees overcame a 7–1 Red Sox lead to win, 9–7. Before the final game of the series, a plane flew overhead towing a sign that said THE GREAT DIMAGGIO. As good as Dominic was, there was no doubt which brother the banner was referring to, and Joe delivered again, this time driving a fastball from Mel Parnell against a light standard over the left-field wall for a three-run homer to key the Yankees' 6–3 win. The Clipper later said those three days in Boston were "the most satisfying in my life."[2]

The Yankees' sweep left the Red Sox eight games back and their season teetering. But as the weather warmed, so did the team. They sliced two games off the Yankees' margin by the end of July, then went on a 42–13 tear in August and September. DiMaggio caught pneumonia, and the Yankees slumped. The Indians had faded to third place and were not a factor. Things had jelled for Boston. The hitting and pitching had come together at the same time, and the Red Sox were loose and having fun.

Three of the players perhaps most responsible for the team's harmony—and, in particular, for keeping Ted relaxed and happy—were Birdie Tebbetts, the catcher acquired from the Tigers in 1947, Mickey McDermott, the flame-throwing left-hander whom McCarthy had belatedly brought up from Louisville in June, and Lou Stringer, the backup second baseman.

Tebbetts, whose first name was George, was one of the leading bench jockeys in baseball, and he loved to needle his own teammates, too, especially Williams. Birdie liked to say that when he was catching in Detroit, Ted was a better hitter than he was now. Williams would always take the bait: "What the hell do you mean?" he'd ask indignantly.[3] Tebbetts also knew he could easily irk Ted just by reading the papers to him. So he'd sit in the clubhouse, casually scanning the day's baseball news. "God, Ted, did you see what they wrote about you today?" he'd ask. "I wouldn't put up with that crap if I were you."[4]

Ted also had had a soft spot for Mickey McDermott since 1947, when McDermott was up briefly to throw batting practice and had decked Williams in the cage at Yankee Stadium. Mickey was throwing bullets over and behind the hitters' heads. "Bush, take it easy," Ted had impishly told him then. "Batting practice pitchers come and go. Making it in the game is what counts."[5]

At spring training in '48, the nineteen-year-old McDermott made a splash — both for his live but still wild arm and for being a character. That spring in Sarasota, a photographer had taken a shot of McDermott smiling broadly while a trainer rubbed ointment on his sunburned neck, and the photographer sold the shot to *Life* magazine, which published it as a generic exhibit A of the wide-eyed rookie. That picture was said to have been the inspiration for Norman Rockwell's famous painting *The Rookie,* which later ran on the cover of the *Saturday Evening Post.* The painting depicts Williams, Dom DiMaggio, Jackie Jensen, and Billy Goodman staring skeptically at a gawky, freckle-faced kid carrying a worn suitcase and wearing a poorly fitting sport jacket.[6]

The Red Sox sent McDermott down again in 1948 because of his control issues, but when he was brought up for good in June of '49 he was being hailed as the freshest face to hit the Red Sox since Ted himself in 1938. Ted, after perusing a headline that already proclaimed the rookie a star, had seen fit to call McDermott over and remind him that there was only one star on the team, and that was the Kid.

Once, after Mickey won a game, he wanted to take a girl back to Ted's hotel room. Ted said, "Yeah, but get out by midnight." Arriving with his date, McDermott was impressed with the suite and the arrangements Williams had made for him: "The lights were low," he wrote in his book. "Candles flickered romantically. A tray of hors d'oeuvres awaited along with champagne chilling in an ice bucket." After tending to his primary business, McDermott fell asleep, not to awaken until morning. Later he apologized profusely to Williams, saying, "Ted, where were you? All you had to do was knock on the door."

"Bush," he replied, "I know you. No way you'd be out of there by midnight. I rented another suite."[7]

Stringer, who'd played for the Chicago Cubs before being acquired by the Red Sox in '48, told the late David Halberstam he liked to pump up Williams around the batting cage, knowing that his mood improved as he hit the ball better and better in practice before a game.

"Ted, you're looking great!" Stringer would say as Williams took his cuts. And Ted would reply, "You're goddamned right. You see that wrist, you see that swing, you see that power? I'm the best goddamn hitter in the world, kid, you goddamn better believe it. The best goddamn hitter who ever lived."

Stringer's wife, Helen, was attractive, and Ted seemed to have a crush on her. "Hey, Bush, we'll keep you around just to keep her around," he had told Lou after meeting Helen. The next time Ted saw Helen, at

Back Bay Station, she engaged him skillfully. Had he heard about the new prospect the Red Sox were bringing up? No, said Ted.

"He's gonna be better than you, he's gonna take the sun away from you."

"Who's that?" said Williams, growing more anxious. "Who's that?"

"Lou Stringer," said Helen proudly.

Ted roared with laughter and said to Lou, "I wish I had a girl like that, who loved me that much."[8]

As the Red Sox approached the last two days of the season—against New York, inevitably, in the Bronx—they led the Yankees by a single game.

The Yankees chose October 1 to stage a day for DiMaggio. The players warmed up, then sat for an hour as the Clipper was honored. His mother and Dominic stood next to Joe as he was showered with gifts. "I'd like to thank the good Lord for making me a Yankee," he told the sellout crowd.

New York started Allie Reynolds against Boston's Mel Parnell. McCarthy was taking no chances after his Galehouse gambit of a year ago. Parnell had had a career year, winning twenty-five games to that point. Tom Yawkey, meanwhile, was feeling confident enough to have put a special train on standby in Boston to bring the team's wives down to New York to celebrate a pennant.

Dom DiMaggio and Ted got things going for the Sox in the first inning with singles. Williams's ball was hit so hard that it bounced off both first baseman Tommy Henrich and umpire Cal Hubbard. Junior Stephens knocked in Dominic for the first run of the game. In the third, Reynolds pitched around Williams and walked two others to load the bases. Yankees manager Casey Stengel's instructions were to pitch carefully to Williams at all times, though he had a hard-and-fast rule to give him nothing he could hit in the late innings if the game was on the line.[9]

Bobby Doerr singled to knock in one run, whereupon Reynolds was lifted for Joe Page, who walked two more batters, and the Red Sox were up 4–0. But DiMaggio led off the fourth with a double, and the Yankees rallied for two runs, then struck for two more in the fifth to tie the game. In the bottom of the eighth, Johnny Lindell, facing Red Sox reliever Joe Dobson, slammed a pitch into the left-field grandstand to make it 5–4. Page hung on, and the Yankees won.

Then, just as in 1948, two teams were tied, and the final game was for the pennant. Stengel chose one of his mainstays to pitch—Vic Raschi, who was then 20–10—while McCarthy tapped Ellis Kinder (23–6), who hadn't lost a game he'd started since June 6.[10]

Raschi got the first two Red Sox he faced to make outs, walked Williams, then retired Stephens. Shortstop Phil Rizzuto led off for New York. He faked a bunt to draw Johnny Pesky in slightly at third, then slapped the ball over Pesky's head down the left-field line. The ball got stuck in a gully and rolled past Williams, who'd been shading Rizzuto to left-center. Rizzuto made it all the way to third. With the infield held back by McCarthy, Henrich grounded to Doerr at second, and Rizzuto scored with the first Yankees run.

Improbably, that run loomed larger and larger as the game wore on. Kinder was holding the Yankees in check, but the Red Sox could do nothing with Raschi. Entering the eighth inning, it was still 1–0, Yankees.

After Birdie Tebbetts made the first out for Boston, Kinder was up next. Though Kinder wasn't a bad hitter for a pitcher, and though McCarthy had little confidence in his bull pen, he decided to send out Tom Wright, the only left-handed batter available on the bench, to pinch-hit. Wright, who had only recently been brought up from the minors and had just three at bats with Boston, walked, but Dom DiMaggio hit into a double play to end the inning. McCarthy then brought in Mel Parnell, who had pitched four innings the previous day.

Parnell had nothing left. The first batter he faced, Henrich, walloped a home run. Berra singled, and McCarthy belatedly brought in Tex Hughson to face DiMaggio, who grounded into a double play. But Lindell singled, as did Billy Johnson. Williams juggled Johnson's ball, allowing Lindell to reach third. Then Cliff Mapes walked to load the bases. Jerry Coleman, the number eight hitter, came up. With the count three and two and all three runners on the move, Coleman hit a little flare off his fists to right field. It was a do-or-die play for Al Zarilla, who raced in, dove, and caught the ball, but then watched it squirt out of his glove as he slammed to the ground. He got up and threw Coleman out at third, but not before all three runners had scored to make it 5–0, New York.

Johnny Pesky led off for the Red Sox in the ninth and fouled out. Raschi again pitched around Williams, walking him. A wild pitch sent Ted to second. Stephens singled sharply to center, Williams stopping at third, then Doerr tripled over DiMaggio's head, driving in two. Zarilla popped to shallow center, forcing Doerr to hold at third, but Billy Goodman singled to make it 5–3 and keep the Red Sox alive. Tebbetts, representing the tying run, came to bat, but popped up to Henrich at first to end the game.

The loss was devastating for Boston, a team that had run away with the 1946 pennant only to lose the seventh game of the World Series, then the playoff game of '48, and now this de facto playoff game. The loss crystallized emerging Red Sox lore that would remain firmly entrenched until 2004: Boston was a club that for all its talent always found a way to lose in critical situations.

McCarthy's decision to pinch-hit for Ellis Kinder in the eighth, when it was still 1–0—while defensible and certainly no Galehouse-like gaffe—was nonetheless immediately the primary topic of discussion among players, writers, and kibitzers. Kinder was beside himself in the losers' clubhouse, openly flashing the choke sign at his manager. The way Kinder spun it to the writers, had McCarthy not lifted him at such a key moment for the untested, raw Wright, he would have pitched two more shutout innings and the Sox would have later won, 3–1. On the train ride home, Kinder burst into McCarthy's compartment and railed at him further.

Williams and his teammates were crushed. "It was like a damn funeral train," Ted wrote in his book. "Everybody was stunned. We had come so far, had made up so much ground.... The whole team was heartbroken. Sick. To come that close twice in a row was an awful cross to bear."[11]

Individually, Ted had had one of his most stellar seasons. His 43 home runs led the league, as did his RBI total of 159. He came within a whisker of winning another Triple Crown, but after going 0–2 against Vic Raschi he lost the batting title to George Kell of the Tigers on the last day of the season, .3428 to .34275. The writers did name Williams the runaway winner of the American League's Most Valuable Player award, his second MVP—slight balm for the 1947 calumny.

Ted's archenemy in the press, Dave Egan of the *Record,* seized on his performance in the final two games against the Yankees to make the charge that in the ten biggest games of his life—the seven World Series games of 1946, the playoff game for the pennant against the Indians in 1948, and the last two games of the 1949 season—Ted had failed in the clutch, his big-game average just .205.

It was a deceptive artifice, of course, to cherry-pick ten games out of more than two thousand in a career and ignore the scores of other instances in which he did come through—like the time when he hit a homer and three doubles to drive in five runs while reaching base eight out of ten times in the final two games against the Yankees in 1948 to propel Boston to the playoff game against Cleveland. Or his critical role in the Sox's eleven-game winning streak—including three over New York—at the end of the 1949 season, which put them into first place. Williams had won four of those games himself with home runs. The Egan analysis also failed to take into account the number of times pitchers took the bat out of Ted's hands in key situations by walking him, intentionally or otherwise.

Still, the sting and hurt of that final loss to the Yankees lingered, more difficult for Williams to accept than the '48 playoff loss to the Indians. He gave Lou Boudreau his due for a phenomenal performance that year. But he thought the '49 Yankees, besides getting a brilliant half season from DiMaggio, had mostly been lucky.

After a few weeks of moping, Ted, Doris, and little Bobby-Jo repaired to Minnesota, where they would again spend the winter in Princeton. Williams quickly went off with friends to the wilds of the Superior National Forest, in the northeastern tip of the state, for a month of fishing and hunting. Then it was down to Stuttgart, Arkansas, for what he considered to be the finest duck hunting in the country. (Asked to be a judge in a duck-calling contest, he marveled at the way the locals could summon mallards at will.) Ted returned to Minnesota for some ice fishing through Christmas and New Year's, then it was time to head for Florida.

Doris and the baby took the train down while Ted drove his brand-new powder-blue four-door Cadillac. They rented a cabin in Everglades City, and Ted got in another month of fishing, this time for tarpon and snook in remote Lost Man's River.

Williams and the Red Sox agreed on a one-year contract that made him the highest-paid player in the history of the game: a base salary of $90,000 (representing a $15,000 raise from 1949), with attendance escalators topping out at $100,000 if Boston drew 1.6 million fans to Fenway Park. Total home attendance in '49 had been 1,596,650.

Ted was now thirty, arguably still in his prime, but acutely aware that he was starting the second half of his career. He'd already lost three years' salary to the war, so he wanted to maximize his income on as many fronts as possible. In his first column of the upcoming season—this time writing for the *Boston Herald*—Williams noted that he was struck by the short length of the normal baseball career when he arrived at spring training. There, he realized that only one player, Bobby Doerr, remained from the time he had first arrived in Sarasota in 1938. He authorized Fred Corcoran to aggressively seek outside income opportunities, such as endorsement deals for Quaker Oats, Ted's Root Beer, and even Chesterfield cigarettes, though he didn't smoke and knew it set a bad example for kids.* He turned down a book and movie offer, but gladly accepted a two-week gig that paid him $10,000 to appear at the Boston and New York sportsmen's shows, where he put on fly-casting exhibitions. He also decided to buy his first home—in Miami. Williams was increasingly comfortable in Florida, where there was good fishing and it was always warm.

Corcoran had also gotten Ted interested in the stock market, and he now read the *Wall Street Journal* regularly, as well as *Forbes* and *Barron's*. Becoming conversant in market lingo, using expressions like "book value," "dividend yield," and "holding company," he confined his investments to blue-chip firms such as General Electric, Standard Oil of New Jersey, and Union Carbide—but would take an occasional flier if he got a good tip. He even mused about becoming a trader once he retired.

Before leaving for spring training, he decided to spend a few days bonefishing in the Keys and was thrilled by the experience. "Brother, that's the biggest fishing kick I ever got," he told a *Time* reporter—one of five the magazine had dispatched to hang out with Williams during spring training and report an April cover story on him. "One of those ten-pound babies will damn near jerk the rod out of your hand—just take off like a jet airplane. From now on, I'm a Florida bonefish man. I'm going to be down here every winter."

Arriving in Sarasota with Doris and Bobby-Jo, Ted checked into a deluxe furnished two-bedroom apartment in Florasota Gardens, an ivory-and-yellow apartment-hotel complex covering three square blocks, which was billing itself as the city's newest and smartest address. Ted's apartment, for which he was paying $350 a month, looked out on a sweep of lawn, a lagoon, and native Florida pine trees.

Per usual, his first-day arrival at Payne Park was chronicled minute-by-minute by a pack of writers and photographers who generally were struck by Ted's healthy appearance and sunny disposition. Ted said he wasn't predicting anything; he just hoped he and everyone else on the

---

* Other players, such as Joe DiMaggio, were heavy smokers, even in the dugout during games.

team would have a good year. He also said he planned to play for as long as he could. "It's the greatest game there is and I want to stay with it just as long as I can. It's done everything for me."[12]

The *Time* team paid careful attention to Ted's daily routine from the moment he entered the clubhouse until he left. Appearing at noon for a 2:00 p.m. game, he usually announced his arrival by whistling loudly and greeting the first teammate he saw with, "Hey, ham head" or several variations thereof, including lunkhead, mule head, mutton head, or fart head, uttered with either affection or annoyance, but generally the former.

Ted's greetings for closer pals were usually more profane or simply an equally filthy complaint about something mundane—like the wind blowing in that day or his inability to find one of his extra pairs of spikes. Accustomed to such minitirades, his teammates would let him blow off steam, then one, often Birdie Tebbetts, would sing out, "Hey, that's telling 'em, good Kid. Yes, sir, good Kid."

As Williams arrived at his open locker, his distinctive number 9 road-gray uniform was hung neatly near various personal accoutrements, such as a lanolin preparation for his curly hair and some suntan lotion. Johnny Orlando, always carefully attuned to Ted's wants, would check in to see if he needed anything else.

Dressing for the game, Williams first tended to one of his three pairs of spiked shoes, making sure the laces were tied just so. The first pair was old and soft for pregame warm-ups. The second and third were harder and stiffer for better ankle support during games. Then he would fuss for quite a while putting on his uniform pants, adjusting the elastic to hold the pants far down on his shin. Some critics thought Williams wore his pants far lower than most players as a way to draw even more attention to himself, but his friends knew that the real reason was to make his skinny, pipestem legs look a bit more substantial.

When Ted stepped into the batter's box, *Time* took detailed notes on his every move: he planted his left toe a few inches behind home plate, then dug in the spikes of his left heel, but more gingerly than some of the other hitters, who often pawed big holes in the dirt. Then he placed his right foot a yard ahead of the left, anchoring it less solidly. He extended his bat across the plate, assuring himself he had proper coverage. He wiggled his left hip back and forth, setting himself more firmly. His right leg flexed and unflexed. His long hands rotated in opposite directions on the handle of the bat until he was ready. When he swung, his left heel came out of its hole slightly while his right toe turned toward right field as he followed through on his swing. Unlike most hitters, he did not stride into a pitch. His power was in his wrists, hands, and forearms.

Ted told the reporters he was in good shape. "I always am, but I've never felt better than this year. I'm really relaxed." Asked about his ambition and what kept him going, Ted turned earnest: "That's easy. I want to be as good a hitter as ever came along." Then he paused and added: "And I want to be the best ballplayer Joe McCarthy ever managed." Which, of course, included the great DiMaggio. When assessing his legacy, Williams almost always talked in terms of wanting to be regarded as the best hitter, not the best all-around player, which would have to include fielding. But he didn't make the distinction in this case. McCarthy, however, told one of the *Time* writers that Ted was paying much more attention to his fielding and had generally matured as a player.

Not that he was going to crash into a wall chasing a fly or anything. "What's the sense of it?" Ted asked. "You hit the wall and maybe you don't get hurt, but you're out of position to play the ball and the guy takes the extra base. . . . If you get hurt bad, you're out for a long time and how the hell does that help your ball club?"

On March 19, returning to Sarasota from Miami on a chartered DC-4 with the rest of his teammates, Ted was in fine fettle. He'd hit a big home run to power the Sox to a 10–7 Grapefruit League win against the Yankees. He sang a song in falsetto, bowed in good humor after he was roundly jeered, then went up to the cockpit and flew the plane for a while. He returned to his seat just before landing and announced: "Don't be scared, you guys. I'm going to let the regular driver take it in." A Boston writer who'd had his scraps with Ted watched all this and said quietly to a nearby *Time* reporter, "You know, I'm falling in love with that character. He's never been so nice. He can be a terrific guy and he's always terrific copy, nice or not. I hope the stiff hits .494."[13]

The Red Sox had a horrific opening day on April 18. Playing New York at Fenway Park, Boston jumped out to a 9–0 lead, only to have the Yankees storm back and win the game, 15–10. "The Red Sox went from the heights of sublimity to the lowest depths of ridicule," as Jack Malaney put it in the *Boston Post*.[14]

Any writers who might have been prone to rip the team after this woeful exhibition were given more reason to seethe when, upon assembling outside the clubhouse to interview the players after the game, they were told there was a new policy in effect: the press was now banned before games and for an hour afterward.

The catalysts for barring the writers were Ted and Dom DiMaggio, but it was Williams who controlled the locker room and enforced the ban—with great relish. Usually dressed only in a towel, he would stand by the clubhouse door, counting the seconds until the hour was up, then say, "Okay, now all you bastards can come in." By then, all the other players were typically gone—it would be just Ted and the clubhouse boys.

The writers complained to general manager Joe Cronin, who ducked the issue, saying it was the players' clubhouse and they could do as they pleased. Joe McCarthy went along. Ted had long felt that the Red Sox didn't do enough to insulate him from the writers and the stress they created by poking, prodding, and trolling for trouble, so he'd finally taken matters into his own hands. He even posted a sign by his locker that said, NO WRITERS. (Harold Kaese wondered if Williams, the new *Herald* columnist, would be restricted from entering the clubhouse along with the other newspapermen.) Of course, the eight Boston papers (the *Transcript* by then had folded) could have banded together and boycotted coverage of the team, but who wanted to risk losing the readers who bought copies specifically to follow the Red Sox? Eventually the post-game ban was dropped to thirty minutes for the remainder of the 1950 season and to fifteen minutes for years after that.[15]

The Red Sox again started slowly. Ted wasn't hitting up to his standard. Mel Parnell and Ellis Kinder were the only pitchers who were even somewhat reliable, and McCarthy soon found himself increasing their workload by using them in relief, between starts.[16] But no one else was playing particularly well, either. When the Tigers came to Boston for a doubleheader on May 11, they were tied for first with the Red Sox. In the sixth inning of the first game, Ted dropped a routine fly ball. The error was meaningless in a 13–4 Tigers blowout, but the fans booed Williams as he trotted into the dugout after Detroit was retired. Piqued, the Kid extended the middle finger of each hand and gave the paying customers what for.

In the second game, with the Sox leading 2–0, Detroit had the bases loaded with two out in the eighth when Vic Wertz hit a sharp grounder into left field. Ted charged the ball, trying to keep the tying run from scoring, but it took a bad hop and skidded past him, rolling all the way to the wall. All three runners scored, and at the end of the inning, the crowd of 27,758 jeered Williams mercilessly as he ran off the field. Ted responded by again extending his finger to the fans, this time in three separate dramatic gestures to different sections of the park.

"Ted began, 'You in left field, fuck you!' and he saluted," recalled Walt Dropo years later. Dropo was the six-foot-five-inch, 220-pound slugger who had been called up from Louisville in early April to replace Billy Goodman at first base after Goodman broke his leg. "And then he went to center field and then to right field, and then, 'You Black Knights of the Keyboard, take this,' and he gave them the finger.... That day Ted just had had enough. It had been building over a period of time. He just vented his emotions right then and there in front of everybody."[17]

For good measure, as he was waiting in the on-deck circle to hit in the bottom half of the inning and the boos continued, Williams turned around and spat contemptuously at the crowd. Boston went on to lose, 5–3.

It was by far the biggest and most extreme tantrum of his career, and the papers savaged him for it. Baseball "never wallowed lower in the muck than it did on a softly wonderful day in beautiful Fenway Park," wrote Dave Egan, trotting out a new nickname for Ted after his finger display: "the Pantomimist."[18] Austen Lake wrote that Williams had "removed himself from the ranks of decent sportsmen. Yesterday he was a little man, and in his ungovernable rage, a dirty little man."[19] The *Post* said it had pictures of Ted's crude gestures but wouldn't publish them "for the sake of the children, ladies and normal persons."

In the clubhouse after the game, Ted was unrepentant. "I didn't mind the errors," he said, "but those goddamn fans, they can go fuck themselves, and you can quote me in all the papers."

The next morning, Tom Yawkey called in his star for a tongue-lashing. He demanded that Ted apologize and made him promise he would never do such a thing again. The team then issued the following statement: "After a talk with Mr. Yawkey, Ted Williams has requested that this announcement be made to the fans. Ted is sorry for his impulsive action on the field yesterday and wishes to apologize to any and all whom he may have offended."

The statement would have been more effective if it had dropped the *may have*. Williams was chastened, mortified, and ashamed. It had been a Tourette's-like outburst that he couldn't control but regretted immediately. After cooling off, he wanted to apologize, but the circumstances of being called in by Yawkey and the statement being issued in his name rather than in his own words made it look less than sincere. Or, as Gerry Hern put it in the *Post,* it looked "somewhat like a mother dragging a reluctant child to a neighbor's house after breaking a window."[20]

When the din died down a bit, Commissioner Happy Chandler summoned Williams to his office for a private talk, which was kept quiet at the time. Chandler liked Ted and wanted to see if he could help soothe the slugger's frayed nerves.

"Ted kept saying about the Boston fans, 'What do they want me to do?'" Chandler said years later. "He said, 'I hit the ball into the stands for them. I hustle. I make the catches. But they boo me. Or those sportswriters blast me.' He's a good boy. Trouble with Ted is, he's got a persecution complex. He can't understand why people boo him. That's why I called him in. I thought I'd try to help him. When a fellow needs a friend, a fellow needs a friend. But I just couldn't reach him."[21]

Jimmy Cannon, the prominent *New York Post* columnist, played off the tantrum story and wrote on June 1 that Ted wanted to be traded—to Detroit. Though Cannon was one of the few writers Ted liked, he panned the story and the next day issued a denial in his own column: "I never said I want to be traded. I don't want to play baseball anywhere except in Boston, and I don't want to play for anybody except Tom Yawkey."

In a seminal piece later that month, Roger Birtwell of the *Globe,* writing from Chicago on June 20, referred to the Red Sox as "baseball's Country Club Set" who didn't seem the least bit upset to have just lost five games in a row in Cleveland and Detroit, or to be idling nine and a half games out of first place. "The Country Club boys, who receive half a million dollars a summer to play ball games, were relieved to escape from Detroit and Cleveland—two towns where the players are simply low-brow roughnecks," Birtwell wrote. "Besides, they play too hard there." This listless, fat-and-sassy image of the Boston players as pampered and overpaid by Yawkey would linger and define the team for a generation.

As always, Ted was central. The scene on the train ride from Detroit to Chicago was "the picture of contentment." There was Junior Stephens asleep on a parlor chair, Mickey McDermott sprawled across six or seven seats, and Williams off by himself, sitting next to a porter in a separate smoking car, reading the sports pages and checking on his investments in the *Wall Street Journal.* Wrote Birtwell, "One of the players told Williams some time ago, 'You buy every newspaper you can get, and spend half your time reading them—just to find someone to get mad at, each day.'"[22]

Sure enough, Ted popped off to Birtwell six days later: "Before the war, I hit .400," he said. "When I hit 50 points lower after the war, the writers say it's because I can't hit against teams like the Yankees. But it could be that the Yankees have better pitching, couldn't it? A guy can't hit .400 every year." Then he added this cruel postscript: "I'll be able to retire in a couple of years or so. I'll be hitting around .350. And I hope the baseball writers are up in the press box with the temperature at 121....Men die at 120."[23]

The *Globe* quoted that vicious remark in an article prominently placed on its front page. The piece ran just beneath the lead story, which reported that North Korea had invaded South Korea the previous day. President Harry Truman quickly ordered a Naval blockade of the Korean coast on June 29 and authorized General Douglas MacArthur to send American troops into Korea. By early July, 6,500 Marines set sail from San Diego, bound for Pusan, Korea.

As the ground commitment escalated, the need for tactical air support also grew. The Marine Corps was short on pilots, so it made plans to activate hundreds of its pilots who had served in World War II and who were still carried in the inactive reserve ranks. One of the pilots who stood to be recalled was Williams. After being discharged from World War II, he had remained in the Reserves and now held the rank of first lieutenant, an appointment he'd accepted in writing on June 30, 1949. He had casually signed up for the Reserves while filling out his discharge paperwork in 1946—and would later assert he did so unwittingly. He had agreed to allow the Corps to use his name to promote recruiting, and he'd recorded radio commercials for the same purpose, but he certainly hadn't given serious credence to the notion that another war could be on the horizon or that becoming a reservist could make him vulnerable to be recalled to fight in it.

On July 12, Brigadier General Clayton C. Jerome, director of public information and recruiting for the Marine Corps, wrote Williams to tell him that since "the recruiting picture has indeed changed completely," the Corps would be delaying the rollout of a generic poster featuring Ted's photo to instead focus on a pitch that encouraged volunteers to join the "service which selects its men."

Meanwhile, manager Joe McCarthy's drinking had gotten out of control. He would go off on benders and miss a few games, then the writers would cover for him, reporting that he had the flu. Some days, he'd fall asleep in the dugout. Joe Cronin finally warned McCarthy that if he appeared at the ballpark drunk one more time he'd be sacked. When it happened in Detroit in late June, the club announced that McCarthy was resigning for health reasons. Coach Steve O'Neill took over as manager for the rest of the year.

Boston was eight back at the All-Star break. Williams had started slowly, but by that midpoint, he was cooking, at .321 with an impressive 25 homers and 83 RBIs. "I was hitting better in the month before the All Star game than I had ever hit in my life," Ted later said.[24]

The other Red Sox joining Williams at Comiskey Park in Chicago for the All-Star Game on July 11 were Dom DiMaggio, Bobby Doerr, Junior Stephens, and Walt Dropo, the rookie who had emerged as a power-hitting force, batting fifth in the Red Sox order behind Williams and Stephens.

In the top of the first inning, Pirates slugger Ralph Kiner hit a deep drive to left-center. Williams raced back for it and made a spectacular one-handed catch before crashing into the scoreboard, bracing himself for the collision with his left elbow. He rubbed the elbow hard on his way into the dugout, and American League manager Casey Stengel asked him if he was all right. Ted said he was.

In the bottom half of the inning, he laced what appeared to be a single to right field, but Jackie Robinson, playing well out on the grass in the Williams shift, grabbed the ball on one hop and threw Ted out at first. In the third, Kiner again smashed a line drive to left, and Ted made another nice running catch, continuing to belie his reputation as a poor, indifferent defender.

Kiner turned the tables on Ted in the bottom half of the inning, making a leaping catch of a scorcher Williams hit to right. In the fifth, with the score tied 2–2, Williams singled in the go-ahead run for the Americans. Stengel kept asking him how his elbow was. "I kept nodding, 'OK, OK,' because I wanted to play...but by now the elbow's a balloon and I'm in great pain," Williams recalled in his book.[25] Ted struck out in the eighth, whereupon Stengel pulled him from the game, which the NL went on to win in fourteen innings, 4–3.

Williams was in agony on the flight home to Boston, Dropo remembered: "Ted was holding his hand in his shirt, and he said, 'This goddamn thing, I think it's broken.' It was a four-hour flight from Chicago to New York, and all that time Ted was sitting there the heat of his body is going out. We got into LaGuardia—we had about an hour layover—and we went upstairs to the rotunda to have a drink. Ted said, 'Give me a double Jack Daniel's....He kept saying, 'This son of a bitch is broken. It's killing me....' We landed in Boston, and I went to the hotel where I was living. I got up in the morning and I read the paper: 'Williams's Elbow is Broken. He'll be out two months.' Imagine."[26]

On July 13, Ted was operated on, and seven bone chips were removed from his elbow. Williams was praised in the papers for courageously playing eight innings with a broken elbow—and playing well, at that. It was surprising that he'd violated his own dictum of not crashing into walls in pursuit of a fly ball—they didn't pay off on fielding, he'd said. Now he wasn't just out for a few games, he was out for a few months and had placed the balance of his career in jeopardy by breaking his elbow, a key cog in the willowy Williams swing. Ted would later say that the injury was one of his biggest disappointments, and he said that he was never the same hitter again because he would always have stiffness in the elbow, was never able to get full extension in his left arm, and as a result lost some of his power.

After immobilizing his arm for a period, Williams began an exercise and physical therapy regimen for his elbow. On the sixteenth, he told Joe Cashman from his hospital bed that though the Red Sox were now eight and a half games out, he still thought they could catch up and win the pennant without him. He said he hoped to return in five or six weeks, adding: "I would like to play enough games to drive in seventeen runs to reach the one-hundred-RBI mark," a plateau he hadn't missed since his rookie year in 1939. The Kid seemed blithely unaware that the rather crass and baldly stated individual RBI goal might appear at odds with the team goal of winning a pennant.

While he was out, Williams would sometimes appear in the Red Sox dugout for home games, but he didn't travel with the team. He tried to remain upbeat, but he could not have been cheered by a small item in the August 8 *Globe,* which reported that he was now eligible to be recalled to active duty by the Marine Corps under its latest reserve mobilization plan. A Corps spokesman was quoted as saying there were no plans to activate Ted "at this time," but an obviously worried Williams fired off a letter the same day to Major General M. H. Silverthorn, director of the Marine Corps Reserve. "In view of the present situation I believe it important that I have my complete service record at hand," Ted wrote, using official Red Sox stationery, in case Silverthorn had any doubts that he was receiving a letter from anyone other than *the* Ted Williams. Ted wanted to see precisely what he'd signed and confirm for himself the extent to which he was still on the hook.

Billy Goodman, his broken leg healed, had replaced Ted in left field and went on to have a career year at the plate, hitting .354 to win the batting title. With Goodman hitting for average and Dropo for serious power (he would hit .322 with 34 homers and 144 RBIs on the year), the loss of Williams was concealed. Starting August 15, the Sox won eleven in a row and sixteen of seventeen at Fenway Park to get back in the race, just two and a half games out of first place.

In the midst of this streak, Williams went up to Maine on a five-day fishing trip. This outing took place during the five- to six-week time frame within which Ted had estimated he would return to playing, so the specter of him fishing leisurely in the wilds of Maine rubbed some the wrong way. Colonel Egan, for one, let him have it: "T. Wms. Esq., who usually is considered part Ruth and part Shakespeare, has chosen the high point of the baseball season to become Izaak Walton and to throw all his energies into bagging a five-pound bass."[27] He went on to write his column from the point of view of a bass terrified at the prospect of being stalked by Ted. HOW THE FISH FEEL AS TED DESERTS SOX, the headline read. Others, including Harold Kaese, wondered if Williams's teammates were irked by his fishing getaway. If he couldn't play, could he not at least come to the ballpark and cheer his team on?

In fact, Williams was ambivalent about playing again. When he took his cast off, he couldn't extend his left arm to within four inches of his right. He still had considerable pain, and wasn't sure if he would help or hurt the team. Many argued that the club's recent winning streak was evidence enough that the Red Sox were better off without Ted.[28] But Steve O'Neill wanted Williams in the lineup and argued he should test the elbow now rather than wonder all winter what he could have contributed. So Ted was eased back, first with a pinch-hitting appearance against the Yankees at Fenway on September 7. When he bounded out of the dugout in the fifth inning and strode to the plate, making his first appearance in more than eight weeks, the crowd of 29,897 erupted. "No one ever received a greater ovation," wrote Alex MacLean in the *Record*. "No appearance was ever more dramatic."[29]

There were men on second and third and one out. Yogi Berra walked to the mound and looked into the dugout for instructions as the cheers continued to thunder down from the grandstand and the bleachers beyond. Casey Stengel, predictably, ordered an intentional walk. Ted was lifted for a pinch runner, then he showered and left the park before the writers could get to him. The Sox went on to win, 10–8, and were now within one and a half games of the Yankees and the Tigers, who were tied for first.[30]

O'Neill held Williams out for another week before pinch-hitting him again on September 14 against the Browns in Saint Louis. Ted doubled in a 6–3 loss. He returned as a starter the following day. It was hot and humid at Sportsman's Park, so Williams was able to get his elbow good and loose. He hit a long home run over the fence in right and out onto Grand Avenue, as well as three singles, to lead the Sox to a 12–9 win.

But Ted's barrage of hits amounted to false hope. His elbow still hurt, his timing was off, and he wasn't in game shape. He could manage only two hits in his next seventeen times to the plate. "At times he seems afraid to swing," remarked Hank Greenberg after watching the Sox play the Indians at Cleveland.[31]

By the nineteenth, Boston went back within a game and a half of the top, but then they crashed, losing four in a row in Cleveland and New York despite two homers by Ted in the second Yankees game. They finished third, four games behind the Yankees.

In their postmortems of the season, the press noted that the team had gotten close without Williams and sunk when he returned—to be precise, Boston had been 44–17 without Ted and 8–8 after he came back. Some players were quoted anonymously as saying they "could have won it without Ted" and that he had only created tension when he returned. Such conflict was fuel for the hot-stove season, of course, and soon there were renewed rumors that the Kid might be traded, even though, despite missing sixty-seven games, he'd still hit .317, with 28 homers and 97 RBIs.

Williams retreated to Florida for a winter of bonefishing in the flats of the Florida Keys. He would pole the boat four or five miles each day, stretching his elbow and building it up again in the process.

"In the spring, I began to feel a little strength coming back," he said.[32] But it was still sore and stiff. As a result, Williams, now thirty-two, announced that he would set his own schedule in spring training and play a limited number of Grapefruit League games. That struck Steve O'Neill, who was anxious to put his own stamp on the team in his first full season, as a direct challenge to his authority, and he decided to publicly face Ted down on the issue, declaring that the star would play whenever he, O'Neill, said so. Williams, grumbling all the while, capitulated and played a full exhibition schedule.

O'Neill, fifty-nine, was no naïf. Before being named to succeed Joe McCarthy, he had been a manager for nine years—with the Indians from 1935 to 1937 and the Tigers from 1943 to 1948, compiling an overall record of 708–582. He'd won a World Series with the wartime Tigers in 1945. But O'Neill would turn out to be Williams's least favorite manager, and they sparred throughout spring training over his playing time. When Ted asked to be let out of a March 18 game in Tampa against the Reds because of a cold, O'Neill refused, whereupon Williams went into his diva routine—pouting, loafing, and generally going through the motions, earning boos and jeers from the crowd as a result. He responded by spitting at the fans on three different occasions, the last time as he crossed home plate after belting a homer. Assessing Ted's new nadir, John Gillooly of the *Record* gave him a new name: the Splendid Spitter.[33]

The Red Sox started slowly, per usual, and Williams slower still. On May 20, Ted was hitting only .226, prompting alarmist whispering from the press box and elsewhere that he was done. Naturally, that kind of talk was just the motivational tonic he needed to go off on one of his tears. In the last ten games of May, Williams went 26–53, including 4 homers and 22 RBIs, to raise his average to .321. The Sox won ten in a row and by mid-July were in first place. Ted was hitting to all fields, fielding well, and hustling—even scoring from second on a bunt in a game against New York. Boston stayed competitive through August, but collapsed again in September as the Yankees surged to another pennant. Boston finished third, eleven games out, and Williams slumped at the end to post what for him were subpar final numbers: a .318 average, with 30 home runs and 126 RBIs. The punctuation mark came in his final at bat of the '51 season, when his two-out pop-up in the ninth gave Yankees pitcher Allie Reynolds his second no-hitter of the season.

For the Red Sox, the 1951 season marked the end of what many prognosticators, starting in 1946, had thought would be a dynasty in the making. Key pitching injuries had derailed the 1947 season, but pennants were lost on the final days of 1948 and 1949, while the '50 and '51 teams contended into September and could have won. Now the nucleus was aging, with Williams, Dom DiMaggio, Pesky, Stephens, Doerr, and Kinder all in their thirties.[34] Doerr, bothered by a chronic bad back, announced his retirement following the '51 season, and DiMaggio followed in early 1953. The team wouldn't be a pennant contender for the rest of the '50s, a decade in which Williams was virtually the only reason to come to the ballpark. These would be years in which Ted, lacking even the semblance of a supporting cast, no longer bothered to eschew the role of individualist, the role that his critics had long cast him in.

12

Ted and Joe

On December 11, 1951, Joe DiMaggio announced his retirement in New York.

The fabled Yankee Clipper, who had just turned thirty-seven, said his decision was prompted by advancing years, a spate of physical ailments, and the simple realization that as a player, "I no longer have it."

Addressing a gaggle of reporters, photographers, and newsreel cameras at the Yankees offices in Manhattan's Squibb Tower, Joe said that "when baseball is no longer fun, it's no longer a game. And so I've played my last game of ball."

Responding to questions, he said his greatest thrills had been the fifty-six-game hitting streak of 1941 and his smashing return to baseball in Boston that summer of 1949, when he'd missed the first sixty-five games of the season because of a heel injury. Asked who he considered to be the greatest of present-day hitters, Joe replied: "Ted Williams. He is by far the greatest natural hitter I ever saw."[1]

After some more questions, the large room suddenly went dark after fuses blew under the strain of all the cables and wires powering the newsreel and radio feeds. When the lights came back on after several minutes, Joe was gone.

The heir to Ruth and Gehrig, DiMaggio had personified a certain graceful nobility as well as the Yankees aura of success and invincibility during his relatively short career, which spanned 1936 to 1951, with three years out for World War II. In Joe's thirteen seasons of supple but sparkling defensive play and prodigious clutch hitting, the Yankees won an astonishing ten pennants and nine World Series, a record that served only to put a sheen on his skills and reputation and define him as a winner. DiMaggio came to transcend baseball as a cultural icon: the Hemingway hero, the Joltin' Joe celebrated in Simon and Garfunkel lyrics, the megawatt star who married his equal in Marilyn Monroe. In his latter days, he assumed less dignified roles as the omnipresent Mr. Coffee TV pitchman and, finally and less visibly, the rapacious memorabilia hawker obsessed with making money.

DiMaggio's acknowledgment of Williams at his farewell press conference was fitting, since the two were by far the dominant players of their era—baseball's golden age—and came to be joined at the hip in fan discourse. During their careers and into their retirements, there were endless debates about who the better player was and who was most valuable to his team, and both men remained rivals for the rest of their lives. For Ted, the rivalry was friendly. For Joe, it was fierce.

The two were opposites in many respects.

DiMaggio was shy, backward, and hardly spoke at all. Traveling in a car across the country in 1936 to his first spring training as a Yankee with fellow San Franciscans Tony Lazzeri and Frankie Crosetti, Joe never uttered a word until he was asked if he would like to share the driving, whereupon he said he didn't drive.

Williams, on the other hand, was a chatterbox, with a boisterous, voluble personality and a curious mind. Joe, whose teammates called him the Sphinx, was stolid. Where Ted was explosive and colorful, Joe made it a point to conceal his emotions.

Ted came from a troubled home; Joe a strong one.

Joe always dressed immaculately, usually in a tailored suit and sporting a fresh manicure. As Roy Blount Jr. once wrote, when they saw Joe in the flesh, people would always say to him, "You look good, Joe." And when the Clipper was out of earshot, the people would say to themselves, "Don't he look good?"[2]

But the Kid was a rumpled, unmade bed who almost always wore a casual, open-collared shirt.

"DiMaggio was regal," wrote Tom Boswell of the *Washington Post*. "But Williams was real. Joe D met the world like an icy myth of a starched man and liked it that way. Ted wore his rough edges and his opinions on his sleeve."[3]

When Joe returned to Yankee Stadium after he retired, he would demand an appearance fee and insisted on being introduced last, after Mantle and other stars.[4] Williams never made any such demands, and he stayed involved in the game far more than DiMaggio did. Joe didn't have any modern-day favorites, the way Ted did in Tony Gwynn and Nomar

Garciaparra—or any baseball causes, such as trying to get Dom DiMaggio and "Shoeless" Joe Jackson into the Hall of Fame.

Ted often argued with the fans, whereas Joe did what he could to cultivate their goodwill. Joe knew how to tip his hat deftly, just enough to acknowledge the crowd but not enough to annoy the other team. Ted, of course, did not tip his hat at all.

Both were proud. When photographers wanted a joint picture, they'd have to get both of them to meet in neutral ground, behind the backstop. Neither would go to the other's dugout.

Ted enjoyed being Ted more than Joe enjoyed being Joe, and Williams had a more satisfying post-baseball life.

Ted never demanded sycophants and had a healthy distrust of people who sucked up to him. Joe could cut you off if you didn't call him Clipper and insisted that everything be done for him. He was surrounded by coat holders and fixers; he expected freebies or others to pay his tab. Ted always insisted on picking up his own check and paying for others.

Joe smoked incessantly—even in the dugout. Ted never smoked. Joe loved nightclubs, Ted loved the outdoors.

Ted had a significantly longer career—seventeen full years and two partial seasons, which were interrupted by the Korean War. Since Williams aspired to be the world's greatest hitter and was largely an indifferent fielder, DiMaggio, who was perhaps peerless in the outfield, certainly must be considered the better all-around player. But Williams was clearly the superior batter, statistically.

Ted was better in average, homers, and RBIs as well as on-base percentage and slugging percentage. Ted won six batting titles to Joe's two, four home-run titles to Joe's two, four RBI titles to Joe's two, and six runs-scored titles to Joe's one. Ted won two Triple Crowns, Joe none. Interestingly, though DiMaggio is generally thought to have been faster than Williams and a better base runner, Joe only had thirty career stolen bases compared to twenty-four for Ted, whose six runs-scored titles suggest he was at least not a liability on the base paths. DiMaggio was harder to strike out. He had only 369 strikeouts in 6,821 career at bats compared to Ted's 709 in 7,706: Joe struck out just 5 percent of the time compared to Ted's 9 percent.

Ted hit from the left, Joe from the right. Joe was still at the plate. Ted was jittery and moved his hips from side to side.

Ever the disciplined hitter, Ted took far more walks than Joe, who was willing to swing at bad pitches to drive in a runner. That was a key difference in their hitting philosophies, and even some of Ted's team-mates gave the edge to DiMaggio on this issue.

Eddie Pellagrini, a Red Sox utility infielder in 1946 and 1947, recalled that when he was stationed in Hawaii during World War II, playing ball with other major leaguers, the Williams-DiMaggio debate was a hot topic among Red Sox and Yankees players: "All the Red Sox guys would say, 'Aw, shit, Williams is the better hitter.' I'd say, 'Williams might be a better hitter for average, but let me ask you a question. Who would you rather have up there with the winning run on third, Williams or DiMaggio?' This was in forty-five or so. Ted had hit his .406. I said, 'Joe would hit that ball when it was way outside. Williams would take the walk.' I met DiMaggio at some Old-Timers' Game years later. . . . I said, 'With runners on base, you'd hit a ball that far outside.' You know what he said? 'Farther than that.' He wanted to hit the winning run in. Even on a bad ball."[5] But Johnny Pesky, Ted's longtime friend and team-mate, dissented, saying simply that Williams was the better hitter and DiMaggio the better all-around player. "That's the way we always set-tled it. I've been calling Ted the greatest hitter that ever lived for the last fifty years."[6]

New York writers were given to fawning, over-the-top depictions of Joe. "He's an artist in the exact sense of the word, a Cezanne with a fin-ger mitt, a Van Gogh with a Louisville slugger," gushed Joe Williams of the *New York World-Telegram* in 1948.[7] And while Joe was protected by the press to conserve his standing as a hero, Williams was not. "The New York writers both respected [Joe] and feared that he would cut them off," wrote David Halberstam in *Summer of '49*. "They generously described his aloofness, born of uncertainty and suspicion, as elegance. . . . No such protection was offered Williams."[8] It was thanks in part to his good press and strong relationships with the writers that Joe won three MVPs to Ted's two. Despite Ted's .406, the 1941 vote in favor of DiMag-gio was defensible because of Joe's streak and because the Yankees won the pennant, but the narrow 1947 tally for DiMaggio, in the face of Wil-liams's overwhelmingly superior numbers, was not.

"The New York temperament rallied around Joe," John Updike, the writer and longtime Williams admirer told author Peter Golenbock. "You cannot say that about the Boston fans and Ted. But the run of us certainly were for Williams, and admired him all the more because he seemed to be carrying all these handicaps, broken bones, angry *Herald* columnists, all these loud fans, double war service, divorce problems. . . .

He never had a smooth season where he just played ball and everything just fell into place."[9]

As Ted made his mark in the Pacific Coast League he'd been touted by Lefty O'Doul, Joe's manager with the San Francisco Seals, as the best prospect to come out of the PCL since...DiMaggio. Ted demurred: "I've never even seen DiMaggio play but from all I have read about him, I know I'm not in his class yet," he said in 1938.[10]

The two first laid eyes on each other in Yankee Stadium on opening day of 1939, Ted's first big-league game. Williams was a bit starstruck and made sure to play the Clipper deep. Over the years, they would play in nine All-Star Games together, but never became particularly friendly. There was that famous picture of the two sluggers in the clubhouse after Ted's winning home run in the 1941 game, both beaming, Joe's right arm around Ted, his left fist pumping Williams in celebration. But Joe would generally keep to himself at those affairs, not talking much to anybody.

"It was either Ted or it was me," DiMaggio would say years later about the rivalry between him and Williams. "In a sense it was flattering. What people were saying was that, at the time, we were the two best."[11]

Williams had been aware of DiMaggio since 1933, when Joe began starring with the San Francisco Seals. In 1936, the year Ted graduated from high school and joined the San Diego Padres, DiMaggio had his magnificent rookie season with the Yankees, batting .323 with 29 home runs and 125 runs batted in. That fall, Joe—the fisherman's son who couldn't stand the smell of fish and had spurned the entreaties made by his father, Giuseppe, to join him at sea—returned home to San Francisco and a hero's welcome. Giuseppe's fishermen friends hoisted him on their shoulders and carried him along the wharf in triumph.[12]

In his public comments about DiMaggio, Williams was unfailingly generous. "It took the big guy to beat me," Ted said after Joe beat him out as the 1941 MVP. Of the streak, he said: "I believe there isn't a record in the books that will be harder to break than Joe's fifty-six games. It may be the greatest batting achievement of all." And assessing Joe's career, Williams wrote in one of his books on hitting: "I can't say enough about DiMaggio. Of all the great major leaguers I played with or against in my 19 year career, he was my idol. I idolized Joe DiMaggio!"[13]

Joe's public comments about Ted, on the other hand, ranged from gracious ("There's no question in my mind—I've always said he was the greatest hitter in the game"[14]) to damning with faint praise ("Best left-handed hitter I've ever seen"[15]) to sharply critical ("He is a crybaby. You can write that for me"[16*]).

And, privately, when speaking to his friends or sympathetic writers, DiMaggio was contemptuous of Williams. "He throws like a broad and runs like a ruptured duck," Joe would say. According to Joe's agent and lawyer, Morris Engelberg, who in 2003 wrote a book entitled *DiMaggio: Setting the Record Straight,* the Clipper considered Gehrig, Ruth, Hornsby, and Cobb better hitters than Williams and was dismissive of Ted for never having won a championship. "'Tell him to hold up his hands. Where are the rings?'" Engelberg wrote, quoting Joe.[17] "He thought Williams was a selfish player because he concentrated on one thing, his hitting, and neglected to improve his base running and fielding." Joe was also critical of Ted for taking too many walks. He even undercut Ted's .406 achievement, telling pals that he could have achieved the milestone himself in 1939 but for his manager, Joe McCarthy. He'd been over .400 late in the season when he came down with an infection in his left eye. He couldn't see the ball properly, but McCarthy insisted on playing him, and his final average dipped to .381. After the season, Joe said McCarthy told him he'd left him in the lineup because he did not want DiMaggio to be a "cheese champion."

Williams would read about Joe's private comments, or friends would tell him about them, but Ted would turn the other cheek—or even be sympathetic to Joe. "Ted would put a positive light to it, like, 'Well, we were competitors; what do you want the guy to say?'" recalled Al Cassidy, Ted's friend and the executor of his estate. "Or he'd sit there and say, 'You know, I didn't throw the ball very well.' He justified why Joe would say it. I never knew Ted to be condescending to anybody, even in conversations like that, whether we said it or someone would say it to him."[18]

When both men attended events, Ted would be solicitous of Joe and sometimes defer to him. Dan Wheeler, a friend of Williams, recalled the interplay between the two men at a New York fund-raising event for Major League Baseball in the '90s: "We were in the green room. Joe Garagiola was the emcee. Sandy Koufax and Whitey Ford were in the room, and then Joe D came in, and Ted and Joe talked. Garagiola came

---

* The latter remark was made in August of 1949, after a Red Sox–Yankees game in which Ted, criticized for not stretching a double into a triple at Fenway Park, replied defensively that no one had criticized Joe when he didn't stretch a single off the wall into a double in the same game. That evening, DiMaggio summoned Dan Daniel, the *World-Telegram* syndicated columnist, and handed off the crybaby quote. The writers raced back to Ted the next day and prodded him for a response, but Williams only smiled and said he had nothing to say.

over to Ted, and said, 'Ted, we're gonna introduce you last,' and Ted said, 'No, second to last.' He pointed to Joe and said, 'Introduce him last, this is his town.' "[19]

Jonathan Gallen, a memorabilia dealer turned investment banker who had business dealings with both Ted and Joe, confirmed the differences between what each man said about the other privately: "Joe D could never hand out a solid compliment. It would be like, 'Yeah, he could hit, but he couldn't field.' The general tone of it all was negative. Ted loved people. He never ran them down. He saw the best in people. He loved baseball. He had a giant appetite for life. There was no one whose public perception was more different than the reality than Joe DiMaggio. The reverse was true of Ted. Joe was cheap as hell. Ted could not say no. Ted would give you everything, and Joe would give you nothing. Ted would want you to do well. But Joe—if you were making more than he thought you should off a deal, Joe wouldn't do the deal. Joe was stingy and unhappy."[20]*

As he got older, DiMaggio became fixated on making money from the memorabilia market. Williams dabbled in it, mostly as a way of reconnecting with his son, John-Henry, to whom he would entrust most of his business dealings.

The man who coordinated most deals for both men over a span of about fifteen years was one of the nation's leading memorabilia brokers, Jerry Romolt of Arizona.

"I had Joe and Ted both, but I never promoted shows for them together," Romolt said. "They were friendly when they crossed paths, in social activity, but they were not particularly close. Ted loved Joe, and Joe respected Ted. Joe was not a giving, gregarious person like Ted was; he was not as open as Ted was to him. Joe had a very competitive streak, and I know he was envious of Ted. Williams was my favorite of all time. He was rough on the exterior. But on a personal level there wasn't a better human being. He was eminently reachable. There was an exposure to his soul that Joe could never bear."[21]

Sometimes, DiMaggio would agree to do a promotional deal for a certain price, then insist on getting paid more when the event was actually being held.

---

* DiMaggio's frigidity and greed extended to his own family. Joe's image was on the cover of his brother Dom's memoir of the 1941 season, *Real Grass, Real Heroes,* but Dom never asked his brother's permission, Joe said, because he knew Joe would have said no. Engelberg wrote in his book that Joe and Dom didn't speak to each other for five years before Joe's death.

Once, the Bowery Savings Bank in New York had hired DiMaggio to help it persuade Italian customers not to take their money elsewhere. "They called in Joe to reassure people, and to endorse the bank," recalled former John Hancock Financial Services CEO David D'Alessandro, who at the time worked as an executive for an advertising firm retained by the bank. "He agreed to ten thousand dollars a day for two days. Then, after being told they had a full house and were turning people away, he said: 'You guys are getting too good a deal,' and raised his fee to twenty thousand dollars a day."[22]

In his dealings with Bowery Savings, DiMaggio was always looking for ways to get extra money or merchandise, D'Alessandro said. For one advertising campaign, the bank wanted the Clipper photographed in his old Yankees uniform with assorted vintage equipment, so D'Alessandro arranged to borrow the precious gear from the Hall of Fame in Cooperstown. "After the photo shoot, the son of a bitch started packing the stuff up and was going to walk away with it!" D'Alessandro said. "I said, 'Mr. DiMaggio, we borrowed this from Cooperstown. We have to return it all.'

"Joe said, 'What are you talking about? I played with these things.' Only after I told him that I would lose my job if I didn't return the stuff did he give it back. The problem with Joe—he was always nickel-and-diming. You had to send him two first-class air tickets to bring him in from San Francisco. He would use one and cash the other."[23]

According to Dr. Rock Positano, a leading podiatrist who began treating DiMaggio for his aching heels in the early 1990s and then became a Clipper intimate, Joe always stayed competitive with Williams and remained keenly aware of what Ted was doing.

"There was always this immense rivalry, even fifty years after they played ball," Positano said. "Joe wouldn't make a move without Ted doing it first—like going to the White House. Joe did not want Ted to get any of the publicity." In 1991, President George H. W. Bush wanted to honor Joe and Ted on the fiftieth anniversary of the streak and Williams's .406 milestone, and then fly them to the All-Star Game in Toronto aboard Air Force One. "Joe had a trepidation about it. He said, 'Doc, Williams is doing it, so I've got to do it.'"

When DiMaggio introduced Rock to Ted at the Marriott Marquis hotel in New York, Positano was enamored with Williams and thought he was "larger than life." But Joe didn't want him to get too friendly with Ted. "He said, 'Listen, Doc, he's a little different than I am. He's not as friendly as I am.'

"Joe really did not like Ted, that's the bottom line. He respected him as a hitter. Joe thought Ted was a one-dimensional player. Just a hitter. He always judged his contemporaries on how many championships they won. But he did think Williams was the best natural hitter in baseball. And he had great respect for someone who served in the military.

"Ted was a lot easier on Joe than Joe was on Ted. I told Joe once, 'Look, you have to be easier on this guy. He didn't have an easy life. He was a war hero.' Joe would say, 'Listen, Doc, you have to understand, I'm still a competitor. Just because we stopped playing ball doesn't mean we don't have a competitive drive. I respect him as a hitter, but when it comes down to it, he should respect me more.' "[24]

Whenever the Yankees played the Red Sox at Fenway Park, Joe wanted to be sure to perform especially well, because he was not only going up against Ted but against Dominic as well. The Clipper was irritated by a ditty that Boston fans would serenade him with whenever he came to town. Sung to the tune of "O Tannenbaum," it went: "He's better than his brother Joe, Dominic DiMaggio!" Joe knew that wasn't true, of course, but he thought Dom never gave him enough respect, and he didn't like that Ted and Dom were friends.

"Joe felt his brother was too close to Ted," Positano said. "He felt Ted had his attention. Joe always said that bothered him a little. He never asked Dom to pull away, but he'd say, 'He may be your teammate, but I'm your brother.' "

Once, two of Ted's friends were spending the night at his house in the Florida Keys. In the drawer of a bedside table was a small notebook of Williams's, and inside was written: "Ways I'm better than DiMaggio."[25] The note probably revealed more about Ted's insecurity than it did about his rivalry with the Clipper, which never reached the level of nastiness DiMaggio seemed to give it. In the end, Williams maintained his grace.

13

Korea

After the 1951 season, Ted added a new wrinkle to his winter routine by taking up golf, inspired by a tip from Ty Cobb, who'd confided that the game had been good for his conditioning and had helped him stay in the big leagues into his forties. After two weeks of lessons, Williams made his debut on the Florida links in December, losing fifteen balls on the first nine holes.[1]

Mostly, he remained in his preferred fishing-dominated seclusion, tuning out baseball, though when he heard that one of his favorite umpires, Cal Hubbard, had injured an eye in a hunting accident, Ted immediately sent flowers and a droll telegram that stood the traditionally deferential player-umpire relationship on its ear: "Get that peeper in shape for April," Williams wrote.[2] "You're my boy — Ted."

Williams was indifferent to rumblings out of Boston that he would be traded, rumors that had spiked in October after Lou Boudreau was hired to take over as Red Sox manager for Steve O'Neill. On being introduced, Boudreau had said: "There are no untouchables on my team. I'll trade anyone on the club, including Ted Williams, if we can get what we want."[3] Ted had a cool relationship with Boudreau, who'd joined the Red Sox as a free agent for a final, lackluster season as a player in 1951. ("Well, if it isn't a Boudreau shift!" Williams had said to his former nemesis when they met that spring.)

Shortly after the turn of the New Year in 1952, the idle rhythms and concerns of Williams's off-season ended abruptly. On January 9, while fishing in the Keys, Ted received a phone call from his agent, Fred Corcoran, informing him that he had officially been recalled for service in Korea by the Marine Corps. News reports from Washington had it that Ted was one of several hundred Marine fliers being summoned to replace pilots being discharged from Korea. Assuming he passed a physical on April 2, he would begin eight weeks of training on May 2 and then serve seventeen months in Korea.

Williams was incredulous. Despite the ominous notices of the previous year that he was eligible to be recalled, Ted never thought it would actually happen. After all, he had already served in World War II and missed three full seasons of his baseball prime as a result. He'd done his duty. Now, at thirty-three, he would have to miss two more seasons of a career that only had limited time left. That seemed punitive. Weren't there others available who had not already served? Did they really need *him?* Williams was not alone in suspecting a Marine ploy to use his star power as a recruiting tool.

Details of precisely how Williams came to be recalled remain murky to this day. A captain directly involved in the selection process later told friends that when officials chose Ted, they didn't realize it was *the* Ted Williams. Another Marine, Williams's squadron commander in Korea, said that was initially true, but before orders were issued, officials did know they were dealing with the ballplayer. The commander also asserted that the Marines reneged on an informal agreement that then–Commandant Alexander Vandegrift had reached with Ted at the end of World War II, which provided for Williams to remain in the Reserves and help with recruiting with the understanding he would not be recalled to active duty.

Ted was furious, but Corcoran counseled calm. The agent, mindful of his client's image, issued a conciliatory, gung-ho statement on Williams's behalf that was totally inconsistent with what he was actually thinking and feeling at that moment. The statement said: "If Uncle Sam wants me, I'm ready. I'm no different than the next fellow." But on a parallel track, Ted decided to privately explore all his options to contest the order.

Williams called Joe Cronin with the bad news. They determined he should go to spring training as usual and participate until he was actually called up for duty. It was a long shot, but there was a slim chance he could fail his physical because of his bum elbow.

Man-on-the-street reaction in the papers mostly mourned the loss of a great star. The writers thought the call-up likely spelled the end of Ted's career, while his teammates said they thought he was getting a raw deal. "We all thought that was unfair," remembered Dom DiMaggio. "We thought they were making an example of him. Using him for public relations. Baseball years are so short, and he had already served."[4]

The raw deal view was taken up and flogged for all it was worth by columnist Dave Egan, usually Williams's archenemy. But the libertarian Egan, who had also supported Ted's right to a deferment in World War II as sole supporter of his mother, again thought Williams was being treated unfairly.

Egan wrote, "I cannot rid myself of the feeling that he has been called back to the Marines, not because he is a reserve officer, but because he is Ted Williams...and because he can guarantee the press agents—pardon me, the public relations experts of the Marine Corps—plenty of front page publicity, and because he will stimulate recruiting."[5]

But the Marines strongly denied they had singled out Williams.[6] A spokesman revealed that Ted had been notified on June 30, 1951, that he had been promoted from first lieutenant to captain and that while he could have declined the promotion he did not. Instead, he submitted to a physical exam, which the boost in rank required, then accepted the promotion in writing. The spokesman noted that Ted had long been involved in recruiting—posing for photographs, recording radio promotional spots, and giving interviews designed to spur enrollment. A Marine recruiting poster in the late '40s featured a photo of Ted in his Red Sox uniform and the message: "Ask the man who was one!"

Colonel Egan retorted the following day that any suggestion that Williams, by accepting a promotion, somehow was signaling that he wanted to be restored to active duty was a "Stalinesque fabrication" on the part of the Marine Corps. In this provocative analogy, Egan invoked none other than President Harry Truman, who in 1950 had famously dismissed a congressman who demanded that the Marines be given their own general on the Joint Chiefs of Staff by observing that the Corps already had "a propaganda machine that is almost equal to Stalin's."[7] After an uproar ensued, Truman apologized for the remark, but Egan clearly believed the president was right the first time.

When the Korean War broke out, the regular Marine forces, and the crews of aviators needed to support them, were manned at levels far below what was needed to wage a battle halfway around the world. The Reserves were quickly called up, and they played a key role in early campaigns, such as the Inchon Landing. In November of 1950, as the American-dominated United Nations forces met with increasing success, China entered the war to bolster North Korea. Soon some sixty thousand Chinese troops had thirty thousand UN forces encircled at the frozen Chosin Reservoir. Still, during fierce fighting from December 5 through December 10, the UN troops managed to escape the trap and inflict crippling losses on the Chinese in a battle that remains etched in Marine lore as one of the Corps' finest hours.

After being released from active duty at the end of World War II, reserve officers such as Williams had automatically been assigned to the Voluntary Reserve unless they specifically requested otherwise, which Ted did not. The goal was to build up an experienced standby force. Congress tried to make service in the Reserves more attractive by increasing benefits and adding new ones. By 1950, the Marine Corps was offering its active, or organized, Reserves longevity pay tied to their rank and increased pay for the required two-hour weekly drill, as well as for the two-week active-duty summer program. Promotions were generally easy to come by, and retirement benefits were enhanced.[8]

The volunteer, or inactive, Reserves to which Ted belonged were required to do no weekly or annual drills and were essentially a group that could be recalled in the event of a war or national emergency. Williams had not participated in any such drills as a member of the Reserves, and had only flown once since the end of World War II. Enrollment in the inactive Reserves was high because servicemen had assurances that they could quit when they wanted to and that they could only be recalled under certain parameters. Specifically, prior to the outbreak of hostilities in Korea, the Marine Corps was guided by the Naval Reserve Act of 1938, which provided that a member of the Reserves "may be ordered to active duty by the Secretary of the Navy in time of war or when in the opinion of the president a national emergency exists...but in time of peace, a reservist may be ordered to or continued on active duty with his consent only."[9]

But that policy changed after the Korean War broke out on June 25, 1950. President Truman's decision to commit US forces the very next day prompted Congress to approve the Selective Service Extension Act. Now Truman was authorized to "order into the active military or Naval service of the United States for a period not to exceed 21 consecutive months, with or without their consent, any or all members and units of any or all Reserve components of the Armed Forces of the United States."

Under draft rules then in effect, college students could avoid being called up as long as they were enrolled, a policy that eliminated an entire class of able-bodied men. Furthermore, it soon became apparent that, at least among fighter pilots, a high percentage of career enlisted fliers were being assigned not to combat duty but to positions as instructors, in which they could train others to operate a new generation of jet aircraft.

That meant that a disproportionate share of the combat duty was falling to older reservists who were veterans of World War II (many of whom were immediately resentful).

Williams secretly retained a lawyer and instructed him to pursue any legal recourse he might have against the recall order, though there seemed none, since Congress had eliminated voluntary reservists' ability to resign in 1950, following the start of the Korean War. There was a personal hardship exemption, but that was defined as having four or more dependents. Ted only had two—his wife and daughter—or three, if you still counted his mother.

The other avenues of pursuit were medical and political. Ted's elbow still hurt him, especially in cold, damp weather, which Korea had in abundance, but he recognized that if he could play baseball with it, using the elbow as an excuse to get sprung from the military would seem both far-fetched and crass. Still, Williams was certainly open to a discreet inquiry from someone of influence who might make the case to a correctly situated official in the military hierarchy that Ted had already served his country and that asking him to do so again was asking too much.

Joe Cronin tried first. Cronin would tell his daughter, Maureen, a lifelong admirer of Williams, that he had called a friend who was an admiral to arrange a meeting at which Ted could go and make his case. "Ted went to visit this guy, to argue he had already served his time," Maureen Cronin said. "I assume the meeting did not go well."[10]

Ted wrote in his book that at spring training that April in Sarasota, a fan he described as "a big cheese man from Ohio" who thought the recall to Korea was unfair approached him and offered to ask his senator, Republican Robert A. Taft, to help. But after looking into his case Taft declined to intervene, telling the intermediary: "I have some reservations as to the fairness of it, whether these fellows should be going back, but I don't interfere with a thing like that." Taft, son of William Howard Taft, the twenty-seventh president of the United States, was then mounting an unsuccessful bid for the 1952 Republican presidential nomination himself. Ted said the senator wrote him a letter about the issue, which he did not keep. Another prominent politician, John F. Kennedy, then a third-term Massachusetts congressman running for the Senate, "tried to do something" for Williams but was unable to, Ted later claimed.

Concluded Ted, "I didn't say anything, but I was bitter because it wasn't fair. I think if it's an emergency everybody goes. But Korea wasn't a declared war, it wasn't an all-out war. They should have let the professionals handle it. A lot of the professionals on duty for Reserves didn't go...."

The unfairness of the Selective Service is obvious when you know how the draft laws and the exemptions work. There's only one way to do it, of course, if you're going to have a draft, and that's to draft everybody."[11]

The Marine Corps still insists that Williams's selection was fair and square, as was that of other major leaguers summoned to Korea, including Jerry Coleman of the Yankees, Lloyd Merriman of the Reds, and Bob Kennedy, then of the Indians. (Kennedy was later granted a hardship discharge for having at least four dependents.) In any case, even if Williams did have an informal deal with Vandegrift at the end of World War II, he had no one to blame but himself for not having gotten out of the Reserves before the 1950 act of Congress froze him in place. He knew, or should have known, that he could have resigned any time before that. In 1948, the Marines had even given him a reminder in writing. In an October 29 letter that year informing him that he had been given a "permanent commission" as a first lieutenant, Ted was told: "Should you decide, subsequent to the acceptance of this appointment, that you are unable to continue the obligations your commission entails, you should submit your resignation to the Secretary of the Navy...and the Commandant of the Marine Corps."

But the fact remained that he had served in World War II, and his peers felt he was getting a raw deal. "He was pissed off to no end that he had to go back the second time," said Ted Lepcio, a Red Sox infielder from 1952 to 1959. "He was very resentful. Breaking records kind of gnawed at him. He was always indicating to me, 'Do you know what I could have done with those numbers?' Then it would have been everyone chasing him."[12] Bob Feller sent Ted a sympathetic letter: "Personally, I cannot get too much enthused about the way they handled your particular case," Feller wrote. "In fact, I do not like it."[13]

Williams seethed at what he considered the injustice of it all, but he kept his rage bottled up. It wasn't until four years later, when he lashed out at the induction of Brooklyn Dodgers pitcher Johnny Podres, and the year after that, when he popped off about his own case, that the depth of Ted's resentment at being recalled for Korea became publicly known.

Podres had been the star of the 1955 World Series, winning twice to lead the Dodgers over the Yankees in seven games. Though before his Series heroics he had twice been rejected for the service because of a bad back, Podres was inducted into the Army in early 1956. When Williams was asked innocently that March if the Dodgers would miss Podres, he was off to the races: "Gutless draft boards, gutless politicians and gutless baseball writers—that's what we've got," said Ted. "Here's this kid who was deferred three years ago for a bad back and then what happens? He wins a couple of games, gets famous and some two-bit draft board puts the arm on him. It's a damn shame and something should be done.... They've taken 20 percent of his baseball life, his earning life, away from him, and for no other reason than he gets famous by beating the Yankees in the World Series."[14]

Then during spring training of 1957, Williams went nuclear about his own case, revealing for the first time that he had sought outside intervention to keep from being called up to Korea. Following an exhibition game in New Orleans on March 31, as the Red Sox were at the airport preparing to return to Florida, Crozet Duplantier, executive sports editor of the *New Orleans States* newspaper, approached the *Globe*'s Hy Hurwitz and asked to be introduced to Williams. Like Hurwitz, Duplantier had been a Marine. He was still in the Reserves and told Hurwitz he hoped he could get Ted to say something that might give the Reserves a boost.[15] After Hurwitz made the introduction in the airport restaurant, Duplantier asked Williams if he harbored any resentment against the Marine Corps for having twice interrupted his baseball career. Ted ignited. "You're damned right I do," he said. "Resentment against the Marine Corps and the whole damned government." At that point he got up, left the restaurant, and stalked out into the terminal. Duplantier followed. "You think Senator Taft was a great man?" Williams continued. "Well, here's what I think of him." Then he turned to spit on the floor. "He was afraid to even try to do anything for me. He said he wouldn't mind going to bat for some other guy. But not me. I was too important."

"And the same goes for Harry Truman!" Ted added, whereupon he spat on the floor again. "And the whole damn government is phony." Asked if he was still in the Reserves, Williams replied: "Boy, you know, I'm not. When I got out this last time and they gave me a chance to pick up that [discharge] paper, I grabbed it."

Ted's blast ricocheted across the front pages of the country. The next day, Ted confirmed to the Associated Press that his remarks to Duplantier about the Marines and Taft were accurate, but he denied bashing Truman and the government. Then he took another swipe at the Corps. "I'll tell you about the Marines," he said. "They got the government to appropriate a lot of money. They said they had the pilots but they needed planes for them. Actually, they had no pilots, so they called 1,100 guys like me back. Most of us hadn't flown a plane for 11 years, but the Marines wanted to make a good show. That's why they grabbed a big name like me."[16] A spokesman for the Marine Corps said it would have no comment because "we take the position that Williams is a private citizen and can say what he wants to."

As the publicity intensified and Ted came in for increasing criticism as a selfish lout who had tried to pull strings and expected to be treated differently from the average guy, Williams retreated and grudgingly apologized—after a fashion. In a statement issued under Red Sox letterhead, he was contrite toward the Marines but implied that Duplantier was a drunk and therefore not trustworthy. Then, inexplicably and ineptly, he opened up a new line of attack against what he saw as government overreach and excess for its handling of a tax case against boxer Joe Louis: "Look at this terrible treatment Joe Louis is getting," Williams said. "Here's a guy who's been a credit to his race and to his country. If some big shot phony politician was in the same predicament, they'd allow him to settle it by paying two cents on the dollar."[17]

In issuing Ted's rambling rant on team stationery, the Red Sox did themselves and their star no favors, again calling into question the club's lack of public relations acumen and its inability to play the clearheaded adult in dealing with another of Williams's petulant pop-offs.

Ted showed up in Sarasota for spring training on March 1, 1952, characteristically late for the first workout but cheerful enough for someone ticketed for Korea the following month. He joked with Lou Boudreau, met with Joe Cronin to sign his contract, then posed for pictures with both men. The writers asked how he felt about his pending Marine physical exam, scheduled for the following month, and Ted said he needed to get in shape for the season in case he flunked the physical. In response to such speculation, the Marine Corps had recently noted that Williams had passed a physical the previous fall upon his promotion to captain. Ted suggested, hopefully, that the April checkup would be more thorough.[18]

Some around Williams were urging him to put up a fight on the medical front, to marshal his own doctors, who might attest that his elbow still caused him significant pain and would interfere with his ability to function as a Marine. One of those pushing him on in this regard was Evelyn Turner, a National Airlines stewardess with whom Ted had become romantically involved. Ted and his wife, Doris, were estranged by that time. They had been drifting further and further apart, and among the bevy of women who frequently crossed his path, Ted had taken a particular shine to Turner, an attractive blonde three years his senior, starting in early 1950.

Doris never really confronted Williams about his philandering, and Ted received any questioning about other women with dismissive, slightly bemused, nondenial denials. After all, he was Ted Williams—of course there were other women, and lots of them. They were a star's entitlement, and he indulged himself. On the road, Ted would often use visiting-team clubhouse attendants to facilitate his assignations. In his engaging memoir of life as a Detroit Tigers batboy, Danny Dillman tells a colorful story about a delicate errand he ran for Williams in 1949.

"Hey, kid!" Ted yelled at Dillman, who was then fifteen.

"Yes, sir, Mr. Williams."

"Here's thirty-five dollars. Take a cab downtown and get me the best five-pound box of chocolates you can find and a big box of rubbers. Can you do that for me, kid? This is very important. I've got a heavy date this weekend. Don't let me down."

"No, sir, you'll have them before game time," replied Dillman confidently, though he immediately began wondering how he would persuade a pharmacist to sell a pack of condoms to a fifteen-year-old.

Getting the candy at a Fanny Farmer store was the easy part. Then Dillman entered a nearby drugstore and approached the pharmacist with great trepidation. Did he need a prescription filled? the proprietor asked the boy. No, he didn't, Danny stammered. Unable to speak his request, he asked for a piece of paper and wrote it down. He worked for the Tigers and was on a mission for a famous ballplayer. He needed a big box of condoms. The pharmacist chuckled and said, "You're kidding, aren't you?" Danny said he wasn't, and then had the presence of mind to suggest that the man call his boss in the visitors' clubhouse at Briggs Stadium, "Fat Frank," who could verify the assignment. The pharmacist made the call, Fat Frank vouched for his batboy, and Danny got his rubbers.

Returning to the clubhouse, Dillman, who would go on to get his PhD in geography and become a university professor, a job he held for forty-four years, proudly placed the chocolates and condoms at the top of Williams's locker, along with an envelope. Ted eventually ambled over, held up the envelope, and shouted, "Hey, kid, what the hell is this?"

"I put the change there from the thirty-five dollars you gave me," said Danny.

"Well, I'll be goddamned. This is the only fuckin' time I ever got money back from an errand. People usually keep what's left as a tip."

"Mr. Williams, we want this to be the best visitors' clubhouse in the American League."

"Well, it sure as shit is, kid. You keep the money for yourself." It was $6.50, more than two days' pay for Danny.

His romantic plans on track, Williams could return to his pregame routine: rubbing his bats on a soup bone to remove any dirt or resin accumulated from the previous game and weighing them on special scales to confirm they were his preferred weight. Then, wearing only his jockstrap, a sweatshirt, and shower clogs, Ted would stand in front of a full-length mirror and begin swinging a bat.

"My name is Ted Fuckin' Williams and I'm the greatest hitter in baseball," he'd say, then swing.[19] "My name is Ted Fuckin' Williams and I'm the greatest hitter in baseball," he'd repeat, teeth clenched, and swing again. He would continue this swing-and-proclaim routine for several minutes, interrupting it only occasionally to offer a lecture on the finer points of hitting to anyone who cared to listen.

"That was his mantra," says Dillman. "He did that before every game. . . . He was psyching himself up. He wasn't quite as confident as he appeared."[20]

But Ted did not lack confidence with women. If Baseball Annies, starlets, models, and assorted others fell into his orbit because of his celebrity, plenty of other women came on to him merely because they thought he was good-looking, without having a clue that he was the Red Sox star, Williams confided to friends.

Ted had met Evelyn Turner on a National Airlines flight when she'd asked him to sign a baseball for her. "To Ev, a sweet chick, Ted Williams," he wrote. From 1950 to 1954, Turner obsessively documented her affair with Ted, saving such commemorative shards as airline tickets to cities where they rendezvoused, hotel receipts, and ticket stubs from various American League ballparks.[21] She inventoried some of the gifts she'd received from Ted, such as a gold wristwatch. There were snapshots she took of Ted, photos of them together, and a series of pictures of her striking sexually provocative poses. There was even a July 1951 shot of Williams in front of his house near Miami as well as one of his daughter Bobby-Jo, three years old at the time, holding two parrots. Doris was nowhere in evidence. Turner assembled all these mementos in an album, which she would decide to send to Bobby-Jo after Ted died. Evelyn even kept some of Ted's clothes — such as shorts, boxers, shirts, and trousers — folded and boxed for fifty years. Ted wrote Turner thirty-nine letters during their time together, and she kept them for the rest of her life in a box marked PERSONAL, PRICELESS LETTERS FROM TSW, according to Joe Bastarache, a friend and neighbor of Turner's in Blowing Rock, North

Carolina, where she would retire in the 1980s.[22] Bastarache, who became Turner's guardian after she moved into a nursing home and then the executor of her estate when she died in 2004, said Evelyn told him she and Ted lived together in Miami for a while — apparently after Williams and Doris were formally separated in 1954. "They would go for rides in Miami in Ted's Studebaker convertible," said Bastarache. "Often they'd go to a drive-in, until Ted got recognized, and then they'd peel away. Ted seemed to enjoy this game."[23]

Turner had a son, Albert Christiano, from a first marriage and would ultimately be married three more times. Recalled Christiano: "My mother was very much in love with Ted. She told me several times that he asked her to marry him, but she said no because of Ted's priorities. She told him she'd marry him if he assured her she would be his number one priority. He said, 'It's baseball first, fishing second, and you third.' She regretted till the day she died that she didn't accept that offer and try to work her way up the priority list."

Christiano said Evelyn told him she was responsible for Ted's breakup with Doris Soule. "She wasn't proud of it. But she also said it didn't matter because he was going to leave his wife anyway."[24]

In a meandering, sixty-six-page account of her time with Ted, much of it quoting from the letters he wrote her, Turner told of her role as an interlocutor between Ted and the doctor he was consulting with just before he was scheduled to take his final physical, which would decide if he'd be sent to Korea or not. "I was given the message to relay it to Ted," Turner wrote in her manuscript.[25] She told him his doctor, Russell Sullivan, chief orthopedic surgeon at Boston City Hospital, had contacted a sympathetic admiral in Baltimore who planned to put in a good word with a Marine commander. But the doctor insisted Ted submit to a medical examination to justify his claim, and in the end, Williams decided not to play this card. While he'd lost about a third of the bone that rotates in the socket of his left elbow following surgery, he'd built much of his strength back, he'd played all of the previous season with the elbow and been productive, and he was swatting the ball with authority in spring training. Basically, using the elbow as an excuse wouldn't fly.

"When I passed the important information to him, he listened thoughtfully, but then and there, I knew his fierce pride would not allow him to take the necessary steps for dismissal from his duty," Turner wrote. "As the future later proved for itself, Ted was 100 percent correct in his judgment. Had he followed through with the plan to excuse himself from duty, never would Ted have held his head so high or be able to face his loyal public with the same air of confidence as he now can."

Accompanied by Yankees infielder Jerry Coleman, Ted appeared for his physical at the vast Naval Air Station Jacksonville on April 2 at 10:00 a.m. Coleman and Williams were the only two men examined at that time. A medical board consisting of a handful of officers headed by a Captain J. C. Early conducted the exam, which lasted two hours. Commander L. S. Sims, who assisted Early, was first out of the examination room. "Both boys are in," Sims said to six reporters waiting outside. Sims watched with amusement as two of the reporters collided and nearly knocked each other down as they raced for a phone in the lobby nearby to spread the news. He suggested they wait just to be sure, because the X-rays of Williams's elbow hadn't been developed yet.

That seemed a mere formality. Soon Captain Early appeared with the ballplayers in tow. "Meet Captain Coleman and Captain Williams, boys," Early said, adding that X-rays and an examination of Ted's elbow had shown "no significant limitations." Both players seemed resigned to the decision. "Well, I'm back in the Marines," said Ted. "I'll try to be a good one. After that, who knows?"[26]

Williams's orders were to report on May 2 to the Marine Air Reserve Training Command at Willow Grove, Pennsylvania, for a four-week refresher course and then go to Marine Corps Air Station Cherry Point, in Havelock, North Carolina. Before then, on April 30, the Red Sox staged "Ted Williams Day" to commemorate what was to be their star's last game of the season and—who knew?—perhaps of his career. Just under twenty-five thousand fans turned out on a sunny and warm Wednesday afternoon to say their good-byes to Ted, who before the game was feted with an assortment of gifts ranging from a new Cadillac donated by a handful of friends to hundreds of "memory books" containing the signatures of some 430,000 admirers, which had been collected by the *Herald* and *Traveler* newspapers. Though it was not announced, the Red Sox also moved to mitigate the sting of his recall by paying Ted's full $85,000 salary for 1952.

There were tributes from Massachusetts governor Paul Dever, Boston mayor John Hynes, and other dignitaries as Williams listened, head down, hands clasped behind his back, nervously pawing the ground with his left foot. When emcee Curt Gowdy gave him the microphone, Ted said: "I've always believed that one of the finest things that could happen to any ballplayer was to have a day for him, and my being so honored today with such little advance fanfare makes me feel humbly honored. Little did I realize in 1938 that I was joining such a wonderful organization and that I was to be with so grand an owner. I wish I could remain all summer for I feel sure the Sox will surprise a lot of people. I do hope you fans stick with them. This is a day I'll remember as long as I live, and I want to thank you from the bottom of my heart."[27]

As the crowd roared and Williams bathed in the cheers, a friend standing just behind him, *Herald* sports editor Ed Costello, whispered to him: "Tip your hat." Ted yanked his hat from his back pocket and held it aloft, first to the right-field grandstand. The fans cheered louder still. Then he turned to home plate and finally to left field. The Kid thought he was done, but Costello leaned in again and whispered: "Center field. Don't forget center field."

"Not those [expletives] too!" said Williams, laughing.[28]*

With that, the Red Sox and their opponents that day, the Detroit Tigers, joined hands. Williams was in the middle: on his left was Dominic DiMaggio; on his right was Private Fred Wolfe, an injured Korean War veteran confined to a wheelchair. Then the players and fans sang "Auld Lang Syne."

Amid all the huzzahs for Ted, which included a resolution from the Massachusetts Senate praising him for being an "inspiration...to the youth of the country," the only discordant note was struck by Dave Egan, who, after blasting the Marine Corps for recalling Williams, had reverted to form by castigating the Red Sox that very morning for hosting a day in honor of someone he considered ill-mannered and a terrible role model for kids.

If Ted was aware of the blast—and he almost certainly was, since he always paid close attention to Egan—it didn't appear to bother him. Rather, he seemed to revel in the adulation that poured down on him. He was applauded for anything he did: running to his position in left field, catching a fly ball, running back to the dugout, coming out to the on-deck circle, singling his first time at bat off Virgil Trucks—even striking out in the third inning.

But in the bottom of the seventh, in what figured to be his final at bat that season—and possibly, many thought, his final at bat ever—Williams jolted the crowd past polite applause and into frenzy. With the

---

* Reporters, ever alert to any Williams gesture, would later ask him if he had not violated his own ban on hat tipping. Ted of course said he had not. It had been merely a wave of thanks and farewell, hat held aloft, not the traditional baseball hat tip—hand to brim with cap on head—given to acknowledge a home run or other applause. For Williams, this was not an insignificant parsing of differences.

game tied 3–3 and a man on base, Ted dug in against Dizzy Trout. He fouled off the first pitch. Then Trout snapped off a knee-high curve, and Williams drove the ball into the wind and six rows deep in the right-field grandstand.

"No crowd ever was paid off with a bigger thrill as Ted raced around the sacks," wrote Arthur Sampson in the *Herald*. "When he ducked into the dugout to get away from the applause as quickly as possible, as is his custom, his teammates pounded him heartily in their elation."[29]

There was no tip of the hat, as was also his custom. "I said I wouldn't tip my cap right along," Ted told the writers afterward, "and I had no intention of doing it. That's the way I feel about it." And how did this homer compare with the other thrills he'd had in his career? "Oh, it was a thrill," Williams replied. "But it didn't compare with the one I hit off Claude Passeau in the All Star game in Detroit in '41. That will always stand as my top thrill in this game." Still, his teammates were incredulous at the calling card he had left them. "He never said it out loud, but I'm sure he wanted to hit a home run before he went to Korea," recalled Ken Wood, a utility outfielder on the Red Sox for part of 1952, who was at Fenway that day. "He did it. It was almost to say, 'I'll leave you with something to remember me by.'"[30]

That night, Ted threw a good-bye party for himself at Jimmy O'Keefe's, the Boylston Street saloon he frequented, run by his pal Bill Greeley. Not a single teammate or anyone else from the Red Sox was invited—no big shots at all, in fact, which was how Williams liked it. The core group was the so-called Thirteen-Year-Olds, a reference to eight Bostonians who had been close to Ted for the thirteen years he had been with the Red Sox, since his rookie year of 1939. Besides Greeley, this regular-guy crowd included theater manager John Buckley; state cop John Blake; former Red Sox batboy Freddy Stack, who by then was a fireman; Ted's dentist, Dr. Sidney Isherwood; former Sheraton hotel bellhops Dave and Chick Hunter; and Johnny Benedetti, who had lived in the suite next to Williams's in the old Canterbury Hotel. Also attending were Ted's manager, Fred Corcoran, and Dr. Russell Sullivan, his medical confidant on the Korean call-up. "There isn't a soul here who hasn't helped me appreciate the friendliness of Bostonians," Ted remarked to George Carens, a trusted *Traveler* writer whom Williams had allowed in to chronicle the evening.[31]

The next morning, Ted set out for the Naval Air Station in Willow Grove, Pennsylvania, outside Philadelphia, where he would begin his training on the SNJ fighter plane. Ted hitched a ride with Raymond

Sisk, the Boston friend he had served with in World War II at Chapel Hill, Bunker Hill, and Pensacola. Sisk had also been recalled for Korea duty.

They arrived at Willow Grove that evening, and all looked quiet. Remembered Sisk, "Ted said, 'Just drive by at first. These Philadelphia reporters are the worst in the world.' On the first pass there was no one in sight. Then they came out of the woodwork. By the time we got back, there were ten or twelve all of a sudden, coming up and taking pictures. The colonel came out and said Ted had to check in, then they could sit down and talk to him."[32]

"I hope very much that I can play when I get out," Ted later told the writers. "I'm going to do the best I can. This is a really wonderful looking base. The best I've ever seen." The next day, the Marines could not resist staging a photo op. They had Williams stand next to the old recruiting poster he'd put out for the Corps that featured his photo and the message "Ask the man who was one!" A smiling Ted was shown changing "was" to "is."

Before long, Doris and Bobby-Jo arrived and moved into a hotel in nearby Doylestown. Ted easily got the hang of flying again and was assigned an instructor, Bill Churchman, who had also been his instructor at Pensacola during World War II.

"Ted and I became the closest of friends when he became my student at Willow Grove," Churchman said. "I knew him well enough to say hello, and we reminisced about Pensacola. I challenged him to a dogfight, needling him. You climb to five thousand feet flying SNJs. You decide who takes the altitude advantage and who goes below. Higher directs the order of the scissoring. I said to Williams on my radio, 'Where the hell are you?' And he was right in my rearview mirror, ready to shoot me down. I relaxed a little bit, and he beat the hell out of me. We'd have a lot of fun, and [we'd] bullshit together. I never found an indication he wasn't one hundred percent with the program. He never complained."[33]

After three weeks, Commander Clarke Ingraham reported that Williams was doing "very, very well. Not only has he done well, but he's extremely popular here."[34] Ingraham said Williams would soon be going to Marine Corps Air Station Cherry Point for advanced instruction and operational training.

Marine Headquarters was thrilled, and no doubt relieved, that Williams was adapting well and being a good soldier, at least in his public statements. The hierarchy almost certainly would have known that Ted had hired a lawyer to explore his rights and that he had consulted with

Dr. Sullivan, who had put out feelers to Marine officials he considered sympathetic. Lemuel Shepherd, then the Marine Corps Commandant, may also have heard that Ted felt he had had a deal with Commandant Alexander Vandegrift after World War II that specified he was not to be recalled.

In any case, on May 22, four days before Commander Ingraham gave his glowing progress report on Ted, Shepherd wrote Williams an extraordinary private letter on official Marine Commandant's office letterhead.

Dear Captain Williams,

Regardless of the heading on this stationery, please consider this letter as a purely personal one. I have never met you and have only seen you play ball a few times before you became a Marine. Nevertheless, I do want to tell you that I greatly admire the true Marine Corps spirit that you have displayed since your orders to active duty were issued.

I recognize the tremendous personal sacrifice that this turn of events involves for you, and I know that in similar circumstances a man of less character might have protested his orders, made complaints to the press, solicited outside influence, or taken some other action which might have been embarrassing to the Marine Corps. However, you recognized the realities of the situation, took your assignment like the man you are, and in so doing have proven yourself once again to be a good Marine.

I personally regret that it was found necessary to recall you to active duty at the height of your baseball career. However, it was a situation beyond our control, brought on by the continuation of the Korean War and the shortage of pilots. I am extremely proud of the way you have stood up to this difficult situation. It adds further justification to the respect and admiration borne you by your countrymen.

I hope someday to have the pleasure of meeting you in person. Meanwhile, and with all good wishes for success in your present duties, believe me to be

Most sincerely,
LEMUEL C. SHEPHERD, Jr.
General, U.S. Marine Corps
Commandant of the Marine Corps

When Ted reported to Cherry Point, the largest Marine Air Station in the country, located in Havelock, a small city in eastern North Carolina, he was called in to see the commanding general of the Second Marine

Aircraft Wing. The general said the station was fielding a baseball team and they'd love it if the Red Sox star would join the club.

"Of course that was anathema to Ted, and he viewed it as child's play," recalled Tom Ross, then a major at Cherry Point who also had been recalled for Korea duty after serving in World War II and who became a friend to Williams.[35] "He said something to the effect that, 'Well, my fee for baseball is about ten thousand dollars a game,' which of course closed the discussion."

It was at Cherry Point that Williams learned to fly jets—the Grumman F9F Panther. He took to the new plane quickly, marveling at how easily it handled and how much faster and more powerful it was compared to what he had been used to flying. He would frequently ask Ross and others technical questions: What was the procedure for a restart during a flameout? What about the oxygen system, which had some peculiarities as you went up in altitude? The fuel control system?

If Ross took to Ted, Hoyle Barr, the squadron commander, did not. "He was a spoiled-brat type," Barr said of Williams. "He had too much money and had too many people rooting for him. By the time I got ahold of him there was no straightening him out. He was thoroughly spoiled. But he was one of the best pilots I ever knew. He had instant reflexes as good as I'd ever seen. He was very talented."[36]

The attempt by the general to recruit him to play baseball had only made Williams more suspicious of the Marines' motives in recalling him, so he continued his efforts to explore ways to get released. "His lawyer was calling him about every other day," remembered Bob Ferris, another major at Cherry Point who became a friend of Ted's.[37] Ferris said he never asked about the lawyer's strategy, but he assumed the man was trying to build a case for loss of income, because a professional athlete had only a relatively short time to make his money—a variation of the hardship defense. "Ted did mention it several times. He'd look at his watch and say, 'There's another hour. I just lost five hundred bucks.' He wasn't too happy about his career being interrupted again in his prime, but he did not act real bitter. He was pretty well resigned to it. He liked flying and fishing." Indeed, if Williams had any free time, he would go to Slocum Creek, off the Neuse River. Or to Camp Bryan, a privately owned hunting and fishing preserve.

The wealthy businessmen around Cherry Point were always entertaining and assisting him. Among them was a car dealer who had arranged a house off base where Doris and Bobby-Jo could stay with Ted. Irv Beck ran a local drive-in theater then, and would see the

Williams clan when Doris and Bobby-Jo were in town. "We showed popular movies, mostly westerns and musicals," Beck said.[38] "His wife and daughter used to come into the theater, sometimes with Ted, but mostly by themselves."

Ferris, who would chat with Ted about life as the two men drove around in Williams's new Cadillac, quickly became aware that Ted and Doris were having problems. Once, Ferris was visiting when Ted and Doris got into a big row over who was going to take Bobby-Jo out to dinner. "Doris said, 'Ted, you're taking her to dinner.' He let loose at her with every four-letter word you could think of, and I just slunk down. I told him he should watch his language in public, but he didn't care who heard him swear."

It was obvious that Williams wasn't thinking about Doris much. One time, as Ferris and Ted were checking out new fishing gear at the base PX, Ferris was startled to watch Williams respond aggressively to a flirtatious salesgirl. "Every gal was making eyes at Ted. This one girl behind the counter, who had a reputation of trying to make half the pilots on the base, said something to him, and he said to her, 'How would you like me to grab you right by the snatch?'"

Ferris learned about Evelyn Turner when Ted let his involvement with her interfere with his duties. Ferris and Williams were down in Puerto Rico at the Roosevelt Roads Naval Station, practicing bombing and strafing maneuvers. Ted claimed his plane had mechanical problems and took it to a Marine base in Miami for servicing.

"Ted was dragging his feet in Miami," Ferris said. "So Barr sent me up there to get him. I flew up to Miami. I told the bartender at the base I needed to find Captain Williams. Ted had left a phone number. I called the number, and a girl answered. She was a stewardess. Ted came on the phone, and I said, 'Ted, there's a plane early in the morning, [and] you got to be on it.' At six thirty the next morning the blonde dropped Ted off at the base. He wasn't too happy."

Turner, who wrote about this episode with some delight in her account of her time with Williams, had been receiving regular letters from her lover since his arrival at Willow Grove and, subsequently, at Cherry Point. Mostly, Ted's correspondences were filled with newsy, perfunctory updates scrawled out amid a hectic schedule. But there were occasionally tender, and ribald, terms of endearment as well, which suggested that Williams regarded his stewardess flame as something more than merely a zealous groupie:

[5/22/52:] Dearest Ev—How's my sweetheart?... You don't know how sweet you are Ev but I think your [sic] as sweet as a gal can get and your [sic] forever on my mind. Keep me on yours. Promise. All my love, T.

[7/31/52:]... am going to get to Jacksonville or Miami. Now get this. I'll call you when I'm going so's you can meet me. Can't wait cause I'll love your little body to death....all my love, T.

Turner excitedly devoted more than three pages of her manuscript to her extended rendezvous with Ted when he was supposed to be in Roosevelt Roads, a time she said was extended to nearly two weeks because of bad weather and a sympathetic conspirator. Williams "wanted so much to have a bit of time away from the rigors of training," Turner wrote. "The radio man who was to check over Ted's jet was nearby, so after Ted buzzed a few whispers in his ear, the radio man motioned that he understood and had the situation well in hand. Of course, it was a surprise to some the next day when Ted's plane developed 'radio trouble.'" But by the end of two weeks the Marine Corps had grown "a bit curious as to where their prize pigeon had dropped by the wayside," as Turner put it, and dispatched Bob Ferris to pick him up and ferry him back to where he was supposed to be.

On November 14 it was announced that Williams had received his orders for the Pacific—the Corps' euphemism for Korea. He would be detached from Cherry Point on December 8, granted a leave until the end of the year, and then report to the Marine Air Station in El Toro, California, near Los Angeles, on January 2 before being sent overseas.

Two days later, Ted received word at Cherry Point that his father, Sam Williams, had died in a convalescent home near Oakland at the age of sixty-six. Williams flew out for the funeral and burial at the Masonic Cemetery in San Francisco. On the flight home, Ted wrote Evelyn that burying his father had been "the most heartbreaking moment of my life and made me feel guilty that I hadn't been more considerate and been out to see him more often....I know now you never realize how much you loved them till after there [sic] gone."[39]

Williams returned home to Miami to begin putting his affairs in order. He wrote a friend that he expected to be killed in combat, but that he was "going to give it a battle."[40] The day after Christmas, in a move that reflected his growing uncertainty about his baseball future, Ted announced that he had acquired a 25 percent interest in Southern

Tackle Distributors, a Miami-based fishing-tackle firm, which served the Southeast, the Caribbean, and South America. Ted said he needed to start thinking about life after the big leagues, "something I can get my teeth into after I'm no longer able to swing a bat."[41]

On New Year's Eve, Ted and Fred Corcoran set out for Los Angeles on a National Airlines flight that was scheduled to stop in New Orleans. Corcoran's main job was still to serve as promotional director for the PGA, whose first golf tournament of the season was the LA Open. There, Corcoran hoped to show off his star baseball client to Bing Crosby and the like, if Ted's schedule permitted.

Evelyn joined the two men for the first leg of the flight. "As I deplaned in New Orleans," she wrote, "Ted and I had a few moments in which to chat and say farewell. Neither of us knew, or could even slightly predict the destiny that the future held in its invisible hands....I prayed fervently for his safe return." She said Ted bet her that he would fly his first combat mission by February 15, 1953.

El Toro amounted to a high-level review and final tune-up on the F9F Panther, coupled with an arduous side trip to the Sierra Nevada mountains for cold-weather survival training. In 1951, the Marines had established the high-altitude Cold Weather Battalion in Pickel Meadows on 46,000 acres of the Toiyabe National Forest, near Bridgeport, California, by the Nevada state line, one hundred miles south of Reno. The idea was to prepare Ted and the other pilots—who would arrive in the midst of the harsh Korean winter—in case they were shot down and had to fend for themselves behind enemy lines. Williams described the experience in his book as "living on canned stuff, spruce sprouts for beds, parachute for a tent and I almost froze my tail off."[42]

As he was prone to do, Ted picked up a virus, and he carried it with him all the way to Tokyo, where he was to lay over for a few days before going on to Korea. Soon, however, Williams was feeling well enough to inquire about female companionship. He bumped into Dick Francisco, the Marine pilot he'd trained with at Pensacola during World War II. Francisco had been recalled for Korea, too. He'd flown eighty-four missions, and was now on his way home.

"I hadn't seen him since we were cadets," Francisco recalled. "The first thing he says to me is, 'Francisco, what can you screw around here that's safe?' I said, 'You son of a bitch, you probably haven't showered from your last encounter.' He was a great cocksman. He always had pretty girls with him. He had a good line of baloney, too. He had a philosophy that you seduce them with words first."[43]

Rejuvenated, Williams flew on to his base in Korea, at Pohang, a port city on the Sea of Japan in the southeastern part of the country. The Japanese had used the base in World War II—now the Marines called it K3, one of fifty-five American air bases in use throughout South Korea. The landing strip was six thousand feet long and had a corrugated mat. Williams looked around and didn't like what he saw: "Crummy quarters, a real dog box. Cold and damp and awful," he wrote in his book.

There were two fighter squadrons based at K3: VMF-115 and VMF-311. Ted was in 311, which had been the first land-based Marine squadron in Korea to be used for close air support—to bolster the operations of Marine and Army forces on the ground. The squadron used WL as its code letters, which were prominently displayed on the jets' tails. The letters were spoken phonetically as "William Love," from which came the squadron nickname Willy Lovers and the adoption of the heart as part of 311's insignia. Pilots wore baby-blue scarves with pink hearts and the squadron name printed on them.[44]

The base itself was on a bluff overlooking the sea. Ted was assigned to officers' quarters. These Quonset huts, each of which had two or three rooms, were square and made of corrugated metal. Some had sandbags on the roofs to keep them from blowing away. Each hut was serviced by a rancid six-hole outhouse.

Williams was in hut 1-C with two roommates: Major Jim Mitchell of San Francisco and Captain Lee Scott of Ellensburg, Washington, both of whom seemed charmed by their new celebrity companion and delighted in needling him.[45] Ted's bed consisted of two two-by-six boards, set three feet apart, with box springs fashioned from the inner tubes of a jet's tires. Over the bed was a pinup calendar from a Columbus, Ohio, auto parts firm. A predecessor had brought the calendar with him, and Ted opted not to disturb it.

K3 was 180 miles south of the bomb line—the front where ground troops had dug-in positions. Most flights were run in support of the First Marine Division. Generally, four or eight planes would go on a mission; sometimes it would be a squadron of twenty-four. Career officers and reservists were supposed to be paired together within the groups. Unlike the newer and faster F-86 Sabre jet used by the Air Force to engage the Soviet MiG-15, the Marines' F9F Panther was heavier, less agile, and geared for ground support. It carried a three-thousand-pound bomb payload and five-inch-diameter high-velocity aircraft rockets, or HVARs. It was equipped with four twenty-millimeter cannons and could carry napalm.[46]

The Joint Operations Center in Seoul, which coordinated all air activities in Korea, would assign the missions, specifying enemy targets and the payload each jet would carry. The orders would come down in late afternoon for the following day. The operations officer for K3 would then do the scheduling. A flight would usually go out early in the morning, at first light, with each pilot carrying aerial reconnaissance maps and a photo of the target. Occasionally there might be another flight later in the day. Half the missions were generally close air support—low-altitude strafing of targets using bombs, HVARs, napalm, or a combination thereof. The other half would be interdiction missions carried out farther north, behind enemy lines (or in Indian Country, as the Marines called it), targeting manufacturing plants, ammunition dumps, or bridges.

Williams flew his first combat mission on the morning of February 16, 1953, the day after the deadline he'd set for Evelyn Turner—a thirty-five-plane strike involving both VMF-311 and VMF-115, targeting a tank-and-infantry training school along Highway 1, fifteen miles south of Pyongyang, the North Korean capital.

Ted was assigned to be the wingman for Marvin "Pinky" Hollenbeck, then a major who was to lead a four-plane division. Hollenbeck knew this was Ted's first combat. They discussed the mission in the ready room before takeoff. "We were after a heavy target that day," Hollenbeck remembered. The two squadrons would fly about two hundred yards apart in designated sectors. "We had to dive, and when we came off the target go directly west to a river, then due south, climbing toward Seoul and the base. I said, 'Ted, this is your first mission. I don't care if you hit the target or not. I just want you to be safe.'"[47]

After Hollenbeck dove steeply, Williams followed, but in the haze and smoke from the bombs he soon lost sight of Hollenbeck. Ted dove in low at about forty-five degrees, dropped his bombs, then climbed out and headed toward a prearranged rendezvous point. But as he approached five thousand feet, red emergency lights lit up on his instrument panel, and the throttle stick began shaking hard. Though he hadn't heard it or felt it, he'd been hit by small arms fire. Instead, thinking that he had a hydraulic leak, he called for help, but his radio was out.

Williams was heading the wrong way, northwest, farther into North Korea, when he was spotted by Larry Hawkins, who was the leader of a two-plane section of Hollenbeck's division. Hawkins had just turned twenty-two. He was from a small town in Pennsylvania and so gung-ho that his parents had had to sign a waiver so that he could enlist in the Marine Corps at age seventeen, after graduating from high school.

Ted's "plane was sputtering, streaming fluid," Hawkins recalled. "If it had been hydraulic it would have been finished, so I knew it was leaking fuel. By this time I had him turning west, heading to the Yellow Sea. I patted my head and took the lead. He indicated he had no radio. We were climbing at a high rate of speed. I think we were up to twenty thousand or twenty-five thousand feet. I wanted to get out of range of antiaircraft fire, which could reach nineteen thousand to twenty thousand feet."[48]

Hawkins didn't know right away that it was Williams. He radioed Hollenbeck and told him he had a pilot in trouble. Hollenbeck instructed Hawkins to head south and guide him toward the nearest safe landing area, which was the Air Force base in Suwon, designated as K13. Soon Hollenbeck picked up Williams and Hawkins.

"I moved up on Williams on his starboard wing," Hollenbeck remembered. "He never did look right and see me. I wanted him to eject and save his life, because his landing gear was not down, but I still couldn't get his attention. The tower called and said, 'Your landing gear is not down, your landing gear is not down!' But of course Ted couldn't hear because his radio was off."

Williams considered ejecting, which was normal procedure in this situation, but quickly dismissed the idea. He was nearly six-four and had to be shoehorned into his Panther jet. Crew chiefs on the ground literally had to stand on his shoulders and jam him into the cockpit with their boots. The ejection systems were still primitive. If he ejected, he could have broken his back or seriously injured his knees, ruling out the possibility of any more baseball, so he decided to try to land the plane.

It was this likelihood of serious injury, not the possibility of being taken prisoner, that concerned him about ejecting. Williams would tell one interviewer years later: "If I was floating down on a parachute, if any of those slanty-eyed little fuckers came up to me, I'd have said, 'I'm Ted Williams. I'm a big deal baseball player. . . . How may I help you?'"[49]

South of Seoul, Hawkins got Williams into a landing pattern. "We kept talking by hand signals," Hawkins said. "He kept signaling he was getting lower and lower on fuel. I knew if I started to slow down, fuel would pool and he'd break into fire. He came in doing about two hundred knots. I was flying about a hundred and fifty feet over him off to the side."

It had been about fifteen minutes from the time Hawkins first spotted Williams in trouble to the time he was preparing for an emergency landing at K13. By then the word had spread among the other pilots that it was Williams.

"The word went around like wildfire," recalled Woody Woodbury, who was on the mission that day. "Everybody knew it was Ted. It was a fright. He got hit. He got hit hard. Nothing worked. His radio was out, everything was wrecked, couldn't get his wheels down, his flaps down, only the engine was working, but not much else. He had to be scared shitless. That's all there was to it."[50]

Around 11:00 a.m., Williams came streaking over the K13 base at three hundred feet, traveling from east to west, and started a wide sweep toward a final approach to the nine-thousand-foot dirt runway. He watched as Koreans from a nearby village looked up at the plane, with its thirty feet of trailing fire, then scattered and ran for their lives.

Then, as he crossed the airfield, a metal panel from the bottom of his jet broke loose and crashed on the mess hall roof. To Williams, the panel popping off sounded like an explosion. "Now there was fire and smoke underneath the plane," he wrote in his book. "Why a wing didn't go was just an act of God. The plane was still together and flying, but I knew something bad was happening. All I cared about was getting on that deck."[51]

He shut off the master fuel switch to try to slow his speed a bit. He estimated he was going 225 miles per hour. He tried again to lower his wheels for landing, but now they were locked. He would have to belly it in. Then Williams, nominally an atheist who often took the Lord's name in vain, nonetheless shouted what for him passed for a prayer. His exact words, as he related them later to his cousin Frank Venzor, were: "If that son of a bitch up there believes in me, he better save my ass now!"[52]

"I hit flush and skidded up the runway, really fast. No dive brakes, no flaps, nothing to slow the plane. For more than a mile I skidded, ripping and tearing up the runway, sparks flying. I could see the fire truck, and I pressed the brakes so hard I almost broke my ankle, and all the time I'm screaming, 'When is this dirty S.O.B. going to stop?' Geez, I was mad. I always get mad when I'm scared, and I was praying and yelling at the same time. Further up the runway the plane started sliding toward a second fire truck, and the truck tried to get out of the way, dust flying behind it. I stopped right at the end of the runway. The canopy wouldn't open at first, then I hit the emergency ejector.... Boy I just dove out, and kind of somersaulted and I took my helmet and slammed it on the ground, I was so mad."[53]

Williams skidded about eight thousand feet, nearly the full length of the runway. By the time the plane stopped, the fire had gone out, but fire crews quickly sprayed the plane down with foam just in case. The base operations officer and his assistant, Robert Veazey, sped out in a car and tended to Williams, who had sprinted away from his plane, expecting it to explode.

"He wasn't shaking like a leaf or anything, but you could tell that he was somewhat agitated," Veazey said. "We asked him, 'Are you okay?' He said, 'Yeah, I got bumped up a little bit.' He was not talking a lot at that point. We didn't even ask his name—we didn't have his name until we got to the base hospital, and he still had his helmet on, with his oxygen mask hanging to one side, and that's where we found out it was Ted Williams. We'd had no idea who he was."[54]

Doctors examined Williams, but except for a sprained ankle from pressing on the brake so hard he had barely a scratch. Veazey then took him back to base operations, and before long a crowd of about forty pilots had shown up to gawk at the Great Man, who posed for pictures and signed autographs. Eventually, a C-47 turned up to ferry Ted back to his home base at K3.

The Associated Press got word to Doris Williams back in Florida that her husband had been in a crash but was fine. "Oh, my gosh," she said to the reporter. "I think it's awful. It's an awful close call—too close. And he just got there.... Golly, I'm glad he's safe."*

Ted thanked the AP for calling Doris, but he seemed to be thinking more of Evelyn Turner. He dashed off a letter to her the day after the crash, saying, "No doubt by now you've heard about my 'hairy' experience of the 16th. I had holes all over the plane and I was riding on all the prayers people say for me 'cause I was awfully lucky. My plane was burning like hell when I crash landed. Everyone around here now is calling me lucky. Anyway I'm missing you. Every inch of you 'cause I know how sweet you are. Love, Ted."

That same day, the seventeenth, Williams—his crash not twenty-four hours distant—went on another mission, unloading six bombs in a four-plane attack south of Pyongyang. Marine policy was that a pilot who had been involved in a crash should be grounded for a few days at least, but Art Moran, Ted's squadron commander, decided it would be

---

* Marty Keough, a Red Sox utility outfielder from 1956 to 1960, recalled that one of his favorite memories of Ted concerns the time when a plane carrying the team was struck by lightning in the late '50s. "They had a cracked window and the priest was up saving everyone," Keough said in an interview. "We were supposed to land in Florida at eleven at night and didn't get in until three or four in the morning. Ted was the calmest out of anyone. He didn't say a word, just sat there. Everyone else was freaking out, especially the ones who didn't like to fly in the first place. He was probably thinking, 'Shit, this is nothing. Just imagine doing this every day in Korea.'"

best to send Ted right back up lest he lose his confidence. Moran was called on the carpet for this decision by Major General Vernon McGee, commander of the First Marine Aircraft Wing in Korea, and Williams was subsequently grounded for three days.

News of Williams's flaming crash landing—and survival—reverberated around the United States, especially in the Boston tabloids. (TED WILLIAMS IN WAR CRASH, screamed the front page of the *Record*.) In turn, the Marines facilitated the surge of interest in their celebrity pilot by making Ted available for interviews with the wire services and other news outlets. There, Ted offered modest accounts of how he'd managed to bring his jet in. He said he was lucky and gave credit to Larry Hawkins.*

But fanned by purple prose and numerous breathless accounts of the event, Williams's feat of derring-do would settle in the public consciousness as a bookend to his baseball prowess. Although Ted was no Audie Murphy, his valorous, dauntless deed in combat was magnified by his status as one of the most famous athletes of his time.

Still, that would be for history to sort out. For now, Williams tried to settle into a routine of sorts in Korea, knowing that crash landings wouldn't happen every day. He set about getting to know his squadron mates. Like Ted, most were reservists who had served in. World War II. One pilot Williams quickly formed a friendship with was John Glenn, the future astronaut and US senator from Ohio. Glenn had arrived at K3 shortly after Ted and took over as operations officer for VMF-311, assigning pilots to the daily missions. After Ted introduced himself in the pilots' ready room, Glenn, an avid baseball fan, was thrilled. He found Ted genial and likable, and noted that he devoured the chocolate fudge sent over by Glenn's sister-in-law.[55]

Glenn, who lived in the same Quonset hut as Williams, began to choose Ted to serve as his wingman. "He was excellent," Glenn said. "He didn't shirk his duty at all. He got in there and dug 'em out like everybody else. He never mentioned baseball unless someone else brought it up. He was there to do a job. We all were. He was just one of the guys."[56]

Once, the two flew an early-morning reconnaissance and bombing run together that Glenn initially feared would result in his being court-martialed. The North Koreans moved troops and supplies to the front at

---

* Dave Egan pounced on the crash news to reprise his argument that Williams had only been recalled for PR purposes, and now that those aims had been achieved in spades he should be released.

night, and Glenn and Williams took off in darkness, hoping to spot the enemy still on the road at dawn. Glenn's plane would fly about one hundred feet off the ground while Ted's would stay up fifteen hundred feet so that he could see farther up the road and give instructions to Glenn, who would be looking for trucks and troops. Then every ten minutes they would switch positions.

The HVARs on the Panther jets had had some problems with their proximity fuses, causing explosions when the plane landed, so if they weren't needed on the mission, the pilots were on orders to fire them off before landing. Recalled Glenn, "I unloaded all my HVARs—squirted them off. Ted's coming along behind me. I turned around to see where he was. He went around again and fired all six of his HVARs. At the time, there had been some HVAR drops that had accidentally hit American troops. I looked on my charts and I thought Ted's shots were on our lines. I was so mad at him. I thought I was going to be court-martialed. We looked at a more accurate map back at the base. I plotted where I thought Ted's rockets had hit. It turned out the lines had changed and had been redrawn back to the south, and Ted's rockets hit in what was still enemy territory." Williams claimed he knew it all along.

Ted liked to play acey-deucey, poker, and pinochle to pass the time, and he was an occasional visitor to the officers' club, the center of K3 social life. Woody Woodbury would preside at the O club, as it was known, playing a piano that he and Glenn had brought in from Japan. Woodbury, who would go on to a successful career as a singer-entertainer and comedian, played each night at happy hour, leading improvised songs like "On Top of Old Pyong-Yang" (sung to the tune of "On Top of Old Smoky") and "I Wanted Wings 'Til I Got the Goddamn Things." ("Ted would join in once in a while, but he was certainly no boy soprano," Woodbury said.)

In Korea, Williams also got serious about photography, which his father had taught him and which he had dabbled in. While he took reconnaissance photos as part of his job, he eagerly took pictures of villagers around Pohang and people he encountered on trips to Japan, where he'd buy the best cameras. He would develop his own prints in the K3 photo lab and eagerly display the pictures to his roommates and other pals.

But Ted's favorite thing to do in Korea was to go duck hunting. The local ducks were huge. "My God, they were as big as a C-47," recalled Woodbury.

Duck hunting was the domain of one Edro Buchser, a self-described "hillbilly from Kentucky" whom Ted befriended. After Buchser had flown eighty-seven missions, they made him provost marshal of K3, a position he took to with great zeal and humor.

Buchser had been there about a year when Ted arrived. He supervised scores of men, was in charge of several roving patrols, and was responsible for a fleet of Jeeps, which he mostly used for speeding around the rice paddies to keep tabs on the ducks.[57] Ted had difficulty going anywhere on base without people trying to talk to him. Buchser had an office in a tent, where Ted would come to get some privacy.

Buchser also helped Williams evade another enemy—the Boston press corps: "Those sons of bitches. One sportswriter from Boston came one night at three a.m. and found his hut, woke him up for an interview, and he had to fly at six a.m."

When it came to hunting, Buchser would usually go all out for Williams. First he'd dispatch a few patrols to find the ducks, and then they'd get going. "We'd get a hundred ducks in, say, an hour and a half or two hours. He'd get sixty-five and I'd get about thirty-five. He could outshoot me, and I was very proud of the way I could shoot."

Sometimes the brass would ask Buchser to take them hunting, and if Williams was along, so much the better. One day, Major General Vernon McGee was the featured guest, and he brought along his aide-de-camp, a zealous Ivy Leaguer. Ted insisted on absolute quiet, and the aide was making too much noise. "I put the general downwind of the rice paddy, the best place," said Buchser. "Ted was upwind. When a flock of ducks came, the aide stood up and said, 'There they are, General!' I heard Ted grumbling. Next time the kid did the same thing. Ted jacked one in the chamber, stood up, and said, 'You son of a bitch, you do that one more time I'm going to shoot you.'" Instead of giving Ted a dressing-down, McGee sent his aide back to the Jeep.

Williams generally found his superior officers obsequious, and he preferred the company of enlisted men. The officers were either groveling or demanding inside baseball tidbits; sometimes they asked Buchser to arrange dinner with Williams. Ted would reluctantly agree, but would not be afraid to use the occasion to speak his mind about whatever was bothering him—such as the rules of engagement, which he considered too restrictive, or even the brouhaha surrounding his recall.

Williams had one other misadventure. It happened on a late-April bombing run when the fuselage of his plane was hit by a rock that had been dislodged by the bomb explosions. But Ted was able to return to base and make a routine landing.

Increasingly, the sudden drops in altitude necessitated by combat fly-ing maneuvers, coupled with the cold, damp weather, were causing Ted serious health problems. He was hospitalized with pneumonia for three weeks aboard a Navy hospital ship off Pohang. After returning to K3, his head was all plugged up, he couldn't hear the radio, and flying was painful. He wrote his friend Bill Churchman in Philadelphia that he was nearly totally deaf in one ear. Churchman told the press, which prompted a flurry of stories.

Further testing revealed that his eustachian tube, connecting his mid-dle ear to his throat, was inflamed and would require more specialized treatment than was available in Korea. So the Marine Corps decided to cut its losses with Ted Williams after he had flown thirty-nine missions. He would be mustered back home to the Bethesda Naval Hospital in Maryland and eventually released.

On June 28, as he was packing his bags to go home, Williams gave an inflammatory interview to the International News Service in which he made public the sentiments he had expressed privately to several officers: the Americans were holding back in Korea and not fighting to win. "The United States ought to be ashamed of itself the way this thing is going on out here," Ted said. He described Korea as the "forgotten war" to all but the families of the men fighting and those close to them. He wondered why the United States kept its forces at the 38th parallel and the atom bomb went unused, asking rhetorically, "Do you think we are trying? We're not trying one-tenth of what we could." Finally, asked about his baseball future, Williams said it depended on "how the Red Sox feel about it and how I feel about it."

After stops in Tokyo and Honolulu, Ted landed at Naval Air Station Moffett Field, outside San Francisco, on July 9, along with thirty other Korean War veterans. Navy and Marine Corps commanders had arranged a full-dress press conference for Williams with writers, pho-tographers, and TV, radio, and newsreel reporters all waiting. Several hundred sailors had also assembled to watch in the wings.

Ted said he didn't expect to return to the Red Sox that year but would be ready for the following year. He joked that his ear problems might help with those hecklers in left field. He said the only time he had swung a bat while he was away was when he and Lloyd Merriman of the Reds had given a baseball clinic—in a rough field, equipped with only twelve balls—on orders of the commanding officer. Ted said he was struck by how important baseball was to the enlisted men in Korea, and that they had hounded him for news of their teams because he received the *Sporting*

News regularly. He was able to keep up on daily scores and games through shortwave radio broadcasts.

Ted heaped praise on the men he'd served with, saying he'd never met a better bunch, and adding cryptically: "I only wish I fitted in better into their ways and feelings." Asked to elaborate on his blast against US war policy in Korea, Williams wisely begged off, saying, "I was in a bad mood that day." On reflection, he'd likely realized (or had been counseled by agent Fred Corcoran) that his off-the-cuff ruminations, those of a line officer, on the weightiest of national security issues—whether to deploy the atomic bomb—had come off as ill-considered, to say the least.

Before leaving for further tests on his ear at the Oak Knoll Naval Hospital in Oakland, Williams was told that Ford Frick, the commissioner of baseball, was on the phone for him. Could he come to the All-Star Game in Cincinnati on the fourteenth and throw out the first ball? Frick wanted to know. Certainly he could, Ted replied.[58]

Then Corcoran called from New York, telling Ted he should start thinking about returning to baseball *this* season, not next. "There's still two months left in the season," Corcoran said. "Everybody wants you back."

"Hell, Fred," Williams replied. "It's the middle of July. The Red Sox aren't going anywhere. I'm not ready to play baseball. Mr. Yawkey says I can do what I feel like doing. I feel like fishing."

"You're not a fisherman, you're a ballplayer."

"You've never seen me handle a fly rod. I'm the best there is."

"I'm serious, Ted. You've got to get started. It'll be the best thing in the world for you. Work yourself in gradually, then be ready for a full season next year. Listen, baseball is your *business*."[59]

That got Ted's attention. Baseball was, in fact, his business, and he needed to tend to it again. Of course he would have to be released from the Marine Corps first, following a ten-day evaluation in Bethesda, but that was looking more and more like a formality. Having taken him out of baseball for more than a year in a questionable calculation, the Corps was plainly getting ready to face reality and spring him.

Ted's appearance in Cincinnati for the All-Star Game, where he was greeted like a returning messiah and stole the show, only made him more eager to return to baseball soon.

He had checked into Bethesda, then arrived in Cincinnati with

Corcoran on the overnight train. Tom Yawkey had a car waiting to bring Williams to a private breakfast meeting with him and Joe Cronin. Both told Ted they wanted him to play as soon as he felt ready. Appearing in the stands at Yawkey and Cronin's box, he was engulfed by autograph hounds and brought batting practice to a standstill. When Ted's name was announced before the game, the 30,846 fans gave him an ovation of several minutes' duration, and then he tossed out the first ball, a crisp strike to Roy Campanella. Ted, dressed in civvies (dark brown slacks, light brown blazer, and an open flyaway collar), was cheered again as he made his way to the American League dugout, where Frick had decreed he could watch the game. Ted delighted in greeting some of his teammates, such as George Kell and Billy Goodman, as well as old rivals like Bob Lemon of the Indians and Yogi Berra, Phil Rizzuto, and Allie Reynolds of the Yankees. Casey Stengel welcomed Williams back warmly and thanked him for his service to the country.

About playing again, Ted said it was possible the Marines might release him in a few weeks, in which case he'd like to return to the Red Sox that year. "I do not hear as well as I used to," he said. "As a flier, I am of no use to the Marines. A lot of fellows flying jets have the same kind of ailment." He said that his eyesight was still twenty-fifteen; that it would take him about a month to get into playing shape; that he was sure he could hit but unsure about the other aspects of the game. Yawkey, when asked about Ted's return to baseball, said he was just happy that the Kid had returned alive.[60]

On July 27, after more than three years, the so-called "police action" in Korea ended with the signing of an armistice agreement. The next day, Ted was formally discharged at a morning ceremony at the Marine barracks at the Naval Gun Factory in Washington. As he handed Williams his official papers, Colonel K. G. Chappel, commandant of the barracks, said, "I'm sure that what you have done will be an inspiration to thousands of young men who have left their careers and families in order to help their country in these trying times." Then, smiling broadly, Chappel added: "I guess now your home will be Fenway Park." Williams, wearing his Marine uniform for the last time, thanked the colonel and said he was headed to Boston right then.[61] He promptly drove to New York and spent the night at Fred Corcoran's apartment, then pulled into Fenway late in the morning of July 29.

The Red Sox were playing the White Sox that afternoon. Ted avoided the players' parking lot, where hundreds of fans had arrived early to greet him, and burst into Tom Yawkey's office unannounced. Interviewing the owner at that very moment was George Sullivan, the former Red Sox batboy who had once cleaned up the dead pigeons Ted shot.

Sullivan by then was a student at Boston University and a stringer for the *Traveler*. He'd written a flattering profile of Yawkey the previous winter and sent the owner a clipping down at his plantation in South Carolina. Yawkey wrote Sullivan a thank-you note — "best story ever written about me" — along with an invitation to come by his office the following summer to see him.

"A few days before," remembered Sullivan, "I saw Ted was due back in Boston from Korea. That morning I called the secretary and I said, 'I see Ted's due back, and I understand if Mr. Yawkey wants to reschedule.' She checked with Yawkey, and he said, 'Let's go ahead.' So I was in with him, and all of a sudden Ted comes busting in like John Wayne.

"They get caught up a little, then finally Yawkey says to Ted, 'Why don't you go down and hit a couple?' Ted says, 'No, I haven't hit for a year.' They go back and forth like that for a minute or so, and Ted finally agreed to go down to the batting cage. A lot of times Ted wanted you to outlast him and talk you into something. I made a beeline for the batting cage because I wanted a box seat for this.

"This is the scene I remember most about Ted. It was long before the game. Ushers were there and concessions kids. I don't think they'd opened the gates yet. Some of the players were out playing catch.

"All of a sudden Ted comes striding out in those long, loping strides, and there's a roar from the concessionaires and even the ballplayers. They used to have a wonderful batting-practice pitcher — Paul Schreiber. He was in there. Everyone is clapping.

"Ted hit a couple of line drives. Then he hit one out, next to the bull pen. This is the first time he's hit since coming back from Korea. Schreiber threw another. Ted hit it out. Then a third that went way out. Schreiber was following the flight of the ball. 'Never mind watching,' Ted screams at him. 'Throw the fuckin' ball!'

"He must have hit about twelve out. Then I noticed that blood was coming through his clenched fingers. His skin was tender. Finally, after, like, the thirteenth one, he just went back to the dugout.

"It was the greatest display I ever saw."[62]

The Kid was back.

14

Transitions

To keep hitting while the blisters simmered on his still-soft hands, Williams began wearing golf gloves, a habit that other players later picked up and that would eventually lead to the use of batting gloves by most hitters today. He quickly signed a contract for the remainder of 1953 and the entire 1954 season, announcing that he would work out twice a day, aiming to begin pinch-hitting in ten days and to return to the starting lineup in three weeks. He was eager to play but didn't want to disrupt a team that, while still in third place and nine and a half games out, had won eighteen of its last twenty-four. So he decided to take batting practice alone some of the time to minimize distractions.

But of course Williams couldn't help making his presence felt, and the dynamic around the team changed immediately, as if the carnival were back in town. Taking batting practice one day, Ted caused a stir by announcing that home plate was out of line by a hair. Joe Cronin happened to be in the vicinity, and he responded that they had, in fact, reset home plate recently. Cronin thought Ted was crazy, but to humor his star with the renowned eye, he agreed to bring in a surveyor. Sure enough, the point of the plate was off-kilter by an inch.

They brought in extra clubhouse kids to tend to Ted as he got in shape—to shag flies in batting practice and to generally be his gophers. Two of them were the Murphy brothers—John and Tom—sons of Johnny Murphy, the former Yankees pitcher who had joined the Red Sox front office in 1948 as farm director.

Tom was nineteen that summer, John just twelve. They couldn't wait to finish their chores on the field and get into the clubhouse so they could listen to Ted hold court. Topic A for Williams was still Korea.

"We'd be usually sitting in the trainer's room," John remembered. "Ted would be getting a massage, telling stories about Korea—Truman sticking him in the war, the vendetta Williams felt Truman had against professional ballplayers. He had a deep-seated hatred for the government for fucking up his career. 'They didn't know what they were doing. Nobody told us about the antiaircraft fire in some fuckin' valley. The reconnaissance was pathetic. They were putting lives at risk unnecessarily. They never warned us.' These were angry, derisive outbursts, but terribly funny, too. He was a great raconteur. Me and my brother, the clubhouse boys and batboys, we were enthralled all the time. Players would wander in and out."[1]

Ted made his pinch-hitting debut on August 6, popping up to first in the ninth inning of a ten-inning 8–7 loss to the Browns before just 6,792 fans. But the small crowd nonetheless roared appreciatively, both as Ted was introduced and as he made his way back to the dugout. Leo Monahan of the *Record* called the innocuous pop-up the biggest news of the week in the American League.

Williams's next appearance, three days later, in a game against the Indians, was more auspicious. Sent up by Lou Boudreau as a pinch hitter against Mike Garcia with one on and two outs in the seventh, Ted drilled a 3–1 fastball 420 feet into the center-field bleachers, sending the crowd of 26,966 into a frenzy.

Boudreau called it "the greatest ovation I've ever witnessed on a ball field." The dugout was a mob scene as all his teammates pounded Ted with gusto and glee. Harold Kaese of the *Globe* ranked the homer as Williams's third best, behind the 1941 All-Star blast and the farewell shot before he left for Korea. Ted downplayed the crowd reaction, telling the writers: "I'm working on a new theory this year: I'm not going to take too much for granted when things are going good, and I'm not going to get down in the dumps when they're bad."[2]

Williams decided he was ready to make his first start on August 16, in the second game of a doubleheader against Washington at Fenway. He doubled and homered in three at bats, leaving after five innings with tired legs and the Red Sox one run down. His replacement, Hoot Evers, was booed.

With their star and main gate draw safely in the fold again, the Red Sox were eager to stage a welcome-home-Ted event of some kind, but Williams rejected the idea. He just wanted to get back in shape and down to business. Yet when someone suggested a $100-per-plate banquet to raise money for the Jimmy Fund, the Boston charity to benefit cancer research, Ted agreed.

The Jimmy Fund had become the official charity of the Red Sox earlier that year. (The team's sponsorship replaced that of the Boston Braves, who had succumbed to declining attendance and moved to Milwaukee.) Williams had already spent countless hours on behalf of the Jimmy Fund and at various hospitals around Boston, visiting sick children and bringing them good cheer. In fact, he was always on call, especially for patients with leukemia, which in those days was nearly always fatal. Without exception, the visits came with the same string attached: there could be no publicity. Williams's compassion was genuine, and if his visits were hyped in the press he worried that it could look self-serving.

But sometimes word of these appearances would leak out, and in the run-up to the dinner, writers like Harold Kaese of the *Globe* and Austen Lake of the *American* detailed some of Ted's acts of kindness. Kaese, concluding that Williams preferred the company of children to adults, told the story of a mechanic who was surprised to find that Ted had paid his child's hospital bill after taking a liking to the boy. The mechanic admitted he used to be among those who would "ride Williams just for the fun of it" at Fenway.[3] Lake wrote that Ted gave away thousands of dollars every year, "often to insignificant people," and said that when he visited sick kids, he would come laden with gifts, including TV sets and autographed baseballs.[4]

The dinner was set for August 17 at Boston's Hotel Statler. A motorcade of forty cars left Fenway Park at 5:00 p.m., with Ted in the twenty-fourth car. He was preceded by Commissioner Ford Frick, American League president Will Harridge, Tom Yawkey, and Braves owner Lou Perini, as well as television's Ed Sullivan, singer-entertainer Morton Downey, and actress Elaine Stewart. The rest of the Red Sox players followed Williams.[5]

Some one thousand people attended the dinner, which was televised live locally. A total of $150,000 was raised, including $50,000 from the Kennedy family, a check for which was presented by twenty-one-year-old Ted Kennedy, then still nine years away from being elected to replace his brother John as a US senator from Massachusetts. In a short speech, which he wrote himself, Williams declared, "All the bullets and all the bombs that explode all over the world won't leave the impact—when all is said and done—of a dollar bill dropped in the Jimmy Fund pot by a warm heart and a willing hand."[6] Williams wore a tie at the beginning of the festivities, but he took it off during dinner and was later photographed with the tie dangling from his pocket.

The Red Sox finished a distant fourth in 1953, sixteen games behind the Yankees, but the summer had been redeemed by Ted's return. He hit

.407 in 91 at bats, with 13 home runs and 34 RBIs. His on-base percentage was .509, his slugging percentage an astonishing .901. Yogi Berra of the Yankees remarked in September that Ted "don't look like he used to. He looks better."[7] And one writer, Jerry Nason of the *Globe*, concluded that Ted's superlative performance after returning from the battlefield had made a mockery of spring training.[8]

Korea was a watershed for Williams, both in terms of how he viewed baseball and how he came to assess his own life.

"When I returned late in '53, [the Red Sox] were no longer a factor," Ted would write late in his life. "For the rest of my career we always finished back in the pack. Baseball was never as much fun for me after Korea as it had been before."[9]

That summer of 1953, in a reflective, as-told-to piece for the *American Weekly,* the now-defunct Hearst Sunday supplement magazine, Williams made clear he'd been seared by the Korean experience. "It was good to be home again, back in a ballpark, but I wonder if anyone ever leaves Korea, even when you're thousands of miles away from its filth and mud, and its nauseating stench no longer fills your nostrils," he said.[10] "The forgotten men who have stood or fallen there come home with you in spirit, I believe. And all the unanswered questions and confusion of this strange conflict—the war that is not a war—continue to haunt you, and you wonder if there is a solution at all. I'm not bitter. Any guy who has been in combat knows that bitterness vanishes quickly when you gamble with death—and win."

Yet he *was* bitter. The bitterness came in his rants to the clubhouse kids, in his plaintive, private talks with friends and teammates about what his total numbers might have been, and in the public explosions to come in the 1956 Johnny Podres affair and the New Orleans airport meltdown of 1957.

Still, in time, Williams would come to realize that the positives of being called back—taking his medicine, sacrificing career goals to serve his country, and surviving a spectacular crash landing—outweighed the negatives of time missed, the lost at bats, and the lost chances to set records. Korea was an undeniable plus, as it gave him heroic legitimacy. So gradually, that bitterness evolved into an ambivalence about his military service and finally into a sense of great pride and accomplishment. Fortunately for Williams, his quiet efforts to avoid being recalled and the unappealing bitterness he later expressed publicly would be largely forgotten or ignored.

*   *   *

Ted spent most of the off-season in the Florida Keys. Since the end of World War II, he had gravitated to Islamorada, a village in the Upper Keys about seventy-five miles from Miami, just down from Key Largo.

He'd come at first to fish with Jimmie Albright, a saltwater fly-fishing pioneer and legendary Islamorada guide who schooled Williams in the ways of bonefish and tarpon. It was Albright with whom he'd been fishing two years earlier, when word came that he'd been recalled for Korea.*

Now, in the fall and winter of 1953 and early 1954, Ted was back in Islamorada, still a disciple of Albright and, more recently, of Jack Brothers, a Brooklyn transplant who was quickly becoming a formidable, though friendly, competitor of Albright's. Brothers concentrated on bonefish.

Williams was alone on the island; Doris was up in Miami. They were now effectively separated. But although they hadn't functioned as a married couple for years, Ted was in no hurry to get a divorce. There was still a stigma associated with that, which he wanted to avoid. And of course there was the couple's daughter, Bobby-Jo, now six. A divorce couldn't be good for her, either, he thought.

But Doris had decided she'd had enough of Ted. So on January 19, she filed a formal separation petition in a Miami court that accused her husband of beating her and making her life "an intolerable burden and physical impossibility." The petition cited six years of marriage "in which he mistreated and abused" her and used "language that was profane, abusive, and obscene...swearing at her both in private and public." Doris further asserted that Williams hit, beat, and struck her, even though she had done all she could to be a "kind and dutiful and loving" wife. She asked for "reasonable sums" of money for support, the use of their Miami home and Ted's Cadillac, as well as custody of Bobby-Jo. A hearing was set for February 19.

Today, of course, such allegations of physical abuse would have ignited a multimedia maelstrom, but the press of 1954, especially the baseball writers, gave Ted a pass on the issue. Within days, they were back to speculating on how many spring training games Lou Boudreau would let Ted sit out. And the public seemed to care even less about his marital problems. On February 6, eighteen thousand adoring fans turned out for

---

* When Williams returned to his home outside Miami, he found a mob of reporters waiting for him. So he made a U-turn and headed straight back to Islamorada, to Albright's house. Could he lie low there for a while? Sure he could. Albright's wife, Frankie, prepared a meal, and just as they were sitting down to Key lime pie for dessert, two reporters knocked on the door, looking for Williams. Ted jumped up and hid in a closet. Albright, rather than shoo the scribes away, invited them in for pie and coffee and made Ted sweat it out in the closet for a bit.

Ted's annual fishing and casting exhibition at the sportsmen's show in Boston and mobbed him with autograph requests.

Doris's filing did have the effect of outing Evelyn Turner. Gossip maven Walter Winchell revealed her romance with Williams on his February 7 radio show and speculated that the couple would soon be married; then the wires picked up the story. Evelyn professed shock at the reports. "Ted's a real wonderful fellow and we've been friends for a long time—but strictly friends," she was quoted as saying. "After all, he's still married."

Asked many years later whether she knew if her father had ever struck her mother, Bobby-Jo said she had been assured by her grandmother—Doris's mother, Ruby Soule—that he had. Ruby told her it had happened in Boston in late 1947, when Doris was about seven months pregnant with Bobby-Jo. There had been an argument, some pushing, and Doris had fallen down the stairs, though it was unclear if Ted actually intended to push his wife down the stairs.

Ruby had flown in from Minnesota to be with her daughter after the stairs episode. Doris "had a big bruise on the side of her stomach, and a bruise on one side of the arm, big bruise," Bobby-Jo said. "Grandma said it was black."[11]

"I doubt that he meant to push her down the stairs," Bobby-Jo recalled. "I mean, I'm almost positive of that, but that's the way it happened, and I don't know." But Bobby-Jo thought the language Doris's attorney used in the petition was accurate, not hyperbole. While the details of the physical abuse allegations were murky, there was no question that her father had verbally abused her mother—Bobby-Jo had witnessed a lot of that and had often been on the receiving end of Ted's wrath herself: "He could hurt you as much with his mouth as he could if he punched you in the mouth. He could."

One indication of the troubled marriage, though certainly not the major cause of the breakup, was that by the time Williams returned from Korea, Doris was a full-blown alcoholic. Her problem would only get worse as she aged.

Doris's brother, Donald Soule, recalls her drinking hard as a young woman, too, and the problem only intensified after her marriage to Ted. It didn't help that he was on the road so much playing ball, and away fighting two wars. "She started drinking early in life, and I guess it got to where she couldn't handle it," Soule said. "She drank all the time. It's awfully sad. She told me she used to hide her bottle in the vacuum cleaner. She had to be worried about Ted catching her."

The drinking was hard for Ted to accept. Though late in life he came to enjoy a stiff cocktail, in the early- to mid-'50s he was still a relative teetotaler who would take only an occasional glass of wine, usually sparkling Burgundy.

"Two very difficult, volatile people got together and made a lousy job of it," Soule said in assessing his sister and Ted's marriage.[12]

Now that Ted's wife had asked for a formal separation, a marriage that had been largely a sham for the previous several years began its official unraveling, and for the rest of the decade, Williams would revel in the single life—both the diligent pursuit of other women and the tending to his own whims. Not that being married had ever stopped him from either.

Doris's decline continued after the breakup. One of Bobby-Jo's daughters, Dawn Hebding, remembered visiting her grandmother in Miami after she'd divorced Ted and gone through another marriage. By then Doris had a heart condition and was aging less than gracefully. She'd become a lonely, pathetic figure, living alone in an apartment, mostly just smoking and drinking. Once, her apartment had caught on fire because of a carelessly discarded cigarette. She developed Alzheimer's and died in 1987, at the age of sixty-eight.

It was in Islamorada, in the fall of 1953, several months before Doris's court filing, that Ted met Louise Magruder Kaufman. Louise was the daughter of an Ohio industrialist and by this time was quickly becoming a leading lady in Islamorada. She and her husband, Bob, had inherited 75 percent of her father's metal cookware manufacturing company in Carrollton, Ohio, near Canton. Bob had joined the family business, and the couple and their five children lived on a 650-acre horse and dairy farm near Carrollton.

The Kaufmans had first come to Islamorada in the winter of 1948 and lived aboard their forty-two-foot sportfishing yacht, which had a full-time captain. Then they upgraded to a fifty-foot Chris-Craft before they tired of living on a boat and built their own house in 1952. By then, Louise, an avid and accomplished fisherwoman, had grown increasingly enchanted with the Keys and bored with Ohio. So she began spending most of the year in Islamorada, and she and Bob, who stayed back in Carrollton, drifted apart.

Islamorada was then just a sleepy village of about one thousand people on Route 1, halfway between Miami and Key West. It had a tidy harbor, a grocery store, a gas station, a construction company, a two-room schoolhouse, and a few restaurants and motels, including the Whale

Harbor Inn and the Green Turtle Inn, which featured sea-turtle steaks, soups, and chowders.

Louise was forty-one years old, five foot three and 120 pounds, with shoulder-length light brown hair—attractive but not striking. She immersed herself in the fishing life and soon was catching all the important game fish in the Keys and beyond. She caught a 152-pound tarpon, a woman's world record for bait casting. She would catch bluefin tuna in Bimini as well as white marlin, sailfish, and wahoo off Islamorada. She also enjoyed cruising around the island in her black 1952 Buick convertible, which had red upholstery.

One night Jimmie Albright, the ace fishing guide, called Louise and said there was a big boxing match on television. Could he and Frankie come over and watch the fight? (Kaufman had one of the few TVs on the island.) Jimmie said they'd be bringing a friend—Ted Williams. Louise had heard of Ted, but she wasn't much of a baseball fan. Still, she was struck by how handsome Williams was. "The physical attraction was there immediately," Louise would tell an interviewer years later. "The way it happens. He was the most gorgeous man I'd ever seen."[13]

They discussed fishing as equals. Ted liked Louise's vibrant, forceful persona and seemed impressed that she was putting down roots in Islamorada, mostly alone. But he wasn't particularly attracted to her. For one thing, she was six years older than he was—he'd just turned thirty-five that August. True, Evelyn Turner had been three years older than Ted, but Louise was quite different from the archetypal younger bombshell type Williams was coming to prefer.

Yet Ted and Louise began hanging out together. Islamorada was so small they'd bump into each other at the marina, the grocery store, or the gas station. Everyone seemed to know everyone else. They'd go fishing. It was low-key, casual, comfortable.

Soon, Louise wanted her best friend from Ohio, Evalyn Sterry, to come down and meet Ted. When Evalyn arrived, Louise (most of her friends called her Lou) said they were going to a meeting of the Islamorada Fishing Club. Evalyn wasn't interested in fishing, but she went along. Ted was giving a talk. "Lou said, 'That's Ted Williams.' And I thought that was the handsomest man I ever saw. You can't believe how handsome he was," Evalyn recalled.[14]

The next night Louise said they were going to meet Ted for a drink. It turned out Ted had a special guest staying with him: Benny Goodman. The King of Swing himself. Goodman was dressed casually, in khakis, and Evalyn assumed he was a fishing guide.

By 1955 Ted and Doris were divorced. Later Ted decided to buy a small, rudimentary house in Islamorada, on the ocean side of the island, about six blocks from Louise's place, which was on the bay side. Bobby-Jo would come and visit Ted, and Louise's five kids would visit her. The families mingled freely.

Meanwhile, a complicating factor for Louise was the emergence of another married woman who was smitten with Williams: Lynette Siman. Lynette, a petite brunette who was then thirty, was from the Boston area. She and her husband had arrived in Islamorada in 1953 and built an eight-room motel called The Sands. She was thrilled to be in the Keys.

"Oh, it was delightful," Lynette said.[15] "In September, you could stand in the middle of US 1 and shoot a cannon and you wouldn't touch a soul. It was just a group of people who loved that tropical island living."

Lynette eagerly jumped into Ted and Louise's orbit. They fished, dined, and socialized together. Lynette grew romantically restless, and within five years she had divorced her husband and married a retired Iowa feed manufacturing executive who was twenty years her senior. She drew him into her Islamorada circle, and of course he was quite enamored of Williams, too. "A lot of us loved Ted," she said.

While Lynette certainly wasn't above flirting rather boldly with Ted when her husband and Louise weren't around, she tried to be careful. "I didn't wear a badge saying 'I love Ted' or anything like that. I was married; Louise was separated. We were neighbors. We were all friends. There was something always there, but the timing was not right." Summing it up, Siman said, "I think we both knew there was a tremendous attraction, but there was never any hanky-panky, if you want to call it that."

Lynette said she never told her close friend Louise of her feelings for Ted, but admitted it's doubtful that Louise could have been oblivious to what was going on. As for Williams, he seemed to enjoy all the attention, like a star quarterback sitting back to watch two cheerleaders vie for his favor. Lynette knew that Louise had the circumstantial advantage over her with Ted, so she deferred to her friend and watched anxiously as he and Louise went back and forth to each other's houses, often with their children.

If Williams and Kaufman were casual and warm with each other, such coziness did not carry over to their children. Ted had a routine with Bobby-Jo that Louise loved. In a mock military drill, he would make his daughter stand for a cleanliness inspection before dinner. Ted would tell

Bobby-Jo, who was then about six, to address him thusly: "Yes, sir, daddy dear sweetheart, I love you in the major leagues." The terms eventually changed so that this response was required not just before meals but whenever she was spoken to.*

Living close by, spending a lot of time with Ted, and getting to know his daughter perhaps gave Louise a false sense of security. She knew she wanted to spend the rest of her life with him, and while Williams didn't encourage her, he did put her in touch with his divorce lawyer in Miami. Louise flew up to Boston a time or two around 1955 to watch Ted play. When she was there, she stayed at the Somerset Hotel, where the Kid by then resided. Once, when Bobby-Jo was visiting, the three of them posed together for a picture.

Then, in 1957, Louise decided to make the leap and divorce Bob Kaufman, but Ted was not there to catch her. The baseball seasons of 1953 through 1957 yielded exciting, new, gorgeous—and much younger—women, some of whom Ted developed strong feelings for. It was unclear how much Louise knew of this; Williams of course compartmentalized the in-season romances, which were mostly for Boston and the road. Louise was for Islamorada—warm and comfortable, like a pair of slippers, not sexy high heels.

Ted would jilt Louise at least twice more by marrying two other women, even though each time Louise thought she would be the anointed one. Still, even spurned, she would never go far, always remaining at his beck and call, adoring, almost worshipful. Kaufman would love Ted for forty years, staying involved with him through all three of his marriages and persevering through all the rejection and heartache until he finally returned to her. It would be on his terms, however—not as a fourth wife, but as a live-in companion.

Louise could live with that. Indeed, that was the secret to living with Ted, after all—doing it his way. You had to be willing to let him run roughshod over you, to endure outbursts and crude insults. Louise would put it more diplomatically: you just had to know Ted and let him blow off steam. These were just passing squalls, and he would forget about them as soon as they happened. He really didn't mean to hurt. But sometimes the hurt didn't go away.

---

* Years later, when Bobby-Jo met Ted's son, John-Henry, for the first time, they compared notes on this practice: "We went alone into a room to talk. The first thing he said—we closed the door, this was 1991—he said, 'Did you ever have to say...' and he started to say it, and we both picked up the phrase at the same time, and I said, 'Holy shit!'"

After Louise persevered and finally landed Ted later in life, when she was in her early sixties, Lynette Siman was happy for her old friend because she knew how much Louise had suffered along the way. Lynette was seemingly blocked again, but she knew a thing or two about perseverance herself. "After my husband died and Lou passed away, things took their normal course, I guess," Lynette said.

As a boy, Williams could not have been less interested in girls. He was single-minded in his pursuit of baseball, and little else mattered. He was shy, gangling, and awkward around girls and only had one date during his entire time in high school. That was when his pal Bob Breitbard insisted they double-date at their senior prom in 1937, and Ted escorted Alberta Camus.

As Williams put it in his autobiography: "A girl looked at me twice, I'd run the other way.... I never went out with girls, never had any dates, not until I was much more mature-looking."

According to Ted's ghostwriter for his autobiography, former *Sports Illustrated* writer John Underwood, it was not until his rookie year with the Red Sox, in 1939, that Ted decided he was ready to have sex for the first time. He was twenty or twenty-one, and the team was playing the Tigers in Detroit. A young woman about three years his senior came on to him at the ballpark and then at the team hotel. Ted suggested a movie, but was wary of anything more. "I was scared of those things then," Ted told Underwood thirty years later, in 1969. He thought "sex could screw up my career if I got gonorrhea."

But the woman was ardent in her pursuit, so Williams procured a condom and agreed to do the deed. What should have been a delightful experience turned into merely an embarrassment. Ted was so inexperienced he didn't know what to do with the condom, so the groupie had to show him. When he finished, he told Underwood, he felt "degraded. I said, 'Geez, I'm never going to do that again until I get married.'"

The same woman stalked him again the following season, when the Red Sox arrived in Detroit. Ted ignored her messages until she sent him a two-page telegram claiming that she'd gotten pregnant during their 1939 encounter and she was now going to have his baby. Terrified, Williams consulted his older roommate, Charlie Wagner, who advised that they bring the problem to manager Joe Cronin. Cronin called in the cops, and it turned out to be a scam this woman had tried on Tigers star Hank Greenberg as well.[16]

Later in life, Ted told different versions of the story of how he lost his virginity. In 1985, chatting with *The New Yorker*'s Roger Angell at the Red Sox spring training facility in Winter Haven, Florida, Williams complained that the modern player was thinking far more about sex than about hitting. "They're fucking their brains out," Ted said. "They're just kids but they're all married, and the ones that aren't have got somebody living in with them, so it's like they're married. They're just thinking of that one thing." Williams then asked Angell if he had not had pretty decent seasons in 1938, when he was with the Minneapolis Millers in the American Association, and in 1939, his rookie year with the Red Sox. "Of course you did," Angell replied, knowing full well Ted had hit .366 with the Millers and won the Triple Crown, then hit .327 and led the American League in RBIs with 145 the following year in Boston.

Angell was wondering where this conversation was headed when Williams proceeded to make an explicit link between hitting performance and abstinence: "Roger," the Kid said, "I didn't get laid for the first time until the All-Star Game break of my second year in the majors. I was thinking about hitting."[17] That would place his rite of passage in Saint Louis in 1940, not in Detroit in 1939, as Ted had told Underwood.

Not long before he died, Williams offered still another version—time and place not specified—to one of his lawyers, Eric Abel, though this story, too, was linked to performance on the field. "He was about twenty," recalled Abel, who later would marry Ted's younger daughter, Claudia. "He told me he was in a hotel room, traveling with the team. There were girls waiting outside. Groupies. But he was very shy. He said he couldn't imagine taking a girl, just like that, going up and having sex. But his buddies took the women up. He'd be up there, and one said, 'Send someone up.' Finally one of the guys said, 'You gotta do this, Ted. Just do it.' So I think one of his buddies called the bellhop. Ted's telling the story, and he says, 'I'm nervous, but Jesus, it's pretty good. This is pretty good. Whoa!' Next day he goes three for four. 'I'm telling you what, this is the ticket. I've got to do that again tonight.' Next day two for four. 'This is it. I love this. Feels pretty good.' Next day, oh for four. Another night, then oh for four. After that he rules it out as helping his hitting. He was more concerned about its effect on his hitting than he was enjoyment."[18]

It wasn't long, however, before Ted lost all his sexual inhibitions. Johnny Lazor, a backup outfielder with the Red Sox in the '40s, recalled an awkward moment in Detroit in 1946: "In Detroit, the hotel was within walking distance from the ballpark, and we were walking back after a game. There were four of us walking down the street. I don't know if I should be saying this, but there were four women on the sidewalk. And Ted, he picked out one girl and walked up to her and tapped her on the shoulder and said to her, 'Do you fuck?'" The girl and her companions scurried away.[19]

At games, Williams would happily join his teammates and play what was known as "shoot the beaver," a game in which the players would scan the stands for the best-looking talent in attendance. Plenty of women would be checking Williams out, too. Once, in Washington, an overzealous girl decided to crawl out on the top of the Red Sox dugout during pregame warm-ups and gaze into the dugout at Ted.

"Her head's upside down, six feet in front of us," remembered George Sullivan, the former Sox batboy turned baseball writer, who was sitting next to Williams at the time. "She propositioned him. Told him what she'd do for him. She had long, dark hair, hanging way down. A brunette."[20]

Such incidents, as well as the ready assistance of ushers and clubhouse attendants, would often lead to dates. If Ted and one of his Red Sox friends double-dated, Williams wouldn't hesitate to hit on the teammate's girl if he decided she was more attractive than his own date.

Eddie Pellagrini, the backup shortstop in 1946, recalls a time that year on the road when Williams suggested they go out. "Hey, dago," Williams said, using his preferred name for Pellagrini. "I've got a date with my girlfriend, and she's got one for you. She's supposed to be a gorgeous chick."

Ted and Eddie picked up Ted's girl at the hotel. "Ted says to his girl, 'Where we going?' She says to the theater. I was thinking, 'Oh, Christ, who is my girl going to be, a popcorn girl, a ticket taker?'" Pellagrini recalled, laughing. "So we get there and this girl walks up and Ted says, 'Is that her?' His girl says, 'Yeah, that's my friend Heidi.' Ted is carrying on in the front. I just said, 'She ain't bad.' She was actually gorgeous. Heidi says, 'Well, I have my own car. Eddie, why don't you come with me and we'll go in my car?' I said, 'Why not?' She was prettier than Ted's girl. *Gorgeous!* Oh, yeah, shit. So we go to some restaurant, and Ted's putting the moves on my girl the whole time. He was really workin' her. Oh, yeah, he was a good-looking kid, but Heidi's paying attention to me, not him. Anyway, she took me home and nothing happened. I might have put my arm around her. I don't remember if I kissed her or what. To make a long story short, I got back to the hotel, Ted was in the lobby. He says, 'Hey, dago, how did you make out?' I said, 'Wooooo, oh, baby!'"[21]

Williams was less on the prowl in Boston than he was when the Red Sox were on the road. At home, his hotel room was his base and refuge. He shunned the limelight, preferring to be alone. He'd decompress after a game, watching television and tying intricate flies to add to his collection for fishing.

When he returned from Korea, Ted moved back into the Shelton Hotel on Bay State Road off Kenmore Square, near Fenway Park. The two-hundred-room hotel was on the banks of the Charles River and had an eclectic, mostly residential clientele that included Eugene O'Neill, the playwright. When the Sonnabend family, who owned the Shelton, sold the hotel to Boston University in 1953 so it could be converted to a dormitory, Paul Sonnabend, the manager, told Williams he was leaving to become general manager at the Somerset, a much larger hotel nearby, overlooking Commonwealth Avenue. "Can I come with you?" said Ted.[22]

Sonnabend made sure his staff at the Somerset zealously catered to Ted and ensured his privacy. He settled into a second-floor suite, room 231, which had a sweeping view of Commonwealth Avenue, one of Boston's grandest boulevards. There were elegant brownstones on either side of the street, which was divided by a median lined with trees. Williams also took another room on the sixth floor for guests, or to use as a getaway for added privacy. The Somerset was the only hotel in the city at the time that had a swimming pool, and it had two good restaurants, the Rib Room and the Polynesian Village, which would each carve out some breathing room for Ted if he wanted to come down and eat in peace.

Williams soon grew close to the Somerset assistant manager, the doorman, bellhops, bell captains, parking lot attendants, the valet, television repairman, and telephone operators, all of whom went the extra mile for him. He took exceptionally good care of them financially, too, and came to regard some as close friends.

Williams had asked for a room on the second floor so that he could reach his suite easily by using a back stairway, without anyone seeing him. He wanted to avoid walking through a crowded lobby to take the elevator, which he would need to reach a room on the upper floors. The hard-core Ted groupies were of course aware that he lived at the Somerset and would sometimes congregate in the lobby hoping for a sighting, but the staff was vigilant for this and would shoo them away whenever they reached critical mass. (Mae Carney, the lead telephone operator, was under strict instructions never to put any phone calls through to Ted, only to take messages, which the bellhops would slide under the door of room 231.) If Ted expected female company he would usually alert the parking lot attendant or one of the bellhops, who would facilitate her arrival via the back stairs.

Arthur D'Angelo came for his laundry, and Andy Giacobbe was the TV repairman. D'Angelo had a key to Ted's room and would come and go several days a week, picking up and dropping off laundry. He was an Italian immigrant who had come to Boston in 1939 with his twin brother, Henry, and launched a dry cleaning business that serviced several of the hotels, including the Somerset.

Starting in 1946, Arthur and Henry had opened a side business selling souvenirs around Fenway Park, which would mushroom years later into the highly lucrative Twins Enterprises Inc. across from the ballpark, which now sells all manner of Red Sox paraphernalia. So Ted already knew Arthur. Back then, he'd see the brothers on the street and say, jovially, "You two guys are making a fortune on me and you're not giving me a penny, but I don't give a shit."

Later, at the hotel, Ted and Arthur would continue the banter. "When I saw Ted at the Somerset, we'd talk about the usual stuff," Arthur said. "What did he do when he was out of town, did he pick up any broads, nothing big. He was an ice cream freak. He had just a room with a refrigerator, and his place was always filled with candies and ice cream. He liked Baby Ruth candy bars. He was interested in where I came from. He'd say, 'You little greaseball, you came from nothing in Italy and you made a fortune.' He'd talk like that. I think he liked me. I think he trusted me."[23]

Andy Giacobbe was startled one day when he walked into Williams's room to check on his TV. "Would you like to be my best friend?" Ted asked him. "This TV is my life. I eat all my meals in front of the TV, I tie fishing flies in front of the TV, I don't go to theaters, I don't go to dinner. I want you to check it for me every day, whether we're here or on the road." Following instructions, for the next several years, Giacobbe would go to his room seven days a week. "He was a lonesome guy who hungered to have friends," Andy recalled. "He used to insist I have breakfast with him, he gave me tickets to day games, and over the years I got to know him pretty well." When he was in town, Ted would look forward to Andy's daily visits. "If you're not busy, stay a while," Williams would tell him. "You'll never overstay your welcome." Once, when Andy stopped by a pet store and the owner told him he was about to throw out a sick canary, Andy took it, plucked its feathers, and presented them to Ted to use for his fly making. "I thought he was gonna kiss me, he was so elated, and he told me what kinds of flies he made with them, and he still remembered that fifty years later," Andy said.

Usually the chambermaids kept his suite immaculate, but one day, in 1957, Andy came in to find the room a shambles. Ted had thrown the cushions on the floor and there was crumpled newspaper everywhere. "Eleven years!" Williams screamed. "Eleven years and Egan won't get off my back about the 1946 World Series!"[24]

Another regular visitor to room 231, though he was not an employee of the Somerset, was Jim Carroll, who had emerged during the '50s as one of Ted's closest friends and his man Friday. The two had met accidentally in 1950 on Cape Cod when both turned up for a fishing trip at the wrong dock. Carroll noticed the famous man sitting in his beige Cadillac Coupe de Ville with Minnesota plates, reading the paper. It was a Monday, an off day for the Red Sox. Ted asked if Jim wanted to get some breakfast.

Carroll was the top liquor salesman in Boston in his day. He had seventy-six bars and fourteen package stores on his route, mostly in his home territory of South Boston. In case his visitors wanted a drink, Ted would order a case of Cutty Sark regularly from Jim, and before long Carroll had a key to Ted's room to make his deliveries.

They would hang out in the suite and talk, watching Ed Sullivan as Ted sipped on a ginger ale. Jim routinely met Ted at the airport when the team came home from a road trip, pulling up to Logan in Williams's Cadillac, which Ted let him use when the Red Sox were away. Carroll got a big kick out of showing the car off to his friends, and it wasn't bad for business, either, as he made his rounds of the bars and package stores. (Ted declared Jim's own 1958 Ford convertible a shitbox.)

Sometimes when Williams got restless at night he'd ask Jim to go for a walk. They would leave the hotel, cross Commonwealth Avenue, make their way to Marlborough Street, go down to Arlington Street on Boston Common, then head back on Beacon Street to Kenmore Square. Often they'd stop outside the Howard Johnson there and Ted would send Jim in for a chocolate and vanilla double cone.

They would talk about politics, especially later, when the Kennedy-Nixon presidential campaign heated up. Ted was a big Nixon man, of course. They also discussed more metaphysical subjects. Once, when the two were out walking, Carroll dropped his rosary beads. Ted noticed and said, "You're one of them?" Ted questioned him about Catholicism and what he believed. Williams said he wanted to be cremated. Did the Catholics have a policy on that?

Ted had been in Boston for years, but he didn't know the city well, so sometimes Carroll would drive Ted around town and take him to neighborhoods he'd never been to, like South Boston.

The two men wouldn't eat out much, but when they did, Ted liked the Union Oyster House, near Faneuil Hall, or the Linwood Grill, on Kilmarnock Street, near Fenway. "They gave him a good steak there, and no one bothered him," Carroll said. Not being bothered was as important to Williams, if not more important, than the food. Once, Ted suggested they go see a western, but when about fifty people surrounded him and started to create too much of a scene, Williams said, "Let's get the Christ out of here." Carroll complained he had just paid for the tickets. Ted said, "You want the money back?"

Sometimes Ted would go to Fenway for extra batting practice and invite Carroll along, sending him out to right field to shag flies. Jim remembers line drives whistling over his head. If he was lucky enough to catch a ball, his hand would burn with pain.

One day in June of 1955, Ted asked Carroll to drive him to visit Harry Agganis at the Sancta Maria Hospital in Cambridge. Agganis, then twenty-six, had emerged as a power-hitting first baseman for the Red Sox in 1954, unseating Dick Gernert and hitting eleven home runs that year, eight of them at Fenway, as a left-handed batter. In 1955, he was hitting .313 in the cleanup spot behind Ted when he was suddenly hospitalized with fever and chest pains. The son of Greek immigrants, Agganis had been raised in working-class Lynn, north of Boston, and had gone to Boston University, where he starred as an All-American quarterback and came to be known as "the Golden Greek." Drafted by the Cleveland Browns, he chose to play baseball instead and signed with the Red Sox. Williams had grown close to Agganis and was shaken by the hospital visit, as it was apparent his teammate did not have long to live. Ted and Carroll got to talking about what his funeral would be like. Carroll noted that Agganis was Greek Orthodox, and the church customarily had an open casket. "I'm not gonna lay in a goddamn box and have people gawk at me," Ted said, reiterating that he wanted to be cremated. Agganis died of a massive pulmonary embolism two days after the visit.

There were more pleasant outings. In February of 1957, Carroll was hanging out in Ted's Somerset suite. Reading the paper, Jim noticed that James Michael Curley was seriously ill. Curley was the legendary rogue who had served as a congressman, the mayor of Boston, and the governor of Massachusetts. In 1947, during his fourth term as mayor, Curley had been imprisoned for his role in an influence-peddling scandal, but he had been pardoned by President Truman after five months behind bars.

"I got a good idea," Carroll said. "Why don't we go visit Curley. I know where he lives. What a thrill that would be for the old man." When they arrived, they were escorted to Curley's bedroom. He was lying on a twin bed. Ted sat on the other bed, talking baseball and Babe Ruth. People and the press congregated outside after learning that Williams was inside. Ted stayed about forty minutes and invited the old gent to opening day in April.

"Curley lit up," said Carroll. Afterward, Ted asked Carroll, "Did you ever see such piercing eyes for a man like that? And what a voice!" When opening day came, Curley told the writers he was at the game as Ted's guest. Declaring that it made him feel young again to be at the ballpark, he warmly recounted Williams's visit in February. "Ted is in a class by himself," Curley said.[25]*

In August of 1957, Ted asked Jim to drive him to Lynn to visit a sick child on behalf of the Jimmy Fund. They were supposed to leave early in the morning, but the previous night, Carroll's mother had had a cerebral hemorrhage. Jim was with her in the hospital and got home so late he overslept and missed his date to pick up Williams. Ted called him, mad as a hornet. Where the hell was he? Jim explained that his mother had had a stroke.

Ted hung up, embarrassed. He'd met Jim's mother, an operator for New England Telephone, once before and charmed her. Ted called the Somerset doorman, asked directions to Carney Hospital in the Dorchester section of Boston, and jumped in his car to visit Mrs. Carroll. He got lost on the way, then, exasperated, started driving too fast. A cop pulled him over. He asked for Ted's license, then looked at the driver for verification. "Oh, my God almighty, it's Ted Williams," he said. When the Kid explained his predicament, the officer gave him an escort to the Carney.

Ted presented Carroll's mother with a carnation and visited for a half hour or so. By then, word was all over the hospital that Williams was there, and the corridors were jammed with doctors, nurses, and nuns clamoring for autographs. He obliged as many as he could, left a check for $5,000 at the front desk to pay for Mrs. Carroll's care, then had the cop who had pinched him escort him to Fenway Park for an afternoon game against the Chicago White Sox.

Carroll learned of the visit later that day when he came to the hospital and one of the nuns handed him Ted's check. Jim returned it to Williams,

---

* Curley died the following year, at the age of eighty-three.

who was not amused. "I left the goddamn money there, and it was none of your business!" he said. Jim thanked him but explained his mother had health insurance through her job at the phone company.

The following year, when Williams was turning forty, Carroll decided he wanted to do something special for his friend's birthday. When they were talking one day, Jim asked Ted if he had a hero. First he said he didn't, then, after thinking about it awhile, said he did: General Douglas MacArthur, the supreme commander of Allied forces in Korea when Ted served there. "Good man," Williams said. "Never should have got fired."

MacArthur lived at the Waldorf Towers in New York. Using the Somerset bellhop network, Jim wangled the general's home number. He called, and Mrs. MacArthur answered the phone. He explained that he was giving a party for Ted Williams's fortieth birthday and wanted to get an autographed picture of the general.

"Land sakes, my husband would be so pleased to hear that," Mrs. MacArthur said. "He thinks Ted's a great American." She gave him an office number in New Jersey. Jim called, and a man answered. He recognized the voice.

"I don't go to any birthday parties," MacArthur said.

"I wonder if I can get a picture of you, because Ted Williams idolizes you," Carroll replied.

"I'm really flattered. I think he's a true American and one of the greatest baseball players I've ever seen." What, MacArthur suggested, if he sent an oil painting of himself? He had hundreds of them that admirers had sent him. He told Carroll he'd be happy to inscribe it to Williams and send it up to Boston. MacArthur chose a painting among the many and wrote in the lower right-hand corner: "To Ted Williams, not only America's greatest ball player, but a great American, who has served his country in two wars. Your admiring friend, Douglas MacArthur, General of the Army." Jim presented the painting at the party. "He took a look at that, and the guy melted," Carroll remembered. "He was thrilled. He said he was going to put it in his living room in Islamorada."[26]

In the 1960s, when the feminist movement emerged in earnest, Williams would not know what to make of it. He was a product of his times in that he saw women primarily as sex objects or glorified domestics. He was unenlightened, to say the least. (Perhaps the only thing he had in common with some feminist thinkers was a deep dislike of women wearing makeup—but of course this consensus was reached from nearly opposite directions.)

Ted's retro view of women and what they were capable of frustrated his daughter Claudia. "You had to really fight to gain Dad's respect as a woman," Claudia said.[27] "Even as a sexual object, most women were still out for something else. They were using that as their power, and he would instantly disrespect them for that, too. I think in Dad's world and in his experience, there were very few women that had beauty and brains and independence. I mean, I can remember every time he would ask about what I'd want to do in life, I would tell him X, Y, and Z. 'I want to do the Tour de France' or 'I want to be a professional triathlete.' He'd be, like, 'Why don't you just become an English teacher? Go to school. Be a teacher. That's a really good job. Gives you great benefits.'"

While Ted could be charming and courtly with women when it suited him, he could also be crude and cruel. From his twenties, after he discovered sex, through his thirties, post-Doris, when he greatly expanded his female repertoire, Williams, while successfully forging meaningful relationships with a handful of women, generally hopped from one sexual encounter to another. "After he was turned on to sex, he only viewed it as sex, not as a commitment or part of a relationship," said Steve Brown, who became a close friend of Ted's late in life. "He felt there was no permanence in the institution of marriage. He loved beautiful women, and usually he would get them whenever he wanted them."[28]

But sometimes, if he was just feeling randy, Williams became less discriminating in his tastes, and less than beautiful would do just fine. This surprised some who assumed that a star of his magnitude would only deign to date perfect tens. "Once, in Santa Barbara, I was with him when he came on to some broad," remembered Ted's cousin Sal Herrera. "I said to him, 'That bitch is uglier than a mud hen. What are you making out with her for?' 'Well, I haven't had some in a while,' Ted said."[29]

Arthur D'Angelo, who had the Somerset Hotel laundry account, visited Ted's room so often he wouldn't always knock. Once or twice he interrupted while the Kid was busy with a woman. "They'd get covered up, and Ted would say, 'You son of a bitch, you could have knocked at the door," D'Angelo recalled, laughing. "He wasn't too upset about it. I think I knew his personal life better than most. Some of the women he was with were homely. Later I'd kid him and say, 'Hey, Ted, look at DiMaggio. He has Marilyn and gets the cream of the crop. How come you got dogs?' He'd laugh and say, 'A hole is a hole.'" Others were struck by the harshness of his language. "He would talk about women in awful ways," said Jonathan Gallen, who worked closely with Ted in the memorabilia business in the early 1990s. "Everyone was a 'fuckin' cunt,' or a 'fuckin' bitch.'...He'd talk about women in ways I'd never heard before."[30]

Friends and family members linked Williams's misogyny to his mother, a classic case of transference: the deep resentment that Ted harbored toward his mother for tending to the poor of San Diego at the expense of him and his brother was deflected onto women he met, and it colored his relationships with them.

Claudia called her father's resentment of his mother "the seed that grew to be the disrespect Dad had for women." There was also frustration, she said, that Williams couldn't always control the dynamic with women. "He couldn't control his mother. She was never around. He couldn't control a woman. 'They're good for nothin'.'"

Added cousin Manuel Herrera, Sal's brother: "Ted had vicious hate for women because of his mother.[31] He had no patience for anything. When I visited him in eighty-nine or ninety, he said, 'My father should have got the medal of honor for putting up with that son of a bitch.'"

Bobby-Jo thought her father grew angrier with women as successive relationships failed and as marriages kept ending in divorce. "After his last divorce, he was angry for a good couple of years," she said. "Real down on women. Boy, he could be laughing, watching TV, or watching a game, and it hit him in his head, and he'd go off."

At the same time, he couldn't do without the opposite sex. He was keenly aware of the effect of his celebrity on women, which, combined with his looks, seemed to give him carte blanche to have whomever he wished whenever he wanted, and he reveled in asserting this power. He would be in a restaurant and notice a nice-looking waitress. He'd get up, and as she approached he'd put his hand on the wall so she couldn't pass by. Then he'd stand there talking to her for ten minutes while the trapped woman was pinned against the wall. "He was addicted to women," said Bobby-Jo. "I think it's absolutely amazing—you would never wish superstardom on anyone that you really cared about, because something happens to you. My dad was as handsome as they come, he really was, and he had an air about him that—it was just an air. And maybe it was because he was such a big guy and he carried himself like somebody. He'd walk in and everybody'd just go—it was like they'd drop their box off the cart."

Even when he was married, Ted preferred to leave his wife at home whenever he went out, the better to preserve his options. "He wanted other women to think he was available," said Claudia. "It was more exciting that way. Are you kidding? You got the little wifey next to you, it's, like, 'I gotta behave.'"

Williams would milk his iconic status as leverage for flirtations or propositions well into retirement. Maureen Cronin, Joe Cronin's daughter, who always had a crush on Ted, tells of the time in the '70s when the Kid attended a Red Sox luncheon. An elegant matron of a certain age from upscale Wellesley, west of Boston, approached him and asked him to sign a baseball. "Ted Williams, room 305," the Kid wrote.[32]

At Old-Timers' Days at Fenway Park, the bobby-soxers who had screamed for Ted back in the day would return and come down close to the field, still starry-eyed, yoo-hooing number 9. There would be women waiting on the charity circuit, too. Once, in the '80s, he attended a golf tournament to benefit the Jimmy Fund out in Springfield, in western Massachusetts. The tournament was being played on several courses, and at one point Ted asked to go to the course where the ladies were playing. His host was Jim Vinick, a pal from Springfield who had acquired Ted's film rights in hopes of doing a movie on his life. They roamed the course in a golf cart. "We stop at all the different foursomes, and he's hugging the women and kissing them, and 'Thank you for coming to the Jimmy Fund, we're gonna raise a lot of money this year,' and on and on," said Vinick. "He was in his glory. He was very cordial and just loved the adoration." Then all of a sudden, Williams said, "Uh-oh." "What's the matter?" said Vinick. Said Ted: "See that fat little old lady with the white hair over there? Let's get the hell outta here. Every time I come north she finds me." Vinick asked where she was from. Ted anxiously replied that she'd probably come from "the Somerset Hotel, for Chrissakes! Let's get outta here. She's there with her son. That could be my son!" Williams added, "You're with them once and they think they own you forever."[33]

At times it could seem like all Ted was interested in was getting his share. Recalled Red Sox outfielder Jimmy Piersall, "One time we were playing in a mostly empty stadium, but there was this one pretty lady sitting in the upper deck that we were both looking at, and Ted dropped a fly ball. I gave him shit, and he said to me, 'C'mon, Jim, I lost it in the moon.' Bullshit: he lost it in the broad in the upper deck."[34]

For all his amorous adventures, Williams was keenly aware of his shortcomings when it came to sustaining a successful relationship. He would always refer to himself as "a three-time loser" in marriage. While he was disappointed by his daughter Bobby-Jo in many ways, he admired the longevity of her marriage to her second husband, Mark Ferrell. On a visit once in the late '90s, Ted asked Mark how long they had been married. Mark said twenty-six years.

"Jesus!" said Ted. "That's a long time. What's the secret of staying together that many years?"

"You give and take, you love each other," Mark said.

The next morning at breakfast, Williams told Mark and Bobby-Jo wistfully: "I thought about you guys all night. What the hell is the secret?" So they went through it again. "'Give and take, compromise. You stay truthful to one woman,' I should have said, but I didn't," Mark noted.[35]

The eight years between 1953, when Williams returned from Korea, and his second marriage, in 1961, were filled with romantic belt-notching, intrigue, and fulfillment—so much so that he felt vindicated in his decision to brush off Louise Kaufman. First, there was still a lot of catting around to do, but second, he had significant relationships with three women during this period—two of whom, Nelva More and Isabel Gilmore, he would propose to. The third, Nancy Barnard, Ted ardently pursued but could never land. She would be a mysterious woman in his life, one who got away—one who rejected him at a time when others flocked to him constantly. Yet all three women carried tender memories of Ted with them and would stay in touch with him and care for him for the rest of his life.

Nelva More was a stunning brunette whom Williams met not long after his return from Korea. A mutual friend had introduced Ted to Nelva, a model and fledgling actress, on August 30, 1953, in Cleveland, following a Red Sox–Indians game.

Nelva, who was then twenty-two, had been born and raised in Greensboro, North Carolina. She left home suddenly after she was raped and everybody seemed to know about it. She went to South Carolina and started working as a carhop. A dress designer spotted her and asked if she wanted to model in Miami. After a stint there, she graduated to New York, modeling clothes and suits in the garment district, then she did runway work. She got a role in *The Fifth Season*, a Broadway play about the fashion business. Then came small movie roles, including one with Henry Fonda in *Stage Struck*. On television, she appeared with Jackie Gleason and the June Taylor Dancers.

Nelva had been in Cleveland on a modeling job when a friend who knew Williams invited her to come with him to the game and meet Ted. She said she knew nothing about baseball but went along anyway. She met Williams after the game, and they talked for a while. "I thought he was a rugged diamond in the rough," Nelva recalled. "Not the kind of person I was looking for. I like men who like to dress elegantly. Not Teddy." But there was a spark. "Ted and I just liked the way we looked at each other, I guess, or I probably gave him a kind of look that [made him decide] to call me back."

They decided to meet again a week later in Philadelphia, where the Red Sox were scheduled to play the Athletics and where Nelva had a modeling date. They ordered room service at the Warwick Hotel for dinner, made plans to meet again in New York, and the romance was on. Nelva was married but separated from her Brazilian husband when she began her relationship with Williams. Before long she called and told her husband she wouldn't be returning to Brazil.

Instead she came to Boston to spend a week with Williams. The suite at the Somerset was modest, she thought. "It was about what you'd expect Teddy to have," she said. "It wasn't the Plaza or the Waldorf." Williams wanted her at Fenway Park every day she was there. Sometimes she'd arrive late, and that irritated Ted. "You always arrive late and come sashaying in and want everyone to notice you," he told her. "I wait until after you a hit a home run," Nelva replied. "You don't seem to hit one when I'm there."

Still, she was thrilled to watch him: "Everyone around probably knew I was with Teddy, but no one stared at me. It was just like I was at any ball game, but as he was going into the dugout he'd give me a smile. I felt kind of proud because I was with him. All the people would lust to get an autograph or photograph. Women were always coming up to him in the hotel lobby or at the ball games. They'd be hollering silly things like women do sometimes. Throwing notes down to the dugout. I think he liked for people to see that he had one on his arm. Or he liked for people to know he could have them."

At the end of the season, Ted invited Nelva down to Islamorada and, inevitably, they ran into Louise. They were at a restaurant, and Kaufman came right over and sat on Ted's lap—and just stayed there, Nelva be damned: "I got upset because he didn't tell her to leave," Nelva said. "He seemed to be enjoying it."

Travel to road games meant Williams and More couldn't spend much extended time together, but they stayed in close touch by phone. "We'd talk on the phone just about every day," Nelva said. "I might call him or he might call me. Mostly he'd call me." Nelva found conversation easy. Neither wanted to discuss their families or childhoods, because those were unhappy times for them both. Instead they talked about their likes and dislikes and what they wanted to accomplish in the future, not what happened in the past. (Doris was a no-go area. Ted didn't even tell Nelva about the divorce until it was official.) Williams also took her fishing. Once, off Montauk, at the tip of Long Island, Nelva caught a fish and was straining to bring it in. Ted said, "Aw, Nelva, that's just a little snapper. Hell, you're working it like it weighs a ton. It's just a little fish." So she gave him the rod, and he jerked it once, and it turned out there was a mud shark on the line with the other fish. "Teddy was such a perfectionist in what he chose to do. I had all kinds of his fishing gear. He showed me how to do everything. But once he showed you he expected you to have it and pay attention. If you did not, he said, 'Forget it; you're not going to make it if you can't even pay attention.'"

Ted usually insisted they stay in rather than go out to a restaurant, where his presence would cause a scene, but Nelva thought he secretly liked the attention he got at restaurants. "You're not the greatest if you're not getting the attention," she said. "He wanted to be private, but he couldn't be. It came with the territory. He wanted to have his cake and eat it, too."

Nelva would stand up to Ted when she thought he was wrong, and his reactions lacked the volcanic quality other women (and men) had encountered after confronting him. She was at Fenway Park once when he spat at the fans after they got on him. She asked why he did that and told him it was stupid.

"I got tired of them booing me," Williams said. "I thought, 'Who needs them?'"

"You do," Nelva replied.

They had an understanding that they could date other people, but as Nelva understood the deal, it meant that they couldn't be intimate with anyone else. She said Ted couldn't hold to that. When she called him at the Somerset, sometimes she could hear a female voice in the background. "I'd confront him, but he'd just laugh and say, 'Well, do you not go out with anyone while you're in New York?' I said, 'Yes, but not in my apartment.' I couldn't be that stubborn about it. I didn't want to take a chance on losing him."*

---

* In 1954 they went to see a horror movie called *Creature from the Black Lagoon*, starring Richard Carlson and Julie Adams. Ted emerged from the theater a bit too enthused about Adams for Nelva's liking. "What a body!" he said. "How pretty!" Ted promptly asked Fred Corcoran to arrange a meeting with Adams, the sort of request from Williams that Corcoran was accustomed to receiving. Ted and the actress went out, and the news hit

When the Red Sox were on the road, Nelva once told Ted that she supposed he was like a sailor, with a girl in every port. Ted said she could go on the road with him anytime. "He did not say he didn't have a girl in every port," she noted.

Still, such dalliances notwithstanding, Williams was enamored enough with Nelva to keep coming back to her. In January of 1957, he called her in New York before he left Islamorada for Boston and, in his own way, proposed.

"Why don't you meet me in Boston and we'll talk about something more serious?" Ted said.

"Like what?" Nelva wondered.

"How would you like to get married?"

That was the proposal.

At the time, More was sharing an apartment in New York with her stepmother, who had heard Nelva's end of the conversation, concluded that a marriage was imminent, and promptly alerted the New York gossip columns.

The next night, Ted called Nelva and couldn't reach her. He kept calling and calling, assuming the worst, that she was out with another man. Actually, she was at the Brazilian consulate for a party and after that had gone out for breakfast. "He thought I was with someone else. He was very jealous. When he finally reached me, he said, 'Who the hell were you sleeping with last night?'"

She promptly hung up on him. He called back, cursed some more, and again she hung up. If he knew that news of their plans to marry had made the papers, he didn't mention it.

When Ted arrived in Boston, the reporters were waiting at the airport to ask about news of the nuptials. Williams replied that while Nelva was a nice girl, he wasn't going to marry her because he'd "had it" with marriage. He then spelled it out: H-A-D I-T. Wounded by Ted's quote, Nelva struck back when called by a reporter for a response. "I said he wasn't really my type, wore baggy pants, and I didn't like his mannerisms," she said.

They tried to hash things out. Ted finally accepted her explanation about simply going to the party and then breakfast. He said he hadn't meant the "had it" quote to be as harsh as it appeared—he just didn't have her explanation at that point. But when Ted told More she'd have

---

the gossip columns. "Ted Williams is the kind of man that makes you glad you're a woman!" Julie told the *New York Daily News* on July 12, 1954. "I've really only had one date with him, but it was one date I'll never forget if I live to be a million."

to give up her job if they were going to get married, Nelva replied that she wasn't ready to do that.

For Williams, that was enough. "I never saw him again," said Nelva. "I had every desire to go up there and be with him, but I knew it wouldn't work out."

Four years later, on the night before Ted was to be married to another woman, he called Nelva to tell her the news. "I wished him all the luck in the world. He said we had some great times. I felt a little pang. I really cared for him. Some people you just don't get over."[36]

Nancy Barnard met Williams in Sarasota during spring training of 1956. She had just turned twenty-five. She was a Tufts University graduate with a geology degree who had a job in Boston advising investment bankers on where oil might be found. "Famous people were brought into my office," she said. "I had maps all over the wall with pins on them, and people thought I was a curiosity."

Nancy was attractive — five foot five, with blue eyes and dark hair cut in a pageboy. She loved baseball and had had a box seat at Fenway behind the Red Sox dugout since 1953. (In those days, the box seats behind the dugout were metal folding chairs arranged seven seats across to form a row.) One day in Sarasota, Nancy and a guy she knew from Boston who had a seat near hers at Fenway were chatting in their front-row box at Payne Park when Ted wandered over. All business, he didn't say hello. He looked at Nancy.

"You have a roster card?" he asked her.

"Yes," Nancy replied.

"Can I see it?"

"Yes."

Williams took it and wrote the name of his motel, his bungalow number, and "7:30."

As it happened, Nancy was staying at the same motel, in a modest room above the office. But she was taken aback by his bold overture. "I did not follow up," she said. "I don't automatically wander over to men's bungalows." Nevertheless, she saw him around the motel and at the pool. Ted at one end, Nancy at the other. They never spoke. Nothing happened.

The last day Nancy was there she went into a drugstore in town that had a soda fountain. Ted was there having breakfast. He came up and asked her out to dinner. Nancy said she was sorry, but she was flying back to Boston that afternoon. Ted said he'd call her when he returned.

About three weeks later, at a regular-season game in Fenway, an usher behind the dugout came up to Nancy and said, "The Man wants your phone number."

"Oh, yeah?" she replied, in a tone that suggested he was fresh to have asked, but that she would be happy to comply. She gave the usher both her home and work numbers. A few days later Ted called her office. When the switchboard operator put him through, Ted didn't say who he was, but she of course recognized his voice.

He asked what she did, and she told him. They spoke for about a half hour, mostly about what exactly a petroleum geologist did. Ted didn't ask her out exactly, but hinted at it. "See ya at the park," he said. "Over the top of the dugout."

There were more telephone calls, notes back and forth from the clubhouse — where would Nancy be at such and such a time? Innocuous stuff, and unproductive. Several attempts at getting together failed for one reason or another.

Then Nancy had a date in New York with Red Sox pitcher Mel Parnell.

Ted heard about it, because Parnell knew that Ted was attracted to Nancy and wanted to rub it in by telling Ted that he'd had a delightful time with her. She hadn't been back home five minutes when her phone rang. It was Ted, demanding to know why she had gone out with Parnell. "I told him it was none of his business what I did. I had no arrangement with him. I was an independent person and a very independent woman, considering the job I had and the traveling I did. I didn't feel like I had to answer to anybody." Williams made no effort to disguise his anger, telling Barnard that her behavior was unconscionable. "I figured I could go to dinner with a twenty-game winner," said Nancy. "What's wrong with that? It was just one dinner in New York at Mamma Leone's, for cripe's sake. At least he wasn't a Yankee!"

The next obstacle was put in place by Ted when he began seeing one of the singers on Arthur Godfrey's show. She would come up from New York and sit near Nancy at the games, and the two became friends. The woman would say she was going to meet Ted at the Polynesian Village in the Somerset Hotel and ask Nancy to wait with her for him. When Williams showed up, Nancy would leave. "She was obviously crazy about him. I didn't want to hurt her feelings. So I just backed away," said Nancy.

In the meantime Nancy didn't remain idle. She went out with another Red Sox player, catcher Sammy White. Ted of course quickly learned of that and called her to announce, "I don't know what you see in him. He can't hit!"*

That was priceless, Nancy thought. A classic Teddy Ballgame retort. She told him, "You wouldn't understand." For the next several years, this pattern would repeat itself: whenever Ted heard that Nancy was going out with someone, he'd call to berate her.

"I assume I was the burr under his saddle," Nancy concluded. "A couple of years we played this game, that's all. I don't know if Ted ever wanted me. I think he just thought I didn't show him the proper respect. Most girls were falling down dead in front of him. I guess I seemed mysterious to him."

For the rest of his career, Ted would glare at Nancy as he came in from left field on his way to the dugout between innings. She was in the stands for Ted's last home run, then she got married, moved to Michigan, and went on to have three children. She had no contact with him after that until she began writing to him in the mid-to-late '90s, after he became seriously ill. She'd become an avid fisherwoman, and she wrote him about her experiences fishing in Kenya and Alaska, enclosing pictures. An assistant would write back on Ted's behalf, saying he was tickled to hear from her.

"All I knew," she commented wistfully, was that Williams "was someone I was very fond of. If I could give him something to think about besides being sick, I would write. I think I was a disappointment to him. I wasn't that nice to him, and I think he was hurt, and I'm still sorry about it."[37]

Of Williams's three significant romances in the post-Korea period, the one with Isabel Gilmore would turn out to be the most important. Forty-five years after they met, when Ted lay on his deathbed, Isabel would be at his side, a source of love and solace.

They had met during spring training in 1957, one year after Ted had encountered Nancy Barnard. Isabel taught art at a private school in Sarasota. Her true name was Isabella, and friends called her Izzie, but Ted settled on Isabel, with one *l*. She'd been born in Crozet, Virginia, outside Charlottesville, where her father grew apples on a 350-acre orchard. She was five foot four, a brunette with a pleasant Virginia lilt in her voice. She was divorced with two sons, and she later would settle in Alabama, where her southern accent grew more pronounced.

---

* White had hit .245 in 1956, with 5 homers and 44 RBIs.

Gilmore met Ted at a performance of the Sailor Circus, Sarasota's youth circus, also known as the Greatest Little Show on Earth. Isabel was there watching her boys—one was a clown, and the other played in the band. Ted was there with friends and was introduced to Isabel.

"He was very nice and polite, but I didn't think anything further, because I wasn't a model," she remembered. "I was a schoolteacher. And baseball players go for Marilyn Monroe–type looks. I was shocked when he called: the very first thing he did is he showed up at the front door unannounced with a quart of ice cream and said he'd like to talk to me and get to know the family better. It was quite a surprise." She thought it would be impolite not to invite him in, so she did.

Isabel found Ted charming and solicitous of her, not at all the bad boy he was cracked up to be. They'd go for long walks, play checkers and chess, and dine out if Ted could avoid causing a hullabaloo. "I didn't think of him as a celebrity. He was a nice, attentive person who enjoyed my company and the children's."

There were some things about Ted that Isabel and her boys—Grant, then ten, and Marshall, then seven—did find jarring, like his swearing. Isabel would cheerfully say, "Not in our presence, please!" Once, Marshall heard a few choice words upstairs as he was getting ready for bed and yelled down, "Mr. Williams, we don't allow curse words in our house." Ted blushed and said okay.

Isabel was an active Presbyterian, and one Sunday she suggested to Ted that he come to church with her. "He enjoyed it, but I don't know that he agreed with it. He was not really an atheist. I think his vocabulary made people feel that. He'd always say, 'Aw, Jesus Christ!' I believe he used those expressions because a lot of the baseball players do. They're not using it sacrilegiously, but out of habit. I think also because his mother was so overly religious, he was fighting back." Once, Isabel took the boys to Key West, and Ted invited them to visit him in Islamorada on their way back. "He thought that was the most wonderful place in the world. We were talking about how beautiful it was, and he said when he died he wanted to be cremated and have his ashes sprinkled in the sea there."

Isabel could really only see Williams play during spring training, not during the regular season, because she had to be home for the boys. But she loved watching him play and followed him closely when he was away. "I'm very practical and down-to-earth and sincere," Gilmore said, "so I didn't do a lot of oohing and aahing and carrying on. He appreciated that. Everything in our relationship was very refined and on the up-and-up. I wasn't running after anyone."

She liked the way his mind worked. Ted was curious, a reader who could stump her on any history question. (They didn't agree on politics, so they avoided that topic.) She did, however, get him to talk about his childhood a bit and could tell it had been painful. Doris also came up. He'd tell Isabel "how he'd made mistakes and she made mistakes, and they were young. The life he was living was just too much for her. But he never said anything unkind about her. He never said anything unkind about anyone."

Isabel thought Ted respected women "if they demanded it. I demanded it. I expected it. If I didn't get it, the heck with him. I wouldn't care if he was president of the United States. But there are times when one person has to give in to another, and Ted expected a woman to give in to him." Yet he also loathed the fluttering surrender of the sycophant.

As things heated up, they saw each other as often as possible and spoke on the phone two or three times a week. He'd send her gifts, such as flowers and perfume, a plastic statue of himself swinging a bat, and even a painting of himself holding a salmon, which he inscribed: "To Isabel, with all my love, Ted Williams." The boys got boxing gloves, plus bats and balls, even though they weren't serious about baseball and didn't know much about the game. Still, Ted tried to interest both boys in baseball and had them come up to the summer camp that he ran in Lakeville, Massachusetts, south of Boston. Ted made a splashy arrival and took Marshall and Grant off in a limousine, making the other campers jealous, and he gave them other perks, such as arranging for a major-league scout to evaluate them. It was for naught. The boys asked to leave the camp after just a few weeks.

But Williams didn't seem to mind, and he tried to engage them in other ways. He gave the boys their first fishing rods and plenty of tutorials in how to use them. And in the summer of 1958, he took them to the Smithsonian National Air and Space Museum in Washington. Grant was interested in aeronautics and was dazzled by Ted's knowledge of planes. He later did a painting of the Panther jet Ted had flown in Korea and presented it to him.

"Ted always asked me a million questions about everything," Grant explained. "For two reasons—one to find out more information, but the other was to test me, to see what I knew."

Marshall also felt Ted's warmth. "When Ted was connecting with you, you could tell he really liked kids. Yet he was a perfectionist, and he was playing ball. So there was a bit of him that was hard. He was a star and a celebrity, and that gives you an essence that makes it hard to be around. But he could click that off." And years later, when Marshall's own son came down with Hodgkin's lymphoma, Ted would be there for him as well. "My son came down with this cancer out of nowhere. Ted called and talked to him and gave him his words of encouragement. To my son this was a god from baseball calling."[38]

"We were without a father," said Grant. "My mother had divorced when I was two years old. I'll always remember Ted as very honest and straightforward and generous. He represented, to me, striving for perfection and doing well in whatever you do in life."[39] But though Ted genuinely cared about Grant and Marshall, as he got more and more serious about their mother, he couldn't picture them all living together under one roof. He was still a major leaguer, flying hither and yon. If he was going to be with Isabel, he wanted to be able take her on trips and go wherever they pleased. The boys would prevent that. So in 1959, when Williams asked Isabel to marry him, the proposal came with a big condition: that the boys would have to be sent off to boarding school.

"It sort of came out of the blue, because I thought that he would probably marry someone in the spotlight, too," Isabel said. "I can't remember where he did it. He didn't get down on his knees or anything! Just in a conversation."

Isabel thought it was a compliment that Ted proposed, but she explained that she intended to personally raise her boys and was not going to send them to boarding school. Isabel told him she wanted a conventional home with her boys—along with Bobby-Jo. Indeed, she would have said yes, she made clear, if he'd agreed to living with the kids. They were all about the same age, and Bobby-Jo needed a good home, too.

"You're the first person that's ever said no to me," Ted said, not mentioning Nancy Barnard. But maybe he thought she was in a different category. He'd never proposed to Nancy, after all.

"No, I don't believe that," said Isabel.

"Yes, it's true. You are. I can get anybody I want."

Isabel thought Ted, though disappointed, respected her decision. After all, in her commitment to her sons, she had shown precisely the sort of loyalty and devotion that his mother had failed to show him and his brother when they were growing up.

Ted never forgot Isabel, and she never forgot him. "I thought Ted was a terrific person and very, very kind," she said.

15

1954–1956

Not ten minutes into his first day of spring training on March 1, 1954, Williams broke the collarbone on his left shoulder.

He had been shagging flies in left field when Hoot Evers hit a line drive in his direction. Ted jogged in for it, but when the ball started to sink he tried to catch it off his shoe tops with both hands. Losing his balance, he did an awkward quarter-gainer, then tried to rescue himself with a somersault, all to no avail.

"I heard something pop when I fell," he told the writers later.[1] "I knew I had a broken shoulder." Dr. Russell Sullivan, the Boston orthopedist who had driven up to Sarasota from Islamorada with Williams that morning after completing a fishing trip, rushed onto the field to tend to his friend. After X-rays revealed the collarbone break, Sullivan estimated that Williams would be out for two months.

Some of the writers noted that at 215 pounds, Ted was the heaviest he had ever been, and they chided him for not doing enough off-season running to keep his weight down and his legs fit. "At least he was hurt hustling," wrote Harold Kaese of the *Globe,* stretching for a silver lining. Kaese did some further research and found that only in 1949 had Williams been able to play an entire season without missing a game.[2] Various injuries had kept him out of 138 games thus far in his career, and in thirty-five others he had been relegated to pinch-hitting duty because of one ailment or another—more than a season's worth of games in total.

Ted flew to Boston for surgery, and his collarbone was reinforced with a four-inch steel pin. Restless while recuperating, Williams decided to stir the pot by giving a long interview to two New York writers, one of whom—Joe Reichler of the Associated Press—was a favorite of his.

Reichler and his collaborator, Joe Trimble, turned the interview into a three-part series in the *Saturday Evening Post,* for which Ted was reportedly paid $25,000.

In the first installment, Williams made big news by announcing that 1954 would be his final season. "This is my last year in baseball," he began.[3] "Even before I broke my collarbone on my first day of spring training last month, I had made up my mind to quit at the end of this season." He said if it weren't for the Korean War, he probably would have already been out of the game, claiming that he'd told Tom Yawkey he initially intended to have 1953 be his last season. He noted he would be thirty-six years old that October (actually, his birthday was in August). That would make him "an old man" as ballplayers go, and he didn't want to embarrass himself. "I have a lot of pride in my .348 lifetime batting average," Williams said. "The minute I find I can't go at top speed or that baseball is no longer fun, I'll know it's time to quit. That time will come next fall." Then he'd go back to Miami and tend to his fishing-tackle business, he said.

Williams's retirement announcement roiled Boston, but it was greeted with widespread skepticism by fans, teammates, and a press corps that quickly concluded that one of Ted's true motives in the story was to stick it to them yet again by giving his scoop to two out-of-town reporters. Harold Kaese said Williams could easily change his mind if he had a good season and would come under considerable pressure to do so from Yawkey, Cronin, and Fred Corcoran, "who also has to eat."[4] Kaese's *Globe* colleague, beat writer Hy Hurwitz, predicted that Ted would keep playing as long as he could be in the lineup regularly, hit well, and draw a top salary. Hurwitz noted that Williams himself had said as much earlier that year at the sportsmen's show: "When the day comes that I have to sit on the bench, to hell with it, I'll quit." And, predictably, the columnists teed off on him.[5] Bill Cunningham said Williams was still a "sour, mixed up kid," while Dave Egan wrote that "the Red Sox would be well served by Williams if he should make his retirement retroactive."

In fact, while Williams always delighted in antagonizing the Boston writers, that was just a collateral benefit of the story; his main goal in the piece was likely to force his wife's hand in court. Doris and her attorney, Earl Curry, had been taking a hard line in the increasingly contentious divorce proceedings, moving to attach a share of Ted's future baseball earnings. If he retired, there would be no future earnings available, and Doris might be more motivated to negotiate a settlement.

Ted began taking batting practice in late April, about six weeks after his surgery. When he returned to the starting lineup on May 16 in Detroit for a doubleheader against the Tigers, he put on a show. After getting three singles in four times up in the first game, Ted surprised his team-mates by opting to play the second game, too, and he proceeded to go 5–5, with two home runs and a double. That was 8–9 on the day—"the greatest batting show I have ever seen," said Curt Gowdy.[6] "Here's a guy who had had no spring training. I don't think he ever had a better day." The Sox lost both games, 7–6 and 9–8, but few seemed to care.

The team would mail in the rest of the season and finish fourth, forty-two games out of first place. Indeed, in 1954—and throughout the rest of the decade, until the end of Williams's career—the Red Sox would be a case study in mediocrity, never finishing higher than third and never less than twelve games behind the winning team. And the winning team would always be the mighty Yankees, except for 1954 and 1959, when the Indians and White Sox respectively captured the pennant. It was Ted who supplied virtually all the sizzle, the only reason for most fans to come out to the ballpark during those seven sullen seasons.

After his May 16 star turn, Williams supplied more dramatics the following month when the Red Sox traveled to New York for an exhibition game against the National League Giants at the Polo Grounds on June 28. As was customary in such matchups, there was a home-run contest beforehand. Ted and three of his supporting cast would go against Willie Mays, who was just emerging as a superstar, and three other Giants.

Each player would have a chance to hit five fair balls, and the one with the most home runs would be the winner. None of the first three Giants hit more than two, then Mays came up and hit three. The first two Red Sox each hit one home run, and the third hit two. Then Williams strode to the plate, the last to bat, and the air crackled with expectation as he dug in against his favorite batting-practice pitcher, bull pen coach Paul Schreiber, a right-hander. Ted let the first two pitches go by, as was his wont, to size up Schreiber's stuff and to get acclimated. He smashed the next pitch into the lower deck in right field. Ted pulled Schreiber's next offering down the line just inside the foul pole for home run number two. Then came a shot into the upper deck to tie Mays at three. The crowd rose to its feet, and players in both dugouts moved to the top step as the drama built. In came the pitch, and out flew the ball, deeper into the upper deck this time. That was four swings, four home runs. Could he make it five for five? Williams let one pitch go—too low. Then he turned on the next one and crushed a rising line drive high in the sky. The ball struck off the base of the light towers and bounced down into the stands. The fans and players from both sides gave Ted a five-minute standing ovation. "Unbelievable!" said Red Sox rookie pitcher Russ Kemmerer. "I've never seen anything like it and most likely never will."[7]

Kemmerer's shock and awe were typical of the way Williams's teammates viewed him. Most were much younger than he, the product of a youth movement begun by manager Lou Boudreau in 1952, when Ted went off to Korea, and now they were getting their first extended time with the Great Man. For his part, Williams, in his first full season back since the war, was still adapting to all the new faces. He missed his old pals Bobby Doerr, Johnny Pesky, and Dom DiMaggio. (Doerr had retired after the 1951 season, Pesky had been traded to the Tigers in June of 1952, shortly after Ted went back into the service, and DiMaggio had retired suddenly in 1953.) Instead, there were players like Milt Bolling, who took over the starting shortstop job in 1953 at age twenty-two and stayed with the Red Sox until he was traded in 1957; Billy Consolo, the California bonus baby who came directly to the team in 1953 from high school, at the age of eighteen, and would remain the team's utility infielder until 1959, when he was traded to Washington; Ted Lepcio, the starting second baseman in 1954 who had debuted in 1952 at age twenty-two; and the talented and voluble Jimmy Piersall, who had become the starting right fielder in 1953 at twenty-three and would move over to center, adjacent to Ted, by 1955.

Of course Williams gave his young teammates hitting tips. He would always counsel against swinging at the first pitch. Better to let the pitcher show you as much as he was willing to. And look for the fastball, then adjust if you get the curve, Ted would say. The players noticed that Williams was so quick he could do the reverse: look for the curve but catch up to a fastball if it came. "I stayed in baseball for forty-three years," said Bolling.[8] "I saw a lot of players, and he made it seem like the rest of us were Little Leaguers and he was the only major leaguer."

Consolo was closely attuned to the clubhouse dynamics surrounding Williams. The players all had a single wire-cage locker, but Ted had a double-width steel locker in addition to his chain-link unit. The players were each issued two white home uniforms and two gray uniforms for the road. One day while Consolo was idling in front of his locker, he noticed an Italian tailor come in and start tending to Ted. He was tailoring the Kid's uniforms. None of the rest of the players had fitted uniforms. Then there was the matter of leaving Fenway. After the game Ted would go to his car and try to drive out of the parking lot. Inevitably, there would be a sea of people, and it would take him a minute to move barely a foot, so Williams got in the habit of leaving the ballpark early if the game was decided, or if there was basically no chance he'd get up again. Consolo might often be called to pinch-run for him, then Gene Stephens would go in and play left field.

When he played, Consolo would usually bat leadoff. "When I played and I got out, Ted would be waiting for me. He was going to ask me what pitch I got out on. I was only nineteen and I didn't know what it was. I was just happy when I hit the ball." Consolo soon learned another Williams idiosyncrasy after he got on base and Ted hit a home run. "I'm standing at home plate all excited like it was a high school game. I put out my hand and he went right on by me. I didn't know what to do so I ran back to the dugout. I went to one of the trainers and told him what happened. He said, 'No, the Kid don't shake.' I learned my lesson."[9]

Williams was the team's de facto hitting coach years before there was any such official position. He would critique a teammate's swing or a time at bat, try and help someone out of a slump, share information about enemy pitchers, and expect his fellow hitters to give him any morsel they could in return. "I learned to listen to Ted because I might pick up some things that could help me out," remembered Frank Malzone, the longtime Red Sox third baseman who came up in 1955 and was a starter from 1957 to 1965. "Like being patient at the plate, not being too anxious, or swinging at the first ball you see. When I would swing at the first pitch from a relief pitcher, Ted would say, 'You dumb dago, how do you know what he's throwing?' I was an aggressive hitter, and I couldn't wait all of the time. He hated that."[10]

Williams would be brutally frank in his assessment of a hitter's performance. Lepcio, a Red Sox infielder from 1952 to 1959, would be ready for Ted's comments when he returned to the dugout after making an out. "I used to tell him the truth," Lepcio said. "If [I'd been] shitty, I'd tell him. And most of the time he'd agree: 'You're right, it was a real horseshit swing,' he'd say."[11]

If Ted was on deck, there wasn't always time for a full debriefing if the hitter ahead of him had made an out. But he still expected that the hitter, on his way back to the dugout, would give him some sense of what the pitcher was throwing. If Williams then failed at the plate, he sometimes would blame his teammate for inadequate reporting. Once, in 1957, Indians reliever Don Mossi had just struck out Billy Klaus, then the Red Sox starting shortstop. "As I was heading back to the dugout, I told Ted, 'I don't have shit today, he's throwing good and hard,'" Klaus recalled. "Ted had a serious look on his face as I went into the dugout.

Mossi struck out Ted, too, and he was furious when he came back into the dugout. He said to me, 'Billy, you little shit, you didn't tell me he was throwing that hard.' "[12]

When Ted's pupils weren't receiving his tips, they would watch him carefully when he came to the plate, both during batting practice and in games. During one game, Consolo and Lepcio were sitting on the bench next to Mickey Vernon, the longtime Washington Senators first baseman who had come to Boston in 1956 and 1957. They watched as Ted hit a line drive so hard it nearly beheaded the opposing first baseman. When Consolo and Lepcio wondered how it was possible for anyone to hit a ball that hard, Vernon piped up: "Listen, when this guy first came up he used to hit three shots a day like that. I remember when I played first base against him, I used to ask the manager not to let me hold the runners on first because that s.o.b. hit them down there so fast you didn't have a chance."[13]

Since he was Ted Williams, Ted expected due deference from his teammates, and when he didn't get it, he might throw a snit. In batting practice before the game, for example, each player was supposed to get two bunts and eight swings, but Ted considered the eight-swings rule elastic. If the Kid wanted nine, ten—or as many swings as he wanted, really—what teammate would dare challenge him?

One day Don Buddin did. At the start of his rookie year in 1956, when he became the starting shortstop at the age of twenty-one, Buddin was waiting to hit after Williams. "Ted did his two bunts and eight swings, then went for a ninth swing," said Buddin, who would be tagged with the nickname Bootin because of his penchant for making errors. "I stepped in the cage and said, 'What are you doing? Eight swings and out!' He laughed and said, 'Fuck you, you cocky little son of a bitch.' I didn't know any better. But he was a team man. Everybody admired him, and everyone liked him. He always gave a hundred percent and never criticized his teammates. Having my locker next to him was one of the biggest thrills of my life."[14]

Other teammates seemed struck as much by Williams's panache and presence as by his talent. Pete Daley, a substitute catcher from 1955 to 1959, remembered a scene early in the 1955 season. "A sportswriter came in, and Ted was sitting on a training table. The writer said, sarcastically, 'Well, what do you think you'll hit this year?' He said, 'If I don't hit over .350, I'll kiss your ass.' [He would hit .356.] I don't think there was anybody in the clubhouse. He was always quick with that tongue. He had to be one step ahead of them."[15]

One player who had grown up idolizing Williams but who came to have a somewhat contentious relationship with him as a teammate was Jimmy Piersall. Piersall was the starting right fielder in 1953 and 1954 and the center fielder from 1955 to 1958. A better-than-average hitter (.272 over seventeen major-league seasons), Piersall was brilliant defensively. He played a shallow center field, often made seemingly impossible catches, and had a rifle arm. But Piersall, who suffered from bipolar disorder, was best known for the nervous breakdown he had in 1952, when, following a series of meltdowns on and off the field, he was institutionalized and given shock therapy. When he returned to baseball in 1953 — a time when mental illness and the issues surrounding it were largely ignored — Piersall faced merciless taunts from rival fans and players who would call him cuckoo, gooney-bird, and worse. Courageously, he wrote a book about his experience in 1955, *Fear Strikes Out,* which later became a movie.

Piersall noted that Williams took a lot of abuse from the fans, too — for different reasons. "They were tough on him, but you know why? They sort of sensed that when they got on him, he played better," Piersall told one interviewer. "He hit better. Ted used to say to me when I got mad about something, 'I'll take care of it kid. Don't worry.' He used to talk through his teeth when he got mad. I said, 'Ted, why are you getting so mad all the time?' And he said, 'You know why? Because I've got to be good every day. You don't have to be.'"[16]

After his breakdown, Piersall sometimes played to type, seeming to delight in pulling zany stunts. He was traded to Cleveland after the 1958 season, and on a visit to Yankee Stadium with the Indians he hid behind the monuments in center field. In 1960, on a return trip to Fenway Park, Piersall began jumping around in center, trying to distract Ted when he came to the plate. Williams, who couldn't abide any distraction while hitting, asked home plate umpire Ed Hurley to "put the chains on him." Hurley walked toward center and gestured at Jimmy to stop, but Piersall merely began imitating Hurley's gestures, prompting the ump to toss him. Piersall had a fit and had to be escorted off the field by his teammates.[17] In 1963, after hitting his hundredth home run while playing for the New York Mets, Piersall ran around the bases backwards. "Probably the best thing that ever happened to me was going nuts," he once said. "Who ever heard of Jimmy Piersall until that happened?"

Piersall's antics made him Ted's rival for fan and press attention, which was probably one source of the tension between the two men. Ted didn't like any teammate to challenge him in those departments. Piersall, who liked to flaunt his defensive prowess, also openly bossed Williams around in the field, whistling over to him and positioning him to the right or left, deeper or more shallow. Sometimes Ted would ignore the instructions and tell Jimmy to fuck off, but over time, he came to appreciate Piersall's skills in the field and deferred to him, letting Jimmy roam as far as he pleased into left-center for fly balls.

Toward the end of the 1954 season, with the Red Sox floundering well back in the pack, the team decided it would fire Lou Boudreau over the winter and hire a new manager for 1955. Joe Cronin approached Ted and asked if he would be interested in the job.[18] Hell, no, Williams replied. He had declared in the *Saturday Evening Post* in April that this was to be his last year, and as the games wound down he was sticking to that line publicly. But he told Cronin if he did come back it would be as a player, not a manager. He could still hit, after all.

Cronin persisted, arguing that Ted had the respect of the other players and would make a fine manager. Ted said he didn't know any of the subtleties, like when to replace a player. He didn't even know how to make out a lineup card. Cronin assured him he'd get him all the help he needed. Later, Tom Yawkey made the same pitch, but Ted turned him down, too, saying he knew it would be a disaster. He'd get into one kerfuffle after another with the writers, and before long he'd be fired.

As the season wore on, there were more and more stories in the papers speculating on whether Ted would really retire as he had claimed he would. Harold Kaese reported that fans were mounting petition drives urging Ted to come back.[19] The *Boston Post* took this a step further by printing a blank coupon daily, headlined PLAY NEXT YEAR, TED!,[20] in which fans would write down in ten words or less why they thought Ted should return, and mail it back to the paper. The Boston Chamber of Commerce backed the *Post*'s campaign with a ten-word submission, saying Ted should keep going because "the youth of Greater Boston need him as an inspiration."

One ardent Williams fan who was reading accounts of Ted's imminent retirement with alarm was Ed Mifflin, a thirty-one-year-old sales manager for an upholstery firm in Swarthmore, Pennsylvania. Mifflin, a forerunner of the statistical geeks now ubiquitous in modern baseball, chanced to run into Williams in mid-September in the rotunda of Baltimore's train station. The Red Sox had just finished a series with the Orioles, and Williams was reading a newspaper, waiting for a train to take him to Washington for a game against the Senators.

Mifflin spotted him and walked right up. "Excuse me, Ted," he said. "But I've been bothered by all that talk about your quitting baseball. You were kidding, weren't you?"

Ted looked up and saw a short, stocky man holding a bulging briefcase. "Why should I kid about a thing like that?" he said, then went back to reading his paper.

But Mifflin was on a mission. "Look here, Ted," he said. "You're crazy if you think you're going to quit baseball now. You're not! You can't!"

"What do you mean I can't?" Ted snapped. "That's *my* business."

"It's a lot more than your business. You're not just an independent operator. You're public domain. You owe it to baseball, if not to yourself, to reach certain milestones before you quit." Mifflin proceeded to lecture Williams as if he were a baseball naïf and began citing specifics of his career totals in various key hitting categories.

"Do you know how close you are to having 2,000 hits, 400 homers, 1,500 runs batted in, and 1,500 runs scored? None of the really great players stopped when they had any of those goals in sight. Do you realize you have 1,400 RBIs, and only twelve men in history have gone over 1,500? In my book, you're one of the finest hitters the game has ever known. But if you quit now, the record books will never show how great you were. Did you ever stop to consider how you're going to stack up in baseball history if you call it a day without trying for four thousand total bases? Joe DiMaggio didn't make it. But you can."

"Well, now, listen here—" Ted began to sputter.

"What do you actually know about your lifetime records, Ted?"

Williams said he knew how many home runs he had and what his average had been each year.

"Just as I thought," Mifflin said. "You really have no idea where you stand. Why, there are sixteen offensive departments in which you're approaching milestones—and all you've kept track of are your home runs. Do you know how many hits you've racked up?"

"No."

"You've got 1,930 in all, including yesterday. It won't take much to reach two thousand. And in home runs, you're not even among the first ten in lifetime totals. But if you stick around . . ."

Mifflin, who was also a Republican Party leader in his hometown of Swarthmore, had Ted's attention now. "Who are you, anyway?" he asked. Just then Ted's train arrived. Mifflin only had time to reply that he was "a helluva fan of yours" before Williams had to board. But Ted had been intrigued by this stranger's pitch.

"Get in touch with me!" Williams yelled as the train pulled away.

Not long afterward, the two met again over dinner in New York, and Mifflin laid out in more detail a series of realistic hitting goals that Ted could attain. "Before our meal was over, Ed Mifflin had given me a reason for playing baseball," Ted told Leslie Lieber in 1958 for an article in *This Week* magazine, the now-defunct Sunday newspaper supplement, that disclosed the Mifflin intervention. "By showing me how close I was to bettering my lifetime records, Mifflin had set up goals that made sense to me. He had given me a baseball blueprint for my whole remaining career."

By the time the Lieber story appeared, Mifflin had surfaced as the statistician behind a 1957 *Look* magazine spread entitled "The Case for Ted Williams," which said Ted had a higher percentage of game-winning home runs than Ruth and ranked second only to the Babe as a slugger and hitter for average.

During the six more years that Williams played, Mifflin would send him scores of telegrams and postcards alerting him to various "approaching milestones." He took special care to point out whenever Ted had passed one of DiMaggio's records. In September of 1956, for example, Williams learned he had passed the Clipper's RBI total and, later, that he had bettered Joe's total-bases mark.[21] But Ted would disclose nothing of his dealings with Mifflin for four years, so as the final game of the 1954 season approached, on September 26, he was giving no public indication that this would not be his final appearance at Fenway Park.

There were only 14,175 people in attendance for the game against the Senators. The first prolonged ovation the fans gave Ted came when he stepped to the plate in the seventh for what figured to be his last at bat, with the Sox leading 4–2. Washington pitcher Gus Keriazakos refused to take the mound until the applause died down. Ted then swatted a home run into the right-field stands. He trotted around the bases with his eyes fixed to the ground and without tipping his cap, of course. When the Red Sox blew the game open on the way to an 11–2 win, Ted got up again in the eighth and made an out. Boudreau pulled him from left field with two outs in the ninth to give him a curtain call.

Williams had finished his injury-shortened season with a .345 average, 29 home runs, and 89 RBIs in 117 games. For the eighth time, he led the league in walks with 136, a number that prevented him from getting the requisite four hundred official at bats to qualify for the batting title.* In the clubhouse, Williams insisted he'd just played his last game. "I've decided that this is the end," he said.[22] "You think I'm kidding, but I'm not." He would have his fishing business and plenty of other projects to keep busy, he said. Then Williams shook hands with all the writers, smiled, and declared, "There was only one guy among you I really hated"—presumably Dave Egan. Tom Yawkey, Joe Cronin, and Lou Boudreau all said they hoped Ted would change his mind and return to play next year.

Ted went off to Maine to fish, a tune-up for his trip to Peru in December, when he was to fish for marlin in the waters of Cabo Blanco, then considered one of the most prolific big-game fisheries in the world. Cabo Blanco was five miles off the coast, where the cold-water Humboldt Current merged with the warm-water Equatorial Current in a stretch known as Black Marlin Boulevard.

Williams would fish for six days. On the first day, he hooked a big marlin, but it got away. ("I never felt so low in my life," he said later.) On the sixth day, though, December 10, Ted caught a bigger one. For thirty minutes he dueled with the fish, strapped to a chair with a harness and wearing gloves, while several Inca guides looked on. The marlin jumped some thirty feet in the air several times in an effort to escape as Ted furiously reeled it in. When the fish was finally gaffed and hauled alongside the boat, Williams popped his harness and danced for joy. It was a fourteen-foot, 1,235-pound behemoth, then the eighth-largest black marlin ever caught in the world. "I always thought that 1941 All Star homer was my biggest single sports thrill," Ted said, "until I caught that marlin."[23]

The catch was documented, it later emerged, by a film crew doing a public service announcement for the General Electric housewares division. The 16mm color film was acquired by the International Game Fish Association and later digitized and released as a fifty-four-minute DVD in 2005. "This is the story of the biggest fish I ever caught," the Kid said in the introduction, proudly.[24]

As 1955 began, Williams had decided—if there was ever any doubt— that he was, in fact, returning to baseball, despite his statements to the

---

* Toward the end of the season, Boudreau began hitting Ted second in the order to get him more at bats, but he still fell fourteen short with 386, and Cleveland's Bobby Avila won the batting title with a .341 average. Casey Stengel, always a Ted booster, spoke out against the four-hundred-at-bats rule, saying it was "never meant for a guy like Williams. It's for Humpty Dumpties trying to steal a batting championship on half a season's work."

contrary the previous season. The problem was that he couldn't announce his intentions because he was still locked in negotiations with Doris and her lawyer over how large her divorce settlement would be. Once spring training began and opening day approached, Doris hoped that Ted would get antsy, report for duty, and sign a new contract, which she could then take a healthy percentage of. But Williams was determined not to let that happen: either he would reach an agreement with Doris before he signed his new contract or he would sit out the entire year, if necessary.

Doris's lawyer, Earl Curry, took to the press to try to pressure Williams. "Ted shows no eagerness to reach a settlement," Curry told Austen Lake of the *American* in early April. "He's in no hurry. So we'll wait too, at least until after the baseball season starts. Then we'll consider the next move.... He's the sort who will chop off two inches of his own nose to cut off an inch of ours." Curry added that in the couple's last two negotiating sessions, Williams had stated emphatically that he did not intend to play baseball again. Furthermore, his attitude during the conferences was one of "total indifference. He sat slumped on the end of his spine and just snorted. He is completely uncooperative.... We hope that when the ball season opens, he'll have a change of mind."

Ted's lawyers—Daisy Bisz of Miami and Cornelius Hurley of the white-shoe Boston firm Hale and Dorr—were under strict instructions from their client to say nothing to reporters. Bisz was among the first women to practice law in Florida and would be a friend to Williams for fifty years. (She was also the attorney Ted had recommended to Louise Kaufman several years earlier.)

Hurley, a Holy Cross graduate and prominent Catholic in Boston, received criticism from some of the Jesuits at his alma mater and from others in the Archdiocese of Boston for taking on such a prominent divorce case. But he brushed off the carping and defended his faith during long, animated discussions with Williams, who was skeptical of any religion. During lulls in the divorce case, and later in life, Ted would pepper Hurley with questions about what it was like to be Catholic, why he believed what he did, and what it was like to have gone to Holy Cross and later to Georgetown for law school. "My dad thought Ted was the most intelligent person he'd ever met," said Hurley's son, Cornelius Hurley Jr.[25] "Not from reading books or getting a formal education. But because of the penetrating questions he asked of people." (Hurley would end up an equity partner in Ted's fishing business, and the two would later make an unsuccessful investment together in a magnetized pin-setting mechanism for bowling.)

In the end it was Doris who blinked first. On May 9, Miami circuit court judge George E. Holt granted the couple a divorce and two days later announced the financial terms: Ted would pay Doris $50,000 within two years and $125 per week until the lump sum was paid; she would receive the couple's $42,000 home in South Miami and the Cadillac; Ted would pay $12,000 in court costs and $100 per month in child support for Bobby-Jo.

According to the *Miami Herald,* the Red Sox agreed to pay the $50,000 to Doris as an added inducement to lure Williams back, but Joe Cronin denied this. In any case, the terms were widely seen as a strategic victory for Ted, an assessment Judge Holt himself seemed to encourage when he remarked of his ruling: "That ought to get him back in baseball." And it did—immediately after the judge announced the financial specifics, Ted called Joe Cronin and said he would join the team in two days. He told reporters from Islamorada, where he was fishing with Bobby-Jo, that "altered circumstances have cleared the way for my return."[26]

The Red Sox, who had lost sixteen of their last nineteen games, were thrilled at the prospect of Williams's return—both for the offensive punch he would bring to the lineup and for his impact at the gate. Attendance was off seventy thousand so far that year. Harold Kaese guessed that Ted would boost the team two rungs higher in the standings and about $200,000 higher in ticket revenue.[27]

Around the American League, reaction to the Williams news was just as enthusiastic. "It's the best possible thing that could have happened to our league," said Yankees manager Casey Stengel.[28] White Sox general manager Frank Lane went further, saying he would have been willing to pay part of Williams's salary, since his presence at a Red Sox series at Comiskey Park would mean five thousand more fans per game.[29]

Ted arrived in Boston and met with Joe Cronin to sign what was widely reported to have been an $80,000 prorated contract for the balance of the 1955 season. In fact, the contract was for $60,000, according to official Major League Baseball records.[30] But Williams wrote in his book that he signed for $98,000 that year. The discrepancy resulted from the fact that, starting in 1955 and continuing into his retirement, Williams would opt to defer a portion of his salary in order to conceal income from Doris.

"I was going into a divorce proceeding with my wife, and since the alimony was going to be determined by my income, it just seemed like common sense to limit my income as much as possible," Williams admitted to a friend years later.[31] Ted may have been the first professional athlete to sign a deferred payment contract; Hale and Dorr worked out details with the Red Sox after consulting the Internal Revenue Service, which approved the plan as long as Ted agreed to provide certain unspecified services to the team after he retired.

His contract signed, Williams took the field and in short order swatted three home runs in batting practice—the first time he'd hit in more than seven months. His clubhouse confidant, Johnny Orlando, crowed to the writers that he'd known all along that Ted would be back, then casually predicted Williams would play in one hundred games and hit .350. New manager Mike Higgins, the former Red Sox third baseman who had been promoted after a successful run at Boston's top farm team in Louisville, knew enough not to rock the boat, saying Williams would set his own timetable on returning to the lineup.

Ten days later, Ted made his debut in an exhibition game against the New York Giants at Fenway, and he belted a home run into the bleachers. His first official start came on May 28 at home against the Senators, and he singled to center off Camilo Pascual in his first at bat. With that—the Red Sox twelve games out—Williams settled into another regular-season grind.

One pleasant respite came on July 28, when Bobby-Jo Williams, then seven, came to Fenway Park to watch her father play for the first time. She sat in Jean Yawkey's box with John Buckley, his wife, Vivian, and Mrs. Yawkey herself. Buckley was the local movie-theater manager who had been a Williams chum for years. He and his wife would play an increasingly important role as surrogate parents for Bobby-Jo when she visited Ted in Boston after the divorce. Ted couldn't muster any heroics for his daughter, managing only a single in the eighth inning, after which he was lifted for a pinch runner.[32]

Bobby-Jo said her parents' divorce had little impact on her other than causing friends in school to make fun of her. After the split, Ted and Doris got along much better than they had before, making an effort for her benefit. Bobby-Jo would see as much of Ted as she ever had, perhaps more. She'd visit him on weekends, during school vacations, and for the entire summer in Boston, except for three weeks at the end, when she'd go to Albany, New York, to see her grandmother—Doris's mother, Ruby Soule.

Being with her father was always unpredictable. He loved her, she thought, but she never knew how he was going to treat her. "I was like a dog," she recalled. "You know, if a dog doesn't know if you're gonna screech at it or if you're gonna come over and give it a good ol' scratchin' and make it happy—I was just kind of, 'Whoa, where we gonna go this time?' He was a perfectionist, and he wanted me to be that way, too. Only that's not how I was geared. Like he wanted me to play tennis, but I wanted to swim. The better I got in swimming the more he bitched about it: 'Aw, shit, you oughta be playin' tennis.' You know, that's the way it was. I was good at art. 'Yeah, but what the hell do you know about math?'"

Sometimes, they would drive up to Boston from Florida together, and Bobby-Jo would dread those trips. "It was like two and a half, three days of school in that car. And he'd pack the same stuff that we used to pack to go fishing. It was very strange. Two pieces of bread with peanut butter on it, no jelly, no butter, and we'd have a little-bitty old Thermos of water—we'd share it—and an apple. He'd pack three or four sandwiches each, twelve apples, and we'd go. Boom." They'd pull over at a motel for the night, but Ted would insist on getting up at four in the morning and hitting the road again. He would have her read whatever she was reading in school to him, then quiz her on it. Nancy Drew was her favorite, and Ted seemed to like those stories, too.

In Boston, her base was the Somerset Hotel: Williams had a twin bed brought into his suite, and Bobby-Jo moved right in. "As I grew older I realized that was really a lot for him to do. He was a good dad." She recognized that she was putting a crimp in his social life, so after a while she would get farmed out to stay with the Buckleys for two or three days at a time, and they would bring her to Fenway for the games. Bobby-Jo preferred to sit down near the field, but Ted thought she could get clipped by a line drive, so he always arranged for her and the Buckleys to sit upstairs in the Yawkey box or in one of the other front-office boxes. Bobby-Jo had the run of the place, running out to chase foul balls or going to get a hot dog or a Coke. Thirty-nine years later, when Ted opened his hitters museum in Florida, he would invite some of those concessionaires, and they greeted Bobby-Jo as though she were a celebrity. "I watched you when you were a little girl," they'd say. "I watched you grow up." And then they asked for her autograph.

During the games, Ted would keep an eye on his daughter, both from the field and from the dugout, and flash signals to her. When he pulled his cap down low over his eyes, that meant she was being too rambunctious and had to sit down. "I liked the games," she said. "I still try and figure out if I would have if I hadn't been thrown into this situation—born into this situation. But I loved ball."

Growing up in Florida, though, she loved fishing more. Ted took her to the Everglades when she was two, and she grew to be so skilled that her father was delighted. But fishing with Ted was intense—especially going for tarpon or bonefish, where he would stand and pole the boat and insist on absolute silence. If she made one false move, he could go off. But she proved herself: on her ninth birthday, Bobby-Jo caught a nine-pound bonefish. Ted took a picture of her holding the fish, had it framed, and hung it on the wall.

The next year, when Ted asked her what she wanted for her tenth birthday, Bobby-Jo asked him to take her fishing for snapper. They'd go farther out in a bigger boat, and he'd be much more relaxed and much less guarded than he was going for bonefish or tarpon. When they'd snagged enough fish, Ted and Bobby-Jo would pull up to an island, build a fire, and fry up their catch, along with some hush puppies. "We did this every year after that—just he and I," she recalled. "It was really good. That's what I loved. I loved it."

The Red Sox won forty-four of sixty games after Ted returned, and in early September were only three games out of first place, part of a four-team race. But the pitching collapsed, and the team finished fourth at 84–70, twelve games behind the Yankees.

As for Ted's numbers, Johnny Orlando's prediction was just about right. He played in 98 games, not 100, and hit .356, not .350, along with 28 home runs and 83 RBIs. Ted's .356 average was the highest in the American League, but because of another shortened season, he was well short of the necessary 400 official at bats—he had just 320, with 91 walks—so Al Kaline of the Tigers won the championship at .340.

But Williams could have no beef. After all, he had missed almost all of the first two months of the season—not because of injury but because of a conscious decision to protect his finances—and in so doing, he put his own interests ahead of those of his team.

Perhaps only Ted could have gotten away with this. Neither Yawkey nor management ever complained. Neither did his teammates. The writers gave him a pass, too—even Dave Egan concluded that Williams had played the best baseball of his career in 1955, not because of his hitting but because of his fielding, hustling baserunning, and his presence: "He was a team player and a mighty inspirational force for the first time in his long career," the Colonel wrote. The team succeeded as long as he did, and swooned after Labor Day only because Ted tired in September. So Egan suggested he should skip spring training altogether, because he'd proven he didn't need it, and pace himself for the long haul.

But Williams did not skip spring training in 1956—he reported, upbeat and frisky, anxious to get in shape and lay the foundation for a healthy and complete year that would contrast with his previous two abbreviated seasons. Ted actually enjoyed the Sarasota ritual as long as he was allowed to set his own pace and not play every exhibition game. That was fine with Mike Higgins, whose laissez-faire style fit well with his star's wishes and whims.

Yet the year would not go as Williams hoped. A freak injury in late spring would significantly cut into his playing time. The Yankees' Mickey Mantle burst into superstar status by making a concerted run at Babe Ruth's single-season home-run record on the way to a Triple Crown year, a year that far eclipsed Ted's. And Williams's combustible personality would trigger a spate of humiliating pop-offs and meltdowns that generated far more attention than his performance on the field.

Ted's warm-up in the controversy department came in mid-March. He was asked by a group of visiting San Francisco writers to comment on the case of Johnny Podres, who after pitching the Brooklyn Dodgers to two wins in the 1955 World Series had seen his draft status reclassified from 4F to 1A. The case reminded Ted of his own adventures with the Selective Service System in World War II and Korea, so he ripped politicians, draft boards, and the writers for exploiting Podres's sudden fame. "Podres is paying the penalty for being a star," he said. The Boston writers struck back with critical commentary, annoyed at being tarred by Ted's broad brush and perhaps even more peeved that he had again seen fit to use out-of-town reporters to deliver his blast.

In April, Ted slipped off one of the clogs he wore in the shower and hurt the arch in his foot, an inglorious injury that sidelined him for five weeks. "As the 1950's wore on, I was just plain wearing out," he said later.[33] "I kept hitting, but I suffered one damn injury after another."

He didn't return until May 29, and then he started slowly. Mantle, meanwhile, was on fire, and by mid-June he had hit his twenty-fifth home run. Clif Keane of the *Globe* suggested that the torch had been passed. "When the ballplayers start to talk about another player like the Sox were talking about Mantle tonight, you know he's great. They're talking about him the way they used to talk about Williams years ago."[34]

Ted started to hit, but erratically, and he began to hear a smattering of boos, which he always blamed the writers for, feeling that his critics in the stands were unduly influenced by what they read in the papers. But the boos turned to cheers on July 17 at Fenway, when Williams hit the four hundredth home run of his career in a game against Kansas City. As he crossed home plate, Williams snapped his head suddenly toward the press box and pursed his lips as if he were preparing to spit. The on-deck hitter, Mickey Vernon, approached and extended his hand to congratulate his teammate on the milestone.

"Now, Ted didn't go for shaking hands after a big play," Vernon remembered.[35] "If you stuck out your hand he would just slap it. But when he hit his four hundredth I figured I would shake his hand. It was appropriate. So I stick out my hand as he crosses the plate and he leans over and just spits on the ground, like he was disgusted."

Williams was lucky the story ended as it did. According to the Kansas City players, before he crossed home plate and cocked his head at the press box, Williams had spit at the fans in the left-field grandstand as he approached third base, but this was overlooked in the papers.[36] As is, the Associated Press captured Ted craning his neck toward the press box, poised to spit, in a marvelous photograph that ran on the front page of the *Boston Herald* the next day, but the writers were slow to pick up on the story. Only the *Traveler*'s George Sullivan, the former batboy turned sports reporter, asked Williams about it in the clubhouse. Ted angrily said he had intended to spit at "you bastards" but stopped short because he was afraid he'd hit Vernon, the on-deck batter. The other writers heard a commotion and asked Sullivan what the Kid had said, and he told them.

Three nights later, Williams continued his waterworks and other antics, spoiling a night in which general manager Joe Cronin was honored in advance of his induction into the Hall of Fame the following week. Ted participated in the pregame ceremonies honoring Cronin, then retreated into his own inner world of festering sores. The show started at the end of the top of the seventh, when Williams, after initially misjudging a line drive hit toward him in left field, backpedaled and made a nice leaping catch. Running in toward the dugout, he flung the ball high in the air toward second base, then as he came into the infield, he tossed his glove skyward to the Red Sox batboy. With the boobirds now in full voice, Ted, who happened to be leading off the inning, grabbed his bat and appeared ready to spit at the press box again, but the wind was blowing in his face, so he turned and spat downwind, toward the right-field stands.

Baseball commissioner Ford Frick, who had come to the game to honor Cronin, watched the entire spectacle, but quickly ducked out to avoid commenting to reporters and took a cab to the airport to return to New York. As for Cronin, he was furious that the man he had nurtured since he was a brash rookie had marred an evening held in his honor. (Cronin hadn't actually seen any of the spitting. He'd been entertaining friends and family in his box. It was George Sullivan who came in and told him, looking for a comment.)

In the clubhouse after the game, Williams ranted and raved incoherently, vowing to continue to spit to show his contempt for Boston writers and those fans who booed him unjustly. "I'm going to continue to give it to those characters," he said. "Nobody's going to make me stop spitting. The newspaper guys in this town are bush. And some of those fans are the worst in the world. What do they want from a guy? I've hit over .340 for 17 years in this league, and every time I walk up there, they give me the business. What do they expect me to do, smile at them?"[37]

The writers, in deference to Cronin, largely held their fire, but Ted was not done with his spitting jag yet. He was saving his most outrageous display for a few weeks later.

On August 7, the Red Sox played an afternoon game against the Yankees that drew a post–World War II record crowd of 36,350. Boston was in third place, eight and a half games behind New York, and showing few signs they could mount any sort of meaningful run. But the Yankees always drew a large crowd, and Mantle was having his Triple Crown season, which would ultimately include a prodigious fifty-two home runs.

Despite Mantle's presence, the game was a gripping pitchers' duel between the Yankees' Don Larsen and Willard Nixon of the Sox. After ten innings, the score was 0–0. With two outs in the top of the eleventh, Mantle lifted a routine fly ball to short left field. Williams ran in to catch it, but the ball popped out of his glove, and Mantle reached second. The crowd let Ted have it. Then Yogi Berra hit a drive to left-center, which off the bat looked like it would at least be off the wall, but the wind was blowing in and knocked the ball down enough to allow Ted to reach up and spear it at the scoreboard. It was a nice catch in a key situation, and the boos moments earlier now turned to ringing cheers. But Williams hated this fickle fan behavior—front-running, he called it—and he seethed as he trotted in for the bottom of the eleventh.

After crossing the first-base line, Williams spat contemptuously at the fans behind the dugout. Just before entering the dugout, he turned his head toward the press box and let fly with another glob. While he was in the dugout and the crowd howled, Ted picked up his glove and waved it toward the Yankee bench and the area between home and third, then he hopped out of the dugout and spat a third time in that direction. "Oh, no, this is a bad scene!" said Red Sox announcer Curt Gowdy on the radio.[38]

For all the furor, the Red Sox still had to hit. Pitcher Nixon led off and reached on an error. Billy Goodman laid down a bunt toward first. Moose Skowron fielded it, but his throw to second sailed wide, and the runners were safe. Billy Klaus worked a walk to load the bases for... none other. As Williams strode to the plate, the crowd was in a fully lathered frenzy, with boos dominating the cheers. Those booing seemed to want to provoke Ted into another outburst.

Casey Stengel lifted Don Larsen and brought in left-hander Tommy Byrne to face Ted. Figuring Williams would be overeager to paste one, Byrne pitched around him and got behind in the count. But Ted, disciplined as ever, refused to offer. Byrne kept nibbling, then lost him—ball four. The winning run was forced in.

It was such an anticlimax. Ted had lusted to hit and cared not a bit that the Red Sox had won the game. Frustrated, he took a few steps toward first base and flipped his bat fifty feet high in disgust.[39]

Done for the day, Williams continued to vent out of sight. On the way to the clubhouse, he attacked a watercooler and ripped it off the wall, causing a flood in the tunnel leading from the dugout to the locker room. The deluge meant that the players had to go through the stands to get to the clubhouse, and when they arrived, they made sure to give Ted a wide berth. Billy Consolo remembered the silence being broken by the clomping of Mike Higgins's cleats as he walked over to Ted's locker. "Kid, that wasn't a good thing to do," the manager said. (He probably meant the spitting, but he could have been including the bat throw and the watercooler assault as well.) Higgins walked away. Ted pointed to Gene Stephens, his substitute, and said, "Bush, you're the left fielder tomorrow."

The players continued to sit there in silence, stunned at what they'd witnessed earlier. No one took a uniform off or was in any hurry to get to the showers. "You could hear a pin drop," said Consolo.

Tom Yawkey was in New York in his suite at the Pierre hotel, but had listened to Mel Allen's call of the game on the radio for the Yankees, so he knew of the entire fiasco and was appalled. After the game ended, he quickly called Joe Cronin and ordered that Williams be fined $5,000—a huge sum at the time.

Cronin called Ted at the Somerset and gave him the news, then announced it to the writers. Cronin said the fine was just for the spitting, not the bat throwing, and the watercooler incident was not addressed. "We cannot condone such actions," Cronin said, adding that Ted could not explain his behavior. "Ted was sorry he did it. He told me he didn't know why he did it."

But Williams sounded a totally different tune to a few writers who ventured to the Somerset. Ted was still so mad he refused to leave his room, and he conducted the interview from behind a closed door. One of the writers outside the door was the *Globe*'s Bob Holbrook. Five days earlier he had been sitting in the Red Sox dugout talking with a Detroit writer before a game at Fenway against the Tigers. After finishing batting practice, Ted flung his bat toward the dugout. It hit the dirt in front, bounced off a girder near where Holbrook and the Detroit writer were sitting, and broke off at the handle. Williams apologized to Holbrook, saying he wasn't trying to hit him.[40]

Now, inside his room, Ted was defiant.

"I'd spit again at the same people who booed me today," he said.

"Why do the boos bother you?" Holbrook asked.

"I just can't help it."

"Don't you think you are a little bit to blame for this situation?"

"Not a damned bit! You writers are responsible for this whole thing. I'm no rock head, you know. If it didn't bother me, I wouldn't be as fired up as I am right now."

Williams wanted to be sure they had taken down what he said correctly. "Now you got that quote? Two things. First, I'd spit at the same people who booed me today. Second, I wouldn't be at the ballpark tomorrow if I could afford a...$5,000 fine every day. Got it? Read it back to me."[41]

If the writers had largely given Ted a pass on his spitting episodes in July, there was no holding back now. The papers played the story with unrestrained zeal. The *Record* featured Ted on its cover in midspit, while the *Globe* showed Williams's bat throw and ran four front-page stories under a screaming banner headline. The headline even eclipsed coverage of the trial of eight members of the gang accused of robbing the Brink's Building in Boston six years earlier of more than $2.7 million— the largest heist in US history at the time.

Williams's case came to be called the Great Expectoration, and the press excoriated him. "Ted Williams should do himself a favor," Harold Kaese wrote. "He should quit baseball before baseball quits on him." The spitting incidents of the last several weeks had been "displays of unrestrained rage. What he may do the next time he blows up is not pleasant to contemplate. It could be more than embarrassing. He should quit before it happens."[42] Dave Egan was even blunter in the *Record*. "Williams is sick."[43]

Prompted by the latest explosion, some sought to plumb his psyche, looking to explain the inner rage. Austen Lake of the *American* called Ted a psychotic personality who, as he grew up, erected a defensive wall and developed "ingrown animosities toward grownup society, suspicion for adult motives, so that now, at the age of 38, he still turtles into his shell or foams up in tantrums.... Ted is a divided personality, two distinct people, little child, big man. Nothing malicious! Just confused in his emotional standards, a small lad's yearning to be liked and a grown man's fear of ridicule!"[44]

On the one hand, Williams was self-reliant, authentic, and liked to chart his own course. Yet at the same time he craved—and, based on his record of excellence, thought he deserved—the cheers and adulation of society, as represented by the fans and the writers. When he did not get that approval, he would regress to childlike behavior and throw tantrums. He felt remorse for his outbursts, and knew they were infantile and outrageous, but rarely could express regret, because to do so might have been seen as a sign of weakness, and that would be another humiliation.

At his essence, Williams was a performer, one who cared almost as much about looking good as about performing well. "The one thing I want to do when I'm out there is look good," Ted told *Sports Illustrated* writer Joan Flynn Dreyspool for a 1955 profile in the magazine. "I hope I do the best I can, and I hope I don't look lousy doing it. I hope I don't boot a ball or look bad swinging. You hope to hell you're gonna win the game, but the thing I worry about is that I don't look bad. If I do, it makes me mad and I'm a little better the next day."[45]

Yet he was used to being the center of attention, to having all eyes on him, and felt most comfortable in that place. If his hitting was off, and thus was not reason enough to keep him in the headlines, he would look for other ways to get back in the news—maybe stir up a spat with the writers, get aggrieved, or go on a tear.

But the root of his problem was not the writers. Rather, it was the slings and arrows he'd endured in his youth, which festered still. "You know, I was born on the wrong side of the tracks," Ted told a friend in the late '40s. "Everybody was always against me. The other kids used to throw rocks at me and I'd throw rocks at them. Well, it's the same way now. I keep thinking everybody is against me."[46]

★   ★   ★

On August 8, the day after Ted's tirade, the Red Sox were playing the Baltimore Orioles at Fenway, and of course there was enormous interest in what might happen next with Williams. Would he even come to the ballpark? Or would he stay at the Somerset in a snit? If he showed up, would he play? And if he played, what other pyrotechnics might he be contemplating? As it happened, it was Family Night, so the Red Sox were especially worried that their X-rated star might offend the sensibilities of the G-rated crowd.

As a precaution, the team decided not to sell tickets to a section of the left-field grandstand where the worst Williams wolves usually congregated, and extra cops were deployed with instructions to toss out any rowdies. Anticipating trouble nonetheless, several of the writers covering the game decided to do so from the left-field seats so they could have a bird's-eye view of any heckling contretemps that might break out. One writer, Bill Liston of the *Traveler,* even decided to heckle Williams himself and report on how the fans reacted to him.

When Williams appeared in the clubhouse before the game, he seemed in a good mood. His teammates kidded him about his shenanigans the day before, and he smiled broadly, and wisecracked with Johnny Orlando. Harold Kaese witnessed the scene and wrote: "Williams was grinning because his name was back in the headlines, and his [name] was on everyone's lips. For a few hours, at least, he had made people forget about Mickey Mantle and Babe Ruth's home run record. He was the center of attraction once more, and he was happy."

When Williams went up to the dugout and poked his head out to look around, the fans cheered. Billy Loes, an Orioles pitcher, happened to be walking by and said to Williams: "They're cheering me, Ted, not you."

When Ted's name was announced in the starting lineup, he received a loud ovation from the 30,338 fans with only a smattering of boos. Tom Yawkey, who had rushed back to Boston from New York, looked on nervously from his box.

The reception was the same after he came to bat in the first and grounded out. A nice running catch in left-center in the second off a line drive by Tito Francona won him more applause. Williams didn't look at the crowd directly, particularly the left-field section, but all eyes were on him, even when he took a stroll to the wall to chat with the scoreboard operator, who told him Mantle had hit another homer, in Washington against the Senators.

Soon Ted had them all out of their seats. Leading off the sixth inning with the game tied 2–2, he unloaded a bomb twenty rows back into the right-field pavilion. The crowd screamed its approval as he circled the bases, then quieted as he crossed the plate and approached the dugout, his preferred venue for spitting. Then, with the timing of a skilled showman, and knowing that sixty thousand–odd eyes were riveted upon him to see what he would do at that moment, Williams extended his right arm and covered his mouth with his hand, self-mockingly, to confirm that he wouldn't be spitting this time.[47] The cheers turned to empathetic laughter. It was a disarming, self-deprecating gesture that had the effect of turning even some of Ted's harshest critics among the fans to his corner. A new, more rounded and appreciative view of the thin-skinned hero began to emerge. Sure he was too sensitive, temperamental, outrageous, and prone to fly off the handle — if not his rocker — at times. But who among the fans, after all, had his skills? Who among them had been in the pressure-filled arena for more than seventeen years, and how would *they* react to the acerbic attacks of abusive patrons and nettlesome sportswriters?

This shift in public opinion manifested itself in different ways. Grassroots fund-raising drives sprang up around Boston and Massachusetts to raise money to pay Ted's $5,000 fine. A state representative, James Condon of South Boston, filed a bill in the legislature barring spectators at sporting events from making profane or obscene remarks to participants. The *Globe* ran a full page of letters to the editor, all of them either pro-Ted, antipress, or anti–loudmouth fan. "A non-understanding, cruel press has gone the limit in crucifying a brave man," wrote one resident of the West Roxbury section of Boston. "Ted had two hitches on combat missions. Ted had marital trouble. Ted had several severe injuries. Ted received a continuous barrage of abuse in the papers. Ted was booed while hitting .372. If the above facts aren't enough to ruin anyone's 'nerves,' I'll eat a regulation bat, ball and catcher's equipment. In my opinion, Ted deserves a rest, a good doctor and a little help, not censure."[48] And the *Sun* newspaper of suburban Lowell, north of Boston, editorialized that "the verdict is that the Boston typewriter jockeys in the press box — not one of whom could carry Williams's bat — ought to leave the guy alone, stop tormenting him and start behaving like decent human beings instead of literary jackals seizing each and every opportunity to pounce on him and tear him to shreds."[49] Even Happy Chandler, the former baseball commissioner who then was serving a second term as governor of Kentucky, jumped into the fray, telling syndicated columnist Bob Considine that Ted was "a good boy," and that the Boston writers would "hit their grandmothers with the bases loaded."

Those writers, slow to detect the new mood, continued to pound away at Ted for a few days, but when the breadth of criticism emerged, they got defensive. Privately, many of the newspapermen thought Ted was a churlish lout and that the public had no idea of the raw abuse he subjected them to in the clubhouse. But the die was cast. The fans had crossed the Rubicon in their warts-and-all acceptance of Williams as a tormented talent, and their appreciation of him would only grow with time. Gradually, the writers would reflect this shift in their own coverage. As for the $5,000 fine, Tom Yawkey apparently never bothered to collect it.

The Red Sox coasted to a fourth-place finish, thirteen games behind the pennant-winning Yankees. The only interesting factor in the final days of the season was the race that developed between Mantle and Williams for the batting title, but since Ted had missed so much time at the beginning of the season because of his foot injury, there was again the question of whether he would have the necessary four hundred official at bats.

Mantle idolized Williams. "I was like everybody else — when he took batting practice, I got up and watched," Mantle told the writer Ed Linn. "He was the best hitter I ever saw." When they were in the clubhouse together at All-Star Games, Mantle could barely bring himself to speak to Williams, he was so awestruck. After Mickey retired, he was vacationing in Florida one year and decided to drop in on Ted in Islamorada. He found the house but didn't dare ring the bell. He knew Ted guarded his privacy and feared he would resent the intrusion.[50]

Mantle wanted the Triple Crown desperately, and knew that to get it, he had to beat Williams for the batting title. The two teams closed the season with another series in New York, and Williams, forced to chase bad pitches and minimize walks so he could make his four hundred at bats, continued to struggle. Ted finished with four hundred official appearances exactly and a formidable .345 mark, but well behind Mantle's .353. "If I could run like that son of a bitch, I'd hit .400 every year," Williams said of the Mick, admiringly.[51]

16

Late Innings

If his .406 season stands today as the young Williams's historic masterpiece—a grand achievement of callow youth—then 1957 would become his classic in the gloaming, a dazzling reassertion of pure hitting skill that was in many ways more remarkable than his 1941 feat.

Given the physical and emotional rigors of the previous three seasons, Ted had reported to Sarasota for spring training thinking that 1957 would be his last year. He was in good shape and relatively fine fettle.[1]

But his affability didn't last long. In late March, the Red Sox were on their way back to Florida from an exhibition swing to the West Coast and stopped in New Orleans on a layover. The *Globe*'s Hy Hurwitz introduced Ted to Crozet Duplantier, sports editor of the *New Orleans States,* who, like Ted and Hurwitz, was an ex-Marine. Though he perhaps thought the Marine connection would save him from being quoted, Ted was soon blasting the Corps, President Truman, and other "gutless politicians" for allowing him to be recalled to serve in Korea after he'd already interrupted his career for three years of service in World War II. In the ensuing furor, Ted was forced to apologize for his remarks.

Still angry at Hurwitz for his role in the Duplantier affair, Ted threatened the writer several weeks later during a confrontation in the Fenway clubhouse. Hurwitz and another writer were minding their own business, commiserating with catcher Haywood Sullivan after learning that Sullivan had been demoted to the minors.

"Be careful what you say to those cocksuckers," Ted told Sullivan as he passed by. "They'll twist it around and fuck you up."

Hurwitz had had enough. "You're nothing but a cocksucker yourself," he said to Williams.

Ted seethed. "If you were a foot taller I'd knock your block off!"

"If I were a foot taller, you wouldn't try," Hurwitz replied.

"I started the season mad and I finished mad," Ted said later.[2] "I didn't say two words to the Boston writers all year, and in between, I probably had the most amazing season any near-forty-year-old athlete ever had."

Traditionally a slow starter in the cold weather, Ted busted out early that year, and after two weeks was batting .474, with nine home runs. Three of the homers had come on May 8 in Chicago off Bob Keegan, the first time in a decade Williams had hit three such clouts in one game. On June 13, Ted cracked three more home runs against the Indians — off Early Wynn and Bob Lemon yet — in Cleveland. That left him with seventeen homers on the season and a still-scalding .392 average.

There had been minor setbacks and routine controversy for Williams to that point. On May 16 at Fenway, for example, Ted struck out three times against Jim Bunning of the Tigers. Enraged on returning to the dugout after one of the whiffs, Williams punched out the bat rack, bloodying his hand. After another plate appearance in which he popped out, Ted flung his bat high into the air in disgust and was fined a paltry $25.

Then on May 24, during an off day, Ted went to empty Fenway Park for some target practice against pigeons. This time he took his shotgun and set up camp on a chair in front of the bull pen in right-center field. There he proceeded to pick off between thirty and forty of the birds over the next few hours. One writer chided Williams for carrying out a "slaughter" at his "sit-still safari," and the Massachusetts Society for the Prevention of Cruelty to Animals was predictably outraged.[3] But the rest of the press, chastened by the fact that Ted now seemed immune to its darts, largely gave him a pass, and the episode quickly faded. Furthermore, the Red Sox's other leading sportsman, owner Tom Yawkey, had participated in the hunt, a mitigating circumstance for Williams.

Ted stayed focused. His engagement with Hurwitz was an aberration, and he adhered to his pledge to avoid the Boston writers. The one exception was his pal Ed Rumill of the *Christian Science Monitor,* who once had thrown batting practice for the Sox and was a confidant of Yawkey's as well. Whenever the writers tried to get a quote from Ted on his 1957 surge, Williams would dismiss them, saying, "You know I'm not talking to you guys." So the reporters relied heavily on Rumill to be their interlocutor with number 9. Rumill would interview Ted and then distribute the quotes to his colleagues.

Williams withheld from Ed Rumill and everyone else a key adjustment he had made that spring that had paved the way for his success in

1957. It would not be for another twelve years, with the publication of his autobiography, *My Turn at Bat,* in 1969, that Ted revealed he had been using a heavier bat, which enabled him to beat—and, finally, effectively end—the vexing Boudreau shift. He'd experimented with a 34.5-ounce bat in Sarasota, which was an ounce and a half heavier than he normally used. He choked up a quarter inch and noticed that the balls seemed to be ringing off his bat and going to all fields. As the team headed north after spring training, Williams went to the rack one day, ready to switch back to his usual lighter bat, but decided to stay with the heavier one since he was hitting so well with it.

On opening day at Fenway against the Yankees, Ted got two hits to left field. As most teams continued to use the shift against him, he noticed that the heavier bat slowed his swing just enough to enable him to naturally hit line drives to the left of second base into vacated zones. Unaware he was using the heavier bat, the rest of the league concluded that Williams was simply aging and could not turn on a fastball the way he used to. So gradually, most American League teams began abandoning the shift. The most dramatic example of this came in late April, when the Red Sox went to Kansas City to play the Athletics. Lou Boudreau, the architect of the shift, had moved on to be the manager of the A's, and when Williams came to bat, Boudreau played his defense straight.

As the weather warmed—traditionally, the time when Ted got loose and began to hit in earnest—he switched back to his lighter bat and started to pull the ball like the Williams of old. But now there were plenty of holes, since the defenses were no longer packed onto the right side of the diamond.[4]

After his second three-homer outburst, on June 13, Williams cooled down and went into the All-Star break in July in a certified 1–16 slump. Yet he had hit so well in the chilly months of April and May, when he historically had fared poorly, that his average stood at .340, with twenty-two home runs. Williams went hitless at the All-Star Game in Saint Louis, then flew off to Detroit to await the Red Sox and the second half of the season. Tired, he remained in his hotel room for nearly two days and got plenty of sleep. When he went to Briggs Stadium on July 11, he felt reinvigorated.

Then he learned of an ill-considered column in the *Globe* that morning written by Bob Holbrook, headlined TED'S BATTING BAROMETER DECLINES and accompanied by a subhead that posed the question: "Nearing End of Trail?" Holbrook was playing off the undeniable fact that Williams's average had dropped more than fifty points in June (albeit from .392), and he wrote that "observers are looking for those tell-tale signs that Number 9 is reaching the end of the trail.... Will it happen fast? Or will there be a gradual deterioration in his productiveness[?]" Holbrook tried to cover himself by noting that no one "is foolish enough to come right out and say" that Ted is nearing the end, and that he "has a way of coming back to make such statements look ridiculous."[5] But the cheap shot had been taken, and it was just the added motivational fodder Ted needed to go off on one of his hot streaks.

In his first game back, Ted cracked two doubles, and on the following day he took his revenge against Jim Bunning for the May 16 humiliation at Fenway, when Bunning had fanned him three times. His first time up, Williams blasted a home run off the top of the third deck, and the second time up he cracked another rocket, this time into the second deck.

Ted stayed hot. When the Cleveland Indians came to Fenway for four games in late July, Williams went 8–12, and he finished the month with a 3–4 night at home against the Tigers. He was hitting .550 since the All-Star break, and his average on the year now stood at .384. Approaching his thirty-ninth birthday and with two months left in the season, Williams was again flirting with the .400 milestone.

Fan interest in each one of Ted's at bats was now intense, as was keenly evident in the July 31 game against Detroit, when he got three hits. But one of those hits was initially deemed an error on the part of Tigers shortstop Harvey Kuenn by the official scorer, old friend Hy Hurwitz. Ted had scorched a line drive slightly to the right of second base, and Kuenn, playing there in the shift, couldn't handle the ball and dropped it. When an error was announced, the crowd roared its displeasure. "Never before had Boston come so close to a baseball riot," wrote the *American*'s Mike Gillooly in *Sport* magazine. "Fans glared at the press box. They shouted insults and made threatening gestures. It was an unprecedented display of anger, and it seemed to refuse to subside. The earmarks of a mob riot were all there. An hour after the game ended, people were still lingering around the exit from the press box, jeering at the writers as they came out."[6]

Hurwitz changed his ruling and gave Williams a hit after interviewing Kuenn in the clubhouse afterward.[7]

Ted's average was up to .391 by August 9, when Boston's newspapers went on strike for three weeks. During this information blackout, the papers were flooded with calls each day asking what Ted had done. The Red Sox were more than twelve games out, and few seemed to care about the team's fortunes.

At the end of the month, Williams's average had come down to .377, one point ahead of Mickey Mantle, who was having another monster season, though he led Ted by only one home run — thirty-four to thirty-three. Then Williams came down with another one of the acute viruses that had plagued him throughout his career, and he was forced out of the lineup for two weeks. At the same time, Mantle went down with shin splints.

Ted actually had pneumonia. While he was recovering, Hy Hurwitz obtained Williams's medical records and reported that he had a "chronic lung condition."[8] On September 14, Hurwitz wrote that it was "quite possible" Williams would miss the rest of the year.

Ted read the story and went ballistic. "I'll get back now even if they have to carry me out there on a stretcher," he promised. "I'll get back there just to show that little so-and-so up."[9]

Three days later, with the Red Sox at home against Kansas City, Williams told Mike Higgins he was available to pinch-hit. Higgins called on his star in the eighth, and as the crowd roared, Ted popped out of the dugout and strode to the plate for his first at bat in seventeen days. Facing Tom Morgan, Williams promptly crushed a ball four hundred feet through a stiff wind ten rows up in the right-field bleachers to tie the score at 8–8, and the Sox went on to win the game, 9–8.[10]

It was another dramatic moment in a career laced with dramatic moments. Ted basked and thrived in the limelight and proceeded to prove it again and again for the rest of the season. He pinch-hit the next day and walked. Then the Red Sox were off to Yankee Stadium for a series, and in another pinch-hitting appearance, Ted homered in the ninth inning off Whitey Ford in the first game of a doubleheader. Williams started the second game, hit a grand slam off Bob Turley (the fifteenth of his career), then walked three times. In the final game of the series, Williams walked, homered, singled, and walked again.

On September 23 in Washington, Ted singled, was walked three times, and was struck by a pitch. When he grounded out his first time up on September 24, it was the first out he had made in a week. He had hit four home runs in four official times at bat since returning on the seventeenth, and he had reached base safely his first sixteen times up. After grounding out to end the streak, he homered his next time up, giving him five home runs in his eight official at bats since the seventeenth.

Ted finished the season with a luminous .388 average and thirty-eight home runs, a number he had only surpassed in 1949, when he hit forty-three. But it was the .388 figure that astonished the baseball world and marked what Williams himself considered the grandest achievement of his career, surpassing his .406 in 1941. After all, he was now thirty-nine years old, increasingly prone to injury and illness, and still slow. With just five more hits, he would have reached the .400 mark, and if he'd had half of Mantle's speed, those could have been measly infield, or "leg," hits. Of course there were no such hits among Ted's 163 in 420 official times at bat, making his .388 all the more remarkable. The .388 figure was a full forty-eight points higher than the .340 mark, which stood as the average winning number for the previous five American League batting title holders.

From his return in mid-September until the end of the year, Williams hit .647, and after the All-Star break, he hit .453. Yet the writers snubbed him again for the Most Valuable Player award and voted it to Mantle by a tally of 233–209, even though he had four fewer home runs than Williams and a final average of .365 — impressive, but twenty-three points lower than Ted's. Mantle did have ten more RBIs than Williams, and the Yankees won the pennant, as usual, but Mickey said he was shocked by his selection. "I thought Ted Williams would have made it easily," he said.[11]

The culprits were two unidentified out-of-town writers who mischievously slotted Williams ninth and tenth on their ballots. The Boston writers spoke out against the vote, and even Ted's archenemy Dave Egan called it disgraceful. But while his teammates, Tom Yawkey, and others criticized the decision, Williams took the slight in stride and held his tongue.

"All the American League's got is me and the Yankees," Ted quipped, not incorrectly. "When I leave this league, it's going to be pretty damn dull."[12] Examining the Red Sox's final season attendance figure — 1,181,087 — Harold Kaese wrote that the Sox drew 181,087 and Williams the million.[13]

Ted's brilliance in 1957 reverberated well into 1958, producing a burst of glowing press and national recognition. The Associated Press named Ted its 1957 Male Athlete of the Year, and the influential New York chapter of the Baseball Writers' Association of America voted him its Player of the Year. Both awards, especially the latter, served to somewhat mitigate the injustice of the American League MVP award going to

Mantle. And there were fresh assessments of Williams as an all-time hitting great. Besides the eight-page "The Case for Ted Williams," a statistical analysis published by *Look* magazine,[14] other statisticians poring through the detritus of the '57 season found more nuggets: Ted's three pinch-hit home runs in September, for example, gave him seven for his career, which was an American League record. And his thirty-three intentional walks for the year were the most ever recorded in a season.[15]

All this was further evidence that the tide of public opinion—which had begun to shift in favor of Williams in late 1956, after his deft, self-deprecating mime following his spate of spits—was now surging in his direction, buoyed both by the brilliance of his '57 season and by a popular backlash against the MVP vote for Mantle. What had long been portrayed in the press as Ted's ill-mannered, crude, and self-centered behavior now mostly came to be seen as principled nonconformity, a willingness to take unpopular positions and stand up for what he believed. People came to appreciate his assertion of independence—his insistence on flouting convention and going without a tie, his daring to give the writers and even the Marine Corps what for.

Seemingly bulletproof now, Ted drew 150,000 people to his annual fly-casting exhibition at the sportsmen's show in Boston during the first week of February. On the sixth, Williams popped over to Fenway for his annual contract signing and joust with the now-cowed writers. His salary for 1958 was described in all the papers as the largest sum ever given to a professional baseball player. The amount was not officially revealed, of course, but the writers colluded and set the figure at "an estimated" $125,000. If true, then $65,000 of it was deferred, since the team reported to Major League Baseball that it was paying Ted just $60,000 for the season.

Speaking to a horde of reporters and flashbulb-popping photographers, Williams offered détente on his terms. "I'm looking forward to a great summer and I'm going to be as fair as possible with you fellows," he said. "But the first time I read one of those stinking, detrimental, dishonest, prejudicial stories, then don't come around me. You know what I mean. Those stories which disrupt my playing or disrupt the club. Just keep out of my way. And don't be yelling to have me benched if I'm only hitting .280 in May."[16]

Then Ted picked a bone with the New York writers who had given him their Player of the Year award for 1957. He'd been unable to go to New York to pick up the prize because he had a conflict, which he'd explained in a telegram while expressing his appreciation for the honor. But the writers had put the blast on him for being a no-show and hadn't bothered to read his telegram at the banquet, which featured Vice President Richard Nixon as a headliner. "Strictly bush," said Ted. "I have confirmation that the telegram was delivered to the chairman at 5:30 p.m. the day of the dinner. It wasn't even read. Bush, bush, bush."

As for his physical condition, Williams allowed that he was ten pounds overweight but said he'd sweat it off in spring training without any problem. He planned to take up tennis to help get his legs in shape before reporting. He'd slipped on a rock while fishing up in Labrador the previous fall, and his ankle was sore, but it was responding to diathermy treatments, he said. Joe Cronin broke up the press conference by echoing Williams's own words about his news-making prowess. "It'll be damned dull when you're not here, Ted," Cronin said.[17]

Williams's stellar 1957 performance hardly carried over to the early part of the 1958 season. He would turn forty later that summer and was feeling his age: he'd hurt his side in spring training, and swinging the bat was painful; his off-season ankle injury lingered and nagged; every ache and pain seemed magnified. He found batting helmets, newly mandated by the league for protection, bothersome.

Ted had missed opening day in Washington because he'd eaten a bad batch of oysters and come down with food poisoning.[18] When he returned to the lineup, nothing seemed to click, and his hitting was anemic. On May 20 he was batting .225, the worst start of his career. The next day, Ted's longtime bête noire, Dave Egan of the *Record,* died at the age of fifty-seven, succumbing to heart trouble, the accumulated ravages of the bottle, and related ailments. The Red Sox were on the road in the Midwest at the time, so Ted was spared the tributes for his harshest critic as well as the pomp and circumstance of the funeral, which were considerable. Boston archbishop Richard Cushing (who would be elevated to cardinal the following year) presided over the service. Pallbearers included Joe Cronin, star Boston Celtics guard Bob Cousy, former world welterweight boxing champion Tony DeMarco, former Massachusetts governor Robert Bradford, and former Notre Dame football coach Frank Leahy.

Ted finally got his stroke going and by late June had raised his average to nearly .300, but that was not enough to make the All-Star team. Über–Williams fan Casey Stengel later chose him for the American League squad anyway.

In July, Williams regressed on the spitting front, this time in Kansas City. After failing to run out a routine ground ball, Ted was roundly booed, and he spat at fans along the first-base line. The league fined him just $250, and Ted issued a tepid apology. ("I am principally sorry about the $250," he said.) The writers, inured to such flare-ups and by then thinking it futile to take Ted on, made little of the episode.

By September, the Red Sox were twelve and a half games out and going nowhere, but Williams was again keeping things interesting, this time by competing for a batting title with a teammate, banjo-hitting second baseman Pete Runnels, who had been traded to the Sox over the winter by the Washington Senators. Runnels, an affable Texan, bene-fited from batting second in the order, in front of Williams. "To tell you the truth, I was pulling for Runnels," Williams said later. "But I wasn't about to give it to him. Baseball isn't charity."[19] Runnels credited Wil-liams with teaching him how to be a good hitter, especially mentally: "Ted taught me how to be a successful hitter, a thinking hitter. And bat-ting in front of him certainly didn't hurt, either. Pitchers gave me plenty of good balls to hit. They couldn't afford to walk me and have to face Ted. . . . He'd show me which umpires called strikes on high pitches and which umpires called strikes on low pitches. What kinds of pitches to expect from certain pitchers, and what kinds of pitches to expect on dif-ferent ball-and-strike counts. He was masterful."[20]

Williams slumped a bit in the middle of the month, and by the time the Red Sox hosted Washington on September 21, he was 0 for his last 7. Facing pitcher Bill Fischer, Ted made an out his first time up, and on his second trip was called out on strikes by umpire Bill Summers. That almost never happened, and Williams flung his bat in frustration. He had meant to throw it toward the Red Sox dugout, but because of the sticky pine tar he'd begun rubbing on his hands to get a better grip while hitting, Ted lost control of the bat and it sailed seventy-five feet into the box seats just to the left of the dugout, striking a sixty-year-old woman named Gladys Heffernan in the head.

The papers had dramatic photos of Williams's immediate reaction to this sickening spectacle: first he raised both arms, clenched his teeth, and raised his left leg, as if he were preparing to break an imaginary bat across his knee in a fit of pique; then he hung his head, arms at his side, knees bent forward in utter despair; then he raced over to the seats to check on Mrs. Heffernan and express his sorrow for what he'd done. He could see that his bat had struck her on the left side of the forehead and that she was bleeding.

"Don't worry about me, Ted," Mrs. Heffernan said. "I'm all right. I know you didn't mean it."

The lady was taken off to a first-aid room under the stands to be bandaged before leaving for the hospital. A shaken Williams followed her down and spent a few minutes with her while his teammates continued to bat.

When it was time for the Red Sox to take the field again, Ted remained in the dugout, crying. Bill Summers, the umpire who had called Ted out on strikes, walked over to the dugout and urged him to resume play. Williams finally took the field to a chorus of boos.

"I told Ted to get out to the outfield and play ball and to forget it," Summers said after the game. "I don't think he wanted to play because he felt so badly about it."

Williams faced the writers in the clubhouse. "I just almost died," he said. "I was almost sick when I went out to the outfield. I'm very thankful it wasn't a serious injury. I was mad and threw the bat, but I didn't mean to throw it that way....I started to flip the bat along the ground, but the sticky stuff kept it in my grip just long enough so the bat left my hands on the fly instead."

Mrs. Heffernan, who happened to be Joe Cronin's housekeeper, had her own press conference from her room at Sancta Maria Hospital in Cambridge as a smiling Cronin sat by her bedside. "Why did the crowd boo Ted Williams?" she asked. "I don't see why they had to boo him. I felt awfully sorry for him after it happened. He came right into the first-aid room to see me, and you could tell by the look on his face how badly he felt. It was an accident. It all happened so fast I don't actually know what happened." Cronin seemed to enjoy his housekeeper getting the star treatment. "Gladys," he said, "you're going to feel like Liz Taylor before this is over."[21] Mrs. Heffernan laughed and gave the photographers permission to take her picture. Ted later sent the lady a $500 wristwatch, likely endearing himself to her further.

As for the batting race, Ted did rip a double to center field his next time up, but Runnels had three hits on the day and led Williams .323 to .314 with six games left. Then Ted went on a spurt, and the two entered the final game of the season in Washington with Williams ahead .327 to .324.

They bantered around the batting cage an hour before the game as if nothing were on the line that day. "I'm getting me some land-locked salmon in Canada tomorrow," Ted told Runnels. "They'll run to 25 pounds, almost as big as those deer you shoot."

"I'll have me a buck deer before you get your first bite and start yelling about the big one that got away," Pete replied.[22]

Williams stayed nice and loose, popping a double and a home run off Pedro Ramos to finish at .328, while Runnels went hitless in four trips and ended at .322. It was Ted's sixth—and last—batting championship.

One day over the winter, at his house in Islamorada, Williams was sitting outside in the shade of a coconut tree talking to a friend about the upcoming 1959 season. He spoke broadly of his goals and said he felt rested and healthy. As if to prove it, Williams got up, grabbed a bat, and began swinging it easily. After several swings, he felt a twinge in the back of his neck, but thought nothing of it, assuming it would pass or be just another kink to work out in spring training.

That year the Red Sox were to leave Sarasota and train in Scottsdale, Arizona. Tom Yawkey thought his team could draw more fans out west, and one of the economic highlights of the spring, the team hoped, was to be three exhibition games against the Cleveland Indians in Ted's hometown of San Diego. It would be the first time Williams returned to play ball in the city where he grew up since his barnstorming tour with Jimmie Foxx eighteen years earlier.

Ted reported to Scottsdale on March 1, three days late, causing his usual stir among writers and teammates and delighting the locals, who weren't used to such star wattage. He put on a show when he took his first licks of the year in the batting cage, casually swatting two homers.

Williams settled into his Cactus League routine and before long pronounced himself happy with Arizona. "This place is better than Florida for a training site," he said. "The weather is great, really great. . . . The people here are wonderful too. Why, they're the most friendly and hospitable group I've seen in years."[23]

The fans in Scottsdale soon learned that if they wanted to see Williams in action, they would mostly have to come and see him practice, for the Kid followed the same spring training regimen he'd established in recent years, which was to play as few exhibition games as he could get away with. Mike Higgins and the front office were fine with this approach, saying that Ted knew his own body best and concluding that it was an acceptable trade-off for the team to hold back their star from Cactus League games in the interest of saving wear and tear and maximizing his availability for the regular season.

The Arizona writers questioned this philosophy and complained that local fans who had bought tickets to spring games expecting to see the Great Man were getting stiffed. One fan in nearby Mesa voiced this very complaint to Harold Kaese of the *Globe* when Williams failed to appear with his teammates for a game against the Chicago Cubs. "He should have come with all these people here," said the local retiree, none other than Ty Cobb himself.[24]

Cobb and Williams had a prickly relationship. The Georgia Peach had been critical of Ted earlier in his career for failing to hit to left field more often to beat the shift, and he'd written him private letters offering to counsel him on his hitting technique. In addition, Cobb had been outspoken in arguing that the players of his era were superior to those in Ted's time, a contention Williams considered ridiculous.

But Ted and Ty seemed to patch things up at a pleasant photo op around the batting cage in Scottsdale. Cobb, then seventy-two, leaned on his cane, wrapped his left arm around Ted's right shoulder, and both men beamed. The photographers, in their captions, wrote that the two legends "discussed hitting."

Williams had a pal out for spring training whom he knew would be thrilled to meet Cobb. Joe Lindia owned a restaurant in Cranston, Rhode Island. In the winter of 1955, Lindia's brother and his wife had been vacationing in Islamorada and chanced to meet Ted, who invited them out fishing with him. That night back in Cranston, Joe, a huge Williams fan, received this news in a phone call from his brother. Beside himself with jealousy, Joe said he would beat it down to Islamorada as quickly as he could. Williams was waiting for him in good cheer: "So you want to go fishing, Bush?" A friendship developed, and before long Joe was hosting annual fund-raisers for the Jimmy Fund at his restaurant with Ted as the star attraction. Sometimes, Ted would invite Joe to go on a road trip with the Red Sox, and the two men would room together at various hotels. Joe was thrilled.

Back in Scottsdale, Ted and Joe were walking one evening when Ted said he had someone he wanted Joe to meet. They got in the car and drove to a seedy motel nearby. Then they knocked on a door to one of the rooms, and Ty Cobb appeared—dressed only in his boxer shorts. He seemed happy to have some company, and within minutes, Cobb and Williams were talking baseball, arguing about which era was better, and debating the relative merits of this pitcher or that hitter. Invariably they disagreed, and frequently they would turn to Lindia and ask him what he thought. Joe thought he was in heaven.[25]

★   ★   ★

There was a new face on the Red Sox that spring—a very different face: Elijah Jerry "Pumpsie" Green, a switch-hitting infielder from California who also happened to be the first black player ever to play for Boston, the last major-league team to integrate. Tom Yawkey and Joe Cronin, who had left the team earlier that year to become president of the American League, had long denied any racist intent and weakly insisted they had been unable to find a suitable black player.

Green was still being forced to live in different quarters from the white players in Scottsdale because of the segregation policies of the day, and the Red Sox were unable or unwilling to leverage their new presence in town in support of Pumpsie. One obstacle was the manager, Mike Higgins, who did little to disguise his antipathy to blacks, telling a Boston writer, Al Hirshberg, sometime after being named manager in 1955, "There'll be no niggers on this ballclub as long as I have anything to say about it."[26]

After arriving in Scottsdale, Williams had gone out of his way to introduce himself to Green and to make him feel welcome. One of the ways he did this was by asking Green to warm up with him before games, a gesture Pumpsie remembered fondly.

"He treated you like you should be treated," Green said of Ted. "He didn't put stuff on it that shouldn't be. He wasn't forcible or anything. He was a friendly person. I found him to be a very well-liked person among the ballplayers."[27]

Spring training ended, and Green appeared to have made the team, but as the club headed back to Boston, Higgins suddenly announced that he was cutting Green. "Another season or half season in Minneapolis is what this boy needs," Higgins said. The Boston chapter of the NAACP and two other local groups charged the Red Sox with racism and asked the Massachusetts Commission Against Discrimination to investigate. It did, but cleared the team of any wrongdoing.

Williams made a sentimental return to San Diego in mid-March for the three exhibition games against the Indians at Westgate Park. Ted grounded out twice and walked in the first game before 7,358 fans, and afterward hosted a party that lasted into the wee hours for about fifty of his childhood friends. The next night he got an infield hit and cracked a double that was inches from being a home run; he went 0–2 in the third game. The series drew more than twenty-two thousand fans, making it a financial success for both teams, but Ted had aggravated the neck injury he'd sustained lazily swinging his bat in Islamorada over the winter.

Returning to Scottsdale, he tried to work out the kinks by throwing some batting practice, but that only made things worse. He went to a Phoenix hospital and was diagnosed with a pinched nerve. It was decided that he would fly back to Boston and be admitted to New England Baptist Hospital, where he would be fitted for a medical collar and put in traction. He ended up staying in the hospital for three weeks, his neck immobilized, and started the season on the disabled list.

Williams made his return at home on May 12 against the White Sox and went 0–5, a performance that would set the tone for the rest of the season. His neck was still killing him, and it was all he could do merely to face the pitcher squarely after he stepped into the box. During the next week, he had one hit in twenty-two times up and was batting .045.

Then on June 13, the unthinkable happened: Williams was benched. He'd brought his average up a bit, but only to .175. Mike Higgins explained that he thought Ted could use a rest. This development prompted Harold Kaese to wonder how and when the Red Sox would eventually get rid of Williams—perhaps by turning him into a manager. In fact, Tom Yawkey did ask business manager Dick O'Connell to sound Ted out on whether he had any interest in the job. "He told me that he would never give the Boston writers the chance to second-guess him," O'Connell recalled. "I've never really been sure whether he understood that the job was really being offered to him."[28] But Ted knew, recalling that Joe Cronin had asked him to manage at the end of the 1954 season. He also knew it was easier to fire a manager than a player, especially one of Williams's stature. As manager, he could have been dismissed if the team had a lousy record, as seemed likely, or even for blowing up at the writers, which seemed even more likely. He could then have been eased into the front office in some capacity as a gesture of respect, but there would be no hiding the fact that he'd failed.[29]

Ted returned to the lineup on June 23 and brought his average up to .244 over the next three weeks, enough for Williams booster Casey Stengel to again name him to the All-Star Game. Ted said he appreciated the gesture.

On July 3, the 31–42 Red Sox deflected attention from the Kid's woes by firing Mike Higgins as manager and replacing him with Billy Jurges. With Higgins gone, it was easier for the Red Sox to finally elevate Pumpsie Green, who was hitting .320 in Minneapolis and had been named a Triple-A All-Star for the second consecutive year. The Sox had finally integrated.

Green was used only as a part-timer, but a week later, another black player, pitcher Earl Wilson, was also brought up, though neither man had much of an impact, as Boston finished 75–79, in fifth place, nineteen games out. Williams had his worst season ever, hitting only .254 with 10 home runs in 103 games. After the Red Sox's final game, Tom Yawkey summoned Ted to his apartment at the Ritz. After some chitchat, the owner got to the point.

"What do you think you ought to do next year?" he asked his star player.

"What do *you* think I ought to do?" Williams replied.

"Ted, I think you ought to quit," Yawkey advised. "You've had a great career. You were hurting this year, and I don't want to see you hurt more. Listen, why don't you just wrap it up?"

Hearing this "kind of burned my ass," as Williams put it later. He had no intention of quitting on a sour note. He knew he could still hit. He had posted averages of .345, .356, .345, .388, and .328 in the five seasons previous to 1959. Now he'd hit .254 while clearly hurting. "Well, I'll tell you, Mr. Yawkey," he said. "I'm going to wait until next spring to decide. I still think I can hit. If I feel I can't do it by spring, I'll let you know."[30]

A few days later, Yawkey fired Johnny Orlando in a move that the writers speculated would infuriate Williams and perhaps influence his decision to retire. The reasons for the dismissal were not announced, but Orlando's drinking had gotten out of hand, and he was showing up late to work, generally neglecting his duties, and leveraging his position for personal gain—getting the players to sign autographed balls and then selling them, for example.[31]

Ted seethed at Orlando's firing but kept his feelings to himself. Nevertheless, he grew less certain that he would come back if the team didn't want him. When he returned to Boston for the sportsmen's show in January, he stopped in unannounced to see Dick O'Connell at Fenway Park to discuss his 1960 contract. "Dick, if there are any doubts the club wants me back this year, hell, I'll quit," Williams told him. "I think I can still play. I told Mr. Yawkey I'd go to spring training and find out. But I don't want to play unless the management *wants* me to." O'Connell was surprisingly reassuring. "Aw, Ted, don't be silly," he said before pulling out a contract calling for the same salary Williams received in 1959: $125,000, with $65,000 of it deferred.

Ted was relieved, but he had a different idea: he would take a pay cut. "Dick, look. I had a lousy year, the worst I ever had. I was injured and suffered for it, but I don't deserve what I made last year. I've had the biggest raises a player ever had. I've gone up from nothing on this club to $125,000 a year. I want to take the biggest cut ever given a player."[32] He agreed to play his final season for $90,000—$60,000 on the books and $30,000 deferred—nearly a 30 percent drop.

When he arrived in Scottsdale on March 1, Williams was not exactly exuding confidence. He complained to the writers that his neck still hurt him and declared that if the pain didn't subside, he doubted he could play that year after all.

The day after that pessimistic assessment, manager Billy Jurges announced that in addition to his duties as a player, Williams would also become a batting instructor. This of course fueled speculation that the Red Sox were preparing a soft landing for Ted if he no longer could take the field.

One of the rookies Jurges wanted Williams to mentor was a twenty-year-old named Carl Yastrzemski. Yaz (as he was known) found Ted moody and his teaching style esoteric. "I didn't know what the hell he was talking about," Yaz would recall. "I'd listen and not say a word, hoping he'd get finished soon." The rookie's theory of hitting was simply to wait for a good pitch and try to hit it, and he was baffled by Williams's talk of hip rotation and the like. When Ted asked him questions about what he'd just said, Yaz remained silent, fearing he'd give the wrong answer. When reporters would ask him what Ted was teaching, Yaz would just vaguely respond that he was learning a lot. Fearful of reprimands, he tried to avoid Ted, but that was impossible because they were assigned adjoining lockers.[33]

In retirement, when Williams would return to the Red Sox as a spring training instructor, Yaz remained largely unresponsive to the Kid's teachings. Future team CEO John Harrington remembered witnessing a Williams–Yaz tutorial in the '70s: "Ted was giving Yaz a lecture about his bat being too long and big. Ted was talking physics and bat speed and calling Yaz a dumb Polack for not grasping the intricacies of the aerodynamics. It was Greek to Yaz."[34] But, in 1960, Ted liked what he saw of Yastrzemski and commended him to Ty Cobb, who lingered at the Red Sox camp, still annoyed that Williams wouldn't take his hitting counsel.

A week into camp, Ted's neck loosened enough to let him pop a long homer in an intrasquad scrimmage, prompting encouraging headlines and reportage. "There is still plenty of zing in Ted's swing," wrote Bob Holbrook of the *Globe*.[35] Over at Hearst's *Evening American,* there seemed no doubt the Kid would have a prosperous season, as the paper sprung Johnny Orlando from his forced retirement to write a twelve-part ode to Ted, as told to Mike Gillooly, who just two years earlier had weighed in with the fifteen-part "The Case for Ted Williams." While Ted surely missed Orlando, he apparently viewed the *American* series as a betrayal of sorts, even though the clubhouse nuggets Johnny dished out were all complimentary, almost fawningly so. A month later, Gillooly's brother John, who had taken over for Dave Egan as the lead sports columnist for the *Record,* wrote that Williams had yet to contact Orlando: "Now Williams is treating him like one of the Boston press—just because Johnny O had a byline?"[36]

Ted sought out a favored writer, Milton Gross of the *New York Post,* to further lower expectations for the season: "I keep thinking, 'Williams, you're dying hard.' I keep saying to myself, 'Your ankle hurts, your neck hurts and your back hurts, and you are dying so damn hard....' Playing is still fun, but it's harder. God, how much harder it is."[37] So why did he continue? Gross asked. Ted said he needed the money, plus he wanted to redeem his lousy 1959 season and attain five hundred career home runs. He had 492 at that point.

Three days after this column appeared, Williams got word that his brother, Danny, had died of leukemia at the family home in San Diego at the age of thirty-nine. Ted had written his brother and Danny's wife, Jean, a letter from Scottsdale, again complaining how sore he was but hoping for one more good year. Ted said he hoped Danny's new medication was helping him, and that the summer heat would be therapeutic.

But Danny's condition had deteriorated rapidly in 1958 and 1959. After getting leukemia, he'd moved back into the Utah Street house where he'd grown up, accompanied by his wife and sons. As he grew sicker and weaker, the living arrangements became untenable for May, and she went to Santa Barbara to move in with her sister Sarah. Danny had wasted away to just ninety pounds at the end.

"He died tough," Ted later wrote. "I got his little pistol. I always thought he would shoot himself because he suffered so much.... There wasn't the closeness between us there should have been. I regret that. After I left for pro ball, I never saw much of him."[38]

Funeral services were held at a mortuary in San Diego, and Ted flew

With Joe DiMaggio at Yankee Stadium on July 2, 1941. (National Baseball Hall of Fame Library)

Getting mobbed by fans, circa 1941. (Ted Williams Family Enterprises)

Inspecting the lumber at Louisville Slugger's bat factory, circa 1942. (San Diego Hall of Champions Sports Museum)

Working on his form in the Fenway clubhouse, circa 1942. (Brearley Collection)

With Dom DiMaggio, Bobby Doerr, and Johnny Pesky, 1942. (Red Sox photograph)

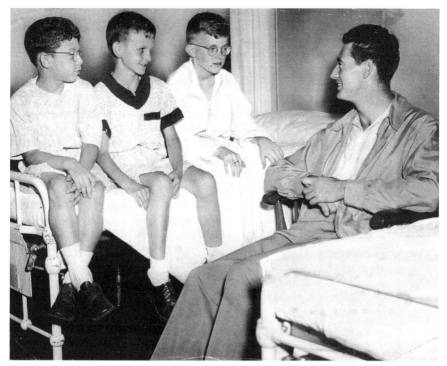

Visiting sick kids in Boston, 1942. (*Boston Globe* photograph)

Getting sworn in to the Navy on May 22, 1942. (Courtesy of the Trustees of the Boston Public Library / Leslie Jones Collection)

With *Daily Record* columnist Dave Egan after enlisting in the Navy, May 1942. (Rogers Photo Archive)

In World War II. (May Williams Collection)

Boxing with his instructor at the Navy Pre-Flight School, summer 1943, at the University of North Carolina, Chapel Hill. (North Carolina Collection, University of North Carolina at Chapel Hill, Wilson Library)

Tossing a football at the Navy Pre-Flight School, summer 1943. (North Carolina Collection, University of North Carolina at Chapel Hill, Wilson Library)

With the Babe
at Fenway Park
before a wartime
exhibition game,
July 1943. (Rogers
Photo Archive)

On the flight line at Pensacola with another pilot, July 3, 1944. (Defense Department photograph)

With Eddie Pellagrini, Hank Greenberg of the Detroit Tigers, and John F. Kennedy at Fenway Park as Kennedy was running for Congress in 1946. (*Boston Globe* photograph)

Tackling one of his columns for the *Boston Globe* in 1940. (*Boston Globe* photograph)

The center of attention during the 1946 World Series. (Brearley Collection)

At the throttle of the *Merchants Limited,* leaving Boston for New York, September 1949. (Leslie Jones photograph)

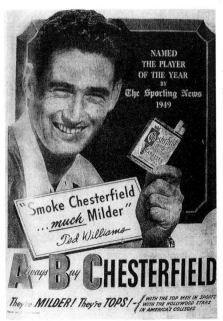

Williams always regretted doing this cigarette ad since he didn't smoke and knew it set a bad example. (Ted Williams Family Enterprises)

Holding court with the writers, 1950. (Courtesy of the Trustees of the Boston Public Library / Leslie Jones Collection)

Addressing the Fenway Park crowd before leaving for Korea, 1952. (Red Sox photograph)

In Korea, preparing to deliver a message. (May Williams Collection)

With Larry Hawkins, the Marine pilot who guided the disoriented Williams in for a crash landing when his plane was shot down on a mission in Korea. (Ted Williams Family Enterprises)

Entering the cockpit in Korea, 1953. (National Baseball Hall of Fame Library)

Meeting a Korean *papa-san* while touring the countryside. (Defense Department photograph)

Ted and Bobby-Jo, circa 1953. (Ted Williams Family Enterprises)

With Howard Cosell at spring training in Sarasota, mid-1950s. (National Baseball Hall of Fame Library)

With Red Sox owner Tom Yawkey, circa 1955. (National Baseball Hall of Fame Library)

Spitting toward the press box after hitting his four hundredth career home run on July 17, 1956. (Rogers Photo Archive)

With Jackie Robinson in Boston, 1957. (The Sports Museum)

With Mickey
Mantle, in Florida,
circa 1955. (Ted
Williams Family
Enterprises)

With Richard
Cardinal Cushing,
Archbishop
of Boston, in
1958. (Red Sox
photograph)

Reacting with fury and anguish on September 21, 1958, after seeing that a bat he had flung in disgust after striking out had struck an elderly woman. (National Baseball Hall of Fame Library)

Gladys Heffernan is tended to after being struck by Ted's thrown bat. (Rogers Photo Archive)

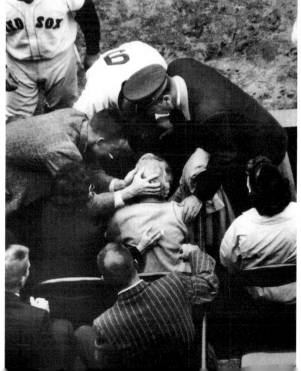

With Ty Cobb at spring training in Scottsdale, 1959. (Red Sox photograph)

Hooking a babe for a gag shot at spring training in Scottsdale, 1960. (Rogers Photo Archive)

Heading to the field before his last game, September 28, 1960. (The Sports Museum)

out from Scottsdale to attend. Williams spent tens of thousands of dollars on Danny's medical care toward the end of his life, including flying him on charter flights and private jets to the Mayo Clinic and even to Mexico for treatments.

"When my father was sick and couldn't work, Ted supported my whole family," said Danny's son Ted, whose college education would later be paid for by his famous uncle. "And May, too. Ted comes across as being hard-assed and arrogant and aloof. But he helped a lot of family members. Certainly with money. He knew he had a special place in the world and had the opportunity to help people less fortunate than he. The whole family besides him were just ordinary people who never accomplished much. The rest of the family really saw him as a hero. I don't think he ever forgot his family. That's probably missed."

The Red Sox opened the season in Washington on April 18 before 28,327 fans and assorted dignitaries, including President Eisenhower and Vice President Nixon. When Williams first came to bat in the second inning, Nixon was heard to tell Eisenhower: "This is probably his last season. Let's root for him," according to the Associated Press. "That's a good idea," Ike responded.[39].

Williams worked the count to three and two off Senators ace Camilo Pascual, then crushed a fastball to dead center. The ball took off on a rising line and in just a few seconds cleared the thirty-one-foot fence, landing at least 420 feet away. The president and vice president were delighted, and they rose to give the Kid an ovation as he rounded the bases. Ted's 493rd homer tied him for fourth on the all-time list with Lou Gehrig. They were trailing only Mel Ott, Jimmie Foxx, and Ruth. Another looming milestone that season, the press noted, was Williams's two thousandth walk. He would reach that mark after he gained fifty-seven more bases on balls. Ruth again had that record with 2,056.

The next day in Boston, in the home opener against the Yankees, Ted blasted another pitch into the right-field grandstand in the eighth inning off Jim Coates. Williams proved how creaky he really was, pulling a leg muscle as he rounded the bases in his home-run trot. Then he caught a virus, to boot, and didn't return to the lineup until late May.

As Ted rode the bench, there was managerial and front-office intrigue aplenty. With the Red Sox floundering, a pro–Mike Higgins faction among the writers had been reporting that there was dissension among some players over how Billy Jurges was handling the team. Alarmed by the reports, Jurges called a team meeting in New York on April 26 to clear the air, asking any player who had a beef with him to speak out. No one did.

Williams scoffed at the dissension stories and strongly backed Jurges. "It's a lot of horseshit!" Ted told his pal Joe Reichler of the Associated Press. "It's those damn Boston writers again. They're always starting trouble."[40]

But a cloud remained over Jurges. At the end of May, UPI reported that Tom Yawkey was on the verge of replacing the manager with Williams, but both Yawkey and Ted denied the story.* Then the owner, along with Joe Cronin's replacement as general manager, Bucky Harris (Harris had been the Red Sox field manager in 1934, when he was replaced by Cronin), issued a strong statement saying that "Billy Jurges is our manager and no changes are contemplated." After its release, a furious Yawkey walked over to a group of writers at Fenway Park and said that while he believed in freedom of the press, "sometimes it goes beyond the bounds of human dignity and reason. I don't put up with it. I don't have to. How many of you guys think you're qualified to manage a ball club?" No one spoke up. Yawkey picked out one reporter and looked him in the eye. "Do you?"

"No, I don't think I'm qualified," the reporter said.

"You're damn right you're not."[41]

But the anonymous sniping persisted, and the skittish Jurges called another clubhouse meeting, this time inviting the writers to attend as well. Most of the players looked at the floor nervously. Williams glared at the reporters, still protective of Jurges. The manager asked that the player whom the wire story had quoted off the record as saying that Jurges had lost control of the team step forward and identify himself. Of course no one said a word. Then, astonishingly, Jurges turned to the writers and asked *them* to identify the culprit. "We're all in this together," he told the reporters. "We're all working for the City of Boston and the Boston Red Sox."[42]

After another long silence, the *Globe*'s Roger Birtwell piped up and, in his best Brahmin-Harvard accent, proceeded to give Jurges his lecture on the journalistic ethics of the day, such as they were. The writers covered the team; they were not *part* of the team, he said, and the manager was exceeding his authority by even asking them to come to this meet-

---

* In 1958, United Press had been renamed United Press International (UPI) after taking over the International News Service (INS).

ing. Most of the players giggled through Birtwell's separation-of-church-and-state discourse. Ted slowly boiled.

On June 14, two weeks after Yawkey's nearly Shermanesque statement that Jurges was his man, the manager was fired and replaced by old standby Mike Higgins.

Williams returned to the lineup rejuvenated, with the pain in his neck mostly gone. On June 17, he belted his five hundredth home run in Cleveland. With that, after the game he told a Cleveland writer, Hal Lebovitz, that this was definitely his last year.*

Ted proceeded to hit for average and power, and by July 4, Harold Kaese declared Williams the hottest hitter in the league, with fourteen home runs on the season and twelve in his last eighty at bats, the most potent power streak of his career.[43] Three days later his average stood at a sparkling .345, though it was clear he would yet again not have enough at bats to contend for another batting title.

On August 10, in Cleveland, Ted hit his 512th career home run to surpass Mel Ott's 511 for third in the all-time rankings, behind Foxx at 534 and Ruth at the seemingly unattainable 714. Later the same game, Ted swatted number 513.

"I'm happy and delighted over these two homers," Williams told the writers in the clubhouse. "I wasn't going for the long hit either time. . . . I got to know Mel Ott when he was traveling as a broadcaster with the Tigers. We used to talk hitting a lot. I can hardly believe that I have finally hit more homers than he did."[44]

On the flight to Baltimore, Boston's next stop on that road trip, Williams shocked the writers by sending them champagne. "So scientists think getting to the moon is an accomplishment?" wrote the *Globe* the following day in noting Ted's gesture. "Know what happened to the baseball writers yesterday on the flight here from Cleveland?"[45]

Soon he collected his two thousandth walk on the way to what would be a final total of 2,021 — forty-one less than Ruth's record. Ted's walk-is-as-good-as-a-hit credo was still not yet firmly established, but the stats mavens who would later emerge as a force in the game blessed his base on balls numbers as a key cog in the vital on-base percentage statistic. Williams's .482 on-base percentage (OBP) remains a major-league record.

With each milestone reached, with each record tied or broken, there

---

* The Boston writers were annoyed they had to follow the Lebovitz scoop, but they contained their grievances in light of the five hundred milestone.

was inevitable press speculation about what might have been had Ted not lost nearly five years of his prime to World War II and Korea. The *Globe*'s Jerry Nason calculated that his service in both wars cost Williams 2,534 times at bat, or 169 home runs, based on his lifetime average of one home run every 14.9 times up. At that rate, his five hundredth home run would actually have been his 669th had he kept playing straight through, Nason wrote. But Ted brushed off the might-have-been talk. Others who went off to war had their numbers affected, too, after all. "Nobody is more grateful than I am to have played as long as I have," he said. "I've been lucky."[46]

The *Sporting News* announced that it had named Williams baseball's "Player of the Decade" by acclamation in a vote of veteran players and writers in major-league cities around the country. This was effectively a lifetime achievement award, an acknowledgment that Ted had set historic records and fully redeemed himself in his valedictory season. Williams told *Sporting News* publisher J. G. Taylor Spink that to be recognized ahead of the likes of Mantle, Mays, Musial, and Aaron was meaningful to him, and it helped alleviate the sting of various MVP snubs.

The Red Sox mailed in the rest of their season and finished in seventh place with a record of 65–89, thirty-two games behind the pennant-winning Yankees. It didn't matter—the story, as ever, was Ted. He resisted offers from other AL teams to hold days in his honor as he took his final trip around the league. Instead, Ted underscored his longevity by homering off the Senators' Don Lee, prompting old-timers to recall that twenty-one years earlier, he had also homered off Lee's father, Thornton.

Williams tried to keep his mind on baseball—even though he'd had to deal with the news that his home in Islamorada had been destroyed by Hurricane Donna on September 11, along with many of his trophies and a set of custom-made four-foot-by-five-foot scrapbooks containing personal photographs and clippings. His final numbers—a .316 average in 113 games with 29 home runs and 72 RBIs—validated the story line he had hoped for entering his final season: that even at forty-two years old he could put together a season worthy of his excellent career and prove that 1959 was an aberration resulting solely from injury.

On September 25, the Red Sox made official what Ted had already announced—that he was retiring. The announcement, which was made after the Yankees clinched another pennant, also said that Williams would serve as a batting instructor at spring training in 1961, and after that, he would assume "other duties best suited to his talents." Four days earlier, Yawkey had offered Ted the general manager's job for the following season, but Williams had turned it down and suggested the hitting coach role instead.[47]

His final game at Fenway Park as an active player would be against the Baltimore Orioles on September 28, a Wednesday afternoon.

17

Last Ups

The Red Sox didn't play on September 26, and Ted used the free time to make a half-hour instructional film to be released in 1961 entitled *How I Hit, by Ted Williams*. He smashed balls off an elevated tee, then faced live pitching from Jerry Casale, a third-year right-hander. Rookie Jim Pagliaroni, who idolized Williams, served as the catcher, while another rookie, Don Gile, shagged out in right field.

Ted bantered with some hovering writers, and said with a smile that this was "some private business. The boys are just taking pictures of my swing. They got an idea that it might make a film." One writer asked him if he was sorry to be retiring as a player. "Yes, I am," Williams replied. "Baseball has been very good to me over the years, and I'll be forever grateful. Sure, I'll miss it as a player. That's only natural after all these years, but it had to come."[1] Such innocuous stuff provided adequate fodder for a press corps hungry for any off-day morsels about Ted. The news, such as it was, was featured in all the papers the following day, alongside accounts of the historic first televised Kennedy-Nixon presidential debate the previous night in Chicago as well as a report that Nixon would be boldly campaigning in JFK's home state of Massachusetts later that week.

Ted's penultimate home game, on September 27, was a forgettable 17–3 shellacking at the hands of the Orioles in which he grounded out, popped up, and walked. On the twenty-eighth, the weather was overcast, chilly, damp, and bleak, with little wind. Ineptly, the Red Sox chose this very day to step on the Williams valedictory story line by announcing the firing of general manager Bucky Harris and the return the following season of slugging outfielder Jackie Jensen, who had quit the team in 1959 because of a fear of flying. The news meant that before the game most of the writers were preoccupied in the executive suites. That left more running room for Ed Linn, who had been assigned by *Sport* magazine to cover Ted's last stand.

Linn had grown up in the Dorchester section of Boston as an ardent Williams fan who had watched with delight from the Fenway bleachers in 1939 as the rookie made his debut in right field and captivated the crowd with his youthful exuberance. After serving in the Army during World War II and attending Boston University on the GI Bill, Linn began a career as a freelance writer that was anchored by his association with *Sport* and his status at the magazine as a Williams aficionado. He had first been assigned a piece on Ted in 1954, following the spring training mishap in which the Kid broke his collarbone. Linn showed up at the clubhouse and heard Williams's response inside the training room when he was asked if he would receive a man from *Sport*.

"Send the son of a bitch in," said Ted.

Linn entered and introduced himself, whereupon Williams immediately said he would not talk to him. But he would tell him why. He had been nursing a grudge against *Sport* since 1948, when he had failed to show up for a luncheon the magazine had invited him to following the World Series and *Sport* had retaliated by dispatching a reporter to do a hatchet job on him. He couldn't remember the writer's name, but it would come to him, Ted said.

Linn mumbled something about the magazine having new ownership now and a new editor.

Who was the editor? Ted asked.

Ed Fitzgerald, Linn replied.

"Ed Fitzgerald! *That's* the son of a bitch" who had maligned him, Williams roared.

Having given up on getting his interview, Linn asked if he could at least ask one question. Williams, now feeling some empathy for the inexperienced young writer, who after all had had nothing to do with the 1948 retribution, answered at length. Linn ended up staying on to interview Ted and his teammates over a period of three days. When his teammates asked if it was okay if they spoke to Linn, Ted would respond, "Yeah, yeah. Talk to the son of a bitch." Linn modestly concluded that neither his technique nor his interviewing skills had had anything to do with Williams changing his mind: "Ted could see that he had someone there who had not the slightest idea what he was doing. And Ted has always had a thing about lending a helping hand to the disadvantaged."[2]

Every year after that for the rest of the decade, *Sport* called on Linn to write an article on Williams, and now here he was for the ending.

On his last day, Ted arrived at the park at 10:50 a.m., nearly four hours before game time. He was wearing dark brown slacks, a yellow sport shirt, and a tan pullover sweater. When Williams saw Linn, who had finagled his way into the Red Sox clubhouse in violation of the team rule that barred reporters for two hours before the game, he snapped: "You're not supposed to be in here, you know."

"It's your last day," replied Linn. "Why don't you live a little?"

Williams started to the trainer's room, but then wheeled around. "You've got a nerve coming here to interview me after the last one you wrote about me."

What was the matter with the last piece? Linn asked.

"You called me unbearable, that's what's the matter."

Linn noted that the full quote was actually that he "was sometimes unbearable but never dull," which had a different connotation.

Williams then reverted to bashing *Sport* for its original sin — the 1948 piece, now twelve years old. What he objected to in that article, it turned out, was the mere fact that the reporter had deigned to interview his mother to elicit a complimentary quote about him. As far as Williams was concerned, his family was off-limits, even if they said nice things about him.

"Why don't you just write your story without me?" Williams suggested to Linn. "What do you have to talk to me for? What can I tell you now that I haven't told you before?"

"Why don't you let me tell you what the story is supposed to be? Then you can say yes or no," Linn said before realizing this phrasing invited only one reply.

"I can tell you before you tell me!" Ted shouted. "No! No, no, no."

Linn retreated, hoping Williams would largely forget he was there and just let him observe. He proceeded to spend the entire time before the first inning with Ted, and later walked him out of the park when all was done. His lead piece, published in February of 1961, entitled "The Kid's Last Game," would be the definitive behind-the-scenes account of Williams's finale.

As his teammates dressed and went out on the field, Ted remained in the clubhouse and read his mail. Then he took his spikes into the trainer's room and began shining them. A photographer came by and asked him to sign a ball. "Are you crazy?" Ted sneered before demanding that the clubhouse boy throw the offending photographer out.

Williams did not leave the clubhouse for the dugout until 12:55 p.m., just thirty-five minutes before the game was scheduled to begin. He'd decided to skip batting practice—the better to make a dramatic entrance, Linn thought. As he climbed the stairs to the dugout, he bumped into his fishing pal Bud Leavitt, sports editor of the *Bangor Daily News*. Spotting Williams, a group of photographers closed in and began firing away. Ted leveled a few choice obscenities at them and guided Leavitt to the far end of the dugout. "Let's sit down so we don't get bothered by all these blasted cameramen," he said.

Leavitt let Ted know that he had brought Cornelius Russell III and a bunch of his friends to the game. Russell was a friend of Leavitt's, a young man from Bangor who had broken his neck in a sports mishap and was now confined to a wheelchair. Several years earlier, while Ted was in Bangor, Leavitt had taken him to meet Russell, an avid Red Sox and Ted fan known as Connie. Ted and Connie became friends, and Williams would visit him whenever he came to Bangor to hunt or fish, and he would call him on holidays to offer good wishes. Connie had never seen a major-league game, so now Leavitt had invited him and several of his friends to Fenway for Ted's finale. They were all sitting behind the Red Sox dugout. Ted told Leavitt to bring Connie and his friends around to his suite at the Somerset Hotel after the game.[3]

As Leavitt walked away, a young, attractive redhead peered into the dugout from her box seat and asked Ted if he would sign her scorecard.

"I can't sign it, dear, league rules. Where are you going to be after the game?"

"You told me that once before," the woman said.

"Well, where are you going to be?" Williams shouted.

"Right here."

"All right."

Joe Cronin, Ted's first manager and now the president of the American League, came into the dugout to greet his old charge. They talked quietly for a while, and as Cronin left he said to Ted, "Behave yourself."[4] Then Williams came onto the field to do a television interview with a local anchorman, Jack Chase of WBZ-TV, and his colleague Betty Adams. By this time, most of the surprisingly small crowd of 10,454 in attendance that day were in their seats, and they let out a lusty cheer at the sight of Ted. It was foggy and dark with a threat of rain.

Chase asked Ted how he felt. "You can't get blood out of a turnip," Williams replied. "I know I've gone as far as I can go as a player. I wouldn't try to go any further." Betty Adams followed up with a question about his future plans. "Sweetheart," Ted said, "all I know is I'm going to spring training. After that, I don't know what I'll be doing."[5]

Williams pushed his way through a gaggle of photographers who had been taking pictures of him doing the interview and headed back to the dugout. Someone asked him to pose with Cronin, and he did. Then Ted grabbed his glove and went out to play catch with Pumpsie Green, as he generally did during pregame warm-ups. At this the photographers closed in again. "Why don't you cockroaches get off my back?" Ted sneered at them. "Let me breathe."

A bell rang to signal the end of warm-ups before Ted could make more than a few dozen throws to Green. Most of his teammates went back into the clubhouse, but Williams stayed in the dugout and put on a jacket to ward off the chill. An older photographer asked him to pose, but Ted would have none of it. "Get lost," he said. "I've seen enough of you, you old goat."

Curt Gowdy, the Red Sox broadcaster who would preside over a pre-game ceremony honoring Williams, stopped by to go over the script. Then an old woman leaned in from the box seats with a plaintive wail: "Don't leave us, Ted! Don't leave us!" Williams was unmoved. "Oh, hell," he said, turning his back on her with disdain. When the young redhead saw this, she said to him: "Why don't you act nice?" Ted ambled over to her, smiling broadly, and said teasingly: "Come on, dear, with that High Street accent you got there."

Williams noticed Ed Linn soaking in the scene from a seat in the dugout. "You getting it all?" he asked him sarcastically. "You getting what you came for?"

In watching Williams's serial displays of rudeness and bad manners since his arrival that morning, Linn had concluded that Ted was determined to go out with his hardness on full display, without betraying even a hint of sentimentality.

Gowdy called the proceedings to order at home plate. "As we all know," he said, "this is the final home game for—in my opinion and most of yours—the greatest hitter who ever lived, Ted Williams." There was loud applause. After some more preliminary remarks from the broadcaster, the chairman of the Boston Chamber of Commerce presented Williams with a silver bowl "on behalf of the business community of Boston." Another chamber representative offered a plaque in appreciation for Ted's visits "to kids and veterans' hospitals." Boston mayor John Collins then proclaimed it Ted Williams Day and handed Ted a $4,000 check for the Jimmy Fund.

As this was going on, the Orioles starting pitcher, Steve Barber, a twenty-two-year-old rookie left-hander, limbered up on the sidelines, trying to stay warm. Pitching coach Harry "the Cat" Brecheen, the former Cardinals ace who had owned Ted in the 1946 World Series, supervised Barber. Williams fidgeted nervously—head mostly down, with one foot pawing the ground—waiting for the ceremony to wrap up.

Gowdy said, "Pride is what made him great. He's a champion, a thoroughbred, a champion of sports.... I don't think we'll ever see another like him." He then asked for another round of applause "for number nine on his last game in Boston." At that, Williams gave Gowdy a hug and whispered in his ear that he'd like to get a copy of his remarks.[6] Gowdy told him he'd ad-libbed it. "Aw, shit!" Ted said, then he grabbed the microphone and addressed the crowd.

"Despite the fact of the disagreeable things that have been said about me by the Knights of the Keyboard—and I can't help thinking about them—despite these things, my stay in Boston has been the most wonderful thing in my life. If I were asked where I would like to have played, I would have to say Boston, with the greatest owner in baseball and the greatest fans in America. Thank you."

The crowd roared and applauded. Williams walked back to the dugout, where his teammates were standing and waiting for him, also applauding. He smiled and winked at them, bounded down the steps, and took a seat on the bench.

Of course the writers were not thrilled at Ted's "Knights of the Keyboard" dig, but they had grown accustomed to his scorn over the years and well knew that his retirement also meant the passing of a reporter's dream. No one, after all, was better copy than Williams. In fact, John Gillooly of the *Record* had announced his own mock retirement that morning. "Dear Boss," he wrote. "This is it. Deal me out. I am through. Get another boy and give him a new ribbon and let him take over the keyboard. This is my official resignation. Williams has retired.... The loss of Williams to a Boston sports columnist is like a bad case of athlete's fingers to Van Cliburn. You just can't pound the keys any more. The song has ended." Gillooly said Ted was "our Hemingway. Oh, the stories he has written for us."[7]

Besides Ed Linn, there was another keen follower and admirer of Williams in attendance that day, a different kind of writer who had already established his bona fides as an ascendant man of letters: John Updike. Updike—who died in 2009 after producing a vast collection of fiction, poetry, essays, and criticism that established him among the leading lights of American literature — was then twenty-eight, just six years removed from Harvard, where he had graduated summa cum laude. He was firmly ensconced at *The New Yorker* magazine, for which he had already written more than one hundred articles, essays, short stories, and poems. In addition, he'd already published three books: a collection of poems, a collection of short stories, and a novel — *The Poorhouse Fair.*

The married Updike was at Fenway Park that day only by chance, he later admitted. He had come up from New York to rendezvous with another woman, but when he went to her apartment on Beacon Hill he learned that he had been stood up. So knowing this was Williams's last appearance in Boston, he went to the ballpark instead and ended up writing a piece for *The New Yorker* entitled "Hub Fans Bid Kid Adieu," which is considered by many to be the best sports essay ever.

Growing up in Shillington, Pennsylvania, near Reading, Updike loved baseball but was uninterested in either Philadelphia team — the Phillies or Athletics — but he latched onto the Red Sox. In a 1986 article for the *Boston Globe* entitled "Loving the Sox," Updike wrote that he had become aware of the great Williams before World War II, though it was the 1946 World Series that turned him into an enthusiastic Boston fan. He had a vivid memory of sitting in his father's Chevrolet at the age of fourteen and listening to the seventh game.

Working for *The New Yorker* after college, he would take the subway to Yankee Stadium to watch the aging Williams duel with Mantle. Then in 1957, Updike and his family moved to Ipswich, on Massachusetts's North Shore, where he would listen to Sox games on the radio. He loved Curt Gowdy's voice, "with its guileless hint of Wyoming twang," and became such a devotee of the team that he once got stranded in the Vermont wilderness after pulling over to listen to a game and draining the car battery.

In a 2008 interview, Updike told *Globe* sports columnist Bob Ryan, "No other sports figure has moved me as much as Ted Williams."[8] He was drawn to Ted's fragile persona, his constant warfare with the fans and the writers, and the sense of drama that seemed to always surround him. "The fact that he had these detractors in the stands and in the press just made Williams all the more appealing," Updike said. "It made you like him more and root for him harder. It gave him a heroic ethos....He never had a smooth season where he just played ball and everything just fell into place. There was always something going wrong."[9]

For Ted's last game, Updike arrived early and bought a good seat, near the Orioles dugout, behind third base. For his *New Yorker* audience, he immediately set the scene: "Fenway Park, in Boston, is a lyric little bandbox of a ballpark," he wrote, a description that would be quoted ad nauseam in the ensuing years and etch its way firmly into Red Sox lore.[10]

Batting third as usual, Ted came to the plate in the bottom of the first inning. There was one out and a runner on first. Willie Tasby — the center fielder acquired from the Orioles that June in a trade for Gene Stephens, Ted's caddy — had walked. Barber started Ted off with a curve that was inside; then a fastball was low. The crowd began to boo, wanting to see Williams hit. But the next two pitches were balls, too, and Ted trotted to first with a base on balls. After a hit batsman and a wild pitch, Williams found himself on third. Lou Clinton then lined out deep to center fielder Jackie Brandt. Ted tagged up and slid into home past catcher Gus Triandos as Brandt's throw hit him in the back. The crowd, which was cheering Ted's every move, was delighted by the uncharacteristic sliding hustle play.

When Ted returned for his second at bat in the third inning, Barber had been replaced by Jack Fisher, a twenty-one-year-old right-hander in his second year. Williams drove a one-and-one pitch to deep center, but Brandt drifted back and made the catch easily.

It was then announced over the public-address system that Ted's number, 9, would be retired by the Red Sox "after today's game." That meant that Williams had decided not to accompany the team to its final three games of the year at Yankee Stadium. So this would not just be his final home game but his final game, period.

In the fifth inning, with two out and nobody on and the Sox trailing 3–2, Ted came to bat for the third time. By then a fog was coming in, and an east wind had kicked up. He lashed a ball hard and deep to right-center. Off the bat it looked gone, but the right fielder, Al Pilarcik, raced back as far as he could, and with his back against the bull-pen wall, out from the 380-foot sign, caught the ball chest high. "I didn't think I could hit one harder than that," Williams said after the game. "The conditions weren't good."[11]

In the sixth inning, the lights were turned on to counter the advancing darkness and gloom. Jack Fisher was having few problems with the Red Sox and appeared in command as he took a 4–2 lead into the bottom of the eighth. Williams was due up second for what figured to be his last major-league at bat.

Willie Tasby, the first batter, came out of the dugout, followed quickly by Ted, whereupon the crowd roared. Tasby, rather than do the customary dawdling by the on-deck circle to swing a bat or two, proceeded directly to home plate, as if he couldn't wait to cede the spotlight to Ted. He hit the first pitch on the ground to shortstop for a routine out.

Williams had barely settled into the on-deck circle on one knee, swinging the lead bat to limber up, when it was his time. As he strode to the dish, everyone in the ballpark stood, but the cheers heard all afternoon now stopped in favor of more respectful sustained applause. Home plate umpire Ed Hurley—who, like all the umpires, admired Williams and who would stop by the clubhouse after the game to pay his respects—called time as the applause swelled and continued with no sign of dying down. Ted stood in the box, swishing his bat back and forth and staring at Fisher, all business, ready to hit. He seemed oblivious to the fans' acclaim and did nothing to acknowledge it. After about two minutes, Hurley signaled for Fisher to pitch, and he did so, even as the applause continued. Only after he threw his pitch—a ball, low—did the ovation stop.

The second pitch was a fastball, neck high. Williams swung mightily—and missed. The fans oohed, but they seemed to take some satisfaction in seeing that he was obviously going for the downs—neither he nor they would be cheated. Ted said later he couldn't believe he missed it. After the first pitch, he'd thought Fisher "humped up, as if he were going to try and fire the ball by me. I *knew* he was going to try and pump it right past. And gee, here comes a ball I should have hit a mile, and I *missed* the son of a gun. I don't miss, *completely* miss, very often and I don't know yet how I missed that ball."

He'd swung a tad late, so he told himself to be quicker on the next pitch: "Fisher couldn't wait to throw the next one," Ted remembered. "He must have thought he threw the last one by me, and maybe he did, but all my professional life I had been a fastball hitter, and whenever I had an inkling one was coming it was that much better for me."[12] But even guessing fastball and getting it, there was still the matter of delivering: he had hit the ball in the fifth inning on the screws, and it had not gone out. Then there was the singular pressure of this moment, the last at bat of his career, and the keen strain to satisfy his own yearning—and those of legions of others—to go out in style.

Fisher was confident. "I had just thrown a fastball right by him," he remembered. "So I came right back with another one. He hit it real good."[13]

Yes, he did.

The pitch came in waist high—on the outside corner, but still too fat. Williams turned on it and sent the ball screaming on a grand trajectory out to deep right-center. Jackie Brandt, who'd denied him in the fifth, couldn't reach this one. The ball sailed into the Red Sox bull pen and struck an aluminum canopy that covered the bench where the relief pitchers sat, making a loud racket.

"It was in the books while it was still in the sky," as Updike put it.

Deafening cheers, tinged with pure joy, rejoined the applause now as the Kid rounded the bases quickly, head down, expressionless. As he passed second, he thought of tipping his cap, he said later. If he were ever going to do it, this would be the time, his last chance. But he didn't.

As he approached home plate, Gus Triandos, the Orioles catcher, greeted him with a big smile, and Ted smiled back. The on-deck hitter, catcher Jim Pagliaroni, had dropped his bat and started to cry. "This was my idol," he recalled, "and no one will understand how special this was to me." Beside himself with excitement, he reached out his hand to congratulate Williams, a routine Ted never liked, even then. So Williams didn't extend his hand in return, but Pagliaroni reached out and grabbed it anyway.[14]

Said Pagliaroni of the moment, "It was my biggest thrill. I caught Catfish Hunter's perfect game and Bill Monbouquette's no-hitter. When Ted did that it was overwhelming."[15]

Williams entered the dugout and was swarmed by his teammates, who hooted and hollered and thumped his back. Ted took a seat on the bench and put on a jacket, assuming he wouldn't reenter the game. The fans were on their feet, delirious, and the park shook with cheers, which later turned to chants of "We want Ted! We want Ted! We want Ted!" Williams let all the adulation wash over him, and a satisfied smile came over his face. His teammates and Mike Higgins urged him to pop out to the field for a curtain call. Even the first-base umpire, Johnny Rice, motioned for him to come out, but Ted never budged. "Gods do not answer letters," Updike famously wrote, in what became the most quoted line of his seminal piece.

But Higgins wanted to give Williams one more chance to acknowledge the crowd. So at the end of the inning, he ordered Ted to take the field for the top of the ninth. Williams scowled at the manager, ripped off his jacket, grabbed his glove, and ran out to left. As soon as he arrived, he noticed Carroll Hardy running out to take his place and recognized Higgins's ploy, his nod to theater.

The crowd screamed anew, but Ted ran right through the cheers, still unwilling to bow to convention. As he passed shortstop, he said to Pumpsie Green, "Isn't this a crock of shit?" Green laughed.[16]

Nearing the dugout, he still was not showing a trace of emotion. First baseman Don Gile challenged him to show *something,* even to show off. "Put it on, you big shit!" Gile said.[17] But Ted just smiled as he passed by.

The ninth inning continued without Williams, and the Red Sox went on to score two runs to win the game, 5–4. As his teammates finished out the formalities on the field, the first thing Williams did when he reached the clubhouse was to go to a phone and share the news of his heroics with one Lee Howard, a fetching blond model from Chicago whom he had been seeing.

Howard had been born Lee Houda and raised in the affluent Chicago suburb of Riverside. Her father ran a cookie and cracker business in the city. Lee—tall and slim, with blue eyes—became a fashion model for Marshall Field's and various high-end ladies' clothing stores along Michigan Avenue. In the early '40s, she did a brief stint in Hollywood as an MGM starlet, during which time it was suggested she change her surname to the more mellifluous Howard. She appeared in small roles in a few films, at one point as a Ziegfeld girl. In 1945 she married William Charley, a wholesale food distributor, who enlisted Ronald Reagan to serve as his best man at their wedding. The couple had two children, but the marriage ended in divorce after three years. Lee resumed her modeling career, and in 1955 was named one of the dozen most beautiful models in the country.

Ted's pal John Blake, the state trooper based outside Boston, had introduced Lee to Williams in February of 1959, in Florida. Blake and some trooper friends had been lounging around the hotel pool and chanced to meet the divorced Lee, who was there with her young daughter and parents. By and by, Blake, who enjoyed being something of a talent scout for Ted, insisted that Lee meet his good friend Ted Williams.

"I had heard of him but did not know about baseball," Lee said. "I wasn't a fan. Anyways, I said to Blake, 'Is he a nice person?' He assured me he was. I think it was love at first sight on both sides. He called me every day after that, and he couldn't have been nicer for the next year or so that we were going together." Ted flew her out to spring training in Arizona, and she would see him play when the Red Sox came to Chicago, or nearby Detroit, and occasionally when she came to Boston.

"These were the first professional games I had seen. It's funny I think of it now, how great he was at the game."

Lee was delighted to get his call in Chicago from the Fenway Park clubhouse on the day of that final game. "He said, 'Well, I did it! I hit a home run the last time I was up!' I said, 'Well, isn't that great!' And he said—he volunteered it—'I didn't tip my cap to the sons of bitches, either.' And I said, 'Oh, Ted, you should have.' And he said, 'Oh, no!' "[18]

Williams showered, then told a batboy to bring the bat he had just hit the homer with upstairs and present it to Tom Yawkey as a gift. Some of Williams's teammates were awestruck by what they had just seen. Pete Runnels wandered around the clubhouse, repeating: "How about that? How about that? How about that?" By the time the writers were allowed in, after the obligatory fifteen minutes had passed, Ted was waiting for them with a towel around his waist. The old-timers, those with the best relationship with Williams, approached first. Among them was George Carens of the *Traveler,* the only reporter he had invited to attend his periodic dinners with close friends. Ted threw his arm around Carens and said, "This guy has always been in my corner."[19]

Williams was gracious to this first group. Had he been trying to hit a home run? "I was gunning for the big one," he said, smiling. "I let everything I had go. I really wanted that one."

Was he sure it was gone right away? "I knew I had really given it a ride."

Asked about his immediate plans, Ted said he would take care of some business in Boston, cover the World Series for *Life,* then return to the Keys to assess how much damage the hurricane had inflicted on his house.

Ed Linn, now reporting the end of his story from the clubhouse, thought Ted seemed a bit dazed. After the first group of writers left, he kept walking back and forth to the trainer's room from his locker. Once, departing from his usual postgame fare of two quarts of milk, Williams grabbed a bottle of beer and downed the whole thing with relish.

He answered more questions from other reporters, those whom he did not consider friends. Some did not venture over to interview him at all, perhaps wary of a final clash or a public dressing-down for some perceived past slight. Finally, when all the other writers had drifted away and Ted was getting dressed, Linn approached him.

"Ted, you must have known that when Higgins sent you back out that he was giving you a final chance to think about tipping the hat or making some gesture of farewell," Linn said. "While you were running back, didn't you have any feeling that it might be nice to go out with a show of good feeling?"

"I felt nothing," Williams said.

"No sentimentality? No gratitude? No sadness?"

"I said *nothing*. Nothing, nothing, nothing!"

As Linn was totaling up the number of nothings, Williams again berated him about the alleged unfairness of that *Sport* article of a dozen years earlier. It was clear that he'd slipped back into his hard, mean veneer. A photographer from one of the papers asked him to pose for one last shot, but Ted would have none of it. "I've been here for twenty-two years," he snorted. "Plenty of time for you to get your shot."

"This is the last time," the photographer pleaded. "Cooperate just this one last time."

"I've cooperated with you," Ted snapped back. "I've cooperated too much."

Don Fitzpatrick, the clubhouse man who had replaced Johnny Orlando, escorted Williams to the bleacher entrance and ordered the door opened, whereupon a driver pulled up in Ted's powder-blue Cadillac. Fitzpatrick scurried around to the passenger door and opened it for Williams. Just then, three young women who happened to be walking by noticed who had just hopped into the Caddy. "It's him!" one of them exclaimed. Another simply screamed, while the third went weak at the knees and fell mute. Hearing the noise, a group of men and boys ran down the street and pursued the car as it pulled away. The car turned the corner, but it was forced to stop behind a bus at a red light. As the group closed in, the driver pulled around the bus and sped away.[20]

Back at Ted's suite at the Somerset, Bud Leavitt was waiting with Connie Russell and his pals from Bangor, and the group settled in for the evening. Said Leavitt: "The way he celebrated his departure from major league baseball was opening up a couple of bottles of wine back at the old Somerset Hotel, while the police protected him from crowds trying to get a last look, and spending it with this kid in a wheelchair."[21]

In the papers the next day, some of the writers speculated that Fisher may have grooved the last pitch to Ted to give him a nice send-off. But Fisher strongly denied this. "No way, Jose, that I grooved that pitch," he said. "I was going to go after Ted, and I wasn't about to walk him. Nobody had to tell me that. You never want to face the tying run. You've got to make 'em hit their way on. It's common sense." Still, Fisher was moved by what had happened, even if it came at his expense. "I called

Ted that night at the Somerset Hotel, and we talked for about five minutes. I told him that I was happy for him, but not so happy that I had lost the game. He said he appreciated the fact that I had tried to challenge him, not mince corners or walk him."[22]

Updike was delighted by the reaction he received to his story and always remained proud of it. He continued to follow Ted with interest later in life, and wrote about him for various publications. Williams, of course, loved "Hub Fans," and when it came time for him to publish his autobiography, in the late '60s, he had an intermediary ask Updike if he would write the book. But Updike—no ghostwriter, he—politely declined. Still, Ted wanted to meet the man of letters and in 1982 wrote him a note asking if he would like to go fishing. Updike again begged off but expressed in his typed reply that he loved getting a letter from the Kid, particularly as it came just after he had listened on the radio as Williams returned to Fenway for his first Old-Timers' Game. "For a lot of people that piece on you is the best thing I ever wrote—even the only good thing I ever wrote," Updike told Ted in his letter. He explained that Williams's invitation was wasted on him since he was not a fisherman, but his letter was not, and concluded by thanking Ted for enhancing his life and all he had done to give him "some notion of excellence to shoot for."[23]

18

Kindness

When Williams finished his playing career, his excellence as a hitter was firmly established. But he had also established another legacy, which he would nurture and develop for the rest of his life—his work for the Jimmy Fund to help children with cancer.

His innate kindness to sick kids and to others who were having a hard time in life was Ted's most redeeming quality—the quiet counterbalance to all those moments when he boiled with rage and became unhinged.

The outbursts—like the spitting, the gesturing at fans, the rants at writers—tended to linger longer in the public memory, in part because much less was known about Williams's good deeds, which he did, after all, go to great lengths to conceal. It was harder to grasp Williams's softer side, but that part of him provided an equally compelling window into his character and helped him forge a lasting bond with fans in Boston and around the country.

While the Jimmy Fund was the main vehicle through which Ted performed his acts of kindness, he quietly showed his charity in other ways, including offering generous financial support to his mother, father, brother, and other family members; using a trusted courier to dispense hundreds of dollars in cash to people he knew were in need, with explicit instructions not to reveal where the money came from; soliciting a small check for the Jimmy Fund from friends he knew were struggling financially, then using the account number on the check to wire the people substantial sums of money anonymously; and spending hundreds of dollars annually to buy Red Sox tickets, then giving the tickets out to bellhops, cops, cabdrivers, and others of modest means.

But children were Williams's principal focus, and not all the kids he cheered up were seriously ill. In the spring of 1947, for example, nine-year-old Thomas Sessel of Chattanooga, Tennessee, a huge Ted fan, had been promised by his father that they would see the Red Sox when the team came through town on its way to Boston following spring training. But when the day came, Tommy had the flu and his parents ordered him to bed. He would have to miss the game.

"My father happened to see Ted Williams on the street that very day, before the game," Sessel said. "Now my father was a salesman. He stopped, approached Ted, and told him the story. He could sell anything, so he sold Ted Williams on getting into a car in a strange city, with a strange man, going God knows where. All of a sudden, into my room walks Ted Williams!...What made it interesting was that he was regarded by some as a misanthrope who would hardly give anybody the time of day. His actions really belied that reputation. He sat down and we talked for a little while. I forget how it came up, whether he offered or whether I asked for him to hit a home run for me that day. But he did."[1]

Promising home runs, then delivering, became one of the trademarks of Ted's visits to kids. Besides Sessel, there was double amputee Glenny Brann of Massachusetts. After visiting Glenny at a hospital outside Boston in May of 1947, Williams promised the boy a homer in his next game, then hit not one but two—the first balls he hit over the left-field wall at Fenway. And in 1949, his first homer of the season was dedicated to a fourteen-year-old polio victim.

These were Ruthean, outsize feats, and in his dealings with kids, Williams was following the Babe's tradition of being a source of comfort for needy children. Like Williams's parents, Ruth's mother and father had made little time for him when he was a boy and had actually abandoned him when he was seven years old, awarding custody to a Jesuit missionary order. Both men's experiences as neglected children colored their decisions as adults to get involved in the lives of kids in need.

While Williams nursed great resentment of his mother, the Salvation Army zealot, he admired her dedication and selflessness. Those qualities must have shaped Ted's own charitable impulse.

Williams grappled with a range of emotions throughout his life, including a taut discipline and drive to succeed, rage, shame, and tenderness—all amplified by a kind of narcissism, which drove his need to be admired and in control so as to further avoid the shame and hurt he carried with him from childhood.

He had a soft side but also a wish to fight or lash out, which hitting thousands of baseballs helped to sublimate. The Jimmy Fund work was a good counterweight to a life spent smacking a ball, dropping bombs as a fighter pilot, and struggling to contain a burning anger. Helping kids with cancer was an acceptable way to show that softer side.

Growing up, Williams had been an emotionally deprived, almost feral child. As an adult, the Jimmy Fund kids who worshipped him served as a soothing balm. If you wanted to be Ted's friend you gave him a refuge, and the Jimmy Fund served as a refuge for him, a place where he could relate to kids on his own terms.[2]

Williams's traumatic, neglectful upbringing left part of him longing for the love and attention he should have gotten early on but never did. Later, the praise he received for being a great hitter never made sense to him. He did not like sycophants. But he liked underlings who could be willingly subservient to him, idealize him, and idolize him. He needed the hero worship and connected with people through what he did rather than who he was.

Ted had lifelong friends. But most were fond of him, at least initially, because he was the great Ted Williams. And he gravitated toward people who were not his social equal, people like the TV repairman, the liquor salesman, and the clubhouse attendant—those whom he wasn't threatened by and felt safe with.

Williams felt uncomfortable if he was not in control of a situation. The rage attacks came on like a fever, usually triggered by loss of control—such as when he was booed by fans or ripped by writers for reasons he felt were unfair. One reason he connected with the Jimmy Fund kids and some of his trusted friends was because he was always in control. The charity work was compelling to him altruistically, but it also made him feel powerful. He was tall, athletic, and famous, but he didn't always feel powerful—he felt vulnerable. And the Jimmy Fund kids were helpless and dying. These were uneven relationships, but Ted could relate. After all, he had been a disenfranchised, neglected kid himself. And if on some deep, emotional level he didn't feel good about himself, maybe being in the company of people who were really suffering made him feel better. The Jimmy Fund kids could bring out Ted's tenderness, and he—at least the part of him that needed his mother, who was out on the streets—craved such an outlet. And if he knew that someone was dying, maybe he could give even more freely: no future obligation would be due. The kids couldn't hurt him. He had few situations like that. Not with the fans, the press, or even his own children.

But Ted had a good heart. Even as a schoolboy, he had often donated his thirty-cent daily allowance to kids less fortunate than he. High school teammates recalled Williams befriending outcasts, including handicapped people and a boy who stuttered.[3] In the minors at Minneapolis, he would visit sick and impaired kids in hospitals, and this carried over to his arrival in Boston in 1939.

Don Nicoll was in the hospital that year with a ruptured appendix, in the days before penicillin. He'd had surgery and was in serious condition. "My father, who was an avid baseball fan, somehow got to Ted Williams and asked him to see his boy in the hospital," Nicoll remembered. "Ted, who was then in his rookie year with the Red Sox, said yes, so he came to see me, and after I got out of the hospital, he came and visited us at our home on a number of occasions. I think he found ... [our] home a place where he could be where he wasn't under the gun, he was not being badgered, nothing was expected of him except that he'd enjoy himself."[4]

On his own initiative, Williams would often call on other children like Nicoll until 1947, when the Jimmy Fund launch gave him an organized way to focus his efforts. The Variety Club of New England, an association of people in show business, decided that year to adopt Boston Children's Hospital as its favored charity so that they could spotlight the problem of cancer in children, not just in adults. They raised $47,000 through a raffle and established the Children's Cancer Research Foundation, headed by Dr. Sidney Farber, a renowned pediatric pathologist at Children's Hospital, who is credited with being the father of chemotherapy.

Farber's early work attracted wide attention, and to build on that success, the Variety Club arranged for Ralph Edwards to feature the Boston effort on his nationally syndicated *Truth or Consequences* radio program in 1948. On the air, Edwards telephoned the Children's Hospital room of a young cancer patient. The child chosen by Farber to talk with Edwards was twelve-year-old Einar Gustafson, who was from a small town in northern Maine, near the Canadian border. His identity was not revealed on the broadcast, which assigned him the pseudonym Jimmy.

Since Einar was a Boston Braves fan, it was arranged that Edwards would steer the discussion to baseball, and that some of the Braves players would be standing by to make a surprise appearance in the boy's hospital room.

The players—including Johnny Sain, Warren Spahn, Eddie Stanky, and Earl Torgeson, as well as the manager, Billy Southworth—assembled around Einar's bed and presented him with a raft of baseball loot, including a uniform, bats, and balls. A piano was then brought into the room, and the boy led everyone in a rendition of "Take Me Out to the Ball Game" in an animated, off-key voice. Edwards concluded the broadcast with a fund-raising appeal, and when he bluntly suggested to Farber that the clunky Children's Cancer Research Foundation was too long a name for people to remember, Farber quickly came up with a handier two-word alternative: the Jimmy Fund.

The radio show struck a chord. People in Boston walked in off the street to give cash, while letters containing checks arrived from various parts of the country. Jimmy Fund collection canisters began popping up throughout New England and became fixtures at Little League games, movie theaters, bake sales, and wherever large numbers of people gathered. By the fall, more than $231,000 had been raised, and the following year, ground was broken on a five-story Jimmy Fund headquarters building in Boston, which replaced the tiny lab Farber had been working out of.[5]

The Red Sox's first major event was the fund-raiser starring Williams in the summer of '53, following his return from Korea, and Ted was effectively the spokesman for the charity from that point on.

After Einar Gustafson went into remission and left the hospital, Jimmy Fund officials lost track of him over the years, and many assumed he had died. But Gustafson would later reemerge dramatically and identify himself as the original "Jimmy" more than fifty years later, as the charity prepared to celebrate its golden anniversary.

Williams remained closely linked to the Jimmy Fund from 1947 until his death—a span of fifty-five years. That marked one of the longest associations of any public figure with a charity—rivaling or surpassing Jerry Lewis's work for muscular dystrophy and Bob Hope's for the USO. During Ted's involvement, the Jimmy Fund became a New England phenomenon, raising more than $200 million for the Children's Cancer Research Foundation, which later became known as the Dana-Farber Cancer Institute. Williams was the impetus behind a significant portion of that total.[6]

He was the public face of the Jimmy Fund, personally attending fund-raisers at American Legion halls, drive-in theaters, local police stations, Little League games, temples and churches, department stores, fish fries, bake sales, and cookouts. He would also lend his name to major pledge drives and endorse any checks sent to the Jimmy Fund—a creative way for fans to get his autograph. At speaking engagements, in lieu of a fee,

Ted would ask whoever had invited him to send a check to the Jimmy Fund. He also made movie trailers for the charity, along with stars such as Bing Crosby, Spencer Tracy, and Joan Crawford.

But his most important work was unheralded—the quiet visits Williams made to the bedsides of dying children, which he insisted could not be publicized. Ted came to call because he cared, that was all. He feared that if the papers wrote about the visits, the authentic would look inauthentic; that his compassion would appear to be a calculated attempt to soften his bad-boy persona. Reporters knew about the visits, but whenever one broached the subject, Williams warned him not to write about it or he would never talk to the writer again.

Michael Cioffi was one of the many children Ted came to see. Although Cioffi later died, Ted's visits lingered as a loving comfort to Michael's family, which included seven brothers and sisters. Michael was four years old and had leukemia when Williams first saw him at Children's Hospital in 1954.

Michael's brother, Ernest Cioffi, remembered: "I was there with my mother, and Michael said to me, 'Know who that guy is over there?' He had his back toward me, so I said, 'No; who is that?' So my brother yelled up to him, 'Hey, Ted!' and the guy turned around, and my jaw dropped to the floor. Ted Williams came over and talked to Michael and me, and he spoke to my mother, and my mother asked if he'd like to come over to the house for an Italian dinner." A week later, Williams appeared at the Cioffi house, in the Charlestown section of Boston. Michael, by then blinded from a tumor in his eye, had gone home to die. Ted stayed for two to three hours. "There's eight of us, so that's why he was there all that time. It was an honor, a day I'll never forget. Michael would always say, 'Ted Williams says I'm gonna get better, to keep fighting.' Things like that. Ted was a modest person, very nice, and he was really down and hurt when he came to the house, because looking at my brother, he had a tumor in his eye and in his brain, and his head was almost twice the size of a normal head."[7]

Mike Andrews, the former Red Sox second baseman who went on to become the Jimmy Fund chairman, told of a time when a little boy wouldn't let go of Williams's hand, so Ted had someone pull up a cot, and he slept next to the boy.[8] Saul Wisnia, publications editor at Dana-Farber and the author of a book on the history of the Jimmy Fund, told a similar story of Williams spending the night on a bed next to another boy. Then when the boy's family went to check him out of the hospital and pay the bill, they were told Williams had taken care of it.[9]

Even four days before his final game, Williams had gone to Rhode Island to make four appearances for the Jimmy Fund. Before he left, he stopped at Children's Hospital in Boston to visit a dying boy. The boy, who presented Williams with a belt he had made for him and buckled it around Ted's waist, died a few days later.[10]

While reporters respected the news blackout Williams imposed on live coverage of his Jimmy Fund visits, fans generally became aware of what Ted was doing because people such as Farber and Richard Cardinal Cushing, of the Archdiocese of Boston, would talk about Ted's kindness publicly. And sometimes the grateful parents of a child Ted had helped would call the papers and sing his praises as well.

Assessing Williams's impact on his cancer patients, Farber said in 1958: "I've seen Ted with them and he's better with the children than a collie-dog. He comes in quietly to visit them. He comes without publicity. And I have to respect the man for it. This is his contribution to society. When you put together the whole case for Ted Williams, it's then you find a wonderful human being who has done a great deal of good."[11]*

One mother said that in the late '40s, Williams helped her young son pull through a delicate operation in which a metal plate was inserted in his skull. "You can't imagine the tender sincerity with which Ted talked to the lad," she told *American* columnist Austen Lake. "It was amazing how he could put himself on childhood's level, the direct simplicities of which my boy understood and which smoothed away his fears. You know children are quick to detect adult artificiality or a false note, like in a cracked bell. Here was a spiritual therapy beyond medical science. It gave my little one courage to face his ordeal, which restored him to health with a silver plate in his head. . . . So in the impressionistic mind of a boy, there is a little bit of God about Ted."[12]

In 1957, Williams visited a fifteen-year-old boy at Children's Hospital who died shortly afterward. Nevertheless, the boy's father was so touched by Ted's visit that he wrote the *Boston Globe* to suggest that a ward at the hospital be named after Williams. "If he could prolong even for a day the life of a child, he would give up all his baseball trophies, honors and records," the man said of Williams. "It hurts me to hear him condemned, knowing all the good he has done. I don't care whether he throws his bat, expectorates, wears a necktie or not. Let us not forget the good

---

* Reflecting on Williams's emotional outbursts, Farber compared Ted to General George Patton, also known for a raging temper—a "man of greatness under strain" whom people didn't take the time to fully understand.

things about this gracious man....I know what he has done to try and keep my child and others alive."[13]

Once, in the '40s, when another admiring father sent Ted a letter saying he had named his son after him, Williams sent out a silver cup to the young boy engraved: FROM TED WILLIAMS TO TED WILLIAMS.[14]

On at least three occasions, Williams responded to appeals to boost the spirits of seriously ill or dying children who lived out of state by quickly chartering a plane and flying to visit them.

In the late 1940s, when the Red Sox were in Washington to play the Senators, Williams received a telegram from a doctor in North Carolina who was attending a dying boy. The doctor said the boy talked about Ted constantly and wondered if Williams could send him an autographed ball to give him a lift. Ted flew down to deliver the ball in person and returned to Washington that night.[15] On another occasion in the capital, before the Red Sox were to start the season, a Richmond, Virginia, man reached Williams by phone and told him his son was seriously ill in a hospital there. "Can I see him this afternoon?" Ted asked. He hired a plane and returned in time for opening day.[16]

Then in the early '50s, broadcaster Bud Blattner, in Boston to televise a Game of the Week for ABC, told Williams he'd visited a ten-year-old boy with leukemia in a Midwest hospital. Ted was the boy's hero—would he sign a ball for him? Williams said he'd do better than that—he'd charter a plane and go see the boy, on two conditions: Blattner could say nothing of the visit on television, nor could any local press in the boy's hometown be alerted. Ted made the trip, and the boy died later that year.[17]

Throughout the rest of his career, Williams kept up a schedule of frequent visits to Jimmy Fund patients and public appearances on the charity's behalf. In 1957, in Baltimore, when the Orioles wanted to honor Ted on his birthday with gifts, he refused and asked for contributions to the Jimmy Fund instead. In 1958, following a Sunday afternoon game at Fenway, Williams made a dramatic entrance by helicopter at the Suffolk Downs racetrack in East Boston to preside over what was billed as the "world's largest spaghetti dinner," at which fifteen thousand people turned out to donate money for the cause.

Until Ted died, he would stay in touch with, and be a mentor to, some of the children who had survived. He always considered most of his Jimmy Fund work—certainly the visits to sick kids—to be private expressions of cheer and goodwill, and he disliked anyone suggesting that he was some sort of saintly benefactor.

"Look, it embarrasses me to be praised for something like this," Ted said years later. "The embarrassing thing is that I don't feel I've done anything compared to the people at the hospital who are doing the really important work. It makes me happy to think I've done a little good. I suppose that's what I get out of it. Anyway, it's only a freak of fate, isn't it, that one of these kids isn't going to grow up to be an athlete, and I wasn't the one who had the cancer?"[18]

Williams also thought of his younger brother, Danny, with that same there-but-for-the-grace-of-God tinge to his voice: "My brother had cancer of the bone marrow or some damn thing. He threw a ball or an orange at somebody and broke his arm. Aw, shit. Could have been me, you know?"[19]

19

Real Life

With his final home run, Ted's lifetime average stood at .344407 — a sliver higher than Tris Speaker's .344338. That put him fourth on the all-time list, behind Shoeless Joe Jackson at .356, Hornsby at .358, and Cobb at .367. He was then third on the home–run list at 521, behind Foxx's 534 and Ruth's 714. He was first in all-time on-base percentage at .482, ahead of Ruth's .474, and second in slugging percentage, with .634 to the Babe's .690. *Globe* stat guru Harold Kaese calculated that Williams had won a remarkable ninety-eight games with home runs for the Red Sox over the course of his career — a higher percentage than Ruth. He had made the dramatic seem almost routine, and his team came to depend on him so much that his failures — in the 1946 Series, the 1948 playoff game, and the last two games of 1949 against the Yankees — stood out all the more.

Obviously, losing nearly five years in his prime to two wars affected Ted's numbers dramatically, and now the "what if" games began in earnest. Kaese, adding his projections to those of others, wrote that if Williams had played the 727 games he missed during World War II and Korea, he would have finished with 165 more home runs at 686, 403 more RBIs at 2,242, and 842 more hits for 3,496.

Beyond the numbers, Updike's essay reverberated and served to put a sheen on Ted. Having one's heroics celebrated — even with dollops of clubhouse cruelty and vulgarity — in *Sport* magazine was one thing, but having them exalted in the pages of *The New Yorker* was quite another. Now Williams had transcended the sports pages and mass-circulation monthlies and entered the realm of *literature,* a development that only helped propel him on his way to Cooperstown and formal designation as an immortal.[1]

On a practical level, however, Ted now had to come to terms with just what he would do next, and his heroic departure from baseball helped elicit a spate of offers. The Yankees—presumably trying at least in part to embarrass their rivals in Boston—asked Ted to pinch-hit for them in 1961 at a salary of $125,000. He said no. The Tigers inquired as to whether he'd have any interest in managing their team. Ted said no. If he were going to stay in baseball, he wanted it to be with the Red Sox, and though he'd agreed to a part-time job helping out the hitters at spring training, he was ambivalent about a continued association with Boston. He didn't think he was suited to be a manager, but felt that if they'd wanted to, the Red Sox could have fashioned a full-time job for him, combining being a hitting coach with scouting, perhaps. "I thought for a long time the Red Sox wanted to keep me in some capacity, but as I look back I have to think there was a faction that didn't want me around, that kind of undercut me a little bit," Ted later wrote. "I never felt I was really wanted, so the hell with it."[2]

Of course, it wasn't imperative that Williams take any job. Ted Williams Enterprises, created by Fred Corcoran in 1946, had been generating well over $100,000 annually for years. There was a clothing and product line: Ted Williams hats, shirts, belts, and hunting boots. There was baseball card income, and there were various endorsement deals. Williams, who didn't smoke and couldn't abide the habit, had hypocritically done advertising campaigns for Lucky Strike and Chesterfield in the '40s. One Lucky ad showed Ted with a cigarette dangling from the left side of his mouth, and he was quoted as saying: "Luckies are really a great smoke. They give me what I'm looking for in a cigarette." Williams later regretted doing the ads. "I always said I was going to give that money back to cancer research," he said. "I always said I was going to, but I never did."[3]*

There was a contract with the Wilson Sporting Goods company that produced a five-figure annual fee, and a similar deal with the Horton Manufacturing Company of Bristol, Connecticut, which made fishing tackle. The annual fly-casting exhibition at the sportsmen's show, which he would continue, was lucrative. Publishers were clamoring for his autobiography whenever he wanted to clear enough time to talk into a

---

* While Ted kept his distance from his mother's side of the family, one of his endorsement deals, with Wheaties, meant that hundreds of boxes of cereal were regularly delivered to 1008 Chino Street in Santa Barbara. The extended family was effectively raised on the cereal. "I remember I ate Wheaties until I was blue in the face, and I can't stand them now," said Ted's cousin Rosalie Larson, Paul Venzor's daughter.

tape recorder and let a ghostwriter weave it all together. And Hollywood had a standing offer with Corcoran to produce a feature film, *The Ted Williams Story.*[4]

Now television also beckoned. Would he do color commentary on the Game of the Week? Ted said no. ABC took an option on Ted's services to host one or more shows on either baseball or fishing.[5] Fishing remained Williams's great passion outside baseball. In late 1952, he'd invested in a Miami-based fishing-tackle business, then several years later, Ted and the golfer Sam Snead had started their own tackle firm, Ted Williams, Inc. In November of 1960, Ted wrote a rather presumptuous letter to L.L.Bean, the venerable Maine-based outdoor clothing and equipment store, asking if it would consider merging, or being acquired by, Ted Williams, Inc. The overture got nowhere.

Ted Williams, Inc., made a good rod and reel, Ted felt, but it couldn't generate any sales volume. Earlier in 1960, while fishing with Karl Smith—his roommate at Pensacola during World War II, whom he'd stayed friends with and who had a sales background—Ted asked Smith how he could expand his fishing business.

"Have you heard of Sears?" Smith asked.

"You think they can sell fishing tackle?" Ted said.

"They've got ten thousand stores. Next time you go to Chicago and have some time off, go to the Sears building and tell 'em who you are and that you want to see a person that sells fishing tackle."

So Williams did and made a contact, George Struthers, a vice president in charge of merchandising. Then the day after Ted's final game, Struthers sent Williams a telegram saying he wanted to talk with him about his future. Several days later, Struthers and a colleague were in Ted's suite at the Somerset in Boston to finalize a contract for Williams to develop and test a range of baseball, fishing, hunting, camping, and boating equipment for the company as well as to do some marketing and promotion. Ted would become chairman of Sears's "Ted Williams Sports Advisory Staff."

Ted flew to Chicago for the announcement, two days after Christmas. The deal was for five years at $125,000 a year, but that was just a base figure; Williams also got a percentage of anything sold with his name on it, according to Ted Rogowski, a lawyer who represented him on the Sears deal. And while Ted would be required to drop his association with Wilson, a competitor, he could keep his fishing-tackle business.

A few weeks after the deal was announced, Williams called Karl Smith to thank him for giving him the Sears idea.

"It's the biggest robbery since Brink's," crowed Smith. "It means you're gonna go hunting and fishing anywhere you want to and Sears will pick up the tab for it."

Ted laughed and said, "You've always been a wise son of a bitch."[6]

The deal was a coup for Williams. It paid well and linked him to a major company and the recreational sports that he so enjoyed. Moreover, he wouldn't have to work that hard: all told, the time required of him would not be more than two months a year.

Ted enjoyed the interaction with members of his "sports advisory staff," all of whom were leading lights in their fields. Sears was then at the forefront of an effort by the merchandise sector to recruit celebrities as endorsers of its products, and Williams was the company's celebrity in chief. Under him were about a dozen active or former "sportsmen," including Sir Edmund Hillary, the New Zealander who in 1953 had become the first to scale Mount Everest; Bob Mathias, the Olympic decathlon winner in 1948 and 1952; basketball's Jack Twyman, then captain of the Cincinnati Royals; and, later, pro tennis star Butch Buchholz.

Sears quickly became the biggest buyer of Ted Williams, Inc., gear and launched an aggressive advertising campaign that was the first of its kind. It featured two-page layouts in *Life, Look,* and other magazines that showed the Kid, dressed in a white jacket, dark tie, and dark slacks, standing in front of Sir Edmund and the others. The ad copy said that Sears had signed Ted as a "playing manager" who would "add a cold, professional viewpoint on the quality of every piece of Sears sports equipment *before* it gets into the Sears catalog or any one of the...Sears department stores."[*]

Williams and his advisory group gathered at least twice a year; they met with manufacturers to discuss equipment (Ted might recommend putting stronger wheels on a camp trailer, lighter soles on hunting boots, or softer leather on baseball gloves to improve their feel) and visited new Sears stores when they opened. On those occasions, Ted would put on fly-casting demonstrations, setting up garbage cans in a parking lot and dropping a line into them from two hundred feet away.

"We were not just endorsees; we had to test and be satisfied and proud of the products, and Ted was very much the leader of that philosophy,"

---

[*] Though it was hard to imagine Hillary not having the first say on how to make the best sleeping bag, one early ad presented Williams as the idea generator: "Most sleeping bags seem to be made for midgets. Let's make them longer and a whole lot wider—so that people can really stretch out. Who wants a sleeping bag that fits like a straitjacket?"

said Buchholz, who joined the group in the early '70s. "Ted was a very strong individual. He led by example, and if he didn't like something, boy, he made sure the manufacturer would fix it. I saw him break fishing poles over his knee if they weren't good enough."[7]

The advisory group was filled with type A personalities who liked to hold forth on the intricacies of their sports, and they each commanded attention. Jack Twyman and Williams hit it off particularly well. Williams nicknamed the six-foot-six-inch basketball star the Glandular Case, and Twyman called Ted the Swollen Splinter. Besides Williams, Twyman was struck by Hillary. "Sir Edmund Hillary: he was a tiger.... Just imagine climbing Everest like he did! He was the toughest man I have ever seen; I wouldn't tangle with him." Twyman recalled that Williams would grab a fork during dinner, simulate a bat, and talk for hours about the art of hitting. "There was no one that studied it like him or could articulate it like him," and he would brook no challenges. " 'You don't know anything about it,' he'd say."[8]

Ted was just as expert at fishing. He would analyze the butt of the rod for strength, the middle for flex, and the tip for feel. His boss at Sears, Carl Lind, recalled that at a sporting goods show in Houston, a buyer introduced Ted to a group from Daiwa Seiko, the Japanese fishing-tackle manufacturer. "Ted became the center of attention when he began to dissect their reels down to the last screw, showing them how to reconfigure the parts to improve their function," Lind said. "It was a sight to see three Japanese engineers furiously taking notes. They got a free fishing lesson that day from the master." When Lind introduced his boss to Ted, the man excitedly volunteered that he had just bought a new fishing pole. "We only deal with rods in this business," Williams informed the executive curtly. "Poles are for catfishing."

Ted was also involved with a Sears division that made fishing boats, motors, and marine safety equipment. One key corporate goal, Lind said, was to produce an unsinkable boat. Their designers used plastic to shape the hull and deck and poured expandable foam in between. Williams was chosen to be the centerpiece of a TV ad campaign for the boat and was shown drilling a hole through the bottom, but the boat sailed on. Then, in the climax, he sawed the boat in half, and still half of it kept planing along. "This was a merchandising utopia," Lind wrote in a short reflection on his time with Ted.

To promote the boat and its other products, Sears invited a group of writers from various outdoor magazines, like *Field & Stream, Outdoor Life,* and *Sports Afield,* to come to its test base at Fort Myers Beach, Florida.

One of the writers asked Williams: "Did you really saw that boat in half in the TV commercial and still ride in it without sinking?"

"Hell, yes!" said Ted. Then he pointed to the manager of the test base. "Get me the half boat we used in the commercial. I'll show them." The manager retrieved it from storage, attached a motor, and took it to the dock. Ted hopped in, fired up the engine, sat well back in the stern to ensure the craft would plane, and off he went—just as he did in the commercial. But as he made his way out into the Gulf, Ted inched forward, curious to find the tipping point where the boat would no longer plane. He went an inch too far, and suddenly the boat capsized, and Williams was hurled into the ocean. Fearing his star attraction might drown in full view of the outdoor press, Lind dispatched a motorboat to the rescue, and Ted was fished out. When he docked, he emerged laughing, as if he'd thoroughly enjoyed the entire spectacle.

Williams also made his presence felt in hunting. Once, on a trip to Arkansas to visit the factory that manufactured Daisy BB guns, carried by Sears, Ted watched a demonstration of point shooting, in which a rifle is fired from the hip as opposed to the shoulder. He then tried firing at a series of objects such as coins, keys, and buttons that were dangling from a line tied between two trees. "From about 20 feet away, it was remarkable, after a few trials, how many of those objects Ted was able to hit," Lind wrote.[9] On another outing in Illinois, a skeet-shooting competition was arranged between Williams and decathloner Mathias. Each shot a perfect twenty-five for twenty-five.

As Ted established himself with Chicago-based Sears, he was also spending more time there courting Lee Howard. During one of Ted's visits, when Lee had to cut the evening short to relieve her parents, who had been babysitting her children, he suddenly proposed. Actually, it was more of a directive, she recalled: "I told him I had to leave. He said, 'This is ridiculous. We're getting married!' He didn't ask me. He told me. I thought it was great. I kind of liked it that he didn't ask."

Ted made it clear he didn't want to have any more kids. "No, he did not want children. It didn't matter to me. I had mine, so I didn't care if we had any more children. I didn't try to push that at all."

Ted told her a little about his childhood, but not much. "He would just grit his teeth and clench his jaw over the fact that he used to have to stand around on corners with his mother and collect money. That really, really bothered him. I suppose it was embarrassment."

May Williams died on August 27, 1961, in a Santa Barbara nursing home at the age of seventy. Ted flew out and took charge of the arrangements. Bobby-Jo, who by then was thirteen, called her father to say she was sorry that May had died. Her mother had instructed her to call him and express her condolences, but he seemed uninterested. She'd never met her grandmother. There was a simple graveside service conducted by the Salvation Army.

Ted and Lee got married less than a month later, on September 19, in Cambridge, outside Boston. Ted was forty-three, Lee thirty-eight. Ted wanted absolute secrecy, so his old pal John Buckley, who ran a movie theater in Cambridge by then and was well connected at city hall, had a friend—an assistant court clerk who was also a justice of the peace—marry the couple in his office at the courthouse.

The ceremony lasted ten minutes. "It was the second wedding for both of us," said Lee. "We wanted something low-key, and of course Ted wanted no publicity, if he could help it." Williams was dressed in a cream-colored sport shirt, a blue checked sport jacket, blue slacks, and white buckskin shoes. Lee wore an understated but elegant cream-colored dress. In the wedding paperwork, Ted listed his occupation as "public relations."

The couple was forced to scrap plans to honeymoon in Bermuda because of Hurricane Esther, which was then raging up the Atlantic, so after a celebratory dinner with the Buckleys at the Carriage House in nearby Lexington, Ted and Lee got in a car and drove north to Maine, on their way to Canada, where Williams had bought some land along the Miramichi River in New Brunswick and planned to build a cabin. The river was known for having some of the best Atlantic salmon fishing in the world.

Lee, the Chicago fashion flower, was no outdoorswoman, but Ted set out to make her one. Though she'd barely fished a day in her life, it wasn't long before Williams had her decked out in rubber hip boots in the pools of the Miramichi, on the prowl for salmon. When she didn't perform to Ted's liking in that first test, he assigned her a task for which he deemed her more suitable: picking out furniture for the new cabin. "It was very nice furniture, very tasteful for a cabin," she remembered, but it was too luxe for Ted. "He said, 'Jesus Christ, you'd think you're trying to furnish a penthouse on Fifth Avenue!'"

Soon there were more fishing trials. When they went to Islamorada for the winter, Ted was up at 5:30 each morning and would wake Lee with a mock reveille, sung through his fist over his mouth. "Rise and shine!" He'd insist she go out on the boat with him and adhere to a strict protocol. "He would take you out on that boat for nine hours at a crack, and he didn't want you to sit, you had to stand up—something about the fish making a fool of you, don't ask me, I have no idea. One day I was complaining about having to stand, and he is saying, 'Stand up! Get up!' whenever I'd sit. So I'm facing out the back of the boat and I'm holding a rod and I heard a splash and I say to myself, 'Oh, gosh, he's got a big one,' and I turned around and he'd fallen overboard. I just roared with laughter. He wasn't too happy with me."

Williams had a workshop in the back of the house where he would spend hours tying extremely intricate flies. "He'd have me out there and try to teach me," Lee said. "He was very good at it. It's difficult, very difficult. I didn't find it too exciting, though."

She liked golf better, and sometimes they would go over to the Cheeca Lodge, an Islamorada resort, where there was a course. "That's where he used to throw the clubs whenever he hit a bad shot," she said with a chuckle. "He would get so violent with the temper when he played golf. At one point I had him taking calcium pills. It was supposed to calm him down, but it didn't work. Now, if they had had Prozac at that time, that's what the man should have been on."

Lee also had to adjust, in Islamorada, to the presence of Ted's old flame Louise Kaufman, who lived just a few doors down from the new house Williams had moved into after the hurricane destroyed his old one. Louise had been devastated when Ted informed her that he was marrying Lee—after all, Louise had left her husband, with whom she'd had four children, on the hope that she would eventually marry Ted. Louise warned Ted that Lee would just get pregnant and take all his money.

Lee, in turn, teased her husband about his attraction to the older Louise. "I used to kid him and say, 'Do you have a mother fixation or something?'" she said, laughing. She was less amused after she caught Louise prowling in the bushes outside at night, trying to peek in their bathroom window. She told Ted, who just shrugged it off, bemused.

Ted was fully aware how different Lee and Louise were. Just before they married, he had invited Lee to join him at the summer baseball camp for kids he had started in 1958 in Lakeville, Massachusetts, a rural community about forty miles south of Boston promoted with typical chamber of commerce gusto as the "gateway to Cape Cod." One evening Ted was holding forth to his pupils under a tall oak tree. Lee remembered: "I walked out there and Ted said, 'Listen to what I am going to ask you now, fellas.' I was standing right there. 'If you had two gals, one that loves you just for yourself and the other one that loves you but wanted parties and mink coats, which one would you choose?' And I spoke up and said, 'The smart one!' He was talking about Lou Kaufman as the other one. He was saying that that's what I wanted, parties and the mink coat, but the other one just loved him for himself." Lee convinced herself that Ted had been kidding—after all, it had been he who'd bought her a $5,000 mink coat in Chicago after the wedding. He insisted, so she took him to a furrier she knew from her modeling days. "He wanted everyone to know he'd bought me a mink coat. I wasn't asking for one." And it was Ted who wanted her to have all the jewelry she needed, ordering a Boston jeweler he knew to send a selection of pieces for her to inspect down in Islamorada. "He had them send a bunch of bracelets, gold bracelets, and a chain with a diamond, a pendant. I could pick out what I wanted." Less glamorously, Ted also bought Lee a sewing machine and asked her if she'd make him some Bermuda shorts.

Sometimes they would go for long walks in the evening and have good talks. Once, they discussed what would happen when they died. "It was one of those foolish things where he said, 'I want to go first, and I don't want to be here without you.' And I said the same thing, blah, blah, blah. And that led to him saying that he wanted to be cremated."

When they were courting, Ted had been on his best behavior, and his temper hadn't been an issue. She knew he swore like a trooper, and after they were married, in jest she had tried to get him to curb the habit by instituting a fining system. She put a jar on the table, and every time he uttered a four-letter word, he would have to put a dollar in the jar. But Ted was familiar with that exercise, and there would be ten dollars in the jar within the hour, so it was pointless.

Still, the swearing seemed to mask a deeper anger that she hadn't been aware of and that soon became troubling. "I always used to wonder how someone who had such talent and had been given so much could be so angry," Howard said. "And I asked him that many times, and he wouldn't answer."

After fishing, golfing, and walking, Lee ran out of things to do in the Keys, and she yearned for a taste of mainland civilization, so she would drive up to Coral Gables and go shopping. Williams wouldn't want her to go and angrily accused her of sneaking around and flirting with other men. The nearly instant lurch into ferocity alarmed Lee. "It would just be nothing to set him off," she recalled. "You never knew when it was going to happen. It was incredible." One Thanksgiving, Lee had worked all day preparing the meal and announced that the turkey was ready. But when Ted opened the oven, he was enraged—the bird wasn't nearly brown enough, he said. "I would say it was his childhood, but that couldn't have made you that angry to all of a sudden just go berserk. He'd rip phones out of the wall at the house. He hated phones. He would throw phones and break them. I told him, 'I am not calling the phone company anymore.' I was embarrassed."

Williams's temper could also flare when Bobby-Jo visited. In the summer of 1962, Ted, Lee, and Bobby-Jo were at Williams's baseball camp. One evening there was a dinner for the camp counselors and other adult staff and their families. Bobby-Jo noticed that Ted was getting increasingly agitated because he felt people were not finishing the food on their plates. Williams had such an aversion to wasting food that he had carved the words "It's a sin to waste food" on a small tree planted inside the camp dining hall. Bobby-Jo wasn't sure why Ted felt so strongly about this. Her husband, Mark Ferrell, thought it dated to his childhood, during the Depression, when sometimes he'd be home alone and there wasn't enough food. Bobby-Jo remembered the time Ted had taken his friend John Buckley out for Chinese food. Buckley kept ordering one dish after another. "You'd better eat every bite of that," Ted warned him. Then he said it again, more angrily. When Buckley added still another dish, Williams said, "You'd better eat every bite of that, you dirty son of a bitch!" Bobby-Jo and others had to help Buckley finish all the food to forestall another tirade from Ted. "We were, like, bloated," she remembered.

Now, at the camp, she could see her father doing another slow boil. Then he threw his napkin on the floor in disgust, something Bobby-Jo knew he sometimes did at the dinner table if something displeased him. Afterward, he expected that someone would pick up the napkin and somehow rectify the affront, so Bobby-Jo did what she knew he expected of her. When she gave the napkin back to her father, Williams suddenly spit a mouthful of food in her face.

"I was absolutely and totally so mortified that I remember sitting there, and I did nothing for a few seconds," Bobby-Jo said. "Then I hit the outside, running, and I ran and it was cool and I didn't know what to do. I didn't want anybody to see me. I got back to the car, and I'll never forget this: one by one, and two by two, they started coming out to me.

All the women. They were all at the car. And they said, 'Your father didn't mean that, but he wasn't right.' And you know, he never apologized."

"There could be no mistakes," Bobby-Jo said of life with her father. Around the same time, one night when Ted and Lee had taken Bobby-Jo out for dinner and were bringing her home to her mother's house in Miami, Bobby-Jo forgot her keys, and Doris wasn't home. It was late at night. Ted got out of the car, screaming and calling his daughter a dumb little bitch. He tried to open a window or two in the house without success. Then he ordered Lee back into the car and pulled away, leaving Bobby-Jo cowering in the bushes, alone, waiting for her mother to return.

"It was so absolutely obvious that he had a mental problem," Bobby-Jo said. "But my father loved me, you know what I'm saying? He was so far ahead of his time as far as wanting to be a good dad, and he was good at it. The thing he wasn't good at was, he had no control over his temper. It got progressively worse and worse and worse."[10]

Lee thought one explanation for Ted's unpredictable, abusive behavior was that he simply wanted attention—good or bad. "He was a very private person and cherished his privacy, yet at times if he didn't get attention, he wanted it. He was kind of like a Jekyll and Hyde, to tell you the truth. When he didn't get attention and wanted it, he would be very loud and obnoxious so everybody had to give him the attention. There was no two ways about it. A lot of things he did was just to shock people. Because in front of others, if he was nasty to me, he was usually winking at me. In other words, he was letting me know that 'I don't even mean this,' that he was putting on a show. But the other people would be saying, 'Oh, my God!'

"His friends knew how he was, so they accepted it. He didn't stay mad at them or me. A lot of times when he would try to embarrass me in front of people by doing things, he would come back to me and say, 'I love you more than anything.'"

Lee was also struck by Ted's insecurity. "He used to say to me, 'If I was an elevator operator'—why he chose that profession I don't know—'If I was an elevator operator, you wouldn't even look at me.'" That insecurity could morph easily into jealousy. At airports, Ted would insist that Lee walk in front of him so he could see which oncoming men were staring at her. Once, driving along the highway, they passed a car and Lee looked over, as passengers often reflexively do. There were two men in the car, and Williams suddenly erupted. Recalled Lee, "He flew off the handle. Why was I looking at them! And he hit me in the arm with his fist. I was all black-and-blue. But that's the only time he ever touched me."

Yet sometimes he would be so good to her, so attentive. He'd bring her coffee in bed in the morning, for example. "So he could be soft and kind and turn around and be a son of a gun. It's so hard to explain how he could be half one way and half the other way." But the son-of-a-gun side flared too often. Once, she had to lock him out of the bedroom because he'd gone into some rage. The next day he said he was sorry. That was the only time she could remember him apologizing.

She was always on pins and needles, never knowing when he was going to blow—either at her or at his friends, Lee recalled.

"In the end, I'm not sure he liked women too much," Lee concluded. "Maybe because he was always using the word 'bitch.' 'Unappreciative bitch' is what he named me. I couldn't figure out why he had all this rage in him. I wondered if he had a hatred for his mother. He must have. It caused him such embarrassment. That's all I can see."

Finally, after two and a half years, Lee decided she'd had enough. One morning in January of 1964, while Ted was out fishing, she jumped in the car and drove home to Chicago. Ted called her. He said he would do anything she wanted him to do if she came back, even go to church. She found that an odd statement, since she wasn't particularly religious and hadn't been asking him to go to church. The first Christmas they were together she'd wanted to take him to a Presbyterian service, but he wouldn't go. Maybe he'd been thinking of that. Lee said no, she wasn't coming back. "He kept telling me, 'I'll change.' I said to him, 'Ted, I can't do anything right.' That's the way it was."[11]

In the winter of 1961, the Red Sox announced that in addition to his hitting-coach duties at spring training, Williams would become "special executive assistant for player personnel." This would involve making the rounds of the Sox farm system to help develop players, sign prospects, and scout National League teams to help identify players Boston might trade for.

In March, Ted arrived in Scottsdale and immediately upstaged the return of Jackie Jensen, who was coming back to the Red Sox after a year's sabbatical because of his fear of flying. Proving he'd lost none of his snark for the writers, Williams encountered Harold Rosenthal of the *New York Herald Tribune* and berated him for a piece he'd written three years earlier, which had compared Ted unfavorably to Mickey Mantle. Then, just warming up, Williams approached Larry Claflin of the *Record-American,* who was sitting in the Red Sox dugout, and teed off on him. Ted claimed that Claflin had called his ex-wife, Doris, in December to inquire what Williams had given Bobby-Jo for Christmas. His right fist clenched and his face white with rage, Williams told the terrified Claflin, "I'll punch you right in the nose." Claflin vigorously denied Ted's charge and called it a monstrous lie. He said he had never called Doris to ask about Williams and his daughter, offered to take a lie detector test, and bet Ted $1,000 that he would pass it. Red Sox traveling secretary Tom Dowd guided Williams away before he could commit further mayhem as the rest of the writers watched the scene, transfixed.

Ted, after cooling down, then held a press conference, the first Red Sox batting coach ever to do so. "I know I'm going to be happier for the next 20 years than I have been for the past 20," Williams said. "For one thing, I won't have to read a lot of garbage about me in the sports pages." One writer mildly challenged him: "Well, wouldn't you say that the past 20 years furnished you with more compensation than annoyance?"

Ted had to agree: "I really did have a wonderful time. Baseball has been very good to me. But I think I had to take a lot of abuse I didn't deserve. Of course, I also did things I shouldn't have done. I regret that."[12]

Williams made his debut as a scout that May, returning to San Diego and his alma mater, Herbert Hoover High School, to watch a young pitcher named Dave Morehead. Morehead would sign with the Red Sox and go on to throw a no-hitter against the Indians in 1965. Ted said he was impressed with the changes at Hoover since he'd been a student there, and the players on the baseball team seemed thrilled when he stopped by to schmooze with them.[13]

That summer of 1961, Williams focused most of his baseball attention on the camp he had launched three years earlier in Massachusetts. The camp consisted of 180 largely wooded acres on the shores of Loon Pond. A Boy Scout camp that owned the property in the mid-'50s had decided to sell. The town didn't want the site developed, so Albert H. Cassidy, who was part owner of a Lakeville drive-in restaurant, had the idea to start a boys' camp. Cassidy didn't have enough money to fund the venture on his own, so he approached a local bank for a loan. The bank told him the only way his project would fly would be if he could get a celebrity involved whose cachet might attract customers.

A friend introduced him to the boxer Rocky Marciano, who had retired in 1956 as the undefeated heavyweight champion of the world and lived in nearby Brockton, Massachusetts. Cassidy figured if he could get the backing of the Brockton Bomber, that would give him his requisite star appeal. After much cajoling from Cassidy, the champ agreed to lend his name to the venture. Thrilled, Cassidy went back to the bankers, but they were dismissive. A boxing camp? What mother would send her son off to get beaten to a pulp? They suggested Cassidy try to land Ted Williams.

Cassidy was back to square one. He didn't know anyone who knew the great Williams. But he knew someone who knew Eddie Pellagrini, the former Red Sox infielder in 1946 and 1947. Pellagrini had stayed in touch with Williams and agreed to put in a good word with the Kid about the camp idea. Meanwhile, Cassidy did more homework, taking pictures of the campsite and preparing a scrapbook. He arranged to go to Fenway Park and meet Williams in the summer of 1957, when Ted was well on the way to his glittering .388.

According to the story Cassidy passed down to his son, Albert B. Cassidy—who would later become the executor of Ted's estate—the visit to Fenway came about because he decided he needed more than Pellagrini's introduction in order to make an effective presentation. Getting to the park early, he slipped an usher ten bucks to let him hang out in the lower box seats until Williams appeared for batting practice, when he would try and intercept him as he emerged from the dugout on the way to the cage and talk about his proposition.

"Hey, Ted!" Cassidy called out as Williams approached. "Hi; my name is Cassidy. Can I have a few minutes of your time?"

"Let me finish hitting, and I'll come and see you," said Ted.

After taking his rips, Williams returned and joined Cassidy in the lower boxes. Cassidy pulled out his scrapbook filled with pictures of the campsite and began talking—fast. He said he had an idea to start a baseball camp for boys in Lakeville on this beautiful site next to a lake. He displayed the photos. The problem was, he didn't have any money or any credit. He needed someone like Ted Williams to come in as the catalyst for the project. Ted listened to the pitch and was intrigued, but he was in the middle of the season and couldn't focus on it now. He suggested they talk in the fall.

Cassidy felt deflated. He'd gotten his meeting and a polite hearing, but he felt the chances of Ted contacting him again were nil. Yet not long after the season ended, the phone rang, and it was Williams. When could he come down to Lakeville and tour the property?

After walking around the proposed site and hearing added details from Cassidy about his plans, Ted was even more impressed. It was baseball and kids. What was there not to like? He said he would do it. He thought Fred Corcoran would not like the idea, but Williams called him right then and there and said this was something he'd like to do.

Beside himself with joy, Cassidy returned to the bank and announced that he had Ted Williams as a backer. The low-level loan officer he had been dealing with didn't believe him. The man consulted his boss, who consulted *his* boss, who went to the president of the bank. Before long, Cassidy was meeting with a group of executives in the president's office. The men said they needed proof that Williams was, in fact, signed on to the venture. Cassidy, enjoying the moment immensely, reached for the phone and dialed a number. Ted's unmistakable loud voice came on the line. Yes, it was him, he said, and he was in.

The bankers were incredulous. For years, they had been trying to get Williams to back a promotional venture of their own, without any success. So how was Al Cassidy, part owner of a local drive-in, able to get him? Still, the bankers said they felt that even with Ted, the venture was too risky, so they again turned Cassidy down.

Cassidy relayed the bad news back to Ted. Annoyed, Williams said he knew the head of the savings bank in nearby Middleborough and would call him. He did, and the man promptly approved the loan. The camp cost $60,000. Ted put up a down payment and took a 25 percent interest. Cassidy and his two brothers each got 25 percent without having to put any money down.

"Ted did this deal even though he didn't know my dad at all," said the younger Cassidy.[14] "That's the kind of guy that Ted was. He was not one to check people out. But he said, 'Al, there's only one thing I'm going to ask of you.' He took his hands and put them on the top of the table and said, 'Al, where are my hands at?' Dad says, 'On top of the table.' 'That's right, and that's always where I want to see your hands. I never want to see them under the table.' That was Ted also. He always insisted on the truth. No matter how bad it hurt or how embarrassing it might be to Ted, he would always tell you the truth. Whether it was a personal deal or a business deal, if you robbed a bank, he'd give you a second chance. If you lied to him, he was done with you."

The camp, for boys between the ages of eight and nineteen, cost $125 for two weeks, $250 for four weeks, and $490 for eight weeks. By the mid-'60s, there were about two hundred boys in camp, including some from Canada, Mexico, and Japan. Later, girls were included and the activities expanded beyond baseball to include swimming, boating, volleyball, basketball, soccer, and the like.

At night, they would play a game called blooperball on a Little League field, using a deflated softball that couldn't be hit too far—unless you were Ted Williams. Just fooling around, Ted could hit the ball over the trees behind the fence. "One night we were playing an away game in town and lots of locals were watching because Ted played," remembered Charles Zarrell, a camper in the late '60s. "In a very memorable at bat, the pitcher lobbed the ball to him and he blasted a homer over the left-center-field fence. Ted was livid that he didn't pull the ball and cursed himself as he trotted around the bases, saying if he couldn't goddamn pull a friggin' blooperball, he shouldn't play this goddamn game."[15]

Not surprisingly, Ted insisted on military-style rules for the camp. Reveille would be at 7:00 a.m. Everyone would line up in a horseshoe at the flagpole. The national anthem would be played and the flag raised. During the day, the boys would move from one instructional station to the other for hitting, pitching, baserunning, and infield and outfield drills. Ted would make it a point to go to each station to talk to the kids and offer tips—especially at the hitting station, of course. The kids were in awe and hung on his every word.

Don Brown, a former counselor at the camp, recalls that one kid who wasn't awestruck was Joe Coleman, a local high school pitching phenom who would go on to the major leagues. Coleman was also the son of the Philadelphia Athletics pitcher of the same name who had been Ted's roommate in 1942 at Amherst College, Williams's first stop during World War II. "Joe Coleman was pitching and striking everyone out," said Brown. "Ted came over in his street clothes and Coleman was taunting him: 'You couldn't hit me, old man!' Ted never said a word. He just went up to the plate and hit the next four pitches out, into the oak trees four hundred feet away, then put the bat down and walked out. Never said a word. He was about five years out of the game. In street clothes."[16]

Ted hadn't been able to spend much time at the camp while he was still playing, but now his engagement showed signs of classic Williams intensity. Driving around in a golf cart, the Lord of Lakeville would carry out rigid inspections every Saturday. He would start at his favorite locale, the dining hall, which overlooked the lake. He insisted on a clean kitchen and asked that there be plenty of Lawry's seasoned salt on hand. Then he'd head for the living quarters, where beds had to be crisply made and everything in order. A stickler for short hair, Ted, in loco parentis, would check behind the campers' ears and order up haircuts for those he deemed shaggy.

When not in the golf cart, Williams sometimes drove the camp bus, always wanting to be the center of attention. He'd say he was the greatest driver in the world, and if he wasn't driving, he would give backseat critiques constantly—bantering and barking orders. He even instructed a receptionist on how to leave a message on an answering machine: not too fast.

Ted would usually dress in chinos and a white polo short with white sneakers. Some days he added a light blue jacket with "Ted" stitched on the arm. "I love this place," he told a *Globe* reporter who was doing a story on the camp. "I like being here with the kids. You see them grow up from year to year and hope that you might help them become better men."

He'd start the day at 6:30 with nine holes of golf. (Williams claimed he shot around eighty-five and carried a fourteen handicap.) Then he would stop at a local greasy spoon for a mammoth breakfast of three or four eggs and six pieces of toast, washed down by a coffee milk shake. He bemoaned the influence of golf on baseball. "When I was a kid, there weren't 300,000 golfers in the whole country. Now there's 8 million," he said. "When I was young, guys in their 30's would still be playing sandlot ball. You never see that anymore. They're out playing golf, and it's rubbing off on the kids."[17]

Williams was comfortable in Lakeville. After a while, he decided to buy a house surrounded by some land so that he and Lee would have a nice place to stay. "He did a heck of a lot for the community there in Lakeville," remembered Al Palmieri, the camp director at the time. "He seemed to enjoy doing things for young people, and he loved young people. We always had local priests, dentists, doctors, and people come out to talk to Ted, wanting him to play golf with them, but he would say he was busy at the camp. But if you wanted him for a benefit for the Jimmy Fund or something, he'd be there." Palmieri said that despite Ted's 25 percent stake, he never took a dime from the camp, plowing everything he was entitled to back into everyday operations.[18]

Besides Al Cassidy and his brothers, Williams surrounded himself with a staff he liked and was comfortable with. In addition to Al Palmieri, the baseball director was Joe Camacho, an elementary school principal in neighboring New Bedford who had played minor-league ball. Ted also brought in Wos Caldwell, his Hoover High coach, and Roy Engle, who'd been the catcher and captain of the team while Ted was at Hoover.

Camacho thought one of the reasons he got along well with Williams was that he stood up to him. "I think the first day I met Ted, I got into an argument and wouldn't give in to him, something about baseball. I don't remember what it was specifically. I wouldn't kowtow to him, I wouldn't be a yes guy, and he liked that."

On the early-morning golf outings, Williams's temper would usually be on full display as he'd fling various clubs around the course in disgust after a missed shot. Camacho remembered, "One day he threw his club up into the tree, and he says to me, 'Go get it.' And I told him, 'You go get the goddamn club.' ...Al Palmieri and I, we used to tell him, 'You don't behave, Ted, we're leaving.'"[19]

"Ted was happiest as an adult at that camp," Camacho's son, Jimmy, said. "He was really in an element kind to his personality. He enjoyed the company of children, the structured atmosphere. It was structured like school or a military academy, with uniforms, and everybody was organized by team and always going everywhere together. There was a logic and predictability to it. Observing him, he looked enormously happy, comfortable."[20]

The oldest and best players at the camp would play American Legion teams in the area, and Ted would show up at these games and of course root for his team. Kevin Flanagan remembered what happened the day he was pitching for his New Hampshire Legion team against the camp club: "We were actually beating Ted's camp team, 7–2, in the fifth inning when a sedan pulled up to the field and out pops Teddy Ballgame. He took a look at the scoreboard and started cursing up a blue streak. 'How the fuck can my guys be losing to a little New Hampshire team?' He was loud and kept muttering to himself as he made his way to his team's side of the field. For three innings, Ted actually sat and watched us play and beat his boys."[21]

Williams was out and about as much as possible, preferring to spend as little time as he could in the camp office fielding phone calls. He hated the phone and wouldn't even get on the line for most people. One person who called him regularly in those early years at the camp, and whom Ted would always talk to, was young Carl Yastrzemski, who had succeeded him as the Red Sox left fielder. Yaz was still insecure as a hitter, and whenever he got into a slump, he would call Williams for advice. "Ted was quite loud, and you could hear him all over camp, yelling," said Al Palmieri. "He would give Yaz hints about standing forward or back more, the usual thing about picking out a good pitch to hit, and he would yell this at him." If Williams felt Yaz wasn't taking his advice, or comprehending it fully, he would call him a dumb Polack—not unaffectionately. At midyear, Yaz was hitting only .220 and called Williams in a panic, saying he wasn't sure he could make it in the big leagues. Ted, who was in New Brunswick fishing at the time, flew to Boston immediately and worked with the rookie for three days, restoring his confidence. Yaz hit .300 for the rest of the season.

As for returning phone calls after messages were left for him at his camp, Ted was hopeless. He would get a stack of messages every day, come in the office, look at the first three or four, and take all of them and throw them away. One summer day in 1961, Al Cassidy took a phone call from the White House: John F. Kennedy, the new president, would be in nearby Hyannis Port soon and wanted to invite Williams to come down and see him. Cassidy took the message and put it on Ted's desk. Williams threw it away. After not hearing back, the White House called again to see if Ted got the message, and Cassidy said he'd try again. This went on for three or four days, with Williams still not calling back. Cassidy was embarrassed—the president of the United States wanted to see Ted—so he wrote the message on a big piece of paper and put it on his desk on top of everything. Ted came in, looked at it, and threw it away.

Cassidy decided he had to speak up. "You know, I usually wouldn't want to be nosy, but did you see that message from Kennedy?"

"Yeah," said Ted.

"He wants you to come and meet him. You have to call him back."

"I don't have to."

"You have to let him know. I have to tell them something next time they call. I'm not going to tell them you just don't want to talk to them."

"Well, just tell them I'm not coming."

"Ted, I've got to tell them something more than that."

"Well, tell them I'm a Nixon fan."[22]

So Cassidy did.

Williams had admired Richard Nixon for years. A mutual friend introduced them in Miami in the mid-'50s, when Nixon was vice president, and the two hit it off immediately. When the Red Sox came to Washington to play the Senators, Nixon and Ted would often have lunch together in a private dining room at the Statler Hotel.[23]

Kennedy, meanwhile, had been courting Williams politically since 1946, when he ran for Congress and arranged to have his picture taken with Ted twice. And along with his aide Dave Powers, JFK was a great fan of the Kid's. On September 29, 1960, the day after Ted homered on his final at bat, Kennedy, then in the homestretch of his run for the presidency against Nixon, used Williams as a foil to knock down the Republican argument that he lacked the necessary experience to be president. "I read in this morning's newspaper that a great hero of my hometown, Ted Williams, was retiring," the candidate said at a speech in Syracuse, New York. "And I was also interested to read that he was too old at forty-two. Maybe experience isn't enough."

Less than three weeks later, on October 18, Kennedy and Nixon each flew into Miami to address the American Legion convention. As Kennedy's plane was taxiing to the gate, he looked out the window and saw Williams getting out of a private jet. Nixon had asked that Williams appear with him at the Legion convention, and Ted had gotten a fishing buddy who was a pilot, Stu Apte, to fly him up from the Keys for the occasion.[24] Kennedy called out to Dave Powers with excitement, "Dave, look, there's Ted!" As their plane drew closer, however, JFK, who apparently didn't know of Ted's history with Nixon, was crestfallen. "Look," he said. "The son of a bitch is wearing a Nixon button."

According to David Pressman, the Chelsea, Massachusetts, doctor on whose advice Ted had heated his bats over the second half of his career, the Catholic Church, through Richard Cardinal Cushing of Boston, made a late effort through Pressman's father to convince Williams not to endorse Nixon. Pressman said he relayed the request, to no avail.

After Kennedy won the election, Williams groused that JFK's father had bought him the presidency. Ted nursed a personal grudge against Joe Kennedy for having once given him a bum stock tip, and he also considered the old man a glorified bootlegger who had acquired much of his wealth through ill-gotten gains.

Executives at Sears were happy with how their contract with Williams was working out, but they decided they should look for ways to maintain his visibility now that he had retired from baseball. The company's press agent, Bill Doll, suggested a syndicated newspaper column, periodic short radio spots, and a sports cartoon strip for smaller weekly papers in rural parts of the country, where Sears had a presence. Williams was agreeable to each idea. He made it clear that he'd need a ghostwriter, but he insisted on choosing him and on approving each column in advance. He would record the radio spots, which would be lighter in tone than the column, from an approved script, and he wanted to sign off on the cartoon panels as well.

For the column, Doll approached a dozen sportswriters and asked them to submit a sample from which Williams would then select his favorite, without being shown the name of the writer. Given Ted's tense history with the Boston press, Doll ruled out anyone from that city and focused instead on a group of New York and Chicago reporters. As a lark, Doll asked one of his assistants, Jordan Ramin, to submit a column, knowing that Ramin had grown up in Boston and was a huge Williams fan. Ted ended up choosing Ramin's entry, telling Doll: "This guy writes like I think."

The columns ran from June of 1962 to March of 1967 and were syndicated in ninety daily papers, including the *Boston Globe,* which Ramin considered the flagship paper and which carried Ted's first piece on the front page. The columns were sent out weekly under the heading SWINGING WITH TED WILLIAMS, though each paper was free to use any headline it wished. A paper was also free to run the piece immediately, every two weeks, or even once a month if it wanted. Ramin would think of an idea and get Ted's approval by phone. Then he'd write a draft of a column and mail it to Williams in Islamorada. "Ted would either approve or disapprove," said Ramin. "He even corrected the grammar sometimes. Jesus, he was smart! He knew a lot about a lot of things. I never knew about his interest in music, for example. He loved Stan Getz and Erroll Garner for jazz, and Streisand for pop music." The topics centered on baseball, but they would dabble in other sports, such as basketball and boxing. There would also be softer fare, like Ted's New Year's resolutions and his enjoyment of cooking, as well as excursions into politics — some of which were surprising for those who thought they knew Williams.

"He had a thing about the American Indians," remembered Ramin. "He thought they really got shafted." In one column, Williams cited the disparities in Indian education levels and life expectancy compared to other citizens and called this situation "un-American. . . . It's about time we start making amends to our own people. . . . If you're a real American, you should be angry, insulted that this kind of treatment has been allowed for so many years."

In September of 1963, Ramin received a letter from President Kennedy's aide Dave Powers, the über–Williams fan, asking to be put on a mailing list for a copy of Ted's column. Two months later, JFK was dead. Ramin suggested to Williams that he write a column on the assassination, and Ted agreed. In a piece headlined THE WOUND, distributed four days after the slaying, Williams issued what amounted to a kumbaya call, saying that not just the assassin but also everyone in the country was to blame because there was too much hate in the land. "It will take more than just time to heal our nation's deepest and most tragic wound," the column began. "In this case, time can only be a scab and not a healer. The wound is still open and sore and it hurts, it hurts so much.... We must stop this terrible hating that has been going on in our country during the last few years. We're supposed to live in a civilized society, we're supposed to live in the greatest country in the world. Well, let's start acting like human beings.... If, through this horrible tragedy, we can act toward our fellow human being with more understanding, then President Kennedy's death will not have been in vain."

The blunt political commentary expressed in these columns was unusual terrain for a professional athlete. Williams's ringing support for the downtrodden Indians, and the can't-we-all-get-along ethos he expressed in the Kennedy column, belied the archconservative Republican views he was generally thought to hold. "He may have been a Republican, but not like they are today," said Ramin. "He was what they call a Rockefeller Republican. He would have ridiculed the Christian right, for example." The columns also revealed the Williams who was obscured by his own angry outbursts: yes, he hated the Boston press; yes, he had serious issues with women and his family—but when it came to the broader culture and his sense of protecting the underdog, he could be generous and courageous.

But his temper still flared. The radio spots were aired as part of the NBC national program *Monitor*. Ted might record several in one sitting in New York, and Ramin remembered going to the baseball camp in Lakeville to tape some of the spots. "He was very impatient about things, almost like a kid wanting instant gratification," said Ramin. "When he rehearsed the scripts, he sometimes would have difficulty pronouncing a name, like the ballplayer Ted Kluszewski. Then he'd say, 'Who wrote this shit?' and slam the script down. We'd try to placate him. Bill Doll was good at that. He was from West Virginia and had a drawl like Red Barber. Whenever Ted got upset, Doll would say, 'Ted, ain't that the truth.' Then Ted would calm down."[25]

The cartoons—given free to 2,200 weekly papers and marketed separately from the column, under the heading TED WILLIAMS SAYS...— consisted of one panel containing a drawing below an innocuous quote from Ted. In one sample from 1964, he said: "I knew it was time to hang up the spikes when I hit a home run off Don Lee and someone reminded me I had hit a homer off Don's father, Thornton Lee, many, many years ago."*

On April 3, 1964, Lee Howard filed for divorce in a Miami court. She charged in her lawsuit that Williams had routinely cussed her out in temper tantrums so frequent that she couldn't stand living with him anymore. She said such explosions "violated her sensibility" and that his behavior was "erratic, irresponsible and wholly unpredictable."

"I was with him two and a half years, and it took me another two and a half years to get a divorce," Lee said. "The reason was that he was never available. He told me later he never wanted the divorce, and the reason it took so long was that he wouldn't ever answer the phone. He knew that it was going to be a lawyer."

A few months earlier, in late February of 1964, several weeks after Lee left him, Ted had invited her to join him on a trip to New Zealand. The New Zealand trip was yet another Sears initiative to promote Williams, this time in collaboration with the New Zealand government, which wanted a famous figure like Ted to help showcase the country as a fishing and hunting destination for tourists. Lee knew he hoped to use the exotic locale to rekindle their romance, so she refused to go.

Dubbed the Sportsman's Marathon, the plan called for Ted to try and catch a big-game fish at sea, then go inland to catch a trout, and finally shoot a deer—all within a twenty-four-hour period. Williams, it turned out, accomplished the feat in ten hours and twenty-five minutes.

On the flight home in early March, somewhere over the Pacific en route to San Francisco, Williams looked around the first-class cabin after he'd had a few cocktails and allowed his eyes to rest on a beautiful brunette sitting across the aisle a row behind him. Her name was Dolores Wettach, a five-foot-nine-inch *Vogue* model returning from a shoot in Australia.

Williams got out a piece of paper, wrote "Who are you?" on it, then crumpled it up and threw it at Dolores, like a child might throw a spitball. Dolores, tired of her *Vogue* group and game for flirting with a hand-

---

* Besides the column, the radio spot, and the cartoon panels, George Struthers, the Sears executive who had first reached out to Williams, also thought the company should produce a television documentary on Ted's life. To that end, Struthers paid $10,000 to hire four researchers who combed through newspaper archives and put together two huge three-ring notebooks filled with clippings and notes chronicling Williams's career. A script was written, and Ramin even wrote a song for the film. Then Struthers died suddenly of a heart attack. His replacement was less of a Ted booster, so the documentary project was dropped.

some stranger, wrote that she was a model, and who was he? She threw the note back at him.

"Sam Williams, a fisherman," was the reply Ted tossed back to her. "What's your name?" Dolores wrote her name down and threw the paper again. The final written exchange came from Ted, who suggested they have dinner after they arrived in San Francisco.

Dolores didn't answer that one and eventually got up to go to the bathroom. Ted followed her down the aisle and was waiting when she emerged from the toilet.

"You are meant to be bit and sucked," Williams told her as she passed him.

"I was gonna haul off and slap him one, but I held back," Dolores recalled. She remembered considering him "an intoxicated gentleman."

When the plane landed, Dolores was having second thoughts about dining with Ted and walked off briskly until they got separated in the terminal crowd. Besides, she was supposed to meet a doctor friend for dinner. After a while, however, the doctor sent a telegram saying he couldn't make it, and Dolores promptly booked a flight on to New York. Then, to her amazement, a phone call came in for her at the airline counter she was standing in front of. It was Ted. She had no idea how he knew where she was at that moment or how he could arrange a call to that very desk. He wanted to know if she was still there, he said. She was, but she was returning to New York, she told him. Then came word from the airline that the flight would be canceled because of bad weather in New York. Soon Ted called again. Worn down, Dolores said yes to dinner. She still had no idea who he was.

Williams took her to a Polynesian-style restaurant, where the coat-check girl immediately recognized him. "I know who you are," she said. "You're Ted Williams."

"Nah, I just look like him," said Ted.

Dolores had only heard of three baseball players. "I'd heard the names Ted Williams, Babe Ruth, and Joe DiMaggio," she said. "I realized afterwards that this really *was* Ted Williams."[26]

20

Bobby-Jo

After Ted and Doris were divorced in 1955, Bobby-Jo's visits to her father began to wear on her, not just because they were stressful and she couldn't make one false move without risking an outburst from Ted but also because her friends were where her mother was. "You know, going to Fenway Park, sitting at the games—it's cool for a while, but it's not what you want to do," Bobby-Jo said.[1]

Not that life with Doris was easy. Her alcoholism had only gotten worse after the divorce. She'd bought a beauty shop in Coral Gables to try to become more economically independent, but that didn't work out. Then she worked part-time at various funeral homes, doing dead people's hair, mostly the ladies.

Despite the difficulties with her father, Bobby-Jo liked the attention that being Ted Williams's daughter brought her, so she didn't hesitate to let her friends know of the connection. Once, in third grade, after her classmates asked her for some autographed balls, she got Ted to give her a dozen, then excitedly reported back to him that she had sold them for twenty-five cents each.

Ted's chief role as a father seemed to be the mostly absent provider and disciplinarian. Enforcing proper hygiene was always a priority. "He wanted to watch me brush my teeth for four years to make sure I was doing it properly," said Bobby-Jo. "And then every once in a while, right on up till I was driving, he'd say, 'How do you brush your teeth?' He was a tooth fanatic. It was the cleanliness part of him. He wanted to see everybody's nails, too." Once, at a fancy Boston restaurant, he exploded at a waiter whose nails were not up to his exacting standards.

Williams could be generous and slip his daughter extra cash when she visited, but he was a stickler with Doris on child support, insisting that she manage with what he gave her. "He gave my mom a hundred dollars a month for child support. But that was for everything. He didn't want to know about any additionals. He wanted to know why you couldn't make do with what you had. But a hundred dollars a month wasn't cutting it." And paradoxically, while Ted preached the importance of education, he refused to give Bobby-Jo a set of encyclopedias she told him she needed when, around fifth grade, she'd been assigned written reports for the first time.

Still, Williams was there for at least some of the big events in his daughter's life—including her confirmation, when she was thirteen, at an Episcopal church in South Miami. Ted showed up underdressed, as usual, and a priest slipped him a tie to put over his Ban-Lon shirt.

That year, 1961, Doris got married to an insurance salesman named Joe Tridico. Bobby-Jo thought he was nice enough, but Tridico hardly dared intrude on Ted's discipline domain, even though Doris, burdened by her alcoholic haze, left Bobby-Jo unchecked.

"Poor Bobby-Jo—it was awful," said Daria Stehle, a friend of Ted's and Doris's in the '50s. "Doris let her do whatever she wanted. She wasn't receptive to help. She just never stayed sober. There was no control. Then Bobby-Jo would go down to see her father, and he was very strict, and it was such a change for her. She couldn't handle it."[2]

Not long after Bobby-Jo got her driver's license, Ted agreed to buy her a car, a surprising decision given his stated desire not to spoil her and his penchant to pinch pennies when it came to less extravagant items on his daughter's wish list. Then, exploiting the vacuum left by Doris, Bobby-Jo took to tooling around in her new car, relishing a new sense of freedom and life as a sexually precocious teenager. She dropped out of high school, and in the summer of 1965 got pregnant at the age of seventeen. The father was a local boy she'd been hanging out with but didn't feel a particularly close attachment to.

When Ted got the news from Doris, he—predictably—went ballistic. Bobby-Jo, who lived for her father's approval, could not bear his scorn. She went into the bathroom at home and slashed both her wrists. Doris found her before it was too late.

Williams quickly decreed that the pregnancy would have to be aborted—no discussion was to be had, though neither Doris nor Bobby-Jo mounted any serious objections. A safe abortion was still hard to obtain in those days, but it was legal and relatively easy to arrange if the procedure could be done under the auspices of a psychiatrist, Ted learned.

"Ted called me up and said, 'Can you help me?'" remembered his World War II and Korea Marine buddy Bill Churchman, from Philadelphia.[3] "He explained to me that Bobby-Jo had attempted suicide. There was this institute here run by the University of Pennsylvania. This was not a penal offense. I hooked Ted up with a good friend of mine who was a psychiatrist, and they got her admitted. Ted had the impression that if he went to a Florida hospital, attempted suicide might be considered a criminal offense."

Churchman met Bobby-Jo at the train station and took her to the Institute of the Pennsylvania Hospital, a noted psychiatric facility in Philadelphia that had treated Marilyn Monroe and Judy Garland, for what would end up being a convalescence and psychiatric evaluation of several months' duration. She wore a sweater in the summer heat to try to cover up the scars, which extended from her wrists to her elbows, but Churchman couldn't help noticing the wounds. She checked into a private room on the fifth floor and was placed on a suicide watch, under the care of Dr. Silas L. Warner, a specialist in personality disorders.

After a while, Bobby-Jo was allowed to come and go as she pleased, as long as she returned to the hospital at night. One evening, she and a young man who was also a patient at the institute went to a party on the Main Line. There she met eighteen-year-old Stephen Tomasco, the son of a truck driver for the *Philadelphia Inquirer* and the *Philadelphia Daily News*. Tomasco had graduated from high school earlier that year and was working at a local racetrack selling tip sheets.

Bobby-Jo homed in on Tomasco immediately. "She was a good-looking girl," Steve remembered. "The way she carried herself, she was very friendly, easy to talk to. She showed within minutes of talking to her that she liked you. The night we met, she said real fast, 'Why don't we leave here?' I said, 'What about the fella you came with?' She said, 'He's a screwball.'

"I was a virgin when I met her. One night when she was in the hospital, we took a ride to a park, and she said, 'Come on, let's do this.' You know how a young guy is. I figured, what have I got to lose?"[4]

Bobby-Jo had quickly told Steve who her father was, and he'd been intrigued. He was a baseball fan, though not a rabid one. Over time, Steve noticed that she would reveal the Ted connection early on when they met new people, trying to build on his success.

Bobby-Jo also readily told Steve all about her abortion and slitting her wrists. "When I saw her wrists, that scared the hell out of me," he said. "What a sight. She said she couldn't deal with Ted's reaction to her being pregnant." But Steve liked that she was honest with him, and he started visiting her at the hospital regularly. "She got real serious, real fast. She'd been around the block before, and I hadn't. We kind of fell in love real quick. We spent every day together. I was working, and I'd go and visit. We'd stay out all night, mostly in my car, and I'd take her back to the hospital at four or five in the morning, then go to work."

When Ted came to Philadelphia to see Bobby-Jo, he would stay at the Warwick Hotel. Since he didn't like to go to the hospital, Bobby-Jo would have Steve drive her to the hotel to see her father. Williams was primed to meet Steve because his daughter had announced that she wished to marry him, an idea that Ted was strongly against, given Bobby-Jo's fragile condition. There was also the fact that she was not yet eighteen.

"Ted interviewed me, asked what I did, asked about my family," Steve recalled. "But he didn't flip out on us. He wasn't loud, like I've seen him. He wasn't mean. He was forthright. He said he thought it was a mistake, and he didn't think we should do it. We spent the whole time in the hotel and ordered room service."

Steve had problems convincing his parents, too. His mother, especially, was not wild about Bobby-Jo—or Barbara, as Steve usually called her. The mother thought Bobby-Jo had a sharp tongue and could be disrespectful. Finally, Steve's parents gave their consent because he convinced them this was what he wanted to do. "I was just young and didn't have any better sense," he said now of his decision.

Bobby-Jo was released from the hospital in the late fall of 1965 and returned home to Florida, but with marriage now firmly in her mind, she found living with Doris increasingly untenable. Doris didn't seem to care if her daughter got married or not. It was Ted whom Bobby-Jo had to convince, and eventually she did. As Steve put it: "She talked him into marriage, saying it wouldn't be too horrible."

That was a pretty low bar, but Williams became resigned to the idea and, in a phone call to his friend Bill Churchman to share the news, managed a pinch of gallows humor: "Here I entrust my daughter to you, and what do you do? You let her run off with a dago kid!" Ted said.[5]

Bobby-Jo returned to Philadelphia and moved in with Steve's parents. In January of 1966, they went to Elkton, Maryland, on the north side of Chesapeake Bay. In the 1920s and '30s, Elkton had been a marriage mecca for the Northeast, cranking out more than ten thousand newly-weds a year because it had no residency requirement or waiting period. Later, concerned that the town was developing too trashy an image, local officials mandated a forty-eight-hour waiting period.[6]

Steve and Bobby-Jo were married by a justice of the peace on January 17 — eleven days before her eighteenth birthday. Since Bobby-Jo was still a minor, one of her parents (Doris did the chore) had to submit an affidavit giving consent. Steve was by then nineteen. Only his mother attended the ceremony.

To help make ends meet, Steve took a second job, slicing cold cuts behind the deli counter of a supermarket. Later, Doris invited twenty or thirty of her friends to a reception for the new couple down in Coral Gables. Ted wasn't there.

After Doris's reception, Steve and Bobby-Jo went to Islamorada for a few days to visit Ted. He still wasn't happy about the marriage — as was apparent from his decision to attend neither the wedding nor Doris's gathering — but he offered to get Steve a job at Sears. Eventually, Steve did go for an interview, and was offered a salesman position, but he decided not to take it, worried that he'd always be known as Ted Williams's son-in-law.

Steve thought computers were the future and noticed an ad in the Sunday paper for a training course in computer programming. Before long, Ted was on the phone with the head of the training school trying to get the lowdown on the curriculum. He agreed to pay the tuition for Steve to attend school full-time and to support him and Bobby-Jo in the interim. Steve graduated high in his class and got a job as a computer operator at Temple University. "My career has been very successful, but I feel indebted to Ted for getting me started," Steve said.

From the moment he first met Steve, Ted insisted that a certain proto-col be observed. "Ted said, 'Steve, you can call me Mr. Williams. I think respect is in order.' I didn't argue with him. Even after we were married, I always called him Mr. Williams, and Barbara always called him Daddy. He had that piercing glance when he looked at you. Kind of tilted his head and stared right at you. It demanded your attention. It was, 'I'm going to give you advice now, and here's what you ought to do.' 'Just keep your eye on the ball,' he'd say. 'That's what old Teddy Ballgame would do. Teddy Baseball.' He talked about himself in the third person."

Steve had a beard at the time, and Bobby-Jo smoked too much — a pack and a half of Kents a day. Williams wasn't happy about either. He told Steve to lose the beard and advised his daughter to stop smoking.

"Ted was very threatening—a big guy," said Steve. "His facial expressions and his loud voice were enough to get your attention. When he got angry, the only thing you could do was watch. One night in Islamorada, a space heater wasn't pumping out enough heat, so he tore it apart. He went on a rampage, cursing it. It was mounted on a wall. He kicked it, tried to tear it out of the wall. He had a hair-trigger temper. When he went off, he'd get loud and animated very quickly. The arms, cursing, and facial expressions. That's what scared a lot of people. He was always an angry guy."

Steve had a front-row seat from which to observe the relationship between Ted and Bobby-Jo, and he reached several conclusions: that she was largely successful in manipulating her father financially, despite his nearly constant complaints that he was giving her too much money; that Bobby-Jo could never get enough of Ted's time; that he wanted a son and wasn't happy with her as a daughter; and that he felt she was a nuisance to him and not independent enough.

"I think early on, Barbara got into a habit that whenever she needed something, she got it from her father," Steve said. "Barbara had a split personality. She was perfect in front of Ted, but different in front of everyone else." She would spend hours on the phone and rack up hundreds of dollars in long-distance bills that Steve couldn't begin to pay for. Bobby-Jo said Ted would. He'd pay for them. She'd run up a big credit card bill at Sears; Ted paid. She also maintained a virtual hotline to Ted's Boston accountant, Paul Brophy, who oversaw a trust fund that Williams had created for his daughter. Brophy couldn't make any disbursements at her request, of course, but Bobby-Jo often found him sympathetic to her cause, and he would occasionally persuade Ted to cut another check.

Ted had been very strict with Bobby-Jo when she was growing up, but he had hardly any time for her. He was always on the road. When he called her he'd ask about her weight and how she was doing in school. He wanted to be sure she was thin.

"Barbara never got enough of his time, and she resented that. She went along with the program of, 'Yes, Daddy, no, Daddy.' She probably wanted to hug him. She was always trying to gain his approval but never quite made the grade. When he called, she'd get really nervous and run for her cigarettes and her Diet Pepsis."

Steve found his early life with Bobby-Jo difficult. First, she quickly became pregnant, which should have been a happy occasion, but she always seemed stressed-out. She hated to go to bed and hated to get up. She began abusing the Darvon she'd been prescribed by Dr. Warner at Pennsylvania Hospital. "I had to watch the bottle, because she'd think nothing of taking three or four pills at a time," Steve said. "She overdosed at least two times and had to be hospitalized. She'd call me at work and want me to come home for lunch. If I couldn't, she'd threaten to take a handful of pills unless I did. Once, I came home and found her unconscious, and I had to call the rescue squad."

Bobby-Jo had inherited a temper, though in her case it led to depression as opposed to ferocity. She would do drugs; not care; not eat.

"I always found myself like an investigator with Barbara," Steve explained, "probing, trying to find the truth. I used to spend countless hours questioning [her]." Much of the questioning concerned what he quickly came to discover was her promiscuity. "I counted seven or eight relationships she had when we were married," Steve said. "It was obvious how she acted. Sometimes with my friends."

He didn't tell Ted about that, of course, and he found that Williams was of little assistance when it came to Bobby-Jo besides being a ready source of money. "Whenever we talked about Barbara's problems with Ted, he'd always tell her, 'Jesus Christ, it cost me seventy thousand dollars for all that time you were in the hospital. You should be better by now.' That's what he expected. I think he saw her as a thorn in his side who couldn't stand on her own two feet. It was always, 'She's asking me for something.'"

21

"Inn of the Immortals"

Three days after Bobby-Jo and Steve got married, Ted would find out whether he'd been elected to the Hall of Fame.

It was widely assumed that he would easily receive the required 75 percent of the vote from the Baseball Writers' Association of America. The only question would be his margin, and whether some writers would nix him from their ballots out of spite to avenge his shabby treatment of them over the years. A minority felt it was possible Ted would fall short, simply because even the greats don't always get in the first year they are eligible. Joe DiMaggio, it was noted, failed twice before he made it.

The *Traveler*'s Tim Horgan, responding to a story in his own paper headlined WILL SCRIBES PAY TED BACK?, said he would be voting *for* Ted. "I'd rather help reserve T.W. for posterity than get embalmed myself," Horgan wrote. "The inference is clear. This isn't an election. It's a grudge match. And if the scribes don't vote Teddy into the Hall, tar and feathers will be among the many public terms applied to them.... We'll become the Knives of the Keyboard."[1]

Arthur Daley of the *New York Times* called for a unanimous selection of Williams and warned his brethren against any vengeful behavior. "If the Baseball Writers let pettiness or spite imperil them to default on a solemn obligation, they would stand revealed to the world of sports as men too small-minded to be worthy of the trust imposed in them," Daley wrote.[2] Williams guru Harold Kaese of the *Boston Globe* opined that a first-ballot induction was a given, and that the only real question was whether the vote would be unanimous—unlikely, since no previous player had gotten a unanimous vote.[3] (Ty Cobb had been the highest rated, at 98 percent, followed by Ruth and Honus Wagner at 95 percent and Bob Feller at 94.[4])

John Gillooly of the *Record-American,* heir to Colonel Egan, told his readers he had voted for Williams but gave voice to the wounds still nursed by many of the writers who had felt Ted's lash: "This of course, is not a popularity contest, but it is a little difficult to go into the booth, pull the curtains and put an X after the name of a person who has often gone out of his way to demean your profession."

Gillooly thought it possible that the writers might make Williams cool his heels for a few years. "DiMaggio had to wait, wait and wait some more before the room clerk found him a space at the Inn of the Immortals," Gillooly wrote. "So don't be startled if the Kid is asked to sit in the lobby for a while." And, noting that the Hall voting instructions required writers to judge a candidate's "playing ability" and his "contribution to the team," he reprised the essence of Egan's critique: "I'm trying to tell you that Williams, a great buster, was shy of several essential talents (running, fielding, throwing) and that the Red Sox record of Williams's era (one flag) indicates that he wasn't a tremendous leader, a team-man as was Joe DiMaggio. Yes, The Kid could be put on a stand-by basis."[5]

Just after 10:00 a.m. on January 20, Williams walked into the Fenway Park press room before a throng of writers, cameramen, commentators, and assorted courtiers. ("The lamb in the lion's den," Ted cracked, smiling, as he surveyed the majority before him.) The *Globe*'s Hy Hurwitz, who had sparred with Williams many a time over the years, called the proceedings to order in his capacity as secretary of the Writers' Association. He took out a manila envelope, ripped it open, and announced that Ted had been elected to the Hall of Fame with 282 votes, or 93.3 percent.

No other player had been elected on that cycle. Of the 302 ballots cast, twenty writers had not included Ted's name in what was seen as a token protest. Hurwitz said the 282 votes were the most that any player had received since Hall of Fame balloting began in 1936.

Williams took to the microphones, clearly touched. "This completes everything a ballplayer ever dreams about or hopes happens to him," he proclaimed. "I can't begin to tell you how pleased I am to have been elected to the Hall of Fame. My only regret is that some great ballplayers couldn't make it at the same time." He cited in particular Red Ruffing, the old Yankee whom Williams had faced in his first major-league at bat at Yankee Stadium. Ruffing had received 68.8 percent of the vote. Then Ted thanked the writers he had once scorned for electing him, especially in the first year he was eligible. Inevitably, he was asked to comment on his tumultuous relationship with the newspapermen. "My 'feud' with the baseball writers?" he said with a grin. "A great, great majority of the press was always with me, on my side. It was the small minority which was against me. If anything, their criticism helped. It irritated me and spurred me on."

Assessing his career, Ted rated the 1941 All-Star Game home run as his biggest thrill and the loss of the 1949 pennant to the Yankees as his lowest point. "The longest train ride of my life was that one, returning to Boston." And he declared that hitting .388 in 1957 gave him more satisfaction than hitting .406 in 1941. "I was an old man and near the end of it all when I hit .388," Ted said. "It was a real struggle for me all the way—yet I think I really hit the ball better that year than when I hit .406."[6]

Reaction to Williams's ascent among players, public, and press was almost universally favorable. A notable dissenter was Jim Murray, the gifted *Los Angeles Times* columnist, who broadened the Egan-Gillooly critique to the national stage. Ted was an objet d'art who belonged in the Louvre, not Cooperstown, Murray felt. He wrote that Ted was "probably the greatest pure striker of the baseball who ever lived. But this translated out into exactly one pennant for his team in 19 years. . . . His main adversary was a decimal point. He fought the public, the press, the Marine Corps—but not necessarily the New York Yankees. He was a stylist, not a struggler.

"I know it would be easier to keep snow out of Alaska than Ted Williams out of the Hall of Fame," Murray continued. "I wouldn't if I could. As I say, he was unique. I only hope they keep his trophy case well aloof from that of the rest of them in there, well away from the Frankie Frisches, Lou Gehrigs, Joe DiMaggios, Ruths, Robinsons and Cochranes—so that nobody will get the idea he's part of a team, and will know that it's just another All-Star appearance."[7]

But Murray was decidedly in the minority. Generally, Ted was showered with kudos, and the newspapers were filled with fawning tributes, series, and retrospectives on his career. Soon, Williams would also be hailed for his forward thinking and his surprising decision to leverage his induction to help right a wrong.

The ceremony was held six months later, on July 25, a Monday. Ted hadn't been in Cooperstown since 1940, his second year, when the Red Sox played an exhibition game against the Cubs on June 13. He had belted two home runs, one of them landing on the porch of a house on nearby Susquehanna Avenue. Still a boy, dreaming, he'd thought that day how great it would be to have a career that would make him worthy of the Hall of Fame. Now he was about to be inducted, along with Casey Stengel, who had been voted in separately by the Veterans Committee as a manager.* The Stengel-Williams relationship was a mutual admiration society. "I don't think anybody contributed more to baseball than Casey Stengel," Williams wrote in his book. "He ranks right there with Ty Cobb, Babe Ruth and Judge Landis. He was in baseball 50 years and caused as much copy to be written about the game and about himself as anybody."[8] And Stengel, for his part, loved Ted. "I wouldn't let my pitcher throw to Mr. Williams, because he could see the ball better standing sideways than the umpires could standing straight ahead," said Casey, who was about to turn seventy-six. "Williams was the most aggressive hitter I ever saw."[9]

On Sunday, the day before the ceremony, Ted, in his capacity as a Red Sox executive, joined farm director Neil Mahoney in Oneonta, New York, about twenty miles south of rustic Cooperstown. Williams had originally planned to watch the Sox's minor-league club play a game, but he begged off and decided to stay in his room at Oneonta's Town House Motor Inn. He began writing his acceptance speech on the hotel's stationery.

That night, Ted rendezvoused for dinner with about twenty friends, as well as with his quite pregnant daughter and her husband, at the Otesaga Hotel in Cooperstown. The Otesaga, with its thirty-foot columns and striking federalist architecture, is located on the southern shore of Otsego Lake—the Glimmerglass of James Fenimore Cooper's novels. It's the grande dame of Cooperstown, where all the immortals stay when they're in town.

The Williams circle included old teammate Bobby Doerr; war pal Bill Churchman of Philadelphia; Ted's accountant, Paul Brophy; and his agent, Fred Corcoran. Sometime girlfriend Lynette Siman of Islamorada made the cut, along with her husband. Bobby-Jo wore her hair up in the then-fashionable beehive. Ted had to excuse himself early from dinner to continue working on his speech. "I've never seen him so nervous," Doerr remarked to a reporter.[10]

Some seven thousand fans turned out the following morning on a hot, cloudless day, swarming the village of Cooperstown in what was

---

* The Veterans Committee is a voting arm of the Hall of Fame empowered to induct managers, umpires, baseball executives, and players retired at least twenty-three years who have not been admitted by the writers.

said to have been the largest crowd ever to come to an induction. The ceremony is usually held on the front steps of the museum and spills over onto Main Street. But that year the stage was set in Cooper Park, behind the museum, where there was more space—though, it turned out, still not enough to accommodate everyone. People sat in folding chairs and packed the slopes overlooking the lawn; others hung from the nearby elm and oak trees to get a better view of the platform. The spillover crowd in front of the building could hear the proceedings via loudspeakers but could not see the goings-on.

Williams, characteristically tieless despite the august occasion, was dressed in a white knit polo shirt buttoned to the throat, slacks, and a plaid sport jacket. He had requested to speak before Stengel, not wanting to follow the eccentric, comical former manager. Prior to the ceremonies, Hall of Famers Joe Cronin, Joe McCarthy, Bill Dickey, and Bill Terry were introduced to the crowd from the platform. Williams had connections to all four. Cronin and McCarthy were two of his managers, Dickey had been a Yankees rival, and Terry one of his childhood heroes with the New York Giants. Also introduced were the widows of Babe Ruth, Christy Mathewson, and Eddie Collins, who had scouted Ted for the Red Sox.

William Eckert, a former Air Force lieutenant general who had been named commissioner of baseball the previous year, introduced Ted and was forced to stop and wait several times as the crowd erupted in cheers when he cited Williams's litany of hitting accomplishments. "He gave five years to the service of his country and if he hadn't, probably would have hit one hundred and fifty more home runs," Eckert said. A voice from the crowd yelled, "Two hundred and fifty!" "Okay, two hundred and fifty," Eckert replied, laughing.

After Eckert handed Ted his Hall of Fame plaque and the crowd roared its approval, the photographers called for him to hold the plaque up in triumph. He obliged. Finally, after a suitable interval, he approached the microphone.

"Mr. Commissioner, baseball dignitaries, and fans, I'm happy and I want to emphasize what a great honor it is to have the new commissioner of baseball here, General Eckert," Williams said. "The general and I have at least one thing in common. We each did some flying. He was in the Air Force and I was a Marine, and I want you to know that no matter what you might have heard, there were many times when the Air Force went out first and the Marines had to go out and hit the targets they missed." The crowd erupted in laughter.

"I guess every player thinks about going into the Hall of Fame. Now that the moment has come for me, I find it difficult to say what is in my heart. But I know that it's the greatest thrill of my life.

"I received two hundred and eighty–odd votes from the writers. I know I don't have two hundred and eighty–odd close friends among the writers." Again there was laughter and applause, and Ted chuckled. "I know they voted for me because they felt in their minds, and some in their hearts, that I rated it. And I want to say to them, 'Thank you. Thank you all from the bottom of my heart.'"

And then Ted stepped into dicey terrain for the Hall of Fame. He had come to thank — but also to chide.

"The other day, Willie Mays hit his five hundred and twenty-second home run. He has gone past me and he is pushing ahead, and all I can say to him is, 'Go get 'em, Willie.' Inside this building are plaques to baseball men of all generations, and I'm privileged to join them. Baseball gives every American boy a chance to excel — not just to be as good as someone else but to be better than someone else. This is the nature of man and the name of the game, and I've been a very lucky guy to have worn a baseball uniform; to have struck out or hit a tape-measure home run. And I hope that someday, the names of Satchel Paige and Josh Gibson in some way can be added as a symbol of the Negro players that are not here only because they were not given a chance."

Williams spoke for a bit longer, about Stengel and about his own hope to stay involved in baseball. When he was done, the crowd rose to its feet and gave Ted a long, loud ovation. The six-minute speech, which Williams read from the handwritten text he'd composed on the Oneonta hotel stationery, had been delivered flawlessly, with grace, humility, poise, and humor.

There had been only one hiccup. After Commissioner Eckert introduced Ted and handed him his plaque, a fan sitting in the first few rows called out to Williams, "What would Dave Egan think of this?" Ted, standing about five feet behind the microphone as he waited for the applause to subside, then scowled, put his head down, and muttered a remark about Egan, his onetime nemesis, who had died in 1958.

Tim Horgan, the *Traveler* columnist, was sitting about twenty rows back and was quite sure he heard Williams say: "Fuck Dave Egan." Henry McKenna, Horgan's colleague from the *Traveler*'s sister paper, the morning *Boston Herald,* thought he heard the same thing.

Horgan, recalling the incident years later, said two Red Sox officials, Neil Mahoney and Ed Kenney, who worked with Mahoney in minor-league operations, spun around immediately to see if any of the writers had heard what Ted said. He also noticed others in the crowd whispering about it. "That gave me more confidence about the thing because I wasn't the only one who heard it," Horgan said.

He filed his column for the afternoon paper without mentioning Ted's remark about Egan, but he told his editor about it, and the editor decided that the obscenity should be the lead of Horgan's piece and proceeded to write the first four paragraphs himself.

"Red Sox slugger Ted Williams, apparently unawed by the solemnity of his elevation [to] baseball's Hall of Fame, cast a vulgar tone on today's ceremonies by making an obscene response to a heckler which left a majority of the crowd of over 10,000 stunned," the first paragraph read.[11] That was a clear overstatement, since only a fraction of the crowd sitting near the front had heard the remark, and the person who had called out to Ted about Egan was an admirer, not a heckler. McKenna's ten-paragraph account of the incident the next morning in the *Herald* added some detail the *Traveler* did not include, such as characterizing Ted's quote as "- - - - Dave Egan," so the reader could easily figure out which offending four-letter word had been involved. He concluded that "the profanity detracted from a noble day."[12]*

No other newspaper reported on the incident, and in his book, Williams denied that he had cursed out Egan. After the fan called out asking what Egan would have thought, "I made a face and said, 'Yeah, that Egan' and mumbled under my breath, carrying the joke out," Ted wrote. "It was one of the few times in my memory when I *didn't* use a few choice words to describe Egan. I was in too good a mood to let his memory spoil my day."[13]

Tom Yawkey thought that the *Herald* and *Traveler* had unconscionably sullied Ted's fete and was outraged. Though the *Herald* had written about the episode in more detail and more extensively, Yawkey focused his ire on Horgan and the *Traveler,* perhaps because the evening paper had come out first and thus began stirring the pot. Three or four days later, Horgan was at Fenway and received word that Yawkey would like to see him in his office. Horgan went up. Yawkey was sitting behind his desk, and to his right sat two Red Sox executives, Haywood Sullivan and Dick O'Connell. Fifteen or twenty feet away were a chair and a tape recorder.

---

* Ironically, the *Herald*'s editorial page that day differed from McKenna's assessment. In a short editorial entitled "The Honest Man," the paper decided that the Williams remark was a refreshing example of his candor.

"It looked like the electric chair," Horgan said. "Yawkey asked me to sit down and play the tape. It was a tape of Ted's speech. I played it several times, but I couldn't pick up exactly what he said about Egan."

Then Yawkey leaped out of his chair and began screaming and cursing at Horgan, saying he had maligned Ted and ruined his grand occasion. Horgan let him vent, then walked over to O'Connell and Sullivan, both of whom he knew better than the owner, and said, "I don't care who this guy is. If he keeps talking to me that way I'm gonna punch him." O'Connell and Sullivan smirked.

Finally Yawkey calmed down and said to Horgan, "Ted wanted to handle this, but I said I would."

"What do you want?" Horgan asked.

"I want a page-one retraction."

Horgan turned to leave, and as he did, Yawkey reminded him that the *Herald-Traveler* corporation owned WHDH radio, which broadcast the Sox games and made the newspapers a lot of money. The inference was clear: he might give the broadcast rights to another station. "If you give us the retraction, you'll never hear from me or Ted again," Yawkey said. "I promise you."

Back at the paper, Horgan told his editors what had happened, and they quickly folded. "They realized the awkward position the paper was in," Horgan said. "So they said to go ahead and write the correction. I had no recourse if I wanted to keep my job. I wrote the correction myself over my byline. From that day on, Yawkey and I were pals."[14]

Under the headline ANOTHER LOOK AT TED'S TALK, Horgan wrote: "Nobody likes to eat crow, but this time I don't mind. This time it's better that I, rather than Ted Williams, be wrong."[15] He said he'd thought Williams had made a vulgar remark, but after hearing the tape, he'd concluded that Ted had said "Let Dave Egan..." with the rest of what he said muffled in background noise. He had to fall on his sword. The *Herald* followed the next day with its own front-page mea culpa, headlined TED WILLIAMS, WE APOLOGIZE.[16]

Though little remarked upon at the time, the most significant section of Williams's acceptance speech was his totally unexpected and surprising call for the Hall of Fame to induct the Negro League greats, who had been deemed ineligible because they didn't have the requisite ten years of major-league experience. This, of course, was a catch-22 restriction, since the color line had barred them from playing in the first place.

Ted's remarks amounted to a bold and courageous political statement.

Most ballplayers are inherently apolitical. Williams, the iconoclast, was opinionated and willing to speak his mind when asked, but he certainly wasn't in the habit of calling for fundamental policy changes in baseball. And while his brand of Republican conservatism didn't seem consistent with a call to break down racial barriers, he was a strong believer in the egalitarian, democratic ideal. He might have hidden his own ethnicity from the public, but growing up as part of a Mexican-American extended family, he had witnessed discrimination firsthand. In addition, Williams had a basic sense of fairness. He'd heard about the exploits of Negro League old-timers since he was a kid, and at age fourteen he had gone to see Satchel Paige pitch, marveling at how hard he could throw. He'd competed against black players in high school, including Jackie Robinson in the 1936 tournament in Pomona. And while he was in the Pacific Coast League, and at least once in the majors, Ted had faced barnstorming Negro League players, including Buck O'Neil, who would go on to become a pioneering coach and scout in the major leagues and work in the commissioner's office. Williams, O'Neil recalled, always treated black players as equals.

Though Williams's statement at the Hall of Fame certainly caught the baseball establishment and most everyone else off guard, his actions and statements about black players and civil rights generally—both during his career and in the six years before his induction—actually foreshadowed it. When Robinson broke the color line with the Dodgers, Williams had sent him a letter of congratulations. When Larry Doby integrated the American League the following year, Ted had befriended Doby, going out of his way to make him feel welcome and frequently offering him batting tips. When Doby and his black Cleveland Indians teammate Luke Easter came to visit Ted in the hospital in 1950 after he broke his elbow, and were initially not allowed in to see him, Williams had insisted they be sent up to his room.

He'd touted black players to the *Saturday Evening Post* in 1954, declaring, "These fellows are not only great players but also a credit to the game." In 1957, Ted had met with Robinson in Boston when Jackie was visiting as part of an NAACP tour, and Robinson said he considered Williams "a fine person."[17] When the Red Sox finally integrated in 1959, with Pumpsie Green, Williams had taken the lead in welcoming Green, making sure to set an example by playing catch with him in front of the dugout during warm-ups before each game.

In 1963, at the beginning of his retirement, Ted, writing in his syndicated column, had called for network executives to televise more basketball and thereby showcase black players. Noting the rioting in Birmingham,

Alabama, earlier that year, an outgrowth of the civil rights movement, Williams wrote, "There should be room to show the world...there is another side to our country. Sports do not ask what a man's color is."[18] A few years later, after learning that a young black pitcher for the Kansas City A's, Johnny "Blue Moon" Odom, couldn't get a room at the team's hotel in Florida, Williams went to the front desk and quickly forced his accommodation.[19]

On a private hunting trip around the same time with his longtime friend Joe Davis, a Florida businessman, Williams made it clear what kind of talk he would and would not tolerate. "There were some boys from Georgia with us, telling stories about taking the doors off of black families' homes if they couldn't pay the rent," Davis recalled. "Ted got up and wouldn't listen to their talk. He didn't think it was funny."[20]

And there was Williams's sense of honor and the generosity that followed. Theodore Roosevelt Radcliffe had once managed a black All-Star team that played against Ted's San Diego Padres in the Pacific Coast League. Years later, Williams, the major-league star, encountered Radcliffe and asked him, out of the blue, "Are you broke, Ted?" Radcliffe didn't answer directly, but Williams knew that, as Radcliffe put it, "We didn't make much money in the old Negro Leagues." Williams took a photograph of Radcliffe and paid him $900 for the privilege.[21] Williams could be abusive, nasty, and narcissistic, but when he encountered the unlucky — be they those denied a chance because of racism or children denied a chance because of disease — he followed his heart.

Curt Gowdy, the longtime radio and TV voice of the Red Sox, said he considered Williams to be one of the most honest and fair men he'd ever met. "That's one thing I admired about him — that he was really open. And he said to me, 'You watch for that day that the major league players will be fifty percent black.'" When Gowdy asked why he thought that, Williams replied in the politically incorrect vernacular of the day: "Well, they'll go play in the minors for a hundred bucks a month and work their way up, get out of their element. Their bodies are stronger, they walk everywhere, they lift. They're great athletes."[22]

Ted's prediction that the major leagues would be half black proved way off the mark. The number of black players would peak in 1975 at 27 percent and has been in steady decline since, hitting 8 percent as of 2012.[23] Still, Williams's speech — along with the 1970 publication of Robert Peterson's pioneering history of the Negro Leagues, *Only the Ball Was White* — forced baseball to reassess its exclusion of the old black stars from Cooperstown. Bowie Kuhn, who in 1969 had succeeded William Eckert as baseball commissioner, admired Williams and considered him the greatest personality in baseball.[24] At first, Kuhn proposed only to give special recognition to the Negro League greats, not full membership in the Hall of Fame, since none of the players satisfied the requirement of ten years of service in the big leagues. It was a clumsy move akin to invoking a separate-but-equal doctrine, and there was strong backlash from the press, fans, and some leading black players, most notably Jackie Robinson himself. "If it's a special kind of thing, it's not worth a hill of beans," Robinson said. "It's a lot of baloney. It's the same goddamned thing all over again. If it were me under those conditions, I'd prefer not to be in it. They deserve the opportunity to be in it but not as black players in a special category.... Rules have been changed before. You can change rules like you change laws. If the law's unjust..."[25]

Kuhn and the Hall relented. A special committee was appointed to select Negro Leaguers it deemed worthy of full Hall of Fame member-ship, and on July 7, 1971, the committee announced its first inductee: Satchel Paige. Paige would be followed later by Josh Gibson, Buck Leonard, Monte Irvin, James "Cool Papa" Bell, Oscar Charleston, Martin Dihigo, William "Judy" Johnson, and John Henry "Pop" Lloyd. More former Negro League players would be enshrined in subsequent years.

Two days after the Paige announcement, Williams was honored in Washington by historically black Howard University for his role in opening up the Hall of Fame. "I've been thankful for baseball," Ted told the crowd, which included Buck Leonard, the former slugging first baseman for the Homestead Grays, and track great Jesse Owens. "It's what I've done best. It's what I know. But a chill goes up my back to know I might have been denied this had I been born black. I think it's time we realized that these great players were not just great black players, they were great players period. They should rightfully be enshrined next to the Musials, Alexanders, Cobbs and Ruths."[26] That statement brought a standing ovation from the crowd.

Former Negro League stars also praised Williams for giving their ranks a key boost. Monte Irvin, a standout outfielder with the Newark Eagles before signing with the New York Giants in 1949, and who two years later sparked that team to its historic comeback pennant win over the Dodgers, was the fourth player admitted to the Hall of Fame after Paige, Gibson, and Leonard. Irvin credited Ted's statement for his induction: "There are eleven men from the old Negro Leagues who are now in the Hall of Fame due to the fact that Ted spoke out, and when Ted speaks, people listen, and so everyone was very grateful that he made that statement."[27] Added Buck O'Neil, who was there the day Ted entered the Hall, "He really got the ball rolling.... We all knew it needed saying by someone like him. Regardless of how much we black ballplayers were saying it, it didn't mean much. He said it because it's the way he felt."

Williams's statement in Cooperstown had added resonance and significance because he'd played for the Red Sox, the last major-league team to integrate and the club with the worst record on race.

Owner Tom Yawkey had been among the thousands cheering for Ted that day when he was inducted, but he must have been taken aback by his star's detour into the subject of race, for not only had Yawkey's team been the last to integrate, Yawkey had been one of the leaders of baseball's segregationist old guard, one of the authors of that secret 1946 report advising then-commissioner Happy Chandler to keep the game white.

Even putting aside the sham tryout the team gave to Jackie Robinson and two of his Negro League compatriots in 1945, and its passing over Willie Mays in 1948, the Red Sox record on race continued to be dismal. In 1966, four months before Williams's remarks in Cooperstown, Earl Wilson, a black pitcher on the Red Sox, was subjected to an ugly incident in Florida for which he was given no support by the club. Wilson, who had thrown a no-hitter in 1962, had gone to a bar in Winter Haven, the Red Sox spring training site, with two white teammates and was told: "We don't serve niggers." Wilson reported the incident to team officials, who told him to forget about it and to say nothing to the press. But Wilson did go to reporters, and in the ensuing uproar was traded away to the Detroit Tigers.

As far as the public knew, Ted's remarks at Cooperstown were his first about race. He was a baseball player, after all, and what ballplayer spoke out on political issues of the day, much less on the tinderbox of race relations? Few, if any, knew of his acts of kindness toward Robinson, Doby, Pumpsie Green, Blue Moon Odom, or Theodore Roosevelt Radcliffe. His 1954 quote touting black ballplayers in the *Saturday Evening Post* had been buried in a larger piece about Williams himself, and the 1963 column in which he wrote that "sports do not ask what a man's color is" was otherwise forgettable.

Since Williams, not Tom Yawkey, was the public face of the Red Sox in the '40s and '50s, and since he seemed to be so powerful, many in the black community actually suspected that Ted had played a role in keeping the franchise white far beyond its time. Such critics "believe Williams to have been the secret engine behind the Red Sox' reluctance to integrate during the 1950's," said Howard Bryant, author of the 2002 book *Shut Out: A Story of Race and Baseball in Boston.* "I think it is illustrative of many blacks' need to 'find some plausible explanation' for why the Red Sox were so recalcitrant during those times." Yet there was no evidence to indict Williams for this, Bryant noted. In fact, the record proved the opposite, and Bryant rejected the hypothesis as "absurd" when discussing his book in a forum.[28]

According to Al Cassidy, the executor of Ted's estate, Ted, later in life, regretted that he had not done more to use his influence with Yawkey to speed up the integration of the Red Sox. "Ted didn't feel he had the standing to force this change," Cassidy said. "He said, 'Who am I?' He knew he had status as a player, but Ted had a strict rule with Yawkey. Yawkey was the owner of the club. Ted drew a line, and he would not have crossed that line. Still, it was one of those things that truly bothered him. Not just the Pumpsie Green case but the other Negro League players. Inequalities hurt him."

Once, Cassidy's father, with whom Ted had started the baseball summer camp in Lakeville, asked Williams directly why he had not done more to help the black cause. Recalled the younger Cassidy, "I was there when Dad asked him point-blank: 'You were so powerful back then; you could have made it an issue.' Ted said, 'Looking back, you're right, but back then I didn't think I had any authority with Mr. Yawkey.' He said that was one of his regrets—that he didn't do more."[29]

Certainly for Williams to have lobbied his club owner on a major policy issue like integration in that era would have been unusual. "Ted challenging Yawkey on race, or anything else, would have been like a guy on the Ford factory line going up to Henry Ford and saying, 'You know, I think you need this in your V-8,'" said Martin Nolan, former editor of the *Boston Globe* editorial page and a lifelong Red Sox fan.[30] Buck O'Neil agreed. "Ted had nothing to do with the Red Sox decision," he said. "Ted was a ballplayer, not the owner."[31]

Yet Williams was not just any assembly-line worker and certainly was not just any ballplayer. He was a superstar to whom Yawkey had shown great deference: moving Fenway Park's right-field fence in for him, making sure he was the highest-paid player in baseball, tolerating his temper tantrums and outbursts, backing his demand that writers be temporarily kept out of the clubhouse after games, condoning his ploy to miss two months of the 1955 season and conceal income so he could get a better divorce deal, and offering to make him a player-manager. So it is not implausible to argue that since he knew Yawkey gave him a wide berth and admired him greatly, Williams might have leveraged his status to prod the owner on race—especially in the '50s, after the color line had been broken and it would have been easy to mount an economic argument, not just a moral one. Red Sox teams were consistently dismal that decade, attendance was in decline, and the addition of black players could have made the team far more competitive. As his early acts of compassion to Robinson, Doby, Pumpsie Green, and others attested, Ted knew better, but he went along. "He framed it as being a different world back then," Cassidy said. "It embarrassed him it took so long. But he said prior to Robinson, it was just accepted that blacks had their league and whites had theirs. It was normal. He looked at Robinson coming in as a good thing, but not necessarily as a call to arms. It was the times."[32]

Williams's comments to the Cassidys suggest that his failure to at least broach the question with Yawkey festered within him, perhaps contributing to his decision to take a stand on racial equality in his Hall of Fame speech.

There was a footnote to Ted's big day at Cooperstown: After being presented with his plaque, the Kid decided that he didn't care for his bronzed likeness. The features were off, and it just didn't look like him, he felt. So he asked that the artist have another go at it.

There are no records kept at the Hall of Fame in the category of inducted players demanding that their plaques be redone, but suffice to say it was a rare, if not unprecedented, request. But this was Ted Williams, so officials agreed.* Williams found the likeness on the second plaque an improvement, though he told friends he was not thrilled with that one, either. Still, he could hardly make another stink about it.

Years later, in 1985, a life-size wooden statue of Williams by the sculptor Armand LaMontagne would be dedicated at the Hall of Fame and situated in a place of honor in the lobby, next to the statue of another remarkable hitter also sculpted by LaMontagne: Babe Ruth. When Ted pulled the covering from the statue, the crowd cheered, and scores of flashbulbs went off. Williams gazed at his likeness and absorbed the moment, then wept, overwhelmed by his proximity to Ruth.[33]

"The comparison with the greatest physical force in the history of the game was too much for me," Ted remarked later, explaining his tears.[34]

---

* Hall of Fame president Jeff Idelson later told the *Boston Herald* that the first casting was not destroyed, as it should have been. It was tossed in a Dumpster, then pilfered and sold on the memorabilia market to an unknown buyer.

22

Dolores

Three months after Ted's enshrinement, he was officially divorced from Lee Howard. Before issuing his decree, Miami circuit court judge Harvie DuVal asked Lee if she thought there was any chance of a reconciliation. "Are you kidding?" she replied.

DuVal awarded her $50,000, plus $10,000 in attorneys' fees.[1] Ted, after initially trying to win Lee back, had become resigned to the divorce and was ready to move on. And there were other family doings. In December, he became a grandfather when Bobby-Jo gave birth to a girl, Francine Dawn Tomasco, who became known by her middle name, Dawn. As she grew up, Dawn would look forward to visiting Ted, partially just to escape life with her mother, which she described as tumultuous and unsettled. "I used to love going to Islamorada and being with Grandpa," she said, "because I knew everything would be okay—that's where I felt safe."

Dawn and her younger sister, Sherri, who was born in September of 1968, would play on a hammock and a tire out back. Then they'd watch Ted tie flies by the hour in his workshop.

"He wanted to know about my grades in school, how long my finger-nails were, how much I weighed," Dawn recalled. "He'd say my hair was a bit long. He was very loud. He used to cook breakfast. He was a terrible cook. He'd make eggs, and they'd still have the whites in them. They'd be raw! 'Aren't those the best damned eggs you ever had? You want some more?' He'd be gritting his teeth. He was always intense. Then he'd make us baked beans from a can. He'd call them Ted Williams's famous baked beans!"

Ted had the girls give him a list of all their friends in school, then he would send the friends autographed balls. He'd take Dawn and Sherri out for Key lime slushies. And when he visited in Philadelphia, they'd go shopping—to Radio Shack for the latest electronic gadgetry, or to buy Bass shoes, his favorite. The shoes had to be Bass, Ted said. "He'd spoil us terribly. He loved obedient children. Visiting us with Mom, he'd want us to help her with her chores, then he'd stick hundred-dollar bills in our pockets. 'Don't tell your mom,' he'd say."

On August 26, 1968, less than a month before Bobby-Jo was to give birth to her second child, she got a call from her father informing her that she now had a little brother. "There's a gal by the name of Dolores," Ted said.[2] Dolores Wettach, the *Vogue* model Williams had met on the plane home from New Zealand in March of 1964, had been helping him tend to his love life after his breakup with Lee Howard. After their San Francisco dinner, he'd invited her to join him at spring training. She declined, but an intermittent courtship began. Ted was traveling, busy with Sears, his Red Sox duties, and fishing. Dolores was traveling, too, from her base in New York, pursuing a fledgling acting career in addition to the modeling work that was her mainstay.

They were a combustible mix of sexual tension and emotional volatility. Dolores was smart, sensuous, and sassy. She had a back-to-the-land sensibility leavened by urban sophistication. She told him about her experiences as a nurse, model, and actress. She told him that she'd had a daughter by a hometown boyfriend she was never serious about and that she'd decided to give the girl up for adoption. The two had little contact now.

At first, Ted liked it when she refused to play the sycophantic bobby-soxer to his Great Man. Dolores seemed to delight in asserting her independence and standing up to him when he was outrageous or too casually asserting his will. They'd be lucky if they went three days without a fight, after which there would be an eruption followed by a tender reunion. Dolores got used to the cycles. "I was smitten with him," she said. "He was easy to love."

In the spring of 1968, Dolores told Ted she was pregnant with his child. Williams was incredulous. He asked her if she was sure he was the father. Dolores said she was quite sure. But Ted wasn't. Uncertain what to do, he called his second wife, Lee Howard.

"I got a call from him one day, and he was crying on the phone," Lee remembered. "He was saying, 'It's not mine, sweetie, it's not mine!' Dolores was threatening to expose the pregnancy, and he was with Sears, and that would have been bad. Ted told me she was threatening to go to the papers. He kept saying, 'It's not mine. It's not mine.'"

Lee was unmoved. "Don't tell me, Ted!" she said. "Tell her!"[3]

Dolores denied she pressured Williams or threatened to go public with her pregnancy. "That's silly. No one threatened Ted. You didn't force him to do anything." She said she'd been hoping he'd propose for three years, but she hardly entrapped him. "I'm not going to throw myself at someone," she said. "I'm not going to try and finagle them. You like me or you don't like me. That's it."[4]

Reluctantly, Ted decided he would have to marry Dolores, and he told her they would elope to Jamaica, though first he insisted that she sign a prenuptial agreement. When they met at the airport for their flight to the island, he carefully looked her over. She was six months along but still barely showing. "Maybe you're not pregnant," Ted said hopefully.

It was not the most romantic way to start the trip, and the chill continued when they arrived in Jamaica. Williams nixed Dolores's proposed wedding dress. (She'd brought a formal gown that she considered jazzy and elegant, but Ted thought it was over the top given the circumstances.) She settled for a simple white wraparound knit number, and Ted wore just an Izod sport shirt over a pair of baggy slacks. "He'd say, 'I like a little ass room in my pants,'" Dolores recalled.

The wedding, on May 7, was held in a remote section of Kingston Parish. He didn't want a lot of fanfare, he'd told her, and there was certainly none of that: they were out in the middle of nowhere. "He whisked me off down into the hinterlands of the island," Dolores said. "We went in there to get married. The chickens were crowing. I thought it wasn't a professional place." The justice of the peace waved in a few locals to be witnesses. When the justice asked for the ring to put on Dolores's finger, "Ted said, 'She doesn't get a ring.' So the man, he looked at my stomach as if to say, 'She must be pregnant or something. . . .' And then, after being married, Ted took me to spend the night, and the mattress sunk way down, and I couldn't sleep in the bed because I kept rolling onto Ted. So I got up and slept in the bathtub."

Dolores Ethel Wettach was the oldest of four children. Her mother was Swedish, and her father, Karl Joseph Wettach, was Swiss-German. Karl had come to the United States at the age of twenty and headed for Montana, aspiring to make it as a cowboy. He rode Brahman bulls and broncos for a while, but decided it wasn't as glamorous, or lucrative, as he had hoped. Back east, he married Ethel Erickson, and they settled on an eighty-acre farm in Westminster, Vermont, a town of about three thousand people on the banks of the Connecticut River, some twenty-five miles north of the Massachusetts line, near Brattleboro. Karl made a go of it as a mink farmer.

As a girl, Dolores would walk a half mile to a one-room schoolhouse. She had to drop out for a while during World War II, when her mother was working and Dolores was needed at home to help take care of her two sisters and brother. She'd get up early and do chores on the farm, including taking care of the minks. They had to be fed ground-up horse-meat and watered five times a day, and Dolores would drag pails of water up a hill from the well to the barn.

She went to the regional high school in Bellows Falls, and then on to the University of Vermont, over the objections of her old-fashioned father, who saw no purpose in girls pursuing higher education. Dolores majored in nursing with a minor in animal husbandry, since she wanted to be able to help her father run the farm. A professor suggested she compete for the Miss Vermont title, part of the Miss USA pageant. Dolores didn't need much convincing. In high school she'd thought of herself as a tall, gangly ugly duckling, but she'd blossomed in college. Being Miss Vermont would be a validation of her adult beauty.

She won that first title, becoming Miss Vermont in 1956, then it was off to Long Beach, California, and the Miss USA round, where she sized up the girls from what were then the other forty-seven states with trepidation. Pageant officials, meanwhile, pored over her vital statistics like commodities brokers: she was a blue-eyed brunette, 37-24-36, five foot nine, and 130 pounds. (Her enormous feet—size 11AAA—were not officially noted.) For local color, she donned a Vermont Green Mountain Boys costume and a white swimsuit with rhinestones around the bust, but the Miss USA crown went to someone else.

Returning to the University of Vermont in the fall of 1956, Dolores got involved in politics, helping host a visit to Burlington by Tennessee senator Estes Kefauver, who was the Democratic nominee for vice president on the ticket with Adlai Stevenson. After graduating in 1957, Dolores took a job as a nurse at St. Clare's Hospital in New York, where a few chance encounters soon broadened her horizons, first in acting and then in modeling. One day, as Dolores was riding a crosstown bus, the producer of an off-Broadway play, taken by her beauty, approached and asked if she would like to audition for the play—in his apartment. "My girlfriends told me it was just a line and I shouldn't go, but I thought he looked sincere," Dolores told the *New York Journal American* in 1959 for a saucy feature the paper did on her unlikely evolution from nurse to actress.[5] She was given the role of a sorceress in *Shakuntala*, an Indian stage classic about a king who falls in love with a maiden commoner. *Variety* archly noted Dolores was "lithe and lovely, and most expressive when she is mute."[6]

Despite the theater experience, she had to work as a waitress to supplement her nurse's salary. Two fashion photographers spotted her in the restaurant and told her she'd make a great model. They asked her to come to their studio for a shoot, after which *Vogue* quickly snapped her up.

It was 1961, and the country was infatuated with Jacqueline Kennedy. Fashionistas coveted the "Jackie look," and Dolores was deemed nearly a dead ringer for the new First Lady. Both *Time* and *Newsweek* had articles on the surging Jackie trend and said that models who looked like her were prospering. Dolores was pictured striking an elegant pose in the *Newsweek* spread, while in *Time* she was touted as "lush and Lorenesque... the newest, most dewy-eyed model this year." The only negative was that she was deemed to have "too much figure." Translation: she was too buxom. "I'm made to wear a flattening bra," Dolores was quoted as saying. "Otherwise, I take away from the dress."[7]

While a regular in *Vogue*, Dolores was also featured in *Look, Esquire, Pageant,* and other magazines. Soon, she was being sent all around the world. "It was good money, but you couldn't take it seriously," Dolores mused. "You were selling garments. The girls were very competitive. I didn't really like it that much."

In 1964, the year Dolores met Ted, Carlo Ponti, the famed Italian producer, was captivated by her modeling photos and offered her a costarring role in one of his movies, *Controsesso* ("A Woman of Affairs"), a wry sexploitation comedy filmed in Rome. Dolores jumped at the offer and was amused by the interaction between Ponti and his legendary wife, Sophia Loren, who towered over him and was twenty-two years his junior. That same year, Dolores nearly became one of the James Bond girls when she was considered for the part of Pussy Galore opposite Sean Connery's Bond in *Goldfinger*. The Bond people had sent for her after seeing her pose in *Vogue*, putting on a pair of hose alluringly. She says she was initially offered the part, but the producers changed their mind and gave the role to Honor Blackman. In Ian Fleming's novel, Pussy is a lesbian. In the film, Bond seduces her, but only after a sexually ambiguous scene in which Pussy fends him off by saying she is "immune" to his advances. "They just said, 'I'm sorry, Dolores, but you won't pass for a dyke,'" she recalled, laughing.

There had been other movie-business encounters for Dolores—a meeting with the director Howard Hawks, a correspondence with Marlon Brando, a dinner date with Anthony Quinn—but those memories, those possibilities, receded abruptly as her relationship with Ted Williams developed. They had to. She knew how possessive Ted was, how he wouldn't brook any sort of perceived competition or sharing of center stage. "He told me, 'Don't try to steal the limelight,'" Dolores said.

At the time of the wedding, Dolores was thirty-three, sixteen years younger than Ted, but she liked to be coy about her age. Being in the beauty business, she found it prudent to keep people guessing about how old she actually was, so she carried three different birth certificates. On her marriage certificate, she listed herself as twenty-seven. Ted correctly said he was forty-nine, and gave his marital status as divorced. Dolores, with a touch of whimsy, reported that she was a "spinster."

Her parents disclosed the wedding to the press in June of 1968. Fibbing, they said the union had taken place the previous fall rather than the previous month.

That Christmas, Ted tried to rectify his wedding-ring slight. The first several presents she opened from him were innocuous. Finally, Ted produced a small box with a rose on it, which contained the wedding band. Ted himself declined to wear a wedding ring. Of course he hadn't bothered to get her an engagement ring before the wedding, either. Years later, he would try and make amends on that score by giving her his MVP trophies instead.

Their son was born on August 26, 1968, in Brattleboro, Vermont. Ted wanted to call him John, with the middle name Henry. Dolores suggested they combine John and Henry into a hyphenated first name. They both liked the legend of John Henry, the black former slave who, in the nineteenth-century push to lay railroad tracks to the West, became the greatest steel-driver of them all and who died victorious in a contest to beat an automated hammer touted as a replacement for the men on the line. Someone teased Williams about naming his son John-Henry because it was considered "a colored name," Dolores said, to which Ted responded, "Oh, yeah? Well, so is Williams." Dolores added a middle name: Dussault, after a friend of hers and Ted's, Ding Dussault, the track coach at Tufts University, outside Boston, and a neighbor of Ted's at his fishing camp in New Brunswick. Dolores called the boy Dusey.

Just as he did with Bobby-Jo, Ted missed the birth of his son, again because he was away fishing. When he showed up at the hospital, Dolores said, Ted took a long look at his son and said: "Yeah? Well, he'll never be the ballplayer I was."

Though Dolores now had a full-time job tending to John-Henry, Williams hoped she could help him deal with Bobby-Jo as well. His daughter was having serious problems coping with marriage and with being a mother, and Ted didn't have a clue what to do about it. He still cared about Bobby-Jo—his house in Islamorada was filled with pictures of her taken when she was a baby girl and when she was a young mother and at every stage in between—but he was frustrated by her various meltdowns, for which he had no patience or understanding.[8]

Bobby-Jo certainly needed help: she was now abusing drugs, having moved on from Darvon to Seconal. The Seconal didn't mix well with alcohol, which she had also begun using with increasing frequency. Sometimes she'd just announce to her husband that she was taking a handful of pills, hoping to end it all. And then there were the affairs. "Her promiscuity—that's what led us to a divorce," concluded Steve. At one particularly low point, she announced that she was in love with one of their neighbors and that she was pregnant. Not sure if the baby was the neighbor's or Steve's, Bobby-Jo tried to abort herself and botched the job badly. She had to be rushed to the hospital and have a hysterectomy. They went to Florida and spent a month with Doris. Things calmed down, and Bobby-Jo promised not to see the neighbor again, yet she later ran off with him, taking the girls.

"We moved to Miami and lived in an apartment," Dawn recalled. "My mom was basically a hippie. We were always on Miami Beach, and we'd never go home. I always felt more secure with her friends. They played guitar, and the only song Mom knew was 'Row, Row, Row Your Boat.' When it was just us and my mom, she was unpredictable, and she'd get mean. She smoked marijuana. Her drinking got worse. I became more of the caretaker than Mom. I'd take care of Sherri because Mom couldn't.

"She'd go on drinking binges. She'd wake us up in the middle of the night, and we'd call my dad in Philadelphia. He had an unpublished number. She'd call the police and fire departments and say there was a family emergency and they had to get in touch with him. She'd say there's something wrong with the kids. She wanted more money, and she'd make us get on the phone and ask our dad for more money."

Then one day Bobby-Jo called Steve, crying, and said her lover had beaten her up, hit the kids, and thrown them all out on the street. She told her husband she still loved him and begged him to take her back. Ignoring the advice of his friends and family, Steve agreed. He rented a trailer, drove to Florida, picked up his family, and drove home. "The kids were thrilled," Steve recalled. "They were elated. It was almost as if not a lot had changed. In a short time it felt like old times. Barbara acted as if nothing had happened. It was like we'd taken a trip and we were coming home. So I felt great."

But Bobby-Jo lapsed again. Steve says she had a fling with a 7-Eleven attendant, then took a handful of pills and had to have her stomach pumped. After she took another fistful of pills, Steve had her committed. When he called Ted and asked him for advice, Williams ducked the issue and sent Dolores to Philadelphia instead. She gave Steve a sympathetic ear, but delivered a tough message as well. "Dolores said Ted could no longer be financially responsible for the trouble Barbara got into," Steve said. "It was unfortunate, but she pretty much said, 'You're on your own.' I wasn't looking for money, really, just support and advice."

Dolores says Ted hoped that with her nursing background, she could perhaps instill in Bobby-Jo a greater sense of maturity and "straighten her out." But the new Mrs. Williams wasn't seen by Bobby-Jo as neutral. "If anything, she resented my being in her life because she needed her father for her," Dolores recalled. "She needed all she could get and then some." And Ted, Dolores added, "couldn't stand" Bobby-Jo anymore. "She just didn't behave the way he wanted a kid of his to behave, that's all. She was a spoiled brat. She was looking for attention. She didn't care how she got it." Bobby-Jo, for her part, dismissed Dolores as an interloping gold digger. "I just thought she was different from *anybody* my dad had been around," she said. "Different from anybody."

After several months, against doctors' advice, Steve took Bobby-Jo out of the hospital. In her absence, he had put their daughters in a foster home because he worked and said there was no one else to take care of them. When Bobby-Jo came home, they regained custody of the girls.

Seeking some sort of reconnection, Bobby-Jo and Steve went to visit Ted and see her new half brother. At one point they were standing in the living room of Ted and Dolores's apartment, and John-Henry crawled out onto a balcony, ten floors up. Bobby-Jo darted out to scoop him up, worried he might fall. "Dolores came over to me, and she grabbed him, and she said, 'Don't you *ever* touch my child again.'"

Not long after they returned home, Bobby-Jo took another lover, and that was the last straw for Steve. He moved in with his parents. When she moved to Florida with still another man, again taking the girls, Steve had her served with papers, and they were divorced in 1971.

Bobby-Jo's daughter Dawn Hebding said her mother never told her why she and her father split up. "My mother broke up the marriage, according to my father. But after growing up with my mother, no sane person could have gone through that. I think my father felt he was going to have to let us go in order to have a life without us burdening him." Nor did Bobby-Jo ever discuss why her own parents, Ted and Doris, got divorced, or the strains that placed on her. "She has so many secrets, she holds so much in," Dawn said. "I'm sure that's contributed to her problem. I love my mother, but she's very ill, emotionally."[9]

If Bobby-Jo had been less than thrilled by the arrival of Dolores on the scene, there was another woman who had a far stronger reaction: Louise Kaufman.

Nursing her wounds from the Kid's earlier rejections, Louise had spent time in Paris and Ireland, but when Ted and Lee divorced, she and Williams reconnected in Islamorada and, before you knew it, Louise had moved her clothing into Ted's house. But when Dolores got pregnant and Ted announced he would marry her, Louise had been jilted yet again.

After Ted gave her the bad news, Louise called a friend of theirs, John Underwood, and begged him to talk some sense into Ted. "She felt she'd waited long enough, and asked me to intervene," Underwood said. But he declined. "I said that was Ted's decision."

Underwood was a writer for *Sports Illustrated,* then in his early thirties. A year before, in the summer of 1967, he had spent two days fishing in the Keys with Ted, then written a sparkling feature for the magazine called "Going Fishing with the Kid." He was a facile writer, and the piece was a revealing look at Williams's fishing expertise as well as his demanding, perfectionist persona.

Williams liked the story and sent Underwood a note. "Way to go," he wrote. "You captured the real me." Underwood and his editors at *Sports Illustrated* saw an opportunity. Williams had never told his life story to anyone. He plainly liked Underwood. Why didn't they approach the Kid about doing a series for the magazine?

Williams was coy. "A lot of guys want to do that, but maybe you're the one," he told Underwood without committing. Ted put him off for a while longer, but eventually agreed. The two men met for weeks at a time at various places, such as Ocala, Florida, where the Red Sox had their minor-league training camp, or they'd go hunting and fishing.

Recalled Underwood, "He'd call me and say, 'I'm going somewhere, you want to go?' We went fishing in Costa Rica once. I was, in effect, becoming his brother. I taped as much I could, probably half tape and half notes. Ted was totally candid. There was nothing he wouldn't delve into. He had a way of talking that was peculiar to Ted. He'd not only expose something, he'd go back over it. He had a very analytical mind. He'd analyze his own actions, even when they weren't so nice."[10]

The result was a four-part series about Williams's life and a stand-alone article about hitting a baseball. The series began on June 10, 1968, after Ted and Dolores had been married a month. Simon and Schuster then asked Underwood to turn the *SI* series into Ted's autobiography, which he did. *My Turn at Bat* was published the following year and became a bestseller. The hitting article was also later turned into a book, called *The Science of Hitting* (a title Ted chose), and remains today perhaps the foremost batting tutorial. Adding to his Williams oeuvre, Underwood would also crank out a third book with Ted, this one on fishing, called *Ted Williams: Fishing the Big Three,* a guide to going after tarpon, bonefish, and Atlantic salmon.

In a July 18, 1968, letter to Williams, Underwood said that Simon and Schuster had committed to a $75,000 advance for *My Turn at Bat.* No figure was mentioned for the hitting book, but they were aiming for $25,000 for the fishing story. No fishing book had ever earned a $25,000 advance, unless it was *The Old Man and the Sea,* Underwood assured Ted in the letter, which began, "Dear G.C." This was a reference to G. C. Luther, an alias Williams had told the writer he often used to register at hotels when he traveled.

There were some sloppy mistakes in the autobiography, such as misspelling Ted's mother's maiden name (it was Venzor, not Venzer), getting the score of the Red Sox's playoff-game loss to the Indians in 1948 wrong (it was 8–3, not 4–1), and incorrectly naming the *Boston Globe*'s Mel Webb as the one writer who had failed to nominate Ted in the controversial 1947 MVP balloting, when Webb didn't even have a vote. Underwood also glossed over Williams's first two marriages and chose not to explore his Mexican heritage, even though Ted had not put anything off-limits. But the book, written in the first person when Williams was forty-nine, amounted to a revealing first cut of his life to that point, and was especially effective at capturing Ted's voice. "Obviously he didn't say all those things the way I wrote it," explained Underwood. "You get all his things in bits and pieces. If you can capture the lexicon and argot, then you could go off on tangents. I felt like I was inside his mind, and I could write the way he would speak, so I weaved it together."

During the year he spent with Ted on both the fishing story and the magazine series, Underwood got to know Dolores well. "Ted met his match with Dolores, in terms of her ability to cuss and stand up to him," he said. "In many respects, she was probably the right woman for him, but she was also too similar, and they were constantly at odds."[11]

Unsurprisingly, Dolores quickly found herself at odds with Louise Kaufman. When Dolores arrived in Islamorada, Louise didn't concede defeat immediately. Instead she tried to use her status as Williams's next-door neighbor to her advantage by inventing excuses to remain in touch with Ted. According to Dolores, some of these bordered on the ridiculous, such as Louise tossing her dog over the fence onto Ted's property, then asking him to bring the dog back to her house, saying it had escaped. It was the first Dolores had heard of Louise, and so she worried: "He had said I meant more to him than any dame he ever met, but then I wondered, did I really? Because I couldn't quite understand the patience he had with these other women."* Finally, Louise appeared to give up. She sold her house in Islamorada and moved up to Delray Beach, Florida, to be near her friend Evalyn Sterry.

Ted and Dolores, meanwhile, had no fixed home; they moved with the seasons. They'd spend the summers at Ted's baseball camp in Massachusetts, the fall at his fishing cabin on the Miramichi River in New Brunswick, the early winter, until Christmas, at Dolores's house in Vermont, then return to Islamorada for the rest of the winter, until spring training.

Williams taught Dolores to fish on the Miramichi, and not only did she quickly get the hang of it, she also became quite confident, if not cocky, about her ability. Dolores thought she was especially accomplished at fly casting, and Ted got annoyed when other fishermen admired her stroke — sometimes too annoyed. He was extremely possessive of Dolores on and off the water. If she was out when he called, he always wanted to know where she'd been and what she was doing. If ever she was with a man Ted did not know, he would say, "What are you doing with that clown?"

Williams prided himself on his ability to tie intricate flies, and he'd

---

* Dolores's use of the plural was indicative of a broader trail she'd noticed, just as Ted's previous wives had.

spend hours in his workshop at the Miramichi. Dolores told him the lacquer on his flies had an odor, and if she were a fish, she'd never bite it because of the smell. She tied her own flies au naturel, using chicken feathers. Once, a big salmon he had spotted upstream eluded him and came downstream, where Dolores caught it, though it got away. Ted groused, "You'll never be that lucky again." And she thought some of their happiest moments as a couple were when he'd take her out on the flats in Islamorada to fish for tarpon. "He liked my casting. I got a lot of respect, peace, and calm from him, which meant a lot. He said, 'You're not a dumb dame.'"

Dolores loved Vermont and considered it home. She had a sixty-acre farm near her parents' home, but Ted didn't like it there. Whenever he got annoyed with her, he'd call her "Cow Hampshire." The state was wrong, but the point was clear: she was a hick. He kept complaining he was freezing his ass off and there wasn't enough to do. Dolores didn't even have a television. (She hated TV and considered it decadent. Every time Ted bought a TV when they were in Vermont, Dolores would move it out when he left town.)

"Ted much preferred to be down in the Keys, where it was warm and there was fishing," Dolores said. "Vermont also cramped his style. There were no girlfriends up there. He couldn't take other girlfriends out." But for Dolores it was home, and she spent as much time there as she could. At one point, she built a stone wall on her property and called it her "Ted frustration wall. If I had Ted on my mind, I'd get extra energy to push a heavy rock up a little bit further." And she took shooting lessons. Ted kept shotguns and an automatic pistol at the house. She wasn't worried about intruders, because she had two German shepherds, one of them trained to attack on German commands.

Dolores went to extreme measures to try to get her husband to like Vermont. Once, when he was away, she hired someone to put her house up on wheels and tow it up the hill to provide a more sweeping view. The next time Ted was there, he was confused and called Dolores. "Where the fuck is the house?" he asked.[12]

"I'm *in* the house," she responded from up the hill. It didn't do any good. Ted still didn't like being there, but he got a kick out of telling friends what Dolores had done: "Not only does she move the furniture, she moves the whole goddamn fucking house!" he said.

Dolores didn't mind Williams's swearing. In fact, she found it rather endearing. "I thought his way of swearing was very colorful. I didn't mind it at all. I thought it was the most acceptable way for a gentleman to be cursing. You know, it was okay to hear him saying, 'As long as I have a hair on my ass, so help me...' That's nice, instead of using those four-letter derogatory terms that people can use. He didn't insult people personally to their face."

She also found a silver lining in her husband's crass view of women. His favorite line was, "They're a pain in the ass, and if you couldn't fuck 'em, they wouldn't be worth anything."

Said Dolores: "That was Ted. But he had a clever way of being abusive that was forgiving. He really didn't point-blank debase the person. He didn't attack the individual per se. It was all women. 'Christ, you couldn't please them if you were Jesus Christ himself.' And it just made it okay."

Yet it was certainly a form of abuse, and, like her predecessor, Lee Howard, Dolores soon learned that Ted had far more anger than she'd known before she married him.

"He was a tornado," she said. "You never knew what he was going to be like. He was volatile. He had easy, nice, calm sessions, and then, boom! A storm would blow up. You either walked out or—you certainly didn't try to talk him out of it. You played all your psychiatric training you ever had in nursing. You never go running into the beehive if somebody's upset. He knew how to hurt. He was rough about it. The timbre of his voice was rough. Growly."

To cope, she tried to be optimistic: he was explosive, but he had sensitive enough antennae to tell when he'd pushed too far, and then he'd say he didn't mean it and that he loved her, after all. She noted, too, that Ted could channel his anger in constructive ways. "It was his best friend, because it gave him power to do things which saved him, which was important. If he had to swing the bat, and he was angry, that ball would fly. If he was fishing, and he was angry, that fly would just fly, and the fish didn't stand a chance."

But the difficulty came in social situations, when his loved ones and his friends felt the lash. Dolores and Ted might be playing chess, for instance, and if he lost, he'd gather up the pieces and send them flying into the venetian blinds. Ultimately, Dolores felt the source of Ted's rage was his inability to satisfy the perfectionist ambitions that he set for himself. When he failed to meet his own expectations, no matter how innocuous the activity, he could snap.

23

The Splendid Skipper

It was the winter of 1969, and Bob Short had a problem.

Short, a wealthy Minneapolis businessman who loved sports and politics, had recently bought the lowly Washington Senators for $9.4 million, beating out the comedian Bob Hope. It was Short's second stint as the owner of a professional sports franchise. In 1957, he and more than one hundred other businessmen had put up a mere $100,000 to acquire the floundering Minneapolis Lakers of the National Basketball Association. Then, as the Lakers continued to lose money, Short gradually bought out his other partners, assumed sole control, and moved the team to Los Angeles. He sold the club for $5 million in 1965.

The sale netted Short about $3 million, but it was in the trucking and hotel industries that he had made his fortune. He'd hoped to make his mark in Minnesota politics as well, but he lost runs for Congress in 1946 and lieutenant governor in 1966. His friend and fellow Minnesotan, Vice President Hubert Humphrey, had installed him as treasurer of the Democratic National Committee, and Short had also been one of Humphrey's most prodigious fund-raisers during the latter's failed presidential campaign of 1968.

In early 1969, Short immersed himself in running the sad-sack Senators, who the previous year had finished tenth — dead last — in the American League with a record of 65–96. Short's challenge — to rekindle excitement in the Senators among Washingtonians, traditionally far more interested in their Redskins and pro football than in baseball — was magnified by the coup that the Redskins had just pulled off. They had lured Vince Lombardi, the legendary Green Bay Packers coach, out of retirement and installed him as the Redskins head coach.

To counter the buzz that the hiring of the fabled Lombardi had generated, Short, who had given himself the general manager portfolio and fired the previous manager, Jim Lemon, determined that the Senators needed a "storybook manager, the kind people dream about."[1] There were only two people Short could think of who met that criterion: Ted Williams and Joe DiMaggio.

Short quickly gravitated to Williams, whom he had revered ever since watching the Kid slug for the Minneapolis Millers at Nicollet Park in 1938, when Williams had torn up the American Association and won its Triple Crown before moving on to Boston.

"Washington was not only last in terms of the American League, the sport was practically dying in the town," Short would say later in explaining why he went after Williams. "You don't go after anything less than the divine when you're trying to raise the dead."[2]

At first blush, the notion of Williams as a manager did not compute. After all, he had turned down the Red Sox when they offered him the job in 1954 and again in 1959, when he was still a player. Then he had said no to the Detroit Tigers in 1960, after he retired. "All managers are losers; they are the most expendable pieces of furniture on earth," he had written in his autobiography, which was to be published later, in 1969. And temperamentally, the job seemed a bad fit. How could a perfectionist like Williams tolerate as much imperfection as he would see in the Senators? He was a loner and a brooder who could be volatile and combustible. How would those traits play out in a job that required patience and tact? Also, Williams had never been a leader on the Red Sox. He had been the practiced individualist who, if he led at all, did so only implicitly, through the brilliance of his hitting, rather than by exerting his influence on behalf of the team. Then there was the press. Ted had spent his career feuding with the writers. Could he change his stripes for a job that would require daily press conferences and interviews, public relations skills, and the need to forge amicable relationships with reporters covering his team?

Moreover, there were the Senators themselves to consider. The team was an expansion club that had started in 1961 after Calvin Griffith had moved the old Senators from Washington to Minnesota and renamed them the Twins. The new Senators were known to be one of the worst organizations in baseball, with a weak farm system and a weak scouting operation. Washington had never supported baseball adequately, and the stadium—which had been renamed for Robert F. Kennedy, to honor the recently assassinated senator—was located in the ghetto.

Williams was surprised when Short called him in Islamorada. The owner said he could name his terms. Ted replied that he knew nothing about managing and hardly even knew who played for the Senators, other than the huge slugger Frank Howard and a few others.

Short plowed ahead, conceding that Williams would be inheriting the worst team in baseball but arguing that if the players got no better, people would say they were just lousy and he would not be blamed.[3] If the team improved, however, he'd get the credit. Then Short appealed to Williams's love of the game and his desire to see the sport prosper: it was vital that there be a viable, successful franchise in the capital. Given his stature as a baseball icon, he had a responsibility to help. Short even turned his pitch to patriotism and politics: Williams returning to baseball would be good for the country and for Richard Nixon, the new president, whom Ted held in such high esteem. Nixon, after all, loved baseball and was on record as wanting to see the Senators thrive.

Ted was flattered but unmoved. He politely declined the offer.

Then Short called Joe Cronin, by then president of the American League, and asked him for help. Cronin, drawing on his long history with Williams, called Ted and leaned hard on him. He said it was especially important that baseball have a healthy team in Washington, where Cronin himself had been named player-manager in 1933. After Mickey Mantle's retirement at the end of the 1968 season, the American League could use a shot of Ted's glamour and sizzle, even as a manager. The league needed him, Cronin said. So did baseball.

Short called Williams again, proposing to fly to Florida and drive down to Islamorada so that they could meet face-to-face. Ted, now weakening, said that wouldn't be necessary: they could meet in Atlanta, as Williams had to stop there en route to South Carolina on a trip for Sears. His answer was still no, but he agreed to make a list for Short of people he thought would be best for the job.

Ted's list had his own name on top.[4]

Williams called his bosses at Sears to ask if they would support his taking the Washington job, and they immediately said yes. His $100,000-a-year Sears contract ended in 1970. Becoming a manager would get him back in the limelight, something Sears had already thought was important. That's why they were having him do his syndicated column, radio spots, and the cartoon strip. Williams realized that managing would bring him far more attention than any of those activities and would position him well when it came time for Sears to decide whether to extend its contract.

Talking with John Underwood, his ghostwriter, the night before he was to fly to Atlanta to meet Short, Williams was still leaning against taking the job, but he said that "the one thing, the only thing, that could make me change my mind is m-o-n-e-y."[5] Ted had played his last six years with the Sox on a deferred salary, so his last deferred payment had been made, a factor that caused him to be more concerned about his finances.

Short and Ted met at the Marriott hotel in Atlanta. Williams thought Short was bright, dynamic, and an ardent salesman. As they talked late into the night, the Minnesotan further endeared himself to Ted by telling the story of watching as a young man when Williams was starring for the Millers. Short laid it on thick, and then, rather than have Williams fly commercial for his meeting with Sears in Columbia, South Carolina, Short flew him there in his own plane and used the extra time to lobby some more.

Williams had changed his mind-set. Instead of thinking of why he should *not* take the job, he began thinking of why he *should*. First, he had to admit he was bored. It had been great to indulge his love of fishing, for which he had traveled to many exotic locales, but he'd had his fill. At fifty years old, he was too young to do that for the rest of his life. Second, baseball remained his first love; it was what he knew best, and he could still make a significant contribution. Maybe Short and Cronin were right: the game did need him. And truth be told, Ted missed the action and the limelight.

He would be a good teacher, he thought. As a player, he had been constantly giving his teammates and his opponents tips on how to hit. He'd been doing the same thing for young kids at his baseball camp for more than a decade, as well as for Red Sox minor leaguers in spring training throughout the '60s.

Then there was the lucre. Short was offering a five-year contract at $65,000 a year, plus an option to buy 10 percent of the team for $900,000.[6] He would get ten years to exercise the option. He also would be given the title of vice president, an unlimited expense account, and a free apartment at Washington's Shoreham Hotel. He could quit, but not be fired, and would be free to assume a front-office position at any time.

This was a generous package worth a bit less than $1.5 million. Williams had about $400,000 invested in the stock market and owned some Florida real estate, but this deal could go a long way toward making him financially secure for life, he thought.[7]

Williams consulted several friends and associates, most of whom advised him to accept the offer. One notable whom Ted called was Tom Yawkey, the Red Sox owner, a man he had worked for in one capacity or another for thirty-one years. Williams was still on the team payroll as an executive/celebrity responsible for showing the flag at spring training, and this and that. Technically, Yawkey had to release Ted so he could pursue the Washington job, though that was just a formality. Yawkey was an important figure in Ted's life, and Williams wanted his blessing. He also wanted the owner's candid view on whether he thought Ted could actually be a manager. Yawkey told him he thought he could do a good job.[8]

In fact, privately, Williams was disappointed that once he retired, the Red Sox had never asked him to be their manager. When he turned down the job before, the main reason was he felt he could still be productive as a player and didn't want the distraction of being a manager at the same time. After he retired, Ted felt the team never showed him the proper respect, and toward the end of his life, he confided to friends that he had wanted to return to Boston as manager. But if Yawkey had ever seriously considered Williams to lead the Red Sox after he retired, the year 1969 was certainly not the time. After all, Boston had won its first pennant in twenty-one years in 1967 under Dick Williams, who still was firmly established in the dugout with the club.

Ted finally signed his contract with the Senators on February 21, in Short's suite at the Washington Hilton, after a battery of lawyers on both sides took more than a week to hash out the stock-option details.

When everything was just so, Williams and Short emerged to face more than one hundred writers, radio and TV people, and photographers for what was said to have been the largest sports press conference in the city's history. "This is Ted's night, and Washington's night, and the Senators' night, and America's night," Short said in his grandiose introduction.[9] "I have a world of confidence in Ted as the manager of our ball club. I know it's traditional in baseball that great players never make great managers, but if anyone can, I believe he has the ability to become the exception."[10] Williams said he regarded his former manager Joe McCarthy as his role model. He said he believed in discipline and would institute a curfew for his players. He ruled out pinch-hitting at age fifty. He promised to try and get along with the writers and said his troubles in that regard had only been with a handful of antagonists. He suggested he was wiser and humbler now than he had been in his playing days. "I hope I've matured a little, that my thinking's better," Ted said. "I did not feel I was qualified when I could have managed the Red Sox, and I feel the same now to a degree, but I am ten years older. I took the job, I think, because of Bob Short, and because it happened to come along at the right time."

Williams fielded nearly seventy-five questions deftly and with humor. At one point he was asked, "Will manager Ted Williams be able to tolerate a player like Ted Williams?" The new manager replied, "If he can hit like Ted Williams, you're damn right."[11]

Harold Kaese, the *Boston Globe*'s veteran Williams watcher, came down for the press conference and wrote that Ted's return as a manager was the most exciting off-the-field development in baseball since Jackie Robinson broke the color line in 1947.[12] That level of interest was evident four days later, when Ted took the field for the first time as manager at the Senators' spring training facility in Pompano Beach, Florida. A throng of reporters and photographers surrounded him as he settled into the dugout and prepared to hold court. He was wearing his familiar number 9, having usurped it from Frank Howard, the team's six-foot-seven-inch, 255-pound slugger, but the numeral was invisible beneath the baggy blue Senators warm-up jacket Williams wore to disguise the forty extra pounds or so he had packed on since his playing days, mostly in the gut.

Williams projected enthusiasm and energy and was candid about his weaknesses and strengths. "I'm going to try," he said. "I may turn out to be a horseshit manager, but I'm going to try. I'm going to be the last man out on that field every day if that will help." He was perhaps more revealing than he was wise, given the need to inspire confidence in his cellar-dwelling team.

"I know my weaknesses. I don't know infield play, that's my special little bugaboo. I don't know how to run a game—at least I don't feel I do. I never even made a lineup card. It's something I don't know about— when to do certain things. Get too interested watching a pitcher or batter and you're two moves behind before you know it. But I'll have somebody right beside me helping me with that part of the act. The thing I know about, the most important part of baseball, is that game between the batter and the pitcher. I know I'm going to be able to help those hitters. I am sure of that."[13]

Williams said he had just told his players in a meeting that there would be a midnight curfew during spring training. He would also require them to turn in two hours after night games during the season. "I told them this was for their own good and I told them of the many players I knew who missed big opportunities in the majors by misbehaving. I hope it registered."[14] He also said there would be no players in the hotel bar, no serious card playing, a three-beer limit on plane flights, and—increasingly convinced that swinging a golf club corrupted good batting mechanics—a $1,000 fine for hitting the links during the season.[15] There would also be a dress code—jackets and ties while traveling. For Ted that would mean his familiar blazer and bolo tie. He even tried to insist that his players have a two-hour nap before each night game.

He said he would engage in "trial and error," hoped to make "an intelligent and meaningful contribution to the team," and was "intent to use the powers of observation."

Many of the writers who knew Williams from covering him as a player were skeptical that he had the patience to be a manager. One said to him that first day: "I know you well, Ted, and you might chuck this whole thing in 90 days." Ted looked at the writer with a cold stare and replied: "You don't know me as well as you think."[16]

He reminded the press how much patience is required to be a good fisherman, and added: "Don't you forget that ol' Teddy Ballgame is the best fuckin' fisherman anywhere." And this: "Look, I'm the guy who says that the hardest thing to do in sports is to hit a baseball. I know damn well that is true, so how can I be impatient of those who haven't yet learned to do it? No one knows better than me how much time it takes."[17]

Ted pointedly told the writers he would help his players deal with *them*: the prodding press corps. "You know who's the least prepared of all to cope with you guys?" he asked them. "Young ballplayers, that's who." Williams could have been thinking of himself, the naïf who landed with the Red Sox in 1938 and 1939 and was thrown to the writers without protection or advice from the club. "If I ever get a kid like that," Ted continued, "I'm going to school him. You better believe it."

Ted was still carrying a letter he had received from an old friend advising him not to take the job, and he took it out now and read portions to a few confidants. It was clear that, at least this once, Ted was enjoying bantering with the writers and giving as good as he got. Besides getting to know his players, half his time over the next few months would be devoted to accommodating the unceasing demand from one newspaper, magazine, radio station, or TV station after another, each of which wanted to do its own variation of the "Teddy Ballgame Returns" story. The reporters swarmed Pompano, and Short was delighted, knowing no one was better copy than Ted and believing that his instinct to hire Williams had been validated. His slogan for the season was: "It's a Whole New Ball Game."

The Boston writers all showed up, of course. Ted was willing to let bygones be bygones, but he seemed to enjoy resuming the joust as well. "You know, when the Braves moved to Milwaukee, those Boston papers never fired any of their baseball writers and they all came at the Red Sox," he said one day, a twinkle in his eye.[18]

Frank Howard was a holdout that season and arrived late to spring training. Short took him into the clubhouse to introduce him to Ted. They shook hands, and Williams said: "Geez, are you strong. If I'd been as strong as you, I would have hit a thousand home runs.... You hit the ball harder than anyone I've seen, though you don't hit it as far as two I've seen—Mantle and Jimmie Foxx."

Williams told Howard he wanted to sit down with him and talk hitting. The two had polar-opposite styles: Ted insisted on the self-discipline to wait for a good pitch to hit, while Howard swung at virtually any pitch from his eyes to his shoe tops. Howard had only had fifty-four walks the previous year; Ted said he could have at least a hundred by being more selective. He should spot the pitcher a strike, even two, in an effort to get a better pitch to hit. Howard demurred, noting that even when he did get his pitch, he didn't always make good contact the way Ted did. Still, he offered to try Williams's approach.

After two weeks, Howard reported back that he didn't think he could spot the pitcher two strikes—the risks were too high that he'd strike out, because he wasn't a reliable enough contact hitter—but he would be willing to take one strike as part of an effort to become more selective. "Well, all right," Williams said, content with the compromise.

Howard had heard so much about Ted's temper he thought he'd be popping off at the players all the time, but he found Williams to be patient. When a hitter would walk back to the dugout after whiffing, Ted would just say, "Don't be anxious. Get a good ball." And Howard thought Williams's enthusiasm was infectious. "Are you ready?" Ted would shout to the starting pitcher in the clubhouse before the game. Of course, the pitcher would reply that he was. Then Ted would yell at the rest of the players: "All right, let's go, let's be ready, let's have a little ginigar."[19] (The word *ginigar*—not a word at all but a Williams concoction meaning "pep" or "energy"—puzzled the players at first. "What do you drink that with, tonic?" the utility infielder Tim Cullen would ask Ted.[20])

Williams liked to stake out a perch behind the batting cage and issue running commentaries on the hitters he watched in the form of nonstop chatter. "Be quick," he'd say. "Don't be big. Go to right.... Go to right three straight times and you get a Cadillac."[21]

Williams tried to be upbeat with the players. Meeting someone new, he'd say, "What did you hit last season?"

"Oh, .204," the player might say.

"You did? With that swing of yours, you got to be better than that."[22]

Ted quickly took on Mike Epstein as a special project. Epstein, a big, left-handed-hitting first baseman, had been a bust his first two seasons, hitting in the low .200s with a total of eighteen home runs. "He wants to hit the ball 550 feet instead of 380 feet," Williams explained to a reporter. Epstein, a bright University of California at Berkeley graduate, liked engaging with Ted. "There's interaction," he told the same writer. "I think that makes for a terribly healthy environment. If you think you have a solid basis for argument, he'll listen to you. He'll discuss it with you. He is always trying to make you think a little bit."[23]

Epstein, like virtually all the other Senators, held Williams in awe, at least at the beginning. Opposing players came to kiss the ring, too. Epstein recalled one day when the Cincinnati Reds were in Pompano for an exhibition game, Pete Rose, who in 1968 had won the National League batting title with an average of .335, came over to the Senators dugout with a ball in his hand.

"Excuse me, Mr. Williams," he said. "I'm Pete Rose. Can I have your autograph?"

"Is it for you, Pete?" Ted said.

"Yes, sir."

"I'll sign it."

Epstein was sitting next to Williams and saw that he signed the ball: "To Pete Rose, a Hall of Famer for sure, Ted Williams."

Then Johnny Bench came over with a ball, and he asked for an autograph.

"Is it for you, John?" Ted asked.

"Yes, sir."

Again Ted signed the ball: "To Johnny Bench, a Hall of Famer for sure, Ted Williams."

"So I'm thinking, 'I gotta get in on this,' so I reach in the ball bag and get a baseball, lean over, and ask Ted to autograph the ball for me, and he signs it, 'Ted Williams' and gives it back to me," Epstein said, laughing. "That's Ted. Ted was the most honest person I've ever known. He wouldn't lie to make you feel good."[24]

For his coaching staff, Williams chose to keep two major-league veterans he had inherited: Nellie Fox, an All-Star infielder for twelve years with the White Sox, was the first-base coach, and Sid Hudson, who had won 104 games with the Senators and Red Sox and played with Ted from 1952 to 1954, was the pitching coach.

Then there was Wayne Terwilliger, a journeyman second baseman in the majors for nine years who was slated to manage the Senators' Triple-A team, the Buffalo Bisons, in 1969. Terwilliger was at Pompano Beach helping out, and Williams had been impressed by his energy, enthusiasm, and knowledge of the game. One day Ted approached Terwilliger, who was known as Twig, and asked: "Did you coach third base when you were managing in the minors?"

"Yes, sir," Twig replied.

"Is there any reason you can't coach up here?"

"No, sir."

"Okay, you're my third-base coach."

Just like that. Then, right before the season started, they had another chat. Obviously, what he knew best was hitting, Ted said. He didn't know much about stealing a base, or when to hit-and-run and bunt, so Twig should handle all that and flash the signs as he saw fit.[25]

As for that "person right beside me" Ted had told the writers he needed, he created the position of bench coach, first trying to recruit his old Red Sox pal Johnny Pesky. But when Pesky turned him down, Williams turned to Joe Camacho, the former minor leaguer who had taught at Ted's baseball camp and was currently an elementary school principal.

There was an official rule book on the desk of his office at Pompano, and Williams kept saying he had to read it, but meanwhile, his coaches helped expand his knowledge of the game beyond hitting and its converse, pitching.[26] Still, Ted always made it clear what his first love was. One day, Fox and Camacho were conducting a run-down drill and after several minutes got into a heated argument about the preferred technique for fielders to use when they had a runner trapped. The argument got louder and louder and attracted a crowd. Finally, Ted ambled over to see what the commotion was all about. "What the hell's going on here?" he demanded. Terwilliger explained, and Williams threw up his hands, bored by what he considered an insignificant phase of the game. "Fuck it," he said. "Let's hit." And the batting cages were rolled out.[27]

Of course, Williams also felt he had something to say to pitchers—

after all, he had studied them carefully all his life. He knew their tendencies, what they liked to do when, but he also liked to needle them. He'd make remarks like: "Pitchers are the dumbest sons of bitches in the world." This was a variation of the same flippant remark he had made for years as a player, but now that he was a manager, it had a different connotation, especially if it had been heard by a pitcher. The pitcher usually wouldn't see any humor in the crack and take it as evidence that Ted the manager still had the one-dimensional, hitter-only mind-set he'd had as a player.[28]

Before the Senators' opening game, at home against the Yankees on April 7, Ted was pacing back and forth nervously in the clubhouse. Frank Howard called out to him, "Hey, Skip, I bet you would like to be 20 years younger today." Williams grabbed a bat and went into his batting stance. "Oh, geez," he said. "Would I? You bet I would."[29]

The weather was sunny and pleasant, with temperatures in the sixties. President Nixon was on hand, in a box near the home dugout, seated next to Bowie Kuhn, the new baseball commissioner, and Bob Short, confidant to the man Nixon had just beat, Hubert Humphrey.

The presidential seal was affixed to the outside of the box on the field, but a key word was misspelled. For that day, Nixon was the "Presidnt of the United States." When Kuhn handed a ball to Nixon so he could toss out the ceremonial first pitch, the president booted it and had to rummage beneath his seat to make the recovery. The press quickly called it the first error of the new season. Finally, Nixon lobbed first one pitch, and then two more for the benefit of the photographers, out to the sixty-odd players and coaches from both teams who had assembled in wait.

Nixon was an unabashed Senators fan after spending so many years in Washington, first as a congressman and senator from California, then as vice president, and now as president.[30] A beaming Williams was right by Nixon's side, and Ted pointedly told the writers that he had voted for the president and contributed to his campaign. "I don't think too many people are any happier than I am that he is President," Williams said.[31] Nixon loved Ted too. He had invited Williams to the inaugural ball in January and sent him a handwritten note in March congratulating him on being named manager. "It's good to know that we share the same goal: to make Washington a first place city," Nixon wrote, signing off, "Sincerely, R.N."[32]

Underscoring his stature as the star of his team, Ted was the last member of the Senators to be introduced to the crowd—a rarity for a manager. He received a standing ovation from the 45,113 fans, a record number, and then he did something he had not done since 1940: he tipped his cap.[33] The game itself was an anticlimax: the Senators lost to the Yankees 8–4, despite getting fourteen hits. But they won the next day, 6–4, and the day after that, too, 9–6, behind sixteen hits. That made thirty-six hits in the first three games, so the press speculated that maybe some of Ted's hitting magic was rubbing off. SENATORS SHOW WILLIAMS TOUCH was the headline in the *New York Times*.[34]

In the second series, at Baltimore, Washington won the first game but lost the next three by a combined score of 20–0, prompting Short to panic and call a meeting with Ted and his coaches. Short was furious at the way things were going, but Williams was more furious with the owner's attitude. The two started screaming at each other, and Williams cussed Short out.

"I ought to fire you!" Short exclaimed.

"I'll quit first!" Ted screamed back.

There was an awkward silence, then Short asked if the coaches had any thoughts. Wayne Terwilliger offered a face-saving way out for both men, saying he thought the Orioles were the best team in baseball. They were going to win a lot of games that year, and some of them inevitably would come against the Senators. Williams walked out of the room and slammed the door as hard as he could.[35]

On his return to Yankee Stadium on April 15, Ted got the loudest ovation,[36] and in Boston, of course, the goodwill tour continued in earnest. More than a hundred writers, broadcasters, and photographers were waiting outside the visitors' dugout at Fenway Park for Ted, and when he poked his head outside, he received his first standing O of the day. The second came when he walked his lineup card out to home plate before the game started. Then the 28,972 stood again and cheered, but this being Boston, Ted did not tip his cap.

The Senators won the game, 9–3, and afterward, one of Williams's more controversial policies came in for a vigorous debate. He had reinstituted his rule—originally started when he and Dom DiMaggio pressured Red Sox management decades earlier—barring reporters from entering the clubhouse for fifteen minutes after a game to give his players a "cooling-off" period. Dick Young, the *New York Daily News* columnist who was president of the Baseball Writers' Association of America at the time, had written Williams a letter of protest, which Ted had ignored. Now Young was banging on the clubhouse door, yelling at

Ted to open up.[37] Williams screamed back at Young that he could go fuck himself.

When the doors were finally opened, Young walked right up to Ted. "What's this, after a 9–3 victory?" he asked.

"What's what?" replied Williams.

"Making these men wait. It's not dignified."

"Oh, you're going to make a project out of that?"

"Yes."

"Nothing's going to be done about it."[38]

Bob Short was in the clubhouse, watching this scene unfold with amusement. The Washington writers had also groused about the policy, but Short, though sensitive to the need for good press, was not about to cross his manager on something that was obviously important to him. The Senators players loved the fifteen-minute ban, and it helped establish Williams in their eyes as a players' manager. Even President Nixon, who of course had spent his career jousting with reporters, weighed in on the issue—in support of Williams. That helped Ted finesse the mild pressure he was receiving from Bowie Kuhn, who, after receiving a copy of Young's protest, had written Short and Williams asking if anything could be done about the situation.

"Neither Kuhn, Nixon, or Jesus Fucking Christ could change this goddamn ban!" Ted gloated to Shelby Whitfield, the radio and TV broadcaster for the Senators, adding he'd resign before relenting.[39]

If the Senators played poorly, Williams didn't hesitate to let them know. Once, after an especially sloppy performance, he locked the clubhouse door and let them have it. "Gentlemen," he said, "that was the worst exhibition of baseball I have ever witnessed. I'm afraid we're going to have to start over at the beginning." He reached for a ball and said, "Now this, gentlemen, is a baseball."

At that moment, Frank Howard raised his hand from the back of the room to interrupt. "Uh, Skip," he said, "would you mind taking that a little slower?" Everyone laughed, and the tension was broken.[40]

But tension remained. Williams was consistently annoyed because his hitters often couldn't remember what kind of pitch they'd faced against a given pitcher—either when they struck out or got a hit. (Williams claimed to recall the key details of all of his 521 home runs.) He was not always shy about making his bewilderment known.[41]

Still, by July 1, Williams had the Senators just over .500 at 40–39. In Washington, accustomed to decades of losing badly, this was enough to have the writers give Ted rave reviews in their midyear assessments of the club. "Stop the clock, right now, and baseball's manager of the year, no dispute permitted, is Theodore S. Williams," wrote Shirley Povich, lead sports columnist for the *Washington Post*.[42] Povich noted that Williams had improved virtually all the players' batting averages, commanded their respect, had them hustling, and was making strategic moves with the self-assurance of a polished veteran manager rather than the rookie he was.

Forgotten now, it seemed, were the preseason concerns about Ted's churlish, mercurial personality and his reputation as an impatient loner. Even with the fifteen-minute rule, he had won the writers over with his witty charm. He was proving to be a hands-on leader who didn't hesitate to trot onto the field and argue a call with an umpire, something he hardly ever did as a player. Once, he even had an assistant call the press box to lobby for a scoring change on behalf of one of his starters. He said he was finding that the hardest part of managing was knowing when to take a pitcher out: if anything, he was tending toward an early hook rather than leaving someone in until he was gassed and prone to being shelled. But otherwise, he seemed confident and expert. Asked at midseason how he was enjoying managing, Ted replied, "Well, a lot of it's fun. A lot of it's horseshit. When it gets to be more than fifty percent horseshit, I'll quit." Ted said the percentage was currently about fifty-fifty.[43]

Ted got another burst of publicity at midseason with the publication of his autobiography, *My Turn at Bat*. He promoted and signed the book for fans zealously, both at home and on the road. By now, Williams was even getting more attention than that other new coach in town: Vince Lombardi. Life was good.

In his relationships with the players, Ted was helped significantly during his first season by his iconic status. He leveraged the awe he received from virtually all his charges to maximum effect. The players relished merely being in his orbit, so they strove to learn from the Great Man and please him.

"I remember the pedestal that Ted was put on," said Dick Billings, an infielder on the 1969 team who was later converted to a catcher. "It was an unbelievable feeling to be around him, not just for me but for everyone. He was so dynamic and animated about everything. It didn't matter if he was talking about hitting, fishing, cameras, or whatever. That first year, when he walked in a room, everything just stopped."[44]

Billings and the others had never heard the sorts of stories about hitting that they heard from Ted. Recalled Billings, "He'd say that when he was playing, in the early innings, he'd try to hit the top half of the baseball for singles and doubles. Then from the seventh inning on, he tried to hit the bottom of the ball for home runs. We're all looking around at each other like, 'Yeah, right.' But he was adamant about it."

If that was a bit of esoterica, another was Ted's continued infatuation with Bernoulli's principle, so whenever he was bored, Ted delighted in gathering a group of players, especially the pitchers, since this was their department, and asking them if anyone could tell him what made a curveball curve. "They'd answer, 'Well, it has to do with the spin and the grip,'" Billings recalled, chuckling. "Ted would scream, 'I'm not talking about that blankety-blank crap. I'm talking about the physics of it.' No one knew."

Bernoulli's principle was also central to a friendship Williams forged that first year with a most unlikely species: a sportswriter. Dave Burgin, then thirty, wrote a column and was sports editor of the *Washington Daily News,* a now-defunct, Scripps-owned afternoon tabloid.

Burgin had been sitting in the dugout at Pompano Beach during spring training with about thirty other writers, talking with Ted. Williams was saying that he'd asked one of his pitchers, Notre Dame graduate Jim Hannan, what made a curveball curve. He said, "Even the fuckin' college boy didn't know the answer." Ted wondered if any of the writers did.

Burgin had been raised in Dayton, Ohio, home of the Wright brothers, and if you grew up there, chances were you might know something about aerodynamics. "It's differential pressure," Burgin piped up meekly.

"Jesus fuckin' Christ, I don't believe it!" Ted bellowed. "A sportswriter knows that?"

Then one night at the bar in the hotel where the players and writers were staying, Ted had spotted Burgin sitting with his wife, a dark-haired beauty, and had come over to introduce himself, teasing the writer about how he could have landed such a girl. Not long afterward, Ted was driving back to Pompano from Palm Beach after an exhibition game, going about ninety miles an hour in his Cadillac, when Burgin screamed by him in his Porsche Targa, going well over a hundred. Williams tried to catch him, to no avail, and when Burgin arrived first at the hotel, Ted came over to him and said, "Goddamn! What is that thing?"

Burgin's car, his wife, and his knowledge of Bernoulli's principle had marked him as an intriguing character in Williams's eyes. During the Senators' first homestand, Burgin got a phone call. "This is Teddy Ballgame," said the voice on the other end of the line. "What are you doing for dinner tonight?" Of course, Burgin could have had a dozen different plans and would have canceled them all immediately. "It was like that all summer long," Burgin said. "He'd always call me. We must have had dinner twenty times."

Williams never specified if any of the sessions were off the record, though Burgin considered them so and never burned his new friend. He only told his wife and a few others about the dinners he was having with Ted and the friendship they were developing—never his staff at the *Daily News.* He took no notes at each session they had, nor did he ever write about the experience. "I kept it private. First of all, I did not think anyone would believe it. I kind of thought he wanted something, but that wasn't the case at all. He just liked me, and here's a guy that's supposed to hate sportswriters." Ted was not reticent in the least, either. "He loved to argue. He was right-wing, but he didn't know right-wing. If you said he was a right-winger, he didn't know what you were talking about. It was just, 'America's great, dammit.' He was an optimist." Burgin was especially interested in hearing about Ted's service in Korea, but they also talked about newspapers, managing, and women. Recalled Burgin, "I wanted to know all about being a pilot in Korea. He told me a hundred stories about what it was like doing that. I really enjoyed it. He did it with gesticulations and sound effects. He'd grab the stick and *rat-a-tat-tat* the machine guns. He was in the jet and they were supposed to cross the Yalu River. He's saying, 'I'm going across and I see a convoy of trucks crossing a bridge. I see it's gooks. They don't see me till the last second. I put five trucks on fire.' He said, 'I betcha I killed a hundred gooks. Worthless commie cocksuckers.'"*

As they met over the course of the season, Burgin got the impression that Williams felt managing the Senators was becoming a chore. He was frustrated with the level of talent but liked what he'd done with it. He took pleasure in teaching people how to hit, but he made it clear he wasn't going to last too long. And after initially being enamored with Bob Short, Ted was souring on him.

They discussed the concept of team chemistry, and Williams said he thought it was "bullshit," Burgin recalled. "He thought team chemistry was playing your heart out. Didn't mean you had to love the guy playing first base. Team chemistry was winning."

A fundamental psychological point about Williams, Burgin thought,

---

* Burgin mentioned that he'd served in the Army for three years, and Williams teased him by saying, "A scribe in the fuckin' Army? Jesus Christ, so much for military secrets."

was that he always seemed angry. "He reminded me of the grandfather or father who tells his kids, 'You don't know how tough life can be. I had to walk to school three miles in the snow.' Something was bugging him. It ran deep, and I have no idea what it was, and I never asked him."

Burgin—who later would become editor of the *Orlando Sentinel,* the *San Francisco Examiner,* the *Dallas Times Herald,* and the *Houston Post*—said he remained dazzled by what seemed in hindsight like the fleeting moments he had with Williams that summer of 1969. "Other than the Babe himself, is there another ballplayer more likely to tongue-tie a kid from my generation?"[45]

Dolores had thought Ted becoming a manager was a good idea. She knew her husband was basically bored with the Sears job and that helping the Red Sox with spring training and assorted other chores, along with going fishing, wasn't challenging enough. Baseball was what he knew best, and as a manager, he could make a contribution and have a real impact. "I said he should take the job," she remembered. "He wasn't going to take it."

Of course, Dolores didn't have a clue about baseball and had never even attended a game before. She liked the idea of learning about it, but soon found that Ted had no interest in teaching her any of the fine points. And while part of Williams's motive for taking the job was surely to get back in the limelight, Dolores, already uncomfortable in the role of celebrity wife, soon became even more distressed by the concomitant effects of fame as she watched the spotlight shine brighter and brighter on her husband.

Once, she went to a game only to find a beautiful girl sitting in one of her seats. "I wondered, 'Who is she? How come she's in my seat?' But I didn't introduce myself to her and ask her to leave. Maybe that could have been Lee Howard or someone. I don't know. I let it go. I didn't want to look for a confrontation. If someone didn't want me, that's fine. Let me go my way."

And of course, people were more curious about her now. The press wanted to talk with the wife of the new Senators manager. Her first encounter with a major newspaper, her first interview as Mrs. Ted Williams, did not go well. She spoke with Myra MacPherson of the *Washington Post* at Ted's house in Islamorada. It was a soft setting—at home with Mrs. Williams—but Dolores misread the situation. She turned up dressed to kill, offered champagne to the reporter at lunch, swore occasionally, and then stirred the pot by suggesting that Ted was not easy to live with and that he had a hard time getting along with people.

MacPherson wrote that Dolores, clad in low-slung, hip-hugger jeans and a shirt tied at the midriff, "looked about as much like a housewife as Zsa Zsa Gabor looks like a nursemaid." When she opened a bottle of French champagne for lunch, she remarked, "It's not too early for wine. Some people have it for breakfast." And about Ted's new managing job, Dolores said: "It's about time he learned to get along with people. He's up and down like the weather. I go from being extremely happy to extremely unhappy. Just when I'm ready to give up, he'll say, 'I love you and I didn't mean it.' "[46]

Ted was mortified by the *Post* story and barred her from giving any more interviews. But in late September, at the end of his first season as manager, Dolores, without telling her husband, decided to open up to someone else. Don Newbery was the antithesis of a *Washington Post* reporter. He was not even a reporter per se but a high school teacher and coach in Silver Spring, Maryland, who did some freelance radio work on the side. He'd go to Senators games and Washington Redskins games and practices, then hustle interviews with players and coaches and try to sell his pieces to area radio stations. Newbery had interviewed Ted and met Dolores at the ballpark. He asked her for an interview. At first she ignored him, but at the end of the season, she told him to call her and arrange a time to come by and talk. They met where she and Ted lived in Washington, at the Shoreham Hotel. When he arrived, she suggested they do the interview on the roof.

As they spoke, it was obvious that Dolores was dying to unburden herself of various pent-up frustrations about life with Ted: how he wouldn't deign to discuss his Senators job with her, how insecure he was, how jealous she was of the other women who flocked around him, how much of the romance had left their relationship since they got married.

"It's the toughest relationship going when you live with someone as famous as he is and with someone as volatile as he is and someone who is as expressive and can work under these pressures. He's very insecure. He wants badly to be able to do something right the first time. Nothing can get in his way. If I even ask a question it turn[s] into an argument. They say you always hurt the ones you love, but when he would come home and just take everything out on me, it was tough, and of course, I don't know baseball, and for someone like me to show some interest it was more irritating than anything. Like you don't have time for the greenhorn. This now became *the* most important thing in his life, and that was difficult.

"I think in the beginning I was kept out of everything. I was told I couldn't go to the training, I wasn't allowed at practice, I wasn't allowed at the games, I couldn't travel, and I had all of these imaginations of why, why, why? What's happened? Why doesn't he want me? I was trying to think of where I failed. Then he'd come home with all of this tension. I began—oh, dear, all of these women! The female plague—jealousy. Of course, they were mobbing him. He is charming; he could charm the leaves off a tree. And of course this was eating at me. His hostility that he's capable of. . . . When you're not married to someone you don't know how unpleasant it is to be married sometimes. I had the best relationships when marriage wasn't involved, but as soon as it happened, the romance went right out the window. I'm not an equal anymore." Plaintively, she added, "I'd love to be able to make mistakes and have Ted say, 'I love you anyway, sweetie. I love you for your faults, too.' "[47]

This was poignant but explosive material. Newbery knew that if he had aired his interview at the time, it would have made front-page news around the country. But he was not a reporter and lacked the scoop mentality. He was more teacher than journalist, and as a human being, he was worried about Dolores. Worried that Ted would go ballistic when this came out, and worried about Dolores's welfare as a result. So Newbery decided to pack away his cassettes and not release them until after Ted died.[48]

Williams tried not to play favorites among his players, of course, but if he had a pet, it was probably Mike Epstein, the young power-hitting first baseman whom his teammates called Super Jew.

Scanning his roster after he took the job, Williams had concluded that Epstein was too heavy at 230 pounds. So he wrote him a letter and asked him to get down to 210 by spring training. Epstein dieted like mad and reported to Pompano twenty pounds lighter.

"I'm Ted Williams, who are you?" Ted said to Epstein, introducing himself.

"Mike Epstein."

"Jesus Christ, you look awful. Jesus, are you sick? You better put on some weight."

"But you told me to lose some!"

"Well, I didn't know you had that big a frame."

Williams gave Epstein extra time in the cage that first spring, and after practice, he would take him to the Howard Johnson on Route A1A in Pompano Beach and bulk him up with milk shakes. Ted would usually have a shake or two himself.

Williams liked the kid's company, and during the season, he took him hunting. "On days off, we'd go to Sharpsburg, up in Maryland, and we'd hunt groundhogs," Epstein said. "We'd come off a road trip at three or four in the morning, and he'd say to me, 'Aw, shit, there's no reason to go to bed. We've got an off day tomorrow—let's go shooting.' So we'd go up and wait for the rock chucks, and we'd fall asleep by two p.m. with our rifles in our hands, out in the grass."

Epstein was always picking Williams's brain and firing questions at him about hitting. Ted had asked lots of questions, too, of course, as a young player and throughout his career, so in that sense Mike reminded him of himself. Many of the great hitters didn't have a clue about how to teach others, Epstein said: "I'll talk hitting with Hall of Famers, and you don't get any answers. Joe DiMaggio is a classic example. He said to me, 'One day you'll wake up and realize you're born with it or you aren't.' That was the extent of Joe getting into hitting technique." Epstein thought Williams was better at teaching the mental part of hitting than the mechanical side. Ted could dissect a swing and demonstrate proper technique, but Mike found years later when he was starting a hitters' school that Williams sometimes couldn't explain the why of it all. "He'd say, 'Hips lead the way,' but in his book he never tells how that would happen. So I asked him one day, and he says, 'Well, it just happens. When you've got good mechanics, it just happens.' And I said, 'But if some kid comes up, and you're a hitting instructor, and he says, "You say the hips lead the way," and I say, "They just do," I'm not Ted Williams. They're not gonna take a lesson from me.' "

Ted couldn't really resolve that. Sometimes teaching seemed to only go so far. Mentally, he would encourage his hitters to guess in certain situations and advised them to adapt to how they were being pitched to so they could turn what the pitcher perceived as their weakness to a strength. "He would tell you things like, 'If they're pitching you inside, look for that pitch, look for the pitch that's giving you the most trouble,' and then he'd walk away," Epstein said.

On July 21, Major League Baseball celebrated its hundredth anniversary with a lavish dinner in Washington attended by 2,200 people, including six members of President Nixon's cabinet and thirty-five members of the

Hall of Fame. The Baseball Writers' Association of America selected Babe Ruth as the greatest player ever, while Joe DiMaggio was voted to the all-time team and named the outstanding living player. Williams was left off the all-time team and voted to the all-time living team. Piqued that he had been bested by DiMaggio, Ted refused to attend the dinner. DiMaggio did come. Williams sent Dolores to accept his award for him, and she tried to explain away her husband's absence by citing his aversion to dressing up for such fetes.

"You all know Ted's sentiments on formal occasions," Dolores said. "Well, he hasn't changed any, and that's what makes him great."

Not so great, actually, in the eyes of the writers, Bowie Kuhn, and the other lords of baseball, who saw Williams's absence for what it was: a petty snub.

The following day, President Nixon, the überfan, hosted a reception at the White House in honor of the centennial, and this time Ted, wearing his bolo tie, showed up, waiting in a long receiving line with some four hundred other baseball dignitaries to greet Nixon.

Williams's and the president's mutual admiration society was one of the more intriguing subplots of Ted's term as manager of the Senators. Ted hardly disguised his feelings for Nixon, going so far as to hang a large photo of the president in his office at RFK Stadium for all the writers to see, a bald political statement that might have been a first for a major-league manager.*

Nixon came to a handful of Senators home games each season, and Williams would have Ed Doherty, the former Red Sox public relations man whom he had brought down from Boston to serve in the same capacity, sit next to the president and tend to his every need. Doherty had been hired by Tom Yawkey in 1939 and was so hostile to reporters that the writers in Boston viewed him as the anti–press agent, but that reputation helped him with Williams. Ted and Doherty made sure the president got a good in-house press. A smiling Nixon even ended up on the cover of the team program for the 1970 season alongside the words "Our No. 1 Fan."[49]

---

* In 1970, Nixon arranged for his son-in-law, David Eisenhower, to be the statistician for the Senators. According to Shelby Whitfield, Eisenhower was a diligent worker who would report for duty in the press box wearing a dark pin-striped suit. In a tell-all memoir of his two years with the Senators, Whitfield wrote that during the seventh-inning stretch, Eisenhower would ask a press-box attendant to get him a bowl of ice cream, as the writers sent out for beer. On road trips, some Senators players took Eisenhower out on the prowl, determined to test the strength of his relationship with Julie Nixon, but without success.

During Nixon's reelection campaign, in 1972, Williams, who thought Watergate was much ado about nothing, made sure that writers covering the team knew how he felt about Democrats such as George McGovern, Ed Muskie, and Hubert Humphrey. "As politicians, they make me puke," he said. In the presence of Bob Short, however, Williams had to tone down his extreme anti-Democratic views. After a game in 1969, Short, the Democratic Party luminary, asked Ted and Dolores to join him for dinner at the Occidental Restaurant with Eugene McCarthy of Minnesota, who had lost the Democratic presidential nomination to Hubert Humphrey the previous year. Williams was diplomatic and contained his enthusiasm for Nixon.[50]

Ted was also a devotee of Spiro Agnew, the vice president, and loved the way Agnew gave the press hell. In addition, he publicly supported the National Rifle Association and proudly displayed one of the colorful law-and-order bumper stickers on his car that helped fan the culture wars in the divisive late '60s: IF YOU DON'T LIKE POLICEMEN, THE NEXT TIME YOU NEED HELP CALL A HIPPIE.[51] After Nixon resigned the presidency in disgrace, he and Ted would remain in touch. In 1977, Nixon invited Williams to visit him in San Clemente for a few days, but Ted had a prior commitment and had to beg off. In the summer of 1984, the president saw Williams interviewed on TV and dashed off a fan note: "Dear Ted: Last night I had a choice between listening to the Democratic National Convention and your superb interview on Channel Nine. You won in a landslide! You were intelligent, articulate and informative."[52] And in 1994, on the opening of Ted's museum in Florida, Nixon submitted a videotaped testimonial in which he said he "cherished" Williams's friendship. "In politics," he said, "I've learned that you win and you lose. When you win, you hear from everyone, and when you lose, you hear from your friends. I always heard from Ted Williams. He's a role model. I'm one of his fans, as millions of Americans are, not just because he was a great baseball player but because he was a fine human being."

During the season, Ted would occasionally call his managerial mentor, Joe McCarthy, for strategic advice. Then in early September, when the Senators had two off days in a row, Williams and Ed Doherty went to visit McCarthy at his home outside Buffalo. Ted had his team at 71–66, the best record the Senators had had in decades. Still, he wanted to pay his respects to McCarthy.

As a writer for the *Buffalo Evening News* who had been invited to sit in looked on, the two men reminisced about their years in Boston and about McCarthy's kind words to Ted after the devastating loss in the 1948 playoff game against the Indians. McCarthy had said they surprised everyone by getting along so well.

The Kid said he'd appreciated McCarthy's defense of him to the press on another issue that year. "When criticism grew over my taking a base on balls instead of swinging at a pitch just off the strike zone, I went to you for advice," Williams said. "And I told you that you knew the strike zone better than anyone else in baseball and that you should never change," McCarthy replied.

As Williams prepared to leave, McCarthy wished him luck and said, "You're the only manager I light candles for." In the car as they drove away, Williams asked Doherty what the candles reference meant. Doherty explained that McCarthy was a Catholic, and it was common to light a votive candle in church for someone you are praying for. Ted, who was, at best, ambivalent about religion, pondered that in silence for a while, then said: "How can I miss with a man like McCarthy praying for me?"[53]

Williams went on to lead the Senators to their best season in seventeen years. The team finished in fourth place out of six teams in the new American League East division, with a record of 86–76. Not since 1952 had the club finished above .500, and this team had had essentially the same players as the 1968 club, which had won twenty-one fewer games. It was not hard to conclude who had made the difference.

Williams "bubbles with enthusiasm and it's contagious," said shortstop Ed Brinkman,[54] whose average spiked up 79 points from the previous season to .266 in 1969. Frank Howard ended the year with a career-high 48 home runs, a .296 average, and 102 walks, nearly double his previous year's total. He also cut down on his strikeouts with 96— 45 fewer than in 1968. Mike Epstein raised his average 44 points to .278 and hit 17 more home runs than he did in 1968 to finish with 30.

While batting averages improved by eleven points throughout baseball in 1969 as a result of rule changes that had lowered the pitching mound by five inches and decreased the size of the strike zone, the Senators' twenty-seven-point increase was much more pronounced. Even the pitching was improved—Dick Bosman led the American League in earned run average, and the team ERA dropped from 3.64 in 1968 to 3.49 in 1969.

In Washington's baseball renaissance, fans appreciated the difference in the 1969 club, too. Attendance shot up to 918,016 from 546,661 the year before, even though Short's ticket prices were the highest in the league.[55]

In gratitude, the 17,482 fans who attended the last home game of the season against the Red Sox gave Ted a standing ovation when he walked his lineup card out to home plate. On his way back to the dugout, Williams did not tip his cap but threw his arms out to the side in a knock–it–off gesture and smiled.[56] The Senators went on to win, 3–2, and in the clubhouse afterward Ted let his satisfaction show, especially since some of the writers standing before him had predicted he would flame out and quit before the season ended. "Enthusiasm and hustle — that's all I wanted," he said. "A lot of times a ballplayer's got enthusiasm, but he's playing for a dead-ass coach, so he doesn't put out, but you put him with an enthusiastic coach, he's a charger." Someone with a tape recorder held out asked about the Washington fans: "Let me say that no one has been more enthusiastic than the nine hundred thousand fucking fans. Keep that on your fucking tape if you can, buddy."

The writers later rewarded Williams by voting him American League Manager of the Year. Williams was on a safari in Africa when Bob Addie of the *Washington Post* called him with the news. He was stunned.

"Manager of the Year?" Ted bellowed on the phone from Lusaka, Zambia. "Me? Forget it. Come on. Really? It's true? Well, that's just another example of you writers being all wet again. I'm terribly honored. What does a guy say in a situation like this? I'm flabbergasted. I'm honored, but I'm terribly disappointed that Billy Martin and Earl Weaver didn't get it. Both of them did a helluva job and both of them deserved the honor. You're not kidding me?"[57]

Weaver had led the Baltimore Orioles to the American League pennant, while Martin took the Minnesota Twins to a division title in his first season as manager. Martin initially offered Ted his congratulations, but a few years later, he told a reporter what he really thought: "I took a seventh place team and won my division, and they voted Ted Williams manager of the year," Martin complained. "Then I find out that Williams doesn't even give the signs from the dugout — Wayne Terwilliger gives them. I told Williams he should give the trophy to Terwilliger."[58]

The Manager of the Year rode high all winter.

With delight, he flaunted his fashionable Christmas present from Dolores. Mrs. Williams told a reporter that in an effort to spruce up "Mr. Baggy Pants," she had taken Ted's favorite ten-year-old black cashmere coat and asked a New York furrier named Mr. Fred to spice it up by stitching in an otter collar. Ted was now wearing his new coat around like a "Czarist," according to the *Boston Globe*.[59] Williams reciprocated by going to Mr. Fred's to buy an opossum-lined maxicoat for Dolores that tied on like a bathrobe.

Ted returned to Boston to do the sportsmen's show after a four-year absence and was treated like a conquering hero. He spoke his mind freely, as usual, putting the knock on one of his own pitchers, Joe Coleman, for not realizing his potential. He also came out strongly against Curt Flood's historic challenge of baseball's reserve clause. Baseball had been going on for a hundred years, "and the first one who thinks he is a slave is Curt Flood," said the Kid, in one of his more impolitic quotes.[60]

Williams arrived for spring training in 1970 still dining out on the rousing success of 1969. "I don't think I'll make all the mistakes I made in the '69 season and I expect improvement from everyone—even the writers," he said. He fielded some renewed, perfunctory complaints from the press about his fifteen-minute ban, but waved them away with a father-knows-best air. "I know how to handle the Knights of the Keyboard better than anyone else in this business," he said.[61] "I ought to, after all the experiences I've had with them."

But Ted had a sense of foreboding about his second season as manager. Over the winter, during a long evening of eating and drinking in Washington with Shelby Whitfield, with whom he had grown close, Williams confessed he was worried about how the summer would play out. He knew he'd been at the peak of his power in his first year, when everything was new. He was granted an extended honeymoon—the press and players hung on his every word while paying homage to the prevailing story line: the legend had come out of retirement to save the day. He had owned the town. Yet this was a new season. He knew he could get only so much mileage out of the previous year and that there soon would be a what-have-you-done-for-me-lately reckoning. The Senators had probably played over their heads in 1969. It was an older club, without much young talent and little that was promising in the farm system.[62]

One of the first indications that things would be different in 1970 came in April, when the Washington writers, who had fawned over Ted the previous year and rarely challenged him, questioned him aggressively on April 26 after a loss to the Angels. Williams answered their questions but thought the reporters did not adequately reflect his responses in print the next day. So he popped off and blasted them for "second guessing" him.

"It is bush, just plain bush!" Ted thundered. "I'm going to refuse to discuss strategy with you guys if you keep on second guessing me in the papers.... After the game, you guys come down here and ask me why I did this or why I did that, but none of my quotes ever get in the paper. You guys only print what you think I should have done."[63]

While Ted had a point if indeed his explanations were not being reported, to object to second-guessing at all when baseball had a long tradition of it came off as arrogant, and the writers ripped him. "Williams has a valid case against the writers, a witless group who are without understanding that Pope Theodore II is above criticism and not to be confused with the other 23 major league managers who are subject to post-game comment and other hazards of the trade," wrote Shirley Povich of the *Washington Post* in a scathing column that could have been written by Ted's old nemesis, Dave Egan. "Let there be no second-guessing by those wretches in the press box with their 20-20 hindsight. There can only be one oracle in the stadium and he wears a No. 9 on his back."[64]

Then Williams caused another stir on May 20, when, after a 2–0 win against the Yankees in New York, he explained that even though his starting pitcher, Dick Bosman, was throwing a shutout in the seventh inning, he had taken him out because he'd lost some stamina since getting married. "Bosman is only good for 100 pitches or so," Ted said.[65] "Last year he used to go to 120. He just got married." Actually, Bosman had been married seven months. Williams later tried to soften his remarks by noting that Mrs. Bosman was "a real cute thing," but Dick Bosman himself was piqued and went on the record disagreeing with what he called Ted's "theory," as did two other married players. Mike Epstein dismissed it as nonsense, while Rick Reichardt, an outfielder and a bachelor, said he thought "a guy gets less sex after he's married."

According to Shelby Whitfield, who spent two seasons traveling with Williams and the Senators, Ted was a "fanatic" about sexual abstinence and did his best to enforce celibacy for the players on the road.[66] He thought women were a distraction during the season and that sex sapped energy that was properly saved for baseball. There was growing resentment among the players toward Williams's puritanical views on sex (especially given their assumption that he had been no wallflower as a player), and they groused that his curfew after games was too early.

Another beef was that Ted, in his eagerness to teach hitting, was giving opposing hitters too many tips. Once, Ken Harrelson of the Indians was in a slump and asked Williams for help. Ted told him he knew what he was doing wrong but wouldn't tell him until after the four-game series was over. However, after Washington won the first three games, Ted took pity on Harrelson and told him his problem: he wasn't clearing his hips quickly enough on his swing. Harrelson thanked Williams and promptly hit two home runs, the second one the game winner. As he rounded the bases, Harrelson looked into the Senators dugout, smiled at Ted, and nodded. Williams was enraged and embarrassed in front of his players.[67]

Then there was that $1,000 fine for anyone caught golfing. Some of the Senators who liked to golf asked their player representative, infielder Bernie Allen, to talk to Williams about the rule. Allen, who also liked to golf, went to see the manager and would delight in recounting the exchange that followed:

ALLEN: Golf is for relaxing, to get away from baseball.
TED: It'll hurt your swing.
ALLEN: It won't hurt mine. I bat lefty and play golf righty.
TED: That's dumb. Why do you do that?
ALLEN: I don't want to hurt my golf swing.

Allen was a wiseacre who enjoyed antagonizing Williams because he didn't think Ted let him play enough. He particularly resented what he saw as Ted's imperiousness and failure to communicate with players or explain his rationale.

"I really like the way you swing," Williams had told Allen after first meeting him in the clubhouse.

"You should. I read every book you put out," Allen replied.

"You really hang in there good against lefties. Do they bother you?"

"Some do, some don't."

"Well, I like the way you stand in there. Oh, by the way, I'm not gonna play you against lefties."

And then Williams walked away.

"I have no idea why he did that," Allen said. "He did that the whole three years I was there. That first year I faced lefties ten times, got four hits, and you'd have thought I'd done something wrong from the way he looked at me. I tried to prove him wrong, but he never communicated things. He was that way with most of the players. He told me he liked me, and I thought, 'Man, I'm glad he doesn't hate me.' "[68] Allen demanded to be traded, and eventually he was—to the Yankees, after the 1971 season.

Toward the end of June, his team mired in fifth place with a record of 30–40, Williams picked another public fight with pitcher Joe Coleman, who was 5–6 with a 3.76 ERA. Williams complained that Coleman was reluctant to throw a slider (the pitcher said it gave him a sore arm) and should have developed faster. "I've tried everything with him," Ted said. "I've cuddled him, hugged him, mothered him, lectured him, but nothing seems to work. He's a young, starting pitcher and he should be doing better than .500 for us."

Williams made these remarks in Boston, where he knew they would have maximum effect, or embarrassment, on Coleman, who had grown up in suburban Natick. The pitcher, irked by Ted's remarks, responded in kind to a *Boston Globe* reporter, saying he disagreed with his manager. "He doesn't talk often to the pitchers," Coleman said. "He's a hitter's man."[69]

Williams's continued sarcasm about the supposed inferior intellect of pitchers was wearing on them. "He considered pitchers nonathletes," said Dick Bosman. "I remember once he'd made sure one of us was around, he'd raise his voice around a sportswriter. He'd say, 'What do you think is dumber than a pitcher? Two pitchers.'" Bosman also noticed that Williams had a needling personality. He'd lob a gratuitous insult at a player, then saunter off, seemingly oblivious to the grenade he'd tossed. "He'd say things like, 'You working out right? That uniform's starting to fit a little tighter on you.' He'd walk away, and you'd think, 'Why would he say something like that?' I think he was bored."[70]

One day, as infielder Tim Cullen was taking batting practice, Ted asked him what he did in the off-season. "Stocks and bonds," said Cullen, one of the few Senators who had seen his average go down under Williams in 1969, not up. He'd finished the year at .209. "I hope you're good at that, because you can't hit," Williams replied.[71]

Williams began giving the impression he was increasingly disengaged. Asked in Boston, just after his public tiff with Coleman, if he expected to manage the Senators for years to come, Ted replied: "Hell, no! I don't want to stay in this managing business any longer than I have to. Maybe Bob Short will decide otherwise, but I'll tell you one thing, I'm not going to seek out the job next season."[72]

By mid-July, the Senators had dropped to last place in the American League East. President Nixon decided to come out to RFK Stadium on July 20 to try and give the Nats, as the club was affectionately known, a shot in the arm. The team beat the Milwaukee Brewers, 2–0, for its third win in a row. "I think you're on a streak," Nixon told the players after the game. "Win six in a row." A beaming Williams took Nixon around the room and introduced him to each player.

The writers sarcastically noted that the president had been allowed into the clubhouse right after the game ended, in violation of Ted's fifteen-minute ban. But Nixon made it a point to boost Ted on that front, too. "I'm one of the few people who approve of your rule about 15 minutes," Nixon told Williams. "After a game, win or lose, fellows are a little wrought up so it's good to give time to cool off and then let them talk to the press." The president added he thought it would be a good thing if politicians cooled off before talking to the press as well.[73]

Ted grew frustrated that he couldn't get through to some players on things that he thought should have been basic, like the need for a hitter to guess in certain situations. The players thought Williams didn't understand that not everyone could be as good as he was. "Ted would talk about mental approach," said Joe Camacho, the bench coach. He'd say, 'If you're in a count, you should be looking for a certain pitch. So you should be guessing properly. If you're not, you're hitting defensively.' He would talk to them like that, but they'd say, 'I'm not Ted Williams.'"[74] Casey Cox remembered once sitting on the bench with Williams as Ken Harrelson of the Indians was coming back from an injury. Harrelson was struggling in batting practice, and Williams couldn't understand why he couldn't get right back in the groove. "Christ, I was gone five years, and it didn't bother me," Ted said.

"Yeah, but how many could do that?" asked Cox. "You're Ted Williams."

"It doesn't make any difference."

"Well, the fuck it doesn't."[75]

Ted knew his 1969 sheen was wearing thin. He was losing the confidence of a number of players and squabbling openly with some of them. Also, the writers were criticizing him on his handling of several phases of the game, such as platooning too much, burning out his bull pen, playing percentages too rigidly, not bunting enough, and not paying enough attention to fundamentals. Williams confided to Shelby Whitfield that he regretted not taking a front-office job that year and quitting managing while he was ahead.[76]

Ted had bonded with the broadcaster and began spending more and more time with him. They'd hit it off from the first time they met, after Williams took the job. Whitfield—who had worked for radio stations in the Southwest and been sports director for the Department of Defense's Armed Forces Radio and Television Service—helped Ted get up to speed on the Senators players. Over the next two seasons, they sat together on the plane during road trips and often took meals together.

When the team traveled, Ted and Whitfield looked for ways to pass the time. Sometimes they'd go to gun shows or even art shows. "The art shows were a little out of character," said Whitfield, who was seventeen years younger than Ted. "He'd look at the paper, or somebody would tell him about a show, and we'd go. He looked for places to get away. I never knew him to buy a piece, but he was always the center of atten-tion, and he enjoyed that. He also valued his privacy, but I think deep down, if he did not have that recognition he was unhappy about it."

Ted loved to talk politics with Whitfield and enjoyed making the uphill argument that Herbert Hoover was the greatest man of all time. "Not Lincoln, Washington, Alexander Graham Bell, Julius Caesar, Napoleon, Attila the Hun," Ted would say. "Not Jefferson, Wilson, Churchill, not even FDR, but Herbert, by God, Hoover. Every cure of the Depression was thought up by Hoover. Here is a man who is blamed for things that are not his fault, yet he never complained, and continued to help his country for the rest of his life. To me, that's a real man."[77] After Hoover, Ted told Whitfield, the five other men he respected most were Nixon, General MacArthur, Tom Yawkey, Richard Cardinal Cushing—the Catholic archbishop of Boston in Williams's day—and Marine general Louis B. Robertshaw, Ted's commanding officer in Korea.

Williams would often vent to Whitfield about having been called back to Korea and being stuck at 521 career home runs. He would name each hitter who had more than five hundred and talk about what might have been. "He'd say, 'If I hadn't missed so many at bats, no one would have been close to me.' Without the two wars, he meant, not just Korea. 'If I'd been able to play those years, this guy and that guy and that guy wouldn't be close to me.' He was very ego-driven, but this was never something he would dare pop off to the media about." Whitfield thought it interesting that Ted's public image never reflected that career bitter-ness. He was seen as the fighter pilot hero, akin to a John Wayne stick figure. "That always surprised me, because it was not accurate. You'd think the media, hating him the way they did, would have picked up on it more."

At home, Whitfield and his wife, Lora, would dine out with Ted and Dolores. Whitfield liked Dolores: "She was quite a gal," he said, "a tall beauty, outspoken. I could tell that marriage was not long for this world. She had her own mind. And Williams was probably one of the worst people to be married to that you could imagine. He was the most pro-fane guy I've ever met. His favorite adjective was 'syphilitic.' As in, 'syphilitic Jesus,' this and that. I thought he drew the worst connotation he could think of."[78]

And despite his restrictions on his players, on the road, Williams, while discreet, had a voracious sexual appetite, Whitfield said: "Besides hitting a baseball, fishing, eating, and fucking were Ted's favorite things to do—not necessarily in that order. A pretty girl always turned his head. When we walked together in cities or in airports, he would always say, 'Look at that, look at that! I'd screw her in a minute, wouldn't you?' That was frequent dialogue." Unpacking her husband's suitcase after a road trip, Dolores would tell Lora Whitfield that she'd found lipstick on his shorts or a package of condoms. When jousting with Ted during dinners with the Whitfields, Dolores threatened to write a sequel to his book. She would call it *My Turn at Bat Was No Ball*.[79] "She repeated that quite a bit. She was flirtatious. We had a good relationship. She'd confide in me about how difficult life with Ted was. She'd say, 'How do you put up with him when he's on the road?'"

As the 1970 season drew to a close, Whitfield told Ted and Dolores that he was having more and more difficulty with Bob Short. He said the owner expected him to "learn to lie" on the air in the interest of promoting the team. To boost attendance at home games, he would have to predict good weather even if the forecast called for driving rain. He couldn't mention the number of men the Senators left on base after an inning lest it reflect poorly on the club's hitters. He couldn't mention the size of a crowd unless it was more than twenty-five thousand. And he couldn't talk about losing streaks or poor player performance. Short also expected Whitfield to give back to the club any money he made from speaking engagements.[80]

"When it looked like Short was getting rid of me, Dolores, who was always a rebel anyway, said, 'Why don't you write a book?'" Whitfield remembered. When Short did fire him at the end of the year, he went ahead and wrote a kiss-and-tell memoir of his years with the Senators, *Kiss It Good-Bye,* that was filled with behind-the-scenes detail and included two chapters on his relationship with Williams. Whitfield dedicated the book, published in 1973, to his wife—and to Dolores, whom he credited with suggesting that he write it.

Whitfield spent a lot of time in the clubhouse observing the dynamics of Ted's relationships with the players, and he found the differences between the first year and the second year to be stark. He thought Williams plainly got bored and that the players grew to dislike him—especially toward the end of the 1970 season, which spiraled out of control with the loss of fourteen straight games. The team finished last in the American League East. After their 70–92 season, Williams suggested that more than half the team should take stock of themselves and perhaps look for another line of work before returning the following year.[81] Over Ted's objections, Short then pulled the trigger on a major trade. He sent the starting left side of his infield—shortstop Eddie Brinkman and third baseman Aurelio Rodriguez—as well as starting pitcher Joe Coleman and reliever Jim Hannan to the Detroit Tigers for troubled pitcher Denny McLain and three other players.

McLain had made history in 1968 by winning thirty-one games for the Tigers, along with the MVP and the Cy Young Award. Then in 1969, he'd won another Cy Young by posting a 24–9 record. But in 1970, McLain tumbled to 3–5, and he was suspended three times: first by Commissioner Bowie Kuhn for gambling violations, then by the Tigers for throwing a bucket of water at some writers, then again by Kuhn for carrying a gun on a plane. Apart from the behavioral issues, McLain, though still only twenty-seven, was having serious arm problems and was taking cortisone injections in secret so that he could keep pitching. Still, Short was thrilled. "McLain is the greatest pitcher in baseball," he proclaimed. "This is my trade."[82]

Williams, in highly unusual public remarks distancing himself from his owner, made his position clear. "This is not my trade," he said. "It looks now that he gave up more than he should.... I'm really disappointed to have our two best infielders leave our club."[83]

When spring training for the 1971 season started at Pompano Beach, Dolores learned she was pregnant. Ted was not happy to receive this news, because he and his wife had been fighting frequently and were on the skids. The prospect of a third child was so troubling to Williams that, to make sure there would not be a fourth, he decided to have a vasectomy.[84]

Dolores confirmed that her pregnancy was "unplanned," and that Ted was unhappy about it. She left for Vermont, and for the baseball season they were effectively separated.

On October 8, in Brattleboro, Dolores gave birth to a girl, whom she named Claudia, after her friend and New York agent, Claudia Franck. (The agent inspired young Claudia's middle name as well: Franc.) Ted was absent for the birth again, making him three for three in that department. "He came around after he was finished with his fishing," Dolores remembered.

By this time, Dolores was considering her options. "It was getting rough with Ted," she said. "I had been to see a lawyer, and the lawyer advised me to hang in there as long as possible."[85]

On one occasion during his first year as manager, Williams had humiliated his wife publicly when she joined the team for a road trip to Minnesota. After the game, as the team bus was preparing to go to Bob Short's house for a party, Dolores was talking to a few people, apparently unaware the bus was waiting for her. "We'll get going as soon as this fuckin' cunt gets on the bus!" Williams said, loud enough for all to hear. Dolores boarded, and there was awkward silence during the trip. Russ White, the beat reporter for the *Washington Daily News,* later told Dolores: "I really felt sorry for you back there. There was no need for that."

"He'll get his," Dolores replied.[86]

Once, during a private argument in Washington, Dolores said, Ted had punched her in the jaw. "It hurt to open my mouth," she recalled, "and I figured the next time he tries that, I was going to do like the Aborigines do in Australia. I was going to grab him with my teeth around his throat and not let go." That next time wasn't too long in coming, but this time Ted "checked his swing. He didn't slug me that time—the second time. His cheeks started jumping, his veins were bursting. I thought, 'This time I'm ready. I'm ready.' I must have just looked wild in my eyes. I was going to just launch for him, just put my teeth right on his throat and hang on for dear life. He didn't do it. He checked his swing and brought it back."[87]

The arrival of Denny McLain changed the dynamic of the 1971 Senators substantially and further eroded Williams's influence. Ted couldn't stand McLain, and the pitcher couldn't stand him.

McLain was a free-spirited prima donna who chafed under authority, played the organ, and sang at Las Vegas lounges. He made a dramatic arrival at Pompano Beach in his own plane, and before long he was taking his new teammates on joyrides over to the Bahamas. Williams viewed him as an over-the-hill troublemaker. McLain was predisposed to dislike Ted after reading that his new manager had stressed that this was Bob Short's trade, not his own. McLain said that he was further turned off by his first meeting with Ted when Williams did a variation of his pitchers-are-stupid shtick: "What's dumber than one fucking pitcher? I'll tell you what. It's two of you dumb fucking pitchers."[88]

When McLain said he liked to pitch every fourth day, Williams replied he preferred that his pitchers be on a five-day rotation. "All I could say in response was that I had won 117 games and lost only 62 in the major leagues before I came under the guidance of one of the game's great hitting experts," McLain wrote in his 1975 memoir, *Nobody's Perfect,* in which he savaged Williams.

After an early losing streak, Ted called a practice one morning when the team was scheduled to play that night. The players were angry, and McLain led a minirevolt in which they went to the practice on their own, not on the team bus. When the bus left the hotel for the field, it carried only Ted and his coaches. "Williams was seething," McLain said. "For a couple of days, he went around like a wild ship captain looking for the culprit who stole his strawberries. Ted wanted to know who organized the bus boycott."

One of McLain's next capers was to flout Ted's no-golf rule. He pulled together three other players who liked to golf, and they called themselves the Touring Pros. They hit the links as a foursome every day on the road. "Our baseball was so pitiful, the golf couldn't hurt it," McLain said. The Touring Pros also thumbed their noses at the $1,000 fine their manager had imposed. "Williams never got a dime from me, or from anyone else in the foursome, as far as I know," McLain added.

Another time, Ted, who generally sent coach Sid Hudson out to the mound when he wanted to remove a pitcher, instructed Hudson to go out and yank McLain. McLain told Hudson: "If that fat fucker wants me out, you tell him to come take me out." So Williams, steaming, came out to the mound, and when he got close, McLain flipped him the ball and headed to the clubhouse.

"I'd never seen Ted so mad," said infielder Dave Nelson, who witnessed the scene. "I could hear the veins in his neck pumping, and I was on the field, not in the dugout."[89]

Late in the season, McLain ratcheted up his treachery by forming what he called the Underminers' Club, the purpose of which was simply to sabotage Ted's tenure as manager. The other members were Bernie Allen, Tim Cullen, Dick Billings, and first baseman and outfielder Tommy McCraw. "We were the people dedicated (in our minds anyway) to the overthrow of Ted Williams," McLain said. One night, McLain and his wife had a team party at their house in which they inducted six new members of the Underminers' Club in a spoof of a Ku Klux Klan ceremony. McLain and his crew dressed up in sheets and carried crosses as they inducted the new members.[90]

McLain went 10–22 on the year with a 4.28 ERA, including a twenty-one-day stint on the disabled list, which he said "may have been the most pleasant days of the season."[91] With the team floundering and losing money, Bob Short announced in mid-September that he was moving the club to Arlington, Texas, outside Dallas. The Senators would become the Texas Rangers.

President Nixon said he was "distressed" that Washington would again be without baseball. But Ted said Short had little choice but to move the club. "There was a hard core of fans here all right, but there were only six or seven thousand of them," he observed. "Basically, Washington is a city of transient people. Most people didn't give a damn."[92]

The Senators finished fifth in their division with a record of 63–96, thirty-eight and a half games out of first place. About the only positive in the year for Ted (besides Sears extending his contract for another nine years, to 1979) was the publication of his second book, again with John Underwood, *The Science of Hitting*. The book did little to help Williams as a manager, since it only reinforced the perception that his approach to baseball was one-dimensional.

Surprisingly—given the performance of his team and its near insurrection—Ted signed on for the move to Texas. He still retained Short's support, and the press wasn't on him much. The writers, in fact, seemed more interested in Williams's upcoming second safari to central Africa than they were in the performance of the Senators. Ted said this time he hoped to bag a lion, a buffalo, a leopard, and maybe an elephant.[93]

In the off-season, McLain and two other ringleaders of the Underminers' Club, Bernie Allen and Tommy McCraw, were traded away, while a fourth, Tim Cullen, was released. Williams hoped that getting rid of most of the clubhouse lawyers would ease his passage to Texas. To help herald the move, Ted donned the obligatory ten-gallon hat in a photo op demanded by the photographers, but from the beginning, he hated the Dallas area and had largely checked out as manager.

"In Texas, Ted didn't act like a guy that liked to manage," said Tom Grieve, an outfielder on the 1972 team. "You could talk hitting or pitching with him, and then the enthusiasm bubbled over. But the managing, the traveling, being part of the team—he couldn't wait to get out. I don't think he was frustrated with himself, he was frustrated with all of us. We all felt a little embarrassed and guilty to know we had the greatest hitting instructor ever and couldn't do better."[94]

Williams lived in a hotel and began spending more time with his third-base coach, Wayne Terwilliger. There was a pizza place outside

Arlington that showed Charlie Chaplin and other old movies that Ted enjoyed, so he would ask Twig to join him there. Another time, they went to a jazz club in Dallas to listen to Erroll Garner, long a Williams favorite. They sat near the piano, and Ted would talk to Garner between tunes. "Ted would say that the sound of the bat hitting the ball was as beautiful as listening to Erroll Garner," Terwilliger wrote in his book.[95]

Once, in Cleveland for a game, the two men came across a peep show. They went in, got behind separate curtains, fed quarters into the slots, and watched dirty movies together. Sometimes Ted would sing out, "Hey, this one's not too bad," so Twig would go over and have a look.[96]

The highlight of the year, unquestionably, came August 25, when the Rangers came to Boston to open a three-game series. It was a Friday night, and there was a full house at Fenway for a game in which all proceeds were to go to the Jimmy Fund. As an added draw, several Red Sox old-timers, including Johnny Pesky, Eddie Pellagrini, Ted Lepcio, Haywood Sullivan, Dom DiMaggio, Sam Mele, Frank Malzone, and Walt Dropo, were to engage in a hitting contest.

There had been an announcement in the press box earlier that Williams would not be among the Sox veterans to hit. But before the game, Rangers trainer Bill Zeigler spotted Tom Yawkey going into Ted's office in the Rangers clubhouse, presumably to lobby his former star. After Yawkey left, Ted emerged and said he was going to hit in the contest after all. He would turn fifty-four in five days.

In the dugout, Williams rummaged through the bat rack and couldn't seem to find anything he liked. His players looked on carefully, taking in the moment.

"No wonder you fuckin' guys can't hit," Ted said. "These bats are terrible."

Then Zeigler, who revered Williams so much that he had named his son Ted Williams Zeigler, handed him some of Tom Grieve's bats. Grieve used the Louisville Slugger W183. The W stood for Williams, and 183 was the model number Ted had used for the last several years of his career. Williams picked the bats up and flexed each one before he found one to his liking. "Give me some pine tar," he barked to Zeigler, and then he began working the bat until he got the grip just the way he wanted it. Williams glanced out at his former teammates hitting soft-serves from Red Sox coach Lee Stange, who was known as Stinger. "He's gonna have to throw harder than that to me," Ted muttered to Zeigler. "I can't hit that slow shit." When the last Red Sox veteran finished batting, there was a lull for a few minutes. Then the crowd began to chant: "We want Ted! We want Ted! We want Ted!" Williams let them chant a bit longer, psyching himself up and letting the drama build. "I'll show these cocksuckers," he said quietly. Williams walked out of the dugout and began striding to home plate in his distinctive gait, head down, as the crowd stood and roared. He still had on the silky warm-up jacket he'd been using to conceal his girth since becoming a manager, but he ripped it off and let it fall to the ground before reaching the batter's box.

Stange threw his first pitch, but Ted let it go by. He always took the first pitch.

Then he pulled the next ball hard, but way foul.

"Goddamn it, Stinger," Ted barked. "Put some juice on the damned ball."

Then Ted began hitting line drives all over right field and center field. They were all ropes. One ball cleared the right-field fence by Pesky's Pole. Another hit the bull-pen wall on a short hop. After ten or twelve swings, Ted flipped his bat in the air dramatically and walked back to his dugout in triumph, as the entire park cheered deliriously. Players from both benches also stood to applaud.

"It was the most electrifying experience in my life," said Dick Billings, the onetime Underminer. "I've never in my life heard an ovation like that. We sat on the bench with our mouths open. He never hit in spring training or during our batting practice. The Boston fans absolutely loved him. For him to be able to do that, he's the best or one of the best ever. What I saw that day, he still could have hit .300 if he didn't have to run."

Williams skipped down the dugout steps with a big smile on his face. "I guess I showed those cocksuckers I can still hit," Ted told Zeigler.[97]

The Rangers lost a hundred games that season, winning but fifty-four, and finished last in the American League West. Williams had had enough. "I had another year on my contract, but that was it," he said later. "I had managed my last game."[98]

24

Young John-Henry and Claudia

Ted saw little of Dolores and their two children, John-Henry and Claudia, that spring and summer of 1972, when he was off in Texas. His relationship with his wife had deteriorated into a series of acrimonious exchanges punctuated by characteristic outbursts of anger from Williams. When Ted quit the Rangers and was home full-time, nothing changed, so Dolores decided to file for divorce in Miami, asserting in her suit that Ted had "made life unbearable" for her with his "constant obscene criticism."

Williams had hardly spent any time with his two youngest children thus far, and the divorce would not change that pattern. Just as his own parents had largely been absent, Ted proved an indifferent father at best. His career and the demands of celebrity were mitigating circumstances, perhaps, but even out of baseball he remained preoccupied with himself, not his kids.

Years later, driven by a basic love and mutual need, Ted, John-Henry, and Claudia would rediscover each other—Claudia having done all she could to forge her own identity, John-Henry having subsumed himself in his father's shadow.

If there was a triggering event that made her decide to file for divorce, Dolores thought, it came one day when she and Ted were arguing, and John-Henry, then about five, intervened on her behalf and confronted his father. "You don't talk to Mommy that way!" he said with chest puffed out. Then, turning to Dolores, the boy added: "There, Mommy, I served him. Now, let's go, and if you're not ready, I'm going without you."

"I think when John-Henry said that, I knew I had to get a divorce,"

Dolores concluded. "It just wasn't working. I didn't have the courage to tell him directly, so I had a lawyer do it for me. Ted reacted with frustration. He told me, 'I couldn't please you if I was Jesus Christ himself.'"

As the case awaited trial, there were moments when Dolores felt Ted was reaching out to her. On March 15, 1974, for example, he wrote her a short, whimsical note on his Sears stationery offering to pay her $10,000 if she could take two out of three sets from him in tennis. "Please bring knife when this happens," he added, before signing the letter "Ted Williams, of sound mind."[1]

But as she went ahead with the divorce, his letters were no longer lighthearted. He told her he regretted ever meeting her, accused her of entrapping him by deliberately getting pregnant with John-Henry, and of sleeping around once they were married. She retorted that he was a lousy lover and gathered ammunition for her lawyers—such as soiled clothing that she said proved Ted had his own collection of infidelities and a series of telephone messages left for him by presumed girlfriends.

The divorce was finalized on November 25, 1974. Under the terms, Ted waived the prenuptial agreement Dolores had signed before they were married, six years and seven months earlier. He agreed to pay her $20,000 to renounce any further claims on his property and $16,000 per year in alimony for the rest of his life. If Dolores remarried, the alimony would drop to $6,000 a year and end altogether in 1987. Dolores was to get full custody of John-Henry and Claudia, and child support would be $2,000 annually per child. Ted also agreed to pay college and medical expenses for the children and to leave each one not less than one-quarter of his net estate after he died. In addition, Williams gave Dolores two cars and paid her legal fees.

Now thrice divorced, Ted was fifty-six years old. The idea of spending the rest of his years alone had no appeal, so he quickly began looking for other options. His first choice was to try to reconcile with Lee Howard, wife number two.

Lee had spent the last few years in California managing a 365-unit apartment complex in Marina del Rey. Ted had reached out to her a few times while he was still married to Dolores—to touch base, or perhaps to hedge his bets. "Things weren't going too well with Dolores, apparently, so he would call and say, 'How are you? Have you found anybody?'" Lee remembered. "He told me to write to him, and he gave me a post-office box. I wrote a letter or two, but what was I going to say?"

After the divorce from Dolores, Ted and Lee arranged to have dinner in Florida, and he asked her to come back to him. She said no. Williams, no longer wanting to start from scratch with someone new, then turned to his old reliable: the long-suffering Louise Kaufman, who had been holding out for Ted for more than twenty years, since first meeting him on Islamorada in 1953. Now, after Lee spurned his request to give it another go, Ted summoned Louise back to Islamorada from Delray Beach, where she was still living near her friend Evalyn Sterry. Thrilled, Louise promptly appeared at Ted's door with all her clothes and furniture. She was sixty-two when she finally won her man.

Since he had been married three times and had made a hash of things on each try, Williams told Louise up front that there could be no fourth marriage for him. Though she ached for the status and legitimacy of a Mrs. Williams title, she accepted Ted's terms. Louise also realized that they would probably fare better as a couple if Ted felt less bridled, so she settled into her own bedroom.[2]

Louise knew to give Ted plenty of rope and, most important, to let him explode when he had to. She hated these outbursts of rage, but knew she couldn't stop them and that it could be even more dangerous if he weren't able to blow off steam. She would try to temper his behavior by not being a doormat and by calling him out on his excesses. He respected her for that, but he also respected her for letting him blow and not holding it against him, as his three wives had. He needed his loved ones not to nurse grudges toward him, even when he knew, down deep, that his tantrums were unwarranted.

Ted didn't tell Louise about his final overture to Lee, of course, and tried to make it appear that he wasn't just settling for her. He tempered his no-marriage edict by promising Louise that he wouldn't jilt her a fourth time. And he tried to adapt to her wishes, such as saying grace before a meal. "When we'd go down to stay with Ted, Louise would always say a blessing," said Bobby Doerr, a devout Christian. "You always doubted Ted was religious. But he'd grab your hand and say, 'Come on,' while she said the blessing. So you wondered down deep if he had any religious feeling. It was at least a show of respect for her."[3]

Dolores, meanwhile, had rented a house on the other side of Islamorada from Ted and enrolled John-Henry and Claudia at the Island Christian School, a new private school. But before long, the island felt too small for both her and Ted, and bumping into Louise around town was more than Dolores could abide, so she took the kids and moved back to Vermont, on the farm next door to her parents. They established a routine in which Ted would call Claudia and John-Henry on Sunday mornings, and the children would spend Christmas vacation in Islamorada and a few weeks during the summer at Ted's cabin on the Miramichi River in New Brunswick.

That wasn't a lot of time, but the kids weren't used to seeing much of Ted anyway. As manager of the Rangers and a spokesman for Sears, he'd been away almost constantly. Louise at first urged Ted to spend more time with John-Henry and Claudia, but they resented her immediately as an unwanted intruder who only got in the way of access to their father. And Louise, despite her initial good intentions of wanting Ted to engage more with the children he barely knew, would come to deeply resent John-Henry and Claudia as well.

"I still remember going to the Keys and seeing Louise there for the first time and wondering, 'Who is this woman?'" Claudia said.

When Claudia was about four or five years old, she and her brother were in Islamorada on one of their periodic visits. Claudia had just learned to braid her own hair, and Dolores had told her to make sure it was braided when she went out on the boat to fish with Ted, otherwise it would get knotted up and tangled. "Dad, when he goes fishing, he goes, and there's no waiting around. I could hear him just bellowing: 'Come on!' In walks Louise, just barges in the bathroom, yanks the hair out of my hand, braids it up real fast, and she pushes me out the door. She said, 'Don't you ever make your father wait!'"

In addition, Claudia had a fair complexion. When she got out on the boat she realized she'd forgotten her sunbonnet and sunscreen. She started to get out of the boat to run back to the house, but Louise pulled her back in. "I was very intimidated by my father at that young age," Claudia recalled. "He was very loud. Not very patient. Now we were going fishing, and there was no other focus, no other goal. I didn't dare say, 'I need to put on sunscreen.' Well, my mom was so mad when I got back because my whole back was just sun blisters and peeling and red. I just hid it the whole time because I didn't want Dad to get mad. I remember the guest room where we stayed, John-Henry and I. We were in the two twin beds, and every night he was putting aloe or cream on my back. I'd be crying, and he'd say, 'Don't cry. Don't cry. Don't get Dad mad.'"

Conflict was to be avoided at all costs lest Ted get provoked. "If he called and I was sick, he'd say, 'Well, Jesus Christ! Why'd you get sick?'"

"I didn't mean to get sick," Claudia would reply.

"Well, goddamn it, get in bed and stay in bed and drink vitamin C."

Despite her resentment of Louise, Claudia said she wanted to love her, "but it just couldn't happen. Every time I tried to do something nice, she'd be extremely critical, or she would twist it. She was out to make me [out] to be a bad person. She was very threatened by the relationship that John-Henry and I had with our dad. Because when we did visit him, it was just us. We'd just climb all over him. John-Henry was on the right, I was on the left, just piled on top of him on the recliner chair."

The next Christmas, John-Henry and Claudia arrived to find that Louise's daughter Barbara Kovacs was there with her children. "Now not only do we have to share Dad with Louise, but we have two grandkids," Claudia said. "I remember hating that. And they were constantly being compared to us. 'Oh, so-and-so was on the honor roll this week. Claudia, how are *you* doing in school? John-Henry, how are *you* doing in school?' It was never pure dad-and-kids time. It was always competition."

Time with Ted meant they would watch TV, go fishing, get an ice cream. Another favorite activity was watching movies together. Ted would send John-Henry and Claudia out to the video store and have them bring back a handful of John Wayne classics. Ted loved Oreos, and one Christmas, Claudia gave him a fancy tin filled with the cookies, and it was his favorite present. "He loved it. 'Get the milk!' We dunked the cookies in the milk. He loved us kids for a kid reason: he could be a kid, too."

Yet Williams's tin ear regarding offense to those close to him was evident in one of his terms of endearment for Claudia: "little shit"—as in, "C'mere, you little shit, you," when he wanted to give her a hug.

She preferred visiting him in Canada to going to the Keys. The Miramichi was remote. There was no phone, which seemed to relax Ted further. When Louise had one installed, Williams had the phone listed under "Spaulding Trappers Association" to throw off any unwelcome callers.[4]

Claudia conceded that it was difficult for Louise. "That's hard. That's hard for a woman when she's first in the relationship with Dad, and here we come." Mary Diver of Baltimore, who had a cabin on the Miramichi near Ted's and was a friend to him and Louise, said Louise "couldn't stand John-Henry, and I don't think she liked Claudia that much, either." She recalled a scene in which "Ted was on the couch, and Claudia was fussing over him and messing with his hair, and Lou comes in and says, 'Look at that little hussy.' I don't know if it was jealousy or one-upmanship."[5]

While Claudia said she tried to get along with Louise, to no avail, John-Henry didn't even bother to try, and he could get away with it because he had a different relationship with Ted from the one his sister had.

"John-Henry just had such a tight bond with Dad. Nothing Louise could do or say could sway Dad. Whereas me, I would easily be labeled whiny or bitchy or whatever. But boys don't do that. I'd go running to Dad: 'Louise did this, Daddy.' And he'd be like: 'Shut up! I don't want to hear it.' John-Henry just wouldn't do that. He didn't care. He got to go where Dad went, and Louise couldn't go, either. Girls aren't allowed in the dugout.

"I think Dad probably always wanted a son. And when he finally got one, especially after Bobby-Jo, he loved him so much. He just adored him. And when I came along? He was probably going, 'Please, God, don't be like Bobby-Jo!'"

Louise was jealous of John-Henry's relationship with Ted, according to Janet Franzoni of Vermont, who, along with her late husband, Bob, was a close friend of Ted and Louise. "John-Henry would spend time with Ted, and she didn't like it," Franzoni said. "She also didn't trust him."[6]

When Claudia and John-Henry visited Ted, their older sister, whom they had not even met, was little discussed. When Bobby-Jo was talked about, it usually was when Ted was mad. "I just knew that whoever this Bobby-Jo was, I didn't want to do what she had done," Claudia said, "because Dad would say awful, awful things about her. He probably saved the *c* word if the kids were around, but 'bitch' and 'whore' and 'tramp' and just 'lunatic' were common. Dad would never be so direct as to name something specific that she did, but I remember many times going to Mom and saying, 'Who is this Bobby-Jo? Why does Dad hate this Bobby-Jo?'

"She'd tell me, 'Well, that's your half sister. She's about twenty-five years older than you are, but she's done some things where she's hurt your father and made him very upset.'"

Claudia never dared ask Ted what those things were. "I didn't want to talk about something that made him upset. My time with Dad was limited. I wanted it to be happy."

Claudia and John-Henry watched their father walk all over Louise. "We didn't like her, but we respected her because she was with Dad so long," Claudia said. "We saw that woman get absolutely chewed up. He'd call her 'a dried-up old cunt,' 'an old bag.' We thought, 'Oh, my God! She'll go now.' But she hung in there."*

Claudia and John-Henry thought that one way Louise kept Ted's

---

* Claudia knew from experience how to hang in there, too, having been on the receiving end of coarse insults from Ted. "Yeah, it hurt the first time I heard my father say to me: 'As long as I have a hair in my ass, you'll be a pain in it,'" she said. "And I'd be like, 'Oh, my God!' Just devastated. I'd go off to my room, bawl, pout, do whatever I had to do,

excesses in check as he aged was to let him drink too much, and this became another point of conflict with the children. Ted basically didn't start drinking until he was in his late fifties, and while it could have the relaxing effect Claudia said Louise wanted, it could also facilitate his mean streaks.

Ted did show Louise kindness, like buying her rings and new cars, but the kids noticed few displays of physical affection. He might throw his arm around her after a day of fishing, but there would be no hugging or kissing. Part of her father's physical reserve, Claudia thought, was because he was a germophobe. "If he thought he had a stink on him, boom, in the shower," Claudia said. "And he always had fresh breath. Watching him brush his teeth was a twenty-minute ritual. He'd literally grab his tongue and brush it, then almost throw his back out gargling. Then he'd slap on some Drakkar Noir cologne. Finally, when he was finished primping, he'd wink and smile at the mirror. If I was in there and he saw me, he'd say, 'What do you think of Ted Williams, huh? What do you think of your old dad?'" Then, getting dressed, Ted would put his shoes on first to avoid wrinkling his pants when he sat down to lace his shoes. Claudia assumed this was a carryover from the service.

Williams liked a regimented life; he liked order. When an emotional issue developed, that posed a problem. Once, when she was away at a boarding school in ninth grade, Claudia wasn't getting along particularly well with her mother and called Ted instead, saying she was homesick. He didn't have a clue what to do.

"Well, Jesus Christ!" he told her. "What's the matter? What the hell's wrong? Call your mother!" Then he hung up the phone.

"He couldn't deal with emotions. He couldn't deal with someone being upset. He couldn't deal with me crying. I think part of the reason was because he couldn't do anything about it. Every time I remember Dad getting mad about something, it was something he had no control over," Claudia said.

If the phone rang during dinner, Ted might go off the deep end, but afterward he wanted to know who called and what the person said. "It was control," Claudia said. "He couldn't control the call coming in during dinner, so he wanted nothing to do with it.

"If you talk to a psychiatrist, most people's problems derive from not being in control of a situation. Leads to anxiety, leads to depression, leads to anger. That was Dad."

---

come back out to the kitchen: He loved me! He loved me! But I don't think I ever heard my dad say, 'I'm sorry.' Never."

Claudia thought she understood how her father's mind worked. She, too, learned to let him vent, even if she was bearing the brunt of one of his outbursts. "I don't think I have a moment in my mind that I can think of right now where I resented my father. Maybe at the moment for a brief second I'd be like, 'Why is he doing this? Why?' I can remember when he would get mad or scream at me and say something. I'd be like, 'Dad, why are you doing this? Settle down. Don't be so mad! It's no big deal.'"

She said she didn't resent his absence when she was growing up. And on significant occasions, he *was* there for her. For a big cross-country invitational Claudia was running in, Ted was there. She was in an opera. Ted was there. She was misdiagnosed with lupus one year when she was twelve. Ted was there. She got a hernia. Ted was there. And he reliably called her and John-Henry on Sunday mornings between eight and nine o'clock. Then the kids would take turns getting on the phone. He'd ask Claudia if she had any boyfriends yet, and she would always say no. Pity the poor boy who might have to pass muster with Ted, she knew. Then he'd want to know how much she weighed. How was her appetite? He wanted her to eat well and grow, but she knew she couldn't be overweight.

Claudia would grow to be five foot eleven and was always thin, but Ted kept her on guard. Once, she bought a white miniskirt and wanted to try it on for John-Henry and Ted. First she asked her brother if he thought it made her look fat. He said no, it looked fine. When Ted saw her he said, "Get the fuck outta here, you fat bitch." She rolled with the blow.

Sometimes she would ask her father about his childhood, but he refused to talk about it. "Nah, read my book," he'd say, waving her off. "The time with Dad was so short, or so it seemed, that we totally focused on each other. Ourselves. He'd never ask me about my aunt or my cousins, and I'd never ask him about his parents or his mother or brother or anybody else. It was just, 'How you doing in school?' Here and now."

While John-Henry and Claudia let it be known that they disliked Louise, most of her five children weren't exactly taken with the Kid, either. The exception was Louise's daughter Barbara Kovacs and her children, who adored Ted. But Louise's oldest son, Rob Kaufman, thought Williams was a boorish, loud bully who was insecure and wholly lacking in the social graces.

"He reminded me of a typical very successful athlete, and I'm not sure what else he brought to the table," Kaufman said. "I know he was loud. My mother thought Ted walked on water, and she was very protective of him. He was a very important person in her life and stayed that way for her last forty years. She had what she wanted out of life when she had Ted. She characterized him as John Wayne — sound- and look-alike."

Rob thought his mother and Williams probably had a 60 percent loving relationship and a 40 percent angry one, filled with turmoil. She mothered him. Neither one of them was easy to get along with. They both had mood swings. Maybe that's why they were a good match. Louise only feared him moving on again. She didn't fear him in other ways. "One time I was visiting, and he was ranting and raving like a two- or three-year-old, and she left the room. I looked at him and said, 'You know, she divorced Bob Kaufman for acting like an asshole, like you are now. What makes you think you're any different?' From that time on, when I called he always said, 'Hi, Rob, your mother's fine; here, would you like to talk to her?' I challenged him, and I was right. It was at his table, in his house, and it went away."

Rob thought Ted's anger was initially a cover-up for being unsophisticated, something he used as a young athlete to hide his feelings of social and educational inadequacy. "People ran for cover, and that became a method and later a lifestyle. He started arguing with people and bullying people. They either succumbed to it or left the situation. He was totally lacking in social skills. He spent too much time in the locker room. He was intelligent, but he didn't learn any of the skills that his peers learned."

As for Ted's kids, Rob thought John-Henry and Claudia were spoiled, especially John-Henry. "I think John-Henry very early on was impressed that he had a famous father. And that was worth something to him — maybe not to win friendships. The father might not have been there, but the name was. My mother's relationship with him was that John-Henry decided he didn't have to listen to her. If you were picking on John-Henry, you were picking at the heart of Ted. He would have defended him to anybody else."[7]

Williams must have known that John-Henry and Claudia disliked Louise, but occasionally he let them know how important she was to him. Once, when the three of them were having dinner at a restaurant in Boston along with Ted's lawyer, Bob McWalter, John-Henry and Claudia were watching pretty women walk by and rating them on a scale of one to ten. Ted was annoyed. "Claudia, John-Henry, when we get home, I want you to look at Louise Kaufman," he said. "There's no number high enough for Louise Kaufman."[8]

For John-Henry and Claudia, there were relatively few forays to see their father. Home base was rural Vermont, where they led a simple, rustic—even austere—life under the rigid supervision of their mother. Their old farmhouse, high on a hill, had a sweeping view of the woods and, on the horizon, the Connecticut River. The house had creaky, wide-pine floors and was heated by a woodstove. John-Henry and Claudia slept upstairs in a loft lit by oil-burning lamps. There were chores to be done. Every fall, they would head out to the woods and cut down enough trees to yield four or five cords of firewood for the winter. Dolores and John-Henry took turns on the chain saw, and Claudia would help stack the wood, first onto a truck and then in their cellar. They had to tend to chickens, geese, sheep, and a horse. Television was still not allowed. In fact, there was no TV in the house, and when Ted sent them one for Christmas, Dolores promptly threw it out.

"She was very tough," Claudia said. "Very tough. We never did drugs, never smoked. We were straight kids."

Dolores encouraged John-Henry and Claudia to read and immerse themselves in nature instead. They collected sap and made maple syrup. They studied Polish one year, Swedish another. They took singing lessons, piano lessons, learned the violin.

Ted liked Dolores's style—as a mother. "Dad would often say, 'You can't make your mother happy' or 'Your mother's a pain in the ass.' But till the day he died, he also said, 'Your mother—I've got to give her this: she was a great mother. She did a great job of raising you kids.'"

Over the years, as Claudia and John-Henry felt increasingly alienated by Louise, they would subtly push their parents to reconcile. But Ted wouldn't hear of it, and while Dolores in her heart yearned for a second chance, she realized it could never work out. "Yes," she said, "the kids wanted a reconciliation, but Ted and I never discussed it. Besides, there were still enough women vying for his attention. I would have had to have been involved in a briar patch again, and I didn't want to have to do that. I didn't need to be scrambling like a bear on the street for pennies."

Dolores and Ted had different notions about what was best for John-Henry. She wanted to make him more worldly and have him follow an artistic bent. Ted wanted to toughen him up and encourage him to play sports, including baseball. But after her experience with Ted and the

Senators, Dolores thought baseball people were crude and uncouth. She yanked John-Henry off his Little League team after learning that one of his coaches had sworn at him.

That incident became fodder for a lively family discussion. Ted, the dean of foul language, seized on the story as much ado about nothing and used it to suggest that Dolores was coddling John-Henry. And he needled his son about it by way of suggesting that he needed to toughen up and develop a thicker skin.

John-Henry had shown little appetite for baseball to this point. Once, he'd attended Ted's camp in Lakeville and had been hit twice on the thigh by pitches while batting. Missing his mother, he asked to go back to Vermont early.[9]

When John-Henry was in the sixth grade, Dolores promoted her vision for her son by sending him off to France on an exchange program. The following year, 1982, the Eaglebrook School—John-Henry's boarding school in Deerfield, Massachusetts—sponsored a spring-vacation trip to a more exotic locale: Brazil, where students would explore the Amazon River. Dolores had her doubts, but Ted boosted the idea, seeing it as a rite of passage that might help make a man out of his son. To Dolores's consternation, however, John-Henry returned home early from the Amazon, riddled with mosquito bites.

Landing in Florida, he spent the rest of his vacation with his father at the Red Sox spring training camp in Winter Haven, where he was given a uniform and designated a "junior batboy." He loved the atmosphere: while Ted made the rounds, instructing hitters and holding court, John-Henry found himself the object of considerable attention. Fans and press alike were able to get a gander at "the Kid's kid," as the press quickly dubbed him—tall, slender, and handsome.

"I'd like to be a hitter," John-Henry told a TV interviewer. "The same as my dad."

"He'll be a pitcher," said Ted, playing along. "He's got the perfect build for a pitcher."[10]

Williams's friends—like Al Cassidy and his father, who had started the baseball camp in Massachusetts with Ted—observed the dynamic between him and his son with interest. "The kid when he first came down did not have the best of experiences," said the younger Cassidy.[11] "Ted did not know how to be a father to John-Henry. He was the public Ted with him. Me and Dad would sit with Ted and basically tell him, 'You have to stop being Ted Williams with John-Henry. You're not Ted Williams—you're his dad.'"

Over the winter, the Red Sox had called and told Ted they wanted to stage their first Old-Timers' Game in May, but they would only do it if Williams appeared as the lead attraction. The game was the idea of George Sullivan, the former Red Sox batboy who later became a sportswriter—much to Ted's dismay—and then publicity director for the team. Sullivan knew that unless he could convince Ted to play, the team ownership felt the game would be pointless.

"I called him," Sullivan remembered, "and of course he said, 'Jesus Christ! I always said I'd never play in one of those goddamn games,' and blah, blah, blah. I let him rave on for a few minutes. Then he said, 'When do you want me to be there?' He said, 'The Yawkeys are the only people I'd ever do it for.' Next spring, we go to spring training, and after practice one day I heard the crack of the bat, crack of the bat. I said, 'Geez, I wonder who's taking extra hitting.' I went out, and there was Ted in the cage by himself. Getting ready. He was hitting some shots."[12]

John-Henry, fresh off the positive spring training experience, asked his mother if he could watch his father in action at the Old-Timers' Game. Dolores refused to let him go, and Ted, still in the doghouse over the Amazon trip, backed her decision. John-Henry then appealed to Ted's old teammate and close friend Johnny Pesky, whom the boy considered his godfather, to intervene. Pesky did, strongly urging Williams to permit the visit and use it as another stepping-stone with which to forge a relationship with his son. Dolores relented, on the condition that she accompany John-Henry.

Winter Haven was one thing, but seeing his father at Fenway Park was quite another for John-Henry, who again served as a batboy. It was the first time he began to fathom how big a figure Ted had been. The crowd cheered the sixty-three-year-old Williams's every move wildly, starting with his emergence from the dugout on his way to the batting cage, where he ripped the first pitch thrown to him into the right-field stands, on one bounce. In the game, Ted went 0–2 at the plate but raced into shallow left field to make a nice shoestring catch off Mike Andrews, the second baseman on the pennant-winning 1967 Red Sox, who would become chairman of the Jimmy Fund in 1984.*

After the game, as Ted was holding court in the clubhouse with his buddies, Sullivan came by to see him. "When Ted saw me, he said, 'There's the SOB I want to talk to,'" Sullivan remembered. "His big

---

* The headline in the *New York Times* the next day was TED WILLIAMS: GOOD FIELD, NO HIT.

booming voice. I worried something was wrŏng. He said, 'Come on, let's go into the office.' He shut the door. He said, 'You remember when you called me last winter I said I told you I'd never play? This morning I woke up in the hotel, and I looked at myself in the mirror. I'm fat and out of shape, and I was cursing you. But right now, I want to tell you,' he said, 'this is one of the greatest days in my life. I really, really enjoyed myself.'"

The Williamses, father and son, each met someone at the 1982 game who would become a significant figure in their lives. For Ted it was Sam Tamposi, a minority owner of the Red Sox who was a major real estate developer in New Hampshire and Florida. For John-Henry it was Michelle Orlando, the granddaughter of Red Sox equipment manger Vince Orlando.

Tamposi told Ted that he and his partner, Gerry Nash, were getting ready to build a retirement community on twenty thousand acres of land they had been sitting on since the 1960s in Citrus County, Florida, some seventy miles north of Tampa and sixty-five miles west of Orlando. The demographic they were trying to attract was seniors in New Hampshire, extending down into Massachusetts and the Boston area—just the kind of people who had grown up under the Williams spell. They needed a pitchman for the development, someone who could serve as its public face and vouch for the premise that Citrus Hills, as it would be called, was a slice of heaven on earth. Ted was intrigued and said he would be glad to receive Tamposi and Nash down in Islamorada to discuss the idea further.

Ted hadn't been to the development site, but he knew and liked the fishing in and around the Gulf Coast towns of Crystal River and Homosassa Springs, ten or fifteen miles to the west. Tamposi and Nash came down and spent more time with Ted, and they met Louise. Williams especially liked Tamposi, a self-made hustler who had been raised on a farm and sold salve and vacuum cleaners door-to-door before making it big in real estate. Tamposi was also a kindred Republican spirit, Ted learned, having long been active in New Hampshire politics, and he'd been a major fund-raiser for Barry Goldwater, Richard Nixon, and Ronald Reagan.

Tamposi and Nash were catching Ted at an auspicious time. First, Sears had not picked up his contract again, so he needed a new source of income, and second, he was tiring of the Keys. Islamorada, the remote island he had been coming to since the late '40s, was by then overrun with tourists, and its character had fundamentally changed. All manner of boats now prowled Ted's favorite fishing spots, and Route 1 was getting so congested that he sometimes had to wait several minutes just to turn onto the highway. Ted asked Louise what she thought of moving up to north-central Florida. She was game.

"When I first went up there, I thought, 'I can't imagine moving to this godforsaken place,'" remembered Louise's friend Evalyn Sterry. "There wasn't anything there. It looked like the middle of nowhere. But wherever Ted wanted was fine with Lou."

By December of '82, Ted, Tamposi, and Nash had thrashed out a deal: in return for providing promotional services for Citrus Hills, Williams would receive one-half of one percent of all real estate sales in the development, which would yield him an annual income of about $300,000. In addition, he received options to buy forty lots at predevelopment prices, options that he would exercise. He would be required to move to Citrus Hills, meet with prospective buyers, live in the most expensive home, and allow visitors to gawk at his house from a distance.[13]

John-Henry and Michelle Orlando fell for each other with puppy-love excitement. She was his first girlfriend, and he was her first boyfriend. Michelle was a lively, pretty brunette who had grown up hearing Ted Williams tales of yore from her grandfather Vince Orlando, Johnny's younger brother.

Vince was the less prominent Orlando and deferred to Johnny, the clubhouse manager, but he had established his own relationship with Ted. He loved to tell his family about how he and Williams used to go on double dates together when the Kid was starting out, and how Ted would speed around Boston in his big Buick, terrifying Vince. When they went to the movies, Ted would want to sit as close as he could to the screen; Williams said he liked to imagine the dirt flying out and hitting him in the face when the horses flew by. Or how Ted, at his first Red Sox spring training in 1938, bought a bat for $1 at a drugstore on his way to Sarasota and hit with it the entire first week.[14]

After meeting at the 1982 Old-Timers' Game, John-Henry and Michelle began hanging out together at spring training. By 1984, they had become close. She thought he was a bubbly country bumpkin, a clueless innocent when it came to city life.

He asked her questions about his father as a player, and she would answer, drawing on what Vince Orlando had told her. "One of the things I had to help John-Henry with was that when it came to bonding with his father, he saw him as being mean. If he heard Ted call his name — 'John-Henry!' — he'd shiver. I said, 'Why don't you look at old videos and see him as you are today?' I think through us he got to see the warmer side of his father. And as time went on, I think by understanding his father, the more he loved him."

One day in the spring of 1984 at Winter Haven, Michelle and her family were going to Epcot Center for the day, and she invited John-Henry to come along. He said he didn't think his father would let him. When Michelle asked why, John-Henry said Ted was afraid he would be kidnapped. Michelle's grandmother Mary Orlando overheard the conversation and thought she could help. She went over to Ted, explained the situation, and assured him John-Henry would be safe with her family. Ted agreed.

"Nana, why is Ted afraid John-Henry will be kidnapped?" Michelle asked Mary after Williams had left.

"For a ransom," her grandmother replied. "You're too young to remember the Lindbergh baby. The boy was stolen and murdered just because his father was famous. Don't worry; that was a long time ago. You'll all be safe today."[15]

John-Henry told Michelle he liked working with clay and enjoyed taking art in school. Back in Vermont, he showered her with letters and called her constantly. He told her he loved her. Once, he took a bus down to see Michelle at her home outside Boston without telling Dolores where he was going. He showed up at the house and told Michelle's mother, Candace Orlando Siegel, that he was on a school vacation and had permission to be there. "So the next day I got a phone call from Ted," Candace remembered. "He said, 'Is my son there?' 'Yeah.' 'Well, he's not supposed to be. He's supposed to be home.' He was furious. I had to bring him back to the bus."

John-Henry liked Candace and confided in her about wanting to become an artist. "He said, 'I don't want to be in sports or business. I want to be an artist, but my father won't let me.' His father stifled it. Ted didn't think that was a real career."[16]

Candace wondered if John-Henry had any sort of spiritual life. He didn't. "We used to talk to him about God, and he'd say, 'You really believe that stuff?' 'Yes! Come to church with us.'" John-Henry would brush the suggestion away. He also would say he thought he was going to die young because his uncle, Ted's brother, Danny, had.

If being an artist was impractical, his other dream, John-Henry told Michelle, was to play the young Ted Williams in a movie about his father. Then came an accident on his farm that seemed to make an acting career out of the question.

It happened in November of 1984. John-Henry had noticed a small cat on the side of a road near his house. He brought it home, but it died the next day, and the local vet advised burning it in case it had an illness that could be contagious to the other animals. John-Henry went next door to his grandparents' house, where they burned trash in a barrel. Pouring gas on the cat, he didn't realize he'd spilled some of the fluid on his hand. When he ignited the animal, flames leaped up to his hand and onto a polyester shirt he was wearing, which melted on his chest and hands. Claudia screamed at him to roll on the ground, and as soon as the flames were extinguished, they went running home. Dolores thought the burn didn't look too bad and put some aloe on it, but then they decided to go to the Brattleboro hospital, where they were told the burn was severe — too severe for them to handle — and that John-Henry needed to be transported to the Shriners Hospital in Boston. The sixteen-year-old was hospitalized for weeks and had skin grafts. He now had a big scar on his chest and hands, which he was acutely self-conscious about. Ted came to visit. John-Henry and Michelle talked on the phone a lot. "He sounded very sad and said he was lonely," she remembered. "He'd have a crack in his voice."

John-Henry had recently started tenth grade at a new school near his house, Vermont Academy, and he and Michelle drifted apart. A few years later, when John-Henry ran into Michelle's grandmother at a golf tournament and asked after Michelle, he was told she was married. John-Henry nearly fainted.

Their timing was off, but they stayed friends. "He said we were young, we'd lead long lives, and get back together again. He said, 'You're my Louise Kaufman,'" Michelle recalled.[17]

The cat-burning incident was one of two factors that greatly complicated John-Henry's first year at Vermont Academy, a small private school just down the road from his house in Westminster, which had about 250 students, 180 of them boarders. John-Henry was one of the seventy day students. The second difficulty was that John-Henry had broken into the coin box of a video game on campus and stolen about $150 in quarters. The theft was the talk of the school. Parents were notified. An investigation was conducted without turning up the culprit. Then Dolores found the quarters in her son's possession at home. Furious, she marched him into the office of the headmaster, Bob Long, dropped a huge bag of quarters on his desk, and said, "John-Henry wants to turn this in."

"This was completely out of the blue," Long remembered. "There was no suspicion at all." Though expulsion was virtually automatic for theft, Long and school officials found a way not to dismiss him "because of the honesty factor," Long said. He had, after all, admitted the theft and returned the loot. Or Dolores had done it for him.

Long did not know why John-Henry had stolen the money, but it was clear to him that things were not going well at home. "There were difficulties—I'm assuming with his mom. But a lot of it was a young kid who's coming into early and later adolescence, inquiring and concerned more about how his dad should, and could, be more of a player in his life."

Sometimes John-Henry felt the Ted void acutely. One day when he was about fifteen or sixteen, John-Henry called a family friend, Brian Interland, in tears and asked him, "Why doesn't my dad love me?"

Interland hemmed and hawed, wanting to make the most plausible excuse he could for Williams.

"John-Henry, your dad talks about you so much—maybe not when you're around—and he loves you as much as I love my kids," Interland said. "You can just see it in him, in the way he expresses himself."[18]

"Well, how come I don't know that?" John-Henry replied.

"Well, you're young, and you're not with him. If you were with him, you would have known that a long time ago. But Ted's different than a lot of people. He's very independent, he loves to fish, and why you guys don't see each other more than that, I don't know. I just know one thing, and any of Ted's friends would tell you the same thing: he loves you more than you know."

Ted rarely made it to Vermont Academy. Once, he turned up to watch John-Henry play in a JV baseball game. Though Williams just sat and watched, the mere presence of Teddy Ballgame cowed the inexperienced coach. Dolores, on the other hand, was a frequent presence at the school, and Long found her a handful. "Dolores came into the office frequently—three, four, five times in a semester—to ask about, or complain about, something with John-Henry, and she would unfortunately spend a good piece of time ranting about Ted and how poor of a father he was."

It was decided that John-Henry would live on campus for his final two years, and after that he had no other serious discipline problems. Young Williams was an average student and an average athlete. "Overall,

John-Henry was a gregarious, friendly kid," Long said. "He didn't stand out particularly. He was not a doper, not a drinker, a pretty straight kid who seemed more comfortable with adults than kids. Not that he was ostracized by kids, but he was more of an adult person than a kid person."[19] Once, he snuck off in a car with a bunch of other boys and went into town looking for girls, only to run into Dolores, who ordered him out of the car and hauled him back to school.

One of the adults John-Henry gravitated to in this period was Ferd Ensinger, an executive for the Bigelow Company, a Portsmouth, New Hampshire, mergers and acquisitions firm. One of Ferd's clients was a New Hampshire bank that Betty Tamposi—daughter of Ted's new confidant Sam Tamposi—was a director of. One thing led to another, and before long Ted met Ensinger—a former teacher—and asked if he would take John-Henry under his wing. Maybe Ferd could sharpen the boy's writing skills, help steer him to the right college, and just generally be a mentor.

Soon, John-Henry was spending almost every weekend with Ferd and his wife, Mary, at their home near Portsmouth, more than a hundred miles away. Ferd thought John-Henry had a lot of energy and a short attention span. He was Hollywood handsome, slender with dark hair, and growing like a weed. In the ninth grade, he had been five foot ten; a year and a half later, he was six two; and by his senior year, he would be six five, more than an inch taller than his father.[20] He was not a good writer, and so they would practice on a subject he was familiar with, perhaps something in his past or baseball trivia. Most of all, Ferd was struck by how lonely John-Henry seemed. It was hard to tell why, but he had no friends. So Ferd and Mary became his friends. He called Ferd "Dear Buddy" and Mary "Mrs. Old Buddy."

Getting to know John-Henry, Ferd talked of his own early years as a baseball fan, how he was drawn to Ted, what Williams had been like in his prime, and what he had meant to him. On his wedding day, Ferd had said to Mary, "Honey, you know what? Ted Williams hit three home runs today." Ted loved that story, and so did John-Henry.

The Ensingers came to regard John-Henry as an adopted son, giving him love and affection. "I like to think we represented a source of elder counsel, mature counsel," Ferd said. "We had a background of communicating with young people from strength and maturity, and I think John-Henry found that rewarding, satisfying, and comforting."[21] And it worked: after much time working with Ferd, John-Henry applied for early admission at Bates College, in Maine, and was accepted. That

Christmas in Islamorada, Claudia remembered, John-Henry wrapped his acceptance letter from Bates in a green velvet envelope with a red velvet rope and gave it to his father as a present. Ted was delighted, and Claudia snapped a photograph of him holding up the letter in triumph.

When he arrived at Bates in September, John-Henry went to see varsity baseball coach Chick Leahey. Leahey had contacted John-Henry's coach at Vermont Academy and received what he termed "a modest evaluation" of the young man's baseball skills. Leahey said there would be a two-week tryout period indoors in the early spring, followed by a cut.

Before the season rolled around, Ted came for a visit, and John-Henry asked Leahey if he could set up the batting cage in the field house so his father could watch him hit and give him some tips.

Leahey agreed, more than curious to see Teddy Ballgame himself expound on the art of hitting.

"So at three o'clock Sunday afternoon they came in, and Ted barged into my office and said, 'What's it all about here? What kinda things do you do?'" Leahey recalled, chuckling. "So I talked about the baseball program, reminded him that I had a cut day but everybody had an opportunity for two weeks of daily practice and then the hammer came down, and he understood that. He had such an image, you were taken aback by this guy."

Leahey set up the pitching machine and watched John-Henry hit. Ted was standing outside the netted area and watched as his son put on an indifferent performance. Leahey wondered what Ted would say, but he offered only neutral, measured comments, like "Keep your head in there"; "Don't lunge"; "Let the ball come to you." After about a half hour, Ted told John-Henry to wrap it up, take a shower, and meet him in the coach's office.

Williams, taking over, then quizzed Leahey about the hitting technique he taught. "Now, what's this about the top-hand thing you're trying to sell to these kids?" he asked.

"If you're right-handed, your right hand is doing two to three times the amount of work as your left hand, picking up things, opening doors, et cetera, so your left hand is passive while your right hand does the work," Leahey said.

"That wouldn't have done much for me. I was a left-handed hitter and I was a right-handed person." Ted threw that out, as if to say, answer that one.

Leahey paused for a moment and said: "I have no problem figuring that out, because there's only one Ted Williams." It was a nice answer. He wasn't going to get into the weeds of a discussion on batting with the last of the .400 hitters. Ted laughed, John-Henry appeared, and they said good-bye.

When the tryouts were held, John-Henry didn't make the cut.[22]

The Ensingers came to visit John-Henry at Bates. Ferd suggested they go to a basketball game, but John-Henry seemed uninterested. Indeed, he didn't seem to know anyone and didn't introduce them to any other students. "I was just shocked that John-Henry wasn't more involved," Ferd said. "He was still pretty much a loner. And at the end of that first year, his grades suffered badly. I think he was on probation." Soon afterward John-Henry called Ferd to say that he was transferring to the University of Maine.

Ted had felt things slipping away for his son at Bates. In the fall of 1986, he'd asked Sam Tamposi and Al Cassidy to meet John-Henry in Boston for lunch during the World Series, when the Red Sox were playing the New York Mets. Williams wanted his two successful business friends to preach the importance of college to the boy and give him a pep talk. But neither man had been to college, and they didn't deliver the pitch with enough verve, much to Ted's dismay.

Before John-Henry moved on to the University of Maine, Ted thought he needed the discipline of a job to help him focus and get serious about his education. So he went back to Tamposi for help, along with his daughter Betty, who had a leading role in the Tamposi Company real estate development firm, based in Nashua, New Hampshire. Sam said the boy could live with him at his home and Betty, who was helping manage the development of a five-hundred-unit residential complex, would create a job for him. It was the spring of 1987 when Ted came to Nashua to discuss John-Henry with the Tamposis. He had his dog with him, a Dalmatian named Slugger—the same name as his previous dog. Louise's grandchildren had given him the pet as a Christmas present. Ted groused at the time that the last thing he needed in his life now was a dog, but he had quickly come to love the animal.

Betty took Ted on a boat ride along the Nashua River. It was a sunny day, and she wanted him to see how beautifully it had been cleaned up after being contaminated by textile mills and a cannery. The river used to be covered with a fluorescent green coating. Now you could fish in it.

"We came back, and in the car driving back to my office, Ted had Slugger in the back," Betty remembered. "He started to get upset about

John-Henry, and I was asking him what was going right and what wasn't going right. He said he wasn't taking his education seriously, just being cavalier about everything, he wasn't able to stick with anything, he was all over the map, and he needed to get focused. He was getting angry talking about it, and out of nowhere he turned around and he punched Slugger.

"I said, 'Why did you hit the dog?' and he didn't answer me, he just sat there fuming, but that was an indication to me that he had real demons, real problems containing his anger, his hostility. I was just in my early thirties. It was difficult to figure out how to handle both Ted and John-Henry."

Betty found the younger Williams charming. So she decided to have him meet and greet prospective customers at the development they were building. He could also give them an overview of the project and perhaps help determine if the buyers were qualified. But it was hard for John-Henry to keep a regular schedule. Some days he didn't show up at all; other days he'd breeze in late. Then, after the first month, Betty got the phone bill for the sales and marketing department, and it was thousands of dollars higher than it should have been. John-Henry had been making personal calls all over the country, and she made him pay the money back by docking his salary.

When shortly thereafter the Tamposi partners were coming in to inspect the project, Betty chose John-Henry to greet and attend to them. But on the appointed day he was nowhere to be found, and Betty was forced to make do by herself. Finally, as they were finishing up their tour, they came upon John-Henry lying on a chaise lounge and sunbathing with some friends as hot dogs and hamburgers sizzled on the grill.

His entitled behavior continued. At Fenway Park, he would saunter into the owner's box uninvited, often with an entourage. Once, Betty heard Tom Yawkey's wife, Jean, say to him: "John-Henry Williams, all you're doing is using your father's name to get a passport into these places. You don't have any reason to be here, you're not allowed to be here because you're not an owner, and I don't want to see you in this box again."

In 1988, during the American League Championship Series, when the Red Sox were playing the Oakland Athletics, John-Henry, lacking a ticket, assumed he could work his connections at the Fenway gate to get in. He left his car directly in front of the main entrance on Yawkey Way with the red hazard lights flashing and called Betty, who was inside with her father, sitting in an owner's box.

"It was a mob scene pregame, and everybody was just walking around the car with the hazards on. I knew he was trying to get into the park and he didn't have tickets. So I said to him, 'John-Henry, listen, you can't just park on Yawkey Way, on the sidewalks, nobody does that,' and he was laughing and said, 'Come on, lighten up, it was fun.'" Then John-Henry decided to go over Betty's head and call her father to appeal for help in getting into the game. "I was standing with my father, he picked up, and it was John-Henry, and he said, 'Mr. Tamposi, no one will let me into the park. My usual people won't let me in.'" He added that Dom DiMaggio and his wife were also outside and having difficulty getting into the park for some reason. Sam Tamposi went downstairs and waved the DiMaggios in, but not John-Henry.

"What was endearing about him is he really wanted to do good, the intention was there, but it was heartbreaking to watch when he started to unravel, to a trajectory where bad things were going to happen," Betty concluded.

By now, John-Henry was questioning why he needed to be in college at all. Recalled Betty, "He'd say, 'I don't understand why I can't just start developing. I want to make money.' So we had discussions about money. It was just important to him, a way of accomplishing things. He saw the money as an end in and of itself. John-Henry could be extraordinarily thoughtful. He had a depth and richness to the way he thought about things, and he really did have charisma. He was beyond his years in some ways, but John-Henry's dictum was 'Anything goes as long as you don't get caught.'"[23]

One positive for Williams about John-Henry going to the University of Maine was that its principal campus, in Orono, was just north of Bangor, so Ted's old friend Bud Leavitt could keep an eye on the boy. Also, the baseball coach at Maine, John Winkin, was a pal who had been an instructor at Ted's camp in Lakeville, Massachusetts. Winkin had spent twenty years as the baseball coach and athletic director at nearby Colby College and had come to Orono in 1975. Ted had called Winkin and asked him to facilitate John-Henry's transfer to Maine.

Not that he had any reasonable chance of playing varsity baseball at Maine. After all, he had not made his team at Bates, a Division III program; Maine was in Division I and had gone to the College World Series in Omaha six times since Winkin arrived.

Winkin said he had talked to the Bates coach about John-Henry, so he knew what sort of player he was. Winkin had also talked to Sam

Tamposi. "Sam and I exchanged views about John-Henry, and he told me that he had difficulty getting him to really work, that he was kind of a lazy kid," Winkin recalled.

There were two baseball diamonds at Maine. At the first practice, Winkin's policy was to have the returning lettermen go on the varsity field and the new players report to the freshman field. John-Henry showed up carrying several of his own bats and walked over to the varsity field. Recalled Winkin, "I said, 'John-Henry, you go where the new guys go,' and I guess he was upset about that, and he left the field. I got a call from Ted that night, and I explained it to Ted, and he said, 'Oh, well, that's the way it should be.'

"So John-Henry came back the next day, and he said, 'Did Dad call you?' And I said, 'Yeah.' I think he thought his dad had made it possible for him to go to the regulars' field. I said, 'No, you've got to go with the guys who are starting out fresh,' and he was disappointed. He decided not to come out for baseball. I think he was looking for special treatment. To be honest with you, he was a difficult kid to deal with. He was hard to trust."[24]

John-Henry never told Ted that he had walked out. One day, Ted called Jim Vinick, a longtime friend of his from Springfield, Massachusetts, who had purchased the movie rights to *My Turn at Bat*.

"I was going to North Miami," Vinick remembered. "I have friends down there—and Ted says to me, 'While you're down there, why don't you go to see Miami play? They're playing against Maine. John-Henry's on the team,'" Vinick said. "Well, I got to my buddy's house in North Miami, and I said, 'Let's take a ride down to Coral Gables. John-Henry Williams is playing for Maine against Miami.' These guys are big Miami fans. We get down there, and I knew one of the assistant coaches. I walked out onto the field, talking to the guy, and I said, 'Where's John-Henry Williams?' And he looked at me and said, 'What do you mean?' And I said, 'Isn't he on the team?' And he says, 'No, he never made the team.'

"He'd lied to Ted. He told Ted he made the team. He never made the team. So I called Ted and I said, 'Got down to see Maine play Miami, but John-Henry wasn't there.' He said, 'What do you mean he wasn't there?' And I said, 'Ted, he never made the team.' He went freakin' nuts on the phone."[25]

By now, John-Henry was clearly chafing at Maine. His grades were decent, but he annoyed some of his professors by bringing his cell phone to classes, and it would often ring, causing a distraction.[26] He was living alone, off campus. He was restless and again not making many friends. So in January of 1989, he called Ferd Ensinger and told him he'd decided to take the spring semester off and go to California. "He said, 'I've made up my mind. I've got to hit baseballs. I have to find out if I really can hit baseballs,'" Ensinger remembered.

John-Henry headed to Santa Barbara to stay with Ted's second cousin, Manuel Herrera. Manuel was a Vietnam veteran who then worked construction, running a bulldozer. He'd been orphaned as a boy when his mother, Ted's first cousin Annie Cordero, was murdered by Manuel's father, Salvador Herrera, who then killed himself.

Manuel's grandmother, Mary Venzor, had been the sister of May Williams, Ted's mother. And Manuel had been one of the points of contact for Ted when it came to his dealings with the Venzors. He got John-Henry a tryout with a local sandlot team. "He batted ninth for the team, but kept trying to tell everyone what to do," Manuel said. "I saw him play. He was slow, had a pretty nice swing, but was an average ballplayer. He had no confidence." Next, Manuel got John-Henry a job at the local Radio Shack, which he quit after two weeks without informing his supervisor. He stayed at home watching TV and making long-distance phone calls. "John-Henry, when he stayed with me, was calling everybody. His phone bill was three to four hundred dollars a month. I couldn't afford that."*

Added Manuel, "I got tired of him. He was always trying to manipulate people. Money was always his focus. He told me he was waiting for his dad to die so he could be a millionaire." Manuel was particularly struck by how entitled John-Henry felt. "He said, 'I can have anything. My dad will pay for it.' He had dreams of being a NASCAR driver. He thought his dad could buy the car for him, and he could step right in. He wasn't ready to work his way up." After a few months, Manuel got fed up with John-Henry and threw him out. "I was probably the only one who ever did," he said. "Because he was Ted Williams's kid, no one had ever stood up to him that way."[27]

That June, Manuel wrote Ted and Louise a letter, reflecting on John-Henry. "He tries to be Ted Williams when he should be J. H. Williams," Manuel wrote. "Ted, sir, your son needs help. I am sorry."[28]

Then Manuel's older brother, Salvador Herrera Jr., took John-Henry in. Sal and his wife, Edna, a retired Los Angeles police officer, lived in Porterville, California, north of Bakersfield in the San Joaquin Valley.

---

* Manuel said Ted eventually sent him $1,500 as reimbursement.

Sal, then fifty-four, was a rough-and-tumble ironworker with a hair-trigger temper who had played minor-league ball in the Milwaukee Braves organization. He had his own batting cage and moonlighted as a hitting instructor. He took one look at John-Henry in action inside the cage and thought he was pathetic. Sal's style was confrontational and in-your-face. He told John-Henry that if he wanted to get serious about baseball, he was starting far too late. "I said, 'You're twenty-three years old or something. You're a mama's boy and you're a daddy's boy. You don't know how to do anything.'"

But after a while, John-Henry began to respond to Sal's drill-sergeant persona, and his hitting started to improve. Sal kept Ted apprised of his son's progress. The pair liked each other and talked on the phone every month or so. They needled one another, spoke candidly, swore up a storm, and one would often hang up abruptly in a snit if he felt the conversation was not going his way. The aggrieved party would then promptly call back and say, "Don't you *ever* hang up on me again"—and then hang up.

"I told Ted, 'You don't know how to teach guys to hit. You'd rather tell them how *you* hit,'" Sal said. "We used to argue about that shit. I told him, 'I taught your kid something. I make it simple: you throw it and you hit it.'"

John-Henry stayed with the Herreras for three months. He greatly admired the way Sal could still turn on a ninety-mile-an-hour fastball and back up the abuse he dished out. John-Henry was further enamored of Sal because he had arranged a token tryout for him with the Toronto Blue Jays in Los Angeles by calling in a favor with a Blue Jays scout he knew. (On the way home, Sal said to John-Henry, "You might be a doctor or a lawyer, but you're not going to be a professional baseball player."[29]) John-Henry respected Edna, too, and soon found himself confiding in them in a manner that surprised the couple. They couldn't believe what they were learning about the young man.

The first thing they learned came from Dolores, who called to inform them that her son had stolen several paintings from her house before leaving for California. "His mom called me up, and told me he got in her house and stole all her paintings and sold them," Sal said. "He was a thief. The people he sold the paintings to told her. He admitted it to his mother. He told me, too. I said, 'Hey, man, your old lady told me'—he laughed. That kid was the most money-hungry piece of trash I've ever seen."

Next, John-Henry mocked the Herreras' religious beliefs. Sal and

Edna displayed a cross in their house. "He saw that and said, 'Hiss-hiss,'" Sal remembered. "He said, 'I don't believe in God. It's all bullshit. There is no God.'" Added Edna, "The part that surprised me about him was his utter lack of standards. I try to run the center of my home on a some-what spiritual basis. He had none. He had no direction at all. He had no moral standards at all."

One day, Sal said, John-Henry bragged to him that he was selling Ted Williams–autographed balls and bats at a healthy profit. But Ted hadn't signed the merchandise—John-Henry had forged his father's name. "He told me he'd forged a bunch of bats and balls and he could prove it to me, and that's when he started to write Ted's name on a pad of paper. John-Henry was sitting at my table showing my wife and I how he could duplicate his dad's signature so good. He was showing off. He said, 'I can write my dad's name to a tee. I've practiced this.' He used to sign baseballs and bats and have the trunk of his car loaded and sell them. He spent hours and days doing it. He did it right in front of my wife and me. I said to him, 'You're crazy. You're just like your uncle Danny'"—Ted's brother. Concluded Edna, "He had no idea of things you do and things you don't do. I don't think he ever got any guidance. John-Henry's focus was on money. I said, 'That's not all there is to life.'"[30] When one of Edna's coworkers at a local hospital asked for a Ted Williams–autographed ball, she said John-Henry simply signed it in his father's name.

John-Henry also fretted to the Herreras that his inheritance would be severely diminished now that Louise Kaufman had reentered Ted's life. "He was afraid Ted was going to leave all the money to Louise," Sal said. "He said, 'Louise has got my dad wrapped around her finger. He's going to leave her everything.' So he was actually trying to find out how to have her killed. He talked to my wife about that. He said, 'How can I kill her and get away with it?' She was retired LAPD, and he figured she'd know. He was serious about that shit."

Edna was shocked. "John-Henry did tell me that he was convinced Louise was after Ted's money, and if he could think of a way to get rid of her, he would. I said, 'That's evil thinking, pal.' I said that to him. He was waiting for Ted to die. He was counting early on what he was going to be getting. He was so concerned he was not going to get his share. He said that. He was very open."

If John-Henry followed a traditional path from a prep school near home to college, albeit with detours, Claudia decided to do something different. After spending the ninth grade at Northfield Mount Hermon, a private school in western Massachusetts just over the Vermont line from Brattleboro, she set out for Paris. She would finish high school at École Active Bilingue, a prestigious bilingual studies program that attracts students from around the world.

"I think I was struggling very hard to find out who I was," Claudia said. "Where I was at home didn't seem big enough for John-Henry and I. We so badly wanted our father's approval and recognition that we strived hard to do something exceptional. For me, because John-Henry had right from the start such a tight, tight relationship with Dad, I had to go a different direction to get Daddy to notice me." In addition, Claudia felt that Dolores was smothering her. "It got to a point where Mom and I just started bashing heads. And I couldn't get far enough away."

Her maternal grandfather was Swiss-German, and Claudia had taken a school trip to Switzerland and Germany when she was thirteen. She had grown enamored of Europe, and loved the idea of becoming fluent in at least one foreign language. Dolores came around to the idea and asked a friend in Switzerland to go to Paris once a month to keep an eye on Claudia. Ted was fine with her plan, which required little effort on his part.

Claudia moved in with a Parisian family near the school as a *fille au pair,* and that took care of her room and board. She would come home twice a year, usually once at Christmas and once over the summer. She traveled widely in Europe, including in England and Austria. She had gotten interested in bicycle racing at home and now trained with a group of French cyclists, even aspiring to be the next Jeannie Longo, the French women's cycling champion.

While cycling was a bit too exotic for Ted to relate to, he was alarmed when he learned of another of Claudia's offbeat interests: parachuting. Once, she showed up at his house fresh from a jump. Williams thought her outfit was strange.

"What the fuck kind of shorts are those?" he asked her.

"Parachute shorts."

"Jesus Christ! I hope you never do that."

She then pulled out a photo of herself skydiving. Ted soon forgot his admonition and turned proud, introducing his daughter to friends as someone who "jumps out of airplanes."

Being in Paris was a formative experience for Claudia. At home she'd always wondered, "Are they liking me for me or for who my dad is? In Europe, nobody knew who Ted Williams was. So every kind of compliment or accomplishment or recognition that I got over there, I earned it one hundred percent. And that was so character-building for me, especially at that age, because I was so desperately trying to figure out, 'Who am I? Am I ever going to be able to even get close to who my father was or what he accomplished?' That's a pretty big shadow to grow up in. And I liked the people in Europe, the realness of it. When you make a friend there, they stay a friend. I find America fake and caught up in celebrity."*

If she had had her druthers, Claudia would have stayed in Europe for a while after graduating from her Parisian school rather than go to college right away. She wanted to pursue cycling to see if she might be able to make it as a professional, but Ted wouldn't hear of it. "He was constantly on us about the need to go to college, to get our education," Claudia said. "There were two reasons for this. One of them was because he didn't do it. He always used to say, 'I'm just a dumb ballplayer.' He wanted to have that certificate for his kids that said, 'No, my kids have had their higher education.' And I also think he wanted us to be different than Bobby-Jo. If his first child was a failure, then he didn't want his next children to make the same mistakes."

Claudia had hoped to go to Middlebury College in Vermont to pursue her love of languages, but was rejected, so she went to Springfield College in Massachusetts. After her first semester, she kept trying to apply to Middlebury, this time as a transfer student, but to no avail, despite her fluency in French and strong grades. One day she told Ted of her frustration. "So for the first time, Daddy said, 'What's with this Middlebury?'" Unbeknownst to Claudia, Williams called John Sununu, the former governor of neighboring New Hampshire, and asked if he might help his daughter at Middlebury.

"A week later I got a call from the admissions office saying they'd apparently overlooked my application. I said, 'I'm so disappointed in Middlebury. You get a call from a governor and only then do you check out my application? I had great grades and speak fluent French, and only after a politician calls do you want me?'" She turned them down and stayed at Springfield, graduating in three years. Claudia called her father and chewed him out for calling Sununu. Ted said, "Well, Jesus Christ, all I wanted to do was help you, goddamn it!" and hung up the phone.

---

* When Claudia came back from Paris, Ted would always ask her to speak French to him, and when friends came over, he would demand that she give them a command performance. "Until the day Daddy died, he'd ask me to talk French."

But in the meantime, Ted told all his pals how proud he was of Claudia going her own way.

"He told fifty people, 'My daughter, I'm so damn proud of her. She did this. She did that. I called up Sununu, got her into Middlebury. She turned the fuckers down! She's gonna do it her way.' He loved that."

But Ted never told Claudia how proud he was. "If there was one thing that I wish my dad had done when I was growing up, I wish he could have been able to tell me how proud he was that I was so independent. How proud he was that despite having him open a door for me, I said, 'No, Dad, I'm gonna show you I can do it this way.' I always felt like I was constantly waving flags, going, 'Notice me!' He would tell other people. And these people would even come to me and they would tell me these stories, and I'd be like, 'Why doesn't he just tell me?'"

At Springfield, no one knew she was the daughter of Ted Williams until graduation day, when he showed up. When she spotted him in the crowd, Claudia bolted from the line of students awaiting their diplomas and raced over to give Ted a big hug, causing a stir as people recognized the Kid. Delighted, Williams told her with a smile, "Well, Jesus Christ! Get back in the line!"

"When I graduated from Springfield, there wasn't a brighter face in the audience than my dad," Claudia said. "It was so awesome to see how happy my father was sitting in the audience." She graduated cum laude, with a major in psychology. When the president of the college handed Claudia her diploma, he quietly asked if he could meet Ted after the ceremony.

Claudia returned to Europe after college for another five years, this time to Germany, where she worked for a publishing house and gained fluency in German to go with her French. She fell in love with a German named Roman, whom she brought home to meet her father.

Ted took a break from his fishing and received Roman. Of course the Kid was rough on the young man, and later, when Claudia told Ted that Roman had dumped her, Williams said: "That fuckin' Kraut! Just be glad there's no kids involved. Where is he, back in the Fatherland?"

25

The Fishing Life

During and after his baseball career, Williams's other great passion was fishing.

Ever since he was a kid starting out with a split bamboo pole — first going for bass in a lake outside San Diego, then surf casting for corbina at Coronado, then snagging a raft of barracuda on a deep-sea outing off Point Loma in 1934 — Ted had simply been captivated by fishing. "I was just carried away with the whole damn thing," as he later put it.[1]

His desire to fish only grew as he prospered in baseball. Playing for the Minneapolis Millers in 1938, he loaded up on walleyes and northern pike throughout Minnesota. By the time he got to Boston the following year, Williams made sure to carve out time for fishing around his baseball commitments. In his rookie season, he went fly-fishing for the first time on Lake Cochituate in suburban Natick, and a girl he had with him lay prone in the boat to avoid being hit as he cast, prompting an inquiry from another curious fisherman who wanted to make sure everything was okay.[2]

Well into the late 1940s, whenever the Red Sox were playing at home, Williams would often get up early in the morning and go fishing at various local hot spots before coming to Fenway Park. On off days, he might make a run to Cape Cod, or head north of Boston near Cape Ann, where he made headlines in 1949 by catching a 394-pound tuna. At night, he'd unwind after a game by tying flies in his room at the Somerset Hotel for hours. Over the five-year period after he returned to baseball following World War II, he claimed that he tied twenty-five hundred flies.[3]

Ted's love of fishing was well noted in the press during his playing days, and some fans took an interest in his interest. One day during a game, a harmless drunk came out of the stands, ambled out to Williams in left field, and announced: "I just wanted to tell you that the fish are really biting at Cape Cod Canal."[4]

What was it about fishing that enthralled Williams? For one thing, it gave him solace and a refuge from the celebrity glare. But it was much more than that. He loved the beauty and authenticity of the outdoor life: "No stuffy characters. No formal dinners. No tight ties around your neck. Just good, clean, fresh air and the gamest opponents in the world," as he put it in 1952.[5] That was a sharp contrast to how he felt about people. Williams liked to call himself "a Will Rogers fisherman: I've never met a fish I didn't like."[6]

He bathed in the beauty of isolated streams, rivers, ponds, and the sea. He loved "just being there, away from the telephones, away from people. I can't think of anyone who had more fun out of life than Zane Grey. He had that big three-masted schooner, and he just traveled the world, hunting and fishing."[7] Until he died, Ted would harbor his version of the Zane Grey fantasy: to buy a seventy-five-foot shrimp trawler, equip it with a crew and a small skiff or two for excursions away from the mother ship, and then cruise around the world at his leisure, looking for fish he hadn't caught before.

Like the novels that Grey wrote, the trawler would remain a romantic fiction. As it was, however, Williams did live out a fisherman's fantasy, catching a 1,235-pound black marlin off Peru, a five-hundred-pound thresher shark off New Zealand, salmon in Russia, and tigerfish in Zambia. (Other foreign destinations included Iceland, Panama, Costa Rica, Belize, Mexico, Australia's Great Barrier Reef, and the Fiji Islands.) He'd fished all over the United States — catching albacore off San Diego, muskie in the Midwest, trout in Montana, bluegill in the Arkansas River, bass in Maine's Pocomoonshine Lake, and snook in the Everglades. But mostly he favored the Florida Keys and his adopted Islamorada, where he helped put saltwater fly-fishing on the map in the late '40s and early '50s while trolling endlessly for tarpon and bonefish. Those two, plus his beloved Atlantic salmon, which he caught for years on the Miramichi, were Ted's favorites.

He exalted those three fish in *Ted Williams: Fishing the Big Three,* his 1982 book with John Underwood. It had been Underwood's 1967 *Sports Illustrated* piece, "Going Fishing with the Kid," which pleased Williams so much that he picked the writer to do *My Turn at Bat.* In 1981, Underwood wrote a *Sports Illustrated* sequel about Williams going for Atlantic salmon on the Miramichi, which, along with the 1967 piece, formed the basis for *Fishing the Big Three.*

Just as he had approached hitting as a science, Ted brought to fishing the same spirit of inquiry, energy, and intensity, as well as a thirst for knowledge of whatever fish he was after and its habitat. And just as he had studied the habits and tendencies of pitchers, he studied the ways of fish and strove to develop the most refined technique for catching them, adding his own skill, endurance, and patience to the mix. As it turned out, the drive for excellence that made him want to be known as the greatest hitter who ever lived evolved after he retired from baseball into another goal: not literally to be known as the greatest angler, but to master the art of fishing totally—fueled by his love of the outdoors, an insatiable curiosity about fish, and his innate competitive drive. Ultimately, Williams became so esteemed in the fishing world that he was inducted into both the National Fresh Water Fishing Hall of Fame and the International Game Fish Association Hall of Fame. He was delighted by these honors, almost as proud of being designated an angling immortal as he was of his enshrinement in Cooperstown.

Long before leaving baseball, Williams had been able to turn his love of fishing into a paying avocation. In 1952 he'd bought an interest in a Miami fishing-tackle firm. In 1953 he launched a TV show that aired weekly in Miami on outdoor life. In 1955 he made a thirty-minute fishing film for General Electric, which brought him to the Miramichi in Canada for the first time. Then, over several years, he filmed thirty-nine 15-minute TV spots on fishing in which he served as the narrator and sometimes appeared with guests, such as Bing Crosby and Sam Snead. The films were syndicated by Beacon Television of Boston, which Ted and his business manager, Fred Corcoran, held stock in.

In January of 1960, before starting his final year with the Red Sox, Ted unveiled a line of fishing gear for the Bigelow & Dowse Company of Boston, a hardware retailer that dealt in fishing tackle. The line included a spinning reel that was praised for its effectiveness and ease of use, combining the best aspects of the manual and full-bail pickup reels. When he went to work for Sears after finishing his baseball career, Ted had a broad platform from which to develop effective fishing tackle. He could test his ideas and help build the sort of equipment he wanted, and he played a role in the technological advances of rods, reels, lures, and lines. He watched rods evolve from bamboo to fiberglass to graphite-boron and other synthetic composites; he saw lines go from braided linen to the finest monofilament.

For years, Williams showcased his fishing skills by serving as the headliner for the annual sportsmen's show at Mechanics Hall in Boston.

Tens of thousands packed the hall to watch Williams put on fly-casting demonstrations, sometimes with the former heavyweight boxing champion Jack Sharkey as his friendly foil. There was a carnival atmosphere at the shows, which ran over the course of nine days in February and which featured logrolling, archery, performing dogs, hooded falcons, canoe-handling exhibitions, a "catch 'em and keep 'em" trout pool, and Williams casting to a spot about twenty-five yards away while Sharkey heckled him from the sidelines.

After the 1946 baseball season ended with the Red Sox losing the World Series in seven games, Williams was dying to go fishing. He called a guide in the Florida Keys: Jimmie Albright. Through word of mouth, Ted had heard that earlier that year Albright and his client Joe Brooks had become the first to catch a bonefish using a fly rod. Bonefish cruise in shallow water and are relatively small, weighing seven to twelve pounds and extending close to three feet in length. But they are a widely prized game fish and considered, pound for pound, the strongest and fastest of saltwater fish. Catching bonefish on a fly was unheard of at the time, and it caused a stir in the fishing world. Albright, who lived in Islamorada, soon made his mark as a saltwater fly-fishing pioneer. He took Williams out, the two formed a lasting friendship, and Ted quickly became smitten by Islamorada.

Albright, who was two years older than Williams, had already established himself as a fabled guide, fishing with the likes of Zane Grey, Ernest Hemingway, former president Herbert Hoover, the actor Jimmy Stewart, and the actress Myrna Loy.[8] A native of Indiana, Jimmie had come to Miami in 1935 and caught on as a mate for an offshore charter boat. After a stint in the Navy during World War II, Albright settled in Islamorada with his new wife, Frankie Laidlaw, who was an accomplished fisherwoman in her own right.

Jimmie and Frankie built a house and guest cottage on the water. There was no electricity or running water in the village, and the population numbered about seventy-five people—mostly so-called Conchs, descendants of the white Bahamians who fled the American Revolution as Crown loyalists. Jimmie had a charter boat, The Rebel, and a handful of fifteen-foot skiffs that were powered by 7½-horsepower Mercury engines. In the big boat, he fished the Gulf Stream for marlin, dolphin, sailfish, wahoo, and kingfish. He'd use the skiffs to pole the flats for bonefish and permit.

Besides his nose for fish, Albright was also a knot-tying savant credited with developing two knots considered indispensable to anglers: the nail knot and the Albright Special. The nail knot used a nail or tube to tie two lines together, while the Albright Special linked two lines of different diameters.

But it was Ted who became Albright's longest-lasting and most notable client. They would fish together perhaps fifty times a year, and while other guides were more than willing to fish with Williams free of charge for the cachet it could bring them, Ted always paid Jimmie aboveboard. It had been Albright who introduced Ted to Louise Kaufman, and it was at Jimmie's house where Ted hid from reporters in 1952, when he was called back for service in Korea. Albright would protect Williams from interlopers who wanted to gawk at him or otherwise invade his privacy—unless it was someone Jimmie thought Ted might like to meet, like Jack Nicklaus, whom he once brought around.

Albright was the guru of guides, but it was Williams's heralded fishing presence on the Keys that provided a significant jolt to the local economy, and Islamorada soon took to billing itself as the "sport fishing capital of the world." It certainly was for Ted: by the mid-1960s, Williams had caught more than one thousand bonefish, the species that had first brought him to the Keys. For his next challenge he began to focus on the tarpon, one of the great saltwater game fish. The "silver kings," as they are known, range from five to eight feet in length and usually weigh anywhere from twenty to 150 pounds. They are best known for their leaping ability and fighting spirit. To boost tarpon fishing, Williams persuaded the Islamorada guides to stage an elite, invitation-only tournament called the Gold Cup. At the first tournament, in 1964, Williams caught the biggest tarpon, but the fish broke free after Ted insisted on using a spinning rod—against the advice of his guide, Clifford Ambrose, who urged him to use a fly rod.[9] Williams used Albright as his guide the following year and won the tournament with a fly rod. Ted couldn't make it in 1966 because he was being inducted at Cooperstown, but he won his second Gold Cup in 1967, again with Albright. "After Ted won the Gold Cup a couple of times he quit fishing it, because everyone was groaning that he'd won it twice," said Islamorada guide Buddy Grace. "He said he was too damn good for it, that's all."[10]*

Though Ted got the glory, as far as Albright and the other guides were concerned, they were the ones who did the heavy lifting and deserved the credit. Of course Williams would have none of that.

---

* The Gold Cup Invitational Tarpon Fly Tournament, as it is officially known, continues to be held every year in June and is known as the Wimbledon of tarpon competitions.

After a day on the boat, Ted and Jimmie would retire to a round table at the Islamorada Yacht Basin, which later became the Lorelei restaurant, and hold court. This central perch became known as "City Hall," and by the mid-to-late '50s, it was further enlivened by the addition of Jack Brothers, who would become the second most important guide in Islamorada after Albright. Brothers was a Brooklyn transplant who had arrived in 1953, married a Conch, and after a stint at a local marine park set up shop as a guide.

Like Ted and Jimmie, Jack could be rather crotchety and cantankerous. Business was good by now, and the guides could fish with whomever they wanted to whenever they wished. One day, approached by two oversize men who wanted to go out bonefishing, Brothers told them: "If you think I'm gonna pole your fat asses around all day you're crazy."[11] Williams got a kick out of that and quickly cottoned to Brothers. Ted took Jack's son, Frank, under his wing, too. When Frank got to be about sixteen, Williams would take him out on Saturdays and pay him $5 an hour to pole him around after bonefish. Frank was overweight and, unsurprisingly, Ted felt no need for sensitivity. Criticizing the young man's poling technique, he blurted out, "Jesus fuckin' Christ, Porky!"[12]

In the '60s and '70s, a new generation of fishing guides arrived in Islamorada. They revered Albright, Brothers, and Williams and observed their dynamic at the Lorelei and elsewhere with keen interest — not daring to crash the inner circle but eager for any crumbs of wisdom or acceptance that might be thrown their way.

For all his camaraderie with the guides, though, Williams mostly fished alone. One of his favorite spots — still known as Ted's Hole — lies south of Islamorada, about half a mile off Long Key. He knew that on certain tides, he could count on plenty of fish running through there, and guides would frequent the Hole, too — but only when Ted wasn't there, of course. He'd also fish an area called the Pocket, on Buchanan Bank, seven miles southwest of Islamorada, a highly desirable spot that was occasionally the source of turf disputes among the guides. The Pocket was where they sprinkled Jimmie Albright's ashes after he died in 1998 at the age of eighty-two.

Ted could also be seen poling himself around the mudflats and the mangroves like a gondolier, or even just sight fishing off his dock on Florida Bay. One friend of Ted's from Boston who wintered in Islamorada for years, Dan Pitts, marveled at the show Williams put on one afternoon off his dock, pulling in one bonefish after another.

"You have to see them in order to catch them—if you don't you're just throwing the line in," said Pitts. "We were out there one day, and Ted said, 'Here they come, two o'clock, forty feet out.' I've got polarized glasses on, and I don't see a goddamn thing. So he throws his line out, and *boom!* Bonefish are the fastest-hitting fish in the ocean, so he got that one. Once again we're waiting, and they call it mudding, they put their jaw in the sand, so you see that little wave of cloudiness, that's how you see them. So the second time he says, 'Here they come again, one o'clock, fifty feet out.' Again, I can't see them. He says, 'Jesus Christ, are you retarded!' And *bam!* He pulls a second one out. Then here we go again: 'You ready? Thirty, thirty-five feet at three o'clock.' I didn't see them, but I know where three o'clock, thirty to thirty-five feet out is, so I cast it out there, and he says, 'About friggin' time!' But I still couldn't see the fuckin' fish anyway. That guy had eyes like there's no tomorrow."[13]

As Pitts's experience suggests, Williams was less than tolerant of people who couldn't fish well after he'd taken the time to show them how. He exploded at a local kid who, he felt, hadn't listened closely enough, screaming and declaring the boy illiterate. Another time, local artist and neighbor Millard Wells was visiting Ted at his house when the phone rang. On the line was a friend who wanted to go fishing. "Ted said, 'Well, if you can't fly-fish any better now than you could last time, why don't you just stay home?' and he slammed the phone down so hard it bounced off the cradle."[14]

But those flare-ups were leavened with acts of kindness that became well known on Islamorada. When guide Gary Ellis wanted to launch a fishing tournament to benefit those who suffer from cystic fibrosis, Williams provided key support, which attracted other big names, and today the tournament generates more than $1 million each year. When a local boy, Billy Bostick, needed money for a lung transplant, Ted got involved and helped raise $250,000 for the operation. When Jimmie Albright fell on hard times toward the end of his life and needed a new roof on his house, Williams gave a contractor $10,000, along with instructions not to tell Albright where the money came from. And when Frank Brothers, Jack's son, got married and needed to buy his first house, Ted gave him $10,000 as well.

To fish with Williams was to understand four things: he was a perfectionist, he was better than you were, he was a needler, and he was in charge.[15] If you were a guide or otherwise an expert, fishing with Williams could be delightful. Otherwise, it would likely be disastrous. He despised fishing dilettantes and thought the only way to fish was to be all in, to be well prepared, and to know what you were doing. "Ted's major problem, with his famous personality, was he was not tolerant of anybody who was not really good at what they did," said Ellis.* "He was a tremendously precise fisherman. He was a scientific angler who knew everything about every piece of tackle, knew every monofilament, the oscillation of every fly rod. He was just the way he was at baseball. He was very analytical about fishing. He did it very carefully."[16]

As soon as he felt a tug on the line, Williams would switch to battle stations. "When he was pulling on a fish he would use more expletives in one sentence then I'd ever heard in my life," said Ellis. "It was almost poetic. It was lyrical, like him singing a song. He didn't do it vindictively or in anger, he was just being himself, always trying to top himself. It was your mother, my mother, his mother, Jesus fucking Christ, he could have put everybody in there. He wanted the fight, he wanted to see them eat the fly, he wanted to see how quick he could turn 'em around and stop 'em. He just wanted to pull on 'em and then turn 'em loose."

Catching a fish, Williams would pull the rod quickly in three quick bursts to set the hook, then he would check the drag. During the fight, he would use his own body as a check against the fish's strength and work to decrease its supply of oxygen. He thought using heavy equipment was taking the easy way out, and that the challenge lay in doing the job with lightweight tackle.

Ted came to prefer fly-fishing to other kinds of fishing, but he was not a purist who insisted on a fly. He enjoyed, and was expert at, all kinds of fishing, whether it was for marlin, tuna, or bonefish. He was not just a fisherman. He was an angler who mastered everything associated with catching a fish.

In Islamorada, when he was not fishing or shooting the breeze with the guides, Williams could generally be found in the small shed in back of his house, where he would spend hour upon hour tying flies. Occasionally he would receive guests there who could talk fishing with him or trade gossip on the comings and goings of tarpon and bonefish.

Ted was known for a particular kind of tarpon fly that he made. He would drill a hole one-sixteenth of an inch in diameter in the tail of a

---

* In the early '60s, while shooting a film for Sears, Ted had expertly maneuvered a tarpon directly into his boat for the benefit of a photographer stationed in an adjacent boat, only to find that the photographer hadn't been ready and had missed the shot. Enraged, Ted paid the man on the spot and sped off, telling him to find his own way home.

wooden plug, then tie a variety of colored feathers on different nails that would be inserted into the hole. So there would be a yellow feather, a red, a black, a brown—a variety. Tarpon are known to favor particular colors depending upon the light or whatever their whim may be at a given time. If a fish refused yellow, Ted would take it out and push in a red, and so on. It was a method of giving the fish what it would take, offering it options. In his shed, he also liked to demonstrate his skill at tying knots, which, he would tell visitors, were the envy of any guide.

Other serious fishing discussions were held in Williams's second-floor den, where he liked to entertain. There were plenty of fishing photos on the wall but few that featured baseball. The living room downstairs was a neutral zone he shared with Louise Kaufman. Ted's pals hoped to be invited up to the second floor. If they stayed on the first floor, they realized it would be a short visit. There was a phone in the house, but it usually was not plugged in, so Williams could avoid the distraction of incoming calls. If he wanted to call someone, he'd plug the phone in.

Fishing dominated the conversation, certainly, but Ted was also intellectually curious, and when visitors came to call, he liked to engage them in a free-form discussion on a variety of topics. For example, when John Underwood arrived in the summer of 1967 to report his "Fishing with the Kid" piece for *Sports Illustrated,* Ted wanted to talk about the Vietnam War, technical aspects of photography, boxing, and the recent book on Ernest Hemingway by the celebrated author's friend and confidant, A. E. Hotchner.

Edwin Pope, the *Miami Herald* sports columnist who was there that day, said Williams opined that Hotchner's book *Papa Hemingway: A Personal Memoir* was "good stuff."[17] The book, besides revealing that Hemingway's death in 1961 was a suicide, contained remembrances of what Hotchner and his friend discussed over the years—including Hemingway's view that the Yankees' Whitey Ford must have had a "death wish" when he pitched to Williams and that Ted and Joe DiMaggio knew how to quit when they were on top. If Ted was resentful that Hemingway had omitted him and touted "the great DiMaggio" in *The Old Man and the Sea,* he didn't say so. Williams once had a date to fish with Hemingway in Cuba, but, as he told friends, the rendezvous was "broken up by Fidel Castro."[18]

Ted's two-story, two-bedroom white stucco house on Florida Bay, separated from the road by a chain-link fence and a grove of rubber trees, was his second on Islamorada. The first, on the ocean side of the

Overseas Highway, was largely destroyed by Hurricane Donna in 1960, after which Ted sold the property to a Chicago businessman for $28,500.

Williams was a fixture around the village, at the drugstore, and at the grocery, where his booming voice signaled his arrival and could be heard two or three aisles over. He usually dressed in long khaki pants and a white T-shirt, an outfit he was reluctant to change for anyone or any occasion. At the Cheeca Lodge, Islamorada's upscale resort, the women wore long gowns at night and the men were required to wear ties. One evening when Williams showed up in his usual khakis and T-shirt getup, he was turned away. So Ted went home, put on a tie, and returned, still in the same khakis and T-shirt. They let him in, and after that, the Cheeca dress code was effectively broken.

By the early 1970s Williams had caught more than one thousand tarpon to go with his one-thousand-plus bonefish, so he began to turn most of his fishing attention northward, to his camp along New Brunswick's Miramichi River, one of the most important breeding grounds for Atlantic salmon in the world.

Ted was increasingly enamored of the Atlantic salmon, and he was fond of saying that if he could only choose one fish to pursue, that would be it. It had size, it put up a terrific fight, it took great skill to catch one, it was good eating, and it had that great spawning story: hatching way upriver, maturing for about three years—if it could survive an array of natural predators in and around the river—then shooting downstream and out to sea, only to contend with another raft of threats. If it withstood the new dangers, after a few years it returned to the very same river it came from, making its way against astronomical odds to the exact same location from which it was spawned.[19]

The prime fishing season on the Miramichi went from June until October, and as the season got under way in 1978, Williams—who kept a handwritten journal spanning two volumes detailing his catches and conditions along the river over the years—wrote that he had caught 947 Atlantic salmon.

When he first traveled to the Miramichi in the mid-'50s to promote fishing for New Brunswick tourism officials and to make the film for General Electric, Ted hadn't particularly liked it. It seemed too crowded with other fishermen. "But then I made another trip and got a big one, a 20-pounder," he told a reporter from the *Los Angeles Times*. "It was quite apparent that if I really liked it I'd better get a place of my own because everything was private property. So I bought a mile of river. I spend the summers there and leave in the fall and can't wait for June. I live the whole year for those three months."[20]

Non-Canadians had to hire guides to fish the Miramichi, and Roy Curtis, two years younger than Williams, was the one assigned to Ted on a 1958 trip. Thus began Curtis's thirty-year hitch—along with his wife, Edna—as guide, caretaker, and custodian of Ted's camp overlooking the Miramichi. Roy died in 1988.

As he did with the Islamorada guides, Ted developed a close relationship with Roy based on competition and needling. Williams would keep a running tally in his log of how many more fish he caught than Roy, reporting with relish the daily or seasonal score to family and friends. At times, Ted felt that Roy had not shown him the proper respect or deference after he executed some skilled maneuver or another on the river, and the result would be a standard Williams broadside.

Once, early on, after Ted popped off at something or other, Curtis announced, "Mr. Williams, I'm not going to take this from you," and started walking away. He didn't understand that Ted wasn't mad at *him,* just mad at the world over whatever it was that was frustrating him at that moment. As Curtis walked away, Claudia Williams recalled, Ted was mortified. "Dad was like, 'Don't leave! Come back! I'm not mad at you!' He was just mad that the car stopped, or mad that the car got stuck, or whatever it might have been. He wasn't mad at you, but he would still scream and curse a streak that people would say, 'Oh, my God. I've got to get away from this.' "[21]

Over the years, Roy, a native guide and student of the salmon, came to be amazed at how accomplished a fisherman Williams was and duly gave his opinion to visiting journalists who came to chronicle the Kid's exploits along the river—among them John Underwood, who was told, "Forty years and I ain't seen none better, no. There's days a feller can beat him, maybe. But day in day out he's the best. He can do it all. He can tie the best flies, rig 'em just right. He can cast to the toughest spots. He can cover more water than anybody. He knows exactly how to play a fish and he has a fine steady hand to release 'em, and that's an art, for sure. Sometimes I sit on the bank and never lift a finger.... And persistent? Oh, my. He'll stay out there all day, any kind of weather. Stay and stay."[22]

If Curtis quickly recovered after experiencing Williams's brusqueness, it took some of the other locals considerably longer to accept Ted. "When he first came up here, he was a little arrogant—that's what people on the river felt," said Jack Fenety, former president of the Miramichi Salmon Association, a conservation group Williams became involved with. "He wouldn't speak to people, and if he did, it was to say, 'Get the hell out of the way; what the hell are you doing fishing my water?' He was antisocial, and people knew his record with the press in Boston, so they took him at face value. I think people thought if the press did not like him and he doesn't like them, he can't be a good fellow."[23]

Another early Williams faux pas on the Miramichi came when he had a run-in with W. W. Doak, owner of one of the leading tackle shops in the area. Recalled W.W.'s son, Jerry Doak, "The altercation occurred because Ted had quite a mouth on him; he was brash and profane, so my dad drew his attention to it a couple of times when he was in the store and told him, 'If you can't control your mouth you'll have to leave.' . . . Ted was used to doing whatever he wanted whenever he wanted and wherever he wanted, and it didn't work like that up here. That was pretty much the river's approach to Ted—it was not impressed by his celebrity. Had he been a hockey player maybe it would have been different."[24]

Williams belatedly picked up on criticism that he was putting off some of the locals and made some adjustments to become more welcoming. He got to know his neighbors along the river and stopped shooing away people who fished in his pools. But the main reason that Ted grew to become a highly respected figure along the Miramichi was that he turned into an ardent, if not militant, conservationist on behalf of the Atlantic salmon.

Williams had become involved in fishing conservation early on. As far back as 1961, he was calling for limits on saltwater game fishing and was using his platform at the annual sportsmen's show in Boston to urge outdoor writers to crusade against pollution in rivers, streams, and oceans. Then in 1971, Williams and Bing Crosby headlined a gala at the Waldorf Astoria in New York to focus attention on the fact that Danish commercial fishermen were killing huge numbers of salmon in their North Atlantic feeding grounds.

"I'm here because I want to try and help save the greatest fish that ever swam," Williams said. "The problem is simply this. A small number of Danish commercial fishermen operating off the Davis Strait near Greenland are taking huge quantities of young salmon in their North Atlantic feeding grounds. If something isn't done to stop it, there will be no more salmon for the sports fishermen in North America and Europe."[25]

The Danes eventually agreed to phase out the fishery off Greenland, but Williams kept up his advocacy on behalf of the Atlantic salmon, making speeches to business groups from his platform at Sears and assuming a leadership role in the Miramichi Salmon Association. The association held its annual meetings in a Boston suburb, and Ted helped generate extensive news coverage of the many threats to the Atlantic salmon: abuse by Indians of their traditional fishing rights, poaching, and excessive incidental catching by commercial fishermen off New-foundland of salmon bound for their home streams. Williams would also talk with local game wardens regarding the need to educate people about the importance of Atlantic salmon to the economy of New Brunswick. To raise the chances that a released fish will survive, he told *Popular Mechanics* in 1989 that he had recently started to file the barbs off his hooks, and he advocated mandatory saltwater licenses for all sport and commercial anglers with a fee that would cover "hard-nosed law enforcement and restoration work." Though he said he was "basically conservative" and "against government meddling whenever possible," he felt these steps were needed to save American sportfishing.[26]

In the fall of 1993, Williams told the *Telegraph-Journal* of Saint John, New Brunswick, that he was "going to cut my throat right here" if the Canadian fisheries department and law enforcement did not do a better job of enforcing existing laws. Canada required fishermen to release adult salmon to bolster the breeding stock, but Ted said too many anglers were keeping the fish. "All they're thinking of is getting the big fish now," he said. "Screw the river, get the fish."[27]

This over-the-top outburst caused a flap throughout New Brunswick and beyond, leaving Jack Fenety of the Miramichi Salmon Association to put out the fire. "Ted made these wild statements to the press, and they were all over me," said Fenety. "So I said to them, 'He's a John Wayne type. No matter what he says, it's good publicity for conservation and good for the salmon.'" But Williams was who he was, and toning things down was not always his style. When a local judge let off a salmon poacher with a slap on the wrist, Williams railed against the judge and said he should be "hanged," and that caused another fuss. When the Canadian Broadcasting Corporation did a program on the endangered state of the salmon, Ted gave the network an earful on abuses by com-mercial fishermen.*

---

* In appreciation of his conservation efforts, the Canadian government later gave Williams a fishing license, enabling him to avoid the requirement that foreigners hire local guides, but Ted continued to use Roy Curtis. After Roy died, Ted employed his son Clarence.

In the winter, Williams would give Roy Curtis $10,000 to keep an eye on the camp and shovel snow off the roof. In season, besides serving as Ted's fishing guide, Roy would do chores around the house. In the mornings, Ted would usually be up by five o'clock and head to his work-bench in the basement to start tying flies. The Williams-preferred fly for the Miramichi was the double-hook Conrad, size 8. Another of Ted's favorites he called the Stoplight, which was a variation on the multi-colored fly he made in Islamorada for the tarpon, and then there was the Whore, though his journal entries didn't explain why he called it that.

Roy and his wife, Edna, lived two or three miles down the road and would appear by 7:00 a.m. or so, and Edna would fix a huge breakfast. If he had guests, Ted would emerge from his basement and rouse them for the meal by playing reveille — without a bugle — which would often morph into "The Marines' Hymn." Edna, who also did the housekeep-ing, cooked three meals a day for Williams, and they would all eat breakfast and dinner together. For lunch, she would fix Ted and Roy salmon-salad sandwiches that they took out on the river with them. For breakfast, Williams liked Red River oatmeal, or eggs, or French toast, and lots of bacon, no matter what the main dish was. For dinner, Edna would make meat loaf, pork chops, steak, roast beef, chicken, or liver. Ted loved liver. They would eat early, around 4:00 p.m., because Wil-liams liked to go back out and fish until dark. Then, returning home, Ted would plop down on a king-size couch facing a Franklin stove and listen to the Red Sox game on the radio. The reception in eastern Can-ada was usually poor, and sometimes he'd have to strain to pick up the voices of the broadcasters.

Of the various pools along the river that Williams owned or leased, his favorite was called Swinging Bridge, named after a working foot-bridge that had spanned the river at that point but was destroyed by an ice storm in 1970.

Ted and Roy would take the pickup truck to reach Swinging Bridge, about fifteen minutes away, and Williams made sure to load the neces-sary equipment: waders, angling vests, rods and reels, rain gear, and an extra rod. You never knew when a tip might break, and an entire day of fishing could be ruined without a spare.[28] He was a stickler about his fishing tackle. Before going out, he would take reels apart to make sure all the bearings were free, leaving nothing to chance.

In 1972, Ted told a crew that was making a film of him for Sears that he usually fished eight hours a day and made a thousand casts. He cast right-handed — the way he threw, not the way he hit — with power and ease.

He said his normal cast was sixty-eight to seventy feet, but occasionally he would go to ninety if he needed to, depending on the conditions. He used an eight-and-a-half-foot rod, and usually cast at a forty-five-degree angle from the direction of the river, or the direction of the wind.

On August 30, 1978, his sixtieth birthday, Williams reported in his log that he had caught his one thousandth Atlantic salmon a few days earlier. Red Smith, the *New York Times* sports columnist, had been a guest of Ted's a month earlier and wrote three columns from the Miramichi, using as one of his pegs the Kid's approaching Triple Crown of fishing. Smith concluded that Williams's "fly rod is a deadlier weapon than his bat used to be."[29]

Williams's camp sat in a grove of white birch trees on a hill overlooking the fast-moving river about 150 feet below. There was a main lodge and a small guesthouse. In the main cabin, over the front door leading out to the porch, was a wooden sign that read: GIVE US THIS DAY OUR DAILY SALMON.

Guests were a fixture at Ted's place, and they all had to be mindful of the house rules: this was his camp, his river, and things had to be done his way. One had to totally submit to the Williams treatment. Typical was the experience of Sammy Lee in 1993. Lee is a bass fisherman from Alabama who hosted a syndicated radio show on fishing called *Tight Lines with Sammy Lee*. He'd gone to Ted's house in Florida to interview him for his program. What Lee expected to be a thirty-minute inter-view lasted eight hours, then Williams invited him up to the Miramichi.

Lee was an expert bass fisherman, but he had never fly-fished, so he consulted some friends in the know and bought some brand-new fly rods and related gear for his trip to New Brunswick. When he arrived, Ted said to him: "Let me see what kind of junk you brought. Hell, you can't catch a fish with that. It's not worth a damn."

After breakfast the first day, at which Lee said Ted ate five eggs and a dozen pieces of bacon, it was time to go fishing. Lee gathered up his gear and headed toward the river when Williams stopped him short.

"Where you going?" Ted said. "You ain't getting in my river today. You haven't earned the right to get in my river."

"I just flew halfway around the world to get here," Lee protested mildly.

"Sit on the bank and see what you learn by watching," Williams said.

So Sammy grabbed his camera and spent his first day wading out into the river to take pictures of Ted fishing. Williams, also an accomplished photographer, proceeded to question Lee about his camera technique.

The second morning, Sammy finally got his chance to fish, but Williams refused to let him use the new gear he had bought. "You're not gonna use that crap," Ted said. "You're gonna use my rod and reel." Williams then kept up a running commentary and critique lasting the next two hours. No matter how good the cast, no matter how long the distance, there was always something deficient. Finally, Williams evicted Lee from his position: "Kid, fish down to the bend of the river."

"So I'm making casts," Sammy recalled, "stripping line, and I come to a rock in the river, and not thinking, instead of backing up I try to step over it, and just as soon as I raised my left leg the undercurrent caught me and flipped me upside down. My head was straight down and my feet were straight up, and my only thought was, 'Even if you drown, do not let go of this rod and reel,' because it was Ted's, and I was not about to lose Ted Williams's personal rod and reel. I lost my sunglasses, my hat, my waders were full of water, and I get up finally, and I look over at the beach." Williams was looking on, bemused, along with his guide, Roy's son Clarence.

"Get your ass up here," Ted called out to him. "That was good for you. Teach you some respect for the river." When they took their lunch break, Lee asked Clarence why he hadn't come out to help him. "Clarence said, 'I jumped up to help you, but Ted said, "Let the son of a bitch drown—as long as he doesn't lose my rod and reel. If he loses it, I'm gonna kill him, and he'd better hope he drowns." ' "[30]

At the end of fishing season on the Miramichi, it was always difficult for Ted to leave. The river closed on October 16—always too early for Williams.

"Every fall going home, he'd leave crying, almost," said Edna Curtis. "He'd just have to leave, get out the door, and go. There'd be tears in our eyes, too. He'd give me and Roy a big hug. I worked with him for thirty years. He really thought a lot of us—we a lot of him, too. He'd be awful lonesome, leaving. He really loved to fish."[31]

26

Being Ted Williams

If fishing was the act of a loner, much of Ted's life in retirement had a decidedly public dimension in which he happily starred in the iconography of being Ted Williams.

He did not recede, out of sight and out of mind. On the contrary, after baseball, Williams had a vibrant second act. While most star athletes, or the stars of any endeavor, fade into obscurity in retirement, Williams, paradoxically, saw his fame grow after his playing days were over.

Visiting Boston later in life, he was always surprised but gratified by the affection with which he was received. The tide of public opinion had shifted in his favor abruptly in the late '50s, toward the end of his time with the Red Sox, after he had ridden out the uproars caused by his rages—the gesturing, the spitting, the popping off. And then his popularity surged again as he took his leave.

Williams "succeeded in bending life to his own prodigious will," as the writer Michael Gee put it in a prescient 1983 piece for the *Boston Phoenix*. "The spectacle of someone forcing his own terms on the world around him is rarer by far than the sight of a home run. The most famous baseball heroes have often come to sad ends. Ruth and Gehrig died prematurely and in horrid pain. Ty Cobb died alone, a clinical psychotic. In their 50s Mickey Mantle and Willie Mays, while hardly sick or broke, are less than imposing figures as casino shills in Atlantic City. But in 1983, Ted Williams flowers. His public recognition of his status as a revered elder statesman isn't the act of a man coming to terms with age, but rather a kind of gracious acceptance of the world's inevitable surrender to Ted Williams."[1]

Ted remained an active fan of baseball and became one of the game's leading goodwill ambassadors. He returned to the Red Sox as a hitting professor emeritus after a decade's absence, during which he managed the Washington Senators and Texas Rangers, then awaited an invitation home to the club he had spent his career with. He came back to Coopers-town as an involved immortal, and to Fenway Park to be reembraced by Boston again and again. He returned to San Diego to reconnect with his roots and with childhood friends. He dabbled in, but was not consumed by, the memorabilia business. He continued, and finally was acclaimed for, his mostly anonymous good deeds on behalf of the Jimmy Fund and kids stricken by cancer. And in 1991, the fiftieth anniversary of his sub-lime .406 season was celebrated at the White House and beyond, kicking off a decadelong spate of honors for Williams in which he was hailed as a national monument and "Father Baseball." In the process, he learned how to receive and return love.

It was the exalted .406 milestone, of course, for which Ted was most acclaimed. After posting the number in 1941, he had never thought he might be the last major leaguer to hit .400. Yet years went by, then decades, and no one else had done it. In some ways, this was unsurpris-ing. The rise of relief pitching as a specialty has meant that fewer pitchers go a full nine innings and that hitters have to face fresher arms. Hitters have also had to contend with new pitches, such as the slider and the cut fastball, and they face each pitcher fewer times, thereby getting less of an opportunity to learn their tendencies. Other factors in the demise of the .400 hitter include the fact that hitting for a high average has lost some of its luster as players see that more prestige, money, and glamour flow toward the home-run hitter and as other measurements, such as slugging percentage and on-base percentage, have come to be considered better indicators of hitting ability. More night games and more demanding travel have also probably militated against higher batting averages. Finally, today's season runs 162 games — eight more than Williams and his .400 predecessors played. But Ted would constantly be asked if he thought some player or another was up to the challenge, and Williams would say yes, he thought so.

In the summer of 1977, when Rod Carew, the Minnesota Twins first baseman, was making a serious run at the .400 mark, Williams indulged *Sports Illustrated* and his pal John Underwood by doing a feature for the magazine (which Underwood ghostwrote) headlined I HOPE ROD CAREW HITS .400. Ted said there were three reasons he felt this way: First, he wouldn't have to answer any more questions about whether he thought it could be done, and he could fish in peace. Second, he'd been saying for more than thirty-six years now that someone would hit .400, and he'd like to finally be proven right. And third, he said, "Carew's a damn good hitter and a deserving one, and if he does it, it has to be a great stimulus for baseball. I have a feeling he might."

Ted critiqued Carew, calling him the best hitter for average in the majors but one who flew under the radar because he was a prototypical singles hitter. Yet he had good form, good plate coverage, and a quick bat, and was a classic straightaway hitter—the kind of player who traditionally attains the highest average. Hitting ran in cycles, Ted pointed out, rising or falling with the quality of the pitching. In 1941, he had benefited because a lot of the name pitchers in the American League were past their prime. By 1977, major-league expansion and a decline in minor-league quality had diluted pitching. In addition, the ball seemed livelier, and they had lowered the pitching mound and reduced the size of the strike zone in an effort to boost hitting. All these factors augured well for Carew.

But in general, Williams was less hopeful about his record being easily broken, claiming (as he had for many years) that the current crop of ballplayers had numerous distractions, too much time on their hands, and made so much money they could be complacent. "In my case, nothing else mattered but the hitting," Ted said. "I lived to hit. I was willing to practice until the blisters bled. And then I practiced some more. A trip to the plate was an adventure—and a time to store up information too. I'm as dumb as a lamppost about a lot of things, but I think I learned a lot about hitting."

As it turned out, Carew, who was then thirty-one, fell short and finished the year with an average of .388, the same figure Ted hit in 1957, when he was thirty-nine. Williams's sentiments and good wishes toward Carew were nonetheless gracious, especially since comparing the two men was an apples-and-oranges exercise. After all, Ted had 429 more career home runs than Carew, a slugging percentage more than two hundred points higher, and an on-base percentage nearly one hundred points higher. But Ted's cheerleading for Carew and his willingness to participate in the magazine feature revealed a beguiling selflessness, his love of the game, and a desire to stay involved in it—especially when measured against Joe DiMaggio, who never did anything comparable when anyone hit safely in thirty-odd games and had designs on his streak.

★   ★   ★

In the winter of 1978, Williams was attending the annual New Hampshire writers' dinner in Manchester and gave a radio interview in which he said he'd like to get involved in baseball again as a coach working with young hitters. Al Rosen, the Yankees president, was on hand and heard Ted's remarks. He approached Williams after the interview, and the two had an animated discussion.

Rosen took down Ted's contact information. Three days later, New York owner George Steinbrenner was in Boston proclaiming a great scoop: the pride of the Red Sox was going to work for the Yankees. Boston general manager Haywood Sullivan, racing to avert a public relations fiasco, quickly called Ted and said he thought his place was with the Red Sox. Williams, who hadn't signed anything with New York yet, agreed. He'd just been waiting for his old team to ask.[2]

When Ted showed up in Florida for the first day of spring training at the Red Sox camp in Winter Haven, it was like the old days. Scores of writers were on hand to see and photograph the Kid put on a Red Sox uniform again for the first time in eighteen years. At 245 pounds, he was more than fifty pounds north of his playing weight, so equipment man Vince Orlando fit him into a pair of pants with an elastic waistband to accommodate his girth. The players and Sox manager Don Zimmer were totally upstaged as a smiling Williams held a full-dress press conference in which he said it felt "pretty damn good" to be back in a Boston uniform, "the only uniform I'll ever want to wear."

Elaborating on his return to the Sox, Williams told Thomas Boswell of the *Washington Post* that he'd missed baseball since quitting as a manager in 1972, and he'd especially missed the Red Sox. "This is the uniform I should never have taken off," he said. "You're always a fan of this game after you played it. You enjoy being around it, listening to the young guys in the clubhouse. This is my chance to be up close to the game for a few weeks. I'll leave when the rookies are shipped out. But it's enough to give me an interest in the game again."

Getting down to business with Red Sox hitters, Williams focused his attention on first baseman George Scott, who was known as the Boomer. Sporting a necklace that he said contained "second basemen's teeth," Scott demonstrated his stance for Ted and insisted that he, George Scott, was "one of the greatest hitters that ever lived."

Smiling, Ted said: "Well, you'd be a hell of a lot greater if you'd open up your front foot so you can clear your hips and get that big rear of yours into the ball."

"Right on, Number Nine," said the Boomer.[3]

Williams had taken up tennis, and when he checked into camp, he'd asked Vince Orlando who the best player around was. Carl Yastrzemski, came the answer, whereupon Ted challenged his successor in left field to a match. This contest attracted plenty of interest—about fifty spectators, some of them reporters—and George Scott volunteered to be the ball boy. There was considerable betting, and most of the money was on Yaz, who, at thirty-eight, was twenty-one years younger than Ted. Though both men had hit left-handed, they played tennis right-handed.

Williams, who took the court wearing a blue warm-up suit and a light blue visor, quickly fell behind, 5–0. But Ted, using chops and spins, came back to make it 5–5. Yaz tried talking some trash.

"You hit [.344] lifetime?" he shouted. "You had a [.634] slugging percentage? You play like a broad."

"Just keep playing," Williams said.

Yaz took the first set 8–6, the second 6–1, and the third 7–5. The match took an hour and a half. Yaz had done the most running and afterward seemed to need toweling off and liquid refreshment more urgently than Williams did.

"The only reason I won was age," he said. "If he wasn't...older than me, I don't think I would have handled him."

"He runs pretty good," Williams remarked. "Better than I thought. But you know what? I play him again, I gotta bet on me. And this time we're going to play for something. No more playing for nothing."[4]

In the summer of 1980, Williams returned to Cooperstown for the first time since his induction into the Hall of Fame fourteen years earlier. This time, he was appearing on behalf of Tom Yawkey, the longtime Red Sox owner who had died of leukemia four years earlier, at the age of seventy-three. Yawkey had been voted in to the Hall posthumously by the Veterans Committee, and his widow, Jean Yawkey, asked Ted if he would accept the award on her husband's behalf.

Williams didn't hesitate. The two men had had a convivial, though not especially close, relationship over the course of Ted's playing days and into his retirement. Yawkey had thrilled to his star's heroics, and Williams had been grateful for the owner's generosity and kindness. They enjoyed talking about baseball, politics (serious Republicans both), fishing, and hunting. Ted had always had a standing invitation to come up to Yawkey's private bar, under the roof along the third-base line, after games. There was a ticker-tape machine there on which the out-of-town scores came through, and these smoke-filled boozefests—where Yawkey, Joe Cronin, their minions, and assorted guests held court and talked baseball—would last until the wee hours of the morning.

Williams liked Yawkey's zest for the game and the fact that he didn't hesitate to avail himself of the boyish perks of ownership. Every morning, for example, Yawkey would get dressed in a baseball uniform (number 44, for the year in which he married Jean) and play pepper with the clubhouse boys. After that he would take batting practice—he was a right-handed batter who could occasionally reach the left-field wall but never clear it. Then he would shower, and if his team was away he and Jean would take a blanket down to the field, spread it in the outfield, and have a picnic lunch while listening to the game on the radio. Fenway Park was their backyard.

Commissioner Bowie Kuhn began the ceremony in Cooperstown by calling Yawkey "one of the most storied executives in the history of our game." Not mentioned, of course, was the owner's most shameful legacy—the fact that, during his tenure, the Red Sox became the last team in Major League Baseball to integrate, in 1959.

Instead, Kuhn and Ted stressed Yawkey's charitable efforts on behalf of children with cancer at the Jimmy Fund as well as his contributions to a hospital and a home for wayward boys in Georgetown, South Carolina, where he had had his twenty-thousand-acre estate.

In his remarks, Williams said that Yawkey was "someone that I loved, and above all he was one of the greatest sportsmen and humanitarians of any era anywhere." Ted added, "There never was a more considerate, kind, or more respected person in the vast empire of baseball."

Williams also offered his congratulations to the three players being inducted that day—Duke Snider, Al Kaline, and Chuck Klein—but the rousing cheers Ted received suggested that he, again, was the real star of the show. After the ceremony, he was mobbed walking through the Hall of Fame and through the streets of Cooperstown, and he seemed delighted to acknowledge being the Kid again. Jean Yawkey later prevailed on him to get involved in baseball's shrine. He joined the Veterans Committee and would become one of its leading voices, using the platform to push his favored issues and causes.

After giving Yawkey his due at Cooperstown, Ted resumed his retirement routine of sporadic forays into the spotlight, the routine of being Ted Williams. Four years later, Williams was back at Fenway to have his number, 9, retired in a ceremony, along with Joe Cronin's number, 4—the first numbers the Red Sox had ever retired. Speaking at second base, near a cluster of well-wishers—including Jean Yawkey and former teammates Bobby Doerr and Johnny Pesky—Ted took the microphone and said, "I wish I had the ability to say what's in my heart tonight." Then waving up toward the seventy-seven-year-old Cronin, who by then was in ill health and in a wheelchair, watching the proceedings from a roof box, Ted said, "I can't tell you how important he was to me. I had understanding from a very, very wonderful man. . . . Baseball is the greatest in Boston and the fans are the greatest—and I salute you."[5] Ted was then driven around the ballpark in a golf cart as he held up a plaque bearing his number and waved to the crowd.

Few lives had been filled with as much pure drama as Ted Williams's, and so there had long been talk of a Ted movie.

Since the early '50s, Warner Brothers had had a standing $250,000 offer on the table for Williams to play himself in a Hollywood spectacular. But he had nixed the idea because the filmmakers naturally wanted to include certain dramatic elements—his personal life, his war service, his tussles with the press, and his efforts on behalf of the Jimmy Fund—that the Kid preferred to avoid. Instead, he wanted only his baseball and fishing prowess featured. Over the years, however, he was persuaded that he would have to agree to more drama if he ever wanted to see his story—at least the version he could control—hit the silver screen. And so in March of 1986, a press conference was called at the Red Sox spring training headquarters in Winter Haven to announce that Ted had signed off on a movie about his life and that the $6 million production would get under way later that year.

James Vinick, an investment banker from Springfield, Massachusetts, with no experience in making movies, had acquired the rights to Ted's life story by giving him a check for $125,000 with the promise of more to come when the film started production and at the back end, depending on how much money it made.[6] Vinick and Williams had become friends through their involvement with the Jimmy Fund (Vinick's son Jeffrey had died of cancer in 1982), and some of the proceeds from the film would benefit the charity.

Vinick recruited an executive producer, Skip Chernov, and, to write the script, John Underwood, who seemed to remain ubiquitous when it came to Williams-related literary and artistic endeavors. Underwood's script would be adapted from *My Turn at Bat,* the book he had ghostwritten for Ted.

Williams took a break from his duties at spring training and showed up for the press conference, along with Vinick, Chernov, and Underwood. "I think it should be honest and fair," Ted said of the movie, which had the working title of *Hitter*. It was apparent he had changed his mind about what could be included in the film: "I've had my ups and downs, good and bad, and I think it all should be in there. However, I know who the bad guys will be," he added, looking at the Boston writers and drawing a laugh.[7]

Of course the reporters wanted to know who would play Williams. "Sam Shepard is the perfect Ted Williams," replied Chernov. "He's moody, antisocial, controversial, introspective and he's had his problems with women. A guy who plays Ted Williams has got to look like Ted Williams. I didn't want Don Johnson to play Ted Williams, no matter how popular he is. We don't want Magnum, P.I. to play Ted Williams. You go down the list of stars, and there's not that many that could handle the role." Ted ventured that he had met James Garner in 1963. "He told me that if they ever made my life's story, he'd play me, but he's gotten older now....I just hope whoever they choose is good looking and a helluva athlete." He said he'd be able to give the actor a hitting consultation. "I'll make a comment if he doesn't get his ass into the ball," Williams said, "but nobody else will know the difference."

Underwood said he would try and keep four-letter words out of the script, as Vinick had promised to avoid an R rating.

Summing up, Ted said the movie would be "the story of a desperate, dedicated kid who wanted to play baseball more than anything else in his life."[8]

Williams knew how he wanted the movie to begin. "It's in a fighter plane, see, flying, from the pilot's eye, over KOREA. Seoul," he told the writer Richard Ben Cramer earlier in 1986 for the memorable *Esquire* profile in June of that year that captured the Kid's voice precisely. Cramer used capital letters to underscore the volume Ted used when saying certain words.

"And it's flying, slow and sunny and then *bang* WHAM BOOOOMMM *the biggest goddamn explosion ever on the screen. I mean* BOOOOOMMM. And the screen goes dark. DARK. For maybe ten seconds there's NOTHING. NOTHING. And then when it comes back there's the ballpark and the crowd ROARING...and that's the beginning."[9]

But the movie was never made. Vinick and Underwood had a parting of the ways. Other scripts by other writers and tentative deals with various studios all fell apart when executives who had been pushing the film jumped to rival studios.[10]

★   ★   ★

In 1987, Ted left the Keys and moved to central Florida, fulfilling the terms of the deal he had made five years earlier with the New Hampshire developers Sam Tamposi and Gerry Nash to be the live-in spokesman for their Citrus Hills development. Islamorada had grown too congested for him, anyway. Besides, now that his Sears contract had not been renewed, he needed the money, and Citrus Hills represented an easy source of income.

Ted was an enthusiastic pitchman. "Hi, I'm Ted Williams," he said, looking into the camera for a short promotional film that Tamposi and Nash ordered up. "If you always dreamed of a place in the sun, come to the outdoor wonderland of Citrus County. Citrus Hills. On Florida's Gold Coast. It's truly a sportsman's paradise. Fishing, golf, tennis, and more. Citrus Hills has something for everyone. Including a spacious country club with the best dining around. I love it. I know you would, too."

Of course there had been many failed and colorful outtakes before that one—aborted attempts in which Ted had botched his lines, kicked over a light stand or two, and railed at "cocksucking, fuckin' syphilitic Jesus." But never mind. It was the finished product that counted, and the lots sold briskly—despite the fact that Citrus Hills really was in the middle of nowhere, a cultural wasteland peppered with strip malls and ominous billboards calling on sinners to repent while they still could: the apocalypse was approaching.

"When he moved to Citrus Hills, we said, 'Dad, there's nothing here,'" Ted's daughter Claudia said. "But he loved it. He moved here for Sam."

Louise Kaufman was happy to have the change of scenery, too, even though some of her tonier friends, like Evalyn Sterry, considered Citrus Hills a crude backwater. As long as Ted was happy, Louise was. They moved into a modest condominium at first, then a model home built along a golf course, and in 1991 to what was considered the prize in the development: a four-thousand-square-foot ranch-style house with three bedrooms, a pool, and a lanai on four and a half acres of land that was surrounded by a grove of tall oak trees dripping with Spanish moss. The house sat atop a hill that was one of the highest points in all of Florida—at 230 feet.

The developers carved out a special street that led to the house and named it Ted Williams Court. In case visitors had any doubts about where they were going, there was a huge gate with a big red number 9 on it blocking access to the driveway. Friends knew the keypad code to make the gate swing open: 1941, the year the occupant hit .406, of course.

One of the first new friends Williams and Louise made was Ted Johnston, the young contractor who built their house on the golf course, and later, the bigger one on the hill. After moving into the first house, Ted had called Johnston, who was in his early thirties, and asked him to come over for a drink. They talked for a while, and as Johnston was getting ready to leave, Ted handed him an envelope. "I want you to have this money," Williams said. "I know you didn't make a lot on this project." When Johnston was about a block down the street, he pulled his car over to look inside the envelope. "It was twenty-five hundred dollars, and it was the smartest twenty-five hundred dollars Ted ever spent," Johnston said. "Every time he called with a problem I went right over there, so he got his money back and more. The longer I was around the better friends we became. They treated me like a son."

Ted took Johnston under his wing and took him fishing in Islamorada, Mexico, the Bahamas, and Belize. Williams advised him to start a travel business focusing on fishing destinations, and Johnston did. "He had a hot temper for some people, but he never raised his voice to me," remembered Johnston. "He was eager to teach, and I was eager to learn. The guy was good with things the general public was not aware of, such as hunting and guns. He could go into the detail of the graining of a bullet, the machining of a barrel, ballistics, velocity, and so on."[11]

Some of Ted's new friends took due note of his temper. "He used to get these terrible tantrums," recalled Frank Inamorati, the local tennis pro, who also became a friend. "He had a loud voice, very penetrating. Once, he got upset in a restaurant and I just put my head down. I told him, 'I'm not gonna subject myself to that anymore.' It was not often, but it did happen."[12]

Ted would call Joe Rigney, a Citrus Hills property manager, if he needed something done around the house, and the needs were frequent, since Williams wasn't exactly handy. "Ted Williams couldn't hammer a nail straight," said Rigney, who as an ex-Marine, a retired Boston cop, and a big Red Sox fan bonded quickly with Ted. "I don't think he'd ever had to, so I got to do a lot of work for him and we hit it off pretty good." One of the reasons they did is because Rigney didn't grovel around the Kid. "I never asked him to autograph balls or pictures, because I knew that bothered him," said Rigney. "A lot of people took advantage of that, and they'd sell them."[13] Williams got friendly with Rigney's son, too. When the boy was killed in a car accident in 1993 at the age of seventeen, Ted went to both the wake and the funeral, one of the few funeral services he had ever attended.

Besides the new friends, there were some familiar faces. Monte Irvin, the former Negro League great who had joined the New York Giants in 1949 and later the Cubs before making it to the Hall of Fame, lived nearby. Ted convinced his old friend Joe Lindia, the Rhode Island restaurateur, and his wife, Dorothy, to move down. And Andy Giacobbe, who had faithfully tended to Ted's televisions at the Somerset Hotel in Boston, moved to Citrus Hills, smitten by his hero's sales pitch.

Other friends found Citrus Hills too isolated to consider buying a home there, and the remote location made for fewer visitors than Ted and Louise had received in the Keys. But Williams still went out on the road a fair amount, continuing to take his bows.

That same year, 1987, Ted returned to San Diego to attend his fiftieth high school reunion. He made the rounds of Hoover High, reconnecting with classmates, signing autographs, and speaking to students.

Several months later, in February of 1988, the year Williams would turn seventy, Sam Tamposi recruited his friend for another endorsement mission — to pitch not another housing development but a presidential candidate.

Vice President George H. W. Bush had just lost the Iowa caucuses decisively to Senator Bob Dole of Kansas. Even the Reverend Pat Robertson had finished well ahead of the vice president and claimed second place. To revive his flagging candidacy, Bush had to win New Hampshire.

Tamposi was close to John Sununu, then the governor of New Hampshire, who was chairman of the state's Bush campaign. When Tamposi suggested to Sununu that they bring in Williams, the governor quickly embraced the idea.

"We tried to take advantage of Ted wherever we could, to be blunt," Sununu remembered. "Just put Ted anywhere there was a line or a lure." The crowds would reach the thousands. "I remember going to a gun show or something in Manchester," Bush recalled with a laugh, "and hell, it was like I did not exist. 'Hey, Ted's coming!' I thought to myself: Wait a minute, the vice president of the United States is here, too." At one event, Ted signed autographs using Bush's back for support.[14] "Ted was what I call a uniform Republican," said Sununu. "His heart and soul was military. He viewed the country as an old soldier would, and as such had a very strong, positive feeling about George Herbert Walker Bush — the Marine and Navy flier."[15]

Bush was thrilled to have the Kid stumping for him. As a teenager at Phillips Andover Academy, outside Boston, Bush had gone in to Fenway Park occasionally, and Williams had been his favorite player. Then their paths crossed in the run-up to World War II, in preflight school at Cherry Point, North Carolina. "I was there in the First Battalion, and everybody was excited that the big hero Ted Williams was coming," Bush recalled. "Then in 1988, we came into New Hampshire really having to win it. Ted came up there and he was great. We'd go out to dinner, and he could be pretty cantankerous, and bawl out the waitress if she did not respond fast enough. He could get a little feisty. Barbara commented on it. But he was a fun guy. With me he was down-to-earth. We talked about sports; politics some, but not a lot. He was fairly conservative and not all that steeped in the particulars."[16]

In the end, Bush won the primary going away, with 37.6 percent of the vote to Senator Dole's 28.4 percent, gaining the momentum he needed to eventually capture the Republican nomination and the presidency. "That's the greatest story of Ted's life — greater than anything he did in baseball," the younger Al Cassidy said. "Ted won that election for Bush."[17] Sununu, a more astute and dispassionate analyst of New Hampshire politics, would not go that far, but judged the "Ted effect" to be considerable.

Bush would always be grateful for Williams's help. He would honor him twice at the White House in 1991, and in 1989, four months into his presidency, he invited Ted to join him in Baltimore for the Orioles' opening day.*

Continuing his goodwill tour following the New Hampshire political interlude, Ted came to Boston to attend a ceremony in which a twenty-mile stretch of Route 9 running west of the city was renamed the Ted Williams Highway. "Over the past many years, I've had a lot of difficulty finding Route 9," he told the assembled crowd, "but if I don't know how to get there now, I won't know what my own name is."

That August, the Kid turned seventy, and in Massachusetts, Governor Michael Dukakis proclaimed it Ted Williams Day. Three months later,

---

* The new president's other guest that day made for an unlikely companion for Williams: Egyptian president Hosni Mubarak.

Ted made one of the most meaningful stops on his Being Ted Williams tour: he came to Boston to be honored for the forty years of work he had put in for the Jimmy Fund. He had been visiting the Dana-Farber Cancer Institute regularly in retirement, sometimes bringing John-Henry and Claudia with him. "When Dad met the kids, it was heartbreaking," Claudia remembered. "He was so careful and gentle with them. Dad was not normally delicate or careful. He would ask them if they liked baseball—even the girls. And if they said no, he'd ask, 'Why not?' in a goofy, sarcastic, smiling way. When we walked the hospital halls, Dad was pretty quiet. I only remember him asking, 'Is he going to be all right? Is he going to make it? How is he feeling? Are they in a lot of pain? Do the parents have insurance to cover all this?'"

When he departed, Williams would glance at the heavens and rage at the injustice of it all. "When we left the hospital Dad was *so* mad," Claudia added. "It was scary to be around him when he got like that. He ground his teeth down and clenched his teeth, and God forbid if anyone around him did anything wrong at that moment. Because then the anger would flow all over us, even for something stupid like dropping our fork at the dinner table."[18]

The Jimmy Fund event on November 10, 1988, was called An Evening with Ted Williams, Number 9, and Friends, and 4,200 people turned out at an ornate old theater in Boston, the Wang Center, to see Williams feted by a slew of admirers ranging from his old pal John Glenn to the Red Sox–loving writer Stephen King.

"It took an awful, awful, awful, awful lot to get me here," Ted told the press before the program began. "I just thought there were millions and millions of people who've done a lot more for this than I have." But friends had leaned on him to accept the honor, not least because $250,000 would be raised for the Jimmy Fund, so there he was, even wearing a tie—though it was a bolo tie, sporting a silver oval clasp with a gold salmon embossed on it.

Besides Glenn and King, the friends of Ted who offered testimonials about him included his old teammates Dominic DiMaggio, Bobby Doerr, and Johnny Pesky; rivals Joe DiMaggio and Bob Feller; fishing pal Bud Leavitt; former House Speaker Tip O'Neill of Boston; President Ronald Reagan and president-elect George H. W. Bush (both via video); and baseball ambassador-at-large Tommy Lasorda, the former Dodgers manager.

Perhaps the most memorable of the testimonials was Joe DiMaggio's. The Yankee Clipper, in contrast to some of the disparaging remarks he'd made about Ted privately, gave Williams his due in public that night: "Absolutely, he was the best I ever saw," Joe said. "I've never seen a better hitter. Not just hit, but power. He was feared."[19]*

John Glenn, who had become a US senator and Ted's favorite Democrat, told the crowd about his fellow fighter pilot's excellence in Korea and of surviving that crash landing. "Let me say just one thing," Glenn said. "Ted only batted .406 for the Red Sox. He batted a thousand for the Marine Corps and for the United States."

When the testimonials were finished, Ted's son, John-Henry, then twenty, appeared onstage with a five-year-old boy named Joey Raymundo. Dressed in a tuxedo and acting on behalf of the Jimmy Fund, Joey, who had leukemia and was being treated at the Dana-Farber Cancer Institute, presented Williams with the fund's gift of an oil painting depicting the Kid in baseball action.

At that, it was Ted's turn to speak. He took out some notes and, to everyone's surprise, a pair of reading glasses, his famed vision having dimmed a bit. "Not a lot of people have seen these," he said of his specs.

Ted spoke of how lucky he had been, and when the emcee asked a question that Williams thought cut too deep, he replied: "You're not gonna make this old guy cry." Then he looked around at his friends who had come to praise him, then out at the audience, and said: "This has been an honor, and I'm thrilled and a little embarrassed." Then he paused and added: "And I want to thank you." There was a catch in his throat, and his eyes welled up a bit.[20]

Being Ted Williams had always meant signing autographs, but starting in the 1980s Ted began charging a fee for his signature as the memorabilia industry emerged to offer aging sports heroes an unexpected source of money.

In his retirement, Williams had constantly been asked if he begrudged modern ballplayers the multimillion-dollar contracts that even .250 hitters were getting. He always said he did not, and more power to them. Still, the windfalls that the red-hot, baby boomer–driven memorabilia market suddenly produced in the late '80s and into the '90s for icons like Ted and DiMaggio had the effect of leveling the playing field somewhat

---

* When Dominic was asked his opinion, he gave his standard diplomatic reply, all the more so because his big brother was watching and listening carefully: "Well," he said as the audience laughed sympathetically, "the best *right-handed* hitter was Joe. But the best left-handed hitter by far was Ted Williams."

and letting the storied old-timers catch up financially with the modern mediocrities.

There were card shows, personal appearances, and various other permutations of the market to be taken advantage of. By the early-to-mid '90s, the Kid and the Clipper could make up to $250,000 for a weekend of signing. Ted couldn't believe how easy the money was, yet unlike DiMaggio, he declined to game the system for all it could bring him.

Williams had started out in 1983 doing a few appearances—one in Connecticut, another in Kansas City—for $1,000 an hour. By 1989, he was making a minimum of $5,000 an hour and attending more shows, like one in Atlantic City that featured all the living players who had hit five hundred or more home runs. DiMaggio refused to sign bats or balls, but Ted would sign anything. Joe didn't bother to look up when he signed to acknowledge his fans, while Ted was engaged, chatty, and willing to pose for pictures.

In February of 1989, for example, more than a thousand people, middle-aged or better, assembled outside Chicago to wait four hours for Williams to sign autographs at $20 each. People were ready with their autograph books, photos, bats, balls, and even an old sign bearing the legend TED's CREAMY ROOT BEER. One man in a Red Sox uniform thrust a baby in Williams's arms and started snapping off pictures, while a blonde posed with him and kept clinging to his arm well after their photo was taken.[21]

Sometimes, if the spirit moved him, Williams would do a signing show for free, as he did in October of 1989 for Eddie Walsh, a retired Boston cop who had gone into the memorabilia business. Ted wanted to help Walsh because the officer had been kind to John-Henry. "The guys in charge of security wouldn't let John-Henry into the ballpark because they thought he was a pain in the ass," Walsh recalled. "I told them his father built Fenway Park and they should let the kid in." Williams's complimentary signing went on for more than two hours.

"I made fifteen thousand dollars," said Walsh. "Ted wouldn't take any money. I gave the Jimmy Fund five thousand dollars. I gave John-Henry five thousand dollars—he was still in college—and the rest to one of my daughters. We had one thousand seven hundred and eighty-three people. Ted was talking to everyone. Sometimes they don't let these guys talk at these shows."[22]

In the early-to-mid 1990s, Ted would ratchet up the number of signing shows he did annually, because John-Henry had taken over his business affairs by then and wanted him to be more active. While Williams often grumbled about the escalating demands on his time, especially as his health started to fail, he was generally a willing participant, motivated by a desire to leave a significant inheritance for his children.

The son's entrée to a position of power and influence over his father was facilitated by the fact that Williams had fallen victim to a memorabilia swindle in 1988, a scam that would cost him dearly.

One day that year, Ted had gotten a call from a man named Vince Antonucci, who ran a baseball card shop in Crystal River, Florida, just down the road from the Kid's new home in Citrus Hills. Though Williams didn't know it at the time, Antonucci was a con man who had been convicted of various charges ranging from fraud to larceny. Antonucci lured Ted to his store, which was called Talkin' Baseball, by saying there was a package there for him that he had to sign for.

After arriving, Williams quickly learned there was no package and that the purpose of the visit was to give Antonucci and his partner, Barry Finger, a chance to talk Williams into entering the memorabilia business with them. Ted was bored and looking for something else to do. He was also naive and credulous, and Antonucci had a clever line of patter. His pitch essentially was that Ted could get off the autograph-show grind and just sign bats, balls, and other items for Talkin' Baseball, which Antonucci and Finger would then market and sell.

Ted agreed to take a one-third interest in the company. Soon Finger and Antonucci were arguing about the direction of the business, and Finger wanted out. Williams bought out his share, at which point he owned two-thirds of Talkin' Baseball.

Ted gave Antonucci $38,700 to buy one hundred cases of baseball cards, but Antonucci promptly put the money into his own checking account and spent it. When Williams noticed that the cards never appeared and that other inventory they had assembled was also unaccounted for, he went to civil court to dissolve the partnership. Antonucci countersued, claiming Ted owed him money from various signings he had done.

Williams went all out and hired Washington superlawyer John Dowd, best known for representing Major League Baseball as chief investigator and author of a report that led to the banning of Pete Rose for betting on games. Dowd, who had grown up in Brockton, Massachusetts, and served in the Marine Corps, regarded Williams as a hero and was thrilled to meet him. But he tried to persuade him to drop the litigation. "I told him it would be very expensive," Dowd said. "He 'goddamned' me a few times. He wanted to do it. I told him he shouldn't. I didn't take the case." Williams called Dowd back a few weeks later. "I was getting this 'Goddamn it, I checked you out. You're the man. You gotta do it.' I said, 'Ted, it's crazy. You don't need to relive this thing.' I went through the costs. 'I don't give a good goddamn' about the money." Dowd tried again to distance himself. "Then he showed up in my office in Washington without an appointment. Down the hall there was all this noise. The place was going crazy. He was signing autographs. The word went through this place like lightning that Ted Williams was here. We've got Red Sox fans all over the place. He said he was not leaving until I took the case."[23]

So Dowd signed on—and, as he predicted, the cost of the case quickly reached the point of diminishing returns for Williams. Ted's legal fees for chasing Antonucci exploded to nearly $2 million, and in the end only a portion of the missing memorabilia was recovered.

In February of 1992, Antonucci was found guilty of grand theft for taking the $38,700 and sentenced to five and a half years in prison and ten and a half years of probation. He got out of prison early, in August of 1993, then violated his probation and began crisscrossing the country selling Williams's forged signatures. He was finally captured in Washington State in 1995 after being featured on television's *America's Most Wanted* program.

After the Antonucci saga, John-Henry would successfully argue that in order to continue to play in a business filled with cheaters and sharks, Ted, a gullible sort anyway, would need to rely on someone he could trust totally. And who could he trust more than his own son?

The Antonucci affair and its attendant expensive misery represented an anomaly from the exalted star turns commonplace in Ted's retirement routine. But the everyday acclaim intensified in 1991, the fiftieth anniversary of his .406 season, for which he would be honored by the Red Sox and by the Bush White House—twice. Harvard University had also hoped to use the anniversary as a peg upon which to hang an honorary degree they wanted to give Williams, but Ted declined the invitation, a decision that underscored his lingering insecurity about not having an education beyond high school.

Harvard and Williams had extensive talks that progressed to the point where the university sent him a detailed letter in February, spelling out the logistical arrangements for the day he would receive his honorary degree—he would have a limousine at his disposal while staying at the Ritz-Carlton in Boston, the president of Harvard would host a dinner the night before for him and the other honorees, at which no press would be allowed, and at the commencement itself, Ted would stand while a citation was read and bask in the applause without having to make a speech.

"This will be a unique occasion in your life," Jack Reardon, associate vice president for university relations, wrote Williams in a February 26, 1991, letter. "Harvard has recognized unique achievement in all fields of endeavor; and you are as deserving of this special recognition as any other winner of a Harvard honorary degree." But Ted ultimately said no.

"We had several conversations," recalled Reardon. "He was always coming back to, 'This isn't the right thing for me. I'd be very uncomfortable. I did not earn it.' And he'd say, 'The biggest mistake I ever made was not getting a college education.' I told him he joined Fred Astaire and Katharine Hepburn among those who turned us down. He laughed and said he thought that was pretty good company."[24]

On May 10 and 11, during a homestand against the Texas Rangers, the Red Sox hosted a weekend Tedfest. On the first day, the team paid homage to the great DiMaggio as well, saluting his famed hitting streak of 1941. The Kid and the Clipper met underneath the center-field bleachers and had a few quiet moments together before they emerged in separate golf carts—Ted's heading toward left field and Joe's through center toward right—and rendezvoused at home plate, where they shared a poignant embrace.

Ted had John-Henry, then twenty-two, and Claudia, nineteen, there that day. He'd arranged for them to throw out the first ball and insisted they spend some time practicing the day before. As their father beamed, they both delivered crisp pitches.

The following day was just for Williams, and 33,196 fans turned out. Each received a folder containing a collage of photos and news clippings commemorating Ted's career. In the Red Sox clubhouse before the game, as Williams bantered with manager Joe Morgan, players like Roger Clemens and Wade Boggs, who had also gotten the Ted folders, were lined up, waiting for him to autograph them. Williams signed and chatted with Boggs, telling him he watched Sox games through his satellite dish in Florida now. He asked why Wade had chased a bad pitch on a three-and-one count the other day. Boggs was stunned to be asked such a specific question, but knew which pitch Ted meant.

"Well, Ted, it was 3–1 and I was looking for a fastball in, and sometimes a fastball can look like a slider, you know, Ted," Boggs explained.[25]

Two of the opposing Rangers also came over to pay their respects. Williams asked one, Julio Franco, how he could hit with such a contorted stance, and he quizzed the other, pitcher Scott Chiamparino, on his knowledge of Bernoulli's principle.[26]

Curt Gowdy, who had called Williams's last home run and toasted him before that game, was to be the master of ceremonies again this day, and Ted had thought carefully about what he wanted to say and do when he addressed the fans. One nice touch, he decided, would be to finally do something he had stopped doing as a player for twenty years: tip his cap to the fans. He confided his plans to John-Henry the night before with instructions not to tell anyone and to get him a Red Sox cap when the time came.

But as he accompanied his father onto the field for the ceremony, John-Henry suddenly realized he'd forgotten to get the hat, so he raced into the clubhouse and borrowed the cap of Red Sox closer Jeff Reardon. Then he came back to the field and discreetly slipped the hat to Ted, who stuffed it in the back pocket of his pants, beneath his sport jacket.

After Gowdy introduced him and the cheers rang out, Williams soaked up the moment, smiled broadly, and, like the showman he was, delivered one of his signature imaginary swings of the bat, clasped hands slashing through the air as the wrists rolled over and the hips turned, still smoothly.

In his remarks, and with the intended hat tip, Williams wanted to bury the hatchet forever with his public, but as he did when he retired that day in 1960, he couldn't resist taking another dig or two at the Boston press.

"I used to get just a little annoyed when some of my teammates would kid me about how lucky a hitter I was, and I didn't mind that because I knew how lucky I was," Williams announced. "But when they started writing, or when they would even intimate in any way that I was hard-headed, that did bother me a little bit. And it really annoyed me when the Knights"—he pointed up to the press box—"elaborated on it in print. That did annoy me a lot."

Then the Kid started his windup. "So they can never write ever again that I was hard-headed, never write again that I never tipped my hat to the crowd"—at this he pulled out the hat from his hip pocket, threw his head back, and laughed, perhaps both in delight at the cleverness of his own gambit and at himself as he could sense the crowd catching on to the caper—"because today, I tip my hat to A-A-ALL the people of New England, without question the greatest fans on earth."[27]

Williams and DiMaggio made another joint appearance on July 9, this time at the White House. The appearance came about because the

All-Star Game that year was to be played in Toronto on the same day, and then-commissioner Fay Vincent had invited President George H. W. Bush to be his guest at the game. Bush suggested to Vincent that they honor Ted and Joe at the White House first with the Presidential Medal of Freedom, then they would all fly together to Toronto on Air Force One for the game.

A problem emerged. It seemed Joe had already received a Medal of Freedom—from Gerald Ford in 1977. "Please thank the President, but I already have one," DiMaggio told Bush's chief of staff, John Sununu—with some delight, according to Morris Engelberg's book.[28] It was agreed both men would be given presidential citations instead, and Williams would get his Medal of Freedom separately later that year. Vincent recalled that when he invited DiMaggio to attend, Joe responded: "Do you want me to come, Commissioner? Is it personal to you?" Joe made it quite clear he was keeping track of favors.[29]

Ted needed coaxing, too. Sununu invited Williams by letter, but received no reply. Vincent suspected that the reason Williams hadn't answered was because he didn't want to wear a tie. Sununu said he wouldn't have to, whereupon Vincent called Ted with that message, and he accepted.

Ted had brought Louise Kaufman with him, and they spent the night before the ceremony in the Lincoln Bedroom. Rob Kaufman, Louise's son, said that was the highlight of his mother's later life. Late that night, Bush suddenly appeared in the Lincoln Bedroom. He wanted to talk fishing with Ted and took him to the adjacent room, to two large dressers. Bush opened a drawer and revealed a gorgeous collection of fishing flies, all beautifully tied in a variety of colors—red, green, orange, and yellow—and made of goose feathers, sealskin, and other exotic materials. Then Bush showed him a collection of reels, and they talked about those. Williams liked a president who knew his fishing.[30]

The morning of the ceremony, a Marine, saying he was risking going to the brig, asked Ted and Joe to sign his white glove. Then Sununu appeared and gave each of them forty-eight balls to sign. Ted cheerfully obliged and plunged into the assignment with gusto, but Joe turned to Vincent and asked, "Is he kidding?"

"He's not kidding," Vincent replied.

Joe fumed, but gave in. "I'm going to do it, Commissioner, but I don't like it."[31]

After a private meeting and photo session in the Oval Office, Bush, Ted, and Joe emerged for the ceremony in the Rose Garden, where a throng of senators, congressmen, White House staffers, and guests, most of a certain age, had gathered for a glimpse of the two great men. Also present was the Louisiana State University baseball team, which was being honored for winning the College World Series. DiMaggio looked characteristically elegant in a tailored dark blue suit, white shirt, and purple paisley tie. Ted wore an ill-fitting gray sport coat, his bolo tie, and blue-gray slacks over brown-and-tan suede saddle shoes.

Bush, the good-field-no-hit former Yale first baseman, was plainly delighted to be in the presence of baseball royalty. He recalled that in 1941, when Ted and Joe had had their sterling seasons, he'd been seventeen, "and like many American kids in those days...I followed those box scores closely, watched the magnificent season unfurl." Then the president turned to DiMaggio. "In those days I was, Joe, a Red Sox fan." The Clipper nodded as Bush, hoping to make amends, added that his brother had been a Yankees fan. "Fifty years later, that '41 season just remains a season of dreams.... Who even now does not marvel at the Splendid Splinter and the Yankee Clipper?

"These genuine heroes thrilled Americans with real deeds," Bush said. "Both men put off their baseball careers to serve their country. Their service deprived them, I think every baseball lover will tell you, of even greater statistics, but also enhanced their greatness in the eyes of their countrymen." Williams, the president added, was "John Wayne in a Red Sox uniform," while DiMaggio "bespoke excellence."

Ted accepted his citation first. "I've always realized what a lucky guy I've been in my life," he said. "I was born in America. I was a Marine. I served my country. I'm very, very proud of that. I got to play baseball. Had a chance to hit. I owe so very, very much to this game that I love so much. And I want to thank you, Mr. President." Williams, the staunch Republican, then looked at Bush and added: "I think you're doing a tremendous job. And I want you to know that you're looking at one of the greatest supporters you'll ever have." The bipartisan crowd laughed.

Then it was Joe's turn. "Thank you Mr. President, ladies and gentlemen," he said. "I'm honored. Thank you so much. And to you LSU players out there, congratulations on your championship. I know the feeling. I've been in one or two myself."[32]

After the ceremony, it was off to Toronto for the All-Star Game aboard Air Force One. Joe was awed by the plane, later describing its interior in great detail for his agent, Morris Engelberg. And the Clipper was anxious to tell Ted that he had already received a Medal of Freedom, to which, as Joe later wrote in his diary, Ted responded that they were now even when it came to medals.[33] This was apparently a reference to the fact that Ted's service record, when all was said and done, was longer and far more substantive than Joe's, because the Clipper had mostly sat out World War II playing ball.

Williams also enthused over the plane and inquired how much thrust the engines put out. While they were airborne, Bush placed a surprise call to Ted's daughter Claudia, who thought it was a prankster on the line.[34] Barbara Bush brought some more baseballs back for Ted and Joe to sign — mostly for the traveling press corps. The amiable Mrs. Bush was harder for DiMaggio to resist than Sununu, so he complied without a fuss this time.

The two talked baseball with anyone who asked. "It was unbelievable," remembered Sununu.[35] "Here were two icons of baseball talking and reminiscing. They were friendly. By that time they had accommodated themselves to each other."

Canadian prime minister Brian Mulroney was on board, and Williams seized the occasion to lobby the startled Mulroney, demanding to know what he intended to do about Indians overfishing the Miramichi for Atlantic salmon.

When the day was finished, DiMaggio told Vincent bluntly that while he'd enjoyed himself, he would never do it again.[36] Later, taking inventory of his various awards, Joe couldn't find the Medal of Freedom that he had received in 1977, so he called Sununu to see if he could get another.

"I said, 'That's almost impossible to do, but I'll do it,'" Sununu said. "I had also gotten Williams and Joe to sign a picture of them and Bush for the president, and I wanted one for myself. So I sent Joe the new Medal of Freedom and the picture, asking that he sign it. He returned the picture unsigned, saying he couldn't sign it." He said when he told Bush about this, the president gave him his own signed photo.

"DiMaggio was revered during his playing years and became more of a difficult personality as years went on, and [it] hurt his reputation," Sununu said. "Ted was aloof during his playing years, but his heart got bigger than ever as he aged. They were just the opposite."

Bush remembered another mercenary moment concerning Joe and the pictures they had taken at the White House. "That one famous picture of DiMaggio, me, and Ted, we had a hundred signed copies and agreed that each would get a third. One of us got thirty-four. Joe didn't want his share." Williams was happy to take the extras, and DiMaggio was happy to provide them — for $500 each. Ted paid.

That November, the president wanted Ted to return to the White House to accept a Medal of Freedom along with nine others, including Betty

Ford and William F. Buckley Jr. But Williams was tardy in responding to the official invitation, again wary of attending another spectacle that would require his wearing a tie.

Commissioner Vincent intervened and, after consulting with Sununu, brokered a deal whereby Williams would attend without having to wear a tie.

John Dowd, Ted's lawyer in the Antonucci affair, greeted Williams at the airport, and they repaired to the Hay-Adams Hotel. Dowd, who, like Williams, was a retired Marine captain, had a stricter sense of decorum than Ted when it came to proper attire when visiting the president of the United States, their commander in chief.

"The morning comes, Ted's wearing gray slacks and a powder-blue shirt, and he's saying, 'I'm not wearing a tie,'" recalled Dowd. "I got everybody out of the room. I said, 'This is your commander in chief. I'm not going over there with you if you're gonna look like Joe Shit the Rag Man.' Then he weakened a little and said, 'I don't even know how to tie the fuckin' thing.' So I tied it. He's mumbling out of the side of his mouth, 'This is the last time.'" Dowd even persuaded the Kid to add a handkerchief to his ensemble.

"At the White House, we go in the north gate. A Secret Service guy yells out, 'Yo, Mr. Williams, you look terrific.' 'I don't want to hear that,' says Ted. Then we're in the receiving line waiting to meet the president. No one can be more gracious than the Bush family. Ted puts me in front of him in the line. I meet the president. Bush says, 'I don't recognize this fellow with the tie on.' Ted had steam coming out his ears.'

"He had a ball. Then, when it was time to leave, as soon as we got out, he ripped that tie and handkerchief off and threw them at me. You can imagine the calls I got asking for the tie. I gave it to John Sununu. I kept the handkerchief."

About two weeks later, Ted suffered a mild stroke.

He had driven the seventy miles from Citrus Hills down to Tampa to meet with Stacia Gerow, his longtime secretary. She lived in the vicinity, and they were scheduled to spend a few days catching up on his mail and other paperwork. When he arrived, he developed a severe headache, which was unusual. Ted liked to brag that he never got headaches.

He checked into a motel and took two aspirin. When the pain persisted, he took two more, and after a while, another two. Then he noticed that he couldn't see normally, especially with his peripheral vision. Though it was only afternoon, he went to bed, and he didn't get up until the next morning, when he decided to drive home and see an ophthalmologist. The ophthalmologist told him he had lost his peripheral vision permanently and recommended that he go to the hospital to determine if he had had a stroke. At the hospital, he was told that he had, and after tests, Williams's carotid artery was found to be 95 percent blocked. He would have to have surgery to clean the vital artery out.[37]

The surgery was booked for mid-January, after the holidays. In the meantime, Williams began pondering his own mortality and decided to take care of one piece of business that was important to him. Though he had talked with his personal attorney in Boston, Robert McWalter, about the sort of arrangements he wanted to have when he died, Ted thought now would be a good time to formalize his wishes in writing.

So he wrote McWalter a letter on December 19, 1991:

Dear Bob,

This letter is to confirm our discussions over the years relating to my desires for funeral and burial arrangements. I feel strongly about what I want and do not want, and I hope you will make my wishes known to Louise and my family at the time of my death.

It is my wish that no funeral or memorial service of any kind be held and that my remains be cremated as soon as possible after my death. I want you to see that my ashes are sprinkled at sea off the coast of Florida where the water is very deep. Naturally, I understand that others may want to have some sort of memorial service, but I do not want it sponsored by my family or you, my friend and professional advisor.

From time to time as we talk, I will give you further details, but for the moment I want to document my present thinking.

Sincerely,
Theodore S. Williams[38]

Ted used "Ted Williams" when he signed autographs. "Theodore S. Williams" was for legal documents or other papers of serious intent. And concerning the arrangements after he died, the Kid appeared to be quite serious.

27

Enter John-Henry

Two days after laying out his wishes in writing for his lawyer, Williams was feeling well enough to travel to Orono, Maine, for John-Henry's graduation from the University of Maine.

It was the first time any one of his three children had graduated from college, and Ted was filled with pride. Dolores, John-Henry's mother, did not attend, perhaps because of tension between her and Ted, but Claudia was there, along with Ted's fishing buddy Bud Leavitt, family friend Brian Interland, Williams's lawyer, Robert McWalter, and Rodney Nichols, a young Maine state trooper who had become acquainted with John-Henry the year before.

When he watched his son walk across the stage to get his diploma, Ted cried. "I had never seen him cry, and I didn't think he knew how," recalled Interland. "But the tears were spurting out, and unabashedly. It was unbelievable to see. He was always a very proud man, and it just hit him—that his son did something that he never did, that nobody ever did in the family."[1]

But when John-Henry showed his leather binder to his father, there was no diploma inside. John-Henry said there must have been a mix-up.

It turned out he was just shy of the necessary credits to graduate, but the university, knowing Ted would be there, let John-Henry walk the line anyway to avoid embarrassment. For Ted, this latest misstep reminded him of John-Henry's previous faux pas—his pretense that he had made the University of Maine baseball team and his entitled escapades in California while living with his Herrera cousins—and it would also be a harbinger of egregious errors in judgment to come. Despite his genuine love for his father, John-Henry would consistently display a pattern of using Ted's famous name to enrich himself or to skate through difficulties caused by overconfidence in his business acumen. This behavior would be abetted by Williams's own love for his son and by the long slack Ted extended John-Henry in an effort to make up for years of neglect.

After young Williams made up the credits the following summer, he presented the diploma to his father with fanfare. "John-Henry put his cap and diploma in a gold-laminated frame, with the graduation program included," Claudia remembered. "Well, you would have thought Dad got the best present of his life. He loved it! Hung it right in the middle of the best place in his office. 'That's my son! He went to college.'"[2]

A year before graduating, John-Henry had gotten his first significant press coverage, a coming-out of sorts, when he was the subject of a feature story in glossy *Boston* magazine entitled "The Kid's Kid." (The phrase would always remain the default position for any headline writer charged with dressing up a piece on John-Henry.) Interviewed while watching a Red Sox game at Fenway Park, Ted's son — described as six foot five and "movie star handsome" — was depicted as privileged but searching for his identity. He was said to be a fixture at Fenway who was allowed to park his car in the players' parking lot and was well known to the front office — as well as to secretaries, ushers, and concessionaires — walking around "as if he owns the place."

The *Boston* writer thought the son was struggling to find a way to make his own mark. "Let's not kid ourselves — Ted Williams's son, that's why you're here," John-Henry told the reporter. "It's going to be fun when — and it will happen some day — when Dad's going to say, 'I'm *his* dad.'" At times, John-Henry's haughtiness was striking: he said he argued with his father about hitting technique, but Ted always had the ultimate comeback: "Oh is that so? I don't see *you* in the Hall of Fame." He knew that escape would be nearly impossible. "I don't know," he told the reporter. "Maybe it's better the way it happened. It's kind of sad sometimes. Not sad, but what the hell. Everything will fall into place. I'm sure of it. Dad's looking out for me. There are a lot of opportunities out there."[3]

Seven months before his college graduation, John-Henry had seized his first opportunity to make money off his father's reputation. In the run-up to Ted Williams Day at Fenway Park in May, he decided to try dabbling in the memorabilia business by exploiting the hoopla surrounding the fiftieth anniversary of .406. Ted reluctantly gave his consent but advised his still-green son to accept the counsel of Brian Interland. Interland had first met Ted in 1951, when he and two other members of his Little League team were plucked out of the stands at Fenway Park to pose for a picture with the Kid and Lou Boudreau. Years later, when he was in college and interning for a Boston television station, Interland tagged along with a reporter who was doing a feature on Williams. The reporter told Ted that Interland had compiled an array of statistics on him over the years. Williams arranged a time for Interland to meet him at his hotel and show him what he had. A friendship developed, and Interland eventually purchased a condominium in Islamorada so he could be close to his hero. Later, he served as a mentor for John-Henry as he grew up.

Interland was as excited as John-Henry about going into the Ted business — if not more so. He fawned over Williams and told him he needed to be marketed as the legend he was. "We were going to do something that nobody had ever done before," he said, "which was really represent a former athlete in a way that no one had. I mean, we'd walk through airports and it was amazing. People thought he was a god." Interland took a leave from his job in the recording industry and he and John-Henry formed Grand Slam Marketing, financed with $60,000 in start-up funds from Interland's business partner, Jerry Brenner.

At the time, the Antonucci debacle was still playing out in the courts, and Williams's legal bills were piling up. He was receptive to the argument that he needed people he could trust to run his affairs. "I just took over where Antonucci kind of was," John-Henry told the *Boston Globe* in 1995. "What I wanted to do was take the fear out of Dad's mind of someone else trying to scam him. If he can't trust me, he can't trust anybody. I'd do anything for him."[4]

Grand Slam started with the limited goal of producing Ted Williams Day T-shirts, and then it expanded into marketing and licensing all things Ted. On May 16, 1991, just five days after the Red Sox honored Williams, Interland seized the commercial moment and arranged for the Kid to appear on the Home Shopping Network to hawk his wares, including baseball cards, autographed balls, a replica of a 1941 Red Sox jersey ($498.75), a commemorative plaque of Ted and Mickey Mantle ($159.75), and a replica of a 1946 World Series press pin ($99.75).

It was jarring to see Williams on the Home Shopping Network, long relegated to the remote precincts of the cable television dial. As a perfectly manicured and bejeweled female hand incongruously caressed each ball and card up for sale, a fast-talking announcer extolled the virtues of the pieces and the value of memorabilia as investment vehicles. An earpiece in Ted's left ear allowed him to communicate with callers. He gave them some inside tidbits, like how he used to weigh his bats constantly and how he used to be able to smell the burning wood on his bat when he hit a ball on the screws.

Other ballplayers—like Pete Rose, Reggie Jackson, and Mantle—had gone on the Home Shopping Network before, but some observers thought Ted should not have stooped. "It was if John Hancock were selling commemorative copies of the Declaration of Independence, as if Ernest Hemingway were hawking signed copies of *A Farewell to Arms,* as if Clark Gable or Humphrey Bogart or Spencer Tracy were peddling plastic replicas of Oscar," wrote *Sports Illustrated*'s Leigh Montville at the time. "The eye had trouble convincing the mind about what it was seeing."[5]

Later in 1991, as John-Henry finished up college, Interland negotiated a deal for Ted with Upper Deck, the baseball card company. The agreement, which was signed in November and ran through the end of 1993, called for Williams to sign up to 2,800 cards over the two-plus years and make himself available for occasional promotional duties. Upper Deck was starting a new line of cards called Heroes of Baseball, for which Ted's card was to be the centerpiece, or "chase card," as it is known in the trade. When a buyer of a Heroes set drew Williams's signed card in the mix, it was said to be worth $500 or more. Ted also agreed to appear at two Heroes of Baseball games sponsored by Upper Deck, the first of which was the 1992 All-Star Game in San Diego.

These were no-heavy-lifting deals, grossing Williams $250,000 for the first thirteen months and $250,000 for the subsequent year. During the negotiations, both sides also discussed a second, even more lucrative agreement. Upper Deck wanted to use Ted as the springboard to start a second company known as Upper Deck Authenticated, which would move beyond baseball cards and enter the larger autograph market of so-called flats—such as photographs, postcards, and lithographs—as well as signed balls and bats.

The Upper Deck arrangements were in sync with John-Henry's plans to broaden his father's commercial horizons. He and various other partners would launch four more companies tied to Ted besides Grand Slam Marketing: Major League Memorabilia, which handled the sale of Ted stuff on the Home Shopping Network; the Ted Williams Card Company, which made specialized themed baseball cards; Global Electronic

Publishing, which produced CD-ROMs about the Kid; and the Ted Williams Store, which sold Ted paraphernalia in a shopping mall outside Boston. Such entrepreneurial flurry represented an attempt to capitalize on the sports collectibles craze of the early-to-mid '90s, a market that was driven in no small part by Williams. "Ted Williams was the first one who made autograph prices soar," said Phil Castinetti, owner of Sportsworld, the largest memorabilia store in the Boston area. "After Ted Williams's autograph got to be hundreds of dollars, everything else went up."[6]

But John-Henry's quick build-out was an overreach, an effort to do too much too soon without a coherent, interconnected business strategy. Among the things he had ignored in his rush to riches was that memorabilia prices were (like prices in general) dependent on scarcity, and the more Ted memorabilia he put out there, the less collectors were willing to pay for it and the fewer items they were willing to purchase. As the saturated market peaked, John-Henry suddenly declared in the press that fully 80 percent of Ted Williams signatures were fakes. With little evidence that this was so, John-Henry proceeded to launch a mostly self-serving jihad to clean up the industry.

"He just burned bridges every place he went," Castinetti said. "Everybody he talked to, everything had to be his way. He'd go to card shows and say, 'That's a forgery; where'd that come from?' And the dealer would say, 'I bought it from you two months ago.'" John-Henry would visit a store, approach a salesman, and demand to know the provenance of a Williams-autographed ball or simply label it a phony in a preemptive strike. He'd do the same at card shows, further alienating a large slice of the collectibles industry.*

Some of John-Henry's tough-guy tack seemed designed to impress his father and convince him that he could succeed in the business world.

"He was a kid who really was wanting his dad's approval, wanting to impress his dad that 'Dad, I'm a good businessman, I'm gonna be here to look after you like nobody else will,'" said Interland, who had watched John-Henry grow up. "He would go down to Florida to be by his dad's side. He'd come back, and they ended up developing the relationship that I think John-Henry always wanted."

---

* Many concluded that John-Henry's effort was merely a ploy to eliminate some Ted signatures from the market in order to enhance the value of the autographs he was generating, but the son denied that. "It's the furthest thing from the truth," he told *Sports Illustrated* for its November 25, 1996, issue. "It doesn't matter what type of forgeries are out there. It's not going to affect the amount of money I make. But when I see people devaluing his autograph, that's not fair."

Ted and his son bonded further in July of 1992 on a trip to San Diego. John-Henry was agog as he watched his father throw out the first ball at that year's All-Star Game and attend a ceremony at which a local highway was renamed the Ted Williams Parkway. Williams made his arrival at the highway ceremony in a black 1940 Ford convertible, and a big crowd surged around him. At another event, Ted donated several of his most important trophies to his childhood friend Bob Breitbard's museum, the San Diego Hall of Champions.[7]

But the highlight of the trip for John-Henry came when Ted took him on a tour of his childhood home on Utah Street.

"There was never a bigger thrill in my life than going into the house where he grew up," John-Henry told Ed Linn for Linn's 1993 book on Williams. "I saw his room. I saw where he slept, and I was there with Dad to see it....I mean, I saw his roots. And that was tremendous."

As for Ted, he looked pained to be back in his old house, filled with all the bad memories. "I remembered how rundown it was until I made enough money so that I could send home and get it fixed up...so that I wasn't ashamed to have anybody come to it."

But Williams brightened up when talking about John-Henry. "We're so close. God, I enjoy every minute of the time I look at him. He's so bright and honest. And so nice. I want all my friends to get to know him."

John-Henry said that starting Grand Slam Marketing had facilitated a new beginning for him and Ted. "I'm spending an awful lot of time with Dad now, which is great. One reason we started this company, it keeps him very involved with me, both ways, and Dad enjoys watching me grow up, and I get to enjoy Dad's company....I want to take good care of Dad. I'm going to be watching him, making sure he's protected. He's too easy, too nice to everybody. I'm a buffer zone for him."[8]

Learning on the fly, John-Henry immersed himself in Grand Slam Marketing. The company rented an office in Woburn, Massachusetts, north of Boston, and John-Henry commuted to work with Interland, with whom he was living. Also in the office were Interland's partner, Jerry Brenner; his lawyer, Albert Cullen III; Anita Lovely—a former Miss Massachusetts in the Miss USA pageant, with whom John-Henry would become romantically involved—and a handful of others.

An early business adviser for John-Henry was an accountant named Clifton Helman. "John-Henry was schizophrenic," said Helman, who was Ted's age and a longtime Williams fan. "One minute he could be the nicest young man and the next the ugliest SOB. Psychologically, he was beaten by his father. I think Ted's fame and greatness had a tremendous effect on John-Henry. I think he suffered tremendously from what he and others thought he should accomplish by comparison. I always told him he shouldn't have to meet those expectations."

Helman soon came to realize that Ted was under financial strain as a result of the Antonucci affair. He would listen in on conversations between Ted and his son when John-Henry put the phone on speaker. "One day, driving home from a meeting with stockholders in Woburn," Helman recounted, "we got Ted on the phone in the car. John-Henry said, 'Dad, we just had a good meeting.' Ted said, 'Son, never mind that. Did you collect any money?' Money was Ted's prime interest."

Money was of considerable interest to John-Henry as well, and he now found himself in a business environment where he could indulge his expensive tastes. He drove a BMW 740i as well as a high-end Porsche. He and others at Grand Slam traveled first-class and stayed in fancy hotels, using expense accounts ultimately drawn on Ted's funds. Said Helman, "His attitude was, 'I'm Ted Williams's son.' He was entitled." He acted as such in ways that were minor but all the more annoying because of their trivial nature.[9]*

In 1993, according to Helman, Ted had a net worth of $2.6 million. This included investments in orange groves, a quarter interest in 2,020 acres of land along the Peace River in southwest Florida, a stake in hotels owned by Sam Tamposi and Al Cassidy, a share in a Boynton Beach, Florida, bank, and investment income. His annual income was $504,208, but his expenses were $522,655. When various other obligations were added—such as gifts, alimony, and support for his children—Williams was paying out $119,000 more per year than he was taking in.[10]

But John-Henry continued to be aggressive—with Ted's money. In December of 1992, he heard that former Boston Bruins great Bobby Orr and Larry Bird, the Boston Celtics star, were going on television to be interviewed together on a popular late-night sports show in Boston hosted by Bob Lobel. John-Henry asked Lobel how he'd like to have the biggest Boston sports icon of them all on his show with Orr and Bird: Ted Williams. Lobel jumped at the offer and agreed to John-Henry's demand that he get exclusive rights to all still photographs coming out of the interview. John-Henry turned the resulting photos of the three legends into a commercial venture in which the "Boys of Boston" shots

---

* Once when Ted was in town and staying with his son, John-Henry borrowed a window air conditioner from the Helmans so his father would be more comfortable. Helman didn't get the unit back until he asked for it two years later.

were marketed by Grand Slam. Orr later complained that John-Henry was shortchanging him on royalties from the photos.

In February of 1993, John-Henry negotiated, with Interland, a new contract with Upper Deck that would pay Ted $2.75 million over three years. This deal superseded the old agreement and allowed the company, under the name Upper Deck Authenticated, to use Williams to expand its franchise into the larger autograph market, covering not just baseball cards but bats, balls, pictures, jerseys, posters, and assorted other paraphernalia. Under the terms of the contract, the seventy-four-year-old Williams had to sign up to twenty thousand autographs the first year and twenty-five thousand each of the following two years. He would get $875,000 in 1993, $875,000 in 1994, and $1 million in 1995.

A few months later, Grand Slam announced the formation of the Ted Williams Card Company, which would market a line of themed baseball cards under the Ted rubric. To set itself apart in the saturated card market, the company would offer a limited number of cards and dispense with the usual statistics on the back in favor of a story about the player or a remark about him from Ted—such as his impression of the short and stocky Yogi Berra the first time he saw him: "I looked at him and wondered who they were trying to fool."[11] Further expanding, the company issued a set of football cards in April of 1994 that featured O. J. Simpson—just two months before he was arrested and charged with murdering his wife, Nicole, and Ronald Goldman.

Realizing that Upper Deck might consider the Ted venture into baseball cards a threat, John-Henry and Interland had gotten the company to sign off on it as part of the three-year deal Ted signed in February. Yet Upper Deck had no idea that John-Henry and his team had been making plans for their own card company for months or that the rollout would happen so quickly. Exacerbating the issue for Upper Deck was the fact that one of its former executives, Tony Loiacono, had been tapped to be a lead player for the Ted card company, based in California.

Ted had told John-Henry that he was happy to help out with the card company—with one big exception. "Ted said, 'Do whatever you want, John-Henry, and if I can help you with my likeness or my autograph, or with anything you want, I'll be glad to help you,'" said Robert McWalter, Williams's lawyer. "'But don't you dare get me financially involved. I don't want anything to do with that card company.'"

However, shortly after this admonition from his father, John-Henry secretly approached Bob Breitbard, Ted's old friend from San Diego, and asked for a $500,000 loan on behalf of the card company. Breitbard, who had inherited a family dry cleaning business, was a wealthy man. He built the San Diego Sports Arena and the Hall of Champions sports museum in Balboa Park, owned the National Basketball Association's San Diego Rockets before the team moved to Houston, and owned a minor-league hockey club. "John-Henry told me he and his father were going to buy out two partners in their card company, and he told me the money would be paid back in four months," said Breitbard. "I did it because of Ted Williams. I didn't consult with him."[12]

There was virtually nothing Breitbard would not do for Williams, so he gave John-Henry a $500,000 check. In turn, John-Henry signed a promissory note on May 23, 1993, pledging to repay the money less than four months later. It was this unsecured, interest-free loan that launched the new card company. Further ensnaring his father, John-Henry, totally unbeknownst to Williams, made Ted the company's primary stockholder.

Like Brian Interland, McWalter was one of the people whom Williams had asked to keep an eye on John-Henry as he started his business career. McWalter had long worked for the Boston law firm of Sherburne, Powers & Needham. Since the early '70s, Williams had been represented in his personal financial affairs by one of the firm's senior partners, William Andres, but by the mid-'80s, Andres handed off the Ted account to McWalter. McWalter established trusts for Ted's children, drafted his will, and worked on various estate planning issues. He came to have relationships with Bobby-Jo, John-Henry, and Claudia, as well as with Dolores Williams and Louise Kaufman. He kept detailed notes on his dealings with Ted and the rest of the Williams clan.

An official at the card company told McWalter he thought the firm was being seriously mismanaged, and when the lawyer began examining its books he found the numbers didn't add up. McWalter set up a meeting with John-Henry at his Brookline apartment and began questioning him closely. After a while, John-Henry told him about the Breitbard loan.

"Dad is the largest shareholder," the son said.

"How did he become the largest shareholder?" asked McWalter.

"I borrowed some money from Bob Breitbard. I told him this money was going to make money real fast, and he'd have his money back fast. He'd be doing it for Dad, and Dad would make a substantial profit."

McWalter reminded John-Henry that Ted had specifically told him he did not want to invest his personal funds in this venture.

"When he sees how much money he'll make, it'll be okay," John-Henry said.

After September, and then October, came and went without the loan being repaid, Breitbard began to get nervous and called McWalter.

"I received a series of calls from Bob saying he had obligations to make. That cash would come in handy, and he couldn't get John-Henry to return a call. I tried to make some excuses for John-Henry," said McWalter. "I asked Bob if he'd had any conversation with Ted about the loan. He said no."

McWalter confronted John-Henry, telling him that he had to liquidate the company. "Your father gets stock worth nothing, and you owe Bob Breitbard $500,000. Look what that's going to do to your father." John-Henry claimed the money would be repaid, and demanded that McWalter not tell Ted anything about the situation. McWalter stated that he had a lawyer-client obligation to explain what was going on to Ted.

John-Henry's face turned ashen. "If you do," he said, "I'm going to jump out this window."[13]

Tension between young Williams and McWalter had been building for some time. An early flash point came in June of 1989 at Ted's cabin on the Miramichi River. McWalter would visit Ted there for days at a time and would sometimes drive John-Henry and Claudia up with him. John-Henry had been staying with Ted's cousin Manuel Herrera in California, and Herrera had thrown him out after he racked up a $1,500 phone bill and generally behaved badly. Herrera had written Ted a stinging letter saying John-Henry was adrift and needed his father's attention. Williams had shown McWalter the letter and asked his advice. "The sense I got was Manny was trying to do John-Henry a favor by telling Ted so that Ted could help him," McWalter recalled. "Ted called John-Henry into the house in Canada and some sort of a battle took place. John-Henry was in tears when he came out."

McWalter also fielded complaints from Dolores about her son during this period. "When John-Henry was in college, I got phone calls from his mother that he was selling memorabilia. He wanted me to distribute money to him from his trust, and I couldn't get a good reason from him why he needed it. He was already getting an allowance. At one point he wanted to open up some kind of a store in Bangor. Bud Leavitt told me we should start a club of all the people burned by John-Henry."

As he got more deeply involved with Ted's memorabilia operations, John-Henry began to question—and resent—the far-reaching power that McWalter, who was the managing trustee of the various Williams trusts and held Ted's power of attorney, had over Ted's affairs.*

Despite this tension with the son, McWalter maintained a close relationship with Williams himself. Ted had his legal affairs in order, so much of their time was spent bouncing ideas around. Bob spent extended time in Citrus Hills and worked out of Ted's condo there.

While McWalter usually slept at the condo as well, sometimes Williams would insist he stay at the big house with him and Louise, and the lawyer observed the Kid's domestic routine with interest. McWalter saw Williams have many a tantrum, then bounce back immediately and be exceedingly nice—often when walking with his beloved Dalmatian, Slugger. Some of this felt familiar to McWalter: "I've had a series of burnouts throughout my career. There was a psychologist specializing in what they call executive stress. I was seeing this doctor, and a lot of Ted stuff was going on. I was relating how difficult it was to be with Ted in his household—anger one minute and love the next. The psychologist said, 'That's what we call a swinging-door, bipolar personality.'"

One task Ted entrusted to McWalter was dealing with his third wife. Dolores would call Bob regularly and claim that Ted was stiffing her on this payment or that, or that the alimony was insufficient. "Ted wouldn't talk to Dolores," recalled McWalter. "He'd do it through me or John-Henry. He'd tell me, 'Help her out, but don't let her think it happened easily. The dumb shit, she needs someone to take care of her. She's been good to those kids.'" That help included minor sweeteners like donating one of Ted's cars to Dolores after he'd bought a new one and dealing with her health insurance, but Williams made sure to keep his distance.

Dolores, John-Henry, and Claudia each held Louise Kaufman at least partially responsible for breaking up the marriage. Ted, not surprisingly, didn't care what his children or his ex-wife thought of Louise. He had finally cast his lot with her and seemed to be quite happy about it. He knew Louise accepted him for who he was. She tempered his excesses and helped smooth out his rough edges.

But with the passage of time Claudia felt her relationship with Louise had only gotten worse. "I'm not going to lie," she explained. "Louise did not like me and I did not like her. We did our best to be civil to one

---

* John-Henry also challenged some of McWalter's moves, such as his decision to settle a minor dispute that arose after Williams bought out Barry Finger, Vince Antonucci's original partner. "John-Henry said, 'That isn't the way the Ted Williams family does business. When someone crosses us, we get him! We don't settle with him, we get him. You're not our kind of person.'"

another, but the older she got the nastier she was to me, and the older I got, the less I put up with her."

John-Henry, for his part, felt Louise's enmity toward him on his Florida visits to see Ted, and he did little to conceal his own hostility to her. After all, only four years earlier he had openly discussed the idea of killing Louise with his cousin Salvador Herrera and Sal's wife, Edna, the former Los Angeles police officer, when he was living with them in California.

In the summer of 1993, Louise was bothered by a bowel obstruction, a problem she'd had surgery for years earlier. But she told her best friend, Evalyn Sterry, that she felt up to going to the Miramichi in Canada with Ted. She knew the trip was the highlight of his year, and she wanted to be with him.

Around the first of August the bowel obstruction flared up again, and doctors in Moncton, New Brunswick, determined it could not wait until Louise returned to Florida. She needed surgery immediately. Her daughter Barbara Kovacs flew up for the operation from her home in Columbia, South Carolina. Louise, who had just turned eighty-one, reacted badly to the surgery and slipped into a coma.

Ted, fretting, sought comfort by calling his friends and loved ones. Claudia, who after college had returned to live in Europe, tried to reassure him. "I said, 'Daddy, that's one tough broad. She'll make it.' I was cheering him on. I could hear he was worried."

Williams also found solace from an unlikely source: a man of the cloth. The man who frequently referred to Jesus as "that syphilitic Jew bastard" was comforted by Barry Craig, a priest at the Episcopalian parish that Louise frequented near Ted's camp on the Miramichi.

"Nineteen eighty-five was the year I met Ted and the year I arrived as priest," Craig recalled. "One day after service, Louise invited me down to their camp. I was a lifelong Red Sox fan, so of course it was great to meet him. Early on, Louise was keen on getting Ted to talk about spiritual things, since he'd been estranged from religion—all forms of religion. The story was that his mother had forced it on him, and Louise wanted me to talk to him about God, maybe get him to stop swearing. She always wished that he would go to church but had long since given up asking him. Her way was to invite the priests down there and hope something would rub off on him."

Louise's illness prompted Ted to reach out to Craig for support, and in the process he made a startling admission. "We were having a drink on his porch overlooking the river," Craig recalled, "and I said, 'Louise always hoped that you would pray,' and he said, 'Father, I pray every day of my life at night.' When he and I were in the hospital standing over Louise's bed, he'd ask me to say prayers for Louise, and we'd stand together and say a prayer."

This was not only a side of Ted that Craig hadn't seen before but also a side that few others had ever seen. Given Williams's routine blasphemous rants ("cocksucker in the sky" was another of his favorite terms of endearment for God or Jesus), most everyone who encountered Ted assumed he was an atheist. Beneath his vocal disdain for God, however, Williams was more ambivalent, even curious, about religion, and once, in the mid-1970s, he had even accepted an evangelist's invitation to acknowledge Christ as his savior.

There had been various ways in which Williams acknowledged God in his life. When his plane was shot down over Korea, Ted begrudgingly asked for heavenly help in landing safely, and publicly admitted his entreaty later. At his Hall of Fame induction speech he said part of the reason for his success was "because God let me play the game and learn to be good at it." He queried believing friends about why they believed what they did, and he kept a photograph of one prominent man of the cloth he admired, Boston's Richard Cardinal Cushing. He acknowledged saying a prayer for his friend John Glenn before Glenn became the first American to orbit the earth in 1962, and he told one friend, Doyle Carlton, that he thanked God every day for his blessings. He tolerated and was even respectful of overt religious displays, such as saying grace before a meal (though Claudia Williams recalled that if Louise Kaufman's blessings went on too long, Ted might get antsy and say, "Yeah, that's right, fuckin' amen!"). And while Williams certainly eschewed any form of organized religion, his comfort of and devotion to the Jimmy Fund kids and his general willingness to help the down-and-out suggested there was a spiritual dimension to his life.

His tirades against God were likely due in part to festering resentment against his mother for her service to the Lord through the Salvation Army, which Ted believed came at his expense. And he would regularly, if simplistically, blame God for the unjust suffering he saw in the world (if there was a God, why would He allow such suffering?) and even for his own failing health as he aged. But this was largely misdirected anger, which allowed him to ignore the role of man and nature—as well as his own dysfunctions—in his grievances.

Ted's little-known encounter with the evangelist, which took place on Islamorada in 1975, suggests that he was more open to religion than he ever let on publicly. It happened at the Island Christian School, then a new private elementary school that John-Henry and Claudia were attending following Ted and Dolores's divorce the previous year.

One day Ted was in the school talking with Bruce Porter, founding pastor of the Island Community Church on Islamorada, which the school was affiliated with. Porter liked to invite outside speakers to address his isolated congregation, and the day he was talking with Ted, the Reverend Jack Hyles was visiting. Hyles was the fire-breathing pastor of the fundamentalist First Baptist Church in Hammond, Indiana, one of the first megachurches in the United States. In the mid-1970s the church boasted that it had the highest Sunday school attendance of any church in the world, with some thirty thousand students. When Porter spotted Hyles walking through the school, he waved him into his office to meet Ted. As it happened, Hyles was an avid baseball fan, and Williams had been his hero. He knew the highlights and the lowlights of Ted's career and proceeded to engage the Kid in animated conversation. After a while, Hyles, Ted, and Porter moved outside to talk, along with the school principal, Tony Hammon. There, leveraging the chink in Ted's armor—his anger—Hyles steered the conversation to the matter of Williams's salvation and, to the amazement of Porter and Hammon, got him to pray and say that he accepted Jesus Christ as his savior.

When he got back to Indiana, Hyles couldn't wait to tell his flock about his triumphant encounter with the great Williams in Islamorada and how he had saved him. "And to my complete surprise, there was my hero, my number one sports hero, Ted Williams," Hyles said in remarks that were tape-recorded. "I could not believe that I saw Ted Williams! And I walked to him. I said, 'Hey, Ted! You know who I am?' He said, 'No, who are you?' I said, 'I am your number one fan in the whole world.' I said, 'Ted, the way you hit .406 in 1941...,' I said, 'Ted, boy I appreciate that [.344] lifetime batting average you had and the five hundred and twenty-one home runs you had.' And I said, 'Ted! I remember that time when you got mad at the umpire and got mad at the manager, too, and...you just put your right hand down, took a swing with your left hand, and knocked the ball against the center-field fence for a double.' And 'Ted, you remember the time that you got mad and threw your bat and hit a lady in the head over there in the front row?' He looked at me and he said, 'If I ever run for president, you'll be my campaign manager.'

"Then I saw it. He liked me. He knew that I was human. And then I said, 'Ted, not a single hit that you got will help you when you stand before God. Not a one of those five hundred and twenty-one home runs, not the .406 batting average, not the lifetime [batting average], not all the RBIs you've got.' And there, standing on a street corner, about four hundred people gathered around, I got to win Ted Williams to Jesus Christ."

Porter and Hammon confirm the essence of Hyles's story, save the part about four hundred people. Porter said there were actually about forty, and they were students in a class passing by outside who paused respectfully when they saw a group of men with their heads bowed in prayer.

"Hyles prayed for a moment or two, and then he asked Ted Williams to reach out his hand and shake Hyles's hand if he truly wanted to receive Christ," said Porter. "I looked up a little and saw that Ted did that, and then he repeated a prayer out loud that Hyles repeated."[14]

Hammon, the school principal, was especially startled by what he saw: "I remember standing there with my mouth agape watching as this evangelist put his arm on Ted's shoulder and Ted bowed his head and prayed. I expected Ted to blow him off. I remember holding my breath, thinking, 'He's gonna rip you apart.' But there was a much more tender side to Williams than others knew. If I was Baptist evangelist I would tell you his life changed from then on, but Ted Williams went on being Ted Williams, and maybe that's good."[15]

Ted did go on being Ted—certainly never behaving as if he had been "saved" or, heaven forbid, nudging others to accept the Word. He continued his diatribes against the divine and continued to pop off at his loved ones occasionally. In New Brunswick, when the Reverend Barry Craig offered solace to Ted as Louise Kaufman declined, he couldn't help but remember the times he'd seen Williams be harsh with his live-in companion. "I had a lot of anxiety about Louise," Craig said. "Ted could be so gruff. He'd yell at her to bring him a drink, or he'd yell for her to do something else, and she would respond. She'd bark back, or roll her eyes, and I always thought, 'I don't know.'...But when she was ill, Ted's love for her was so evident. I remember standing in intensive care over her bed, and there were tears running down his cheeks as he looked at her, and it was pretty clear to me then that he loved her, however awkward he was about being demonstrative about it."[16]

Louise came out of her coma for a day and seemed to be fine. She spoke with her daughter and with other family members by phone, but then she went back into the coma and never came out. She died on August 10.

John-Henry prepared to fly up to New Brunswick to be with his father and called Claudia in Switzerland to give her the news. She flew to Canada, too. "When I saw Daddy after Louise died," she recalled, "he said to me, 'You mean more to me than any other woman in this world now. You need to be around me.' That was how he talked."

Back at his camp the following day, Ted asked McWalter to help him with a letter he was writing to President Bush. Bush had sent Williams a sympathy note upon Louise's death. Ted wanted his lawyer to proofread the letter, correct any grammatical mistakes, and generally buff it up a bit. "Ted handed me his draft and asked me to rewrite it, saying he couldn't do it well," McWalter recalled. "He told Bush how sad he was. I said, 'Ted, put that in the envelope just the way it is. It's beautiful, just a masterpiece.'"

Louise's funeral service was on August 17 at a Lutheran church in Columbia, South Carolina, as Barbara Kovacs wished. Ted's closest friends were there, as were his three children. As guests began arriving, Claudia heard Ted yelling. "I listened carefully to decipher whether that was a bad yell or a good yell. Was he just greeting somebody? But I remember doing that attentive perk-up listen—be careful before you approach it, because you don't know whether it's friend or foe. And out of the corner of my eye, I saw the same reaction out of this woman. And I just looked right at her. Not to mention she looks a lot like Dad. But I looked at her and I said, 'That is Bobby-Jo. I know it.' And I walked right up to her and I said, 'You must be Bobby-Jo.' She goes, 'Claudia?'"

It was the first time Bobby-Jo and Claudia had met.

"We were friendly. Very friendly. We were practically sitting in each other's laps on the way over to the cemetery. Holding hands. She was overly affectionate with me. I didn't see anything wrong with it. I didn't have a problem with it. I was like, 'What's so wrong with this lady? She's nice!' And I can even remember Dad when we all got back to the hotel, saying, 'That was very nice that you were so sweet to Bobby-Jo.' I didn't think twice about it."

At the funeral, Ted was weeping inconsolably. Bobby-Jo, who hadn't seen her father in six years, was struck by that.[17]

"I never saw my dad cry like a baby," she said.[18] "And he put himself into a corner, because he didn't know what to do. He literally started bawling so hard he felt naked, and he just turned and walked into a corner. This was after the service."

Rob Kaufman, Louise's son, though no Williams fan, was touched by his display of emotion. "Ted was very despondent and in tears, feeling miserable," Kaufman remembered.[19] "He was professing his love. 'I love this woman more than anything in the world. She was the most wonderful person I knew. I miss her so much that I don't know what I'm going to do.' It was nice because he sounded like a husband after being widowed after a long, happy marriage."

It was an open casket. Ted had tied one of his special fishing flies and pinned it on the lapel of Louise's dress. At the church, he reached out and grabbed her hand. Claudia was standing next to him at the time and felt squeamish about touching a corpse. "I thought, '*Eech,* I couldn't do that,'" she said.

The sisters had talked about staying in touch afterward, and Bobby-Jo got into the practice of calling Claudia a few times late at night. "I said to myself, 'Gee, this is awfully late to call me.' I kept listening to her and thought she sounded really tired. But she was actually really drunk. She was talking to me about, 'I always wanted to have the relationship that you've had with Daddy. And it's not fair.' She was going on and on, and I was like, 'Bobby-Jo, you've just got to let that go. That's how Dad is.' I was trying to console this woman, and then all of a sudden I didn't like it anymore. It was starting to feel uncomfortable to me." Claudia changed her phone number.

For the twenty-four-year-old John-Henry Louise's death represented a significant turning point. Louise had long been a burr in his saddle — not only a rival for Ted's affection but also a roadblock to the son's ambitious plans to take charge of his father's life.

"When Louise died, Ted had another nine years," said Ferd Ensinger, the family friend who had been a mentor to the young John-Henry and taken him to visit various colleges. "But those years would not be easy for him, and that nine-year period, of course, is when John-Henry would make his mark."[20]

28

Ted Failing

After Louise's funeral, Ted repaired to the Miramichi and listlessly finished out the fishing season in despair.

He donated a new steeple for Louise's local church in her memory and canceled a trip to Paris with John-Henry and Claudia that had been planned before Louise died, in no mood for any "gay Paree" frivolity.

Ted's seventy-fifth birthday, at the end of August, was muted, to say the least. And his malaise was exacerbated when he slipped down an embankment near his cabin and broke a rib. Returning to Florida in the fall, Williams sank further into despondency. He closed the shades on his big house at Citrus Hills, brooded, and started to drink heavily.

"When Louise died I went to visit Ted, and he was sitting in his house alone in the dark, all full of sadness, and we talked for three or four hours about death, how you're remembered, the things that you do, the legacy you leave, and I made sure I left with the lights on, trying to get his spirits back up," recalled Williams's fishing buddy Sammy Lee.[1]

Also working overtime to brighten Ted's mood was Lewis Watkins, an accomplished painter, sculptor, and printmaker who lived in nearby Brooksville. After meeting Williams in the late '80s, Watkins had been commissioned to make a print of a photograph of Ted's 1936 San Diego Padres team and then a print of a vintage poster of Fenway Park. Ted liked Lewis, who was nearly thirty years his junior. They would go fishing with some other local guys, country boys, then play liar's poker with dollar bills. Williams would invite Watkins to come over for breakfast, and at the end of the meal he'd want to make plans for dinner. The two men became good friends, and Watkins would emerge as a significant figure at the end of Ted's life—a doer, a fixer, and a key intermediary for those who wanted to reach the Kid by end-running John-Henry.

"John-Henry hated my guts, probably because I had a close relationship with his dad," said Watkins.

Williams opened up to Lewis, talking frankly about his childhood—how he'd gone hungry as a kid and how people couldn't get a quarter off his mother but she could get a dollar off them. Once, he said, he'd given her $5,000, and she turned around and gave it to the Salvation Army.

Man-to-man, Ted cracked the door open on his marriages a bit as well, even confiding to Watkins that the best sex had been with Lee Howard but that she was also the most jealous and possessive of his three wives.

Soon after Williams's return from Canada, Watkins came up with an idea to perk his friend up. Two years earlier, Lewis and Ted had been talking about presidential museums when Williams, in an unusual display of hubris, allowed as to how he wouldn't mind having his own museum, too. So, earlier that summer of 1993, when Ted and Louise were at the Miramichi, Watkins had arranged for ground to be broken on a prime lot in Hernando, where Citrus Hills was located. The land had been donated by Sam Tamposi, the Citrus Hills developer, who had also funded about $500,000 worth of construction. For their part, the Red Sox chipped in $150,000.

Now Watkins drove Ted over to the construction site to show him the building taking shape amid the jumble of bulldozers and busy hard hats. Williams started to tear up. He said he'd never imagined anything so nice. Watkins told Ted they were on track for a grand opening three months later, in February of 1994. It would be the first museum ever built for a living American athlete.

The museum served as a nice diversion from the Louise blues for Williams. His spirits were buoyed further by the reappearance of Lynette Siman, Louise's longtime friend from Islamorada, who had been longing for Ted since the early '50s. Over the years, Lynette, a petite brunette originally from the Boston area, had worked to contain her ardor for Ted in deference to Louise—and because she was married, of course. But now Louise was dead, and so was Lynette's husband.

Lynette lived about forty miles east of Hernando, in Yalaha, Florida, but soon was spending more time at Ted's house. Eventually she brought some clothes with her so that she could spend the night. Concerned about appearances, Ted asked Watkins if it was too soon after Louise's death, and Watkins waved him off: Williams should do what he wanted.

What he wanted was companionship, and so Lynette was in. They reminisced about life in the Keys circa 1953—how Lynette and her first husband built a small motel called The Sands; how, with Louise, they had all fished and socialized together; how Lynette had divorced her husband and married an Iowa man twenty years her senior, who of course was also enthralled by Ted. And they talked about how things might have been different if Lynette hadn't been married and if Louise hadn't been on the scene.

"Then Ted said to me, he said, 'We should have been married thirty years ago,'" Lynette said. "I told John-Henry this one day. His mind went so fast, and he said, 'I wouldn't have been born if you had.'"

Within a few months, Lynette maintained, she and Williams decided that they would get married after all and make up for all the years that they could have been together. "Ted and I were going to be married. No one has to believe it, but I know it. He knew I wasn't going to practically live there if there wasn't something permanent about it."

Lynette was not a John-Henry fan. "Let's just say we weren't bosom buddies. He did everything in the world to keep us apart. He thought, 'If I can get rid of you, I could have him all to myself.' He didn't want anyone close to his father." But when Lynette complained mildly to Ted about John-Henry, he turned on her. "The only thing I said was that I don't think John-Henry likes me. Do you know what Ted said? 'You disappoint me.' I almost started to cry, and I said, 'I don't know why I disappoint you. He's the one who doesn't like me.' I don't think Ted had any idea in the world that John-Henry was exactly like he was. He had blinders because it was his child. That's the only answer.

"That boy was probably the most malevolent person I've ever seen," Lynette concluded. "He loved the money, and he loved the fame. When these two things enter into it, I don't know where love does. But Ted did love him. He wouldn't entertain a bad word about him."[2]

The opening of Ted's museum—officially named the Ted Williams Retrospective Museum and Library—on February 9, 1994, was surely the biggest thing to have ever happened in Hernando, Florida. The festive, mini–Oscar night atmosphere included red carpets, bright lights, fleets of limousines coming and going, and hovering news helicopters.

The museum was 5,200 square feet and laid out in the shape of a baseball diamond, with various phases of Williams's life illustrated and displayed at each base. There were memorabilia and scores of photographs, as well as video testimonials on a loop from various players and from Presidents Nixon, Ford, Reagan, and Bush (the elder). A new wing was to be added the following year for the Hitters Hall of Fame, whose members would be personally selected by Ted.

More than two thousand people turned out for the opening ceremony, which was held in a large tent near the museum. The headliners, besides Ted, were Joe DiMaggio and Muhammad Ali. Ali, by then struggling with Parkinson's disease, showed up a few days early and helped drum up publicity for the opening. There were a total of thirty-seven Hall of Famers there, including DiMaggio, Stan Musial, Bob Feller, Bobby Doerr, Al Kaline, and Brooks Robinson. Country singer Lee Greenwood performed, along with the United States Marine Band.

The night before, Ali and Ted had dinner at a local restaurant. Also attending were Howard Bingham, Ali's longtime photographer; John-Henry; and Robert McWalter, Ted's lawyer. Williams had boned up for days on each of Ali's fights, and the dinner conversation consisted mostly of Ted asking the Champ specific questions about his various bouts. A bunch of Ted's local pals hovered around at tables nearby watching the scene, wishing they'd been invited to the table.

Watkins said that when touring the museum, Ali had cried when he read Williams's Hall of Fame induction speech calling on Cooperstown to admit Negro League stars. Perhaps knowing of Williams's reputation, Ali felt comfortable enough with Williams to venture a provocative joke when the two were seated alone. "Ted," he said, "did you just call me a nigger?" Williams was shaken and didn't know how to respond. Then Ali laughed and said, 'I'm only kidding you, Ted.'" Williams delighted in telling this story to friends later.[3]

Although Claudia wasn't there for the museum festivities, Bobby-Jo was, invited by Ted after he reconnected with her for the first time in years at Louise's funeral. Bobby-Jo came with her second husband, Mark Ferrell, a copyright enforcer for ASCAP, the American Society of Composers, Authors, and Publishers. They had met at an Orlando bowling alley in 1975 and later moved from Florida to Nashville, where Bobby-Jo dabbled in country music and once recorded a song she proudly presented Ted called "I Love You, Dad." Now Ferrell was about to retire, and the couple planned another move—to remote Franklin, North Carolina, in the Smoky Mountains.

Bobby-Jo was thrilled to be remembered and fawned over at the museum opening by a host of Ted's old pals, including the longtime Fenway Park ushers and concessionaires whom Williams had invited down. "It freaked me out," she remembered. "They said, 'I watched you grow up,' and they even lined up for my autograph."

Bobby-Jo said John-Henry looked on warily as Ted's friends greeted her. "And I just knew that right then, John-Henry considered me the enemy. Right then is when I know he said, 'She's gonna be a problem to my plans.' Everybody knew me at that thing. He'd never seen that before."[4]

DiMaggio, dapper in his tailored dark suit, introduced Ted by saying: "Some people like to set goals, and Ted did this. He said he wanted to be the greatest hitter that ever played the game. Well, I can't vouch for that completely…" He cited some greats, such as Ruth, who had preceded Ted. But from the time Williams came up in 1936 until the present, Joe said, "I can truthfully say I've never seen a better hitter than Ted Williams."

If that represented a slight retreat from previous unequivocal DiMaggio testimonials that Ted *was* the greatest, Williams, taking the podium dressed in a light blue short-sleeved shirt, seemed fine with the assessment.

"I go to some of these places in life and I'm sitting someplace and somebody at the microphone starts hollering and yelling to everybody that I'm the greatest hitter that ever lived, and I'll tell you something, I get a little lower in my seat and I want to hide if I can, but I can't," Ted said. "Because I can't believe that myself either.… I never saw those guys, so I feel the same way, Joe, that to single one guy out is tough. But if they'll put me in the select company of Ruth, Gehrig, Simmons, Foxx, Hornsby, DiMaggio and some of the others—Aaron, Mays—that suits me to a T."[5]

After the ceremony, Williams, DiMaggio, and Musial—escorted by a gaggle of sheriff's deputies more interested in genuflection than protection—went back to Ted's house and talked baseball late into the night: the Kid, the Clipper, and Stan the Man.

Ten days after the museum opening, Ted and Lynette were sitting around watching TV at night when Williams said he wanted to take a shower before bed. After he had been gone for what seemed to Lynette like a long time, she started to go check on him and heard Ted calling for her. Entering the bedroom, she saw Williams lying on the floor, unable to get up. He had emerged from the shower, put on a pair of shorts, and was walking around his bed when he'd suffered a stroke and collapsed. A blood clot from his heart had gone to his brain.

"My legs gave way," Ted said later. "There was no pain, but I had no strength. I couldn't get enough push from my legs to get up."[6]

A distraught Lynette said she would call 911, but Williams told her to call Lewis Watkins instead. She did, but she summoned an ambulance as well, and soon Ted was taken away to the local hospital, Citrus Memorial, before being transported to Shands Hospital, a teaching facility at the University of Florida in Gainesville, sixty miles to the north.

Williams stayed at Shands for nine days and underwent a spate of tests, after which doctors determined that he had just suffered his third stroke, not his second. In early 1992, not long after he had his first stroke—the one he suffered in December of 1991, which had robbed him of some of his peripheral vision—Williams had had another mild stroke without realizing it. Now this third stroke had taken away all his peripheral vision and about 75 percent of his remaining eyesight. Now the hitter and fighter pilot with the renowned vision could only see straight ahead: he had tunnel vision.

The doctors concluded that Ted's strokes and vision problems were linked to an irregular heartbeat, so he was given an electric shock treatment to stimulate his heart and his sight. As a result, Williams thought what he could see became 30 percent brighter.[7] But the left side of his body was numb, which affected his balance and required that he begin using a walker and, later, a cane, after intensive rehabilitation therapy. The balance and vision problems required adjustments around the house to help him navigate. Frequently traveled hallways were marked with his old uniform number—9: 9 to the bathroom, 9 to his bedroom, 9 to the living room.[8]

Williams did his physical therapy at a clinic in Ocala, about twenty-five miles from Citrus Hills. His mood was dark, and he was feeling sorry for himself, but then he met seventeen-year-old Tricia Miranti. When she was five, Tricia had had a brain hemorrhage that left her confined to a wheelchair and impaired her speech. She and Ted were assigned the same therapist, who had them play a game of checkers as a rehabilitation exercise.

Williams assumed that because Tricia had difficulty speaking she was mentally impaired as well, so he thought he'd let her beat him at checkers. But she was not mentally impaired in the least. He noticed that she was making a series of skilled moves, and before long she really *had* beaten him.

Ted learned that Tricia lived in Inverness, just five minutes from Citrus Hills. He visited her house and invited her to his. Tricia needed water therapy, so Ted insisted that she use his pool.

Vicki Miranti, Tricia's mother, a teacher's assistant, said Williams was "always nice and helpful. It was, 'Whatever I have you're welcome to it.' He loved to make her giggle and laugh."

Williams learned that Tricia attended a local junior college, and he said he wanted to pay her tuition. Vicki thanked him but explained that because Tricia was disabled, the state paid. Ted asked what else he could do. Vicki told him that Tricia could use a live-in caregiver, and Williams promptly started a 501(c)(3) nonprofit organization for the teenager's benefit, which he called the Ted Williams Citrus County Scholarship for the Physically Impaired.

Soon Tricia became Ted's local cause célèbre, a mini–Jimmy Fund project. He told all his friends about her and urged them to meet her and chip in to help. When *Sports Illustrated* came to town to do a big piece on the Kid in his dotage, Ted said he'd do it on one condition: that Tricia be in the story and get paid, to boot. "They paid her two thousand dollars," Vicki recalled. "All the money was used for the caregiver, rent, living expenses. Ted would say, 'If the damn little girl wants to get a dress, I wanna make sure she can goddamn get a dress.'"

As for why Williams got so involved in Tricia's case, Vicki Miranti said Ted told her: "'I was sitting there feeling sorry for myself, and she's struggling to take a step, sweating, fixating, concentrating, and she still had a little smile, and it inspired me to not feel sorry for myself.'"[9]

Tricia, for her part, teared up when she talked about Ted. "He was, and always will be, my angel."[10]

Ted's three children convened in Florida to be with their father after his stroke. Claudia flew in from Germany, where she was living after becoming romantically involved with a young German man. Bobby-Jo was furious that John-Henry had not called her with the news, which she had seen on TV. When she confronted him about it, he said he hadn't been able to get to a phone but would try to keep her in the loop in the future.

"When he told me that, he was walking around with three cell phones: one around his neck, one on his face, and one in his hand," Bobby-Jo said. "So whatever." She soon returned to Nashville.

John-Henry had come from Boston with Anita Lovely, the former beauty queen. They had been dating since January, and John-Henry had named her vice president of Grand Slam Marketing. She was twenty-nine, nearly four year his elder, tall and attractive with brown hair and a distinctive port-wine stain on her left arm.*

Meanwhile, Lynette Siman was still in the house and trying to adjust

---

* Anita had initially turned down the Grand Slam job but finally accepted it on the condition that she would work for Brian Interland, not John-Henry. Interland was older, and she felt she could learn more about business from him than the inexperienced young Williams.

to poststroke life. She said Williams told her he was no longer interested in getting married: "He said he wouldn't marry me under his health condition. He said he was an invalid and didn't want to saddle me with that, but I didn't care. I loved him." But John-Henry and Claudia, as they surveyed Ted's life and sought to bring a new order to it, quickly decided to send Lynette packing. "Lynette was a duplicate of Louise," said Claudia. "I was like, 'Jesus, we gotta deal with another one?' I don't think Dad was sleeping. He was getting very irritable. Lynette couldn't cook. Dad hated her food. And it was like she was taking over. She was bad for Dad at that time. He was lonely, no question, but we finally just told Lynette she had to leave. John-Henry and I high-fived after she left."

Protecting Ted became a top priority. "John-Henry made some other changes," Claudia added. "All of a sudden there were codes on the doors. The numbers were changed. Joe Public just couldn't come walking up to the door and knock and proclaim themselves as the greatest fan of Ted Williams, and 'Won't you please sign this?' I mean, it had to be like that."[11]

With Ted increasingly infirm, John-Henry would move to consolidate his growing power—and keeping a close eye on his father was crucial to that end. John-Henry told Claudia that he planned to move to Citrus Hills. He would run the various Williams enterprises and oversee the caretakers who would watch over their father from down there. At first he and Anita lived in the condo that Ted kept at Citrus Hills, then they moved into a house that John-Henry bought at nearby Black Diamond Ranch, a gated community with golf courses. Anita described the house as a "small villa."

She helped hire the caretakers for Ted, monitored an office for Grand Slam Marketing at a strip mall in Hernando, and oversaw the Ted Williams Store outside Boston, all while taking on more responsibility within Grand Slam. And when John-Henry decided that Ted was no longer able to run his own bank account or write his own checks, he had Anita take the checkbook and issue checks on Williams's behalf.

Following Williams's first stroke, in December of 1991, John-Henry had obtained his father's health proxy and with it the legal authority to make life-and-death decisions for Ted if he were incapacitated. Now, in May of 1994, he obtained a power of attorney authorizing him to make any move he wished with respect to Ted's various memorabilia companies, and that power would be strengthened two years later to include all his father's finances.

Both documents were drawn up by Eric Abel. Abel, then thirty-one, was house counsel for the Citrus Hills development where Ted lived, but he was also playing an increasingly important role as a Williams family attorney and a trusted confidant to John-Henry.

"When Ted first agreed to give John-Henry his power of attorney, I had to have a discussion with him about how powerful this is and what can happen," Abel said. "I presented it to him right down to the exaggerated 'John-Henry, if he wants to, can empty your bank account.' Ted would look stunned and say, 'Would he do that?' He'd pause and say, 'Fuck it, let's do it. If I got it, he can have it.' "[12]

Anita and John-Henry still had one foot in Boston as they worked to move their various businesses to Florida but, increasingly, remote Citrus Hills became home, and she found it quite an adjustment. There wasn't a decent restaurant for miles—not even an Outback Steakhouse or an Applebee's. They played golf and tennis and drove to the coast to try scuba diving. They were fixtures at the nearest movie theater, in Inverness. She would take Ted out in a golf cart and drive him around Citrus Hills. They might go watch John-Henry play golf or tennis, and Ted would comment on his son's shots. Anita would let Ted drive the golf cart, even when he could no longer drive a car. He could still see straight ahead.

For his part, Ted was thrilled to have John-Henry's operation nearby, Claudia recalled. "He loved to just surprise John-Henry. Drive on down to the office. Just barge in. Half the employees would go gawking because Ted Williams just walked through the office. Dad loved it."

Anita thought John-Henry yearned for his father's approval and wanted to prove to him that he could run the various memorabilia businesses. "He wanted to be in his dad's favor, definitely, and he was very protective of his father. I think that he looked at a lot of people as trying to take advantage of Ted, and he wanted to protect him from that. He thought he could help to grow a business for his father, but there was a money element for John-Henry, too. He definitely was attracted to money. He wanted to earn a lot, and he wanted to spend a lot."

She thought this desire for money stemmed from his austere life growing up in Vermont, where he'd been deprived of most luxuries. Now he was seeing what money could buy and what comfort it could create. But John-Henry was essentially using the various businesses as his own bank account, sometimes running up tens of thousands of dollars in monthly bills for personal expenses.[13] "All of a sudden he went from having nothing to being able to buy whatever he wanted," Anita recalled. "You could not quench his desire to have the latest gadgets. It was unbelievable." She thought Ted, had he been aware of the expenses John-Henry was running up, would likely have found it inexcusable. "Cost control was always a problem," Anita said. John-Henry "just didn't think too much about it."[14]

However, Bob McWalter, Ted's lawyer, *was* concerned about cost control in the Williams businesses, and he was beginning to raise more questions about John-Henry as a manager.

In November of 1993, McWalter had created a new entity, Ted Williams Family Enterprises, to guard against non–family members, especially Grand Slam Marketing's Brian Interland and Jerry Brenner, reaping any benefits that should accrue to Ted alone.

"We wanted to make it clear that Ted owned everything," McWalter said. "I was very concerned that intellectual property rights would get in the hands of Jerry and Brian. I was afraid that the right to give permission to use Ted's likeness was slipping away from Ted himself. I thought, 'Let's get this under one hat.' So we formed TWFE, with one hundred percent of common stock owned by Ted. We transferred all of these rights to that corporation. I was also concerned that John-Henry was throwing things in front of his father to sign, and Ted would be signing away this and signing away that. Now we would have a center of gravity." McWalter made himself president of TWFE as further protection from those who might take advantage.

That December, Ted persuaded McWalter to quit his job at Sherburne, Powers and come work for him full-time. John-Henry was opposed, but his father insisted. He was comfortable with McWalter, and they had been working together for years.

In his new full-time capacity, and as president of Ted Williams Family Enterprises, based in an office on Boylston Street in downtown Boston, McWalter began to comb through the books and determined that a large amount of cash was unaccounted for. He concentrated on the three facets of the operation he was most familiar with: Grand Slam, the Ted Williams Store at the Atrium Mall in Chestnut Hill, outside Boston, and several days of so-called private signings that Williams had done with McWalter in Boston in February of 1994, just before his stroke. At the signings, Williams would autograph pictures that fans sent him and affix a personal message, as requested.

"No money ever came in from the private signings of photographs that people sent in," McWalter said. "On the retail store in the Atrium

Mall, I was out there a lot watching. I saw stuff going out but no money coming in to Ted. Anita was dropping hints. It might have been just a sigh. Then I got some information on the sales at Grand Slam. For a long period not only did no money come in to Ted but nothing came in to Grand Slam. I had a meeting with Interland and Brenner, and they said they hadn't seen John-Henry for three or four months. They admitted they could have cut expenses more, particularly Interland. He charged two new Lexuses to the corporation. They were always flying first-class, the three of them: John-Henry, Interland, and Brenner. Even Ted never flew first-class."

When McWalter added it all up, he discovered that $1.8 million was missing. First he reported his findings to John-Henry, who attempted to quickly shift blame to Interland and Brenner, but McWalter thought the two men weren't culpable. "They were very dedicated to Ted and caught in the middle," McWalter concluded.*

After meeting with John-Henry, McWalter flew to Florida to talk with his client, Ted. Williams was in his bedroom.

"Ted, this is very painful," McWalter began. "But as best I can figure, you have autographed stuff and not been paid what you are owed. I'm not sure who owes it — Grand Slam, John-Henry, or a combination — but you are owed about 1.8 million dollars."

"Where the hell is it?" Williams said.

"Jerry and Brian have said that except for excess spending, they don't have it, and that only leaves John-Henry. I think you ought to raise that issue with him."

McWalter decided to get all the bad news out at once. "There's something more," he told Williams. "Do you realize John-Henry has borrowed a great deal of money from Bob Breitbard and invested it in the Ted Williams Card Company?"

Ted didn't seem to comprehend.

"Ted, Bob Breitbard has called me and said he's owed five hundred thousand dollars," McWalter explained. "Money was borrowed by John-Henry to invest in the card company in your name. I know it's a painful thing to hear. I know how you feel about Bob, particularly about money from Bob, and I know this isn't easy, but I have an ethical obligation to tell you."

---

* Interland said the Lexuses were leased, not bought, and he acknowledged significant expenses, but denied knowing about any missing funds. "On the $1.8 million, that's unbelievable," he said. "I have no idea of that. That's shocking. I don't recall that at all. When we were involved, we were not billing anything like $1.8 million."

Williams shook his head in sadness and lay quiet for a while. Finally, he said, "Okay, we've got to get that resolved in a hurry."[15]

Ted confronted his son with what McWalter had told him and insisted that he repay Breitbard. John-Henry brushed off the lecture, but was furious with McWalter for causing him problems with Ted. They had had other clashes—over the lawyer's involvement in the 1989 letter that Manuel Herrera had sent Ted criticizing John-Henry and over McWalter's decision to settle, rather than litigate, the minor memorabilia dispute with a business associate of Ted's. And after his father's latest stroke, John-Henry resented the way McWalter used his power of attorney to sign document after document on Ted's behalf. But now John-Henry had taken the power of attorney for himself, and he was not about to let McWalter be a further impediment to his own plans.

In April of '94, McWalter flew out to San Diego to meet with Richard McWilliam, president of the Upper Deck company. Ted, since his stroke in February, had been unable to keep pace with his obligation to sign twenty-five thousand autographs a year under Upper Deck Authenticated's 1993 deal with Grand Slam Marketing. Now McWilliam wanted to review the status of the contract and to express his continued frustration that the Ted Williams Card Company was effectively acting as an Upper Deck competitor. John-Henry had been expected to go on the trip but decided not to at the last minute.

"It was the day of President Nixon's funeral, April twenty-seventh," McWalter remembered. "The Upper Deck president kept me sitting for four hours. Then he blasted me for John-Henry, as if John-Henry was sitting there. He said he loved Ted and enjoyed doing business with him. I was finally dismissed. I was not used to being treated this way."

Later, back at his hotel, McWalter got a call that a fax had arrived for him. The fax was from John-Henry. Acting under his new power of attorney, John-Henry told McWalter he was fired. Everyone the various Ted companies were doing business with was also being notified that he had been fired and was no longer authorized to represent Ted.

McWalter began fielding calls from startled clients. The first call was from John Harrington, head of the JRY Trust, which owned the Boston Red Sox. Ted had been doing some informal consulting with the Red Sox, and McWalter had been discussing the possibility of a formal arrangement for Williams with Harrington in hopes of leveraging a limited-partnership stake in the team. The stunned McWalter had to say he had no idea what John-Henry was doing.

Then Ted himself called McWalter, as if nothing were amiss, wondering about the status of the Harrington negotiations. McWalter told him that given the stroke, he didn't think Ted could put in enough hours on consulting to make a deal viable. Ted also asked about the status of the missing $1.8 million McWalter had told him about earlier. McWalter said he thought they should do a formal audit to develop more specific information. Williams clearly had no knowledge of McWalter's termination, and McWalter held his tongue.

The lawyer flew back to Boston and prepared to meet with John-Henry, who had consulted with his accountant, Clifton Helman, and told him he intended to fire McWalter. "I said, 'You can't do that. He just left his law firm,' " Helman recalled. "John-Henry said, 'I don't care. I don't need him. I don't like him.' "

Helman reminded John-Henry that just five months earlier, Ted had made a commitment to McWalter that if he left Sherburne, Powers and went to work solely for him, he would pay him $100,000 a year. John-Henry acknowledged that Ted had made this offer, but he said he could no longer accept the authority and power that McWalter held. He had not told his father that he was going to fire him.

As the meeting with McWalter began, John-Henry was nervous and had a hard time getting to the point. He was discussing business as usual when McWalter interrupted him.

"Are you trying to tell me, John-Henry, that my job here is terminated? I tell you, I've had a magnificent run with your dad. He's one of the finest men I've ever known. I'll never forget that." Then he cited the poster Williams had given him with the inscription: "To my friend and lawyer and confidant."

"Oh, hell," John-Henry said, "he writes that to everybody."

McWalter was steaming, waiting for the inevitable. "Why are you wasting time?" he asked. "Did you come to fire me?"

"I guess that's why I came," John-Henry replied. Then he stood up, as if aware that his reply lacked the dramatic impact the moment seemed to call for. He looked directly at McWalter and said: "You're fired!" McWalter stormed out of the room. "I don't believe Ted would do that to me," he said as he left.[16]*

In a few days, after John-Henry had finally given his father the news, McWalter called Ted, who seemed anguished. "Bob, I don't know what I'm going to do," Williams said. "He's put me in the middle. He told me

---

* John-Henry stopped payment on a few paychecks that were in the pipeline to McWalter, but a sympathetic Helman found a way to make the checks good, unbeknownst to young Williams.

I have to make a choice between you or him." McWalter didn't try to reverse the decision. "Ted, if that were me, I'd pick my son," he said.

A few weeks later, John-Henry called McWalter to a meeting at his apartment in Brookline. There, McWalter was asked to help the Williams companies make the transition to new management without him. His replacement was to be Steve Southard, a Florida business consultant close to Al Cassidy, the longtime Williams family friend whom Ted would name executor of his estate. Ted flew up for the meeting, which was run by Southard.

"They put me in a straight-back chair, and they surrounded me, sitting in comfortable chairs," McWalter remembered. "Ted was polite, but I felt he thought he was a fox. He would say things he obviously didn't mean. He said, 'Bob, I want you down at my house like you have been. I want our friendship to continue.' I did not believe a word of it." McWalter resigned from the trusts that Ted had asked him to help oversee and was given a modest severance package.

In early July, Williams sat down with the *Boston Globe*'s Dan Shaughnessy to assess his changed life. Shaughnessy had revealed in an April column that his eight-year-old daughter, Kate, had recently been diagnosed with leukemia and that Williams had called her in the hospital to wish her well. Kate didn't have a clue who Ted was when he called. She passed the phone to her father, saying, "Daddy, there's a loud man on the phone, telling me I'm going to be okay."

When Shaughnessy got on the line, Williams told him: "Dr. Sidney Farber used to tell me, 'Ted, we're going to find a way to cure these kids.' Sure enough, he did it. You tell your daughter she's going to be fine. Tell her I'll come visit her."[17]

Williams told the columnist that he should have seen his third stroke coming. "If there was ever a candidate for this, it was me because I was involved in 40 different things," Ted said, speaking from the new Grand Slam office that John-Henry had set up in Hernando so that his father could more conveniently autograph memorabilia. "That museum was a big project and...I was just trying to do too much. They want me to go so many damn places. I had too much going on and too many stresses and worries and stuff. It was harder as I got older, because no matter what, there [were] more demands on me." And why were there so many demands on him at the age of seventy-five? Shaughnessy asked. "They think you're going to die, I guess," he said with a laugh. "Let's get him before he dies."[18]

Then Ted shared a dream he'd had recently. "I was laying there and I was having a lousy night. I was kind of resting and then I started to dream. Randy Johnson was pitching. I said, 'Geez, I can't hit him. I just had a stroke and I'm not even seeing very good.' But they kept teasing me and I thought, 'Aw, Christ.' So I started to get up there and he's throwing a couple and I'm saying, 'Geez, he's got pretty good stuff.' So I said to myself, 'I'm not going to try to pull him.' That's the first thing I said in my dream. 'I'm not going to try to pull him, I'm going to try and hit it hard through the middle.' He threw one ball and it was a ball. I seen his speed. He threw another one and another one and it was right there and I just punched it through the middle."

Three weeks after Shaughnessy's piece ran, Ted made his first public appearance since his stroke. He flew up to Boston to attend an event at the Ted Williams Store, John-Henry's memorabilia shop in suburban Chestnut Hill. He signed autographs with his friends and former teammates: Dom DiMaggio, Bobby Doerr, Johnny Pesky, and Eddie Pellagrini. All six hundred tickets for the event were sold in a few hours. "The Splendid Splinter looked fatigued and walked with a cane, but his voice was loud and clear," the *Globe* reported. "His vision is probably permanently impaired, but his signature was bold and authoritative."[19] The event was essentially the swan song for the Ted Williams Store: by December, it had closed down so that John-Henry could complete his move to Florida.

As for the various other Ted-related businesses that had been launched a few years earlier, Major League Memorabilia, which supplied material for the Home Shopping Network, was closed; the Ted Williams Card Company went bankrupt in 1995; and Grand Slam Marketing moved to Florida and continued to operate as Grand Slam Sports, Inc. Brian Interland and Jerry Brenner, who each owned a third of Grand Slam, considered asking John-Henry to buy them out, but decided to walk away and cede their interests to the Williams family rather than risk alienating Ted.

As some companies closed, others opened. John-Henry started Green Diamond Sports to license and market Ted memorabilia, further refining what was being done by Grand Slam and Ted Williams Family Enterprises. Then, swerving in a totally different direction, he started a gun company, called Full Auto, Inc. John-Henry loved guns and was a collector, and he decided that starting a business would be a logical extension of that hobby. He also liked cops and enjoyed flashing a sheriff's badge from Middlesex County in Massachusetts, which he had received as a member of the Reserve Deputy Sheriffs Association, a volunteer group. He had some law-enforcement friends and contacts who, he thought, could help him in business. "Like anything, when he had an interest, he went head over heels to understand it, to see what he could do," said Eric Abel. "It started as having some guns, then he wanted faster, more powerful guns." First he collected .357 handguns and 12-gauge shotguns, then a black, light handgun with a laser sight that he described as the kind Navy SEALs would use, then a .45-caliber, fully automatic machine gun, and finally a grenade launcher.

John-Henry and Abel liked to take an automatic, go out on a remote tract in the Citrus Hills development that had a sandpit, and blast away. "We'd set up a target," Abel said. "It was incredible, how fast it fired. You could pull that trigger and it unloaded some shells. The clip maybe held fifty rounds. Tension got harder and harder as you loaded them in there. John-Henry was very safety-conscious. He wasn't some wild man. He made sure I knew what I was doing, and I was gun-experienced. You hold it down at your hip. He thought it was a wonderful piece of machinery. The technology amazed him. We each fired it twice and went through about fifty dollars' worth of shells in two minutes."

After the old businesses were put to rest and the new ones launched, John-Henry no longer felt any need for Steve Southard. He thought Southard's $125,000 salary was too high, and, more important, he was becoming an obstacle. Southard, for his part, was frustrated dealing with Ted's son, privately commiserating with Bob McWalter about John-Henry's irresponsibility. Al Cassidy came up to try and act as a mediator between his friend Southard and John-Henry, to no avail.

"Steve came home and just said, 'I'm not working there anymore. John-Henry came in and said he'd used me as much as he wanted to,'" recalled Carol Southard about her husband, who died suddenly in 2003 at age fifty-seven. "He said he wasn't paying him anymore, and therefore he was just done. I think John-Henry was very much a user of other people. When he called at first to offer Steve a job, I answered the phone and said, 'Why do you want Steve to work for you?' John-Henry said, 'Because he's the smartest man I ever met.' But after Steve straightened out all his messes, and it was just the running of the business, he said, 'I don't need this guy.' That was John-Henry. When he was done with you, he was done."[20]

With the hiring of a number of caretakers for Ted, a new phase of life began for Williams. Their arrival meant that his independence was gone: not only were these strangers walking in and out of his house, some actually lived there, effectively working twenty-four-hour shifts five to seven days a week. Most of the caretakers clashed with John-Henry, whom they considered imperious and entitled. Some described instances in which he privately mocked Ted behind his back, and almost all said the younger Williams pressured his father into signing autographs to generate income even as Ted grew more frail. But Claudia Williams and family friends insisted no one could force Ted to do anything he did not want to do, and that he was anxious to generate money that he could leave to his children. Most of the caretakers, they added, had an ax to grind because they were either fired by John-Henry or left under duress.

Over time, Williams bonded strongly with some of his new room-mates. Ted's favorite caretakers were George Carter, a former Marine and Pawtucket, Rhode Island, cop; Frank Brothers, a jack-of-all-trades whose main qualification was that he was the son of Jack Brothers, the late Islamorada fishing guide and Ted pal; and Judy Ebers, a transplanted New Yorker who sassed Williams in a way that charmed and delighted him. Carter, fifty-four, and Brothers, thirty-eight, were the live-in mainstays who would play a key role at the end of Ted's life. Amid the gloom of Ted's unrelenting decline, these three provided considerable comic relief. Ebers liked to come to work wearing a Yankees hat to needle Ted. Carter once reported for duty wearing only his underpants, apparently in homage to Williams, who often took his meals wearing only his briefs and a T-shirt. When Ted hired a French chef, Ebers, Carter, and Brothers set about teaching him the American vernacular, especially one important word in the Williams household: *bullshit.* "Bool-sheet, bool-sheet," the chef kept saying.

Carter and Ted related to each other as former Marines. They loved to tease and cuss each other out. Carter had heard of Williams but was not a real baseball fan and certainly no hero-worshiper. "I've seen people who if they would touch Ted Williams, they'd have an orgasm," he said dismissively. But George had to admit he was taken aback when, on one of his first days on the job, he answered the phone and it was Joe DiMaggio calling to check in on Ted after his stroke.

Carter had problems dealing with Ted's ex-wife Dolores, who, now that John-Henry was in charge of Ted, was coming down from Vermont more frequently. Ted tolerated her, but barely. He usually imposed a three-day limit to her visits, but gradually, as he began to develop symptoms of dementia, she would extend her stays beyond that limit. Then when Ted saw her, he would have forgotten she was there in the first place. "When did you get in town?" he would say. "Well, how are ya? How are the animals? How is it in Sticksville?"[21]

Carter got into a memorable scrap with Dolores one day, and she kicked him hard in his rear end, prompting him to briefly quit. Ted and Dolores were looking for John-Henry, but he couldn't be found. "So Ted started yelling at me, 'Where's John-Henry?'" Carter recalled. "I said, 'Goddammit, I don't know where the little bastard is, okay? I've got too many things to do without keeping an eye on that little prick.' Well, his mother was sitting there. And she grabbed me by the arm and dragged me into Ted's bedroom. She slammed the door and locked it. She says, 'Who the hell are you to talk to Ted Williams like that?' I said, 'You better open the goddamned door or I'm going to call the cops.' I went over and grabbed her wrist and took her hand off the knob, opened the door, and walked up the hallway. As I was walking up the hallway, she gave me a swift kick in the ass. Claudia was there with her German boyfriend. Claudia was on my side, and not even speaking to her mother at the time."

Dolores's eccentricities were no secret. She would sunbathe in the nude outside, oblivious to the caretakers or any workers who might wander in and out. Another time, Carter was in the kitchen cooking a meal for Ted when Dolores bounded in, just out of the shower, with only a towel wrapped around her. She was going out for the evening. She had a roll of tape and ordered Carter to tape her breasts apart so that they could better conform to the plunging neckline of her dress. Bemused, Carter obliged.[22]

Carter was off duty when, in November of 1994, Ted fell and broke his shoulder while walking near his house with Kay Munday, who had been hired by Louise. Munday had asked Williams to use his wheelchair, but he refused. They plodded along slowly, with Ted occasionally flipping a ball for Slugger the dog, when all of a sudden his legs gave way and he fell. Munday ran into the house to get the wheelchair, and a plumber who happened to be working at the house hauled Williams into it. Before long, he was in the hospital having surgery.

When Frank Brothers moved in and started to help take care of Ted in June of 1995, Williams gave him $10,000 to help buy a new house for his family in Citrus Hills. Brothers was touched by the gift, which he said John-Henry tried unsuccessfully to turn into a loan.

"John-Henry was all about the money," Brothers said. Once, when a Cleveland Indians old-timer of Ted's vintage asked Williams to sign one of his game-used bats, John-Henry tried to stop his father from doing it. Brothers recalled, "In the late fifties, when the Red Sox were playing the Indians, Ted had cracked a bat. The guy asked Ted if he could keep the bat, and Ted said sure. Now, years later, this gentleman called the house and wanted to see Ted, so I set up a breakfast meeting for them. John-Henry was out of town, and he heard that this guy was coming up for breakfast, and he calls his dad, saying, 'I know this guy's got a game-used bat, and you'd better not sign it.'" When the two men had breakfast, the visitor asked Ted if he would sign the bat. Williams did. That afternoon John-Henry got home and exploded.

"You know what, Dad? You just made that bat worth ten thousand dollars," he snapped at his father.

"I don't care; he's an old ballplayer," Ted replied. "You know, I hope he can get fifty thousand for it. He needs the money. I'll do anything for an old ballplayer."

When John-Henry persisted in arguing, Ted cut him off. "It's my signature. Fuck you!"

Ted would continue to sporadically end-run John-Henry and give autographs to whomever he wanted to. When Williams appeared at a memorabilia show in Atlantic City in November of 1996, a show that featured all the living players who had hit five hundred or more home runs, Brothers was with him, along with Dave McCarthy, the New Hampshire state trooper, and some of McCarthy's friends who had served as Williams's informal security detail on trips. Ted didn't really need the security. It was just an excuse for McCarthy and his pals to hang out with their hero, and they did so at their own expense, without being paid. One of their perks was that Ted would give them memorabilia with his signature. "But these guys also knew that John-Henry would go nuts whenever Ted gave an autograph away, so one of them would be watching the hallway in the hotel on the lookout for the kid," Brothers said. "Ted would be signing stuff for these four or five cops. It wasn't a lot, ten or twelve pictures and whatever. But even Ted knew the kid was gonna be furious about him signing. So one of the guys in the hallway said, 'Here comes the kid, here comes the kid!' And me and Dave were throwing stuff under the bed to try and hide it from John-Henry."[23]

Ted's daily routine was to wake up each morning around 6:30. He'd sit in his room and talk to Brothers or Carter, maybe watch some news on TV. Then he liked to make phone calls. John-Henry often got the first call, but he hated to get up early and generally wouldn't answer the phone, irritating Ted. ("I'm fuckin' up, goddamn it, get your ass up!" he would bark into his son's answering machine.) Then he might call Joe Camacho, his bench coach with the Senators, Dominic DiMaggio, Joe Davis, or old friend and divorce lawyer Daisy Bisz. Bob Breitbard would usually be phoned later in the morning because of the time difference in San Diego.

After the calls came the food. Breakfast had long been Williams's favorite meal, and it continued to be a high point of his day. Ted loved eggs and sausage and was very particular about his grapefruit, which had to be cut just right and eaten last to "cleanse the palate." (Williams would force visitors to eat grapefruit even if they didn't like it.)

There would be physical therapy in Ocala three days a week, on Mondays, Wednesdays, and Fridays, and a personal trainer would come to the house a few other days. When Brothers started, Ted would usually stop at the Grand Slam office in Hernando on the way back from physical therapy and sign for an hour or so. John-Henry might have some special items for Ted to sign on Tuesdays and Thursdays. To further maximize production, John-Henry enlisted Carter and Brothers to get Ted to sign routine items, like photos, any time they could around the house. He put them on an incentive plan, saying each man would get fifty cents for every signature they could get Ted to produce. Carter balked, telling John-Henry it was a conflict of interest for him and Brothers. They were supposed to be taking care of Ted. The staff at the office was supposed to be working with him on signatures. But John-Henry insisted, so George and Frank went along, though they were soon miffed because John-Henry rejected half the signatures that they turned in as not good enough.

Judy Ebers, forty-six, worked for Ted for about eight years starting in 1994. Nominally a cleaning woman, she would fill in for Carter and Brothers in caring for Ted and became a soul mate of sorts for Williams: seeing her in the morning, he would announce, "Forget the cleaning," and ask her to come sit at his bedside, and they would talk for hours. He told her about how his father had all but ignored him growing up but then tried to cash in when Ted signed his first pro contract; about his crash landing in Korea; even about his date with the actress Julie Adams in 1954. At one point, suffering from a serious cold, Ted told Judy, "You know, if you weren't married, you could be my wife." Replied Ebers, "We'd kill each other, but what a ten minutes it would be."

In fact, Ebers was happily married and the mother of five children.

Williams would visit her house regularly and ask Judy's husband, Herb, to sneak him a martini. Twice a year, Judy and her husband would host a party she called Sullivan County Days, named after her home county in the Catskills region of New York. They would have about fifty people over, mostly all Yankees fans, but Ted would be the star of the show, of course. ("They may be Yankee people," Williams told her, "but they're good people.")

Before long, Williams was letting his inhibitions down with Judy. One day, when she was filling in for Frank Brothers while he ran an errand, Ted wandered into the living room stark naked and announced he wanted to take a shower. She thought this either represented the dementia in fuller bloom, an immortal's sense of entitlement, or both. She told him he'd have to wait until Brothers returned.

Ebers watched John-Henry and Ted clash frequently over signing autographs. She thought it was a case of an ill-equipped son trying to exploit his famous father. "John-Henry just did things the wrong way. He was trying to be a businessperson in a little kid's brain. Ted was an old man who didn't need to be doing this. He wasn't stupid. He knew his son wasn't making anything of himself—just using his name."

Sometimes, when Ted argued with his son, he would yell out "Wet-tach!" in frustration. That was Dolores's maiden name, and Williams was linking his son's shortcomings to her. "She's fucking crazy, and so is he!" Ted would shout.[24] "Something was wrong with the way John-Henry was raised," Ebers said. "When he grew up, his father was on the road, and his mother was nuts. How Dolores got along in public life without being certified I don't know."

Besides memorabilia, John-Henry, armed with his power of attorney, was also frequently having Ted sign various documents. Ted, his vision virtually gone, would ask what he was signing, but John-Henry would usually say it was just routine business and not give a specific reply.

"John-Henry was a wheeler-dealer, and Ted was mainly in oblivion to everything that went on—he really didn't know what he was sign-ing," said Ebers, who quit for a time after John-Henry installed surveil-lance cameras throughout the house.[25]

Claudia Williams said the cameras were installed after the baseball that Babe Ruth had autographed for Ted was stolen along with a pair of boxing gloves that Muhammad Ali had given Williams, inscribed TO THE GREATEST FROM THE GREATEST. But the cameras caused resentment among the help, whose integrity was clearly being questioned.

Caretaker John Sullivan—like Carter, Brothers, and Ebers—witnessed regular flare-ups between Ted and John-Henry over signing memorabilia, but one argument stands out in his memory. Brothers and John-Henry had designed a device to facilitate Ted's signing of bats. The bat would be clamped in, and there was an armrest so he could sign it at just the right angle, without strain. "There were two of these so-called bat carts or racks to place bats in, and they had a chemical that was used to wipe off a bad signature," Sullivan recalled. "One day John-Henry was pushing Ted to sign, kind of getting on his case. Ted reacted by defying him. Once, Ted said, 'That's enough. Not now. I'm not gonna sign.' John-Henry took that bat rack and threw it across the room, and bats flew all over."

Sullivan, a former Marine who was in his sixties, thought that as Ted continued to fail he was growing more despondent. Religion was hardly any consolation, recalled Sullivan. "Ted would gaze heavenward and say, 'You black, bearded, Jew son of a bitch and your whore mother....I don't believe in you anyway.'"[26]

Several of those who worked for Ted said they witnessed John-Henry occasionally mock his father behind his back, imitating his strained gait and smirking.

"I was in the kitchen one day; Ted was walking out to the car, and he kind of teetered on his feet," recalled Marion Corbin, who worked part-time for Williams as a cook. "He couldn't see. He was staggering. His son mocked him. It made me so mad I like to spit. The first time he did it, Ted said, 'What are you doing, John-Henry?' He said, 'I'm just playing.' John-Henry was walking like a drunk across the garage. He didn't know he was going to be seen. And another time at the dinner table, we saw him shake his fist behind Ted's head. He was a disrespectful, ugly man."

Marion also said she saw John-Henry forge Ted's name on memorabilia. "He'd be sitting and signing Ted's name. Sometimes he did it in the house, and sometimes he did it in his office....He had his daddy's signature down pat. He signed correspondence for Ted, and I saw him do this on pictures and balls. He'd tell Ted they had to sign stuff, and what Ted didn't finish, John-Henry did. I wouldn't want to buy anything, because you wouldn't know they weren't forged."[27] Her husband, Jim Corbin, said that he once saw John-Henry sign his father's name on several bats at the museum and on shirts at Williams's house. "He didn't seem to care if I was watching," Corbin said. "I saw him do that at least a half dozen times."[28]

Anita Lovely, however, doubted that John-Henry ever signed Ted's name on memorabilia. "I can assure you that from my experience...he never, ever, produced autographs," she said. "We really guarded that— the authenticity of his dad's signature so the public could understand that all of those pieces were authentically signed by his dad." But she could not be 100 percent certain: "Could John-Henry have done something like that? Possibly. He could have. But he wouldn't say something like that to me if he did that. I don't think he would, anyway."[29]

Claudia Williams, who returned from Germany in 1996 and settled in Saint Petersburg, some seventy-five miles south of Citrus Hills, was absent when most of the memorabilia signings took place. But she said the caretakers' criticisms should be viewed skeptically. "They wanted to hate John-Henry and didn't approve of what he was doing to our father," Claudia insisted. "They would say, 'He's going to die anyway. Let him eat what he wants to eat.' Or, 'He's too old. He doesn't need to sign anymore.' What they failed to recognize was, Dad wanted to live longer. He wanted to sign. He wanted to do stuff for John-Henry. It made him feel alive. He no longer cared about making money for himself. He wanted to make money to help John-Henry succeed." Not surprisingly, Claudia felt that John-Henry was right to take action against any caretaker insolence: "When things got out of hand, out of control, John-Henry didn't like how it was going, and he fired some of these caretakers, like any good employer would. They were disgruntled. And they decided, 'How can we get back at him? Let's say something mean, say something wrong. Base it loosely on fact; maybe something that might have happened, but let's turn it around and twist it.'"

Ted now left his house less often because of his failing health, but in December of 1995, he flew up to Boston for a major honor: a $2 billion tunnel running under Boston Harbor and connecting Logan Airport to the Massachusetts Turnpike extension was being dedicated in his name.

Williams was driven through the tunnel for the official inaugural ride in a 1966 Thunderbird convertible by then-governor Bill Weld, a Republican. In the backseat were two former Democratic governors who also had had a hand in the project, Michael Dukakis and Ed King, though they despised each other and barely spoke, even on this joyful occasion. With John-Henry at his side, Ted appeared before a crowd of about three thousand fans, politicians, and hard hats still putting the finishing touches on the tunnel. In the winter chill, Ted, walking with a cane, was dressed in a who-gives-a-shit blue knit ski cap and Windbreaker that unceremoniously said RANGER BOATS, FLIPPIN, ARK. on its back.

"Certainly, the last few weeks, I thought of me being in front of all you Bostonians," Williams said. "And everyplace I go, they're waving at me, sending out a cheer...and I can't help but keep thinking, Geez, for people to be so...nice and respectful and enthused...I've only seen that when somebody looks like they are gonna die—or they are gonna die. And I'd just like to say this one thing today....I'm a long way from that."[30]

But excursions like that one were increasingly the exception. Ted mostly stayed at home, ever more reliant on John-Henry, Anita, and the caretakers. Once Claudia arrived on the scene, she began spending more time with her father. From her new base in Saint Petersburg, where she was competing in triathlons under a sponsorship, Claudia would get on her bicycle and bike the seventy-five miles to Citrus Hills, stay for the weekend, then bike back again.

"I think it impressed him that I could do that," she said. "I would get off the bike and just go right back—cleats and all, go right back into the bedroom—crawl right into bed, and give him a big kiss. He'd be like, 'Jesus Christ, you stink! Go take a shower.' But he was just so happy to see me."

Claudia had been away for years, and now she was acutely aware that her father was getting old. "Dad was like a grandfather to me, not really a dad," she said. "We skipped generations. When we were together, we were all like kids, playing. Dad was never the dad to say, 'Did you do your homework?' It was playtime, and the happier you were, the better. But if you showed any sign of weakness, it infuriated him."

Now, though, she was pulled into his inner circle with John-Henry. "I was finally included in the group, and we became the Three Musketeers. At breakfast he'd be saying, 'Where's John-Henry?' It was John-Henry, John-Henry, John-Henry. Then finally it was Claudia, too."

Claudia had been largely uninterested in her father's memorabilia ventures, but now that she was back in the United States she began to consider her own finances. She was comforted by two thousand signed bats that Ted had given her, which were in storage as a nest egg. Furthermore, Ted planned to either sell or give the balance of the shares in Ted Williams Family Enterprises to her and her brother, with John-Henry (who had already convinced his father to sell him a small stake) retaining the controlling interest.

Eric Abel drafted an agreement on behalf of Ted and John-Henry calling for Claudia to receive 45 to 50 percent of Ted Williams Family Enterprises in return for the company acquiring her two thousand signed bats. Since he was representing Ted and John-Henry, Abel advised Claudia to get her own lawyer to review the agreement and protect her interests. But when Claudia's lawyer questioned the fairness of the deal, Ted went ballistic. "He thought he was helping his daughter out, and now she goes and gets an attorney and they're demanding things," Abel said. "Ted thought it was disloyal or ungrateful. So he said fuck it, and John-Henry ended up with the whole thing."

Claudia was upset and even called Bobby-Jo to commiserate, apparently in an attempt to mount a sisterly alliance of convenience against Ted and John-Henry. Bobby-Jo was surprised to get the call and thought Claudia was nervy asking for her help, given that they had no relationship to speak of. "There wasn't anything I could have done about that anyway," Bobby-Jo said.

So Claudia watched her brother run the memorabilia business from a certain remove, but she was home one weekend when John-Henry made an unusual request of his father. Ted flew a ten-by-fifteen-foot American flag in front of his house. The flag had grown a bit tattered, and a new one had been ordered. Rather than just throw the old flag away, John-Henry decided it would be a good idea for Ted to sign it, then they would sell it on eBay.

"We took this Old Flag and decided to give it a place in History forever," John-Henry wrote in his online sales pitch. "Ted Williams signed it in blue Sharpie on a white stripe in big bold letters. This is the only flag of its kind in existence. The other flags were not as lucky as this one."

The flag drew twenty-eight bids and sold for $3,050.[31]

The press found out, and a mild stir ensued. Claudia said no one thought the issue through. She initially thought it was a great idea until she was told that many would see it as exploitive. "After we decided to get a new flag, we brought the old one into the house, laid it on the table, and John-Henry said, 'Dad, what do you think about signing this?' He was like, 'Get a pen!' Thought it was a great idea. None of us, including Dad—the man who served his country twice—said, 'Don't disfigure this flag.'"

By now, Eric Abel had emerged as a key figure in the Williams circle, a consigliere to both Ted and John-Henry. He extricated the family from the Upper Deck contract after both sides became dissatisfied with the deal, prepared the power of attorney that empowered the son to take legal control of his father's affairs, and rewrote Ted's will. Along the way, Abel served as a right hand and eventually best friend to the isolated and untrusting John-Henry.

Abel could sense that Ted, in his weakened condition, wasn't happy with his lot, so one day, when they were alone, he asked Williams if he was tired of living. "He said he was tired of taking these goddamned pills, but no, he wasn't tired of living. And he said, 'We'll not talk about that again.' The man was happy for every day he lived. But he had dignity. And there were times when he had his fill of being told what to do."

Abel found himself occasionally yanked out of the legal arena into the nitty-gritty task of helping convince Williams to take his daily batch of pills.

"John-Henry would say, 'I'm leaving this fuckin' place if you don't take the pills,'" Abel recalled. "Ted would say, 'Go ahead!' Then I would come up and talk him into it. He was used to total control. Fame gave him that. I don't know if *spoiled* was the word, but that was the way he was used to doing things."

Abel and John-Henry would sometimes stay up all night playing video games. Anita Lovely disapproved of these marathon sessions and worried that they underscored John-Henry's immaturity. Abel also helped facilitate Ted's interest in placing the occasional sports bet, usually on college football, boxing, or the horses. Abel's brother Ken, a quadriplegic, was a bookie and happy to take Ted's money. "Ted had some tipster out of New York, and he would check that information with Ken," said Eric. "Once, they bet on a horse named the Splendid Splinter."

Abel had a front-row seat from which he could watch the relationship between Ted and his son develop.

"Yes, I can describe screaming matches, throwing pots and pans, telling each other to fuck themselves," he said. "There were many times I said, 'What am I doing here?' But thirty minutes would never pass without one of them calling the other back. Early it was John-Henry calling, later it was Ted. But it was always mutual. They were both full of pride, so no one wanted to make the first call. Neither wanted to give in. But someone always did. Some of the moving moments were hearing Ted and John-Henry say that they loved each other. That evolved so they could say that. It was beautiful. They could each say it. Ted's pride went down as he aged." John-Henry, Abel concluded, "became the most trusted person in Ted's life. It got to the point where Ted would rather have John-Henry make the wrong decision than have anyone else do it. Because he knew John-Henry loved him. It was faith and love."

In 1996, Ted and Abel began discussing Williams's desire to revise his previous will, executed in 1991, to make clear that he wanted to be cremated and have no funeral. Then there was another key change. Whereas the 1991 will had divided his estate equally in thirds for each of his three children, now it would exclude Bobby-Jo entirely.

Ted never told Abel precisely why he wanted to disinherit Bobby-Jo, and the attorney never dared ask him. But Abel noticed that when Ted spoke about his oldest daughter, he did so with despair, and he would complain that he had had to support her throughout her life. Abel thought the last straw for Ted came when Anita Lovely discovered that Bobby-Jo's younger daughter, Sherri, was getting money Ted had been sending to pay for college expenses despite having dropped out. Ted blamed Bobby-Jo.

"I tried to dissuade Ted from writing off his daughter," Abel said. "I wanted him to understand the ramifications and that he'd be subjecting John-Henry and Claudia to allegations that they engineered this thing. He and I talked about Bobby-Jo about ten times. There was not one occasion that he did not refer to her as 'that fucking syphilitic cunt.'" Ted also wanted to cut Bobby-Jo out of her one-third share of a $600,000 irrevocable insurance trust he had established for his three children in 1985, but learned that he couldn't, Abel added.

In his revised will, dated December 20, 1996, Williams directed that his remains be cremated "and my ashes sprinkled at sea off the coast of Florida where the water is very deep. It is my wish and direction that no funeral or memorial service of any kind be held for me and that neither my family nor my friends sponsor any such service for me.

"I have purposely and deliberately eliminated my daughter, Barbara Joyce Ferrell, from this will because I have provided for her in my life," Williams added. "For purposes of the operation of this will, it is my intent that Barbara Joyce Ferrell shall be deemed to have predeceased me leaving no issue surviving."

Later, after the new will was filed, Ted called Bobby-Jo and her husband, Mark, in for breakfast to notify them of his decision. Williams had wanted to avoid the unpleasantness of a face-to-face meeting, but Abel and another lawyer involved in changing the will had insisted that he meet with Bobby-Jo to tell her he was disinheriting her so as to prevent her from bringing a claim after he died. Abel advised Ted to soften the blow by telling Bobby-Jo she was still going to get $200,000 from the

insurance trust. And he could remind her that he had given to her gener-
ously throughout her life, but he felt he now had to provide more for
John-Henry and Claudia. Ted then said he didn't want to do the talking;
Eric could deliver the news.

Williams sat at the end of a long rectangular table with Eric on his
left. When Bobby-Jo arrived, she sat on her father's right and Mark sat
next to his wife. After some chitchat, Abel called the meeting to order.

"Bobby-Jo, the reason your father called you here today is because he
rewrote his will." "Oh?" said Bobby-Jo.

"Yes. He made some changes and wanted you to know about it while
he's alive, so there are no questions about it after he dies. You will get
two hundred thousand dollars as your share of an insurance trust that
your dad set up for his kids in 1985. He's provided for you during your
life, but John-Henry and Claudia have not had the same opportunity,
and he wants to make it up to them in his will. So you will not be in the
will."

Bobby-Jo was stunned, but remained stoic and straight-faced. Eric
asked her if she had anything to say.

"That's okay with me, Daddy," she said. "I don't have a problem with
that. But I want to just make sure of one thing. Is that what you want?"

Ted took umbrage at the question. "That's what I fuckin' want," he
replied through gritted teeth.

"Okay, Daddy, if that's what you want, okay." Bobby-Jo was almost
cowering.

Abel returned to his office, typed up notes on the meeting, and then
had them notarized in case Bobby-Jo later decided to mount a legal challenge. He felt badly for her. "It was the ultimate humiliation."

29

Hitter.net

In December of 1996, soon after appearing on the cover of *Sports Illustrated* for a piece entitled "The Kid at 78," Ted tripped over his dog, Slugger, fell heavily, and broke his hip. He went into the hospital for surgery in January and then began another long recuperation.

If the story proved the potency of the so-called *Sports Illustrated* cover jinx—the belief that bad things befall those who appear on the front of the magazine—it was also notable for its attempt to correct the image of John-Henry as someone who was exploiting his father. The article credited the son with giving Ted a renewed sense of purpose, boosting his morale, improving his diet, limiting his alcohol intake, and insisting that he go to physical therapy and use a personal trainer. "If it wasn't for John-Henry, Ted would be dead right now," the Williams family friend Al Cassidy was quoted as saying. Frank Brothers, who privately despised John-Henry, gave him public credit for tending to Ted: "He has taken a lot of hits, but how many kids, no matter who their father was, would drop their lives and move 1,500 miles to take care of him? John-Henry did." Ted himself declared, "I could not have done it without John-Henry."

Young Williams took the opportunity to push back against claims that he had become the new scourge of the memorabilia industry and that he was pushing Ted to sign autographs. "I still make mistakes," he said, "but I'm his son, and I don't know when you ever beat that." He got a bit carried away when discussing his baseball foray after he dropped out of college to train under his cousin Sal Herrera. "I was hammering baseballs, 300 a day," he said. "I'm in Fresno, and I'm hitting off a batting machine cranked to the max, 105, 106 miles per hour. Dad talks in books about how your blisters start bleeding? I knew what that was like. And how you start smelling leather burning off the bat? I knew what that was like. You know, it's all timing...and ooh, I was so strong. I was hitting the ball so good. Crushing it." That his attempt at playing baseball had, in the end, been a complete failure went unmentioned.[1]

In subsequent press interviews, John-Henry boldly picked up the Al Cassidy theme that were it not for the son, the father would not be alive.

"My dad would be dead if it wasn't for me: medically, emotionally, everything," John-Henry told the *Daily Evening Item* of Lynn, Massachusetts, which used the first half of the quote as the headline over the story. "The only reason I ever got involved in this business was to protect Dad. He's 2,000 percent—sometimes not to his benefit—honest, open-hearted and generous."[2]

John-Henry complained that his statements had been twisted in the press, but he added: "I don't mind what people say. Nothing's going to change my mind to make me do anything differently."[3] This was the same stubbornness that Ted always projected with the Boston writers back in the day. Then John-Henry took it a step further and suggested that the Boston press, in particular, was intent on maligning a new Williams generation.

"It's really impossible to fight someone who has an endless ink pen," he told the *Hartford Courant*. "It's funny, because it just seems Boston wants to crucify the Williams name. Dad got crucified his entire career there. I don't know why they have such a bad thing going for me there."

The young Williams, while tiring of the criticism, was also getting bored with the memorabilia business. Intrigued by the early promise of the Internet, he had bought a state-of-the-art computer, but access to the Web at the time in isolated Hernando, Florida—there was only a dial-up connection, with frequent busy signals and disconnects—was spotty at best. He tried an Internet service provider in Orlando, which offered a faster and more reliable direct phone connection, but the resulting phone bill was enormous.

Having experienced the quality of a direct connection, John-Henry began to investigate what it would take to get the same quality in the Hernando area. In July of 1997—using money from Ted Williams Family Enterprises, Green Diamond Sports, and other Ted memorabilia interests—John-Henry acquired some computer servers and a couple of modems and started his own crude network, using a small group of friends, including Eric Abel, to test it out. By the end of August, the group had twelve users, and by September, they had a hundred.

Encouraged and thinking he could fill a local market void, John-Henry opened for business as a Citrus County Internet service provider in October. He called his new venture Hitter, Inc.[4] The domain name was Hitter.net.

Ted was in a funk while rehabbing after his hip surgery, and John-Henry thought it would be good to take him on what probably would be his last fishing trip.

The plan was to go to one of Williams's favorite spots: Ascension Bay, off Mexico's Yucatán Peninsula. Ted asked a friend of his, Brian O'Connor, to join them. O'Connor, a Polaroid executive and Jimmy Fund trustee who had served in Vietnam as a Marine, had met Ted in the '80s, and the two had become friends. Williams considered O'Connor to be a savvy businessman and wanted to ask him to keep an eye on John-Henry and his various ventures.

John-Henry had rented a house with a cook. Ted and O'Connor fished all day, from 7:00 a.m. to 6:00 p.m., in a small boat. John-Henry was on his own most of the time. Williams was still shaky from the hip surgery, so they rigged up a contraption to steady him in the boat. A guide who didn't speak English stood in the back, leading them to bone-fish and permit. O'Connor wasn't a fisherman and devoted much of his attention to making sure Ted didn't fall out of the boat.

O'Connor met John-Henry for the first time on the trip. Then, after returning to Florida, at Ted's request, he began spending more time with young Williams, analyzing his business record to that point and offering him advice for the future. "John-Henry had this high opinion of himself," said O'Connor. "Confidence isn't a bad thing, but it needs to be realistic." Realistic John-Henry was not. According to O'Connor, he thought he might be the next Steve Jobs.

"There was nothing but dead business bodies in John-Henry's wake," O'Connor noted. "He had so many bad deals it was incredible. He never told me he made a mistake or it was his fault." As for Hitter, Inc., or Hitter Communications, as it was also known, Ted had told O'Connor what he knew about it on the fishing trip, which wasn't much. "Ted knew Hitter was an Internet service provider, but he didn't know a computer from a phone," O'Connor said. "He didn't really know what was going on with the business. But I think Ted was aware that a lot of money generated by the memorabilia activities was going into Hitter. Also, the museum was starting up. John-Henry had a captive market there and was selling Ted memorabilia to the museum. There was a lot of commingling of funds going on."[5]

★   ★   ★

As John-Henry was trying to get his Internet business off the ground in the fall of 1997, he became embroiled in a headline-grabbing memorabilia scandal featuring an FBI sting operation to retrieve two supposedly stolen Red Sox rings that had belonged to Ted before he'd given them to his son. The first ring commemorated the team's 1946 pennant, which Ted had been instrumental in winning; the second, which the Red Sox gave to Williams, honored the club's 1986 American League championship.

The key figure in the rings affair was Rodney Nichols, the Maine state trooper who had befriended John-Henry when he was at the University of Maine. After his graduation, John-Henry had stored many of his personal effects in the basement of Nichols's parents' house in Eliot, Maine—including, it emerged, the two rings.

Nichols had left the Maine state police and was working at a car dealership when, in 1997, he found himself owing a New Hampshire bookie $33,000. Unable to pay, he remembered the rings, which he said John-Henry had abandoned in storage at the Nichols family house. Nichols told the *Boston Globe* that he and his father, also a Maine state trooper, had repeatedly asked John-Henry to pick up his belongings, to no avail. Finally, the father notified John-Henry he was going to sell off his possessions at a yard sale. Sorting through the material, he came upon the rings. Rodney Nichols called John-Henry, who said, "I wondered where those things went."

"He never asked for them back or brought them up again," Nichols said.[6]

Nichols, inferring he now owned the rings, gave them to the bookie to settle his debt. The bookie, wanting to ensure the rings were authentic, gave them to an emissary to bring to Phil Castinetti, who ran the largest memorabilia business in New England from his store outside Boston. Castinetti could see the rings were genuine, but he needed to be sure they were not stolen.

"The guy who brought the rings in said to me, 'They're not stolen—call the kid,' meaning John-Henry," Castinetti remembered. "I called John-Henry, and he said, 'I've got to get them back.' I asked, 'Are they stolen?' and he said, 'No, no they're not, but I need to get them.'"

Castinetti told John-Henry he would sell the rings back to him for $90,000. Otherwise he would auction them off. He even called in a local TV crew to show them the rings and publicize his auction. John-Henry decided to call the FBI. But whereas he had told Castinetti that the rings were not stolen, John-Henry told federal agents that they were. A meeting was arranged, and John-Henry, accompanied by an undercover FBI agent, showed up at the Hotel Meridien in Boston with a satchel containing $90,000 in cash.

"Knowing John-Henry was a sneaky little bastard, I brought my lawyer just in case," Castinetti said.[7] The lawyer insisted that John-Henry sign an affidavit confirming that the rings were not stolen, and John-Henry did. Then, after the diamond-encrusted rings with Ted's name carved on the sides were turned over and the money changed hands, a gaggle of gun-toting federal agents burst into the room and arrested Castinetti. He and two associates were charged with possessing stolen property and selling stolen goods that had been taken across state lines. The whole scene was captured by a camera that authorities had hidden in the hotel room. Later, Rodney Nichols was also arrested and charged separately with stealing the rings.

"I'm very pleased with the work the FBI has done," John-Henry told the *Globe*. "Absolutely first class."[8]

US Attorney Donald Stern, in high dudgeon and groping for what he considered the appropriate baseball metaphor, told a press conference: "These guys must have been out in left field to try to sell these stolen rings back to John-Henry Williams. Ted Williams earned these rings, and his son shouldn't be shaken down to get them back."

At the Castinetti trial in March of 1998, John-Henry testified that Nichols had stolen the rings from him. He said he had gone back to the Nichols family home to retrieve his other Ted memorabilia. But Nichols's father, Maine state trooper Robert Nichols, took the witness stand to deny that John-Henry had ever returned, and he produced a box of valuable memorabilia as proof, including hundreds of photos of Ted, signed publicity photos, personal family photographs, handwritten letters from Ted to John-Henry, several plaques given to Ted by the Jimmy Fund, and Ted's handwritten address book. It was in this same box, Robert Nichols testified, that he had found the rings. When he called John-Henry to ask him to pick up his belongings, John-Henry told him to "get rid of everything but my skis and my poles," Nichols said.[9]

After deliberating nine hours, a jury acquitted Castinetti and his two associates on all charges. In a statement, John-Henry said: "I stand by my testimony. The rings are still my property. I never gave them away." Castinetti was bitter. "It just didn't have to happen this way," he said. The arrests and trial only happened "for one reason: Ted Williams, the name, that's it."[10]

But three months later, Rodney Nichols was found guilty by a federal jury in Portland, Maine, of stealing the rings and was sentenced to six months of house arrest. Jurors said they concluded that while John-Henry had been careless with his belongings in leaving them at the Nichols house for so long, the rings were still his property, and Rodney Nichols had no right to take them.

So the rings were returned to young Williams.

One of the pleasures of Ted's life was following Red Sox games via a satellite dish and the forty-six-inch television that the club had given him. He liked to watch the players, evaluate the talent, then call general manager Dan Duquette to kibitz about something he saw or someone else on another team whom he liked and thought the Sox should trade for.

Duquette, who served as general manager from 1994 to 2002, thought Ted's mind was still razor sharp—at least for baseball. "He could go back and re-create an at bat better than anyone I ever heard—what the pitch was, what the count was, what the situation was. Unbelievable." And Duquette loved it when Ted came to Boston and visited Fenway Park. His favorite story was the time Williams reunited with Helen Robinson, the team's legendary telephone operator, whose tenure extended back to Ted's day. "One day Ted was in my office, and after we were finished talking, I said, 'Ted, I'd be remiss if I didn't bring you down to see Helen.' He said, 'Helen Robinson! Absolutely!' So we walked down the hall. Helen sees Ted and said: 'Ted Williams! Come over here and I'll give you a hug.' So he walks over with his cane and said, 'Is that *all* you're gonna give me, Helen?' And Ted put his arms around Helen. Helen was slight. He was hugging her, and all of a sudden I see tears coming down Helen's cheek. Later, I asked her why she was crying. She said, 'He was standing on my foot! I knew he couldn't see that well, and I didn't have the heart to tell him to get off.'"

Ted's favorite Red Sox player, the one he asked Duquette about most, was Nomar Garciaparra, the shortstop who had been named Rookie of the Year in 1997.

"He called me after the first time he saw Nomar and said, 'Where did you get this kid?'" Duquette recalled. "I told him he'd gone to Georgia Tech, been in the Cape League, and so on. Then he said, 'You know, he reminds me of somebody that I've seen. I can't put my finger on it. I'll think of it.' Ten days later I get a call. Voice on the end of the line said: 'DiMaggio.'"

"One day Ted calls again. Nomar's hitting about .380. Ted said, 'Dan, this guy can hit .400. Take his walks and double them. This guy can hit .400 if he wants, but he's got to be a more selective hitter.' Nomar was a notorious first-pitch hitter.

"After Nomar won the batting title for the second consecutive time, I picked up the phone, called Ted, and said: 'DiMaggio.' Ted said, 'That's what I told you.'"[11]

When Williams met current Red Sox players, he'd ask them a range of questions—what pitches they looked for, how they approached a certain pitcher, what they thought about Fenway Park. In Nomar's rookie year, Ted asked Duquette to arrange a phone call so that he could quiz the shortstop on the fine points of the game. Garciaparra had heard about Williams's skull sessions with the players and was nervous before the call came through.

"He pounded me with questions to see how much I knew and what I was thinking about hitting," Garciaparra recalled. "He would ask about certain situations and what am I trying to do in those situations. 'What are you thinking on a three-and-two count? When you're struggling, how do you get out of it?' I just answered him instinctively."

Williams liked Nomar's answers and called Duquette to tell him so. Duquette then called Nomar to report that Ted had said he was the first Red Sox player he'd talked to who answered all his questions correctly.

"From that time on, Ted and I became friends," Garciaparra said. "We would talk numerous times during the season. Even after we took batting practice the phone would ring in the clubhouse. Helen Robinson, the operator, would say, 'I've got your hitting coach on the line.' It was Ted checking in. 'How are you doing? How you feeling?'

"Baseball was obviously our connection, but once we got to know each other it was about life. We had things in common. We were both from Southern California and had played ball in Boston. Then his mom was Mexican, and both my parents are Mexican. So we were talking about family."[12]

Following his brief star turn for George H. W. Bush in the New Hampshire primary of 1988, Williams continued to dabble in politics at both the local and national levels. He endorsed the Citrus County sheriff, Jeff Dawsy, even though Dawsy was a Democrat. And Ted got involved in a Massachusetts sheriff's race on behalf of the incumbent in Middlesex County at the time, Brad Bailey, a Republican whom he had met through John-Henry. Williams filmed a TV commercial for Bailey and even flew up to Boston to attend a fund-raiser for him, but Bailey lost the election.

Ted's next political foray came in the summer of 1997. *Esquire* magazine had asked Arizona senator John McCain, the famed Vietnam War hero and Navy pilot who had been shot down and taken as a POW, who his hero was, and he had said it was Ted. The two had first met in 1993, when John Dowd, McCain's lawyer, who'd also represented Ted in the Antonucci affair, introduced them. Williams signed a baseball, and McCain still kept it on his mantel at home. Now McCain was preparing to run for reelection to a third term in the Senate the following year. After that he planned to seek the Republican nomination for president. A Hernando visit was arranged

McCain waited a while in Ted's house for Williams to appear. Finally Ted came out from his bedroom, using a walker. From the hallway, he bellowed: "Where is that guy that's gonna be the next president of the United States?"

McCain was struck by how much frailer Ted had become in four years. He asked a question: Was it true, as the Williams mythology had it, that he really could see the laces on the ball after it left the pitcher's hand? "Shit, no," Ted replied. "You're reading all these sportswriters. Jesus, that ball looked like a pea coming in there."

They talked about the wars they'd served in and about flying in combat. McCain asked Ted about the time his plane had been shot up in Korea and why he hadn't ejected. Williams had told the story a thousand times, but cheerfully went through it again. He was almost six four and knew that if he'd ejected he would have broken both knees. "I'd have rather died than never to have been able to play baseball again," Ted said.

Williams remarked that McCain looked like a million bucks and should think about running for president. The senator was encouraged. "If Ted Williams thought I could do it, well, why shouldn't I give it a shot," he wrote in his 2002 book, *Worth the Fighting For,* in which he devoted a chapter to Williams.[13]

McCain announced his candidacy for president in September of 1999. Williams liked McCain and wanted to back him, but there was a complication: George W. Bush was also running. Ted loved Bush's father. After he helped George H. W. in New Hampshire in 1988, the president had honored him at the White House twice in 1991, and he'd come down to Hernando in 1995 for Ted's annual museum shindig. Williams knew he had to stay loyal to the Bushes, so he endorsed the Texas governor a few weeks before the New Hampshire primary in 2000.

The endorsement stung McCain, but he would defeat Bush in the primary decisively. John-Henry was concerned that his father had backed the wrong horse. He called Dave McCarthy, the New Hampshire state trooper, complaining that McCarthy had assured him Bush would win. It wasn't good for Ted's brand to back a loser. An annoyed McCarthy assured John-Henry that Bush would go on to win the Republican nomination and the presidency, which he did.[*]

Despite Ted's frail condition, John-Henry still had him out working the memorabilia circuit. In their mind's eye, fans who hadn't seen Williams for a time no doubt assumed that he was still vigorous, so they were startled by what they actually saw. In January 1998, for example, at an autograph show at the Ramada Plaza Hotel near JFK Airport in New York, there were gasps in the crowd as the Kid, pale and sickly-looking, was wheeled into a conference room and helped into a chair on a raised platform to begin his work, for a $225 minimum per signature. "It was a sickening sight," said David Armstrong, then a *Boston Globe* reporter, who was present.

Ted turned eighty on August 30 of that year.[†] "Well, I'm getting along pretty good," he told Dan Shaughnessy while in a reflective mood. Shaughnessy was one of the few writers Williams liked. "I can't run. I can't fish, and I don't see that good. I can't drive. But…thank God there's a television."[14]

Ted, as he mellowed, found that he actually enjoyed doing interviews and staying in touch with his public. Earlier that year he'd flown up to New York to go on television's *Late Night with Conan O'Brien* program. Two months later Ted was asked to throw out a first ball at the first game that the Tampa Bay Devil Rays played at Tropicana Field in Saint Petersburg. The Rays sent a helicopter to Hernando to pick him up from his front lawn.[15][‡]

That October, Williams went over to the Kennedy Space Center to see his old pal John Glenn return to space aboard the shuttle *Discovery*,

---

[*] After the nomination was settled, Ted unsuccessfully lobbied Bush's father to have his son choose McCain as his running mate.

[†] Williams was watching the Red Sox play the Angels at Fenway Park with his cook, Robert Hogerheide, a former Navy chef, when they heard the announcers wish him a happy birthday. So Ted called Fenway, and they patched him straight through to the TV booth. "They broadcast the conversation right on the air as we were watching," said Hogerheide. "It was great!"

[‡] Meanwhile, to honor Ted, the Marine Commandant had recently promoted him from captain to colonel. Williams was thrilled by this and loved for his caretakers or friends to call him Colonel.

thirty-six years after he became the first American to orbit the earth. Williams was introduced to another celebrity attending the launch, rocker Steven Tyler of the Boston-based band Aerosmith, but the name didn't ring a bell. "So, you're in a band, huh? What kind of band?" Ted asked. Tyler, graciously, didn't try too hard to explain, saying simply: "Ted, I think it was more of a pleasure for me to meet you than for you to meet me."[16]

The following month, Ted took John-Henry with him to a reunion of his 1969 Senators team in Chantilly, Virginia. Williams made a dramatic late entrance in a wheelchair pushed by his son. As the crowd stood and applauded, Ted stood up by himself, hobbled to the stage, and began to speak.[17]

On March 8, 1999, Joe DiMaggio died. Ted, quite sick himself by then, was in bed watching the History Channel on television when one of his caretakers came in to give him the news. Soon Dan Shaughnessy called and asked for his thoughts on Joe's death. "I can only tell you that I'm sad, but I'm glad Joe's not suffering anymore," Ted said. "He was an American hero and a legend for sure. I never, ever compared myself to him. I thought there never was a greater player in the history of baseball. For me just to be mentioned in the same breath, boy, I always felt like I was two steps below him. I thought I could hit with anybody, but he was in my opinion as good as any that ever played the game."[18]

Williams did a round of interviews on the occasion of Joe's death, including an appearance on the *Today* show, where he appeared to doze off after being questioned by Tom Brokaw, as Brokaw interviewed another guest.

Ted always considered himself a foodie, so he was delighted, that spring, to be visited by Molly O'Neill, the food columnist for the *New York Times Magazine,* for an in-the-kitchen-with-Ted spread that was headlined WHAT HAPPENS WHEN TED WILLIAMS—THE SPLENDID SPATULA—STEPS UP TO THE PLATE. (Actually, Ted wasn't doing the cooking anymore. He was barking orders at one of the men who cooked for him.[19]) When O'Neill said the best egg she'd ever had was in Paris, Williams playfully erupted, badgering her to admit that his were better.

Besides food, there was another connection between O'Neill and Ted: baseball. Her brother happened to be New York Yankees outfielder Paul O'Neill, who at that moment was 5–50 in spring training, Molly told Ted.

"Get that brother of yours on the phone!" Williams yelled. "I need to talk to that kid. Get him on the phone!"

"Paul? This is Ted Williams. I been thinkin' 'bout you. You're a helluva ballplayer," Ted said before passing on a few tips: hit inside out and swing low to high. "But you know all this. Don't let anybody change ya. Hit the ball hard up the middle. Don't pull it. Wait for your pitch. And remember that the lousier you're hittin', the more you're thinkin' about hittin'. You shouldn't have a worry in the world. I'm tellin' ya right now, you're a helluva player."

That afternoon, Paul O'Neill broke out, going 3–4.[20]

By its first anniversary, in July of 1998, Hitter, Inc., John-Henry's Internet venture, had succeeded in attracting four thousand paying customers in the three-county area around Hernando. In November of '98, Hitter expanded into Gainesville and Orlando, and by the end of the year, to Tampa. John-Henry laid out an ambitious goal of extending the company's reach throughout Florida by the end of 1999 and going national by 2000. Hitter invested heavily in the newest and most advanced computer technology, including a state-of-the-art server and the infrastructure for high bandwidth through ISDN phone lines and T1 lines. Hitter also offered website design and maintenance services, twenty-four-hour technical support, a training center, and a repair store.[21] For his staff, John-Henry insisted on hiring only Microsoft-certified professionals and was willing to pay high salaries to get them.

Soon he found that the funds from the memorabilia companies, while considerable, were insufficient for the ambitious expansion he had in mind for Hitter. So in the spring of 1999, he borrowed about $500,000 from Gerry Rittenberg, the CEO of Party City, the largest retail party-supply chain in the country. Rittenberg was also a leading collector of Ted Williams memorabilia (he had acquired Ted's 1947 Triple Crown trophy, among other items) and a board member of the Williams museum who had become a friend and booster of John-Henry's.

Rittenberg agreed to loan the half million dollars for Hitter on condition that the loan be secured by the equivalent amount of Ted memorabilia. A grateful John-Henry threw in two more valuable items that he said Rittenberg could keep: Ted's newly retrieved Red Sox rings from 1946 and 1986.

But six months later, John-Henry asked for the rings back. "I said, 'Oh, shit.' I liked the rings but understood he should have them," Rittenberg said. "He also asked me if I'd give him the Triple Crown. So we did a deal. The deal was he would buy the Triple Crown and the rings back in return for giving me certain other memorabilia."[22]

John-Henry repaid the $500,000 loan within three months, and Rittenberg said he provided young Williams with other short-term loans secured by memorabilia. John-Henry was apparently able to repay Rittenberg so quickly because he obtained another loan for Hitter in the amount of $570,000 from a local SunTrust Bank on July 6, 1999. The SunTrust loan was in turn secured by an investment account valued at about $740,000 that Ted maintained at the bank.[23] According to Eric Abel, Ted signed off on the loan to Hitter in which his funds were used as collateral.

In moving aggressively to expand Hitter, John-Henry struck deals with a number of major telecommunications companies—including AT&T, BellSouth, Qwest, Sprint, MCI, and Time Warner—to acquire large amounts of bandwidth. Getting the bandwidth to remote Hernando required the companies to invest a lot of money: Time Warner, for example, dug a dedicated fiber-optic line from Tampa to Hernando just to service John-Henry's order for Hitter, and AT&T had to expand its infrastructure in Tampa. These costs were reflected in the companies' monthly bills to Hitter, which were enormous. AT&T alone was charging $1.5 million a month, and Eric Abel estimated that when the other firms' bills were added in, Hitter's monthly costs for bandwidth were $4 million. Though Hitter would grow and eventually attract tens of thousands of subscribers, the customers' monthly payments of about $22, along with revenue from local small businesses, did not begin to generate enough income to service the high bandwidth costs. Faced with this shortfall, and knowing he had lots of unused bandwidth to sell, John-Henry decided to take Hitter in a radical new direction: pornography.

In archconservative Citrus County, this decision was a closely guarded secret. Eric Abel registered Hitter's porn subsidiary, which was called Strictly Hosting, Inc., in Nevada, along with a related corporate shell called Strictly, Inc. If Strictly Hosting were ever to be hauled into court on smut charges, the thinking went, the litigation should take place where the company was registered, in Nevada, where the denizens were presumably more sympathetic to matters of the flesh.

Two Citrus County men were recruited and paid handsomely to help run Strictly Hosting and to agree to put their names on the corporate papers in Nevada. The party line would be that Strictly, which Abel said never produced its own porn, was an independent business simply buying bandwidth from Hitter.

Secrecy was paramount. John-Henry, when he e-mailed about Strictly Hosting, used the pseudonym Eric Good. The town fathers of

Hernando certainly would have looked askance at a porn-trafficking business, and Hitter's regular Internet customers likely would have frowned on the association, too. Then there was the risk of tarnishing the Ted Williams brand. And Ted himself could never know, of course, even though $570,000 of his funds had been used as collateral to help launch Hitter.

It wasn't long before John-Henry's bandwidth suppliers caught on. "I started noticing a tremendous amount of traffic coming out of Hernando, which was highly unusual for a place that isolated," said a sales rep for one of the telecoms that dealt with John-Henry. "Then the Strictly Hosting people I met confirmed it, and John-Henry finally admitted it." Strictly Hosting provided users with links to such websites as Filthy Teens and Hospital Fetishes as well as to other sites that carried numerous graphic images of men and women engaged in sex. Said the sales rep, "At the height of his business there he had almost every site that was on the Internet for porn. He had customers in California, Detroit, the Carolinas, Boston. Hernando is a notch in the Bible Belt, but it became the porn capital of the South."

While the telecom industry might have been reluctant to deal directly with porn companies, they were sometimes quite happy to do so at arm's length through an intermediary like Hitter. Soon the representative, who asked not to be identified, and John-Henry were flying first-class to Los Angeles to meet with leaders of the porn industry, solicit business, and sign contracts. Said the sales rep, "The porn people weren't the most trusting guys, but John-Henry would always tell them, 'You know who my father is? You should go ahead and trust me. Where am I going to go? There's nowhere for me to hide. Look who my dad is.'"[24]*

While the money was nice, not everyone in John-Henry's circle was happy with his new endeavor, especially Anita Lovely, to whom John-Henry had become engaged. The wedding was set for September 9, 1999—or 9/9/99, a date chosen to show off Ted's old Red Sox number to maximum effect. Anita, a devout Catholic, was troubled by the porn business, to say the least, but knew she couldn't stop it.

"It's funny, in retrospect this stuff looks naughty and bad, but at the time it was just pure business," said Abel. "John-Henry was being a busi-

---

* The sales rep also accompanied John-Henry on several fruitless nonporn sales pitches in which the son tried to leverage the father's name to get business for Hitter, including proposals to the Detroit Tigers owner, Mike Ilitch, and to the Jimmy Fund in Boston. John-Henry was trying to persuade both organizations to hire Hitter to provide their Internet services and website design.

nessman. He wanted what could be profitable, and didn't have the same moral concerns that others might."

On June 11, 1999, Ted made a trip to New York. New York Mets owner Nelson Doubleday had wanted to honor Williams while the Red Sox were in town to play the Mets, so a thin pretense was created: a celebration of the sixtieth anniversary of Ted's rookie year. After paying tribute to New York baseball fans and saying the best team he ever played for was "the US Marines," Ted prepared to throw out the first ball. Steadied by legendary pitcher Tom Seaver and another former Met, Rusty Staub, Williams then lobbed one in to Mets catcher Mike Piazza, who had received hitting tips from Ted as a teenager.[25]

Tommy Lasorda, the former Dodgers manager and Ted pal who was on hand for the ceremony, witnessed John-Henry take advantage of the moment by demanding that his father be compensated for the event. Recalled Lasorda, "Doubleday really got upset. He said, 'Listen, you young squirt!' I asked Doubleday later what that was about, and he said, 'The guy wanted me to pay an appearance fee!' They were honoring Ted, for Chrissakes. Doubleday said to me, 'That young punk! That SOB!'"[26]

Years later, asked about the incident, Doubleday said he didn't recall clashing with John-Henry. "I don't have a memory of it, but I was prejudiced against the kid beforehand. I'd heard so many bad things and that he was ruining Ted's life."[27]

In any case, as far as John-Henry was concerned, the Shea Stadium appearance was a mere dress rehearsal for what he hoped would unfold in Boston the following month. On July 13, the All-Star Game was to be held at Fenway Park. To celebrate the end of the century, Major League Baseball was planning to announce an All-Century Team. The thirty-odd living players chosen for the hundred-man team would be flown to Boston and introduced by actor Kevin Costner in what was intended to be a re-creation of Costner's *Field of Dreams* leitmotif. Old-timers like Stan Musial, Willie Mays, Hank Aaron, Bob Feller, and Yogi Berra would join the current All-Stars, including Nomar Garciaparra, Mark McGwire, Sammy Sosa, and Derek Jeter. But to anchor the show, the Red Sox knew they had to have Ted throw out the first ball. So the team, and the league, assigned Dan Duquette to line the Kid up. "He wasn't sure if he could come because of his health," recalled Duquette. "I kept talking to him. I said we'd get him a private plane. All his friends would be there. The fans wanted to see him. He had to come."

Part of the problem was that it now was getting increasingly hard to persuade Ted to go anywhere. Claudia Williams said he would work himself into a tizzy before he was scheduled to appear somewhere. "Two or three weeks before an event, he'd be a bear. 'This is the last fuckin' event I'm ever gonna go to!' But then after it was over he'd say, 'Wasn't that great, and wasn't it great to see so-and-so?'" She said the buildup to an appearance became so fraught that John-Henry would only tell him about an event two or three days in advance to curb the Sturm und Drang.

Duquette wasn't the only one having a hard time closing the sale. John-Henry wanted his father to go to Boston both to burnish the Williams legacy and to reap the attendant commercial benefits. John-Henry told Peter Sutton, a Boston lawyer who helped represent the family's interests, that he had fielded offers from a few corporations to pay Ted six figures if he were willing to wear their corporate logos on the field. John-Henry and Duquette both asked Sutton to get involved in persuading Ted to come. "I called Ted, and when I mentioned that there were some corporations who wanted him to wear their logo, that didn't interest him, but then he turned to John-Henry, who was in the room, and said, 'If I went for you, would that help your company?' John-Henry said yes. So Ted said, 'I'll go for my son.' John-Henry and I laughed later and said, 'Why didn't we think of that before?'"[28]

Claudia said: "At key moments in Dad's life, we got him to do things by making it a personal appeal. 'Will you do this for us, Dad? Me and John-Henry.'" If the question was framed in personal terms, she said, Ted's attitude was, "'Well, if you put it that way, sure I will!' To protect Dad in that context meant to make everyone think he was going to the All-Star Game to see all the old players and all that. Really he was doing it for John-Henry."

It was unclear initially how Ted would demonstrate his support for Hitter.net, but John-Henry soon confided his plans to the telecom sales representative: Ted would be making a series of appearances in and around Boston leading up to the game. He would wear both a polo shirt and a baseball cap emblazoned with the Hitter.net logo at each event and, finally, at the game itself.

"I said to John-Henry, 'There's no way Ted will wear the hat at the game. The guy never tipped his hat to the fans when he played. What makes you think he's gonna wear your baseball cap?'" the sales rep recalled. "And John-Henry said: 'Oh, I'm going to get him to do it. Blood is thicker than baseball.'"

*   ★   ★

Ted arrived in Boston several days before the game and checked into a suite at the Four Seasons Hotel overlooking the Public Garden. Traveling with him were John-Henry, Anita, and a caretaker, Jack Gard.

The first event on the schedule was at the Jimmy Fund, where Ted was to meet Einar Gustafson, the sixty-three-year-old Maine truck driver who was the original "Jimmy," the pseudonymous boy who had become the poster child of the charity back in 1948. Brian O'Connor, the Polaroid executive and Jimmy Fund board member, had arranged the event, which he knew would be a publicity bonanza for the charity: Williams, its chief benefactor, was meeting its original namesake.

But O'Connor had nearly failed to get John-Henry to agree to the visit. "He didn't think it was practical," O'Connor said. "He didn't see the benefit of Ted going to the Jimmy Fund. He didn't see what he would get out of it, so I laid the law down. I said there was more to this than monetary benefit. He just didn't see that. He was a cold kid."

As it turned out, John-Henry was delighted when a swarm of media turned up for the Ted and Jimmy show. "Where's this guy, Jimmy?" Williams shouted on arriving at the Dana-Farber Cancer Institute, wearing a powder-blue Hitter.net shirt and a red Hitter.net baseball cap. Ted was taken to meet some dignitaries first, but eventually caught up with Gustafson. "How are you, Jimmy baby?" Ted fairly shouted. "This is the biggest thrill of my trip, right here! Geez, you look great! You're an inspiration to everybody!" The two sat in rocking chairs and reminisced about the Jimmy Fund's early days, and then Williams made the rounds to visit the sick kids as he used to do.

"Boy, oh, boy, what a good-looking kid you are!"

"How are you doing with school now?"

"I bet you're not here too long."[29]

The next day, Ted traveled to Loudon, New Hampshire, to serve as grand marshal for the Jiffy Lube 300, a stop on the NASCAR circuit at the New Hampshire International Speedway. Ted, dressed in his Hitter .net finery again, fit right in with the NASCAR drivers, all of whom looked like human billboards, hawking motor oil, soft drinks, car companies, and various tire brands.[30]

Williams was introduced to a loud ovation from a crowd that he was astonished to learn numbered fully ninety thousand. Then he was taken for a spin around the oval in a green Chevy. He shook hands with each of the forty-three drivers, did an interview with the television announcer, and, when the time came, took the microphone and said the magic words of car racing: "Gentlemen, start your engines!" Then John-Henry brought his father up close to the rail for a taste of the energy as the cars roared past.

On the day of the All-Star Game, Ted and John-Henry went to Fenway Park to go over the logistics of Williams's appearance that night. His limousine would get a police escort from the hotel to the park and enter in a holding area underneath the center-field bleachers, off Lansdowne Street. Then, after the other old-timers were introduced, Ted would make his grand entrance from center field in a golf cart driven by Al Forester, a member of the Red Sox grounds crew who had been working for the team since 1957. Williams knew Forester well and had often used his name as an alias over the years when checking into hotels.

During this walk-through, John-Henry asked Brian O'Connor what he thought about Ted wearing the Hitter.net hat. "I said I thought it was more appropriate that he wear the Red Sox hat, but if Ted wants to wear it, that's his business. Ted had told me during those few days, 'I'm up here to promote Hitter, period.' So the hat, in that context, made sense."

Jack Gard, the caretaker on the trip, was repulsed, but not surprised, by the decision. "It was disgusting. That really made a lot of Ted's friends back away because they could see the kid was exploiting him."[31]

Gard and John-Henry had a tense relationship. In 1998, Gard had filed a formal complaint with Florida's Department of Children and Families alleging that Ted was being abused by his son. A department investigator responded by going to Ted's house, accompanied by a sheriff's detective. After questioning Williams, the official decided the complaint was unwarranted. Ted said he enjoyed working with his son and helping him out.[32]*

Not long before the start of the game, Ted's limo, escorted by a squad of policemen on motorcycles, eased down Lansdowne Street, behind the Green Monster, and pulled to a stop at an entrance behind center field. Spotting Williams, a crowd surged around him, chanting, "Ted! Ted! Ted!"

New Hampshire state trooper Dave McCarthy sprang into action with his two friends Eric Goodman and Dan Wheeler, each dressed in Hitter.net polo shirts. They formed a circle around Ted and got him out

---

* Gard was fired in 2000 for allegedly getting Ted to sign autographs and then selling them without permission, according to Eric Abel, the Williams family lawyer. Gard denied he was fired and said he quit for health reasons.

of harm's way into a garage area where Al Forester was waiting in his golf cart.

Williams climbed into the passenger seat and chatted with well-wishers, then Forester drove over behind a red curtain that was covering the open garage door. In a few minutes Ted would emerge from the curtain and make his entrance on the center-field warning track. The other members of the All-Century Team had already walked onto the field to be introduced.

As John-Henry waited, he took McCarthy aside. The son was having a last-minute twinge of doubt about putting his father in the Hitter.net hat. Someone from the Red Sox had brought a team hat for him to wear on the field. Ted was already wearing the company shirt. McCarthy thought the hat would be overkill. John-Henry said he still thought Ted should wear the Hitter hat, but was looking for reassurance.

McCarthy said this was the All-Star Game, a national showcase, and each player was expected to wear his team hat. If he put Ted in the Hitter.net hat, John-Henry should expect a heavy backlash. John-Henry noted that Carl Yastrzemski, Ted's successor in left field for the Red Sox, had just been introduced as a member of the All-Century Team wearing no hat at all. Recalled McCarthy, "He said, 'You know, millions of people are gonna be watching this on TV. It's good for Dad and good for me and the company. Watch how many hits we're gonna get on the website.'"[33] So John-Henry put a sparkling white Hitter.net hat firmly on his father's head and sent Ted out into the night, into the roaring crowd.

Forester took a slight left and headed his golf cart along the two right-field bull pens. He drove slowly to give the 34,187 adoring fans, and Williams himself, plenty of time to soak up the moment. Then he took a hard right at Pesky's Pole, went past the Red Sox dugout, behind home plate, and past the visitors' dugout. The American League and National League All-Stars all applauded as they stood along the baselines, as did the All-Century players. Ted waved the unfamiliar white hat early and often to the delirious crowd—hat tipping, after all, was now routine for him since he'd shattered his own taboo against the practice back in 1991.

Then Forester took a right around third base and headed to the pitcher's mound, where Ted was engulfed by players young and old in a memorable tableau of spontaneous joy and adulation. The younger players seemed especially eager to bask in Ted's aura, and he happily greeted some of his favorites, including Tony Gwynn, of the San Diego Padres, and Nomar Garciaparra. Mark McGwire pressed in for a blessing and

Ted asked him if he had ever smelled burned wood when he fouled off a pitch. "All the time," McGwire replied.

The players kept crowding around and wouldn't leave, despite pleas from the public-address announcer to do so. "Everybody said no," recalled Garciaparra. "Nobody wanted to leave."

It was a magical moment, one of the greatest nights in Ted's life. "I'm a rather emotional guy, and when I got up there, tears were coming out of Ted's eyes," said Larry Walker of the Colorado Rockies. "I kind of turned away. It almost brought tears to my eyes. The greatest player in the world is surrounded by more great players. It was outstanding to see."

Finally Tony Gwynn helped Ted out of the golf cart and pointed him toward home plate so he could throw out the first ball. As Gwynn took firm hold of his left arm, Williams stood in front of the mound and tossed a ball in on the fly to Carlton Fisk, the former Red Sox catcher. A giddy Fisk then jogged out to hug Ted.[34]

After the ceremony, Al Forester drove Ted up to luxury box L–22, the Polaroid suite, overlooking left field, which had been rented by Gerry Rittenberg for four days during the All-Star festivities. Rittenberg was there with his father and two sons. John-Henry was there, thrilled, along with Anita. Actor Matt Damon came by with his father. The four pilots who had buzzed Fenway in their jets during the pregame flyover dropped by to pay their respects, and Ted quizzed them on what altitude they'd been cleared for. The pilots said twelve hundred feet.

"You weren't at twelve hundred feet, you were at seven hundred feet, right?" Ted said.

"You're right, sir," the pilots replied sheepishly. Then they talked in detail about the specs of the jets: their engine thrust, how fast they could go, and how they compared to those Williams had flown in Korea.[35]

Predictably, John-Henry took a shellacking in the press for his Hitter.net play. Even some of his close friends and his sister Claudia questioned the move. But Claudia said her father himself later told her he'd been all in. "Dad said, 'I wouldn't go out on the goddamn field if I wasn't wearing the hat.'"

However, at Williams's next public appearance, that October—a cameo at the second World Series game in Atlanta, which John-Henry did not attend—Ted took the field in his Red Sox hat.

30

Spiraling

Ted's joy at the reception he received at the All-Star Game was short-lived, tempered by the death, that same month, of his long-time faithful dog, the Dalmatian named Slugger.

Williams had grown so attached to the dog that he had told many of his friends that he wanted to die before Slugger did. He'd even said so publicly. "I've got a dog I absolutely love," Ted told the *Boston Globe* in 1998, just a year earlier. "I asked that guy in heaven to drop me dead before my dog. That's how much I love my dog."[1]

But Slugger had already been operated on for cancer, and now, at the age of thirteen, was struggling with kidney failure. And so the local vet, Charles Magill, who had been caring for Slugger for several years, was summoned. The dog was lying on his bed in the garage when Magill put him down.

Williams "was very stoic but quite verbal about his attachment to the dog," Magill recalled. "'Dogs are a lot more loyal than people and a lot nicer,' he said."

When talking with friends or his caretakers about his hope that he would die before his dog, Ted would usually go on to say that he and Slugger would both be cremated and their ashes tossed in the sea. That's what he told his *My Turn at Bat* ghostwriter John Underwood five months after Slugger's death, when Underwood visited with his wife just before Christmas. "Once, Ted paused in front of a picture of Slugger and said, 'Yeah, he's dead, and I'm going to have my ashes mixed with his and thrown out to sea,'" Underwood said. "We have a videotape of this."[2]

Three years later, after Ted died, Magill was shocked to read a quote from John-Henry in the local paper in which the younger Williams said that he had buried Slugger's ashes in Ted's backyard. Actually, John-Henry had never picked up the dog's ashes, and Magill still had them. "Ted loved Slugger so much," Magill said. "I think John-Henry may have been a little jealous of the dog."

Magill contacted Ted's estranged daughter, Bobby-Jo, and gave the ashes to her.[3]

Since John-Henry's arrival in Citrus Hills in 1994, he had narrowed Ted's circle of friends to those he deemed necessary or would never dare exclude, such as old Red Sox pals Dominic DiMaggio and Bobby Doerr. John-Henry could monitor who was calling the house from his office in Hernando, and he decided that certain calls and messages for Ted would go undelivered and thus unanswered.

"Ted had a huge network of friends from all walks of life," said Rich Eschen, who helped with the memorabilia business in Hernando. "Military friends, baseball friends, local schmucks, and he loved us all. I think John-Henry resented that. I think he wanted that attention. When John-Henry came down here, some of the people that Ted used to consider friends felt shut out. Friends of Ted's for fifty years who would come visit and shoot it with him—that all stopped around ninety-four."[4] Mail stacked up, and many Christmas cards and birthday wishes to Williams remained unopened or never given to him. As a result, Ted gradually felt more isolated. Buzz Hamon, a former director of Williams's museum, said Ted would call him and complain that he felt like a prisoner.[5]

Ted used the same word—*prisoner*—with two closer friends: Elden Auker, his former Red Sox teammate, and Tommy Lasorda. "John-Henry wouldn't let anyone get near Ted," Lasorda said. "Ted said to me, 'I'm like a prisoner. I can't get to see any of my friends.' He was in that house, and he couldn't get out. He couldn't do anything about it. I think I was one of the few he let in at all times. Me and Elden Auker."[6]

In March of 2000, Lasorda arranged to spring Ted from his house and fly him over to Vero Beach in a private plane to watch a Dodgers spring training game. Williams met with the Dodgers players in the clubhouse before the game and seemed offended when only about a dozen of them said they had read his book *The Science of Hitting*. "There are, what, sixty of you in this room, and only twelve of you have read that book? That's horseshit!" Ted said as the Dodgers laughed.[7]

In the stadium, Williams was introduced to the crowd, and Lasorda, mindful of Ted's failing vision, supplied a pitch-by-pitch account of the game as Auker sat next to them and looked on. "Afterwards, Ted said to me, 'Tommy, you made me the happiest guy in the world taking me down here today,'" Lasorda said.

Williams's deteriorating vision was also making it more difficult for him to see the Red Sox games on his big-screen television. He told Dom DiMaggio about this, as well as about his feelings of isolation, and DiMaggio found a way to address both problems: "I said, 'Teddy, how many guys do you see—you get a lot of guys coming?'" DiMaggio recalled. "He said, 'Dommie, I don't see anybody, and I have a hard time getting information on the game. I've got a big-screen TV, but I'm having trouble seeing it. People around here don't understand the game. I know when they win or lose, but I don't know the details.' I said, 'Teddy, this is what I'm going to do. I will call you every morning and give you the report in detail of the Sox game.' He said, 'Oh, that would be good.' So I called him every game except for a day off. Sometimes I would forget, and I'd kick myself."[8]

The press sensed Ted was nearing the end of the line, and Williams probably did, too, so he gave several valedictory interviews in which he offered some insights on his career and his persona.

Talking to Bob Greene for a *Life* magazine spread in February of 2000, he confessed, "My most disappointing things all my life were always related to baseball. I didn't feel good because I did something successfully—I felt bad if I failed to do something that I was expected to do." Williams said that while he always wanted people to think he was the greatest hitter who ever lived, he never believed it himself. "I didn't believe it then, and I don't believe it now," he said. "Babe Ruth, Hank Aaron, they were so good."

And what made him happy these days? The sound of birds, Ted said. "I've got five clocks in my house, and they all sing different songs, on the hour. At 10 a.m., I might hear eight or ten birds sing at the same time. I've learned to love to hear those clocks sing. The beautiful songs."[9]

In July, Williams explained to Paul Reid of the *Palm Beach Post* that before he was a fisherman he'd been a hunter. "I think the most peaceful times of my life were spent at dawn, in a duck blind somewhere," Ted said. "Manitoba. Minnesota. You wait for the flocks, it's quiet, a breeze maybe. So quiet. So majestic. But then the great bird migrations got not so great. The birds disappeared. People did that, yes? Not hunters, but mankind. What a wacky bunch we humans are."

Ted complained, quite forcefully, about getting old. "The so-called golden years. What a lot of bull. I think you ought to get a pill when you turn 72, a pill to take if and when you think it's time. I call it the Kevorkian pill."

More than anything, Reid was struck by Williams's curiosity. Ted asked the writer who he thought the most important American of the century was. Knowing Ted's conservative politics, Reid thought he would tweak him by answering FDR. While Williams mustered a few kind words for Roosevelt, he said he had someone else in mind.

MacArthur? Reid guessed.

"That's the ticket," said Ted. "Douglas MacArthur. There's a book about him, a book I read and then picked right up again and reread. *American Caesar* I think is the title. It's written by...ah, written by..."

"William Manchester," Reid said.

"Yes. What a writer."

Reid told Williams that he and Manchester had a few things in common. Manchester had been a Marine, wounded in Okinawa, and he was a lifelong Red Sox fan. Then Reid asked Ted if he'd like the renowned biographer's phone number. Reid was a good friend of Manchester's and before long would be chosen by the ailing writer to finish the third volume of his trilogy on Winston Churchill. Manchester would die in 2004.

Williams, always sensitive about his lack of formal education, asked Reid if he thought Manchester would really want to talk to him. Reid said he was quite sure the answer would be yes.

So the phone call was arranged, and it turned out that Ted and Manchester had something else in common: they had both faced Vic Raschi, the late New York Yankees pitcher. Manchester told Williams that he and Raschi had grown up in Springfield, Massachusetts—Manchester a light-hitting second baseman for Springfield's Classical High School and Raschi a flamethrower for Springfield Technical. Raschi made quick work of Manchester the one time he faced him, striking him out easily. "He threw so hard I couldn't even see the ball," said Manchester. "I feared for my life."

Back in Ted's kitchen, Reid watched as the Kid picked up a baseball in his right hand and gazed at it "with all the intensity of Hamlet with Yorick's noggin." Then he sighed, rolled the ball across the table, and said: "I was a ballplayer."

"Like a Ferrari is a car, Ted," Reid said.

Williams smiled at that. Reid thought Ted knew he was going to die soon.[10]

★   ★   ★

As John-Henry had hoped, following Ted's appearance at the All-Star Game, Hitter.net received a surge of interest, not only in the form of hits on its website but also in the form of some inquiries about buying the company. The most serious potential buyer was Duro Communications, a large Internet service provider near Orlando that had raised more than $100 million in equity and had quickly acquired dozens of smaller ISPs. But one issue soon emerged: Duro was only interested in the dial-up, ISP portion of Hitter, not its Web hosting component—that is, porn— and it concluded that the businesses were too intermingled.

Still, talks continued for almost a year through various fits and starts, but no deal would be had. "John-Henry was a sales and marketing guy with little regard for finances or understanding of finances, in my opinion," said Ted Taylor, head of Duro's investment bank. "The numbers didn't prove out all the time. His accountant would have some problems trying to reconcile John-Henry's numbers, and Duro was very thorough in their due diligence, and there were always things that came to light each time we would get close to a deal."

At one point, Taylor, who participated in the negotiations, said the company offered John-Henry a figure that was "north of $5 million" for Hitter. Peter Sutton, Williams's Boston-based lawyer, said that the figure was about $7 million, and that he and others advised John-Henry to "take it and run."

But John-Henry chose to hold out for more, believing he could ride the dot-com boom higher. However, the Internet bubble peaked in March of 2000 and went downhill, bursting by 2001. At the same time, interest rates increased, and the economy slowed.

"At the end, it fell apart because the numbers just wouldn't support the minimum price John-Henry wanted," Taylor said. "We kept trying to make it work, and it didn't. The fact of the matter was John-Henry was an excellent salesman, but he wasn't focused enough on what he was trying to do. We told him Hitter would go under, but he was in denial. He had the forethought and vision to build that business at first, but he should have found a techie and a business partner who would manage it for him. He was a nice guy, he commanded a presence; he just didn't know his own limitations."[11]

Duro's warning that Hitter would fail was prescient. Though his porn business was still healthy, John-Henry had acquired new and bigger computer equipment using leveraged money, and his bandwidth costs had increased substantially. He had postponed paying a growing list of creditors, assuming that Hitter would be sold, but when Duro walked away, he felt he had no alternative but to protect his company and himself, so on July 21, 2000, Hitter filed for bankruptcy in Orlando, listing assets of $1,293,183.92 against liabilities of $5,518,608.71.

John-Henry delegated Anita Lovely to deliver the bankruptcy news to Ted. Williams was upset, naturally, and as it happened, Bob Breitbard, Ted's boyhood pal from San Diego, was visiting at the time. Ted and Breitbard exchanged annual visits, with Williams usually going to San Diego in the winter and Breitbard coming to Florida in the summer, around Ted's birthday. As pained as Williams was to learn that Hitter had gone bankrupt, Breitbard had another John-Henry issue to raise: young Williams had only repaid him $250,000 of the $500,000 Breitbard had loaned him in 1993. Frank Brothers, who was present for this discussion, recalled Breitbard saying, "Ted, I'm gonna be honest with you. Your son has never paid me a dime of the $250,000 he owes me. And the only reason I'm telling you this is I have children. As long as I'm alive, nothing's going to happen. But if I die before you, my children are going to go after your son for that money. The only reason I'm telling you this is because I love you."[12]

Ted tried to absorb this second blow. John-Henry had assured Breitbard that he was going to repay him in full, but Williams was now frantic. Over the next few days he worked the phones, trying to determine what he might sell immediately to repay his friend. The likely choice was his place on the Miramichi River in Canada.

Ted might also have been pondering his own financial condition. Not only would he have to find some way to pay the $250,000 he'd just learned John-Henry still owed, but the $570,000 he had put up as collateral for John-Henry's Hitter loan from SunTrust had been quickly seized by the bank after the bankruptcy filing. And God only knew how much money John-Henry had taken from the memorabilia companies — Ted Williams Family Enterprises and Green Diamond Sports — to invest in Hitter.

Ted had willingly given John-Henry his power of attorney, but some of the caretakers and aides say that Williams was pressured into signing papers even though he didn't know what he was signing. "Once, John-Henry was having Ted sign papers that were blank," said John Sullivan, a caretaker from 1997 to 2000. "He was signing pages for a larger document. Ted said, 'I want you to tell me what it said!' John-Henry said something that didn't satisfy him, and they got into a shouting match."[13]

Another time, when Mary Dluhy, an aide to John-Henry from 1997 to 2001, was sitting with Ted at his kitchen table, having him sign a document, Williams said to her: "Mary, tell me I still own my own house."[14]

"Of course," Dluhy replied, tearing up as she recalled the story.*

Within a few days of being told that Hitter had gone bankrupt and that John-Henry still had not fully repaid Bob Breitbard, Ted developed angry red blotches on his chest and under his left arm. "Ted came down with a case of the shingles and was in great pain," George Carter said. "The stress really got to him. It was pitiful to see what this kid did to his father. It was just pitiful. When Ted got the shingles, that was a turning point. He spiraled down after that. I seen it happen right before my eyes."[15]

A few weeks later, Hitter's link to pornography was partially revealed. The *St. Petersburg Times* reported that a man who worked for Strictly Hosting, Hitter's dummy corporation, had been arrested and accused of raping a teenage girl. The article said that while the ties between Hitter and Strictly Hosting were unclear, when a reporter called Hitter and asked for Strictly Hosting, he ended up being put through to Hitter CEO John-Henry. John-Henry was quoted as saying that Hitter merely provided Strictly Hosting with high-bandwidth access to the Internet, and he denied that the two companies had any corporate links. Fortunately for John-Henry, Ted never heard about any of this and thus was spared further strain.[16]

In early October, the Red Sox announced that the team was for sale. John-Henry—not lacking for chutzpah less than three months after Hitter had filed for bankruptcy—was one of the first to call John Harrington, who ran the Sox on behalf of Jean Yawkey's JRY Trust, to express an interest in acquiring the club. John-Henry said he would be forming an investor group with his father as the titular head and wanted to let Harrington know that the group would be a contender. Harrington never took him seriously. "We looked at it as John-Henry saying to the world, 'Hey, you want the inside track? Bring me in,'" Harrington said.[17]

---

* Actually, Dluhy believed she was fibbing in giving that answer. She and some of the caretakers knew that Ted's big house on the hill, which he had built in 1989, had been refinanced, and they assumed he no longer owned it. But he did. Records show the original mortgage was for $260,000 in 1989. The note was paid off in 1998 and a new $240,000 mortgage taken out, still in Ted's name. The purpose of the refinancing was to take advantage of lower interest rates, not to take out equity, according to Eric Abel.

Still, John-Henry called Dan Shaughnessy of the *Globe* to fan interest in his bid. "There's an awful lot of work ahead to make something like this come off," he told Shaughnessy, whose story appeared under the headline A SPLENDID IDEA: TED CONSIDERS SOX. Said John-Henry, "We've had some positive people looking at all of our options regarding this, and over the next few weeks we're going to have to put together a group. Unfortunately, Dad and I don't have $400 million. But something that we do have is something that cannot be bought, and that is the Ted Williams name and the Ted Williams legacy and the Ted Williams feeling about baseball." The Hitter bankruptcy, little known outside of Citrus County, was not mentioned in the *Globe* story.

Baseball commissioner Bud Selig reacted favorably: "I will say that there is no name more synonymous with the Red Sox than Ted Williams." But Ted himself—still staggered by Hitter's bankruptcy, the lingering debt to Breitbard, and that painful case of shingles—hardly sounded as though he saw himself as a baseball baron. "John-Henry's talked to me about it, and he's got his own ideas," Williams told Shaughnessy less than enthusiastically. "It's gonna take a lot of dough, I don't know how much. I'm a little peon down here. I might be able to buy the strap that holds third base."[18]*

In fact, on the night of October 30, just eighteen days after the *Globe* trial balloon, Ted was taken to Shands Hospital in Gainesville after having a hard time breathing. Williams had barely slept for two days and was showing symptoms of Cheyne-Stokes respiration—an abnormal breathing pattern alternating between slow, deep breaths and short, quick breaths, sometimes followed by a temporary stoppage of breathing altogether. Paged by Ted's caretakers Frank Brothers and George Carter, John-Henry drove over quickly from his house at nearby Black Diamond Ranch. Eric Abel soon appeared as well. John-Henry called an ambulance, but when it arrived, Ted balked, saying he wouldn't get in. The ambulance driver said that without the patient's consent he couldn't go anywhere. So Frank and George lifted Ted into Williams's Suburban and drove the sixty-odd miles to Shands as John-Henry and Abel followed in John-Henry's BMW.

---

* One deep-pocketed member of the embryonic Ted–and–John-Henry group was Gerry Rittenberg, the Party City owner and Williams memorabilia collector. Rittenberg tried to round up some venture capital tycoons he knew, and he said they expressed interest, but only if they could meet with Ted himself. Williams, however, was in no condition physically to meet with any possible investors, so the John-Henry gambit never got off the ground.

Since Cheyne-Stokes breathing can be associated with heart failure, Williams's cardiologist, Rick Kerensky, had been alerted and was waiting for Ted when he arrived at the emergency room. It was quickly determined that he should be admitted to the hospital. John-Henry told Frank and George to check into a motel across the street. They would be based there but take turns staying in Williams's room to help with his care and, on alternating twelve-hour shifts, keep him company. Carter asked John-Henry if he wanted him to inform his sisters, Claudia and Bobby-Jo, that Ted had been admitted to the hospital. No, John-Henry told Carter; he would call his sisters.

Around 2:00 a.m., John-Henry and Abel were hungry, so they drove to a nearby Chevron gas station off Interstate 75 and picked up some snacks from the station's all-night convenience store. As he ate in the car, John-Henry's mind was racing. He realized his father was declining quickly. In two days, Kerensky would be performing a catheterization procedure on Ted's heart, likely a precursor to installing a pacemaker several days later. John-Henry decided it was time to revisit with Abel, his best friend, a delicate subject he had first raised with the lawyer three years earlier: cryonics.

Cryonicists, operating on the margins of society, believe people can be frozen after they die in the hope that advancing science and medical knowledge will one day be able to bring them back to life through a process they call reanimation.

John-Henry was intrigued by the practice, which operates under the Uniform Anatomical Gift Act, a law that allows people to donate their bodies to medical schools or laboratories for research. He had watched a documentary about cryonics on the Discovery Channel, conducted some research on his own, and was mindful that cryonics, while still widely viewed as a highly improbable theory subscribed to by several hundred eccentrics, had nonetheless seeped into popular culture through numerous science-fiction stories and movies like Woody Allen's *Sleeper* and *Forever Young,* starring Mel Gibson.

Now, as Ted Williams neared death, John-Henry was getting increasingly serious about freezing his father's remains.

The first time he raised the subject of cryonics with Abel, in 1997, they were at Ted's house, fooling around online. John-Henry went to various cryonics websites. He showed Abel the two leading practitioners: the Alcor Life Extension Foundation, in Arizona, and the Cryonics Institute, in Michigan. "They freeze you on the chance they can bring you back," John-Henry explained. Abel told him he was out of his mind.

In fact, young Williams had casually broached cryonics directly with Ted back in 1997. Frank Brothers was there at the time, along with another aide, Donna Fleischmann. "They were just finishing breakfast when John-Henry said, 'Dad, you ever heard of cryonics?' Ted goes, 'Yeah, I've heard of it; they freeze your body,'" Brothers recalled. "John-Henry goes, 'Well, you want to be frozen?' and Ted goes, 'No.' But John-Henry kept pushing. 'They can freeze you; they can only freeze your head,' and Ted's like, 'I've already signed my will, John-Henry. I want to be cremated.' The kid kept pushing it, and finally Ted just pushed himself from the table, and he got up without his walker and started walking back to his room. Oh, he was pissed."[19] Fleischmann confirmed the conversation: "Ted had a few choice words for the cryonics idea. He said it was never going to happen."[20]

Brothers said there were two other occasions when he and Williams discussed cryonics after John-Henry first raised the subject. And from those encounters, Brothers gathered that John-Henry was still talking to his father about the idea. Later in 1997, Brothers and Ted were watching a documentary about cryonics on TV. "We watched the thing, and Ted goes, 'That's a crock of shit.' Then he said something like, 'I can't believe John-Henry still wants to have me frozen.'" The second conversation with Williams occurred in 1999 as Brothers was putting him to bed one night: "Ted brought it up to me that 'John-Henry talked to me again about that cryogenics crap.'"

As he grew more interested in the subject, John-Henry asked various family friends, including Dom DiMaggio, what they thought of cryonics. "I remember him talking about it in Ted's kitchen," DiMaggio recalled. "I didn't pay much attention to it. Then he said to me, 'What do you think of it?' I said something like, 'That's way off. Only a dream.' I never dreamed he was thinking of that for Ted."[21]

But he was—and seriously, as Abel realized after sitting with John-Henry in his car for two hours in the early morning of October 31, 2000, near Shands Hospital.

"I'd say John-Henry was probably ninety-five percent there, maybe ninety-eight percent, by the time we had that late-night meeting," Abel said. "At that point it was real to him. It was a decision he wanted to make. I beat him up on the mockery that was going to be made of him. He brushed that off. It was like, 'That I can live with. I can handle that. It's worth it, I believe.'"

Abel then began to discuss various legal options to prepare for a cryonics scenario. The first was that if John-Henry could get Ted to accept it, they simply could write a new will and have him affirm that he no longer wished to be cremated—he wanted to be frozen. But this option was quickly rejected. "Changing the will would have raised competency issues," Abel said. "No one wanted to jeopardize the will that had already been redone. With cryonics, the existing will could have been thrown out, and he would not get any of his intentions done. We already assumed Bobby-Jo would be a nightmare. We didn't want to give her more ammo."

The other options, Abel told John-Henry, would be to convince Ted and have him submit an application to Alcor or the Cryonics Institute; or he could sign a notarized statement saying he wished to be cryonically preserved. Or his three children could legally dispose of their father's body as they wished. Ted would not have to apply to a cryonics facility himself, Abel added. Either all three children could submit an application on his behalf to a cryonics facility, or two out of the three—a majority—could do so.[22]

On November 3, Dr. Kerensky catheterized Ted's heart in a routine diagnostic procedure. It was determined that his heart was beating too quickly and that the condition could be corrected by installing a pacemaker.

John-Henry was the only family member present during the catheterization procedure, according to Kerensky's assistant, Nancy Carmichael, who was watching from the control room behind a glass wall. Soon after that, John-Henry developed a case of the chicken pox and was put under quarantine, barred from returning to the hospital for several days. One thing Carmichael found troubling was that young Williams had given instructions to Ted's nurses not to put intravenous lines in his right arm. "He didn't give a reason that I know of, but we assumed that it was because it was Ted's signing hand."[23]

The pacemaker surgery was scheduled for Monday, November 6. Claudia arrived the day before and got into a minor auto accident, rear-ending another car as she was getting off the highway near Shands. She hadn't known that Ted was in the hospital again and had called George Carter earlier on the fifth, furious at him for not informing her. Carter replied that John-Henry had told him he would call her.

The pacemaker was installed by Dr. Anne Curtis. Later on November 6, after Ted recovered from the surgery, he filled out an absentee ballot to vote in the presidential election the following day. He voted for George W. Bush, the Republican, of course.

Williams stayed in the hospital for another two weeks, trying to get his strength back, and he made friends with various nurses. One, Debbie Erb, had a house in the Keys and liked to fish. One day in mid-November, she brought in some pictures of herself fishing there. That prompted Ted and Frank Brothers to discuss their adventures in Islamorada. Frank noted that his late father, the famous guide and Williams pal Jack Brothers, had been cremated, and they'd sprinkled his ashes in what the locals called the Pocket, off Islamorada. "Ted said he wanted to do what his friend did, and that is be cremated and have his ashes scattered in the Keys," Erb said.[24]

John-Henry knew he was going to need some extra help for his father, since Carter and Brothers had each worked twelve-hour shifts daily for three straight weeks and would need time off. So on November 19, the day before Ted checked out of Shands, John-Henry arranged for Becky Vaughn to come to the hospital.

Vaughn, a critical-care nurse at Citrus Memorial Hospital, had taken care of Ted after he fell and broke his hip in 1997. John-Henry remembered that Ted had liked her, so he called Vaughn and asked if she could come visit Ted to get reacquainted. Then they could discuss whether she'd be able to provide some care for him when he got home. Vaughn said she'd be happy to as long as she volunteered. A former model and amateur boxer who was married to a successful lawyer, Vaughn didn't need the extra money, plus she'd grown fond of Williams after tending to him when he broke his hip. "I always got the feeling that somebody wanted something from Ted," said Vaughn. "I didn't want that. At the hospital in ninety-seven, people would ask me if I could get Ted to sign a baseball for them. I said no! I was like a mother bear to him because he needed to be protected. I was determined not to see him as a famous person. I was determined to treat him like a human being. People would do extra EKGs on him and pocket them. It was ridiculous. I wanted to protect him from that."

When Williams arrived home after the pacemaker procedure, Vaughn set up a medical area at the house, designed a rehab program, and put him on an herb-and-vitamin regimen that she and John-Henry both thought was beneficial. She would come over three or four days a week, take his blood pressure, check his medication, and they would talk.

On Christmas, Ted had one of his aides call Vaughn. "He said, 'Hi, sweetheart; I just called to say Merry Christmas. You have such a nice family. I wish I could have a family like that.' I said, 'Are you having anybody over?' 'I don't know. John-Henry is in charge of that.'"

Vaughn got to know John-Henry well. She thought he looked like

John F. Kennedy Jr. and was charismatic, but she also thought he was extravagant, wasteful, entitled, and behaved oddly. "We sat down to order some medical supplies once," she remembered. "One of the things was a physician's desk reference that tells you about the side effects of meds and other things. You can buy it for thirty dollars. Instead he bought the computer program that hospitals use for [between] three thousand [and] five thousand dollars. If he went out to buy one thing he'd buy fifty of them instead. He was wasting a ton of money." And if he wanted something, patience was not an option. "Money and people were nothing to him," she continued. "If he had a question for a doctor he'd call him at three a.m. No respect. He called me once at two a.m. and asked me about Ted's blood pressure. It was as if he had an impulse-control problem. He could not see consequences for actions."

Vaughn also thought John-Henry had a childlike quality. Once, at night, when they went outside to get something from her car, John-Henry stopped in his tracks. "He said, 'Look at those stars! Don't you wish you could travel to those stars?' He was like a kid."

One day in late December, Vaughn was sitting with Ted in his bedroom when John-Henry came in and asked her if she had ever heard of cryonics. She had, and she mentioned a lab in Orlando where he could get more information about it.

"Then John-Henry, in his Peter Pan way, said, 'Just think of it: a thousand years from now, people could say their child could have a piece of Ted Williams.' He said, 'They could clone my father's eyes, and a child could have Ted Williams's eyesight. And they could bring him back to life, and he could feel great.'"

"What makes you think Ted would want that?" Vaughn asked.

Ted stirred in his bed, having heard the conversation. "John-Henry!" he said. "Stop talking about that bullshit!"

But John-Henry now felt free to talk in front of his father about sensitive issues, knowing that he drifted in and out and would forget what they were talking about by the next day anyway.

"What does your father want?" Vaughn asked John-Henry again.

"In his will he doesn't want a funeral. He wants to be cremated and sprinkled over where he used to fish in the Keys."

"If that's what his will said, then that's what he wants."

"There are ways to get around things like that," John-Henry said.

Vaughn said he went on to say "how cool it would be to clone Ted's eyes, kind of a scenario where he and his dad would wake up and his dad has no aches and pains and he could go off and play baseball. He said he'd also sell pieces of Ted's DNA. I remember him saying, 'Wouldn't it be great if parents could have a child that could see like Ted Williams and hit a ball like Ted Williams?'"

In the end, Vaughn thought, John-Henry's cryonics notion was more fantastical than exploitive.[25]

"I felt he was this little boy who wanted to make his dad happy but never dealt in reality. A little boy in a man's body. He was going to make people happy by cloning his dad's eyes. Who thinks like that? I think he felt this was how they'd make their money in the future. I don't know if he was thinking, 'Hey, I can take advantage of this old guy.' I thought it was more: 'I'm gonna do this for my dad and we'll live forever.' It was Peter Pan."[26]

31

Alcor

It soon became apparent that Ted's cardio issues were more serious than a pacemaker could address, for on January 11, 2001, he suffered renewed shortness of breath and an apparent heart seizure. Becky Vaughn was on duty at the house and accompanied the ambulance over to nearby Citrus Memorial Hospital.

Soon Williams was back at Shands, in Gainesville, where doctors debated, along with John-Henry and Claudia, whether they should put the eighty-two-year-old Ted through open-heart surgery. Further testing had shown that the mitral valve on Ted's heart was not closing properly when his heart pumped, causing blood to leak from his left ventricle into his left atrium. So the valve needed to be replaced. Ted asked his cardiologist, Rick Kerensky, what the chances of surviving the operation were, and Kerensky said fifty-fifty.

"Let's go for it," Williams told Kerensky.

The surgery would be done at New York–Presbyterian Hospital by Dr. Wayne Isom, chief of cardiothoracic surgery, who had operated on comedian David Letterman and violinist Isaac Stern.[1] Kerensky had actually recommended a heart surgeon in Birmingham, Alabama, but John-Henry liked Dr. Isom's celebrity cachet: if he was good enough for Letterman, he was good enough for Ted.

Williams met with all three of his children at Shands before leaving for New York. Bobby-Jo and her husband, Mark Ferrell, had moved to Citrus Hills in 1999 from North Carolina and had built a house on one of the fifteen lots in the development Williams had taken options on before giving five to each of his children.

Bobby-Jo had been in only sporadic contact with Ted in recent years.

She had been dealing with various issues: she continued to struggle with alcoholism and also had lupus, a chronic autoimmune disease. She and her husband had moved to Citrus Hills at her father's urging, she said. But according to Bobby-Jo's oldest daughter, Dawn Hebding, the move was primarily intended to curry favor with Ted. "Mom and Mark would say, 'John-Henry and Claudia are making their move!'" said Hebding, laughing. "They wanted me and my sister to call Grandpa more. They'd say not to say this, and not to say that."[2]

Hebding, who had a rocky relationship with her mother and stepfather, said she visited a downbeat Ted in January of 2001, shortly before his seizure. "He talked about death, about being cremated and having his ashes thrown in the ocean," Hebding said. "That was the last time I saw him."

Now, on January 14, Bobby-Jo and Mark entered Ted's room at Shands. John-Henry and Claudia were already there. Bobby-Jo, who barely knew her half siblings, already felt like a third wheel in the family. She had not been consulted on whether Ted should have the surgery and was against it. She knew her father was near death and thought it folly to undergo such a major and risky operation at this stage.

Truth be told, she had not even wanted Ted to have his heart catheterized or the pacemaker implanted in November. Whereas John-Henry and Claudia were pursuing an aggressive course of treatment and care for their father, Bobby-Jo wanted no heroic measures and to let nature simply take over. "Bobby-Jo said to John-Henry, 'Just let him die,'" Claudia recalled. "She wanted him to be in hospice and to just die peacefully. We were throwing her out of the picture."[3]

There was a certain formality and awkwardness as Ted spoke to Bobby-Jo, whom he had written out of his will. Yet he wanted to summon some kind words now, knowing that they might be the last ones he uttered to his oldest child. "He said out of nowhere, 'I sure do love you, sweetie,'" Bobby-Jo said. "And he just said, 'I wish I'd been around more to have appreciated what a loving, sweet, wonderful person you are.'"

Then they wheeled Ted down to an ambulance that drove him to the Gainesville airport. John-Henry, Claudia, Bobby-Jo, and Mark followed in a caravan, right out onto the airport tarmac. There was another round of good-byes there before Williams was deposited in a Learjet, accompanied by John-Henry, two paramedics, and Nancy Carmichael, Kerensky's assistant. After a few hours, the plane landed at Teterboro Airport in New Jersey, and Ted was taken by ambulance to Manhattan.

The surgery the next day lasted nine and a half hours. Dr. Isom and a team of a dozen others replaced the mitral valve in Ted's heart with a tissue, or "pig," valve, and while they were at it they repaired his tricuspid valve, which they found to be faulty. While it was initially thought Williams would remain in the hospital for about fourteen days, his recuperation turned out to be much more arduous than planned and dragged on for more than a month. He was on a respirator for an extended time and had to be heavily sedated.

On January 20, Ted acknowledged John-Henry for the first time since the surgery and reportedly enjoyed watching George W. Bush being inaugurated as the forty-third president on TV. But after that, the medical updates were few and far between. The Boston press, on high alert for even the most incremental Ted development, was forced to find other story lines, such as questioning why John-Henry chose New York over prestigious Boston hospitals for the heart surgery and whether it was appropriate for an eighty-two-year-old to have such traumatic surgery in the first place.

At the one-month mark of convalescence, doctors issued a gloomy report that said Williams was still on a respirator, spent most of the day sleeping, and that when he finally was released from the hospital he would need to spend several additional months in rehabilitation. A few days later, John-Henry chose a facility in San Diego for the rehab phase over others in Boston and Gainesville. On the morning of February 19, Ted was taken by ambulance back to Teterboro Airport, where he was lifted onto another Learjet and flown across the country, accompanied by John-Henry, a surgeon, and two paramedics. He checked into San Diego's Sharp Memorial Hospital, not far from 4121 Utah Street, where he'd grown up.

Bob Breitbard, Ted's boyhood chum, was thrilled to have Williams back in town, infirm as he was. Breitbard arranged for apartments for John-Henry (who still owed him the $250,000) and Ted's two Florida caretakers, Frank Brothers and George Carter, so that they would have places to stay while they were in San Diego.

Meanwhile, as Ted faded, John-Henry was pressing ahead with cryonics, broadening the circle of people he sought advice from and narrowing his search for the right facility. In mid-December of 2000, John-Henry had contacted the Alcor Life Extension Foundation in Scottsdale, Arizona, the leading practitioner of cryonics in the country, and asked the company to send him its brochure. He asked his secretary, Eleanor

Diamond, to be on the lookout for the package and, when it arrived, to send it to Peter Sutton in Boston after reading it herself and letting him know what she thought. Diamond, then fifty-seven, had moved to Florida from her native Brooklyn and still spoke with the accent of her old neighborhood. "I said, 'John-Henry, I'd never do that to my parents, but maybe there's something in it for you. Nobody thought you could transplant a heart years ago, so maybe it's something down the road.'"[4]

Anita Lovely soon confided to Diamond that she, too, thought cryonics was crazy and said she was upset by John-Henry's interest in the practice. John-Henry's wedding to Anita, originally set for the Kid-happy 9/9/99, had been postponed, and there was no new date. John-Henry continued to resist any commitment, much to the consternation of Ted, who adored Anita and had once offered his son a $500,000 inducement to marry her. John-Henry still cared for Anita, and they had been through a lot together, but he seemed now to see her more as a friend and business partner than as a lover or future wife.

Sutton, a senior partner in the litigation department of the Boston law firm Riemer & Braunstein, reacted to cryonics the same way Eric Abel did when John-Henry had initially broached the subject to him: "I said, 'Are you fucking crazy?'" Sutton recalled. "John-Henry's approach was, 'If I'm wrong, I don't lose anything; but if I'm right, boy, do I win.' He said it's like a lottery ticket. You won't win unless you buy it, but what if you win the two hundred million? He'd say, 'How do you know it won't work? How do you know there's a God?'"

Sutton, a pugnacious Greek-American who relished a legal scrap, was a big Ted Williams fan who met John-Henry in 1994 while visiting the Ted souvenir store in Chestnut Hill, outside Boston. Later, when John-Henry tripped on an icy step outside his Brookline apartment and broke his ankle, Sutton filed a lawsuit against the landlord and got young Williams some money. Then he became a troubleshooter for John-Henry on the memorabilia front, working on licensing, royalty, and forgery issues. Sutton never charged Ted and John-Henry much, if anything. He liked being in the Williams orbit.

As they discussed cryonics further, John-Henry told Sutton that he, too, planned to join his father and be frozen when he died. Would Sutton himself ever consider the practice? "He wanted me to be a part of it because when they got thawed out, he and Ted wanted their lawyer! I think my answer was I'd rather have my family keep the hundred and fifty thousand dollars...than give it to those snake charmers. I went home and told my wife and said, 'Hey honey, you want to be frozen with the kids?' She's Greek Orthodox, and we had a good laugh about it."

Sutton said he wasn't concerned about whether Ted himself wanted cryonics because Williams, after he gave John-Henry his power of attorney, had said that whatever his son wanted was fine by him. "If John-Henry had gone to Ted and said, 'We're going to jump out of a plane holding hands without a parachute,' Ted would have said, 'Okay.' So there was never a thought in my mind that Ted wouldn't go along with whatever John-Henry wanted."[5]

As for Claudia Williams, she, like everyone, was skeptical of cryonics at first, but it wasn't long before John-Henry had his sister on board. "I think the thing that certainly sold me on it was first and foremost his enthusiasm for it and his belief," Claudia said. "He had faith in it, and it made him so much more ready for when Dad died. I knew that John-Henry had cryonics to hold on to. And that's what sold me on it. And you know, after he'd educated me on it, talked to me about it, yeah! There might be a chance!"

She conceded that early on Ted was dismissive of cryonics. But she says he gradually evolved on the issue and became interested in it. He was not religious; rather, he was curious, and he listened to John-Henry's occasional updates. "At first Dad reacted just like everybody else. He said, 'That sounds a little kooky to me.' Then John-Henry would tell him a few things. He'd be like, 'Do you know, Dad, that they can now freeze a kidney for up to two days or twenty-four hours, and there will be absolutely minimal damage?' And Dad would be like, 'Really? Who discovered that?' And then when Dad started to realize that all these latest little discoveries, if you will, that John-Henry was presenting were all from cryonics, he would every so often ask, 'What's the latest on that cryonics thing?'"

As Ted continued his recovery in San Diego, John-Henry took advantage of the city's proximity to Arizona to take a short flight over to Phoenix and visit Alcor, in suburban Scottsdale.

Founded as a nonprofit in 1972, Alcor had been located there since 1994, after moving from Riverside, California. Its headquarters is at 7895 East Acoma Drive, a gray stucco building in a nondescript industrial park just down the road from the Scottsdale airport. The front door is always locked to guard against unwelcome visitors. At the time of John-Henry's visit, in the spring of 2001, Alcor had frozen—"suspended" is the official term—forty-six people and several pets. Most of the humans, by a factor of three to one, are "neuros": those who had chosen to preserve only their heads.

One of the first things a visitor notices in the lobby is a photo of Robert Ettinger hanging over a plaque that reads, FATHER OF CRYONICS. Ettinger, a physics teacher and science-fiction writer, was the author of the 1964 book *The Prospect of Immortality,* which caused a media sensation at the time and launched the cryonics movement. Ettinger's credo was that "life is better than death, healthy is better than sick, smart is better than stupid, and immortality might be worth the trouble!" His surmise was that death is only a transit station and that quick-freezing a corpse and preserving it that way offered the hope of resuscitation sometime in the future, when rapidly advancing science and medicine could cure whatever disease the person died from, and when cell damage now deemed irreparable might be fixed.

Ettinger went on to found the Cryonics Institute in Michigan and the related Immortalist Society, an education and research group. Soon most cryonics followers paid homage to Ettinger by calling themselves "immortalists." Alcor displayed Ettinger's picture to acknowledge his status as a cryonics pioneer, even though his Cryonics Institute was the Arizona company's main competitor. Ettinger conceded in an interview, however, that Alcor was better organized, better funded, and further along in research than his group, thanks to the contributions of two wealthy benefactors: Saul Kent and Bill Faloon, both of whom John-Henry was soon introduced to.[6]

Kent and Faloon, both multimillionaires, were Alcor leaders assigned to recruit John-Henry hard, with the goal of landing his commitment to deliver Ted Williams when the time came. In 1980, Kent and Faloon founded the Florida-based Life Extension Foundation, which sells vitamins and dietary supplements and promotes antiaging research.*

Kent became infamous in 1987 for presiding over the beheading of his eighty-three-year-old mother, Dora, and having her head frozen at Alcor. The procedure took place two days after Kent took his mother out of a Riverside, California, nursing home and brought her to Alcor—ailing but quite alive. The case garnered international attention after Riverside County coroner's investigators questioned whether Mrs. Kent

---

* In 1991, Kent and Faloon were indicted on multiple counts of importing drugs not approved for sale in the United States, conspiracy, and dispensing drugs without prescriptions. The two men had a long wrangle with the Food and Drug Administration and the Justice Department, but the US attorney's office in Fort Lauderdale ultimately dropped the charges against both.

was still alive when the "neuro" procedure began. A death certificate, signed by a procryonics doctor who was not present when Mrs. Kent was said to have died, listed the cause of death as heart disease and pneumonia. The local district attorney's office ultimately decided not to file any charges, and Saul Kent denied any wrongdoing, saying his mother had been a cryonics supporter and had died shortly before the procedure began. This episode would later be memorialized in a short, not unsympathetic documentary by the filmmaker Errol Morris entitled *I Dismember Mama*. Adding to Kent's allure for cryonicists was the fact that he had a dog named Franklin whom he had experimentally frozen then successfully revived after a few hours.

Kent and Faloon's Life Extension Foundation took most of its name from the Alcor Life Extension Foundation. Kent was on the Alcor board, and the groups had other interlocking ties though no official corporate relationship. Life Extension also funded various companies doing cryonics-related research, including Suspended Animation, Inc., in Florida, and 21st Century Medicine, in California. The eccentric Kent was also deeply involved in finding a site for a construction project he called Timeship, which would be a mecca for cryonics research and the long-term storage of people who choose to be frozen after they die.

It was the Life Extension Foundation through which John-Henry obtained the various vitamin and herbal concoctions that he insisted his father take, and his dealings with the foundation provided a catalyst for his interest in cryonics generally and Alcor specifically, according to Claudia Williams.

Dr. Jerry Lemler, Alcor's CEO, was another aggressive suitor of John-Henry's. An ardent baseball fan whose motto is "You only live twice," Lemler, in conducting a tour of the facility for a *Denver Post* reporter, pointed to the huge cylinders known as Dewars that contain four bodies and up to five heads and said: "These people aren't dead. They are only at a point where contemporary medicine has given up on them. We're not about raising the dead. . . . We're about extending life further into the future than ever before."

The fiftyish, bearded Lemler, who liked to quote Robert Frost and Woody Allen and smoke a cigar, saw himself as an adventurer. "I've pushed limits and mostly been better for doing so," he said. "So the future offers virtually limitless possibilities."[7]

John-Henry also met two Alcor lifers so devoted to the organization that they lived in the building: Hugh Hixon and Michael Perry. Hixon, a former Air Force captain, started working for Alcor in 1982 and had attended virtually every cryopreservation procedure since then, includ-ing that of his own father. Perry is a computer science PhD who has worked at Alcor since 1987 as a computer programmer and writer. He also is an ordained minister in the Society for Venturism, an obscure quasi church based in Arizona that touts cryonics while practicing its "immortalist" philosophy.

John-Henry learned more about the demographics of the cryonics movement: the average cryonicist is a middle-aged white male, gener-ally from an engineering or technical background, college educated, fairly affluent, and the kind of person who recognizes and admires the impact that technology has had in his life.[8] Of the people frozen at Alcor, the ratio of men to women is four to one; a third were gay, and a third were Jewish. About 90 percent of Alcor's clients—those who have signed up to be frozen when they die—are concentrated in Florida, California, and New York.[9]

Returning to California, John-Henry continued his research and met with several other cryonics activists and researchers. Then, several weeks later, when Alcor's next client was about to die, Alcor called John-Henry and asked if he'd be interested in watching a cryonics procedure. This was virtually unheard of and indicative of the lengths to which Alcor was going to woo the young Williams.

John-Henry not only made the trip but filmed the procedure. He returned to San Diego and asked Claudia, who was visiting Ted, if she wanted to see his film. She didn't.

John-Henry, now wildly enthused with cryonics and with Alcor spe-cifically, was ready to tell some of Ted's old friends, including Bob Breit-bard and Eddie Barry, the former Boston Bruin and Ted pal who wintered in Citrus Hills, about his plan. Both men told him they thought he was mad.

Undaunted, John-Henry was comforted by the fact that he had Clau-dia in his corner on the cryonics plan for Ted. He thought it would be even better if he could win the support of Bobby-Jo so that all three of the Williams children might be on board.

In early June, John-Henry called Bobby-Jo from San Diego. She was in the garage of her new house in Citrus Hills having a cigarette when the call came through. There was some brief chitchat before John-Henry asked her if she'd ever heard of cryonics. In fact, Bobby-Jo, having recently seen a documentary on the subject, knew quite a bit about it. Furthermore, her mother's side of the family had been in the funeral business. She knew about death and its attendant rituals. John-Henry told her that he was impressed—and then dropped his bombshell: "How would you like this for Dad?"

Bobby-Jo exclaimed that her father had wanted to be cremated, but John-Henry confidently told her everything could be worked out. He also let her know that he had witnessed a cryonics procedure and could arrange for her to do the same.

Bobby-Jo was shocked. "Where?" she asked.

"In Scottsdale. And I want you to come out here, and they'll show you one."

This was too much for Bobby-Jo to absorb. She told John-Henry she had to go to the bathroom. "I went in and got Mark and I said, 'You've got to come out here now!' I said, 'John-Henry's talking about cryonically freezing Daddy!'" They went back to the phone, and Bobby-Jo angled the receiver so that Mark could hear what her brother was saying. John-Henry excitedly explained that they wouldn't even need to freeze Ted's entire body but could simply cut off his head.

"'Think about this,'" Bobby-Jo said he added. "'The way the science is going, we can make a whole lot of money. If we can get them to take Dad's DNA, think about it. How many people would buy Ted Williams's DNA to have little Ted Williamses running around?'"

Six months earlier, John-Henry had also raised the possibility of selling his father's DNA in discussing cryonics with Becky Vaughn, the critical-care nurse who had tended to Ted. Claudia Williams, who said she was with her brother when he called Bobby-Jo, acknowledged that John-Henry did mention DNA during the phone call, but only in answering a question Bobby-Jo asked about cell damage during the freezing process. "He was like, 'No. They can now regenerate cells, and all we need is one DNA or one cell particle, and it sends the message and it completes the DNA chain and it makes it again.' That's how that came up." Besides, Claudia pointed out, John-Henry hardly needed to go through cryonics and freeze Ted to get his DNA. He could have taken some of Ted's hair or a vial of his blood anytime he wished.

For Bobby-Jo, the phone call and her brother's plan were horrific. But Claudia got a different impression of her sister's view. "I was right there with John-Henry," Claudia said. "When he got off the phone he was sky-high. He was like, 'This is great. She actually knows a lot about this. She's coming out.' He was all excited."

The next day, Eleanor Diamond, John-Henry's secretary, called Bobby-Jo to say that her brother had bought her a plane ticket to fly to Arizona. Recalled Bobby-Jo, "I said, 'No. John-Henry and I have already discussed this, and I don't want that ticket.'" John-Henry called Bobby-Jo back to try to get her to change her mind, but a disgusted Mark answered and he wouldn't put his wife on the phone.[10]

Bobby-Jo and Mark Ferrell moved quickly to put John-Henry's inner circle on notice that they knew of his plan to freeze Ted and objected to it. Bobby-Jo called Peter Sutton, nearly hysterical. "I remember her calling me and saying, 'They want to cut my daddy's head off!' and I called John-Henry and said, 'What are you doing?'" Sutton said. "He said Bobby-Jo had freaked out when he talked to her about cryonics for Ted. He couldn't believe it. He said calling her had backfired and he thought he'd made a mistake." And Ferrell called Al Cassidy, whom Ted had chosen to be the executor of his estate. Ferrell vilified John-Henry's cryonics plan and told Cassidy there was no way Bobby-Jo would approve of it.

John-Henry had already let Cassidy know of his intentions. "I strongly recommended that he talk to Ted about it. It was a touchy subject, obviously," Cassidy said. "Every conversation I had with him, I said, 'Have you talked with your father?' 'Not yet.'

"He told me they had several conversations about it leading up to the [2001] heart surgery. And he finally affirmed to me before the surgery that Ted had agreed to it." Cassidy took this claim as truth; after all, he said, "John-Henry never lied to me."[11]

For John-Henry, Bobby-Jo's rejection of his request to consider cryonics for Ted, and her and Mark's subsequent harsh complaints to Sutton and Cassidy, were watershed moments. He decided to sever whatever ties he had to Bobby-Jo, then he went further: he would deny her permission to ever visit Ted again, and if she came to their father's house, he would have her arrested.

John-Henry had Eric Abel deliver that message. When Abel called, Mark answered the phone, as he was doing increasingly, wanting to act as his wife's spokesman. Ferrell, who despised Abel, questioned whether John-Henry could legally do that. Abel said the power of attorney that Ted had given his son was broad and empowered him to make such a decision. Soon Ferrell was venting about John-Henry's cryonics plans for Ted, and issued his own threat.

"You all do this shit, and we'll go to the press," he said.

Abel paused for a moment or two, then replied, "You'd do that?"

"You're goddamned right we would."[12]

32

Foreboding

John-Henry hardly let the negative reaction from Bobby-Jo and some family friends deter him from cryonics or from digging in with Alcor as his preferred provider when the time arrived.

And though his own brief career in business thus far had been checkered at best, he did not hesitate to give the Alcorians advice on how to run a tighter ship. John-Henry pressed the company on its finances and on the ways in which the arrival of Ted Williams could turn things around. He even raised the possibility of making an announcement while Ted was still alive, prompting Dr. Jerry Lemler, the Alcor CEO, to gush, in a June 2001 letter to John-Henry, about the advantages of a "pre-mortem disclosure." Lemler treated the young Williams as a princeling.

"We at Alcor are most assuredly grateful to you for your abiding interest and sincere concern regarding not only the optimal rescue and long-term care of your father, but the security and stability of our organization in toto," Lemler wrote John-Henry in his June 12 letter.

As for what it might mean to announce that Ted would be coming to Alcor, Lemler thought "it would be huge. In nearly three decades of providing biostasis services, we've had a few so-called 'heavy hitters' look us over, but we've never had a .400 hitter as a member. It's a genuine first for us! Stated bluntly, the Williams name can be expected to provide Alcor with a fund-raising and membership enhancing leverage wedge it has never possessed."[1]

Ted's rehabilitation in San Diego lasted four months and was difficult. He was still prone to infections. In New York, he'd developed a staph infection for which vancomycin, a powerful antibiotic, was prescribed. The vancomycin had killed the infection but damaged Williams's kidneys, and he had to go on dialysis. The same pattern recurred in San Diego, where he'd registered at the hospital under the alias Luke Jackson. He was still on a ventilator, often uncooperative in his rehab, and listless, despite visits from John Glenn, Dom DiMaggio, and the third Mrs. Williams.*

A visit from Tommy Lasorda perked Ted up, however. "Ted always kept his eyes closed at that point in time, but he opened one eye briefly and closed it again," his doctor Allan Goodman recalled. "When Tommy saw Ted respond he pulled me aside and he stepped up. He spent about an hour and a half in the most motivational session I'll ever see. He leaned over Ted and said, 'Ted, open those eyes,' and Ted shook his head no. So he said, 'Ted, I want to see those beautiful eyes I love so much,' and Ted said no again, but within five minutes he was opening his eyes, and Tommy wouldn't give up. I told him, 'Tommy, we need to get him walking,' because at that time he wasn't walking. So Tommy said to him, 'Let's see you move those legs.' And he hadn't moved his legs in months, but he finally wiggled his toes, and Tommy said, 'That's not enough, I wanna see those legs move!' And before you know it Ted was kicking his legs, just going to town."

Then Lasorda told some doctor jokes at Goodman's expense, and Ted began rolling in his bed, laughing. The visit was a breakthrough, and Williams became a more willing partner in his rehabilitation. "When we walked out of the room, I said, 'Tommy, I now see how every time the Dodgers came to San Diego, you beat the Padres,'" Goodman said.[2]

Despite this progress, John-Henry and Claudia had philosophical differences with Goodman over Ted's care. Goodman was a friend of Bob Breitbard's and had grown up in the Boston area a big fan of Williams. They thought Goodman was too passive in his approach and that he belonged to the Bobby-Jo school of letting nature run its course.

"We thought we were going to lose him in San Diego," Claudia remembered. "As soon as we moved out there, Breitbard and the doctors started saying, 'Let's let him go.' Finally we said, 'We're out of here.'"

So in mid-June, preparations were made to fly Williams back across the country to Florida, where he would be readmitted to Gainesville's Shands Hospital. Before leaving San Diego, John-Henry decided to fire

_____

* Dolores caused a stir at the hospital after she slipped Ted some sort of homeopathic remedy that caused various monitors and machines attached to Williams to light up in alarm. She was asked to leave.

Frank Brothers and George Carter, Ted's longest-serving caretakers. While he knew his father loved Frank and George, the young Williams continued to have a tense relationship with both men, and he thought they were undermining him.

Ted returned to Shands, signing in as Chris Rivers, and was gradually weaned off the ventilator. "We're convinced Shands saved Dad's life," Claudia said. "He looked so bad John-Henry wouldn't allow visitors because he didn't want Dad to be embarrassed."

But Bobby-Jo visited, tipped off by a sympathetic nurse that Ted was back. John-Henry, who had been deliberately keeping his older sister in the dark, was furious when he learned she had been at the hospital, and he issued orders that she was not to be allowed back.

Ted was released from Shands in time for his eighty-third birthday on August 30, the first time he had been home for nearly nine months.

Bobby-Jo, forgetting or ignoring the fact that John-Henry had banned her from coming to Ted's house, called her brother and left a message on his cell phone saying she would be over to celebrate Ted's birthday. He called her back that evening to bluntly tell her that she was not a "team player" and that he didn't think she was going to see her father again.

Bobby-Jo and Mark complained to the local sheriff but were told it was a civil issue, not a criminal issue, and that John-Henry was within his rights under the power of attorney Ted had given him.

In late October, Ted had a delightful and often emotional two-day interlude—a visit from two of his oldest Red Sox pals, Dominic DiMaggio and Johnny Pesky.*

Teddy and Dommie (as they'd come to call themselves) had grown closer as they'd aged. Ted admired the richness and fullness of Dom's life: After retiring from baseball abruptly in 1953, he had founded two successful manufacturing businesses—one that made carpeting for automobiles and another that made foam padding for car seats. He and his wife, Emily, had been married for more than fifty years and had three children. He was a good citizen who gave back to his community.

Ted had told his friend once that by comparison, he had made a hash of his personal life with his failed marriages and absentee fatherhood. Dominic had scolded Williams for coming to such a gloomy conclusion:

---

* The meeting would be chronicled in David Halberstam's engaging, short book *The Teammates*.

Ted was an undisputed icon who had achieved so much in his life—the greatest hitter in baseball, a war hero, and a champion to sick kids. But Ted could not shake the comparison.

And now it was Dominic, more than any other friend, who took the initiative in staying in touch with Ted. He would call to deliver his Red Sox reports, and they would shoot the breeze as Williams's health permitted. In turn, Dominic would relay Ted's news to Pesky and to the fourth member of their gang, Bobby Doerr, who these days was preoccupied with tending to his ailing wife, Monica, at their home in Oregon.

In early October, Dominic and Emily had been having dinner at a restaurant with their friend Dick Flavin, a former television reporter who had become a well-known humorist and toastmaster in Boston.* The DiMaggios, who lived in Marion, Massachusetts, on Buzzards Bay, were discussing their annual winter move to Florida. Emily said she would fly down soon to get their place ready, but Dom said he was thinking of driving. Emily said she forbade him to drive alone—he was eighty-four, after all—so Flavin volunteered to keep him company. Wonderful, said Dom, who then called Johnny Pesky to see if he wanted to go, too. Pesky said he was game, so the three men set out on October 20 in Dom's gray Jaguar sedan. Flavin and Dom shared the driving. Pesky was in the backseat and agreed not to smoke his cigar.

Flavin, who was about twenty years younger than Dom and Johnny, was beside himself with excitement. There he was, a lifelong Red Sox fan who never had been able to hit the ball out of the infield as a kid, embarking on a road trip with two of his heroes, on their way to see the great Williams.

Flavin felt like he was in fantasy camp as he listened to Dom and Johnny spin baseball yarns—like the one about the play they used to work together. Dom would be on first and Johnny would be up. If Pesky felt the situation was right—usually with no one out—he would signal to Dom by rubbing his nose, and then he would drop a bunt down the third-base line. Dom would be off with the pitch and race all the way to third, which would be vacant after the third baseman had come in to field the bunt. They worked this so often that the papers wrote about it.

---

* Flavin was also a fixture at Fenway Park, where he was known as the Poet Laureate of the Red Sox. In that capacity, Flavin was best known for his rendition of "Teddy at the Bat," his knockoff of Ernest Lawrence Thayer's timeless "Casey at the Bat," wherein Flavin substituted the Kid for Casey—but, of course, Ted did not strike out. In 2013, Flavin was named the Red Sox's lead public-address announcer.

Then one day, against the Yankees, the play backfired. Pesky dropped his bunt down and duly drew the third baseman in, but by the time Dom got to third, catcher Bill Dickey was waiting to tag him out. "I read the papers too, you know," Dickey said to the startled DiMaggio.

The three travelers arrived at Ted's house on Tuesday morning, October 23, around ten o'clock. When no one answered the door, Dom and the others just walked in. As they entered the living room they spotted Ted in silhouette from a distance. He was on the other side of the room near a sliding glass door, slumped in his wheelchair.

"He was alone, and it was just so jarring," Flavin said. "Christ, this was Ted Williams, and here is this poor invalid. I can remember Johnny actually gasping."

DiMaggio took the lead and almost ran to his friend. "Teddy, it's Dommie! Teddy, it's Dommie!" he cried. "And Johnny Pesky is here! And Dick Flavin!"

Williams stirred. "Hello, Dommie," he said.

Pesky couldn't speak for the first twenty minutes and seemed on the verge of tears. Dom started chatting away and telling Ted about the ride down. Williams's vision had so declined that at one point he looked at Johnny and said, "Who are you?"

"Ted, I'm Johnny Pesky!"

"Needle!" Ted said with conviction, using his favorite nickname for Pesky, a reference to his long nose. Then Williams greeted Flavin, whom he knew a bit. They had conspired on the phone together about how best to boost Dominic for the Hall of Fame. This had been a pet cause of Ted's from his perch on the Veterans Committee, to no avail. Dominic, after all, had fallen just short of the .300 mark as a hitter (.298 lifetime), and while he'd been a scintillating fielder, they didn't pay off on fielding, as Ted himself had famously said.

Dom noticed several ceramic knickknacks in the kitchen that paid tribute to Ted's beloved Dalmatian, Slugger.

"That was a helluva dog, right, Ted?" Dom said.

"Helluva dog," Ted agreed.

"What kind of dog was it?"

Williams paused for a moment or two to think about that. "A German shepherd," he said.

Then Ted, livening up a bit, said he had a trivia challenge for his guests. He was thinking of a Yankee who was a great clutch hitter. His initials were PT. Dom, Johnny, and Dick racked their brains but couldn't come up with anyone who had the initials PT.

"Paul O'Neill," Ted finally told them.

The guests graciously failed to point out Ted's mistakes and moved on.

During lunch, Williams had to be helped with his food, and this infuriated him, underscoring as it did his lack of independence. When he went off on a swearing jag, one of the nurses handled him kindly and skillfully. "Now, Ted," she said, speaking to him as if he were her naughty son.

John-Henry appeared and said hello. Flavin looked askance at the cameras the young Williams had stationed around the house but said nothing. "He apparently wanted to make sure none of the caretakers got an autograph from Ted or something."

That night, over a glass of wine, Dominic announced that he was going to sing an aria for Ted. Williams sat and listened, rapt and smiling. After Dom finished, he explained what the song was about. A guy was in love with a girl, but he was too afraid to tell her, so he had his friend do it. The friend did and stole the girl. An exuberant Ted asked Dom for another rendition. After the second aria, Flavin, not to be outdone, said he, too, had a song for Ted, and he launched into one of his favorite Irish ballads, "I'll Take You Home Again, Kathleen." "Ted thought my song was pretty good, but he said, 'Dom's better than you,'" recalled Flavin, laughing.

From time to time during the course of the two-day visit, Flavin noticed that Ted would quietly weep—especially on the first visit in the morning, when he appeared overwhelmed that his two old Red Sox teammates had come to see him. Once, Ted, who always liked to measure himself against the great DiMaggio, asked Dom if Joe had ever cried. "He did toward the end," Dom said. "But there was a difference. Joe was never going to get out of his bed again. You're getting stronger and better."[3]

John-Henry was still bruised by the Hitter.net failure. Its success could have helped him at least partially emerge from Ted's considerable shadow and forge his own identity outside the memorabilia business, which was dependent upon his father's famous name. Paradoxically, John-Henry was also acutely aware that Ted had only limited time left, and he felt a strong need to do his father proud in some way while he still could.

The 9/11 attacks had helped trigger this soul-searching, the taking stock of where he was in life. Someone had called Ted's house that day to let him know that a plane had crashed into a skyscraper in New York. John-Henry and his father turned on the TV. "He and I just sat there, stunned, watching it, watching the aftermath, and seeing how precious life all of a sudden is again," John-Henry recalled later. "I just sat there and got a sense that life is...passing me by and that motivated me. I think it motivated a lot of other Americans too, to get off their tush and start doing something positive. And that's what I did."[4]

What he decided to do—improbably and, some would say, ridiculously—was embark on a career as a baseball player at thirty-three years of age.

John-Henry, who had failed to make his college baseball teams and whose foray to California in 1989 to train under his cousin Sal Herrera had been a bust, now wanted to give it one last serious shot. His goal, his fantasy, would be to become a good enough hitter, and a passable enough fielder, to be able to sign a minor-league contract. Then, if he progressed and rose through the ranks, who knew? Maybe he could make it to the majors. Maybe he could get just one at bat with the Red Sox.

John-Henry presented his plan to Ted and asked for his blessing. Williams must have realized that the idea was hopeless, but he loved his son and knew how deeply John-Henry needed his approval, so he gave it.

There was only one hitting instructor in the land, Ted said, who could deliver the crash course necessary to give John-Henry even a remote chance of success: Steve Ferroli. Ferroli was a Williams disciple who had been an instructor at Ted's baseball camp in Massachusetts and then had established a business on his own teaching the Williams theory of hitting. He had practically memorized Ted's book *The Science of Hitting* and then had self-published his own book: *Disciple of a Master: How to Hit a Baseball to Your Potential,* for which Ted had written a foreword. Ferroli liked to say that he was the successor Ted anointed to teach the Williams theory of hitting to future generations.

So in November, following the visit by Dick Flavin and the teammates, John-Henry called Ferroli out of the blue and said: "I want to try and hit baseballs." Ferroli, who was then in his early forties, had known John-Henry for years and regarded him as something of a kid brother. In his sporadic displays of interest in baseball growing up, young Williams had attended some of Ferroli's instructional clinics and later had been supportive of Ferroli's desire to preach the Ted gospel.

John-Henry proposed that Ferroli come down to Florida for thirty days and see how things go. He could live at Ted's house or at his condo. Ferroli had a wife and kids and a business, but he knew he had to drop everything and go.

"Ted Williams was my hero," Ferroli said. "It's, like, who does Elvis send his kid to for singing lessons? It was the ultimate compliment. How could I have turned my back on that?"

When he arrived, Ferroli took one look at John-Henry—dressed in casual business clothes, driving his BMW—and wondered what he had signed up for. He took his pupil down to a local high school field and ran him through his paces to make a baseline assessment.

"The first practice, we had a machine that pitched to him," Ferroli said. "Out of thirty pitches he might have fouled off one of them. The machine was probably throwing seventy to seventy-five miles an hour, like a high school fastball. He was horrible in every way, shape, and form. He didn't throw right, he had no conception of ground balls, bunts—he didn't understand where the ball's supposed to be bunted; he didn't understand baserunning at all. At the plate, he had good hip rotation, he seemed to see the ball well, but he had no sense of timing."

Before long, Ted cornered Ferroli and started grilling him: "How's the kid doing? Is this a bunch of bullshit or what?" Ferroli would be as encouraging as he could. "I'd say, 'He's pretty good; he's coming along.'"

Soon the first thirty days were up, and Ferroli settled in for an extended stay, into the new year—2002. Then John-Henry decided to buy a batting cage. He and Ferroli drove over to Orlando, where John-Henry bought a $75,000 cage, practically the most expensive one on the market. It consisted of a pitching machine placed behind a life-size screen featuring a virtual pitcher throwing toward the plate. The ball would come out of a hole in the screen where the pitcher's hand was. The machine could throw fastballs at speeds up to the high nineties as well as curves, sliders, and other pitches. John-Henry had the cage installed amid a grove of trees in front of Ted's house. He wanted it positioned near the window of his father's bedroom so Ted could hear the rhythmic crack of the bat. A concrete path was built from the front of the house to the cage so that Ted could be wheeled out to watch his son flail away. Floodlights were installed for night sessions. Over the next several months the frail Williams would regularly emerge to check in on John-Henry's quixotic quest and to offer commentary that ranged from encouraging to acerbic. "Keep your elbow in, and turn your wrists," Ted would say. If John-Henry resisted his father's suggestions in any way, or said he wanted to try something his way, Williams was dismissive: "Yeah, okay, do it your way. See if you hit .400." But Ted would generally try to keep his remarks from sounding too harsh.

Soon the Kid looked forward to coming out to the cage each day. "That would be his reason to get up," Claudia Williams said. "To get up out of bed, to get dressed, to get in the wheelchair—you've got to understand, that could take close to an hour to do. Then he'd go rolling out and just watch John-Henry." The daily hitting sessions around the cage became prime entertainment not just for Ted but for the whole household and any guests who might be present.

"John-Henry made a great tape of him talking with Dad around that time, and he let me hear it," Claudia added. "John-Henry said to Dad, 'Do you think there'll ever be another .400 hitter?' Dad said, 'Yeah, I think there will be. Probably our boy in Boston.' I think he meant Nomar. Then there was a pause, and John-Henry goes, 'Do you think I could?' And Dad goes, 'And you. And you. Yeah, you could, too.' It's just precious. Precious."

To supplement Ferroli's hitting tutorials, John-Henry decided he needed a conditioning and speed coach, someone who could teach him to be quicker, run faster, and develop better technique. He called another old friend, Steve Connolly, then sixty-two, who had an eclectic background: he'd played baseball and run track at San Jose State University, become a Marine, and made his mark professionally as a paparazzo, taking photos and digging for dirt on celebrities for various tabloids and movie magazines.*

"It became a circus at the house," said Connolly, who moved in with Ted and established a training regimen for John-Henry, running him on golf courses, sand dunes, and high school fields to improve his speed. When Connolly first timed John-Henry in the sixty-yard dash, he ran it in 8.4 seconds. When he finished with him, in April of 2002, his time was 6.9, which was the average for major leaguers.[5] John-Henry also ate well and lifted weights vigorously to build his strength.

Meanwhile, on the hitting front, Ferroli was noticing steady progress as well. He put John-Henry in a local semipro league, where the kid was hanging in there and getting the bat around regularly against pitchers throwing eighty to eighty-five miles per hour.

One day, Ferroli was throwing batting practice and beaned John-Henry.

---

* Connolly—who'd worked the Bill Clinton–Gennifer Flowers beat, among others—had employed John-Henry as his legman in early 1989, when he was stalking Jane Fonda on behalf of *Star* magazine. John-Henry was in California trying to play baseball at the time, and Connolly knew that young Williams had dated Vanessa Vadim, Fonda's daughter from her first marriage, to the French director Roger Vadim. *Star* was chasing a story that Fonda was soon to divorce her second husband, Tom Hayden, and Connolly asked John-Henry to meet with the actress, whom he knew via Vanessa, to see what he could find out. He came up with enough information to help the *Star* story, and Connolly paid him $3,000 in cash. Fonda and Hayden were divorced later that year.

"I drilled him. I can't believe he stood there and watched it hit him right in the head. He just didn't think that I would ever hit him. I didn't mean to. I tried to throw him a high inside fastball, and it got away from me. I just kind of put it in his ear, and he stayed there and it hit him. Bam! He got up and looked at me, and I said, 'Sorry. Part of the game.' We got that out of the way."

Ferroli would give Ted almost daily progress reports, and he told him about the beaning. "I hit your fuckin' kid today," Ferroli said. "It was like a deer when you put the headlights on him—he just stood there." Ted shrugged it off as a rite of passage.

Sometimes Ted would summon Ferroli from his room down the hall to talk at three in the morning. Williams would be restless and couldn't sleep. After talking about John-Henry for a bit, they'd talk baseball in general.

"He'd say, 'What do you think of Greenberg?' And we'd start talking about Hank Greenberg, the old Detroit slugger. And he'd start picking apart all sorts of old-time hitters. He'd say, 'Who was the best push hitter of all time? And you better fuckin' get it right.' I'd say, 'Cobb; I told you last year.' 'Jesus, you're right. What did he hit?' '.366.' You know, it was fun." And Ferroli learned some of Ted's personal quirks: he used to iron his money so he could hand out crisp bills; he always put his shoes on before his pants. Ted also told Ferroli he'd never get married again.

"I don't go 0 for 4," he explained.

In the spring of 2002, John-Henry suddenly brought in a strength and conditioning coach from Colorado named Jim Warren. Warren had trained Barry Bonds, who was widely suspected of using steroids to inflate his record-setting home-run totals for the San Francisco Giants. He had hit seventy-three in 2001.

Ferroli and Connolly were surprised by the move and found Warren's Bonds connection alarming. Soon enough, John-Henry was asking them what they thought of steroids. Both men, though they understood the allure of a shortcut for John-Henry, told him they strongly opposed the substances. "I just said, 'If you're going to cross that line, I'm out,'" Ferroli said.

Neither Ferroli nor Connolly thought John-Henry went on to take steroids, but they couldn't rule out the possibility that he did. "If God came down and asked me, 'Did John-Henry Williams take steroids?' I would say no, but I can't say for sure," Ferroli said.

But Dom DiMaggio was suspicious: "He took all kinds of tablets and pills. God knows what he was taking. He had me feel his arm. It was like steel. He was a big guy."

★   ★   ★

Two of the most important women in Ted's life—two of his loves—
came back to him toward the end: his second wife, Lee Howard, and
Isabel Gilmore, the art teacher he had met in 1957, during spring training at Sarasota, and later proposed to. She'd turned him down because
Ted's offer came with a big condition: that she send her two sons off to
boarding school.

Lee and Isabel had surfaced again in 1994, around the time of Ted's
big stroke. They had never stopped loving him, really, and reached out
not to try to rekindle a romance but simply to reconnect in the way that
any two people who care about each other deeply would want to do—
especially since Williams was infirm and obviously in rapid decline.
Dolores, Ted's third wife, would make forays to Citrus Hills from Vermont and was a presence at the end, too, but her access was facilitated by
her children, John-Henry and Claudia, both of whom still liked seeing
their mother and father together. While Ted regarded Dolores as something of a wacky nuisance, he also felt affection and admiration for her.
But he viewed Lee and Isabel differently—as two of his loves that could
have been lifelong.

Lee had been visiting her friend Dotty Lindia in Citrus Hills, and one
day they decided to drop in on Ted.

"We went to the door, and Ted answered, and he was surprised as he
could be to see me," Lee recalled. "We visited for quite a while that
afternoon. He told me to stay in touch, to keep calling him, but to call
collect. He didn't want me to pay, and he had trouble dialing at that time
unless he asked the guy that was taking care of him. So when I'd call I'd
call collect, and it worked a few times, but then John-Henry started getting in on the act and refused to accept the charges."

When they were able to talk on the phone, Lee noticed that Ted
would speak louder than normal. "He wanted John-Henry to hear. He'd
say, 'I still love you and always will,' and then he would repeat it even
louder."

Lee still loved Ted, too. "If he would have just been the way he was
near the end, when he was sick, if he was like that all the time, it would
have been perfect. I've said many times that I probably should have been
a little more patient when he said he would change, and maybe I should
have went back and tried it, but who knows if he would have changed?"
But Ted was now part of a package deal—one that worried Lee, as it did
so many others. "Ted's big mistake when he got sick was giving John-
Henry power of attorney," she said. "One of the last times I talked to

him, he said, 'I wish I had a lot of money to give to you.' And I thought, 'Why is he saying this?' He paused and said, 'But it's all gone.' So he had to know what John-Henry was doing."[6]

Isabel had reappeared suddenly and attended the opening of Ted's museum in 1994. Following Louise Kaufman's death the previous year, and after John-Henry and Claudia had dispatched Lynette Siman, they had pondered how to get a woman involved with their father again. They considered Isabel but felt she wasn't the right match. "She was very nice and sweet, but too soft for Dad," Claudia said. "He'd talk of 'dames and broads.' Though he acted more the gentleman with her, I think they knew it wouldn't work out." But before long, Isabel, who was living in Alabama then, began driving over to see Ted once a month, and they would talk on the phone regularly. Williams would send her flowers on her birthday and on Valentine's Day.

"He was in a pathetic condition at the end, with tubes and wires everyplace," Isabel said. "He should have passed on when he was ready to, in peace. John-Henry kept him alive for financial reasons."

When Isabel visited, she'd check into a local motel and stay for a few days. She'd go up to Ted's house and sit with him. They'd have lunch, and sometimes John-Henry and Claudia would be there.

"Ted would always thank me for coming," Isabel said. "He'd tell me what a dear friend I was. We'd reminisce. And he'd smile. He'd say, 'I was so dumb not to have married you.'

"At the end, I called him every few days. He couldn't talk, really, but he'd say a few words. 'Thank you for calling and thank you for loving me.' The nurse would hold the phone for him."[7]

In January of 2002, John-Henry excitedly went to see *Vanilla Sky,* a new movie starring Tom Cruise in which cryonics plays a significant role. He knew the power of the arts, especially film, to shape public perception, and he was curious to see how Hollywood would treat the controversial practice to which he was now committed. He was also curious to see how the young woman he was taking to the movie would react.

Jenna Bernreuter was a twenty-nine-year-old critical-care nurse from Mississippi who was giving dialysis to Ted at night in his house. She had started in October of 2001, and she and John-Henry began dating in December, after which Jenna resigned her position because she felt she had a conflict of interest. Anita was shattered by John-Henry's betrayal and returned to Massachusetts.

After the film, John-Henry started telling Jenna about cryonics. "I'm from a nursing background," she recalled. "I'm thinking, 'Dead meat doesn't beat.' I watch people die every day. But in John-Henry's mind, cryonics meant you'd never be apart and still be together someday. He said he wanted to do it for himself, that his father was very interested in it, and they'd talked about it. He said Ted didn't believe in God. John-Henry didn't, either, so the only thing they could believe in was science. His philosophy was: 'I'm not going to heaven—I'm going to Alcor.'"

John-Henry later took Jenna to meet Saul Kent and Bill Faloon, the leading cryonicists and Alcor figures. And after that, she met Jerry Lemler, the Alcor CEO.[8]

Meanwhile, Alcor was shifting into high-alert mode for Ted's death. John-Henry had told officials at the company that it was a done deal: they were getting the Kid. So Alcor hired a public relations strategist to deal with the anticipated flood of media attention when the news broke. The company also began to make logistical arrangements for a team of specialists to race to Citrus Hills when the time came to pack Ted's body in ice.

The PR man was Bill Haworth from Los Angeles. Haworth had worked on the 1992 and 1996 Clinton presidential campaigns before easing into the cryo milieu by working with Saul Kent on his project to build Timeship, a cryonics megafacility.

"It was a closely held secret that Ted was coming to Alcor," Haworth said. "Board members and some of the key staff knew. What I'd been told by Jerry Lemler and Saul Kent and John-Henry was that under the right circumstances and at the proper time, there would be a news conference in Boston to announce that Alcor had Ted Williams. I knew Ted was the man of the hour, that everyone thought he could change Alcor's fate. I'd get reports in the spring of 2002 that Williams's health was failing. There was discussion that we could make hay with this. That this was an ideal opportunity if it was handled right."

Haworth drafted a five-page statement for Lemler to read at the anticipated Boston press conference. "Jerry Lemler was the most ardent baseball fan I've ever met," Haworth said. "I can't describe how clearly delighted Jerry was at the prospect of Alcor attracting not only a true celebrity but a celebrity from *his* pastime. Jerry was a PR man's dream. He wanted to do anything and everything to promote the case for cryonics. I was given a blank check to do whatever I needed to do to bring the media in line with cryonics, to spin the thing out."[9]

As Haworth contemplated how best to manage the PR, Alcor hired Suspended Animation, Inc., of Florida to see to it that Williams's body was as well preserved as possible when it arrived in Scottsdale to be dismembered and frozen. Suspended Animation, then based in Boca Raton, worked to develop equipment and techniques to minimize cell damage after death.

John-Henry would give Alcor frequent updates on Ted's condition, and Alcor would relay the information to Suspended Animation's chief operating officer, David Hayes. "We were given certain parameters we had to prepare for," Hayes said. "If Ted got sick or ill, we'd go into different levels of standby. We'd be prepared to get on the road, bags packed; or the other level of standby was to go to Citrus Hills and sit where the patient was for weeks on end. Crews went to wait near his house. There were many discussions about where to park the ambulance so it wouldn't draw attention."[10]

As he neared the end, Ted had had enough of life in his debilitated condition and asked one close friend, Steve Brown, to pray for him to die. Brown, an ardent Christian but not pushy about it, wanted to talk to Williams about God but didn't know how.

"It hurt me not to bring a good argument about God," Brown said. "I didn't know how to present it. Ted was open to being convinced. My secretary prayed with Ted, and Ted prayed with her. He asked me what made me believe and think there's an afterlife. I said I didn't know, but I kind of look at it as an insurance policy. If there is, and all I have to do is ask His forgiveness, how can you not? I think he took it to heart. When I told him I couldn't pray for him to die, he said, 'That's not the answer I was looking for, Bush, but it's a good one.'"[11]

A few of Ted's caretakers were zealous Christians as well. When they saw that Williams's days were numbered, the caretakers looked for an opportunity to bring him to Christ, even though they knew that he was skeptical of religion at best and that John-Henry and Claudia were firm nonbelievers.

The leader in this effort was nurse Virginia Hiley-Self. Since October of 2001, when she started working for Ted, she had raised the subject several times with him, but he had declined to bite. "I'd say, 'Jesus Christ is my savior; are you interested in sharing about it?' He'd say, 'Not now,'" Hiley-Self recalled. "It wasn't something I did every day. I just felt when the time was right I'd bring it up because it was important to me that before he died he did accept Christ. I wanted him to go to heaven. I felt God led me to that house for that reason. I felt my purpose was served there, not only taking care of him but also eternal."[12]

Hiley-Self enlisted the help of a friend who also was taking care of Williams, Donna Van Tassel, a nutritionist whom John-Henry had brought in to administer an herbal regimen for Ted. Van Tassel was also deeply religious and looked for ways to interact spiritually with her clients. "I go in there with people thinking they need herbs, but I do a lot of emotional healing, and a lot of times people have an experience with the Lord," she said.

Van Tassel had never been to a baseball game and knew nothing about the sport when she first met Ted in January of 2002, but she said they bonded, and after a while, she "could see more of a reason for me to be there than for an herb," so she concluded that Williams was ready for a spiritual approach.

One day (Hiley-Self recorded it in her journal as January 21), when Ted was alert and in the living room, sitting in his wheelchair, Van Tassel began to lead him in the sinner's prayer. "I said to him, like with everybody, 'Do you want to ask Jesus to come into your heart as your savior?' He said, 'Yes.' So I said, 'I'll lead you, but you have to be the one to say it: Heavenly father, I know I'm a sinner.' Then he'd say, 'Heavenly father, I know I'm a sinner. . . .'

"I talked with him, and as I was talking, I was saying what I could see, and it was like we were on a baseball field, just me and him. It was very real. I was standing there on the base. It was spiritual baseball. That's never happened to me—I could not have come up with these words. God knew what Ted needed, so He put it in terms that he could relate to. I'd say, 'Okay, this is the greatest hit you've ever hit,' and he's playing along in the game, I'm throwing the ball and he's at bat. It was very back and forth, together. He kept receiving. I'd say, 'Okay, you're up to bat,' and he kept playing this spiritual baseball game, until the end. And they were cheering him, the fans, and in the spiritual field, the angels were rejoicing."[13]

Thrilled, Van Tassel reported the exciting news to her friend Hiley-Self. Two days later, January 23, Virginia followed up with Ted. "I asked him who his Savior was, and he said, 'Jesus Christ is my Savior,'" Hiley-Self said.

Claudia Williams was highly skeptical of these accounts and resentful that Hiley-Self and Van Tassel approached her father about such a personal issue. "I came to learn that some of the caretakers tried to enlighten Dad with God, and he'd be just squirming in bed, screaming, 'John-Henry!'" Claudia said. "Dad at that point was either too tired to fight them and argue with them or was trying to be respectful of someone who was wiping his butt and cleaning his wounds, or doing whatever they had to do, [and was trying] to not say something degrading to them. Even on his deathbed, he swore to God. 'Why are you putting me through this?'"

On February 17, 2002, Ted made his first public appearance since his nine-hour heart surgery more than a year earlier. It would also be the last time he was seen in public.

The occasion was the annual induction ceremony at Williams's museum, where Cal Ripken of the Baltimore Orioles, Don Mattingly of the Yankees, and Dwight Evans of the Red Sox were being honored. It was a last-minute decision by John-Henry to have Ted appear. Tommy Lasorda, the master of ceremonies, had already begun the program when he got word that Williams was on his way.

"We have a special guest," Lasorda said. "Let's wait a few seconds until he gets here."

Outside, a van pulled up. The sliding door was opened, and the Kid, in his wheelchair, was lowered to the ground by a hydraulic lift. As John-Henry and Claudia guided their father onto a stage, Lasorda said: "Ladies and gentlemen, the greatest hitter that God ever put on earth, Ted Williams!" Nearly two thousand people, including Johnny Pesky, Dom DiMaggio, Elden Auker, and other old-timers—such as Enos Slaughter, the former Cardinal who had figured so prominently in the 1946 World Series against the Red Sox—rose to their feet, many weeping.

Ted wore a blanket around his legs and a sweater underneath his blue blazer despite the Florida heat. The ninety-one-year-old Auker bent down and kissed his friend of more than sixty years on the forehead. "I love you," Williams said softly to Auker in response. Then Bob Lobel, a Boston TV sportscaster there to help with the awards, gently wiped a tear away from Ted's cheek.

Lasorda turned the microphone over to John-Henry. "We knew this day was coming for a few weeks," the young Williams said. "We never clearly realized what it would mean to be here on the same stage with my dad and my sister, breathing the same air everybody else is breathing and knowing how valuable life is and what love is. . . . I don't think there are two children luckier in the whole wide world than my sister and I. All I want him to know is that I know the hell he and I have gone through in the last year and a half, and I and my sister could not have done it without him. Dad, we love you." Claudia embraced her father, then Ted waved weakly to the audience without speaking.

Afterward, Auker made it clear to the *Boston Globe*'s Gordon Edes that he disapproved of the way John-Henry was handling his father's care and suggested that the public appearance had been exploitive. Ted "can hardly talk," Auker said. "He's got this thing in his throat, he's on dialysis every night, and now he's lost his appetite and is losing weight. His face is very pale. They're just keeping him alive. It just isn't right. He doesn't want to live. He's in a wheelchair, he can't take care of himself, he's got someone around him 24 hours every day. It's very, very unfortunate, sad to see."

Auker said he thought Ted's appearance at his museum was inappropriate. "It's like he's on display. Of course, people were thrilled to see him, but to see him in that condition, to see him like that?"[14]

In June, after nearly eight months of working with John-Henry, Steve Ferroli concluded that while the kid could never hit major-league pitching, he might be able to pass muster in rookie ball. But this would require signing a contract with a major-league team that sponsored a club in a rookie league.

John-Henry asked Ferroli what he should do. Ferroli suggested the obvious: approach the Red Sox. The team had just been sold to John W. Henry, a commodities trader who had previously owned the Florida Marlins. John-Henry should just call John Henry and ask for a meeting, Ferroli advised.

Henry, after acquiring the Sox, had gone to Citrus Hills to introduce himself to Ted and pay his respects. Now he sat down for a meeting at Fenway Park with Williams's son, who was accompanied by Ferroli. Henry's new Red Sox CEO, Larry Lucchino, who had held equivalent positions with the Baltimore Orioles and San Diego Padres, also attended.

"John-Henry was a nervous wreck," said Ferroli, whose role was to be supportive, to attest to how hard his pupil had worked over the previous eight months, and to argue that he deserved a chance, despite his advanced baseball age.[15] Everyone in the room understood that this scheme would have been a nonstarter absent the Ted connection, but the Red Sox agreed to give John-Henry a basic minor-league contract out of respect for the Kid. Henry warned the young Williams that he would likely be subjected to snarky and occasionally ruthless coverage from the press and even fans, but John-Henry was undeterred.[16]

Lucchino actually was attracted to the entertainment and curiosity aspects of the John-Henry gambit. "I've always been open to a vaudevillian approach—the Bill Veeck school of baseball, if you will—if it's not going to hurt anyone," he said. "Ted was near the end of his life, and we saw it as a gesture of respect to the father. I called our farm director, Ben Cherington, then, and suggested that he be given an opportunity. It was not that big a deal. We're in the yes business. We didn't see it as that big an imposition on the organization, given his bloodlines."[17]

The Red Sox announced the John-Henry signing on June 20, 2002, and said he would be assigned to the club's Class A Fort Myers affiliate in the Gulf Coast League. With a few exceptions, press reaction ranged from skepticism to cruelty. Gordon Edes of the *Globe* called the signing a "ridiculous publicity grab."[18] The *Boston Herald*'s Steve Buckley ripped the Sox for perpetrating "this disgraceful, embarrassing sham." He referred to John-Henry as "Thanks Ted" and said every inning of playing time he received would be an inning taken away from a legitimate prospect. "Let's face it," Buckley added, "the kid is a clown. If he's going to play for the Red Sox, he might as well have red hair and a red nose."[19]

In his first game for the Gulf Coast League Red Sox on June 26, John-Henry—wearing number 37 and batting eighth as the designated hitter—went 0–3 but acquitted himself honorably. He hit a slow roller to shortstop, popped up to short, and lined hard to the third baseman.[20] In his second game, he played first base, where he recorded ten putouts and one error while again going 0–3, though he reached base when he was hit by a pitch.[21] In his third game, John-Henry started at first once more, but had to leave the game before getting an at bat after running into a railing while chasing a pop-up and breaking a rib. The Red Sox said he would be sidelined for six weeks.[22]

Shortly after 9/11, Ted told an old friend that while he still wished to be cremated after he died, he knew that John-Henry wanted him to be cryonically preserved and that whatever his son wanted was okay by him. But several months later, in the spring of 2002, Williams told one of his caretakers that he did not want cryonics.[23]

In his final months, Ted began to feel a general sense of foreboding, of disquiet and unease. He told five friends, including Bob Breitbard and Isabel Gilmore, that he was unhappy with his isolation and that he wanted to see a lawyer. He also said he was concerned that John-Henry had made a mess of his finances, and he was worried that his wishes were not being carried out.

One of the first to receive these anxious calls from Williams was Billy Reedy, an old friend from Detroit whom he had met through Islamorada fishing guide Jimmie Albright. Reedy, who owned two bars near Tiger Stadium, had helped arrange the meeting between John-Henry and Detroit Tigers owner Mike Ilitch to discuss Hitter.net. Reedy would send Ted a shipment of sausage each year, and he had clashed with John-Henry once when young Williams said to mail packages like that through him. "I said, 'You go fuck yourself,'" Reedy recalled. "'I knew your father before you were born. I wouldn't send anything to you unless Ted told me to.'"

Starting in late 2001 and extending into the spring of 2002, Reedy said Ted called him about a half dozen times to complain that he was feeling increasingly isolated. He asked Reedy if he could come live with him in Detroit. "He called me one Saturday and started talking to me about coming out here to live," Reedy said. "That I was the one guy who could get him out of there. I called Bob Breitbard about it right away. Bob said there was no goddamn way."

Williams told Reedy that he felt like he was being held captive, cut off from many of his friends. "I wondered if he was senile," Reedy said. "When I told my wife about it, she thought he was hallucinating." But Ted persisted: "By the second or third call he said, real quiet, 'Do you remember what we talked about? Can you do it? You're the guy who could do it.' About a week later I got another one, then another one. One day I called him. He was really bad that day. I said, 'How are you?' He said, 'I can't talk right now.' I said, 'Do you remember talking to me about a few things?' 'Yes.' 'Is that why you can't talk now?' 'Yes.'"

Reedy said he never actually told Ted no. "I was hoping it would just go away. But he kept saying, 'I'd just like to come up there and live with you.' I had a small house on a lake. Nothing fancy. He sounded weak. He'd cry a little bit when he talked to me. I'd say, 'How we gonna do it, Ted? The weather up here? We got winter.' The second or third time he called I told my wife, 'I don't think he is hallucinating.'"[24]

In the spring of 2002, Ted reached out for help from his old friend Daisy Bisz, who besides having helped represent him in his first divorce had drawn up an early version of his will.

"He called me in May and asked me to get an attorney for him to get his property back from John-Henry," said Bisz. "He said John-Henry had taken everything over, taken everything he had. He asked me to come to his house. I told him I'd come as soon as I could, to hang in there and I'd try to help. He was just upset. He wasn't nutty. He was clear. Not crying."

But Bisz, then ninety-two, was recovering from recent surgery and was not able to visit Williams or, it would turn out, arrange for another lawyer to help before Ted died. "I was saddened by the call, and it turned out that was the last time I got to talk to him."[25]

On May 28, 2002, Ted received a visit from John Burgess, a Greenville, South Carolina, business executive who had been working with him to champion the cause of getting Shoeless Joe Jackson admitted to the Hall of Fame. Ted had contributed to the building of a bronze statue of Jackson that had recently been dedicated in Greenville, Shoeless Joe's hometown, and Burgess wanted to show Williams a photo of the statue. He'd flown down for the day on a private plane along with his friend and lawyer Mike Glenn, who wanted to meet Williams.

While they were at Ted's house, Bob Breitbard called and was talking with George Carter, who was back working for Ted occasionally, despite having been fired by John-Henry the previous year. Carter told Breitbard that John Burgess was visiting. The two men knew each other through Ted, and Breitbard asked Carter if he could speak with Burgess. Carter handed Burgess his cell phone. Breitbard told Burgess that Williams had called him the other day, upset. He had said: "I really need a lawyer. Things aren't going well here."

Burgess said he happened to have Glenn with him and offered to put the lawyer on the phone. They took the cell phone outside for privacy.[26] "Bob told me that Ted felt like his son was doing things that were not appropriate, that he didn't want," Glenn said. "He was unhappy with the circumstances. . . . I told Bob I didn't think he could do anything as a friend unless one of Ted's other kids wanted to intervene." Added Glenn, "It was pretty clear to me the day I was there that Ted would not be able to go to court and help himself. There were times during our visit when he was as sharp as he could be, and a few minutes later you'd think he was in a coma. He went back and forth that way."[27]

Glenn wondered why Breitbard, a wealthy man with many resources at his disposal, didn't consult an attorney on his own.[28]

On June 18, 2002, Buzz Hamon, a friend of Williams's who ran his museum from 1994 to 1999, called Ted to gauge his interest in doing a book about the last twenty years of his life. The book would be written by former Williams collaborator John Underwood. Hamon said Ted was interested, but John-Henry nixed the idea. "Then Ted told me, 'I need a lawyer. I've made a mistake.' After that he went silent, like somebody had walked into the room. Our conversation ended."[29]

Ted's expressions of angst to Reedy, Bisz, Breitbard, and Hamon were delivered over the telephone, but he spoke to Isabel Gilmore in person about his fears during her visits. "He begged me the last three or four times I was down there that he needed a lawyer," Isabel recalled. "He said, 'I need a lawyer. Things aren't going right.' Ted could hardly talk." But she was unsure how seriously to take what he said. "I didn't know whether it was just his being sick, and also I knew if I did anything I'd be sued by John-Henry and Claudia for interfering." She consulted her son, a lawyer, and he advised her to stay out of it—this was a family problem, and she wasn't part of the family.

"I didn't know what it was about. I said, 'Why do you want a lawyer?' He said, 'I just do.' I thought it was something running through his mind. This happened three different times on three different occasions over two months in the spring of 2002. He said something like, 'I need a lawyer. My wishes not carried out.' I didn't know what he was talking about. His wishes. No one had ever mentioned this cryonics to me. I never dreamed of it, never heard of it until I read it in the paper after he'd died. I said, 'What wishes? Can I take care of it? What's the problem? Can I help?' 'No, I need a lawyer. I'm not going home.'

"That's it. He meant he was not going to be cremated. He wanted to be cremated and his ashes put in Islamorada. He'd told me that back when we were dating, and he told me that again in 2002, but now he knew he was not going to be cremated, and it was bothering him as he was getting closer to death. He said this to me as I was holding his hand on one of my visits. I would say it was about a month before he died.

"I never told John-Henry or Claudia what he was saying because they had a family lawyer, and John-Henry had power of attorney. He was doing everything he could to make his father comfortable, so it never dawned on me there would be anything other than what Ted wanted."

33

July 5, 2002

Williams now had a virtual intensive care unit set up in his house with what seemed like platoons of nurses monitoring his every move. One of them, John Butcher, a paramedic and RN who had started training to become a firefighter, didn't like what he saw when he started his shift at 2:00 a.m. on Friday, July 5.

"Ted was having a restless, difficult sleep, and I couldn't do anything to comfort him," Butcher recalled. "He seemed to be starting to show the signs and symptoms of shock; he was sweaty and pale, his oxygen level dropped, so I tried suctioning and ventilating manually." But without success.[1]

Butcher tried to get a pulse but couldn't. Then he asked a nurse's aide who had come on duty, Joshua Poulin, to try, but Poulin couldn't detect one, either. "There was absolutely no point of consciousness the whole night," Butcher added. "He thrashed a bit and made noises, which he often did at night if he was having a dream."

Then Kathleen Rolfingsmeier entered the room. She was the live-in nurse who coordinated all Ted's at-home care. A Kansan with red hair and green eyes, Rolfingsmeier had been on the job for two months. "We turned him over, we tried different things and put him back on the ventilator, and it just didn't look good to me, so I called 911," Rolfingsmeier said. It was 8:10 a.m. She told Butcher to ride in the ambulance while she and Poulin followed in her car.[2]

Rolfingsmeier called John-Henry as she drove to let him know his father was being taken to the hospital, and it didn't look good. "I could hear the terror in his voice," she remembered. John-Henry was still in Fort Myers, two hundred miles to the south, nursing the broken rib he'd sustained on June 27. His new girlfriend, Jenna Bernreuter, was with him.

John-Henry struggled to contain his emotions and to prepare to implement his cryonics plan of action. Over the next half hour, he would make a series of cell phone calls to Rolfingsmeier, Butcher, Josh Poulin, Dr. Joseph Dorn (Ted's primary care physician), Alcor officials, and others. One person he could not reach was his sister Claudia, who had left Tampa early that morning to fly to Boston for the weekend.

Arriving at the hospital at 8:30, Rolfingsmeier still had John-Henry on the line and handed her phone to Butcher, who had been in the ambulance and had more recent news. Butcher told John-Henry that they had done CPR on Ted on the way to the hospital, and now he was being worked on in the emergency room.

"I told him they were doing everything they could, but it didn't look hopeful, and he instructed me that if they terminated resuscitation efforts to pack him in ice so he could be transferred to the cryonics place in Arizona," recalled Butcher.

Ted was pronounced dead at 8:49 a.m.

Butcher called John-Henry back with the news. "He was upset— very, very upset, but he still had it together that he wanted his dad prepped for Alcor. He was very explicit with those instructions."

Butcher walked back into the ER and relayed John-Henry's instructions that Ted should be packed in ice. This was no everyday request at Citrus Memorial, so the staff looked at Butcher quizzically.

"I told them first, and they're looking at me like, 'What?' They weren't moving as quickly as John-Henry wanted them to to get him packed," Butcher said.

Then Joseph Dorn arrived. Dorn had been Ted's doctor since 1996, and the two had become friendly. Dorn, who was also a Methodist missionary, had occasionally made house calls, and he and his family had socialized with Ted. John-Henry had felt comfortable enough with Dorn to have confided in him about his cryonics plan more than a year earlier, so when Dorn spoke by phone with John-Henry that morning, the doctor was not surprised, and he helped facilitate young Williams's wishes.

Someone ran down the hall and returned with a garbage bag containing crushed ice. "They put a large bag of ice on his body, but he really needed to be encased," Rolfingsmeier said. "So I remember telling them that they had to totally surround him. It was just a bag sitting on his abdomen." Soon the blood thinner heparin was being pumped into Ted's veins per the instructions of Alcor and John-Henry.

★   ★   ★

Several miles away, Bobby-Jo and Mark Ferrell had heard the siren of an ambulance but hadn't thought much of it; they lived in an elderly community, and people were always being taken to the hospital, it seemed.

It had been ten months since Bobby-Jo had seen Ted. During that time, she had confided to three of her friends that John-Henry was planning to freeze their father when he died. Now one of those friends, who coincidentally was at Citrus Memorial Hospital when Williams arrived, called. Mark answered the phone.

"He said, 'Tell Jo her worst nightmare is happening. They're pumping Ted full of blood thinners and icing him down,'" Mark said. "Then I had to go and tell my wife that her father was dead. I mean, they were gonna try to hide it, sneak him out of here. But I got that call."[3]

To pick up Ted's body, the hospital called Dwight Hooper, proprietor of Hooper Funeral Homes & Crematory, to which the local newspaper, the *Citrus County Chronicle,* had given its Best of the Best award each year for as many years as anyone could remember. Hooper was thirty-two, the newest generation in a business that had been family owned and operated since 1946. He had never handled a cryonics case before. "I talked to people at Alcor," Hooper said. "They gave simple instructions on packing: 'Cool the body off as best you can, and we'll take it from there.' I'd assumed they would want dry ice, and that might be hard to find on short notice, but they said just regular ice." Hooper sent someone down to the local Winn-Dixie to purchase the necessary amount.[4] He was told to take the body to the Ocala airport, where he would meet the private plane that Alcor was sending. Hooper pulled his hearse out of the funeral home around noon for the thirty-minute trip to the airport, driving alone with Ted.

John-Henry got in his car and raced north on Interstate 75 from Fort Myers. Jenna followed in her car. "John-Henry felt terrible guilt and also denial," she said. "He wasn't there when his dad died. He'd been there for Ted so much, and then the day it happened he was not there."[5]

When John-Henry arrived at the airport, he was wearing Ted's navy blue blazer. He was all business, cell phone glued to his ear, pacing back and forth, organizing, talking to Alcor, and still trying to reach Claudia. Ted had died when she was in the air, and John-Henry desperately wanted to give her the news himself rather than have her learn about it on television.

Jenna and John-Henry didn't talk much. "I gave him a big hug. He'd have moments where he'd break down, crying and crying. I sat with the Ziegler [the steel case often used to transport dead bodies], and he would come up to touch it." When he did so, she would leave so that he could have some private moments with his father.

Then Dave Hayes, the Suspended Animation official who was serving as Alcor's field representative, arrived. He introduced himself to John-Henry; told him how sorry he was. Hayes opened up the Ziegler and tended to Ted, assisted by Jenna, with her nurse's training. He injected more heparin through Ted's dialysis catheter, which was still attached to the body.

Jenna made sure John-Henry didn't see any of this. "I told him I didn't think it was a good idea for him to see his father like that," she said. "At that point he'd been dead six or seven hours. That wasn't his dad anymore, and he needed to let Dave Hayes and I do this. So we got screwdrivers, opened up the case, and put more ice in. I wrapped Ted's head in a towel, and I just looked at him and said, 'Bye.'"

Hayes still had a raft of paperwork to take care of before he could legally take possession of the body. Unlike virtually everyone else whose bodies were frozen at Alcor, Ted had never submitted an application or signed up for the procedure himself. Nor had John-Henry ever observed that formality on behalf of his father. Hayes called his girlfriend in Atlanta, who went online and directed him to a nearby notary. After about a half hour, Hayes and John-Henry returned to the Ocala airport, where the plane had arrived.

The jet chartered by Alcor was small, with only a pilot and copilot. One of the pilots, Howard Lopez, served as a witness to some of the paperwork John-Henry was now feverishly completing. At 2:44 p.m., about six hours after Ted was pronounced dead, John-Henry faxed an application to Alcor in his father's name. Then Hayes, Hooper, Jenna, and the pilots loaded the Ziegler case on the plane, strapping it into an open section in the middle. There were four seats in the back. John-Henry and Jenna debated whether one of them should accompany the body to Arizona, but John-Henry decided he had to drive to Tampa to meet Claudia, who was now on her way back from Boston. Jenna preferred to stay home. Hayes convinced them everything would be fine. The plane took off around 5:45 p.m.

Hooper was instructed by Eric Abel to say nothing to the press about what he did that day or how Ted's body was disposed of. And the death certificate would be deliberately vague on that point—the place of disposition, it said, was "undetermined."

*   *   *

Bobby-Jo, meanwhile, was desperately trying to find out where her father's body was. But John-Henry wasn't taking her calls, so she and Mark called John Heer, a lawyer in Cleveland whose wife was a friend of Bobby-Jo's from the time both families had lived in Nashville.* Six months earlier, Bobby-Jo had confided in Heer about John-Henry's plans for cryonics and about the fact that he had barred her from visiting her father. Hearing that the cryonics plan was on, Heer told Mark to contact law enforcement to see if there was any way they could help. He then advised Bobby-Jo to send an e-mail to Alcor warning the company not to proceed with plans to freeze Ted. Heer, a specialist in environmental law, was not familiar with the specifics of the relevant laws, but he decided there was no harm in putting an adversary on written notice.[6] Bobby-Jo went online to the Alcor website, took down the name and contact information of the first official she saw, and then, at 1:25 p.m., more than four hours before Ted's body left Florida, sent the following e-mail to Jennifer Chapman, then Alcor's member services administrator:

> *My name is Barbara Joyce Williams Ferrell, the daughter of Ted Williams. It has come to my attention that you and your organization may be in route to Citrus County Florida, to pick up my Father's body. I am letting you know now, "DO NOT go any further—I am opposed to this procedure and you are 'On Notice' at this time." John-Henry Williams is not taking care of my Father's last wishes. This was never my Father's wishes, ever!*

Getting off the plane in Boston late that morning, Claudia Williams noticed large clusters of people grouped around TV sets, the telltale sign of a big breaking news story. She walked over to see what it was, only to learn her father had died.

"I landed, saw it on the TV, turned right around at the gate, got back on the plane, and came home," Claudia recalled. "John-Henry had been trying to get ahold of me, but my cell phone wasn't working. I called him, and he said he'd meet me at the airport in Tampa."[7]

Claudia had sensed Ted was close to death, and she would speculate later that he had not wanted her or John-Henry to be with him when he died. Ted had called her early on the morning of July 3—to say good-

---

* Heer's wife was a singer and had once helped Bobby-Jo record her country song in honor of Ted, "I Love You, Dad."

bye, she felt in retrospect. "He called up, and he was having trouble breathing. It was five thirty or six in the morning. He said, 'Claudia? Claudia? I love you! I love you! Don't you ever forget it!'"

When John-Henry met her in Tampa, Claudia was struck by how apologetic he was for not having been able to reach her. "I was afraid to ask him questions," she recalled, "because he was driving, and I didn't want him to cry. But he just went on, we were driving home, and on his own, he just told me everything that went down—the phone call that he got from the nurses from the house before the ambulance came and how Dad was struggling. And John-Henry was just telling me all this and crying, and I asked him, I said, 'Did you talk to Dad at all?' And he said he did, on the phone, in the ambulance on the way over there." He had, he explained, called John Butcher, the attendant who was riding with Ted in the ambulance. Then Butcher had placed the phone to Ted's ear, and she said John-Henry "yelled to him that he loved him."

It warmed Claudia to hear this dramatic story, and she cried as she told it years later. But according to Butcher, the story wasn't true. There was no call from John-Henry then. "I cannot substantiate that" was the way Butcher put it—diplomatically—reaffirming that he did not speak with John-Henry until they had already arrived at the hospital and Ted was in the emergency room. The paramedic in the ambulance at the time, Teresa Fletcher, confirmed Butcher's account.[8] It was a puzzling piece of hyperbole, since while he'd been away playing baseball, John-Henry had dutifully called in daily to check on Ted, including once on July 4.

John Heer finally reached Eric Abel in the early evening, but Abel refused to tell him what was going on or where Ted's body was. "I remember saying, 'Eric, you've got to be kidding me. This is the daughter, and she's entitled to know what happened to her father.' He said, 'Well, that's what John-Henry and Claudia want me to tell you.'"

Heer appealed to the local sheriff's office for help, as Mark Ferrell had that morning, but Heer was again told this was a family matter and that John-Henry, holding Ted's power of attorney, had broad authority.

At that point, Heer, Bobby-Jo, and Mark felt they had no other option but to go to the press. "We agreed if anyone can get to the bottom of this it's going to be the press," Heer said. "We knew time was of the essence. Alcor had a certain window of time to do what they were going to do. We didn't know they'd already done it by Friday night."

Heer had grown up a Red Sox fan and knew the Boston newspapers:

the *Globe* and the *Herald*. He called the *Globe* first. "I just called in to the news desk. They were saying, 'Yeah, right!' They didn't believe me for a second. They thought I was completely nuts. I said, 'I know you're going to think we're nuts, but we're not, and we need help.'"

Eventually, his call was routed to Joe Sullivan, then the assistant sports editor. An amazed Sullivan consulted with other editors, and it was decided that because the tip involved cryonics, a science reporter, Beth Daley, should pursue it. "We were really suspicious," said Daley, a tall, thin blonde with high energy who speaks in staccato bursts. She was assigned the story between 7:30 and 8:00 p.m. "It sounded so insane. I didn't believe the editors when they told me Ted Williams's daughter was accusing her brother of freezing Williams's head. That's how it was presented to me. I thought the whole thing was ludicrous and a crank."[9]

As reporters do, Daley tried to make herself an expert on the subject immediately. Wanting to get some background before interviewing Bobby-Jo, she surfed the Internet and checked past news stories about cryonics and Alcor. She called Harvard and MIT to try to round up an expert who could speak about cryonics generally, but it was after hours on a Friday night, and she got nowhere. Another reporter, Raja Mishra, gave her a quote from a cloning expert who said that while it was possible to freeze tissues and organs, they could not be thawed out without causing severe damage.

Then Daley called Alcor. "The woman on the other line was excited and implied she couldn't talk because she was waiting for an important phone call. She refused to say from whom. I asked her if it was about Williams, and she said, 'I gotta go.'"

After interviewing Bobby-Jo, Daley thought she sounded scared, furious, and legitimately aggrieved, but the whole story still seemed so wild. "Bobby-Jo was upset with John-Henry, alternating between tears, disbelief, anger, and assuring me her father loved her. She sounded credible, but I had never heard of this woman before, and when someone starts saying their half brother was trying to cash in on their dead father by freezing his head and selling his DNA, well, who wouldn't be skeptical?"

Given the lack of secondary confirmation, the *Globe* decided to be cautious, write a short story, and place it inside the paper, with a tease off page 1. For one thing, the front page would have to be dominated by the overarching news that Ted had died: the main obituary, reaction stories, and a piece on his legacy. And while Bobby-Jo was named and on the record as making the charge that Ted had been frozen, John-Henry, whom she was accusing of doing the deed, could not be reached for comment. In addition, Alcor wouldn't confirm it had Ted.

Still, Daley's story made for gripping reading: "Ted Williams's estranged daughter said the baseball great's son is freezing the hitter's body in hopes of reviving him in the future—a decision that goes against Williams's wishes to be cremated," the first paragraph said.

Back at Ted's house, John-Henry ignored all calls from reporters requesting comment on his father's death. Instead, Eric Abel issued a statement to the Associated Press saying that the Williams family was grateful for the "overwhelming display of love and support" from Ted's fans and friends. It said Ted was a private person in life and wanted to remain so in death, so there would be no funeral, and in lieu of flowers, the family requested that donations be made to the Jimmy Fund or to the Ted Williams museum in Hernando.

At the time the statement was drafted, John-Henry and Abel didn't know that Bobby-Jo had already given interviews to the *Globe* and the *Herald*. They assumed they were still in control of the cryonics story and that Ted's presence at Alcor remained a closely guarded secret. "Our goal was not to have this in the public arena," said Abel. "It was for no one else's consideration. Probably the world would have concluded we had a private ceremony, be it cremation or burial. They could have reached whatever conclusion they wanted to, in a vacuum."[10] But late that night they learned via the Internet and local television that Bobby-Jo had gone public. Abel recalled that "there was a collective 'Oh, shit!'" from him and John-Henry as well as from the others present: Claudia; Al Cassidy, Ted's executor; and Cassidy's wife, Gloria.

When reporters started calling Ted's house for comment on the cryonics angle, Claudia shouted, "It's none of their fuckin' business! If that's what we wanted and that's what Dad wanted, then why don't they leave us alone?" But they decided not to respond right away. They would wait and offer a considered reply the next day. "We didn't want to be hasty," Abel said. "We wanted to make a statement that addressed it all." So for the moment, they tried to find consolation in watching the wondrous archival footage of the Kid in his prime that was being broadcast on television.[11]

There was an undercurrent of tension between Claudia and John-Henry that flared occasionally. Three months earlier, John-Henry had taken the extraordinary step of suing his sister in a Florida court and winning a temporary injunction that prevented her from selling the two thousand bats that Ted had autographed and left to her as a nest egg. John-Henry, who had two thousand signed bats of his own from Ted, claimed the deal violated an agreement he had with Claudia whereby she would give him the right to buy her bats before she sold them. Claudia countersued John-Henry, and the litigation was pending. Ted had not been told about this unseemly bit of sibling rivalry.

Now Claudia couldn't resist remarking on the absurdity of the situation, Abel said. "Claudia would take a poke: 'I don't know why we're fighting. We've got enough on our hands without fighting about the bats.' Then John-Henry would jab back. That was a distraction, and Al Cassidy worked hard to resolve it." Cassidy put John-Henry and Claudia in separate rooms and started a round of shuttle diplomacy to try to bring them to their senses. "It was one of those shocking moments in life in which I said, 'Did I just hear that?'" Cassidy recalled. "Claudia was on the floor and John-Henry on the couch and I about fell off the couch. I called them in one at a time." John-Henry seemed to enjoy the process. He told Cassidy he actually admired Claudia for standing up to him and fighting to support her bats deal. And with an almost cultish devotion to cryonics, he remarked to Gloria Cassidy that Al, knowing Ted was at Alcor, must be regretting the fact that he had not had his own dead father frozen.

Before Ted's cryonics procedure began in the operating room at Alcor headquarters in Scottsdale, Dave Hayes, who had accompanied Ted's body on the plane from Ocala, briefed about a dozen technicians, support staff, and two surgeons on what had happened to that point. According to the operating room notes, the "team leader" that day was Mike Darwin. A former Alcor president, Darwin was an influential cryonicist who was presiding over Williams's procedure as the lead surgeon. But Darwin was a dialysis technician by training, not a surgeon. Jose Kanshepolsky, a retired local surgeon under contract to Alcor who normally officiated at the group's suspensions, as they were called, was relegated to a secondary role, assisting Darwin.

After the procedure began and Darwin announced that they were ready to cut Ted's head off, Hayes called a halt to the proceedings. He told the group that when he had flown to Ocala to pick up Ted's body, John-Henry had told him he was still trying to decide which kind of procedure his father should have: the whole-body or the neuro. There were pros and cons associated with both options. One of the last things he asked of Hayes was to promise him that he would not let Alcor sever his father's head until he was called first to give his final approval. Hayes promised.

So Jerry Lemler, the Alcor CEO, picked up his cell phone and called John-Henry. Lemler put his cell phone on speaker. "Four or five of us were talking to John-Henry," said Hayes. "Jerry said, 'This is what we want to do. I want everyone to hear.' Most science surrounding cryonics thought a neuro was better, and so we discussed with [John-Henry] the benefits of it, and he agreed the neuro would be the way to go."

When Lemler's call came in, it was after 11:00 p.m. in Citrus Hills, and John-Henry walked out on the patio to speak privately, motioning for Eric Abel to come with him. The young Williams didn't want Claudia to hear the details of this gruesome discussion. He put his Nextel phone on speaker so Abel could be a witness and participate if he wished.

"John-Henry thought neuro was best, but there were social considerations, too," Abel said. "I said, 'Whole-body sounds better. If this gets out, it's bad enough that it's cryonics, but neuro only is even worse. Doesn't it sound better to say whole-body? That at least brings up an image of the whole body being together.' So we decided to preserve the body as well. Otherwise they would have cremated it. But he did authorize the neuro. And he wanted to make sure they did as good a job as possible. In John-Henry's mind that was most important—to get the head right."

But Alcor quickly picked up on the PR value of preserving Ted's body as well. "It was initially planned to be a cephalic isolation, as they call it," said Bill Haworth, Alcor's strategist, referring to only the head being cut off. "But then John-Henry said to Lemler, 'Jerry, do you really think the public would ever stand for my father, the Splendid Splinter, to have his arms not being preserved?' So a decision was reached: not only would they separate the head, but they'd preserve the body as well."

With these fundamental issues resolved, Darwin picked up a carving knife and began to slice off Williams's head. Two of the Alcorians, Charles Platt and Bobby June, had been taking pictures of all this. In addition to June and Platt, there were a gaggle of other people around and about, taking pictures of the dead Ted Williams going under the knife in a chaotic scene that was a gross breach of traditional operating room protocol.

"Many people photographed the subsequent surgical procedure," Platt would write of the scene in a July 30, 2003, memo to the Alcor board that criticized Lemler's performance as CEO. "None of them signed any non-disclosure form. None of them agreed that Alcor would own the pictures. We do not know what happened to all these people with their cameras and photographs.... Security in the operating room during this case was grossly negligent."

Added Haworth: "From talking to people that were there and directly involved, like Lemler and others, at one point in that OR there were as many as thirty people in scrubs—cameras clicking, video cameras, and house cameras videotaping it as well. It was controlled pandemonium. I mean, everyone was there. They drove in. They flew in. Anyone with credentials, any heavy-duty cryonicist who wanted to be there was there. The plane was met at the airport by a small motorcade. I've seen pictures of that scene. You had sixty to seventy percent of the board, all the staff, all the big contributors. It was a who's who list of Alcorians. I think it came as a surprise that there were so many people there taking pictures, and there was a lot of concern about the supermarket tabloids. Any tabloid would have paid six figures for one of those pictures. They had to have been skulking around, yet nothing ever appeared."

Also present were Alcor members in the Scottsdale area who wouldn't have missed Ted Williams's procedure for the world. Many of these members naturally gravitated to Alcor whenever a new patient arrived anyway. After all, there were only two or three procedures a year, on average, so each took on the trappings of a social event as well as what some critics thought was an overly festive atmosphere.

"The problem I had was that when you had a suspension, it was like a circus," said Tom Brown, an Arizona mortician who worked at Alcor for most of 2002 but did not attend the Williams procedure. "People were getting food and drink. You had about twenty or thirty people in there when you only needed about eight. It was always like a circus atmosphere. 'We got somebody! We got somebody!' I was disappointed to see this atmosphere of a carnival. The party was on."[12]

Back in Citrus Hills, it was time to call it a night. John-Henry walked back to Ted's room and lay down on the king-size bed, which had a remote control that could lift the head and feet. He decided to spend the night there. It seemed a good way to stay close to his father. After he got settled under the covers, he called Jenna Bernreuter.

"He said, 'I'm wrapped up in Dad's sheets,'" Jenna recalled.

34

The Pact

News of Ted's fate stirred national outrage. John-Henry was vilified as the bad seed who had flouted his father's well-documented wishes to be cremated and have his ashes sprinkled in the waters off Florida. There was widespread sympathy for Bobby-Jo, who quickly vowed to go to court to "rescue my father's body."[1] John-Henry and Claudia promised to resist her there.

Journalist after journalist went after John-Henry's subzero plotting: "Make no mistake: The Kid's kid is Very Bad News, and he has saved his best/worst move for last, managing to besmirch...his father's truly remarkable life," wrote Bob Ryan, the *Boston Globe* sports columnist.[2] "Because of something Ted Williams could have absolutely no control over—the dispute in his family about his remains—he has been turned into a joke," Bob Greene lamented in the *Chicago Tribune*.[3] In the *Sporting News,* Dave Kindred picked up on the same theme: "No honor attends Ted Williams frozen.... The loss of dignity comes because Williams specifically and repeatedly made known his wishes to be cremated."[4]

Reporters and camera crews staked out John-Henry, hungry for any explanation he cared to offer about why he had dispatched his father to Alcor, but he remained hunkered down in Ted's house, saying nothing. Bobby-Jo and her husband, Mark, on the other hand, granted interviews to virtually all comers, happy to stoke the flames of the emerging narrative that portrayed John-Henry as the devil incarnate.

Most of Ted's old friends were appalled, though in retrospect some would note that John-Henry was tremendously persuasive, especially with his father, and might indeed have convinced Ted to accept cryonics. Still, such sentiment was barely reflected in any of the press coverage.

Major League Baseball announced on July 8 that it was renaming its All-Star Game Most Valuable Player Award after Williams, and John-Henry and Claudia were invited to come to Milwaukee for the game. But the reaction against John-Henry was so virulent that he and Claudia were quietly disinvited the next day.

Then on July 10, as the conflict appeared headed to court, John-Henry made a phone call that seemed to have little to do with the business at hand. Ringing up Shands Hospital in Gainesville, he asked for the date on which Ted had his heart catheterization procedure performed — the one he underwent before the pacemaker was installed. Nancy Carmichael, the assistant to Rick Kerensky, Williams's cardiologist, called John-Henry back with the date — November 3, 2000 — and expressed her condolences on the occasion of Ted's death. After the call, she wondered why, as he grieved for his father, John-Henry wanted to know the date of a surgery that had happened nearly two years earlier.

The media swarm in tiny Citrus County, Florida, was more than matched by the crush of reporters and cameramen who gathered outside Alcor headquarters in Scottsdale, Arizona, looking first for confirmation that Ted's remains were inside and second for illumination into the strange world of cryonics. Alcor was prohibited by its own confidentiality rules and by its agreement with John-Henry from acknowledging that it had Ted. But it was determined to take maximum advantage of the attention it was receiving to tout the company and cryonics generally. And since it was so widely assumed that Williams was at Alcor anyway, the company looked for a way to make the unofficial official.

"To get ahead of the curve a bit, to answer the 'Is he at Alcor or not' question, and to make a positive case for cryonics, we thought, 'Let's see if we can let the *New York Times* do something,'" recalled Bill Haworth, the Alcor PR man. "It was probably one of the best placements I ever did — below the fold, front page, on July tenth. It was basically constructed as 'The *Times* has learned from sources close to the family that Williams is at Alcor.' This at least provided the authority of the printed word, the words that we could not utter officially. I was tickled with that one, and while we didn't know what John-Henry's reaction would be, the day it ran, he called and said, 'Great story in the *Times*.' Then we opened the door selectively, one-on-one, to media. We still couldn't acknowledge officially, but 'Let's talk about cryonics,' and 'You want to do the tour?' That's how I spun the media out from that time on."[5]

Jerry Lemler, the Alcor CEO, and other officials gave certain reporters a tour of the facility, including the "patient care bay," where the massive stainless steel tanks known as Dewars, which contain the frozen bodies, hang from the ceiling. Officials would linger near Dewar number 6, sometimes nodding their heads, so reporters could feel confident in providing the rich detail that that was where Williams's remains resided. Alcor officials took care to conceal the grisly fact that Ted's head had been cut off and was sitting in a can inside a "neuro column." All the press attention seemed to have its intended effect: Lemler crowed that whereas, pre-Ted, Alcor had only averaged about five thousand hits a day on its website, since the news broke it was getting six hundred thousand hits daily.

At the request of John-Henry and Claudia, Bobby-Jo agreed to try mediation in an effort to end their dispute. They gathered on July 15 at the office of Richard "Spike" Fitzpatrick, one of Bobby-Jo's attorneys, located near the Citrus County courthouse, where reporters were assembled to await the filing of Ted's will.

The mediator, David C. Brennan, a lawyer from Orlando, greeted the three Williams children and passed out copies of Ted's 1996 will, wherein he said he wanted to be cremated and wherein he excluded Bobby-Jo from his estate. Then Brennan presented Bobby-Jo and Mark Ferrell with a piece of paper they had never seen before. It appeared to have been written on a sheet of 8½" x 11" paper, turned sideways, with one end ripped off. Creased, handwritten, and oil-stained, the document was presented by John-Henry and Claudia as a private pact that offered incontrovertible proof that their father did, in fact, want to be cryonically preserved: "JHW, Claudia and Dad all agree to be put in bio-stasis after we die," it read. "This is what we want, to be able to be together in the future, even if it is only a chance." Below this declaration were three signatures: John-Henry's, Ted's, and, on the final line, Claudia's. The document was dated November 2, 2000—the day before Ted's heart catheterization procedure at Shands Hospital.

Bobby-Jo, Mark, and their two lawyers tried to make sense of the document. Mark quickly concluded it was fraudulent, raising the possibility that it had been built around an existing Ted Williams signature. He knew from the caretakers that John-Henry had been in the habit of having his father warm up before signing sessions by writing his signature on blank pieces of paper to make sure it was of adequate quality. Mark also pointed out that the date, written as 11/2/00, had an anomaly. The 11 was darker than the other numbers, and there was a line between the two 1s, so it looked like a capital *H*. It appeared that the number might originally have been a 4 that was changed to an 11, Mark thought. He also noted that whenever Ted signed a letter or any kind of a formal document, he used "Theodore S. Williams," not the informal "Ted Williams," which appeared on the pact.

During breaks in the long day of mediation, Bobby-Jo's team thought of ways to undermine the written pact. They began looking for people whom Ted had told he still wanted to be cremated *after* November 2, 2000. Bob Breitbard said Williams had told him so in November of 2001 and again in February of 2002. Nancy Carmichael of Shands said she remembered Ted talking of being cremated just weeks after the pact was supposedly signed, when he was still in the hospital recovering from his pacemaker surgery. Frank Brothers, also there at the time, along with another nurse, Debbie Erb, corroborated. Caretaker George Carter said Williams told him he still wanted to be cremated when recuperating from heart surgery in San Diego in the spring of 2001. Becky Vaughn, the nurse who cared for Ted in December of 2001, following the catheter and pacemaker procedures, had been present when Ted told John-Henry to stop talking about the cryonics "bullshit." Bobby-Jo's daughter, Dawn Hebding, had seen her grandfather in January of 2001, just before his seizure, and he had told her he wanted to be cremated. And Isabel Gilmore said Ted reaffirmed his wish to be cremated in 2002, not long before he died. Those eight, at a minimum, stood to be witnesses on behalf of Bobby-Jo if her challenge made it before a judge.

John-Henry and Claudia, feeling Mark was too angry, volatile, and controlling, wanted to speak to Bobby-Jo alone at the mediation session. Though reluctant, she finally agreed.

Claudia decided to do the talking, and she thought things were going well.

"I was thinking: 'John-Henry, she doesn't like you. Let me talk. Girl to girl. We might relate.' Bang, we hit it off. I'm like, 'Bobby-Jo, let's be together on this. Please! This is what Dad wanted. This is what we did. We were there, Bobby-Jo. We were there! You weren't there. We're sorry.' I even said to her, 'I'm sorry you didn't have the relationship with Dad that you may have wanted. But please, don't take this away from us. Let's be together. Let's be a family.'

"She looked right at me and John-Henry and said, 'You know, that's all I've ever really wanted. To be included.' She was being really nice. We were blown away! John-Henry's sitting there. He finally said, 'All the time, Bobby-Jo. We will be as one. Come on, let's make it happen.'

We were so ready to just welcome her in. 'Let's just be united on this. Let's be united.'"[6]

When Bobby-Jo came out of the room and reported back to her team, Cleveland lawyer John Heer, who was also there representing Bobby-Jo, thought she seemed "shell-shocked. She didn't know what to think. She said they were being very nice."

That night, the two sides were near an agreement, according to a memo Fitzpatrick dictated at the time. Bobby-Jo wanted assurances that John-Henry would never sell Ted's DNA, as she said he had threatened to do in their first phone call, and he agreed, saying that was never his intention. One sticking point, however, was that John-Henry and Claudia did not want to attach a copy of the written pact to the will when it was filed. It was too crude, and they were embarrassed by it. But Heer and Fitzpatrick thought the document was a fake, and they felt it was in their interest to have it revealed.

The next day, any hope of a resolution was dashed when the mediator invited Mark to participate, and the effect was like tossing a grenade into the room.

"I said, 'Are you sure they want me in there?'" Mark recalled. "'Because if I go in there it's gonna be over with, because I don't like what they've done, and they're not gonna convince me this is what Ted wanted.'" When he sat down at the table with John-Henry, Mark promptly announced, "I've lived through sixty years, and you're the most despicable piece of human garbage I've ever met in my life, you son of a bitch." He then turned to Claudia and told her, "You're just his little puppy dog."

John-Henry's face grew flush as he let Mark vent, but he held his tongue. Finally, he said, "I'm sorry you feel that way." Claudia recalled that she had to contain herself to keep from lunging across the table at Mark, but in the end she, too, said nothing.

After the talks broke down, Al Cassidy, the Winter Haven real estate developer whom Ted had appointed as his executor, asked a judge to settle the issue of what Ted's wishes were. But Cassidy had already made up his mind. "Based on what I know and believe, after the time of his will, Ted chose to have his body preserved via cryonics," he said in a statement. "While many people may not make the same choice for themselves, I hope people will respect this as a private family matter."

On the night of July 22, the Red Sox staged a tribute to Williams at Fenway Park. This Tedfest came as a welcome respite from the lurid cryonics story and gave people a chance to say good-bye to the Kid and revel in their warm memories of him.

There were 20,500 paying fans who turned up. A huge number 9 hung from the center-field wall. On the left-field wall were large blown-up photographs showing Ted hitting, flying his jet in wartime, and kneeling while talking to children. In left field itself was a 77' × 36' number 9 made of white carnations. Bouquets of roses and other flowers filled the carnation borders.

After the national anthem and a flyover by Marine jets, the evening began, and more than a score of people who had been friends of Ted and had known him at various stages of his life took turns coming to home plate and telling stories about their experiences with him. The guests included Williams's old pals and teammates Dominic DiMaggio and Johnny Pesky; John Glenn; Carl Yastrzemski; and Nomar Garciaparra, then the Sox shortstop and public face of the team. Noticeably absent were Ted's three children, all of whom had declined invitations to attend. Given the public mood, John-Henry and Claudia's absence was not surprising, but Bobby-Jo would later say she regretted not attending and seizing the moment to make a public plea for getting Ted's remains out of Alcor.

Dom DiMaggio served as her surrogate, however, and he elicited a standing ovation from the crowd when he said: "I am saddened by the turmoil of the current controversy. I hope and pray this controversy will end as abruptly as it began, and the family will do the right thing by honoring Ted's last wishes as to his final resting place. And may he then finally rest in peace."

After the speakers finished, nine white doves were released from a box at home plate and then flew out over the outfield and beyond. For the finale, the lights were turned off, and a number 9 formed by a pattern of lights inside the Prudential Tower, behind right field, appeared. Then a group of Red Sox old-timers, led by DiMaggio and Pesky, and a handful of current players, led by Garciaparra, went out to the left-field garden, and each laid a red rose amid the white carnations that shaped Ted's 9. Finally, Curt Gowdy, the former voice of the Red Sox, came to home plate and reenacted his call of Williams's final home run, on September 28, 1960. Gowdy was helped by Jack Fisher, the former Orioles pitcher who had served up the pitch that Ted hit out that day. Fisher walked out to the mound and obligingly wound up and pretended to throw a pitch, happy to play the willing victim.

★   ★   ★

On July 25, John-Henry and Claudia released a statement about their decision to have their father frozen, announcing that Ted had been skeptical about cryonics but had gradually come around, and that "when we were together prior to his surgery, he embraced the idea as his own."[7] They also disclosed the written pact in a court filing after all, thus supplying the first written evidence that Ted had changed his mind about cremation and committed to cryonics. But the document's authenticity was met with widespread skepticism by the commentariat.

Responding to questions from reporters about the chain of custody of the pact after it was purportedly signed on November 2, 2000, representatives of the younger Williams children told the media that John-Henry had folded it up, put it in the trunk of his car with other papers, and forgotten about it. The note remained in the car for the next seventeen months, collecting oil stains, and only recently was recovered and stored more carefully after its significance in the cryonics dispute became apparent. Bobby-Jo's lawyers pointed out that the pact had not been notarized or otherwise witnessed, and they also questioned whether Ted was mentally competent at the time, given his age and hospitalization for congestive heart failure.

"It's authentic because my clients were there," Robert Goldman, a Naples, Florida, attorney representing John-Henry and Claudia, said. "I can tell you unequivocally that it's an absolutely authentic document." As for whether Ted was of sound mind at the time of the pact, Goldman said Shands doctors could testify that he was, though he somewhat oddly added that Florida's standard was so low that "literally, there are many zoo animals that could" be found competent.

On August 8, Al Cassidy formally dropped his request on behalf of Williams's estate that the court settle what Ted's wishes were, saying he had concluded that the written pact was genuine. Cassidy noted that a handwriting expert, whose selection was approved by both sides, had concluded that Ted's signature was authentic, and he also said he had been influenced by a new sworn affidavit from Claudia in which she said she was present in the hospital room on November 2, 2000, when Williams "verbally indicated he wanted to be cryonically preserved in bio-stasis."★

★ The expert, Linda J. Hart of Miami, concluded that both the pact and Ted's signature had been written before John-Henry folded the document and stored it in his car. She said Ted and John-Henry had signed using the same pen, while Claudia used a different pen. And though two samples of Ted's signature included in the report—samples from the night of October 30, 2000, when he checked into the hospital—appeared to the naked eye to be much weaker and different in several respects from the signature on the pact, which was dated three days later, Hart concluded in her report that there were "no significant differences observed."

Lawyers for Bobby-Jo said she would continue to press her court challenge, though her financial ability to do so was in question. She had already appealed to the public for donations to help finance her legal expenses, indicating that her own funds were limited.

When Nancy Carmichael saw the date of the pact—November 2, 2000—she immediately thought she knew why John-Henry had called the hospital after Ted died, wanting to know the date of the catheterization procedure: to date a forged note plausibly, he needed to place himself in the hospital before the surgery. Any kind of surgery for Ted at his age and in his condition was risky, so it would have been natural to have a discussion about committing to cryonics before that time. And he could not have chosen a day or two before Williams's pacemaker was installed, on November 6, because John-Henry had been barred from the hospital during that period as a result of his chicken pox. "I just thought, 'Oh, my God. That's why he wanted to know the date,'" Carmichael said. "I guess he figured I'm too stupid. I'd never figure it out. I immediately thought it was a phony. First because of the conversations about cremation—I was present when Ted and Frank Brothers were talking about Islamorada, and Ted said he wanted to be cremated. That was just after the time John-Henry was saying Ted signed this paper that he wanted to be frozen. Secondly, the state of the document. I don't keep my very important documents in the trunk of my car with grease on them. Plus it wasn't notarized."

Carmichael told John Heer her story and offered some supporting evidence. When John-Henry had called the hospital asking for the date of the catheterization procedure, he had reached Michael Johnson, a clinical social worker with whom he was friendly. It had been Johnson who asked Nancy to get the information, and she still had on her pager the text she had received from him on July 10 at 10:58 a.m.: "Nancy, please call JHW about his dad. He wants to know when the heart catheterization [sic]."[8] Carmichael read the text to Heer on the phone. She also said that while she recalled seeing John-Henry on November 3 for the catheterization procedure, Claudia was not there. Carmichael declined to talk to reporters about all this, concerned about violating patient confidentiality regulations, but she told Heer she would testify in court if she were subpoenaed.

Heer and Spike Fitzpatrick, Bobby-Jo's other lawyer, turned their attention to Claudia. If she had not been there for Ted's catheterization procedure when it occurred at 7:50 a.m. on November 3, a Friday,

The Women in Ted's Life

Ted and his first wife, Doris, in San Diego, January 1946, after he returned from World War II. (May Williams Collection)

Evelyn Turner, circa 1952. (Courtesy of Albert Christiano)

Nelva More, circa 1956. (Courtesy of Nelva More)

The Women in Ted's Life

Isabel Gilmore
in Sarasota, 1959.
(Courtesy of Grant
Gilmore)

With his second
wife, Lee
Howard, 1961.
(Courtesy of
Lee Howard)

The Women in Ted's Life

Dolores Wettach modeling, circa 1963, about five years before she became Ted's third wife. (Ted Williams Family Enterprises)

Ted with Louise Kaufman at his camp on the Miramichi River, 1993. (Courtesy of Rob Kaufman)

Delivering his induction speech at Cooperstown, July 25, 1966. (Red Sox photograph)

With Senators owner Bob Short after signing to manage the team, February 1969. (Rogers Photo Archive)

President Nixon throws out the first pitch at the Washington Senators' home opener on April 7, 1969, as Ted, left, looks on. (*Boston Globe* photograph)

With Dolores at the ballpark, 1969. (Ted Williams Family Enterprises)

Taking his rips as manager of the Texas Rangers during a hitting contest with other Red Sox old-timers at Fenway Park on August 25, 1972. (*Boston Globe* photograph)

With Claudia and John-Henry, circa 1974. (Ted Williams Family Enterprises)

Getting fitted for his uniform after putting on a few pounds, spring training, 1978. (Red Sox photograph)

With Red Sox manager Don Zimmer, 1978. (Red Sox photograph)

With Carl Yastrzemski after a spring training tennis match in 1978. Yaz won the match, 8–6, 6–1, 7–5. (*Boston Globe* photograph)

Heading onto the field at his first Red Sox Old-Timers' Game, 1982. (Red Sox photograph)

John-Henry is given his father's number at spring training. (Red Sox photograph)

John-Henry and Claudia as teenagers. (Ted Williams Family Enterprises)

Bobby-Jo and her second husband, Mark Ferrell. (Ted Williams Family Enterprises)

At the unveiling of his statue in Cooperstown, 1985. (Ted Williams Family Enterprises)

The Kid in repose at
spring training, circa 1985.
(Red Sox photograph)

Then vice president George H. W. Bush and Ted campaigning in New Hampshire,
February 1988. (White House photograph)

Casting in the Miramichi. (Ted Williams Family Enterprises)

Ted tips his hat to the Fenway Faithful on May 11, 1991. (*Boston Globe* photograph)

Ted and John-Henry, circa 1991. (Ted Williams Family Enterprises)

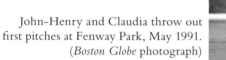

John-Henry and Claudia throw out first pitches at Fenway Park, May 1991. (*Boston Globe* photograph)

With DiMaggio, being honored by President George H. W. Bush at the White House in 1991. (Ted Williams Family Enterprises)

With Bobby Orr and Larry Bird, December 1992. (Courtesy of Brian Interland)

With Slugger, circa
1993. (Ted Williams
Family Enterprises)

With daughter Claudia on his eightieth birthday, August 30, 1998. (Ted Williams Family Enterprises)

Taking a victory lap and tipping his Hitter.net hat at the 1999 All-Star Game at Fenway Park. (Ted Williams Family Enterprises)

Ted being kissed by Claudia and John-Henry at his last public appearance, February 17, 2002. (Ted Williams Family Enterprises)

H-2-00
JHW, Claudia, and Dad all agree To be Put into Bio-Stasis after We Die. This is What we want, To be able To be Together in The Future, even if it is only a chance.

The pact. (Ted Williams Family Enterprises)

would she have been there the night before to sign the pact? She had, after all, been working in Clearwater, some 150 miles south of Shands, in Gainesville.

Caretakers George Carter and Frank Brothers, who had been alternating twelve-hour shifts and staying with Williams throughout the day, told the legal team that Claudia had not been there on November 2. Carter remembered easily, because he said Claudia called him on Sunday the fifth, furious he had not told her that Ted was in the hospital. Brothers was also present when Claudia called, and he talked with her as well that day: "I was right there when Claudia called George on the fifth, screaming and yelling, 'I thought you were my friend,'" he recalled. "She'd just found out her father was in the hospital on the fifth. And George is trying to explain to her, 'Look, John-Henry said he would call you.' And I got on the phone and told Claudia that as well, and she said, 'You guys should've known better. You should have just called me.' Now, how could she have been in that room to sign that on the second when she didn't even know her father was in the hospital on the second?"[9] Furthermore, Brothers and Carter stressed that between them, they were with Ted twenty-four hours a day, and at no time during his Shands hospitalization were John-Henry and Claudia with him alone.

Rick Kerensky, Ted's cardiologist, had introduced Claudia to his assistant, Carmichael, on the morning of November 6 before the pacemaker surgery. "When Kerensky introduced me to Claudia, she made excuses why she had not been there for the catheter because of her work," Carmichael said. "Her work wouldn't let her off or whatever. I remember that very well. She also told me about a car accident she got into the night before, on the fifth—she rear-ended someone at the bottom of the exit ramp near the hospital after driving up."

Nevertheless, as the controversy over the authenticity of the pact raged in the press, John-Henry approached Kerensky and asked him to sign a statement attesting that Claudia was at Shands on the night of November 2. The doctor agreed. Several years later, Kerensky concluded in an interview that he no longer could be sure his letter was correct. "I felt signing the letter was the right thing to do at the time," he said. "But I've got to admit, I was very naive. I wasn't thinking, 'This was why he was doing that.' Can I absolutely recall that date? No. I did the best I could."[10]

During the course of several taped interviews with me that began in 2004, Claudia spoke for the first time in detail about how the pact came to be signed, saying in the end that Ted did agree to the procedure and that it was easy to get him to do so simply by framing the issue as something that was vitally important to John-Henry and to her. She stressed that the crude note had never been intended for public consumption, and she vigorously defended her and her brother's right to do whatever they wanted with their father's remains—as is the general legal standard for next of kin. She also insisted that she was at Shands Hospital on November 2, 2000, and disputed the accounts of Carter, Brothers, and Carmichael, who each said she was not. But one key piece of evidence that she said would prove she was there on the second—her car accident—had the opposite effect when the accident report showed that the mishap occurred on November 5.

Claudia said she, Ted, and John-Henry had not discussed cryonics as a threesome before, nor had she and her brother planned to sign a pact with their father. It just happened spontaneously the night of November 2, though they were mindful of his failing health and his surgical procedure the next day. When she arrived, she said she did not see either Brothers or Carter and that they were not in Ted's private room within the intensive care unit at the time.

According to Claudia, Ted was sitting up in his bed with a tube of oxygen attached to his nose when the following conversation ensued:

"Dad, remember all the conversations we've had about cryonics, and I would want you to do that?" John-Henry began.

"Yeah," said Ted.

"You know, I've talked to Claudia about it. We've talked a lot about it, and we really want to do it, too."

Williams turned to Claudia and said: "You're in on this, too?" She smiled and nodded.

"We really want to do it," John-Henry continued.

"I know, I know."

"And you know we're really worried about you, and you know we really love you."

"I know you do, and I love you, too."

"Will you please promise us that we can do this, that we will do this as a family?"

Ted paused before answering, closed his eyes, and seemed to get annoyed that he was being pressed on the subject. But Claudia was sure this was just a pose that he affected to assert his control, a drumroll before he replied.

"You can do whatever you want with me," he finally said. "I've had a great life. Whatever you want to do with me is fine."

John-Henry brightened. "Okay," he said. "Let's all sign it. Let's all make a pact. Let's all agree, among us, that we'll do this. We'll promise each other right now that we'll do it."

"And that's exactly how it went down," Claudia said. John-Henry "reached over, and he grabbed a piece of paper and ripped off the bottom because it had something written on it that was from the hospital. Then he wrote out the words right there, using that portable tray that hospitals use to serve food, you know?

"He grabbed it and wrote it, just like that. He read it out loud to Dad and me, and we signed it. This was for us. It was a moment. It was a very private moment that was for us. It was our Bible, okay? It was ours to have, to know it was okay, that we were all going to do it."

John-Henry signed first, then gave the pen he used to his father. Then Ted signed. Claudia said she grabbed a different pen that was closer to her, and she signed. "I'm glad we got that out of the way," Ted said with what Claudia interpreted as loving sarcasm.

She conceded that her father had said many times that he wanted to be cremated, but she said that he changed his mind as he grew closer to his younger children. "It's true he said he wanted to be cremated often. But what a lot of people don't realize is that the last year and a half of his life, Dad changed a lot, and it was because he was with us, and because we were living with him, helping him, working with him, loving him, caring for him, you know? And he knew that. And he knew that John-Henry and I both were struggling with the fact that right when we were starting to get to know him and love him and understand him, we were losing him, you know? And it was awful. We didn't want that to happen. So I know he did it for us. There's no doubt in my mind. And he's like, 'What the hell, who knows, it might happen,' you know."

Ultimately, Claudia thought, getting Ted to agree was "easy. It was easy! If your kids came to you and said, 'Dad, please. Dad, please. We're going to miss you so much. Give us something to hold on to. Just sign this.' Are you going to say no to your kids?"

After the pact was signed, John-Henry looked at his sister and held it up with a smile, almost in triumph. Then he tucked the note in his pocket.

The very crudeness of the pact attests to the fact that it was never meant for public consumption, Claudia said—merely as a private expression of a decision taken. "John-Henry and I never wanted to bring that note out. We were praying that we would never have to bring that note out. Because we knew it's crude. It's stained. But we never thought we would have to use it. Never! Never! It was among us. It was us. And there were three people in that room: John-Henry, me, and Dad. Then after Dad died it was for two of us to hold on to when we lost the third leg of our stool. The only reason we brought out the note was because we were afraid Bobby-Jo was going to take it all away. It wasn't meant to be shown. It's a pact. It was our little secret."

She bitterly resented that they were forced to reveal that their father's remains were frozen in the first place, that their privacy was invaded, their beliefs questioned. "Why do I have to prove anything to anybody? I'm certainly not going to tell you that you have to cremate your mother. I wouldn't say to someone, 'Give it up. God doesn't exist.' Don't stomp on my faith. I'll stomp on yours. It's private, personal family business, and people forget that but for a jealous, estranged daughter, it never would have been made public.

"Everybody wants to say something bad about John-Henry and I. What we did! What did we really do? Think about it. What did we really do? We loved our dad. There was no greater love, in my opinion, that existed than between John-Henry and his father. No greater love. And then you have someone like Bobby-Jo, who resented it and was going to fight it the only way she knew how: by telling vicious, mean lies. She did whatever she could to just tear us down. She got an awful lot of people out there thinking John-Henry was an awful boy. I'm 'Fraudia' and John-Henry's 'Freezer Boy.' I mean, that's pretty crude. It was just awful."

After the pact was signed, Claudia said John-Henry put it in a folder he carried with him in his car and apparently forgot about it. "He lived in his car."

Seventeen months went by. In the days following Ted's death, as pressure mounted to prove what Williams's wishes truly were, John-Henry and Claudia met at Ted's house with Goldman and with Eric Abel, who was helping to map out a legal strategy. Goldman said the way he read Florida law, they were going to need something in writing from Ted saying he wished to be cryonically preserved.

"When Goldman left the house, John-Henry said to me, 'You know, Claudia and I and Dad signed something, but I don't know if it's what Goldman's looking for,'" Abel recalled. "I said anything Ted signed, even on a napkin, would help their case. He started telling me about this note. I asked him where it was. He didn't know. Next day, John-Henry said, 'I looked here, looked there, couldn't find it.' I said, 'Keep looking.' Finally he found it and showed it to me. I was like, 'Holy shit!' It was just amazing he had it in writing. It was like finding a gold mine. The crudity of the document meant nothing to me. He said it was in the trunk of the car."[11]

On why Ted signed the pact as Ted Williams rather than Theodore S. Williams, which had been his habit when signing any kind of official document, Claudia said: "Dad for the last probably five years of his life didn't have to sign any more official documents because John-Henry did that for him. All Daddy had to do was practice 'Ted Williams' so that he could sign memorabilia for John-Henry. It was easy. Dad at that time could barely see. But he could basically close his eyes and sign 'Ted Williams.'"

On why John-Henry called Shands Hospital on July 10 and asked for the date of Ted's catheterization procedure, Claudia said she had not known that he did. "Let's just assume for a second that John-Henry did make that phone call, and he asked for the date because he wanted to make sure he had the right date on the note, and the whole damn thing is forged, you know? With that aside, what is so wrong with what he did? Dad died, okay? Dad died. He left two children behind that were heartbroken that they had lost their father. Two children behind that for the last good three years of his life were around him all the time, okay? What is so wrong? Why, why do people want to just say, 'Aha! Look at that! They're bad. They did something wrong.' The fuck we did!"

And Claudia bristled when considering Carter's and Brothers's accounts that she could not have been at the hospital on November 2. "I can't believe that they have the nerve to say I wasn't there then, because I had an accident that day on the way up to be there. So I mean, it is crazy. I was rushing to get up there and I had a car accident. Right off the exit, near the hospital. I had to go see a doctor while I was there just to make sure I was okay." Yet when Claudia learned that the accident report placed her in Gainesville on November 5, not November 2, she was devastated and burst into tears. "I know it happened," she said, referring to the written pact. "But now you won't believe me! I know what I felt, saw, and lived."[12]

Bobby-Jo's lawyers thought the fact that Ted, when he was alive, had never applied to Alcor himself cast further doubt on what his true wishes were. And the fact that John-Henry had not bothered to fill out an application on his father's behalf until after Ted died raised an interesting legal question: while the son's power of attorney clearly empowered him to deal with Alcor on Ted's behalf while he was alive, after Williams died, didn't John-Henry's power of attorney expire as well? This was an issue that young Williams's attorneys were not anxious to litigate. One of them, Peter Sutton, acknowledged that the power of attorney did die with Ted, while Eric Abel thought John-Henry still might have some wiggle room. "Many lawyers would say no, the power of attorney does die on his death," Abel said. "But that doesn't mean some attorneys wouldn't argue that there are residual powers. If it helps my client, I would argue it."

As John-Henry and Alcor waited for the question of Ted's wishes to be resolved in court, they were facing other difficulties, since it appeared that their compliance with multiple sections of Florida law regulating anatomical gifts could be challenged unless the pact was accepted. The law at the time said that if a decedent did not execute an agreement to make an anatomical gift while he was alive, as Ted had not, certain "classes of persons" could make the donation for him upon his death. The first class was the spouse, but Ted was not married when he died. The second class was "an adult son or daughter of the decedent." But the law went on to say that a person in this class could only make the donation "in the absence of actual notice of contrary indications by the decedent or actual notice of opposition by a member of the same . . . class," such as Bobby-Jo.*

Moreover, the Florida law placed restrictions on the "donee," in this case Alcor, if the children were making the gift. The statute said: "If the donee has actual notice of contrary indications by the decedent or . . . actual notice that a gift by a member of a class is opposed by a member of the same or prior class, the donee shall not accept the gift."

Alcor seemed particularly vulnerable on the question of whether it had been given notice of Bobby-Jo's opposition to the cryonics procedure, since early on the afternoon of Ted's death, hours before his body left Florida, she had e-mailed Alcor to notify it that she was opposed to her father being frozen. But the company went ahead anyway. In accepting Ted's body, Alcor also seemed to have violated its own policy. The company had a clause in its "Third Party Application for Membership," filled out by John-Henry for Ted, that explicitly stated that if an appli-

---

* Eric Abel said he doubted John-Henry was aware of restrictions governing the transfer of Ted's body to Alcor under Florida law, but he acknowledged that he hadn't advised John-Henry of those restrictions.

cant had a will specifying that he wished to be cremated, the agreement to freeze the person would be invalid. Included in the Alcor application were two questions, each followed by Yes and No boxes to check: "Does Donor have a will?" and "If 'Yes,' does it include any provisions contrary to cryonics?" John-Henry did not answer either question.*

Abel said that the night Ted died, Alcor called John-Henry and asked him to sign some of the documents again. "They were making up the agreement and wanted it resigned, making it more specific to the case," Abel recalled. "Then they wanted Claudia as next of kin also." That was probably because Alcor knew that, unlike Florida law, the Arizona statute on anatomical gifts had language specifying that in the event of a conflict between the decedent's children over whether to donate the body, the majority ruled. Claudia signed her set of papers and faxed them to Alcor between 9:10 and 9:33 p.m. eastern time on July 5, 2002. More than twelve hours after Ted's death, she officially became the majority vote.

And there were still other problems: though Ted's body was flown from Florida to Arizona, only Florida law likely governed the transaction under the legal test of "significant contacts." When the laws of two states might conflict, the law of the state where the principals involved have the most "significant contacts" takes precedence. Ted lived in Florida, his estate was probated there, and all three of his children lived in Florida.

When the cryonics news became public, John-Henry entered into a negotiation with Alcor, asking for concessions on its $170,000 bill ($120,000 of the bill was for Ted's "whole-body" procedure, which covered his trunk, and $50,000 of it was for the "neuro"). John-Henry thought a deep discount was appropriate, if not a waiving of the fees altogether, given the publicity boon the company was getting—indeed, he was even willing to consider waiving the confidentiality provision to let Alcor speak about Ted publicly if the price was right.

But Alcor balked, pointing to its costs in chartering the private jet that flew Williams's body from Florida to Arizona and arguing that it was incurring extra costs because of new security demands and having to add people to handle all the phone calls they were getting. The company knew it had the upper hand, since John-Henry had failed to negotiate any price concessions when he had far more leverage—when Ted was alive. Now Williams was dead, and Alcor had his body.

---

* While Alcor provided me with a tour of its facility and made its chief operating officer at the time, Tanya Jones, available to discuss its general practices, it declined all comment on the Williams case, citing patient confidentiality restrictions.

The Alcorians were worried about Bobby-Jo going to court, and when John-Henry and Claudia produced the written pact, there was considerable relief—and a touch of skepticism—in Scottsdale. "When the note was revealed it buttressed our position internally that even though we never met Ted Williams and no one ever spoke to Ted Williams, this at least indicated that John-Henry had talked to Ted and Claudia in this bemusing note hidden in the trunk," said Bill Haworth. "But the note seemed so bizarre. You had to question it. It didn't pass the smell test, but that's what we ended up with. Alcor and Jerry Lemler were just so thrilled with the prospects of someone like Ted Williams becoming a patient, as they called him, they didn't want to even suggest that John-Henry didn't discuss it with his father. They wanted to believe it was the truth because that validated what Alcor wanted to gain. We were also worried about John-Henry's power of attorney and whether it could survive Ted's death. Was he carrying out his father's wishes or his own?"

John-Henry thought there was a real possibility that Bobby-Jo would win her legal challenge and that Ted's body would be ordered out of Alcor. But, he confided to his girlfriend at the time, Jenna Bernreuter, he had a contingency plan in place: if Bobby-Jo succeeded, he would move Ted's body to a cryonics facility in Germany, where, his research indicated, the legal climate was more favorable.[13]

"If Ted's body had been ordered out of Alcor, it would have sent John-Henry off the deep end," Peter Sutton said. "That was the key to the whole situation. That's why we fought Bobby-Jo so hard—because Ted would not have wanted to have his son blow his brains out over this problem. I sent Al Cassidy over there to watch him right away. It was scary. Very scary. He was losing it. I think it was the weight of the whole thing, the stress. Bobby-Jo was attacking him. The press was attacking him. It was just too much for him."

But John-Henry, backed by Ted's estate, had key financial advantages that Bobby-Jo did not, allowing him to string out the legal proceedings to drive up his sister's legal fees. By September, Bobby-Jo signaled the end was near. John Heer told reporters she had spent $50,000 so far, mostly from her retirement savings, and he anticipated it would take another $60,000 for the case to go to trial. She had been able to attract only $2,500 through the fund-raising vehicle she had set up, Ted Williams's Last Wish Fund, mostly in $10 to $25 contributions from the public.[14]

John-Henry could have prevailed through attrition, but he had another key chit at his disposal, which he used to settle the issue. Under the terms of an irrevocable 1986 insurance trust, Ted had left $600,000 to his three children, to be distributed equally. John-Henry asked the three trustees of the trust—Eric Abel, Al Cassidy, and David McCarthy, director of the Ted Williams museum—to give Bobby-Jo her $200,000 share immediately if she agreed to drop any legal challenge and let Ted's body remain at Alcor. Abel said that Ted, in revising his will in 1996, asked him verbally not to distribute Bobby-Jo's full share in a lump sum because he was afraid she would spend it all, recklessly. But Abel said he persuaded the other trustees to go along with paying her the full $200,000 immediately if she would drop her objections to Ted's final resting place.

In December, five months after her father's death, Bobby-Jo agreed. Her share, with interest, came to $211,000. (Peter Sutton said Bobby-Jo also received thirty-seven Ted-signed bats from the same trust, worth $2,000 each, "as part of the deal to get rid of her.") A bitter Bobby-Jo and Mark Ferrell used much of the money to buy a new trailer, and they took off on an extended trip around the country.

Forged or not, the written pact and the sad cryonics coda showed that Ted reaped what he sowed as a father and underscored the fact that Williams never fully escaped the family dysfunction that had ensnared him as a boy.

Eager to atone for neglecting John-Henry in his youth, Ted welcomed his son back into his life as an adult and gave him the keys to his kingdom. John-Henry took his father's trust—and his power of attorney—and ran with them.

Their relationship was symbiotic and mutually fulfilling. Ted grew to love his son and in the end relied on him totally as his caretaker, though Williams's appeals to several close friends for help just before he died showed that he came to have second thoughts about having delegated so much power to John-Henry. But it was too late.

Young Williams, for his part, plainly exploited his father but was also devoted to him. Consumed by his father's considerable shadow, the son never made any attempt to escape it. Taking over Ted's memorabilia business was virtually a license to print money, and John-Henry used it fully, keeping Williams hustling long past the time it was comfortable for him to sign autographs. He also deceived his father, as when he borrowed $500,000 from Bob Breitbard without telling Ted and went into the porn business to try and grow Hitter.net.

Yet John-Henry certainly loved Ted. Where he easily could have let the nurses and caretakers look after his father, in the end he took part in the nitty-gritty himself: showering with Ted so he wouldn't fall, grooming him, administering his oxygen and medications, and even, according to Claudia, learning how to insert his catheter. The son's bizarre but poignant decision to mount a pro baseball career at the age of thirty-three was all about paying homage to his father. And John-Henry's cryonics decision for Ted seemed less about exploitation than it was about not wanting to let go.

In the fallout from the cryonics affair, people were reminded of the fact that Williams was not just the greatest hitter who ever lived, not just the war hero, and not just the man who had helped sick children but also a man with all the same human frailties that his fans had. He had never really shaken the shame he carried from childhood—about his mother, the Salvation Army zealot, who had time for street urchins but not for him; about his absent and indifferent father, who finally abandoned the family; about his jealous, thieving brother; and about his own bloodlines and ethnicity. Despite harboring bitterness toward members of his immediate family, Ted stayed loyal to them in the way he felt he could: by supporting them financially. The money represented both needed assistance and a means to replace deeper interaction.

The controversy over Ted's wishes, which burned so intensely at his death and for months thereafter, faded over time. He was dead, after all, and wasn't coming back—or so most thought. Only John-Henry and Claudia knew for sure what their father signed or didn't sign, but among those following the Williams saga, there came to be a more forgiving discussion of the notion that all families have their peculiar dynamics. "People assume either he wasn't competent or he was the victim of a family situation rather than, 'Oh, Ted went goofy at the end,'" said Bob Costas, the sports broadcaster, who knew Williams well and had dealings with John-Henry and Claudia.[15] In that climate, questions about a tarnished legacy receded. The mind's eye—and history's—gradually readjusted to the image of Ted Williams in his prime on a ball field. Yet for all his exploits as a batsman, one of the most striking things about Ted is how much he excelled at almost anything he undertook in a serious way, like flying, fishing, and photography. His innate talents took him only so far. His drive, determination, curiosity, and passion for learning took him the rest of the way. This notion of being distinctive at anything he undertook resonated with people.

Memories of Ted's grand reception at the 1999 All-Star Game at Fenway, his public farewell, still linger warmly and attest to his status as a baseball god with cross-generational appeal. He was someone whom fathers told their sons about, generation after generation, and thus he served as glue in the social fabric. The lasting image remains one of radiant youth, Williams attaining .406, the perfect swing, the swagger, and the heroic, Bunyanesque deeds, like hitting a home run in his last at bat—the Kid, once and forever.

Epilogue

In August of 2002, John–Henry informed the Red Sox that he would not be returning to its farm team in the Gulf Coast League. Ted was now gone, and there was no sense pressing his luck or trying the patience of a front office that had graciously indulged him.

But he was not through with baseball. He left Florida, moved to California, and began working out again to try to resume a career as a professional. Starting in the spring of 2003 and going into July, John–Henry played briefly for three teams at the lowest reaches of the minor leagues: the Schaumburg (Illinois) Flyers, in the independent Northern League; the Southeastern Cloverleafs, of the unaffiliated Southeastern League of Professional Baseball; and the Baton Rouge River Bats, of the Southern League of Professional Baseball. He made about $700 a month along with a $12 per diem.

John–Henry quit the River Bats in July after he began to feel increasingly weak and fatigued. It was a chore to even warm up and do calisthenics. Back in Los Angeles, he picked up two bags from the airport luggage carousel and couldn't walk far before he had to sit down on the bags and catch his breath. An examination at the UCLA Medical Center revealed that he had myelodysplasia, a blood disorder that is often a precursor to acute myelogenous leukemia, a cancer that starts in the bone marrow. Soon the leukemia was confirmed, and John–Henry began chemotherapy treatments in October. In December, his sister Claudia gave him her bone marrow in a painful transplant procedure. The oncologist deemed Claudia a perfect match and was optimistic that her brother could make a full recovery.

Meanwhile, John–Henry had met and fallen in love with Lisa Martin, a twenty-four-year-old dental hygienist from Santa Cruz. The relationship grew serious quickly, despite his bleak diagnosis, and both John–Henry and Lisa were optimistic he would beat the illness and thrive. Around Valentine's Day of 2004, they decided to get married. John–Henry wanted to do it right away—that night, even. Lisa told him he was crazy; that they should sleep on it and wait at least a few days.[1]

Peter Sutton had a friend in California who was a judge, and she agreed to perform the ceremony on February 19, at sunset, near the pier in Santa Monica. Steve Connolly, who had helped train John-Henry for his baseball fling when Ted was still alive, served as best man and took photos. No other friends or family were present.

For Lisa, the marriage was far from a deathbed decision. "He was going to live for another fifty years at that point," she recalled. But within days, John-Henry was back at UCLA Medical Center in rapid decline. Claudia flew out to be with him, along with their mother, Dolores; Eric Abel; and Anita Lovely, the jilted fiancée with whom John-Henry had nonetheless remained close. Young Williams asked Abel and Peter Sutton to make sure his affairs were in order. At the top of the list was making sure his body would quickly be taken to Alcor so he could join Ted. Proceeds from John-Henry's $2 million life insurance policy would be used to pay for his procedure and to settle Ted's remaining bill, which still had not been paid.

Shortly thereafter, John-Henry's brain began to hemorrhage, forcing urgent surgery to relieve pressure. The procedure was of limited success, and he was put on life support, allowing Alcor's emergency responders plenty of time to be on hand with ice and the other equipment their protocols required.

John-Henry died on March 6, 2004, at thirty-five years old. His body was driven by ambulance to Alcor headquarters in Scottsdale, where he was admitted as patient A-2063. Like Ted, John-Henry underwent both the "whole-body" and the "neuro" procedures. Finally, his remains were placed in the same tank, or Dewar, as those of his father.

After settling her court challenge in the cryonics affair, Bobby-Jo decided to leave Citrus Hills and its painful memories and move back to Tennessee with her husband, Mark. They wanted to begin a new chapter in their lives and, to that end, virtually went underground, changing their e-mail addresses and phone numbers after settling in the small city of White House, some twenty miles north of Nashville. They severed all ties with friends in Citrus Hills as well as with others who had helped and worked with them during the cryonics controversy.

Then on July 28, 2010, Bobby-Jo died in isolation and obscurity at the age of sixty-two. Her death certificate listed the cause as end-stage liver disease. Told of her death, her Florida friends and associates said they had not previously heard the news, nor was there any obituary or other notice of her passing. The mercurial Mark Ferrell continued to guard the couple's privacy zealously—including threatening those he felt were intruding.

Claudia Williams moved to Citrus Hills after Ted died and still lives there. She married Eric Abel on January 9, 2006, and has taken his last name. She is studying to become a registered nurse and is becoming less shy about embracing the Williams legacy she spent most of her early life rejecting. At an auction of Ted's personal effects at Fenway Park in 2012, she delivered a fluid speech about her father, and later the same year she accepted an invitation from the Red Sox to throw out a first ball before a nationally televised Yankees game at Fenway. Besides working on a small book of remembrances about growing up with Ted, Claudia also looks after her mother, Dolores Williams, who suffered a stroke in 2008 and then moved from Vermont to Citrus Hills. Claudia is planning to have her own remains sent to Alcor when she dies so she can join her father and brother, as she pledged in the pact.

Acknowledgments

I am deeply indebted to many people for their help during the decade it took me to research and write this book, but perhaps foremost among them is Dan Golden, a fantastic journalist who used to work for me at the *Boston Globe* before moving to the *Wall Street Journal* and later Bloomberg News. At the *Journal,* he won a Pulitzer Prize for a series of stories documenting favoritism in college admissions for the children of rich alumni donors. He later expanded the series into a bestselling book called *The Price of Admission.* Dan generously agreed to give me a rigorous edit on *The Kid* before I submitted the book to Little, Brown, and in the process provided me with numerous insightful comments and suggestions for which I will always be grateful.

I'd also like to offer my special thanks to the following people:

My friend Jack Connors—founding partner of Hill Holliday, the superb Boston advertising agency—who offered me a desk and a place to hang my hat after I resigned from the *Globe* to begin work on this book. I had privacy, tech support, a copier that always worked, and other advantages of being part of a big organization. Jack gave me a nice "family rate" and probably thought I would be out of there in a year or two at most, but the book took me far longer than I imagined, and I kept working away, never looking over my shoulder. When Connors retired, his successor, Mike Sheehan, along with the agency's president, Karen Kaplan, both continued to cheerfully welcome me with no questions asked, despite my nonstaff outsider status. My run of luck there lasted about eight years, far longer than it had any right to last, and I will always be appreciative. Others at Hill Holliday besides Mike and Karen who welcomed me and offered their hospitality include: Donna Vallois, Will Keyser, Joe Berkeley, Dave Gardiner, Scott Cheyne, Phil Chadwick, Amy Hardcastle, Johnathan Ng, Sam Mullins, Dave Majeau, Mike Moran, and Beau Phillips.

When I left Hill Holliday, Ed Reilly, a friend of more than thirty years and a former Boston politico who went on to a rich and rewarding career as a strategic consultant to businesses around the world, arranged an office for me at his company, FTI Consulting, just a few blocks away along State Street. I finished the book there, thanks to the gracious hospitality provided by Bob Duffy, FTI's head man in Boston, and by senior managing director Stephen Coulombe. The office was ideal: spacious and quiet, with all the amenities. In addition to Bob and Steve, I'd like to thank others at FTI, especially Maria Dillon, who could not have been more helpful to me; Brian Quinn, who was always ready with tech support; and my two office neighbors, Mark Murphy and Gabe Bresler.

Thanks also to three researchers who helped me a lot along the way: John McDermott, Allen Vaughan, and Matt Herrick. John stationed himself at the Boston Public Library microfilm department for months on my behalf, no doubt straining his eyes as he reviewed and copied old newspaper articles about Ted Williams dating from 1939 to 1960. This was no easy job, as there were sometimes as many as nine papers published in the city during that period. The result was what has to be the definitive clip file on Williams, organized by year, which provided me with the organizational spine of his years with the Red Sox. Allen Vaughan, a graduate student at Northeastern University's School of Journalism, helped me track down and interview some of Ted's old Red Sox teammates. Talking to these old-timers was my first order of business, since they were all, of course, old, and one couldn't be sure how long they would live. One measure of how long I worked on this book is that, of the six-hundred-odd people interviewed, more than thirty, as of this writing, have since died. Matt Herrick, a brilliant young Wheaton College graduate who loved baseball, was a right hand to me from 2004 through 2007 — transcribing interviews, helping me cross-reference my burgeoning files by subject area, creating detailed time lines of what Williams did each year from 1937 to 2002, helping me track down and interview a spate of new people I discovered in Ted's private address book, and also conducting substantive interviews himself, such as those with some of the Washington Senators players Williams managed as well as with some of the people who took care of Ted at the end of his life. Tragically, Matt died suddenly while hiking in Maine in January of 2009. I think of him often and miss him, so this book is in part dedicated to his memory. Thanks also to my old friend Steve Burgard, director of the Northeastern University School of Journalism, who, with the help of Professor Link McKie, put me in touch with Allen Vaughan and another Northeastern journalism student, Sam Perkins. On deadline, Sam quickly and skillfully helped me put all my chapter notes in order after I betrayed my lack of computer skills and submitted them to Little, Brown in the wrong form when the book was nearing completion.

Claudia Williams, Ted's younger daughter, overcame her initial reluctance and gave me lots of her time and precious access to her father's private papers, letters, journals, wartime pilot's logs, fishing logs, and family photos, among other material. Thanks also to Claudia's husband, Eric Abel, a lawyer who was a confidant both to Ted and to his son, John-Henry. Eric generously gave me as much time as I needed and was always available to answer any question I had, however minor. Peter Sutton, the Williams family lawyer based in Boston, also gave me a lot of his time, opened doors, and was a constant source of encouragement. Thanks also to Al Cassidy, a longtime Williams family friend who served as the executor of Ted's estate, for the many interviews I conducted with him.

Bobby-Jo Williams Ferrell, Ted's older daughter, also gave me considerable time and access to family photos as well as to poems written by her mother, Ted's first wife, Doris Soule. Thanks also to Bobby-Jo's lawyer in the cryonics case, John Heer, who was always accessible and helpful to me; her husband, Mark Ferrell; and her daughter Dawn Hebding.

Ted's nephews, the sons of his brother, Danny—namesake Ted Williams and Sam Williams—were generous with their time, and Ted kindly let me use historic photos from the May Williams collection. Williams cousins Manuel and Salvador Herrera, Dee Allen, Gino Lucero, Charles Venzor, Daniel Venzor, and Frank Venzor all contributed helpful interviews, as did family members Virginia and Ron Amidon and David Ronquillo.

In addition, I am grateful to Ted Williams's loves, including two of his wives and three of his girlfriends, two of whom he proposed to. Ted's second wife, Lee Howard, gave me a lot of time, and over the years she would kindly call me to say hello and check on my progress. Ted's third wife, Dolores Williams, the mother of John-Henry and Claudia, was helpful and thoughtful in discussing her years with Ted. Thanks to Nelva More and Isabel Gilmore, who candidly discussed their romances with Ted in the 1950s and his marriage proposals to them. And I'm grateful to Nancy Barnard Cafiero, who played hard to get for Ted in Sarasota and Boston. Rob Kaufman gave me insights into the relationship between his mother, Louise Kaufman, and Ted, who lived together from 1974 until Louise died in 1993. Thanks also to Joe Bastarache and Albert Christiano for discussing details of the relationship between Williams and Evelyn Turner in the 1950s. Bastarache was the executor of Turner's estate, and Christiano is her son.

Ted's former Red Sox teammates Dom DiMaggio, Bobby Doerr, and Johnny Pesky, Williams's closest friends on the team, provided especially useful stories and details. Elden Auker, Milt Bolling, Don Buddin, Billy Consolo, Walt Dropo, Dave "Boo" Ferriss, Don Gile, Pumpsie Green, Billy Hitchcock, Billy Klaus, Ted Lepcio, Tony Lupien, Frank Malzone, Sam Mele, Bill Monbouquette, Mel Parnell, Eddie Pellagrini, Jimmy Piersall, Dave Sisler, Gene Stephens, Mickey Vernon, and Charlie Wagner were also helpful.

Dick Bresciani, team historian of the Red Sox, generously allowed me access to the club's collection of Ted Williams photos and helped put me in touch with a host of former players. Thanks also to others in the Red Sox organization, notably Pam Ganley, Meg Vaillancourt, Tom Werner, Sam Kennedy, John Henry, Larry Lucchino, and Dr. Charles Steinberg for their help and courtesies along the way. In addition, George Mitrovich, chairman of the Great Fenway Park Writers Series—a novel and engaging forum where writers of all types can come and discuss their new books, a program unique in professional sports—was a welcome source of encouragement during this project. George's four chief Writers Series wingmen, Dick Flavin, Donna Cohen, Diane Tiernan, and Janet Wood, were always interested and helpful supporters.

Nine former sportswriters who covered Ted Williams—Bob Ajemian, David Burgin, Bud Collins, Tim Horgan, Will McDonough, Bob and Leo Monahan, Dave O'Hara, and George Sullivan—told me about their experiences for a chapter I devoted to the Williams-press dynamic, a subject I found rich and important in understanding the Kid. Thanks to Maria Badaracco, who told me about her friendship with the late Dave Egan, the *Record* columnist and Williams nemesis, and to Dave Egan Jr., the Colonel's son, who spoke candidly about his father and loaned me an enormous scrapbook containing hundreds of his old columns. Four of my former colleagues at the *Boston Globe*—Tom Mulvoy, Marty Nolan, Jack Thomas, and Peter Mancusi—kindly read my first draft of the writers chapter and offered thoughtful critiques.

Nancy Carmichael, a physician's assistant at Shands Hospital in Gainesville, Florida, took care of Williams when he was at the hospital and provided me with important information on her dealings with John-Henry after Ted died. Debbie Erb, a nurse at Shands, was also helpful, as was Becky Vaughn, a nurse who took care of Ted at home toward the end of his life. Vaughn told me about a key discussion she had with John-Henry about cryonics, in Ted's presence.

Former Washington Senators who served under Ted when he managed the team from 1969 to 1972—including players Bernie Allen, Casey Cox, Tim Cullen, and Tom Grieve, coaches Joe Camacho and Wayne Terwilliger, and trainer Bill Zeigler—contributed keen observations. And team broadcaster Shelby Whitfield was especially helpful.

I am also grateful to the following childhood friends of Ted: Bob Breitbard, Les Cassie Jr., Frank Cushing, Roy Engle, Swede Jensen, Ben Press, Bill Skelley, and Joe Villarino. My gratitude extends to these long-time friends as well: Joe Davis, Buzz Hamon, Brian Interland, Gene Moore, Billy Reedy, and Lewis Watkins.

Many thanks to Ted's fishing pals: Stu Apte, Hank Brown, Gary Ellis, Jack Fenety, George Hommell, Joe Johansen, Sammy Lee, Jerry McKinnis, Rick Ruoff, and Millard Wells. Edna Curtis, the cook and house-keeper at Ted's cabin on the Miramichi River in Canada, was very helpful, as were her two sons, Clarence and George Curtis. Thanks also to my friend Steve Woodsum, an expert angler himself, for reading my fishing chapter and making sure I had my terminology straight.

I appreciate the assistance provided by Ted's friends from World War II and Korea: Edro Buchser, Bill Churchman, Dick Francisco, John Glenn, Larry Hawkins, Marvin Hollenbeck, Samuel Hynes, Bob Kennedy, Frank Maznicki, Ken Poth, Tom Ross, Raymond Sisk, Karl Smith, and Woody Woodbury.

The people who took care of Ted at the end of his life, some working twenty-four hours a day for a week at a time, came to know Williams well and gave me a valuable perspective on the family dynamic. The lead caretakers, Frank Brothers and George Carter, provided important information and insights. Also helpful were Geedee Bond, Marion and Jim Corbin, Jack Gard, Virginia Hiley-Self, Robert Hogerheide, Kay and Bill Munday, Kathleen Rolfingsmeier, John Sullivan, and Donna Van Tassel.

The following doctors who took care of Williams toward the end of his life shared their experiences: Jeffrey Borer, Anne Curtis, Arthur Day, Ed Dodge, Joseph Dorn, Allan Goodman, Richard Kerensky, Joseph Layon, William Stalcup, and Robert Watson.

The late David Halberstam was a great source of encouragement for me on this project and gave me access to his papers at Boston University, which included his interview with Williams for *Summer of '49*. He also sent me copies of key interviews he conducted for his marvelous small book *The Teammates*. David was always generous with other writers, and he is missed.

Former *Boston Globe* editor Marty Baron gave me a leave of absence to start the book before I resigned; I am grateful to him as well as to his successor, old friend Brian McGrory, and the terrific Lisa Tuite, head of the *Globe* library.

Thanks also to the one and only Bill Brett, who helped me gather some wondrous photographs for the book.

My friend Mitch Zuckoff, a former *Globe* colleague and now a Boston University journalism professor and bestselling author, offered me important early advice on organizing the book, and was a ready consultant throughout.

Thanks too to another former *Globie,* Carol Beggy, who has a comprehensive understanding of the book business, and shared valuable marketing ideas.

I am grateful to Henry Scannell, curator of microtext and newspapers at the Boston Public Library, for his help in assembling all the reels of microfilm containing the old Boston papers. Thanks also to the BPL's Aaron Schmidt, Jane Winton, and former president Bernard Margolis.

I'd like to thank the following people for providing significant interviews or otherwise helping me during the course of the book: Janet Amphlett, Mike Andrews, Roger Angell, Bob Aquilina, Ken Auletta, Brad Bailey, Doug Bailey, Teresa Barker, Eddie Barry, Jack Bean, Jenna Bernreuter, Yogi Berra, Daisy Bisz, Jerry Brenner, Bobby Brown, Don Brown, Tom Brown, Ken Burns, former president George H. W. Bush, John Butcher, Phil Castinetti, Josh Cook, Peter Corbett, Jack Corrigan, Bob Costas, Bob Cousy, Barry Craig, Kit Crissey, Maureen Cronin, David D'Alessandro, Beth Daley, Arthur D'Angelo, George Daniels, Eleanor Diamond, George Digby, Danny Dillman, Emily DiMaggio, Mary Dluhy, Jerry Doak, Edward Donovan, Marguerite Donovan, Nelson Doubleday Jr., John Dowd, Ted Doyle, Patrick Drane, Earl Duffy, Kevin Paul Dupont, Dan Duquette, Nan Ellis, Ferd Ensinger, Rich Eschen, Robert Ettinger, Bill Faloon, Cindy Felix, Tommie Ferguson, Mark Ferrell, Pat Ferris, Steve Ferroli, Jack Fisher, Donna Fleischmann, Dr. Michael Foley, Ralph Ford Jr., Al Forester, Lane Forman, Janet Franzoni, Jonathan Gallen, Peter Gammons, Joe Garagiola, Nomar Garciaparra, Marea Gardner, Andy Giacobbe, Bob Gillespie, Eric Goodman, Hill Goodspeed, Herbert Gordon, Lou Gorman, Curt Gowdy, William Gutfarb, the Reverend Tony Hammon, John Harrington, Sid Hartman, Ernie Harwell, Bill Haworth, David Hayes, Clifton and Robert Helman, Jack Hillerich, Jon Hoffman, Dwight Hooper, Sid Hudson, Charles and Ruby Hughes, David Hunt, Cornelius Hurley Jr., Mike Ilitch, Eli Jacobs, Bill James, Larry Johnson, Michael

Johnson, Richard Johnson, Ted Johnston, Tanya Jones, Frank Jordan, Jim Kallas, Eddie Kasko, Kasey Kaufman, George Kell, Tom Kennedy, Steve Kurkjian, Sheldon Kurtz, Tom Lasorda, Wallace Lawrimore, Chick Leahey, Jane Leavy, Bill Lee, Sammy Lee, Bill "Lefty" LeFebvre, Sandy Levinson, Dorothy Lindia, Hildy Linn, Marty and Sam Linsky, Bob Lobel, Bob Long, Barry Lorge, Anita Lovely, Fred Lynn, Michelle Orlando MacIntyre, Bud Maloney, Don Marinari, Lisa Martin, Willie Mays, Dave McCarthy, Robert McWalter, David Mercer, Tricia and Vicki Miranti, Leigh Montville, Joe Mooney, Joe and Dot Morgan, John and Tom Murphy, Sean Murphy, Jerry Nash, Alan Nathan, Don Newbery, Don Nicoll, Bill Nowlin, Tony Nunziante, Brian O'Connor, Dan Okrent, Buck O'Neil, Thomas P. O'Neill III, Marc Onigman, Jim Pagliaroni, Al Palmieri, Sam Perkins, Charles Pierce, Charles Platt, Gloria Poston Player, Johnny Podres, Bruce Porter, Frank Porter, Dr. Rock Positano, Bob Posner, Leo Pratt, Dr. David Pressman, Jordan Ramin, Jack Reardon, Jerry Remy, Gerry Rittenberg, Bettye Roberts, Ted Rogowski, Roselle Romano, Jerry Romolt, Charlie Rose, Mary Jane Ryan, Morley Safer, Alex and Zoe Sanders, Ed and Judy Schoenthaler, Beverly Schultz, George Scott, Dan Shaughnessy, Phil Shimkin, David Shribman, Candace Orlando Siegel, Don Skwar, Daria Stehle, Glenn Stout, Joe Sullivan, John Sununu, Bill Swank, Betty Tamposi, Steve Tamposi, Larry Taylor, Dick Thicket, Stew Thornley, Paula Tognarelli, Stephen Tomasco, Della Truax, Chip Tuttle, Jack Twyman, John Underwood, Vanessa Vadim, Bob Veazey, George Vecsey, Jim Vinick, Cheryl Walsh, Eddie Walsh, Phil Wilkinson, John Winkin, Saul Wisnia, Charles Zarrell, Rachel Zarrell, and Don Zimmer.

Thank you to my agent, the formidable Bob Barnett.

Geoff Shandler of Little, Brown is a brilliant editor. I want to thank him for acquiring the book; for being patient and supportive with me, as the research and writing took me far longer than I had originally thought; and for using his red pencil so effectively. I must admit it was daunting to see so many red marks in the returned first draft. But he cut out the fat, improved the organization, and sharpened the prose. If Geoff thought even a single sentence in the back of the book worked better toward the front, he didn't hesitate to recommend the change, and he made sure that the transitions worked as a result. But it was never his way or nothing. He was always willing to work with me if he knew I felt a certain passage was important. Thanks also to Geoff's able assistants, Brandon Coward and Allie Sommer; crack Little, Brown publicist Michelle Aielli; and Hachette Book Group CEO Michael Pietsch, a skilled editor in his own right. Senior production editor Karen Landry, eagle-eyed copyeditor Barbara Clark, and fact-checker Jeffrey Gantz were all fantastic. The Boston-based Little, Brown copyediting operation is second to none.

Finally, I'd like to thank my wife, Jan, for maintaining her support and enthusiasm for this project throughout the decade that it took me. She read portions of the manuscript and, as a public relations pro, helped me think about marketing the book when I finished it. Thanks also to my three terrific children—Greta, Joe, and Anna—who often asked how the book was progressing, even though I rarely had a satisfactory answer. It was coming along was about all I could ever say!

My apologies to anyone I've inadvertently forgotten.

APPENDIX I

Ted Williams's Lifetime Statistics

Year	G	AB	R	H	2B	3B	HR	RBI	BB	SO	BA	OBP	SLG	OPS	TB
1939	149	565	131	185	44	11	31	145	107	64	.327	.436	.609	1.045	344
1940	144	561	134	193	43	14	23	113	96	54	.344	.442	.594	1.036	333
1941	143	456	135	185	33	3	37	120	147	27	.406	.553	.735	1.287	335
1942	150	522	141	186	34	5	36	137	145	51	.356	.499	.648	1.147	338
1943	Did not play in major leagues (military service)														
1944	Did not play in major leagues (military service)														
1945	Did not play in major leagues (military service)														
1946	150	514	142	176	37	8	38	123	156	44	.342	.497	.667	1.164	343
1947	156	528	125	181	40	9	32	114	162	47	.343	.499	.634	1.133	335
1948	137	509	124	188	44	3	25	127	126	41	.369	.497	.615	1.112	313
1949	155	566	150	194	39	3	43	159	162	48	.343	.490	.650	1.141	368
1950	89	334	82	106	24	1	28	97	82	21	.317	.452	.647	1.099	216
1951	148	531	109	169	28	4	30	126	144	45	.318	.464	.556	1.019	295
1952	6	10	2	4	0	1	1	3	2	2	.400	.500	.900	1.400	9
1953	37	91	17	37	6	0	13	34	19	10	.407	.509	.901	1.410	82
1954	117	386	93	133	23	1	29	89	136	32	.345	.513	.635	1.148	245
1955	98	320	77	114	21	3	28	83	91	24	.356	.496	.703	1.200	225
1956	136	400	71	138	28	2	24	82	102	39	.345	.479	.605	1.084	242
1957	132	420	96	163	28	1	38	87	119	43	.388	.526	.731	1.257	307
1958	129	411	81	135	23	2	26	85	98	49	.328	.458	.584	1.042	240
1959	103	272	32	69	15	0	10	43	52	27	.254	.372	.419	.791	114
1960	113	310	56	98	15	0	29	72	75	41	.316	.451	.645	1.096	200
Totals	2292	7706	1798	2654	525	71	521	1839	2021	709	.344	.482	.634	1.116	4884
162-game average	162	545	127	188	37	5	37	130	143	50	.344	.482	.634	1.116	345

People Who Were Interviewed for *The Kid*

Abel, Eric (Williams family lawyer; Claudia Williams's husband), **Aitken, Melanie** (military spokeswoman), **Ajemian, Bob** (reporter who covered Williams), **Allen, Bernie** (Washington Senators player), **Allen, David** (husband of Dee Allen), **Allen, Dee** (daughter of Saul Venzor), **Allen, Jerry** (childhood friend of Ted), **Allison, Patti and John** (did physical therapy with Ted), **Altshuler, Justin** (his father was Ted's dentist), **Amidon, Ron** (son of Virginia Amidon), **Amidon, Virginia** (widow of Chester Amidon Jr., Ted's first cousin and the only son of Sarah Venzor, May Williams's sister), **Amoroso, Sarah** (daughter of hitting expert Bert Dunne), **Amphlett, Janet** (psychologist), **Andres, Ernie** (played fifteen games for the '46 Sox), **Andrews, Mike** (Jimmy Fund head; former Sox second baseman, notably for '67 Impossible Dream team), **Angell, Roger** (acclaimed *New Yorker* baseball writer), **Antignano, John** (Ted's Citrus Hills fishing buddy), **Apte, Stu** (Ted's Miami and Keys fishing buddy), **Aquilina, Bob** (Marine Corps historian), **Armstrong, Eleanor** (longtime friend of the Yawkeys), **Atkins, Jim** (pitched briefly for Red Sox in 1950 and 1952), **August, Steve** (former Red Sox traveling secretary), **Auker, Elden** (pitched in the majors for ten years, including Ted's rookie year, 1939, with the Red Sox), **Avila, Tito** (president of Hispanic Heritage Baseball Museum), **Ayoub, Philip** (Ted acquaintance; spring training visitor in the '80s)

Badaracco, Maria (godmother of Dave Egan Jr.; friend of the Colonel's and his wife, Verda), **Badgett, Rogers** (Ted friend; former part owner of the Red Sox), **Baker, Floyd** (played for Red Sox in '53–'54), **Balbini, Paul** (salesman who installed Ted's TV satellite dish at Citrus Hills), **Ballard, Mariclaire Dunne** (daughter of hitting expert Bert Dunne), **Barber, Michael** (*Citrus County Chronicle* reporter who covered John McCain visit to Ted in '97), **Baroni, Peggy** (cleaned for Louise and Ted for fifteen years along with her sister, Peg Smith), **Barr, Hoyle** (Ted's former squadron commander at Cherry Point when he was recalled for Korea), **Barry, Eddie** (close friend of Ted; former Boston Bruin and amateur golf champ who wintered in Hernando, Florida), **Bastarache, Joe** (friend of Evelyn Turner), **Battersby, Adam** (sold John-Henry a pitching machine), **Batts, Matt** (backup catcher for BoSox from 1947 to 1951), **Baumann, Frank** (pitched for the BoSox from 1955 to 1959), **Bays, Michael** (State Farm insurance agent who handled Ted's insurance for fifteen years; close friend to Ted and John-Henry; served as trustee on some of Ted's trusts), **Bean, Jack** (old Minneapolis friend of Ted), **Beck, Irv** (met Ted and Doris in summer of 1943, when Ted was at Cherry Point; owned a drive-in theater), **Beeland, Maggie** (Winter Haven tennis instructor; friend of Ted), **Bell, Leonard** (childhood friend and Hoover teammate), **Berberet, Lou** (played for Sox in 1958), **Bernreuter, Jenna** (John-Henry's girlfriend), **Berra, Yogi** (Hall of Fame catcher for the Yankees for seventeen seasons [1946–63]), **Billings, Dick** (came up with Senators in 1968, then stayed with Washington and Texas until 1974), **Bisz, Daisy** (lawyer and longtime friend of Ted), **Blaikie, Bill** (Ted's former flight instructor at Pensacola during World War II), **Blasband, Charles** (Citrus Hospital CEO), **Blood, Allen** (former Jimmy Fund patient; met Ted at Fenway as a boy), **Bolling, Milt** (played all three infield spots for the BoSox from 1952 to 1957, when he was sent to the Senators; was Red Sox scout for forty-three years), **Bond, Geedee** (former Ted caretaker), **Boone, Ray** (thirteen years in the major leagues, including thirty-four games with the Red Sox in 1960; was a few years behind Ted at Hoover High in San Diego), **Borer, Dr. Jeffrey** (Ted's cardiologist; witnessed Ted's open-heart surgery in New York), **Borland, Tom** (pitched sparingly for Red Sox in '60 and '61), **Bosman, Dick** (pitched for Senators and Rangers from 1966 to 1973), **Bradley, Rex** (Louisville Slugger sales rep), **Branom, Mike** (AP reporter who covered Ted's death), **Breitbard, Bob** (longtime friend of Ted), **Brenner, Gerald N. (Jerry)** (worked with John-Henry in Grand Slam, Ted Williams Card Company, and Major League Memorabilia), **Bresciani, Dick** (longtime Red Sox spokesman, now their historian), **Brewer, Tom** (pitched for the Red Sox from '54 to '61), **Broberg, Pete** (starting pitcher for Senators and Rangers from 1971 to '73, **Brothers, Frank** (son of Jack Brothers; Keys friend; Citrus Hills caretaker), **Brow, Dick** (helped Ted on 1988 campaign for George H. W. Bush in New Hampshire), **Brown, Bobby** (played for Yankees from 1946 to 1954; was American League president from 1984 to 1994), **Brown, Carl** (Maryland friend of Ted's; would send him soft-shell crabs), **Brown, Don** (hitting instructor at Ted's camp; was at Ted's last game), **Brown, Hal** (pitcher for BoSox from 1953 to 1955), **Brown, Hank** (Islamorada fishing guide), **Brown, Joy** (wife of Hank Brown), **Brown, Steve** (artist; fisherman; close friend to Ted at the end of his life), **Brown, Tom** (Arizona mortician who worked at Alcor for most of 2002), **Buchholz, Butch** (former tennis great; served on Sears sports advisory staff with Ted), **Buchser, Edro** (Marine flier; met Ted in Korea), **Buddin, Don** (played for Red Sox from 1956 to 1961), **Burgess, John** (knew Ted because of effort to get Shoeless Joe Jackson into Hall of Fame; hired Buzz Hamon after he left Ted's museum), **Burgin, David** (former sports editor of now defunct *Washington Daily News* in 1969, when Ted became manager of the Senators), **Burkart, Peter** (Huck Finnegan's nephew), **Bush, President George H. W., Butcher, Don** (a student of Williams's service in World War II), **Butcher, John** (nurse who was with Ted when he died)

Cafiero, Nancy Barnard (was courted by Ted and was one who got away), **Caldwell, William E.** (son of the late Wos Caldwell, the Hoover baseball coach), **Caligiuri, Fred** (pitched for the Philadelphia A's in 1941; started second half of doubleheader in which Ted went 6–8 to hit .406), **Caliri, Victor** (witness to the 1939 fight between Ted and Doc Cramer), **Camacho, Jimmy** (son of Joe Camacho), **Camacho, Joe** (Ted friend; Lakeville camp instructor; Senators bench coach), **Canales, Fred Ponce** (grandson of Frederico Ponce, who married Eulalia Hernandez, Natalia's sister and May's aunt), **Carmichael, Nancy** (Shands Hospital physician's assistant), **Carpenter, James** (serviced Ted's satellite dish in Citrus Hills), **Carroll, James** (close friend of Ted), **Carroll, Kenneth** (a flight instructor with Ted at Pensacola), **Carroll, Thomas** (son of Ted's Hoover baseball teammate Bernard G. Carroll Jr.), **Carter, George** (Ted caretaker), **Cashavelly, Chris** (friend of Ted), **Cashman, Brian** (grandson of *Boston Daily Record* beat writer Joe Cashman), **Cassidy, Al** (longtime Ted friend and associate, and executor of his estate), **Cassie, Les, Jr.** (boyhood friend of Ted), **Castinetti, Phil** (memorabilia dealer in rings case), **Ceballos, Dolores** (youngest sister of the late Joseph Urezzio of Mount Vernon, New York, who is listed as the informant on the death certificate of Ted's aunt Mae [born Veacy Williams] Grey), **Chakales, Bob** (pitched for Red Sox in last part of 1957), **Chittum, Nelson** (pitched for Red Sox in 1959 and '60), **Christiano, Albert** (Evelyn Turner's son), **Churchman, Bill** (Ted's longtime friend; Pensacola and Willow Grove flight instructor; mentor to Bobby-Jo), **Cioffi, Ernest** (Ted visited Michael Cioffi, Ernest's four-year-old brother, who was dying of leukemia, on 7/8/54 in Charlestown), **Clark, Doris** (church friend of Louise Kaufman), **Clark, Errol** (Ted's accountant for several years from the late '80s to the early '90s), **Clark, William "Otey"** (pitched for Sox in 1945, his only year in the big leagues), **Clarke, Harriet Poston** (oldest daughter of Harry Poston, who managed the Yawkey plantation for several years in the early 1950s), **Cleary, Bill** (former Harvard hockey coach and athletic director), **Cleary, Jim** (friend of Ted), **Clevenger, Tex** (pitched for Red Sox in 1954, then went on to play for Senators), **Cohen, Jeff** (former Brandeis athletic director and son of longtime *Record* sports editor Sammy Cohen), **Coleman, Jerry** (former Yankees great; World War II and Korea veteran), **Coleman, Joe, Jr.** (went to Lakeville camp; pitched for the Senators under Ted), **Collins, Bud** (reporter who covered Ted), **Colson, Bill** (former *Sports Illustrated* editor), **Connolly, Steve** (trainer of John-Henry), **Consolo, Billy** (played for Red Sox from 1953 to 1959), **Contreras, Teresa Dolores Cordero** (twelfth child of May Williams's sister Mary Venzor and Albert Cordero; Ted's first cousin), **Cooper, Alice** (member of the Hernandez side of the family whose father, Rayo Hernandez, was the brother of Natalia Hernandez Venzor, Ted's grandmother and May's mother), **Corbett, Peter** (reporter who wrote most of the Alcor stories for the *Arizona Republic*), **Corbin, Jim** (husband of Marion Corbin), **Corbin, Marion** (Geedee Bond's sister; also worked part-time for Ted), **Cordero, John** (son of Mary Venzor, May's sister), **Corea, Larry** (Red Sox clubhouse assistant, nephew of Johnny Orlando, and husband of Mary Jane Corea), **Corea, Mary Jane** (sister of Johnny Pesky's wife,

Ruth), **Cornblatt, Bruce** (Boston native; producer for Bob Costas at HBO Sports), **Costas, Bob** (the broadcaster), **Coughtry, Marlan** (played second and third base for 1960 Red Sox), **Cousy, Bob** (former Boston Celtic; honorary pallbearer at Dave Egan's funeral), **Cox, Casey** (Senators and Rangers pitcher 1966–72), **Coyle, Bill** (friend of John Sullivan; also went to Lakeville camp as a boy), **Craig, Barry** (the Episcopalian priest in the parish on the Miramichi River), **Cramer, Ruthie** (Islamorada neighbor of Ted), **Crissey, Kit** (expert on military baseball), **Crockett, Woodrow** (former Tuskegee Airman; interviewed about Korea), **Cronin, Corky** (one of Joe Cronin's three sons), **Cronin, Maureen** (daughter of Joe Cronin), **Cronin, Mildred** (widow of Joe Cronin), **Cullen, Albert, III** (Grand Slam clerk and Ted Williams Card Company director), **Cullen, Tim** (played for Senators from '66 to '71), **Curtis, Dr. Anne** (Shands Hospital doctor; did pacemaker surgery on 11/3/00), **Curtis, Clarence** (son of Roy and Edna Curtis; brother of George), **Curtis, Edna** (housekeeper at Ted's Miramichi cabin; widow of Ted's beloved guide Roy Curtis), **Curtis, George** (son of Roy and Edna Curtis; brother of Clarence), **Cushing, Frank** (younger Hoover graduate, longtime friend of Ted)

D'Alessandro, David (former John Hancock chairman; interviewed about his dealings with Joe DiMaggio), **Daley, Beth** (*Boston Globe* reporter; covered the cryonics story), **Daley, Pete** (caught for the Red Sox from 1955 to 1959), **D'Angelo, Arthur** (head of Twins Enterprises Inc.; used to run a dry cleaning business that serviced hotels in Boston, including Ted at the Somerset), **Dangleman, George** (Naval flight instructor who served with Ted in World War II), **Daniels, George B.** (financial adviser to Hazel Weisse, who owned the South Carolina brothel financed by Tom Yawkey), **Davis, Joe** (business partner and friend of Ted), **Dawsy, Jeff** (sheriff of Citrus County, Florida), **Day, Arthur** (doctor who treated Ted after his strokes in 1992 and 1994), **Dayton, Joan** (friend of Ted from the Keys), **Deal, Ellis "Cot"** (pitched briefly for Red Sox in 1947–48), **Dennis, Jeff** (flew with Ted in Korea), **Desmond, John** (Pensacola flight instructor), **Diamond, Eleanor** (former assistant to John-Henry and witness to Claudia's signing of Alcor consent forms the night Ted died), **Dickson, Eugene** (nephew of Minnie Williams, Sam Williams's second wife), **Dickson, Floyd William** (nephew of Minnie Williams, Sam Williams's second wife), **Digby, George** (longtime Red Sox scout who tried to sign Willie Mays), **Diles, Dave, Sr.** (former sportscaster; author; wrote a book on Denny McLain), **Dillman, Danny** (former Detroit Tigers batboy who ran errands for Ted), **DiMaggio, Dominic** (former Ted teammate and longtime friend; brother of Joe), **DiMaggio, Emily** (Dominic's widow), **Diver, Mary** (Miramichi friend of Ted and Louise), **Dluhy, Mary** (former John-Henry aide), **Doak, Jerry** (son of W. W. Doak, late owner of the Miramichi tackle shop), **Dodge, Ed** (Williams family doctor ca. 1990–96), **Doerr, Bobby** (former Ted teammate and longtime friend), **Donovan, Edward** (fireman who was there the day Ted visited his uncle John C. Smith at the Mount Vernon firehouse in August of 1939), **Donovan, Marguerite** (friend of Ted and widow of the late Red Sox executive John "Deals" Donovan), **Dorn, Joseph** (Williams family doctor '96–'02), **Doubleday, Nelson, Jr.** (former owner of the New York Mets who honored Ted at a game between the Red Sox and Mets at Shea Stadium in June of 1999), **Dowd, John** (Ted's lawyer in Antonucci case), **Doyle, Danny** (caught for Red Sox in 1943), **Doyle, Ted** (did public relations for Ted and John-Henry for ten years starting in 1991), **Drane, Patrick** (assistant director of Baseball Research Center at University of Massachusetts at Lowell; interviewed about Ted heating his bats), **Dropo, Walt** (played for Red Sox from 1949 to 1952), **Duffy, Earl** (assistant manager of Shelton Hotel, where Ted lived after Korea), **Dunn, Floris** (widow of Jim Dunn and mother of Jimmy), **Dunn, Jimmy** (son of the late Jim Dunn, a former Navy firefighter who helped pull Ted out of a plane that had crashed while practicing carrier landings in Jacksonville in 1945), **Dunne, Mike** (son of hitting expert Bert Dunne), **Dupuy, L. J.** (general manager of Baton Rouge River Bats, for whom John-Henry played briefly), **Duquette, Dan** (Red Sox general manager from 1994 to 2002), **Durrell, Dick** (Minneapolis acquaintance of Ted)

   Ebers, Judy (one of Ted's favorite caretakers), **Edwards, Daniel** (sculptor of "death mask," a crude impression of Ted's frozen head), **Edwards, Dyterius "Digz"** (befriended John-Henry on the Schaumburg Flyers), **Egan, Dave, Jr.** (son and namesake of the legendary "Colonel" Dave Egan), **Ehrenreich, Rich** (managing owner of Schaumburg Flyers), **Elderkin, Phil** (friend of Red Sox beat writer Ed Rumill), **Ellis, Gary** (fishing guide), **Engle, Roy** (boyhood pal of Ted), **Englund, Craig** (Ted's Citrus Hills neighbor), **Ensinger, Ferd** (longtime friend of Ted and John-Henry), **Epstein, Mike** (Senators slugger; "Super Jew"; now teaches Ted's hitting methods), **Erb, Debbie** (one of Ted's nurses), **Eschen, Rich** (friend and associate of Ted and John-Henry), **Ettinger, Robert** (pioneering cryonicist), **Evanish, Hank** (flight instructor of Ted's in World War II), **Ezelle, Reverend Dawn** (gave Ted a Bible embossed in gold with her name on it)

   Faloon, Bill (cryonics figure and Saul Kent associate), **Feigner, Anna Marie** (widow of softball legend Eddie Feigner, who knew Ted), **Fekeshazy, Margaret** (wife of Alex Fekeshazy, a fishing guide for Ted on the Miramichi), **Fekeshazy, Walter** (son of Alex Fekeshazy), **Felix, Cindy** (former facilities operations manager at Alcor), **Fenety, Jack** (former director and president of the Miramichi Salmon Association; friend of Ted), **Ferguson, Tommie** (former Boston Braves batboy and Angels traveling secretary; longtime friend of Sox clubhouse man Don Fitzpatrick), **Ferrell, Bobby-Jo Williams** (Ted's daughter and his oldest child), **Ferrell, Mark** (Bobby-Jo's husband), **Ferris, M. P. "Pat"** (owner of fifteen hundred acres on Cat Island in Georgetown, South Carolina, next to Tom Yawkey's South Island), **Ferris, Robert** (served with Ted at Cherry Point before his recall to Korea), **Ferriss, Dave "Boo"** (pitcher for the Red Sox from 1945 to 1950), **Ferriss, Miriam** (Boo's wife), **Ferroli, Steve** (John-Henry's hitting coach), **Finger, Barry** (memorabilia collector; partner with Ted and Antonucci in Talking Baseball), **Finnegan, Brian** (son of Huck Finnegan, *Boston Evening American* writer), **Fisher, Jack** (Orioles pitcher; gave up Ted's final home run), **Fitzpatrick, Spike** (lawyer for Bobby-Jo in her litigation against John-Henry and Claudia), **Flanagan, Pat** (former Red Sox front-office employee), **Flavin, Dick** (humorist and friend of Ted), **Fleischmann, Donna** (worked for John-Henry), **Fleming, Bill** (Red Sox pitcher in 1940 and 1941), **Fletcher, Teresa** (EMT who was in the ambulance with Ted the day he died), **Foley, Michael** (former Red Sox doctor and friend of David Pressman, below), **Ford, "Jeep"** (longtime family friend of Tom Yawkey in Georgetown, South Carolina), **Ford, Ralph, Jr.** (son of Ralph Ford, a fine-foods grocer who was Yawkey's best friend in Georgetown, South Carolina), **Forester, Al** (longtime Fenway grounds crew member; drove Ted out on golf cart at '99 All-Star Game), **Forman, Lane** (former memorabilia dealer; involved in lawsuit against John-Henry), **Frakes, Bill** (longtime *Sports Illustrated* photographer; did the shoot for the 1996 cover article on Ted), **Francisco, Dick** (Marine Corsair pilot in World War II and Korea; served with Ted at Pensacola during World War II), **Franzoni, Janet** (friend of Ted and Louise; widow of Bob Franzoni, fishing buddy of Ted), **Fredo, Joanne** (youngest daughter of Joseph Urezzio, friend of Ted's uncle John Smith in Mount Vernon, New York), **Friend, Owen** (infielder; played fourteen games for the Red Sox in 1955)

Gallen, Jonathan (did memorabilia work with Ted for ten years), **Garagiola, Joe** (former Cardinals catcher; caught against Sox in '46 Series), **Garciaparra, Nomar** (former Red Sox shortstop and friend of Ted), **Gard, Jack** (one of Ted's caretakers), **Gardner, Marea** (widow of Tom Yawkey's nephew Bill Gardner), **Gartlan, Robert** (made two thousand collectible porcelain Ted figurines, which Ted signed), **German, David** (military records specialist), **Gernert, Dick** (played for Red Sox from 1952 to 1959), **Gerow, Stacia** (Ted's longtime personal assistant), **Giacobbe, Andy** (former TV repairman at Somerset Hotel; knew Ted; later moved to Citrus Hills and volunteered at Ted's museum), **Gile, Don** (played for Red Sox from '59 to '62), **Gilmore, Grant** (son of Isabel Gilmore), **Gilmore, Isabel** (Ted's lover in the late '50s who rejected his marriage proposal but remained close to him late in life), **Gilmore, Marshall** (son of Isabel Gilmore), **Gleason, Jim** (former San Diego Padres pitcher who used to throw to Ted on the playground when they were growing up), **Glenn, John** (former astronaut, senator, and friend of Ted who flew with him in Korea), **Glenn, Mike** (lawyer friend of John Burgess, above, and Buzz Hamon, below), **Godwin, Rebecca** (teacher at Bennington College and author of *Keeper of the House,* a novel based on the Sunset Lodge in Georgetown, South Carolina), **Gonzalez, Ruth Ponce** (Ted's first cousin once removed), **Goodband, Clifford, Jr.** (his father was the veterinarian to Ted's dogs in the 1950s; took batting practice as Ted pitched), **Goodman, Allan** (Ted's doctor at Sharp Memorial Hospital in San Diego, 2001), **Goodman, Eric** (friend of John-Henry; worked on Ted's security detail), **Goodspeed, Hill** (Navy historian), **Gordon, Herb** (bought Ted's house in Islamorada), **Gorman, Lou** (former Red Sox general manager), **Gowdy, Curt** (longtime Red Sox announcer and friend of Ted), **Grace, Buddy** (Keys fishing guide who knew Ted), **Green, Pumpsie** (first black Red Sox player; infielder from 1959 to 1962), **Grieve, Tom** (played with Senators and Rangers under Ted), **Grinold, Jack** (polio victim in the late '40s; visited by Ted in Boston), **Gumpert, Randy** (pitcher with the Sox for part of 1952; pitched for the Yankees from 1946 to 1948), **Gunn, John** (former reporter and editor involved in military baseball), **Gutteridge, Don** (played for Red Sox in 1946–47)

Hammon, Reverend Tony (started Island Christian School, John-Henry and Claudia's grade school in Islamorada), **Hamon, Buzz** (former Ted museum director), **Hardy, Carroll** (outfielder for Red Sox from 1960 to 1962; known as only man to pinch-hit for Ted), **Harrington, John** (former Red Sox CEO), **Harshman, Jack** (played the first half of '59 with the Red Sox), **Hartman, Sid** (Minnesota sports personality; as a boy, saw Ted play with the Millers; befriended him), **Harwell, Ernie** (longtime Tigers announcer; knew Ted as a young reporter in Detroit in the '40s), **Hash, Herbert** (pitched with the Sox in 1940 and '41; briefly Ted's roommate), **Hatton, Grady** (played for the Red Sox from 1954 to the early part of 1956), **Hawkins, Larry** (Marine pilot who led Ted home safely in preparation for his crash landing in Korea), **Haworth, Bill** (Alcor PR man), **Hayes, David** (escorted Ted's body from Florida to Alcor, in Arizona), **Hebding, Francine Dawn** (Bobby-Jo's daughter and Ted's granddaughter), **Heer, John** (Cleveland lawyer who represented Bobby-Jo in cryonics litigation against John-Henry and Claudia), **Helman, Clifton** (CPA and business adviser to John-Henry and Ted), **Helman, Rob** (Clifton Helman's son, who worked with his father and also dealt with John-Henry), **Henry, Bill** (pitched for Sox from 1952 to 1955), **Henry, John** (Red Sox principal owner), **Herrera, Edna** (wife of Sal Herrera; retired LAPD officer), **Herrera, Manuel** (Ted's first cousin once removed; brother of Sal), **Herrera, Salvador** (grandson of May Venzor's sister Mary; first cousin once removed of Ted and older brother of Manny Herrera), **Hiley-Self, Virginia** (one of Ted's nurses), **Hill, Peter** (lawyer who took Hitter.net through bankruptcy), **Hillerich, Jack** (longtime president and CEO of Hillerich & Bradsby, makers of Louisville Slugger bats), **Hillman, Darius "Dave"** (pitched for the Red Sox in 1960 and 1961), **Hinrichs, Paul** (pitched four games in 1951 with the Red Sox), **Hisner, Harley** (pitched one game for the 1951 Red Sox), **Hitchcock, Billy** (infielder for Red Sox, 1948–49), **Hoeft, Billy** (played five games for the 1959 Red Sox between stints with the Tigers and the Orioles the same year), **Hoffman, Dick** (he and his brother Tom, now dead, spent time with Ted in Minneapolis in 1938), **Hoffman, Jon** (retired Marine colonel, Marine historian, and writer; interviewed about Ted's military records), **Hogerheide, Robert** (former Ted chef), **Holcombe, Ken** (pitcher for 1953 Sox), **Holetz, Jean** (Doris Soule's childhood best friend), **Holland, John** (flight instructor with Ted during World War II), **Hollenbeck, Marvin** (former Marine who flew with Ted in Korea), **Hommell, George** (friend of Ted; neighbor in Islamorada), **Hooper, Dwight** (proprietor of Hooper Funeral Homes & Crematory), **Hopper, Peter B.** (founder of Internet company Duro Communications; discussed buying Hitter.net with John-Henry), **Horgan, Tim** (longtime sportswriter for the *Boston Herald* and *Boston Evening Traveler*), **Hoskins, Herb** (state investigator in the Antonucci case), **Howard, Lee** (Ted's second wife), **Howard, Roy** (Princeton, Minnesota, mail carrier who knew Ted a bit), **Hoyt, Carl** (eighty-one-year-old Weare, New Hampshire, hunter and fisherman; knew Ted since 1950), **Hudson, Sid** (pitcher for Sox from '52 to '54; pitching for Senators in '41, he grooved pitches to Ted in the next-to-last series of season to aid in Williams's quest for .400; also pitching coach with Senators under Ted), **Hughes, Charles** (son and only child of Hazel Weisse, madam of the Sunset Lodge), **Hull, Bill** (nephew of Minnie Williams, Sam Williams's second wife), **Huntsinger, Elizabeth** (author of *Ghosts of Georgetown,* which contains a chapter on the Sunset Lodge brothel), **Hurley, Cornelius, Jr.** (the son of Cornelius Hurley, a former partner in the old Boston firm of Hale and Dorr and confidant of Ted's who died in August of 2002 at the age of ninety-six), **Hynes, Samuel** (professor of literature at Princeton who served as a Marine aviator with Ted at Pensacola during World War II)

Inamorati, Frank (tennis pro at Citrus Hills; Ted friend), **Interland, Brian** (friend of Ted and business partner with John-Henry in Grand Slam and the Ted Williams Card Company), **Irvin, Monte** (Hall of Fame player, first with Negro Leagues then with New York Giants)

Jackson, Ron (played for Red Sox in 1960), **Jacobs, Eli** (former Orioles owner; friend of Ted), **James, Bill** (baseball's sabermetrics guru), **Jensen, Swede** (Ted's old chum from Hoover High; played on the Padres from 1939 to 1949), **Johansen, Joe** (Islamorada fisherman), **Johnson, Larry** (Alcor whistle-blower who wrote a controversial book about his time at the cryonics facility), **Johnson, Michael** (Shands Hospital clinical social worker and friend to John-Henry), **Johnson, Richard** (director of the Sports Museum in Boston and coauthor of two coffee-table books on Williams), **Johnston, Ted** (Ted's friend and the contractor for his first and second houses in Citrus Hills), **Jones, Tanya** (former Alcor chief operating officer), **Joost, Eddie** (Sox utility infielder, 1955), **Joyner, Robert** (caretaker of the Yawkey estate in South Carolina)

Kaiser, Joyce (niece of Minnie Williams, Sam Williams's second wife), **Kallas, Jim** (Princeton, Minnesota, fishing and hunting buddy of Ted), **Kasko, Eddie** (former major-league player, Red Sox manager, scouting director, and friend of Ted), **Katz, Bob** (runs My Grandma's of New England, a coffee cake company; would send cakes to Ted; did a brief business deal with him), **Kaufman, Rob** (elder son of Louise Kaufman), **Kaufman, Ruth Banash** (a Jimmy Fund volunteer who knew Ted), **Kell, George** (beat Ted to win the Triple Crown in '49; played on Red Sox in 1952–53 and part of '54), **Kelly, Jack** (friend of Don Fitzpatrick; batboy; spent time in Sox clubhouse), **Keltner, Autumn Durst** (daughter of late Cedric Durst, Ted's teammate and mentor on the San Diego Padres), **Kemmerer, Russ** (pitcher for Red Sox in 1954, '55, and part of '57), **Kennedy, Bob** (major leaguer and World War II pal of Ted), **Keough, Marty** (Red Sox outfielder from 1956 to 1960), **Kerensky, Richard** (Ted's Florida cardiologist, who attested to Claudia being present on the day the pact was signed), **King, Lori** (Ted dialysis nurse), **Kingsley, John** (saw Ted take batting practice at Harvard in the 1950s), **Klaus, Billy** (Red Sox infielder from 1955 to 1958), **Klein, Carol** (niece of Minnie Williams, Sam Williams's second wife), **Knowles, Darold** (Senators pitcher from 1967 to '71), **Korba,**

Harry (friend of Ted from 1954 to 2002), **Kunzman, Alan** (former Riverside, California, coroner's investigator who wrote a book critical of Alcor), **Kurth, Judi** (daughter of Joe Dulak, deceased Minnesota and World War II friend of Ted; consulted with John-Henry on his businesses), **Kurtz, Sheldon** (University of Iowa College of Law professor and expert on the Uniform Anatomical Gift Act)

Larson, Rosalie (Ted's first cousin; daughter of Paul Venzor, May's brother), **Lasorda, Tommy** (longtime Dodgers manager and friend of Ted), **La Spada, Carmella** (founder, No Greater Love, charity of which Ted was president), **Lawrimore, Wallace Hampton** (son of Hampton Lawrimore, Tom Yawkey's chief mechanic in residence at South Island from about 1929 to 1951), **Layon, Joseph** (Florida doctor who treated Ted at Shands Hospital), **Lazor, Johnny** (played for Red Sox from 1943 to 1946), **Leahey, Chick** (former Bates College baseball coach who had dealings with John-Henry), **Lederman, Mort** (worked security at Jimmy Fund and dealt with Ted in the 1950s), **Lee, Bill** (eccentric Red Sox pitcher in the 1970s who knew Ted from spring training), **Lee, Sammy** (television and radio fishing personality; knew and hosted Ted on his programs), **LeFebvre, Bill "Lefty"** (Red Sox pitcher in 1938–39), **Lemler, Jerry** (former Alcor CEO), **Lenhardt, Don** (played for Red Sox in 1952 and 1954), **Lepcio, Ted** (Red Sox infielder from 1952 to 1959), **Levinson, Sandy** (friend of Daisy Bisz, lawyer to Ted), **Lewis, Lana** (had polio as a child; Ted helped her), **Liebster, Jerry** (John-Henry's baseball agent), **Lind, Carl** (ran Sears staff advisory program with Ted), **Lindia, Dorothy** (widow of longtime Ted pal Joe Lindia, a Cranston, Rhode Island, restaurateur), **Lindia, Frank** (Joe and Dorothy Lindia's son), **Linsky, Sam** (wrote essay entitled "Ted Williams and Excellence" in his application to Harvard and was admitted), **Lobel, Bob** (Boston sportscaster), **Lodigiani, Dario** (former Pacific Coast League and American League player; opponent of Ted's), **Long, Bob** (former Vermont Academy headmaster), **Longo, Al** (Boston businessman with an office at Somerset Hotel while Ted was there), **Lorge, Barry** (former *Washington Post* sportswriter and *San Diego Union* sports editor), **Lovely, Anita** (John-Henry's onetime fiancée and longtime confidante), **Lucchino, Larry** (Red Sox CEO), **Lucero, Gino** (cousin of Ted's on the Hernandez side of the family), **Lucier, Lou** (pitcher for the Red Sox in 1943–44), **Lupien, Tony** (played for the Sox in 1940, '42, and '43), **Luscomb, Brian** (nephew and godson of Rod Luscomb, Ted's playground mentor), **Lynn, Fred** (Red Sox outfielder from '75 to '80; met Ted at spring training), **Lyons, Kirk** (worked with Ted trying to get Shoeless Joe Jackson into the Hall of Fame)

MacIntyre, Michelle Orlando (John-Henry's first girlfriend), **Magill, Charles** (veterinarian to Ted's dog Slugger for six years), **Mahoney, Jim** (Red Sox infielder, 1959), **Mallett, Jerry** (played briefly for 1959 Red Sox), **Maloney, Bud** (younger schoolmate of Ted at Hoover High; *San Diego Union* sportswriter), **Maloof, Ferris** (scoreboard operator at Fenway from 1949 to the late '50s), **Malzone, Frank** (played third base for the Red Sox from 1955 to 1965), **Marinari, Don** (a friend of Ted from the 1980s on), **Martin, Lisa** (John-Henry's widow), **Masterson, Walt** (pitcher with Red Sox from 1949 to 1952),

Maxwell, Charlie (played outfield in parts of 1950, '51, '52, and '54 for the Red Sox), **Mays, Willie** (Ted rooted for the all-time great in his Hall of Fame induction speech), **Maznicki, Frank** (Ted was his flight instructor at Pensacola; played baseball and football at Boston College and football for the Chicago Bears), **McCall, John "Windy"** (pitched sparingly for the Red Sox from 1948 to 1949), **McCarthy, Dave** (former New Hampshire state police officer and now director of the Ted Williams museum), **McCauley, Andy** (manager of Schaumburg Flyers when John-Henry played for the team), **McDonald, Jim** (pitched nine games for the 1950 Red Sox), **McDonough, Will** (*Boston Globe* columnist), **McDougal, Elaine** (daughter of Hampton Lawrimore, Yawkey's chief mechanic), **McKinnis, Jerry** (host of *The Fishin' Hole,* program on ESPN; went to Russia on a fishing trip with Ted), **McWalter, Robert** (Ted's longtime lawyer), **Meehan, Bobby** (worked for Tim McAuliffe, who provided Red Sox uniforms for years), **Mele, Sam** (played two stints for Red Sox from 1947 to 1949 and from 1954 to 1955), **Mercer, Bobby** (rector at Miramichi church from 1974 to 1981), **Minarcin, Rudy** (pitched a handful of games for the Red Sox in 1956 and '57), **Miranti, Tricia** (disabled Florida girl whom Ted took under his wing), **Miranti, Vicki** (mother of Tricia Miranti), **Mitchell, Ramona** (friend of Doris Soule), **Mitrovich, George** (president of the City Club of San Diego; interviewed about the Red Sox beat writer Ed Rumill), **Moford, Herb** (pitched four games for the 1959 Red Sox), **Monahan, Bob** (former *Globe* reporter who covered college sports for the paper for forty years; brother of Leo Monahan), **Monahan, Leo** (longtime *Record* reporter who worked closely with Dave Egan), **Monbouquette, Bill** (pitched for Red Sox from '58 to '65), **Montgomery, Bob** (former Red Sox catcher and broadcaster), **Mooney, Joe** (longtime Red Sox groundskeeper; groundskeeper at RFK Stadium in Washington when Ted managed there), **Moore, Gene** (friend and business partner of Ted), **Moore, Jimmy, Jr.** (lawyer in Georgetown and Myrtle Beach, South Carolina), **More, Nelva** (Ted's fiancée until they broke off their engagement in 1957), **Morgan, Chris** (young promoter from Manchester, New Hampshire, who participated in a panel discussion with Ted, George W. Bush, and former Red Sox pitcher Dennis Eckersley in January of 2000, prior to the annual Granite State Baseball Dinner in which Ted endorsed Bush), **Morgan, Dot** (wife of Joe Morgan), **Morgan, Joe** (former Sox manager and Ted pal), **Morton, Guy** (played one game for 1954 Red Sox), **Moscato, Arthur** (Sox ticket manager; started in the '40s, took requests for Ted), **Moss, Les** (caught for the Red Sox in the last part of 1951), **Mueller, Gordie** (pitched in eight games for the Sox in 1950), **Muggeo, Louis** (lawyer for Lane Forman in memorabilia case against John-Henry), **Mulcahy, Joe** (Warwick, Rhode Island, Little Leaguer who was hospitalized on 8/30/58 after being beaned while batting; Ted sent him a birthday cake and an autographed ball), **Muller, Virginia** (sister of Joe Urezzio, friend of Ted's uncle John Smith; aunt of Joanne Fredo, above), **Munday, Bill** (former Ted caretaker), **Munday, Kay** (Bill's wife; also a Ted caretaker), **Murphy, John** (younger son of former Yankees and Red Sox relief pitcher Johnny Murphy, who helped out around the clubhouse in the 1950s), **Murphy, Sean**

(accountant for John-Henry and Ted), **Murphy, Tom** (older son of former Sox and Yankees pitcher Johnny Murphy)

Nash, Jerry (Sam Tamposi's partner in Citrus Hills; founding director of the Ted museum), **Nathan, Alan** (expert on the physics of baseball; interviewed about Ted heating his bats), **Nathan, David** (Jimmy Fund president emeritus; hosted Ted on '99 All-Star Game visit to the hospital), **Nayfield, Casey** (veterinarian to Ted's dog Slugger for a short time), **Nee, Peter** (Ted's banker at BankBoston; Brookline neighbor of John-Henry), **Nelson, Dave** (played under Ted for the Senators and Rangers), **Newbery, Don** (radio reporter who did an in-depth interview with Dolores Williams in 1969, which he released only after Ted died), **Newman, Roberta** (teaches baseball history at NYU; specializes in baseball advertising), **Nicoll, Don** (first sick boy Ted visited, at Boston's Faulkner Hospital, in 1939), **Nolan, Martin** (former *Boston Globe* Washington bureau chief and editorial page editor), **Nowlin, Bill** (record executive and prolific baseball author)

O'Connor, Brian (friend of Ted; Jimmy Fund board member; adviser to John-Henry), **O'Hara, Dave** (longtime AP sportswriter in Boston), **Oliver, Dell** (Ted's Hoover High teammate), **Olson, Karl** (Red Sox outfielder in 1951 and from '53 to '55), **O'Neil, Buck** (Negro Leaguer; baseball historian; worked in commissioner's office), **O'Neill, Thomas P., III** (former Massachusetts lieutenant governor and PR executive), **Ortiz, Carolyn** (Ted's first cousin; Paul Venzor's daughter; sister of Rosalie Larson), **Owens, Gary** (director of golf at Black Diamond Ranch; knew Ted and John-Henry)

Pagliaroni, Jim (caught for Red Sox in one game in '55, then played from 1960 to 1962), **Palmieri, Al** (counselor at Ted Williams camp in Lakeville), **Parnell, Mel** (Red Sox pitcher, 1947–1956), **Patel, Dr. Dinesh** (chief of arthroscopic surgery at Massachusetts General Hospital), **Patterson, James T.** (Brown University professor; interviewed about Senator Robert Taft), **Pellagrini, Eddie** (played for Red Sox 1946–47), **Perez, Bill** (son of Connie Matthews, sister of Ted's cousin Ernest Ponce), **Perskie, Joe** (HBO producer; did a program on the cryonics controversy), **Pesky, Johnny** (longtime friend; Ted's former Red Sox teammate), **Phelps, Hazel** (Ted's secretary when he was with the Washington Senators), **Pierce, Charles** (former *Boston Globe* writer), **Piersall, Jimmy** (Red Sox outfielder from 1950 to 1958), **Pitts, Dan** (knew Ted at Islamorada), **Platt, Charles** (onetime Alcor executive), **Player, Gloria Poston** (daughter of former Yawkey plantation manager Harry Poston), **Plews, Herb** (infielder for Red Sox in 1959), **Podres, Johnny** (former Dodgers pitcher), **Ponce, Mary** (widow of Ernest Ponce, Ted's cousin), **Porter, Bruce** (former pastor at Island Christian School in Islamorada; introduced Ted to Jack Hyles; witnessed their evangelical encounter), **Porter, Frank** (Marine Corps veteran; interviewed about Ted's military records), **Positano, Dr. Rock** (Joe DiMaggio pal), **Poth, Len** (served in World War II with Ted and played on the Pensacola baseball team with him), **Pratt, Leo** (bell captain at the Somerset Hotel from 1950 to 1960), **Press, Ben** (Ted's childhood chum), **Pressman, David** (as a boy, befriended Ted and persuaded him to start heating his bats), **Proia, Loretta** (sister of longtime Red Sox clubhouse attendant Donald Fitzpatrick), **Psaute, Alice** (member of San Diego's

Salvation Army who knew May Williams), **Puiia, Anthony** (brother of Dominic Puiia, who played ball with Ted in the Marines)

Ramin, Jordan (ghostwriter for Ted's syndicated column in the mid-1960s), **Reardon, Jack** (Harvard official who offered Ted an honorary degree), **Reedy, Billy** (longtime friend of Ted from Detroit), **Remy, Jerry** ('70s Red Sox infielder; currently a Sox broadcaster; met Ted in spring training), **Renna, Bill** (outfielder for Red Sox from 1958 to 1959), **Richter, Al** (played shortstop for Red Sox in parts of 1951 and 1953), **Rigney, Joe** (Citrus Hills community association manager; knew Ted), **Rittenberg, Gerry** (trustee of Ted's museum and a friend of John-Henry), **Roberts, Bettye** (with her late husband, Jack, bought the Sunset Lodge in South Carolina after it went out of business; friend of Hazel Weisse), **Rogde, Ruby and Russ** (Princeton, Minnesota, residents who knew Doris Soule), **Rogowski, Ted** (lawyer for Ted's marriage to and divorce from Lee Howard; also did his Sears contract), **Rolfingsmeier, Kathleen** (live-in nurse who coordinated Ted's at-home care), **Romano, Roselle** (Miami Beach woman originally from Fort Lee, New Jersey, who befriended Sam Williams's half sisters, Ted's aunts), **Romolt, Jerry** (memorabilia dealer and friend of Ted), **Ronquillo, David** (San Diego lawyer who was a cousin of Ted's on the Hernandez side of the family), **Rose, Charlie** (TV broadcaster who interviewed Williams), **Roselli, Mike** (Fenway vendor from 1954 to 1960 who occasionally shagged flies for Ted), **Ross, Jim** (former reporter with *St. Petersburg Times,* now with *Ocala StarBanner;* cowrote a story in August of 2000 linking John-Henry and Hitter.net to pornography), **Ross, Tom** (pilot in Korea with Ted), **Ruoff, Rick** (Islamorada neighbor of Ted; fishing guide and writer), **Ryan, Mary Jane** (former Red Sox secretary; grew up in Vermont near the Wettach family)

Safer, Morley (CBS newsman who did a piece about Ted for *60 Minutes*), **Sanders, Alex** (former Democratic candidate from South Carolina for Strom Thurmond's seat in the US Senate; worked as an environmental lawyer for Tom Yawkey; friend of Ted), **Sanders, Zoe** (Alex Sanders's wife; friend of Barbara Kovacs, Louise Kaufman's daughter), **Satz, Vivian** (AT&T Internet specialist assigned to Hitter.net account), **Schafrann, Jay** (Miramichi neighbor and friend of Ted), **Scherbarth, Bob** (was catcher in one game in 1950 for the Red Sox), **Schoenthaler, Ed** (husband of Judy Schoenthaler), **Schoenthaler, Judy** (daughter of Lee Howard, Ted's second wife), **Schultz, Beverly** (niece of Minnie Williams, Sam Williams's second wife), **Scott, George** (played for the Red Sox from 1966 to 1971 and 1977 to 1979; knew Ted from spring training), **Sheridan, Neill** (played in two games for Red Sox with one at bat in 1948), **Sherman, Steve** (John-Henry's employee at Atrium Mall store), **Shimkin, Phil** (Morley Safer's *60 Minutes* producer), **Siegel, Bruce** (husband of Candace Siegel; worked for John-Henry at Grand Slam), **Siegel, Candace Orlando** (daughter of Red Sox clubhouse man Vince Orlando, Johnny's brother), **Siman, Lynette** (former Ted girlfriend; friend of Louise Kaufman), **Sisk, Raymond** (served in World War II with Ted and trained for Korea with him), **Sisler, Dave** (pitched for Red Sox from 1956 to 1959), **Skelley, Bill** (neighborhood friend of Ted who played on the 1937 Padres with him), **Smith, Bob Gilchrist** (came up with Red Sox in 1955 and pitched one game), **Smith, Karl** (longtime Ted friend; met as roommates at Pensacola), **Smith, Mike** (former Pawtucket schoolteacher; friend of Ted), **Smutko, Michelle** (Ted's dialysis nurse), **Sonnabend, Paul** (manager of the Shelton Hotel and Somerset Hotel), **Soule, Donald** (brother of Doris Soule), **Southard, Carol** (wife of Steve Southard), **Springstead, Jack** (presiding judge in Antonucci case), **Stalcup, William** (doctor who did Ted's hip replacement), **Stehle, Daria** (widow of Jim Stehle, a Marine pilot and friend of Ted who served in Korea at the same time), **Stephens, Gene** (backup outfielder for Red Sox from 1952 to the end of 1960; was known as Williams's caddy), **Sterry, Evalyn** (Louise Kaufman's best friend), **Storton, Alan** (childhood friend of Ted in San Diego), **Stout, Glenn** (coauthor, with Richard Johnson, of coffee-table books about the Red Sox and Ted), **Stringer, Lou** (infielder for Red Sox from 1948 to '50), **Sturdivant, Tom** (pitched for Red Sox in 1960 and for Yankees from 1955 to 1959), **Sullivan, Frank** (pitched for Red Sox from 1953 to 1960), **Sullivan, George** (Sox batboy turned sportswriter), **Sullivan, Joe** (*Boston Globe* sports editor; interviewed about the cryonics story), **Sullivan, John** (former nurse and personal assistant to Ted), **Sununu, John** (former governor of New Hampshire and former White House chief of staff), **Sutton, Peter** (Ted and John-Henry's lawyer), **Swank, Bill** (San Diego Padres historian)

   Tabor, Jim (son of Jim Tabor, Ted's combative teammate on the Minneapolis Millers and the Red Sox), **Tamposi, Elizabeth "Betty"** (daughter of Sam Tamposi, Citrus Hills developer and Red Sox limited partner; assisted John-Henry), **Tamposi, Steve** (son of Sam Tamposi; CEO of Citrus Hills), **Taylor, Larry** (Ted friend; former Marine general), **Taylor, Ted** (identified Hitter.net for acquisition by Duro Communications), **Terwilliger, Wayne** (Ted's third-base coach with Senators), **Thalassites, Leo** (Marine Corps friend of Ted), **Thicket, Dick** (Lakeville, Massachusetts, pharmacist; friend of Ted from his baseball camp), **Thomson, Bobby** (hit "shot heard 'round the world" for the New York Giants in 1951; after playing fourteen seasons in the National League, he moved to the American League in 1960 and played for the Red Sox), **Thrift, Roger** (played pepper with Ted when he was stationed at Chapel Hill prior to flight school in 1943), **Tomasco, Stephen** (Bobby-Jo Williams's first husband), **Trank, Mary** (executive assistant to Tom Yawkey and Dick O'Connell at the Red Sox), **Tridico, Mary** (widow of Doris Soule's second husband, Joseph J. Tridico), **Trimble, Joe** (pitcher for Red Sox in 1955; appeared in two games), **Truax, Della** (Ted Williams Family Enterprises secretary), **Trucks, Virgil** (Detroit Tigers pitcher in '40s and '50s; friend of Ted), **Truitt, Kathy Moran** (daughter of Art Moran, Ted's squadron commander in Korea), **Tulley, Vin** (Nashua, New Hampshire, car dealer; friend of Ted), **Tuttle, Chip** (did public relations for John-Henry), **Twyman, Jack** (former Cincinnati Royal, basketball representative on the Sears sports advisory staff with Ted)

   Umphlett, Tom (played outfield in 1953 for the Red Sox), **Underhill, Emerson** (Miramichi fly tier; friend of Ted), **Underwood, John** (ghostwrote Ted's autobiography, *My Turn at Bat,* in 1969, and other Ted books), **Unser, Del** (played for Senators from 1968 to 1971)

Vadim, Vanessa (Jane Fonda's oldest child; early John-Henry girlfriend), **Van Tassel, Donna** (naturopath and nutritionist who says she brought Ted to God at the end of his life), **Varian, Bill** (former reporter with the *St. Petersburg Times,* now the *Tampa Bay Times,* who cowrote a story in August of 2000 linking John-Henry and Hitter.net to pornography), **Vaughn, Becky** (nurse and caretaker of Ted), **Veazey, Robert** (assistant to the base operations officer during Williams's crash landing in Korea), **Venzor, Charles** (Ted's first cousin; son of Saul Venzor and brother of Dee Allen), **Venzor, Daniel** (Ted's first cousin; son of Bruno Venzor), **Venzor, Frank** (Ted's first cousin; son of May's brother Paul Venzor and brother of Carrie Ortiz and Rosalie Larson), **Vernon, Mickey** (played for Red Sox in 1956–57), **Villarino, Joe** (Ted's childhood pal), **Vinick, James** (bought Ted's movie rights; worked with him at the Jimmy Fund)

Wagner, Charlie (former Red Sox pitcher; he and Ted were roommates for seven years), **Walley, James** (former Marine pilot who flew with Ted in Korea), **Walsh, Eddie** (former Boston policeman who went into the sports memorabilia business and became friendly with Ted and John-Henry), **Watkins, Lewis** (Ted friend; artist; one of the founders of his museum), **Watson, Bob** (Ted's neurologist at the University of Florida), **Watson, Mary** (daughter of Bob Watson), **Webster, Ray** (played briefly for Red Sox in 1960), **Weisbrod, Frank** (knew Ted in Princeton, Minnesota, and hunted with him), **Wells, Millard** (Ted fishing pal in the Keys and on the Miramichi), **Werle, Bill** (pitcher for the 1953 and '54 Red Sox), **Wheeler, Dan** (former New Hampshire state trooper who provided security for Ted), **Whitcomb, Dick** (high school chum of Dolores Williams), **Whitfield, Shelby** (former radio and TV broadcaster for the Washington Senators in 1969 and 1970; friend of Ted), **Widmar, Al** (played briefly for Red Sox in 1947), **Wight, Bill** (pitched for Red Sox in 1951 and '52), **Wilkinson, Phil** (resident biologist for Tom Yawkey on his South Carolina plantation from 1966 to 1977), **Williams, Claudia** (Ted's youngest child and second daughter), **Williams, Dolores** (Ted's third wife), **Williams, Sam** (Ted's nephew; son of his brother, Danny), **Williams, Ted** (namesake nephew of *the* Ted; son of Danny), **Wilson, Archie** (played eighteen games for 1952 Red Sox), **Winkin, John** (longtime University of Maine baseball coach; Ted friend from Lakeville camp; cut John-Henry from the Maine baseball team), **Wisnia, Saul** (publications editor at Dana-Farber Cancer Institute; author of several books, including one on the history of the Jimmy Fund), **Wood, Ken** (played outfield for the 1952 Red Sox), **Woodbury, Woody** (served in Korea with Ted; witnessed his crash), **Worthington, Al** (played in six games for the 1960 Red Sox), **Wowk, Brian** (cryobiologist; Alcor board member), **Wright, Tom** (outfielder for Red Sox from 1948 to 1951)

Zarrell, Charles (former camper at Ted's baseball camp in Lakeville), **Zeigler, Bill** (Washington Senators trainer under Ted), **Zimmer, Don** (Red Sox manager when Ted started doing spring training with the team again in 1978)

Notes

Please refer to the bibliography for complete source information.

Introduction

1. Johnson with Baldyga, *Frozen,* 201.
2. Ibid., 200–2.
3. Interview with Cindy Felix, May 18, 2006.
4. Interview with Tanya Jones, January 25, 2006.
5. Interview with Eric Abel, January 13, 2006.
6. Interview with Claudia Williams, March 29, 2006.
7. Interview with Tim Horgan, October 5, 2005.
8. *Boston Globe,* March 23, 1947.
9. Williams with Underwood, *My Turn at Bat,* 161.
10. Interview with Bobby-Jo Williams Ferrell, May 5, 2004.
11. Interview with Jerry Romolt, July 21, 2004.
12. Interview with Johnny Pesky, October 7, 2002.
13. Interview with Milt Bolling, August 13, 2003.
14. Interview with Bobby Doerr, March 7, 2006.
15. Interview with Johnny Pesky, October 7, 2002.
16. Interview with Dave McCarthy, January 3, 2003.
17. Interview with Steve Brown, November 12, 2004.
18. Interview with Elizabeth Tamposi, September 22, 2005.
19. Interview with Dave Sisler, August 20, 2003.
20. Interview with Bob Costas, June 7, 2005.
21. Interview with Manuel Herrera, October 29, 2002.
22. Interview with Gino Lucero, January 16, 2006.
23. Interview with Tom Wright, June 27, 2003.
24. Interview with Ted Lepcio, August 19, 2003.
25. Interview with Jimmy Piersall, July 16, 2004.
26. *Saturday Evening Post,* January 10, 1942.

Chapter 1: Shame

1. Nowlin, *The Kid,* 252.
2. Interview with Frank Venzor, February 10, 2005.
3. Interview with Al Cassidy, December 5, 2002.
4. Interview with David Ronquillo, June 2, 2006. (Ronquillo was told the story at a 1997 family reunion by a now-deceased relative, Priscilla Wade, who was at the train station in 1939.)
5. Interview with Carolyn Ortiz, November 17, 2002.
6. Interview with Rosalie Larson, November 15, 2002.
7. Interview with Salvador Herrera, November 2, 2005.
8. Williams with Underwood, *My Turn at Bat,* 28.
9. Nowlin, *The Kid,* 260.
10. Interview with Teresa Cordero Contreras, February 9, 2005.

11. Nowlin, *The Kid,* 280.
12. Interview with Manuel Hererra, October 29, 2002.
13. Interview with Dee Allen, November 15, 2002.
14. Interview with David Allen, November 15, 2002.
15. Interview with Ruth Gonzalez, February 10, 2005.
16. Nowlin, *The Kid,* 297.
17. *San Diego Union,* July 7, 1980.
18. Interview with Alice Psaute, November 1, 2002.
19. *San Diego Union,* July 7, 1991.
20. Linn, *Hitter,* 73.
21. Williams with Underwood, *My Turn at Bat,* 33.
22. Interview with Edward Donovan, April 23, 2004.
23. Interview with Roselle Romano, April 14, 2005.
24. Williams with Underwood, *My Turn at Bat,* 31.
25. Ibid., 30.
26. Nowlin, *The Kid,* 265.
27. Ibid., 225.
28. Mills, *San Diego,* 65.
29. David Halberstam interview, January 1988, made available to the author.
30. Williams with Underwood, *My Turn at Bat,* 22.
31. *Time* file.
32. Ibid.
33. Ibid.
34. Williams with Underwood, *My Turn at Bat,* 24.
35. Ibid., 23.
36. *Boston Evening American,* July 14, 1941.
37. Linn, *Hitter,* 4.
38. Williams with Underwood, *My Turn at Bat,* 24.
39. *Time* file.
40. Society for American Baseball Research, *A History of San Diego Baseball.*
41. Nowlin, *The Kid,* 79.
42. *Boston Evening American,* July 14, 1941.
43. Williams with Underwood, *My Turn at Bat,* 29.
44. Interview with Bobby Doerr, October 14, 2002.
45. Interview with Steve Brown, November 12, 2004.
46. Interview with John Cordero, February 10, 2005.
47. Interview with Manuel Hererra, October 29, 2002.
48. Ibid.
49. Interview with Jim Vinick, May 18, 2004.
50. Interview with Swede Jensen, January 20, 2005.
51. Williams with Underwood, *My Turn at Bat,* 22.
52. *San Diego Union,* July 7, 1991.
53. Prime and Nowlin, *Ted Williams,* 7.
54. Interview with Joe Villarino, October 25, 2002.
55. Linn, *Hitter,* 31.
56. Interview with Roy Engle, October 25, 2002.
57. *San Diego Union,* November 12, 1977.
58. Bob Holbrook, "Ted (Yes, Our T. Williams) Started as Righthander: Imagine What He Would Have Done to LF Fence," *Boston Globe,* August 14, 1958.
59. *Sports Illustrated,* August 21, 1967.
60. Interview with Bud Maloney, February 7, 2005.
61. Interview with Ben Press, May 21, 2006.
62. Williams with Underwood, *My Turn at Bat,* 21–22.
63. Linn, *Hitter,* 3.
64. Connor, *Baseball for the Love of It,* 21.
65. Williams with Underwood, *My Turn at Bat,* 25.
66. *Time* file.
67. Ibid.
68. Interview with Jerry Allen, July 30, 2007.
69. Nowlin, *The Kid,* 78.
70. Louis Lyons interview, *Boston Globe,* September 7, 1941.
71. *Baseball Digest,* September 1949.
72. Nowlin, *The Kid,* 56.
73. *Christian Science Monitor,* September 11, 1957.

74. Interview with Bill Skelley, January 21, 2005.
75. Williams with Underwood, *My Turn at Bat,* 33.
76. Interview with Bob Breitbard, October 23, 2002.
77. Interview with Jerry Allen, July 30, 2007.
78. Nowlin, *The Kid,* 237.
79. Ibid., 240.
80. Williams with Underwood, *My Turn at Bat,* 30.
81. Linn, *Hitter,* 34, and *Fresno Bee and Republican,* July 12, 1939.
82. Interview with Fred (Ponce) Canales, February 11, 2005.
83. Williams with Underwood, *My Turn at Bat,* 38.
84. Ibid., 31.
85. Interview with Steve Brown, November 12, 2004.
86. Interview with Les Cassie Jr., October 25, 2002.
87. Williams with Underwood, *My Turn at Bat,* 28.
88. Interview with Les Cassie Jr., October 25, 2002.
89. Linn, *Hitter,* 35.
90. Ibid.
91. *Time* file.
92. Williams with Underwood, *My Turn at Bat,* 27.
93. Society for American Baseball Research, *A History of San Diego Baseball.*
94. Williams with Underwood, *My Turn at Bat,* 30.
95. Interview with John Sullivan, January 7, 2003.
96. Nowlin, *The Kid,* 240.
97. Williams with Underwood, *My Turn at Bat,* 30.
98. Interview with Beverly Schultz, December 14, 2004.
99. Interview with Frank Cushing, October 25, 2002.
100. Interview with Joe Villarino, October 25, 2002.
101. Interview with John Cordero, February 10, 2005.
102. Williams with Underwood, *My Turn at Bat,* 31–32.
103. Linn, *Hitter,* 33.
104. Williams with Underwood, *My Turn at Bat,* 31 and 32.
105. Interview with Al Cassidy, October 9, 2002.
106. Nowlin, *The Kid,* 312.
107. Interview with Sam Williams, October 30, 2002.
108. Interview with John Theodore Williams, October 1, 2002.
109. *San Diego Tribune,* May 15, 1978.
110. *Boston Globe,* September 8, 1946.
111. Nowlin, *The Kid,* 92–94.
112. Williams with Underwood, *My Turn at Bat,* 33.
113. *Time* file.
114. *Boston Globe,* September 8, 1946.
115. Society for American Baseball Research, *A History of San Diego Baseball.*
116. Nowlin, *The Kid,* 55.
117. Williams with Underwood, *My Turn at Bat,* 21.
118. Prime and Nowlin, *Ted Williams,* 5.
119. Nowlin, *The Kid,* 77.
120. *Boston Evening American,* December 14, 1950, as cited in Prime and Nowlin, *Ted Williams,* 28.
121. Nowlin, *The Kid,* 63.
122. Ibid., 54.
123. Linn, *Hitter,* 40.
124. Nowlin, *The Kid,* 62.
125. Ibid., 80 and 81.
126. Prime and Nowlin, *Ted Williams,* 4.
127. *Boston Evening American,* July 14, 1941.
128. Williams with Underwood, *My Turn at Bat,* 34.
129. *San Diego Union,* May 31, 1936, as cited in Nowlin, *The Kid,* 118.
130. Nowlin, *The Kid,* 78.
131. Ibid., 82.
132. *San Diego Union,* February 23, 1935.
133. *San Diego Union,* July 6, 1980.
134. Linn, *Hitter,* 71.
135. Interview with Ray Boone, November 14, 2002.
136. Cataneo, *I Remember Ted Williams,* 12.

137. Williams with Underwood, *My Turn at Bat,* 37.
138. Interview with John Underwood, April 14, 2003.
139. Letter from Elmer Hill to Ernest J. Lanigan, November 24, 1957, on file at the National Baseball Hall of Fame, Cooperstown, New York.
140. Williams with Underwood, *My Turn at Bat,* 36.
141. Ibid., 39.
142. Ibid., 37.
143. Nowlin, *The Kid,* 83.
144. Williams with Underwood, *My Turn at Bat,* 39.
145. Ibid.

Chapter 2: "Fairyland"

1. Nowlin, *The Kid,* 82.
2. Interview with Autumn Durst Keltner, September 27, 2004.
3. *Boston Evening American,* July 15, 1941.
4. Bud Tuttle interview in Nowlin, *The Kid,* 85.
5. Nowlin, *The Kid,* 23.
6. Bill Swank newsletter, December 1999.
7. Williams with Underwood, *My Turn at Bat,* 40.
8. Ibid.
9. To Joe Cashman in *Boston Evening American,* July 16, 1941.
10. Williams with Underwood, *My Turn at Bat,* 40 and 41.
11. Interview with Bobby Doerr, October 14, 2002.
12. Halberstam, *Summer of '49,* 177.
13. Ed Linn's papers, provided to the author by Linn's daughter, Hildy Linn Angius.
14. Williams with Underwood, *My Turn at Bat,* 41.
15. *Time* file.
16. Ibid.
17. Prime and Nowlin, *Ted Williams,* 28.
18. *San Diego Tribune,* June 8, 1966.
19. Williams with Underwood, *My Turn at Bat,* 41.
20. Linn, *Hitter,* 53.
21. In return for one dollar and "other good and valuable considerations," Williams signed a contract with Hillerich & Bradsby on April 21, 1937, giving the company his trademark rights for twenty years in return for an unlimited supply of bats, paid for by his team. Jack Hillerich, who retired as the bat company's CEO in 2003, said Williams would be given new golf clubs annually as well as other sweeteners. "Whatever he wanted, he got."
22. Sampson, *Ted Williams,* 28.
23. Robinson, *Ted Williams,* 33.
24. Prime and Nowlin, *Ted Williams,* 14.
25. *Baseball Digest,* April 1950.
26. Associated Press, April 11, 1939.
27. *San Diego Evening Tribune,* May 4, 1937.
28. Swank, *Echoes from Lane Field,* 25.
29. Nowlin, *The Kid,* 123.
30. Ibid., 124.
31. *San Diego Union,* August 11, 1936.
32. *Boston Sunday Advertiser,* July 13, 1941.
33. *Time* file.
34. Interview with Johnny Pesky, October 7, 2002.
35. *Boston Sunday Advertiser,* July 13, 1941.
36. Hirshberg, *From Sandlots to League President,* 117.
37. Nowlin, *The Kid,* 124.
38. *San Diego Union,* October 5, 1941, as cited in Nowlin, *The Kid,* 91.
39. Nowlin, *The Kid,* 126.
40. Williams with Pietrusza, *Ted Williams: My Life in Pictures,* 17.
41. *Time* file.
42. *San Diego Tribune,* June 8, 1966.
43. Swank, *Echoes from Lane Field,* 26.
44. Nowlin, *The Kid,* 89 and 90.
45. *Boston Globe,* September 8, 1946.
46. Swank, *Echoes from Lane Field,* 19 and 20.
47. Ibid., 29.
48. *Boston Globe,* August 13, 1948.
49. *Baseball Digest,* July 1948.
50. *San Diego Evening Tribune,* January 7, 1937.
51. *Boston Daily Record,* February 19, 1948.
52. Interview with Dominic DiMaggio, October 2, 2002.

53. Williams with Underwood, *My Turn at Bat*, 42 and 43.
54. *Boston Evening American*, July 16, 1941.
55. Bill Swank, "Ted Williams, Earl Keller, and the 1937 San Diego Padres," 2003 research paper, 16, 17, and 23.
56. *Boston Globe*, September 8, 1946.
57. *San Diego Evening Tribune*, September 1, 1937, as cited in Swank, "Ted Williams," 23.
58. *San Diego Evening Tribune*, September 2, 1937, as cited in Swank, "Ted Williams," 23.
59. *Boston Globe*, December 7, 1937.
60. *Collegiate Baseball*, April 7, 1995.
61. Sampson, *Ted Williams*, 13–20.
62. *Christian Science Monitor*, August 11, 1958.
63. *Boston Globe*, March 26, 1954.
64. *Boston Evening American*, July 17, 1941.
65. *San Diego Evening Tribune*, December 8, 1937, as cited in Swank, "Ted Williams," 27.
66. Williams with Underwood, *My Turn at Bat*, 43.
67. Ibid.
68. *Boston Evening American*, July 18, 1941.
69. *Boston Sunday Advertiser*, February 28, 1948.
70. *San Diego Evening Tribune*, February 16, 1938, as cited in Nowlin, *The Kid*, 158 and 159.
71. Eddie Collins confirmed to Boston columnist Austen Lake in the February 28, 1938, *Evening American* that he had settled the dispute by giving Sam and May $2,500. "My purpose in visiting the Coast was to settle the Ted Williams affair," Collins told Lake. "His parents felt they were entitled to part of his purchase price. I handed them a check for $2,500 and it tickled their hearts."

Chapter 3: Sarasota and Minneapolis

1. Interview with Bobby Doerr, October 14, 2002.
2. Williams with Underwood, *My Turn at Bat*, 45.
3. *Boston Evening American*, March 21, 1960.
4. *Boston Herald*, March 10, 1938.
5. Linn, *Hitter*, 79.
6. *Boston Herald*, March 10, 1938.
7. *Collier's*, June 24, 1939.
8. *Boston Post*, March 10, 1938.
9. *Boston Evening American*, March 14, 1938.
10. Associated Press, March 18, 1938.
11. *Boston Post*, March 12, 1938.
12. Harold Kaese notes, the Harold Kaese Collection of the Boston Public Library. (Kaese was the leading Boston baseball writer of his era and covered Williams for the *Boston Transcript* and *Boston Globe* from 1938 to 1960 and beyond.)
13. Interview with Bobby Doerr, October 14, 2002.
14. *Boston Herald*, January 24, 1959.
15. Golenbock, *Fenway*, 116.
16. Williams with Underwood, *My Turn at Bat*, 47.
17. Ibid.
18. *Boston Evening American*, March 21, 1960.
19. Golenbock, *Fenway*, 118.
20. *Boston Traveler*, August 16, 1938.
21. *Minneapolis Journal*, March 21, 1938.
22. *Minneapolis Star*, March 24, 1938, as cited in Nowlin, *The Kid*, 165.
23. *Minneapolis Journal*, March 25, 1938.
24. Jocko Conlan and Robert W. Creamer, *Jocko* (Philadelphia: J. B. Lippincott, 1967), as cited in Prime and Nowlin, *Ted Williams*, 22.
25. *Boston Globe*, December 7, 1959.
26. *Minneapolis Star*, March 29, 1938.
27. *Minneapolis Journal*, April 3, 1938.
28. *Minneapolis Star*, April 11, 1938.
29. Williams with Underwood, *My Turn at Bat*, 52 and 53.
30. *San Diego Sun*, May 5, 1938.
31. Seidel, *Ted Williams*, 36.
32. *Minneapolis Tribune* and *Minneapolis Journal*, April 22, 1938.
33. Thornley, *On to Nicollet*, 69 and 70.
34. *Minneapolis Journal*, April 30, 1938.
35. Ibid.

36. Interview with Sid Hartman, June 3, 2005.
37. *Minneapolis Star,* May 10, 1938.
38. Williams with Underwood, *My Turn at Bat,* 53 and 54.
39. Interview with Jack Bean, September 22, 2005.
40. Prime and Nowlin, *Ted Williams,* 25.
41. Interview with Jim Kallas, January 24, 2003.
42. *Princeton Union-Eagle,* July 11, 2002.
43. Interview with Frank Weisbrod, July 16, 2004.
44. Dennis Tuttle, "Still Slingin': The Sammy Baugh Story," unpublished manuscript, as cited in Prime and Nowlin, *Ted Williams,* 20 and 21.
45. *Boston Evening American,* March 8, 1939.
46. Interview with Bill "Lefty" LeFebvre, November 12, 2002.
47. Williams with Underwood, *My Turn at Bat,* 49.
48. Golenbock, *Fenway,* 121.
49. Johnson and Stout, *Ted Williams,* 15.
50. Williams with Underwood, *My Turn at Bat,* 48.
51. Undated 1955 Sid Hartman column in the *Minneapolis Tribune;* and the *Boston Globe,* June 8, 1955.
52. *Minneapolis Journal,* September 5, 1938.
53. Linn, *Hitter,* 91.
54. Williams with Underwood, *My Turn at Bat,* 49–50.
55. Ibid., 50.
56. Ibid., 49.
57. *Boston Globe,* December 7, 1959.
58. *Minneapolis Morning Tribune,* January 29, 1958.
59. Unpublished interview with Donie Bush by *Time*'s Ed Ogle, March 27, 1950.
60. Linn, *Hitter,* 92.
61. Williams with Underwood, *My Turn at Bat,* 55.
62. Ibid., 55 and 56.
63. Nowlin, *The Kid,* 180.
64. Linn, *Hitter,* 92 and 93.
65. Interview with Bill "Lefty" LeFebvre, November 12, 2002.
66. Linn, *Hitter,* 92 and 93.
67. Undated 1955 Sid Hartman column in the *Minneapolis Tribune.*

Chapter 4: Big Time

1. *Boston Herald,* March 8, 1939.
2. Ibid.
3. *Boston Post,* March 7, 1939.
4. *Boston Evening American,* April 14, 1939.
5. *Boston Evening American,* March 8, 1939.
6. Harold Kaese notes, the Harold Kaese Collection of the Boston Public Library.
7. Unpublicized Cramer–Williams brawl. The Cramer–Williams fight was witnessed by the late Charles Caliri, then a Boston high school baseball standout who was attending a tryout staged by the Red Sox for local prospects. As related in an interview with Caliri's brother, Victor Caliri, on September 12, 2007.
8. *Boston Globe,* March 10, 1939.
9. *Boston Daily Record,* March 15, 1939.
10. Dawidoff, *The Catcher Was a Spy,* 119.
11. Ibid., 98 and 105.
12. *Boston Transcript,* March 22, 1939.
13. Associated Press, July 13, 1939.
14. *Boston Evening American,* March 22, 1960.
15. *Boston Globe,* April 2, 1939.
16. *Boston Globe,* April 3, 1939.
17. Williams with Underwood, *My Turn at Bat,* 60.
18. Interview with Phil Wilkinson, March 2, 2005.
19. Interview with Bettye Roberts, October 29, 2005.
20. Interview with George B. Daniels, November 1, 2005.
21. *Boston Globe,* April 6, 1989.
22. Interview with John Harrington, April 7, 2005.
23. Interview with Ralph Ford Jr., November 1, 2005. (Ford died on February 7, 2008.)
24. Interview with John Harrington, April 7, 2005.

25. Interview with Wallace Hampton Lawrimore, November 7, 2005. (Lawrimore died on May 4, 2009.)

26. Williams with Underwood, *My Turn at Bat,* 60 and 61.

27. Undated Williams interview with Dick Hackenberg of the *Minneapolis Star,* the winter after the 1939 season.

28. Williams with Underwood, *My Turn at Bat,* 61.

29. *Boston Globe,* April 22, 1939.

30. *Boston Herald,* April 23, 1939.

31. *Boston Evening American,* April 27, 1939.

32. Interview with Elden Auker, July 14, 2005.

33. Williams with Underwood, *My Turn at Bat,* 75.

34. Ibid.

35. Ibid., 76 and 77.

36. *Time* files.

37. Williams with Underwood, *My Turn at Bat,* 76.

38. *Time* files.

39. Williams with Underwood, *My Turn at Bat,* 76.

40. *Boston Evening American,* March 28, 1960.

41. *Boston Globe,* May 2, 1939.

42. Williams with Underwood, *My Turn at Bat,* 63.

43. Ibid., 64.

44. *Boston Globe,* May 4 and 5, 1939.

45. Blake, *Baseball Chronicles,* 66 and 67.

46. Connor, *Baseball for the Love of It,* 142.

47. *Boston Globe,* May 31, 1939.

48. Undated Williams interview with Dick Hackenberg of the *Minneapolis Star.*

49. *Boston Evening American,* March 25, 1960.

50. Harry Grayson, NEA Service sports editor, in the *San Diego Sun,* July 24, 1939.

51. *Boston Sunday Advertiser,* July 23, 1939.

52. *Boston Globe,* July 19, 1939.

53. *Boston Globe,* July 7, 1939.

54. *Boston Sunday Advertiser,* July 23, 1939.

55. *Boston Daily Record,* August 4, 1939.

56. *Boston Daily Record,* May 22, 1939.

57. *Boston Daily Record,* July 31, 1939.

58. Associated Press, August 8, 1939.

59. *Boston Daily Record,* August 9, 1939.

60. *Boston Globe,* August 10, 1939.

61. *Boston Globe,* August 15, 1939.

62. *Boston Evening American,* July 21, 1939.

63. *Boston Globe,* August 30, 1939.

64. Williams with Underwood, *My Turn at Bat,* 65.

Chapter 5: The Writers

1. *Boston Globe,* February 2, 1940, as cited in Seidel, *Ted Williams,* 64.

2. *Boston Sunday Advertiser,* February 4, 1940.

3. *Boston Sunday Advertiser,* April 14, 1940.

4. Dave Egan, "Ted Williams Gets Spanked," *Boston Sunday Advertiser's Green* magazine, August 18, 1940.

5. *Boston Evening Transcript,* May 22, 1940.

6. *Boston Globe,* May 21, 1940.

7. *Boston Evening Transcript,* May 22, 1940.

8. Linn, *Hitter,* 121.

9. *Boston Daily Record,* June 4, 1940.

10. *Boston Evening American,* August 13, 1940.

11. *Boston Daily Record,* August 14, 1940.

12. *Boston Globe,* August 14, 1940.

13. Seidel, *Ted Williams,* 79–80.

14. *Esquire,* June 1986.

15. Associated Press, August 20, 1940.

16. *Boston Globe,* September 5, 1940.

17. Williams with Underwood, *My Turn at Bat,* 80–81.

18. Johnson and Stout, *Ted Williams,* 39.

19. Holtzman, *No Cheering in the Press Box,* 16.

20. Halberstam, *Summer of '49,* 110.

21. Interview with Tim Horgan, October 5, 2005.

22. Hirshberg, *What's the Matter with the Red Sox?,* 123 and 124.

23. Kemmerer, *Hey Kid,* 46.

24. Interview with Tim Horgan, October 5, 2005, and interview with Bob Monahan, October 7, 2005.

25. Hirshberg, *What's the Matter with the Red Sox?,* 134.

26. Ibid., 23.
27. Ibid., 24 and 25.
28. Ibid., 134.
29. Interview with Don Buddin, September 24, 2003.
30. *Boston Globe,* May 22, 1958.
31. Interview with Larry Corea, January 12, 2006.
32. Interview with Curt Gowdy, October 24, 2002.
33. Interview with George Sullivan, April 27, 2005.
34. Interview with Tex Clevenger, September 25, 2003.
35. Interview with Jimmy Piersall, July 16, 2004.
36. Interview with Charlie Maxwell, June 25, 2003.
37. Linn, *Hitter,* 16 and 134.
38. *Sport,* January 1958.
39. Interview with James Carroll, February 3, 2005.
40. Interview with Jim Cleary, October 7, 2003.
41. McDermott with Eisenberg, *A Funny Thing Happened,* 64–65.
42. Ibid., 92.
43. *Boston Sunday Advertiser,* August 12, 1956.
44. *Boston Globe,* June 11, 1964.
45. Interview with Elden Auker, July 14, 2005.
46. Golenbock, *Fenway,* 129.
47. Hirshberg, *What's the Matter with the Red Sox?,* 18.
48. *Boston Globe,* April 30, 2003.
49. Ibid.
50. *Sports Illustrated,* October 3, 1966.
51. *Boston Globe,* February 1, 1955.
52. Interview with Brian Cashman, Joe Cashman's grandson, October 19, 2005.
53. Cataneo, *I Remember Ted Williams,* 157.
54. Interview with Phil Elderkin, January 18, 2007.
55. Interview with Bob Ajemian, August 8, 2002.
56. Interview with Bud Collins, May 1, 2003.

Chapter 6: .406

1. Interview with Jim Kallas, July 15, 2004.
2. *Boston Evening American,* May 23, 1942.
3. Interview with Donald Soule, March 11, 2003.
4. Interview with Ramona Mitchell, September 9, 2004.
5. Interview with Jean Holetz, July 28, 2004.
6. Interview with Bobby-Jo Williams Ferrell, March 11, 2003.
7. Associated Press, January 23, 1941.
8. Vince Orlando interview in 1967 by the late *Boston Globe* columnist Will McDonough. (McDonough, then a young reporter, was retained by *Miami Herald* columnist Edwin Pope that year to help him conduct research for a book on the 1941 season of Ted Williams. Besides Vince Orlando, McDonough interviewed a variety of other people, including Johnny Orlando, Joe Cronin, Tom Yawkey, Ted Lepcio, and Williams's roommate, Charlie Wagner. The book was aborted, but copies of McDonough's interviews were among Williams's papers made available to the author by his daughter, Claudia. Some of the interviews first appeared in Montville, *Ted Williams*—after Montville obtained them from Pope.)
9. *Boston Daily Record,* March 12, 1941.
10. *Boston Sunday Advertiser,* March 16, 1941.
11. *Boston Evening Transcript,* February 26, 1941.
12. *Boston Daily Record,* March 23, 1941.
13. *Boston Daily Record,* April 1, 1941.
14. *Boston Evening Transcript,* March 25, 1941.
15. Vince Orlando interview, Will McDonough 1967 interviews.
16. *Boston Globe,* April 8, 1941.
17. Williams with Underwood, *My Turn at Bat,* 84–85.
18. *Boston Globe,* June 24, 1941.

19. Associated Press, June 8, 1941.
20. *Boston Globe,* July 1, 1941.
21. Vaccaro, *1941,* 222.
22. *Sporting News,* July 17, 1941.
23. Prime and Nowlin, *Ted Williams,* 40. (Slaughter kept the ball for forty-four years until he was inducted into the Hall of Fame in 1985, whereupon he presented it to Williams, who signed the ball and left it at Cooperstown.)
24. Williams with Underwood, *My Turn at Bat,* 89 and 87.
25. *Boston Herald* and *Boston Daily Record,* July 9, 1941.
26. DiMaggio with Gilbert, *Real Grass, Real Heroes,* 51.
27. Ibid., 86 and 87.
28. Ibid., 87 and 88.
29. Ibid., 136.
30. Will McDonough 1967 interviews.
31. Vaccaro, *1941,* 231.
32. Ibid., 239.
33. *Boston Globe,* September 7, 1941.
34. Vaccaro, *1941,* 241.
35. *Boston Daily Record* and *Boston Post,* September 17, 1941.
36. *Boston Herald,* September 23, 1941.
37. Holway, *Ted Williams,* 268.
38. *Boston Globe,* September 26, 1941.
39. *Boston Herald,* September 26, 1941.
40. Johnny Orlando interview, Will McDonough 1967 interviews.
41. Williams with Underwood, *My Turn at Bat,* 87.
42. Charlie Wagner interview, Will McDonough 1967 interviews.
43. Harrington E. Crissey Jr., "The Splendid Splinter's Splendid Finish," paper in the *Phillies Report,* May 23, 1991.
44. Interview with Fred Caligiuri, September 19, 2003.
45. Linn, *Hitter,* 161.
46. Williams with Underwood, *My Turn at Bat,* 90.
47. Will McDonough 1967 interviews.
48. *Boston Herald,* September 29, 1941.
49. *Boston Post,* September 29, 1941.
50. *Boston Globe,* September 29, 1941.
51. Johnny Orlando interview, Will McDonough 1967 interviews.
52. Interview with Charlie Wagner, October 21, 2002.
53. *Boston Globe,* September 29, 1941.
54. *Philadelphia Evening Bulletin,* September 29, 1941, as cited in Crissey Jr., "The Splendid Splinter's Splendid Finish."
55. Williams with Underwood, *My Turn at Bat,* 83.
56. Holway, *Ted Williams,* 303.
57. Stephen Jay Gould, "Achieving the Impossible Dream: Ted Williams and .406," as cited in Johnson and Stout, *Ted Williams,* 70.
58. *Time* files.
59. Nowlin, *The Kid,* 184.

Chapter 7: 3A

1. Williams with Underwood, *My Turn at Bat,* 97.
2. *Boston Daily Record,* January 6, 1942.
3. United Press International, February 27, 1942.
4. *Boston Globe,* February 28, 1942. (Eddie Collins told Harold Kaese that Williams gave him the news on January 28.)
5. *Boston Globe,* March 11, 1942.
6. *Boston Post,* March 1, 1942.
7. *Boston Daily Record,* February 7, 1942.
8. *Boston Daily Record,* February 23, 1942.
9. Seidel, *Ted Williams,* 108 and 111.
10. Williams with Underwood, *My Turn at Bat,* 98.
11. *Boston Globe,* February 28, 1942.
12. *Boston Daily Record,* February 28, 1942, as cited in Nowlin, *Ted Williams at War,* 22.
13. *Boston Sunday Advertiser* and *Boston Herald,* March 1, 1942.
14. Seidel, *Ted Williams,* 118.
15. *Boston Post,* March 1, 1942.
16. Associated Press, March 3, 1942.
17. *Boston Daily Record,* March 1 and 2, 1942.
18. Seidel, *Ted Williams,* 118.
19. Williams with Underwood, *My Turn at Bat,* 98–99.

20. Seidel, *Ted Williams*, 114.
21. Ibid., 112.
22. *Boston Herald*, March 10, 1942.
23. Seidel, *Ted Williams*, 119.
24. *Boston Globe, Boston Herald, Boston Post*, and *Boston Daily Record*, March 11, 1942.
25. *Sarasota Tribune*, February 23, 2012.
26. *Boston Evening American*, March 22, 1942.
27. Williams with Pietrusza, *Ted Williams: My Life in Pictures*, 49.
28. *Boston Globe*, April 13, 1942.
29. *Boston Daily Record*, April 16, 1942.
30. Seidel, *Ted Williams*, 122.
31. Ibid., 124.
32. *Boston Evening American*, March 25, 1960.
33. *Boston Globe*, May 12, 1942.
34. *Boston Evening American*, May 23, 1942.
35. *Boston Daily Record*, May 23, 1942.
36. *Boston Globe* and *Boston Traveler*, May 23, 1942.
37. *Boston Globe*, July 13, 1942.
38. Seidel, *Ted Williams*, 126.
39. *Boston Herald*, July 2, 1942.
40. *Boston Daily Record*, July 2, 1942.
41. *Boston Globe*, November 3, 1942.
42. *New York Times*, March 30, 2012.

Chapter 8: World War II

1. *Boston Traveler*, November 17, 1942.
2. *Boston Daily Record*, December 1, 1942.
3. *Boston Globe*, December 21, 1942.
4. Williams with Underwood, *My Turn at Bat*, 101.
5. Ibid., 100.
6. *Sporting News*, December 10, 1942.
7. *Boston Globe*, December 5, 1942.
8. *Boston Evening American*, January 11, 1952.
9. Williams with Underwood, *My Turn at Bat*, 100.
10. Interview with George H. W. Bush, March 3, 2006.
11. *Boston Evening American*, January 11, 1952.
12. *Boston Globe*, July 11, 1943.
13. *Boston Globe* and *Boston Sunday Advertiser*, July 11, 1943.

14. *Boston Globe, Boston Daily Record*, and *Boston Traveler*, July 13, 1943, and Dick Flavin, "The Day Ted and Babe Squared Off," article for a Red Sox program, summer 2000.
15. Crissey Jr., *Athletes Away*, 29 and 30.
16. *Boston Post*, July 31, 1943.
17. Interview with Johnny Pesky, October 7, 2002.
18. Williams with Underwood, *My Turn at Bat*, 100–1.
19. *Boston Globe*, December 14, 1943.
20. Williams with Underwood, *My Turn at Bat*, 101–2.
21. Interview with Johnny Pesky, October 7, 2002.
22. Williams with Underwood, *My Turn at Bat*, 101.
23. *Boston Evening American*, January 11, 1952.
24. *Boston Herald*, May 26, 1997.
25. *Boston Evening American*, January 11, 1952.
26. *Boston Evening American*, January 10, 1944.
27. *Boston Evening American*, March 1, 1944.
28. *Boston Evening American*, January 13, 1944.
29. *Boston Evening American*, January 16, 1944.
30. *Boston Evening American*, January 19, 1944.
31. Hynes, *Flights of Passage*, 67–69.
32. Interview with Dick Francisco, December 21, 2004.
33. Interview with Hill Goodspeed, April 20, 2006.
34. *Boston Globe*, April 18, 1953.
35. *Boston Post*, February 25, 1955.
36. Williams with Underwood, *My Turn at Bat*, 104.
37. Interview with Kenneth Carroll, December 8, 2004.
38. Interview with John Holland, April 19, 2006.
39. Williams with Underwood, *My Turn at Bat*, 103.
40. Interview with Bob Kennedy, April 28, 2004.

41. Interview with Len Poth, July 7, 2004.
42. Interview with Frank Maznicki, April 14, 2004.
43. *Boston Evening American,* January 11, 1952.
44. McDermott with Eisenberg, *A Funny Thing Happened,* 218.
45. *Boston Globe,* March 25, 1952.
46. Williams with Underwood, *My Turn at Bat,* 104.
47. Interview with Jimmy Dunn, January 10, 2006.
48. *Baseball Digest,* April 1946.

Chapter 9: 1946

1. *Boston Globe,* January 28, 1946.
2. *Sporting News,* March 14, 1946.
3. *Time,* April 10, 1946, as cited in Seidel, *Ted Williams,* 146.
4. *Boston Evening American,* April 1, 1946.
5. Seidel, *Ted Williams,* 145.
6. *Boston Globe,* April 7, 1946.
7. Turner, *When the Boys Came Back,* 54.
8. *Boston Globe,* March 9, 1946.
9. Corcoran with Harvey, *Unplayable Lies,* 125–26.
10. *Boston Evening American,* April 17, 1946.
11. *Boston Evening American,* April 29, 1946.
12. *Boston Daily Record,* May 13, 1946.
13. Honig, *Baseball When the Grass Was Real,* 255.
14. Turner, *When the Boys Came Back,* 167.
15. *New York Times,* July 10, 1946.
16. Honig, *Baseball When the Grass Was Real,* 257.
17. *Boston Globe,* July 10, 1946.
18. *Boston Herald,* July 15, 1946.
19. Williams with Underwood, *My Turn at Bat,* 107.
20. Hirshberg, *From Sandlots to League President,* 158.
21. *Boston Globe,* September 8, 1946.
22. Williams with Underwood, *My Turn at Bat,* 108.
23. Dunne, *Play Ball!,* 5–8.
24. Ibid., 95.
25. Ibid., 91–94.
26. *New York Times,* October 31, 1946.
27. Dunne, *Play Ball!,* 266.
28. Turner, *When the Boys Came Back,* 199.
29. Williams with Underwood, *My Turn at Bat,* 109.
30. *Detroit Free Press,* May 24, 2005.
31. *Time,* September 15, 1947.
32. Associated Press, December 30, 1947.
33. Einstein, *The Fireside Book of Baseball,* 385.
34. *Life,* September 23, 1946.
35. Williams with Underwood, *My Turn at Bat,* 111.
36. Linn, *Hitter,* 222.
37. Ibid., 214.
38. *Boston Globe,* October 4, 1946.
39. *Boston Daily Record,* October 4, 1946.
40. *Boston Globe,* October 4, 1946.
41. *Boston Globe,* October 6, 1946.
42. *Boston Evening American,* October 5, 1946.
43. *Boston Globe,* October 6, 1946.
44. *Boston Globe,* October 5, 1946.
45. Interview with Joe Garagiola, April 9, 2004.
46. *Boston Evening American,* October 8, 1946.
47. Corcoran with Harvey, *Unplayable Lies,* 135.
48. *Boston Evening American,* October 10, 1946.
49. Robinson, *Ted Williams,* 168.
50. *Boston Globe,* October 12, 1946.
51. *Boston Evening American,* October 14, 1946.
52. *Boston Globe,* October 13, 1946.
53. *Boston Globe,* October 14, 1946.
54. Ibid.
55. *Boston Globe,* October 15, 1946.
56. Associated Press, October 15, 1946.
57. *Sport,* July 1952, and Williams with Underwood, *My Turn at Bat,* 116. (Rice or the unnamed writer told the dinner-with-Williams story to *New York Journal-American* columnist Frank Graham, who wrote about it in the July 1952 issue of *Sport.* Williams also tells of the dinner in his book.)
58. *Boston Evening American,* October 15, 1946.

59. Interview with Dominic DiMaggio, October 2, 2002.
60. *Boston Globe,* October 16, 1946.
61. Ibid.
62. Ibid.
63. *Boston Evening American,* March 29, 1960.
64. *Boston Post,* October 16, 1946.
65. Williams with Underwood, *My Turn at Bat,* 118.
66. Ibid., 105.

Chapter 10: 1947–1948

1. Williams with Underwood, *My Turn at Bat,* 122.
2. Seidel, *Ted Williams,* 169.
3. *Sport,* February 1947.
4. Williams with Underwood, *My Turn at Bat,* 122.
5. Nowlin and others, *Ted Williams: A Splendid Life,* 31.
6. Prime and Nowlin, *Ted Williams,* 240.
7. Williams with Underwood, *My Turn at Bat,* 18.
8. Interview with Buck O'Neil, July 15, 2004.
9. *Boston Daily Record,* April 16, 1945, as cited in Stout, "Tryout and Fallout."
10. Interview with John Harrington, May 21, 2003.
11. *Boston Globe,* September 3, 1971.
12. Writer Marc Onigman was apparently the first to disclose the race section of the report as part of an article on Yawkey in the August 9, 1980, edition of Boston's now-defunct *Real Paper,* an alternative weekly.
13. Interview with George Digby, October 7, 2005.
14. Bryant, *Shut Out,* 1.
15. Article by Jim Bouton for the *Boston Globe,* October 8, 2003.
16. Interview with Pumpsie Green, July 16, 2004.
17. Interview with Curt Gowdy, October 24, 2002.
18. Interview with Larry Taylor, April 29, 2004.
19. *New York Times,* December 18, 1980.
20. Johnson and Stout, *Ted Williams,* 94.
21. *Boston Traveler,* October 3, 1947.
22. *Boston Traveler,* June 2, 1946.
23. *Boston Globe,* January 7, 1948.
24. *Boston Globe,* January 29, 1948.
25. Harold Kaese notes, the Harold Kaese Collection of the Boston Public Library.
26. *Boston Globe,* February 2, 1948.
27. *Boston Traveler,* February 3, 1948.
28. Stout and Johnson, *Red Sox Century,* 261.
29. *Boston Herald,* February 3, 1948.
30. McNaught Syndicate, February 9, 1948.
31. Williams with Underwood, *My Turn at Bat,*161.
32. *Boston Globe,* March 10, 1948.
33. Stout and Johnson, *Red Sox Century,* 263.
34. Tommy Byrne interview with David Halberstam for *Summer of '49,* provided to the author by Halberstam. (Like Byrne, Berra himself enjoyed trying to distract Ted by doing things like flipping pebbles at his feet.)
35. Stout and Johnson, *Red Sox Century,* 263.
36. Interview with Mel Parnell, October 16, 2002.
37. Williams with Underwood, *My Turn at Bat,* 153.
38. Johnson and Stout, *Ted Williams,* 103.
39. Interview with Jack Hillerich, August 29, 2005. (Williams had mostly been using the same bat since 1941, but it took him a few years to find the right model. When he was a rookie in 1939, he'd tried several bats, including Joe Cronin's, Jimmie Foxx's, and Joe Vosmik's. He liked Cronin's the best and stayed with that. Then, in the spring of 1941, Ted had Hillerich & Bradsby change the Cronin model for him by enlarging the barrel and modifying the handle slightly. That was the year he hit .406, and he basically stayed with that same bat through the 1946 season.

Ted did not have his own model Louisville Slugger until 1947. This was because the company changed how it kept records starting that year. Previously, they would record orders by assigning a new design to the name of the player who first used it, and then would record all orders similar to it as "same as [the player's name]" with any modifications following. Then, in 1947, a letter-and-number system was originated. So Williams's own bats were designated as the W148 [1947 and 1948], the W155 [1948–1950], the W166 [1950–1955], and the W183 [1955–1960].

In the late fifties, it was Ted who first concocted a combination of resin and oil to help grip the bat, replacing tape on the handles. Other players followed suit, but they would usually let the sticky substance stay on the handle for a week before scrubbing it off. Ted cleaned his bats with alcohol every night.)

40. Halberstam, *Summer of '49*, 190.
41. Williams with Underwood, *My Turn at Bat*, 56.
42. Johnson and Stout, *Ted Williams*, 170.
43. Interviews with David Pressman on June 12, 2005; June 20, 2012; June 21, 2012; June 27, 2012; July 2, 2012; and July 3, 2012. (Pressman first told writer Bill Nowlin that Ted put his bats in a dryer for Nowlin's 2002 oral history on Williams, coauthored with Jim Prime, *Ted Williams: The Pursuit of Perfection*. The 2002 book, in which various people gave their remembrances of Ted, was essentially the same as Nowlin and Prime's 1997 oral history, *Ted Williams: A Tribute*, with some new interviews, including Pressman's.)
44. Johnny Pesky was interviewed on the heated bats issue on June 25, 2012, through his son, David, who reported that his father, then ninety-two and in failing health, could no longer be formally interviewed but did clearly recall Ted heating his bats in the clubhouse dryer. David Pressman said that he asked Pesky about the issue in the 1980s and that the former Red Sox shortstop confirmed Williams's practice to him at that time. (Pesky died on August 13, 2012.)
45. Interview with Bobby Doerr, June 24, 2012.
46. Interview with Jimmy Piersall, June 25, 2012.
47. Interview with Alan Nathan, July 2, 2012.
48. Interview with Patrick Drane, June 25, 2012.
49. Alan Nathan said in a July 5, 2012, e-mail that he had combined data on the initial speed and angles of the ball coming off the bat with data from the Hittracker.com website, which uses the measured landing point and flight time of home runs, along with an aerodynamics model, to find a batted ball's speed through reverse engineering.

Chapter 11: 1949–1951

1. Stout and Johnson, *Red Sox Century*, 267.
2. *True*, November 1954.
3. Halberstam, *Summer of '49*, 227.
4. Ibid.
5. McDermott with Eisenberg, *A Funny Thing Happened*, 28.
6. Ibid., 34.
7. Ibid., 220 and 221.
8. Halberstam, *Summer of '49* (notes for the book given to the author by Halberstam).
9. Ibid.
10. Stout and Johnson, *Red Sox Century*, 270.
11. Williams with Underwood, *My Turn at Bat*, 159.
12. *Boston Evening American*, March 9, 1950.
13. *Time* files.
14. Johnson and Stout, *Ted Williams*, 108.
15. Hirshberg, *What's the Matter with the Red Sox?*, 9 and 132–33.
16. Stout and Johnson, *Red Sox Century*, 276.

17. Golenbock, *Fenway,* 190.
18. Johnson and Stout, *Ted Williams,* 109.
19. *Boston Evening American,* May 12, 1950.
20. Stout and Johnson, *Red Sox Century,* 277.
21. Pope, *Ted Williams,* 62.
22. *Boston Globe,* June 20, 1950.
23. *Boston Globe,* June 26, 1950.
24. Linn, *Hitter,* 234.
25. Williams with Underwood, *My Turn at Bat,* 167.
26. Golenbock, *Fenway,* 190.
27. *Boston Daily Record,* August 22, 1950.
28. *Boston Daily Record,* August 30, 1950.
29. *Boston Daily Record,* September 8, 1950.
30. *Boston Globe,* September 8, 1950.
31. Seidel, *Ted Williams,* 224.
32. Williams with Underwood, *My Turn at Bat,* 169.
33. Harold Kaese notes, the Harold Kaese Collection of the Boston Public Library.
34. Johnson and Stout, *Ted Williams,* 113.

Chapter 12: Ted and Joe

1. *New York Times,* December 12, 1951.
2. Roy Blount Jr., "Legend: How DiMaggio Made It Look Easy," in Okrent and Lewine, *The Ultimate Baseball Book,* 206.
3. *Washington Post,* July 6, 2002.
4. George Vecsey, "The Clipper and the Kid," in Baseball Writers of the *New York Times* and the *Boston Globe, The Rivals,* 92.
5. Interview with Eddie Pellagrini, October 22, 2002.
6. Interview with Johnny Pesky, October 7, 2002.
7. Johnson and Stout, *DiMaggio,* 166.
8. Halberstam, *Summer of '49,* 175.
9. Golenbock, *Fenway,* 243.
10. Associated Press, March 18, 1938.
11. *Boston Herald,* November 11, 1988.
12. Gay Talese, "The Silent Season of a Hero," *Esquire,* July 1966.

13. Williams with Prime, *Ted Williams' Hit List,* 77.
14. *Boston Herald,* November 11, 1988.
15. Halberstam, *The Teammates,* 48.
16. *New York World Telegram,* August 11, 1949.
17. Engelberg and Schneider, *DiMaggio,* 94.
18. Interview with Al Cassidy, October 9, 2002.
19. Interview with Dan Wheeler, February 3, 2005.
20. Interview with Jonathan Gallen, May 16, 2005.
21. Interview with Jerry Romolt, July 21, 2004.
22. Interview with David D'Alessandro, February 12, 2004.
23. Interview with David D'Alessandro, May 6, 2010.
24. Interview with Dr. Rock Positano, October 4, 2002.
25. Interview with Alex Sanders, September 29, 2004.

Chapter 13: Korea

1. *Boston Evening American,* December 21, 1951.
2. *Boston Evening American,* January 13, 1952.
3. *Boston Evening American,* October 22, 1951.
4. Interview with Dominic DiMaggio, October 2, 2002.
5. *Boston Daily Record,* January 11, 1952.
6. Ibid.
7. *Boston Daily Record,* January 12, 1952.
8. Giusti, "Mobilization of the Marine Corps Reserve," 41.
9. Ibid., 42.
10. Interview with Maureen Cronin, May 27, 2003, and March 16, 2005.
11. Williams with Underwood, *My Turn at Bat,* 174.
12. Interview with Ted Lepcio, August 20, 2003.
13. Courtesy of Claudia Williams.
14. *Boston Globe,* March 14, 1956.
15. *Boston Globe,* April 1, 1957.
16. *Boston Record-American,* April 2, 1957.

17. Ibid.
18. Associated Press, March 1, 1952.
19. Dillman, *Hey Kid!*, 60–62.
20. Interview with Danny Dillman, August 8, 2007.
21. Associated Press, February 8, 1954.
22. Joe Bastarache, a friend and neighbor of Evelyn Turner's in Blowing Rock, North Carolina, made copies of the letters Ted wrote to Turner available to the author. Most were written from Korea.
23. Interview with Joe Bastarache, October 28, 2003.
24. Interview with Albert Christiano, March 14, 2006.
25. Turner's manuscript was made available to the author by her guardian, Joe Bastarache.
26. *New York Times* and *Boston Herald,* April 3, 1952.
27. *Boston Daily Record,* May 1, 1952.
28. Cataneo, *Peanuts and Crackerjack,* 98.
29. *Boston Herald,* May 1, 1952.
30. Interview with Ken Wood, September 24, 2003.
31. *Boston Traveler,* May 1, 1952.
32. Interview with Raymond Sisk, July 6, 2004.
33. Interview with Bill Churchman, May 11, 2004.
34. *Boston Globe,* May 26, 1952.
35. Interview with Tom Ross, June 29, 2004.
36. Interview with Hoyle Barr, December 14, 2004.
37. Interview with Robert Ferris, December 9, 2004.
38. Interview with Irv Beck, July 8, 2004.
39. Letter from Ted Williams to Evelyn Turner, November 21, 1952.
40. Associated Press, March 26, 1953.
41. *Miami Herald,* December 27, 1952.
42. Williams with Underwood, *My Turn at Bat,* 178.
43. Interview with Dick Francisco, December 21, 2004.
44. Sambito, "A History of Marine Attack Squadron 311," 14 and 25.
45. Scripps Howard in the *Boston Herald,* June 28, 1953.
46. Glenn with Taylor, *John Glenn,* 131.
47. Interview with Marvin Hollenbeck, July 8, 2005.
48. Interview with Larry Hawkins, June 29, 2004.
49. David Truby interview with Ted Williams, June 28, 2006. (Truby interviewed Williams about the crash landing and his service in Korea for an August 2006 article in the aviation adventure magazine *Flight Journal.*)
50. Interview with Woody Woodbury, July 9, 2004.
51. Williams with Underwood, *My Turn at Bat,* 180.
52. Interview with Frank Venzor, November 20, 2002.
53. Williams with Underwood, *My Turn at Bat,* 181.
54. Interview with Robert Veazey, April 7, 2006.
55. Glenn with Taylor, *John Glenn,* 130.
56. Interview with John Glenn, October 25, 2004.
57. Interview with Edro Buchser, April 28, 2004.
58. Williams with Underwood, *My Turn at Bat,* 183.
59. Ibid., 183 and 184.
60. *Boston Herald, Boston Globe,* and *New York Times,* July 15, 1953.
61. *Washington Daily News,* July 28, 1953.
62. Interview with George Sullivan, April 27, 2005.

Chapter 14: Transitions

1. Interview with John Murphy, May 11, 2004.
2. *Boston Globe,* August 10, 1953.
3. *Boston Globe,* August 13, 1953.
4. *Boston Evening American,* August 12, 1953.
5. *Boston Evening American,* August 17, 1953.
6. *Boston Evening American,* August 18, 1953.
7. *Boston Globe,* September 7, 1953.
8. *Boston Globe,* September 11, 1953.

9. From "You Take It, Dommie," an undated paper written by Ted Williams as part of his campaign to get Dominic DiMaggio inducted into the National Baseball Hall of Fame.

10. *American Weekly,* August 23, 1953.

11. Interview with Bobby-Jo Williams Ferrell, May 5, 2004.

12. Interview with Donald Soule, March 11, 2003.

13. Louise Kaufman interview by Ed Linn, 1991, made available to the author by Linn's daughter, Hildy Linn Angius.

14. Interview with Evalyn Sterry, February 16, 2005.

15. Interview with Lynette Siman, January 8, 2003.

16. Underwood, *It's Only Me,* 65–67.

17. Angell, *Game Time,* 382. (In an interview on October 25, 2005, Angell said that he had sat on this nugget for seventeen years until after Ted died, and that even the Boston writers told him they were surprised by it.)

18. Interview with Eric Abel, August 10, 2005.

19. Interview with Johnny Lazor, November 1, 2002.

20. Interview with George Sullivan, September 14, 2005.

21. Interview with Eddie Pellagrini, October 22, 2002.

22. Interview with Paul Sonnabend, September 27, 2004.

23. Interview with Arthur D'Angelo, September 15, 2005.

24. Interview with Andy Giacobbe, August 22, 2005.

25. *Boston Herald,* April 17, 1957.

26. Interview with James Carroll, February 3, 2005.

27. Interview with Claudia Williams, May 3, 2004.

28. Interview with Steve Brown, November 12, 2004.

29. Interview with Salvador Herrera, November 2, 2005.

30. Interview with Jonathan Gallen, May 16, 2005.

31. Interview with Manuel Herrera, October 30, 2002.

32. Interview with Maureen Cronin, May 27, 2003.

33. Interview with Jim Vinick, May 18, 2004.

34. Interview with Jimmy Piersall, July 16, 2004.

35. Interview with Mark Ferrell, July 20, 2004.

36. Interview with Nelva More, September 12, 2005.

37. Interview with Nancy Barnard, April 14, 2006.

38. Interview with Marshall Gilmore, March 9, 2006.

39. Interview with Grant Gilmore, March 13, 2006.

Chapter 15: 1954–1956

1. *Boston Globe,* March 1, 1954.

2. *Boston Globe,* March 2, 1954.

3. *Saturday Evening Post,* April 10, 1954.

4. *Boston Globe,* April 7, 1954.

5. Johnson and Stout, *Ted Williams,* 131.

6. Interview with Curt Gowdy, October 24, 2002.

7. Kemmerer with Madden, *Ted Williams,* 51 and 52. Also Tom Meany, "The Feudal Champion," *Baseball Digest,* November–December 1956.

8. Interview with Milt Bolling, August 13, 2003.

9. Interview with Billy Consolo, August 21, 2003.

10. Interview with Frank Malzone, August 19, 2003.

11. Ted Lepcio interview, Will McDonough 1967 interviews.

12. Interview with Billy Klaus, June 27, 2003.

13. Ted Lepcio interview, Will McDonough 1967 interviews.

14. Interview with Don Buddin, September 24, 2003.

15. Interview with Pete Daley, July 22, 2003.

16. Phalen, *A Bittersweet Journey,* 6.

17. Seidel, *Ted Williams*, 324.
18. Williams with Underwood, *My Turn at Bat*, 191.
19. *Boston Globe*, August 13, 1954.
20. *Boston Post*, September 15, 1954.
21. *This Week*, July 13, 1958.
22. *Boston Globe* and *Boston Herald*, September 27, 1954.
23. *Sport*, June 1959.
24. *Orange County Register*, November 16, 2005.
25. Interview with Cornelius Hurley Jr., March 11, 2005.
26. *Boston Globe*, May 11, 1955.
27. *Boston Globe*, May 12, 1955.
28. *New York Times*, May 13, 1955.
29. *Boston Globe*, May 11, 1955.
30. Official Major League Baseball contracts on file with the National Baseball Hall of Fame.
31. Unpublished Ted Williams interview by Ed Linn, 1991, made available to the author by Linn's daughter, Hildy Linn Angius.
32. Interview with Bobby-Jo Williams Ferrell, May 5, 2004.
33. Williams with Pietrusza, *Ted Williams: My Life in Pictures*, 104.
34. *Boston Globe*, June 19, 1956, as cited in Seidel, *Ted Williams*, 280.
35. Interview with Mickey Vernon, October 17, 2002.
36. *Boston Herald*, July 21, 1956.
37. Ibid.
38. Cramer, "What Do You Think of Ted Williams Now?"
39. *Boston Globe*, August 8, 1956.
40. Seidel, *Ted Williams*, 281.
41. *Boston Globe*, August 8, 1956.
42. Ibid.
43. *Boston Daily Record*, August 9, 1956.
44. *Boston Evening American*, August 9, 1956.
45. *Sports Illustrated*, August 1, 1955.
46. *Time* files.
47. *Boston Globe*, August 9, 1956.
48. *Boston Globe*, August 10, 1956.
49. *Lowell Sun*, August 11, 1956.
50. Linn, *The Great Rivalry*, 246.
51. Seidel, *Ted Williams*, 288.

Chapter 16: Late Innings

1. Williams with Underwood, *My Turn at Bat*, 197.
2. Ibid., 198.
3. *Boston Traveler*, May 24, 1957.
4. Williams with Underwood, *My Turn at Bat*, 198 and 199.
5. *Boston Globe*, July 11, 1957.
6. *Sport*, June 1958.
7. *Boston Globe*, August 1, 1957.
8. Linn, *Hitter*, 292.
9. Ibid.
10. Associated Press, September 17, 1957.
11. Associated Press, November 22, 1957.
12. Stout and Johnson, *Red Sox Century*, 289.
13. *Boston Globe*, September 30, 1957.
14. *Look*, July 23, 1957.
15. Johnson and Stout, *Ted Williams*, 148 and 149.
16. *Boston Evening American*, February 7, 1958.
17. Ibid.
18. Williams with Underwood, *My Turn at Bat*, 206.
19. Williams with Pietrusza, *Ted Williams: My Life in Pictures*, 124.
20. *Boston Globe*, May 13, 1988.
21. Associated Press, September 21, 1958, and *Boston Globe*, September 22, 1958.
22. *Washington Post*, September 29, 1958.
23. *Boston Globe*, March 24, 1959.
24. *Boston Globe*, March 8, 1959.
25. Interview with Dorothy Lindia, January 23, 2003.
26. Hirshberg, *What's the Matter with the Red Sox?*, 143.
27. Interview with Pumpsie Green, July 16, 2004.
28. Linn, *Hitter*, 324.
29. *Boston Globe*, June 14, 1959.
30. Williams with Underwood, *My Turn at Bat*, 207.
31. Linn, *Hitter*, 326.
32. Williams with Underwood, *My Turn at Bat*, 207 and 208.
33. Yastrzemski and Eskenazi, *Yaz*, 57.

34. Interview with John Harrington, May 21, 2003.
35. *Boston Globe*, March 8, 1960.
36. *Boston Daily Record*, April 28, 1960.
37. *New York Post*, March 25, 1960.
38. Williams with Underwood, *My Turn at Bat*, 31 and 32.
39. Associated Press, April 18, 1960.
40. Associated Press, April 26, 1960.
41. Associated Press, May 31, 1960.
42. Linn, *Hitter*, 317.
43. *Boston Globe*, July 4, 1960.
44. *Boston Daily Record*, August 11, 1960.
45. *Boston Globe*, August 12, 1960.
46. *Sporting News*, June 29, 1960.
47. *Sport*, February 1961.

Chapter 17: Last Ups

1. *Boston Traveler*, September 26, 1960, and *Boston Herald*, September 27, 1960.
2. Linn, *Hitter*, 11 and 12.
3. Prime and Nowlin, *Ted Williams*, 175–76.
4. *Providence Evening Bulletin*, September 29, 1960.
5. Ibid.
6. Interview with Curt Gowdy, October 24, 2002.
7. *Boston Daily Record*, September 28, 1960, as cited in Montville, *Ted Williams*, 228.
8. *Boston Globe*, September 28, 2008.
9. Golenbock, *Fenway*, 241.
10. *The New Yorker*, October 22, 1960.
11. *Boston Herald*, September 29, 1960.
12. Williams with Underwood, *My Turn at Bat*, 215.
13. Interview with Jack Fisher, April 9, 2004.
14. *Sport*, February 1961.
15. Interview with Jim Pagliaroni, August 19, 2003.
16. Interview with Pumpsie Green, May 16, 2011.
17. Interview with Don Gile, May 16, 2011.
18. Interview with Lee Howard, October 10, 2002. (Howard died on August 31, 2001. She was eighty-eight.)

19. *Providence Evening Bulletin*, September 29, 1960.
20. *Sport*, February 1961.
21. Prime and Nowlin, *Ted Williams*, 176.
22. Interview with Jack Fisher, April 9, 2004.
23. Letter from John Updike to Ted Williams, May 8, 1982, made available to the author by Claudia Williams.

Chapter 18: Kindness

1. Prime and Nowlin, *Ted Williams*, 131.
2. *Boston Globe*, November 11, 1988.
3. Linn, *Hitter*, 269.
4. Interview with Don Nicoll, May 2, 2005.
5. Wisnia, *The Jimmy Fund of Dana-Farber Cancer Institute*, 10.
6. Ibid., 7.
7. Interview with Ernest Cioffi, September 24, 2005.
8. Interview with Mike Andrews, October 4, 2004.
9. Interview with Saul Wisnia, February 25, 2005.
10. Linn, Hitter, 277.
11. *Boston Evening American*, January 10, 1958.
12. *Boston Evening American*, September 27, 1951.
13. *Boston Globe*, May 20, 1957.
14. *Time* files.
15. *Boston Globe*, September 6, 1964.
16. Golenbock, *Fenway*, 128.
17. Prime and Nowlin, *Ted Williams*, 132.
18. Linn, *Hitter*, 273.
19. Shaughnessy, *At Fenway*, 211.

Chapter 19: Real Life

1. Johnson and Stout, *Ted Williams*, 175.
2. Williams with Underwood, *My Turn at Bat*, 217–18.
3. Williams with Pietrusza, *Ted Williams: My Life in Pictures*, 41.
4. *Sport*, September 1951.
5. *New York Times*, September 30, 1960.
6. Interview with Karl Smith, October 26, 2005.

7. Interview with Butch Buchholz, May 6, 2004.
8. Interview with Jack Twyman, June 10, 2004.
9. From "My Friend Ted Williams"— nine pages of reflections by Carl Lind on his time with Williams, provided to the author by Lind.
10. Interview with Bobby-Jo Williams Ferrell, May 5, 2004.
11. Interview with Lee Howard, October 10, 2002.
12. *Boston Herald, Boston Traveler,* and *Boston Record-American,* March 3, 1961.
13. *Hoover High Cardinal,* April 13, 1966.
14. Interview with Al Cassidy, October 9, 2002.
15. Charles Zarrell email to the author, August 7, 2013.
16. Interview with Don Brown, August 21, 2003.
17. *Boston Globe,* July 4, 1965.
18. Interview with Al Palmieri, May 7, 2004.
19. Interview with Joe Camacho, June 4, 2004.
20. Interview with Jimmy Camacho, August 10, 2004.
21. Letter to the *Boston Globe,* July 22, 2002.
22. Interview with Al Cassidy, October 9, 2002.
23. Linn, *Hitter,* 275.
24. Interview with Stu Apte, November 7, 2005.
25. Interview with Jordan Ramin, September 27, 2004.
26. Interview with Dolores Wettach, September 28, 2008.

Chapter 20: Bobby-Jo

1. Interview with Bobby-Jo Williams Ferrell, May 5, 2004.
2. Interview with Daria Stehle, February 16, 2005.
3. Interview with Bill Churchman, May 11, 2004.
4. Interview with Stephen Tomasco, February 25, 2003.

5. Interview with Bill Churchman, May 11, 2004.
6. *Washington Post,* February 13, 2002.

Chapter 21: "Inn of the Immortals"

1. *Boston Traveler,* December 29, 1965.
2. *New York Times,* January 10, 1966.
3. Lou Gehrig was elected to the Hall of Fame by acclamation in 1939 after it was learned that he had been stricken with ALS.
4. *Boston Globe,* January 14, 1966.
5. *Boston Record-American,* January 5, 1966.
6. *Boston Globe,* January 20, 1966.
7. *Boston Globe,* January 30, 1966.
8. Williams with Underwood, *My Turn at Bat,* 223.
9. *Boston Herald,* July 26, 1966.
10. *Boston Globe,* July 26, 1966.
11. *Boston Traveler,* July 25, 1966.
12. *Boston Herald,* July 26, 1966.
13. Williams with Underwood, *My Turn at Bat,* 224.
14. Interview with Tim Horgan, October 5, 2005.
15. *Boston Traveler,* July 29, 1966.
16. *Boston Herald,* July 30, 1966.
17. Rampersad, *Jackie Robinson,* 319.
18. Williams column in the *Boston Globe,* September 22, 1963.
19. Halberstam, *The Teammates,* 113.
20. Interview with Joe Davis, April 17, 2004.
21. *Boston Globe,* July 22, 2002.
22. Interview with Curt Gowdy, October 24, 2002.
23. *USA Today,* April 15, 2012.
24. Kuhn, *Hardball,* 56.
25. *New York Post,* February 4, 1971.
26. *Washington Post,* July 10, 1971.
27. From Monte Irvin's videotape at the Ted Williams Museum and Hitters Hall of Fame.
28. *The Well,* "Inkwell: Authors and Artists, Topic 159: Howard Bryant, *Shut Out: A Story of Race and Baseball in Boston,*" September 19, 2002, http://www.well.com/conf/inkwell

.vue/topics/159/Howard-Bryant
-Shut-Out-A-Story-o-page01.html.

29. Interview with Al Cassidy, October 9, 2002, and November 18, 2005.

30. Interview with Martin Nolan, November 22, 2002.

31. Interview with Buck O'Neil, July 15, 2004.

32. Interview with Al Cassidy, October 9, 2002, and November 18, 2005.

33. United Press International, July 26, 1985, and the *Oneonta Daily Star* (New York), July 27, 1985.

34. *St. Louis Post-Dispatch,* August 12, 1995.

Chapter 22: Dolores

1. United Press International, October 14, 1966.

2. Interview with Bobby-Jo Williams Ferrell, May 5, 2004.

3. Interview with Lee Howard, October 10, 2002.

4. Interview with Dolores Williams, September 29, 2008.

5. *New York Journal-American,* September 1, 1959.

6. *Variety,* September 23, 1959.

7. *Time,* December 22, 1961.

8. John Underwood, "Going Fishing with the Kid," *Sports Illustrated,* August 21, 1967.

9. Interview with Francine Dawn Hebding, November 19, 2002.

10. Prime and Nowlin, *Ted Williams,* 67.

11. Interview with John Underwood, April 14, 2003.

12. Interview with Claudia Williams, April 29, 2005.

Chapter 23: The Splendid Skipper

1. *Washington Post,* February 13, 1969.

2. *Boston Globe,* March 18, 1969.

3. Whitfield, *Kiss It Good-Bye,* 44.

4. *Washingtonian,* March 1970.

5. *Sports Illustrated,* February 24, 1969.

6. Whitfield, *Kiss It Good-Bye,* 44; *Washingtonian,* March 1970; and *Sports Illustrated,* February 24, 1969.

7. *Wall Street Journal,* April 6, 1970.

8. *Boston Globe,* February 22, 1969.

9. Ibid.

10. United Press International, February 23, 1969.

11. *Boston Globe,* February 22, 1969.

12. *Boston Globe,* February 23, 1969.

13. Whitfield, *Kiss It Good-Bye,* 46.

14. *Boston Globe,* February 26, 1969.

15. Whitfield, *Kiss It Good-Bye,* 46.

16. Ibid., 43.

17. Ibid., 35.

18. *Washington Post,* March 2, 1969.

19. Frank Howard, "What It's Like to Play for Ted Williams," *Sport,* March 1970 (Howard's account of the 1969 season).

20. Interview with Dave Nelson, October 10, 2003.

21. *Boston Globe,* March 17, 1969.

22. *Sport,* March 1970.

23. *Boston Globe,* March 17, 1969.

24. Interview with Mike Epstein, July 18, 2005.

25. Terwilliger with Peterson and Boehm, *Terwilliger Bunts One,* 169.

26. *Boston Globe,* March 19, 1969.

27. Terwilliger with Peterson and Boehm, *Terwilliger Bunts One,* 172.

28. Ibid., 175.

29. *Sport,* March 1970.

30. *New York Times,* April 8, 1969.

31. *Boston Globe,* April 7, 1969.

32. Letter from Richard Nixon to Ted Williams, March 3, 1969, made available to the author by Claudia Williams.

33. *Boston Globe,* April 8, 1969.

34. Terwilliger with Peterson and Boehm, *Terwilliger Bunts One,* 176.

35. Ibid., 176–78.

36. *New York Times,* April 16, 1969.

37. Cataneo, *Peanuts and Crackerjack,* 149.

38. *Boston Globe,* April 24, 1969.

39. Whitfield, *Kiss It Good-Bye,* 98.

40. *Wall Street Journal,* April 6, 1970.

41. Ibid.

42. *Washington Post,* July 2, 1969.

43. *Washingtonian,* March 1970.

44. Interview with Dick Billings, October 7, 2003.

45. Interview with David Burgin, October 15, 2005.

46. *Washington Post,* March 4, 1969.

47. Dolores Williams interview with Don Newbery, September 1969.

48. Letter from Don Newbery to Dolores Williams, March 2003.

49. Terwilliger with Peterson and Boehm, *Terwilliger Bunts One,* 182.

50. Whitfield, *Kiss It Good-Bye,* 38.

51. Ibid.

52. Letter from Richard Nixon to Ted Williams, July 18, 1984, made available to the author by Claudia Williams.

53. *Sporting News,* September 8, 1969.

54. Associated Press, October 21, 1969.

55. Whitfield, *Kiss It Good-Bye,* 77.

56. *Boston Globe,* October 2, 1969.

57. *Washington Post,* October 22, 1969.

58. *Detroit News,* September 20, 1971, as cited in Terwilliger with Peterson and Boehm, *Terwilliger Bunts One,* 181.

59. *Boston Globe,* February 8, 1970.

60. *Boston Globe,* January 23, 1970.

61. *Wall Street Journal,* April 6, 1970.

62. Whitfield, *Kiss It Good-Bye,* 31.

63. Associated Press, April 29, 1970.

64. *Washington Post,* April 30, 1970.

65. *Washington Post,* May 24, 1970.

66. Whitfield, *Kiss It Good-Bye,* 47.

67. *Boston Globe,* May 31, 1977.

68. Interview with Bernie Allen, July 16, 2004.

69. *Boston Globe,* July 1, 1970.

70. Interview with Dick Bosman, October 7, 2003.

71. Interview with Bernie Allen, July 16, 2004.

72. *Boston Globe,* July 2, 1970.

73. United Press International, July 20, 1970.

74. Interview with Joe Camacho, June 4, 2004.

75. Interview with Casey Cox, July 23, 2004.

76. Whitfield, *Kiss It Good-Bye,* 55.

77. Ibid., 37.

78. Interview with Shelby Whitfield, December 21, 2005.

79. Whitfield, *Kiss It Good-Bye,* 26.

80. Ibid., 59, 72, and 75.

81. Ibid., 57.

82. Ibid., 114.

83. Associated Press, October 13, 1970.

84. Whitfield, *Kiss It Good-Bye,* 24.

85. Interview with Dolores Williams, September 29, 2008.

86. Montville, *Ted Williams,* 300.

87. Interview with Dolores Williams, September 29, 2008.

88. McLain with Diles, *Nobody's Perfect,* 115.

89. Interview with Dave Nelson, October 10, 2003.

90. McLain with Diles, *Nobody's Perfect,* 122.

91. Ibid., 119.

92. United Press International, September 22, 1971.

93. *Washington Post,* August 26, 1971.

94. Interview with Tom Grieve, October 28, 2004.

95. Terwilliger with Peterson and Boehm, *Terwilliger Bunts One,* 189.

96. Ibid., 188.

97. Williams's batting show at Fenway Park is based on interviews with Bill Zeigler, August 16, 2004, and Dick Billings, October 7, 2003, and the *Boston Herald Traveler,* August 26, 1972.

98. Williams with Pietrusza, *Ted Williams: My Life in Pictures,* 159.

Chapter 24: Young John-Henry and Claudia

1. Letter from Ted to Dolores, March 15, 1974, made available to the author by Claudia Williams.

2. Interview with Rob Kaufman, March 8, 2003.

3. Interview with Bobby Doerr, June 24, 2012.

4. *Sports Illustrated,* June 29, 1981.

5. Interview with Mary Diver, August 21, 2005.

6. Interview with Janet Franzoni, May 2, 2005.

7. Interview with Rob Kaufman, March 8, 2003.

8. Interview with Bob McWalter, September 17, 2002.
9. Linn, *Hitter*, 358 and 359.
10. *Boston Globe*, March 28, 1982.
11. Interview with Al Cassidy, November 18, 2005.
12. Interview with George Sullivan, September 4, 2005.
13. Ted Williams estate planning memorandum, February 8, 1990.
14. Will McDonough 1967 interviews.
15. Michelle Orlando MacIntyre, *A Red Sox Romance: Spring Training 1984*, private reflections on Michelle's relationship with John-Henry, 27 and 43–44, made available to the author.
16. Interview with Candace Orlando Siegel, January 11, 2006.
17. Interview with Michelle Orlando MacIntyre, February 23, 2006.
18. Interview with Brian Interland, May 18, 2005.
19. Interview with Bob Long, March 25, 2005.
20. *Boston*, November 1990.
21. Interview with Ferd Ensinger, August 25, 2005.
22. Interview with Chick Leahey, May 5, 2005.
23. Interview with Elizabeth "Betty" Tamposi, October 21, 2005.
24. Interview with John Winkin, September 6, 2005.
25. Interview with Jim Vinick, May 18, 2004.
26. *Boston Globe*, July 21, 2002.
27. Interview with Manuel Herrera, October 29, 2002.
28. Letter from Manuel Herrera to Ted Williams and Louise Kaufman, June 10, 1989.
29. Interview with Salvador Herrera, November 3, 2005.
30. Interview with Edna Herrera, November 4, 2005.

Chapter 25: The Fishing Life

1. *Orange County Register*, July 11, 2002.
2. *Boston Globe*, July 16, 1964.

3. *Boston Evening American*, April 16, 1949.
4. *Boston Herald*, April 27, 1969, as cited in Cataneo, *I Remember Ted Williams*, 202.
5. *Sport*, February 1952.
6. *Popular Mechanics*, May 1989.
7. Williams with Underwood, *My Turn at Bat*, 163.
8. *New York Times*, January 18, 1998.
9. Prime and Nowlin, *Ted Williams*, 171.
10. Interview with Buddy Grace, August 13, 2004.
11. Interview with Hank Brown, July 16, 2004.
12. Interview with Frank Brothers, February 15, 2003.
13. Interview with Dan Pitts, January 24, 2005.
14. Interview with Millard Wells, April 14, 2004.
15. *Sports Illustrated*, June 29, 1981.
16. Interview with Gary Ellis, April 20, 2006.
17. *Sporting News*, August 26, 1967.
18. *Boston Globe*, July 5, 2002.
19. *Sports Illustrated*, June 29, 1981.
20. *Los Angeles Times*, November 17, 1977.
21. Interview with Claudia Williams, March 28, 2005.
22. *Sports Illustrated*, June 29, 1981.
23. Interview with Jack Fenety, August 3, 2004.
24. Interview with Jerry Doak, August 10, 2004.
25. United Press International, February 6, 1971.
26. *Popular Mechanics*, May 1989.
27. *Bangor Daily News*, October 3, 1993.
28. *Boston Globe*, July 7, 1978.
29. *New York Times*, July 23, 1978.
30. Interview with Sammy Lee, June 27, 2005.
31. Interview with Edna Curtis, July 1, 2005.

Chapter 26: Being Ted Williams

1. *Boston Phoenix*, April 12, 1983.
2. *Chicago Sun Times*, March 14, 1978.
3. *Washington Post*, March 21, 1978.

4. *Boston Globe,* March 6, 1978.
5. *Boston Herald,* May 30, 1984.
6. Interview with James Vinick, May 18, 2004.
7. Associated Press, March 5, 1986.
8. *Boston Globe,* March 6, 1986.
9. *Esquire,* June 1986.
10. Interview with James Vinick, May 18, 2004.
11. Interview with Ted Johnston, August 6, 2004.
12. Interview with Frank Inamorati, September 2, 2005.
13. Interview with Joe Rigney, August 27, 2005.
14. *Chicago Tribune,* February 14, 1988.
15. Interview with John Sununu, February 21, 2006.
16. Interview with George H. W. Bush, March 3, 2006.
17. Interview with Al Cassidy, October 9, 2002.
18. Claudia Williams e-mail to the author, May 9, 2012.
19. *Boston Herald,* November 11, 1988.
20. *New York Times,* November 12, 1988.
21. *Wall Street Journal,* February 10, 1989.
22. Interview with Eddie Walsh, July 25, 2005.
23. Interview with John Dowd, May 26, 2006.
24. Interview with Jack Reardon, May 11, 2005.
25. *Boston Globe,* May 12, 1991.
26. Linn, *Hitter,* 366.
27. Ibid., 368.
28. Engelberg with Schneider, *DiMaggio,* 301.
29. Vincent, *The Last Commissioner,* 6.
30. *Sporting News,* November 14, 1994.
31. Vincent, *The Last Commissioner,* 7–10.
32. *Washington Post* and *USA Today,* July 10, 1991.
33. Engelberg with Schneider, *DiMaggio,* 301–2.
34. Vincent, *The Last Commissioner,* 11.
35. Interview with John Sununu, February 22, 2006.
36. Vincent, *The Last Commissioner,* 12.
37. Linn, *Hitter,* 370 and 371.
38. Letter from Ted Williams to Robert McWalter, December 19, 1991, courtesy of McWalter.

Chapter 27: Enter John-Henry

1. Interview with Brian Interland, May 18, 2005.
2. Interview with Claudia Williams, May 3, 2004.
3. *Boston,* November 1990.
4. *Boston Globe,* August 8, 1995.
5. *Sports Illustrated,* May 20, 1991.
6. Interview with Phil Castinetti, January 21, 2005.
7. The trophies, described as being "on loan for permanent display," were Williams's 1946 and 1949 Most Valuable Player awards, his 1947 Triple Crown, and the Medal of Freedom presented to him in 1991 by President George H. W. Bush (Associated Press and *San Diego Union Tribune,* July 11, 1992).
8. Linn, *Hitter,* 371–73.
9. Interview with Clifton Helman, December 7, 2005, and December 12, 2005.
10. Interview with Rob Helman, December 12, 2005.
11. *New York Times,* May 11, 1993.
12. Interview with Bob Breitbard, October 23, 2002.
13. Interview with Robert McWalter, September 17, 2002, and August 14, 2006.
14. Interview with Bruce Porter, June 9, 2005.
15. Interview with Tony Hammon, June 3, 2005.
16. Interview with Barry Craig, August 15, 2005.
17. Letter from Bobby-Jo Williams Ferrell to Bob McWalter, August 24, 1993.
18. Interview with Bobby-Jo Williams Ferrell, May 5, 2004.
19. Interview with Rob Kaufman, January 21, 2003, and March 8, 2003.
20. Interview with Ferd Ensinger, August 25, 2005.

Chapter 28: Ted Failing

1. Interview with Sammy Lee, June 27, 2005.
2. Interview with Lynette Siman, January 8, 2003.
3. Interview with George Carter, January 6, 2003.
4. Interview with Bobby-Jo Williams Ferrell, July 20, 2004.
5. *Citrus County Chronicle,* February 10, 1994.
6. *New York Times,* May 22, 1994.
7. Ibid.
8. *People,* March 13, 1995.
9. Interview with Vicki Miranti, August 3, 2004.
10. Tricia Miranti e-mail to the author, August 15, 2004.
11. Interview with Claudia Williams, July 19, 2004.
12. Interview with Eric Abel, August 10, 2004.
13. Caretaker Frank Brothers told the author in an interview on March 27, 2006, that he once saw an American Express bill of $38,000 for one month in which John-Henry had bought an expensive underwater camera lens and other luxury items.
14. Interview with Anita Lovely, August 2, 2006, and August 28, 2006.
15. Interview with Robert McWalter, September 17, 2002, and August 14, 2006.
16. Interview with Clifton Helman, December 7, 2005, and December 12, 2005.
17. *Boston Globe,* April 18, 1994.
18. *Boston Globe,* July 6, 1994.
19. *Boston Globe,* July 29, 1994.
20. Interview with Carol Southard, February 1, 2006.
21. Interview with Claudia Williams, May 3, 2004.
22. Interview with George Carter, January 6, 2003.
23. Interview with Frank Brothers, March 27, 2006.
24. Interview with John Sullivan, January 7, 2003.
25. Interview with Judy Ebers, May 16, 2006.
26. Interview with John Sullivan, January 7, 2003.
27. Interview with Marion Corbin, June 1, 2004.
28. Interview with Jim Corbin, June 1, 2004.
29. Interview with Anita Lovely, August 2, 2006, and August 28, 2006.
30. *Boston Globe,* December 16, 1995.
31. Montville, *Ted Williams,* 429.

Chapter 29: Hitter.net

1. *Sports Illustrated,* November 25, 1996.
2. *Daily Evening Item,* December 16, 1998.
3. Ibid.
4. *Lake Today,* December 1998.
5. Interview with Brian O'Connor, April 13, 2005.
6. *Boston Globe,* January 25, 1998.
7. Interview with Phil Castinetti, January 21, 2005.
8. *Boston Globe,* December 6, 1997.
9. *Boston Herald,* March 10, 1998.
10. *Boston Globe,* March 12, 1998.
11. Interview with Dan Duquette, December 6, 2005.
12. Interview with Nomar Garciaparra, November 8, 2012.
13. McCain with Salter, *Worth the Fighting For,* 214.
14. *Boston Globe,* August 30, 1998.
15. Interview with Larry Taylor, April 29, 2004.
16. Interview with Claudia Williams, May 3, 2004.
17. Walker, *A Whole New Ballgame,* 7.
18. *Boston Globe,* March 9, 1999.
19. *New York Times Magazine,* May 30, 1999.
20. Ibid.
21. *Lake Today,* December 1998.
22. Interview with Gerry Rittenberg, October 31, 2012.
23. The SunTrust loan was secured by an investment account that Ted

maintained at the bank valued at about $740,000. (This information was revealed in a lawsuit brought on behalf of Ted Williams against SunTrust Bank in March 2002.)

24. Interview with telecom sales representative who declined to be identified, August 8, 2005; February 3, 2006; and November 13, 2012.
25. *Boston Globe,* June 12, 1999.
26. Interview with Tommy Lasorda, April 6, 2005, and December 19, 2005.
27. Interview with Nelson Doubleday Jr., January 10, 2006.
28. Interview with Peter Sutton, November 19, 2012.
29. *Boston Globe,* July 10, 1999.
30. *Boston Globe,* July 12, 1999.
31. Interview with Jack Gard, January 11, 2003.
32. *St. Petersburg Times,* July 16, 2002.
33. Interview with Dave McCarthy, November 19, 2012.
34. *Boston Herald,* July 14, 1999.
35. Peter Sutton e-mail to the author, September 20, 2006.

Chapter 30: Spiraling

1. *Boston Globe,* March 25, 1998.
2. Interview with John Underwood, April 14, 2003.
3. Interview with Charles Magill, January 21, 2005, and November 27, 2012.
4. Interview with Rich Eschen, January 9, 2003.
5. HBO's *Real Sports with Bryant Gumbel,* June 23, 2003.
6. Interview with Tommy Lasorda, April 6, 2005, and December 19, 2005.
7. *Vero Beach Press Journal,* March 4, 2000.
8. Interview with Dominic DiMaggio, October 2, 2002. (DiMaggio died in 2009.)
9. *Life,* February 2000.
10. *Palm Beach Post,* July 11, 2000, and June 6, 2004.
11. Interview with Ted Taylor, February 3, 2005.
12. Interview with Frank Brothers, March 27, 2006.
13. Interview with John Sullivan, January 7, 2003.
14. Interview with Mary Dluhy, March 28, 2006.
15. Interview with George Carter, January 6, 2003.
16. *St. Petersburg Times,* August 13, 2000.
17. Interview with John Harrington, May 21, 2003.
18. *Boston Globe,* October 12, 2000.
19. Interview with Frank Brothers, March 27, 2006.
20. Interview with Donna Fleischmann, January 9, 2003.
21. Interview with Dominic DiMaggio, October 2, 2002.
22. Interview with Eric Abel, January 7, 2003; August 10, 2005; and June 29, 2006.
23. Interview with Nancy Carmichael, January 28, 2006.
24. Interview with Debbie Erb, April 5, 2006.
25. Interview with Becky Vaughn, April 5, 2006; April 6, 2006; June 27, 2006; and June 28, 2006.
26. Ibid.

Chapter 31: Alcor

1. *Boston Globe,* January 14, 2001, and January 15, 2001.
2. Interview with Francine Dawn Hebding, November 19, 2002.
3. Interview with Claudia Williams, May 3, 2004.
4. Interview with Eleanor Diamond, December 21, 2005.
5. Interview with Peter Sutton, June 11, 2003, and August 24, 2004.
6. Interview with Robert Ettinger, May 17, 2006. (Ettinger died on July 23, 2001. He was ninety-two.)
7. *Lowell Sun,* July 12, 2002.
8. Interview with cryonicist and Alcor member David Hayes, May 15, 2006.

9. Interview with Bill Haworth, February 7, 2006. (Alcor hired Haworth to do its public relations from 2002 to 2003.)
10. Interview with Bobby-Jo Williams Ferrell and Mark Ferrell, July 20, 2004.
11. Interview with Al Cassidy, January 10, 2003.
12. Interview with Eric Abel, January 7, 2003; August 10, 2005; and June 29, 2006, and interview with Mark Ferrell, July 20, 2004.

Chapter 32: Foreboding

1. Letter from Jerry Lemler to John-Henry Williams, June 12, 2001.
2. Interview with Dr. Allan Goodman, May 20, 2005.
3. Interview with Dick Flavin, December 24, 2012.
4. *Boston Herald,* June 26, 2002.
5. Interview with Steve Connolly, February 9, 2006.
6. Interview with Lee Howard, October 10, 2002. (Howard died on August 31, 2011. She was eighty-eight.)
7. Interview with Isabel Gilmore, June 10, 2004. (Gilmore died on March 28, 2010. She was eighty-four.)
8. Interview with Jenna Bernreuter, February 24, 2006.
9. Interview with Bill Haworth, February 7, 2006.
10. Interview with David Hayes, May 15, 2006.
11. Interview with Steve Brown, November 12, 2004.
12. Interview with Virginia Hiley-Self, November 11, 2005.
13. Interview with Donna Van Tassel, November 12, 2005.
14. *Boston Globe,* February 18, 2002.
15. Interview with Steve Ferroli, November 9, 2005.
16. John Henry e-mail to the author, March 8, 2005.
17. Interview with Larry Lucchino, February 27, 2005.
18. *Boston Globe,* June 23, 2002.
19. *Boston Herald,* June 26, 2002.
20. *Boston Globe,* June 27, 2002.
21. *Ft. Myers News-Press,* June 28, 2002.
22. *Boston Herald,* July 3, 2002.
23. Both the friend and the caretaker declined to be quoted by name.
24. Interview with Billy Reedy, July 21, 2004; August 3, 2004; and September 10, 2004. (Reedy died of cancer in 2009.)
25. Interview with Daisy Bisz, January 17, 2003; May 8, 2004; May 10, 2004; and May 21, 2004. (Bisz died in 2007 at ninety-seven.)
26. Interview with John Burgess, August 15, 2005.
27. Interview with Mike Glenn, August 15, 2005, and August 16, 2005.
28. During the course of ten interviews with the author over four years from 2002 to 2006, Bob Breitbard became increasingly reluctant to talk about John-Henry, and then flatly refused to discuss young Williams further. He said he was wary of revealing details that could make waves and be the subject of litigation. Asked in 2006 about his conversations with Burgess and Glenn regarding Ted's desire for a lawyer, Breitbard, then eighty-seven, said he did not recall Burgess and Glenn. (Breitbard died in 2010 at ninety-one.)
29. *Sporting News,* July 29, 2002.

Chapter 33: July 5, 2002

1. Interview with John Butcher, October 27, 2005.
2. Interview with Kathleen Rolfingsmeier, February 9, 2006.
3. Interview with Mark Ferrell, May 5, 2004.
4. Interview with Dwight Hooper, February 9, 2006.
5. Interview with Jenna Bernreuter, February 24, 2006.
6. Interview with John Heer, September 12, 2006.
7. Interview with Claudia Williams, March 29, 2006.

8. Interview with Teresa Fletcher, September 25, 2006.
9. Interview with Beth Daley, June 27, 2006, and Daley e-mail to the author, July 20, 2006.
10. Interview with Eric Abel, January 7, 2003; August 10, 2005; and June 29, 2006.
11. Interview with Al Cassidy, January 10, 2003.
12. Interview with Tom Brown, April 27, 2006.

Chapter 34: The Pact

1. Associated Press, July 6, 2002.
2. *Boston Globe,* July 7, 2002.
3. *Chicago Tribune,* July 22, 2002.
4. *Sporting News,* July 22, 2002.
5. Interview with Bill Haworth, February 7, 2006.
6. Interview with Claudia Williams, July 19, 2004.
7. *Boston Globe,* July 26, 2002.
8. John Heer e-mail to the author, May 12, 2006.
9. Interview with Frank Brothers, March 27, 2006.
10. Interview with Richard Kerensky, May 3, 2006.
11. Interview with Eric Abel, January 7, 2003; August 10, 2005; and June 29, 2006.
12. Interview with Claudia Williams, July 19, 2004; March 30, 2005; and March 30, 2006.
13. Interview with Jenna Bernreuter, February 24, 2006.
14. *Boston Globe,* September 25, 2002.
15. Interview with Bob Costas, December 20, 2005.

Epilogue

1. Interview with Lisa Martin, May 20, 2005.

Bibliography

Angell, Roger. *Game Time: A Baseball Companion.* New York: Mariner Books, 2004.

Auker, Elden, with Tom Keegan. *Sleeper Cars and Flannel Uniforms: A Lifetime of Memories from Striking Out the Babe to Teeing It Up with the President.* Chicago: Triumph Books, 2001.

Baldassaro, Lawrence, ed. *The Ted Williams Reader.* New York: Fireside, 1991.

Baseball Writers of the *New York Times* and the *Boston Globe. The Rivals: The Boston Red Sox vs. the New York Yankees—An Inside History.* New York: St. Martin's Press, 2004.

Berry, Henry, and Harold Berry. *Boston Red Sox: The Complete Record of Red Sox Baseball.* New York: Macmillan, 1984.

Blake, Mike. *Baseball Chronicles: An Oral History of Baseball Through the Decades.* Cincinnati: Betterway Books, 1994.

Boston Herald. *Ted Williams: Remembering the Splendid Splinter.* Champaign, IL: Sports Publishing LLC, 2002.

Bryant, Howard. *Shut Out: A Story of Race and Baseball in Boston.* New York: Routledge, 2002.

Cataneo, David. *I Remember Ted Williams.* Nashville: Cumberland House Publishing, 2002.

———. *Peanuts and Crackerjack.* New York: Harcourt Brace, 1991.

Connor, Anthony J. *Baseball for the Love of It: Hall of Famers Tell It Like It Was.* New York: Macmillan, 1982.

Corcoran, Fred, with Bud Harvey. *Unplayable Lies: The Story of Sport's Most Successful Impresario.* New York: Duell, Sloan & Pearce, 1965.

Cramer, Richard Ben. *Joe DiMaggio: The Hero's Life.* New York: Simon & Schuster, 2000.

———. "What Do You Think of Ted Williams Now?" *Esquire,* June 1986. (After Williams died, the long *Esquire* article was reprinted as a small book with a new introduction and postscript by Cramer: *What Do You Think of Ted Williams Now?: A Remembrance.* New York: Simon & Schuster, 2002.)

Creamer, Robert W. *Baseball in '41: A Celebration of the "Best Baseball Season Ever"—in the Year America Went to War.* New York: Viking, 1991.

Crissey, Harrington E., Jr. *Athletes Away: A Selective Look at Professional Baseball Players in the Navy During World War II.* Philadelphia: Archway Press, 1984.

Dawidoff, Nicholas. *The Catcher Was a Spy: The Mysterious Life of Moe Berg.* New York: Vintage Books, 1995.

Dillman, Danny. *Hey Kid!: A Tiger Batboy Remembers.* New York: iUniverse, 2007.

DiMaggio, Dom, with Bill Gilbert. *Real Grass, Real Heroes: Baseball's Historic 1941 Season.* New York: Zebra Books, 1990.

Dunne, Bert. *Play Ball, Son!* San Francisco: Serra Publishing, 1945, as reproduced in Dunne's *Play Ball!* Garden City, NY: Doubleday & Company, 1947.

Einstein, Charles, ed. *The Fireside Book of Baseball.* New York: Simon & Schuster, 1956.

Engelberg, Morris, and Marv Schneider. *DiMaggio: Setting the Record Straight.* St. Paul: MBI Publishing, 2003.

Giusti, Ernest H. "Mobilization of the Marine Corps Reserve in the Korean Conflict, 1950–1951." Published by the Historical Branch, G-3 Division, Headquarters, US Marine Corps, 1951.

Glenn, John, with Nick Taylor. *John Glenn: A Memoir.* New York: Bantam Books, 1999.

Goldstein, Richard. *Spartan Seasons: How Baseball Survived the Second World War.* New York: Macmillan, 1980.

Golenbock, Peter. *Fenway: An Unexpurgated History of the Boston Red Sox.* New York: G. P. Putnam's Sons, 1992.

Halberstam, David. *Summer of '49.* New York: William Morrow, 1989.

———. *The Teammates.* New York: Hyperion, 2003.

Hirshberg, Al. *From Sandlots to League President: The Story of Joe Cronin.* New York: Julian Messner, 1962.

———. *What's the Matter with the Red Sox?* New York: Dodd, Mead & Company, 1973.

Holtzman, Jerome. *No Cheering in the Press Box.* New York: Holt, Rinehart & Winston, 1973.

Holway, John. *Ted Williams: The Last .400 Hitter.* Dubuque, IA: Wm. C. Brown Publishers, 1992.

Honig, Donald. *Baseball When the Grass Was Real.* Lincoln: University of Nebraska Press, 1975.

Hynes, Samuel. *Flights of Passage: Reflections of a World War II Aviator.* New York: F. C. Beil, and Annapolis, MD: Naval Institute Press, 1988.

Johnson, Dick, and Glenn Stout. *DiMaggio: An Illustrated Life.* New York: Walker & Company, 1995.

———. *Ted Williams: A Portrait in Words and Pictures.* New York: Walker & Company, 1991.

Johnson, Larry, with Scott Baldyga. *Frozen: A True Story—My Journey into the World of Cryonics, Deception, and Death.* Philadelphia: Vanguard Press, 2009.

Kahn, Roger. *The Boys of Summer.* New York: Harper & Row, 1972.

Kemmerer, Russ, with W. C. Madden. *Ted Williams: "Hey Kid, Just Get It Over the Plate."* Fishers, IN: Madden Publishing, 2002.

Kuhn, Bowie. *Hardball: The Education of a Baseball Commissioner.* Lincoln: University of Nebraska Press, 1987.

Linn, Ed. *The Great Rivalry: The Yankees and the Red Sox, 1901–1990*. New York: Ticknor & Fields, 1991.

———. *Hitter: The Life and Turmoils of Ted Williams*. San Diego: Harcourt Brace, 1993.

———. *Ted Williams: The Eternal Kid*. New York: Bartholomew House, 1961.

McCain, John, with Mark Salter. *Worth the Fighting For: A Memoir*. New York: Random House, 2002.

McDermott, Mickey, with Howard Eisenberg. *A Funny Thing Happened on the Way to Cooperstown*. Chicago: Triumph Books, 2003.

McLain, Denny, with Dave Diles. *Nobody's Perfect*. New York: Dial Press, 1975.

Mills, James R. *San Diego: Where California Began*. San Diego: San Diego Historical Society, 1985.

Montville, Leigh. *Ted Williams: The Biography of an American Hero*. New York: Doubleday, 2004.

Nowlin, Bill. *The Kid: Ted Williams in San Diego*. Cambridge, MA: Rounder Books, 2005.

———. *Ted Williams at War*. Cambridge, MA: Rounder Books, 2007.

Nowlin, Bill, and Jim Prime. *Ted Williams: A Tribute*. Indianapolis: Masters Press, 1997.

Nowlin, Bill, and others. *Ted Williams: A Splendid Life*. Chicago: Triumph Books, 2002.

Okrent, Daniel, and Harris Lewine, eds. *The Ultimate Baseball Book*. Boston: Houghton Mifflin, 1979.

Phalen, Rick C. *A Bittersweet Journey: America's Fascination with Baseball*. Tampa, FL: McGregor Publishing, 2000.

Piersall, Jim, with Al Hirshberg. *Fear Strikes Out*. Boston: Little, Brown, 1955.

Pope, Edwin. *Ted Williams: The Golden Year*. Englewood Cliffs, NJ: Prentice-Hall, 1970.

Prime, Jim, and Bill Nowlin. *Ted Williams: The Pursuit of Perfection*. Champaign, IL: Sports Publishing LLC, 2002.

Rampersad, Arnold. *Jackie Robinson: A Biography*. New York: Ballantine Books, 1998.

Robinson, Ray. *Ted Williams*. New York: G. P. Putnam's Sons, 1962.

Sambito, Major William J. "A History of Marine Attack Squadron 311." Published by the History and Museums Division, Headquarters, US Marine Corps, 1978.

Sampson, Arthur. *Ted Williams: A Biography of the Kid*. New York: A. S. Barnes and Company, 1950.

Seidel, Michael. *Ted Williams: A Baseball Life*. Lincoln: University of Nebraska Press, 1991.

Shaughnessy, Dan. *The Curse of the Bambino*. New York: Penguin, 2004.

———. *At Fenway: Dispatches from Red Sox Nation*. New York: Three Rivers Press, 1996.

Society for American Baseball Research (SABR). *A History of San Diego Baseball*, 1993.

Stout, Glenn. "Tryout and Fallout: Race, Jackie Robinson, and the Red Sox." *Massachusetts Historical Review* 6 (2004).

————, ed. *Impossible Dreams: A Red Sox Collection*. Boston: Houghton Mifflin, 2003.

Stout, Glenn, and Richard A. Johnson. *Red Sox Century*. Boston: Houghton Mifflin, 2000.

Sullivan, George. *The Picture History of the Boston Red Sox*. Indianapolis: Bobbs-Merrill Company, 1979.

Swank, Bill. *Echoes from Lane Field: A History of the San Diego Padres, 1936–1957*. Paducah, KY: Turner Publishing, 1997.

Tebbetts, Birdie, with James Morrison. *Birdie: Confessions of a Baseball Nomad*. Chicago: Triumph Books, 2002.

Terwilliger, Wayne, with Nancy Peterson and Peter Boehm. *Terwilliger Bunts One*. Guilford, CT: Insiders' Guide, 2006.

Thornley, Stew. *On to Nicollet: The Glory and Fame of the Minneapolis Millers*. Minneapolis: Nodin Press, 1988.

Time magazine. Files. Nearly one hundred pages of notes from correspondents Ben Williamson, Ed Rees, and Jeff Wylie prepared as part of an April 10, 1950, cover story on Williams. (The notes were in Ted's papers and given to the author by Claudia Williams.)

Turner, Frederick. *When the Boys Came Back: Baseball and 1946*. New York: Henry Holt, 1996.

Underwood, John. *It's Only Me: The Ted Williams We Hardly Knew*. Chicago: Triumph Books, 2005.

Underwood, John, and Ted Williams. *Ted Williams: Fishing "The Big Three"—Tarpon, Bonefish, Atlantic Salmon*. New York: Simon & Schuster, 1982.

Vaccaro, Mike. *1941: The Greatest Year in Sports*. New York: Doubleday, 2007.

Vincent, Fay. *The Last Commissioner: A Baseball Valentine*. New York: Simon & Schuster, 2002.

Walker, Stephen J. *A Whole New Ballgame: The 1969 Washington Senators*. Clifton, VA: Pocol Press, 2009.

Whitfield, Shelby. *Kiss It Good-Bye*. New York: Abelard-Schuman, 1973.

Williams, Ted, with David Pietrusza. *Ted Williams: My Life in Pictures*. Kingston, NY: Total Sports Publishing, 2001.

Williams, Ted, with Jim Prime. *Ted Williams' Hit List: The Ultimate Ranking of Baseball's Greatest Hitters*. Indianapolis: Masters Press, 1996.

Williams, Ted, with John Underwood. *My Turn at Bat*. New York: First Fireside Edition by Simon & Schuster, 1988.

————. *The Science of Hitting*. New York: Simon & Schuster, 1970.

Wisnia, Saul. *The Jimmy Fund of Dana-Farber Cancer Institute*. Charleston, SC: Arcadia Publishing, 2002.

Yastrzemski, Carl, and Gerald Eskenazi. *Yaz: Baseball, the Wall, and Me*. New York: Warner Books, 1991.

Index

About the Author

Ben Bradlee, Jr., spent twenty-five years at the *Boston Globe* as a reporter and editor. As deputy managing editor, he oversaw many critically acclaimed stories, including the *Globe*'s Pulitzer Prize–winning coverage of the sexual abuse scandal in the Catholic Church in 2002. He lives in Cambridge, Massachusetts.